HISTORIANS AND
HISTORIOGRAPHY
IN THE ITALIAN RENAISSANCE

Contents

HISTORIANS AND HISTORIOGRAPHY
IN THE ITALIAN RENAISSANCE

❧ ERIC COCHRANE ❧

THE UNIVERSITY OF CHICAGO PRESS · CHICAGO & LONDON

THE UNIVERSITY OF CHICAGO PRESS, CHICAGO 60637
THE UNIVERSITY OF CHICAGO PRESS, LTD., LONDON

© 1981 by The University of Chicago
All rights reserved. Published 1981
Paperback edition 1985
Printed in the United States of America
94 93 92 91 90 89 88 87 86 85   6 5 4 3 2

Library of Congress Cataloging in Publication Data

Cochrane, Eric W
   Historians and historiography in the Italian.
Renaissance.

   Includes bibliographical references and index.
   1. Italy—Historiography.   2. Italy—History—
1492–1559.   3. Italy—History—1559–1789.   4. Italy—
History, Local.   5. Historiography—History.   I. Title.
DG465.C62   945'.0072   80-16097
ISBN 0-226-11152-0 (cloth)
      0-226-11153-9 (paper)

CONTENTS

Of Historians and Historiographers in the Italian Renaissance: Books VI

In Which are Mentioned All the Works of a Historical Nature Written by Citizens, Subjects, or Residents of the Several Italian Cities and States, Both at Home and Abroad, From the Beginning of the Fifteenth to the Beginning of the Seventeenth Century, That were Then Published or That Subsequently Appeared in Print, and In Which is Described the Emergence of Humanist Historiography from the Preceding Chronicle Tradition, Its Growth in Response to the Political Calamities of the Early Sixteenth Century, Its Diversification in Form, Scope, and Content, Its Extension First to All Parts of Italy and then to the Rest of Europe, and Its Eventual Crisis in the Face of the Disappearance of the Subject Matter Prescribed by Its Ancient Models; Together with a Consideration of Its Relationship to Other Parallel Humanist Disciplines and of Its Lasting Contribution to the Further Development of European Historiography in the Following Centuries; and with A Copious Index of Names, Places, and Subjects.

Written by Eric Cochrane of the University of Chicago and dedicated to Helen. A. Regenstein, founder and benefactor of the Joseph Regenstein Library of the same university

PROLOGUE AD LECTOREM

IT WAS NOT ORIGINALLY MY IDEA TO WRITE THIS BOOK. I WAS INVITED TO DO SO, back in the happy days of academic prosperity, by an enterprising publisher who was anxious to satisfy the constantly increasing demand for new books in apparently ever-growing Renaissance history courses. I accepted the invitation in part because I thought the task would be relatively easy. All I had to do, I surmised, was to complete the bibliographies I had accumulated while offering seminars on related subjects at the University of Chicago and then to reread the texts presented by my students with the help of scholarly monographs we together had dug out of library catalogues and learned journals.

Then academic prosperity gave way to academic depression. Students abandoned the Renaissance first for more "relevant" and then for more potentially profitable fields of study. And cost accountants forced publishers to reject any titles that might occupy costly warehouse space. The general editor of the series into which my book was supposed to fit declined to answer my urgent pleas for further guidance. When the publisher himself finally sent me what I believe to have been the only volume ever actually to appear in the series, I realized that what I had done up until then no longer corresponded either to his original or to his then current intentions. And in the end he was very happy to wash his hands of the whole project.

Thus what started out as another's idea became mine alone. But what I thought would be an easy task turned out to be increasingly fraught with difficulties. First of all, I discovered that the authorities to whom I turned for help had usually derived their theses from the examination of a relatively limited number of texts. Some of them had studied only the historians of a single city—for example, those of Naples in the mid-sixteenth century, of Bologna in the early fifteenth century, of Florence in the ages of Cosimo *Pater Patriae* or of Cosimo I, or of Venice between the arrival of Marc'Antonio Sabellico and the death of Nicolò Contarini. Others of them had studied only single historians: Leonardo Bruni, Bernardo Giustinian, Paolo Sarpi, Giorgio Vasari, or, the most studied of all, Niccolò Machiavelli. In the first case, the results of monographical research were generally placed in the context of the political history of the particular city. In the second case, they were usually connected only with the life and the other works of the particular historian. In both cases the context of Renaissance historiography as a whole was usually missing, or else it was assumed to be equivalent to what had been said about those few other historians whom the author, for reasons seldom fully explained, held to be representative of all the others. Hence, certain characteristics or accomplishments were pointed out as peculiar to one historian or school of historians that were actually shared by their contemporaries or predecessors. Many cities of Italy that had actually produced a respectable body of historiography were almost wholly ignored. And those nonspecialists whose investigations of other subjects obliged them to refer to this one were inevitably tempted to "jump from one historical text to another"[1]—and to impose upon them interpretations that a philological study of the texts themselves would never have yielded.

I then discovered that some of my predecessors had been guided in their study of the texts by critical principles derived from those of the Italian text editors of the nineteenth century. These principles were based on the assumption that the literary products of the independent communes of the Middle Ages were by nature qualitatively superior to those of the principalities of the Renaissance, particularly after the moment when those principalities became subject to a non-Italian hegemony. These principles therefore demanded the condemnation of "that pompous and crippled style [with which] the flamboyant character of the Spanish corrupted the simple elegance of Italian literature," and they encouraged favorable comparisons of "the good chroniclers and ingenuous recorders of events" with "the declamations of so many 'historians' [who] wrote . . . artful, high-sounding periods out of pride or for a price." They also supported a preference for texts that reflected "love of country and of hard work on its behalf" rather than a preoccupation with "purely family concerns and the noble vanity of ancient houses," and they required the rejection of "the particular vanity [of the humanists], with their passion for eloquence and their willingness to indulge in the most shameless adulation of the great."[2] These principles may seem to be more appropriate to the age of nationalism than to the age of the Common Market. But actually they are still very much alive. In fact, the most recent expression of them occurs in a textbook for university students of sixteenth-century political and historical thought published as late as 1973.[3] The fall of the Florentine Republic in 1530, the author affirms, represents "the last flicker of the attempt of Italians to save themselves from the excessive power of the Hapsburg emperor." All efforts at creative thoughts thereafter, he continues, were hopelessly compromised by an all-embracing "decadence" of Italian culture and by the inability of even the best historians to discern any higher purpose for their works than that of "praising the power and the political sagacity" of foreign and domestic despots.

Others of my predecessors seem rather to have been influenced by a critical principle exactly the opposite of the one held by the humanist historians themselves: not "What is badly written probably won't be read," but "What is consciously well written is probably not worth reading." This principle was put forth most eloquently in Eduard Fueter's *History of Modern Historiography*, first published in 1911. It is one that is expressive of a school of historiography that has long since disappeared. It is one that is also very difficult to reconcile with the results of most of the research dedicated to Renaissance humanism during the last thirty years. And it has accordingly been rejected by several recent authorities. According to Alonso Benito Sánchez, Fueter is guilty of having wholly misinterpreted the work of the sixteenth-century Spanish historians who tried to imitate Tacitus.[4] According to Carlo Dionisotti, his treatment of Biondo and Sigonio is characterized by "chronological and logical disorder," and the whole "first part of his book is so visibly disconnected and unbalanced that it is incredible that anyone mistakes it for a seaworthy ship."[5] According to Arnaldo Momigliano, Fueter and those who follow him completely misunderstand the place of rhetoric in literature. "If a historian wants to persuade and convert his reader," Momigliano asks, "why should he not use all the rhetorical devices...he considers suitable?... [After all,] rhetoric can cover incompetence and dishonesty. But so can paleography and statistics."[6]

Still, Fueter's work is even today the most comprehensive survey at least of individual Renaissance historians, and it was reprinted once again as late as 1970.[7] Hence, the principle put forward by Fueter is inevitably encountered by whoever needs to consult a convenient reference book on the subject. Indeed, it is still used as the basis for selecting texts for mention in general surveys of all European historiography. It is still evoked to reproach the humanist historians for having disguised modern cities as ancient cities and for having blinded their readers to the political realities of their times. It has permitted one modern historian to shift the blame for the historical inaccuracies he observed in Vasari from Vasari himself to "the literary (rather than scientific) concepts of historiography current in the sixteenth century." It has justified another in condemning the "facile moralism" of those humanists who sought "to conceal their sources under a flow of Ciceronian rhetoric." And it has led others to denounce the "rhetorical exercises" of those who were "concerned [primarily] with producing works of literary merit" and of those who were "more interested in style than in objective truth."[8]

I was therefore not surprised to discover also that the authorities differ widely among themselves about both the nature and the chronological limits of Renaissance historiography. To some, its principal aim is to present "in beautiful form" the "facts" cribbed from the chronicles of the Middle Ages. It is identified largely with its formal aspects: "narrations . . . embellished with speeches" and long texts divided into shorter "books" and introduced by "general reflections." And its contribution to subsequent historiography is consequently "limited" or even minimal: "humanism is only one of the roots from which modern historiography grew." Whatever cannot be comprehended within that definition must be classified as isolated works of non-Renaissance historiography that happened to have been written during the Renaissance. To this category belong, it seems, all of Guicciardini's historical works and all those of Machiavelli except the first book of his *Istorie fiiorentine* and his only truly "rhetorical history," the *Vita di Castruccio*. For they are identifiable not by form or style but by the European scope of their contents and by the involvement of their authors in practical politics.[9] This category may also include Flavio Biondo, who tried unsuccessfully to prevent his colleagues from "falling into rhetoric," and Paolo Sarpi, who resurrected Guicciardinian historiography early in the following century. But it does not include either Paolo Giovio or Uberto Foglietta. For although the first was admittedly "famous" in his day and although the second may be "worthy of particular consideration" even in our day, neither is "worthy of admiration," and both were adversely affected by the cultural decadence of the sixteenth century.[10]

To some authorities, on the other hand, the principal characteristic of Renaissance historiography is its acceptance of certain fundamental historical ideas. One such idea is "uniformitarianism, or a cyclical view of change in time," an idea to which most Renaissance historians were "almost slavishly" attached. Hence, Machiavelli, Guicciardini, and to some extent Vasari represent the culmination of, not exceptions to, the process by which conflicts between *Fortuna* and psychologically determined individuals, and between ascending and descending curves, were eventually resolved.[11] Another of these ideas is the primacy of fact, with which, it seems, all Renaissance historians were obsessed. As soon as "facts" came to be presented not in themselves alone but as manifestations of an "internal rhythm of life" and of "the organic character of reality"—as they were to some extent in the work of Bernardo Segni and much more consistently in that of Scipione Ammirato and Guido Bentivoglio—then Renaissance historiography gave way to a very different kind of historiography, that of the Baroque.[12]

Still another of these ideas is "secularization," or the exclusion of superhuman and supernatural forces from the historical process. Almost none of the Italian historians between Bruni and Ammirato ever admitted any but human and natural causes for the events they described. Hence, they are all members of the same school. Accordingly, Alberto Tenenti, in one of the most thorough surveys of Renaissance historical literature, has advanced its terminal date from the middle to the end of the sixteenth century. And Emanuella Scarano Lugnani, in a selection of texts representative of several different genres of historical writing, has included Filippo de'Nerli and Carlo Sigonio within the same category usually reserved for Guicciardini.[13] However, when secular interests were replaced by religious interests, when the description and explanation of human events was replaced by the defense of doctrine and the revelation of the role of divine forces in history, then Renaissance historiography gave way to an even more different kind of historiography, that of the Counter Reformation.[14] And this transformation was facilitated by popes and inquisitors of the Counter Reformation, who cooperated with the despots of the age in extinguishing the essential condition for the survival of humanism, free speech.[15]

To this diversity of judgment and definition corresponds a considerable lack of consensus concerning the relative importance of Italian historiography in the context of early modern European historiography as a whole. One of the two historians who have made the historiography of France so well known today credits Italians with having initiated the process that their French successors carried to completion; and he accordingly dedicates an opening chapter to Lorenzo Valla. But the other has traced what were once thought to have been the historiographical innovations of the eighteenth century back to France alone in the sixteenth century; and he accordingly leaves the Italians out.[16] One historian of German historiography has shown Flavio Biondo to have furnished the models used by the sixteenth-century German topographers. But another has limited Italian influence in Germany largely to the diffusion of the forgeries of Annio da Viterbo.[17] None of the current historians of English historiography is willing to admit any non-English influence on the texts they had studied. Hence the one Renaissance historian of England who happens to have been Italian has been isolated from the others precisely on the grounds of his nationality. The outburst of history writing characteristic of the age of Elizabeth has been traced back no further than the age of John Colet, when a "sense of history" suddenly emerged among a few English scholars. And the striking similarities between the work of William Camden and that of the Italian antiquaries of the age of Onofrio Panvinio have been relegated to the realm of the wholly fortuitous.[18]

This lack of consensus is apparent also on the more general question of the place of Renaissance historiography in the context of all the other elements of European culture, then and now. Hans Baron has insisted that the revolution in historical thought first apparent in the works of Bruni was one of the most lasting accomplishments of the age. Paul Oskar Kristeller has included historiography among the several new disciplines that distinguished Renaissance from medieval culture. And Eugenio Garin has credited the historians of the fifteenth century with having first introduced the notion of the historical contingency of law, philosophical propositions, and political institutions that has been characteristic of Western thought ever since.[19] But another student of the period has granted to the fifteenth century only the perception that written sources too might be products of history. The much more important discovery that the past can be the object of "connaissance médiate," he says, belongs solely to the age of Mabillon, the late seventeenth century.[20] Still another student of the period has placed the equally important discovery of a nexus between single events and corresponding historical periods no earlier than the age of Vico, the early eighteenth century.[21] One recent historian of classical scholarship has reduced the Italian Renaissance historiography to no more than four proper names, of which two are barely mentioned.[22] And others have eliminated it entirely either from the history of historical concepts or from the history of ideas about the nature of time.[23]

In order to overcome these difficulties, I decided to turn for help from my predecessors of the twentieth century to those of the eighteenth century, whom I remembered from my earlier studies of the Italian Settecento to have been better informed about all of Renaissance literature in general than most of their successors have been and probably ever will be. I combed through the immense biographical and bibliographical surveys of Giammatteo Mazzuchelli, of Francesco Antonio Soria, of Apostolo Zeno, of Filippo Argellati, and, above all, of Girolamo Tiraboschi in search of names, and I read through the equally imposing collections of Alessandro Aurelio Pelliccia, of Giovanni Gravier, of Joannes Georgius Graevius, and, above all, of Ludovico Antonio Muratori in search of texts. I then turned to the ponderous dictionaries and editions of their disciples of the nineteenth century—from those published in the early volumes of the *Archivio storico italiano* to those included in the second edition of Muratori's *Rerum Scriptores Italicarum*—as well as to the host of local and disciplinary periodical publications so profusely generated by the Italian academic world during the last hundred years. At the same time I set to work tracking down titles in the libraries to which I had ready access: the Regenstein and Newberry of Chicago, the Biblioteca Nazionale Centrale, the Riccardiana, and the Marucelliana of Florence, and, for a few titles I could not find in either Chicago or Florence, the libraries of Rome, Bologna, and Venice. And I soon realized that the quantity of historical literature produced during the Italian Renaissance was far greater than I had ever imagined.

This unforeseen explosion of my bibliography posed a serious question of organization. If I followed the format of Fueter, as have several recent students of certain aspects of this subject, I would end up with an enormous catalogue of single entries in which what was common to several historians would inevitably be lost amid frequently repetitive detail about each of them individually. If instead I followed a format like the one recently applied to certain aspects of German Renaissance historiography,[24] I would be forced to limit myself only to a few of many possible topics and to repeat the same list, not of ten or twenty, but of several hundred names every time I turned from one topic to the next. If, on the other hand, I followed the example of most of my immediate predecessors and based my theses on a selection of representative or qualitatively superior texts, I myself would become a victim of what I had perceived to be their chief weakness, and I would have to justify my selection of a part on the basis of the whole I did not yet know. I did, it is true, permit myself one limitation that I think is justified by the relative autonomy of Italian culture throughout the Renaissance: I excluded all the historical works produced by non-Italians outside Italy that could not be shown to be direct continuations of work begun by Italians inside Italy. I also permitted myself another limitation that can be justified only in terms of the exigencies of time and space: I admitted only those texts that had been printed either in the fifteenth and the sixteenth or in subsequent centuries, and I excluded all those texts still in manuscript that had not been the object of subsequent scholarly investigation. I readily admit that Pellegrino Prisciano's still unpublished history of Ferrara may be superior to some dry *chronichetta* that local patriotism or personal vanity transformed into a wedding-gift brochure sometime in the nineteenth century. But if I tried to track down in half the libraries of Europe even the unpublished manuscripts mentioned in

Kristeller's *Iter Italicum*, I would have had to triple the time I allotted to my research and to expand by at least a third the already formidable size of my book. And if I waited until the philologists finished digging up all the texts worthy of publication, I would never write the book at all, particularly now that printing costs have all but extinguished the four-century-old tradition of European text editing.

While my bibliography diminished on one side, however, it grew on the other. First, I found that the innovations of the humanist historians of the Renaissance were incomprehensible without some knowledge of the works of the ancient historians upon which they sought to pattern their own; and in order to judge how accurately they followed their models, I was obliged to acquaint myself with some of the considerable scholarly research that has recently been devoted to ancient historiography. Second, I found that the Renaissance historians were far more indebted to their medieval predecessors than might be apparent from their conscious rebellion against them; and I was therefore obliged also to consult some of the equally abundant scholarly literature on the subject of medieval historiography.[25] To be sure, I found medieval historiography to be very different from the humanist historiography of the Renaissance. It was at least potentially and often actually universal rather than local in geographical scope. It was limited chronologically only to the creation at one end and the Last Judgment on the other, not by the founding of a particular city or the termination of a particular war. And it was limited in subject matter only by what one writer could see, hear, or read about during the course of one lifetime. Moreover, medieval historians treated individual men as the passive spectators rather than as the active agents of historical change. They considered the realm of the secular to be important only to the extent that it was a reflection of the divine. And they could find no other connection between one event and another than what they might be able to deduce from the words either of ancient or of modern prophets. Moreover, medieval historiography was wholly independent, in character, in form, and in origins, from the whole body of ancient historiography that the Renaissance considered to be normative;[26] and it maintained this independence even when it occasionally borrowed elements from those few historical works of antiquity that gradually became available. Nevertheless, the medieval historians provided their Renaissance successors with much of the specific information about the centuries in which they had lived and written. In occasionally attempting to endow their narratives with what they thought to be literary elegance, they prepared the way for the humanists' restoration of history to the position it had enjoyed in antiquity as an autonomous branch of literature. Still more important, they developed a form of historical writing—a series of single events listed opposite a corresponding notation of dates in no other order than that of chronological succession—that continued to be used, by humanists themselves as well as by writers whose cultural formation was still basically medieval in content, throughout the period of the Renaissance.

I thus had to place the new kind of historiography that appeared in the several cities of Italy during the early fifteenth century against the background of a native historiographical tradition that in some cases went back as far as the eighth or ninth century. I had also to take into account the remnants of that tradition that continued to flourish well after the advent of humanism. In order to avoid a confusion between what I discovered to be not only successive but also contemporaneous forms of history writing, I have adopted a consistency in terminology somewhat more rigorous than that observable in ordinary usage, either then or since. I always refer to those historical works that follow a medieval model as *chronicles* or, when their style and language have been modified in accordance with humanist standards of writing, as *humanist chronicles*. I have taken into English the Italian terms that indicate the *continuation* in the hand of a *continuer* of a chronicle begun by someone else. Conversely, I always refer to those histories consciously written in imitation of an ancient model, or of an authoritative Renaissance imitation of an ancient model, as *humanist histories,* even when the authors in some passages revert to forms of writing that seem rather to be medieval in character. I then discovered that the kind of history written by the best known of the Renaissance historians, Bruni, Machiavelli, and Guicciardini in his earlier history of Florence, was only one of several that conformed to this basic definition of humanist history; and when referring to it specifically I always use the term *Livian,* or *Livian-Brunian* history, as an indication of what were the ultimate models for all histories of a single political community. Those accounts of a single event or of a single series of events that were written in imitation of Caesar I call *commentaries*. Those accounts of contemporary events in many different places that derive ultimately from Thucydides or Polybius I call *contemporary histories, world histories,* or *histories 'ipsius temporis,'* depending on their geographical scope. Those that extend from the earliest times to the present, more or less on a pattern derived from Justin or Orosius, I call *universal histories* or *histories 'ab orbe condito.'* Those that appear to be segments of any of these kinds corresponding to the lifetime or career of a single individual I call *biographical histories.*

Obviously, all these forms of history writing had to be included in a survey of Renaissance historiography as a whole. At the same time, some attention had to be given to three other disciplines which, although they remained independent of all the particular forms of humanist history proper, nevertheless shared with them the basic humanist principle of imitating ancient models. For they provided theses of historiographical importance or proposed alternate ways of understanding the past in relation to the present. To these I refer as *biography, antiquarian studies,* and *sacred* or *ecclesiastical history*.

Recognizing the regional or municipal character of much of Italian culture in the fifteenth century, I arranged the historians included in Books I and II according to the city of which they were citizens or residents, and the cities I arranged according either to their chronolgical priority in the development of humanist historiography or to the particular political problems that the historians were called upon to clarify or to solve. Recognizing the increasingly national character of Italian culture in the sixteenth century, I arranged the rest according to the kind of history they wrote, and I maintained a municipal organization only when a series of historians in one city all wrote basically the same kind of history.

Still, the vast number of authors and texts that had to be included posed a grave problem of method. I could not possibly in several lifetimes have read through all the immense number of volumes for which I had corresponding titles, and I had neither the facilities nor the talent for directing *travaux d'équipe*. The problem was further complicated by the absence of critical editions of the vast majority of the histories written in the sixteenth century: I was usually left on my own to grasp specific references, to identify plagiarisms or uncited sources, and to spot deliberate misrepresentations of fact. It was also complicated by the plethora of overedited texts of many of the histories written in the fifteenth century, which falls within the chronological limits defined by Muratori as the Middle Ages: I did not have the strength to read every word of introductions that are longer than the texts themselves and of footnotes that crowd the text off page after folio page. This problem I solved first of all by developing what I think is a fairly well-trained eye, one capable of skimming rapidly through a seemingly unending stream of unparagraphed prose and lighting on the one or two passages that illustrate or exemplify all the others. I solved the problem secondly by going beyond the often insincere statements of intentions put forth in prefaces and dedications to what is said about the authors and their lives and works in the many biographical dictionaries with which Italian literature has been abundantly illustrated during the five centuries between Lelio Gregorio Giraldi and the *Dizionario biografico degli Italiani*.

Admittedly, none of these solutions is wholly satisfactory. Some of the leading historians of the fifteenth century lived successively in two or more different cities, and many of those of the sixteenth century wrote voluminously in several different historical genres. Hence, what one historian wrote in a former place of residence is often presented as an introduction to what he wrote in another, and what others wrote—Paolo Giovio being the most notorious example—is scattered about in three or four different chapters. Furthermore, many of the historians themselves are still primary sources for the events they wrote about, and invariably much of what I say about what happened in Renaissance Italy really should be considered not as fact but as what the historians stated as fact. Similarly, even a well-trained skimmer cannot grasp what is readily evident to someone who reads in depth; and there is nothing I say about any single text that could not be modified or rejected after a more careful scrutiny. Finally, neither the biographers nor the text editors of the last five centuries are beyond reproach, not even Tiraboschi, who is occasionally guilty of errors and omissions; and anyone who has the patience to go into the archives in search of vital statistics is sure to find some mistake in what I say about all but those very few historians who have already been the object of detailed investigations.

Needless to say, I have taken some obvious steps to minimize these potential imperfections. I have omitted page numbers in my footnote references to articles in journals, and I invite others to do the same. For numbers of this sort can never be checked from memory, and anyone interested in the article in question can easily look it up in the table of contents of the respective volume. I have checked titles and publication dates for those works which at the moment of revision were no longer accessible to me in the printed catalogues of the British Museum and the Bibliothèque Nationale; and I have thus shifted the responsibility for the accuracy of my transcriptions from myself to the catalogues, even though I am perfectly aware that they are not impeccable either. I have made no pretense at presenting a full list of all the editions of all the texts I cite, and I usually refer only to the one I happen to have read. Nor have I sought to list all the scholarly studies of those texts that have been the object of subsequent investigation. I have instead given only the more recent ones or those which contain references to others I do not mention. Better yet, I have passed around earlier drafts of my manuscript to specialists in several of the specific fields it touches upon. I presented the last part of Chapter 10 to a seminar meeting of my department and parts of Chapter 11 to one of the famous seminars conducted by Arnaldo Momigliano at the University of Chicago. I was aided in the composition of Chapter 2 by the suggestions of Massimo Miglio, of Chapters 3 and 4 by those of Gherardo Ortalli (the current authority on Romagna chronicles), and of Chapter 16 by those of Mario Scaduto, S. J. Hans Baron and Hanna Gray read earlier versions of Chapter 1. Julius Kirshner read the penultimate version of Books I and II. John Woods read most of Chapter 12 and gave me a long lecture that the Venetian ambassadors could have profited from on the difference between Turks and Persians. T. C. Price Zimmermann read all of Book V and corrected my errors concerning Giovio. Lech Szczucki read all that I wrote about Eastern Europe and sent me to the Polish Academy in Rome to check names and bibliography. James Michael Weiss read Chapter 14 and pointed out several misreadings of the ancient biographers. All the chapters but the last were then combed over by two of the most exacting and well-informed students of Renaissance humanism, Riccardo Fubini and Anthony Grafton, whose tolerance of sloppiness is nonexistent and whose knowledge of several aspects of this subject far exceeds mine. If on occasion I have failed to make the corrections my critics indicated, it is not because I dare to disagree with them, but simply because I misunderstood their marginal comments.

To be sure, none of these precautions could fully succeed in freeing my treatment of so vast a subject from numerous errors of fact and judgment. It is therefore certain to be the delight of reviewers, most of whom are sure to question the value of the whole after noting all the deficiencies they are sure to discover in the parts they know something about. It is also certain to be the delight of future Ph.D.

candidates—if any are still left after the crisis that is now afflicting Renaissance studies in both Europe and America. For they will easily be able to catch their readers' attention with some variant of the phrase: "It is astonishing that a scholar of such pretensions should have the nerve to affirm that. . . ."

Still, after some eight or nine years I have invested in studying the historians of the Italian Renaissance, I must admit that I myself have benefited—and that I hope others will also benefit—from the chief lesson they have taught me: that history can be both aesthetically pleasing and politically *engagée* without ceasing to be scientifically accurate. I have also come to respect them, if not perhaps as the fathers, at least as the grandfathers of my profession. It was they who first insisted that knowledge about the past had to be discovered, not merely transmitted, and that it could be organized into compartments that correspond both to historical reality and to the conceptual framework of the human mind. Above all, it was they who first proclaimed, at least in modern times, that the effort required to obtain that knowledge was both rewarding to others and satisfying to themselves. And I hope I have been able to express my appreciation of their accomplishments by rescuing many of them from what they all held to be the worst of evils: unmerited oblivion.

I have done my best to realize the aim upon which the chief value of this book will depend: that of accounting for all the historians and all the historical works written within what, from the point of view of historiography, constitutes the chronological limits of the Italian Renaissance; and I am confident of having accounted for at least 90 percent of them. I am also confident that what I say about these works is not so incorrect that it cannot serve as a basis for future study. And in order to force those who would only consult my book also to read it, I have confined all matters of substance to the text alone, and I have mentioned only titles in the footnotes whenever the author's names are mentioned in the text. I have adopted a sixteenth-century rather than a twentieth-century format not in order to perpetrate an amusing anachronism, but because it is more suitable to the subject. Besides, a division into "Books" is no less logical than a division into "Parts," and a title that says what is in the book is decidedly less misleading than a catchy phrase followed by a dully monographic subtitle. I have departed from this format in only two major instances. I have placed the index not before, but after, the text, which is where readers today expect to find it. And I have omitted a formal dedication. Mrs. Regenstein is not particularly interested in being endowed with an illustrious family tree stretching all the way from Lake Michigan to the Aegean Sea. She probably does not care to be compared favorably with Trajan, Nicholas V, Lorenzo de'Medici, and Antonio Magliabecchi. And she certainly does not want to be charged with the responsibility of defending me against invidious reviewers and irate censors. The monument in Hyde Park that bears the name of her late husband is tribute enough to her sincere and efficacious support of the life of the mind among her fellow citizens. I need only add this brief expression of my own gratitude for having been able to do much of the research for this book among the comforts and amenities which that monument has provided me.

Unfortunately, the very nature of the subject has prevented me from adhering strictly to my heroes' principle of *utile-dulce,* and I admit that my prose more often reads like an imitation of Panvinio than of Bruni or Guicciardini. Moreover, notwithstanding the anecdotes I have occasionally borrowed from my sources, I fear that the absence of romance in my book—or at least of passages that are interesting and amusing in their own right—will detract somewhat from its interest. But if it is judged useful by those inquirers who desire a knowledge of a part of the Western cultural heritage that so far has been little known and often misunderstood, I will be content. Indeed, I will be content even if it is used only, as one of my readers thought it would be, as a substitute for Fueter and as a guide to Muratori. In fine, I have written my work not as an essay with which to win the applause even of the scholarly journals of the moment, but as a possession for the dozen or so scholars who will be forced to consult it each year until someone at last finds the time, the energy, and the patience to do the research all over again.

Chicago, 17 February 1979

BOOK I

THE BIRTH OF
HUMANIST HISTORIOGRAPHY

I

FLORENCE

Leonardo Bruni

LIKE MINERVA, HUMANIST HISTORIOGRAPHY WAS BORN FULLY GROWN.

When the last three books were finally presented to the Florentine Republic in 1449, the *Historiarum Florentini Populi Libri XII*[1] by LEONARDO BRUNI (c. 1370–1444) contained all the basic elements that were to identify its successors for the next century and a half. First of all, it was carefully patterned, in language, style, and exterior form, on recognized ancient models—chiefly on Livy's *History of Rome "ab Urbe Condita"*[2] and to some extent also on Thucydides' *History of the Peloponnesian War*, which Bruni had been one of the first Westerners to read in over a thousand years. Bruni's sentences reproduce Livy's somewhat free rendition of Ciceronian periods almost perfectly. His words come almost exclusively from the vocabulary of the late first century B.C., even to the point of rendering "Lombardy" as *Gallia Cisalpina*, translating "Baptistry of San Giovanni" as *Templum Martis* (which modern scholars say it never was), and hiding unavoidable technical and proper names beneath circumlocutions—like "the Other Party" for the Ghibellines. Events are recorded in chronological order, year by year; and numerical dates, which were unknown to the ancient Romans, are introduced only when Bruni wished to correct a previously accepted chronological error or when he could no longer expect his reader to count from one "the following year" to the next. But chronological order gives way to topical order whenever he thought additional information or an account of long-term consequences to be essential to the proper comprehension of a particular event. Thus the submission of Arezzo in 1336 is preceded by a recapitulation of the vicissitudes of Aretine domestic politics during the previous hundred years. Finally, each of the "books" into which his, like Livy's, history is divided, is organized in accordance with the thematic consistency of its contents. Book I ends in 1250, not only because the paucity of information about the previous centuries permitted only a relatively concise treatment, but principally because that date marked the death of Emperor Frederick II and the triumph of the Guelf party in Tuscany. Book VII begins in the middle of the same year, 1342, in which Book VI ends—with the expulsion of the Duke of Athens, and thus with the reversal, in Florence, of the typical northern Italian pattern of political development toward one-man rule. Book X opens with the outbreak of the "Milanese War"; and it ends with the truce of 1391, which put an end to the first phase of the war.

At the same time, Bruni freely departed from his models whenever they seemed to be inappropriate to his subject. Like most other Renaissance humanists, he looked upon models as guides, not as authorities, and he defined "imitation"—*imitatio*—as an incentive, not as an impediment, to originality. Occasionally he abandoned Livy and Thucydides for other ancient authors. His preface is reminiscent of that of Polybius. His first line, as well as his thesis about the corruption of the Roman Republic in its last years, echoes Sallust's *Conspiracy of Catiline*.[3] His sharp contrast between the creativity of republican regimes and the intellectual sterility of monarchies is obviously inspired by Tacitus. At other times, Bruni invested an authorized form, like set speeches, with a new function. He meant his speeches to be much more than what they often were in Livy, a practical application of Isocrates' prescription of history as an *opus oratorium maxime*. Never, even when they are admittedly contrived, do they openly defy credibility—as does, for instance, the speech of the survivor of Cannae in Livy's Book XXV. Some of them, indeed, are verbatim transcriptions or accurate paraphrases of written records, like the letters of Giangaleazzo Visconti in Book IX, of which the originals are still extant. Others of them serve to heighten the dramatic quality of particularly important moments. Still others permitted the author to editorialize—to introduce an ironic contrast between what ought to have happened and what in fact did happen. Or they permitted him to explain the general historical circumstances of a single event, which is what the Florentine exiles do in their lecture to King Manfredi about the origin of the Guelfs and the Ghibellines. But most of the speeches contain what for Bruni was the most important ingredient of history as a distinct literary genre: the *ratio,* or the causes, of the events recounted. Since he limited causality in history to the intentions, desires, passions, and personal idiosyncracies of the individual actors, the causes were most appropriately expounded in the very words that were, or that might have been, pronounced by the agent.

More important still, Bruni endowed the writing of history with a purpose that had been much less frequently emphasized in the historical works of antiquity: utility. History teaches prudence, he pointed out: by reading about what others have done before us, "we may more easily perceive what we should avoid and what we should pursue" in managing our own affairs. And it teaches political wisdom: by learning how given causes have produced given effects in the past, we in turn may be better able to produce the effects we desire in the future. If history was to be useful, it had above all to be "true"; and the discovery of the truth, which for Cicero had been secondary to the achievement of literary quality,[4] became for Bruni the historian's chief obligation. Rather than shrugging off with a Livian *dicitur* the more incredible myths preserved by tradition, Bruni set out to destroy them—particularly those myths that seemed to lend support to political policies he disapproved of, such as the founding of Florence by Julius Caesar, its destruction by Totila, and its rebuilding by Charlemagne. Similarly, he granted only a coincidental, never a causal, role to those extraordinary phenomena that could not be dismissed for want of reliable testimony—such as the instantaneous transmission of the news of a victory over the Aretines in 1289. He therefore introduced an important modification in the treatment of sources that he had observed in Livy. Rather than following one source for one event and then another for the next, and rather than simply changing the subject when contradictions among the sources became all too evident, he carefully checked what he read in his principal source against all the others. Thus, notwithstanding his proclivity for accepting uncritically the authority of the ancient historians, he became aware that they in turn were dependable only to the extent that their own sources supported them. And this awareness, according to today's authority on the history of classical scholarship, marks "the real beginning of historical criticism."[5] Bruni then supplemented what he took from narrative sources by looking up the relevant documents in the city archives—which is where he found, for instance, the texts of most of the laws and treaties he quotes at length. When his main source for more recent times, the chronicles, gave out (as he found they did for the years after 1385), he turned to state papers, *scritture di palagio,* and to the private papers of the principal Florentine families, to whom he appealed for assistance through his banker, Palla di Nofri Strozzi.[6]

History for Bruni was also mongraphic. That is, it was organized about a single theme—in this case, the rise of Florence from an insignificant Roman colony to a great power. And it rigorously excluded all matters not clearly relevant to that theme. He thus began with the foundation of the city; and he ended with the death of Giangaleazzo Visconti in 1402—an event which, in his opinion, radically altered the relation of Florence to the other Italian states and made possible the outburst of its cultural creativity in the following decades. From the abundant information available even in the Florentine chronicles about other parts of Europe he included only those events, like the accession of King Roberto d'Angiò (Robert of Anjou) in Naples and the Great Schism of 1378, which had forced Florentine governments to alter their foreign policy. And he mentioned the arts and letters only in their role as the aesthetic counterparts of the political and military might of the city. Moreover, history could be concerned only with those matters over which men acting collectively were then thought to exercise some control, namely, politics. Economics, Bruni assumed, belonged in the realm of purely individual endeavor; and since the bank crashes of the 1340s did not produce any notable change in the constitution, he mentions them just in passing. Natural disasters were independent of human volition; and he described even the Black Death largely in order to explain why nothing "worthy of memory" occurred in the year 1348. The intervention of divine or supernatural forces taught nothing about the behavior of men; and the nearest he came to a nonhuman cause in history, or even to Livy's Stoic notion of Rome's destiny, was in the assumption (which he shared with almost everyone in his age) that the founders of a city can impress certain indelible characteristics upon all its successive inhabitants.

Finally, history was didactic; and whenever the events themselves, or the speeches of the protagonists, failed to make the lessons of history perfectly clear, Bruni did not hesitate to point them out. Election by lot, he noted, which was introduced in response to a particular political crisis in 1323, ended by promoting mediocrity in office. The effects of the law of 1345 against honorary titles simply proved the validity of the maxim: "Never should anything be considered useful in a republic that discourages the [quest for] dignities." And the expansion of the domain was best promoted by promising peace rather than by threatening violence to prospective subjects—which, he pointed out, is how the Florentines managed to subdue Pistoia in 1334. But in order to be didactic, history had also to be eloquent. That is, it had to be written in such a manner that its intended audience would willingly read it and even more willingly apply its implied and explicit lessons in the form of concrete legislative acts. No one ever has questioned the eloquent qualities of Bruni's prose. But if it ever occurred to Bruni himself that his classical Latin might be something less than comprehensible to the Florentine merchant bankers he was writing for, he apparently let the question drop out of respect for the other declared purpose of history: that of enshrining great deeds in a lasting literary monument. The acts of men of letters could be recorded in the vernacular, which is what he used in his lives of Dante, Boccaccio, and Petrarch. But the acts of men of state and arms had to be recorded in what was still held to be the most lasting, although not necessarily the most expressive, language. When, finally, the didactic purpose was recognized to be no longer fully compatible with Bruni's definition of the monumental purpose, the text was duly translated. And it was in Donato Acciaiuoli's equally eloquent, although somewhat free, translation, which ran through five editions after the first one of 1473, that most readers had access to the *Historiae,* rather than in the twenty-five-odd manuscript copies of the original, which was not printed until 1610.[7]

To be sure, this attempt to adapt ancient models to the exigencies of a later age did not immediately produce history according to nineteenth- or even according to sixteenth-century standards. On the one hand, it prevented Bruni from recognizing the degree to which the motives and aspirations of individual men were determined by the social groups they belonged to. The family, or *casata,* which modern historians have identified as the most cohesive group in Florentine society of the fourteenth century, he largely ignored. Of the economic interests that often pitted one family against the other, he said not a word. He overlooked even the guilds, and with them the very corporate nature of the Florentine constitution, which alone would have given meaning to the reform program of his chief hero, Gian Della Bella; and when, in his account of the revolt of the Ciompi, he could no longer overlook them, he dismissed them, wholly incorrectly, as mere vehicles of mob rule. Bruni artificially divided Florentine society into three social classes: the nobility of feudal origin, the *infima multitudo* of artisans, shopkeepers, and day laborers, and, in between them, a middle class of big merchants and bankers. The second of these "classes" he consistently judged unfavorably—which may be why he passed over the revolt of the Ciompi as if it had been merely a momentary and fortuitous interruption in the normal course of history. The third he always judged favorably —which may be why he could give no explanation for the expulsion of the Alberti in the late 1380s.

On the other hand, this form of history writing led Bruni frequently to attribute to a collective person, "the Florentines," actions which were really due to the ambitions of single men or groups. By "Florentines," he usually meant the incumbents of the urban magistracies constitutionally responsible for making and executing policy on behalf of the commune. But he endowed them with a constancy of purpose and ideology that their brief tenures could never have permitted. He thus overlooked the internal rivalries that all too often kept them at each other's throats, as Machiavelli was to point out. He ignored the abundant evidence in his archival sources for just the opposite of his thesis about unanimity in foreign policy during the Visconti wars. And he attributed those signs of dissension that he could not avoid wholly to outside interference in domestic affairs. Consequently, he was at a loss to explain the spectacular reversal of traditional foreign policy in the 1370s, when Florence was transformed from the most faithful ally of the Papacy into its most determined enemy. Nor could he explain the tardiness with which the government actually reacted to what he defined in retrospect as the most dangerous crisis in the history of the republic: the occupation of Bologna by Visconti troops in 1402.

Stranger still, Bruni said nothing at all about the office of chancellor, the appointed, professional officer who actually guaranteed most of what there was of continuity between one short-lived political government and the next. Yet that was the very office which he had held briefly in 1411 and which he was to hold again from 1427 until his death; and it was the very office from which his mentor, Coluccio Salutati (who is not even mentioned in the text), had worked out the republican ideology of which the *Historiae* were to be one of the most eloquent expressions. He consistently defined as the government of the people what was actually an oligarchy of an increasingly small number of old, established families, and he showed not the slightest interest in the vast majority of the population, which was barred from all political activity except paying taxes. He continued to identify city and state (partially because his classical Latin did the same thing with the word *civitas*), even though, at least after 1406, the Florentine government had become as much a "lord" of neighboring subject cities as the Visconti had ever been. Consequently, he failed to find the least premonition in previous Florentine history for what is now recognized as the most important political change of his own time: the evolution of a government by "corporations" into a government by an "elite," and the transformation of a semiconstitutional oligarchy into a de facto principate. Bruni himself seems to have become conscious of this failure. For with Book VIII, which was written after the triumphant return of Cosimo de' Medici in 1434, his notation of the erroneous decisions of Florentine governments increased markedly in frequncy. But he always attributed these errors to "the Florentines" as a whole, never to the other than patriotic motives of any one group of them, and never to any possible flaw in the structure of government.

At the same time, Bruni's formula for writing history enabled him to arrive at a completely new vision of the relation among the events of the past and between the past as a whole and the present and future. He was the first to evaluate positively the ancient Etruscans, or at least to consider them something more than just the obscure religion teachers of the early Romans. He was the first (at least since Tacitus, whom he read on the subject), to evaluate the Roman Empire negatively and to portray the establishment of the principate as the death blow, rather than as the culmination, of the republic:

> How many of the great lights of the Republic were extinguished! How many great citizens were taken from the city! . . . How much crime, how many prescriptions! (p. 14)

He was also the first discoverer of weaknesses in the empire of the Antonines— weaknesses like the suppression of free speech and local self-government, which, he noted, not even well-intentioned emperors like Trajan were capable of overcoming. He was the first to proclaim the complete demise of the empire in the fifth century ("Occidentale cessavit Imperium") and to separate it generically from the empire of Charlemagne.

Thus history turned out to be composed not of a fortuitous succession of isolated events but of distinct epochs, each of which could be described in terms of an origin, growth, and eventual decline, and each of which could be fully explained through the wisdom and the folly of the men who lived in it. Each epoch in turn was coincident with a particular political community. It could thus be evaluated qualitatively by the degree to which the respective community had achieved the twofold goal of internal tranquillity and individual creativity—by the degree, that is, to which it enabled all of its citizens, under the protection of just and equitable laws, to develop their own individual talents to the fullest. At least one community had approached this goal in the past: the Roman Republic before the conspiracy of Catiline. And the last two centuries of the Roman Republic thus constituted one of the great ages of world history. But only one community, the Florentine Republic, had yet shown signs of eventually being able to achieve it fully. And the early fifteenth century A.D. thus constituted the second great age, one which had already equalled the political achievements of the first century B.C. and which was still progressing upward on an ascending curve. For the Florentines alone had managed to construct the only kind of state in which the goal could be realized. This state was a cross between a medieval commune and a Greek polis. It invested power in a fairly large (although Bruni never said *how* large) number of responsible citizens. And it made lawmakers and subjects equally subservient to the law. Moreover, only Florentines had gradually become conscious of the irreconcilability of any other form of government with their own—whether it was the Roman Empire of antiquity, the universal Christian Empire of the medieval political theorists, or the territorial tyrannies of fourteenth-century Italy. When, then, with the restoration of the mercantile oligarchy in the 1380s, the perfect constitution had been achieved, and when, in the last phases of the struggle against Giangaleazzo Visconti, the self-consciousness of the citizens as the defenders of "the liberties of Italy" had finally matured, the goal was already in sight. All that remained to be done was to beat off the last external aggressors, Ladislao of Naples and Filippo Maria Visconti of Milan.

History, then, was exclusively political history. That is, it was concerned solely with the collective acts of a political community. For they alone could be plotted along a progressive or regressive line with respect to the final goal. As a consequence, the achievement of the goal meant the abolition of history—that is, the replacement of collective or political deeds by purely private deeds, like making money and cultivating virtue, which were not the concern of historians. Thus by urging the rulers of Florence in his own day to complete what their ancestors had so felicitously begun, Bruni was in effect hastening the day when the city would "be quiet"—*conquiescere*—as it had been momentarily in the few years after 1250 and, again, after 1350. And from that day on, his services as a historian would no longer be required.

The Chroniclers

Humanist historiography was thus born fully grown. But at the same time it was born from the union of two very illustrious parents.

The first of these parents was the chronicle. This form of prehumanist historical writing had begun, over two hundred years earlier, as a simple list of city officials. But it had quickly grown into an instrument for the expression of civic pride—one which sought to magnify the events of the present by placing them in the context of the events of the distant past. The anonymous *Chronica de Origine Civitatis* and the *Gesta Florentinorum* of SANZANOME explained the capture of Fiesole—an event which marked the beginning of Florence's predominance among the cities of northern Tuscany—as the last act in an age-old contest between Roman-Florentine civilization and Etruscan-Catilinarian-Gothic barbarism.[8] Toward the end of the thirteenth century this context was further broadened through contact with the universal chronicles of the High Middle Ages. An obscure Franciscan named THOMAS TUSCIS had used these chronicles effectively, while relaxing in Florence between busy diplomatic missions, in order to place "the massacre of the Ghibellines in Tuscany" that he had witnessed into a list of events all over Christendom extending from the time of Augustus to that of Rudolph of Hapsburg.[9] Other Florentines then discovered that the growth of Florence could now be fitted into the standard medieval system of dating by popes and emperors; and the origins of Florence could be deduced from Sallust and Orosius rather than from the romantic popular legends preserved in the *Libro fiesolitano,* the "Deeds of Caesar," and the *Brieve memoria del nacimento di Firenze,* which were accordingly relegated to the rank of sources of inspiration for poets and novelists. The result was the composition of a number of chronicles that were to provide an important source of information for the later humanist historians. The series was inaugurated by RICORDANO MALISPINI (after 1270), who furnished Dante with many of the specific references he included in the *Divine Comedy,* and by DINO COMPAGNI (1260–1324), whose "marvelous precision" is still commended by modern historians of the age.[10] And it culminated, in 1350, in what was then and has ever since been acclaimed as a masterpiece of the genre, the chronicle of GIOVANNI VILLANI (1276–1348).[11]

This outburst of chronicle writing may have been a reflection of the peculiar social and political conditions of thirteenth- and fourteenth-century Florence, conditions that permitted a certain degree of upward social mobility to industrious businessmen and that encouraged criticism of the policies of even the most firmly entrenched regimes.[12] It was certainly stimulated by what seems to have been a peculiarly Florentine custom: that of keeping domestic diaries, or *ricordanze.* These diaries were intended strictly for the use of the diarist and his descendants. They were a means of keeping track of the sale and purchase of property and of the birth, death, and marriages of members of the family; they served also to pass on to future generations an appreciation of the achievements and a knowledge of the accumulated political and moral wisdom of the family's ancestors. Yet within the limits of the individual family, the *ricordanze* were considered sufficiently valuable to warrant their being continued by successive hands for as long as two centuries, and they were occasionally copied out into another ledger in order to facilitate their consultation.[13] A few of the diaries originated as notarial records—e.g., those of ser Naddo (or Naldo) da Montecatini and of Nofri di Piero "dei Riformagioni."[14] But most of them seem to have evolved from businessmen's account books, an evolution that is particularly clear in the records of the grain dealer Domenico Lenzi, who mixed moral reflections with an almost complete list of grain prices from 1320 to 1335.[15] All of them soon adopted a standard scheme: an invocation to the Trinity, the Virgin, and to John the Baptist, a statement of intent by the author, a retrospective genealogy of his family, and then a series of dates in the left margin corresponding to the chronological annotations on the rest of the page. The diaries also multiplied in number until, according to one recent authority,[16] at least one was kept by every even modest family in the city; according to another authority,[17] those subsequently published represent only a small fraction of the hundreds still in manuscript.

While some of the diaries remained strictly domestic in scope,[18] and while a few of them—like that of the Cerchi—concentrated on real estate to the exclusion of the family's extensive commercial affairs, most of them followed the business interests of the diarists into the four corners of Christendom. As a "véritable livre de chevet du mercator," in the words of one recent historian,[19] they included not only what the merchant-authors observed themselves about what happened from day to day in the market and palace of Florence, but also what their agents reported to them about politics, plagues, and prices all the way from Flanders to the Levant. Thus today the diaries have made Florence one of the richest mines for the new discipline of "family history,"[20] and two of them have been considered such faithful accounts of the mores and institutions of the age that they have been translated into English and published in paperback.[21] In the fourteenth and fifteenth centuries, they strengthened the parallel tradition of chronicle writing in part by instilling into the diarists an appreciation for the temporal succession of events. In some cases, indeed, diarists actually turned into chroniclers. One anonymous diarist forgot all about his domestic concerns after the first few pages and thereafter wrote exclusively about the affairs of the city.[22] Benedetto Dei included a glowing description of the city in a eulogy of "the most glorious and powerful Florentine people" for the benefit of potential readers abroad.[23] And one Griso di Giovanni Griselli developed a form of writing very similar to that generally used in the sixteenth century for official reports of diplomatic missions.[24]

Chronicles were not yet history, at least not according to the new definition of history that was to arise from the work of Bruni and his successors. None of them was ever meant to be a work of literature, not even those which, in the opinion of posterity, merit that title. For literature was still thought to be a product of the arts faculties of the schools and hence not the proper concern of the nonacademic businessmen who wrote the chronicles (Green). Hence, one of the most progressive effects of chronicle writing was completely unintended—namely, the apparently conscious refusal to accede to the Latinizing fashions in prose style in the early fifteenth century, and consequently the preservation of the Trecento vernacular in writing until such time as it could be rescued by the linguists of the sixteenth century.[25] Similarly, none of the chroniclers ever suggested that a study of the past might enable their readers to create something better in the future. A few of them were of rather less than patrician origins. BARTOLOMEO DI MICHELE DEL CORAZZA was a wine merchant with a farm in the Mugello, but he never attained any office higher than that of consul of his guild.[26] AMARETTO MANELLI, although a wealthy merchant, never took part in public affairs, and he interrupted his chronicle when he was called to take charge of his company's branch in Valencia.[27] GIOVANNI DI PAGOLO MORELLI was conscious of having risen only to the penultimate level of Florentine society. Yet most of them were closely associated, either as actual or, as in the case of BUONACCORSO PITTI,[28] as temporarily suspended members of the "elite" which, according to the most recent authority on late medieval Florence, gradually monopolized political power in the decades after 1380.[29] Hence, much as some of them might disagree in their judgments of specific issues (Pitti and MARCHIONNE DI

COPPO STEFANI, or DI STEFANO BUONAIUTI, as Palmarocchi says he should be called, [30] were actually imprisoned for "seditious statements"), they were adamant in their resistance to any notion of progressive change, and they were unanimous in their condemnation of the perpetrators of the most notorious attempt to effect such change, the Ciompi, whose occasional merits were to remain unrecognized until the time of Machiavelli.

Moreover, none of the chronicles was ever considered to be the peculiar creation of an individual mind, not even those that contain considerable information about the author, and not even those which remain closest in form to the *ricordanze*. IACOPO SALVIATI kept careful track of "all the things that have been and will be done by me"; but anyone who knew him could have written it as well as he did, for there is not a trace of personal reflection about any of his various political and commercial ventures in his work.[31] Morelli himself stopped writing in 1437; but his heirs continued to add entries—with no formal indication of change in authorship—for another ninety years. Authorship was thought of as a basically passive operation—one which recorded events rather than imposing a conceptual or aesthetic order upon them. Some of the chronicles are thus wholly anonymous,[32] and one of them is called the "Minerbetti Chronicle" only because its eighteenth-century editor arbitrarily gave it that name.[33] Almost all of them include passages and even whole chapters that are actually copied word for word from other chronicles—with the result that modern editors sometimes have difficulty in deciding who plagiarized whom.[34] Many of them are the work of several successive authors, each of whom took up without a break where his predecessor had left off and then yielded to a successor without any fear of being altered or deformed by continuation in another hand.

Furthermore, the chronicles were exclusively chronological in organization. One event was linked to the next solely by the proximity of their respective dates, and the lack of continuity among them was often emphasized by the introduction of title headings like "How the Duke of Lancaster Passed Over into Spain" and "How the Duke of Milan Died" at the beginning of each paragraph. Whatever schemes of periodization were occasionally used did not come from an observation of similarities among the events themselves. Rather, they came from the Six Ages of the world or the Four Monarchies prophesied in the Book of Daniel, none of which reached much farther than the first centuries after the founding of the city. Sometimes they came from astrology, even though Giovanni Villani was somewhat hesitant in admitting what contemporary science assured him to be infallible portents of another periodic intervention of a wrathful God in human affairs. More often they came from the traditional means of dividing up the penultimate age of the world by the reigns of popes and emperors, few of which happened to coincide with any observable pattern of events in purely Florentine history.

Consequently, all the chronicles were universal in time, space, and subject, even those that began *in media res* rather than with Adam or Noah, and even those that were in fact limited to specific events or moments, like the revolt of the Ciompi.[35] All of them assumed that basic modes of life remain constant from one age to the next, and none of them was at all aware of the anachronism involved in identifying the Gauls of the fourth century B.C. as "French" or calling Jugurtha the king of "Morocco." All of them freely mixed matters that were pertinent to Florence with matters that were pertinent only to Antwerp, London, or Constantinople, and none of them ever considered the possibility of isolating a single political commonwealth as the subject of special investigation. All of them included astronomical, meteorological, economic, supernatural, and purely personal events side by side with the political and military events that alone were to interest the humanist historians, and none of them made any qualitative or generic distinctions among what late-twentieth-century historians would call the *faits divers* of *histoire événementielle*. Since none of them had any reason for terminating at any moment before the Last Judgment, all of them broke off abruptly with matters that the humanist historians were to consider relatively unimportant: SIMONE DELLA TESA's purchase of a house in 1346,[36] MATTEO VILLANI's (d. 1363) announcement of an invasion of crickets in 1363,[37] Stefani's observation of a solar eclipse in 1385.[38] Since none of them found any significant pattern of change in the past, none of them could reasonably make any prediction of what might happen in the future—except occasionally for such purely marginal reflections like those in the *Istorie pistolesi* on the rapid deterioration of the world in recent times.[39]

Finally, the chroniclers wrote for purposes very different from those of the historians. "Minerbetti" wanted only to remind himself of those things of the past "that I have enjoyed so much talking about." Morelli wanted to pass his leisure hours agreeably while informing the other members of his family of what he had done. Dino Compagni hoped to induce "the heirs of prosperous times to recognize God as the source of all good things" and "to weep for themselves and for their children . . . over the pride, madness, and ambition that have undone this noble city." Giovanni Villani sought chiefly to show his fellow citizens how to "adopt virtues and avoid vices" and thus better serve the commonwealth.[40] But since the effectiveness neither of entertainment nor of moral counsel depended upon the veracity or the proper understanding of the event recounted, few of them sought to establish causal connections between one event and the next, and none of them anticipated the rules eventually proposed by the humanists for distinguishing between fact and legend. True, they recognized that purely oral tradition was not necessarily binding,[41] and some of them quietly omitted the fantastic stories handed down by the twelfth-century mythmakers about the amorous adventures of Catiline and the military exploits of the Italic founder of Troy, Dardanus. But they assumed that what had been written down was reliable; and whether the writer was a historian, like Sallust, or a poet, like Vergil, or a patriot, like Sanzanome, made little difference. Hence, they usually contented themselves with recording the report of an event rather than the event itself and with recording it under the date on which they learned of the event rather than under the date on which it actually occurred. Whenever they felt impelled, for moralistic or for political reasons, to offer an explanation of what was reported, they never had any trouble finding one in the omnipotent and incomprehensible hand of God or in the omnipresent and tireless hand of the Devil.

Chronicle, then, was not history. Nevertheless, the chronicles of the fourteenth century made an indispensable contribution to the rise of history in the fifteenth century. They did so first of all by providing an easily available, abundant, and often accurate record of what had happened, at least for the years in which they had actually been written. Indeed, their accuracy has frequently been sustained by modern historical research, and, in at least one case, Giovanni Calvacanti's description of the functioning of the oligarchy at the turn of the fifteenth century,[42] it has proven to have been superior to that of subsequent humanist history. All Bruni had to do, for much of what he included after his first book, was to recast in accordance with his new linguistic and critical standards what he found written in the Villanis, Stefani, and Pitti, who were in fact his principal sources for the fourteenth century. The chronicles also contributed to the rise of history by anticipating certain aspects of its form and style. Giovanni Villani came close to a periodic concept when he decided to break his otherwise undifferentiated succession of miscellaneous events in the crucial year 1292. "This alteration in [the structure of] the state . . . had many and diverse consequences," he noted; "and so the reader will not be surprised that we have begun a new book at this point" (VIII,i). FILIPPO VILLANI realized that the chronicle he inherited from Matteo might serve as the basis for another form of narration, one which would "describe the material so prepared in a more polished manner"; and he submitted the text of his own *De Famosis Civibus* for linguistic and stylistic corrections to the leading Latinist of the day, Coluccio Salutati.[43] GINO DI NERI CAPPONI went still further.[44] His day-by-day narrative of the Ciompi revolt, of which he was a witness, begins, in good chronicle form, with a list of the *priori* for 1378, and it incorporates verbatim the first list of demands presented by the insurgents. But, in what was soon to become standard historical form, many of the more important issues are discussed in direct-discourse speeches, and the narrative is strictly limited in time and substance to the episode announced in the title.

Yet the most important contribution the chronicles made to history consisted in providing it with some of its major theses. All the chronicles were to some extent expressions of Florentine civic pride or apologies for one or the other of the various Florentine political factions. Still, some of the chroniclers managed to place the recent rise of Florence into a broader historical context—Giovanni Villani, for instance, who claimed to have first been inspired to write while meditating on the ruins of Rome during the Jubilee of 1300.[45] Some of them managed to give Florentines credit for what was usually attributed to God or the stars: Stefani, for instance, reduced to internal party strife what Villani had described as a local reflection of universal strife, and he elevated the human agents of history into credible, individual men. Finally, one of them, GREGORIO (or GORO) DATI (1362–1435), in his *Istoria* of the years 1380–1406 (but written after 1409), arrived at a conception of Florence's historical mission that was similar to Bruni's. Dati was still interested chiefly in "memorable deeds," and for him the festivities for John the Baptist's Day in Florence were "memorable" enough to take up more than half of one book. He was still impressed by portents and miracles, such as those that had certified the validity of the election of Pope Urban VI. He was still capable of being sidetracked onto purely legal and theological questions, like the right of the church to possess temporal domains. In other words, he was still a chronicler, not a historian. But when he turned Villani's hero, Caesar, into a villain, and when he turned Minerbetti's villain, Giangaleazzo Visconti, into the most recent incarnation of ancient tyranny, he showed that Florentines were not just the modern heirs of the virtues of the ancient Romans. They were, and always had been, the stalwart defenders of political liberty and republican government against the age-old threat of slavery, tyranny, and universal empire.[46]

The Heritage of Petrarchan Humanism

Chronicle, then, was one of history's ancestors. The other, equally illustrious, although posterior in time and completely separated in its origins from the first, was early Renaissance humanism, the school of classical scholarship and ethical and aesthetic inquiry inaugurated by Petrarch in the 1340s, carried on by Boccaccio and Salutati in the last half of the fourteenth century,[47] and further elaborated by Salutati's disciples in Florence in the first decades of the fifteenth century.

What the early humanists contributed to history was, first of all, a sense of change through time and a general scheme on which change might be plotted. This contribution was largely one of their own devising. They found very little precedent for it either in the medieval chronicles, which they studiously ignored,[48] or in the works of the ancient historians, which they read with alacrity. They seem to have come upon it rather as a result of reflecting upon the differences between what they read about the distant past and what they observed in their own times. The culture, customs, and institutions of ancient Greece and Rome, they realized, had flourished, declined, and finally disappeared; and any hope of returning to them or resurrecting them was utterly in vain. "We have changed [since antiquity]," Petrarch sighed; "and all that we see about us seems to have changed as well."[49] The only way anyone could emerge from the thousand-year age of darkness that had followed the demise of antiquity was either to isolate himself from it, as Petrarch suggested, or, as Salutati and later Bruni proposed, to learn from the ancients how to engender a new great age of their own.

The early humanists thus hit upon the division of history into ancient, medieval, and modern that was to become standard for the next five centuries. They also hit upon a justification for the study of history that was largely foreign to the works of the ancient historians available to them: history, they noted, could be of great assistance in encouraging those who read it to realize fully all their intellectual and spiritual capabilities. At the same time, they dug out of the ancient rhetoricians another purpose somewhat similar to the one proposed independently by Giovanni Villani: history could also act as a stimulant to morality. "The knowledge of what has been done [in the past]," insisted Salutati, is one of the best means for "stirring up princes, teaching peoples, and instructing individuals about what should be done [in the present]." But the stimulant became operative through a particular quality of history that Villani said nothing about: its elegance. "Nothing is more ornate, nothing more elegant in expression," said Salutati, "and [hence] nothing is so capable of moving while delighting the spirit." History promoted morality not by providing an occasion for marginal moral reflections, as it did for the chroniclers. Rather, it assumed that men are more apt to do what they see other men have done than they are to put into practice the "tedious" precepts of ethical treatise writers, particularly those of Aristotle. It therefore proposed, in an attractive literary garb, "the example of the illustrious kings, nations, and men for the imitation...of posterity."[50]

At the same time, the humanists drew attention to the classics of ancient historiography as models for the way history ought to be written. Petrarch began the laborious process of recovering and correcting the surviving texts of Livy that was to continue well into the following century, and Boccaccio popularized his efforts by translating the first ten books into the Florentine vernacular.[51] Then, by demoting all the authors of antiquity to the rank of fallible human beings, they demonstrated that history could be written just as successfully in modern times as it had been in ancient times. The ancients were not immune to errors of fact, Petrarch pointed out after checking their geographical descriptions with his own observations. Nor were they immune to errors of judgment: the motives that Sallust attributed to Caesar, he noticed, did not always correspond to what was known of Caesar's actions. None of them was complete: what Livy said about Scipio had to be supplemented with what Suetonius and Valerius Maximus said about him. And some of them occasionally let personal or political considerations obscure the truth, as even Livy did when he acquiesced to the vanity of Augustus. Indeed, there was no reason why modern men could not even surpass the ancients as historians, particularly since they could begin where the ancients had left off, without having to start from scratch with a wholly new form of literary expression. All they had to do was recognize the ancient historians, rather than the chroniclers, as models of historical writing and then use the chroniclers for the same purpose that the chroniclers had used the ancient historians: as sources of information.

Yet the early humanists never got around to writing history themselves. Petrarch's *Rerum Memorandarum Liber* of 1343–45, which comes closest to history in its content, is actually a collection of anecdotes arranged, according to its "model," Valerius Maximus, under such headings as "leisure" *(otio)* and "solitude."[52] Similarly, Petrarch's *De Viris Illustribus,* vastly different though it may be from its nearest late-medieval predecessor, is really a series of disconnected biographies in which the moral and literary purposes of history are isolated from the narrative;[53] and the most famous of his biographies, that of Scipio, was chiefly intended as a factual underpinning for his epic poem, *Africa.*[54] Neither Petrarch nor his immediate successors worked out any other criterion for resolving the discrepancies they noticed among the ancient historians than a well-cultivated, but still rather subjective, sense of the probable. They were therefore in no position to rewrite what the ancients had already written about. At the same time, they were discouraged from writing about later periods. Most of them thought of themselves as still living in the second, or post-ancient age of the world. And their occasional professions of confidence in a better age yet to come usually got no farther than Petrarch's ineluctable cycles:

> vicissitudo temporum suos cursus recursusque peragit, nunquam permanens.[55]

Moreover, many of them took seriously Livy's invitation to use history as a way not of solving the problems of the present, but of escaping from them. "It is over these small remains [of your work]," Petrarch wrote in his letter to Livy, "that I toil whenever I want to forget these regions, these times, and these customs. . . . As I read, I seem to be living in the company of Scipio Africanus, Laelius, Fabius Maximus, Brutus, and Decius. And, if it were my happy lot to possess them entire, from what other great names would I not seek solace for my wretched existence . . . in this wicked age!"[56]

The early humanists lacked neither the ability nor the desire to write history. What they lacked was the recognition that other times and other places than those of the ancient Greeks and Romans were worth writing about. That defect could not be remedied until humanism, which had resurrected ancient historiography, could be brought together with communal patriotism, which had engendered the chronicle. And that was the work of Leonardo Bruni.

Bruni was first of all a humanist. Even as an adolescent he had become so proficient in Latin that he attracted the attention of the leader of the Florentine intellectual community, Coluccio Salutati, who became his closest friend and first mentor. Soon after the arrival, in 1396, of Manuel Chrysoloras, the first teacher of classical Greek in the West for over a millennium, he became so proficient in Greek as well that he could continue himself what Chrysoloras had begun; and he thus set in motion a wave of text-hunting and text-translating that by the end of the fifteenth century was to recover for Latin Christendom most of the surviving corpus of ancient and patristic Greek literature. Indeed, it was as the greatest living authority on ancient literature rather than as a historian that Bruni was best known to his contemporaries. His chief literary activity in the first three decades after reaching maturity consisted of translating into Latin as many as possible of the Greek books he had been the first to read—into a clear, elegant, classical Latin, that is, one free of neologisms, transliterations, and technical terms, and thus perfectly intelligible to the ordinary, non-professional Latin-reading audience for which Petrarch had written.[57] Parts of Plutarch, Xenophon, Demosthenes, and Basil were completed as early as 1403. Then followed a selection of orations from the *Iliad,* the early Platonic dialogues (1405 and 1424), and finally, from 1414 through the 1420s, the *Ethics,* the pseudo-*Economics,* and the *Politics* of Aristotle, which rapidly replaced the medieval translations as authoritative school texts all over Europe.

Bruni's chief purpose as a man of letters was to make accessible to other Westerners all the vast amount of new information about antiquity that he had acquired through his knowledge of Greek. It was this purpose, rather than the consideration of a specifically historical problem, that first led him to history. He found in Xenophon a full narrative of the political history of the fourth century B.C., which hitherto had been known only as the age of Plato and Aristotle. He therefore composed a Latin paraphrase of the *Greek History,* identifying as best he could the proper names, describing rather than naming those Greek political terms for which there was no Latin equivalent, and adding a concluding paragraph at the end, where Xenophon simply broke off, to suggest a thematic unit for the whole work (from the supremacy of Athens to the supremacy of Thebes).[58] He then found in Procopius, the last of the ancient historians in the Thucydidean tradition, much more information about Italy in the age of Cassiodorus and the late Latin Fathers than had previously been known. He therefore extracted a chronicle of events from Procopius's *Gothic Wars,* leaving out the speeches and the causal explanations and adding whatever other details he could find in other surviving records of the age.[59] Finally, he found in Polybius a means of compensating for the loss of most of those books of Livy which describe the Punic wars. He therefore reduced all the surviving narrative books of Polybius to a simple chronology of events. He added whatever other information he could find in Valerius Antiatus, Plutarch, Florus, and Orosius. He took out Polybius's description of the geography of northern Italy, which modern Italians would have found superfluous, and he inserted a description of ancient Sicily, which Polybius supposed his audience would have already read in Thucydides.[60] What resulted was not history, as Bruni himself was the first to point out, since it omitted any explanation of what was recorded and since it never questioned the veracity of the original accounts.[61] Nor was it mere translation, notwithstanding the practice of some modern librarians who catalogue the books under the name of the chief source. For the structure, the order, and the language were wholly Bruni's.[62] Rather, it was a succinct record of all that the ancients, or at least those of the ancients whose works were then available, had transmitted about the political affairs of three little-known ages of antiquity. Thus Bruni's works in ancient history filled several important gaps in the subject that was increasingly claiming the attention of the reading public of his day.[63] They were accordingly elevated to the rank of standard textbooks, in French and Italian translations as well as in the Latin original, and copied or reprinted over and over for the next two centuries.[64] At the same time, they gave the author a chance to study carefully the texts that were soon to serve him as models in his own venture into the history of modern times.

Bruni, then, began his career as a humanist. But he soon became a citizen as well. True, he had been born an Aretine, not a Florentine, and he had first come to Florence because his father had been expelled from Arezzo during a violent civil war in 1384. Moreover, after the completion of his education, he had spent more than ten years as a secretary to the wandering papal court, and he did not finally settle down in Florence until after the deposition of his patron, Pope John XXIII, at Constance. But Salutati had taught him in his youth to look upon Florence, rather than upon Athens, Rome, or Jerusalem, as a model commonwealth; and from an admirer he became an eloquent advocate of the institutions and traditions of the city he soon adopted as his own. In his *Laudatio Florentinae Urbis*[65] of 1403–4, a work patterned on the panegyric of Athens by the still little-known second-century Greek orator Aristides, patriotism became an ideology, and the kind of political constitution that had overcome the Carthaginians in antiquity and the Visconti in modern times was pitted against the kind of constitution personified by Julius Caesar, which even Salutati could not bring himself to reject, at least in theory. In the second of his two *Dialoghi* of 1403–5, he put aside the pessimism of the early humanists about the inferiority of modern to ancient times and transformed Dante, Petrarch, and Boccaccio from isolated heroes into the forerunners of a third major epoch in the history of the world, the epoch that was just then beginning. Then in his studies of Aristotle's *Politics,* he worked out the rest of the ethical tenets of what is today called "Civic Humanism"—the superiority of the active to the contemplative life, of wealth to poverty, of matrimony to celibacy, of political to a monastic vocation. At the same time, he put these tenets into practice. He gave up his clerical benefice and got married. He accumulated enough wealth, through the generosity of his employers and through judicious investments in farms, private banks, and state bonds, to be included in the highest 1 percent of taxpayers in the Catasto of 1427.[66] After his election to several of the most important magistracies, and, above all, after his appointment as chancellor in 1427, he played a leading role in the political and military affairs of the state. "He was called upon [to take part] in all political discussions," as Vespasiano da Bisticci put it, "and his advice was always considered most wise and temperate."[67] He also elaborated upon these tenets in all his subsequent writings—most notably in his eulogy of Nanni degli Strozzi, which amounted to a Florentine version of Pericles' Funeral Oration.

It was his commitment to these tenets, as well, perhaps, as his appreciation of the new practice among Florentine patricians after 1411 of introducing ancient parallels and historical examples into their political debates, that encouraged Bruni at last to begin writing the *Historiae Florentini Populi* shortly after his return to Florence in 1415. His commitment also enabled him, several years later, to introduce the standards he had learned from historiography into an already established literary genre: biography. By cleansing the life of Dante of Boccaccio's romantic tales, he transformed an artificial collection of abstract qualities into a credible, although still somewhat anachronistic, historical personage. By basing his life of Petrarch on Petrarch's own treatises and correspondence, he transformed a bare list of "things done," which had been characteristic of his chief prehumanist forerunner, Filippo Villani, into a carefully documented reconstruction of a whole man.[68]

Finally, Bruni's commitment to the ideals of Civic Humanism led him, in the last years of his life, to create—or rather to resurrect—still another form of historical writing, one which he thought of merely as a "collection of many events" for the use of a future historian, but which soon became an autonomous genre in its own right: the commentary. Unlike history, the commentary had no other necessary chronological limits than the author's lifetime. It included only what came to his attention, not what he might have discovered after a diligent inquiry; and many passages of Bruni's *Rerum Suo Tempore Gestarum Commentarius* are in fact lifted verbatim from his personal and official correspondence.[69] It was bound neither by a single theme nor by a thesis. It could therefore add events that in a history would have been considered irrelevant, like the teaching career of Chrysoloras; and it could omit even momentous political events, like the recall of Cosimo de' Medici in 1434 and the subsequent persecution of his political opponents, which the author felt to be personally or politically embarrassing. It sought only to inform, "to transmit information to posterity," not to explain or persuade. Yet it succeeded well enough in portraying "like a picture, the achievements of the men of the age and the condition of affairs" (p. 423). And since it soon came to be associated with what both Cicero and Lucian had recognized in antiquity as an independent genre of historical writing, it in turn became a model, together with its ancient prototype, Caesar's *Gallic Wars,* for the writers of *commentarii* from then on.[70]

The Reception of the New Historiography

In spite of Bruni's reputation as the most learned and the most eloquent man of his age, and in spite of the round of stirring eulogies that followed his death in 1444,[71] most of his fellow citizens were slow to grasp the significance of the revolution he had wrought in historical thought and writing. Some of them paid no attention to him at all and went on writing diaries and chronicles according to fourteenth-century standards. To one of them, the fall of Pisa in 1406 was important largely because of "the richest and most beautiful procession I have ever seen" that was put on during the subsequent three-day victory celebration in Florence.[72] To another, Buonaccorso Pitti, what really mattered in the great jumble of trivial and important events he set down (to the delight of modern students of the first decades of the century) were those that concerned his own business and family affairs; and his *Ricordi* (1412–29), which were written almost at the same time as the first seven books of the *Historiae,* show no sign of any contact with Bruni, whom the author, as a wealthy merchant and a frequent officeholder, must have known personally.[73]

Some chroniclers, on the other hand, at least took note of what Bruni had accomplished, even if only for the purpose of ransacking his works for information and for one or two stylistic devices. When PIERO BUONINSEGNI decided, sometime in the 1450s, to bring up-to-date the universal chronicle that his father DOMENICO (1384–1465) had broken off abruptly in 1409, he was already committed to the traditional stories about Caesar and Charlemagne that Bruni had tried to destroy, and he was still circumscribed by criteria of selection that put the Ordinance of Justice and the miracles of the Madonna of Orsanmichele in 1292 on the same plane. But he was also encouraged by his father's example "to turn backwards a bit in order properly to understand," and to recognize the significance of, such extraordinary occurrences as the revolt of the Ciompi. He thus limited his inquiries to what news arrived ("Ci fu nuovo come . . .") on what dates, he left to his sixteenth-century editor the task of filling in missing surnames in his lists of officeholders, and he gave no other reason for abandoning his work in 1460, fifteen years before his death, than what might be inferred from the final phrase, "Laus Deo." But Piero also got rid of all but two miracles. He excluded almost all matters that did not have some connection with the political affairs of the commune. And he took a major step toward a humanist system of periodization by beginning Book II with the first rumors of the impending recall of Cosimo de' Medici in 1434.[74]

Similarly, ANTONINO PIEROZZI (1349–1459), better known as ST. ANTONINO, bishop of Florence from 1445, was bound by the methods and theses of the high medieval world-chronicles that his mentors in the Order of St. Dominic still regarded as authoritative. He divided his work into the traditional six ages before the Incarnation and by popes, emperors, and monastic orders thereafter. He explained the succession of dominant states by the traditional Four Monarchies theory. He dissolved individual historical agents into sets of abstract qualities ("fuit hic . . . in bello fortis, corpore insignis, animo constans, moderatus . . .").[75] He gave more space to Florence than to Flanders or Tunis only because he knew more about it, and he inserted charming stories about St. Dominic's conversations with Jesus because his universalism was conditioned by loyalty to his religious order. Antonino was also bound by the general form of a medieval *summa theologica,* since he intended his *Chronicon*[76] chiefly as an illustrative appendix to his voluminous project of updating Thomas Aquinas. Indeed, it is thanks to his reputation as a theologian that his historical work continued to be read and cited well into the period of the Counter Reformation.

Historical events thus became important as examples of divine intervention in human affairs or of the coercive power of moral principles. The troubles of Arezzo and Perugia, said Antonino, were announced by an earthquake in 1298. The unhappy end of Pope Boniface VIII resulted from his having actively sought the Papacy instead of waiting patiently, like Aaron, to be called. The civil wars in Pistoia were the consequence of what Bruni identified as a legitimate goal of civil life: wealth.

Nevertheless, even Antonino, who was intellectually far more attuned to the thirteenth than to the fifteenth century, was not completely deaf to certain of the humanists' innovations. He sought, albeit none too successfully, to conform to their standards of good Latinity, probably with the help of a secretary who had been trained by no less authoritative a humanist pedagogue than Vittorino da Feltre. And he took as much information as possible from what the humanists held to be the most reliable sources—namely, Bruni's *De Bello Gothico* for the fifth century A.D., Bruni's *Historiae* for the thirteenth and fourteenth, and Bruni's *Commentarius* for the first decades of the fifteenth. Thus one later humanist's complaint that "this Antonino is an excessively loquacious . . . and a dishonest liar in all [he writes] about more recent times" is not wholly justified.[77]

Apparently, then, it was not just an anachronistic attachment to traditional modes of thought that permitted the chronicle to survive as an autonomous genre of historical narration, but rather its ability to absorb certain elements of humanist historiography without losing its peculiar character. This development is well illustrated in the work of two of the most voluminous chroniclers of the mid-fifteenth century, GIOVANNI CAVALCANTI (1381–c. 1450) and ALAMANNO RINUCCINI (b. 1419). Neither Cavalcanti nor Rinuccini wrote for reasons that were substantially different from those of their predecessors. Cavalcanti sought only to note down "those things more worthy of being remembered" and thus to kill time after being thrown into prison for nonpayment of taxes in 1427. Rinuccini sought only to carry on the work that his father, FILIPPO DI CINO (1392–1462), turned over to him in 1459 and to pass it on to his son NERI (d. 1508) after his death in 1499.[78] Yet Cavalcanti, in spite of his modest birth and still more modest education, managed to draw out of the miscellaneous events he recorded an ideological program very similar to Bruni's: "Tuscan liberty" versus "Lombard power"—a program which he found threatened in the 1420s by the Albizzi and after 1441 by the Medici. He made this program explicit in the words and actions of three heroes: Gian Della Bella, who was also one of Bruni's heroes; Michele di Lando, the moderate Ciompi leader who was to be one of Machiavelli's heroes; and Giovanni de' Medici, the father of Cosimo, a "most excellent man . . . whose great deeds I will never be able to write enough about." Finally, he organized at least some of his entries into a dramatic progression culminating in the stirring speech delivered by Cosimo de' Medici on the eve of his expulsion from Florence in 1433.[79] Similarly, Alamanno Rinuccini, largely because of his illustrious birth, his humanist education, and his skill in translating from Greek and composing in Latin, learned to avoid some of the practices that his father should have recognized as no longer admissible—practices like plagiarizing most of Bruni's *Vita di Dante* and skipping over the death of Giangaleazzo Visconti in one brief, and incorrectly dated, statement. He also learned the principle of thematic unity in a literary work. Hence his "continuation" became exclusively a chronological record of the debates and decrees of the official executive body of Florentine government, the Signoria, and of the constitutional changes imposed by Piero and Lorenzo de' Medici for the purpose of limiting or controlling its effective authority.

This peculiar advantage of chronicle over history was eventually recognized by the humanists themselves. One of them, NERI CAPPONI (d. 1457), turned what may have begun as a chronicle in the hand of his father Gino not, to be sure, into a humanist history, but into a humanist "commentary." His *Dell'acquisto di Pisa*[80] began by sketching the background of the war in resounding gerundial phrases. It reached a climax in a long lecture by his father, who had been Florentine high commissioner for the war, to the defeated Pisans. And it ended with Gino's return to Florence and the implementation of his policy of clemency toward his former enemies. At the same time, it eloquently expounded an official rationalization of the concurrent shift in Florentine foreign policy—a shift from the new defense of independent city-states against the Visconti empire to the creation of a territorial state under Florentine domination. And, in a postscript of 1420 (which may be just a transcription of what Gino himself wrote), it added a corollary for domestic policy: Florence could maintain its newly acquired dominion only by preventing "any individual citizen, family, or clique [*congiura*] from becoming more powerful than the government." Neri was apparently pleased enough with the reception of this first commentary that he went on to compose two others based on his own experiences as a member and a representative of the Florentine government. One of them was a short memorandum defending the same policy of territorial acquisition in the Casentino, east of Florence. The other, considerably longer but somewhat less polished, described the errors and accomplishments of Florentine foreign policy (while all but ignoring the domestic revolution represented by the emergency of Cosimo de' Medici) from the beginning of the wars against Giangaleazzo's successor in Milan, Filippo Maria Visconti, to the aftermath of the Peace of Lodi in 1454.[81]

Still other humanists wrote chronicles of their own. Unlike Bruni, whom he nevertheless acknowledged as his master, SOZOMENO DA PISTOIA was a scholar, but not an active citizen or officeholder. He supported himself not as a magistrate or a merchant, but as the incumbent of various ecclesiastical sinecures and, for a few years after 1430, as a professor of poetry and rhetoric. After being appointed as the nonresident vicar of the nonresident bishop of Pistoia in 1446, he dedicated himself exclusively to amassing a huge library and to reducing all the histories and chronicles from antiquity to the present to the form of a bare outline.[82] Except for a few asides to advertise his support of the Medici regime, he added nothing of his own: he simply left blank the two-year hiatus between 1364, where Filippo Villani broke off, and 1366, where Buoninsegni began. Nor did he presume to weigh the relative importance of his various insertions, realizing that evaluation was the concern of historians, not of chroniclers. Hence his description of the wooden bridge built for the procession of Pope Eugenius from Santa Maria Novella to the cathedral, a description copied almost verbatim from Bruni's *Commentarius,* takes up far more space than all the proceedings of the Council of Florence. But Sozomeno occasionally backed up what he paraphrased from the chroniclers with the text of a relevant archival document. When written texts gave out in his own generation, he took his information from oral interviews. He recast all his entries in impeccable classical Latin. Better yet, he managed to line up facts with dates both for antiquity, in which dates were still all but unknown, and for the Middle Ages, in which many dates had been recorded erroneously.

Sozomeno thus went beyond chronicle to recast in humanist form the kind of chronological record of historical events that the Middle Ages had inherited from Eusebius and Jerome in late antiquity. The first to realize the potentialities of this form of chronology for humanist historiography was Sozomeno's brightest pupil, MATTEO PALMIERI, one whose attainments in scholarship enabled him to rise to the highest offices in the state and to succeed Bruni as the chief theoretician of Civic Humanism. Palmieri began composing his chronicle in 1446, at a moment when Sozomeno had reached the year 1294; and he worked along with his former teacher until he arrived at the year 1448. He restudied Sozomeno's ancient model and followed it even to the point of accepting its placement of all the events of the first four centuries five years later than when they actually had occurred. He took out the passages that Sozomeno had transcribed from the chronicles. He put in rubrics to indicate the transitions from one to the other of the historical periods identified by the humanist historians ("Romano Imperio continue declinante.... Secuta sunt tempora...obscuritate inscitiaque summersa"). And he arranged his bare statements of each event under dates indicated, for easy reference, in black and red numbers in the margins.

So well did Palmieri's *De Temporibus*[83] meet the needs of students of history for a full and accurate list of dates that an "infinite number of copies" (according to his first biographer[84]) were circulated in manuscript (ten of them still survive in the public libraries of Florence alone), and it ran through at least eight editions between 1474 and 1579. Its success inspired MATTIA PALMIERI of Pisa, a pupil (but not a relative) of Matteo, to carry it down first to 1458 and then to 1483, the year of his death. Mattia had done his apprenticeship in history by translating Herodotus. He had then used Herodotus as a model in composing a still unpublished history *De Bello Italico:* the first five books (written before 1458) describe the wars following the death of Filippo Maria Visconti (1447), and the other books (written after 1464) present an eyewitness account of the preparations for Pius II's crusade.[85] Mattia's scope in his own *De Temporibus* was somewhat broader than Matteo's. He recorded the deaths of all the famous writers of his generation. He drew extensively on information gathered orally during his years in the service of Pius II. And, at least by implication, he contrasted his three heroes—Alfonso d'Aragona, Lorenzo de' Medici, and Pius II, with his major villain, Francesco Sforza, who became duke of Milan during the period he was writing about. But his general format remained the same: an outline of events distributed according to black and red numbered dates.

The success of the *De Temporibus* also encouraged Matteo himself to compose a more traditional chronicle, one in which the bare outline was interspersed with long, and stylistically coherent, narratives and in which a full record of Florentine foreign affairs between 1432 and 1474 was backed up by frequent paraphrases of official documents.[86] His chronicle then encouraged two other humanists to imitate him. Both of them were professional scholars, rather than citizen-merchants or state secretaries. BARTOLOMEO DELLA FONTE, better known as FONTIUS or FONZIO (1446–1513), rose to fame through the schools of Bernardo Nuti in Florence and of Battista Guarino in Ferrara solely on the strength of his intellectual accomplishments—and in spite of the heavy family responsibilities cast upon him when he was left in charge of three siblings at the age of sixteen.[87] LORENZO BUONINCONTRI was a voluntary exile from the subject city of San Miniato who started his career as a soldier in Francesco Sforza's mercenary army and after 1458 became an expert on astrology at the court of Naples. Fonzio returned to Florence from Ferrara in 1471 to work as a translator and a corrector for the printing press at Ripoli. He returned once again after a short sojourn in Rome, in 1481, to take the deceased Francesco Filelfo's chair of rhetoric in the Studio. And he returned once and for all in 1489, after brief visits to Rome and Hungary, to spend the rest of his days writing letters, translating Demosthenes, and commenting on Petrarch in a suburban villa and lecturing on rhetoric and the Scriptures in town. He learned about history by editing and commenting on Livy *(De Locis Livianis)*. He extracted rules for history writing from Lucan and Caesar, upon whom he gave a series of lectures in 1482. And in order to prepare himself to execute what he had learned, he composed, in 1484, a brief account of the principal political and cultural events of Florence and Italy from 1448 to 1483, the *Annales Suorum Temporum*. Buonincontri learned to write history by reading Bruni; and he freely lifted whole passages out of the *Historiae* and incorporated them into a scheme borrowed from Villani which he called *Annales Miniatensis* ("Annals of San Minato"), but which really consist of a chronicle of Florence between the tenth century and the death of his first patron, Alfonso d'Aragona, in 1458.[88]

None of these chronicles was intended to do much more than provide raw material from which the authors might eventually construct a work of history. Palmieri consciously limited his scope to "what was done and how"; and Buonincontri found modern society so much more complex than ancient society that he dared only list the *res gestae* without putting them into any sort of coherent order. Yet all three chronicles came from the pens of accomplished humanists, who thus gave the sanction of humanism to a form of historical writing that was clearly nonhumanist in origin and structure.

Bruni's Heirs

Meanwhile a few Florentines succeeded in understanding completely the significance of Bruni's *Historiae* and deliberately set forth to elaborate upon the heritage he left them. More than a decade before Bruni's death, Matteo Palmieri had enshrined his ethical principles in a treatise *Della vita civile* (1433); and four years after Bruni's death he repeated his master's theoretic statements on the nature and purposes of history in a preface to his own concrete application of the statements, the *De Captivitate Pisarum Liber.*[89] Like the *Historiae,* the *De Captivitate* drew its material from previous narrative sources, although Palmieri's task was greatly facilitated by his being able to use not just a chronicle but a humanist commentary, the *Dell'acquisto di Pisa* of Neri Capponi, to whom his book was dedicated. It was also based on an ancient model: not Livy, to be sure, since Palmieri was writing about only one episode in Florentine history, but Sallust. As Sallust had put the conspiracy of Catiline within the context of Roman history as a whole, so Palmieri began with a long introduction on ancient and medieval Florence, and he ended with a physical description of modern Florence at the moment of the return of the victorious army from Pisa. He thus put in the *rationes* and the *consilia* that he consciously left out of his *De Temporibus.* He elevated the importance of his subject ("quia magnum et memorabile fuit") by imitating Sallust's terse Latin prose and by making subtle comparisons between the Pisan leader Gambacorta and Sallust's Jurgurtha. He added information from Nofri that Capponi had omitted. He filled in the first names that Capponi had forgotten. He translated Capponi's Christian dating style ("Ascension Day") into the Roman style ("about the kalends of June"). And he ended up with an impeccable exemplar of Brunian historical writing.

Two years after Bruni's death, the official orator at his state funeral, GIANNOZZO MANETTI (1390–1459), applied the same historiographical principles to still another subject: not a single episode in the history of his own city, but the whole history of a city under Florentine dominion, Pistoia. The *Historia Pistoriense*[90] gave Manetti ample opportunity to lecture his colleagues in the Florentine government, who recognized his talents as an orator by sending him on all their more delicate foreign embassies until Cosimo de' Medici forced him into exile in 1453. The absence of a native chronicle tradition (even the *Istorie Pistolesi,* the only Pistoian source he could find, was concerned mostly with Florence) forced him to rely largely on Florentine writers, particularly on Villani and Bruni; and the close association of the two cities during the previous century permitted him to denounce the "detestable" Law of Admonitions of 1378, to describe the Ciompi as a band of robbers, and to hold up the history of Pistoia as a poignant example of one of the ills that afflicted Florence as well: civil discord. Yet the principles of Civic Humanism did not yet extend to the particular situation in which Manetti was placed as a republican magistrate charged with governing not his own but a subject city. And when his subjects petitioned the Florentine government in 1446 for a renewal of his tenure, he had to go beyond Bruni to Cicero, particularly to Cicero's letters to his brother Quintus. A city whose citizens had destroyed every vestige of its ancient splendor during the period of independence and who had taken advantage of every subsequent interval of self-government to butcher each other left no room for practicing the one form of the good life that Bruni—and that Manetti, who also translated Aristotle's *Ethics*—could imagine. The best it could hope for was quietly and gratefully to enjoy the peace and prosperity imposed upon it by the virtue generated in a completely external community. Thus Manetti's history led to an ideological conclusion exactly the opposite of Bruni's. But it was not one that particularly displeased the author, able and conscientious statesman though he was. Many of his purely humanistic occupations, like his study of the Hebrew Old Testament and of Augustine's *De Civitae Dei,* had nothing whatever to do with his political career. And after his long life of public service was finally rewarded with a confiscatory tax, he had no trouble learning to enjoy the peace, the pensions, and the undisturbed *vita contemplativa* accorded him at the courts of Pope Nicholas V and King Alfonso d'Aragona.

As Palmieri and Manetti applied Bruni's principles to one war and to one city, so BENEDETTO ACCOLTI (1415–64) applied them to a completely different subject: the Crusades. Like Bruni, Accolti descended from an old Aretine family that had recently settled in Florence, and he too rose through his qualifications as a man of letters and as an expert in the law to become chancellor of the republic. He was drawn to history both by his discovery of the medieval chronicles of the Crusades, principally that of William of Tyre, and by his desire to clarify a pressing political question: Florence's response to the fall of Constantinople in 1453 and to Pius II's call for a crusade against the Ottoman Turks. This was a question that had occupied much of Accolti's attention since his appointment as chancellor in 1458. His elegant Latin reworking of the original texts, as well as his consistent reference to all Muslims as "barbarians," served to heighten the rhetorical effect of the speeches he put into the mouth of Peter the Hermit and his moral reflections on the discord among the Christian subjects ("scelera Christianorum") of the Kingdom of Jerusalem. And although the work failed to inspire Piero de' Medici, to whom it was dedicated, to fly off to Ancona, it eventually served, in the several editions of the Italian translation that first appeared in 1543, as historical background for Torquato Tasso's poetic evocation of the Crusades in the *Gerusalemme liberata*.[91]

Two other Florentine humanists followed Bruni all the way back to classical antiquity, where he himself had begun. They did so with Bruni's warning in mind: that the history of antiquity had already been written and that modern historians could do little more than make summaries or add a few explanatory footnotes to the work of their distant predecessors. ANDREA DOMENICO FIOCCHI (c. 1400–1452), was a little-known notary and then papal secretary who made enough money from his collection of well-paying benefices in Florence eventually to buy a house and retire in Rome. There he finished the most important of his technical treatises, the *De Magistratibus Sacerdotisque Romanorum Libellus*.[92] Fiocchi sought to explain, in short, succinct sentences, the names and functions of a great number of Roman public offices, which even Livy occasionally got mixed up, and which fifteenth-century readers often misinterpreted by using them to make anachronistic analogies with their own institutions.[93] So well did the *Libellus* meet the demand of the many new readers of ancient history for a convenient manual that it was soon attributed to the first century A.D. Roman annalist Fenestella; and under the guise of a rediscovered ancient text rather than an original modern text, it was frequently reprinted, often along with the better imitations it inspired, from 1477 until the beginning of the seventeenth century. The other humanist historian of ancient Rome was BERNARDO RUCELLAI (1448–1514), a wealthy patrician who patronized many of the leading humanists in Florence, including Fonzio, and who, after 1494, became one of the leaders of the aristocratic opposition to the government of the Great Council. Rucellai also composed a *De Magistratibus* on the model of Fiocchi's.[94] But he is best known for his venture into a field that had been cultivated even in the late Middle Ages and that had recently attracted the attention of humanists in Rome: ancient archaeology. Rucellai followed in the footsteps of his father, Giovanni,[95] who had transcribed inscriptions and noted building measurements during the Jubilee of 1450; and he also followed in the footsteps of Giovanni's famous protégé, LEON BATTISTA ALBERTI, who had supplemented his famous *De Architecttura* with a topographical map of ancient Rome. Rucellai's *De Urbe Roma*[96] added little to what Flavio Biondo had already written in his still definitive work on the subject. But it judiciously supplemented what the author had observed in Rome with what he had observed in other Italian cities and with what he had read in all the texts of ancient literature. And it did so in an impeccable Sallustian prose style ("Cripus elegantia, nitore, atque innovatione cunctis in historia praeferendus") that satisfied the tastes as well as the curiosity of his readers.

Bruni's Florentine heirs thus succeeded in extending the new historiography to other fields and other subjects. But when they tried applying it in the area in which Bruni had claimed it to be most appropriate, that is, the history of the political community of which they were members, they ran into serious difficulties. POGGIO BRACCIOLINI (1380–1459) had been one of Bruni's closest companions ever since they had studied together under Salutati and Chrysoloras; and although they had separated, first after Poggio's departure for England in 1418 and then after his return to the Roman Curia in 1423, they had kept in close contact by letter. Poggio understood as well as Bruni that history alone could make the past present, and therefore intelligible, and that it alone could distinguish the good from the bad in order to provide examples of moral behavior to be imitated.[97] Indeed, he was the only one of Bruni's funeral eulogists to recognize the *Historiae* as Bruni's greatest work;[98] and he followed Bruni's example to the extent of drafting historical biographies of several recent popes (for the sole benefit, unfortunately for him, of his successors in the genre).[99] He also knew that modern times were qualitatively equal to ancient times and that the great generals of his day deserved to be remembered for their great deeds as much as Caesar and Pausanias.

But Poggio was interested in all branches of literature chiefly as a means of showing off the witty, down-to-earth, colloquial Latin style that was to make him one of the most widely read authors of his century. He was interested in studying history largely for the proof it furnished for his theses about the instability of all things. And as late as 1454 he was interested in writing history—even the history of a state he knew to be Giangaleazzo's most recent successor as would-be lord of all Italy, Venice—largely as an occasion for decorating his Latin prose with echoes of Thucydides and Xenophon and of settling his sons in a "quiet home." When, in the last years of his life, he finally got around to writing his *Historiae Florentini Populi* (the title is the same as Bruni's), he did so largely because as Bruni's successor in the office of chancellor he felt obliged to imitate his predecessor. He followed Bruni almost page by page through his first three books, while backtracking from Bruni's critical accomplishments with one after another "it-is-said" or *fertur*. Although he once upbraided the hotheads in Florence for the unnecessary disasters of the wars with Lucca and Filippo Maria Visconti,[100] he generally avoided references to anything that might still be polemical, including the Ciompi revolt and the return of Cosimo in 1434. He attributed all political decisions to the "Florentines" collectively, even after the rise of Cosimo de' Medici, whom he mentioned only once—and then only as ambassador to Venice! He buried all of Bruni's dramatic climaxes in a humdrum recitation of events. He broke off suddenly with the Peace of Naples in 1455—which might have provided him with the most dramatic climax of all—as if it were just one more entry in the annals of a chronicler.

BARTOLOMEO SCALA (1424/30–1497), the last of the humanist chancellors of the fifteenth century, was even less successful, though perhaps more ambitious, than Poggio. Like his predecessors, he rose through his literary talents from a poor family in Colle Val d'Elsa to be honored by the duke of Milan, the kings of France and Naples, and the pope; and he was rewarded by the Florentine government with citizenship in 1471, with a priorate in 1472, with the post of *gonfaloniere di giustizia* in 1476, and finally with reappointment as chancellor after his enemies had fallen from power with the Medici in 1494.[101] Scala sought to supplement Bruni, who he admitted "was the first to bring the whole of Florentine history out of darkness,"[102] and Poggio, whom he also eulogized in his preface. He sought to do so by adding more information to their texts and by continuing their narratives, through a total of fifteen books, down to his own day. But when he tried to use Villani, Petrarch, Sozomeno, Platina, and Biondo as sources of additional information without distinguishing among them as to quality, purpose, and epoch, he ended up putting back in many of the legends that Bruni had explicitly rejected. His innovations consisted solely in a more frequent mention of the arts and letters, which nevertheless remained extraneous to his main interest in military and political history, and in a provocative reconsideration of the barbarian invasions in the light of the invasion of 1494. Hence, a lack of enthusiasm on the part of the author, as well as on the part of his prospective readers, may explain why the *Historia Florentinorum* had gotten no further than Book V (1264) by the time the author died, and why it was not published until 1677. It might also explain why no other humanist ever bothered to turn into history the ample material still being recorded day-by-day in private diaries.[103]

To be sure, humanist historiography did not lose its ability to inspire creative efforts in disciplines marginal or supplementary to history. Humanist biography continued to flourish—from Matteo Palmieri's life of Niccolò Acciaiuoli and Manetti's lives of Pope Nicholas V, Dante, Petrarch, and Boccaccio, to Naldo Naldi's life of Manetti, and finally to the three principal biographical collections of "virtuous" or of "learned men" written, generally in dialogue form, by Benedetto Accolti and Paolo Cortesi.[104] Humanist philology, and the search for ancient texts, flourished even more, particularly in the hands of the greatest philologist of the last decades of the century, Angelo Poliziano, who edited Suetonius, translated Herodian, and discovered documentary support for a modified version of Bruni's date for the foundation of Florence.[105] Humanist commentary, reinforced by the addition of an obvious ancient model, Caesar, to the one provided by Bruni's *Commentarius,* eventually produced a small masterpiece: Bernardo Rucellai's *De Bello Italico,* which was written after 1500 while the author was living as a voluntary exile in Provence. The *De Bello Italico* put the blame for the "crimes, wars, murders, and massacres" that had been perpetrated in Italy through the invasion of Charles VIII right where Bruni would have put it (and where Guicciardini was to put it thirty years later): on the "cupidity" of the Venetians, on the ambitions of Alexander VI, on the stupidity of Alfonso II, and on the disastrous machinations of Lodovico il Moro. It also formulated, for the first time, a theory of a "balance of power" very much like the one Guicciardini was able to propose as an explanation for the stability of Italy before 1492. Moreover, it did so with scrupulous fidelity to the "first law [of history]: Say nothing that is false and omit nothing that is true."[106] And it did so with such conciseness and elegance of style that the author was hailed as another Caesar by Fonzio and as another Sallust by Erasmus.[107]

Yet even in these marginal disciplines humanist historiography did not always succeed in realizing the purposes Bruni had assigned to it. Not even Scala paid any attention to the alternative ancient models or to the chronological rectifications proposed by ANGELO POLIZIANO; and solely, it seems, for the purpose of supporting Savonarola's Francophile foreign policy, he put back into history some of the legends that Bruni had taken out. Poliziano, in turn, paid no attention to the purely historical, as opposed to the apologetic and rhetorical qualities of the commentary: after all, his favorite model was Aulus Gellius rather than Livy or Caesar.[108] His *Coniurationis Commentarium* was rushed to the press, in August 1478, as soon as he had finished polishing his Sallustian infinitives and sharpening his comparisons between the Pazzi and Catiline. But it turned out to be no more than a piece of eloquent propaganda commissioned by Lorenzo de' Medici and squeezed from the pen of the unenthusiastic author, for whom history served only as proof of "the instability of human fortunes."[109] It was judiciously omitted from Aldo Manuzio's first edition of Poliziano's *Opera Omnia* published in Venice in 1498. And it is probably just as well that King John II never got around to commissioning the history of Portugal that Poliziano offered to write for him in 1489—without, needless to say, any thought of ever leaving Florence.[110]

ANTONIO IVANI (or HYVANIUS, 1430–c. 1482) was somewhat more conscientious, He was a career notary and communal chancellor, as Coluccio Salutati had been, one who became an enthusiastic admirer of Laurentian Florentine culture after the Florentines had bought his native city of Sarzana from the Genoese in 1468. He had faithfully served the republic, as well as its subject cities, as chancellor first of Volterra (1466) and then of Pistoia (1476). He was a good enough Latinist to merit the admiration of the omnivorous bibliophile Antonio Magliabecchi two centuries later. And he learned by studying Flavio Biondo's *Roma Instaurata*[111] that he should write history only after examining all the relevant material. Yet Ivani was interested enough in his own career to take note of the interests of his patrons, actual and prospective, and to make sure that his name was inserted, albeit illegally, on the list of the citizens of Sarzana. But he was also interested in the theoretical problem of how to adapt to a subject city a form of historiography that had been designed for a dominant city. And he was interested at the same time in a practical problem exactly the opposite of that posed by Giannozzo Manetti: not how a dominant city should act toward a subject city, but how the citizens of the latter might graciously resign themselves to being governed by the former without wasting their energies in wasteful and pointless bickering. He offered a solution in his commentary on the Volterra War in 1472. The blame for the tragedy, he concluded, lay not with Lorenzo de' Medici, "a man of high authority, great wealth, and great virtue." It lay rather with those few hotheads at Volterra who failed to recognize the great advantage of having their "peace, prosperity, and security" guaranteed by someone else.[112]

Even the biographies fell consistently below Bruni's standards. Manetti emphasized the eulogistic purpose of biography at the expense of accuracy in his life of Pope Nicholas, and, with the excuse of rendering his predecessors' work more acceptable to a Latin-reading public, he put back in all the romantic stories that Bruni had carefully weeded out of Boccaccio's lives of Dante and Petrarch. Naldi let the person of his hero get lost in a mass of extraneous detail—so much so that his biography reads more like a section artificially cut out of a humanist chronicle. Accolti used his dialogue very effectively to denounce the "adulteries, crimes, seductions, avarice..." of the modern clergy; and he was one of the first to point out, partially on his own perception of conflicts between eloquence and veracity, the inadequacies and the undependability of the ancient historians. But when he chose as the greatest statesman of all times, ancient or modern, none other than Francesco Sforza, the condottiere who had extinguished the Ambrosian Republic and become absolute master of Milan, he destroyed what for Bruni (whom Accolti regarded as the best historian of all times) had been the sole condition of greatness: the life of a free republican commune. It is not surprising, then, that the humanist biographies failed to supplant such traditional, anecdotal life-stories as ANTONIO MANETTI's (1423–97) life of Brunelleschi, for which—notwithstanding the author's close association with the highest intellectual circles of the city—the model was Boccaccio rather than Petrarch or Plutarch, or even Filippo Villani, whose chronicle Manetti translated rather freely into Tuscan. Nor is it surprising that even historians today prefer to read the less polished, less accurate, but fuller and more convincing portraits of the prelates, statesmen, and men of letters of the age written by that nonhumanist friend of all humanists, VESPASIANO DA BISTICCI.[113]

The humanist historians themselves were partly to blame for this decline. None of them—with the sole exception of Rucellai, who read the recent treatise on historiography by Giovanni Pontano[114]—ever bothered to meditate further on the nature and purpose of history, which Bruni had discussed more by example than by precept; and they contented themselves with repeating the same old formulas of Cicero and Quintillian, neither of whom had been particularly sympathetic toward history. By increasingly restricting their attention to what they held to be political and military affairs, they were forced to ignore what really distinguished their own from the immediately preceding ages and what justified their claims to have surpassed even the ancients: the arts and letters. Hence, periodical concepts, like Manetti's age of Petrarch and Poggio's age of Chrysoloras, came to be expressed not in works of history but in biographies and orations, or even in prefaces to editions of ancient texts, like that of Alamanno Rinuccini in his dedication to Federico da Montefeltro of his translation of Philostratus's *Life of Apollonius* in 1473.[115] To some extent, however, the fault lay with the master of the historians—not because of his defects, but because of his qualities. Bruni, explained Paolo Cortesi in 1490, had so perfectly accomplished in modern times what Livy had accomplished in antiquity that none of his followers had ever managed to equal him; and since history was "the most difficult of all disciplines," it was highly unlikely that anyone would ever equal him in the future.[116]

Yet the main reason seems to lie in the increasingly ahistorical spirit of Florentine culture in the age of Lorenzo de' Medici and Marsilio Ficino. As political power became concentrated in the hands of one man, or at least in the hands of a narrow oligarchy closely allied with one man, the ideal citizen of Civic Humanism became an anachronism. As the intellectual leaders of the city became preoccupied with Ficino's metaphysical absolutes, they gladly left money to the merchants and politics to the oligarchy in order to escape the city (which for Bruni had been the only conceivable focus of intellectual life) and retreat into the Platonic solitude of "a delightful little villa in the middle of the woods."[117] Even DONATO ACCIAUOLI (1429–78), whose scrupulous attention to the duties of his many public offices and whose thorough knowledge of Greek might have made him the successor, rather than just the translator, of Bruni in the 1470s, was interested in history only as a literary exercise. His lives of Hannibal and Scipio are really just adaptations of Plutarch, no more original than the lives of Demetrios and Alcibiades, which are admittedly translations. His life of Charlemagne, notwithstanding its political significance at the moment of its composition (1461) and notwithstanding its subsequent diffusion as an appendix to most Italian editions of Plutarch, is essentially just a reworking of Einhard, with a few details added from Villani and the *Liber Pontificalis*.[118]

What was merely contingent, individual, and particular fell from favor; and *vita activa* came to be defined not as working with other men for the improvement of a community but as climbing all alone up Pico della Mirandola's Ladder of Jacob. As the tragedies of 1494 and 1499 approached, those who searched for an explanation of the incomprehensible and cataclysmic events of the day turned for answers not to the historians but to the astrologers and the prophets.[119] They sought salvation not in an age of liberty and cultural creativity, but in a Joachimite age of the Holy Spirit or in a Savonarolan New Jerusalem. History, they were told, revealed not an ascending curve but one which had reached its lowest point in their own day. "Read all the books of history," Savonarola proclaimed, "and you will find that the Church has never been in such bad conditions as it is today."[120] Man had made the curve go down. Only God could make it go up again. And the most that responsible members of the Savonarolan commonwealth could do to reverse the ineluctable historical process was to prepare themselves spiritually and morally in the hope of being its eventual beneficiaries. When even Fonzio began plowing through the works of Augustine and Gerson in search of signs of the Antichrist,[121] and when the merchant-scholar Francesco da Meleto, a disciple of Ficino's disciple Girolamo Benivieni, was congratulated by the most learned prelates in Rome for having, in his *Convivio*, restored the long discredited Six Ages and Four Monarchies,[122] then humanist historiography was threatened with extinction in the very city in which it had been born.

2

THE ROMAN CURIA

FORTUNATELY, THE SURVIVAL OF HUMANIST HISTORIOGRAPHY DID NOT LONG REMAIN dependent upon the political vicissitudes of one city or upon the literary proclivities of one group of humanists. Even before Bruni had finished writing the first books of the *Historiae,* history had become one of the major concerns of another, equally important group of humanists: those employed by or associated with the Roman curia.

Flavio Biondo

To be sure, what eventually became curial historiography was really not curial in origin. Its most illustrious progenitor, FLAVIO BIONDO (or BLONDUS FLAVIUS, 1392–1463)[1] was connected not so much with the Curia itself, even though for some years he was one of its most influential members, but with the person of one pope, Eugenius IV, for whom he drafted most of the more important papal documents during the Council of Ferrara-Florence and whom he served as ambassador on a number of particularly delicate diplomatic missions. Indeed, Biondo was not really connected with any particular place or institution. For his city of birth, Forlì, he felt a certain tie of filial affection, even after its successive rulers twice banned him and once confiscated his partrimony; but he actually resided there for only a few years. His education took him first to Padua, where he became associated with the second generation of Paduan Petrarchans, and then to Piacenza, to the school that was soon to be transferred as a university to Pavia, where he met, among others, the future historian of the Visconti, Pier Candido Decembrio. The professional career he inherited from his father, that of an itinerant chancery notary, took him, one by one, to most of the cities of the Romagna and the Veneto; and it was during one such mission that he met the most famous of the early Renaissance pedagogues, Guarino da Verona, who introduced him to classical philology. Not until 1427 did he at last enter papal service, as secretary to the governor of the Marca d'Ancona; and no sooner had he entered the papal household itself than he was forced to follow his employer into exile. When Eugenius's successor, Nicholas V, deprived him of his office, he had no trouble adjusting himself to the prospect of residing thereafter in one of the four cities of which he had been made an honorary citizen or at the courts of Milan or Naples, which he visited in part for the purpose of soliciting a job offer. Even after his office was restored to him in Rome, he continued occasionally to travel; and he went to the trouble of putting together the passages from his previous works about Venice in the form of a *De Gestis Venetorum* in the hope of being invited to settle there as historiographer to the Senate.[2]

If Biondo was connected with any intellectual community at all, it was with Florence. It was there that he had resided during the most formative years of his life. It was there that he composed his first literary work, one that supposedly recorded a conversation among his Florentine and curial friends in 1435 and that concluded with a thesis particularly amenable to the former. Classical Latin, Biondo affirmed after a careful review of the relevant ancient texts, continued to be spoken by all Romans down at least until the time of the barbarian invasions. Hence Italian was not the descendant of a corrupt or colloquial form of Latin but a completely autonomous language; and it began to evolve toward its present form only after Latin had been reduced to the status of a language of the learned alone.[3] It was to Florence, moreover, and particularly to Bruni, that Biondo owed what thereafter became his chief literary commitment, history. While he profited from what Bruni had written, he in turn submitted to Bruni for correction and counsel all of what he himself wrote. It was probably also Bruni who taught him the principles that were to guide him thereafter: that history was concerned with the acts of men, not of God; with politics, not religion; with real, not imaginary or theoretical political organizations. And much as he may have admired the precision and occasionally the accuracy of some of the medieval historians to whom he turned for information, he broke with them completely with regard to method, language, subject, and theses.

Yet as a citizen of all Italy rather than of just one city, Biondo remained as independent of the Florentines as he had of the Curia. When, in the late 1430s, he began to compose an account of the events in which he had been a witness or a participant, one roughly comparable to Bruni's own commentary on his times, the scope of his interest was limited neither to Florence nor to the Papacy, which he portrayed as only two of several political powers. Rather, it included the whole of at least northern Italy. When he then noticed that the problem of organization required that he locate one of these powers as the center to which the others could be referred, he abandoned his original opening date, the death of Pope Martin V, whose efforts finally to establish the Papacy in Rome seemed at the moment to have been in vain. He set it instead at the accession of Filippo Maria Visconti, the son of Bruni's counterhero Giangaleazzo, who then seemed to be on the way to fulfilling his father's program of imposing, if not political unity, at least effective political leadership on all his quarrelsome neighbors. And Lapo da Castiglionchio, the bright young disciple of Filefo whose reputation as an authority on ancient literature had been gained by a number of Latin translations from the Greek classics and then guaranteed by an appointment to a chair at Bologna, pronounced the result to be fully consonant with Cicero's historiographical precepts.[4]

Yet Italian unity under Viscontian leadership was hardly comparable to the unity of the whole Mediterranean that Biondo had come to admire through his reading of the ancient historians. And to discover how the one had developed from the other, he went back to the last of the ancient historians of Rome, Orosius, with the intention of beginning with the event for which Orosius was supposed to have offered a historical explanation: the sack of Rome in A.D. 410. But the scope of Orosius's history was universal; and to have followed its example for all the intervening centuries would have required him to travel all over Europe as well as all over Italy in search of historical records that were still available only locally. And for that he had neither the time nor the money. Moreover, by the time he reached the end of Book VII of Decade I,[5] he found himself bereft of anything corresponding to the concrete incarnations of universality that had served his ancient predecessors— Israel, Macedonia, Rome. After reading what Tacitus had said about the Antonines and what Orosius and Jerome had said about Constantine and Theodosius, he could no longer accept Bruni's explanation for this unprecedented state of affairs: that the empire had irreparably undermined what the republic had so felicitously constructed. Indeed, the Christian emperors had very obviously succeeded in patching up whatever cracks may previously have appeared. But he could not avoid Bruni's conclusion. The Roman Empire was not coeval with the last great age of history before the end of the world, as Dante and most other medieval political theorists had maintained and as all the medieval world chronicles had assumed in marking the movement of time by the successive names of an unbroken—or only temporarily broken—line of emperors and popes. Rather, it had come to an end during the hundred and fifty years after the sack. By the time the Goths, the Huns, the Vandals, and then the Lombards finished tearing down even what Theodoric and Belisarius had vainly tried to restore, nothing was left of it—neither its cities, which were "desolate," nor its civilization, which was "buried" *(bonarum artium interitu . . .)*. Biondo thus made definitive a historical concept that had been proposed, but not yet fully tested, by Petrarch and Bruni in the West, and, still unknown to Westerners, by the fourteenth-century Greek historian Nikeforos (Nicephorus), on the basis of his reading of the early Byzantine ecclesiastical historian Evagrios, in the East.[6] It was a concept that soon became a permanent part of the European historical consciousness, first under the name given it by Biondo, *Inclinatio Romani Imperii,* and then under the expanded name given it by Biondo's eighteenth-century successor, Edward Gibbon, "The Decline and Fall of the Roman Empire."

The sixth-century A.D. marked the end of a thousand-year epoch in the history of the world, Biondo insisted. But it also marked the beginning of a new epoch, one characterized not by successive universal empires but by coeval, though separate, nations. His history of the centuries between Orosius's and his own thus became, for historical as well as for practical reasons, a history of only one of the several nations that had risen from the ruins of the last of the universal empires. It was a nation held together not so much by force as by a common heritage, by common interests, and by a common, and original, language. And it was one organized not by the fictitious or purely theoretical institutions like the "Roman Empire" of Rudolph of Hapsburg, "solo nomine imperator," but by real, if illegitimate, institutions, like the very effective tyranny of Ezzelino da Romano. Unfortunately, the disappearance of the last vestiges of national political unity after the rise of the communes made the new nation ever more difficult to locate, much as Biondo tried to limit his narrative to the external, as opposed to the internal, affairs of the various city-states. Moreover, the new age had very little to recommend it to a man of refined tastes and a classical education like Biondo ("horreo considerare atque recensere"). What started out as history soon turned into annals. The attempt to break up the flow of time at significant turning points (the death of Manfredi, the accession of Roberto d'Angiò) gave way to a wholly artificial scheme of ten-year periods ("decades"). And the consideration of what was of interest to Italy as a whole soon got lost in a welter of detail about what was of interest only to single cities or regions. Nevertheless, while following Bruni almost verbatim in his passages about Florence, Biondo went well beyond Bruni in suggesting that the history of a single *civitas* could be understood only in the context of a community of several *civitates*—a suggestion that was to make possible the even more fortunate experiment in national history by Guicciardini some seventy years later. Moreover, by including cultural along with political events, by admitting good letters as well as peace as a legitimate end of political activity, Biondo proposed still another periodic concept, one that the Florentines had managed so far to discuss only in orations and poems: the Renaissance. Peace seemed farther away than ever in the late 1450s, when Biondo added one last book to his *Decades*. But political chaos, he noted, had not prevented the literary movement inaugurated by Petrarch from coming to fruition at the same time. Accordingly, he designated the year 1410, the one-thousandth anniversary of the sack of Rome, as the beginning of still another age in the long history of Italy—an age which was marked not, unfortunately, by the restoration of political unity but at least by a revival of good letters, which the barbarians had destroyed along with the Roman state. And of this age, his own work was soon recognized as one of the greatest monuments. It was hailed in its day as a masterpiece not only of scholarship but also of "felicitous style," one fully worthy of the "orationis eloquentia" that Biondo had consciously imitated from Bruni, "the greatest writer of our times."[7] It was accepted for another century as the authoritative guide to the history of the "middle age" that Biondo had described between one age of good letters and the next. And not until the early twentieth-century was it mistakenly relegated, apparently because of a misunderstanding of the motives that led Pope Pius II to rewrite it in much abridged form,[8] to a separate realm of "scholarly" as opposed to "literary" historiography.

Biondo's personal independence thus enabled him to conceive of history in terms of a temporal and a geographical scope that none of his successors was able even to approach until the time of Guicciardini and Sigonio in the middle of the sixteenth century. But while he remained spiritually distant from modern Rome, and from its principal institutional expression, the Papacy, he could not avoid, any more than the other humanists of his age, the attraction of ancient Rome. And when, in 1443, the reestablishment of papal authority enabled him finally to observe what of ancient Rome was still visible in modern Rome, he began taking tours of the ruins under the guidance of the most learned resident of the latter, Cardinal Prospero Colonna, in whose rich library he did much of the research for the *Decades*.[9] The problem now posed to Biondo was a difficult one: how to put together what he could see with what he had read. It was not a new problem, to be sure. But unfortunately the available guidebooks all belonged to the genre of *Mirabilia Urbis Romae* that had been popular with pilgrims throughout the Middle Ages and that remained the main source of inspiration for its more recent imitators, Nicolas Rosell, John Capgrave, and Nicholas Muffel, well into the fifteenth century.[10] And none of these guide books conformed to the criteria upon which Biondo insisted for the proper understanding of what he observed: that fact be separated from legend and that archaeological remains be studied as historical documents, not as objects for religious meditation.

To be sure, Biondo was not the first to propose these criteria nor to attempt to apply them in practice. The priority in this, as in so many areas of humanist endeavor, belonged to Petrarch. Having noticed that what he read in Giovanni Colonna's *Mare Historiarum*[11] did not correspond to what he read in Jerome's version of Eusebius, Petrarch took a tour around the ancient fora (*Rer. Fam.*, VI, 2); and he was thus able to plan a similar tour for the Carthaginian ambassadors in his epic poem *Africa* that was remakably accurate. Still further observations were made by Petrarch's followers in the next two generations—by Francesco da Fiano, by the pilgrim Giovanni Dondi (1375), by Pier Paolo Vergerio (1398), and above all by CIRIACO PIZZICOLLI, or CIRIACO D'ANCONA (1391–1457), a friend of all the Florentine and curial humanists of the early fifteenth century, who sent back to Niccolò Niccoli careful descriptions of what he had seen in his travels down the Adriatic coast and up the Nile.[12] In 1423 Poggio and Antonio Loschi began the systematic explorations of Rome that were fully reported in Poggio's *De Varietate Rerum* in 1448.[13] In 1425 Martin V commissioned one of their associates Nicolò Signorili, to put together a list of all ancient and modern churches and a collection of inscriptions and documents regarding ecclesiastical jurisdictional rights.[14] And in the following years the task of arriving at correct identifications was greatly facilitated by Poggio's discovery of several important historical texts: Dionysius of Halicarnassus, Frontinus, Aristides, and Ammianus Marcellinus.

Still, the real founder of the scholarly investigation of Roman antiquities was Flavio Biondo, *"the first* of all moderns,"* according to his greatest successor of the following century.[15] In line with Renaissance historiographical rules, Biondo relegated all the identifications he found in the medieval guidebooks to the realm of the dubious—like the original church of San Marco reported "in certain lives of the popes" and like the "field of Venus" mentioned "in a text written some three hundred years ago." He preferred the testimony of early Roman writers to that of later ones—that of Livy, for example, to that of the fourth-century *Regiones Romae*, which he was at last able correctly to attribute to Sextus Rufus on the basis of a manuscript recently discovered at Montecassino.[16] He accepted as certain only what could be established by "ancient and trustworthy witnesses." And he left open, with the conflicting passages cited in full, any question about which the witnesses disagreed. Like Leon Battista Alberti, moreover, who had written a brief *Descriptio* replete with drawings and tables for the benefit of his artist friends in Florence in 1432–34,[17] he took measurements of every monument he observed. He then arranged what he had collected either by genre (gates, baths, theaters . . .) or by place (the Janiculum . . .) and gave a brief history of each item from its origins to his own time. Finally, in a companion volume (with frequent cross-references) begun over a decade later, he went on to discuss the institutional as well as the physical aspects of ancient Rome: religion, government, customs, spectacles, military organization, etc.

Both the *Roma Instaurata* (1443–46) and the *Roma Triumphans* (1452–59)[18] were admittedly incomplete, and both suffered from a still rather arbitrary and illogical scheme of organization. But they remained standard guides to the literature and monuments of ancient Rome for more than a century thereafter. Most of their identifications are still acceptable to modern scholars; and the few that are not (e.g., the confusion of the modern Piazza Navona with the ancient Circus Flaminius) are supported by arguments that are still considered methodologically impeccable. At the same time, these two works turned out to be much more than just reference books, although that was perhaps their main purpose. They were also works of history in the Renaissance sense of the term. They added further support to the scheme of periodization proposed in the *Decades*—chiefly by defining in greater detail the age that had preceded the decline and fall of Rome. Biondo was mainly interested in the magnificence and quality of the visible aspects of Roman culture. Since he took his judgments of Roman politics from Cicero's letters to Quintus rather than from Tacitus, he placed the first great age of Italy not at the time of the Etruscans or of the early republic, as Bruni had done, but in the first and second centuries of the empire, which Bruni had excoriated. Rather than pining for its independence, said Biondo, "the world rejoiced and gloried at being obedient to Roman government." Far from destroying the creativity of its subjects, Rome "brought them civilization and morality." To the single, local polis of Aristotle and Bruni, Biondo opposed a universal polis, one whose accomplishments rendered it worthy of being "placed before the eyes of the learned men of these times as a mirror and image of good living and every kind of virtue"—an opinion he claimed to have found, surprisingly enough, somewhere in Augustine.

What Biondo did for the city of Rome in his *Roma Instaurata* and *Roma Triumphans* he then expanded to the geographical limits of his *Decades* in still another work, the *Italia Illustrata*, as soon as he once again left Rome in 1448.[19] He may originally have thought rather of doing separate studies for only a selection of the major regions of the peninsula. An earlier version of what became the section on the Romagna was dedicated to Malatesta Novello of Rimini, where Biondo was then living, the section on Latium seems to have been at first dedicated separately to Prospero Colonna, and the section on Liguria consisted of no more than a transcription of the second redaction (1442) of the *Orae Ligusticae Descriptio*, which had been sent to him by his Genoese friend Giacomo Bracelli.[20] But in 1453 the fear of being plagiarized led him hastily to rearrange the various sections into a geographically successive pattern: down the Tyrrhenian coast from Genoa to Naples and back up the Adriatic coast to the Veneto, stopping even at minor (Viareggio) or no longer extant (Luni) towns to give a brief history of each since antiquity and a survey of its current geographical site, government, buildings, and culture. To be sure, the work remained far from complete. The history of Florence was considerably abbreviated because, said Biondo, Bruni had already written about it authoritatively. Rome was barely touched, probably because he hesitated to repeat what he had already included in his previous works. Piedmont and the islands were left out altogether, probably because information about them was not readily available. Yet this ingenious combination of geography, topography, and political and cultural history fully satisfied both "the ardent desire of men of our times to know about the history of past times" and their very practical desire to be able to identify by their modern names those places mentioned in the words of the ancients. It was therefore translated, republished, imitated, and expanded in Italy through the sixteenth century, and it became the model for all the various historical-geographical surveys that were to appear in all the other countries of Europe from the *Germania Illustrata* of the early sixteenth century[21] to the *Laponia Illustrata* of 1701.

The City of Rome and the Roman Curia

What made it possible for Biondo's historiographical innovations to become the basis of a school of historiography centered in the Roman Curia was, first of all, the definitive settlement of the Curia in Rome itself and then the admission into the Curia of papal officials whose chief qualification for office was that of being men of letters.

Unfortunately, the city of Rome offered very little from which the kind of civic historiography characteristic of Florence could have arisen. The some seventy years of the Babylonian Captivity and the some fifty years of the Great Schism had, by the time Pope Martin V arrived there in 1425, reduced it to little more than a "cow pasture"—a *terra di vacca*, as Vespasiano da Bisticci put it—in which the few remaining inhabitants were wholly dependent upon the Papacy both for their bread and for protection against the depredations of their own constantly quarreling nobility. Whatever the Romans possessed of an ideology was based on the memory not of their own accomplishments, as it was for the Florentines, but of those of the Scipios, the Caesars, and the Constantines, about whom they knew more legend than fact; and every attempt, during the hundred years between Cola di Rienzo and Stefano Porcari, to use this ideology as the basis of political action invariably ended up not in support of, but in opposition to, the only alternative to chaos, the temporal power of the Papacy.[22]

Moreover, Rome possessed very little of anything like the rich chronicle tradition that furnished the Florentine historians with much of their information and even some of their theses. Only three texts have survived from the fourteenth century that could possibly be called chronicles. The first, by a certain LODOVICO MONAL-DESCO, amounts to little more than a few notations of "the customs and wars of these times" *(le costiume a guerre che furono allo mio tiempo)*. The second, written about 1357, is concerned almost exclusively with the career of Cola di Rienzo. The third consists solely of "a series of disparate news reports without any apparent order," according to the modern editor, from 1374 (although with several flashbacks) to 1409.[23] And none of them, nor for that matter a similar but much fuller record of the years between 1404 and 1417 by one ANTONIO DI PIETRO DELLO SCHIAVO,[24] gives any indication either that the authors belonged to a "school" or a community of local writers or that they were familiar with the chronicle traditions of other Italian cities.

After 1425 local chronicles became somewhat more numerous and somewhat more public in character. PAOLO DI LELLO PETRONE's *La mesticanza,*[25] of which only the part regarding the years after 1434 has survived, seems to have been fairly widely read, at least to judge from the twenty-four manuscripts still extant. PAOLO DELLO MAESTRO's somewhat more personal diary[26] also seems to have attracted some attention: at least ten of its readers thought it of sufficient general interest to make copies of it. The addition of a historical preface covering the some 180 years between Boniface VIII and the Pazzi War gave STEFANO INFESSURA's *Diario*[27] even a certain resemblance to the Florentine chronicles, of which he knew enough, alone among his colleagues, to borrow a few passages from Giovanni Villani; and thanks to its careful recording of canonizations, processions, elections to city offices, and eleva-tions to the cardinalate, it was eventually recognized as an important document of papal as well as of Roman history. The diaries of GASPARE PONTANI (1481–92),[28] ANTONIO DA VASCO, and SEBASTIANO TEDALLINI (1485 [but really 1492]–1517)[29] are much like Infessura's: they are scrupulously objective, even when the authors are known to have been favorable to one or another political faction, and they are usually accurate, as Pontani's editor discovered when he looked up the correspond-ing notarial records in the city archives. But they too were written in Roman dialect or in Lawyers' Latin, neither of which the humanists recognized as a legitimate literary language. And since the authors were notaries, city clerks, or minor papal officials rather than secretaries, prelates, or ambassadors, they moved in social circles that were totally isolated from those which nourished the arts and letters of the Roman Renaissance, of which there is not a word in any of their writings. Indeed, Infessura, the only one of them ever to come into contact with a real humanist, still thought that the chief purpose of historiography was to test the validity of the prophesies of Gioacchino da Fiore.[30]

Hence, the only Roman chronicles that proved capable of serving even as a source of information for humanist historians were written in the circles not of the city but of the Curia, and not by Roman citizens but respectively by a Volterran and by an Alsatian. That of JACOPO GHERARDI (1434–1516),[31] a papal secretary who retired to his native city in 1492, was composed with some attention to style and language; and since the author never got around to recasting it as a formal history, it remains a very thorough record of the life of the papal court during his tenure of office. That of JOHANN BURCKHART,[32] which began simply as "an account of the duties of the office" of master of ceremonies held by the author for over two decades after 1483, is written without the slightest glimmer of literary sensitivity. What has made it ever since an indispensable source for the history of the Papacy at the time of Sixtus IV, Innocent VIII, and Alexander VI is not the skill or the grace with which it is written, and certainly not the almost illegible handwriting of the original manuscript, but the great number of letters, bulls, decrees, and lists of appointments it quotes *in extenso* and the great amount of specific, though not always reliable, information contained in the text.

To the isolation of the city of Rome from curial historiography corresponded the indifference of the historians to the city of Rome. None of them, after all, was really a Roman. Jacopo Ammannati came from Lucca, Pomponio Leto from Basilicata, Giovannantonio Campano from Capua, Matteo Vegio from Lodi; and of course Raffaello "Volterrano" came from Volterra and Gaspare da Verona came from Verona. Indeed, the only one of them actually to be born in Rome, Andrea Fulvio, was the son of a recent immigrant from a small town in Latium. And the only historian of the whole century to descend from a resident, although rather recent, Roman family, Lorenzo Valla, spent most of his active life elsewhere. On the other hand, so many years abroad cut off the curial historians from any ties but those of affection with what they continued to call their *patrie*. When any of them actually did return to their native cities, it was not to participate as active members in a society of fellow citizens in accordance with the precepts of Florentine Civic Humanism, but to represent locally the wholly external interests of papal temporal power or to enjoy a vacation from the "miseries" of curial life, which all of them professed to detest. They were therefore incapable of appreciating what had been one of the most important formative elements in Florentine historiography: an intimate connection between a literary and a political community.

Nevertheless, the historians of the Curia had much in common with their Florentine colleagues. Several of the more important Florentine humanists had spent many of their more active years in papal service: Bruni, Poggio, Manetti, and Leon Battista Alberti; and one of them, Fiocchi, moved permanently to Rome after retiring from his ecclesiastical offices in Tuscany. Similarly, one of the leading curial humanists, JACOPO AMMANNATI (1422–79), studied under Bruni and Carlo Marsuppini and then taught rhetoric in Florence before beginning his curial career as a cardinal's secretary.[33] Another, BARTOLOMEO PLATINA (1421–81), came to Florence to learn Greek in 1457; and by the time he left, four years later, he had also learned enough about Civic Humanism to write a fairly accurate description of what his Florentine hosts meant by a "perfect citizen"—*De Optimo Cive*.[34] It is not surprising, then, that the historians of the Curia were just as committed as their Florentine colleagues to the revival of ancient languages and literature. GIOVANNANTONIO CAMPANO (1429–77) dedicated much of his very limited spare time to preparing critical editions of ancient texts: Dio Cassius, Quintillian, Suetonius, Cicero, and three of Livy's *Decades*.[35] And GUILIO POMPONIO LETO (1428–97) commented at length on the texts he edited—Statius, Caesar, Varro, Sallust, Tacitus—after his appointment to a chair at the University of Rome.[36]

Nor is it surprising that the historians of the Curia were just as insistent upon defining history as a branch of literature. To be sure, Campano pointed out,[37] history is not poetry. It requires "different words, a different order of sentences, and a different kind of speech." Historical prose should be calm rather than arousing *(sedatus, aestuans)*, flowing rather than marked by interruptions. It should describe not only the events themselves but also the decisions *(consilia)* of those who determined the events. It should both tell the truth and give the appearance of telling the truth—"ut historia quam scribas non fabula esse videtur." Hence, the chief qualification demanded of a historian was that he be a man of letters; and the best work of history was expected from an author who had already excelled in all the various literary forms sanctioned by the ancients—like Campano himself. "Who," asked his eulogist, "is better supplied with an abundance of words? Who can excel him in heroic verse, in songs and epigrams, in orations and epistles, and in every other kind of writing?"[38] Platina thus strove to eliminate nonclassical terms when paraphrasing postclassical texts.[39] AGOSTINO PATRIZI cautiously put inelegant technical terms into the mouths of others ("quos ... vocant").[40] And Pomponio Leto extracted a long list of stylistic precepts from the ancient historians on whom he was lecturing. Beauty *(pulchritudo)*, he said, is produced by economy or paucity of words *(economia)*. The infinitive mood is often preferable to the indicative. Speeches should be appropriate to the situation. And so forth.[41]

Like the Florentines, moreover, the historians of the Curia were also men of action. True, none of them ever managed to find a philosophical justification for the *vita activa* they were forced into by economic necessity. When Campano tried to define the duties of a magistrate, he ended up talking about the age of Cicero, not his own; and his *De Regendo Magistrarum* was not considered applicable to any contemporary polity until a little-known Spaniard decided to translate it, a century later, for no less unlikely a republican magistrate than Grand Duke Francesco of Tuscany.[42] When Platina tried to denigrate Pope Paul II's autocratic government by exalting an exact opposite, he ended up denying his own premises; for he dedicated his *De Optimo Cive* to no less aspiring a prince than Lorenzo de' Medici. Indeed, no one could find any other reason for entering papal service than that of eventually being able to retire from it—that is, of being able to exchange an insecure secretaryship for a well-paying and undemanding bundle of ecclesiastical benefices. Still, only a few of the curial historians managed to retire even into academia. Pomponio Leto and RAFFAELLO MAFFEI, usually called IL VOLTERRANO (1451–1537),[43] became university professors. Platina became prefect of the Vatican Library. ANDREA FULVIO (c. 1470–1527) taught grammar (i.e., Latin language).[44] And Gaspare da Verona taught eloquence (i.e., Latin literature). Most of them were kept busy in politics, diplomacy, and administration throughout their lives. Campano began as an academic, with a chair at Perugia. But after he accepted a position as secretary to the general of the Augustinians, Cardinal Alessandro Oliva, he became involved in an endless round of difficult charges—as a member of an embassy to the Diet of Regensburg and as governor of the strife-torn towns of Todi, Assisi, and Città di Castello; and although, in good pre-Tridentine fashion, he paid no attention to his own distant diocese, he conscientiously administered the diocese of his chief patron, Cardinal Francesco Todeschini Piccolomini, later Pope Pius III, at Siena. Volterrano desired nothing more than to be left alone with his books in a monastery. Being the son of a leading papal legal counselor and the brother of two bishops, however, he was sent on difficult diplomatic errands to as far away as Hungary, and he later played a leading role in defending the interests of Julius II in his conflict with King Louis XII. Ammannati spent his declining years not relaxing with learned friends in his Lungotevere salon, as he had hoped, but quarreling with the duke of Milan over his rights as bishop of Pavia and with the tumultous citizens of Todi as papal legate for Umbria. GIOVAN FILIPPO LIGNAMINE of Messina (c. 1420–after 1495) supervised one of the first and most famous printing houses in Rome while serving Sixtus IV as a physician and a chamberlain.[45] And SIGISMONDO DEI CONTI of Foligno (c. 1440–1512), whom Raffaello pictured as a praying patron in the Madonna of Foligno, had to confine his study of history to those rare moments, between his duties as a *scriptor apostolicus* and as ambassador to Belgium and Venice, when he could escape to the quiet of his villa on the Gianicolo.[46]

Enea Silvio Piccolomini and His Heirs

What then made it possible for curial historiography to develop along lines similar to those established in Florence was, first, the adoption of humanism during the pontificate of Nicholas V as the chief source from which the Papacy sought to draw its ideological support and, then, in 1458, the election as Pope PIUS II, of ENEA SILVIO PICCOLOMINI (1405–64), who happened to be a humanist historian.[47] Like the curial historians he encouraged and inspired, Enea Silvio had been involved in *vita activa* since his earliest days—as a secretary first to an exiled cardinal and then to the Council of Basel, to the antipope Felix V, and to the emperor Frederick III. And he then became one of the most enterprising popes since the time of Boniface VIII, presiding over an international congress, beating down rebellions of *condottieri* and local tyrants in the Papal State, and organizing a crusade against the Ottoman Empire. That he had any time left over for reading and dictating so amazed his contemporaries that he felt obliged to preface his *Cosmographia* with a description of his daily work schedule. He thus became fully aware of the practical value of history, at least as a means of "comprehending all the various aspects" of a particular prob-lem and of clarifying the motives of all those persons, himself included, who had previously contributed to its maturation or aggravation, in preparation for propos-ing an effective solution.[48]

To be sure, some of Enea Silvio's works were not specifically dedicated to this end. For instance, the *De Viris Illustribus* (1440–50), which he began when he was still at Basel, was really just an expanded and updated version of the similar compila-tions of Jerome and Petrarch, with the vital statistics, *res gestae,* physical appearance, and moral qualities of each personage listed in page-long entries, and with historical theses limited to marginal comments on those few entries dedicated to men of letters—e.g., to Bruni, whom he credited with inaugurating the current age of good Latinity.[49] Similarly, his *Cosmographia,* completed after his election, was inspired, albeit independently, by an aim similar to that of Biondo's *Italia Illustrata:* matching modern with ancient geography.[50] Since modern geography was still much inferior to what was preserved of ancient geography in the works of Strabo, Ptolemy, and Pliny, Enea Silvio described central Asia and India as if the Macedonians had just moved out. He divided Asia Minor into such provinces as "Cappadocia" and "Galatia" that had long since ceased to exist. And he was the victim of whatever was reported to him orally—like the tall tales about the civil war in Cyprus recounted to him by an ambassador from Rhodes. The *Cosmographia* was also inspired by an aim similar to those of the medieval encyclopedias, an aim Enea Silvio adapted to Renais-sance standards by dismissing as legends those accounts—like those about the Trojan ancestors of the English and the French[51]—that could not be documented in the works of reliable ancient authors. Since he himself had seen more of the world than almost any other European of his age, the work succeeded very well in this aim—so well, indeed, that it was still considered sufficiently informative a hundred years later, when the amount of available information had multiplied many times over, to warrant its being republished in Italian translation.[52]

Yet even the *Cosmographia* had a practical as well as an informative aim: that of furthering the causes to which the author was then dedicated, like the pacification

45

and strengthening of the Papal Sate and the unification and defense of Christendom. It accordingly excoriated whoever stood in the way of the realization of these causes: Filippo Maria Visconti, the "ferocious" Hussites, the "perfidious" Greeks, and the "barbarous, dirty, cruel" Turks. This practical aim is still more evident in his more strictly historical works. The earliest of them, indeed, was essentially an aide-mémoire, a detailed account of the proceedings of the Council of Basel from November 1439 to July 1440, from which the author sought to determine how he might rise from the position of a mere secretary to one more commensurate with his merits. It was also a public document, one in which the author corroborated what he himself had observed by what he apparently read in the contemporary conciliar diary by John of Segovia, and one in which a sense of the dramatic progression of events, from the Conference of Nürnberg to the election of Felix V, was heightened by the elimination of theological arguments that a lay reader might find "too long" or "tedious." So successful was it, indeed, as a work of accurate and elegant reporting, that the author left it untouched when, ten years later, he wrote another history of the Council from the papal point of view to which he had meanwhile been converted.[53] Similarly, his *Germania* of 1457 was aimed at persuading the Germans, and in particular the antipapal chancellor of Mainz, that the Roman Church alone had turned Germany from the poor, barbarous country described by Tacitus into the rich, civilized country that the author had observed with his own eyes.[54] His *Historia Friderici III* and his *Historia Bohemica* of 1458 sought to explain how the Hussites had managed to beat off all the armies so far sent against them and suggest other means by which they might finally be subdued.[55] His *De Captione Urbis Constantinopolitanae* of 1461 sought to stir the consciences of Latin Christians by reminding them of the horrors recently perpetrated upon their Eastern brethren. "I am persuaded," affirmed the author in the midst of plans for another crusade, "that there will be men, perhaps before my death, [who are capable] of avenging the shame inflicted on Our Lord."[56]

This combination of practical and informative aims is best of all illustrated in the greatest of Pius's works, which he began soon after his elevation to the pontificate, the *Commentarii*.[57] Pius sought first of all to clarify in his own mind how he could bring to a successful conclusion the most ambitious of his many projects as pope, the crusade. And he sought to do so by the same method he had used in his earlier historical works: that of studying the particular conditions within which he would have to move. He sought also, with the help of his now fully developed skill in elegant and effective writing, to perpetuate both the fame of his own "distinguished achievements" in promoting the crusade and the infamy of all those acts that thwarted its realization. To be sure, the work was dictated, not written; and the busy dictator apparently forgot, when he was describing the political situation in Siena in one book, that he had already described it thoroughly in another. Moreover, it is based solely on what the author himself had seen, heard, or read, not on what he had consciously looked for. And he apparently felt no need to check what he said, incorrectly, about the foundation of Florence in Bruni, whose *Laudatio* he had followed as model for his own orations, or to check the legend about his Roman ancestors in Biondo, whose *Decades* he was just then abridging. Moreover, the political aims of the *Commentarii* occasionally took precedence over the informative aims. Thus the speech ˜of the Venetian ambassador in favor of the author's chief bête-noire, Pandolfo Malatesta, is deliberately exaggerated in tone in order to draw attention to the speech that the author attributes to himself but never actually delivered.[58] Nonetheless, the subsequent addition of a long preface convincingly put Pius's acts as pope into the context of all that he had done before. His care in describing the geographical and historical circumstances in which each event took place gave his own recollections of that event a heightened impression of immediacy and accuracy. And the inclusion of speeches that were often transcribed rather than invented, as well as the device of referring to himself in the third person, gave to the work as a whole a remarkable, although probably fortuitous, similarity with a recognized ancient model, Caesar. It was therefore acclaimed as a classic of literature equal, if not superior, not only to Caesar but even to Augustine.[59] Campano, whom Pius asked to read it for errors of fact and style, refused to alter a single word. And it might well have become the classic in the fifteenth and sixteenth centuries that it has become only in the twentieth had it not been put aside during the anti-Pian reaction of the following pontificate and had it not been frankly and abundantly expurgated by its only Renaissance editor, Francesco Bandini Piccolomini, in one of the more unfortunate moments of scandal-erasing hysteria in the Counter Reformation (1584).

Thus Pius provided an ideological purpose for the new kind of historiography introduced by Biondo, one that fully compensated for the absence in Rome of the ideologically motivated political community that had inspired the Florentines. It was a purpose to which Biondo himself eventually became sympathetic: when finally, in the 1560s, the Papacy took upon itself the responsibility for saving Eastern Christendom that Biondo had assumed in 1452 to belong to the emperor and the king of Naples, he addressed a plea to the recipients of his *De Gestis Venetorum* that they, reminded by him of the example of their ancestors and "hortantibus Romanis pontificibus," now do to the Ottomans what Attila had once tried to do to them.[60] Indeed, it was a purpose that attracted support from historians outside Rome as well, not only from Benedetto Accolti in Florence,[61] but also from LEODRISIO CRIVELLI in Milan.[62] Crivelli had first come to admire Pius when he was employed as a secretary at the Congress of Mantua in 1459, and he became an ardent disciple after being granted refuge in Rome in 1461 from the wrath of Francesco Sforza. So ardent was he, indeed, that he continued to defend his master after his death, most notably in an *Apologeticus*[63] he directed against his former colleagues in Milan, Francesco and Francesco's son, Giovan Mario Filelfo. After reading Tolosano's *Chronicon Faventium,*[64]

Peter de la Palud's history of the wars in Palestine, and the chronicles of Robert of Chester, Peter of Toledo, and Peter of Cluny, as well as of Mattia Palmieri and Accolti, he became convinced that the Turks were the successors not only of the Saracen opponents of the first crusaders, not only of the Muslim conquerors of Arabia and Syria (as Pomponio Leto suggested in a rather superficial memorandum),[65] but also of the Persian enemies of the Athenian and the Roman Empires. He thus turned Pius's crusade into a climactic moment in an age-old struggle between barbarism and infidelity on one hand, and Greece, Rome, and Christianity on the other. True to Pius's example, he then extracted from history some practical advice on how best to pursue the struggle in the present. The Danube, he suggested, was a more effective line of defense than the Aegean. And his advice might have been taken more seriously had he not thought his work to have been superseded by Pius's *Commentarii,* and had he not then left it in manuscript to be discovered, three centuries later, by Muratori.

So effective was Pius's demonstration of the importance of history as a support for the policies and the aims of the Papacy and as a source of practical lessons in how to carry them out that his example continued to be followed during the succeeding pontificates. JACOPO AMMANNATI dedicated much of the *Commentarii*[66] he wrote in continuation of those of Pius to trying to explain why the crusade had failed. And he concluded with the advice that another one ought not be attempted in the near future. The emperor, he noticed, was powerless in the Empire and unable even to solve the problem of heresy in Bohemia. The king of France and the duke of Burgundy were constantly at each other's throat. No wonder, then, that none of them showed up at Ancona. After describing the ravages that the Malatesta continued to perpetrate with impunity in the Papal State, he doubted that even a pope would now be able to show up there. And after describing the recent sack of Liège, he wondered if a crusade were even justified, for it was no longer clear just who were the barbarians. Similarly, SIGISMONDO DEI CONTI applied much the same form of contemporary history to a defense of the policies of Sixtus IV.[67] Sixtus was not a troublemaker at all, insisted Sigismondo. He was a "vir mansuetudinis et innocentiae apostolicae idem maximi animi," whose first step as pope was to clear up the diplomatic chaos left by his predecessor and to address letters to the princes of Italy urging them to stop fighting. The troublemakers were Niccolò Vitelli, whose dominant trait was "dominandi libido," the "impious" Lorenzo de' Medici, whose greatest desire was to rob church and churchmen, and the bloodthirsty Pazzi conspirators, who dragged Sixtus unwillingly into the war with Florence. That Sixtus then got out of the war with honor was proof that the policies of God's vicar were identical with those of God himself. Or at least such were the policies of that particular vicar: the way Innocent VIII dissipated ecclesiastical property led Sigismondo to have some doubts about his thesis thereafter.

While Pius provided a purpose, he also provided forms for the writing of history.

His fellow countryman and personal secretary, AGOSTINO PATRIZI, learned to write history by taking down the history his employer dictated to him. When his employer's own former employer, Frederick III, came to Rome in 1468, Patrizi applied what he had learned in a detailed but elegant description of the reception ceremonies, together with the texts of all the speeches delivered and with an explanation of the political and historical significance of the event.[68] Jacopo Ammannati learned to write history by listening to it being dictated; and his own *Commentarii* accordingly begin at the very point at which Pius's were interrupted, in the middle of Book XIII. But the most productive model that Pius left behind was not so much his *Commentarii* as his *Cosmographia*. For his chief imitator, RAFFAELLO VOLTERRANO,[69] went well beyond the limits of what one man could hear and observe to include everything that one man could read about in books. In order to find out how much of Christianity had been anticipated in ancient philosophy, Volterrano read not only Aristotle but all the other philosophers whose works had recently come to light. In order to find out how much of ancient philosophy had been incorporated into Christianity, he read all the Greek as well as the Latin Church Fathers, one of whom, Basil, he later translated into Latin.[70] In order to find out what the world had looked like in antiquity, he read all the works of all the ancients that contained passages of geographical significance, from Homer to Procopius, both of whom he also translated,[71] and from Strabo and Pliny to Ptolemy, Sallust, Arrianus, Paulinus, et al,, apparently in something like that order. In order to find out what had happened to the world since antiquity, he read a great number of medieval chronicles, in spite of his distaste for the "amount of inept and illiterate material" they contained; and he himself introduced Westerners to still another medieval source: the huge scissors-and-paste compilation put together on Mount Athos in the twelfth century by the Byzantine chronicler Zonaras.[72] In order to find out what the world looked like in his own day—and he kept sticking in additional notes as *Loca nuper reperta* in Africa and America multiplied before his eyes—he applied for information from as far away as Lisbon.

Thus the *Commentariorum Urbanorum Octa et Triginta Libri*[73] succeeded in covering the whole known world, from the Carribean Sea to the Indian Ocean, although they stopped short of some of Pius's more distant and fabulous lands. They preserved some of the defects of their model, to be sure. Anacreon is presented as the authority for "the purity of the air, the beauty of the landscape, and the abundance of the harvests" that only a poet could imagine in the plains of Castile. And all religious groups not in communion with Rome are denounced with equal disdain, from the followers of "Viklef" to the Jacobites, the Maronites, and the Jews (the Talmud, said Volterrano, is a deliberate corruption of the Old Testament). Yet they add flora and fauna, customs and mores (e.g., the sexual aberrations of the Greeks), and even calculations of longitude and latitude to the subject headings of Pius's geographical descriptions. They carefully distinguish between ancient and modern place-names, which Pius often confused: Gallia Narbonensis, Volterrano pointed out, is now divided into Dauphiné, Savoy, etc. The information is so abundant at times that the main rhetorical thesis tends to get lost: let the Christian princes learn from the consequences of their predecessors' folly to stop fighting among themselves and gang up on the Turks. But the thesis is then reinforced by the author's objectivity concerning everything that is not directly related to it. Lorenzo de' Medici is cleared of complicity in the Pazzi affair in spite of what he did to Volterrano's fellow citizens.[74] Lorenzo Valla's "howling against religion" (i.e., the temporal power of the Papacy, which Volterrano accepted as an article of faith) does not prevent his thesis about the Donation of Constantine from being quietly accepted—as it had been also by Pius. Louis XII, the archenemy of Julius II, to whom the work is dedicated, is praised for his peaceful, effective government. Indeed, Volterrano's objectivity wanes only when he is obliged to portray the pope who represented all that he thought the Papacy ought to be, Pius II, and the pope who incarnated all that he thought it ought not to be, Paul II. The first was "moribus castissimus, religionis amantissimus"; the second was "nec literatura, nec moribus probatus."

In one case, indeed, the models proposed by Pius nearly succeeded in transforming in accordance with historiographical standards a field that had been almost totally immune to them from its very inception: hagiography. True, the results were not always consonant with the authors' expectations. In the absence of trustworthy documentation, LEON BATTISTA ALBERTI was forced to invent dialogues between an imaginary Roman emperor and an abstract second-century martyr—dialogues that effectively underlined the unapostolic behavior of the fifteenth-century clergy, but that had very little to do with any real historical personage. "Despairing of finding anything in which to place [his] full confidence," ANTONIO DEGLI AGLI, formerly tutor to the future Paul II and later bishop of Fiesole and Volterra, let even Bernardino da Siena, whose sermons he had heard in his youth, dissolve into a list of miracles "quae vulgo referentur."[75] Even the ambitious *Martyrium Antonianum* of Ammannati's Florentine correspondent, Francesco da Castiglione, which the current authority on the subject calls a "piccolo saggio di moderna agiografia," was eventually buried, after much discussion between the correspondents, in a collection of other codices in the monastic library of San Marco in Florence.[76] Still, Agli succeeded in exchanging medieval models for recognized ancient ones—Eusebius, Ambrose, and Jerome; and he rearranged his subjects in chronological order, rather than in the order of their feast days in the calendar. GIUSEPPE BRIVIO, a Milanese humanist who moved to Rome as secretary to a bishop in 1445, corrected what he found to be historical errors in the traditional accounts of the life of St. Alexius, MAFFEO VEGIO added the judgments of his humanist predecessors, Bruni and Biglia, and qualified with "ut opinor" whatever was not "testium ... fide et examinatione comperta, probata, atque conscripta." He relegated the postmortem miracles to an appendix. He wrote in the language of Augustine, whose titular church he had helped to restore. And he thus turned Bernardino from a wonder-worker into a credible human being.[77] Similarly, Volterrano wrote a life of the blessed Iacopo di Certaldo in such a way that it was still considered exemplary a century later. And his Venetian friend, the patrician-diplomat FRANCESCO DIEDO (d. 1484), rewrote the lives of the saints of Verona in a form that was still considered definitive by the reforming bishop Agostino Valier in the sixteenth century and by the Bollandists in the seventeenth.[78]

Another of the models provided, not directly by Pius, but rather by Biondo, whose work Pius associated with his own, the *Roma Triumphans,* eventually inspired some imitators, even though its importance was not fully realized until after the middle of the next century.[79] The first of them was GIULIO POMPONIO LETO, the famous Latin philologist. Apparently Pomponio considered the study of the physical remains of antiquity to be secondary to the study of the literary remains. For the *De Magistratibus,* which was really just a supplement to the work of almost the same name by his Florentine friend, Andrea Domenico Fiocchi,[80] began with the surprising assertion that "Romulus was begotten by Mars"; and it went on to contradict, without any explanation, Fiocchi's thesis about the difference between the *foeciales* and the *patres patrati.* His *Compendium* was so intent upon debunking old heroes, like Constantine, and exalting old villains, like Julian the Apostate, that it slipped into several absurdities: Aurelius Caro "would have turned the whole Persian kingdom upside down" had he not been struck by lightning, Pomponio had the nerve to say, and the emperor Julian actually did reappear after his death on the streets of Constantinople. His *Antiquitates* were devoid of inscriptions or illustrations, and they had no more to tell about the Pantheon than the name of the emperor who robbed it of its silver ornaments.[81] Nevertheless, all three of these books had some merit. The first added a special category for "laws" and a key for the proper interpretation of inscriptions. The second straightened out the order of the pre-Constantinian emperors and lined up literary with epigraphic and numismatic references. The third added in an appendix a short dictionary of ancient place-names with their modern equivalents. They thus turned out to be handy reference works for occasional readers of the ancient historians and for busy tourists in Rome. And they were accordingly reprinted several times, in Italian as well as in Latin, in the course of the next fifty years.

The second imitator of Biondo was FRANCESCO ALBERTINI (d.c. 1517–21),[82] four of whose opuscula were actually published out of the fifteen he claimed to have written. The *Septem Mirabilia Orbis et Urbis Romae*[83] tried unsuccessfully to squeeze everything into three sets of "seven wonders," each of which thus ends with a reference to the "many others" of the same kind. The *De Laudibus Civitatis Florentiae* (1502) and the *Memoriale de molto statue et picture sono nella inclyta cipta di Florentia,*[84] which attempted, notwithstanding the linguistic barbarisms in its title, to apply the structure of Roman guidebooks to Florence, show that the author had learned more about art from Ghirlandaio than about history from Naldo Naldi—or from Bruni, also mentioned. The Florentine Baptistry, it seems, was built by Gnaius Pompeius, Julius Caesar, and "other noble Romans." The *Antiquitates,*[85] on the other hand, are full of new inscriptions and careful measurements; and they add to Biondo and Pomponio Leto a note about the subsequent restoration projects undertaken by Sixtus IV as well as a list of current cardinals with the location of their palaces. Of the three remaining imitations of Biondo in the two decades before the sack of Rome, FABRICIO VARRANO's *De Urbe Roma* consists of little more than a drastic abridgment of the *Roma Instaurata,* with the addition of an interesting calculation of the difference in circumference between the imperial and the modern walls.[86] But the *De Sestertio* (before 1503) of the Romanized German, JAKOB AURELIUS QUESTEN-BERG, might have rivaled the epoch-making *De Asse* by Guillaume Budé had anyone before the twentieth century been able to read it.[87] Similarly, ANDREA FULVIO's two major works, the *Antiquaria Urbis* of 1513 and the *Antiquitates Urbis* of 1527, were the fruit of the author's careful rereading of all the relevant ancient texts and of the studies of ancient medals and coins reported in his *Illustrium Imagines* of 1517. They therefore corrected many of Biondo's and Pomponio's errors, they included several institutions not previously studied (like libraries, with a rhapsodic account of the invention of printing), and they offered some further answers to Biondo's question of why Rome fell. They thus represent, according to Roberto Weiss, "the final expression, or rather testament, of . . . Roman humanism." And that expression might have been even more positive had the maps and charts drawn by Fulvio's assistant, Mario Calvo of Ravenna, not been destroyed in the holocaust of 1527.[88]

Biographical History

Still, the form of history writing that became most characteristic of curial historiography owed to Biondo only its commitment to humanist literary standards, and to Pius it owed only its commitment to the several political, or politico-ecclesiastical, causes of the curial humanists. That was history in the guise of biography. Biographical history was to some extent justified by the example of several suitable ancient models, particularly Plutarch, Suetonius, and Curtius Rufus. But what brought the models to the attention of the Curial humanists was the particular historiographical experience first, of the noncurial Florentine historian Giannozzo Manetti, in his life of Pope Nicholas V of 1453,[89] and then of one of their more recent recruits, GIOVANNANTONIO CAMPANO,[90] whose life of the Perugian condottiere Braccio da Montone was hailed by the author's posthumous eulogist as superior to either of the two ancient models it claimed to imitate. The *Vita Bracii*[91] was devoted to a cause—although the cause was not that of the Curia but just the opposite, that of the independent communes of Umbria. It was also committed to the truth, which the author went all the way to Aquila to ascertain; and it qualified with a *fertur* whatever could not be documented by reliable oral testimony or by references in the

Perugian chronicles. Campano's accounts of debates and battles were rendered particularly vivacious by the kind of detailed and evocative geographical descriptions of which he showed himself to be a master in his treatise on Lake Trasimeno. He successfully exhalted his hero and quietly omitted any details that might have tarnished his hero's reputation. And he went well beyond his hero's own feats to embrace "all the things done by sea and by land in Italy in our times," which, in his opinion, were quite as glorious as any recorded in antiquity and thus quite as capable of encouraging the performance of similar feats in the present.

What had been applied successfully to the lives of Nicholas V and Braccio could obviously be applied to Pius II as well. And the urgency of doing so became particularly apparent as the alliance established by Pope Nicholas between the Papacy and humanism was threatened by the anti-Pian policies of Pius's successor, Paul II. Indeed, Platina's life of Pius was written while the author was in prison, and Campano's was written in response to the attacks on Pius's memory by the Filelfos. But both of them were firmly based on the writings of their hero himself, with which the biographers were thoroughly familiar. In fact, Platina was so faithful to his sources that he repeated without qualification Pius's claim to have descended from a noble Roman refugee from the sack of A.D. 410. Both of them thus succeeded in portraying the pontificate of Pius as a golden age in the history of the Church, one to be commended for imitation once again as soon as the present retrogressive pope was succeeded by someone more worthy of his illustrious predecessor.[92] The defense of Pius then made obviously necessary a counterdefense of the pope to whom he had been favorably contrasted, Paul II, who, unlike Pius, took a direct interest in finding a suitable biographer. GASPARE DA VERONA began with a biography which, like Campano's *Vita Braccii,* encompassed most of the political history of Italy during Paul's lifetime. Indeed, it included so much general information that the author himself had to admit, as early as the end of Book I, that it was a bit "prolix." MICHELE CANENSI, whom Paul made bishop of Castro in 1469, sought to incorporate into history the rules of Quintillian for the *laudatio* that he had already successfully applied in a eulogy of Nicholas V. And although he revised the text again after his hero's death, he remained faithful to his original thesis. Platina was wrong, Canensi insisted, in claiming that Paul had rejected the humanists. Rather, it was thanks largely to Paul that modern times had at last surpassed antiquity. "Some laud their ancestors and men of old," he reflected. "I, on the other hand, am led [*me... iuvat*] to praise, venerate, and admire ... my contemporaries."[93]

Histories of individual pontificates, however, were not yet histories of the Papacy; and the second was even more urgent than the first for those curial humanists who wished to render permanent the accomplishments and to fulfill the aspirations of Nicholas V and Pius II. To be sure, there were a few precedents for such a project: such of the medieval chronicles that dedicated a special section to popes, like Riccobaldo da Ferrara's *Historia Pontificum Romanorum,* and the *Liber Pontificalis,* a compilation of biographies first assembled between the fifth and the seventh centuries that had been resuscitated by Petrarch and then continued for the popes of the Schism by Poggio. But none of these precedents was any longer acceptable. The Venetian jurist-bishop Jacopo Zeno tried to appease the ears of his contemporaries by translating the vulgar Latin of the *Liber Pontificalis* into classical Latin; but he failed to make the results palatable to their critical tastes. Giovan Filippo Lignamine gave up trying to appease anyone. In fact, in his continuation of Riccobaldo from John XXII to Sixtus IV he put back not only the emperors but even the dukes of Milan into what became nothing more than a list of miscellaneous dates. And it would probably not even have been published had the author not owned a printing press.[94] What was needed, obviously, was a completely new history of the Papacy written according to Renaissance standards, not those of early or high medieval times, as Platina realized when he decided himself to write one. For only such a history would be able both to meet the ideological requirements of the Curia and, at the same time, to win an appointment for the author as head of the Vatican Library. Since Platina had already written biographical histories of Vittorino da Feltre and Pius II, and since he had already demonstrated his skill as a Latinist in his translation of Neri Capponi's *Commentari*,[95] it is not surprising that he adopted the same form of historical writing that he himself had helped to canonize at the time of Paul II.

Platina did not always live up to the standards he recognized. He said "ut ait Eusebius" when he really meant Jerome's version of Eusebius. He pretended to use Martin of Troppau (Martinus Polonus) when in fact he was following Tolomeo da Lucca.[96] He bothered to look only at those late imperial Greek historians, like Sozomenus, who happened to be available in translations. He ignored all the various accounts of the Gregorian reform that he could easily have found in the Vatican. He passed off as his own long passages that were lifted verbatim from Biondo—or rather, not from Biondo himself but from Pius II's abridgment of Biondo. As a consequence, many of his lives read like paraphrases of Paulus Diaconus, with all of Paulus's disorganized patchwork of plagiarized passages left intact and all of his scruples about what seemed improbable left out.[97] Many of the others read like a classical Latin translation of Tolomeo da Lucca, without a trace of Tolomeo's untiring search for documents. They are full of tall stories—like Tiberius's proposal to the Senate for a temple in honor of Christ, which Platina could easily have checked in Tacitus. They are full of irrelevant details, like those about Gelasius I's taste for elegant orations and Paul II's passion for melons and salt pork. They are full of highly dubious statements barely shielded behind protestations of *nonnulli dicunt*. They omit any consideration of the one subject that interested most of the popes, theology: the Council of Chalcedon is just another *res gesta* of Leo I, and the difference between Thomas and Scotus, Platina dared to proclaim, is just a matter of words. Most important of all, they failed completely to bridge the gap established in late antiquity between the history of the Church and the history of the Empire and its successors. Platina reviewed the feats of Augustus without even suggesting what they had to do with the birth of Jesus, and he inserted a long excursus on the War of Chioggia without even asking what bearing it had on the pontificate of Urban VI.

In spite of these defects, Platina's *Lives of the Popes*[98] was greeted with almost unanimous acclaim. It went through eight editions in the six years after 1479 and many other editions, in Italian as well as Latin, in the following decades. It was continued for the next three pontificates by none other than Volterrano. And it was eventually incorporated by one of the most meticulous scholars of the mid-sixteenth century, Onofrio Panvino, into what became the official Counter Reformation history of the Papacy.[99] This applause was not wholly undeserved. After all, the various lives were historical rather than hagiographical in form and content, and they were written in what, from the fifteenth to the seventeenth century, was considered to be the proper language of communication, classical Latin. They were also relatively objective, and they thus gave at least the appearance of reliability. None of the heroes is without defects, not even Pius II, whose *vita* in this work was a reworking of the longer version Platina had published separately several years earlier. None of his villains is without merit, either—not even Clement V, who took the Church to Babylon and blessed the slaughter of the Templars, but who also paid for the restoration of the Constantinian basilica. This same objectivity was observed by Volterrano in his continuation: Sixtus IV, whom Platina had been obliged to flatter, was blamed for excessive partiality toward the Franciscans, and Alexander VI was credited with appointing several pious cardinals. Moreover, the biographical form did not prevent Platina from occasionally noting transitions from one historical epoch to the next: in the midst of the chaos precipitated by the death of Giangaleazzo Visconti, he observed, the arrival in Italy of Chrysoloras initiated the rebirth of good letters that was the chief characteristic of the present age. Nor did this form prevent him from noticing important changes in the structure of the Church, like those that followed from the decrees of the Council of Constance. Hence, the *Lives* succeeded in doing for the Papacy what Bruni's *Historiae* had done for Florence. By connecting the present with the past, they showed the misdeeds of Paul II to be merely temporary, and far from unprecedented, aberrations in the history of an institution that had lasted for some fifteen centuries. Having been founded by Christ , established by Peter, defended by Gregory VII, aroused by Peter the Hermit, strengthened by Francis and Dominic, restored by the Council of Constance, and brought to the peak of its glory by Nicholas V and Pius II, there was little chance that it would suddenly succumb before the unworthiness of any one of its momentary representatives. Indeed, in the late fifteenth century it seemed to be the only institution in the world capable of bringing peace to Christendom and ruin to the Ottoman Empire. And Platina never once wavered in his loyalty to it. That Luther managed to extract from the *Lives* information to support just the opposite of their principal thesis merely does honor to Platina's humanism.[100] That a modern scholar as late as 1972 could still refer to them as a "pejorative history of the popes" merely does honor to the lasting strength of the post-Protestant belief that all true Catholics are made in the image not of Pius II but of Pius X.[101]

Thus, the historians of the Curia, in a very different historical and political setting, succeeded in producing works of history that were comparable in quality and quantity with those of the Florentines. But they too eventually ran into difficulties that threatened the future development of their enterprise.

First of all, the curial historians never got around to formulating clearly what was one of their most important innovations in practice: the definition of history as the search for, not just the recording of, the truth. Biondo had never been content merely to paraphrase chronicles; indeed, he had written his accounts of the Blacks and Whites and of Cola di Rienzo only after supplementing what he had read about them in Tolomeo da Lucca and in Giovanni Villani with what Dante and Petrarch had said about them in their letters. Similarly, Ammannati kept his secretaries busy for years writing to men of letters and state all over Italy, and he himself kept a *Diario consistoriale* to make sure that his memory did not fail him about what went on in the Curia. But no one ever gave them any credit for their assiduousness. Pius II was not reprimanded for writing authoritatively about England and Germany without having consulted a single local chronicle and without having learned a single local language during his years of residence in those countries. Nor was Platina reproached when he agreed to write a history of Mantua for his friend and protector, Cardinal Francesco Gonzaga, without the slightest intention of ever setting foot outside of Rome. He proceeded to borrow a few periodic concepts (e.g. the age of "libertas civitatum Italicarum"), as well as most of his information, from Biondo and Bruni. He then looked up what Livy had said about the Etruscans. He borrowed a nice story about St. Longinus and Christ's Sponge from Pope Leo III. And he read the appropriate passages on the Congress of Mantua in Pius's *Commentarii*. He attributed the wars of the Lombard communes to nothing more specific than *aemulatio* and *invidia* in order to shield his eyes from the "rudes et ignaves scriptores" in whom the real causes were recorded. And he paid no attention at all to the pre-twelfth-century *monumenta* that his eighteenth-century editor, Muratori, thought he should have studied. He was not at all distressed when the duke of Mantua sent back the first draft with a long list of errors. In fact, he waited until he had finished the cookbook he was then writing (probably without ever visiting a kitchen) before making the necessary corrections. For he was confident that his impeccable Latin would suffice to "celebrate the memory of those who have acted with strength and constancy" and to persuade his readers to "prefer honest labor to base idleness."[102]

Platina was completely justified in being so confident, for historians in fifteenth-century Rome were not expected to find out anything at all. According to Platina himself, they were supposed simply to outdo philosophers in showing princes and private citizens how to be prudent in this world and how to prepare for eternal happiness in the next.[103] According to Pope Pius, they were supposed to give praise to those who deserved to be imitated; and he accordingly applauded Panormita's history of Naples because it proved Alfonso d'Aragona to be more glorious than any of the ancients, including Socrates.[104] According to Pomponio Leto, who found not a word about research either in the ancient rhetoricians or in those ancient historians he consulted on the matter, historians were supposed to teach readers how to "hate the vices . . . and ardently imitate the virtues."[105] And since history was both easy and pleasant to read, he introduced a few lectures on the historians in his course on ancient literature in order to give his students a break between one heavy dose of philosophy and the next.

The second failing of the curial historians was their inability to understand the nature of the Papacy as an institution. The fault was not necessarily theirs. The ancient historians they read yielded them only one institution, the polis, which unfortunately was as completely inapplicable to the one to which they were committed as it was occasionally misleading for their Florentine colleagues. But it was their own disdain for medieval theology that prevented them from learning from the Fathers at Constance and Basel to see the Papacy as one member in the *corpus* of the Church as a whole. Consequently, neither Pius, who had read all the relevant documents, nor Platina, who had carefully avoided reading any of them, could conceive of either the Papacy or the Church as anything but a random succession of individual persons. True, their fascination with "memorable deeds" enabled them occasionally to extract from history solutions to some of the more important problems the Papacy faced in their day. Having studied the rise of heretical movements in the late fourteenth-century, the apparent triumph of Conciliarism in the early fifteenth century, the building of Rome in antiquity, and the spread of the Ottoman Empire in modern times, they came up with some constructive proposals of how to block heresy, circumvent Conciliarism, rebuild Rome, and resist the Turks. But their assumption that the Papacy consisted of nothing but a series of popes prevented them from understanding why the whole *Corpus Christianorum* did not show up at Ancona, why "the Venetians" preferred commerce to glory, and why the duke of Burgundy hesitated to abandon even for a moment the shaky collection of "states" among which he alone provided a bond of unity. The only explanation they could give for the inability of Pius II to evoke in the fifteenth century the same response that had been accorded to Urban II in the eleventh century was very similar to the one that was to be given for very different reasons, by Egidio da Viterbo at the ill-fated Fifth Lateran Council.[106] The Church, they said, suffered from just three ills: war at home, the Turks abroad, and a few unworthy (i.e., uneducated) men in high places. Of clerical absenteeism, bureaucratic corruption, spiritual indifference, theological aridity, popular superstition, and all the other ills that in fact undermined the prestige of the Papacy in the apparently triumphant decades after the reconciliation of Felix V, they said not a word. They were therefore incapable of forseeing either the Savonarolan rebellion against Alexander VI or the Gallican rebellion against Julius II. In fact, they thought that the Papacy was entering another age even more golden than that of Pius II just at the moment when it was really rushing blindly into the tragedies of 1517 and 1527.[107]

3

VENICE AND GENOA

MANY OF THE SAME CIRCUMSTANCES THAT FACILITATED THE RISE OF HUMANIST HISTORI-ography in Florence also existed in the two other major republics of the peninsula at the turn of the fifteenth century. Both Venice and Genoa were governed by more or less closed, but still relatively numerous, oligarchies. Both were committed to preserving their institutions from what they, as well as the Florentines, considered to be their exact opposite: the kind of domestic tyranny with expansionist ambitions that had come to prevail in almost all the cities of northern Italy during the preceding hundred years. Both had economic interests all over the Mediterranean world—interests which, together with their maritime locations, made them more international than Italian in character. And neither had any scruples about letting their flags follow their ships, particularly when the dissolution of the Byzantine Empire opened up the possibility of acquiring extensive territorial holdings in the Aegean and the Black seas.

Moreover, both cities had recently experienced crises equally as disastrous as the bank crash, the Black Death, and the Ciompi revolt in Florence. After years of fruitless attempts to put down rebellions in Zara, Venice had been forced to cede all of Dalmatia to the king of Hungary (1356). The rise of a strong Ottoman state in Anatolia and in the Balkans had rendered increasingly vain the age-old contest between the two cities for control of the Bosporus—even though neither of them was loath to collaborate with their common enemy for their own particular advantage. The War of Chioggia (1379–81) had left Genoa exhausted and more internally divided than ever, and it had almost cost Venice its very existence as an independent state. Yet both cities had quickly embarked on a strenuous campaign to recover from the crises. Instead of tearing up the Treaty of Turin (1381), which neither of them had accepted without reservations, they decided to use it as the basis for negotiating their future differences; and a half-century of violent conflict gradually gave way to a period of reluctant but relatively peaceful coexistence. The appointment of Jean Le Maingre de Boucicault as lord of Genoa in the name of the king of France in 1401 put an end, at least temporarily, to open warfare among the principal families, and the success of his naval expedition to the Levant in 1403 seemed to herald a renewal of the overseas empire. At the same time, the disintegration of the Visconti state provided Venice with an opportunity once and for all to rid its continental trade routes of interference from the constant shifting of unstable tyrannies on the mainland. Like the capture of Pisa by the Florentines, the capture of Padua by the Venetians at almost the same time marked for Venice the beginning of a new policy aimed at building a territorial state in Italy, while the acquisition of Negro-ponte (1390) and the purchase of Dalmatia (1409) marked the reinauguration of its traditional policy of expansion in the East.[1]

The Chronicle Tradition

More important still, both cities were heirs to a long and rich chronicle tradition. In Genoa this tradition seems to have originated in the private initiative of one man, CAFFARO, who, around 1118, began recording the chief acts of the republic since his entrance into political life in 1100. But Caffaro was much more than merely a private citizen. A trip to the Holy Land in 1100–1 had given him a sense of participation in what was then considered to be the most "memorable," and ideologically impec-cable, act since the Incarnation. It also may have given him some contact with the rudiments of what was soon to become one of the most important literary genres in northern Europe: crusade historiography; and his celebration of Genoa's contri-bution to the Crusades, the *De Liberatione Civitatum Orientis,* was still considered important enough many centuries later to be included among Paul Riart's *Historiens occidentaux des Croissades.* A trip to Rome in 1123 prepared him for the numerous embassies he was to undertake on behalf of the republic all over Italy for the rest of his life. In 1144 he commanded the fleet that threw the Saracens out of Minorca; and soon thereafter showed that he could write as well as he could fight by recording his experiences in his *Ystoria Captionis Almaric et Turtose.* Meanwhile, he occupied in turn the highest magistracies of the republic, including the consulate, to which he was elected five times. Hence what he wrote largely from personal observation was remarkably thorough, particularly in comparison to the bare lists of *podestà* that constituted the sole historical records of most Italian cities of the time; and only occasionally did "the politician win out over the historian" and suppress events that he felt to be somewhat less than praiseworthy. Moreover, his chronicle already contained some elements that anticipated the canons of the humanists: direct dis-course speeches, frequent interruptions of chronological sequence to provide back-ground information, and full recognition of the free commune as a legitimate and autonomous political society.[2]

Thus what started out as a private memorandum soon acquired the character of a public record; and when Caffaro formally presented it to the consuls in 1152, they ordered it copied for future reference in the communal archive and read out loud in meetings of the council. After Caffaro's death in 1166, they appointed a successor, OBERTO, a man of equal wealth and rank and of somewhat more polished education, who cast his continuation for the years 1163–73 in the ornate style recently devel-oped in the Roman Curia. Oberto's first successor, OTTOBONA, was too much of a scribe to exercise the independence of judgment required of a statesman, and his second successor, OGERIO PANE, was too much of a merchant-statesman to give much time to writing. Yet uneven and at times obsequious though their additions may be, they succeeded in underlining the long-range significance of such current events as the demise of the consular regime at home, the expansion of Genoese power in Liguria and Sicily, and the establishment of the Latin Empire at Constantinople.[3]

After 1229, the task of continuing the chronicle was turned over to individual members of the chancery and then to special committees of jurists and notaries appointed by the *podestà*. It therefore became more anonymous in tone, more scrupulous in administrative detail, and more sensitive to major changes in the composition and the policies of the government—all while preserving the general form set down by Caffaro a century earlier. In 1280, the chronicle was entrusted once again to a single statesman, JACOPO D'ORIA, whose wide reading in all the historical literature available in his day and whose personal collection of state documents permitted him to make extensive marginal corrections in the text of his predecessors and to describe in dramatic detail the two major political triumphs of medieval Genoa: the massacre of the French in Sicily and the destruction of the Pisan fleet on the Tyrrhenian Sea.[4]

When D'Oria then lost interest in his work—largely, it seems, out of annoyance with his colleagues in government for not implementing the lessons he had drawn from the past—and when the government showed no signs of immediately replacing him, one of his friends set out to recast all the information recorded in the public chronicles in a form more congenial to medieval audiences: that of a chronicle "from the beginning to the present." JACOPO DA VARAGINE (1228/9–1299) was a voracious reader, one who knew all of what was then available of ancient as well as medieval literature and who could quote at random from Livy or from Bede, from Valerius Maximus or from Augustine, from the Bible or from Vincent of Beauvais. He was also a tireless writer, particularly of saints' lives, sermons, and liturgical handbooks. He was a man of broad experience, having served as ambassador for the republic and the Papacy all over Italy. He was a man of high rank and reputation—first as general of the Lombard Dominicans, and then, from 1292, as archbishop of Genoa. Above all, he was a patriotic Genoese citizen; and in the last years of his life he posed a question that few of his predecessors had ever thought of: why the origins of so great a city were all but unknown.

In the absence of concrete documents, Jacopo fell back on an etymological argument—of the kind, alas, that was to remain popular for the next five centuries,[5] "Genoa," he noted, was usually written "Ianua" in the Latin of his day, which he assumed to be the same as ancient Latin. Therefore, the city must have been founded by Ianus, which was the name later given to Noah after he decided to leave the barren slopes of Mount Ararat and retire among his numerous and wealthy grandchildren in Italy. Fortunately, when Jacopo got down to historical times, he limited himself to the concrete references he found in contemporary authors; and when he reached the twelfth century, he merely arranged under such headings "secular government," "ecclesiastical affairs," and "res domestica" what he found in Caffaro and his successors. His information therefore maintained the same degree of accuracy as that of his sources, which were mostly contemporary accounts written, or at least subjected to correction, by eyewitnesses of the events themselves. Moreover, he presented what he found in such a way as to suggest a progressive view of Genoese history. The tiny village that the Carthaginians had destroyed in the third century B.C. and that the Saracens had destroyed in the sixth century A.D. had, by the end of the thirteenth century, become the mistress of the Mediterranean. All that needed to be done to maintain it in this position was to follow the moral and political precepts that he liberally extracted from its experience in the past. Jacopo thus anticipated, unwittingly and for very different reasons, a view of national history that was to be put forth for Florence by Bruni almost 150 years later. And that is probably one of the main reasons why, in spite of its myths and its supernatural explanations, his work was as widely read and respected in the mid-fifteenth century as it had been in the early fourteenth.

In Venice, the chronicle tradition was still older than in Genoa. It went back at least as far as the eleventh century—to GIOVANNI DIACONO (c. 1018), to a chronicle of the patriarchs of Aquileia (1045–53), and to the *Altinate* (after 1081), of which a section is known also as the *Gradense*. It was further elaborated in the thirteenth century in the *Historia Ducum Venetorum* (1229), in the *Histoire venetienne* of MARTINO DA CANAL (1267–75), and in the up-dated version of the *Altinate* usually called "Marco" after the probable name of its unknown compiler.[6] Moreover, rather than simply dying out, as it did in Genoa when the government neglected to appoint another committee and when Varagine's book came to be accepted as definitive, the tradition in Venice continued developing through the fourteenth century and beyond. The question of language—whether the medieval Latin of most of the early chroniclers or the international French of Martino da Canal—gradually became settled in favor of Venetian. And in the *Cronica estesa* (from A.D. 48, in the surviving texts, to A.D. 1280) and the *Cronica breve* (to the year of composition) of ANDREA DANDOLO (1306–54),[7] the Venetian chronicle reached a degree of methodological consistency and literary refinement approaching that of Giovanni Villani.

The Venetian tradition was also quantitatively richer than the Genoese. In 1291 the government ordered that an official record be kept of all its transactions, and it subsequently recognized Andrea Dandolo's chronicle as the equivalent of an official record. But the principal initiative in chronicle writing came from individual citizens, who found it convenient to keep a running account of those past and current events relevant to their business or political interests. Hence chronicles multiplied: over a thousand different codices have survived from the fourteenth century alone. Moreover, almost no two copies of what purports to be the same chronicle are exactly alike. For any household that did not have a chronicle of its own merely borrowed one from another household—and then made whatever alterations, abridgments, or additions it saw fit. The name of the author carried none of the prestige in Venice that it did in Genoa. Consequently, some of the chronicles have been attributed first to one and then to another author—the most recent example being that of the "not very valuable *cronichetta*" once attributed to an unknown twelfth-century Paduan and now restored to the fourteenth-century Venetian IACOPO DONDI. Many of them remain anonymous and are referred to by their call numbers—like "2034" and "87.1."[8] Many of them turn out to be merely transcriptions or paraphrases of other chronicles—to the point, indeed, where one modern authority has decided to classify them not by the names of the presumed authors but by "families"—e.g., *A-latino, A-volgare, Contaminazione-C-b*. PIERO GIUSTINIAN copied most of his first chapters right out of Dandolo's *Cronica estesa* and then permitted his copyist to add further notes of his own for the years 1354–58.[9] Dandolo in turn copied many of his own pages—without acknowledgment—from Paolino da Venezia, except when he decided to pad Paolino—without warning—with passages copied instead from Martino da Canal or Tolomeo da Lucca. Dandolo's own collaborator and then continuer, BENINTENDI DE' RAVIGNANI (d. 1365), so carefully followed the form and style of the *Cronica breve* that within a century no one remembered where one had stopped and the other begun. Even so careful a student as Marin Sanudo thought that he was reading Pietro Dolfin when actually he was reading ANTONIO MOROSINI, whose voluminous journal of the years from 1407 to 1433 was largely incorporated into Dolfin's chronicle.[10]

It is not surprising, therefore, that the similarities among these many chronicles are far more striking than their differences. After all, almost all the known chroniclers were members of the Venetian patriciate—of that class, in other words, which ever since the late thirteenth century had become dedicated to promoting homogeneity among its members and thus preventing the degeneration of aristocracy into tyranny. Andrea Dandolo was a doge—that is, the holder of the highest office in the state, with lifetime tenure. NICOLÒ TREVISAN (from whose memoranda the chronicle later attributed wholly to him was compiled) was successively a member of the Council of Ten and a *procurator* of San Marco.[11] And Piero Giustinian (if that is indeed the name of the otherwise unknown member of the powerful family who wrote the chronicle attributed to him) was the son of a governor of Zara and Chioggia and admiral of the fleet of the anti-Turk league of the mid-fourteenth century. Those unidentified chroniclers who may not actually have been patricians were at least professional lawyers in the chancery—hence all the more sensitive to the views of their political superiors. And the one known chronicler who began writing as an employee rather than as a member of the government, RAFFAINO DE' CARESINI (c. 1314–90), was eventually rewarded for his services as chancellor during the War of Chioggia with a hereditary appointment to the Great Council.[12]

Thus most of the chroniclers were men of action; and that meant, at least until well into the fifteenth century, that they were not men of letters. Few of them seem to have read any of the classics of medieval European historiography for any other purpose than that of picking up a bit of information. They invariably began their accounts not with the Creation or the Flood, but with the first settlers of Veneto or with the founding of Venice. They marked the passage of time, at least after the seventh century, not by emperors or popes, but by doges. They all but ignored major turning points in history—such as those that appear in the work of Iacopo da Varagine. Even the spectacular events that induced one anonymous writer to begin his chronicle in 1402 rather than 1404 were cataclysmic rather than historical in nature: the appearance of a comet, the ravages of Tamerlane, the fall of "the Turkish chief Bajazid," and the death of Giangaleazzo—all utterly unrelated occurrences with no appreciable effect on what happened in the years following.[13] More important still, the chroniclers generally took note of what went on outside of Venice not, as Villani did, because of its intrinsic interest or notoriety, but solely because of its relevance ot the affairs of Venice. Indeed, the only two chroniclers who took anything but specific information from non-Venetian sources were really Venetians only by birth and nationality, not by residence or in spirit. PAOLINO DA VENEZIA (1270/74–c. 1334)[14] borrowed the guidelines of his three historical works from Augustine and Martinus Polonus, just as he borrowed his political theories from Egidio Romano and his geographical concepts from Vincent of Beauvais. But Paolino was neither a merchant nor a patrician; rather, he was a Franciscan theologian who became successively inquisitor for the Marca Trevigiana (that is, mainland, but not yet Venetian, Veneto), ambassador for Pope John XXII, counselor to King Robert of Naples, and resident bishop of Pozzuoli in southern Italy. Paolino's close friend MARIN SANUDO TORSELLO (c. 1270–after 1343)[15] put the information he himself had collected from firsthand experience into the context of the established historiography of the Crusades, and he did so for the very un-Venetian purpose of trying to persuade the pope to launch still another crusade. But Sanudo was brought up on a family barony on the island of Naxos and spent most of his mature years not residing in Venice, but traveling back and forth from Cyprus to Lübeck, from Bourges to Alexandria, from Palermo to Armenia.

Similarly, most of the chroniclers were concerned not so much with deprecating the present—"hoc infortunato millesimo," as Piero Giustinian put it—as with proposing solutions to current political problems. The author of the *Historia Ducum Venetorum* sought to reverse the course of internal institutional development by portraying the doges as repositories of public virtues, and hence as the rightful custodians of public authority. Martino da Canal sought to promote an alliance with the Papacy and the Angevins for the purpose of throwing the Genoese out of Constantinople and restoring the Latin Empire. ENRICO DANDOLO sought to demonstrate the folly of imperialism and the superiority of merchant ships, which made money, to warships, which cost money. Hence, even those chronicles that were composed within the confines of a single family were meant to be read by the whole of the patriciate. "This record of great deeds should be spread around [*propaganda*]," according to one writer, so that others too might be stimulated "to do good for the republic" (Caresini). The proper language of communication, according to another, was the vernacular, for thus the intended audience would "draw more delight and consolation and more willingly read" what was written (Enrico Dandolo).

At the same time, most chronicles were careful to document just what had been done in the past to further or to obstruct the policies they advocated. Thus Andrea Dandolo copied into his chronicles many of the state papers and statutes that he had discovered during the many years he spent before his election as doge imposing some sort of order on the contents of the archive. Finally, all the chronicles were dedicated to the defense of a number of politically significant historical theses. Venice, they insisted, had always been governed by noble families: only the nobility of Troy could have been able to afford the ships that brought Antenore to the mouth of the Po, and only the nobility of the Roman Veneto could have had the means or the incentive to ship their goods to the islands of the Lagoon when threatened by the ravages of Attila. Venice, they continued, had always been sovereign and independent: neither the Franks, whom the Venetians beat in battle, nor the exarchs of Ravenna, to whom they voluntarily gave refuge, nor—least of all—the Byzantine emperors had ever exercised any authority over the Lagoon; and no one paid any attention to the clear evidence to the contrary that Roberto Cessi was to find, six centuries later, in the very same sources that they also used. Venice, they added, was innocent of any wrongdoing in what everyone else considered to be the most scandalous act of the High Middle Ages: the Fourth Crusade. It had a right to what it had grabbed in the partition of the Byzantine dominions because it was the legitimate representative of "the Apostolic Empire in the East"; it owned outright what it now held because no Venetian—notwithstanding the presence of the relevant documents right there in the Venetian archives—had ever made an act of homage to Emperor Baldwin; and anyway, it had acted not on its own initiative but on a specific command of the pope, to whom all the charges usually levied against the Venetians ought properly to be referred.

The Terraferma Tradition

As in Genoa, then, the chronicle in Venice had already developed, well before the advent of humanism, some of the elements that were to be characteristic of humanist historiography. It might have developed others had the chroniclers been able or willing to profit from one advantage that Genoa did not enjoy: proximity to another, equally rich chronicle tradition in the mainland cities over which Venice was soon to extend its dominion. Outside of Genoa, no one in Liguria or Corsica ever seems to have thought the events of his day worth recording—or at least the one Ligurian who is known to have thought differently, an obscure druggist of the Lunigiana in the mid-fifteenth century, could find little else to put in his diary but what he heard from travelers of what went on in the capital city or the papal court.[16] But the citizens of the Marca Trevigiana had become convinced not only of the utility, but also of the necessity, of keeping such records as early as the first decades of the thirteenth century. Their chronicles had been born in the midst of what at the time was considered to be an inexplicable disaster. The main task assumed by the first chroniclers was that of figuring out why neither the only political authority they recognized as legitimate, the Empire, nor the only political authority any of them had ever known in practice, the autonomous urban republic, had been able to maintain internal law and order or to block the advent of the bloodiest, most unscrupulous tyrant of all times: Ezzelino da Romano (d. 1259).[17]

True, at least one of the chroniclers recognized that the collapse of republican institutions and the subjection of all the cities to the authority of one man was inevitable: GHERARDO MAURISIO of Vicenza (fl. 1198–1237);[18] and that Maurisio's most recent editor should denounce him as a servile sycophant for trying to civilize the masters who mistreated him proves nothing but the lasting influence of Risorgimento historical mythology on early twentieth-century scholarship. Certainly in 1236, when Gherardo began to write, the alternative of rule by Emperor Frederick II, who had just torn up Vicenza and robbed the author even of his clothes, did not seem particularly attractive; and in 1237, when he finished writing, Ezzelino's capture of Padua made the new regime seem more durable than ever.

To most of the chroniclers, however, Ezzelino was the devil incarnate—one whose advent wrecked the orderly succession of magistrates and *podestà* that their fathers had probably been recording for several generations and that they continued to use as the chief framework for their narratives. The so-called "Monk of Padua" (who was really a citizen of Verona and not a monk at all) introduced chapter after chapter under such titles as "Of the Qualities of the Terrible Ezzelino"; and he looked forward as a guarantee against the revival of the accursed Da Romano at the end of the century to the rise of the house of Este, whose adventures since the appointment of Azzo as *podestà* of Verona in 1207 provided the main thread through the maze of miscellaneous information contained in his chronicle.[19] ROLANDINO (1200–1276) emphasized the tyrant's "measureless cruelty" by reporting as true the probably fabricated story about the slaughter of the Paduan prisoners at Verona in 1256; and one of the purposes of his work was to celebrate the return to republican legality in Padua in 1262.[20] When Rolandino's solution failed, ALBERTINO MUSSATO (1262–1329) came up with another, one providentially offered by the descent of Henry VII into Italy in 1310–13: submission to the Empire; and he reproduced the texts of the speeches in the council that resulted, alas! not in submission to but in secession from the Empire and in his own exile to Chioggia.[21] FERRETO DE' FERRETI of Vicenza (1297–1337) admired Albertino's dramatic presentation of the problem in Albertino's classical tragedy *Eccelino*. But he found Albertino's solution incompatible with his own loyalty to the memory of the autonomous commune. When the premature death of Henry VII left the Ghibellines with little but empty dreams, Ferreto looked for salvation to another homegrown, but this time already "civilized," tyrant: Cangrande Della Scala, the protector of his much-admired Dante.[22]

Thus the chronicles of the Marca were just as politically engagé as those of Venice, and Venetian readers would have recognized in them many similarities with their own chronicles. In spite of the imprint left on them by several outstanding personalities, most of them were relatively anonymous—that is, the rank and position of the author were considered much more important than his name, and autobiographical information in the text is usually sparse, if not nonexistent. Most of them were the work of several generations of members of the same family: even Rolandino, whose work is literarily and structurally one of the most complete of the age, began by transcribing the extensive notes he had inherited from his father; and he left his sons at liberty to comment as they pleased in the margins.[23] No descendant ever hesitated to rearrange or add onto the text of a predecessor even at the distance of over a century—as did the mid-fourteenth century author of the continuation of PARISIO DA CERETA's chronicle of Verona from 1117 to 1233.[24] At the same time, the chronicles were all the work of what corresponded in the Marca to the ruling class of Venice: not merchants and patricians, to be sure, who were too busy fighting each other to write—or, for that matter, to rule—but rather the lawyer-jurists known as *notai* who, as men of professional training as well as of wealth and prestige, actually administered the government on behalf of their constantly shifting and increasingly ineffective political superiors.[25] The chronicles thus betray the same taste for extraneous miscellany and supernatural explanations common to all other chronicles of the age: even Albertino, who publicly scoffed at miracles, heralded the entrance of Henry VII into Padua with three days of solar and lunar eclipses in France, bolts of lightning from cloudless skies, and the flight of a new species of bird across Lombardy. But they also betray a scruple for accuracy and precision that might be expected of those who were responsible for keeping records. Although few of them were reluctant to make up orations for rhetorical purposes—like the speech GUGLIELMO CORTUSI (fl. 1315–61) put into the mouth of the dying Cangrande—most of the speeches they quote in direct discourse are versions of the verbatim transcriptions they wrote down as part of their official duties—like Cangrande's letters to Marsilio de' Carrara in Cortusi.[26] Finally, although they occasionally insisted that they were writing simply in order to avoid idleness ("ne, si steriles in ocio torpeamus, sacre virtutis opera destituisse videamur . . .": Ferreti), all of them intended their chronicles as public documents. In fact, Rolandino's chronicle was eventually elevated to the rank of an official version of the events of the century by being read out loud, just like the text of a treaty or a statute, at the meetings of the Council of Padua.

By the time the Venetians moved onto the mainland as governors, landowners, and part-time residents, however, the chronicle tradition of the Marca had begun to wither. For one thing, after two centuries of reflection it had come up with no better explanation for the collapse of the commune than the still inexplicable appearance of Ezzelino; and it persisted in explaining the failure to revive the commune as the result of the same old twofold root-of-all-evil theory used by everyone else in the two centuries before and after Dante: leisure and wealth, *otio et opulentia*. For another thing, the chroniclers gradually gave up looking for solutions to their problems. CONFORTO DA COSTOZA (c. 1300–after 1389) pinned his hopes on the Della Scala as a way of saving Vicenza from the Carrara.[27] When Antonio Della Scala then turned out to be just as cold-blooded toward his subjects as he was toward rival members of his own family, Conforto put his hopes in Giangaleazzo Visconti. And when the savior from the outside turned out to be worse than the various saviors at home, even his son did not have the heart to keep the chronicle going. PIER ZAGATA tried to maintain his usual impassivity as he listed once again the crimes of the tyrant Ezzelino.[28] But when the supposedly civilized *signore* Cangrande II had his brother hacked to pieces in 1375, he left to his successor some fifty years later the duty of impassively recounting what appeared to be just more of the same: the sack of Verona in 1390. History, concluded ANTONIO GONDI (d. 1438), as he rewrote what NICOLÒ SMEREGLI (fl. 1262–1312)[29] and Ferreti had already written about the age of Ezzelino (1194–1260), consisted solely of "misery, affliction, oppression, crime, depopulations, villainy, burnings, and calamities."

Why bother with it then? Gondi certainly did not bother too much. He invented a miraculous golden age before the advent of Ezzelino—one in which the Marca enjoyed "all things necessary to men, being fertile and abundant in populous cities." He then let the golden age fade away into incomplete sentences, grammatical errors, and disconnected paragraphs. Gondi's more famous successor of the late fifteenth century, BATTISTA PAGLIARINI of Vicenza (b. 1406/7), bothered even less. The civic defects of the Vicentini, he decided, were congenital and therefore beyond remedy. What Ezzelino did to them was merely the inevitable continuation of what Constantine and Pippin had supposedly done to them; and all Cangrande had to do to assure his dominion was to wipe out whatever "honest customs and rules of good life" might possibly, although not very probably, have remained. Therefore Pagliarini did not write history at all—although almost everyone thought he had until modern scholars began exposing his plagiarisms.[30] He simply copied haphazardly and indiscriminately from a few of his predecessors and from the several long-since forgotten contemporaries conveniently listed on the first pages of his large volume and then added a good number of new errors of his own devising.

Even the advent of humanism failed to revive the chronicles of the Marca. Since history had long since stopped in Verona, one anonymous chronicler of the late fifteenth century[31] filled up most of his 466-page text with news that reached Verona from other cities; and although he made some effort to check on the veracity of the reports he picked up, he simply copied out the documents sent him by a friend in

Venice without ever being aware that they were deliberately censored. Padua no longer had any history either—not even after the "discovery" of the body of its first historian, Livy, on 31 August 1413. When an anonymous chronicler after 1405 sought to reevoke the memory of the great event that might have preserved Padua as an independent state, the War of Chioggia, he could think of nothing better to do than to copy, rather inaccurately, the eyewitness account of his pre-1405 predecessor, GALEAZZO DE' GATARI. When the author of a *Liber Memorialis* finally abandoned his hope of seeing the Este, rather than the Carrara or the Venetians, as rulers of his city, he could find nothing more to write about than the processions of the Flagellanti. When MICHELE SAVONAROLA (the grandfather of the famous Girolamo) took time off from his medical practice in 1440 to look up the "illustrious men" who had lived in the city since the time of "our most worthy King Antenore," he ended up with eulogies, not history; with individuals, not a society; and with no other explanation for their many great deeds than the "wide and fruitful valleys" and the fish-filled rivers of the surrounding country. Giovan Michele Alberto de Carrara (d. 1490) was the well-educated son of a philosopher and an active participant in the mid-fifteenth century wars between Venice and Milan; but neither he nor any of his successors ever saw fit to publish the some forty-book work in which he described what he had seen.[32] Indeed, the nearest thing to a humanist commentary to be produced in the Venetian mainland dominion was the work of a writer completely detached from the class of notaries who had written the chronicles, CRISTOFORO DA SOLDO. And Cristoforo wrote his detailed and elegant account, in Brescian dialect, of the battles he had fought in, not as a nostalgic citizen of a now dependent city, but as a loyal servant of his new masters.[33]

Nevertheless, the Venetian chroniclers might well have profited from reflection upon some of the original elements in the work of their mainland counterparts. For one thing, the notaries were by professional commitment less attached to the communes of their birth than they were usually willing to admit in principle. The prevailing custom in the municipal republics of barring citizens from the office of *podestà* in their native city and the reluctance of the new *signori* to entrust the more delicate responsibilities of state to anyone distracted by their subjects' party loyalties eventually led to the formation of a kind of intercity corps of professional administrators, particularly after a university degree began to take the place of the earlier father-son apprenticeship. Since the best notaries could usually expect to spend some of their career—or, in the case of Antonio Loschi of Vicenza, chief secretary to Giangaleazzo Visconti, all of it—in the service of another city or prince, they eventually became accustomed to think in terms not of one city but of the whole Marca or even of the whole of northern Italy. The geographical scope of their chronicles thus came to reflect the triumph on paper of the policy that the Da Romano, the Della Scala, the Este, and the Carrara tried in vain to implement in practice. Even Rolandino, whose passionate attachment to the old republic grew steadily during the twenty-year regime of Ezzelino, had to admit in the end that his chronicle of Padua was really a *Cronica Marchie Trivizane;* and Ferreti, whose master, Benvenuto de' Campesani, had probably introduced him to the classics of medieval historiography as well as to the currently available classics of ancient poetry, managed to put the events of the Marca as a whole in a context that ranged from Avignon and Germany to Naples.

Thus the chroniclers of the Marca had already overcome the municipal mentality that was still one of the major defects of the chroniclers of Venice. At the same time, they offered Venetians a potentially important justification for the future mainland dominion. Having despaired of finding solutions to their long-standing political problems by themselves, they happily turned over to Venice the task of solving the problems for them. With a sigh of relief they recorded their acts of more or less voluntary submission—as did JACOPO RIZZONI: "on the 23d the people of Verona took the city away from the representatives of the Carrara, and on the 24th they gave it to the government of Venice...."[34] And having already learned to consider themselves Veneti rather than Paduans or Veronese, they had no trouble learning thereafter to consider themselves Venetians.

This transfer of loyalties had begun as early as 1379, when a Trevisan spice merchant named DANIELE DI CHINAZZO (d. 1428), the son of a former captain in Venetian service, wrote a well-informed, carefully documented, and tightly organized account of the War of Chioggia, of which he had been an eyewitness. Besides being a born, rather than a trained, writer, one who knew how to put his subject in the context of mainland power struggles over the preceding three decades, Daniele was a passionate partisan of Venice and an equally passionate opponent of the Carrara and the Visconti, "the worst tyrants that have been for many years in these parts." The transfer of loyalties was even more fully evident in the polished commentary on the siege of Brescia of 1438 by one of Francesco Barbaro's pupils, EVANGELISTA MANELMI, who put his monographic subject into a broader chronological context with the help of Biondo's *Decades,* and in the unpolished jumble of legends and authentic documents compiled a quarter of a century later by JACOPO MALVEZZI. For although Malvezzi spent so much time on the Trojans that he never got around to the second half of the fourteenth century, he made it clear that salvation from the "dira tyrannorum fulmina" and the "scelus horrendum" of misbehaving ecclesiastics that had afflicted the city during the first half of the century could come only from the "most illustrious lords of Venice," to whom his chronicle was respectfully dedicated. The transfer of loyalties was then completed by ANDREA DE REDUSIO, the heir of an old and prominent Trevisan family, a graduate of the University of Padua, and a notary, like his father, whom the Venetian government appointed captain of the Trevisan contingent in the war against Emperor Sigismund and then made chancellor of his native city. Andrea made Venice, not Treviso, the focal point of world history. He took most of his information about foreign lands from reports of his friends in Venice. He denigrated his father's former employers, the Carrara, condemned Bernabò Visconti as a "wild dog," and wrote off Giangaleazzo Visconti's victories as "vanitas vanitatum." He then dedicated his chronicle of Treviso from the Creation to Tamerlane to the doge himself. For it was the Venetians, he noted, who had at last rescued the cities of the Marca from tyrants and civil war. It was evident to him—as it was evident to everyone after the grandson of the chronicler Cortusi won a handsome reward for betraying a futile anti-Venetian plot in Padua in 1438—that Venetian dominion differed in one essential aspect from all preceding attempts at establishing a territorial state in the Marca: it was permanent.[35]

For another thing, the notaries were not only men of law and government. They were also, unlike their Venetian counterparts, men of letters. Practically all of them wrote Latin poetry on the side. Most of them delighted in decorating their narratives with the latest fashions in ornate writing. Few of them could pass up an opportunity for making a German king talk like Cicero or for describing their work as a fragile boat crossing a stormy lake. Rolandino, indeed, may have learned something about history writing as well as chronicle writing from his former master at the University of Bologna, BONCOMPAGNO DA SIGNA (b. 1165/75), the author of a literary exercise entitled *De Obsidione Ancone;* and many of his sentences turn out to be paraphrases of Vergil, Lucan, Horace, and Augustine. Albertino Mussato, whom everyone from Muratori to Giuseppe Billanovich has hailed as the greatest of the pre-Petrarchan rhetoricians, also wrote classical tragedies, odes, and elegies; and the myriad of details in his chronicles about the duchy of Luxemburg and the house of Aragon as well as about the council sessions in Padua are all woven together with a narrative skill approaching that of his professed model, Livy.[36]

To be sure, the style of the rhetorician-notaries was plastered onto the content of their books rather than being, as Petrarch insisted, an expression of it; and their standards of elegance were still wholly medieval or at least pre-Petrarchan. But by the end of the fourteenth century, the chronicle had already advanced sufficiently toward the rank of a work of art that one of the leading post-Petrarchan humanists had little trouble transforming it into history. PIER PAOLO VERGERIO (1370–1444) was a professor of logic, a pedagogue, and an ecclesiastical reformer, not a notary. An outsider by birth (from Capodistria), he was attached to the rulers, not to the whole community of the one city of the Marca, Padua, in which he spent only twelve years of his long career. Yet Vergerio was a close friend of the most eminent notary-chancellor of his generation, Coluccio Salutati, whom he got to know personally during his two periods of residence in Florence (1386–88, 1398–99). He esteemed Albertino ("qui doctrinae gloria et honoribus in republica claruit") enough to overlook Albertino's staunch opposition to his patrons' ancestors. And he appreciated Rolandino and Cortusi enough to take from them most of the information for his *Vita Carrariensium Principum* (1397).[37] Hence, while his work turned out to be more a collection of *res gestae* than a history, and while much of it consisted of little more than an abridged translation of an earlier anonymous chronicle, it banished the legendary origins of the Carrara to the obscurity of Petrarch's "dark ages" ("Post avulsum quidem ex Italia Imperium, afflictumque a barbaris...non erat ullum literarum genus in pretio"). It erased everything the chroniclers had invented about the vicissitudes of Padua before the appearance of the first written documents. It presented as alternatives to the current regime not the resurrection of a defunct republic but the imposition of a non-Paduan tyranny by its very real enemies, the Visconti and the Della Scala. And had the sudden fall of the Carrara eight years later not consigned it to oblivion, it might well have taken the place of the *Historiae Florentini Populi* as the first great work of humanist historiography.

With two exceptions, however—that of the Braidense codex, some of which turns out to have been copied from the *Gesta Domus Carrariensis,* and that of an allegedly "inhonesta et falsa" Paduan chronicle, which the government ordered to be burned—the Venetians paid very little if any attention to the chronicles of the Marca. What had they, after all, the masters of politics, to learn from those whose political incompetence had reduced them to the rank of mere subjects? But they did notice the humanists of the Marca. Andrea Dandolo was a personal friend of Petrarch. Benintendi was familiar enough with Petrarchan Latinity to lace his prose with classical periods.[38] And Enrico Dandolo had heard enough about the difference between ancient history and modern chronicle to deplore the latter as boring and unreliable. Yet instead of advancing toward humanist historiography, as it did in Florence, the chronicle in Venice retreated from it. The traditional myths about the past were subjected to confirmation and elaboration, not to criticism. Still more Trojan exiles were provided with impressive genealogies. The foundation of the city was fixed firmly at March 23, 421—for no other reason than the coincidence in that year of the Feast of the Annunciation with Good Friday. St. Mark was provided with a long vacation in the Lagoons between one mission and another at St. Peter's command. And the passages in the widely read anonymous chronicle of 1350 inconsistent with the late fourteenth-century campaign to apotheosize Andria Dandolo were cut out of all but seven of the many manuscripts in circulation.

The chronicle as a form of history writing did not die out, to be sure. Venetians went on writing chronicles well into the sixteenth century—so many of them, indeed, that the meticulous eighteenth-century historian of Venetian literature, Marco Foscarini, decided simply to list them: "Who," he asked, "would dare risk drowning himself in all those interminable volumes?" But all these chronicles of the age of humanism remained absolutely impervious to humanist influence. PIETRO DOLFIN (1427–1506), for instance, had impeccable qualifications as a chronicler: he had inherited a family chronicle from his father ZORZI or GIORGIO (1396–1458)—one which started with Attila and ended with a tearful account of the death of the unfortunate doge Francesco Foscari (1457).[39] He had been exposed to what fifteenth-century Venetians also considered to be a good education. In fact, he had copied out the standard manual of Renaissance pedagogy, Pier Paolo Vergerio's *De Ingenuis Moribus,* in his own hand, and he had prepared his own amended version of Matteo Palmieri's *De Temporibus.* But when he came to write his own chronicle, he began all over again with the usual crowd of "troiani zentilhomeni," and he ended with a patchwork of passages torn uncritically out of Nicolò Trevisan, Andrea Dandolo, Andrea Morosini, et al.[40] A certain Filippo di Domenico, whose still unpublished manuscript chronicle was first noticed by the same Foscarini, did the same thing: he merely copied what he found in other chronicles and changed only those passages that seemed somewhat less than consonant with his purpose of glorifying the city. It is not surprising, then, that Antonio Carile, who has read all the chronicles, can usually find no other difference between those of the sixteenth and the fourteenth centuries than the handwriting. Indeed, one of the few modifications Antonio Belloni saw fit to impose upon the fourteenth-century *Vitae Episcopum et Patriarchum Aquileiensium*[41] when he decided to polish and update it in the 1520s was to make St. Mark the godson of Peter and to give the date of his death according to the Roman imperial calendar.

The Venetians were not solely to blame for this retrenchment. Petrarch himself had been perfectly content to put chronicle in the same category as law and politics and thus bar it from the category of good letters. His followers in Padua and Verona in the next generation agreed with him. They were interested chiefly in poetry and moral philosophy. Hence, they read the ancient historians either for "the richness, pleasantness, and elegance" of their language or as a storehouse of good examples for imitation by the young.[42] Even Vergerio, who put history at the top of the hierarchical list of disciplines in his *De Ingenuis Moribus* reannexed it two sentences later to ethics. And only two of his many pupils ever bothered with it thereafter: Giovan Andrea Bussi, who edited Livy, and Jacopo da San Casciano, who translated Diodorus Siculus. Even Vergerio's fellow schoolmaster, Guarino da Verona, who extracted all the precepts about history from the writings of the ancient rhetoricians, had to admit, with one of Valerius Maximus's interlocutors, that writing about living persons was a risky, as well as "ardua res"; and he himself carefully avoided fulfilling his wish to adorn with words the memorable deeds of his own times. Giovanni Conversino might have wondered why a city as great as Venice had not yet attracted a history worthy of the eye of the educated man. But in the light of his own dubious forays into what he thought was history—a collection of hearsay remarks about the affairs of Ragusa and a literary reconstruction of Frederick II's attempts to take Ferrrara—it is probably just as well that he himself did not attempt to fill the lacuna.[43]

Still, the fault lay mostly with the Venetians. It was they who decided to raise Dandolo's chronicles to the rank of faultless classics—and thus to encourage Andrea Morosini, a contemporary of Leonardo Bruni, to adhere religiously to the form, method, and language of the text he permitted himself merely to continue. It was they who made their sons put away childish things as soon as their schooldays were over—even after they began attending the new school at the Rialto (1412) and the University of Padua.[44] And it was they who robbed potential humanist historians of a "problem" to solve—by insisting that the occasional plots of the mid-fourteenth century had been merely passing accidents and that the War of Chioggia had proved the internal validity of current Venetian institutions and policies.

The Revival of Genoese Historiography

While the chronicle writers in Venice fortified themselves against the advent of humanism, the successors of the chronicle writers in Genoa appealed to humanism for assistance in reviving the chronicle tradition interrupted since the death of Jacopo da Varagine. Like his predecessors of the twelfth and thirteenth centuries, GIORGIO STELLA (1370/1–1420) was the son of a chancellor, heir to a sizeable estate in Liguria, and notary and secretary to the highest magistracies of the republic. But by the end of the fourteenth century, the intercity corps of professional notaries had come to include Genoa along with the rest of northern Italy; and through his father Giorgio he became a good friend of Raffaino de' Caresini in Venice, Jacopo de Delayto in Ferrara, and, above all, Coluccio Salutati, "whom no one in our age can be said to excel in history, rhetoric, or elegance of speech."[45] He was accordingly brought up on a somewhat scrambled version of a Petrarchan reading list: Jerome, Ambrose, Justin, Bede, Livy, Josephus, Horace, and Orosius—roughly in that order. He also read Hugo of Fleury, Vincent of Beauvais, Sigibert of Gembloux, and Andrea Dandolo, from whom he learned to see Genoese history in the context of European history. He then read Boccaccio, from whom he learned the principles of textual citicism, and Giovanni Villani, from whom he learned to appreciate what Genoa had lost by neglecting its chronicles. The moment was propitious, since Boucicault had finally realized what Stella's father's favorite patron, Simon Boccanegra, had pleaded for and what his own youthful hero, Doge Antoniotto Adorno, had tried in vain to impose: a respite from the usual plague of factional fighting.

But when Stella set out to fill in the century-long gap in Genoese history, he discovered that none of his predecessors—or for that matter any other author between the age of Gregory the Great and the age of Petrarch—could any longer be accepted without serious reservations. The stories about Janus, he pointed out, "rest on no other foundation than that of popular tales": they could be supported neither by the passage in Solinus, which Salutati assured him Varagine had misread, nor by the etymology of *Ianua,* which he himself found to be a purely medieval neologism for the word *Genua* used by Pomponius Mela. He therefore dedicated his whole first book to battering down myths in the name of Petarchan philology: the myth about the Christianization of Genoa in the first century, the myth about the fountain of blood on the eve of a Saracen attack. . . . And only then did he go on to rearrange what he thought to be the credible entries in Caffaro and his successors into topical headings like *De Triumphis, De Conflictibus,* and *De Adventu Summorum Pontificum.*

Stella's *Annales Genuenses* thus turned out to be not merely a continuation of Caffaro, but almost a humanist chronicle. It clearly set forth the principal political weakness of the republic: "Heu quotiens hac urbe armorum acceptio renovatur!" Within the annalistic form adopted for the previously unchronicled period from 1299 to 1305, it included a number of skillfully constructed narrative passages. And it enlivened the succession of political events with amusing anecdotes worthy of the *Decameron*—like the one about Boniface VIII who instead of applying a finger-full of ashes to the head of the archbishop of Genoa at the beginning of Lent, 1300, threw the whole bowlful right in his face with the salutation: "Memento quod Guilbellinus es, et cum Guilbellinis in cinerem reverteris!" But the work was still a chronicle, not a history. The introductory *apologia* was wholly medieval: Aristotle says it's man's nature to learn, and learning about history has the moral effect of encouraging him to "disdain the things of this world." Similarly, a number of entries are simply left blank for want of information. Characterizations are purely conventional (Charles VI is described in almost the same terms as Giangaleazzo Visconti). Important turning points (like the Treaty of Turin) are not distinguished from humdrum routine. And the two remedies proposed for Genoa's ills are hardly original: let the king of France send us more governors like Boucicault (to whom the chronicle was presented in 1405), and let the Virgin set off another round of Flagellant processions (which Stella nonetheless found distasteful), as she had done in 1399, to distract the Genoese from their quarrels. Hence, Stella's attempt to revive the official chronicle tradition lasted only through the lifetime of his brother GIOVANNI (to 1415) and his son BATTISTA (to 1435), both of whom seem to have gone on more out of a sense of fraternal and filial obligation than out of personal dedication to the project. No one knows whether Gotifredo d'Albano, whom the government eventually appointed as Battista's successor, ever carried out his task. Supposedly Lodovico il Moro took the manuscript off to Milan, and it was never heard of again.

What took the place of a continuous chronicle for most of the rest of the fifteenth century, particularly in the absence of private chronicles and diaries like those of the Florentines, was a series of humanist commentaries. Both GIACOMO BRACELLI (1390–after 1466) and ANTONIO GALLI (c. 1440–1509/10) belonged to the same class of wellborn chancery officials as the Stella. Bracelli was appointed chancellor soon after finishing his legal studies at Padua in 1411 and left his office to his son upon his death in 1466. Galli was commissioner, one after another, for half the subject cities of Liguria and chancellor of the Banco di San Giorgio from 1490 on—all while carefully administering his own extensive real estate holdings. Bracelli carried on an active correspondence with Poggi, Ivani, and Giovan Mario Filelfo, as well as with

Biondo, whose *Roma Instaurata* he "avidly read as fast as he could" the moment a copy reached him in 1448.[46] Galli learned the art of history writing by copying Quintus Curtius's life of Alexander the Great.

But since humanism in Genoa remained the privileged preserve of a small number of chancery officials, and since constant squabbling among the jealous oligarchs deprived contemporary Genoese history of the kind of "memorable deeds" required by the canons of humanist historiography, they received little encouragement. What stimulated Bracelli to write was probably not "the sight of the immense sea . . . from slopes embalmed in sharp marine fragrances" imagined by his late nineteenth-century biographer.[47] He wrote—or rather rewrote (the first draft is from 1418)—the geographical-historical description of Liguria (1442) that Biondo, to whom he sent it, transcribed almost word for word into the *Italia Illustrata*. He wrote his brief catalogue of famous Genoese men of state and church at the request of a wealthy nobleman. And he wrote his *De Bello Hispanico* in order to prove that the Genoese actually could, if they wanted to, accomplish a "memorable deed"—as they did when they captured Alfonso D'Aragona and all his court in a naval battle off Gaeta in August 1435. "Probably no other naval victory will ever equal the dignity of this one in fame, in glory, and in the quantity of booty," he beamed. Skillfully, grace-fully, and concisely he showed the battle to have been the culmination of a half-century-old policy of Aragonese expansion in the Mediterranean and of a growing realization among the Genoese of the incompatibility of that policy with their own territorial and commercial interests. If the work turned out to be somewhat less than a minor classic, the fault lay not with the author but with the events, which he was obliged by the rules of the commentary to follow to their inglorious conclusion: Alfonso's sudden release on the command of Filippo Maria Visconti (Bracelli's *bête-noire*), rebellion and then renewed civil war in Genoa, and, finally, a peace treaty that was "less honorable than it was in tune with the times" ("non tam honesta quidem quam temporibus accommodata").[48]

Similarly, what stimulated Galli to write was probably not the innate talents of the "Ligurian race" so admired by his twentieth-century biographer. He wrote his memorandum on the punitive expedition against Barcelona in 1466 at the request of the official state chronicler, Gotifredo. He wrote one commentary and part of a second on the rebellion of 1476 as a service to his fellow citizens (who probably read it, since eight contemporary manuscripts have survived). And he wrote his account of the voyages of Christopher Columbus (1506) as a tribute to his old friend.[49] Galli was occasionally led astray by his taste for the dramatic and by the humanist pre-scription of speeches on important occasions—as he was most notably in the "one more day and back we go" speech he put into the mouth of Columbus on the eve of his first discovery. But he usually kept his narrative close to the documents—in this case, Columbus's letters to his family and friends in Genoa. He convincingly ex-plained the rebellion in terms of the failure of Francesco Sforza's efforts to ingratiate

himself with his subjects. And he brought to the attention of contemporary statesmen, at least by implication, two new, urgent, political problems: the increasing
financial, and hence political, dependence of the state on the Banco di San Giorgio,
and the ineffectiveness of even heroic sea captains when forced to recruit their crews
among booty-hungry, stateless proletarians.

An occasional commentary, however, did not provide the general survey of
Genoa in its relations with the whole Mediterranean world required both by the
chronicle tradition and by the policy-makers of the state. None of the Genoese
humanists paid any attention to the long description of Turkish administration—and
Turkish atrocities—written by the Genoese businessman and occasional magistrate
JACOPO DE PROMONTORIO after his return in 1475 from most of a lifetime at Adrianople.[50] Nor did a succession of commentaries provide a continuous narrative of
political events. Therefore, in 1492, the doge appointed BARTOLOMEO SENAREGA (d. c.
1514), the son of one chancellor, the father of another, and himself chancellor since
1487, not only to write a continuation of his own and to compile a large appendix of
state documents, but to "recast the chronicles [of all his predecessors] in a sweeter
form of speech that will be more pleasing to their readers."[51]

Fortunately, Senarega left Caffaro intact. But unfortunately, he soon lost interest
in his assignment. After consulting the current authority on good history writing,
Giovanni Pontano, after amassing an impressive collection of relevant documents,
and after skillfully describing the fall of Naples (which he had visited in 1491) to
Charles VIII and the Battle of Fornovo (1495), he began leaving big blanks (1497,
of all years, contained "pauca memoratu digna"!), forgetting the dates of embassies
he himself had taken part in, turning the proper succession of important events (like
the civil war of 1506–7) upside down, spoiling his Latin with Italianisms and illogical
sentences, and trying to patch together his disconnected entries with a superficial
coating of humanist conventions—like the Roman dating system. If his chronicle
appears to contain at least some elements of the commentary it claims to be in his
title, it is because his son, while rewriting his father's notes for the last two years
(1513–14), came to envisage the restoration of independence as the result of a process
that had begun with the French invasion of 1494 and the collapse of the Milanese
state in 1500.

The Humanist Historians in Venice

In Venice, on the other hand, the task of introducing, or trying to introduce,
humanist historiography was left largely to foreigners. To be sure, the first historian
who might in some sense be called a humanist was a Venetian at least by citizenship.
But after working his way up through the world of notaries in the capital, LORENZO
DE MONACIS (c. 1351–1428) went abroad—first on an embassy to Hungary, which
inspired his Latin hexameters on the misfortunes of Hungarian queens, and then to
Crete, where, aside from an occasional trip home and one short mission to France

(1388), he served as chancellor for the remaining forty years of his life.[52] It was probably his rank in the intercity community of notary-chancellors, rather than his traditional professional education, that led him to read a few ancient historians, to correspond with Bruni and Caresini, and to add Martinus Polonus and the "Monk of Padua"[53] to his collection of Venetian chronicles. And it was probably the weight of spare time in his colonial outpost that finally led him, in the 1420s, to rewrite the Venetian chronicles in humanist garb.

Unfortunately, the humanism of the *De Gestis Moribus et Nobilitate Civitatis Venetiarum* was limited largely to the garb.[54] The content remained as the chronicles had established it. De Monacis looked up a few details about the sack of Constantinople in the thirteenth-century Byzantine historian Nikitas (Nicetas) Choniatos; but most of what he supposedly took from him was actually a paraphrase of what Andrea Dandolo had already taken from him. He took some information about Michael III Paleologos from Nikitas's successors, particularly from Giorgos Akropolitis, but he apparently knew Greek no better than nineteenth-century British East India Company officials knew Hindi, and he missed completely their special theses and points of view.[55] Hence all the old myths returned intact, from the Paduan consuls to the victory over Pippin—his friend Bruni's *De Bello Gothico* notwithstanding. Ezzelino, decked out in thundering classical adjectives, was held up as an example of what would happen if the Venetians ever admitted the slightest change in their perfect constitution. And the affairs of the mainland states were mentioned mostly for the purpose of letting the Paduan ambassadors deliver a stirring eulogy of their great, unchanging neighbor: "O felix Venetorum civitas! O sapiens et bene fortunatum commune!"

The first serious proposal for a humanist history of Venice—apart from Poggio's, which was not very serious—had to wait for Biondo, who, in 1454, offered his *De Origine et Gestis* to Doge Francesco Foscari as a sample of what he might do if decently subsidized. Unfortunately, the doge was forced to resign three years later in the wake of a family scandal; and the proposal soon broke down into a counter-proposal to hire Lorenzo Valla instead and into a series of job applications from the humanists resident in Venice—one of whom, Giovan Mario Filelfo, eventually (1468) wrote a barely disguised adaptation of Bruni's life of Dante to prove his competence as a historian.[56] In fact, only one senator really responded favorably: Lodovico Foscarini. But Foscarini failed to convince Biondo when he met him at the Congress of Mantua that presenting the Senate with a fait accompli would work any better than requesting a contract in advance. He therefore fell back on one of his former lieutenants, Evangelista Manelmi, at least in the hope of procuring a record of his own glorious deeds at the siege of Brescia in 1438. But Manelmi's commentary vanished from sight soon after it was written, and no one saw it again until it was finally published in the eighteenth century.[57] Nevertheless, Biondo's sample had the salutary effect of making some Venetians realize that a mere repetition of the same old myths, no matter how elegantly Latinized, would no longer stand up before the kind of historical standards evident in the pages of the *Decades*—which had already destroyed the chroniclers' date for the foundation of the city.

Meanwhile one Venetian patrician, JACOPO ZENO (1417–81), had discovered the potential value of applying the new standards in the field of biography. He had learned them, apparently, during a long sojourn in Florence after 1441, where he had become a friend of Bruni and an enemy of Poggio. Upon his elevation to the bishopric of Belluno and Feltre in 1447, he wrote down what he had learned from his own observations and what he had found out in interviews with the future Pope Nicholas V about Niccolò Albergati, cardinal bishop of Bologna and frequent legate for Martin V, who died in the last days of the Council of Florence. The result was a portrait of a saint who was also a man, one whose usual string of virtues was illustrated in concrete acts and whose sanctity was manifested chiefly in his efforts to persuade the Visconti and the Florentines as well as rival factions of Bolognese citizens to stop fighting each other. Thanks to his connections in the Church, Zeno was soon after exposed to another model still unknown in Venice: Pius II's description of Germany. After repeating all the classical commonplaces about the importance of history and after mastering the technique of substituting "templum quoddam Christiana religione Michaeli archangelo dedicatum" for "St. Michael's Church," he managed to show that "love of country and reverence for ancestors" could best be served by a true portrait of a real general, like his grandfather Carlo Zeno (1334–1418), and by a full explanation of the historical circumstances in which Carlo had accomplished his patriotic acts.[58]

At the same time, it occurred to another Venetian patrician, FRANCESCO CONTARINI (1421–60), that his lessons in the Latin and Greek classics at Padua were something more than just youthful amusements. In fact, Caesar's *Commentaries*—along with the works of Pius II, "pereruditum atque in primis studio eloquentiae clarum," and those of Biondo, which probably inspired his sight-seeing tours around all the cities he stopped at—could help to celebrate his own conduct as commander of the Venetian expeditionary force sent to Siena in 1454. Providing that the Sienese did not mind having the *Dii Immortales* invoked on their behalf, and providing that they could be induced to fight for *focos, aras, Deos Penates* like their Roman forefathers, the models turned out to have another use: that of justifying the Venetian position in the mid-fifteenth-century switch of alliances. All Venice wants is peace, Contarini proclaimed—in a speech as stirring and improbable as was Carlo Zeno's exhortation from the deck of a rocking trireme. If Francesco Sforza and the Florentines are constantly causing trouble, what can she do but forget about republics and tyrannies and ally herself with King Alfonso of Naples?[59]

Unfortunately, not for another two decades did any but a very few Venetians begin to take Zeno's and Contarini's suggestions seriously. Lorenzo Zane, who boasted of being fully qualified as a historian, was banished from Venice for having revealed state secrets to Pope Paul II; and he died too soon after the ban was lifted to respond favorably to Lorenzo Valla's plea that he demonstrate his qualifications. Not until 1483 did the leading Venetian humanist, Ermolao Barbaro, begin discussing the problem of historical writing with the historiographer of the duke of Milan, Giorgio Merula. And not until 1484 did he suggest that Merula might find many more great deeds to write about in a "free city" than in a city ruled by princes— a hint that he give up Milan for Venice.[60]

One reason for this delay is that the task of revising all the centuries of Venetian history for the new audiences of Renaissance Italy turned out to be much more difficult than Biondo had imagined—as BERNARDO GIUSTINIAN (1406–89) discovered when he tried to do it in the last twelve years of his life. Giustinian descended from one of the most illustrious families in the city.[61] His uncle Lorenzo was already recognized as a saint—a saint, indeed, as dedicated to "hard work and [the care of] the goods of this world" and as disdainful of the contemplative life and "the clever disputes of the schools" as any other good patrician.[62] His father Leonardo (d. 1443) had learned Greek from Giovanni da Conversino, corresponded with Ciriaco d'Ancona, translated some of Plutarch into Latin, and written a biography of a Greek Church Father from original sources—all while climbing up the cursus honorum to the office of procurator of San Marco. Bernardo, in turn, was educated by the best humanist teachers then available: Guarino da Verona, Francesco Filelfo, George of Trebisond. And as one of the most effective orators of his day, he was entrusted with many of the republic's most delicate embassies: to the emperor in 1451, to the king of Naples in 1459, to the king of France in 1460, and to all the popes of his generation.

As a historian, Giustinian's first task was to knock down the whole edifice of doubtful stories constructed by the chroniclers—before some disrespectful foreigner knocked it down for him.[63] And by the time he finished he had effectively abolished the Paduan consuls, the organized migration of the mainland nobility, Attila's three-year seige of Aquileia, and all the doges before 800. His second task was more difficult: that of restoring those pieces of the former edifice that he found to be supported by written testimony. Since both Vergil and Quintus Curtius mentioned emigrants from Pamphlagonia, he had to put Antenore and his Trojans back in—all while admitting that Casesar may have been right in tracing the Veneti back to the Gauls. Since the Giustinian family really had once been saved from extinction by the decision of a sole surviving male to abandon his monastery, he had to conclude that a sacerdotal virtue ran in the veins of all his descendants. Since Eusebius had mentioned St. Mark's missionary voyages, he had to restore him to his office as chief fieldworker for St. Peter and founder of the first Christian community in the Veneto.[64]

The third task was more difficult still: adhering to the methodological as well as the stylistic principles of his declared model, Thucydides. If certain events could not be traced back to documented causes, then there was no choice but to appeal to God—particularly in the face of such an inexplicable event as the growth of a poor fishing village to the rank of a world power. If contemporary audiences might miss the moral importance of what they read, then the narrative had to be interrupted; and Giustinian invented a golden age in the happily little-documented sixth century just so that the lazy patricians and wild adolescents of his own day would learn to mend their ways. In other words, when the destruction of the old myths threatened to weaken the basic "truths" of Venetian history, then a few new myths had to be invented. For all Italians in the late fifteenth century had to be made aware that Venice had never been subject to a foreign power, that it had been the recipient of God's special favor ever since its foundation, that it had always been inhabited by liberty-loving nobles rather than, like Rome, by booty-loving outlaws. They had also to be reminded that the peace and concord Venice had succeeded in guaranteeing among its own citizens gave it the right and duty to rule whatever other peoples proved incapable of ruling themselves—Greeks, Dalmatians, Paduans, and maybe even Milanese.

Rewriting Venetian history turned out to be still more difficult for MARIN SANUDO (1466–1533) than it had been for Giustinian. Sanudo was almost as fortunate as his older contemporary in his birth and even more fortunate in his education: he had studied with the well-known historian Giorgio Merula; and while still an adolescent he had written many pages of Latin verse, dissertations on Ovid and Petrarch, a guide to ancient mythology, and a collection of *notabilia* taken from the Venetian archives. His first work—an account of his trips around the Veneto in 1483—was patterned on, and frequently paraphrased, Biondo's *Italia Illustrata*. But it departed from Biondo in providing "documentary" support for the foundation of Padua by "the Trojan refugee Antenore" and of Verona by Noah's son Sem and in justifying current Venetian expansionist policies with a glowing report on what had become of the Veneto since the expulsion of the tyrants. "Sed demum," Sanudo noted, "having come under Venetian dominion . . . it has grown steadily in population and wealth and is constantly improving day by day."[65] His second work—a commentary on the War of Ferrara—was modelled on Caesar's *Gallic Wars:* while dedicated largely to a blow-by-blow narrative of the war itself, it began with a brief history of Venetian-Este relations since 1308, and it put the war in the context of all of Venice's foreign relations, in the East as well as in Italy. But it departed from Caesar, who at least admitted having undertaken a war of conquest, by assuming Ferrara to have long been a Venetian protectorate, by pinning the war guilt solely on Duke Ercole, and by quietly skimming over the forcible annexation of Rovigo. Such was the magnanimity of the Senate, Sanudo concluded, that in the end "everyone remained completely happy" with the peace treaty.[66]

These initial essays apparently convinced Sanudo that he was now ready to finish the task that Giustinian had started; and in the years following he reread most of the old Venetian chronicles and some non-Venetian chronicles as well, all while collecting an immense quantity of treaties, reports, and statutes from the state archives, to which he was given free access. He also decided to include information about customs and traditions that was usually omitted by the humanist historians of his generation and to write in the Venetian language of his intended audience—"those patricians and citizens who were not expert in learning." As a result, the *Vite dei dogi* are still an indispensable source of documents about Venetian life at least for the fifteenth century. They include the full text of a report to the Senate of 1416, the results of the census of 1422, and complete lists of all the holders of major state offices.[67] Unfortunately, however, the work turned out to be as unacceptable to non-Venetians as it was satisfying to Venetians. Biondo's revision of the founding date was rejected—because the traditional date was found to correspond also with the centenary of the creation of Adam. The choosing of the sites for the first churches was attributed to Jesus and Mary themselves, who leaned out of the clouds to direct the masons. The first doge was moved back from the ninth to the seventh century—to 697, in fact, with the election of the "wise and honorable," but unfortunately completely legendary, Paulutio Anafesto. And the literary standards proclaimed in the first pages soon broke down into long lists, interminable paraphrases, unacknowledged quotations, and marathon sentences that not even a loquacious Venetian would have been able to unscramble. Sanudo went on adding, patching, and amending his text until at least 1521; but neither he nor anyone else before the eighteenth century had the courage to publish it.

Since the Venetians themselves faltered in their attempt to write or rewrite their own history, the task fell once again to outsiders—none of whom found it particularly difficult. One was a Venetian subject, a Dalmatian nobleman named CORIOLANO CIPPICO, whose commentary on the glorious deeds of a Venetian admiral[68] was immediately accepted as a semiofficial version of the war against the Turks; and it was incorporated, at times almost word for word, in the official version Sabellico wrote a decade later. Another was a little-known Corsican of humble birth who perfected his humanistic Latin after settling in Venice as a type-corrector and proofreader: PIETRO FILICE, or CYRNAEUS (b. 1477). Cyrnaeus began by applying the rules of humanist history to the past of his native island; and since the rules did not oblige him to go look for information where it was to be found, in the archives of Genoa, he had only to pick out what little information was readily available in the standard histories of ancient Rome and modern Italy and add a final book of *res gestae* concerning his own insignificant family. He then applied the rules of humanist commentary to the current War of Ferrara (1482–84): and since the rules permitted him to include only that information which he himself could gather from oral reports, all he had to do was condense into Sallustian infinitive clauses all the considerable amount of information readily available in Venice that Sanudo had left out in deference to the government. Thus Ferrara became a modern Saguntum,

Duke Ercole became a heroic and popular defender of his people, Venice became a ruthless transgressor against the rights of others—and the work was consequently consigned to oblivion for the next three centuries.[69]

For MARC'ANTONIO COCCIO, better known by the penname SABELLICO (1436–1506) that he adapted from the region of his birth ("Sabine"), the writing of history was easier still. Sabellico could rely without hesitation on an impeccable model, Livy; for no historian, he noted, had ever enjoyed more favorable conditions ("celebris patria, . . . temporum felicitas, maturitas studiorum, sublimis ad scribendum materia, summi principis favor"), none had ever been able to combine the special qualities of so many illustrious predecessors ("copiam Thucididis, Heroditi candorem, Polybii diligentiam, . . . brevitatem Crispi"), and none had ever succeeded so well in carrying out the precepts of Cicero.[70] He could also rely on a sure rule for distinguishing truth from falsehood. What the Venetian chronicles said about their own times could be accepted with the same faith that Livy had placed in the Roman chroniclers. What they said about earlier times could be accepted as long as it did not conflict with what was said by the ancient historians. And occasional differences of opinion among the ancient historians themselves (i.e., Strabo versus Livy on the origin of the "Heneti") could be resolved by recourse to the principle of *verosimile*—what seemed to be the truer account. Better yet, he could rely upon a twofold scheme of historical periodization: for Venice, a linear progression from potentiality to actuality, and for the world as a whole, one great age between the reign of Augustus ("quanto . . . satius fuit ea tempestate floruisse . . . bonae artes et disciplinae in precio fuere") and the reign of Arcadius, another great age beginning with Bruni ("vir philosophiae studiis et eloquentia clarus, nec in historia minus celeber"), and a millennium of obscurity and bad Latin in between.[71]

Therefore, history could be written as a holiday pastime. During his harvest-time vacation in 1478, Sabellico combined his own observations with those of Strabo into a geographical-historical description of the area roughly corresponding to the modern region of Friuli-Venezia Giulia. He then drew together ("corpus unum conficiam") what little information he could find scattered about in the admittedly few ("verum non multis") authors who had said anything about it—without really bothering to "explore" the nonliterary sources as promised in the lengthy preface. He added his own recollections of the Turkish invasions of the preceding years. And he ended up, to the delight of the Venetian governor of Udine, with much more historical proof that Venice had always been free and that it alone could save its subjects from the age-old plague of fratricidal conflict.[72] In 1484 he settled down as a guest in the villa of another patrician near Verona. He picked up a copy of Andrea Dandolo, and perhaps one or two other chroniclers as well, and quickly decided that whatever of value they contained had already been extracted by Biondo, Benintendi de' Ravagnani, and Lorenzo de Monacis—the only ones of his predecessors not hopelessly marred by "squalid, filthy barbarity."[73] He then added the notes he had taken from conversations with his host about recent events and subtracted whatever details might have been provocative of ill will rather than goodwill among his intended readers. Finally, he recast all his material into Livian periods and divided it into Livian "books" and "decades." And after just fifteen months of leisurely writing, the *Rerum Venetarum ab Urbe Condita Libri XXXIII* was ready for presentation to the doge.

The one Venetian patrician who happened to be a humanist as well, Ermolao Barbaro, may have had some reservations about the book he applauded for finally getting rid of the chronicles; and Barbaro's chief consultant on historiographical matters, Giorgio Merula, may have confined his citical comments strictly to externals in order not to talk about the content.[74] But the senators were delighted. Venice, they learned, was the "new Rome," more worthy than the old to the same degree that "the sanctity of laws and the equity of justice" were more noble than mere extent of territorial dominion. Its founding fathers were direct descendants of Trojan noblemen and Roman colonists, who supported themselves in their new homeland not by fishing or making salt but by investing their mobile capital in commerce. Their successors in the seventh and eighth centuries had refused to submit either to the Lombards or to the Byzantines and had outdone the Romans by beating off the fiercest Gauls of all, the "Belgian" armies of Pippin. Their successors in 1204 had responded graciously to a plea from the legitimate emperor of Constantinople and had rightly imposed Latin order on the quarrelsome, schismatic Greeks. Their successors in the fifteenth century had come to the rescue of the Florentines when the Visconti threatened their liberty—since the liberty of others was as dear to them as their own; and they had betrayed Francesco Sforza only to avoid being betrayed themselves by a man of such notorious faithlessness. If occasionally one of them erred, it was simply because he had momentarily forgotten the "ancient customs" of the city. But such errors were few: for strict observance of those customs had at last brought Venice to the culmination of its glory. "Seldom," proclaimed Sabellico, "has the city been more secure and more flourishing ... and never has it enjoyed such felicity."

Thus Sabellico managed to combine the principal defects both of Quattrocento humanist historiography and of the Venetian chronicle tradition. First of all, he bothered to consult only those narrative sources that he could procure without trouble and that he could read without offense to his literary sensitivities. He could easily have asked Giustinian what he had found out about the early centuries of Venice, since both of them were working on that subject at the same time. But he did not. He could easily have learned from Ermolao Barbaro that Macrobius and Ptolemy depended upon Pliny and could therefore not be used to correct Pliny's obviously incorrect estimate of the distance between Gibralter and India. Instead, he just crossed out "milia passuum" and wrote "stadium" instead.[75] He could easily have checked the original texts of the many Venetian authors he mentioned—

probably to give the impression of having read them. Instead, he usually quoted them out of context and incorrectly. He could easily have distinguished the more from the less reliable among the very few non-Venetian authors he used; and he could therefore have avoided swallowing Jacopo da Varagine's story about the fountain of blood in Genoa that Giorgio Stella had long since demolished. He could easily have expanded his passages about the East from the several unofficial, but still very informative memoranda that had arrived in Venice during the preceding decades—like the Minorite Bartolomeo da Gianno's appeal to his Venetian brothers of 1438, like Giorgius of Hungary's (1422–1505) account of his experiences as a prisoner at the Ottoman court (1475), or like Emanuele Piloti's description of Egypt and the Levant (after 1420).[76] If he had wanted more information about Hungary, one of the areas of eastern Europe of greatest concern to Venetian foreign policy, he had only to write to his son's former tutor, and his own close friend, Antonio Bonfini, who had recently become the official historian of the Hungarian court. If he had wanted really to understand the causes of Venice's greatest disaster of the fifteenth century, the loss of Negroponte, he could have read any of several recent Greek historians whose works were available in Italian libraries. Instead, he did no more than take a few snippets from the one Greek historian who had written in Latin, on commission from Pius II, Nikolaos Sekoundinos (Niccolò Segundino). And he was content to hurl the same worn-out imprecations at the Turks while the Senate was doing its best to stay on good terms with them. Mythmaking thus replaced analysis in the realm of Venetian relations abroad. It did so also in the delicate realm of Venetian antiquities. Sabellico restored the stories about Antenore and denounced the rival stories in "certain ignoble writers" about the Trojan foundation of Aquileia. He reestablished the foundation date of Venice at 25 March 421 and reprimanded Biondo for having tried to change it. And he put the Paduan consuls and the prehistoric doges back into their niches. He thus saved the myths in advance from Giustinian's disquieting doubts. And he then embedded them as firmly as Livy's rain of stones in the crystalline spheres of his Livian prose.

Sabellico's theses were so well received by his patrons that he was immediately rewarded with a handsome bonus and a well-paying chair at the School of San Marco.[77] He then went on to reinforce his theses in other works: a panegyric of Venice written in the form of a geographical description, a string of orations on ancient language and literature, a table of the various offices of the state with a note on their separate functions,[78] and finally a history of the whole world—*ab orbe,* this time, not just *ab urbe condita.*[79] Fortunately, the *Enneades* turned out to be even easier to write than the *Rerum Venetarum* had been. The first books were largely paraphrased from the Old Testament. Books IV and V were loosely translated from Polybius. The orations of Jugurtha and Cataline were all but copied from Sallust (compare VI. 1 with *Bel. Iug.* 14). And the major and minor events of the author's own times were thrown in, helter-skelter, as they came across his desk. The invasion of Charles VIII was tucked into two chapters in the middle of Book X. A report from the Venetian legate at Cairo led to some current lore about Ethiopia. The voyages of Columbus and the wonders of "Hispana" were placed under the heading of how ancient place names had changed in modern times. And a truce between Louis XII and Ferdinand the Catholic was heralded as the beginning of an age of general peace.

That the man who held all but the title of official historiographer to the Venetian Republic completely ignored the impending crisis of Italy, and that he failed to anticipate what was already clear to his contemporary, Domenico Morosini—the revolution in Venetian foreign policy after the tragedy of 1509—bothered none of his readers. The *Rerum Venetarum* was published in edition after edition in the original and it was twice translated into Italian. It was reduced to a compendium, in Pietro Martello's *De Vitis Principium Venetorum* (1502),[80] and then translated and "continued" in that form from time to time until 1574. A half-century after its appearance, it was broadcast to the rest of Europe by Celio Secondo Curione as the most authoritative history of Venice.[81]

BOOK II

THE DIFFUSION OF
HUMANIST HISTORIOGRAPHY

4

FROM COMMUNES
TO PRINCIPALITIES

The Communes and the Metropolis

THE SAME PASSIONATE ATTACHMENT TO AN AUTONOMOUS CITY-STATE THAT HAD IN-
spired the first attempts at historical reflection in the Marca Trevigiana also seems to
have been responsible for the appearance of chronicle traditions in many of the other
cities of northern Italy. In Milan, this sentiment was nourished from the very beginning by the memory of the city's once having been the ecclesiastical and political
metropolis of the Western Empire—a memory that neither its destruction by the
Goths nor its eclipse under the Lombards and Carolingians had been able to destroy.
Both ARNOLFO's *Gesta Pontificum Mediolanensium* [1] (late eleventh century) and LANDOLFO
SENIOR's *Mediolanensis Historiae* [2] (to 1083) go back for inspiration to the great days of
Ambrose and Augustine. Similarly, the striking resemblance in theme and language
of the *De Situ Civitatis Mediolani* [3] to the idealized topographical description included
in the literary exercises of Paulus Diaconus's contemporaries make it impossible,
even after several hundred pages of scholarly debate, to place the former definitely in
the tenth rather than in the seventh century. To the centralizing policies of the
Gregorian popes, to the universalist ambitions of the Ottonian emperors, and to the
reform demands of the religious radicals of their day, the earliest Milanese chroniclers affirmed the autonomy and the orthodoxy of the Ambrosian Church. As the
bishops gradually lost their political authority to elected lay consuls, they affirmed
just as strongly the autonomy of the nascent commune: such, for example, is the
thesis of LANDOLFO JUNIOR (c. 1077–after 1137—no relation to Landolfo Senior),
even though he was a cleric by profession and a European by education, and even
though his chief purpose was to prove the sanctity of his clerical uncle. [4] As the
growth of the city aroused the jealousy of its neighbors, and as the assertion of its
independence aroused the fury of Emperor Frederick Barbarossa, the last remnants
of universal loyalties dissolved completely into communal loyalties. "SIRE RAOUL,"
or RAUL BOCCARDO (1146–71), GIOVANNI COGNADELLI, and the continuators of the
Annales Mediolanenses of 1154–1230 [5] may well have been obsessed by a belief that
history consisted of nothing but a series of inexplicable disasters. They may have
thought the exact number of soldiers killed in a particular battle more important
than the outcome of the battle. And they may have failed to understand the long-
term significance even of the Battle of Legnano (1176), which finally freed all the
Lombard communes from imperial control. But they were still capable occasionally

of rising above single details to a comprehension of their dramatic potentialities, and they were firm in their conviction, even after the destruction of the city in 1162, that "God was fighting for the citizens."

To be sure, communes did not automatically generate chronicles. In Ravenna, for instance, where the memories of late Roman grandeur were just as strong as, and even more justified than, they were in Milan, the recording of history meant simply transcribing the vital statistics of the bishops and patriarchs, even after the time when effective political power had passed into the hands of lay lords. The one published and the two still unpublished chronicles of the thirteenth and fourteenth centuries[6] do no more than update the eighth-century *Codex Pontificalis*[7] with some bits of extraneous hagiography and a few more miracle accounts. Similarly, Bergamo, which had inherited the rudiments of a chronicle from as early as the ninth century, seemed to be the true heir to the Latin Rome when its nostalgic son, MOSÈ DEL BROLIO, found himself in the Greek Rome in 1120. And its accomplishments in the wars of Barbarossa had seemed worthy of another Vergil to a Bergamese poet of the next generation.[8] But neither their own fellow citizens nor those of the neighboring city of Brescia paid any attention to them. The *Annales Bergomates* of 1167–1241, the three brief *Annales Brixienses* of the same period,[9] and the two anonymous chronicles of Bergamo of the thirteenth century consist merely of a few scattered notes.[10] The mid-fourteenth century chronicle attributed to the early fourteenth century notary ADAMO DE CRENE treats history merely as a series of pious and naively apocryphal stories—about a virgin who committed suicide at the approach of Barbarossa's hard-up Germans, about Ezzelino's thugs who gouged out the eyes of children. The author of the diary of the first period of Visconti government reduces history to lists of names: what counts is not the death of Giangaleazzo or the rise of the independent tyranny of Pandolfo Malatesta, but the names of the citizens appointed to attend Giangaleazzo's funeral in Milan.[11] The diaries attributed to Castello de Castelli and to "Manfredi Zezunone" have turned out to be forgeries of the late sixteenth century. Indeed, the only historical works that might have been worthy of Mosè's appeal, those of Bartolomeo Osa and Giovanni Brembate, disappeared almost as soon as they were written. And none of the diligent document hunters between the age of Muratori and the age of Carlo Capasso has ever succeeded in recovering them.

On the other hand, some communes were too close to Milan, the fastest growing metropolis of northern Italy, to maintain for long either the political autonomy they had won in the late twelfth century or the cultural autonomy they had begun to assert in the thirteenth. True, Como had inspired one of its citizens to write a verse narrative of its war against Milan in 1118–27.[12] Cremona had been celebrated by two successors of its famous chronicler-bishop Siccardo[13] in accurate accounts of the *gesta* of its consuls and *podestà* up to such communal triumphs as the Lodi War of 1270 and the expulsion of the Ghibellines in 1317.[14] Lodi had been even more fortunate. Its alliance with Barbarossa against the hated Milanese had been recorded by three of the most polished chronicle writers before the advent of humanism: OTTO MORENA, whom the Milanese had driven from the city in 1111, his son ACERBO, who had returned as *podestà* in 1162, and an anonymous continuer to 1168.[15] But by the fourteenth century these auspicious beginnings had been all but forgotten. The exiled Pavian monk GIOVANNI MANGANO reduced history to topographical description in 1329–30 solely for the purpose of persuading Pope John XXII to lift an interdict from the city and so permit him to return home.[16] Except for an obscure abbot named ALBERTO DE BEZANIS (fl. 1370), who picked out a few snippets from the better-known universal chronicles, Siccardo's heirs in Cremona wrote history as a dull succession of "marveliosa e dolorosa" plagues, assassinations, and hangings, from which the city was marvelously rescued by the entrance of Francesco and Bianca Maria Visconti Sforza in 1440.[17] BUONINCONTRO MORIGIA (d. after 1349) admitted that his native Monza was important largely because it was part of a larger *res publica,* a term he took from what Augustine said about Cicero in the *City of God.* To the transcript he had made of speeches given in the Monza city council he added whatever he could find about "the miracles performed in my times" in the Milanese chronicles and in the correspondence of his two main heroes, Azzo and Matteo Visconti.[18]

Still, where there were no communes, there were no chronicles either—or at least none of the kind that would eventually provide the foundation of humanist historiography. In the thirteenth and early fourteenth centuries, most of the region now known as Piedmont was dominated by four large feudal dynasties, each of which depended in turn upon its chief vassals; and after 1416, when Amedeo VIII won the title of duke, all of it except for the amoebalike marches of Monferrato and Saluzzo had come under the control of one of them, the house of Savoy. Hence, none of the Piedmontese towns managed to achieve any more autonomy than could be wrung from the unwilling hands of the still powerful local and regional feudal lords. Even Turin eventually abandoned its experiment with communal government in exchange for the honor of being the capital of the appanage of the duke's heir-apparent, the prince of Piedmont.[19] True, Piedmont had inherited at least two monastic chronicles from as early as the eleventh and early twelfth centuries: that of the Cistercian monastery of Novalese[20] and that of San Michele of Susa.[21] But neither they nor any of their three surviving successors of the thirteenth century had inspired continuers. More important, none of them had ever become associated with any particular political community—not even with one of the feudal principalities. The *Chronica Altaecumbae* consists of little more than obituaries of the monastery's superiors.[22] The various scraps that make up the *Chronicon Ripaltae* amount to little more than a few pages of miscellaneous notes.[23] Even the much longer (169 folio pages) *Imago Mundi* of the Piedmontese nobleman-monk JACOPO D'AQUI is mostly copied out of the standard medieval classics. The author's loyalties were focused not on his native country, but on the Dominican order, and his interest was distracted by such marginalia as a fish with fur, feet, and a lion's head that had supposedly been observed by someone during the same year.[24]

Thus when the dukes of Savoy at last decided to decorate their dynasty with suitable ancestors, the historians they commissioned turned for models not to the chronicles of the Italian city-states but to those of the monks of Saint-Denis near Paris. The first of these *croniques de Savoye,*[25] which covered the twelve centuries between a certain "King Ezens" and Amedeo VIII in 382 massive folio pages, was concerned almost wholly with the entertainment value, rather than with the veracity, of the stories it recounted. Its successor, written in the 1470s by the ducal secretary PERRINET DU PIN, was concerned largely with such charming anecdotes as "How Mme. Bonne de Bourbon entered the bedroom of her son and why she then came out of the said bedroom without wishing to speak to him." The somewhat more serious *Chronica Latina Sabaudiae,* which at least managed to put the main events of the years between 1465 and 1487 in correct order, was written, like a preceding one by JEAN SERVION (1465), in the westernmost extremity of the duke's domains, Bresse: and it was probably unknown in Piedmont. The somewhat longer chronicle of IUVANAL DE ACQUINO, which attempted to recall the last three decades of the fifteenth century from the perspective of the second decade of the sixteenth, was written in Turin. But none of Iuvanal's mass of extraneous detail is integrated into his main subject, the comings and goings of the members of the ducal family; and none of it has any bearing at all on the history of the city he lived in. The still longer *Epitomae Historicae* of DOMENICO DELLO BELLO, or MACCANEO (1466–1529), combined the author's own observations with selections from the information he had collected in some ten still unpublished books of Savoyard antiquities; and he was apparently pleased enough with the results to add to it from time to time until the year of his death. But in spite of a few humanistic terminological conventions (Sigismund, "Pannoniae Rex"), which the author picked up while lecturing on Livy, Valerius Maximus, and Pliny the Elder at the university, most of it is filled with interminable accounts of court festivities and with farfetched comparisons between modern Savoyard and ancient Roman heroes.

The quality of the Piedmontese chronicles is to some extent indicated by the rapidity with which they were forgotten. Most of them exist in a single copy, which no one but the seventeenth-century scholar Samuel Guichenon seems to have read before the late nineteenth century. Their place was taken in the early sixteenth century not by a humanist history but by the many pages of amusing and largely apocryphal tales churned out in pompous periods to honor the accession of Louise of Savoy's son, Francis I, to the throne of France by the captain of the French *croniqueurs,* Symphorien Champier (1472–1539).[26]

The two other feudal principalities of Piedmont were somewhat more fortunate, qualitatively if not quantitatively: and they were so largely because both of them had become Italianate in language and hence open to cultural influences from the rest of northern Italy. When GOTTFREDO DELLA CHIESA (c. 1394–after 1453) decided, in his role as vicar-general of Saluzzo from 1424 to 1464, to find support for his foreign policy of unshakable friendship with the Savoia, he turned for guidance to the works of the "historiography e compilatory di croniche" he had picked up during his diplomatic missions up and down the Po Valley. He turned for inspiration to the geographical works of Enea Silvio Piccolomini, which somehow reached him while he was revising his text in the late 1450s.[27] He thus learned to back up his theses "per notte e substantie de instrumenty," carefully translated into what he thought was Italian, and to recognize as the chief function of chronicle that of providing the stuff ("la medulla") out of which true history could eventually be formed. Similarly, when Bonifacio V of Monferrato decided, around 1483, to have done for his family what the Milanese historians had done for the Visconti and the Sforza, the poet he commissioned, GALEOTTO DEL CARRETTO (d. 1530), was forced, for want of a native chronicle tradition, to look up his information in the latest historical works of the Italian humanists—Platina, Biondo, and Sabellico.[28] He thus learned to supplement what he read in books with what he discovered "in the archives of the said princes." He learned to put related events together in continuous—and at times endless— narratives. And he learned to justify his patron's pro-French policy after 1494 with the lessons of the preceding hundred years: Better the kings of France than the dukes of Milan! Yet neither of these chroniclers succeeded in conceiving of history as anything but a record of the completely apolitical feats of a series of abstract heroes. And neither of them inspired imitators. Gottfredo went back to administering his small state and left his manuscript to the mercy of his secretaries. Galeotto went back to writing plays and theological treatises and left his manuscript so well hidden that not even his scholarly descendant a century later could find it.

Indeed, the only town in Piedmont to produce anything like the continuous chronicles of Lombardy and the Veneto was the one town that succeeded in maintaining an independent commune: Asti.[29] Asti had established an episcopal government by the end of the eleventh century and a consular government by the end of the twelfth; and by the end of the thirteenth century it had become the richest and most powerful city in northwestern Italy. It had kept the count of Monferrato locked up in a cage until he died of exposure. It had kept the count of Savoy locked up in a dungeon until his family accepted its terms. It had blocked the expansion of the Angevins in southwestern Piedmont (1275). It had extended its own territorial domains from the Apennines to the Po. And it had then settled down, in good communal fashion, to an interminable civil war between its two chief families.

The first and second steps of this development were recorded in a brief *Parvum Chronicon* for the years 1122 to 1204.[30] The third step was recorded by an enthusiastic observer who, in 1294, attributed to none other than Christ the amazing success of his contemporaries in "overcoming all the above-mentioned evils, extending the

land of Asti, and multiplying its wealth in persons, castles, villas, and villages."[31]
The third step in Asti's rise to power was then recorded even more thoroughly in the
first decades of the fourteenth century by the prosperous spice merchant GUGLIELMO
VENTURA (c. 1250–after 1326), who gathered much of his information from personal
observation during his business trips around northern Italy. Ventura combined a
healthy skepticism about the legends of the past and about the effects of comets in
the present with a well-developed sensitivity to the financial aspects of such pious
projects as the Holy Year of 1300; and he was convinced that the truth lay not in
what was said but in what was written ("infrascripta inveni in antiquis scripturis
quae vera sunt omnia").[32] As a result, his work was considered important enough
after his death to warrant a continuation by his less gifted son, RUFINO. It was
considered important enough a century later to justify one of his descendants, SE-
CONDINO, in recording the snowstorms, the droughts, and the Milanese diplomatic
skirmishes of the years between 1420 and 1457 in exactly the same form used by his
predecessor. And it was considered important enough for another century thereafter to justify its being copied, plagiarized, altered, and amended almost beyond
recognition.

Above all, Ventura's work assured the survival of chronicle writing in Asti even
after the city had lost all but its internal autonomy—first, as a subject of the Visconti
and then, through the marriage of Giangaleazzo's daughter Valentina, as a possession of the French house of Orléans. Unfortunately, it also seems to have stifled the
further development of the successors it inspired. Antonio Atesano (1412–after
1462), a notary turned schoolmaster, recorded in Latin verse the events he had
observed in Paris and Milan as well as in Asti. He did so, in the last few years of his
life, for no greater purpose than that of glorifying his ambitious and unfortunate
patron, Charles d'Orléans.[33] The author of the so-called Solari chronicle was content in many passages simply to translate Antonio into lifeless Latin prose and in
other passages to reduce patriotism to little more than anti-Savoy mudsling-
ing. The author of an anonymous chronicle written around 1471 confused Ventura's
emphasis on documentary support with an injunction to reproduce verbatim transcripts; and after copying out the entire text of a long treaty between Roberto d'Angiò and the commune, he was apparently too tired to make more than a half-dozen
entries of more than a line apiece for the decades in which he himself lived.[34]

Universal Chronicles

Communal patriotism, then, was the principal ingredient of the northern Italian
chronicles of the late Middle Ages. But equally important, at least in enabling the
chronicles to develop beyond the form of merely local records, was the appearance
in the same area of three of the most successful adaptations of the universal chronicles of Transalpine Europe: those of SICCARDO DA CREMONA (c. 1155–1215), SALIM-
BENE DA PARMA (1221–after 1287), and RICCOBALDO DA FERRARA (d. after 1297).[35]

True, these chronicles were subject to many of the historiographical shortcomings of their local counterparts. They accepted as fact even such improbable legends as the one about Charlemagne's trip to the Holy Land (Riccobaldo). They freely mixed historical narrative with moral asides—like Riccobaldo's disquisition *De Rudibus Moribus in Italia*. They plagiarized at will—particularly Salimbene, who copied the whole first part of his chronicle from Siccardo. And they invariably reduced human personalities to lifeless abstractions—particularly when they came to that standard incarnation of the "inhumanus tyrannus," Ezzelino. Moreover, only Riccobaldo's works succeeded in escaping entirely the bonds of communal affection—in part, perhaps, because the author spent most of his life as an alien churchman in Ravenna, a city in which political loyalties were still secondary to ecclesiastical loyalties. Siccardo's and Salimbene's works were almost as communal as they were universal, particularly because Siccardo was the heir of a very prominent family in the city of which he became bishop at the age of thirty and because Salimbene read all the now lost early chronicles of Parma before embarking on his own.

Nevertheless, all three of the universal chroniclers were men whose cultural horizons extended far beyond the walls of their native cities. They had mastered the fundamental texts of European medieval historiography as well as many of the fundamental philosophic and literary texts of the age. Siccardo had written a book on mythology, Riccobaldo had studied canon law, and Salimbene could quote at random from Horace, Juvenal, and Bernard of Clairvaux. Moreover, they had become familiar with many different parts of what they regarded as the single commonwealth of Christendom, and they had also learned something about what lay beyond Christendom. For instance, Salimbene moved from Siena and Pisa to Cremona and Ferrara before going off to study in Paris; and on his way home he procured a report on the Tartars from a fellow friar who had just returned from central Asia. They were thus in a position to temper their communal loyalties with loyalties to other ideals and institutions—to the Empire as it was represented by Frederick II, "super homines prudens, satis literatus, linguarum doctus" (Riccobaldo), to the Papacy, of which Riccobaldo wrote a separate chronicle, or to the prophets, like Salimbene's hero Gioacchino da Fiore.[36] Above all, they managed to place a great amount of specific information (951 pages of it in the most recent edition of Salimbene) in chronological order with the convenient, if historiographically questionable, framework of successive reigns of popes and emperors. They thus provided the local chroniclers of northern Italy with what Martinus Polonus had provided Giovanni Villani: a means of placing the events of one city in relation to contemporary events in other cities and countries. They were accordingly ransacked by their contemporaries and consulted by all their successors, from the age of Biondo to the age of Panvinio and Sigonio.[37]

To be sure, at a time when real political power was rapidly becoming regional and when the Visconti and the Della Scala were taking the place of the Hohenstaufen and the popes as the effective rulers of northern Italy, the universal chronicle as a form of historical writing could not long endure. The occasional attempts to preserve intact the models established by Siccardo and Salimbene thus proved to be failures. IOAN-NES DE DEO (fl. c. 1241) at least had the advantage of having travelled to Bologna from his native Portugal, and his connection with the commune of his residence was limited to the payment of his salary as professor of law. But his professional com-mitment to "harmonizing the discordant canons" was apparently inconsistent with his taste for history, for his chronicle of the popes turned out to be little more than a "tenuis et arida" series of passages cribbed inaccurately from Siccardo.[38] On the other hand, ALBERTO MILIOLI (fl. 1237–85) spent his whole life in Reggio, where his father had been a prominent notary and where he, after successfully running through the *cursus honorum,* was entrusted with the task of revising the city's statutes. He therefore had to achieve universality by the scissors-and-paste method—copying indiscriminately out of the *Liber Pontificalis,* Gottfredo da Viterbo, Salimbene da Parma, and contemporary local chronicles, and then rearranging what he had copied, none too accurately, according to the scheme he found in Salimbene, his chief "source" for the thirteenth century.[39] Similarly, BARTOLOMEO DA FERRARA had to discover the world from inside his suburban monastery of San Bartolo. He therefore had to leave a number of years blank even during the hundred years before his death (after 1377) and to jot down hastily, and without any rational order, whatever "novelties of Tuscany and Lombardy" happened to come his way.[40] FRANCESCO PIPINO was somewhat more mobile. He traveled as far as Milan, where he wrote accurate descriptions of several churches, and he went all the way to Jerusalem, Syria, and Constantinople on a pilgrimage. He also read widely, thanks perhaps to the richness of the library in his Dominican house at Bologna, and he translated Marco Polo's account of the East into Latin. Moreover, he had a thesis to propound concerning at least one subject of current polemics: that the Papacy should give up its territorial domains and pay more attention to the spiritual needs of Christians. Yet Pipino ran into the same difficulties as the other universal chroniclers when he tried to find enough material about the centuries between the first Frankish kings and 1314 to fill several hundred folio pages. He ended up copying what he needed about the past from Vincent of Beauvais, William of Malmesbury, and Martinus Polonus and what he needed about his own age from Riccobaldo and Jacopo da Varagine.[41]

Nevertheless, when brought to bear on the real political problems of a real politi-cal community, the universal chronicle was capable of generating local chronicles even in those cities that never succeeded in maintaining a communal government. That, at any rate, seems to be the only plausible explanation for the appearance of an occasional chronicle in the eastern Romagna, a region famous even in the Middle Ages as the "land of unbridled passions" (Nino Valeri). Before it fell prey to the rapacity of rival branches of the Manfredi clan, Faenza was fortunate in having a cathedral canon, TOLOSANO (d. 1226), who was learned enough to sprinkle his texts with random quotations from Horace, Vergil, and the Bible, and who was discriminating enough to qualify with a *dicitur* the story about Charlemagne's pilgrimage; and Tolosano's heritage was revived at the beginning of the fourteenth century by the notary PIETRO CANTINELLI, who presented a very detailed record of civic strife in the city during the decades preceding 1306.[42] Before it fell victim to a three-way struggle between the Ordelaffi, the Malatesta, and the papal legates, and before a third of its citizens were butchered by British mercenaries in 1377, Cesena was fortunate in having one canon and one notary whose now lost chronicles—along with a collection of papal, imperial, and communal decrees—provided the basis for a compilation put together in the mid-fourteenth century; and the compiler was still confident enough in Cardinal Alburnoz's ability to do for the Romagna what the Della Scala and the Carrara were trying to do for the Marca Trevigiano that he included much information about the neighboring cities as well.[43]

Unfortunately, few of Tolosano's successors were worthy of him. His own continuer was content to copy much of what Salimbene, who visited Faenza off and on after 1263, had copied from Siccardo; and he gave up altogether after having added no more than ten years to his master's text. The early fifteenth-century Dominican friar GIROLAMO DEI FIOCCHI (1346–1433) bothered to record only those "singular and remarkable events" of Forlì that he could learn about without going outside his monastery.[44] His successor among the Dominicans, the author of the chronicle of Sant'Andrea in Faenza, was interested solely in repeating the usual legends about St. Dominic.[45] His successor as chronicler of Forlì, the author of the *Annales Forolivienses* (1275–1473),[46] plundered Tolosano for the twelfth century, the *Annales Caesenae* and Riccobaldo for the thirteenth century, and Orosius for antiquity. It never occurred to him, notary and chancellor though he was, to learn something about good Latinity and historical method from a certain Leonardo Bruni, whose translation of Plutarch he had read with pleasure.

Indeed, one of the few fifteenth-century Romagna chroniclers to rise above the level of inaccurate lists of unverified miscellany was the one who had nothing to do with any of the three social groups from which all the other chronicles emerged. GIOVANNI DI PEDRINO was a painter, and LEON COBELLI was both a painter and a musician; neither of them was a notary, a canon, or a friar. Giovanni wrote down everything he heard about from 1411 to 1464 with as much patience as his fellow citizens of Forlì listened to the long sermons of popular preachers; and he seconded with his observations their apparent desire to settle down once and for all under the dominion ("la qual molto era desiderada da la oniversitade de tutta la cittade e contado") of their Ordelaffi lords. Cobelli, who borrowed liberally from Giovanni, embellished his chronicle with rhetorical orations and inscriptions for one purpose only: that of telling a good story. And his dialect narrative turned out to be as amusing to read as it was doubtfully accurate.[47] Similarly, the one city in the region to produce a series of chronicles of relatively consistent quality was the one that remained subject to the same family of homegrown tyrants for over two centuries, Rimini. Some of the Rimini chronicles are purely local in scope. They begin, for example, with the election of Firantino Malatesta in 1295 or with the earliest memories of the author, and they end with a funeral oration for Galeotto Malatesta in 1385 or with the consecration of a chapel in 1452.[48] Some of them are really local, while pretending to be universal in scope: they claim to "describe and reduce to memory some of the famous and grand things that will take place in various parts of the world," but they really talk mostly about the Malatesta. Only a few of them are written in Latin—most notably the one by TOBIA BORGHI (d.c. 1451), which an anonymous friend continued for the years 1444 to 1470.[49] Sigismondo Malatesta had imported Tobia from Verona for the explicit purpose of lending a bit of cultural decoration to his none too civilized court. But Tobia apparently remembered little of what Guarino da Verona had taught him about history writing. He shrugged off the disagreeable task of doing a bit of research after his arrival with the plea: "The feats and wars [of the Malatesta] are such that they would require another whole book," which he had no intention of writing. And neither he nor his successor bothered to mention the most famous mark of Renaissance culture in Rimini, Leon Battista Alberti's temple. Only one of the Rimini chronicles achieved any recognition in its day: that of Tobia's predecessor MARCO BATTAGLI, (d. after 1374), a counselor and an ambassador of the city government and the nephew of the famous law professor and later cardinal. Marco simply borrowed what he needed from Riccobaldo, Martinus Polonus, and Villani and added a good dose of what his modern editor calls "monstrous repetitions, screeching grammatical errors, and obscure passages." But he also succeeded in getting his work presented to Emperor Charles IV. And publicity procured for it what inherent quality could not: the privilege of being "copied and recopied, abridged, translated, and incorporated into other works" for over a century after the appearance of the pretentious and empty *Nobilissimorum Clarissime Originis Heroum de Malatesta* of 1377–85.[50]

Different as they were, all the Rimini chronicles shared a common purpose: that of glorifying the ruling family, which they traced back successively to Frederick Barbarossa, to the "ancient Romans," to Scipio Africanus (GASPARE BROGLIO TARTAGLIA DI LAVELLO), or to Noah's son, Nembrot *(Nobilissimorum . . . Ystoria)*. All of them proudly asserted that "no man ever bit one of our Malatesta lords without getting rabies" and that "the Malatesta have always been men of great fame and great deeds." All of them denounced the most dangerous opponent of the family: the temporal state of the popes, which, they insisted, was completely incompatible with the popes' spiritual responsibilities. And some of them went to great lengths to exalt the main demons of the Guelph tradition, Frederick II, "at whose death all justice was buried," and Ezzelino da Romano, "noble by descent and by virtue." Finally, none of them accomplished even a first step in the direction of humanist historiography—not even Broglio, who seems to have understood none of the great deeds he reported of "that excellent and worthy noble citizen named Cosimo de' Medici," and not even Tobia, who admitted to doing little more than "tamquam florem sub compendio compilari." The nearest approach to humanist history appeared not in Rimini but in nearby Ravenna. But even DESIDERIO SPRETI (1414–74) could find no better use for his impeccable Latin periods than to contrast over and over again the horrors of the Polentone "tyrants" with the blessings of the Venetians who had thrown the tyrants out.

From Independent to Dependent Communes

In the eastern Romagna, then, the chief stimulants to history writing seem to have been not the communal spirit of the Lombard and Veneto cities but rather the admiration of some citizens for the universal chronicles of the thirteenth century and the admiration of others for the feats of local heroes. In the region now known as Emilia still another stimulant was present: not so much a pride in having established and maintained a commune as a feeling of satisfaction in at least having resolved the principal problem of the commune—civil strife—through submission to an outsider, and therefore to an impartial and effective lord. In two of the Emilian cities, chronicle writing flourished up to the moment of what appeared to be a final resolution; and then it stopped. Salimbene's worthy successor in Parma, an otherwise unknown notary who lived between 1270 and 1340, carefully and abundantly described the implacable feuds between the Rossi and the Correggio families through more than 259 folio pages down to the point where the weary citizens opened their gates to the mightiest lord of the moment, Alberto Della Scala. "De quo," he observed, "maximum gaudium fuit universaliter inter bonos homines, . . . , clamantes 'pax, pax' cum maximo gaudio usque ad sero."[51] Indeed, the citizens were so happy that the definitive incorporation of the city into the Visconti dominions in 1346 seemed anticlimactic; and none of them bothered to write another chronicle thereafter.

Similarly, Alberto Milioli's much more worthy successors in Reggio, SAGACCIO LEVALOSSI (d. after 1353) and Sagaccio's nephew PIETRO GAZATO (c. 1335–1414),[52] gave a full description of the internal strife of their own and of many other cities besides from about A.D. 800 (the first part is lost) to the festive reception of Bernabò Visconti on the morrow of the disastrous sack of 1371. They did so with such thoroughness that copies of their work spread rapidly among the sister houses of Pietro's Benedictine abbey in Reggio and were used as an important source for the period by most of the historians of Lombardy right down to the time of Cammillo Affarosi in the early eighteenth century. Their implied theses—that Bernabò himself would rebuild the city and that the Visconti government would solve all its problems thereafter—apparently won such acceptance that Pietro made only occasional entries for the next two decades and none at all for the following twenty-four years of his life.

On the other hand, in one Emilian city, Modena, chronicle writing survived for a half-century after its submission to an outside lord. But it did so only because the notary called in to draw up the will of the chronicler BONIFAZIO DA MORANO (d. 1349) happened to be curious about his client's collection of historical records. Bonifazio had depended for the years before 1272 on a now lost chronicle—not to be confused with the *Annales Veteres Mutinenses,* which is really the work of the sixteenth-century scholar Alessandro Tassoni Senior (1488–1565). Although he was a well-to-do jurist, and although he made at least an initial attempt at putting his local chronicle into the popes-and-emperors sequence of the universal chronicles, Bonifazio was really interested only in compiling an accurate list of *podestà* and in showing that the nobles were always right and the *populares* always wrong.[53] Thus his long account of Modena's unfortunate experiment with a succession of domestic tyrants between 1306 and 1336 tends to get buried amid reports about the weather, about the extravagant sermons of a certain Franciscan, and about a cross between an ox and a pig with the ears of a man and the feathers of a bird that some Frenchmen supposedly caught in Tunisia.

But Bonifazio's notary, GIOVANNI DA BAZZANO (c. 1285–c. 1364), had plenty of time, after his retirement from active practice, to go over, not his client's text, which he did not know about, but his material; and he dug up a good bit of new material on his own initiative from the public archives. His account of almost two centuries of Modenese history is anything but dramatic.[54] But it does substantiate one important thesis: unlike the Florentines' Duke of Athens, "spiritu diabolico inspiratus et omni ferocitate repletus," the Este were legitimate rulers. Their restoration in Modena in 1336 came about not by force but "per consilia generale communis et populi." Thus Modena had become not only a subject city but a second capital of the Este dominion; and the chroniclers of Ferrara admitted as much by incorporating in their own work long passages from the works of their fellow Estensi in Modena. This somewhat more honorable status proved insufficient to assure the continuation of the Modenese chronicles through the fifteenth century. But it was sufficient to justify the compilation of at least two dialect diaries, one of which has been published. In the eyes of the prominent pharmacist JACOPO DE' BIANCHI or DE' LANCELLOTTI (c. 1440–after 1502), the Este were still lords of the commune of Modena rather than lords of a territorial duchy. Their main service to the commune lay in squelching insurrections before they became dangerous. Their exactions were really taxes freely approved by "el rezimento de Modena." And the only real threat to their dominion came not from the Venetians or the Papacy but from the Bolognese, who kept alive the military virtues of the Modenese by occasionally reviving the age-old quarrel over their common borders.[55]

In still another Emilian city, Piacenza, the chronicle survived largely because it was supported by an older local tradition. The "Guelph Annals" of GIOVANNI CODAGNELLO in the early thirteenth century built upon still older chronicles now lost as well as on contemporary Milanese chronicles; and they in turn were incorporated (with the words changed to yield the opposite political point of view and with the structure altered to fit that of Martinus Polonus) into the "Ghibelline Annals" of the later thirteenth century, which recorded the experiments with various local lordships after the election of Oberto Pallavicino as *dominus perpetuus* in 1254.[56] These chronicles then provided the essential early material for GIOVANNI DE' MUSSI (to 1402), who, at the end of the fourteenth century, had only to borrow a few details from Riccobaldo in order to push the history of Piacenza back to Adam, or, in his *Descriptio* of 1384, to Eridanus, the grandson of Janus. He then went on to account for the rapid alteration of various hereditary lords in the first decades of the century and to celebrate the voluntary accession of the Visconti in 1335. The only remaining threat to the internal harmony and external security of his city, Mussi concluded, like his contemporaries in Rimini, was the proximity of the Papal State. And the best way to remove that danger lay in encouraging the further expansion of the Visconti empire. "It can be clearly seen," he declared, outdoing his predecessors in substituting vague superlatives for concrete facts, "that the said pastors have started innumerable wars for their above-mentioned temporal domains, because of which infinite thousands of Christians have died, and so much evil [*maledictiones*], destruction, hardship, and disorder have come into the world."[57]

The chronicle also survived in Piacenza because it was carried on by succesive members of the same family: PIETRO (d. 1374), ANTONIO (to 1447), and ALBERTO (to 1484) DE RIPALTA.[58] The Ripalta knew from the experience of the past that every attempt to detach the city from the Visconti had ended in disaster. Antonio learned the lesson once again in 1447, when he barely escaped with his life in the violent suppression of one last anachronistic project to restore the commune by the troops of Francesco Sforza. So, apparently, did another notary, MICHELE RUINAGIA, who added the plague of 1450 to the series of dire punishments visited by God on the Piacentines on account of their sins ("Prospexit Dominus de excelso sancto suo et vidit Placentinorum iniquitates adeo multiplicatas..."). But neither Michele nor Alberto de Ripalta, who was educated at Pavia, Ferrara, and Bologna, and who was accomplished enough as a Latinist to be chosen to deliver a ceremonial oration before Duke Galeazzo Maria Sforza—neither the father nor the son could conceive of a chronicle as anything other than a string of miscellaneous facts. What seems like a step toward humanist historiography in Alberto turns out to be merely an updating of the traditional decorative trimmings of the medieval rhetoricians. Thus the chronicle survived in Piacenza; but it remained frozen in its fourteenth-century mold. Instead of turning a record of the Piacentine bishops into a series of historical biographies on the model of Platina, Bishop FABRIZIO DA MARLIANO—even though a Milanese by birth and citizenship—merely produced a list of names and occasional "feats."[59] Instead of recasting what he had inherited on the model of Bruni, GIOVANNI AGAZZARI merely revised the dates for the foundation of the city according to what he found in Jerome-Eusebius. He then added a few more empty superlatives to the well-known horror stories about "infinitis captivis, mulieribus vidius, et filiis orphanatis factis, urbibus locis et castellis depopulatis. . . ."[60]

Independent Signorie: Mantua, Ferrara, Bologna

The cities of Emilia thus resolved their internal problems by submitting to an outside lord. Meanwhile, three of the principal cities of the lower Po Valley—Mantua, Ferrara, and Bologna—resolved theirs by submitting, each of them, to one of their own citizens. In other words, while replacing an unstable with a stable government, and while replacing endemic civil strife with domestic peace, these three cities managed to preserve their status as independent city-states. And it so happens that the writing of history in these cities flourished even more than it did in Emilia, notwithstanding a cultural environment that was considerably less receptive to a historical point of view.

Mantua had produced only one chronicle during the whole communal period: a complete list of *podestà* and *anziani* with a rather sparse and generic ("fuit fames valida in universo") account of the years after 1095 and a fairly full account of the years in which the author probably lived, 1264 to 1299.[61] But the elevation of Francesco Gonzaga as "captain" of the city in 1388 and the success of his heirs in jockeying for position between the Venetians on the one side and the Visconti on the other inspired one of his principal counselors, ANTONIO NERLI (fl. 1380–1414), an anonymous continuer of Nerli (to 1431), and one of his principal financiers, BONAVENTI ALIPRANDI (c. 1350–1417), to extend the chronicle backward to a legendary foundation and forward to their own times. Indeed, Aliprandi was so grateful for the big contracts he received as *masero del comune* that he accomplished what Nerli had once dreamed of doing: translating his chronicle into verse. Some of his lines are as reminiscent of Dante as may others are replete with heroic nonsense:

> Essendo posto di voler cercare
> per cosa che l'animo desidrava
> la dritta via si vieni a falare. . . .[62]

What Aliprandi did in verse for the past, ANDREA SCIVENOGLIA (1414–81), the secretary of Ferdinando IV Gonzaga, did in dialect prose for the mid-fifteenth century.[63] His packed narrative gives a very detailed description of daily life in the golden age of early Renaissance Mantua—the age of the Giocosa, the Camera degli Sposi, Sant'Andrea, and Pius II's crusade congress.

Ferrara was more fortunate than Mantua in its inheritance from the past, an inheritance that included none other than Riccobaldo. It was also fortunate in having resolved its internal political problems almost a century earlier. True, the author of the *Chronica Parva* of c. 1310 could not reconcile the relatively new Este regime with his nostalgia for the old commune.[64] He therefore employed what he had learned from Riccobaldo about chronicle writing and what he had learned from the rhetoricians about contrived dialogues and elegant phraseology ("Ventorum rex Aeolus, incluso miti Zephyro" instead of "the wind's blowing") on behalf of a reactionary rather than a progressive political platform. But even he had to admit that the "benignus et pius" Azzo d'Este had saved Ferrara from Ezzelino and that Obizzo had been elected lord by popular acclamation. His successor a half-century later was an unenthusiastic supporter of the Este. The *Chronicon Estense* (1011–1354, continued in another hand to the death of Alberto d'Este in 1393)[65] also had some literary pretensions, even though the authors never got around to filling the gaps they had left for want of information; and it managed to put the genealogy of the Este family into Riccobaldo's framework of universal history.

The *Chronicon* was apparently successful enough to inspire an imitation in the last decades of the next century—one which added still new stylistic embellishments borrowed from the humanist conventions of the day ("Gallia Cisalpina" for Lombardy) along with all the more recent vital statistics of the Este family.[66] This imitation was followed in turn by two very abundant diaries—one by UGO CALEFFINI (c. 1439–1503),[67] the other by BERNARDINO ZAMBETTI (c. 1460–after 1505)[68]—and by one anonymous annalistic chronicle (written c. 1492).[69] Caleffini was a minor bureaucrat from Rovigo, with frustrated ambitions to become a major bureaucrat, who began keeping an almost daily record of prices, tax levies, appointments, and the affairs of the court at the outbreak of the war with Venice. Zambetti was a well-educated son of a well-to-do family whose uncle, a favorite of Duke Ercole, supplied him with enough public and confidential information to fill 350 folio pages in the modern edition for the years between 1476 and 1504. The anonymous chronicler was a much less well-educated notary ("rudem stilum humilemque," in Muratori's opinion) interested chiefly in remembering names and prices—for instance, the names of the members of the welcoming delegation for an otherwise unidentified "Emperor of the Greeks" in the 1430s and the price of an elephant offered to Duke Ercole in the 1480s. But he at least made some effort to expand his sources; and he succeeded in combining what he borrowed from Caleffini with what he had observed himself in a fairly consistent narrative of the war.

Unfortunately, none of these late disciples of Riccobaldo says anything about what Quattrocento Ferrara has been best known for ever since: its culture—even though at least one of them, Zambetti, was certainly exposed to it. They mention even Battista Guarini only as a "poet" who built a house in 1496. But that was not their fault. Ferrarese culture in their day was concerned almost exclusively with poetry, painting, architecture, and Platonic philosophy. Indeed, even Borso d'Este's magnificent preparations for Pius II's crusade inspired not a history, but a poem: the *Carmen de Apparatu contra Turcum* of Gasparo Tribraco.[70] None of these disciplines, the chroniclers rightly assumed, had anything to do with the conduct of war, the administration of government, the cost of living, and the comings and goings of princes, which constituted the proper domain of history. Moreover, this assumption was reinforced by the Este themselves, who had very few books of even ancient history in their famous library. It was reinforced by Matteo Boiardo, who translated what by then was recognized as fiction as well as what was still held to be fact in Riccobaldo solely in order to furnish his fellow vernacular poets with more stories.[71] It was reinforced again in the eighteenth century when Gianandrea Barotti omitted the chroniclers entirely from his two-volume literary history of the city.[72] And it has at last been confirmed by the most recent successor of the chroniclers, who has restored princes to the position in the history of Ferrara so long usurped by men of letters.[73]

If chronicle writing was encouraged in Mantua and Ferrara by the establishment of authoritarian regimes, it was encouraged even more in Bologna by the much greater effort and far longer time required to find a suitable solution to its political problems. Throughout the fourteenth century as well as the fifteenth the Bolognese had experimented with four possibilities: the granting of real power to their nominal overlord, the Papacy, submission to the Visconti, the admission of the lower classes and the guilds into a "popular" government, or the establishment of a native lordship. The first had failed in 1339–40, when the papal legates provoked a revolt by demanding unconditional surrender. It failed again after 1403 when the Papal State disintegrated under the impact of threefold schism. The second possibility vanished when submission turned out to mean annexation, and when annexation brought not peace but more war and higher taxes ("Bononia era afamata propter guerram et non poterat stare peius illa vice"—Griffoni). The third possibility vanished when the revolution of 1402 proved to be merely a front for a pro-Visconti coup. The fourth, which seemed to be on the verge of success in 1401 and 1416, was constantly blocked by the presence of rival contenders and was not finally adopted until the accession of Sante Bentivoglio in 1446. Thus the Bolognese—or at least the chroniclers among them—were far more conscious than the Ferrarese or the Mantuans of having themselves been responsible for the erection of the new regime. The Bentivoglio, who could not aspire to the imperial titles won by the Gonzaga and the Este, responded by scrupulously acting not as the successors or destroyers of a commune that had failed but as the guardians and the guarantors of a commune that had brought them into power.[74]

At the same time, Bologna benefitted both from an abundant, although now largely lost, heritage of twelfth- and thirteenth-century chronicle writing (Ortalli) and from its possession of a particular institution, its old and famous university. The university stimulated chronicle writing not because any of its usually foreign-born professors had any interest in history, which they most certainly did not, but because it was a source of local pride. Indeed, several of the chronicles give fairly complete notices of appointments and deaths in the faculties. But Bologna benefited still more from the diligence of its greatest fourteenth-century chroniclers, PIETRO and FLORIANO (d.c. 1385) VILLOLA. Floriano rounded out what had begun as a diary with the texts of all the earlier historical records he could find; and his son LEONARDO elevated the diary, which had been interrupted in 1380, into a chronicle. The achievement of the Villola soon attracted the attention of other citizens. One of them translated the whole text, with some variants, into what is known as the *Testo volgato*. Another, BARTOLOMEO DELLA PUGLIOLA (c. 1358–1424), incorporated the first part of it into two different versions, one from 1362 to 1407, and the other, obviously remolded by a successor, from 1282 to 1432. Still another, possibly the otherwise unknown GIACOMO DA VARIGNANI, translated some of it again, then added some passages from the *Chronicon Estense,* and finally continued writing on his own through the first decades of the fifteenth century.[75]

These initial efforts soon inspired imitations by many other citizens of many different ranks and professions. Unlike in Venice, where the chroniclers were all patricians or chancery officials, and unlike in Ferrara, where they were courtiers and bureaucrats, some of the Bolognese chroniclers were merchants (Villola), some were distinguished magistrates (MATTEO GRIFFONI), some were parish priests (MATTIOLO), some were friars (Pugliola and Burselli), one was a patrician archivist (GIACOMO BIANCHETTI—c. 1335–1405), and one was a mason (Nadi). Like Pugliola, who was plagiarized by Villola's translator just as he had plagiarized Villola himself, they liberally borrowed from each other and more liberally altered and amended what they borrowed; and they ended up with over seventy different texts, all of them so completely mixed up with the others that even the most recent editors have at last given up trying to sort out three of the "families" that Muratori, rather arbitrarily, molded into a single text.[76] In some cases, indeed, only calamity could bring a continuation of a continuation to a halt: that, at any rate, is what happened to the BOLOGNETTI chronicle when a tower collapsed on the house of the heirs of GIOVANNI DI DANIELE in 1484 and killed all but two of them.[77] Most of the chronicles went right on into the next century. That of GIROLAMO DE' BORSELLI (or BURSELLI) (1342–97) was carried on by his fellow Dominican Vincenzo Sparagli (1498–1584) for some eighty-eight years beyond the author's death;[78] that of GIACOMO RONCO (d. 1418) was carried on by GIOVAN FRANCESCO NEGRI from 1400 to 1460 and then by GIOVANNI DE' PILLIZONI (b. 1445) past the turn of the century;[79] and the printed text of the Varignana stops in 1500 rather than 1519 only out of respect for Muratori's arbitrary cutoff point. Some of the chronicles are written in the form of universal chronicles. Ronco's almost wholly local record of *podestà,* embassies, and banishments contains a preface about the creation of the world and the foundation of Rome, and Griffoni's extends the calendar of dates relevant to Bolognese history back to no less than 4448 B.C.[80] Some of them, on the other hand, are concerned solely with what went on within the walls. GASPARE NADI's (1418–1504) diary from 1460 to 1504, to which the author added an introduction for the years from his birth and to which a successor added an appendix down to 1514[81] is purely local in scope.

PIETRO DI MATTIOLO's *Cronaca* of the years between 1371 and 1424 rises slightly above the local level only in the author's own fantastic prophecies of future doom.[82] But all the chronicles were packed with information about the trivial as well as the important events of their day, often with the hour as well as the date given for each entry. Moreover, all the chroniclers who had any political commitment at all—from Griffoni, who was converted from a pro-papal position, to GIACOMO DAL POGGIO, who dedicated his work to Annibale Bentivoglio—agree in viewing the Bentivoglio regime as the culmination of Bologna's political development. And since the chroniclers in Bologna, given their social and vocational diversity, more nearly represented public opinion than those in any other city, their unanimity on this point may help to explain the fury with which the statue of Pope Julius II, who overthrew the regime in 1506, was torn down in 1512.

Thus in spite of the secondary importance of one, the tertiary importance of another, and the nearly insignificant importance of the third in the Italian balance of power, the three independent city-states of the lower Po Valley managed to produce a body of chronicle writing that approached in quality as well as in quantity that of such major powers as Florence and Venice; and they did so particularly as a response to political regimes that are usually described as the exact opposites of the Florentine and Venetian constitutions. Moreover, all three of these cities succeeded in accomplishing, in the second half of the fifteenth century, what had proved impossible in the Emilian cities: a transition from chronicle writing to humanist historiography. To be sure, this transition was not necessarily dependent upon the presence of a particular political regime or even, after the diffusion of printing, upon the proximity of a center of humanist culture. For instance, it occurred in the small town of Cuneo in the ahistorical domains of the house of Savoy in the year 1484, when an unknown Latin teacher who had studied Livy and Suetonius at school happened to run across a copy of Bruni's *Bellum Gothicum*. He forthwith composed not a *chronicula,* as he himself and his modern editor too modestly called it, but a humanist history of Cuneo—one which, except for the last unrevised pages, approximated the standards of the still unavailable *Historiae Florentini Populi*.[83] In Mantua, however, a princely regime was indispensable in calling forth a humanist history of the city. For it was the prince himself, and his brother, Cardinal Federico Gonzaga, who commissioned the most prominent local-boy-who-made-good, BARTOLOMEO PLATINA, to write it; and it was they who took the trouble to correct the many errors that Platina, far away amid the comforts of Rome, let slip into the first draft. What they got was far from scientifically perfect, even according to Quattrocento standards. Still, the *Historia Urbis Mantuae Gonziacaeque Familiae*[84] was based on Biondo as well as on the local chronicles the author had sent to him from Mantua. It divided Mantuan history into periods that corresponded to those sanctioned by the humanists for other Italian cities. It proclaimed as the purpose even of local history the promotion of civic virtue ("bene de suis rebus publicis promerere student"). It exalted the Gonzaga as the guardians of civil liberty at home and the protectors of *Libertas Italiae* abroad. And that, after all, is just what the patrons wanted.

In Bologna, on the other hand, humanist historiography was launched not by the prince but by three politically active and well-educated patricians who admired him. BENEDETTO MORANDI seems to have been attracted to history by his study of Livy, whom he defended from the criticisms of the leading Livy expert of the day, Lorenzo Valla. He at least learned from Livy how to pick out proofs from the Bolognese chronicles in support of his campaign against Pius II's decree on the priority of Sienese representatives in public ceremonies.[85] GIOVANNI GARZONI, a leading member of the city council *(Anziani),* seems to have been attracted to history by the introduction of humanist studies at the university,[86] where he was professor of medicine from 1466 until his death in 1500. After trying his hand at poetry, oratory, moral and political philosophy, and poetics, and after practicing the art of history in several saints' lives, biographies of two previous lords of Bologna, descriptions of Saxony and Thuringia, and accounts of recent Italian wars, he at last produced his greatest historical work the *De Dignitate Urbis Bononiae.*[87] It is a formally impeccable humanist commentary, one that recognizes the continuing vitality of Bologna as a community of citizens while crediting its tempered monarchy ("unus sit rex, unus principatus") with having saved the city from Charles VIII. Borselli, a disciple of Cardinal Bessarion and a member of the wealthy Albertucci family who became prior of the Bolognese Dominicans and local inquisitor, seems to have been attracted to history by reading several historical works: that of his ancestor *in religione,* Galvano Fiamma of Milan,[88] that of his contemporary and fellow citizen, Giovanni Garzoni, and the still unpublished *De Civitate Bononiae* of the Bolognese antiquarian Niccolò Perotti. He learned to combine his models in acceptable, though far from perfect, humanist Latin by writing a history of the popes, a chronicle of the Bolognese Dominicans, and chronicles of several cities—all of which have since disappeared. The result of this fusion was a chronicle half medieval, half humanist. It followed its medieval predecessors back to Noah and left to the discretion of the reader—or of a fellow preacher—which of the vast number of specific details might best serve as *exempla* "for exciting others to virtue." At the same time, it rejected as a forgery the document usually cited in support of the foundation of the university by Theodosius. It used archaeological evidence with a care worthy of Biondo. While eloquently describing the greatest benefit of the Bentivoglio regime (the current urban renewal projects), it predicted even more eloquently what would surely happen should the regime fall: murder and plundering, like that which took place in 1399 and 1402 and which almost took place again during the Malvezzi conspiracy of 1488.[89]

In Ferrara, humanist historiography came into being in part for the same reasons for which it appeared in Mantua and Bologna. JACOPO DELAITO was asked to keep an account of the current reign by the young Niccolò d'Este in 1395. GIOVANNI CANALI

DA FERRARA (1409–62), a professor of theology at the university and a former student of Guarino da Verona, dedicated his revision and continuation of Delaito's chronicle to Borso d'Este in 1453.[90] And PELLEGRINO PRISCIANO (c. 1435–1518), who served Borso and Ercole as librarian, ambassador to Venice, and governor of Reggio, was closely associated with the small group of Ferrarese men of letters who, though indifferent to history, enthusiastically cultivated the study of the classics, mathematics, and astronomy.[91] But humanist historiography also came into being through the internal development of the traditional chronicle form. Even though Delaito, a notary from Rovigo who became chancellor during the difficult days of Duke Niccolò's minority, was the Ferrarese equivalent of his contemporary Coluccio Salutati, he was apparently ignorant of Petrarchan Latin. His chronicle is composed of the same lists of disconnected events, the same piles of vague superlatives ("rebellionibus quae infinitae erant"; "infinitus fuit numerus captivorum"), and the same indifference to historical causation that had been typical of all the medieval chronicles. But Delaito picked up a taste for his task as he went along. He learned to illustrate the policies of the Este with a parallel examination of the rise of the Bentivoglio. He learned to put policy statements in the form of direct speeches. And he learned to replace short *eodem anno* statements of fact with connected historical narratives.[92] Similarly, Giovanni da Ferrara was as uncritical about the old legends as any of his Franciscan brothers, and he often confused eloquence with the fantastic flourishes of the medieval rhetoricians (e.g., on poor Frederick III, "cuius nomen terra tremuit, colles humiliantur, maria fremitum ponunt..."). But at least he learned from Sallust what history ought to be, and he tried to persuade Borso that it was more lasting than pyramids and gold statues. Moreover, his Latin style may have tasted like "warmed over cabbage" to Muratori and like "inflated and tiresome" rhetoric to his most recent editor; but it was perfectly consonant with the standards of his humanist friends at the Ferrara court. These two chronicles then gave way, from 1485 on, to the polished prose of the cultivated humanist Prisciano, who travelled from Milan to Rome in search of materials and who amassed an enormous collection of legal and diplomatic documents before beginning to write. Had the text been published, or had the author not prematurely returned to his several dozen other engrossing intellectual pastimes, the *Historia Ferrariae* might have been acclaimed as the Ferrarese equivalent of Sabellico's *Rerum Venetiarum* or of Platina's *Vitae Pontificum*.

The Historians of the Metropolis

The special advantages for chronicle writing enjoyed singly by one or the other of the mainland cities of northern Italy were all present in the greatest of them, Milan. BONVESIN DELLA RIVA (c. 1250–after 1313) revived the late Roman genre of historical-topographical description in the late thirteenth century,[93] just as (to the horror of his liberty-loving modern editor) the embattled commune finally yielded to the popular tyranny of the Torriani family; and he decked out his work in a flowery style that seemed as appropriate to the other students of *ars dictandi* of his day as it was to seem "barbarous" to the dissertation writers of the late nineteenth century. The wandering notary (*not* priest) BENZO D'ALESSANDRIA, during his seven-year residence at Como after 1313, expanded Bonvesin's format into a medieval encyclopedia on the model of Vincent of Beauvais' *Speculum Mundi* and with information gathered from Siccardo, from Siccardo's late-Roman authorities, from whatever bits of classical historiography he could find, and from the writings of all his Milanese predecessors. This mass of material forced him occasionally to be critical. Where Siccardo had gotten his stories about certain of Noah's sons, "God knows," confessed Benzo, "I don't"; and he threw them out along with the stories about the coronation of the Lombard kings about which he could find not a word in Paulus Diaconus.[94] GALVANO FIAMMA (c. 1283–after 1344), in turn, the most prolific and the best known of all the late medieval chroniclers in Milan, took over all the material and many of the sentences, but, alas, none of the critical intuitions of Benzo's and Bonvesin's works. He added still more general information from Jacopo da Varagine and still other legends from modern and ancient times (such as the story about Boniface VIII and the Devil). He then dedicated the last thirty years of his life to rearranging what he had collected, "totum ex libris autenticis," by chronological or topical order. And he wrote it out in a long series of universal, local, and ecclesiastical chronicles all for the purpose of glorifying his city, degrading its enemies (especially the Cremonese), and reconciling his fellow Dominicans, who had preferred pope to prince during the interdict of 1323, with his chief hero, Lucchino Visconti. Whether he was "a writer of vast culture" (Odetto) or "the perfect but not admirable model of that credulous and chattering mob of chroniclers" (Novati) is a question on which modern critics are divided.[95] But at least he was one of the first writers in all Italian history to perceive the importance of art patronage as an element of political power.[96] And for his contemporaries and successors his works constituted an indispensable warehouse of information, which they continued to plunder, albeit somewhat more cautiously than he had plundered the works of others, for the next two centuries.[97]

At the same time, Milan enjoyed two advantages that were not shared by other cities. One of its early fourteenth-century chroniclers, GIOVANNI DE CERMENATE, was apparently associated with the circle of pre-Petrarchan classical scholars to which Albertino Mussato belonged, for his Latin style was so carefully patterned on Livy that even Muratori could find nothing wrong with it. Cermenati's view of history was as apocalyptic as that of Gioacchino da Fiore, his views of politics were as anachronistic as Dante's, and his views of the distant past were as obscured as Gavano's by those prototypes of modern real-estate speculators, the grandsons of Noah. But he succeeded in bringing to bear all of what he said about the past upon a coherent narrative of one single event, the *Romfahrt* of Emperor Henry VII. All of his more dramatic moments are cast in impeccable Livian speeches. And his mono-graph inevitably leads to the same conclusion regarding the same major political question of the time that Mussato had proposed to the Paduan council: the emperor was the savior of Italy and the anti-imperial Guelphs were its scourge.[98]

Similarly, two of the best Milanese chroniclers were citizens not of Milan but of cities which during the course of the fourteenth century were incorporated into the domains of the lords of Milan. Benzo, needless to say, was born in Alessandria. But a trip to the Holy Land in 1283 and a long career thereafter as chancellor to the bishop of Como and to the lords of Verona gradually turned the direction of his loyalties from the city of his birth to the wider dominions of his city's lords. PIETRO AZARI (b. 1312) was born in Novara, of which his uncle was chancellor, and he grew up there amid the civil turmoil that preceded its conquest by the Visconti in 1332. Azari was no more capable than any of his contemporaries of envisaging any other legitimate political entity than the commune and the Empire, and he was no more capable than any other late-medieval chronicler of seeing in the new Visconti state a possible remedy for the "scelera permulta" of his age. "Circumdederunt me dolores mortis," he exclaimed as he covered over his frequent slips of memory with his notarial seal, "et pericula inferni invenerunt me." Nevertheless, his father had worked as a notary and, in 1323, as assistant to the *podestà* in Milan; and his own peregrinations as notary to various mercenary armies and as a Visconti official in various parts of their dominion had transformed him, in sentiment if not in theory, into a citizen of Lombardy. Thus he too was led, like the chroniclers of those cities that had already come under Milanese rule,[99] to recognize Lombardy as a proper object of historical narration, if not yet as a real political community.[100]

The transformations of Milan into the capital of a nascent territorial state may have succeeded, then, in elevating local chronicles to the rank of regional chronicles in the subject cities. But it seemed to have ruined chronicle writing in the capital. The absence of any diaries or chronicles of the kind that the Bolognese and the Venetians were then busy writing during the hundred-odd years after the death of Galvano Fiamma suggests that the communal spirit in Milan had vanished. The attempt to resurrect what had been one of the chief literary expressions of that spirit in the second half of the fifteenth century turned out to be as futile as the attempt to revive the spirit itself during the fiasco of the Ambrosian Republic. The diary that Francesco Sforza's chancellor CICCO SIMONETTA (c. 1410–1480) kept off and on from 1473 until the eve of his fall from office in 1479 was a purely personal account of the author's official business, even though the great number of state papers it contains make it an invaluable source for the history of contemporary politics.[101] The universal and local episcopal chronicles that the notary DONATO BOSSI (1436–c. 1500) spent thirty years of his life compiling seem to have been essentially miscellanies of "memorable sayings and actions" rather than chronological records.[102] The short *Cronachetta* of the Cremonese court official LEONARDO BOTTA did little more than list the feats and vital statistics of the Sforza family from 1369 to 1458.[103] Muratori's *Annales Mediolanensis*—in spite of the resemblance of its language and some of its narrative passages to the Florentine humanist chronicles—was not concerned with contemporary history at all. It ended intentionally with an account of the pious death of its hero, Giangaleazzo Visconti, which occurred some eighty years before it was actually written.[104] Another anonymous chronicle of the same period consists merely of poorly disguised plagiarisms of Galvano, Azari, Villani, and Mussato. For the fifteenth century, in the absence of any available Milanese accounts, it merely transcribes whatever could be found about Milan in the Italian translations of Bruni and Poggio, whose historiographical innovations the author failed completely to notice. Indeed, the only purpose it has ever served then or since is that of giving a late-nineteenth-century critic a chance to let off another round of imprecations about obscurantist friars.[105]

What saved history writing in Milan was not the survival of the commune, but the identification of the commune with the persons of its princes, whose characters and activities became the almost exclusive concern of the historians of the fifteenth century. What permitted the appearance of humanist historiography was not the survival and development of the chronicle tradition in which the past had been recorded, but the application of humanist linguistic and critical principles in describing the present, which was what interested the first Milanese historians. The Visconti had been among the first rulers of Italy to realize the political utility of Petrarchan humanism. It was Archbishop Giovanni who had hired Petrarch when he finally returned from Avignon. It was Giangaleazzo who had entrusted to Petrarch's admirer, Antonio Loschi, the task of providing an ideological basis for his policy of territorial aggrandizement in Italy. And the humanist chancellors at Milan responded by making Giangaleazzo's potentially national state the modern incarnation of the Rome of the Caesars, well before Coluccio Salutati discovered in the Florentine city-state the substance of the Rome of the Scipios and the Ciceros.

Thus the first Milanese citizen to write the history of his city after the time of Galvano was, like his almost exact contemporary Bruni, a scholar-statesman whose scholarly activities were, as they had not been for Petrarch, intimately connected with his political activities: ANDREA BIGLIA (c. 1395–1435). Biglia had mastered classical Latin well enough to reject the rhymed grammars of medieval Latin and to compose an *epistola consolotaria* that is a perfect imitation of the style of Seneca. He knew Greek well enough, within a few years of Chrysoloras's mission to the Italians, to translate Aristotle. He even studied Hebrew—a half-century before Giovanni Pico della Mirandola introduced Hebrew literature to Christian scholars. Biglia was also a man whose deep piety was projected into a history of his religious order, the Augustinians, and into an account of the translation of the body of St. Monica.[106] Above all, he was a man whose political acumen was recognized by his appointment to important administrative and diplomatic posts in the service of his order and of his prince. These posts enabled him to accumulate the great amount of firsthand observation upon which much of his history of the crisis and revival of the Visconti state is based. The result was a work which, had it been published in the fifteenth instead of the eighteenth century, might have brought as much honor to the Milanese principate as Bruni's *Historiae* brought to the Florentine Republic.[107] It was divided into topical books: one on the collapse of Giangaleazzo's empire from 1402 to 1406, the next on the disintegration of the imperial administration in the hands of his heirs. It ended in 1431, not just because Biglia got tired of writing, but because the imminent expedition of Emperor Sigismund into Italy seemed to herald the approach of another historical period. At the same time, the work presented just as convincingly the exact opposite of the Florentine point of view on the events it recounted. While never failing to admit that "the matter is obscure" whenever testimony was conflicting, or to qualify with "in my opinion" ("ego potius cum aliis existimaverim") whenever it was insufficient, Biglia attributed the rebellion of Siena to the instigation of well-paid Florentine agents and the fall of Pisa to the avarice of that "unfortunate merchant," Gambaccorta. He portrayed the constant interference of the Florentines in the affairs of other states as the expression of their intent not to defend the independence of the Italian city-states but to bring all Tuscany under their dominion.

Of Biglia's two successors in the following generation, one, the otherwise unknown ANTONIO MINUTI of Piacenza, wrote what was essentially a historical biography not of a duke of Milan but of the father of the man who had become duke after the extinction of the direct line of the Visconti—and to whom he dedicated his work in 1454. After isolating an obviously fabricated myth about the origins of the Sforza family in a Latin preface, Minuti's *Vita da Muzio Attendolo Sforza*[108] progresses chronologically, in Lombard Italian, from the birth to the death of its hero in accordance with the appropriate ancient models, Livy and Plutarch. It explains the circumstances of the successive events of the hero's life in a pan-Italian context drawn from what the author regarded as the modern equivalents of the ancient models, Bruni and Biondo. The other, the world-famous classsical scholar PIER CANDIDO DECEMBRIO (1399–1477), wrote one historical biography of the duke he served as secretary from 1419 until 1447 and another of the duke he would like to have served after the death of the former in 1447. Decembrio probably learned Greek from his father, also a ducal secretary, who had studied with Chrysoloras. He mastered the whole of ancient literature, from Homer to Orosius; and he did so with such thoroughness that he earned extra fees as book-buyer and library consultant to the godfather of the English Renaissance, Humphrey of Gloucester. He learned to write history by translating Caesar, Polybius, and Curtius Rufus into Italian for his patron, and Appianus and Diodorus Siculus into Latin for Pope Nicholas V. He collected materials for his own historical writing while traveling up and down Europe from Flanders to Rome on diplomatic missions. He learned to put what he had collected into historical perspective by revising his father's epitome of ancient Roman history and drafting chronologies of the popes and emperors. And he practiced what he had learned by composing a series of lives of famous Romans and of Duke Ercole d'Este.[109] Unfortunately, Decembrio's life of Francesco Sforza turned out to be a eulogy in the form of a chronicle—for the good reason that it was written as an appendix to a job application. But the life of Filippo Maria Visconti follows the example of Suetonius in giving a full account of the wars of the mid-fifteenth century and a fairly full description of the duke's character; and it excuses the negative aspects of his internal administration, like ruinous taxation, not by trying to cover them up but by pointing out the positive aspects as well: the defense of the state against the Venetians and the embellishment of the capital with sumptuous palaces and churches.[110]

What Minuti and Decembrio did in the form of historical biography was transformed by two of their junior contemporaries into biographical histories—that is, into histories of the preceding hundred years in which the careers of the reigning duke and his father provide the main thread through the maze of Italian diplomatic and military conflicts. Like their immediate predecessors, both of them were dedicated, high-ranking ducal secretaries. LEODRISIO CRIVELLI (c. 1413–after 1488) had worked his way through the archepiscopal bureaucracy, thanks in part to his mastery of jurisprudence, which he taught for several years at the University of Pavia. He was rewarded for his part in a plot of 1449 against the Ambrosian Republic with a distinguished post in the civil bureaucracy—and the honor of having the duke as godfather to his son—as soon as the republic yielded to a new lord, Francesco Sforza. GIOVANNI SIMONETTA (1410–92) had followed his uncle Angelo and his omnipotent cousin Cicco through the ranks of Francesco Sforza's private bureaucracy. When their master was suddenly transformed from the head of a mercenary army into the head of a state, Simonetta was rewarded with a seat on the ducal council, a feudal estate in his native Calabria, and an episcopal see for his clerical brother. Both these historians also were eventually mistreated by those they served. Crivelli was forced to seek employment in Rome in the wake of a quarrel with the current dictator of Milanese intellectual life, Francesco Filelfo; and his reply to Filelfo's attack on his new employer, Pius II, was sufficient to stigmatize him in the eyes of his former employer as a drunkard, a sodomite, a Turkish agent, and, worst of all, a sloppy Latinist. Simonetta, like his cousin, got caught on the wrong side of the coup d'état of 1480; and although he kept his head, he passed the few remaining years after his release from prison in relative obscurity. Moreover, both of them were accomplished humanists. Simonetta learned to write history by reading all the humanist historians of his age—from Minuti and Decembrio to Biondo, Poggio, Campano, and Fazio. Crivelli was a friend of Francesco Barbaro and admirer of that "homo disertissimus," Leonardo Bruni; and he put into practice what he learned from them by translating John Chrysostom from the Greek and describing Pius II's abortive crusade in impeccable humanist Latin.[111] Hence, their historical works followed the best models of the day. They checked what they found in the written sources with what they had observed themselves and with what they heard in interviews with their heroes. They supported their theses with documents taken from the ducal and episcopal archives. They accepted Biondo's system of periodization "ab inclinatione Romani Imperii." They admitted no other cause of historical events than the plans and passions of men, and they made men's souls subject to no other limitation than the psychological character associated with certain regions—like the congenital weakness of the Neapolitans for "dissentiones atque discordias." Accordingly, Crivelli's uncompleted *De Vita...Sfortiae* was plundered by Marco Attendolo Cotigliolano and Pier Matteo Carranti early in the following century, even though the original manuscript was stolen by the French in 1500. Simonetta's *Rerum Gestarum Francisci Sfortiae* was printed twice in the original during the author's lifetime and three times thereafter in Cristoforo Landino's Florentine translation,[112] and it was used as the basis of one of Bandello's *novelle* (no. 26).

What Crivelli and Simonetta had cast as the history of two men of their own times during the reign of Francesco Sforza was expanded by two principal historians of the reign of Lodovico il Moro into an inquiry into the origins and growth of the city over which Francesco had been called to rule. Both GIORGIO MERULA (1430–97)[113] and TRISTANO CALCO (before 1455–1515) were humanists by profession—that is, what they did as men of letters was far more important in the eyes of their patron than what they did in their official capacity as ducal secretaries. Merula had succeeded his teacher, Francesco Filelfo, as one of the greatest philologists of his day. He had produced emended editions of a score of ancient Latin texts and translations of several ancient Greek authors. He had taken a leading role in exploiting the last of the great manuscript quarries of the Renaissance, Bobbio. And he had thrown verbal mud (or worse, in accordance with the nickname his enemies gave him—*Merdula*) at the best scholars of all Italy before being summoned in 1482 to be the equivalent in Milan of Pomponio Leto in Rome and Poliziano in Florence and the teacher in turn of such leading lights of the next generation as Baldassare Castiglione and Giovan Giorgio Trissino. Similarly, Calco had been responsible for bringing scholars to Milan and supplying the young prince Giovan Galeazzo II with tutors, and he had served as director of the famous library in Pavia before being called to succeed Merula in 1496.

Both Merula and Calco thus sought to provide their patron with the best that humanist scholarship could provide in the field of historiography. Merula reread all the ancient and all the modern humanist historians to discover whatever they might have said about Milan. He traveled all over northern Italy in search of local chronicles and charters. He ransacked the state archives in Milan, persuaded friends to ransack private archives in other cities, and obtained a ducal order giving him the run of the archives in Pavia. Calco then reviewed the same material, added many documents that Merula had not found, along with another category, legal commentaries ("lego in diariis jurispertorum") that Merula had not considered, and obtained another ducal order permitting him "to look throughout our dominions for any chronicles and other writings . . . pertinent to the task of making this a finished and honorable work." Thus the myths vanished. The descendants of Noah were relegated to the realm of "dreams." The history of Milan was traced back no further than the date of the foundation of the city established on the authority of Livy. The achievements of the Visconti were disassociated from their ancestry, which in turn was made much more recent. The fabulous size attributed by their sources to the Gothic armies was hidden behind such phrases as "quidem tradunt." Epigraphical evidence was used to check the accounts of the chronicles, and bulls and charters were quoted at length to bridge the gaps that the chronicles had left. Biondo was excused for his occasional errors by the admission that one man could not adequately cover everything, and Antonino of Florence was pardoned for his many errors of fact and judgment by the observation that theologians ought not to write history.

Had Merula not died while still writing about the mid-fourteenth century, and had Calco not decided to rewrite what Merula had written rather than to complete it for the remaining 150 years, the *Antiquitates Vicecomitum Libri X* [114] and the *Historiae Patriae Libri* [115] might have ranked as the most complete and most mature products of Quattrocento historiography. Merula's prose is more polished—even though it remained in the form of a first draft. Its historical periodization is more sharply delineated: the Gallic period, the Roman period, the Lombard period, the rise of the commune to its destruction by Frederick Barbarossa, the triumph and the crisis of the commune, the resolution of the crisis through the establishment of the Visconti government. Its theses are more forcibly sustained: that Matteo Visconti was a pious prince and that the popes who excommunicated him were power-hungry politicians, that the only alternative to one-man rule is endemic civil war among many little tyrants, and that the ultimate solution to internecine war among the Italian states is the revival of the empire of the Romans or of the national monarchy of the Lombards. Calco's narrative is more precise, more detailed, and more closely dependent upon original documents, which are quoted at length. It is more merciless in its rejection of legend, or even of careless inaccuracy ("this sort of thing not only does not deserve credit, but it removes from those who approve of it any claim to authority"). It usually introduces direct discourse speeches only when they have been preserved in written form (i.e., those of Ambrose). And it puts the history of Milan much more clearly in the context of the history of northern Italy—although it does so less to support a thesis than to permit the author to demonstrate the vastness of his erudition. But both of these works are mines of carefully evaluated information extracted from all the sources then available. And both of them lead inevitably to the conclusion that neither author had time to state fully: that the course of history culminates in the benign and enlightened monarchy of Lodovico il Moro.

In spite of this achievement, however, all the humanist histories of Milan suffered from certain basic defects that prevented them from rising to the status of the works of Bruni and Biondo. First of all, they were committed to a concept of history that valued change through time only to the extent that it was occasionally interrupted by periods of changelessness. To be sure, this concept was supported by the practice of all the humanist historians in limiting the qualification "memorable" to military and diplomatic events alone and in thus excluding from history those periods of peace and prosperity that all of them would have preferred to have lived in. But in Milan the concept was reinforced by the identification of evil solely with civil discord, which the Visconti did indeed manage to suppress and which the Ambrosian Republic had recently come close to reviving. It was also reinforced by the affection of Milanese scholars for that least historically conscious of all ages of peace and prosperity, the second century A.D., which Merula was taught to appreciate by his closest ancient counterparts, Appianus of Alexandria and Dio Cassius, and which he popularized by translating the lives of the great second-century emperors.[116] It was further reinforced by the attempt to place the last, and supposedly permanent, golden age in the present—in the reign of Giangaleazzo (Biglia), or of Filippo Maria (Decembrio), or of Francesco Sforza (Simonetta), or of Lodovico il Moro (Calco).

Secondly, all these histories were committed to a Milanese variant of the humanist limitation of historical causality to the interplay between individual men and *fortuna*—namely, to the supposition that all action proceeded from a prince. After all, many of the historians were not Milanese by birth, and the rest of them had so thoroughly forgotten the commune—except in one or two of Biglia's purely nostalgic reflections—that they were incapable of defining Milan as anything but a pile of masonry in the middle of the Lombard plain. Moreover, as the highest servants and frequent companions of the prince, none of them was able to perceive what some chroniclers of the subject cities had already begun to notice in the Veneto as well as in Lombardy: the rise of a territorial state. None of them could really object if the prince saw fit to alter what they had written—which is what Il Moro did in crossing out the superlatives from Simonetta's characterizations of his immediate predecessors. And since none of them had risen through the ranks, they were completely blind to what turned out to be the most lasting achievement of the Visconti and the Sforza: the transformation of an urban patriciate into a civil bureaucracy.

Thus when one of the humanists, Ambrosio Tegio, tried to write the history of nonprincely heroes, he was forced to fall back on the same old pile of miracles that his colleagues had long since barred from history.[117] When others of them tried to explain what had befallen the great ages in the past, they were forced to fix the blame on certain villains—those dim-witted co-emperors Arcadius and Honorius, who let in the Goths, that barbarian Charlemagne, who overthrew the wise Lombards, that maniac Gregory VII who tried to destroy the autonomy of the Ambrosian Church, or, the worst and most persistent villains of all, those ever-meddling Florentines, who thwarted Giangaleazzo's noble plan to pacify Italy solely for the purpose of being able to lord it over their neighbors in Tuscany.

Luckily, none of these historians was forced to face the full concequences of these defects. Biglia skidded over the embarrassment of Giangaleazzo's coup d'état by denigrating the character of his uncle Bernabò. Simonetta got around Filippo Maria's failure to provide for an orderly succession by changing the subject and talking instead about the Sforza. Merula and Calco avoided a discussion of the murder of one legitimate duke and the kidnapping of another that had brought Il Moro to power by sticking to the past. And all of them continued to repeat the same ideological justification that Giangaleazzo's humanist chancellors had provided for a projected kingdom of Italy, even though it was perfectly clear that none of Giangaleazzo's successors could aspire to anything grander than a duchy of Lombardy.[118] What would happen to the basic assumptions of the historians if the source of confusion was found to be not among domestic dissidents or foreign enemies but in the prince himself? And what would happen to the assumptions if the whole edifice were suddenly to crumble on the morrow of a single battle?

That was a question that the humanist historians left to their much less capable younger colleague, BERNARDINO CORIO (1459–1513).[119] Corio tried to outdo Merula and Calco in the application of their own principles. He presented their scheme of periodization separately in the dedication to make sure the reader would not miss it in the text—where, indeed, it is barely perceptible. He gave good reasons for preferring Livy's authority to Pliny's on the foundation date—which turns out to be almost the same as the one given by the most recent historian of the period on the authority of Justin. He waited until he had enough information about a speech that actually had been delivered—by the Lodi ambassadors to Barbarossa—before composing one for rhetorical effect. He wrote out the inscriptions he himself had found and left in their original language the bulls and charters he included.[120] He exalted Giangaleazzo—with a full inventory of his treasure collection and a four-page description of his investiture cememonies. And he flagellated the Florentines, whose constant machinations had forced Giangaleazzo to overtax his subjects.

But Corio, the son of a distinguished patrician-bureaucrat and a witness to the murder of Duke Galeazzo Maria in 1475, really had no more of a vocation for history than he had for poetics, which he lifted from Boccaccio, or for biography, which he pasted together from passages in the ancient histories and medieval chronicles. He could think of no other reason for writing history—and for thus accepting the pension Il Moro offered him at the age of twenty-five—than a watered-down version of the old arguments about its superior moral value, which he presented in a prefatory essay "In Praise of History." Thus when the armies of Charles VIII poured over the Alps in 1494, he was totally unprepared for the eventuality that the golden age he was happy to live in might not be eternal after all:

> ...[in these times] peace finally seemed to have been established, and
> everyone gave himself over to accumulating riches, for which all the
> roads were now open.... The court of our prince was in all its splen-
> dor... [full of] excellent men brought from the farthest parts of Europe.
> Here there was a school of Greek, here flourished Latin prose and poetry,
> here congregated the most famous masters of sculpture and painting.

All he could do was insert pointed reflections in his text whenever he came across
what now turned out to be precursors of the present invaders: "the destruction, the
ruin... brought upon us by Frederick Barbarossa and... *by other barbarians,* the
natural enemies of the Italian name..." (italics mine). Then when the armies of
Louis XII crossed the Alps in 1499 for the explicit purpose of seizing the duchy of
Milan and sending its "glorious and illustrious" duke to die in a French prison, he
was at a loss to find an explanation. Perhaps it was the fault of Piero de' Medici, who
never should have yielded to Charles VIII in 1494. Perhaps it was the fault of
Alexander VI, who "assumed the pontificate gentle as an ox and administered it like
a lion." More probably it was the fault of Il Moro, who could not be satisfied with
the glory he already enjoyed and who did, Corio now admitted, push his way to the
throne in a somewhat illegal manner. But the faults of one or two men were
obviously insufficient causes for "such an inextinguishable conflagration." Accordingly, Corio retreated from history into chronicle through most of the second half of
his work. And it was largely because he succeeded at least in this form in bringing
his account down to his own day, rather than because of the quality either of his
language or of his narration, that his work, rather than those of Merula or Calco,
was recognized as the Milanese equivalent of Sabellico's "definitive" history of
Venice well into the sixteenth century.

5

FROM COMMUNES
TO TERRITORIAL STATES

THE EXISTENCE OF INDEPENDENT CITY-STATES WAS SOMEWHAT LESS IMPORTANT FOR THE genesis and development of a chronicle tradition in central Italy than it was in the north. Some towns that maintained a considerable degree of autonomy well into the fourteenth century—like Prato, Montepulciano, and Assisi—produced no chronicles at all. One town that had never enjoyed more than purely local autonomy—San Miniato—did produce a chronicle. For a certain GIOVANNI DI LEMMO DA COMUGNORI decided that the funerals, fistfights, and *podestà* appointments at home were as worthy of "the memory of future generations" as those he observed in the well-chronicled metropolis of Pisa, where he spent much of his time.[1] Another town, San Gimignano, produced a chronicle at the very moment of its definitive submission to Florence in 1354. For an otherwise unknown Florentine Dominican decided that its citizens would better appreciate their current state of peace if they occasionally recalled the interminable feuds that had filled most of the 155 years of their independence.[2] Indeed, one town that never achieved a size or prominence commensurate with the masterpieces of high Renaissance art that were eventually bestowed upon it, Spello in Umbria, produced a series of chronicles that pretended to cover over a thousand years of historical time. For a local lawyer in the fourteenth century was fortunate enough to have studied in one of the greatest law schools of the age, Perugia; and several of his descendants, who earned their money and leisure by working as legal consultants elsewhere in Italy, felt subsequently bound by their ancestor's example.[3]

Indeed, the very different political experiences of three of the more important cities of central Italy—Lucca, Orvieto, and Viterbo—suggest that in some cases the appearance of chronicles had nothing to do with municipal autonomy at all. In all three cities the tradition had been inaugurated in the same way: with a local version of a universal chronicle. GOFFREDO DA VITERBO (c. 1120–c. 1200) had been sent as a youth to study in distant Bamberg, which may be where he first read Otto of Freising; and he had passed most of his life wandering back and forth from one end of Germany to the other end of Italy in the service of three emperors. Then, in the 1180s, he retired to the house his cousins had built for him back home. There he brought together what he had learned on his many important diplomatic and administrative missions with what he had read in Jerome and Bede into a vast *Speculum Regum*, or *Genealogy of All the Trojan, Roman, and German Kings and Emperors,* which was to be applauded and plundered by his successors all over Europe for the next two centuries.[4] TOLOMEO DEI FIADONI of Lucca (c. 1236–1327) had traveled all over France on the business of his religious order and had resided for some years as prior of Santa Maria Novella in Florence. He had met Thomas Aquinas, whose unfinished political treatise, *De Regimine Principum,* he completed. He had also met Dante Alighieri, whom he obliged by transforming the patriotism of the ancient Roman republicans from a sin into a virtue, St. Augustine's declaration on the question notwithstanding. Then, while working at Avignon during the pontificate of John XXII, he remembered the admonition of Solomon and Seneca about the effectiveness of historical discourse in the realm of ethics. Accordingly he put together what he himself had discovered in various French and Italian archives with what he had plundered from Riccardus of Cluny, Goffredo da Viterbo, and the most recent of the great papal-imperial chroniclers, Martinus Polonus, into a vast *Annales* of the known world from 1051 to 1303.[5] Similarly, LEONE DA ORVIETO plundered both Goffredo and Tolomeo as well as Martinus. He brought together the observations he himself had made at the papal court about the first decades of the fourteenth century. And he rearranged all this material, according to the standard scheme, by name, country of origin, and length of tenure (but not dates) of successive popes and emperors from Peter and Augustus to Clement V and Henry of Luxemburg.[6] These chronicles were intended to be wholly universal in scope, and they all used history in support of one or another solution to what was then considered to be the most pressing problem of all Christendom: whether the pope was superior to the emperor or vice versa. But all of them tended to view the world as a whole from the particular vantage point of the author's native city. Indeed, Tolomeo often seems more interested in supporting the cause of Lucca against the Florentines than that of Boniface VIII against Philip the Fair; and he found nothing incongruous in according as much space to a fire in a Lucchese monastery as to the abdication of Clementine V.

According to the Florentine and northern Italian model, the heirs of Geoffredo, Tolomeo, and Leone should have been able to build upon what they had inherited in proportion to the success of their fellow citizens in maintaining a self-sufficient political community. But just the opposite occurred. Between the thirteenth and the fifteenth centuries, Lucca managed to survive several attempts by more powerful neighbors to reduce it to the rank of a subject city, several attempts by domestic tyrants to transform it into a monarchy, and one attempt by a native warlord to elevate it to the rank of a dominant city; and in the sixteenth century it emerged as one of the last remaining oligarchical city-states in all Italy. But only one Lucchese ever thought this remarkable achievement worth recording—unless, perhaps, some forgotten manuscript escaped the piercing eyes of the eighteenth-century chronicle hunters only to be consumed by the fire in the communal library in 1822. Moreover, even he, a "simple man of little intellect" ("semplici e di pogo intellecto") named GIOVANNI SERCAMBI (1348–1426), who was awarded an important administrative post in return for his support of Paolo Guinigi's *signoria* in 1400, seems not to have heard of Tolomeo, although by then half the other chroniclers in Italy were using Tolomeo's book as a standard reference. Sercambi was therefore unaware that much of what he wrote about the period from 1164 to 1303 was erroneous even by contemporary standards. He never seems to have heard of Giovanni Villani either. He thus thought of chronicle not as a form of literature but as a harmless pastime for the unlearned ("per non stare ozioso")—one in which even the simplest rules of orthography, consistency, and appropriateness could be happily disregarded and one in which the chronological sequence of events could be interrupted with irrelevant documents and poetic asides. He also seems never to have heard of his senior colleague in Florence, Salutati. Hence, the three periods he imposed upon the history of Lucca are separated only by the insertion of an invocation ("facte le dicte invocazioni, tornerò a dire...."). The establishment of the Guinigi regime is seen not as a solution to long-standing problems but just as one more, though minutely described, event. Political theory is drawn not from an analysis of the vast amount of specific information about the political actions of the Lucchesi but from Dante's *Divine Comedy,* according to which all political authority belongs to such impotent anachronisms as Pope Boniface IX and Emperor Wenceslas. The practical political advice that is plastered onto, not induced from, the record of history is consequently contradictory. The Temporal Domain is the ruin of the Church and serves only to gratify the "pride and avarice" of the papal governors; but woe to those who, like the Eight Saints in Florence, forget that opposition to the Papal State ends inevitably in ruin. Lucca can beat off even the king of France if it will only provision its castles; but then in this "ill-disposed world, full of sin," where Italians quarrel, Turks "multiply" ("e multipricando il grande Turchio"), and kings are governed by vice ("co' vizi ciascuno si governa"), no one actually can do anything at all. Accordingly, the sole manuscript of the chronicle was locked up in the archives for consultation in jurisdictional quarrels; and no one really cared when it was returned by an unknown borrower in the 1520s with several of its pages missing.[7]

Orvieto, on the other hand, voluntarily renounced its independence in 1354 when, after two centuries of vainly trying to exact tribute from Acquapendente, make the rural nobility pay taxes, and keep the resident nobles from slaughtering each other and being slaughtered in turn by the *popolo,* the communal council unanimously bestowed the lordship of the city upon the ruthless and able founder of the Papal State, Cardinal Alburnoz. Yet it was that event, rather than, say, the victory of the Guelfs in 1346, that launched the chronicle tradition in the decades after Leone. To be sure, the anonymous author of the *Discorso Historico* (1342–68) had more to work with than did Sercambi: three more-or-less accurate lists of consuls and *podestà* from the beginning of the century and a rough addendum to Martinus Polonus.[8] Moreover, neither he nor his successors were completely pleased either with the council's decision of 1354 or with its subsequent decision, thirteen years later, to offer the lordship of the city to the pope himself. "The Orvietans," he admitted, "were not happy with being under the rule of the Patrimony." But they all recognized that the brief experiment with guild government in 1315 had broken down after seven years, that the tyranny of Manno Monasleschi in 1334 had quickly dissolved in quarreling among the victors, that the tearing to pieces of what three hours of torture with hot pokers had left of the body of the Ghibelline leader in Rome in 1346 had not brought peace to the Guelfs, that public order often could be maintained only with the help of Sienese or Perugian guards, and that the miracle of warm water in the wells in 1349 had done nothing to alleviate the disastrous effects of the plague of 1348.

Indeed, the chroniclers of Orvieto recognized that Alburnoz alone had kept them from being completely ruined by the mercenary companies in the 1360s. The second fragment of the *Cronica Urbevetana,* which had begun with a denunciation of Boniface VIII ("hic homo malaevitae et famae fuit") ended up with a staunch defense of the equally intractable Urban VI, mostly because Urban alone could keep the Beffati and the Marcorani from tearing the city to pieces. FRANCESCO DI MONTE-MARTE, whose brother had been one of Alburnoz's lieutenants, expanded the scope of what started as a family diary to include all of southern Umbria. And DOMENICO and his son LUCA MANENTI, whose packed record covers the first decade and a half of the fifteenth century, could find only one fault with papal government: during the dark years after the Council of Pisa it could rule only by trying to manipulate local factions, and for several years after the Council of Constance it was forced to surrender the city to Braccio da Montone. But papal authority had been sufficiently restored by 1450 to permit one obscure chronicler to concentrate exclusively on necrologies and executions. And it had been sufficiently consolidated by 1482 to enable the canon-notary TOMMASO DI SILVESTRO to fill hundreds of pages (almost five hundred in the new *RIS* edition) with fascinating minutiae concerning spectacles, feasts, epidemics, rain storms, cases of syphilis (of which he was one of the first local victims), and occasional brawls among the rural nobility—brawls which, thanks to the papal governors, no longer disturbed the tranquillity of the citizens.[9]

Similarly, Viterbo was too close to Rome to enjoy any more than a limited autonomy in internal affairs, particularly during the frequent periods in which the papal court was actually resident there; and most of its citizens were inclined to accept an increase in papal authority as the only alternative to the bloody feuds between the Gatti and the Cocchi that occasional relaxation of papal authority inevitably provoked. Yet when the wealthy merchant and active politician NICCOLA DELLA TUCCIA (1400–1473) began, in 1456, to expand his account book into a day-by-day record of what happened in the city, he did not have to rely solely on the official papers in the communal archive, all of which, nevertheless, he had read ("ho veduti coll'occhi miei propri").[10] Nor did he have to rely upon legend. Indeed, he maliciously ridiculed the traditional legends by making Japeth settle in London, by letting Japeth's Italian descendants destroy themselves in a prehistoric Gatti-Cocchi feud, and by then confining the whole story to a purely decorative preface. He could draw on Goffredo, whose prophesy he found borne out by subsequent events, that "all those who do harm to Viterbo are punished by God." He could draw on the thirteenth-century local chronicler LANZILOTTO (to 1255) and his continuers, on the thirteenth-century chroniclers MAESTRO GIROLAMO and COLA DI COVELLUZZO, and on a family diary kept by the descendants of Giovanni Giacomo Sacchi from 1297 until his own day and beyond. Above all, he could draw on the rough but substantial chronicle of his less well-educated but equally active contemporary, GIOVANNI DA IUZZO (d.c. 1479), a frequent ambassador of the commune to the papal court and "food czar" for Pope Nicholas V during the Holy Year of 1450. From Giovanni he may have learned what few of the traditional chronicles could ever have taught him: how to portray his dramatis personae as individuals rather than as stereotypes; and he certainly shared Giovanni's conviction that "whoever thinks of rebelling against the Holy Church," at least in Viterbo, "will certainly finish badly." But it was his own experience that made him recognize in the recent consolidation of orderly government, the increase in population, and the "studies of grammar, logic, and the other sciences" (about which he knew very little) what almost no other chronicler ever admitted: that things were getting better in the present and would probably get still better in the near future. Had he taken the time to inform himself of what some of those "other sciences" consisted of, he might have recognized in his own vol-uminous work several unconscious anticipations of the humanist chronicles that were then being written in Rome and Florence.

In some cases, the appearance of chronicles seems actually to have depended upon the successful incorporation of a city into a nascent territorial state. Urbino had never really been any more than a village before a dynasty of professional soldiers settled there to spend what they earned fighting wars for other cities in other parts of Italy. History in Urbino thus meant the *gesta* of the reigning dukes; and PIERANTONIO PALTRONI accordingly read Caesar and Decembrio in order to write not "la Ystoria" but "la vita narrare" of the "illustrissimo Federico duca d'Urbino." But not even Decembrian history in the form of biography was very successful. Notwithstanding a few well-described dramatic moments, like the meeting between Federico and Pandolfo Malatesta, Paltroni usually lapsed into vague generalizations ("fu guerra terribili et pernitiosa dove intervero molte et grande occisione de homini, multissime terre fonno saccomannate et destructe, abrusciate....") written according to equally vague rules of grammar and orthography; and his incomplete and lacunary manu-script was forgotten for another five centuries. Neither Federico da Montefeltro nor any of his successors thought worthy of publication the two humanist biographies written for him by temporary residents at his court, Porcelli dei Pandoni and Francesco Filelfo.[11] Federico did not bother to read the polished but derivative biography of his father, Guidantonio, written for him in 1473–74 by a prospective resident, Giovannantonio Campano.[12] And no one bothered to read the Boccacc-esque mixture of prose and verse, fact and fancy, composed by the great Raffaello's father, GIOVANNI SANTI, until long quotations from it translated into French were accepted, for some reason, as a *thèse* at the Faculté des Lettres of Bordeaux in 1971.[13]

Gubbio, on the other hand, had been a commune, one that traced its ancestors back to Japeth and a Roman consul. But what made it worth writing about for GUERRIERO DE LI BERNI (d. 1480/81),[14] who served as a notary for the professional general Piccinino and as a diplomatic agent for Duke Federico before settling down as a local notable in his home town in the 1460s, was not "its liberty," which had been "totally lost" and "ruined" in 1350, but its incorporation into the duchy of Urbino. For it was incorporation, or more exactly, the election of the Montefeltro as permanent lords of the city, that finally rescued it from the "grande divisioni tra cetadini" that had been characteristic of the whole period of its independence. "We must thank God," reflected Guerriero, "that we at present . . . have such a just and excellent prince, who with such fear of God most justly governs the whole state [*Tucto el so stato*]." Little did it matter that Gubbio had had no history in the traditional sense of foreign and civil wars since the election of Antonio da Montefel-tro as *signore* in 1384. It still had plenty of storms, frosts, parades, and epidemics; and what happened there could easily be rounded out with the news that arrived almost daily from Rome, Florence, Urbino, and Milan.

Similarly, during their years of independence, the cities of the Marche and Um-bria had never produced much more than such brief and lacunary annotations as the two-page *Annales* of Rieti (1054–1377)[15] and the bare list of *podestà* padded with snippets from Martinus Polonus put together by the notary BONAVENTURA of Foligno (fl. 1293–1346).[16] But once the cities had accepted the overall jurisdiction of the papal government, chronicles began to flourish. For ODDO of Ancona, who was sent to Viterbo to greet Pope Urban V on his return to Italy from Avignon, history began with Cardinal Alburnoz, who for the first time had made possible the con-ditions of internal peace and tranquillity upon which the livelihood of the merchants of Ancona depended; and the preservation of liberty meant throwing the Visconti out of the fortress in the popular insurrection of 1383 in the name of legitimate papal authority.[17] In other words, chroniclers and publicists elsewhere in Italy often de-nounced the Temporal Domain as the root of all evil in both church and state. But most of its subjects found it infinitely preferable to rule by such wandering warlords as Braccio da Montone and Francesco Sforza or such homegrown tyrants as the Malatesta of Rimini and the Trinci of Foligno. Such, in any case, was the thesis of PIETRUCCIO DI GIACOMO DEGLI UNTI, a merchant at Ancona who became prior of his native Foligno in 1438 and who recorded what he heard of the events of the day on the opposite pages of his family account book from 1424 to 1440.[18] Such was also the thesis of the notary and chancellor ANTONIO DI NICCOLÒ, the author of a chronicle of Fermo since 1176 that is mostly concerned with the forty years of the author's own lifetime, from 1407 to 1447.[19] The antipapal rebellion of 1396 was provoked, said Antonio, by "enemies of mankind" and "sowers of scandals." The only fault of papal government in the fifteenth century lay in its governing, not directly, but through local potentates barely disguised as vicars—vicars like Bernardo Varani, who demanded for himself the revenue of local taxes, and Pippino Malatesta, a "pessimus homo" who "multa enormia commiserat" during his previous vicariate at Ascoli. The great moment in the city's history finally came on November 23, 1445, when the people of Fermo, "inspiratione divina motus," threw the representatives of Sforza out of town and "gave themselves to the Church, with cries of 'Viva Sancta Chiesa et la libertà!'"

Such, finally, was at least the implied thesis of LAZARO DE'BERNABEI (c. 1430–after 1497), the last and the most conscientious of the Marche chroniclers of the fifteenth century.[20] Lazaro was interested less in writing than in collecting and preserving what had already been written. He therefore overlooked the rhetorical and methodological implications of the sources he copied out: Strabo, Boncompagno, Ciriaco d'Ancona, Bruni's *Bellum Gothicum;*[21] and consequently Ancona received not a humanist history, for which it was still culturally unprepared anyway, but another series of chronicles interspersed with inscriptions and documents that the author had diligently dug out of the ground and the archives. Nevertheless, the succession of illustrious visitors and natural and man-made calamities that he witnessed in his own day all supported his pondered conviction: that only the temporal dominion of the popes was capable of protecting Ancona from "the immoderate desire for power [which] leads man"—and particularly such enemies of liberty as the Malatesta, the Visconti, the Sforza, and the Angevins—"into many evils."

The political-constitutional arrangement that turned out to be the most favorable to chronicle writing was one in which the central government tacitly recognized the de facto independence of the city in external as well as internal affairs while always standing ready to intervene whenever the citizens appealed to it. Such was the arrangement that existed in Perugia, one which a modern historian has called a "diarchy." The Baglioni family enjoyed a position of preeminence. But since they owed most of their authority to papal grants of land and military commands elsewhere in Umbria, they generally let the elected magistrates or—before 1484 and after 1500—the *Dieci dell'Arbitrio* collaborate with the papal governor ("Mons. nostro governatore," the chronicles called him) to keep the peace at home while they went off hunting or warring abroad.[22]

Before this arrangement had become fully effective, several abortive attempts had been made to initiate a chronicle tradition. A certain Bonifazio of Verona had composed a verse *De rebus a Perusinis Gestis* in the thirteenth century. Someone had drawn up a sparse list of dates and events since 1194 in the mid-fourteenth century. And the city council in 1366 had ordered—in vain—the keeping of records of its transactions.[23] But not until the middle of the fifteenth century—not until the restoration of the Papal State had permitted the harsh municipal laws against communication between individual citizens and popes or cardinals to be quietly forgotten—did a certain ANTONIO DEI GUARNEGLIE set out to collect all that could be remembered about the years since 1309. Antonio, whoever he was, did not write in response to an official commission, although several copies of his work were made upon his death in 1450. Neither did his continuer from 1450–1491, PIETRO ANGELO DI GIOVAGNIE (or GIOVANNI):[24] although he occasionally got hold of an official letter from abroad, he seldom could find out what the ambassadors whose arrival he meticulously reported said orally in the council. But while the "diarchy" provided enough internal security to enable the chroniclers to write, it broke down just often enough—when the Baglioni quarreled among themselves or when the other great families united long enough to challenge their preeminence—to assure them plenty to write about: the periodic elections of magistrates, the arrival of briefs from and the dispatch of embassies to Rome, student riots and university petitions, lavish receptions at the Baglioni palace, the execution of nine Perugian citizens caught in the Pazzi Conspiracy at Florence, the arrival and departure of an eloquent Augustinian preacher.... Indeed, Pietro Angelo soon surpassed Antonio's record average of twenty pages a year, and by 1455 he was writing an average of eight pages (in a modern edition) a month. Pietro Angelo's example was followed by his successor, the equally naive and loquacious chronicler FRANCESCO MATARAZZO, who has incorrectly been confused with Perugia's first native humanist.[25] None of the Perugian chroniclers ever had the slightest contact with any of the humanists who occasionally passed through the university. But all of them had an admirable gift for storytelling, and together they provided Perugia with a more detailed account of the daily life of the city than can be found almost anywhere else in Italy during the first century of the Renaissance.

On the other hand, dissatisfaction with the consequences of absorption into a territorial state could stifle an emerging chronicle tradition, particularly when the subject cities were frankly governed for the sole benfit of the dominant city—which was usually the case in Tuscany. Volterra in the fifteenth century was the heir to two rather substantial chronicles: one by a certain PARIS DA CEREA, and another by a certain PIER ZAGATA, who extended what he borrowed from Paris back to A.D. 568 and forward to 1375, whence it was continued by an anonymous imitator until 1454. But neither Zagata's continuer nor the author of the *Chronichetta volterrana* succeeded in explaining why Florentine dominion, which seemed to them to be the only way of maintaining the privileged position of the oligarchical class in their native city, proved to be so incompatible with the principles of the "suave lega" to which both dominant and subject cities had freely agreed in 1361 and 1384.[26] The revolt of 1427–28 could not legitimately be blamed solely on "the Enemy of human nature," since it had obviously been provoked by the unilateral imposition of the Catasto.

Loyalty to Florence thereafter did not prevent the countryside from being repeatedly devastated by foreign armies with which the Volterrans had no quarrel; and loyalty to Cosimo de' Medici in particular did not prevent their economy from being ruined by decree of Cosimo's grandson. Hence, these chroniclers were even less successful than Antonio Ivani[27] in trying to whitewash the sack of 1472, since their own accounts made it appear to be the logical consequence of a long-standing policy of the Florentines toward their subjects. The only explanation that ultimately made sense was that of his successor, GIOVANNI PARELLI (d. 1568), from whom the sixteenth-century Florentine historian Benedetto Varchi borrowed much of his factual information about the seige and sack of 1530. Even though Volterra was "not the least of the cities of Italy for the excellence of its inhabitants," said Parelli, it was doomed by some inexorable fate to suffer an unending series of calamities, beginning with the invasion of the Vandals. Or at least Parelli's explanation made sense three centuries later to the Italian patriot Marco Tabarrini, who published the text as a corrective to Varchi's less than enthusiastic account of that favorite Risorgimento hero, Francesco Ferrucci.[28]

In Arezzo, on the other hand, an already established chronicle tradition—one that went as far back as a late-eleventh-century compilation of the cathedral canons—was abandoned as soon as Florentine domination turned out to be less beneficial than the Aretines had hoped it would be. True, the author of the *Annales Maiores* had to admit, staunch Ghibelline though he was, that the treaty of submission of 1337 promised to end the internecine fighting that had plagued the city for over a century. He noted that "almost all the citizens" greeted the Florentine garrison troops as they marched into the city "cum fraschis et ramis ulivarum," as if it were Palm Sunday.[29] But the consequences of Arezzo's dependent status became all too apparent six years later, when the Florentine governor joined with the Aretine Guelfs to round up twenty Ghibelline leaders, tear down their houses, and hang them without trial before the city hall. And except for a three-page *Memoria* on the purchase of Arezzo in 1384 by the magistrate BENVENUTO DE'NOBILI, neither the author of the *Annales Maiores* nor the monk who wrote the barer and more objective *Annales Minores* found any successors after the abortive rebellion that followed in 1343. The sudden revival of chronicle writing in Arezzo during the rebellion of 1502 finally demonstrated the failure of Florentine policy to turn a series of subject cities into a territorial state. For both FRANCESCO PEZZATI, who, as a canon, was probably a bystander, and a certain BASTIANO, who was an active participant, those who were "friends of the Florentines" were automatically "enemies of their country." During the preceding century Florentine government had meant only higher and higher taxes for purposes in which the Aretines had no interest whatever. And its true nature was revealed once again in 1503, when the Florentine captains tore up the capitulation agreement the moment the French expeditionary force, which had ended the rebellion for them, disappeared over the Apennines.

The consequences of submission to Florentine government were still graver in Pisa, partially because there it had been imposed by force, rather than by an initial contract. Chronicle writing in Pisa had been born of reflection on the first great triumphs of the commune at the beginning of the twelfth century: Pisan participation in the first Crusade, the expulsion of the Saracens from the Balearic Islands, the elevation of the bishop of Pisa as metropolitan of Corsica, and the building of the cathedral.[30] It had been carried on thereafter by members of the cathedral clergy—like the landowner and magistrate turned canon regular GUIDONE DE CORVARA[31]—who had access to Isidore and Paulus Diaconus as well as to Lucan and Vergil. Indeed, the fullest account of the Balearic campaign, the *Liber Maiolichinus,*[32] was written in verse as an imitation of the *Aeneid.* It was also carried on by less literate, less organized, but equally prolific and open-minded layman-magistrates, like BERNARDO MARAGONE (1108/10–1190),[33] who, in the 1180s, looked forward to even greater triumphs through Pisa's alliance with Frederick Barbarossa. Most of these early chronicles were continued and imitated through the thirteenth century, as more architectural monuments were erected (the "Pons Spinae" of 1262) and as the fleet returned to celebrate one victory after the other ("et sic cum magno triumpho Pisani ad propria redierunt"—*Chronicon Breve,* 1101–1268).[34] The disaster at Meloria (1284), which permanently transferred maritime supremacy on the Mediterranean from Pisa to Genoa, temporarily stunned the chroniclers into silence. But by the mid-fourteenth century they were so busy once again copying, amending, and adding to each other that Pietro Silva in the 1910s and Ottavio Banfi in the 1960s have had to follow the example of their colleagues in Venice and categorize them not by authors but by families: M, U, R, B, etc. Utility now became the chief criterion of good writing. The myths about Penelope, daughter of Tantalus, and St. Peter's nosebleed in the church of S. Pietro in Grado gradually gave way to a careful reconstruction of more recent history in strict chronological order, usually with help from the current non-Pisan guides to chronicle writing, Tolomeo, Malispini,[35] and Villani. Short entries grew into long narrative accounts of entire episodes—like the expulsion of the Duke of Athens. Florence gradually replaced Genoa as the chief enemy abroad. And the events of Pisa came to be seen in the broader context of all northern Italy.[36]

Unfortunately, the chroniclers generally failed to appreciate the increasing precariousness of Pisa's position in the power struggles of the age. To RANIERI SARDO (1320/24–99), the son of a wealthy merchant and landowner who was several times elected to the highest magistracy in the state, the feuds among the parties in the city and the devastations of the mercenary bands in the countryside seem to have been finally overcome by the elevation of Pietro Gambaccorta as *signore.* But when the Gambaccorta were driven out by the Appiani in 1392, he was forced to put his hope in those traditional but now powerless saviors, the pope and the emperor. And it never occurred to him that the recognition of Giangaleazzo Visconti as *signore* in

1399 ("Iddio ci dia gratia ci ghoverni bene!") could possibly end in the incorporation of Pisa into a Milanese empire.[37] His successors a few years later were at a loss to understand why the Florentines had such a "great desire to force the Pisans into subjection."[38] The only explanation they could give for the Pisans' unsuccessful resistance in the siege of 1406–7 was that Giovanni Gambaccorta had sold them out. And not even Gino Capponi's conciliatory speech, which one of them copied out in almost the same form in which Neri Capponi transcribed it,[39] could reconcile them to their new status. The city had been "deprived of the liberty it had enjoyed for over 300 years"; and after a decade or so of "miserable slavery to the Florentine state," it had been "emptied of its citizens, its riches, its houses, and all its former happiness." For almost a century chronicle writing ceased altogether. When finally an anonymous chronicler took it up again—one who had learned enough about current forms of historiography to include a few speeches and to look up dates in Platina—the answer was still the same.[40] History meant exclusively the history of a city-state, and Giangaleazzo, much as he might have aspired to such an utterly impossible title as "king of Tuscany," could never have been anything but the lord, or perhaps "tyrant," of Pisa and Milan. Since nothing had been done in the meantime to turn conquered subjects into citizens of a larger state, the history of Pisa still ended abruptly with the capitulation of 1407.

When the loss of independence resulted in an unmitigated state of subservience, then, the chronicle died; and when, on the contrary, it was accompanied by a transference of loyalty to the dominating power, the chronicle flourished. But only the preservation of complete independence was apparently sufficient to enable the chronicle to evolve in the direction of humanist historiography. That is what happened in Florence. And that is what happened in the only other commune of central Italy whose independence was never compromised before the mid-sixteenth century, Siena. Chronicle writing in Siena began in the twelfth century with an order of the bishop for the keeping of an ecclesiastical calendar; and by the middle of the thirteenth century this calendar had developed into a running narrative account of the civic affairs of the city—one in which events of long-term significance, like the disastrous defeat of the Florentines at Montaperti, were clearly marked off from such inconsequential spectacles as the burning of the host by a lightning bolt during a mass in the cathedral.[41]

As the episcopal scribes lost interest in the project (only occasional years are recorded in the fifteenth century), more conscientious lay chroniclers took their place. ANDREA DEI (d.c. 1348) carefully collected every bit of information he could discover about the first two centuries of the commune; and by the time he reached his own lifetime he was averaging six of Muratori's columns a year. Like his successor, AGNOLO DA TURA, whose diary was mixed up with passages by Villani by a seventeenth-century compiler, he knew how to break the strictly *podestà*-by-*podestà* scheme in order to narrate a series of related events—such as the career of Castruccio

Castracani. Like Agnolo's successor, the equally prolific NERI DI DONATO (or DONATO DI NERI),[42] who got into the government after the revolution of 1355 and was thrown out during the revolution of 1368, Andrea was scrupulously impartial when elaborating upon the most persistent theme in Sienese history: the interminable struggles first between the Guelfs and the Ghibellines and then among the various *monti*, the political parties that represented both particular social groups and particular solutions to the never-resolved problems of the structure of government.

Unfortunately, some of the fourteenth- and early fifteenth-century Sienese chroniclers were as interested in creating legends as in establishing the truth. Just at a time when the Florentines were checking the stories of their foundation against the texts of the ancient historians, the Sienese were trying to outdo them by inventing biographies of the wandering sons of Remus, Aschio and Senio. Some of them also became so interested in story-telling that the love affair of a certain Anselmo Salimbeni and an Angela Montanini in 1393 took up much more space than all the campaigns of Giangaleazzo. Moreover, some of them were so embittered by what they described as the Florentine policy of setting up tyrants in the cities of Tuscany and so incensed over what they denounced as Florentine atrocities that they ignored completely the reasons behind the occasional revolts of their own subject towns; and they treated the election of Giangaleazzo as lord of Siena in 1400 as nothing but an alliance for the preservation of liberty in Tuscany.[43] For PAOLO DI TOMMASO MONTAURI,[44] the death of Giangaleazzo in 1402 was no more important than the Council of Siena in 1423, and neither was as important as the verses written for each of the five citizens caught collaborating with the Florentines in 1391.

Indeed, these defects became more apparent in the mid-fifteenth century chronicle of TOMMASO FECINI. Fecini was so absorbed in his series of executions and snow storms that even so momentous an event as the election of Siena's own Pope Pius II is noted merely as one more "venne nuova come" ("news arrived that"). But the defects gradually vanish in the diary (1479–83) of CRISTOFORO CANTORI, who included not only the usual lists of magistrates and ambassadors (and even a complete list of all the members of the various *monti*) but an occasional speech and several state documents as well as long gerundic clauses suggesting causes for the events recounted. The defects were amply compensated for by the political reflections that ALLEGRETTO ALLEGRETTI managed to extract from his immense quantity of tiny details about the life of the city during the half-century after the canonization of that other Sienese hero, St. Bernardino, in 1450.[45] It may have been true that the feet of the Florentines executed for burying a crucifix actually curled up on the gallows and that Pope Paul II strangled an evil spirit that escaped from his ring. But what really mattered was the exile of all the opponents of each succeeding regime, which just made a final resolution of the constitutional problem that much more difficult, and the election of Pius II, who bestowed upon the city not only an arm of John the Baptist and the head of St. Andrew, but also a rain of jobs and gifts.

If it seems to have been an important condition for the development of the chronicle as a literary form, political independence, together with a cultural environment receptive to humanism, was an indispensable condition for the appearance of humanist historiography. The one exception proves the rule: Città di Castello. Ever since its seizure by Piccinino in 1442, this not very significant town in Umbria had enjoyed a status similar to Perugia's: the Vitelli family, whose head was usually off fighting as a mercenary general, enjoyed a de facto, but far from complete, supremacy, while the resident papal governor wore himself out trying to keep the other families from fighting among themselves or trying to throw out the Vitelli. It so happened that one of the papal representatives came to admire Niccolò Vitelli more than he respected his employers in Rome. He thus concluded that the rebellion and seige of 1474 were more than just one more in the customary series of violent tumults. They were, he decided, the first clear sign of the new policy adopted by Pope Sixtus IV, a policy that was soon to provoke the War of the Pazzi Conspiracy. He therefore composed, according to standard humanist form, a prefatory geographical and genealogical survey of the city. He invented an antebellum paradise of peace and tranquillity. He fixed the entire blame for trying to destroy this paradise on one villain, the pope, and he gave full credit for trying (in vain, alas!) to save it to one hero, Niccolò—who acted, to be sure, with the external support of such other good men as Roberto Malatesta, the generic enemy of all the popes, and Lorenzo de' Medici, the particular enemy of Sixtus IV. But this model of a humanist commentary cannot be credited to Città di Castello. Its author, ROBERTO ORSI, belonged to the same class of wandering professional jurist-notaries who had written most of the chronicles and many of the histories of northern Italy. He had been born in Rimini, where his father was a chancellor, and educated under Guarino in Ferrara; and he had gotten to know half the humanists of Italy during his travels as a judge and legal consultant from Rome to Florence, from Bologna and Todi to Cremona. Moreover, he dedicated his work not to the citizens of Città di Castello, who probably never heard of it, but to his native prince, who finally rewarded him with a job back home.[46]

Outside of Florence, only in Siena did citizens become humanists; and only in Siena did humanist citizens apply humanist criteria to the history of their city. The first was really a prehumanist, GIOVANNI BANDINI (d. 1422), ambassador of the republic, rector of the university (at just the time when Enea Silvio Piccolomini was acquiring the foundation of his humanist education there), and, in the last years of his life, "consistorial advocate" at the Roman Curia. Being a contemporary not of Bruni but of Salutati, Bandini seems to have learned how to write history from his own reading of the ancient historians and from the contacts he may have made with the Mussato tradition during his student days at Padua. For the *Suorum Temporum Historia* contains numerous errors that could easily have been corrected (Giangaleazzo, it says, was killed by Florentine poisoners); and it omits as empty of anything "memoratu dignum" all those years that the author himself could not remember. Nevertheless, the chronological scope is carefully defined according to a real period of Sienese history: the restoration of "liberty" in 1403. It provides a more acceptable explanation than those of the chroniclers for the election of Giangaleazzo: it took place, Bandini insists, "honestis conditionibus," solely as a temporary defense against the threat of Florentine aggression, and it was rescinded as soon as Giangaleazzo's successors started acting like "tyrants." Better yet, it draws attention to what Bandini discerned as the greatest danger to freedom and independence: factional fighting; and it suggests a connection between the abandonment of the plans to enlarge the cathedral and the fall in the population since 1348. Bandini's work was continued in the same fragmentary manner by his son FRANCESCO TOM-MASO through the years of the Council of Siena. And it was later supplemented with a more polished, if still incomplete, description of the policy debates that took place during the war between Florence and Lucca.[47]

The second citizen-historian was more successful than the first, largely because he could make use of what by then had become fully developed models of historical writing. AGOSTINO DATI (1420–79) had mastered the most humanist of skills, Greek, while studying law at the university. He had taught that most humanist of disciplines, rhetoric, after turning down an attractive offer from the first humanist pope, Nicholas V. He became a good friend of his fellow citizen Pius II while serving as Sienese ambassador at the papal court, and he opened a salon in his own house for those of his fellow citizens at home who were interested in the new learning. He then sought to turn them into a cross between Christians of the Apostolic Age and Romans of the Republic with a number of moral-philosophic treatises *(De Immoralitate Animorum, De Septem Virtutibus),* several orations *(De Amicitia, Ad Discipulos),* and a series of eulogies (on Bernardino, on Catherine of Siena, *De Laudibus Senensis).* When the learned Sienese cardinal Francesco Piccolomini (who had practiced writing history himself) asked him to write a history as well, Dati quickly agreed. For he was already convinced that modern times were as glorious as ancient times: "what wars, what armies, what assemblies of princes, what great events...are there...that can be compared [to those of] our age?" He reviewed the political conditions of all Italy on the morrow of the death of Filippo Maria Visconti in 1447. He identified the two main heroes who had done the most to make possible the survival of Siena during the ensuing confusion, Alfonso d'Aragona and Francesco Sforza. He showed what the Sienese government had done within the context of these general conditions in pursuit of its major political ends: peace with its neighbors and a republican regime at home ("nam...tot iam saeculis dominum neminem Sena cognovit"). Finally, he suggested that the ends could continue to be achieved in the future as they had often been achieved in the past: by relying on the protection of the Virgin in heaven, on an alliance with the Papacy on earth, and on the "vigilance of the best citizens" ("civium optimorum vigilantia"). When, then, in the 1470s, he was asked to write a history of Piombino, the small though "sane non incelebre" domain of the Appiani family opposite Elba, he had no difficulty applying the same formula. A brief geographical survey introduced the historical background from the period of Pisan administration to the establishment of the Appiani. And the effectiveness of a Sienese protectorate in enabling Jacopo III (d. 1473) to keep what his ancestors had won was carefully documented for the guidance of his better educated and potentially even more glorious successor, Jacopo IV.[48]

What Bandini had done for one decade, SIGISMONDO TIZIO (1458–1528) tried to do for two centuries. Tizio was a Sienese only by adoption. He had been born in Castiglion Fiorentino and educated at Perugia before being caught up, first as a student and then as a resident priest, in the two revolutions of 1482 and 1487. He was an observer rather than an actor; but he was openly partial to the Petrucci family, which eventually took advantage of the succeeding political chaos to establish the kind of one-family rule that all the *monti* and all the chroniclers were pledged to prevent at all costs. He was also a scholar—one who at last threw out the legends that scholarship no longer accepted and who concocted as many more based on fantastic Hebrew and Greek etymologies that scholarship in the age of Annio da Viterbo still tolerated. He looked up the broader context of Sienese affairs in the works of Pius II and Bruni, whom he called "historiae pater." And he checked whatever he took from the chroniclers, particularly from his favorite, Allegretti, with the "priscis codicibus" and the modern state documents that he poured over after the communal archive was opened to him in 1485. Unfortunately, he adopted one criterion of humanist historiography—usefulness in the conduct of government—at the expense of another—selectivity. As a consequence, his six volumes contain references to every minute detail that any judge or magistrate might ever wish to cite as a precedent. But even though it was twice edited by scholars in the seventeenth century, what might now be admired as the greatest monument of early Sienese humanist historiography can be read only in the copies preserved in the manuscript collections of the Biblioteca Nazionale of Florence, the Biblioteca Comunale of Siena, and the Bibliotheca Apostolica Vaticana (which is where Riccardo Fubini read it).[49]

6

FROM TERRITORIAL STATES TO NATIONAL MONARCHY NAPLES AND SICILY

The Medieval Heritage

POLITICAL DEVELOPMENT IN SOUTHERN ITALY TOOK PLACE IN A MANNER EXACTLY opposite the way it did in northern Italy. It began not with autonomous city-republics but with territorial principalities—with the successor states of the Lombard kingdom in the center, with the remaining outposts of the Byzantine Empire in the south, and with the Arab domain in Sicily. And it ended not with a network of subject cities under the control of several *signori* or dominant city-states but with a single, centralized monarchy superimposed on an unstable agglomeration of feudal baronies.

Hence, the kind of urban chronicle typical of prehumanist historiography in the North never emerged in the South. Only one southern city ever enjoyed a status similar to that of the maritime republics of Genoa and Pisa: Amalfi. But the only Amalfitan ever to write a chronicle lived almost a century after Amalfi had lost its predominant position on the Mediterranean and had been absorbed into the Kingdom of Naples. His hero was not the city council or the city, but the Norman prince of the territorial state of Capua. He attributed the lasting glory of the city not to the feats of its citizens but to the patrician blood of a group of noble Romans who, regretful of having followed Constantine to the east, finally settled there, after various adventures on the coast of "Schiavonia." Similarly, only one city, Aquila, ever enjoyed a semiautonomous status in the kingdom comparable to that of Perugia in the Papal State. But none of the chroniclers of Aquila—neither NICCOLÒ DI BORBONA (1363–1424), who wrote a prose continuation of the didactic verse chronicle of Buccio (or Boezio) Ranallo (1252–1362), nor Niccolò's successor, FRANCESCO D'ANGELUCCIO (to 1485)—was aware of any connection between the two major themes of their narratives: the castle-dismantling expeditions and party feuds of their fellow townsmen on one hand and, on the other, the comings and goings of the Angevin and Aragonese princes, whose occasional visits to the city are faithfully recorded but never explained. Indeed, what really mattered was not the ordinary but the extraordinary—for instance, the consecrated Host that remained untouched after the earthquake of 1461 had destroyed everything else in the church, including the tabernacle. What mattered to the chronicler's humanist successor, ANGELO DI SANTE

DEL ROSSO, or FONTICOLANO (FONTICULANUS—d. 1503), was to deflate Giovannantonio Campano's account of the battle of 2 June 1424, which was as flattering to
Campano's hero, Braccio, as it was dishonorable to Fonticolano's fellow citizens.
And after an exchange of letters in classical Latin between Braccio and Piccinino, the
commentary ends with a procession of the Aquilani to the *sacra templa* to thank the
Deus Optimus Maximus for what is presented as a wholly exceptional incident in an
otherwise eternal reign of domestic concord.[1]

Yet the absence of communal institutions turned out to be no greater impediment
to chronicle writing in the South than the loss of communal independence was in
Umbria and the Marche. What was accomplished by Paduan notaries in the thirteenth century and by Florentine merchants in the fourteenth was accomplished
between the tenth and the twelfth centuries by the *vestiari,* or custodians, of the
monasteries of the Benedictine order—an institution that managed to preserve the
remnants of ancient culture in the South long after they had disappeared in the
North.[2] The main task of these custodians was to keep track of religious feasts in the
form of what were called *cicli decennovenali,* or "Easter tables," on which the names
of the currently reigning pope and emperor were usually noted in the margins. Some
of the custodians were conscious of the cultural heritage preserved in their libraries
only to the extent of bewailing the present and future as an irremediable corruption
of a rather ill-defined golden age in the past. They stretched the limits of their rough
style in order to glorify their monasteries and their monasteries' benefactors—
benefactors like Charlemagne, whom the monk of Sant' Andrea del Soratte (near
Ponzano, north of Rome) was the first to credit with a pilgrimage to the Holy
Land.[3] Some of them, on the other hand, were specifically instructed by their
superiors to recast the bare records of their predecessors in a more literary form—as
was a nobleman named GREGORIO DI CATINO (d. after 1132), who entered the monastery of Farfa near Spoleto just after it had been reformed according to the prescriptions of the Cluniac movement.[4] But many of them took full advantage of the
availability of the great historical works of late antiquity and patterned the style and
form of what they wrote on the sources of their general information about the age of
their founders—Jerome-Eusebius, Paulus Diaconus, Isidore of Seville, Bede. They
thus acquired at least a rudimentary scheme of historical periodization: from the
foundation of their monasteries to the Lombard invasion, from the arrival of the
Franks to the first attacks by the Saracens.... And they achieved a fullness and
quality of exposition (the *Chronicon Salernitanum* is almost a hundred folio pages in
the *MGH* edition)[5] fully worthy of their consciously imitated models.

Finally, many of the Benedictine custodian-chroniclers realized that the tranquillity of their monastic life depended in large measure on the successful establishment
of a peaceful temporal order around them. What began as monastic history could
easily be adapted to diocesan history—as it was most notably by JOHANNES DIA-
CONUS, who traced the history of the church of Naples, bishop by bishop, from the

first century to the end of the ninth.[6] It could also approach in subject matter what later was to be called "civil" history. Both the earliest chronicle of Montecassino and the *De Gestis Principum Beneventanorum* of HEREMPERTIUS (to 888)[7] sought to explain the Lombard invasion by tracing the invaders back to their original homeland in Scandinavia and to explain the extent of the Saracen raids by reference to the quarrels among the Lombard princes. LUPUS PROTOSPATA of Bari (or Matera) (860–1102)—notwithstanding the numerous Hellenisms in his Latin prose—supported the Normans in their efforts to throw the Byzantines out of Puglia.[8] The *Annales* of the monastery of Santa Sofia, in both of the two extant versions, gave far more space to Duke Romoaldo, who founded the monastery in 788, and to Duke Arichi II, who endowed it, than to the monastery itself.[9] And the short but packed chronicle of a monk of San Severino of Naples was devoted exclusively to the dates and feats of the princes of the four main states of the surrounding area.[10]

Thus chronicle writing in the South grew both in quality and in quantity notwithstanding a political and institutional structure very different from that of the northern Italian communes. True, it might not have grown fast enough to suit certain patriotic scholars of the early eighteenth century, who tried to outdo Muratori by forging a few more texts. But at least it grew fast enough to tax the patience of five centuries of energetic editors, who have still not managed to publish all the surviving manuscripts, and it certainly grew faster than the suspicious compilers of the *Monumenta Germaniae Historiae* were willing to admit in the mid-nineteenth century, when they cast Cartesian eyes on even the most credible texts.[11] Indeed, chronicle writing soon received an impulse still greater than the one originally provided by the liturgical and temporal needs of the Benedictine monasteries. After 1130 it was also inspired by the success of the Normans in uniting the whole of the South under a single government, in making possible the first steps toward the re-Latinization of previously Greek and Arab areas, and in finally guaranteeing what the Lombard princes had long promised in vain: an end to the Saracen raids.

To be sure, not all the chroniclers gave unqualified support to the Norman conquerors. One of the greatest of them, FALCO BENEVENTANO (1102–40), the one called by his sixteenth-century editor the "prince of medieval historiographers," had been a scribe of the Sacred Palace in Rome before Innocent II made him a judge in his native city. Much of his thick (up to eleven Muratorian columns a year by 1113) record of what he observed and heard about in his own day was devoted to the efforts of his temporal lord in keeping the Normans out of Benevento, which the Papacy had inherited after the death of the last duke in 1077, and in keeping the successors of Emperor Henry IV out of Italy. Even the great spectacle of 1137, when the moon momentarily turned red with blood, was interpreted as a sign of imminent divine wrath upon those kings "who ought to defend and aid the Roman See . . . and who [instead] have spread a new heresy throughout the whole world.[12]

Moreover, the strictly monastic chronicle tradition soon began to disintegrate.

The author of the last of the great chronicles of Montecassino made no effort to figure out a connection between the occasional visits of the most revered "Dominus noster rex" on one had, and, on the other, Pope Alexander's trip to Venice in 1177 and Guglielmo I's destruction of Bari in 1156, which he simply recorded without comment for the corresponding years. His two successors, one in the early twelfth century and the other in the mid-fourteenth, were primarily interested in prodigies: more bloodred moons, stars that rattled in the sky at high noon, earthquakes more destructive than that at the time of the Crucifixion, and famine-struck men who ate the leaves off all the trees in the surrounding mountains.[13] Similarly, the authors of the chronicle of Subiaco lost interest in their task once the inspiration of the learned abbot Giovanni VII began to wane; and their text became so "disorderly, uncertain, and stuffed with spurious names," according to the modern editor, that Guglielmo Capisacchi (1507–79) declined to use it even as a guide to the documents he had collected when he introduced late Renaissance scholarship into the monastery after 1550.[14] Even the most ambitious of the monastic chronicles of the Norman-Swabian period, the *Chronicon Vulturnense* (after 1118), which tried to line up the lives of the first eighteen abbots with the corresponding entries of the *Liber Pontificalis,* was misguided from the start by the unhistorical advice of St. James the Apostle—that men look only to God for wisdom.[15] It dedicated so much space to explaining the absence of the sun and the moon during the first three days of the Creation that it never got around to explaining the relevance of the many false charters and privileges it claimed to have copied from the originals. By the mid-thirteenth century, the tradition had all but vanished. One *Annales Siculi* could fill in only a half-dozen years between 1032 and 1220, and the continuation from 1253 to 1260 adds only one or two observations on Manfredi and Carlo d'Angiò.[16]

Other monasteries were still less fortunate. HUGO of Venosia (d.c. 1144) learned how to write what was for the time excellent Latin by studying—and plagiarizing— the prose of Gregory the Great, and he wrote biographies of his predecessors for the almost humanist purpose of inspiring his subjects in the abbey of Santa Trinità of Cava near Sorrento to follow him in instituting the Cluniac reform. But even Hugo was less interested in the possibly exemplary characters of his heroes than in their inimitable stage tricks—like that of one abbot Leone, who kept a dragon at bay in front of his cave by reciting prayers at it until an arrow finally flew out of a cloud and into the dragon's heart.[17] His sole successor a century later reverted to the bare form of the liturgical catalogues, even though he copied his lists of popes, emperors, abbots, kings, and rains of sand and ashes right onto the blank pages of his copy of Bede.[18] Similarly, the Benedictine who tried to put the history of the monastery of Ceccano, or Fossanova, near Terracina in the context of the history of the Papacy and the Empire apparently failed to understand the potentialities of the literary form he had borrowed from his brothers of Montecassino. For the miscellaneous *gesta* of various Norman princes in various parts of the kingdom are interspersed with poems, papal bulls, and other documents that have nothing at all to do with them.[19] Another monk who tried to make the neighboring village of Atena in Basilicata the center of worldwide attention under the successors of Constantine got no further than the romantic adventures of a son of the emperor Arcadius, who had been appointed governor there; and his successor found nothing worthy of recording but a single earthquake between 1202, when Innocent III excommunicated an emperor, and 1356, when three suns appeared in the sky at the same time.[20]

On the other hand, for that current in the monastic chronicle tradition that had already flowed beyond the boundary between ecclesiastical and civil history, the Norman conquest afforded an opportunity for further development. First of all, it extended the geographical-political scope of history from boundaries of the old regional Lombard states to those of the newly unified kingdom. The first of the twelfth-century chroniclers of Puglia limited his account to one great event, the capture of Motula in 1101, which he found worthy of a paraphrase of Vergil's lament over the destruction of Troy. The second, the Benedictine author of the *Chronicon de Rebus in Barensi Provincia Gestis,* began with a bow to tradition in a prefatory reference to the death of Gregory the Great. But he then jumped to what interested him most: the establishment of Norman power in Puglia.[21] He praised his main hero, Bishop Bisantius of Bari, not for asserting the autonomy of his native city but for favoring its incorporation into the new Norman kingdom of Naples—and for thus saving it from the polyglot hords of Russians, Bulgarians, Wallachians, and Turks sent against it by its former master, the emperor of Constantinople. The next major Pugliese chronicler, MATTHEO DI GIOVENAZZO,[22] was just as conscious as his predecessor of the inadequacy of the acts and scandals of his fellow citizens alone as a proper subject of his almost daily annotations. He therefore began his diary with a note about Frederick II's return from Lombardy. He then inserted every scrap of information he could obtain either from passing visitors or from his own occasional trips to the capital about what he assumed to be the sole source of significant novelties, the royal court. And it was not his fault that he did not always have a chance to check on what was reported to him—about the locusts that ate every blade of grass in Calabria and about the cooked pears that killed the emperor-king in 1250.

Thus monastic chroniclers, who, even before the coming of the Normans, had chosen the regional state rather than the universe since Noah or the Papacy since Peter as their locus, had no difficulty accommodating themselves to the absorption of the regional states into the new national state. By the mid-fourteenth century the process was complete. Abbot STEFANO of Santa Maria dell'Alto realized that the Benedictines were in Nardò largely through the grace of the Norman Count Gof-fredo, who had thrown out the Greek-speaking Basilians to make room for them. He also realized that the kings of Naples rather than the barons of the Salentino had been the Benedictines' chief benefactors ever since. And he was mainly interested, in the 1360s, not so much in exalting the holy men of his house or the pious citizens who built the churches of the city as in denigrating the Hohenstaufen and their Saracen soldiers, who "rubbaro et assassenaro omne cosa," and in exalting the Angevins, who "removed all the hardships and taxes imposed by the said emperor," Frederick II.[23] Similarly, the notary DOMENICO DE GRAVINA began his detailed description of the troubles of Puglia in the 1350s, from which he himself suffered the loss of all his property and a long exile from his native city, with an account of their ultimate causes: the unfortunate marriage alliances contracted by the otherwise "excellentissimus" King Roberto d'Angiò and the accession of Roberto's lascivious, irresponsible minor daughter, Giovanna I, whose assassination of her husband he described in all its gory detail. "O quam miserum regnum istud! quod ad regimen mulierum et infantium est deductum!" His "Chronicle of Puglia"[24] thus turned out to be in fact a chronicle of the kings of Naples. It concentrates on Puglia simply because the chief wars of succession took place there; and it concentrates on the author's native city under the general rubric of its capture by one of the claimants to the throne.

The Norman conquest also brought the historiographical tradition born at Montecassino into contact with two hitherto foreign cultures: that of Sicily, to which the Normans gained full title in 1139, and that of northern France, from which they brought many of their principal collaborators. To be sure, these contacts were not always fruitful, largely because the chronicle-writing Christian subjects of the new kingdom turned out to be far less open-minded than their immigrant princes. For instance, none of them seems ever to have noticed the considerable information about pre-Norman Sicily contained in the Islamic universal chronology of Ismael Alcmujadad, and no one before Muratori ever seems to have noticed the short Sicilian Arabic chronicle of the years between 827 and 963.[25] Stranger still, no one ever paid any attention to the minute geographical-historical description of the whole island compiled by Ibn Idrîs (Edrisi) between 1139 and 1154 with the active collaboration of none other than King Ruggero I himself,[26] or to a similar topographical survey compiled in 1182–83 by a pilgrim returning from Mecca to Andalusia, Ibn Grovair, or Giubayr (1145–1217), with the help of King Guglielmo II. Even a century later, when Christian philosophers and theologians were busily appropriating the Arabic translations of the commentaries on the works of Aristotle, the Christian historians remained closed in a Latin-Christian ethnocentrism similar to that which was to blind the Venetians to the potentialities of Byzantine and Turkish historiography two centuries later; and their accounts of their own times are correspondingly the poorer for their ignorance of what their Arabic-speaking contemporaries, like Ibn el-Athîr and Ibn Sab'în, were saying about the partially Arabic-speaking court of their own monarch, Emperor Frederick II.[27]

But a common Christian faith did make possible a fruitful exchange between the grateful subjects of the new monarchy and the former compatriots of its foreign creators. The first history of the Norman conquest was written by a Montecassino

Benedictine, AMATO DI SALERNO, bishop of Nusio, between 1078 and 1080; and in an Old French translation of the since-lost Latin original, it soon procured for Robert Guiscard and Riccardo of Capua a place of honor in the hero galleries of feudal society all over Europe.[28] The second history of the conquest was written by a Norman Benedictine, GOFFREDO MALATERRA, on commission from Count Ruggero;[29] and it so skillfully blended the best of post-Carolingian Latinity with the results of the author's diligent observations of what went on at court and in the provinces of his adopted country that it was to remain a model for historical writing in Sicily for the next two centuries. Indeed, when Fra SIMONE (or SIMUNI) DA LENTINI decided to remind his fellow Sicilians in the mid-fourteenth century of the great deeds of those who had liberated their island from the infidels, he simply cut out what Malaterra had said about affairs on the mainland and translated the rest into Sicilian Italian—for the benefit of those who could not easily read Latin ("Mali si potia intendire").[30] He altered the sense of the original only to the point of adding a few zeroes to the size of enemy armies (as when thirty Norman knights routed an army of thirty thousand horsemen and "innumerable" footmen) and of accentuating the distinction between glory-hungry Norman generals and profit-hungry Genoese merchants ("plui atenti . . . a lo guadagno chi a li armi"), whose offer of assistance during the siege of Palermo in 1071 was rather disdainfully turned down. Malaterra occasionally had doubts about the appropriateness of prose *(plumbea fistula)* to so exalted a subject, and he did his best to embellish it with stretched-out metaphors and verse interludes *(aurea fistula)*. But thanks possibly to his reading of the one other historian he mentions, Sallust, he succeeded in showing the conquest to be the result of a long historical process that began with the landing of the Normans in France; and he followed the process to its logical culmination in the bestowal of legantine powers on the Norman conquerers by the papal bull of 1099, which is quoted in full on the last page.

Not only, then, did the Normans fully satisfy the longing of southern Italians for internal peace and protection against foreign foes, they also provided them with new and, in some aspects, more advanced models of historical writing. And three centuries before the patricians of Florence and the lords of Milan came to realize the political value of history, they encouraged those willing to test the models with moral and material assistance. As a result, Neapolitans and Sicilians of their own age and of the Swabian age that followed produced several masterpieces of historiography, masterpieces which, in literary quality as well as in thoroughness and accuracy, were to remain unsurpassed until the advent of humanism. All these historians about whom something more is known than their names were men of considerable prominence in the royal administration. UGO FALCANDO (fl. 1169–81)[31] was a close associate and dedicated supporter of King Guglielmo I, whom he served at the court of Palermo for fifteen years after 1154. ROMOALDO GUARNA (d. 1181)[32] served as ambassador for the same king and officiated at the coronation of his successor,

Guglielmo II; and after 1153 he accepted his responsibilities as archbishop of Salerno to the point of composing liturgical and hagiographic works for the guidance of his flock. RICCARDO DI SAN GERMANO (d. 1243/4)[33] was the notary and archivist of his monastery—which explains why his chronicle begins with a visit of Pope Innocent III there in 1208. But his brother was a notary for Emperor Frederick II, and Riccardo himself was closely associated with the court for some fifty years.

Moreover, all these historians were as aware as any of their humanist successors that history was a form of literature. They searched through the earlier monastic histories for relevant information, and they studied the monuments of late Roman historiography, as well as the remaining fragments of classical Roman historiography, for guidance in style and composition. Romoaldo may even have been inspired to write by his meeting with one of the chief protagonists of the "Renaissance of the Twelfth Century" in northern Europe, John of Salisbury. Thus, whether they wrote in a more strictly annalistic style, like the author of the anonymous *Historia Sicula* to 1252,[34] or whether, like Romoaldo, they wrote in the form of universal or papal-imperial chronicles in imitation of Jerome and Isidore, they were careful to organize their accounts in accordance with causal as well as chronological order. They generally put major policy statements in the form of direct-discourse speeches. They attributed what happened to the aims and the character of the principal agents. And they allotted space to single events in proportion to their relevance to the same central theme: the erection and maintenance of a viable political organization. Finally, all these historians wrote for the purpose of sustaining one or another variant of the thesis they all adhered to: that the Normans had ushered in a golden age and that the Hohenstaufen had revived it. Not that they were uncritical of their heroes: Riccardo admitted that the reign of Frederick II was marred by the violent confrontation between Empire and Papacy, and Ugo admitted that Guglielmo II's laziness was in part responsible for the occasional "atrocities" he himself had witnessed. But they all agreed that their rulers were exceptionally successful in realizing the main aim of politics: internal peace. They attributed this success not only to political sagacity and the usual roster of moral virtues but also to a recognition of the importance of the arts and sciences ("liberalium artium et omnis approbatae scientiae scholas in Regno ipso constituit"). And they further attributed the success of their kings to a willingness to recognize and reward talent without regard for race, religion, or national origins ("non tamen conditionem originis quam virtutes moresque considerabat")—as illustrated by the remarkable career of one of Frederick II's black slaves.

Unfortunately, this magnificent achievement failed to inspire emulators once the political framework that had made it possible began to crumble. SALA, or SABBA, MALESPINA tried hard to portray the Angevins as the legitimate heirs of the Hohenstaufen;[35] but he could do so only by denying what his nearest predecessor, NICOLA DE JAMSILLA, had consistently affirmed: that the popes had no right to interfere in the internal affairs of the kingdom.[36] And he apparently failed to convince his compatriots that legitimacy could be purchased at the price of the violence perpetrated on the last three direct descendants of Frederick II. Even the supposedly felicitous reign of Roberto d'Angiò, the patron of Petrarch, under whom much of northen Italy was brought within the Neapolitan sphere of influence, managed to evoke little more than a list of frequently erroneous dates.[37] The major chronicler of the civil wars precipitated by the accession of Giovanna I, the author of the anonymous *Chronicon Siculum,* was forced, for want of adequate contemporary records, to rely exclusively on a brief *Informazione* prepared for diplomatic purposes by the royal official Bartolomeo Caracciolo in 1343. His main political commitment lay in encouraging his fellow Neapolitan nobles to beat up on the "stiff-necked" ("erecta cervice") middle classes ("hominibus medianis et populo grasso," as he calls them in his macaronic Latin). His support of the Angevins against the native Durazzeschi put him in the difficult position of having also to support the Avignon Papacy against the Roman Papacy after the Schism. And he could see no other solution to the chaos of the late fourteenth century than an escapist contemplation of the long-lost golden age of the first Normans.[38] The anonymous chronicler's sole successor in the last decades of the century, the author of the *Cronaca di Partenope,* ended up by turning chronicle into "rhapsody": a mixture of fact about his own time and legends about the past rounded out with extensive dialect paraphrases of Giovanni Villani.[39]

While history writing was declining on the Continent, it was given new life in Sicily by the sudden occurrence of the event that all Sicilian patriots ever since have hailed as the greatest in their national history: the Vespers. Unfortunately, the first literary reflection of this event, the anonymous *Ribellamentu in Sichilia,* put forth a thesis that both homegrown patriots and their foreign sympathizers have often found difficult to swallow—namely, that the massacre of every last Frenchman in Sicily in the days following Easter Tuesday of 1282 was the result of the careful planning and tireless diplomatic activity of one man, Giovanni di Procida, rather than an "improvised explosion of popular vendetta,"[40] an expression of the "rage of a people ferociously oppressed," and a manifestation of the "unsubdued pride of the Sicilian people."[41] Consequently, one patriot in the seventeenth century composed a more acceptable chronicle of his own, which he attributed to an otherwise unknown Frate Athanasiu di Jaci; and another one in the twentieth century republished the same text, with a 179-page introduction,[42] insouciant of the solid arguments just previously put forth against its authenticity.

Still, the author of the *Ribellamentu* was a writer of some skill. He apparently wrote in Sicilian not because he knew no Latin but because he hoped to reach a wider native audience; and he made his characters speak in racy dialogues and elegant orations (like Procida's speech before the emperor at Constantinople) in order better to drive home a lesson in politics: "Let all those lords who hold kingdoms, cities, lands, and castles . . . be warned by this example not to commit shameful acts or injuries against their vassals. . . ." RAIMONDO MONTANARA was also a good writer,[43] though apparently by nature rather than by training, since he spent most of his life fighting in the armies of his sovereign, Peter of Aragon. When he began to write, at the age of seventy, his memory sometimes failed him. But he carefully rearranged the detailed eyewitness records of the military campaigns in which he had taken part in order to point out the causal relations among them. BARTOLOMEO DI NEOCASTRO, on the other hand, was a writer of no small learning and of considerable polish. He was a mainlander by origin, but his close observations of Angevin maladministration during his tenure as judge in Messina had led him to adhere to the cause of the islanders. His *Historia Sicula* opens with the fateful event from which all the others followed: the death of Frederick II in 1250. It culminates in a dramatic account of what happened "on the last day of March, 1282, in the tenth indiction." It concludes with what for Raimondo as well marked the triumph of the Sicilian revolution and of Aragonese arms: the surrender of Messina, the last Angevin outpost on the island. And Bartolomeo emphasized the historical significance of the surrender by putting a passionate oration to the Messinese in the mouth of their new king.[44]

Such was the impact of the Vespers, indeed, that it continued to inspire historical writing well into the following century. A *Chronicon Siculum* written around 1343 and then expanded and continued in a Catalan and in two Sicilian versions to 1359, sought to put the events of 1282 into the perspective of all Sicilian history since the Islamic conquest; and although in chronicle rather than in narrative form, it succeeded, by a careful selection of relevant entries, in suggesting a series of major periods—Norman, Swabian, Angevin—that had led up to the heroic initiative of Giovanni di Procida and the glorious deeds, "per mari e per terra," of King Peter.[45] NICOLÒ SPECIALE returned to Bartolomeo's more monographic form—perhaps in imitation of Sallust, whom he quoted at length. He began with a discourse on the importance of history in preserving the memory of great deeds and an introductory book on the sins of the Angevins and on their expulsion from the island. But he devoted the bulk of his 200-folio-page narrative to the reign of Federico III, whom the Sicilian parliament elected king in 1295 and whom Nicolò served as an ambassador. Moreover, he used the narrative as evidence for several important, though not necessarily concordant, theses: first, that the Angevins provoked the rebellion by their "extorsiones, exilia, carcerem, deportationes," and abuse of "alienas foeminas"; second, that they were usurpers anyway, since Peter of Aragon was the legitimate king of Sicily through his marriage to Manfredi's daughter; and third, that the Sicilians would have in the long run to look out for themselves, since even the Aragonese were not wholly reliable.[46]

With his set speeches and careful explanation of the relation of one event to the next, Nicolò might have provided Sicily with what his contemporary Albertino Mussato gave the Veneto: a push in the direction of humanist historiography. That he did not do so was partially his fault, particularly since he could easily have built upon the solid foundation of the great historiographical masterpieces of the Norman and Swabian periods. He still failed to distinguish between prose and poetry in his source material from ancient times—as if Ovid and Vergil were authorities on the first Sicilians. He still believed Isidore to be as worthy a model of historical writing as Sallust. He still thought Christ, rather than political sagacity or respect for legitimacy, to have been responsible for the calling of King Peter. He still thought that a swarm of flies from the tomb of some Catalan saint could send a French army scurrying back across the Pyrenees. And he was still unable to draw from history any better proposal for what to do about the troubles of his own time than a call for public penace: "Scindite corda vestra, universi qui habitatis in Trinacariam.... Induete membra vestra cilicium, sedete in cinere...."

But to some extent Nicolò's own failure was a consequence of the failure of the political adventure launched by the Vespers. In cutting themselves off from Naples, the Sicilians cut themselves off from all Italy as well, and from the culture of northern Italy that was just then being welcomed at Naples by the court of Roberto d'Angiò. In casting their lot with the house of Aragon, they exposed themselves to the constant danger of being sacrificed to interests not their own—as their ambassadors learned (in a scene dramatically recreated by Nicolò) when they found that Peter's successor was ready to sell them out to the Angevins. When they then tried to govern themselves under an elected monarch, they started quarreling: and the political unity which the Normans had once imposed upon them rapidly dissolved into a state of permanent civil war among the big barons.[47] Occasionally, a "great event," like the battle of Lipari, could still inspire a talented diarist.[48] But by 1361 all that remained of the Sicillian heritage of the great southern historiographical tradition was the "trite, plebeian" (Gregorio), though sometimes pretentious, Latin prose of an obscure Franciscan named MICHELE DA PIAZZA about the interminable round of baronial outrages that even a king like Federico, "tamquam Leo rugiens querens quem devoret," was incapable of mitigating.[49] By the early fifteenth century, all that remained of the once-rich Sicilian chronicle tradition was a scattering of miscellaneous dates in which even 1282 received no more than four words: "The French were killed" ("li francesi foro ancisi").[50]

The Court of Alfonso d'Aragona

Thus history writing had been dead for over a hundred years by the time Southerners once again began to take an interest in it in the second quarter of the fifteenth century, and few if any of them seem to have been at all aware of the rich historiographical heritage left them by their ancestors of the age of the Normans or the Vespers. Only one of them had what even in the twelfth century had been considered to be a minimal education. And he, ANGELO DE TUMMULILLIS (b. 1397), a notary who served in the secretariat of Queen Giovanna II and then as *oratore* for the town of San Germano, frankly admitted to being "indignus et indoctus."[51] Only two of those about whom something is known were at all familiar with a reigning monarch. But the first, MELCHIORRE FERRAIOLO, was a goldsmith, not a prelate or statesman, and his accurate and richly illustrated descriptions of court proceedings remained anonymous until as late as 1960. Similarly, the other, JOAMPIERO LEOSTELLO of Volterra, filled the day-to-day diary he was hired to keep for Duke Alfonso with purely personal matters, and he wrote in an almost incomprehensible mixture of rudimentary Latin, dialectical Tuscan, and Neapolitan:[52]

> Die ij novembris 1488. Surrexit e lectulo et anno a vedere Dom Federico
> et vide messa com sua signoria et torno et fece collatione et cavalcho in
> corte del s. Re et vide vespro de li morti. . . .

None of them had any thesis to propound or any political position to justify—none of them, that is, except the French soldier ANTOINE DE LA SALLE, called SALADE in Naples, who was almost totally ignorant of the country he twice visited on behalf of the French pretender to the throne.[53] Both the two LUDOVICOS, SENIOR and JUNIOR,[54] and the much more observant members of the Raimi family[55] were interested almost exclusively in keeping track of the names of those who participated in public ceremonies; and their descriptions even of such significant ceremonies as the entry of Alfonso I into Naples in 1443 and the confiscation of the estates of the rebel barons in 1487 consist largely of lists. Those of them who wrote for others rather than just for themselves were more concerned with entertaining than with informing their readers; and the line between true chronicle and the kind of tall stories that LOISE DE ROSA (1387–1475) included in what he called a "chronicle" is at times hard to discern. In fact, tall stories crowded out what might have been correct among the rumors that LUCIO CARDAMI picked up in Naples during the reign of Ferrante: no distinction is made between the account of Ferrante's wife begging from door to door after the disaster at Nola in 1459 and that of the beheaded Christian body that stood straight up in front of its Muslim executioners.[56] Only one of the Quattrocento Neapolitan chroniclers was dedicated to any cause. And he, the author of the Monteleone diary, managed to get excited about only one event: the fall of Constantinople.[57] Whether King Ladislao realized his ambition of becoming king of all Italy, whether King Ferrante succeeded in sustaining his declaration of independence from the Papacy ("che le Reame e lo mio et non nde havea fare niente"), whether the Florentines monopolized all the financial and commercial affairs of the kingdom—it was all the same to him. And whether Alfonso d'Aragona or René d'Anjou won out in their contest for the throne was merely a matter of who had the most money: "for everyone runs away from poverty" ("la povertade è fuggita da tutti").

In fact, none of the southern diarists of the fifteenth century seems to have been at all aware of what had been the chief concern of their predecessors of the twelfth century: the spiritual and political unity of the kingdom. The voluntary exile DOMENICO DELELLO, whose recollections of his native country in the decades before

1458 were dictated to a Venetian scribe in 1481 and written down in the Venetian language, would rather have seen his own city of Gaeta occupied by the Genoese or the duke of Milan than by the reigning king of Naples.[58] Most of them wrote not about the Kingdom, but about the city of Naples; and they thus made available a great abundance of detail about daily life in the city in their own days. Those of them who were not residents of the capital, like SILVESTRO GUARINO (from 1492 to 1501), the author of the Afeltro chronicle (from 1434 to 1496),[59] GIACOMO GALLO,[60] and ANGELO TAFURI,[61] wrote almost exclusively about what went on respectively in Aversa, Afelto, Amalfi, and Nardò—to the point, indeed, of portraying the Turkish and Venetian invasions of Puglia as purely local conflicts. None of the diarists had any but the foggiest notion of the previous history of the kingdom—not even Angelo de Tummulillis, who claimed to have searched about for "quedam peregrina et antiqua ex relatione predecessorum." Most of what "Monteleone" wrote about the years before 1370 is wrong; most of what NOTAR GIACOMO wrote about St. Peter's visit to Naples and the adventures of Constantine and Sylvester would have made the twelfth-century readers of Orosius blush.[62] None of them had any other notion of the connection among historical events than that of contemporaneity. That Henry V persecuted the Church was just as important to ANTONELLO CONIGER Lecce as the "great rainstorms" that occurred the same year; and the arrival of the "invitissimo" Frederick III in Rome was far more important than the entry of Alfonso I into Naples.[63] Finally, none of them had any other notion of historical causality than the role of chance or providence—which is apparently why Angelo spent so much time consulting prophets and astrologers.

The introduction of humanist historiography in Naples can thus be attributed neither to the initiative of Neapolitans, who had forgotten how to write history, nor to the restoration of a single, and for the moment unchallenged, political authority over the whole of the former Norman kingdom, which few Neapolitans paid much attention to. The first historian to write about Naples according to the new humanist criteria was only an occasional visitor to the kingdom, MATTEO PALMIERI of Florence. Yet Palmieri drew much of his information about the Florentine chancellor of Queen Giovanna I, Niccolò Acciaiuoli, from Florentine rather than from Neapolitan sources (which said nothing about him); and he rearranged his information according to the model of Plutarch (minus Plutarch's "footnotes," since Livy was his model for Latin prose) because of his conviction that the deeds of a great compatriot would enhance the glory of their common *patria*—not Naples, but Florence.[64] Palmieri's immediate successors (none of whom seems to have been acquainted with his work) were only temporary residents of Naples. The most fixed of them, ANTONIO BECCADELLI (1394–1471) was a Palermitan (hence his surname, PANORMITA) of an originally Bolognese family who had gone to Florence in 1419 looking for a job at the papal court; and he had studied in Padua, Bologna, Siena, and Pavia, and worked for the duke of Milan before joining Alfonso's court back in Palermo in 1435.[65]

LORENZO VALLA (1407–57) was a Roman of an originally Piacentine family who had taught at the University of Pavia before entering Alfonso's service; and he remained in Naples only until 1448, when he finally obtained a university chair in Rome.[66] BARTOLOMEO FACIO, or FAZIO (1408–57) was a Ligurian who had first visited Naples as the ambassador of the Republic of Genoa in 1443; and he several times interrupted his residence there after 1446 with extended patronage-seeking expeditions to the papal court.[67]

Sicily produced no historians at all either before or during the reign of Alfonso (1442–58), perhaps because, by reuniting it with Naples, the Aragonese conquest abolished once and for all the precarious independence it had won in 1282. Or rather, the closest that Sicily came to producing history was the speeches copied or imitated from the *Aeneid* and put in the form of a tiresome epic poem by Sicily's first humanist schoolteacher, Tommaso da Chaula.[68] The mainland produced two historians. But one of them, Giovannantonio Campano, left only a brief topographical description of the city of Teramo before emigrating definitively to Rome;[69] and GIANNANTONIO DE' PANDONI (1405–after 1476), better known as PORCELLI, came back only long enough to escape the wrath of Pope Eugenius IV before leaving again to serve first Alfonso and then Federico da Montefeltro, the Malatesta, and Pope Pius II elsewhere in Italy.[70]

What held this diverse group together was thus not a common homeland or a common cultural tradition. In fact, none of them seems to have heard of, and none of them probably would have been willing or able to talk to, the contemporary Neapolitan diarists, from whom, as a matter of fact, they could have obtained much useful information. What held them together was their common employer, King Alfonso d'Aragona, surnamed the Magnanimous, who, even though he had spent most of his life with his army and even though he never learned to speak Italian very well, was the first king of Naples since Roberto d'Angiò to embark on a systematic patronage of the arts and letters.[71] It so happens that the kind of letters he appreciated the most was history—to the point, indeed, of imitating Scipio Africanus and carrying a copy, not of Xenophon, to be sure, but of Livy around with him on his military campaigns.[72] That is why an aspiring courtier named Gaspare Pellegrino spent all of 1443 compiling the *gesta* of Alfonso in ten manuscript books of stilted Latin, even though no one then or since has ever thought them worthy of publication. That is why Valla spent the last months of 1445 and the first months of 1446 working on what he intended to be a full history of the Aragonese conquest, but what is really, in its half-finished form, a historical biography of Alfonso's father, Ferdinando.[73] It was similarly in order to second his patron's literary proclivities that Fazio spent most of the nine years after his appointment as royal historiographer in 1446 on a sequel to Valla's work, a historical biography of Alfonso himself.[74] This same aim inspired Panormita to continue his historical biography of Alfonso's heir, Ferrante, from 1464, when he completed the first part, until the moment of his death.[75] And it also induced Porcelli to recast in the form of a commentary the news bulletins that he had been commissioned to send back from the front during the wars between Venice and Milan.[76]

To be sure, none of the humanists associated with Alfonso's court was primarily a historian. Valla's main interests lay in the realms of classical philology, moral philosophy, and—at least according to the most recent authorities—theology. Panormita was best known in his own time as a poet. And Porcelli earned a living between one diplomatic mission and the next as a teacher of rhetoric. Still, most of them soon found other reasons for writing history than merely that of pleasing Alfonso. In what was to become the most widely read of his works in the fifteenth century, the *Elegantiarum Latinae Linguae Libri Sex,* Valla insisted that the study of words, upon which all philosophy was based, was capable both of correcting current errors about the past and of transforming manners and institutions in the present. And he sought to do just that in his now-famous, but then rather overlooked,[77] *Declamatio* on the Donation of Constantine.[78] He first put forth a historical thesis: that the emperor Constantine had never granted temporal jurisdiction over the Western Empire to any pope. This thesis was by no means new. It had been proposed by several curial canonists as early as the twelfth century.[79] It had been proposed again in the early fifteenth-century—by Ambrogio Traversari, Leonardo Teronda, and Nicholas of Cusa, among others. And it was to be proposed once again, albeit independently, by the English prelate Reginald Pecock thirteen years later.[80] But Valla reinforced the thesis by adding philological arguments to the traditional legal and logical ones; and he proved the document upon which the counterthesis had long rested to have been forged sometime in the eighth century by someone whose knowledge of the language and the institutions of the fourth century was at best rudimentary. Valla's mastery of the "elegances of the Latin language" then enabled him to put his thesis in the form of a passionate appeal for political action. Let the Papacy renounce its illegal and pernicious claim to ultimate temporal authority in the Kingdom of Naples, he demanded, and leave King Alfonso to enjoy in peace what he has won by law as well as by arms. Let it also give up its own temporal domain, which it held only by arms, not by law, and which has long been "the source of the destruction and devastation of all Italy and of many other provinces as well." And let the pope become what he claims to be, "the holy father of all men, the father of the Church." What Valla did for king and church in the Declamation, he then did for all civil rulers in the *Historia Ferdinandi.* The Aragonese conquest of Naples, he showed, had been the result not of fate or of the inscrutable designs of divine forces but of the careful calculations of intelligent men. It could therefore serve as a lesson for whoever in the future sought to be successful in politics: let him be guided by the truth rather than by misconceptions about the past.

History was thus incompatible with eulogy. And when even his tactful toning-down of the programmatic declarations in the preface to an earlier draft failed to persuade Alfonso of the validity of this principle, Valla abandoned the work short of its projected conclusion.[81] History was also inseparable from rhetoric. And Valla supported this principle first with a more correct and more complete version of the emended text of Livy he had inherited from Petrarch through Cosimo de' Medici and then with Latin translations of Herodotus and Thucydides that were to remain standard, notwithstanding the complaints of his sixteenth-century editor, Henri Estienne ("inscitia, negligentia, inelegantia") for another hundred years.[82] The rules of rhetoric that he induced from the ancient historians required the adoption not only of a style capable of appealing to the intended readers but also of a vocabulary that they could readily understand. Since he was writing "for men of the present and the future," rather than for men of the past, Valla did not hesitate to use modern rather than ancient place names (*Ferraria* instead of *Forum Arrii* and *Papia* rather than *Ticinum*) and to avoid the anachronistic overtones of old words *(dux)* by borrowing more appropriate words *(capitaneus)* from the vernacular. Finally, history was identical with the truth—all of the truth, not just that part of it which pleased either writer or patron. Since Ferdinando did in fact snooze during the speeches of ambassadors and since he did in fact use extraordinary means to provoke erections, Valla did not hesitate to say so. For only a real historical personage, with all his defects as well as all his merits, was capable of being "imitated."

It was such statements as these that soon involved Valla in a violent dispute with his colleague Fazio.[83] The main purpose of history, said Fazio, was to provide literary monuments commensurate with the inherent quality of the events recounted. Monumentality could be achieved only by restricting the vocabulary to what had been sanctioned for all times by the ancient classics. If they did not provide a word capable of designating an order of Spanish knights, and if the word *equites* might suggest an incorrect derivation from the equestrian order of ancient Rome, then the modern historian should use a circumlocution. Monumentality was also a function of propriety. If certain of a king's actions seemed to be somewhat less than kingly, the historian should discreetly hide them behind a list of abstract virtues— virtues which, being abstract, could not actually be denied him. To say that Alfonso's face "radiated with the most pleasing majesty united with a gravity of manner and words" protected the king and did no damage to the truth. And to attribute the corresponding and equally abstract vices to his enemies apparently did no harm either; for among them Fazio was forced to include his own Genoese compatriots.

Fortunately, when he himself came to writing history, Fazio remained much closer to Valla than he would admit in the midst of their acrimonious controversy ("cum videam furorem tuum in dies augescere . . ."); and many of the peculiarities of his work can be attributed to his having chosen Caesar rather than Thucydides as a model. After all, he too had prepared for what he intended as his major work of history by translating Arrian's life of Alexander the Great and by writing an account of his own about the War of Chioggia.[84] He was thus able to put what his hero did into the context of what all the other princes and states of Italy were doing at the same time. He kept moral reflections strictly marginal to his narrative. He named and identified the other participants in each major event. And he drew from his record of the wars what he, and the papal legate whose stirring oration concludes the work, perceived to be the most urgent political objective of the years after 1453: the restoration of peace in Italy. Fazio thus succeeded in two of his major aims: flattering his patron and proving that contemporary history was just as interesting as ancient history. Indeed, he succeeded so well that the exigent critic Giovan Michele Bruto still read his work "summa cum voluptate" a century later; and the original Latin version went through six editions between 1560 and 1567 alone.

For Panormita, however, rhetoric took such precedence over the ascertaining of the truth that history threatened not only to be confused with eulogy but to become eulogy. Both the *De Dictis et Factis Alphonsi* and the recently discovered *Liber Rerum Gestarum Ferdinandi Regis*[85] follow the model of Suetonius, even though Panormita himself classified his model among the "mediocres" of ancient literature. But his works omit much of what was most valuable in their model by including only the virtues, never the vices, of their heroes. Thus Ferrante turns out to be a mere shadow, one which none of the author's unending streams of glowing adjectives succeeds in bringing to life: "fortis vir, strenuus, . . . omnibus aequus, iustus, carus. . . ." Not a word is said about his illegitimate birth, which in fact is what forced him to fight for his father's patrimony. What is said about his upbringing is nothing but an idealized version of humanist educational programs. What is said about the real political problems of the day amounts to little more than an unrealistic misunderstanding of current balance of power theories cast in the form of a final speech by Alfonso.

For Porcelli, moreover, rhetoric—or the abuse of rhetoric—was so important that it almost spoiled what was still good enough three centuries later to evoke the applause of Muratori, both for its style and for its content ("Historicus . . . ingenio et Latino stilo multum valebat.").[86] Porcelli succeeded very well in accomplishing his principal aims. He proved to Alfonso that he had done his job as a reporter, and he proved to his humanist audience the very humanist thesis that modern Venetians were morally and politically superior to the ancient Romans. The day-by-day account of everything that he himself saw or heard from reliable witnesses is backed up with classical Latin translations of all the relevant diplomatic correspondence and all the relevant military communiqués. But when each improbable battlefield oration produces the same enthusiastic reaction, when unlettered condottieri are made to exclaim "Testor immortales deos" in impeccable Sallustian periods, and, absurdity of absurdities, when the two protagonists, Jacopo Piccinino and Francesco Sforza, are referred to throughout as "Scipio" and "Hannibal," then the author's sincerety is at least open to question. Finally, when Porcelli started changing his mind about whom to dedicate his work to, when he started switching his superlatives back and forth from one of his protagonists to the other, and when he loaded the Venetian senators with "sapientia, constantia, moderatione, justitia, virtutumque omni genere" merely in the hope that they would come through with the handsome reward that "Divus Alphonsus" seemed reluctant to accord, then history threatened to become the victim of financial bargaining. Porcelli soon got what he deserved. Alfonso had Piccinino murdered and switched alliances from the Venetians to Francesco Sforza: and the *Commentarii* accordingly dropped out of sight for another three centries, until a friend of Muratori's accidently discovered them on a dust-covered back shelf of a bookstore in Verona.

The Reign of Ferrante

Humanist historiography in Naples was thus on the verge of succumbing to its own inherent weaknesses upon the death of the sole patron who had called it into existence. What saved it was to a considerable extent the cultural policy adopted by Alfonso's successor, Ferrante (1458–94). Ferrante was much less versed in humanist letters than his father had been, notwithstanding the humanist educational curriculum that Panormita dreamed up for him. He therefore left the humanists alone to organize by themselves what soon took the place of the royal court as the center of intellectual life in Naples, the Academy, which became known as the Accademia Pontaniana when GIOVANNI PONTANO (c. 1429–1503) succeeded Panormita as its president. Ferrante was also less interested in history—which may be one of the reasons why most of the literary efforts of the Neapolitan humanists in his reign went not into history but into hortatory panegyrics, orations, and political and moral essays: Galateo's treatises on education, hypocrisy, dueling, and how to fight the Turks,[87] Pontano's *De Laudibus Divinis, De Principe, De Fortuna, De Magnanimitate,* etc. More important, he was much less interested in importing talent for the decoration of his court. Except for Pontano, who was nevertheless a Neapolitan by adoption, having lived here almost continuously since his student days in the late 1440s, all the humanists were natives of the kingdom. GIOVAN FILIPPO DE LIGNANIME (b.c. 1428) came from Messina, GIOVANNI ALBINO (d. 1496) from Castelluccio near Salerno, ANTONIO DE FERRARIIS (1444–1517) from Galatone near Otranto (hence his nickname, GALATEO), PIETRO RANZANO (1428–92) from Palermo, TRISTANO CARAC-CIOLO from Naples itself. Most of them spent most of their productive years in the capital—even MICHELE RICCI (1445–1515), who left in 1495 only because he had cast his lot too decisively on the side of Charles VIII. Indeed, humanism at last began to take root in the city of Naples: by the 1480s one foreign observer claimed to have found there some three hundred citizens who could be qualified as "learned" according to humanist standards.[88]

Most important of all, Ferrante was less interested in how much or how well the humanists wrote than in the practical political and administrative services he could get out of them; and if most of their literary work was actually accomplished after his death, it is in part because he kept them so busy during his lifetime. Pontano became president of the Camera della Sommaria and secretary to the wife of Ferrante's heir, the duke of Calabria, in 1474; and after accompanying the duke on his campaigns in Tuscany and Puglia, he was charged with negotiating the peace treaties with the Papacy in 1482–84 and again in 1492. Albino was secretary to the duke himself, and he was subsequently sent off on diplomatic missions to Florence, Milan, Siena, Urbino, Rome, and even Albania. Galateo became Ferrante's physician after having studied in Ferrara. Ranzano became his ambassador to Hungary after having been superior of the Dominican order in Sicily. Ricci was put in charge of the legal affairs of the royal patrimony—while still giving lectures in civil law at the university. Caracciolo had to work most of his life, landholding baron though he was, as president of the Regia Camera, in order to pay the dowries of his innumerable daughters; and he did not even have time to study Latin literature until he was over thirty-five. Lignamine was the only one of them who did not hold a responsible administrative position; but he kept himself busy from dawn to dusk founding, then managing, and finally trying to salvage from the consequences of overproduction (with occasional subsidies from Ferrante) the first printing press in Rome.

History in the reign of Ferrante was just as dedicated to the cause of the House of Aragon as it had been in the reign of Alfonso. But it was so for very different reasons. Only one of the historians, Lignamine, let himself be tempted into panegyrics. For he was not only trying to write an accurate account of the main events of the first decades of the reign, which he managed to do with considerable skill. He was principally trying to convince Pope Sixtus IV that Ferrante did indeed follow the ancient models suggested by his preceptors, that he really was sober in dress and appearance, that he really was charitable to the poor, that he really did admire in his wife a synthesis of all the virtues of Cornelia, Julia, Lucretia, et al., and that the pope should therefore stop giving him trouble. He was also trying to persuade Ferrante himself, as tactfully as possible, to avoid the unfortunate examples of the royal pupils of Aristotle and Seneca, to be a little less concerned with elegant and costly display, to pay somewhat more attention to economic conditions of his kingdom, and to treat his wife as something more than just the politically valuable heiress of the Durazzo claimants to the throne.[89] It was thus his hortatory, rather than his panegyrical, purpose that led him into most of his errors.

Albino, on the other hand, had no reason to indulge in panegyrics at all. For he realized that Ferrante's personal virtues and vices had very little to do with his indispensable role in overcoming the worst scourge of all political communities, civil war. To make his point clear, Albino began by describing what had happened to Rome at the time of Sulla and Marius and what had happened to Florence at the time of Jacopo de' Pazzi and Lorenzo de' Medici. His own employer, Alfonso, duke of Calabria, had unfortunately been dragged into the wrong side of the Florentine affair. But Alfonso's father, Ferrante, soon corrected the error, first by being reconciled with Lorenzo, and then by vigorously and justly suppressing the revolt of his own barons. And it was his just vigor that later permitted his heir, Ferrante II, to recover the kingdom so quickly after the retreat of the French in 1495.[90] Pontano had even less reason to indulge in panegyrics, for he wrote only after his mistake in preferring kingdom to king in 1495 had cost him his position at court. It was not Ferrante's fault that the golden age of Alfonso II ("hoc regnante Italiae res maxime floruere; pax secuta est tranquillitatis atque opulentiae plena") vanished so quickly after his death. It was rather the fault of Calixtus III, "forgetful of Alfonso's benefits," who was looking for an excuse to replace the Aragonese with a Borgia, and of Giovan Antonio, prince of Taranto, "vario et inconstanti ingenio," who wanted the throne for himself.[91] The cause of truth had not therefore to be sacrificed so frequently. And all three authors, but particularly the last two, scrupulously supplemented the accounts of what they themselves had observed with whatever relevant diplomatic correspondence had come their way during their years of public service.

Following the example of Valla and Fazio, and equally loathe to spend their little spare time combing through the chronicles of the past, the historians resident at Naples wrote almost exclusively contemporary history. The one exception was Lignamine, who, during a brief tenure at the court of Sixtus IV, embarked on a continuation of Riccobaldo da Ferrara's world chronicle. But while the nasty epithets he hurled at the Flagellants ("haec pestifera secta") may have pleased Sixtus as much as his stories about the sad fate of preachers who doubt the doctrine of the Immaculate Conception, his dull list of facts and dates confirmed as decisively as his account of the three suns of Eugenius IV the irreconcilability of humanist and medieval critical standards.[92] Moreover, all these historians followed the standard humanist practice of limiting what they said about other contemporary states to what could serve as an explanation for the accomplishments of the ruler of a single state. The one exception in this case was Ranzano, who was not only a humanist, having studied under Carlo Marsuppini at Florence as well as under Valla, Panormita, and Filelfo at Naples, but also a Dominican. Ranzano's attempt to combine the critical and stylistic innovations of humanism and the worldwide scope of traditional Dominican historiography demonstrated just the opposite of Lignamine's work—at least to judge from the small part that has been published of the eight handwritten folio volumes he composed between 1461 and the year of his death.[93] He began the chapters on Hungary with a survey of everything every ancient author had ever said about Pannonia and the Huns. He learned enough Magyar and Serbian to get proper names spelled correctly. During a diplomatic mission in 1488 he read several local chronicles, he interviewed all the local authorities on Hungarian antiquities, and he traveled extensively in order to check on the accuracy of the ancient geographers. The result was an impeccably humanist history of Hungary, one punctuated by stirring speeches, enlivened by heroic portraits, and brought to a climax at the moment of the victory of Matthias Corvinus over Frederick III. Ranzano began the chapters on Sicily by rejecting all the popular legends ("Panhormitanorum animis impressa credulitas") about a Hellenic diaspora after the Trojan War, by throwing out anything in Vergil that could not be supported from Ptolemy or Strabo, and by following Bruni in proclaiming Thucydides (whom he read in Valla's translation) to be the earliest reliable authority. Palermo, he concluded, had been founded neither by Greeks nor by Phoenicians but by Sicani; and he was happy to find his conclusion backed up by Panormita, "vir mea aestate historicus sapientissimus." But he had to admit that it might have been founded instead by Seph, son of Esau. For that was the name that all the local Jews he interviewed read in a well-known Chaldaic inscription. Silly as it seemed, the attribution was apparently confirmed by a document brought from Damascus by a Levantine Jew at the time of Guglielmo II and by a codex owned—and translated for him—by a Pisan Jew to whom he applied for assistance. And since the most advanced documentary criticism of his age could carry him no further, he was forced, in good humanist fashion, to leave the question in suspense. Only when he sought to combine humanist standards with the most recalcitrant of medieval literary forms, hagiography, did Ranzano clearly fail—at least to judge from the two parts of his world history that were subsequently printed in the *Acta Sanctorum*.[94] He scrupulously observed all the humanist externals: set speeches, ancient place names, and a flattering preface to the general of his order. And he chose for his guide an author whom most humanists still held to be as normative as Caesar and Livy—Jerome, in his life of Hilarion. But the feats he attributed to Saints Barbara (1468) and Vincent Ferrer (1455) were so obviously unhistorical that they could have served no other purpose than that of flattering two powerful advocates in the next world.

The task of putting the present into the context of the past thus fell to foreigners. The first was LORENZO BUONINCONTRI (d. 1481), whose family had been exiled from San Miniato in Tuscany for having taken part in a futile appeal to Emperor Sigismund against the Florentine government. Although an astrologer by profession, Buonincontri managed to read enough during his brief tenure at Alfonso's court to suggest, in proper if not in elegant humanist historiographical form, that the golden age of Alfonso had been preceded by, and to some extent prepared for, by the golden age of the Normans. Unfortunately, he took every opportunity to stray off onto subjects more familiar to him (like the history of Tuscany), to use Villani at the expense of Neapolitan sources, and to swallow a good number of discredited legends. It was thus not wholly regrettable that his work was left to be eaten by worms until the eighteenth century.[95] The second was FELINO MARIA SANDEO (1444–1503), a canon lawyer from Reggio Emilia who rose through the academic hierarchy at Ferrara, Pisa, and Rome to become bishop of the southern diocese of Atri and Penna in 1495. Unfortunately, Sandeo visited the Kingdom only once, during an embassy for Alexander VI, for the invasion of Charles VIII kept him from residing in his diocese—if, indeed, he ever intended to—and led him to spend the last years of his life trying to trade it for the better-paying and less distant diocese of Lucca. What he knew of the Kingdom thus came almost exclusively from what he could find in the margins of the standard humanist histories of northern Italy—Biondo, Platina, Poggio, Giustinian—as if Riccardo di San Germano and Fazio had never written a line.[96] The third, GIOVANNI DE CANDIDA (d. after 1506), fared somewhat better. He was a Neapolitan by birth, and he still remembered something of his native country when, some twenty-five years after the exile of his family in 1462, he decided to write a sketch of it for the inspiration of King Charles VIII.[97] Candida's intellectual formation had taken place mostly at the court of Burgundy, and it is fully reflected in the late medieval, prehumanist sketch of French history he wrote on the request of the abbot of Saint-Denis, Jean de Bilhères-Lagraulas. Moreover, what he said about Naples was colored by his commitment to the Angevin cause, which, by defying historical evidence, he traced back to Charlemagne. Nevertheless, he knew enough about recent historiographical standards in Italy to take his information about Naples from Fazio, about the Papacy from Platina, and about the rest of Italy from Bruni; and some of the members of the entourage of Charles VIII, who took him back home briefly in 1495, may well have profited from his account of the new kingdom about which they knew little or nothing.

The last of the foreign historians of Naples never visited the kingdom at all: PANDOLFO COLLENUCCIO (1444–1503). In fact, most of Collenuccio's efforts during the 1490s were directed toward defending the reputation of Pliny the Elder against those who blamed not the copyists but the author himself for the extravagant lore transmitted in his books. Yet his *Compendio de le istorie del Regno di Napoli* (1498)[98] was soon heralded as the Neapolitan equivalent of Sabellico's history of Venice. It was translated into French, Latin, and Spanish; and it went through fifteen partial or complete editions in the Italian original between 1539 and 1613. Collenuccio learned to be an acute observer of interstate political maneuvering while ambassador of the lord of his native city, Pesaro, to Rome and Venice and of Ercole d'Este to Pope Innocent VIII and Emperor Maximilian I. He learned about the details of internal political administration while serving as *podestà* in Florence and Bologna. He proved his mastery of classical and humanist literature by composing dialogues on the model of Lucan and defending the Latinity and honesty of Pliny the Elder. He tested his abilities as a historian by putting together what he himself had observed with what he had read about ancient and modern Germany, and he did this according to the precepts of Poliziano and Pontano.[99]

What then led Collenuccio to apply his talent and his experience to a history of Naples was his quest for a solution to what he saw as the greatest political problem of his age: the problem of good government. Two Italian states had already achieved the double goal he prescribed for all of them: peace and prosperity, and justice and equality before the law. They had done so, he decided, because of their good fortune in being governed by benevolent, intelligent princes who had been brought up by humanist pedagogues. Naples too had been blessed with at least one such prince of late: Alfonso, "worthy not just of one, but of many kingdoms, . . . fierce in battle, merciful in peace, and a great friend of the study of literature." It had been blessed by other good princes in the past as well, most notably Frederick II, whom Collenuccio took considerable pains to rehabilitate. And it had produced a long line of "excellent men in every kind of learning and discipline," from Pythagoras, Horace, and Sallust to Thomas Aquinas. But Naples turned out on closer inspection to be just the opposite of Florence and Ferrara. It was, Collenuccio discovered, "a parade ground for the ambitious, the avaricious, and tyrants, . . . constantly exposed to plunder and the calamities of war." Indeed, "the most sumptuous and stupendous spectacle in the whole world" had become "the misfortune and sorrow of Italy, . . . miserably buried in ruins."

What had gone wrong? Collenuccio read through all the ancient, medieval, and modern historians, from Tacitus and Procopius to Biondo, Platina, and even the "German writers" of the High Middle Ages. He amassed a large collection of personal letters, public decrees, and inscriptions. And he at last found the answer. Part of the fault lay in the character of the inhabitants, whom even Livy had found congenitally desirous of "novelties." Part of the fault lay in weak or incapable kings—like Corradino, "an inhuman and cruel man," just the opposite of his father, Frederick II. Part of the fault lay also in the lasting effects of the Byzantine occupation, which had dealt a big blow to the civilizing mission of Latin letters. Even greater was the fault of the Angevins, whose illegal and unfounded claims to the throne had upset one after another attempt finally to settle the question of succession. But the principal culprits were the ecclesiastics, led by most of the popes from Innocent III to Calixtus III (but not Pius II, one of Collenuccio's minor heroes), who were interested not in the good of the church, not in the apostolic life, but in the material and political aggrandizement of themselves and their families. It was they who had undermined the Normans, who had called in the Angevins, who had opposed Alfonso, who had summoned the barons against Ferrante. And it was another of their ringleaders, Alexander VI, who was now largely responsible for the most recent attempt to upset the Aragonese establishment: the French invasion of 1494–95.

Collenuccio's answer to the problem was similar to the one suggested by Valla in the *Declamatio* (but not in his history of Ferdinando). It was also similar to the one implicit in all the theological opponents of the Temporal Domain since the time of Dante. And it was almost identical with the one proposed, on the basis of a much wider vision of Neapolitan history, by Pietro Giannone in the early eighteenth century. Nevertheless, its inadequacy became apparent within a few years of its formulation—as soon, that is, as the French invasion turned out to be not simply one more challenge to the integrity of the kingdom but the beginning of a new era in the history of the whole peninsula.

Collenuccio's limitations were not his alone. They were those of the whole school of humanist historiography, of which he was one of the most accomplished representatives. Like the Florentines, he ignored economics; he therefore failed to realize that the absence in Naples of anything like the manufacturing, commercial, and capitalist landowning classes of Florence and Ferrara left even the most vigorous kings bereft of allies in their conflicts with the feudal nobility. Like the historians of the Roman Curia, he was blind to the role of institutions. Thus it never occurred to him that the individual clerics he inculpated might be acting not in response to purely individual vices and passion ("given over to secular concerns, drunken with worldly delights") but as members of a clan or a religious corporation. Nor did it occur to him that a precarious balance of mutually suspicious and generally unstable political powers in Italy in itself constituted a standing invitation to whatever better-organized foreign power felt moved to intervene. He blithely assumed that the virtues of one man (like the last of his heroes, Cesare Borgia) would suffice to create an enduring state overnight—without anyone bothering to turn a fortuitous agglomeration of conquered men into loyal citizens and a group of personal followers into an institutionalized administration. All that needed to be done, thought Collenuccio, was to assure princes of a good humanist education. They in turn would see that the clergy behaved like Peter, John, and Pius rather than like Calixtus and Alexander. And all the problems of Italy would forthwith disappear.

The answers proposed by Collenuccio's colleagues in Naples were still less satisfactory. They too knew that men alone made history; but they were wholly incapable of understanding the real, complex, and individual personalities of the men they picked out as historical agents. They too remembered what Valla had said about the ultimate reality of the single and the concrete; but they took every opportunity to withdraw into the abstract—to marvel at "the great variety of food" served at Ippolita Sforza's wedding (Lignamine) without mentioning a single dish, and to attribute the recent growth of Naples to constants: "coeli clementia, situs opportunitas, agrorum fertilitas" (Pontano). Few of them seem to have been troubled by the philosophic and religious doubts that had led Valla to shy away from the full consequences of his commitment to history: if reality is contingent, can anything, even religious dogma, be eternal? But they were just as unsuccessful as the other humanist historians of the fifteenth century in explaining what they were doing and why they were doing it. True, Poggio and Fonzio added the precepts of Diodorus Siculus and Lucan to those of Cicero and Quintillian.[100] Campano added the examples of Curtius Rufus and Vergerio to that of Arrian as a guide to the writing of biography. But they ended up saying much the same thing. History had to be true and avoid flattery (Vergerio).[101] It furnished far more information about the actions of men than any one man could acquire in many lifetimes (Fonzio). It contained an inexhaustible storehouse of moral examples all the more efficacious for being "brisk, grave, and magnificent in the splendor of its words . . ." (Michele Ferno on Campano). It inspired the reader "diligently and honestly to manage his domestic and civil affairs" (Guarino da Verona).[102] *Testis temporum, lux veritatis,* etc., etc.

In other words, the theory of history failed to keep up with the practice of history in all of Italy as well as in Naples. In fact, the only historian to come up with a new idea was Sigismondo de' Conti: man is naturally curious about his own past and will probably read history no matter how clumsily it is written.[103] But actually, no one in Quattrocento Italy would read it unless it followed the current rules of eloquence. And Conti ended up agreeing substantially with the position of Pontano in the single treatise of the whole century dedicated specifically to the problem, the *Actius* of 1499.[104] History, said Pontano, differed from poetry in that its language was more "chaste," that it observed chronological order, that it excluded "fantasy," and that it reproduced rather than "imitated" nature. But since its purpose was the same, that of inculcating civic virtue, these differences amounted to little more than questions of language and form. It is not surprising, then, that the humanist pedagogues had trouble fitting history into their curricula: the best Battista Guarino could do was put it under "grammar."[105] It is not surprising that readers failed to show much interest in it—that a copy of Livy was the only historical title among the 116 volumes owned by Leonardo da Vinci.[106] And it is not surprising that book publishers shied away from it. Of the 55 books printed in Ferrara before the end of the century, none could be classified as history. Of the 284 printed in Brescia, only 5 could; of the 297 printed in Florence, only 11; of the 535 printed in Milan, only 37—less than 7 percent; of the 545 printed in Bologna before 1520, only 9—or 1.65 percent. And most of these works of history were by ancient rather than modern historians—30 out of 37 at Milan.[107]

Thus when all the accomplishments of Alfonso I and Ferrante melted away at the sight of the first French soldier in 1495, the historians of Naples found themselves in exactly the same dilemma that beset the historians of Milan—and, for that matter, all the other historians who elevated real princes into ideal princes and then assigned to them alone the role of historical agents. Galateo ran home to Puglia to mourn the fate of his fellow exile, King Ferdinando, to bewail the "prostitution" of Italy to the "Gentiles," to recall Alfonso I's public works projects and Ferrante's campaign against the Turks in 1481. Finally, he took refuge in a geographic-historical survey of his native province—in a project, that is, as far removed as possible from the national problems that had preoccupied all his predecessors since the Norman conquest.[108] Ricci ran off to France, and he consoled himself on not being able to return by spinning out whatever he happened to have heard, without consulting either the historians or the chronicles, about his native country during the centuries between Ruggero and Ferdinando. He then assembled a collection of legends and unverified traditions about the other kingdoms of Christendom—France, Spain, Hungary, and the "Kingdom of Jerusalem"; and he published them in a series of ninety-page pocketbooks for the sole purpose of comforting the current victims of the same *fortuna* that alone determined the rise and fall of states.[109] He wholly ignored such standard humanist problems as selectivity and periodization. He credited Louis IX with dividing the royal domain among his brothers. He dedicated a third of his chapter on Charles VI to the story about the deer with the gold collar. He attributed the invasion of 1494–95 merely to the whim of Charles VIII.

TRISTANO CARACCIOLO (1437–1519 or 1439–1528—the authorities differ), on the other hand, stayed in Naples—to witness the final extinction of the direct descendants of Valla's King Ferdinando, whose genealogy he reconstructed, and to realize the full consequences of the annexation of the kingdom to the Spanish crown: the revolt provoked by the attempt to introduce the Spanish Inquisition in 1510.[110] Convinced that history could still furnish "egregia exempla" for the inspiration of "the generous souls of the young," he read through all the works of the historians and the chroniclers (although neither he nor his modern editor say which ones) in the hope of compensating for the all-too-evident absence of exemplary men in his own day. Now that events had proved the heroes of his older contemporaries not to have been heroes at all, he dared to look at one of them, Ferrante, not as the hero should have been but as he actually was in his last years: weary of the world, bored with his former pastimes, subject to bouts of mind-wandering, and consumed by chronic illness. Now that the doctrine of the model monarch no longer obscured the truth about real monarchs, he also succeeded in rehabilitating a traditional villain—Queen Giovanna I, whose education turned out to have been as close to future humanist standards as her father's friend Petrarch could devise, and whose equitable administration filled the Kingdom with commerce and wealth.[111] But when he came to explain the crisis of his own day, he fell back on the same old thesis about the succession problem—Angevins against Durazzeschi in the fourteenth century, Angevins against Aragonese in the fifteenth. Just as he came to the point of explaining why outside pretenders had always found support within the kingdom, he retreated not into an attack on, but into a defense of, the feudal nobility—the same nobility which had willingly joined Calixtus III, Innocent VIII, Jean d'Anjou, Charles VIII, or anyone else who might have helped it expand its own powers at the expense of the monarchy.

History, then, might console or distract private citizens—or at least give them concrete details about what they should mourn over. But it could do nothing to help statesmen figure out how to overcome the total and irredeemable tragedy of Naples and Italy in the early sixteenth century: "hominibus infrequentius Regnum et divitiis exhaustum reddidere. . . ." Caracciolo therefore put his manuscript aside; and no one read it until it was discovered and published for the first time over two centuries later.

BOOK III
LA CALAMITÀ D'ITALIA

7

FROM THE FIRST INVASION
TO THE CARAFA WAR

WITHIN SOME SEVEN DECADES OF ITS BIRTH, THEN, HUMANIST HISTORIOGRAPHY WAS dying of inanition. It was suffering from a lack of clearly defined purposes, from a want of appropriate subject matter, from a confusion about methodology, and, above all, from an inability to provide either a meaningful analysis of the present or a reliable guide to the future. What saved it—what prevented humanist historiography from becoming a purely decorative and celebrative form of literature, what finally provided it with political and philosophical utility, and what therefore justified its existence according to humanist canons regarding the function of learning in general—was the *calamità d'Italia,* Italy's calamity.

A Transitory Disturbance

To be sure, many of the chroniclers and diarists of the sixteenth century wrote for reasons that had nothing to do with any calamity. TOMASINO DE'BIANCHI copied out all the letters and edicts he could find that had any bearing whatever on his native Modena between 1506 and 1554; he did so principally to carry on the work of his father Jacopo, who had bequeathed him his famous diary upon his death in 1502.[1] ANTON FRANCESCO DA VILLA put down what he himself observed as a municipal officer at home and what one of his many sons reported to him as an episcopal *auditore* in France; he did so mostly in order to prove the worthiness of the present heirs of the illustrious ancestors whose names he had plotted on a genealogical chart in 1542. BATTISTA PAPAZZONI continued Ingrano Bratti's fourteenth-century chronicle of Mirandola, which he discovered, down to 1536; he did so largely to show that his miniscule *patria* had produced three of the most outstanding men of his generation: Giovanni ("universally resplendent in all the sciences"), Alberto Pio ("not only a very eminent philosopher, but also a great theologian"), and Gianfrancesco Pico ("his divine work and his other infinite virtues . . . made him loved by all princes and men of letters").[2] PARIDE GRASSO kept track of everything that happened in the papal court after his appointment as master of ceremonies in 1504; he did so largely to show himself even more punctilious and far more professional than his predecessor, Burckhart, on whom he had wasted very little affection. Indeed, Grasso's purpose served him well in adding firsthand experience to his studies of ancient ecclesiastical ceremonial procedures, and his treatises were accordingly elevated to the rank of authorities after the Council of Trent.[3] SEBASTIANO DI BRANCA TEDALLINI collected what news of the whole world he could hear in Rome, probably with the intention of continuing the diary of Infessura, although his responsibilities as a minor papal official after 1503 and as a parish priest after 1508 kept him from putting his occasional narrations into chronological order.[4] TESEO ALFANI noted everything that was talked about from day to day on the streets of Perugia for the same reason that had inspired his prolific predecessors of the fifteenth century: he found it personally interesting.[5] ALESSANDRO TASSONI (1488–1562) noted everything that was talked about in the streets of Modena simply because he had learned to do so while copying the historical sources used by his fourteenth-century predecessors, Giovanni da Pazzano and Bonifazio Morano.[6]

None of these writers seems to have noticed that Italy after 1494 was any different from what it had been before. LUCA COSTANTINI found nothing worthy of his attention before 1502 but lists of captured castles and episcopal appointments—even though he pretended to be following the example of his prolix predecessor, Antonio di Niccolò.[7] Only after reading in "the histories" (he does not bother to say in which ones) did Luca's successor, GIOVAN PAOLO MONTANI, discover that 1494 had been a year "in which almost all Italy was ruined"—although in just what way it had been ruined he himself seems not to have understood. The anonymous revisor of the Fermo chronicles (1445–1557) merely elaborated upon Montani's phrases when he called 1494 "the year fateful for the servile status [*servitù*] to which almost all Italy was subjected"; and he was no more able than Montani had been to discover any connection between the "fateful" year and the only issues that really interested him: the maintenance of municipal autonomy and the subjection of the surrounding towns and villages. An anonymous diarist of Cesena described what for him was the greatest event of his times as a happy, not a tragic, one: the capture of the city by Cesare Borgia, who promised to put an end to centuries of civil strife. Tedallini could not remember much more about the sojourn of Charles VIII in Rome when he came to write about it four years later than the magnificent appearance of the French army ("No one has ever seen so much artillery, such splendid soldiers, . . . and horses that cost some 200 or 300 *ducati* each"). The king himself was "small, crippled: the ugliest man ever seen." That he ever got to Rome was due largely to the machinations of his sponsors, Cardinal Giuliano Della Rovere and the dukes of Milan and Ferrara, who had brought him to Italy. Whatever he accomplished soon dwindled in stature before the feats of Cesare Borgia, who escaped from the French army before it had reached the Neapolitan border and who then murdered his own brother with complete impunity. As a monarch, the king was eventually outshone by Julius II, whose magnificent coronation was surpassed only by his triumphant return to Rome after the conquest of Bologna. Moreover, Tedallini was unable to distinguish the behavior of foreigners from that of his compatriots. The French could certainly be cruel, he admitted, as they were at Capua in 1501, where "tutte le donne foro sbordellate." But so could the marchese of Mantua, who killed the prisoners he took at the battle of the Taro. So could Alexander VI, who confiscated the property of the Colonna ("never before has such cruelty been used"). And so could his son Cesare, who left the handsome young Astorre Manfredi to die in the dungeon of Castel Sant'Angelo.

Similarly, none of these writers was able to distinguish the trivial from the histori-cally significant. For Alfani, the entrance of Julius II into Perugia, an event to which Machiavelli was to devote a famous passage in *The Prince,* was no more important than the fireworks display of 1510. For Tassoni, the meeting of the pope and the emperor in 1529 was important only because it increased the traffic along the "strata Claudia" and occasioned magnificent displays, "cum maxima pompa," on the streets of Bologna. For the chroniclers of Fermo, Charles VIII was not nearly as important as Oliverotto Eufreducci, the tyrant who threw babies out of windows and built roads and bridges; and Julius II's campaign to "expel the barbarians from Italy" was far less important than the endless campaigns of the Fermani to punish the arrogance of the Ascolani. For Tomasino, years of war and famine alternated in-explicably with years of peace and plenty. In the winter of 1525 "everyone is intent on celebrating Christmas gloriously, [for] goods are abundant, . . . the artisans are selling their merchandise at good prices . . . , and the citizens are at peace with one another." But in the winter of 1527, for some unknown reason, "the peasants . . . eat such stuff that not even pigs would touch," and in the spring of 1528 the chapels of the city "are so full of dead bodies that they can no longer be buried."

Nevertheless, even the least historically conscious of these chroniclers was affected by the calamity at least to the extent that it gave him more to write about. Paride Grasso became so engrossed with the interminable movements of the papal court under his reckless hero, Julius II, that he began—in accordance with the humanist standards he seems never to have been exposed to—to take careful note also of the motives of the various protagonists of the court ("Deliberatio Papae consistorialis de eundo versus Bononiam . . ."); and the objectivity of his perspicacious observations yielded only when his hero encountered a determined opponent, like that "exec-rabile monstrum ex humanis perdendum," Giovanni Bentivoglio. Montani and his continuators were so impressed by the unending list of horrors they themselves witnessed—the revolt against Oliverotto in 1503, the massacre of two hundred citizens in 1515, and the "new taxes, new billetings, new commissioners" imposed by contending armies in the Marche almost yearly after 1518—that they did not flinch before the still worse horrors reported by a young nun after an hour-long tour of Hell and Purgatory in 1550. Tomasino noted with pride that his native city had become in his day the object of a visit by the king of France, the scene of the wedding of the duke of Ferrara, and the cause of a war between a duke, a pope, and an emperor. His entries grew accordingly longer: 467 pages for the four years between 1525 and 1529, a whole volume for the three years between 1530 and 1532. By the time of his death in 1554 they filled up the equivalent of thirteen quarto volumes in the modern edition. What Tomasino did in Modena, the authors of scores of still unpublished local chronicles and diaries did in the other cities of Italy—Tommaso Donato in Venice, Gianfrancesco Buzzacarini in Padua, the unknown witnesses of "How Pope Julius II took the City of Bologna," "How Duke Ludovico Left Milan and Went to Germany," "What Happened When Charles V and Clement VII Met in Bologna." Only one of them was shocked into silence; but then what he had written up to that point about the rulers of Monferrato was mostly cribbed from Gottfredo Della Chiesa. The physician GIOVANNI CHIABRERA, or ZABRERIA (d. 1498) and the notary GIOVAN ANTONIO CLARO (d.c. 1516) were so impressed by the arrival of the French army on their very doorsteps, so upset about the harsh treatment accorded to the philo-French citizens of Novara, and so apprehensive about the future ("quamobrem tota fremit Italia") that for the first time they admitted more general news reports into the records they had been keeping of local magistrates, storms, and family marriages.[8] Indeed, history writing grew so rapidly in quantity that Tiraboschi, one of the most industrious encyclopedists of the industriously encyclopedic eighteenth century, despaired of ever getting through more than a part of it. "Many [works]," he explained apologetically, "I can only mention briefly; and many others I will have to pass over in silence."[9]

Some historians, on the other hand, were fully prepared to appreciate what many of the chroniclers failed to notice: the unprecedented nature of the events of their day. But they were too obsessed by the spectacular, or "memorable," qualities of those events to pay much attention to their calamitous consequences. ALESSANDRO BENEDETTI (c. 1450–1512) had studied history with Merula. He had read Sallust, the most obvious ancient model for historians of calamities, with Giorgio Valla, the first of the humanists in Venice to realize that the invasion of 1494 was something more than a parade. Moreover, he knew that the popular preachers of the day were confirming from the pulpit the gloomiest predictions of the astrologers; and he soon realized that the behavior of the French troops in Naples confirmed what the papal ambassadors had pointed out to the Senate: that "Italy, formerly mistress of the world, would in a short time be prey to the barbarians." But when, in August 1495, he returned from active duty at the front as a physician to the Venetian army, he thought only of how to make use of an unhoped-for opportunity to outdo Sallust himself. "Quemadmodum Sallustius suum bellum scripsit Iugurthinum, ita tu Carolinem," Valla admonished. Obviously, the battle of the Taro (6 July 1495), which he had just witnessed, was far more "memorable" than any of those described in the *Conspiracy of Catiline* and the *War with Jugurtha*. Better yet, it represented not the penultimate act of a moribund republic but the most recent triumph of an indomitable commonwealth, which justly rewarded itself with a few more bits of land in Puglia. Unfortunately, while editions of Sallust continued to pour from the presses, the *De Bello Carolino* languished for a century in the single Latin edition of 1496 and the single Italian translation of 1549. But that was the fault of the theses, not of the style. For within a few years no one could sincerely accept Benedetti's main thesis: that the triumph of the Venetians had plugged up the last gaps left by nature in the Alpine barrier between France and Italy.[10]

Similarly, JACOPO D'ATRI had been sufficiently instructed in humanist literary standards to merit an appointment as secretary to Francesco Gonzaga, marchese of Mantua. He also realized that the commentary as a literary form, even if written in the vernacular, required a preface on the "causes" of the event to be related (like the family troubles of the Sforza and the Aragonesi) and a brief account of the events immediately preceding it (in this case one and a half pages of gerundic clauses about the march of the French from Asti to Naples). But for Jacopo, the real significance of the battle of the Taro, which he had witnessed and which he described in minute detail, lay in the magnificence of the armies present there. They were "stupendous to behold," he declared. "Everyone affirmed that since the time of the Romans there had never been seen so great a number of men so well ordered." The real significance of the "grave undertaking against Charles VIII" lay in the opportunity it afforded to document the great deeds ("ogni tuo preclaro gesto") of the hero, "for remembrance of things past and no less as an example for those to come." Accordingly, the account of the event itself begins not with the invasion but with the appointment of Francesco as captain-general of the Venetian army. It includes, as Benedetti's does not, an account of Francesco's brief excursion to Naples to help his former employer, King Ferrante, return from Ischia. And it ends, like Benedetti's but independent of it, with Francesco's triumphant entry into Venice after the battle of Novara. That some Italians actually sided with the French, that the efficiency of the Venetian army was impaired by quarrels between the German and Italian mercenaries, that neither patriotism nor ideology but only a personal contract bound the soldiers to the state they supposedly represented: all these were extraneous details that in no way diminished the "summa virtù" of the hero, "in whose hand a decree of fate had placed [the whole responsibility for] the victory over the French."[11]

MARIN SANUDO and DOMENICO MALIPIERO (b. 1428) had also studied with the humanists. Sanudo took the invasion of Charles VIII as an occasion to demonstrate his ability to imitate Caesar: he divided his "commentary" into books, although according to no other apparent criterion than that of length, and he occasionally interrupted his narrative with a bit of background information ("and you should know that the said king of the Romans had for wife *madona* Bianca, sister of the former duke of Milan"). Malipiero took the same event as an occasion for elevating what he had begun many years earlier as a rather sparse diary (four pages for 1485, two short paragraphs for 1489) to the ranks of "annals," with a long digression on "the cause of the coming into Italy of King Charles" at the beginning of the ninety-two pages he dedicated to the year 1494. Both of them appended to what they wrote the complete texts of many official bulletins, letters, and oral communications—like the reports of Caterino Zeno from Persia that were to make Malipiero an important source for twentieth-century historians of the fifteenth-century Near East. Moreover, both of them tried to present the events of the years 1494–95 as a drama—a drama that had been set in motion by the blunders of Il Moro and that was brought to a happy conclusion by the wisdom and the sense of mission of the Senate, which alone was responsible for the victory at the Taro. "What 'Army of the League'?" Sanudo had the doge retort to the Este ambassadors who arrived to congratulate him on Venice's part in the victory. "It is *our* army, and it is *we,* not the league, who paid for it!"

Unfortunately, Sanudo seems to have forgotten his lessons when he turned from Latin to colloquial Venetian. For his prose was so full of run-on sentences and so padded with pointless asides that the Paduan humanist Marco Guazzo had to cross out half of the text and completely rewrite the other half when he tried to make it palatable to the general Italian reading public some fifty years later.[12] Malipiero seems never to have mastered the art of good writing in any language. If the only surviving version of his *Annali veneti* is at least legible, it is because Francesco Longo (d. 1584) completely rearranged the contents in accordance with the more refined tastes of the Italian-reading patricians of the mid-sixteenth century. Moreover, both Sanudo's commitment to thoroughness and Malipiero's honesty detracted somewhat from the strength of their theses. Malipiero had to admit that the Venetians shared some of the responsibility, if not for having provoked the invasion, at least for having permitted it to occur. Sanudo had to admit that Charles's army got safely back to France largely because Venice's much-lauded Greek mercenaries, the *stratioti,* had been too busy packing their booty to follow up their victory. Moreover, Sanudo and Malipiero had to admit that Venice's newly proclaimed policy of maintaining "peace and quiet" in Italy was belied by the actual pursuit of a policy that other Italians had long identified as an aspiration to acquire "the lordship of Italy": rounding out its frontiers in Lombardy and forcing its supposed ally, King Ferrante, to cede them the ports of Puglia. Neither of them could have objected to the thesis implied in the chronicle of another patrician, Pietro Dolfin, who, if not actually educated by humanists, had at least been brought up by a well-educated father. According to Dolfin, the war against Charles VIII was merely one of the several wars that the Venetians had fought, overseas as well as in Italy, for over a half-century. And the next war, the one in which Venice found itself allied with the successor of its former foe against its reluctant ally of 1495, ended triumphantly—and in an all too brief respite from Dolfin's usual plodding style— with the capture and imprisonment of the latter: "Fo per tuta Venetia sonato il campano."[13]

Malipiero may have been aware of these contradictions, for his "annals" drifted back into a chronicle at the conclusion of the year of glory, and they broke off abruptly four years later. But Sanudo eventually became aware that he had mistaken his vocation. When one last foray into acceptable literary forms, a geographical-historical survey of Friuli of 1502, turned out to be as infelicitous as the others, and when still another whining petition to be recognized as official historiographer elicited the same indifferent silence from his fellow senators, he realized that he was much better as a collector of historical materials than as a historian. Accordingly, he dedicated the last three decades of his life exclusively to recording every act of the Venetian government in almost daily entries and to backing up his record with complete texts of almost every document issued by or addressed to the government. By the time of his death in 1533 he had filled the equivalent of the fifty-six thick volumes that were finally published as the famous *Diarii* between 1879 and 1902.[14] And he thus furnished future historians of early sixteenth-century Venice and Italy with an almost inexhaustible source of information.

From the perspective of the capital of a still growing empire, then, the events of 1494–95 represented the climax of over a century of spectacular triumphs. But from the perspective of the chronically misgoverned cities of the Romagna, and particularly from the most misgoverned of them, Forlì, these events represented merely one more of a series of tragedies that had culminated, six years earlier, in the outburst of violence that followed the assassination of Gerolamo Riario, the sole *signore* ever to try turning a tyranny into a monarchy, in April 1488.[15] "Oh reader, open your eyes to our sufferings: I am sure that never in our Italy has there been seen such cruelty as that which took place in Forlì during these two months," moaned LEONE COBELLI. The city "has fallen into such opprobrium, misery, calamity, and poverty; the virtues are no longer esteemed but disdained; and nothing is heard but weeping." Papal dominion offered no solution: "these dogs of priests," noted Cobelli, "enemies of human nature, recognize neither services nor servants." Nor did the advent of "Madonna prudentissima," the soon to be famous Caterina Sforza. She wasted her resources on her lovers, threw Cobelli into jail, and failed to save Forlì from the main local consequences of the French invasion: the occupation of its territory by Neapolitan troops and the sack of several of its subject towns by French troops.[16]

Cobelli's successor, ANDREA BERNARDI, or NOVACULA (1450–1520), the son of an immigrant Bolognese barber who rose to a position of some prominence in the magistracies of his adopted city, was somewhat less pessimistic. Cesare Borgia had just given the citizens some respite from "our great misfortunes, similar to the pains of hell," and "the city [had been] enriched with magnificent and admirable habitations," he noted. Moreover, he so successfully extended his chronicle to include the past of Forlì and the present of all Italy that the pope awarded him the title of "historicus laureatus Forliviensis."[17] Yet even Bernardi realized that something had gone wrong—if not actually since 1479, when a solar eclipse had portended "molte varie e diverse cose," at least since 1493, when the cardinal of San Pietro in Vincula started pressuring the "rei de Ferancia" to come across the Alps. And he too despaired of a solution: "I have written so that those who will be born after us can fully understand our own misfortunes and can guard themselves from such tribulations *infinita secula seculorum,"* he wrote. But just how they might do that, he was at a loss to say.

What to the chroniclers of the Romagna seemed to be merely one more of many calamities soon came to be viewed in other parts of Italy as a turning point between one epoch and another. In Puglia, for instance, calamities were no novelty. The Turkish occupation of Otranto had been followed by the Venetian occupation of the other coastal cities—and by the atrocities, fully worthy of the worst Turks, inflicted upon the inhabitants by the Venetian *stratioti*. The public drawing-and-quartering of an "infinite number" of rebels in 1485 had been followed by King Ferrante's dinner party of 1486—when most of the guests were hacked to pieces before they finished eating. No one was particularly surprised, then, when Charles VIII walked into Naples "without breaking a lance" and when all the towns of the kingdom "opened their gates to him as if he were sent by God." But after Puglia had again been torn apart by another year-long civil war, even ANTONELLO CONIGER was dumbfounded.[18] "Oh power of God," he exclaimed, "how much you are to be esteemed and feared. Who would ever have believed that in less than two years the Kingdom of Naples could have five kings?" In Campania, on the other hand, calamities had long been disguised behind a facade of public spectacles; and whenever such entertainment was lacking at home, a small-town chronicler like SILVESTRO GUARINO could always find it in abundance during his frequent visits to the nearby capital. Hence, his only misgiving about the entrance of Charles VIII into Naples was that it did not quite come up to the standard set by the funeral ceremonies for Ferrante I.[19] But when Charles VIII's soldiers went rampant in Capua, he began to change his mind; and he was fully sympathetic to his fellow citizens who rose in arms against the French garrison in their city. Then when the soldiers of Louis XII emulated their predecessors in 1501, he gave up hope in the ability of the subjects of the kingdom to do anything to defend themselves; and he merely recorded, without a trace of emotion, the arrivals of whatever new rulers destiny chose to send them—a French viceroy in 1501, a Spanish viceroy in 1502, a Spanish king in 1507.[20]

In Naples itself the invasion was first seen as merely one element of a drama that began with the coronation of Alfonso II in 1494 and ended two years later, when King Federico finally captured the last fortress still loyal to the French. Indeed, the climax of the drama was furnished not by the entrance of Charles VIII but by the return of Ferrante II from his exile in Ischia: "and every person, great and humble, shouted 'cut them up!' [*ferro! ferro!*]; and immediately all the Frenchmen they could find were killed."[21] But by 1499 the first invasion was clearly seen to have been the prelude to a second; and what happened in Milan in 1500 was considered prophetic of what indeed did happen to Naples in 1501—when King Federico "displayed to the populace the text of the league concluded between Spain, France, and the pope . . . to divide this kingdom among them."[22] By 1508, when the Kingdom had become a dependency of the Spanish crown, the invasion was finally understood to have wiped out in a few months what the Aragonese monarchs had spent fifty years of untiring labor to construct: national unity and the rule of law. For GIULIANO PASSERO, the reign of "the glorious lord King Ferrante I" and of his collaborator and heir, Alfonso ("no prince of the time had a nobler spirit than he"), had become an irretrievably lost golden age.[23] Those Neapolitans who had not wept with Ferrante II when, abandoned by all, he had slipped out of the Castle on 21 February 1494, soon learned to "desire [his return] as ardently as Jews wait for the Messiah." The hysterical welcome they accorded him on his return ("Since God made the world there has never been on earth such joy") was fully justified by Ferrante's recognition of the popular government that the citizens themselves had created upon the departure of the French. Alas, their joy was short-lived: Ferrante died prematurely, and Federico's coronation was accompanied by "certain prodigies" that heralded the demise of the Aragonese dynasty a few years later. And the prodigies turned out to be more prophetic than anyone imagined when, in 1510, a Spanish viceroy tried to force upon the Neapolitans the Spanish institution they most detested, the Inquisition. If anyone was to blame for this calamity, it was the "baruni" and the "jentil'huomini," whose secret delegation to France in 1502 wrecked any possibility of maintaining the independence of the Kingdom. Eventually even Giuliano succumbed to the inevitable. He left his job as a silk weaver in Naples and went off as a soldier to northern Italy in the army of Naples' most recent foreign ruler.

From Savonarola to the Medici Restoration

In Florence, on the other hand, what turned out to have been a calamity for the Neapolitans proved instead to have been an unexpected opportunity for erecting a new political order. To be sure, the precise judgments expressed concerning the accomplishments of this new order varied according to the rank, education, and temperament of the authors. Some of them were wealthy patricians—like GIOVANNI CAMBI IMPORTUNI (1458–1535),[24] FRANCESCO GADDI,[25] and TOMMASO GINORI (b. 1480),[26] whose social position was recognized by their election to important political offices, after as well as before, 1494. Indeed, Alamanno (to 1499), NERI (to 1508), and ALESSANDRO (1468–1532) RINUCCINI wrote diaries largely out of respect for the family tradition launched by their forefather, Filippo di Cino.[27] And their more famous fellow patrician, FRANCESCO GUICCIARDINI (1483–1540), wrote history as well as a diary, just as he added a law degree, a brilliant marriage, and a spectacularly precocious career in the diplomatic service to the already notable advantages of a good birth, in order to make his illustrious family still more illustrious.[28]

Some of these Florentine historians, on the other hand, were from less prominent families—like Marsilio Ficino's nephew-in-law BIAGIO BUONACCORSI (c. 1472–c. 1526), the author of a polished chronicle as well as of traditional personal *ricordi* and a smattering of verse, who lost his position in the Chancery, and hence all but a fraction of the salary he needed to supplement the rent he received from a small farm, at the same time that his colleague and close friend Machiavelli lost his.[29] Some were men of letters. Gaddi had been a member of the Platonic Academy and the author of several humanist orations; and PIERO PARENTI had been an intimate friend of Ficino, Poliziano, Argiropoulos, and Bruni's translator, Donato Acciaiuoli, all of whom he mentioned in his work.[30] Some were of humbler circumstances— like BARTOLOMEO MASI (b. 1480), the son of a wood seller and the son-in-law of a baker,[31] and LUCA LANDUCCI, a spice dealer who spent most of his time managing his shop at the Canto de' Tornaquinci.[32] Most were men of piety as well as of politics: Ginori reestablished the Confraternity of the Misericordia, Parenti wrote sermons, and both were active members of the Confraternity of San Vincenzo, to which Alamanno Rinuccini also belonged. Some wrote traditional Florentine family diaries. Some wrote vernacular chronicles on the model of Villani, "simply and purely without adornment of words, in order to remember . . . those things that come to my attention" (Cambi). Some wrote humanist chronicles.[33] And one of them, Guicciardini, wrote what has been called a work of political reflection,[34] but what is also a work fully consonant with the canons of humanist historiography, the *Storie fiorentine*.

Few of these chroniclers and historians paid much attention to the arrival of Charles VIII in Italy. But all agreed that his arrival in Florence constituted "one of the most splendid things that had ever been seen" (Masi), "as magnificent an event as [any] Florence had witnessed for a long time" (Guicciardini). Equally splendid was the reception the Florentines provided for the king: "a triumphal affair, [one in which] everything was done magnificently and well" (Landucci). Most of them were a bit disappointed by Charles himself, "for, indeed, he was a very small man," with "an ugly face, an aquiline nose, and fingers that stuck together" (Masi). Some were impressed by the fear that had preceded his arrival ("eravamo tutti spaventati"—Ginori). And some of them were upset by the behavior both of the king and of his soldiers before their departure. But none of them looked upon the French as enemies, not even Parenti, who called them "barbarians without faith or humanity" and who later turned against Savonarola over the question of a French alliance. After all, the duke of Milan had been responsible for sending them into Florentine territory. The Florentines themselves had been responsible for provoking their hostility by hanging onto a senseless alliance with the king of Naples (Ginori). And the soldiers in Florentine service soon proved themselves to be as "cruel and wicked" as the French—most notably when they massacred the inhabitants of Ponte di Secca (Landucci).

The expedition of Charles VIII, then, was an isolated event, even for TRIBALDO DE'ROSSI, who tried, and failed, to turn his diary into a "Chronicle of the Coming of the King of France."[35] It was unrelated to any of the events that preceded it—either to the monster that was born in Volterra in 1489, or to the lightning bolt that hit

Brunelleschi's *lanterna* in 1491, or to the dire sermons of a preacher whose name Tribaldo could not remember in 1407. And any adverse effects it might have had in Florence were quickly checked by Savonarola, "a man held to be a great servant of God and one of holy life" (Ginori), who got the French out of the city in December 1494, and kept them from coming back again in June 1495. What made the year 1494 significant was not the expedition but what accompanied it, apparently coincidentally: the fall of the fifty-year-old Medici regime. Admittedly, that regime had not been without some merit—particularly for those chroniclers, like Ginori, who had been very closely connected with the ruling family. Lorenzo had been "a man of great intelligence and prudence" (Rinuccini), "one of the wisest in all Italy" (Masi), whose death had been "mourned by the populace . . . [and by] all those in Italy who excelled in letters, painting, and similar arts." Even though "under him the city [had not been] free," admitted Guicciardini, "it could not have had a better tyrant or a more pleasant one." Nevertheless, Lorenzo had all but destroyed what his grandfather Cosimo had left of the old republic. He had robbed the public treasury to pay off his private debts. He had ruined the meritorious great—including the father of the chronicler Cambi. And he had raised up the avaricious humble, "sceleratissimi e audacissimi huomini" (Rinuccini), like Piero da Bibbiena, the "uppity peasant" who became "king of the wicked" (Cambi). Moreover, whatever good Lorenzo had done was quickly dissipated by his son. "It is impossible to imagine anything worse," commented Alamanno Rinuccini, than "the proud, greedy, cruel tyranny of Piero di Lorenzo." And his expulsion from the city was accordingly attributed to "the grace of God and of the Virgin Mary":

> Giubiliano con allegro et alto core, Rendialli gratie et laudi et sommo honore che ha vicitato la sua plebe mesta.
>
> (Parenti)

Unfortunately, joy eventually gave way to disillusionment. For all its pretenses to resolving the age-old Florentine constitutional question, for all its consciousness of being the first political manifestation of "the fullness of time" (Landucci), the new *Governo largo* failed to mitigate the disastrous rise in food prices and unemployment in 1496 ("I cannot possibly count the number of women and girls, men and boys, who are wandering around the city in search of food"—Tribaldo). It raised huge sums of money with taxes and forced loans that even Lorenzo would not have dared to impose and then threw it away on futile, or badly managed, projects. It isolated Florence diplomatically from the rest of Italy for the sake of an alliance with the French that the French themselves consistently refused to honor, and it was rewarded for its fidelity in 1499 with another demand for a huge "loan." Worse yet, it betrayed both of the two principles upon which it had been founded: freedom and justice. It sacrificed the first in a desperate effort to snuff out internal dissent. It did so by letting one man, Francesco Valori, dominate elections to the magistrates and by letting a hysterical minority, "the party of the friar," terrorize the reluctant majority into acquiescence. It sacrificed the second when it denied the conspirators of 1497 the right of appeal to the Great Council; and that the conspirators fully deserved their fate could not hìde the harsh truth that their condemnation had violated the very constitution the government was meant to defend.

Worst of all, the government failed to maintain the integrity of Florence's territorial state, notwithstanding the promises of Savonarola that God would soon give it a much bigger one. "How miserable to think that the Genoese, the Sienese, and the Lucchese, who just a short while ago used to tremble before our might, now go about tearing up and taking over our territory," exclaimed Guicciardini. The most disastrous loss was Pisa, the main port of exit for Florentine manufactured goods. An initial campaign against the rebels succeeded only in depopulating some of the towns in the Pisano. Diplomatic pressures abroad produced nothing more than empty promises and the substitution of the Venetians for the French and the duke of Milan as the suppliers of arms and money to the rebels. Finally, in 1500, a large army was dispatched under the supervision of the commissioner Luca degli Albizzi, whose *gesta* were duly recorded in a historical *relazione* by the chronicler Buonaccorsi.[36] But the promised reinforcements from Emilia never arrived, in spite of the huge subsidies paid to the cardinal of Rouen. The general Paolo Vitelli refused to go through the hole that his artillery had blown out of the wall; and the government could only manifest its fury by executing him for disobedience. Then the rebellion of Arezzo in 1502, which was suppressed only with the help of French soldiers, forced besiegers to retreat ignominiously without having accomplished anything. Neither Buonaccorsi nor the government managed to understand the effectiveness of a bold new constitutional innovation adopted by the Pisan particiate. By admitting even peasants to full civic rights, they gave the rebellion a popular support all but unknown in the rest of Italy.[37] The consequent vitality of the Pisan resistance surprised even the fiercely patriotic local chroniclers. For them it was "an incredible feat for a city with such a small population."[38] Their pride helped them put up with the depredations of the soldiers of their much-lauded liberator Charles VIII. And it helped them accept the huge taxes voted by the Senate just at a time when the expulsion of the Florentine business agents left many of their fellow citizens without jobs. Not until the battle of Agnadello in 1509 cut off the flow of Venetian aid did Pisa finally surrender. And while the generous terms of the capitulation silenced the Pisan chroniclers by belying their patriotic rhetoric, it did very little to restore the confidence of the Florentine chroniclers in their own government.

The Florentine chroniclers still remained loyal to the regime, to be sure; and they were somewhat encouraged in their loyalty when, in 1502, the creation of a lifetime president *(gonfaloniere a vita)* seemed at last to provide the kind of consistent political direction that had been lacking since the fall of Savonarola ("Every change in office brings about a change in government," complained Parenti). Yet their loyalty resulted mostly from their reluctance to accept what was then the only possible alternative: a restoration of the Medici. None of them had yet begun to believe in the pre-1492 golden age that had already been adumbrated by Ficino's biographer, Giovanni Corsi, and that was to receive its classic formulation in Guicciardini's *Storia d'Italia* many years later.[39] None of them, furthermore, was yet willing to follow Guicciardini in projecting an ideal alternative some one hundred years back into history.

Then at 18 hours on 29 August 1512 the Florentines were suddenly faced with a calamity that they could not ignore. An Imperial-Papal army broke through the walls of Prato; and by the time it left, three weeks later, most of the peasant militiamen had been butchered. Most of the cloistered nuns had been sexually abused ("sodomitandole bruttamente"), at least one priest had been cut into pieces and boiled, all the houses had been divested of their furnishings, 5,560 residents had been killed, and most of the rest had been tortured—or at least so said JACOPO MODESTI, who had been an eyewitness.[40] Some of the survivors were fortunate—like the resident citizens of Colle, who were ransomed by their city council for the enormous sum of 5,000 *ducati*. But some were less fortunate. ANDREA BOCCINERI and his brother Piero were kept bound to a pillar by the neck, hands, and feet while their father went to Florence in search of money. They were then "bought" by the papal commissar in Bologna; and when their father was unable to repay the purchase price, he promptly put them back in chains, amid fleas, lice, and their own excrement, with nothing but their summer clothes to protect them from mid-November temperatures. They were sold back to the Spanish, who dragged them behind horses to Modena, where their father too was thrown into a dungeon when he turned up with only part of the money. They finally escaped only after tricking a guard into untying them, killing him, and crawling up through a chimney.[41]

> Greece never suffered such tribulation
> No town was ever subjected to such affliction
> As was Prato. . . .[42]

The chroniclers did not hesitate to fix the responsibility for the calamity, not on the "Moors of Granada, a cruel race without a trace of faith,"[43] in the Spanish army, but on the very regime they had once hailed as the solution for all their problems. The regime admitted blind faith, rather than prudence, as the guiding principle of its foreign policy, even after its supposed French allies had once again abandoned them. It had permitted internal opposition to degenerate into open subversion—to the point, indeed, where the commissioners of the army did exactly "the opposite of what they were ordered to do" (Masi). It had sacrificed the interests of its dominion to the interests of the capital city—by sending subjects, not citizens, into Prato and then leaving them there without ammunition. Apparently, concluded SIMON DI GORO BRAMI of Colle, "the obedience and fidelity of our town toward our lords the

Florentines has cost us far too much."[44] Finally, the regime had promoted mediocrity and indecision at the expense of intelligence and action. The Apennine passes were left unguarded. The fortresses of the Mugello were abandoned without a shot. And the professional army was left standing idle just out of sight of the invaders.

Hence, none of the chroniclers was particularly surprised when the regime itself fell victim to the calamity it had permitted to occur. None of them shed a tear over the execution of two hotheads in 1513 "for having wanted to liberate the city"—not even Luca Della Robbia, who, as an editor of Quintus Curtius and Caesar, should have known better than to end a commentary with speculation about whether the plotters were already in heaven.[45] One of the chroniclers was actually happy: BAR-TOLOMEO CERRETANI (1474–1524). For Cerretani owed his family fortune to Lorenzo's patronage of his father, and he himself had been closely associated with the disgruntled oligarchs in the circle of Bernardo Rucellai, "that most singular man" (Cerretani's epithet), whose *De Bello Italico* he apparently read in preparation for writing his own.[46] And none of them found any difficulty accommodating themselves to the regime that was imposed on them in its place, particularly after patriotic enthusiasm over the election of Giovanni de' Medici as Pope Leo X erased the memory of what had been, as a matter of fact, a coup d'état. Some of them accepted offices from their new lords—Ginori entered the Council of Seventy at the moment of its creation in 1513. Some of them followed Cambi's advice to return to "the ancient mode of life, quiet and sedentary," and thus stayed out of trouble. This accommodation was facilitated by their realization that the calamity of 1512 had been the inevitable consequence of a series of calamities that had begun in 1494. What to Cambi in 1508–9 had seemed to be calamities only for the Milanese and the Venetians—who, by the way, richly deserved them—now turned out to be calamities for all Italians, whose interests the Florentines had become accustomed to regarding as the opposite of their own. Similarly, the new constitution of 1495 turned out to be not the beginning of a bright new era, but the end of an era that could not longer be recaptured. This accommodation was also facilitated by the care with which the post-1512 regime avoided committing itself to ideological principles like the ones the pre-1512 regime had notoriously failed to live up to.

Eventually, to be sure, some sort of ideological justification of the Medici government was proposed—not by the Medici themselves but by one of the faithful and able servants they had inherited from Soderini: FRANCESCO VETTORI (1474–1539), a friend and correspondent of Machiavelli and Guicciardini, who took time off from a busy diplomatic career in the mid-20s to write a biography of the younger Lorenzo de' Medici, duke of Urbino. According to Vettori, one-man, or one-family rule in Florence was justified by its efficiency—by its ability to "compose the differences among the citizens" and to "administer correctly the moneys of the commune."[47] But after the Medici regime had proved to be as ephemeral as its predecessor, and after Vettori himself had turned from writing political dialogues and fictionalized travelogues to writing humanist history,[48] he ended up stating explicitly the thesis that his predecessors had come tacitly to accept after 1512. Politics and ideology, he concluded, were compatible only in the imaginations of utopian philosophers like Plato and an Englishman named Thomas More. In reality, all governments are tyrannies, particularly in a city like Florence, which "has always been subject to parties and factions." The only difference among them consists in the distinction between who tyrannizes and who is tyrannized. Anyone who thinks he can find good government in this world, like his friend Machiavelli, should try getting a poor man heard in a French parlement or suing a patrician in Venice. Anyone who thinks Italy will benefit from throwing out the barbarians should note how Italian soldiers quarrel among themselves and how the most prominent Italian prince, the pope, plunders subjects and church alike for the benefit of his family. Constitutional governments inevitably put power into the hands of well-meaning weaklings like Piero Soderini, whose indecision during the sack of Prato Vettori recounted in clipped Sallustian periods. One-man governments depend wholly on the extraordinary tact of such exceptional princes as Lorenzo the Magnificent and Lorenzo duke of Urbino, who are inevitably succeeded by such incompetents as Piero de' Medici and the Cardinal of Cortona. True, the tiny minority of honest and able men are obliged to go on trying; and Vettori lived up to this principle by cooperating with Clement VII, Alessandro, and Cosimo de' Medici to rescue what was left of Florence after the siege of 1529–30. But all they could hope to accomplish in the long run was to mitigate the effects of the calamities that, since the first great calamity of 1494, had become endemic in Italian life.

The French in Milan

What took the Florentine historians and chroniclers eighteen years to discover became clear to their Milanese colleagues in only five years. True, Charles VIII had never set foot in Milan. None of the Milanese historians of the late fifteenth century had given the slightest hint that the current golden age would not last forever. And when the first calamity finally struck the city itself, it was much less severe than the sack of Prato. But the Milanese historians had two notable advantages. First, they were all men of considerable political as well as social prominence and could base much of what they wrote on direct personal observation. AMBROGIO DA PAULLO (b.c. 1470) was the manager of the ducal estates near Crema, who, after a brief term in prison upon the fall of Il Moro, switched sides and thus won his job back.[49] FRANCESCO MURALTI was a patrician of Como who represented his city at the ducal court.[50] GIOVAN PIETRO CAGNOLA (c. 1432–1507) was a jurist, a diplomat, and an army officer.[51] Giovanni Tolentino (1471–1517), whose beautifully copied and illuminated *Commentaria Rerum Potissimum in Insubria Gestarum* has unfortunately not yet been printed, was knighted in 1486, sent on an embassy in 1489, and twice visited by Louis XII at his villa at Bereguardo.[52] Second, the Milanese writers were all humanists by education, and they all at least tried to write according to humanist canons of historiography. Most of them prepared for writing by studying, and sometimes plundering, Corio, the official humanist historian at the court of Lodovico il Moro.[53] GIORGIO FLORIO[54] was so faithful to the rule that limited a commentary to a single "event" that he broke up his history of his own times under separate titles: one "De Bello Gallico" on the expedition of Charles VIII, one on Julius II's campaign against Bologna, one on the civil war in Genoa. Paullo departed from standard commentary form only in occasionally trying to show off by imitating the poetry of Vergil. Muralti departed from a Livian annals form only when the occurrence of a particularly "memorable" event, like the arrival of Charles VIII at Asti, forced him to divide one year into two parts. Indeed, he went beyond his models by including much information on art and economics—on Il Moro's building projects in Pavia and Vigevano and on the establishment of silk manufacturing in Como, all of which better enabled him to judge the character of his age. In spite of his claim to write "not as a wise historian (a title certainly inappropriate to me) but as a citizen more curious than learned," GIOVAN ANDREA PRATO (b. 1488)[55] departed from his model only in resurrecting discredited myths about the origins of Milan, in showing off his knowledge of ancient poetry, and in occasionally succumbing to an irresistible miracle—a statue of the Virgin that moved its eyes in 1499, a poor man whose paralysis was transferred to an arrogant young nobleman in 1504. But he felt obliged to give ancient as well as modern place names in his Herodotean geographical descriptions of Spain and France, since he was sure that most of his readers, like himself, would have known of them only through Tacitus and Caesar.

Thus the literary form they adopted forced the Milanese historians to put current events in the perspective of past events. As early as 1497 one of them began to have premonitions of disaster. Cagnola's survey of the preceding three centuries was governed by a single theme: the efforts of Italians, or at least certain Italians, first to get the barbarians out of Italy ("liberare Italia da le mane de le barbariche et externe nacione che la vexaveno") and then to keep them out. Since the main cause of foreign intervention lay in the tendency of Italians to quarrel among themselves, the main protagonists of this historical process were great princes—those, in other words, who were virtuous enough and strong enough to overcome dissension within the city, dissension among the cities, and the machinations of the chief sowers of all dissension, the Florentines. The first Visconti had stamped out the civil wars between the Guelfs and the Ghibellines, with which the Florentines, according to Cagnola, had infected all Italy. Bernarbò Visconti had helped restore the Papacy to Rome and Italians to the Papacy, in spite of the opposition of the Eight Saints of Florence. Giangaleazzo, "that splendid [*clarissimo*] prince, of handsome aspect and stature, elegant and learned in letters, of eloquent speech and highest intelligence," had brought peace to all of northern Italy. Francesco Sforza, "a glorious, magnanimous, liberal lord, an invincible captain, a man of singular virtue," had saved Milan from the "discord and sedition" among the patricians of the Ambrosian Republic that almost ended in its conquest by the Venetians. And Lodovico il Moro had been largely responsible for saving Italy from the most recent threat to its independence by chasing Charles VIII back across the Alps after the battle of the Taro. Cagnola's historical vision was apparently as optimistic as that of Simonetta or Corio—except, that is, for one minor detail. In deliberately omitting any reference to the questions that most of his contemporaries were debating—namely, how Charles VIII ever got into Italy in the first place—he suggested that the guardians of Italian independence might well turn out to have been its destroyers. And the end of the cycle might return to its beginning, when another foreign army, that of Frederick Barbarossa, "had visited such cruelty" on the guardians' homeland "that nothing more horrible has ever been heard."

What first turned Cagnola's premonition into a fact for his successors was not the second French invasion, which overthrew the Sforza dynasty and reduced Milan to the status of a dependency of the king of France. It was rather the sack of the houses of the pro-Sforza patricians after the flight of Il Moro in 1499 and the sack of the houses of the pro-French patricians upon his brief return in 1500. The barbarians were discovered to be at home, not abroad. They were on the streets of Milan. They were in the palaces and *piazze* of Genoa, where plebians rivaled patricians in committing "homocidia, rapinae, stupra, incestus, adulteria" (Florio). And they were at the gates of Vigevano, where Il Moro's own subjects had to pay some 15,000 *fiorini* to get his soldiers out of town. "A furore populi libera me Domine!" cried Prato. Accordingly, the French army at first appeared to be merely the instruments of Il Moro's exiled rival, the "astute" general Gian Jacopo Trivulzio, who demonstrated his dedication to law and order by hanging three Gascon soldiers for minor thievery on the morrow of his entrance on 6 September 1499. And Louis XII was greeted as Trivulzio's ally two weeks later, when "almost the entire population" turned out to pay him honor in one of the most splendid triumphal entries Milan had ever seen.

It did not take the Milanese historians long, however, to realize that the calamity of their times amounted to something far more serious and more enduring than a momentary return to the days of the Guelfs and Ghibellines or of the Ambrosian Republic. Prato interrupted his narrative of the first occupation of Milan to provide some bits of horrifying evidence in support of the proverb, "There is no fury like that of the French." And Paullo had to admit that peace under French occupation meant that the French commander was free to snatch citizens off the street and hold them for ransom in the castle. Worse yet, the French were soon followed by the "Germans, the Spanish, and a thousand other barbarian nations" (Prato), who violated the law of nature expressed in the Bergamese proverb, "Dio ha fatto le monti per tramontani stia delà et Taliani di zà" (Paullo), and who, "covetous of Italy, have, and still are, tearing it to pieces" (Prato). By 1512 it was possible to reduce the "ruin ... of this poor, miserable, unhappy Italy" to statistics: 146,410 dead from military engagements alone. And Paullo admitted that the figure was probably far short of the true one.

Having identified the phenomenon, the humanist historians of Milan were then obliged to search for its "causes." None of them was yet willing to concede a role to "fortune," which, said Florio, was just a word used by men to cover up their own misdeeds. Only one of them bothered to look in the direction that Il Moro's observant ambassadors might well have indicated: to the invaders themselves. France, noted Florio, was full of generals and soldiers well schooled in arts of war. But now that "all Gaul is at peace," free both "of domestic discord and of annoyance from its neighbors," they had nothing more to do. All the others agreed with their colleagues elsewhere in Italy that the fault lay not abroad but at home. "None of this would ever have occurred," insisted Paullo, "had our gentlemen been united among themselves." The first culprits were the assassins of Duke Galeazzo in 1476, who first sowed the seeds of discord in the ruling family. The second culprit was Duchess Isabella, who, wrongly injured, wrongly tried to get her father to interfere in the internal affairs of Milan. The third culprit was Cardinal Ascanio Sforza, who bribed the College of Cardinals into electing a barbarian as pope in 1492 and then plundered the churches of Milan to pay for his brother's soldiers. But the chief culprit of all was Il Moro himself: "Occasio omnium malorum extitit Ludovicus Sfortia cognomento Mauras" (Muralti). Il Moro surrounded himself with "vile and abject" men, who betrayed him the moment he got into trouble, while "oppressing the good men of noble blood in Milan" (Paullo). He deliberately enticed Charles VIII into Italy with tempting stories about the wonders of Naples and about the ease with which it could be conquered—all of which is recounted in the speech of his ambassadors that Muralti then and Guicciardini later copied from Corio. Finally, he alienated his subjects, first by crushing them with extraordinary taxes and second by assassinating his nephew, who became as popular after death as he had been ridiculous before. And his subjects justly repaid him for his misdeeds by crying "Mora Il Moro!" as he was hauled through the streets of Asti on his way to death in a French prison.

Once the causes were identified, the historians went on to look for a remedy; but at this point they ran into serious difficulty. A return to an independent duchy was out of the question, for it soon became clear that Trivulzio was the servant of Louis XII and not vice versa. Another solution also proved to be untenable: have the Milanese decide once and for all which foreigners they wanted as rulers. In the first place, none of the foreigners seemed particularly interested in what the Milanese wanted, and in the second place the Milanese themselves turned out to be as unable to decide in the 1510s as they had been in 1447 ("some draw to one side, others to the other"—Prato). That left only one possible solution: pretend that King Louis was unlike the rest of the French, and place full confidence in him. "The clemency of

King Louis of France far surpasses our perfidity," asserted Prato. "Whoever rises to dominion through hard work and virtue," insisted Florio, "will be rewarded with prosperity in all things." Because Louis, like the Roman senators of old, "never did anything without virtue," he was sure to bring peace and happiness to Milan as he had already to Genoa. Unfortunately this solution required the historians to skip over much of what actually happened in Milan during the twelve years of Louis's rule. Indeed, Muralti became increasingly preoccupied with his personal affairs in Como, and Prato skipped over the four years after 1501 with barely one paragraph per year. Finally, in 1512, the solution collapsed. And much as Prato would have liked to attribute the restoration of Massimiliano Sforza to the "will of God," he knew that it would last no longer than the ephemeral union of such unlikely allies as the pope, the king of the Romans, the king of Spain, the Venetians, and the Swiss, upon whom Massimiliano's tenure in office depended.

Agnadello

Since they had long since learned how to turn into benefits for themselves the calamities suffered by the Neapolitans, the Florentines, and the Milanese, the Venetians were wholly unprepared for the calamity that at last struck them too in 1509. They had no historians at all, only two diarists: Sanudo and GIROLAMO PRIULI. The diarists responded to the calamity by multiplying the length of their diaries: the three volumes which Priuli had accumulated during the eleven years since his return from a business trip to London suddenly expanded into a whole volume (427 pages in the modern edition) covering only the months between June and October 1509.[56] But Sanudo had long since given up trying to write history; and Priuli, even after a number of vain attempts to correct what his modern editor calls "gross errors of form and substance," and even after having made sure that his work would be preserved for the benefit of "our most wise and worthy readers," felt obliged to appeal to "other [more] elegant and prudent writers" to "supply what is and what will be lacking" in what he himself wrote. Priuli had been aware that all was not well with Venice as early as 1503, when the price of spices dropped precipitously. But he had never suspected that the Venetian government was anything but a model of prudence and virtue. The rewards it had distributed to its veterans of the Taro were "an act most worthy . . . of being praised for all eternity"; and its abandonment of Il Moro in 1499 had been perfectly justified by the danger which that "father of all traitors" constantly posed to their western frontier, even when he was supposedly an ally. Moreover, since he knew nothing of history, since he could not even remember whether Vicenza or Padua had first submitted to Venetian rule, he was incapable of seeing any connection between the wars that were tearing apart the rest of Italy on one hand and the expectations of the German spice merchants and the arrogance of the sultan of Egypt on the other. Indeed, he had hailed the French occupation of Milan in 1500—as did his fellow citizens, "with fireworks, feasting, and expressions of joy for three days in a row"—because he was sure it would guarantee peace in Italy ("non sarà causa de tenir più la Itallia in guera").

Nevertheless, Priuli was at least conscious of the gravity of what had taken place at Agnadello. "I do not want either to go on writing or to stop writing," he exclaimed in one of his typical unstructured periods, about "how the tormented and sorrowful people of Venice cannot desist from . . . lamenting this so great ruin; for the tongue will not go where the tooth is in pain." After all, he may have been only a "modest merchant and banker," who "kept away from political intrigues," as Roberto Cessi insists. But at least his family bore part of the responsibility for what had happened: his father Lorenzo (according to R. Fulin) had held some of the highest offices in the republic—as *avagador di comun* in 1498 and 1500 and as a member of the Council of Ten *(Dieci)* in 1501, 1502, 1505, and 1508. Moreover, he himself was personally affected by the ruin of the republic when it brought about the collapse of his banking firm three years later. What consolation he could find was sparse indeed: the patriotic spirit of the inhabitants of Venice ("everyone prepared himself for every eventuality in order to be able to defend his country bravely"), the loyalty of the lower classes of Vicenza, the sympathy of the Paduans who accompanied the fleeing rectors to their boat. Furthermore, the very gravity of the calamity led him to look for explanations, or at least for scapegoats. To some extent it was the fault of "fortune," he decided, without bothering to define what he meant by that term. To some extent it was the fault of Venice's enemies, who were motivated solely by greed and envy. To a greater extent it was the fault of the Venetians as a whole: they had offended the Paduans by buying up some two-thirds of their land, and they had offended God by showing insufficient respect for his churches and shrines. But above all, it was the fault of the patricians. "Li signori venetiani," Priuli pointed out, "no longer resemble their ancient progenitors." Instead of "defying danger for the honor and exaltation of their country," they "nourish themselves on delicate and soft things and lasciviousness and delicacies" *(sic)* and have thus become "lazy, spineless, and effeminate." Even their decision to reconquer the Terraferma, instead of, as some suggested, to return to a policy of cultivating their commercial interests and their maritime empire, was taken solely for the purpose of recuperating their investments in land.[57]

That was not a very profound explanation, particularly in comparison with those offered by observers in the subject cities. Some of these observers were chroniclers, who took advantage of the crisis to resurrect the once rich but long dormant chronicle tradition of the Marca. One was the Veronese patrician JACOPO RIZZONI,[58] the nephew of an important official in the Roman Curia who followed the model of his Veronese predecessor, Pier Zagata. And other such chroniclers seem to have been the Paduan patricians Gian Francesco Buzzacarini and Jacopo Bruto and the Friulian patricians Gregorio Amaseo and Nicolò Monticoli, whose eyewitness reports, respectively, of the siege of Padua and the sack of Udine (1511) are still available only in manuscript.[59] Some, on the other hand, were humanists. Such was ELIA CAVRIOLI, or CAPRIOLI, of Brescia (d. 1519), whose taste for miscellaneous astrological details made him more "inclined toward fantasy and arbitrary reconstructions" than might be expected from his prefatory appeals to Sallust and Suetonius.[60] Such may have been the chancellor of Padua, GIAN DOMENICO PASSARINI. And such, certainly, was LUIGI DA PORTO (1485–1529), who was educated at the court of Urbino and befriended by the Veneto humanists Giovan Giorgio Trissino and Pietro Bembo while he was serving as a captain in the Venetian army. Indeed, Da Porto went beyond accepted humanist forms of history writing by blending them with a form previously used only for political and philosophical discourse: the personal letter; and the new form that emerged succeeded so well in juxtaposing historical reflections with minute-by-minute news reports that no one ever dared accept the author's challenge to rewrite it "in a higher style and a more praiseworthy language as an open and diffuse history."[61]

At first Venice's former subjects considered their masters' calamity as their own only insofar as it brought to a sudden end an era of peace, prosperity, and architectural embellishment that they had enjoyed ever since their voluntary submission to Venetian rule; and from the calamity they expected nothing more unhappy than an exchange of one master for another. The Brescians looked forward to living "under the tranquil rule of the king" as they decided against putting up a "fruitless and shameful defense"; and within three days of Louis XII's triumphal entry, they had adopted "the manners, the customs, and . . . even the speech of the French" (Caprioli). The Veronese closed their gates to the fleeing remnants of the Venetian army, escorted the Venetian rector out of the city "amorevolmente," and prepared to welcome the first Imperial troops with shouts of "Impero! Impero!" (Rizzoni). None of them managed to distinguish between Italians and barbarians, Venetians and foreigners. For one of the emperor's generals turned out to be the same marchese of Mantua who had been Venice's hero at the battle of the Taro; and Venetian soldiers turned out to behave no better than the French—for instance, when they destroyed the border town of Triviglio and when they emptied half the houses of Padua.

The historians of the Veneto admitted a degree of co-responsibility for the calamity only insofar as they had permitted themselves to believe in Venice's ability to shield them forever from the ruin of the rest of Italy. But the chief responsibility, they insisted, lay solely with the victims. The haughtiness (alterigia) of the Venetians had offended everyone, particularly the pope, whose request for the observance of canon laws that allowed appeals from local ecclesiastical courts to Rome they answered by insulting him to his face. Their self-confidence deafened them to the reports of their own news agents—to the point where they did not become aware of Louis XII's departure from France until he arrived in Milan. Their pride kept them from using their efficient diplomatic service to pit their enemies against each other and so break apart the unnatural coalition of mutually suspicious powers formed against them. Their preference for the sea led them to turn over the defense of their mainland dominions to mercenaries, whose lack of discipline and dedication became tragically evident in the panic that followed the first reversal on the battlefield.

Gradually, however, these historians began to realize that the calamity was affecting them as well. Within a few days of their arrival, the 5,000 German troops quartered in Vicenza had begun to indulge regularly in "strange kinds of violence, theft, invectives against just men, and the torturing and imprisonment of citizens with unheard of cruelty" (Da Porto). The French troops on their way east from Bergamo killed 400 innocent people in Peschera alone. The Spanish and "Burgundian" troops outside Verona "put to sack everything they could find." And the Imperial governor inside Verona imposed an enormous 20,000 *ducati* levy on the citizens while permitting his German soldiers to molest them at will.

Worse yet, the citizens themselves soon began to split into pro-Imperial or pro-French factions on one side and a pro-Venetian faction on the other; and the cities were soon faced with a recrudescence of the kind of endemic civil war from which the Venetians had mercifully rescued them a century earlier. Indeed, civil strife was in part to blame for provoking the incident that finally gave the Terraferma a calamity all of its own: the sack of Brescia.[62] Some Brescian patricians were sincerely convinced that living "happily and quietly as subjects of the greatest king in the world" was preferable to being governed by "a little wind-blown dukelet in a mediocre republic." So was one of the local chroniclers. INNOCENZO CASARI of the Canons Regular went out of his way to blame the Venetians for atrocities of their own and to blame those attributed to the French on the German and Jewish soldiers in their ranks.[63] But other patricians had soon had enough of the "insultas, contumelias, ludibria, rapinas, adultera, stupra, et fornicationes" visited upon them daily by the great king's most apparent representatives. The approach of a Venetian army in February 1512 while the main body of the French army was away in the Romagna gave the pro-Venetian party its opportunity. Under the leadership of the most dramatic chronicler of the sack, GIAN GIACOMO MARTINENGO,[64] they organized a revolt, which immediately won over most of the lower classes in the city and all of the peasants outside ("ingresso urbem Venetorum exercitu et rusticorum copiosa multitudine"—Casari). Then suddenly the revolt backfired. Martinengo was betrayed by one of his closest collaborators, and he escaped from his French captors only after they had dragged him to Bologna and extracted a huge ransom. The arrival of a relief contingent then forced the Venetians to withdraw; and the French troops they had bottled up in the castle rushed forth to vent their fury on the defenseless citizens. A priest was butchered on the altar while the cathedral was relieved of all its valuables. An abbot was tortured while his monastery was ransacked. Women were violated on the bodies of their slaughtered husbands and brothers. In almost every house, according to CESARE ANSELMI,[65] who, as a Bolognese, was allowed to wander about at will, the inhabitants were stripped naked, "hung by their genitals, held with their feet over fire, bound with their mouths pierced with stakes" until with signs they indicated the location of hidden possessions. So horrible was the sack, indeed, that it was considered a valid pretext even as late as 1534 for claiming a reduction in the taxes owed to the Venetian government.[66] From Brescia, the calamity spread to the entire Terraferma. Spanish, German, Swiss, French, and Venetian troops wandered back and forth across the land, alternately capturing, plundering, and looting every town and hamlet in their paths.[67] Even as late as 1522 "this country is still so full of soldiers," as another witness, ASCANIO CANTIERI DA PARATICO (1496–1545), complained after having lost most of his property, "that it is impossible to stay here any longer."[68]

What saved the Terraferma from total destruction was the rapid recovery of Venice from the ruins of 1509 and the gradual reestablishment of Venetian authority, this time not with the passive acquiescence but with the enthusiastic support of the whole population. This amazing achievement, more "memorable" than any since Rome's recovery from the Hannibalic invasion, inspired still another outburst of historical writing. The Milanese patrician-jurist BERNARDO ARLUNO extracted seven books from his vast, and still unpublished, history of contemporary Milan and reorganized them as a separate historical work under the title *De Bello Veneto*.[69] The Venetian patrician ANDREA MOCENIGO applied the standards of humanist historiography he had mastered in a history of Venice's wars with the Turks to a narrative of the collapse and the reestablishment of Venice's mainland dominion.[70] Both historians traced the causes of Agnadello back to the invasion of 1494, which they now regarded as the first of the many calamities of their times rather than merely as a prelude to one more Venetian triumph. Both of them attributed the calamities to "traitors" like Trivulzio and the anti-Sforza faction in Milan as well as to technical defects in Venice's military organization. And both of them attributed the recovery to the solidarity of the Venetian citizens with their government—a remarkable exception to the rule in most Italian cities—and to the high level of civil morality engendered by unquestionable respect for age-old laws and customs:

> By uncorrupted discipline of the laws and by the high level of morality that reigns in that city, Venice has become the powerful and long-lasting republic that so deserves our admiration. It has now existed for more than 1,100 years, with the same respect for public virtue, the same reverence for pure justice, the same regard for the majesty of religion, preserving unweakened both private and public faith under the sanction of inviolable laws ... (Arluno).

To Mocenigo, however, Venice was still an end in itself; and the proof of the sagacity of its leaders lay in their subjection even of such stirring appeals as that of

185

Leo X for the unity of Italy to the sole goal of the good of their own state. Hence, it is not at all "curious," as one recent historian has thought, that Mocenigo ignored the significance of the wars of the preceding century "as a struggle of two republican cities, Venice and Florence, against despotic Milan."[71] For him, the strength of Venice lay in virtue and the laws, not in its dedication to some sort of "republican" ideology. And he could not have cared less that Milan was ruled by a "despot," providing that the despot acted in a manner acceptable to the no less despotic rulers of the Venetian Terraferma. For Arluno, on the other hand, Venice now served the higher purpose of guarding the independence of all Italy in the face of foreign invaders, all of whom, from the German troops of Maximilian to that favorite of his Milanese predecessors, Louis XII, he categorized as "barbarians." It performed that role not by actively mobilizing its fellow Italians in a common crusade but by providing them with the rules of good government that would enable them to defend themselves. And Arluno's eulogy was accordingly directed not only to the current doge, to whom his work was explicitly dedicated, but also to his own current employer, Duke Francesco II Sforza, whose shaky throne still rested more on the convenience of the emperor and the Swiss than on the goodwill and high morality of his subjects.

Unfortunately, the other cities of northern Italy found it ever more impossible to follow the example Arluno proposed to them. Cremona, it is true, was spared a major calamity: the Venetians rescued it from Il Moro's misgovernment in 1499, and the restoration of the Sforza in 1513 saved it from the French, who, "as is their custom, did much damage to the countryside." But its own saviors, noted the anonymous Cremonese chroniclers, could not prevent a revolt of the artisans, who took advantage of the frequent changes of regime to "sack the houses of the gentlemen," or an outbreak of "a terrible malady called *mal franzoso*"; and the saviors in turn did almost as much harm as those they replaced—hanging citizens suspected of disloyalty without trial and confiscating the property of the bishop, "a good man who could not have administered the revenues of the diocese more honestly."[72] Parma, too, was spared anything more tragic than the siege of 1521. But it suffered along with the other tattered pieces of the former Duchy of Milan from all the evils that had followed the fateful assassination of Galeazzo Maria in 1476: the invasion of 1494, which "the imprudent Ludovico Sforza, poorly viewing his own affairs, brought upon Italy," the sack of Trivilio, where "every sex, age, and condition" was subject to "monstrous ferociousness," the sack of Brescia, where all the resident Parmigiani unable to buy their way out were butchered and thrown into the river. Moreover, its turn was sure to come in the near future. For the defeat of the French in 1525 had switched the balance of power in favor of the enemies of its current sovereign, the pope. By 1526 the firm hand of its prudent governor, Francesco Guicciardini, was beginning to weaken. And the aging historian FRANCESCO CARPESANI FLAMINI (b. 1441) all but gave up hope that his younger readers would ever be able to "enjoy a happier age than the most turbulent times" he had lived through.[73]

Elsewhere the calamities multiplied in proportion to the increasing despair of the victims in ever being able to avert them. Ravenna was torn apart by "Gallic depredations" in 1512, and "ferro, flamma, caedeque fere exhausta,"[74] even though neither prince nor citizens had done anything to provoke the depredations. Rhodes, that eastern outpost of Italian civilization, fell to the Turks in 1522 after a "cruel and atrocious battle." Its surviving Christian inhabitants were set adrift "to wander about on a harsh and stormy sea" in midwinter. Meanwhile, their compatriots in Italy looked on indifferently as the king of France blocked a relief expedition belatedly organized by the emperor.[75] "What a disgrace for the princes of Christendom," cried one Milanese historian, "to let such a city fall into the hands of the enemies of the Faith!"[76] Pavia was beseiged for three months and then plundered by the French in 1525. It was occupied—at the expense of the Pavians—by a Spanish army in 1527. And it was taken over—with "enormous destruction of the faculties of the citizens"—by a thousand Italian troops four months later. That, decided the loyal MARTINO VERRI, was not much "recompense for the valor and the fidelity of the city to his Catholic Majesty" and to his vassal the duke. Pavia was finally emptied of its inhabitants and reduced to a status "worse than that of a miserable village."[77]

The War of the League of Cognac

Thus smaller states and subject cities proved incapable of defending themselves, either by resuscitating ancient virtues or by putting their trust in one or the other of the greater powers of the moment. But the chief metropolis of northern Italy did not even try to follow Arluno's model. In fact, its only really apparent response to the series of calamities that began with the second French occupation of 1515 and culminated in the War of the League of Cognac in 1526 consisted in an unprecedented quantity of historical writing: two polished humanist commentaries (Vegio and Capella), two commentaries that occasionally backslid from humanist standards through the inclusion of irrelevant or extraneous passages, one perfect chronicle in the late medieval tradition enlivened by a typically Renaissance sense of historical change (Grumello), and one personal memoir expanded into a chronicle (Burigozzo).

Taken together, these works dedicate some three thousand pages to the years between 1515 and 1535 (Burigozzo's entries for the next seven years are sparse and lacunary). And that they do so with such thoroughness can be attributed largely to the quality of the writers. GIOVAN MARCO BURIGOZZO (b.c. 1494) was a shopkeeper who had traveled at least as far as Venice and who had a sharp eye for the consequences of the calamities on the humbler classes of citizens.[78] ANTONIO GRUMELLO was a high-ranking army officer who served Il Moro at Novara, Louis XII at Agnadello, Massimiliano Sforza at Lodi, and King Francis I and Duke Francesco II as captain of the fortress at Pavia; and he added to his own observations those of his brother, an officer in the imperial army in Naples.[79] SCIPIONE VEGIO (d. 1535),[80] GALEAZZO CAPELLA (1497–1533),[81] and GIOVAN BATTISTA SPEZIANO (d. 1545)[82] were all ducal secretaries, who held positions similar to those of their Milanese predecessors Crivelli and Simonetta under Francesco I Sforza and of their Florentine contemporary Machiavelli under Pier Soderini. They were thus in a position both "to hear many things and see many more" (Capella) and to check what they saw and heard in the official correspondence they were in charge of. Vegio was a physician as well as a statesman and was rewarded for his dual service with a seat in the Senate in 1529. Speziano was a member of the three-man commission entrusted by Charles V with the administration of the duchy during the duke's absence; and he was later a member of the commission charged with drawing up the "New Constitutions" by which Milan was to be ruled for the following century and a half.

Moreover, all the Milanese historians except Burigozzo had been educated according to the standard humanist curricula. Capella supplemented his narrative of the miseries of his own time with a collection of passages from Cicero and Augustine on the miseries of the human race in general.[83] Speziano studied Latin literature, mathematics, astronomy, music, and medicine, as well as jurisprudence, and he carried around a copy of the works of Marsilio Ficino during his diplomatic missions. Even though he frequently forgot the rules of humanist historiography that he must have learned from his friends in the humanist circles of Vigevano and Milan, GAUDENZIO MERULA at least tried to imitate Vegio.[84] And Speziano recognized the value of his intention by beginning his own far more polished narrative where Merula's left off. All but one of these writers then spent the better part of their lives attempting to apply what they had learned from books and experience to the problems of the state of which they were active members. Only one of them ever thought of giving up—of "retiring to some safe and quiet place [away from] the wars that grew everywhere in intensity" in order to "hear about rather than look at all these interminable calamities." But even he, Capella, dedicated his work to his employer in the hope that it might still remain politically useful after he had gone.

It was not the fault of these humanist statesmen, then, that the various solutions they proposed from time to time all turned out to be fruitless. The restoration of the Sforza had initially been greeted warmly by those many Milanese who, after twelve years of the French, were willing even to forget about the misdeeds of Il Moro—or at least, like Grumello, to attribute his misdeeds instead to Alfonso d'Aragona and Ercole d'Este. But instead of trying to cultivate their goodwill, Massimiliano busied himself with imprisoning and torturing everyone he suspected of disloyalty— including the popular bishop of Lodi, who happened to be a member of his own family. He permitted his underlings to fleece the taxpayers; and he himself imposed so many new taxes that he ruined the merchants, "on whose industry cities live," and provoked an open revolt in the Senate. "If the rest of you want to pay," proclaimed a senator in one of Vegio's impeccable humanist orations, "go ahead. I will not, for I have already paid enough." When the crisis finally came, Massimiliano had no alternative but to appeal to the pope and the king of the Romans, now the sole support of his regime, and to plunder his now thoroughly alienated subjects in order to pay his doubtfully loyal mercenaries. Accordingly, the fortress at Novara surrendered without a shot, and Trivulzio was welcomed back in the train of King Francis I with a round of celebrations that lasted through the following January.

Yet the restoration of the French turned out to be no more durable than the restoration of the Sforza had been. It too rested solely *alienis opibus,* as Vegio put it. And the propaganda speeches of the French general lost their effect on the inhabitants of Lombardy as soon as they noticed that his soldiers behaved no better than had those of Louis XII. "O noble country of France," cried Grumello, "put on mourning and call for vengeance upon your king in the sight of God. For he has sent a captain who has torn apart the unfortunate city of Pavia, torn apart its holy places, torn apart the body of Christ, torn apart. . . ." When the new emperor, Charles V, "began to think it dishonorable that the king of France hold the state of Milan, which by ancient right belonged to the Roman Empire" (Capella), the current Sforza pretender was brought back by an Imperial army; and when Francis I tried again to impose the ancient right that made him, not the descendant of two usurpers, the legitimate duke of Milan, he ended up a prisoner on the battlefield of Pavia (1525), an incident to which Capella devoted his entire Book V. "Of all the events that has taken place in our times and has been thought by all judicious persons worthy of memory, there is none so marvelous . . . as the siege of Pavia and the capture of Signor Francesco Angolem," insisted FRANCESCO TAEGGIO, in a commentary that was more celebrative than historical.[85] But even though the people of Milan, while being punished for their sins with another outbreak of the plague, hailed the victors with shouts of "Impero! Spagna!" they soon discovered that the soldiers of the emperor were even worse than those of the king. "Oh Italy," cried Grumello, "there is no need to set Turks and Moors upon you. . . . For God has sent an even more depraved and cruel race of men . . . [who have] destroyed the noble Milanese state; and there is now nothing in that state but cries, lamentation, hunger, pestilence, most cruel wars and unheard-of cruelties."

Meanwhile, the people of Milan themselves gave up any hope of trying to influence the course of events of which they could be nothing but the victims. In times of peace, they distracted themselves with private feuds. In times of crisis, "reiecta pristinae virtutis memoria" (Speziano), they thought only of hiding what they had extorted from their neighbors. When they had nothing better to do, they organized plots aimed at no more noble an end than enriching the plotters at the expense of the community. And for the most famous of the plotters, Bonifazio Visconti, Speziano found even Sallust's words about Catiline insufficiently harsh. The Milanese were thus utterly incapable of organizing a collective defense when they suddenly found themselves at the mercy of the Spanish and German soldiers in the city who were besieging their duke in the fortress while the city as a whole was being besieged by the army of the League of Cognac. "Such was the hate [the soldiers bore the Milanese]," reported Capella, "that they kept not only men and women but also children tied up" in the houses they were quartered in, so as more effectively to "make use of the other members of the family as slaves." The reconciliation between Duke Francesco and Charles V seemed to offer one last glimmer of hope. But when it became apparent that Francesco would die without heirs, even that hope died out. "O unhappy, abandoned fatherland," cried Grumello. "O unhappy city, destroyed and ruined without compassion. . . ."

The Sack of Rome and the Inquisition Revolt

Thus the War of the League of Cognac brought to a climax the series of calamities that had struck the metropolis of Lombardy since 1499. Similarly, the aftermath of the war visited upon the capital of what had been, since 1509, the strongest independent state in Italy one of the greatest calamities of all times. Of the three surviving chronicles of the sack of Rome of 1527, that of MARCELLO ALBERONI, a native Roman, was included in the diary he kept for the years between 1521 and 1536, and it remains in the form of day-to-day notations, without any attempt at explanation or analysis.[86] That of JACOPO BUONAPARTE, a non-Roman eyewitness, was written during or soon after the event. That of LUIGI GUICCIARDINI (the brother of the historian Francesco and the future civil servant of the Florentine Principate) was written shortly after 1530, and it was dedicated to Cosimo I soon enough after his election (1537) to be addressed simply to the "duke of the Florentine Republic," rather than, as Cosimo soon began to call himself, the "duke of Florence."[87] The authenticity of both Buonaparte's and Guicciardini's accounts has been called into question;[88] but the many differences of opinion and presentation between them make it difficult to understand how one could have been derived from the other. True, there are many similarities. Both chroniclers demonstrate, after a prefatory promise to use "only those simple and natural words taught me by my fatherland," a historical perspective and a narrative skill equal to that of the best humanists. Both agree that the events they describe constitute "the saddest, cruelest, most terrifying tragedy that Almighty God has ever shown to this unfortunate Italy." Still, they differ somewhat in assigning the immediate causes. For Guicciardini, the main fault lay in the defects of the League of Cognac, which, although launched for the laudible purpose of "diminishing the greatness of the emperor and liberating Italy from the avaricious and cruel manners of his ministers," was left "without money and without a captain." For Buonaparte, the guilt lay with the two principal protagonists: with Charles of Bourbon (Carlo di Borbone), "a deceptive and ambitious man who did much damage to both France and Italy," and with Clement VII, a man whose otherwise commendable "love of peace and fear of the uncertain outcome of war" led him to disband his army just when his counselors advised him to strengthen it. They also differed over the long-term causes. Buonaparte went back only to 1523, when Francis I's ambition for glory had led him to tear up his treaty with the pope.

Guicciardini went back to 1494, when Charles VIII had first introduced the "barbarian and wild nations" who had been "running around the length of Italy . . . for the past thirty-three years . . . fearlessly attacking this or that city, sacking it impuniously, and happily settling down there as long as they please." Indeed, Guicciardini went back to the causes of the first invasion itself: "a people not united, not used to arms, without a leader, nourished in idleness and lascivious delights." And his view of the calamity was all the more tragic, since his ultimate solution was even more unrealizable in the late 1530s than it had been when Machiavelli wrote his *Discourses*—that is, to fill "the souls [of Italians] with the love of poverty and justice [and thus] make them ready and willing to defend obstinately their lives and their country with their own and well-ordered arms." Only one thought somewhat relieves the sense of inevitable tragedy in these lines: the thought that the Romans, or at least those Romans associated with the Curia, richly deserved their fate. "The avaricious, ambitious, and slovenly government of these modern prelates," proclaimed Guicciardini, with another string of loaded adjectives totally foreign to the style of his brother Francesco, "are pernicious to the people." And his equally disgusted and horrified fellow chroniclers elsewhere in Italy fully agreed with him. "Proud, greedy, murderous, sensuous deceivers cannot endure for long," concluded Francesco Vettori, who had met many of them during his long residence as Florentine ambassador in Rome. "God often punishes them along with their own enemies."[89]

After the calamity of Rome, a reorganization of the League of Cognac once again brought calamity to Naples—this time in the form of one last attempt by the French to claim the kingdom that Charles VIII had failed to hold on to thirty-fours earlier. Unlike the Milanese, the Neapolitans did what they could to avert the disaster. They did so not by attempting to reassert their long-lost independence, nor even by trying to modify the viceregal regime, to which they had by now become accustomed, but by throwing their support to whichever of the contenders seemed at the moment to be the less disadvantageous to their interests. Unfortunately, such a choice proved to be increasingly difficult to make. Along with the people of the capital city, one of the two chroniclers whose names have survived, the notary GREGORIO ROSSO (d. 1542), remained loyal to the emperor. And after the war he was duly rewarded by twice being chosen *eletto del popolo,* the representative of the people in the Neapolitan parliament.[90] The other, LEONARDO SANTORO (1474–1569), first sided with the emperor, even though his family owed its title and its estates near Caserta to the second Angevin king. Then, when the viceroy released the residents of the conquered territories from their oaths of loyalty, he sided with the king. Finally, when the French killed both his father and his brother, he sided once again with the emperor.[91] He was rewarded for his first change in sides by being appointed food supply commissioner *(commissario della grascia)* in the French army; and he was eventually rewarded for the second by having his confiscated estates restored to him and by having two of his sons promoted to important bishoprics. But neither chronicler was fully convinced of the wisdom of his choice. Rosso heaped abuse on the French, whom he held responsible even for the sack of Rome. He excoriated those barons who went over to the French and praised those few of them who, like Giovan Battista Caracciolo, refused to succumb to the French general's offers of honors and wealth. But he also had to admit that the Spanish soldiers mutinied on their way to defend the capital, that they tried to block the creation of a citizen militia in Naples, and that they treated those they were supposed to defend with "enormous insolence . . . , killing, mistreating, impressing men, and violating women." Santoro heaped abuse on the emperor's chief lieutenants. Antonio de Leva was "cruel, greedy, and proud." Bourbon, that villain of all villains, was "a naturally furious man, audacious and cruel, with a face enflamed as if he were drunk." Cardinal Prospero Colonna was "a harsh, proud, vain man of very bad morals [*pessima vita*]." But even Santoro had to admit that some of the Neapolitans in Imperial service were "gentlemen of grave judgment" and that the French commander was "overbearing and intolerant."

Neither the polished humanist Santoro nor the traditional diarist Rosso, who wrote according to the example of Giuliano Passero,[92] nor, for that matter, the anonymous diarist whose work is preserved in a miscellany *(zibaldone)* of 1584,[93] ever thought of describing the calamity as a struggle between Italians and foreigners. True, the foreigners were barbarians—most particularly the Spanish, who regularly "plundered monasteries and churches," and the "Lanzichenette," their fellow veterans of the sack of Rome, who robbed the terrified nuns of San Lorenzo even of their hoods and then beat up the Spanish soldiers who tried to follow them into the wine cellar. But Italians were barbarians too. The "criminal, ungrateful" Florentines threw out the Medici (Santoro), who alone had raised their city from "the ignorance and uncouthness of past centuries" and turned it into a new Athens. The "light-headed" people of Naples completely forgot the firmness of their ancestors, who had resisted Hannibal, the Goths, and Manfredi. The pro-French barons were inspired only by "the hope of better fortune, the desire for more wealth, and the hatred of Spanish rule." The native soldiers of Basilicata were "a cruel race, given to robbery, criminal, and unworthy of the name of militia." And, after the final retreat of the French, the Italians in the Imperial army joined the Spanish in holding up Neapolitan citizens and ransacking the city of Molfetta.[94]

A foreign invasion, a civil war, a plague, a famine, a six-month siege, and a complete breakdown of moral and civic order was without doubt a "funestissima tragedia" (Santoro); and its tragic character was emphasized by a number of spectacular supernatural phenomena: a host of angels descended on the walls of Salerno, the blood of San Gennaro liquified prematurely, unarmed men floated in the sky above Cosenza, and most of the statues in the Capitanata began to bleed. The tragedy was then consummated on a black-shrouden platform in the Piazza del Mercato, where most of the barons in Santoro's six-page list were bereft of their heads. But unlike their Milanese colleagues, the Neapolitian historians did not lose hope in an eventual solution. For one thing, the reconciliation of Charles V and Clement VII seemed to promise an end to what had been the greatest constitutional weakness of the kingdom since 1250: the existence of rival monarchs and dynasties. Rosso compiled a long list of the many Neapolitans who trooped to Bologna in 1529 "to see so rare a solemnity as the coronation of an emperor" who happened also to be their king. And they were probably as happy as was the secretary of Federico II of Mantua (a secretary who may also have been the tutor of his children mentioned by Ariosto) at the prospect of having "all the affairs of Italy pacifically settled."[95] For another thing, neither the war nor the loss of independence had destroyed either the institutions of local government or the determination of the Neapolitans to make use of them whenever they thought their interests to be in jeopardy. When Charles V tried to get them to pay the bill for the defense of Vienna two years later, they reminded him, at a meeting of the parliament at San Lorenzo, "that without their help, the French army would never have been thrown out and defeated . . . [and that] consequently they deserved rather to be repaid than to be asked for another cent" ("che cacciarli uno quattrino da mane").[96] When Cardinal Colonna, whom the anonymous diarist nevertheless looked to as a savior, refused to collaborate with them, they went over his head to the emperor himself; and when they caught the cardinal trying to corrupt the *eletto del popolo,* they rose in rebellion (1532). When the *eletto*'s successor then tried to sneak out of the city and so avoid the emperor's wrath over the refusal of another levy, they forced him to remain.

But above all, the reconciliation of the Neapolitans with the regime that had emerged victorious from the war of 1528 was made possible by the appointment of an able viceroy—one whose permanent tenure in office (1532–53) and whose conscientious administration gave them the impression of once again having a resident monarch of their own. Pedro de Toledo soon became the brother-in-law of Duke Cosimo I de' Medici; and his authority in Italy as a whole thus rested on what came to look like a reincarnation of the Naples-Florence-Milan alliance of the late fifteenth century. At home his authority rested in part on the continuing confidence of Charles V, a confidence that was reconfirmed in 1543, when, accompanied by "all the princes, marchesi, barons, and countless numbers of gentlemen and men of the people," he welcomed Charles, the king of Tunis, and five hundred "Moorish soldiers" into the city for a week of spectacular celebrations culminating in a "giostra moresca."[97] Toledo's authority also rested on his successful defense of the kingdom against Turkish raids in 1537, which he accomplished, in the absence of a sufficient Imperial garrison, by organizing his subjects themselves into a militia. It rested, too, on his determination to use force when necessary—as he did in inaugurating his "reign" with a round of public executions.

But Toledo's authority rested above all on his success in carrying out what at least the historians perceived as the three principal objectives of his government: law and order in the streets, justice in the courts, and urban beautification in the cities. The first objective he realized by tearing down the *portici* into which criminals usually escaped, by banning the private possession of all weapons except swords, and by reforming the parishes and monasteries under royal patronage according to the advice of Girolamo Seripando, the famous pre-Tridentine ecclesiastical reformer and archbishop of Salerno. The second objective he realized by opening his court to all pleaders regardless of class, by appointing to high judicial offices only judges dependent personally on him alone, and by making an example of those great noblemen, like Giovan Francesco Pignatello, who were accustomed to browbeating their inferiors with impunity. "Well informed about everything," noted an anonymous chronicler whose text was finally divested of its seventeenth-century emendations by an anonymous twentieth-century editor,[98] Toledo "applied justice rigorously, without regard to persons . . ., small or great, noble or ignoble. Neither money nor connections [*amistà*] nor rank [*qualità*] counted for anything." The third objective he realized by rebuilding Pozzuoli after the earthquake of 1538, by draining the swamps around the Bay of Naples, and by plowing straight avenues through the jungle of old alleys in the capital, one of which is still the main street of the city and still bears his name, Via Toledo. Better still, continued the chronicler, he cleared the streets of the awnings and benches that made them "narrow, dark, and melancholy"; and he did it so effectively that the discontented merchants became "happy, quiet, and very content. For the streets now seemed [to them] to be another world, spacious, wide, and full of light [*chiaro*]." "Justice has been restored," proclaimed one of the two principal historians of his reign, SCIPIONE MICCIO.[99] "Criminals are punished without remission. Equality is maintained without regard of persons. . . . Truly, it seems as if the Age of Gold has arrived." Miccio's judgment was published by one of his descendants in 1600 as a model for the inspiration of Toledo's then current successor as viceroy. And it was incorporated almost verbatim into the masterpiece of the great eighteenth-century historian Pietro Giannone.

Such was Toledo's success, indeed, that the historians were all at a loss to understand how he could have become involved in the bloody revolt of 1547. According both to Miccio and to the other historian of the viceroyalty, ANTONIO CASTALDO,[100] the presence of heresy in Naples was only an excuse. Castaldo admitted the attractiveness of the first sermons of Bernardino Ochino, who "preached the Gospel not with extravagant philosophical disputations, as most had done until his time, but with a spirit, vehemence, and admirable fervor." He also admitted that Ochino led some people astray by "arguing about justfication, faith, works, papal power, Purgatory, and other difficult questions," and that his arguments were then reinforced by the free circulation of the writings of Erasmus and Melanchthon and of such pamphlets as the *Beneficio di Cristo,* all of them, he said, "full of impiety and heresies." But neither these aberrations, he added, nor the scandal of Ochino's apostasy were important enough to warrant the "violent and odious remedies" promulgated by the viceroy in 1547.

To some extent, Castaldo surmised, the fault lay in a defect of Toledo's character, namely, his jealousy of his own authority and his inclination to reply violently to anyone who questioned it. To some extent, the fault lay in his imperfect mastery of the technique of dividing and dominating used by all his predecessors: his senseless and gratuitous execution of three popular young noblemen in 1547 had no other effect than that of throwing the people and the nobility into each others arms. To some extent, the fault lay in a momentary dislocation of the imperial power structure in Italy. The death in 1546 of that "valorous" specialist in Italian affairs, Alfonso d'Avalos, marchese di Vasto, suddenly left Toledo defenseless before the dominant Spanish and Imperial interests of the emperor; and the murder of Pierluigi Farnese the following year upset the Papal-Imperial coalition upon which peace in Italy had rested since the Congress of Bologna. When Charles decided to deal with heresy in Naples the way it was dealt with in Castile, Toledo had no alternative but to obey.

A somewhat better explanation was provided by UBERTO FOGLIETTA, who, being a Genoese resident in Rome, was able to see the revolt in Naples in the broader context of the two other revolts that occurred at the same time in other parts of Italy.[101] True, Foglietta was somewhat hampered by the commentary form of history writing: it prevented him from making close comparisons between the theses of his three separate books, and it imposed upon him the thesis that all had been peaceful before the troubles broke out. Moreover, the particular circumstances in which the revolts occurred were not identical. In Naples, a resident and at least Italianized monarchy had been replaced by a viceroyalty dependent on a nonresident foreign monarch. In Genoa, a century-long dependence on either the duke of Milan or the king of France had been broken with the establishment of an independent oligarchical republic under the leadership of the most powerful of the oligarchical families. In Parma–Piacenza, a new independent duchy had just recently been forged out of communes that for two centuries had been subject either to the dukes of Milan or to the popes; and its purpose was to further the interests not of the citizens but of the lay leader of the current papal family, the Farnese. But the policies pursued by the governments of these states, or at least the policies attributed to them by Foglietta, were basicelly the same. Like the viceroy Toledo, the doge Andrea Doria and the duke Pierluigi Farnese both sought, first, to rescue their states from the general instability that had been introduced into Italy by the invasion of Charles VIII, and, second, to extend the protection of the law and responsibility to it to all their subjects regardless of class or status. Obviously, such policies ran directly counter to the interests of those who had most benefited from previous regimes. They offended the big landowners of the Piacentino, who, in response to Pierluigi's abolition of tax immunities, sent the assassins into the castle and then fled when the populace responded to their stirring speeches with hostile silence. They offended Lodovico Fieschi, a former comrade-in-arms of the anti-Imperial Neapolitan, Giovanni Caracciolo, who decided that descent from a great and powerful family was incompatible with the status of a law-abiding citizen of a commonwealth. They likewise offended those recalcitrant Neapolitan barons who, having failed to play off the viceroy against the emperor, finally instigated the quarrel over the Inquisition as a way of letting the viceroy destroy himself. Hence, like the revolt of the Fieschi and the murder of Pierluigi, the Inquisition revolt in Naples represented the last gasp of a reactionary opposition to the most important political innovation of the mid-sixteenth century: the permanent, durable state, superior to the special interests of anyone or any one group of its citizens, and one to which all citizens were equally subject.

Still, even Foglietta's explanation was not wholly satisfactory. While Papal diplomacy reestablished the Farnese in Piacenza, and while Andrea Doria chopped the heads off the Fieschi in Genoa, Toledo backed down, notwithstanding the full support of the emperor, and notwithstanding an offer of assistance from Cosimo I. After saving face with a few more acts of public violence, he swore never again to broach the question of the Inquisition. In other words, he sided with his subjects against his superior—upon whom, accordingly, the Neapolitan historians placed all the blame for having provoked the revolt. He therefore had no trouble putting down still another case of baronial disobedience five years later. And his successor easily won all the subsidies he needed from the parliament when, ten years later, one last baronial family tried to take advantage of the position it had won through the election of one of its members to the papacy. Giovanna d'Aragona may have been more beautiful—and more moral—than Helen of Troy, and the duke of Alba may have been a better general than Agamemnon. But the Carafa War was certainly not the glorious event that ALESSANDRO ANDREA, or D'ANDREA, of Barletta (b. 1519) was looking for when, after distinguished service in the Imperial-Neapolitan army, he sought to prove to his humanist friends in Padua and Venice that he still knew how to write humanist history.[102] Nor was it glorious enough to guarantee the success of Andrea's attempt to introduce still another form of historical writing: the Platonic dialogue. Paul IV's call to throw the Spanish out of Italy may have won the admiration of at least one eyewitness, who tried to force his unpolished prose into humanist historiographical forms for the benefit of an unnamed patron. "This pope is very splendid and magnanimous," he declared; "and had he not been abandoned by the French . . . he would never have consented to make peace, since he was sure of being helped even by the angels."[103] But he failed to rally those of his fellow countrymen who, like Andrea, knew about the "terrible, arbitrary government" Paul had created in Rome with the backing of the same anachronistic remnants of the Neapolitan baronage that had caused most of the kingdom's woes in the past.

True, all was not perfect in Naples. The peasants of the Abruzzi still hated the

Spanish soldiers. The provincial barons were still intent on swallowing up the remaining free towns. The nobility of the capital was still determined to obliterate the remaining political rights of the people. The kingdom was still dependent upon a distant monarch who looked upon it largely as a source of revenue. And all these tensions were to explode thirty years later when an arbitrary exportation order from the king sent grain prices up beyond the reach of most consumers.[104] But the two surviving Neapolitan chronicles of the 1560s are really transcriptions of earlier chronicles rather than original works. And the nearest they come to a reflection on current political problems consists in the expression of a vague nostalgia for the good old days of the Aragonese.[105] The one chronicler who thought the insurrection of 1585 worthy of a separate commentary was interested mostly in the character of its protagonist, the "rich, eloquent, white, and meaty" [*pieno di carne*] *eletto del popolo,* Giovan Vincenzo Starace. As soon as he had finished describing the ceremony in which Starace was dragged through the streets by his neck, he jumped immediately to the happy conclusion, a general pardon for all but the ringleaders, without mentioning the ferocious repression that preceded it. Apparently he too, like Andrea, was happy "to remain subject to the tolerant and just government" established by Toledo, which at least had succeeded in saving Naples for some sixty years from the calamities that had struck it between 1495 and 1529. Just as happy was GIUSEPPE MARINELLO of Molfetta, who learned about the horrors of the siege of his native city in 1529 by interviewing the descendants of the victims. Now that "almost all the families of the people [*famiglie popolari*] had identified themselves with the nobles, embracing with great desire and joy the title once so odious to them," civil strife had disappeared. And as Naples turned into "the most civilized and pleasant city in Italy," so Molfetta by 1591 had become "rich, noble, peaceful, beautiful, and full of joy."[106]

8

FROM THE SALT WAR
TO LEPANTO

IN MOST OF ITALY, THE CALAMITIES OF THE FIRST HALF OF THE SIXTEENTH CENTURY WERE provoked by the presence of foreign armies on Italian territory. But in some places they appeared to have resulted solely from a clash between the remnants of medieval communes and nascent territorial states. BARTOLOMEO ALFEO was sufficiently well trained as a jurist to be invited to write the statutes for one of Ancona's subject towns. He was also well enough educated as a humanist to put his rather irregular Italian prose into fairly correct Livian form.[1] He was therefore perfectly aware that Ancona could no longer survive outside the limits of the Papal State. But neither he nor, apparently, his still wholly unpublished compatriot Lando di Piergentile Ferretti could ever conceive of membership in the Papal State as anything but a direct dependence of each single city upon the pope himself. They were therefore unable to understand why they should help repay for the rebuilding of a city which might have been the pope's place of residence but which was certainly not *their* capital city. Nor could they understand why the pope could have surreptitiously built a fortress right under their noses. Even less could they understand why, when most of them were out of town for the harvest of September 1532, he had reinforced the fortress with three hundred soldiers and then had given them the choice of paying up or losing their heads. They therefore put the blame on the resident Florentine merchants, who, they said, were apparently trying to use a Florentine pope to ruin their Anconitan competitors, and on the Florentine governor, Cardinal Benedetto Accolti, whom they accused of fleecing the city in order to pay for his cardinal's hat. That left them completely at the mercy of the pope, who died two years later without having fulfilled his promise to restore their local autonomy.

The chroniclers of Perugia were equally aware that the restoration of communal independence was an idle dream.[2] All of them came from prominent local families, and all of them had some education. GIOVAN BATTISTA CRISPOLTI was an important officeholder with extensive feudal estates in Umbria. GIULIO DI COSTANTINO (c. 1503–after 1550) was not a baker, as has sometimes been supposed. He was a lieutenant to Malatesta Baglioni, whom he served faithfully even during the siege of Florence in 1529–30. CESARE DI GIOVANNI BONTEMPI and his son and continuator (from 1550 to 1563) MARCANTONIO were descendants of popular families important enough to have been exiled by the Baglioni and reinstated by Julius II; and Cesare remained faithful to his antityrannical persuasion even to the point of applauding the murder of Duke Alessandro de' Medici as "a truly great, praiseworthy, and memorable act, comparable to those of the ancient Romans." GIROLAMO DI FROLLIERE was the notary of the Priors from 1535 and of the College of Merchants from 1540, who at least learned something about historical writing by looking for traces of the Baglioni in the commentaries of Volterrano.[3] But none of these chroniclers had paid any attention to the rebellion of Ancona seven years before. And none of them was very surprised when the other cities subject to the pope declined to answer Perugia's call for assistance in 1539.

The so-called "Salt War" may have been "a marvelous thing to see," and the chroniclers may well have been thrilled to "behold the city and the people of Perugia restored to their freedom, everyone most willing to press forward with the war, showing himself able and willing to suffer every extreme danger to his life rather than submit to the authority of the pope" (Frolliere). Unfortunately, there was no real alternative to submitting. The eclipse of papal authority during the sack of Rome had exposed Perugian territory to depredation by the troops of the pope's reluctant "savior," Duke Francesco Maria of Urbino. The restoration of Malatesta Baglioni had been accomplished at the expense of destroying the entire village of Spello and reawakening the jealousies of the Baglioni's former rivals, who now swore to assassinate every one of them. And the election of Ridolfo Baglioni as captain of the city on the eve of the revolt had been followed immediately by the imposition of a huge tax for the payment of his mercenary soldiers. When the Papal army approaching the city turned out to be vastly superior to the one inside, even Frolliere admitted that the defenders were no longer so "ready to sacrifice property, lives, children" to such a hopeless cause, and that "most of them would now be willing to pay much more .han three *quattrini* per pound [on salt]." When Paul III entered the city on October 24, 1540, he was greeted with the usual shouts of "Chiesa! Paolo! Paolo!"—not because he withdrew the salt tax, which he most certainly did not, but because of the many, but unnamed, *grazie* he graciously bestowed on his repentant subjects. Thereafter Perugians, Anconitans, and all the other citizens of the Papal cities quietly paid not only for transforming Rome into the stage set of the Counter Reformation but also for fighting Huguenots, Lutherans, Turks, and Venetians in Europe and for carrying the faith to four of the other continents of the world. And they did so without a murmur. In fact, the only "calamity" considered "worthy of memory" in all of Umbria and the Marche after 1540 was provoked by the refusal of the people of Urbino, "even though well disposed toward their prince," to pay a new tax on meat. And that calamity ended a few months later when, lightened by a score of lopped-off heads and by the great quantity of money spent trying to avoid the inevitable, they happily agreed to pay what they had once denounced as an unsupportable burden.[4]

Unlike the Anconitans and the Perugians, the Aretines were not at all interested in maintaining or reasserting their autonomy with respect to a territorial state. They had learned the futility of ever trying to do any such thing again in 1502. Rather, they were faced with the problem of choosing between two contenders for the dominion of the territorial state—and of protecting themselves from the consequences of open war between the contenders. When Malatesta Baglioni arrived to defend them against the approaching Papal-Imperial army in September 1529, noted IACOPO CATINI, he permitted his soldiers to "take lodging wherever they pleased, to rob many houses, and to sack the stores, doing much damage." When the Florentine commissioner at last abandoned the city, he assured the citizens that they would be treated no less brutally by his enemies; and most of them forthwith fled to the country. Whether the *popolo* or the Medici ruled in Florence, Catani suggested, was no concern of the Aretines—as long as someone really did rule. Hence, they enthusiastically renewed their oaths of loyalty when the commissioner appointed by Clement VII arrived in September 1530 as guarantor against further calamities; and eight years later they built a fortress at their own expense, "to the honor and glory and security of our illustrious lord, Duke Cosimo," as GUASPARRI SPADARI put it, "whom God save and maintain and render happy with all his happy state."[5]

The Sienese, on the other hand, thought they were choosing to remain independent, whereas actually their choice was limited to submitting either to the emperor or to the king or to the ruler of the nearest territorial state, the duke of Florence. Until 1552, when the Imperial captain Diego de Mendoza suddenly ordered them to surrender their arms and started building a fortress on the edge of the city, they had always thought of themselves as free allies of the emperor—as the ambassador Claudio Zuccantini explained in a tearful oration during which he laid the keys of the city before an image of the Virgin. So shocked were they that they tore down the fortress and chased Mendoza's Spanish troops away. But they soon discovered that they could keep Mendoza out only by welcoming a French general as their "liberator." And they also discovered that the French general's rhetoric about Imperial tyranny was merely a cover-up for the transformation of the republic into an outpost of French dominion in Italy and into a temporary campground for hotheaded Florentine exiles. That, in any case, is what was pointed out to them by one of their fellow citizens, GIOVAN MARIA BENEDETTI, who, since he was living in Rome, could judge the events in Siena in the light of the current political situation in all Italy. And that was what might have been told them by the translator and popularizer Ludovico Domenichi, who, in 1556, thought at last of writing a history of his own about a subject which he knew surpassed the limits of a domestic squabble in an anachronistic city-state.[6]

Actually, the Sienese chroniclers had considerable difficulty in understanding just who was on which side. The Florentine exiles their government had sent to defend Chiusi sold out to the Florentine army—at the climax of an intricate spy-and-counterspy story which that polished storyteller GIROLAMO ROFFÌA, who was then with the Florentine army at Montepulciano, told with relish to his friend, the Florentine governor of Arezzo.[7] The exiled Florentine general Piero Strozzi, whom the government, with permission from the king of France, sent off to raid the Arno Valley, took with him a band not of Sienese but of Swiss and Lombard soldiers. Moreover, the atrocities committed on all sides reached such proportions that Roffìa, no longer thought of them as atrocities. Strozzi's soldiers killed all the men and burned down all the houses at Foiano. French soldiers repaid the voluntary surrender of one village by sparing the lives only of the captain and the *podestà*. German soldiers, tiring of the cries of a crazy woman, nailed her to a gate, shoved one stick down her throat and another up her vagina, and then amused themselves by watching her die slowly, in agony. "Un caso notabile," indeed! When the defeat of the French and Sienese at Marciano wrecked the last possibility of relieving the siege of the city,[8] and when Cosimo de' Medici's captains turned back the women and children whom the starving men inside tried to get rid of, the folly of having started the so-called war of liberation became fully apparent. ALESSANDRO DI GIROLAMO SOZZINI knew little more of even Sienese history than what he had misread in certain unnamed ancient chronicles and what he had looked up in the one modern historian he cites, Marco Guazzo.[9] But what he knew fully supported his thesis: that left alone, the Sienese had always, and probably would always, fight among themselves. The nobles had been overthrown by the Nove, the Nove by the Dodici, the Dodici by the Popolo, the Popolo by the Petrucci, etc., etc., until finally "His Catholic Majesty provided for the quiet of the city" by appointing a resident captain to keep it quiet—and otherwise to leave it alone. That was exactly the kind of arrangement that Sozzini thought was being reestablished at the end of the siege of 1554–55, which he described in the most minute detail. The "Imperial" army marched into the Campo bearing "so many cases of food that everyone was stupefied," and the new governor promptly appointed Sienese citizens—including Sozzini himself—to all the usual magistracies. It never occurred to him that the French were on the verge of a final retreat from Italy, that the "Empire" in Italy had already given way to the dominion of the Spanish crown under the king of Spain, Philip II, and that the magistrates could no longer lift a finger without the governor's approval. Not even thirty years later, when he pulled his manuscript out of his desk for a final revision, did Sozzini realize that Siena had become, for all practical purposes, a part of the Medicean grand duchy of Tuscany.

As the calamities of the rest of Italy gradually diminished in number and intensity in the second quarter of the century, those of that ill-defined borderland between Italy and France now known as Piedmont became ever graver. Or at least they seemed to become so, because not until then did any of the local chroniclers begin to take note of them. Only one of them was really a historian: GIULIANO GOSELLINI (c. 1529–87), who also wrote commentaries on such other "memorable events" as the Pazzi conspiracy, the Fieschi rebellion, and the murder of Pierluigi Farnese—as well as a considerable quantity of poetry, none of which apparently has ever been published. He was therefore able to see the events of Piedmont in the five years preceeding the composition of his major work, the *Compendio storico della guerra di Piacenza e del Piemonte*,[10] in the context of the power struggles of all Italy; and he was able to describe with considerable narrative skill the intricate diplomatic negotiations in which he was an active participent. But Gosellini spent most of his career as secretary to Ferrante Gonzaga, the Imperial governor of Milan. Indeed, much of his text is written as if Ferrante had dictated it, and it ends with a stirring harangue against those who tried to blame Ferrante for starting the war. Hence, Piedmont became merely the background for the exploits of a non-Piedmontese hero. On the other hand, neither GIANBERNARDO MIOLO, the notary of Monferrato,[11] nor GIOVAN ANDREA SALUZZO DI CASTELLAR of Saluzzo,[12] nor even DALMAZZO GRASSO of Borgo San Dalmazzo near Cuneo,[13] was able to put the miscellaneous elements of his chronicle into any other context than perhaps that borrowed thirdhand from what someone had told Miolo about medieval local-universal chronicles. Hence, the battle of Pavia appears to have had no more effect on Piedmont than did a sermon by a certain Oecolampadius in Basel. The outbreak of war between England and France in 1542 was no more important than the locust invasion of the same year. The siege of Saluzzo in 1487, which Castellar had seen, meant no more to him than the funeral of his father in 1497. And the repair of the public clock in his home town meant more to Dalmazzo than the election of Pope Julius II.

The first calamity that succeeded in attracting the attention of the Piedmontese chroniclers was not the invasions of Charles VIII, Louis XII, Francis, I, or Charles V, even though these invasions passed right through their country. Rather, it was the sack of the small town of Rivoli west of Turin—first by the French in 1524, then by the Imperialists in 1525, then again by the French in 1527.[14] The next calamity was effected by a certain cutthroat ex-condottiere named Antonio Torresani, who took advantage of a momentary absence of both French and Imperial armies in 1524 and again in 1538 to "enlist all the thieves and roughnecks" in Piedmont and then visit "massacres and total ruin on its [Rivoli's] poor inhabitants."[15] The third calamity occurred in 1547, when Paul III summoned another French army into Italy as part of a pincer movement aimed at forcing Ferrante Gonzaga out of Piacenza. But instead of turning Lombardy into "another Piedmont" in revenge for the murder of his son, he merely provoked the destruction of all the crops in Mirandola and all the cattle in the Piacentino; and he provided Ferrante with the occasion for another of his inimitable, and slightly anachronistic, noble gestures—pawning his own property, amid a flood of high-pitched oratory, to pay for the troops of his penniless overlord (Gosellini). The most spectacular calamity of all was the siege of Cuneo in 1557, when the people of the city, despairing of assistance, held a French army at bay for almost two months, through one stirring morale-building speech after another, until the Marchese di Pescara finally arrived to drive the enemy away.

The heroism as well as the sufferings of the defenders were duly recorded in three successive works: a dialect diary kept by one of the citizen-militiamen (which the modern edition calls "T"), a reworking of the diary by another eyewitness ("P"), and a longer, and fairly well written, *Vera descrittione dell'assedio* ("M"), which was probably commissioned by the city government.[16]

Then, suddenly, the calamities ceased—or at least they diminished to the point where the chroniclers came to regard them as abnormal exceptions and hence not worthy of special attention. In Piedmont, to be sure, the French occupation forces imposed one more big levy in 1559. They tried to impose still another one in 1560. And they hung onto a number of fortified places for several years after they had agreed to give them up. Moreover, in 1560 the restored Duke Emanuele Filiberto decided to use force upon those of his subjects in the Alpine valleys who stood in the way of his policy of religious uniformity; and he abandoned the policy only after the Valdesi (Waldensians) had decided in turn to oppose violence with violence. Still, even in Piedmont the news of the signing of the Treaty of Cateau-Cambrésis was greated with "allegrezze grandi." For like all other Italians, the Piedmontese realized that the treaty had removed one of the chief causes of the calamities: not, to be sure, the presence of foreign armies on Italian soil, but at least the presence of more than one of them at the same time. Emanuele Filiberto's skill in averting incipient calamities thereafter, as he did at the beginning of one famine with a timely shipment of Sicilian grain, soon made his Catholic subjects forget about the salt tax with which he had inaugurated his restoration. Similarly, his skill in bowing to the inevitable with the Treaty of Cavour in 1561 soon reconciled his Valdesi subjects as well. Indeed, they were particularly anxious to minimize the civil war of 1560–61 in order not to offend their Calvinist allies in Geneva, who were already embarrassed enough over the affair of Amboise. Accordingly, both the first two eyewitness accounts and the somewhat fuller account of SCIPIONE LENTOLO of 1562 insisted that the Valdesi had been not protagonists but victims, that they had been forced into resistance not by the duke but by the pope.[17] When, twenty-five years later, the Geneva-trained ex-Dominican GEROLAMO MIOLO of Pinerolo (d. 1593) sought, with the help of the printed works of Flacius Illyricus, to demonstrate in a form half historical and half catechistic that the Valdesi had been orthodox, law-abiding Reformed Christians ever since the days of Valdo himself, he quietly reduced the war to the status of a brief appendix at the end of a list of two centuries of heroic acts. For he was so appreciative of the duke's strict observance of the provisions of the treaty that he was willing to overlook a few minor infractions. And he insisted in attributing the grant of "full freedom of religion and the public exercise of the same" in the valleys solely to the "grace" of the "most serene and clement duke," of whom he professed himself, and all the members of his church in the Val d'Angrognia, to be the most loyal and submissive subjects.[18]

Unfortunately, the end of the calamities on the peninsula robbed local chroniclers and commentary writers of what had for some sixty years been their chief stimulant. Some of them therefore turned their attention to the calamities that still occurred outside the peninsula, on the borderland between Italian and Ottoman spheres of influence. The first one began as a calamity, for the attackers far outnumbered the defenders of Malta in 1567. But it ended as a glorious victory, when the Turks were forced to retire with empty hands. And it provided GIOVAN ANTONIO VIPERANI with an occasion for fitting into no more than thirty-eight pages all the essential elements of the commentary form: a geographical description of the island (which, it seems, had no poisonous snakes and no other domesticated animals than sheep), an account of the origins and the peregrinations of the knights, a calculation of the exact number of men, horses, and ships on both sides, and a smattering of the usual moral and philosophical reflections. "Nothing can overcome the strength and determination [*fortitudine*]" of Christian warriors, Viperani concluded, when these martial qualities are "joined with piety and religion."[19]

The second calamity, on the other hand, began as a tragedy, with the fall of Nicosia and Famagosta in Cyprus. It culminated in a spectacular victory, the Battle of Lepanto. And it ended in bitter disappointment: the failure of the Christian League to follow up its victory, either with the occupation of Greece or with the conquest of Tunis.

To be sure, the specific judgments of the authors regarding the calamity depended to some extent on their personal loyalties. MARCANTONIO MONTEFIORE was a personal friend of Doge Gianotto Lomellini of Genoa, and while fully sympathetic with the cause of Christendom as a whole in its crusade against the infidels, he was equally interested in exalting those of his fellow crusaders who happened also to be his fellow citizens.[20] ANTON MARIA GRAZIANI of Borgo San Sepolcro (1537–1611) was the secretary of his patron, the papal diplomat Cardinal Giovan Francesco Commendone, who eventually rewarded him for his services with a bishopric.[21] BARTOLOMEO SERENO (c. 1520–after 1604) of Recanati had served in the papal army as captain at Poitiers in France and as a recruiting officer in the Papal State, and he fought both at Lepanto and at Tunis before retiring to Montecassino and taking vows as the Benedictine monk Fra Zaccara in 1576.[22] The sympathies both of Graziani and of Sereno thus lay with the pope and the League and with the pope's campaign to revive a crusading spirit among Christians. GIOVAN PIETRO CONTARINI[23] and FRANCESCO LONGO[24] were Venetian patricians, whose main purpose was to justify the policies of the republic; so was GIROLAMO DIEDO, who wrote his eyewitness account at the request of the doge himself.[25] GIORGIO, or GEORGIO, PILLONI of Belluno[26] and ANTONIO RICCOBONI of Rovigo[27] were both lawyers and citizens of cities subject to Venice; and their main interest lay in gathering the news brought back to them by their compatriots in Venetian service. PAOLO PARUTA[28] was a Venetian historian and political philosopher; and his main interest lay in explaining to his fellow citizens how and why a war came about that ended by robbing them of one of their richest possessions. Hence Sereno viewed the war in terms of a contrast between the characters of those he held to be the two major protagonists: Pius V, a man "of unbending doctrinal orthodoxy, of most holy life, of exemplary and irreprehensible morals," and Selim, "wild and bellicose by nature, ... phlegmatic, slow-moving, irresolute," and given to drunkenness notwithstanding the prohibitions of Islamic law. Longo, on the other hand, took the war as an occasion to remind Italians of the fickle nature of their Spanish masters—who had to be forced to enter the Battle of Lepanto and who sailed away at the very moment when, with the Turkish fleet in ruins, all Greece could have easily have been reconquered. "In men of this sort," he warned, "your country can put its trust and hope only in the expectation of an unhappy outcome." He also took it as an occasion to remind them of Venice's new public image. Venice alone, he pointed out, "does not depend upon Transalpine princes. It alone preserves [the memory of] what all Italy once was. It alone keeps up ... the splendor of its ancient grandeur and freedom. With the wisdom of its counsels and arms, it offers protection to all others against the impetuous desires of the barbarians. ..."

Still, most of the historians of the Cyprus war agreed in tracing its origins to a sudden change in Ottoman foreign policy after the death of Suleimān. And, in good humanist tradition, they put the blame for this change on one man: on Selim, who, they said, felt he had to consolidate the power he had seized with an act of glory comparable to the one represented by the new buildings he had erected in Constantinople and Adrianople. Similarly, most of them were willing to admit, like their forerunners ever since 1494, that Italians were also at fault. True, the Senate had taken the precaution of fortifying the outposts of its empire. But, lulled into apathy by a half-century of cordial relations with the Ottomans, it had neglected to clear up the legal status of Cyprus, over which the sultan claimed ultimate sovereignty by virtue of the Ottoman conquest of Egypt. Similarly, the Venetian government in Cyprus had given the Turks just reason to complain by permitting Christian pirates to take refuge in its ports. Indeed, Paruta went so far as to accuse the Venetian authorities of alienating the Cypriots themselves by perpetuating the social injustices of the pre-Venetian regime; and he was not surprised when they openly petitioned the sultan to intervene on their behalf.

All the historians who wrote about the first phase of the war had some difficulty understanding how the Turks, whom they had come to admire as sagacious administrators (particularly under the "wise" Suleimān who "earned the name of the greatest prince of his times"—Contarini), could have resorted to such barbarism at Nicosia and Famagosta, a "miserable and horrible spectacle." They expressed their bewilderment by making the fall of Famagosta the dramatic climax of their narratives. And they dwelt at length on the superhuman fortitude, "worthy of being celebrated ... for all centuries," of the Venetian general Marc' Antonio Bragadino, who, notwithstanding the surrender agreement, was skinned alive in the public square while the Turkish general Mustafā "sat on an elevated place . . . feasting his bestial eyes on this strange and cruel spectacle." All the historians who wrote about the second phase of the war had just as much difficulty understanding its outcome. Depending upon their political loyalties, either they upbraided Venice for making a separate peace with the Turks or they upbraided Venice's allies for not avenging the fall of Famagosta. The Neapolitan—and hence pro-Imperial—historians, like FER-RANTE CARACCIOLO (d. 1596), who fought at Lepanto before becoming governor of Bari and Messina, and TOMASO COSTO, the future historian of the Kingdom,[29] expressed their indignation by exalting the commander-in-chief, Don Giovanni d'Austria, at the expense of the inexperienced armchair admirals of the Venetian contingent. The pro-Venetian historians could not blame the pope directly, since Venice had compromised its traditional policy of self-reliance by asking him for help. But they expressed their indignation quite as forcibly by downgrading the victory at Lepanto to the rank of a dreadful bloodbath—one in which "the whole sea was filled with the blood of an infinite number of bodies" (Contarini). They expressed their indignation also by exalting Sebastiano Venier as the real hero of the battle. And they did so apparently with some justice; for even Sereno admitted his admiration for "the venerable old man, armed like any other soldier, [who] not only encouraged his fellow soldiers to fight, but also gave proof of his stupendous courage with his own hand."

The victory of the Christian navy at Lepanto may have been more memorable than the victory of Themistocles at Salamis or of Philip of Macedon at Scio. But those historians back home who did not have access to special information about it had to be content with much less memorable events. One such might have been the constitutional crisis in Venice in 1582, when the control of finances was shifted from the Council of Ten to the Senate. It might have been, that is, had any of the chronicles and diaries in which the crisis was described ever been published.[30] Another such event might have been the disagreeable repercussions of Genoa's civil war of 1572 on its subject cities. It might have been, that is, had Iacopo Landinelli not waited until the early seventeenth century before composing his comparison between the sufferings of modern Sarzana and the destruction of ancient Luni.[31] Still another such event might have been the War of Gradisca. But Enrico Palladio degli Olivi died before completing the account that he probably intended to incorporate in his monumental history of Friuli.[32] And the future doge Leonardo Donà lost track of the war itself in a scrupulous account that buries any possible memorable qualities amid details concerning bureaucratic bungling and corruption.[33]

Some events, on the other hand, seem still to have been sufficiently memorable to enable those who wrote about them to fulfill the obligation of glorifying the city in which they took place. Turin was rendered illustrious on 10 August 1585 by the magnificent entrance of Princess Caterina of Austria, the bride of Duke Carlo Emanuele; and the communal secretary, GIOVAN ANGELO SILVA, sighed with relief as he noted that the calendar date of this happy event coincided with the date of a tragic event forty-two years earlier: the outbreak of another ruinous war between Francis I and Charles V.[34] Similarly, the tiny principality of Sabbioneta was rendered illustrious, according to NICCOLÒ DE' DONATI, by the splendor of its prince, Vespasiano Gonzaga, formerly a general in the service of Charles V and Philip II, whom peace permitted finally to settle down in his principality and, instead of fighting, to make a pilgrimage to Loreto, to murder his cousin, to receive communion from the hands of St. Carlo Borromeo, and to be elected chairman of his confraternity. The moment he tried to revert to the mores of pre-1559 days—by picking a quarrel with the duke of Mantua—he was firmly told by the Senate of Milan to withdraw his troops from the border.[35]

What made Forlì illustrious, at the same time, was not the famine it shared with the rest of the Mediterranean world in the 1590s, but the memory of greater days long past—of 3 November 1494, when the citizens "rose up and put to sack all the possessions of the French," of 27 August 1495, when they killed Caterina Sforza's governor, of 6 February 1504, when the Ordelaffi were welcomed back. Indeed, the closer SEBASTIANO MENZOCCHI (c. 1535–1600) came to the present, the sketchier became his text: one paragraph each for 1562, 1563, 1564, and nothing at all for the years between 1568 and 1577.[36] Similarly, what made Alessandria illustrious was the appearance of a comet in 1577, the arrival of a Spanish relic merchant in 1578, and the death of one and the accession of another bishop in 1584. But none of these events, RAFFAELE LUMELLO realized, was worthy of the grandiloquent Latin prose he had bestowed on the city's heroic founder, Alexander III ("vir omnibus virtutibus ornatissimus"), four centuries earlier.[37] What made the tiny town of Castro in Lazio illustrious in 1575 was the memory of its near destruction in 1529–30. For the Farnese had fulfilled their promise to prevent the town ever again from being exposed to such danger—at least so thought one of its citizens, DOMENICO ANGELI, who had nothing more to report thereafter.[38] What made Milan illustrious in the 1560s, according to one anonymous chronicler, was solely its "beautiful site and sumptuous buildings." For after the death of Charles V in 1558 he could find nothing else to say about it.[39] Brescia was somewhat more fortunate. In the 1550s it was graced with the erection of a wooden castle in celebration of the election of Francesco Venier as doge of Venice, a castle defended, according to BERNARDINO VALLABIO, by "twenty-five armed soldiers dressed from head to foot in yellow, with yellow feathers in their caps . . . and with pointless daggers" in their hands (if you can't wage war, play it!). In the 1570s it was visited by the plague, which the physician FRANCESCO ROBACCIOLO described in Manzonian detail. It was bereft of its cardinal protector, whom TITO LUZZAGO had met during his student days in Rome. It was momentarily filled with hysterical peasants terrorized by a rumor that a band of Huguenots (whoever they were) were raiding the countryside. And in the 1580s it played host to the same delegation of Japanese notables that made half the other cities in northern Italy illustrious at the same time.[40]

Thus the war gave way to peace, apprehension to security, chaos to order. All the duke of Mantua had to worry about any longer was a possible challenge to his claims over Monferrato. He accordingly hired GIOVAN BATTISTA POSSEVINO, the brother of the famous Jesuit historian-missionary and a professor of medicine at Padua, to support his claims with historical demonstrations. And when these demonstrations proved to rest on documents that Possevino himself had invented, he turned for assistance to one of the ablest and most prolific scholars and polemicists of the next generation, the Italianized German Gaspare Scioppio, who obliged him with a properly documented genealogical survey of the Gonzaga family.[41] No one in Perugia had to worry about anything at all, not even about the new papal governor, who arrived in 1580 with two hundred men on horseback. For the new governor also brought along two well-trained jurists, whose presence guaranteed his subjects against both arbitrary acts of the government itself and inefficiency and insubordination in governmental administration, as one gate guard soon discovered when he spent two days in jail for not having demanded the obligatory medical certificates from two Sicilian monks. Hence, what GIOVAN BATTISTA CRISPOLTI defined as "news" consisted solely of banquets, harvests, murders, grants of academic degrees, and visits of traveling cardinals.[42] No one at Modena had anything to worry about either—most particularly not GIOVAN BATTISTA SPACCINI, master of the wardrobe and chief of "perspective and fortification" for Duke Cesare d'Este. He wrote a diary as full as Lancilotto's only because he was trying to outdo his more fortunate predecessor of more eventful days. If news was lacking, he could always fill in with the words of the latest popular songs and epigrams. If news was disagreeable, he could just ignore it—as he did the big news of 1595, when Duke Cesare was thrown out of Ferrara. How was he supposed to know why Modena was suddenly filled with troops? How was he supposed to know that the century-old duchy of Ferrara had suddenly shrunk to the much more modest measure of the duchy of Modena?[43]

In no place was the paucity of memorable events more noticeable in the half-century after Cateau-Cambrésis than in the city that had produced such a plethora of them in the half-century after the invasion of Charles VIII— namely, in Florence. One chronicler, Lorenzo Poggio, accumulated a huge mass of notes about what had happened during the five decades between 1531 and 1580, during what seems to have been a lifetime spent in the archives. But he apparently judged none of them to be worth even arranging in some sort of intelligible order.[44] Another chronicler, AGOSTINO LAPINI (1515–after 1592),[45] learned to write chronicle by copying scattered passages from those of Villani and Landucci. But he never learned to discern a connection between the arrival of Charles VIII in Florence and his departure from France or to distinguish qualitatively his arrival from the fall of three meteorites the next year. He was well enough educated to have heard of Pier Vettori, "a man very well versed in Greek letters." But he was not so well educated that he could perceive the childish awkwardness of his own style:

> Frate Francesco . . . *disse* che non credeva che il suddetto frate Girolamo
> *dicessi* il vero di quelle sue profezie che *diceva*. . . . (My italics.)

He lived well enough on his salary as chaplain in the cathedral and holder of a benefice in the Casentino not to have any complaints about the new political regime. But he was not socially prominent enough to think of justifying the regime in any other way than by identifying it with his *patria*. Cosimo, he said, had been created by the will of the citizens and by the consent of the whole people. The exiles at Montemurlo had come "to make war on the city of Florence, their *patria*." And the fall of Siena had been as welcome to the Florentines in general as it was to be repugnant to Lapini's freedom-loving post-Risorgimento editor. Hence, Lapini was not ashamed to dwell at length on the reception of the Japanese ambassadors in 1584, on the celebration of the new Forty-Hour Devotions in 1589, on the fortification of Livorno, on the visits of the archbishop of Milan and the "duca di Luzinburg." For all these events, in his opinion, were as worthy of being remembered as any he had read about in the works of his two mentors.

Another of the late-sixteenth-century Florentine diarists, BASTIANO ARDITI (1504–after 1579), was descended from an artisan family well enough established to have been mentioned in public documents since 1238. He was therefore obliged, according to his modern editor, to reflect "the psychology of the popular masses"—even though he actually limited his dramatis personae to foreign and court dignitaries and to Florentine patricians.[46] So well did he reflect this psychology, indeed, that, *pace* Marx, he immediately identified with the Genoese aristocrats who fled to Florence during the popular uprising of 1575, and he was an enthusiastic admirer of the two young Florentine aristocrats who led the rival football *(calcio)* teams of 1576. He was also obliged, the editor continues, to express the "desolate, bitter protest . . . of the passive, enslaved plebeians" of the city—apparently by quoting the same high prices that everyone else complained about in that inflationary age. And he was obliged by his membership in a class that could not but have resented being tranquilized by traditional opiates to be particularly hostile to "the Counter Reformation"—even though he applauded the efforts of the archbishop and the apostolic visitor to enforce clerical residence and to remedy abuses. True, Arditi had as much to complain of as any cranky old man. But the only fault he found to complain of in the reigning grand duke, Francesco de' Medici, was that he kept a mistress in open violation of "a precept given by the mouth of God." And he condemned the wellborn associates of that operatic Brutus, Orazio Pucci, who had much more to complain of in the grand duke, with as much "spagnolesco dispregio" as his editor, in the days when Spain was still out of favor in certain Italian political circles, was to attribute to Arditi's social superiors.

Thus Lapini was left to record what he himself was incapable of defining as anything but trivia, and Arditi was left with a desire to grumble but with nothing really to grumble about. For GIULIANO DE' RICCI (1524–1606), however, the paucity of memorable events was the cause of a personal tragedy. Ricci wanted to be not a chronicler but a historian. He was a nephew of none other than Niccolò Machiavelli, whose letters he copied out in his own hand and whose works he desperately tried to save from the Tridentine Index. He was also a relative and possibly a student of Pier Vettori, and he was an admirer of Vettori's fellow philologist, Bartolomeo Barbadori. From them he learned how to organize his research notes for future reference, how to interrupt the chronological order of his narrative in order to supply background information, and how to increase the dramatic quality of his prose in order properly to describe such dramatic events as the rebellion of an unreformable convent of nuns in Pisa. That Ricci never fulfilled his ambition, that the 540 pages of the modern edition of his diary remain in the form of an incoherent mass of miscellaneous (though often very informative) notations, cannot be blamed on the current political establishment, of which he was a sincere supporter. Grand Duke Francesco, he pointed out, prohibited gambling, forbade the carrying of arms in the city, appointed well-trained professionals to public office, and kept the patricians of Cortona from fleecing their peasants. Grand Duke Ferdinando sent the corrupt director of the hospital to jail, fired the dishonest head of the Wool Guild, and kept food prices within the reach of the poor. Both of them did their best to keep in line the idle, affluent, overdressed youngsters who were the unfortunate consequences of peace and prosperity. And neither of them did anything to inhibit his "intention to write freely what may seem to me worthy of memory, without respect of persons or adulation of anyone." If he (or his son) decided to rip a page or two out of his manuscript, and if Lapini decided to blot out some of his passages, they did so largely for reasons other than a fear of political retribution.[47]

Rather, the fault lay with the times. The object of historiography, Ricci knew, was great events, and he had some hope, in the first years of his diary-writing, that the series of events inaugurated by Cosimo's triumphal trip to Rome and by the battles of Lepanto and Poitiers might continue. But he soon found that history in Florence had irreversibly dwindled to the level of the comings and goings of prelates, to gossip about the grand duchess, to reports of murders and hangings, and to public spectacles. Indeed, chronicles were gradually being replaced by well-subsidized and elegantly printed *descrittioni* of such purely ceremonial "events" as "the baptism of the firstborn [daughter] of the Prince of Florence, with the *intermedi* of the comedy . . . ," "the festivities for the solemn entrance . . . of the most serene prince of Mantua," or "the funeral ceremonies for . . . Cosimo de' Medici . . . on the day XVII of May in the year. . . ." It might be possible, he thought, eventually to discover a connection between such "light matters" and more "general and great matters"; and he himself tried, without much success, to associate the petty crimes he reported from day to day with what he supposed to have been a recent rise in population. But as early as 1573 he had to admit that "the peace established between

Henry II and . . . Philip king of Spain brought such peace and repose to all Italy . . . that it has taken away any opportunity for writing from those who might have had the desire." And some thirty-three years later he had to admit that he himself had written "in vain." "I never have," he confessed, "and I never will be able" to convert the diary into history.

BOOK IV

THE REVIVAL OF
MUNICIPAL HISTORIOGRAPHY

9

DEPENDENCE AND INDEPENDENCE

THUS THE DISAPPEARANCE OF MEMORABLE EVENTS IN THE SECOND HALF OF THE SIX-teenth century eventually robbed the writers of diaries, chronicles, and commentaries of subjects to write about. But in the meantime, the plethora of such events in the first half of the century rescued the writers of municipal history from the dilemma of their predecessors, who had faced a similar dearth of subject matter in the relatively peaceful years before 1494.

The Subject Cities

It did so first of all by destroying the distinction between dominant and subject cities. To be sure, some historians still had doubts about the validity of what they frankly admitted to be "mediocre" subjects. One of them chose to write in Italian rather than in Latin simply because he despaired of ever finding readers outside Italy. Another proclaimed the "weight, majesty, and purity" of his style to be incapable of attracting any readers at all unless he could add the name of a famous patron to his own.[1] Moreover, many of them obviously suffered from the absence of the kind of ancient models that might have been provided them by the once flourishing school of Hellenistic local historiography—the school that Polybius had demolished with his demands for "pragmatic" history.[2] Nevertheless, none of these historians could any longer maintain that the calamities had respected either size or political status. None of them could deny that those cities from which history had withdrawn in the Quattrocento had, in the Cinquecento, suffered as many sieges, sacks, famines, and extortions and had been honored by the visits of as many famous kings, princes, and generals, as any of those to which history had formerly been confined. And they accordingly made no distinction in form or genre between histories written about a dominant city and histories written about even the most obscure of subject cities.*

Such a city was Aquila. It had never been independent, and its relatively recent

---

* Neither, therefore, do I, even though Riccardo Fubini rightly objects to my use of the term *municipal* with regard to a city like Venice. I would rather use a term that elevates Pavia to the rank of Milan than one that reduces Milan to the level of Pavia; but I cannot find one in any of the languages I know—unless it be the nineteenth-century Italian term *storia patria*. Still, I do note that the principle by which all cities are of equal value is recognized even today. Milan, Naples, and several other regional capitals have recently been made the objects of pluri-volume, encyclopedic histories. But so have Mantua and Brescia, which are only *capoluoghi di provincia*.

foundation (1254) excluded it from any ancient glory except what might be borrowed from its association with the region of the Sabines, in which Sallust had been born. But it had experienced enough "seditions, discords, tyrannies, and popular tumults" to have gained the attention of the leading historians of the Quattrocento. And its Cinquecento historian, BERNARDO CIRILLO (1500–1575), could thus write about it not at home but in distant Loreto, where he was serving as apostolic delegate. After the ravages of the Barons' War, which had broken the peace so arduously established by Alfonso d'Aragona, Aquila had suffered still more severely from the invasion of Charles VIII, from the fights between the Orsini and the Colonna, and from the ravages of soldiers on all sides of the War of 1528–29. There was thus no reason why the great value of history recognized by such men as Livy, Polybius, Alexander Severus, and Ptolemy Philadelphus could not as well "be applied to places and cities subject to the dominion of others" as "to republics that recognize no superior."[3]

Another such city was Bergamo. It had been restored to Venetian rule in 1516; and by 1543 it was enjoying such "peace and civil concord" that "the name of war had been forgotten." But its success in surviving first a French and then a German occupation, in raising the huge tax demanded by an Imperial general, and in cleaning up the mess left after his troops ignored his orders, made it fully worthy of FRANCESCO BELLAFINI's (d. 1543) exercises in telegraphic Latin:

> . . . Arnolpho non suggerente, Berengarium foroiulensem Roma oriundum alii Imperatorem, alii Guidonem Ducem Spoletanum creant: inter quos contentione & postmodum pugna, Berengarius victor apparuit, eo vita functo Lotharium filium Spolentani et Etruschi Regem declarant.

Bellafini was so busy during most of his life—as secretary, chancellor, and *oratore* (ambassador) for the commune—that he did not get around to describing the subsequent, as well as all the previous, accomplishments of the Bergameschi.[4] He had time only to mention them in his dedication: cleaning the aqueducts, damming the rivers, building roads, and "restoring the city to its form and dignity" under the benevolent direction of the Venetian governor.[5] But MARIO GIOVANNELLI realized that the nature of history had changed after Volterra had voluntarily submitted to the new Medici regime in Florence. The only military exploits any longer permitted it were those accomplished far off on the Mediterranean by the Volterran admiral in the granducal navy, Jacopo Inghirami. At home, history had to content itself with such mundane exploits as the reconstruction of the city square, the conversion of a Jewish family to Christianity, and the erection of new institutions: a school, an academy, a hospital, several monasteries, and, best of all, one of the first Tridentine seminaries in all Italy. But Giovannelli did not really object. "Rejoice, O citizens of Volterra," he exclaimed, "be merry, you inhabitants of the city!" For Cosimo de' Medici's fortress now protected them once and for all against a repetition of what had been the price of glory in 1530, the sack of the city by a Florentine army.[6]

Cremona had suffered somewhat less than Brescia and Bergamo. Still, the French occupation of 1520 had produced a fair list of atrocities—a child cooked before his parents when they failed to supply the meat demanded of them, two suspected conspirators torn apart with red-hot pokers as they were dragged nude through the streets, and all the citizens drained of their resources by endless levies. The German occupation that followed the defeat of the French in 1525 left the countryside barren of both food and inhabitants. That alone justified the patrician LODOVICO CAVITELLI[7] and the sculptor ANTONIO CAMPO[8] in searching through the histories of ancient Rome and modern Milan in order to express "the love I always bear and the obligation I acknowledge toward my country"; and it justified Campo in persuading the city council to pay for his statue of Hercules, whom he discovered to have been the founder of the city. "Wars and calamities" and "civil discord and sedition" eventually gave way to "the condition [the city] now enjoys, by the particular beneficence of God, under the invincible, most happy Catholic king of Spain." But the memorable events went on: a visit from Charles V in 1541 and from Prince and then King Philip II in 1549 and 1551, the approach of Piero Strozzi's mercenaries in 1544, the funeral of Cardinal Giovan Battista Speziano in 1545. Then, when "the memorable and most happy year 1559" at last inaugurated "the most sincere and stable peace ever contracted," the Cremonese historians discovered that their fellow citizens, who had been the victims of the art of war since the fourteenth century, could now be agents in the art of peace. Not having generals or princes of its own, they pointed out, Cremona owed its glory to the judge Andrea Borgo, the Greek teacher Daniele de Caietani, the senator Agostino Somencio, the architect Giorgio Fondulo, the anatomist Realdo Colombo, and the bureaucrat-poet Francesco Pietranegra. And the history of Cremona thus turned into a Who's Who of Cremonesi who had distinguished themselves in the arts, letters, and civil administration, both at home and abroad.

Casale had suffered still less than Cremona. But it too had been pillaged by the soldiers of Charles V when it refused to submit to its new lords, the Gonzaga of Mantua, in 1530; and it had been captured by the French when, in 1555, the Spanish general charged with defending it was caught in his cups during a carnival party. Yet history in Casale assumed the very practical function of supporting the maintenance of the traditional autonomy of Monferrato against the pretensions of the distant Gonzaga to rule it as "absolute princes." And it proved capable of fulfilling this function when Duke Guglielmo Gonzaga finally accepted the conditions the citizens imposed upon him.[9] Udine, on the other hand, had suffered somewhat more than Cremona. Its leading historian, JACOPO VALVASONE, dedicated himself, in the second half of the century, to excogitating means for preventing the recurrence of the Gothic invasion of the fifth century, the Turkish invasion of 1499, and the civil war of 1512, all of which he described in detail.[10] Since the only remedy to these ills lay in the "exaltation of the lofty dominion" of the Venetian Senate, he supplemented his histories of Udine and the Friuli under the patriarchs with a survey of the fortresses built under Venetian rule; and he ended with a recommendation that the political frontiers of the republic to be pushed eastward until they corresponded to a geographical frontier.

Some historians of subject cities, on the other hand, despaired of finding inspiration in what had happened since the calamities had ended, and they turned instead to what had happened in the ages before the calamities had begun. Nothing much had taken place in Fermo since a popular uprising in the mid-fifteenth century had thrown out the troops of Francesco Sforza and introduced those of the Church. Or at least neither the cathedral canon FRANCESCO ADAMI nor his paternal uncle, Cardinal Ottinelli, who edited and published Adami's manuscript, cared to recall the horrors perpetrated in 1502 by Machiavelli's villain, Oliverotto, and in 1538 by the pope's son, Pierluigi Farnese. So Adami deduced Fermo's antiquity from appropriate passages in Strabo and Procopius and from the archaeological remains excavated by his contemporaries. And he held up for the admiration of his fellow citizens the bravery of their ancestors in fighting off one tyrant after another from the 1390s to the 1450s, the period to which the bulk of his humanist chronicle is dedicated.[11] Nothing at all seems to have happened in Pisa. Or at least BENEDETTO MASTIANI did not consider either the war of 1528–30, which he lived through, or the restoration of the university, where he taught until 1535, to be particularly worthy of notice. He turned instead to "those things done magnificently by our ancestors" when they conquered the Balearic Islands and brought back the widow and the son of the former ruler for a triumphal procession through the streets of the city.[12]

Adami and Mastiani had good reasons for choosing the past over the present. For the past had been charged with a responsibility that the present was no longer able to bear. Thanks to the presence of a firm, outside authority, Cato's injunction, *pugna pro patria,* had now to be carried out with the tongue rather than the sword. Hence the task of defending the *patria* "against the insults of its enemies" passed from soldiers to historians, whom Giovannelli called upon to "praise and exalt" their city by "telling of its ancient beauty and greatness and of the heroic deeds of its illustrious personages."[13] Similarly, the present could offer no greater examples of virtue than the rather humdrum administrative decrees of the reforming bishops of Verona, and it could offer no more glorious acts than the removal of several centuries' accumulation of garbage from the Verona Arena (Della Corte). Hence, the task of teaching morality fell to those who were familiar with the ages in which adequate moral examples could still be found. They alone could penetrate "the temple of immortality" in which were enshrined "the generous and worthy deeds of the illustrious citizens of bygone centuries." They alone could plot out "the sharp, steep, and tiring path by which one arrived at the golden amphitheater of eternal Honor, Glory, and Fame" (Sarayna). They alone could fulfill an important methodological corollary of humanist ethics: that the effectiveness of the moral examples proposed depended on a belief in their historical veracity. For, as Pancrazio Giustinian noted, a historian's credibility diminished rapidly as he approached his own times.[14] Finally, they alone were able to appeal "to the unlettered as well as to the learned" in accordance with the popularizing tendencies of sixteenth-century humanism. For "domestic examples," as Ludovico Della Chiesa put it, those drawn from a past to which a particular audience was bound by ties of kinship and affection, "much more effectively dispose us to love virtue and abhor vice" than those drawn from the history of another city.[15]

The history of subject cities thus acquired a new purpose. It no longer sought, as it had in the fifteenth century, to persuade a pan-Italian audience that a literary monument worthy of Livy could elevate a Treviso or a Cremona to the rank of ancient Rome. Rather, it sought to elevate the moral life of all the inhabitants of one particular community, and they alone were expected to read and profit from it. It scrupulously adhered to the external forms of humanist historiography, since these forms were still held to be indispensable for rhetorical purposes. But it usually abandoned Latin, which only a few at home could read and which could no longer attract the attention of even the learned abroad. It adopted the vernacular in its place, so that, as Sarayna put it, "the deeds, the language, and you [the audience] will all belong to the same country." Indeed, it did so occasionally even to the point of preferring local variants of the vernacular to the rules codified by the followers of Bembo.[16] The final justification was then provided by SCIPIONE CHIARAMONTI of Cesena, when he summed up in the mid-seventeenth century the arguments put forth by all his predecessors since the mid-sixteenth century. Small cities, Chiaramonti pointed out, are far more numerous than big cities. Aristotle studied small animals far more assiduously than he did big animals. And even the smallest city in Italy possessed enough records of "the vicissitudes of fortune" to teach any of its citizens all they needed to know in order "to prevent the occurrence of all [further] calamities in the future."[17]

Vicenza was particularly well supplied with such records, as JACOPO MARZARI discovered between writing a treatise on comets in 1577 and a textbook on criminal law in 1592. The bishop, Cardinal Girolamo Leandro, had assembled a sizeable collection of manuscripts, and many noble families had succumbed to the current fashion for decorating their palace walls with the ancient inscriptions. Except for the erection of Palladio's Teatro Olimpico, it is true, nothing much had happened in Vicenza since its "voluntary reception into the bosom of the great Venetian Republic"—"under whose banners," Marzari added, "it now lives with great contentment." But a vast number of "memorable deeds and brilliant feats" had been performed there in the some five thousand years since Vento, the son of Veneto, of the noble lineage of Cam, had been led to the city's present site by a white dog running around in circles. So many deeds have been performed, indeed, that the memory of them could adequately keep Vento's heirs inflamed with "a desire for glory and virtue" even in the posthistorical age in which they now lived. "There is no doubt," concluded Marzari, "that Vicenza always has"—and therefore that it always will—"enjoy a most splendid reputation."[18] Udine was equally well supplied with such records, as GIOVANNI CANDIDO (d. 1528) discovered after a Venetian army had rescued him from a church tower during the most recent, and, thank heaven, the last outburst of civil war in the city. He began by appropriating material from two assiduous collectors, Giovan Battista Franceschini, who had inherited a voluminous local chronicle, and Antonio Bellone, "one of the most curious and diligent investigators of our antiquities."[19] He then reread the works of all the ancient and modern historians in order to find answers to some long-standing historical problems: whether Aquileia in antiquity had been inside or outside the Roman province of Venetia, whether its name derived from that of Aeneas's companion, Aquilio of Troy, rather than from the Latin name for "the waters"—*Acquae*—that surrounded it, and whether his predecessors had been led astray by the poets. After reordering all this material according to the stylistic rules he had learned from Sabellico at Padua, he arrived at several encouraging conclusions. The quality of the soil and climate of the Friuli was such, he found, that Augustus's wife Livia had prolonged her life just by drinking its *vino pucino*. The accomplishments of those "worthy and powerful men," the Venetians, could be partially attributed to the presence of immigrant Aquileian nobles among their distant ancestors. And rape doesn't pay, as one soldier learned when the Virgin blinded him for committing it right in front of her statue.[20]

Treviso was even more abundantly supplied with records. Between 1575, when he arrived there to marry and practice law, and 1610, when he accepted another job and contracted a second marriage in Padua, GIOVANNI BONIFACCIO, or BONIFACIO, (1547–1635), managed to fill some 527 quarto pages with what he discovered in them.[21] True, the records were uneven: they yielded two whole books for the fourteenth century alone, but only one book for the fifteenth century and only five pages for the half-century between the restoration of Venetian rule and the Battle of Lepanto. And Bonifacio had some difficulty fitting them into the periodization schemes he borrowed from Biondo ("memorable and truly unhappy without comparison . . . was the year 400") and from Guicciardini (the deaths of Innocent VIII and Lorenzo de' Medici "opened the door to immense, calamitous wars"). But the records were quite sufficient to show all the current citizens "the way to live righteously and wisely not only under good princes," not only under the best of all possible princes, the Venetian senators, but also under bad princes, or the "most impious and cruel" of them all, Ezzelino da Romano. "It is good advice in important affairs," he proclaimed, "not to change forms . . . that experience has shown to be even moderately good." "Peace, wealth, and leisure generate rapacity among the nobles . . . and avarice among the unstable plebeians"—as they did most notably in

1214, when the nobles of Treviso put on a mock battle with oranges and perfume bombs.

Verona was better supplied with records even than Vicenza—so well supplied, indeed, that within a half-century they inspired the composition of two major historical works as well as the collection of the many unpublished notes and memoranda catalogued in the eighteenth century by that most industrious heir of the sixteenth-century municipal historians, Scipione Maffei.[22] Neither TORELLO SARAYNA (or SARAINA)[23] nor GIROLAMO DELLA CORTE[24] particularly enjoyed their work, to be sure. The barbarous language of the texts they had to read revolted them. The contradictory accounts in the chronicles puzzled them. The "ancient and torn pages" that Della Corte found in the library of the Gesuati fathers were often unintelligible. And epigraphic evidence was often contradicted by the literary sources—particularly when it was misread by those scholars who were determined to push the foundation date of the Arena back into the reign of Augustus. It was thus impossible to determine with certainty whether Noah arrived in Italy 240, 248, or only 108 years after the Flood, or whether Verona had been founded in Anno Orbis 2770 (from Eusebius), A.O. 2848 (from Josephus et al.), or in the 248th or only the 204th year before the birth of Abraham (from Augustine, C. D., Book VIII). Nonetheless, Sarayna "did not spare any effort in gathering together the surviving fragments and in putting them together to the best of [his] ability"—first in a Latin treatise on antiquities and then in a polished humanist history that extended from the fall of Rome to the fall of the Scaligers. Similarly, Della Corte "dedicated himself with great attention . . . to the study of all the histories, chronicles, . . . and other writings [that might] offer some light in finding the truth." For history showed that Verona had once generated such heroes as "the most magnanimous and powerful prince in Italy," Can Grande Della Scala, and his "pleasant, benign, and very religious" successor, Bartolomeo. The memory of two great ages in the past, one under the Romans and another under the Scaligeri, served admirably to make modern Veronesi fully grateful for the current, and this time eternal, great age under the Venetians. Now at last they could get on with more important matters like music, as ALESSANDRO CANOBBIO (b. 1532/35) noted in a speech to the Accademia Novella in 1571.[25]

Anti-Medievalism

To be sure, as a teacher of morality history had one serious shortcoming: it could provide examples of virtues only as they were manifested in individual persons. It could not hold up as equally exemplary the political and social circumstances that had elicited, or made possible, the expression of those virtues. Not one of the historians showed the least nostalgia for the ages their heroes had lived in, and all of them shuddered at the very thought of reestablishing in their cities a political status similar to the ones they wrote about. "If we compare the present state of our city with that of the past," said Della Corte, "we will see how miserable, unhappy, and calamitous the others have been." For then no one thought "about anything but his own interests, his own comfort, and the satisfaction of his own appetites." Communal independence, they discovered, had inevitably meant tyranny. "Truly miserable and worthy of great compassion" was Vicenza, said Bonifacio, as it groveled before Ezzellino. "Not only was it dispossessed of its freedom, but it also was made the most unhappy subject of most cruel tyrants." Independence had also meant civil strife. "The disunion of the citizens is truly . . . a deadly pestilence," said Campo,[26] grateful for never having experienced it himself. "It not only brings ruin to noble and illustrious families, but it also exterminates even the most powerful and famous cities." The present might be a bit dull, in other words. But at least it was peaceful, prosperous, just, and happy. And the historians were happy to maintain an absolute separation between what they recorded in their books and what they experienced in their daily lives.

This lack of sympathy with just those periods of their own past which were most productive of objects of imitation may partially explain the reluctance of many students of those periods to publish or otherwise make generally available the records they were forced to study. Bernardino Azzurrini (1543–1620) transcribed some sixty chapters from Tolosano together with snippets from other chronicles of Faenza into "a huge disordered scrapbook of local information." But none of it was published until Antonio Messeri discovered its historical value four centuries later.[27] Fabio Montaperto discovered a manuscript of Goffredo Malaterra in 1555 that supported the current papal thesis concerning Urban II's bull on legatine powers in Sicily. It was immediately confiscated by the civil authorities. Giulio de Syndicis insisted that his twelfth-century compatriot Falco Beneventano, whose chronicle he resurrected in support of papal claims to sovereignty in his native Benevento, was "the most eloquent historian we have from the Middle Age [*mezzana età*]." But he left to Antonio Caracciolo early in the following century the task of putting order into a prose that even Muratori found distasteful.[28] Several gentlemen of Cortona transcribed what few diaries they could find about their native city. But their transcriptions were ignored until the members of the Accademia Etrusca ran across them in 1896.[29] A certain Gaspare Fuscilillo (fl. 1531–71) combined what he copied at home, where he was a canon in the cathedral, with what he could dig out of the archives of Naples about the city of Sessa. But none of what he copied was published until it passed into the hands of the great, but not always accurate, text publisher of the eighteenth century, Alessio Aurelio Pelliccia.[30] A certain Lionardo Astrino was approached by several publishers in the 1520s to "reduce to their original simplicity" several "chronicles of the noble Parthenopean City [that had been] corrupted through the iniquity of time." But they apparently backed away when exposed to a prose "foreign to the rules of historiography."[31] The well-known historian Tommaso Costo was careful to "reorder and reduce" to legible form the documents collected by a priest named Vincenzo Verace without any regard for the "rules of historiography."[32] But when the notorious jurist Antonio Feltrio (d. 1562) tried to "reduce" the many documents he had collected in the course of his interminable lawsuits, he produced what even an eighteenth-century editor (Soria) found to be "the most boring thing in the world." Indeed, most of the work of the sixteenth-century chronicle collectors is still today in manuscript: that of Aulo Giano Farrasio, Antonio and Cardinal Girolamo Seripando in Naples,[33] Mario da Erba in Parma,[34] Domenico Ferretti in Reggio, Claudio Paci and Giacomo Antonio Pedroni (d. 1635) in Rimini.

Thus with one or two exceptions—like the "Villani" chronicle published in Naples in 1526,[35] the "fragments of various histories" included in an appendix to Francesco Bardi's *Vittoria navale* of 1584, and Pietro Gerardo's chronicle of Ezzelino first published in Venice in 1543[36]—the principal literary sources of municipal historiography remained relatively unknown until they came to the attention of a few brave editors in the seventeenth century, like Camillo Peregrino of Naples. And most of them remained unknown until the eighteenth century, when their utility in support of a campaign to resurrect an Italian historical consciousness forced the much more competent editors of that time to suspend their stylistic sensitivities and transcribe the texts exactly as they found them.

In fact, the only Italians of the sixteenth-century who seriously promoted the publication of pre-Renaissance chronicles were the Florentines. And they did so for reasons that had little to do with the exigencies of historical research. Filippo and Jacopo Giunti proposed in 1568 the publication of all "those writers who in any manner whatever have left a memory of past times."[37] But ten years later they admitted that the obvious "truth" in such "simpler and less artful" texts as the *Istorie pistolesi* could not qualify them for consideration in the same category as Bruni, Poggio, and Guicciardini, writers who had "restored" historiography "to its ancient quality."[38] What justified those who "for some time now, with such diligence, have been going around looking for old texts in the back of dusty closets" was the resurrection of the impeccable language of fourteenth-century Florence, which the self-proclaimed linguistic dictator Lionardo Salviati was just then seeking to impose on writers all over Italy. Another eleven years later they neglected completely to mention the historical importance even of the one late medieval chronicle that maintained its popularity throughout the sixteenth century, the chronicle of Giovanni Villani. What justified the members of the Accademia degli Alterati in rejecting the editions of Villani previously published at Venice and in establishing a new text on the basis of the earliest manuscripts was its language, which they proclaimed to be as pure as that of Boccaccio. What justified the republication in 1581 of the 1567 "correction" of Lodovico Domenichi's translation of Matteo Villani was its importance as an essential complement to what was recognized as a linguistic and literary monument—and not, as Domenichi had claimed in the first Torrentino edition of 1554, the abundance of information it contained.

This lack of sympathy with what was called the "Middle Age" may also explain the relative failure of historiography in some of those cities that had succeeded in preserving, if not their total independence, at least their status as *dominanti*. Lucca survived the calamities of the first half of the century in part because of the determination with which the silkworkers' riot of 1531 and the Burlamachi plot of 1546 were put down. It survived also because of the success of the oligarchs who ruled it in placating the new regime in Florence.[39] Yet the only Lucchese historian of the whole century, LORENZO TRENTA, did not even mention these accomplishments, and the term "pristina libertà" he used to describe its current condition had nothing to do with the most famous manifestation of its freedom: its refusal to admit the Jesuits. He merely translated, rather poorly at that and without acknowledgment, what Poggio had written about the Florentine wars of the early fifteenth century; and he came up with very little historical support for his concluding "exhortation to my people of Lucca" to stay away from tyrants—which, by the way, was the one thing that the oligarchs had every intention of doing anyway.[40] Milan emerged from the calamities with an Imperial and then a Spanish governor, to be sure, in the place of its now extinct domestic princes, but with all its traditional institutions intact. It had restored its eastern and western boundaries to what they had been before 1494; it had almost reannexed Piacenza after the murder of Pierluigi Farnese; and it eventually compensated for territorial losses in the south with the conquest of the Valtellina in the northeast. Yet its only major historian before the death of the last Sforza in 1534, Bernardo Arluno,[41] left the body of his work uncompleted in manuscript. And its only major historian during the other sixty-seven years of the century failed even to approach either the standards of his Milanese predecessors or those generally accepted by other municipal historians in his own day.

True, PAOLO MORIGIA (c. 1524–after 1603) promised to deliver "an account . . . in good order" of all that had happened in the city "from its foundation to the present year, 1591: with the number of its archbishops, saints, churches, and monasteries, with the antiquities and nobility of many families . . . , and with two very full tables."[42] He offered all the traditional arguments and one more besides on behalf of local history, which, he claimed, was also the foundation of all social order: "without the discipline that we learn from history, everything would be in confusion." He diligently searched through public and private archives for "contracts, privileges, epitaphs, and other authentic [i.e., nonnarrative] writings," from which he quoted abundantly. And he read carefully through all of the ancient and modern historians who had ever said anything about Milan.

But Morigia missed the point entirely. He failed to distinguish qualitatively or chronologically among his sources, which he dumped together in this fashion:

> Strabo, Titus Livius, Cato, Trogus [Pompeius], Berosus, Polybius, Gottfried [Villhardouin], Cornelius Tacitus, Plutarch in the life of Marcellus, Decius Ausonius, [Giorgio] Merula, Bernardino Corio, Ammianus [Marcellinus], Biondo. . . .

He isolated everything that pertained to ecclesiastical institutions in one book and dedicated another entirely to the history of the Gesuati, simply because that was the order he happened to belong to. He increased the potency of the mythical founder, Tubal, son of Japeth—and the availability of unattached women at the time—to the point of giving him 90 children and 3,700 grandchildren. He multiplied the historically verifiable number of soldiers in the Gothic army and dogs in Bernabò Visconti's menagerie to the fantastic figures, respectively, of 100,000 and 10,000. He credited Narses with having "restored order and industry to all Italy and adorning it with vast structures," and he explained the Lombard invasion solely as a result of the jealousy of the empress Sophia. He skipped over Ambrose and Theodosius, about whom there were plenty of documents, to tell a long story about one of their contemporaries who had killed a dragon. He praised Giangaleazzo as extravagantly—and as abstractly ("beauty of body, splendor of life, nobility of soul")—as he condemned Frederick II ("robber of churches and destroyer of the peace of all Italy"). And he made the year 1499 far less famous for the second French invasion than for the birth of a four-eyed pig and the appearance of a pack of horses in the sky. Morigia must have been rather satisfied with his work, for a few years later he re-presented a "really impressive quantity of ancient objects" in a form borrowed not, alas, from Biondo, but from Leandro Alberti, as a geographical-historical description of one of the favorite vacation resorts of the Milanese nobility.[43] But his much more competent successor two decades later[44] politely ignored him. And when his fellow citizens read that "the climate of Milan is agreeable to all the nations of the world," they must have concluded that he was lost in the fog all winter and prostrate from the heat all summer.

Independence Preserved: Venice

Venice, on the other hand, emerged from the calamities as the most self-consciously independent state in Italy—and, after the debacle of the Carafa War had established the limits beyond which the Papacy dared not challenge the power of Spain, as the most independent in fact. It had reconquered almost all of its former Terraferma dominion north of the Po. Although it gave up its pre-Cambrai ambition of obtaining the *signoria d'Italia,* or even its hopes for recovering its lost possessions in the Romagna and in Puglie, it was still determined to play an active role in international politics, from London to Lisbon to Constantinople, in order to preserve what it had recovered. The sharpness of the foreign policy debates of the last decades of the century between the Gallophiles and the Hispanophiles, and the high, although somewhat overrated, standards of its famous ambassadors' reports bear ample witness to this determination; and the reconciliation of King Henry IV as well as the still more specacular resistance to the papal interdict of 1606 give some indication of its success. Moreover, the city of Venice enjoyed the presence of a good number of resident historians, both native and foreigners, as well as a flourishing book-printing business. It also might have benefited from the diligence with which a number of its prominent citizens and residents studied the diaries of their forefathers and then composed diaries of their own in imitation of them, or of Sanudo. Among these diarists were Agostino degli Agostini, who copied out state documents dating from 1275 to 1570, Lionardo Savina, who wove together selections from earlier chronicles to 1521, Andrea Zilioli, who noted down what he observed as a "public secretary" for twenty years after 1508, Alessandro Cegia, who did the same for twenty-two years after 1560, the physician Giancarlo Silvos, the patriarch Giovanni Tiepolo, and the many others whose manuscripts were reviewed by their still more diligent successor in the eighteenth century, Marco Foscarini.[45] The city might have benefited from these efforts, that is, if any of them had ever been published or at least made available to others for consultation. Best of all, history enjoyed the support of the government, which had been pleased enough with what it had received spontaneously from Sabellico to grant a generous subsidy and an official title to those it hoped would continue his work.[46]

Nevertheless, municipal historiography in the Quattrocento tradition was very slow to be revived in Venice. The first obstacle seems to have been the apotheosis of Sabellico. Sabellico had written the definitive history of Venice, thought PIETRO MARCELLO, apparently oblivious to Aldo Manuzio's condemnation of abridgments. Hence, all that needed to be done was to make Sabellico more accessible to the general public by picking out those of his passages that would be most interesting. After all, he noted, Livy was the definitive historian of Rome; and that is just what Lucius Florus, who also qualified as an "ancient," had done to Livy. Alas, many of the passages that Marcello picked out as "interesting" were the very ones that Giorgio Merula and Ermolao Barbaro had objected to—those about the Paduan consuls in A.D. 421, those about the return to the mainland of all but the rich nobles at the time of Theodoric, those about Pippin's flight after the destruction of his pontoon bridge.... That such stories were even less acceptable in the somewhat more critical sixteenth century made no difference. Sabellico was used as a standard reference book by all the most acclaimed humanist historians of the day, and *ipse dixerat*. Furthermore, the stories all confirmed the self-evident axiom that the Venetians had always been noblemen and that they had always preferred "either to die for their country or to maintain its public liberty ..., which is the dearest thing in the world." Marcello was so successful, particularly after Ludovico Domenichi turned his Latin into lively Italian, that he was "continued" by a certain SALVESTRO GIRELLI, who, although an immigrant from Umbria, quickly absorbed the most recent Venetian politcal propaganda. The Venetians refused an offer of help from the Turks in 1509, he said, "because they believed that not to be honorable for Christian men." While the French "put to sack all the villages and towns that resisted them," he noted, the Venetians bothered no one in Padua but the Jews, who were apparently fair game for "Christian men." And it was not their fault that they were forced by the perfidy of the duke of Ferrara to "destroy everything they found" within his dominions and burn Comacchio almost to the ground. Girelli himself was so successful with this sort of contortion of historical truth that he in turn was "continued" by a certain GIORGIO BENZONE, who laid the heritage of Sabellico to a well-merited rest at the feet of Pope Paul IV, currently an ally of the Venetians. For Paul IV "has exhibited an invincible spirit, one truly worthy of the Italic name," said Benzone, utterly unaware of what everyone knew Paul's nephews were really up to; and he asked God to "conserve this sweet state until the consummation of the centuries as a bastion of liberty and as the chief support of the Holy See."[47]

The second obstacle to the revival of municipal historiography in Venice seems to have arisen from a misunderstanding about the substance and the means of historical writing. The senators did not want an accurate explanation of how they had gotten into the debacle of 1509. They had already been given one as early as 1511, when Andrea Mocenigo blamed "the kings of the world" for perpetrating "unheard of massacres" and "cruel murders" on a "most peaceful republic," without any justification and in defiance of solemn treaties.[48] Neither did they want a reliable guide to what they should do in the future, since they already had one in the example they themselves had set during their successful recovery from the debacle. What they wanted instead was a demonstration that whatever they had done or might still do was "worthy of immortal praise and commendation." And they expected the force of the demonstration to lie not so much in the veracity of the evidence as in the literary quality of the prose. What they demanded of a historian, then, was first of all eloquence, by which they meant an ability to write impeccable Ciceronian, or Livian, prose, and second, prudence, by which they meant a willingness to select material according to the criterion of what would best reflect "the honor and glory of our state."[49]

These two qualifications were admirably combined in their first choice for the position of state historiographer, ANDREA NAVAGERO (1483–1529).[50] Navagero had learned Latin from Sabellico and Greek from Marcus Musurus, one of the most famous of the Greek refugees in the city. He had associated with the leading classical scholars of his age, and he had personally supervised the Aldine editions of Cicero, Quintillian, Vergil, and Lucretius.[51] He was also an active and dedicated member of the Venetian ruling class, and he was to die, appropriately, while serving the republic as ambassador to France. Hence, as he had "put forth the deeds done by the most powerful people" in ancient times, so Navagero could be counted on to do the same *(ea similitudine)* for "the greatest and most ancient of all the republics on the face of the earth" in modern times.[52] Unfortunately, writing history turned out to be far more difficult than writing random historical-geographical observations about the places he had passed through during an embassy to Spain and France in 1524–25. And when a mortal illness struck him before he had had a chance to polish the first draft of the ten books he had written in continuation of Sabellico, he ordered them burned.

Whether or not the lost work really deserved the author's harsh judgment will never be known. But it most certainly must have been superior to the contemporary vernacular chronicle that was subsequently filed under his name in the same volume in the Este library at Modena. Navagero might still have been willing to accept Antenore as a Venetian counterpart to the Trojan Franco claimed by his friends in France. He might have allowed St. Mark to pitch a tent on the site of the modern church of San Francesco della Vigna. He most probably would have agreed in blaming the pope for the errors of the Fourth Crusade and Venice's plunder-hungry allies for the incomplete victory at the Taro. And he certainly would have approved of the inclusion of long extracts of important state documents—like the text of the Peace of Lodi—along with formal orations, of which he himself was an acknowledged master. But he never would have permitted a scheme of organization by episodes or by doges' terms of office rather than by the books and chapters prescribed by his ancient model, Caesar. And he never would have tolerated an *incipit* that reflected a conscious preference for medieval rather than ancient models:

> In the name of God the Father, the Son, and the Holy Spirit and of the evangelist *messere* San Marco. . . . In this treatise is the chronicle in brief form of the magnificent and noble city of Venice; which city is all surrounded by the sea. . . .[53]

These two qualifications proposed by the Senate were exhibited even more eminently in Navagero's successor (1530), PIETRO BEMBO (1450–1547). To be sure, Bembo was somewhat less closely associated with the patriciate into which he had been born, and his status as an ecclesiastic, which was fully recognized in his elevation to the cardinalate in 1538, rendered him somewhat suspicious in the eyes of those to whom loyalty to the state was exclusive of all others. Bembo had left Venice after failing in several attempts to launch himself into the standard *cursus honorum,* and the modest results of the several missions he undertook for Pope Leo X then convinced him that he had little talent for diplomacy either. He therefore spent much of the rest of his life enjoying *otio literarum,* the income from an increasing accumulation of lucrative benefices, the companionship of his faithful mistress, and the conversation of most of the learned men of all Italy in his family villa near Padua.

Bembo may not have been a statesman, then; but as a man of letters he had long been recognized by the title that Justus Lipsius still accorded him a half-century after his death: "easily the prince of the learned men of Italy in our times."[54] His *De Aetna* of 1495 gave proof of the skill as a Latinist that had been foreseen by Poliziano as early as 1478, when his father had taken him on a diplomatic mission to Florence. And his appointment as papal secretary in 1513, together with the publication of his manifesto of Ciceronianism, *De Imitatione,* shortly thereafter, established him as the leading authority in the Latin language—and, consequently, the object of Erasmus's biting satire in the *Ciceronianus.* Meanwhile, his *Prose della volgar lingua* of 1525 confirmed the position which he had already earned with his *Asolani* of 1502 as the leading authority on the vernacular as well; and although his Trecento archaisms were frequently attacked by various of the many contributors to the burning *questione della lingua* thereafter, they were established as canonical by the Florentine linguists of the last decades of the century and enshrined in the first edition of the dictionary of the Accademia della Crusca in 1605. At the same time, Bembo's long association with the scholars of Venice, including Navagero, and then his association with the scholars of all Italy who regularly called on him in Padua and in Rome, earned him still another title: that of the "Petrarch of the sixteenth century." And he justified this title by composing hundreds of poems in imitation of the *Canzoniere* that were as applauded at the time as they are, perhaps justly, forgotten today.[55]

Unfortunately, Bembo felt no vocation for history, which, as he protested to the Senate, he had "never had the slightest thought of writing"; and he had always remained "very distant from public life and from those actions that form the material of history."[56] More unfortunately still, he decided to compensate for this disadvantage by reducing history largely to a matter of language. Together with the position of official historiographer, the Senate gave him Navagero's job as librarian of the republic, which put at his disposal a vast quantity of printed and manuscript books. By the decrees of 26 September and 18 December 1530, it accorded him the almost unheard-of permission "to read the letters and the books of the chancery," "the books of the secret affairs," and the records of all the deliberations of the Council of Ten since 1485. But instead of moving to the free house the Senate provided him in Venice and settling down to study this material, instead of procuring the diaries and commentaries of the subject cities and the histories of the other Italian states, instead of sending for a copy of the memoirs of Philippe de Commynes, whom he was to mention frequently in his text, Bembo decided that he could fulfill his commission just as easily by remaining in Padua—or in Rome or in Gubbio, his first episcopal see. "All that work would be impossible for me," he declared. "And even if it were possible, it would be infinite." He hired a research assistant to go through a few volumes of the Senate's records and send him whatever extracts seemed approriate, or "memorable." He borrowed copies of the works of Sabellico, Bernardo Giustinian, and Pietro Marcello. He then got the Senate to order Sanudo, much against his will, to turn over to him the already-famous diary; and Sanudo was left with the meager consolation of a miniscule pension and the very prophetic assurance that "no writer will ever get very far in the history of modern times without seeing my diary." He then reread Caesar, not for form, to be sure, since his limits were merely chronological rather than those of a particular "event," but for language and style. And finally he set to work recasting in Ciceronian or Caesarian—and then in Petrarchan—language what he lifted from the "sources" he had selected.

The senators should have been pleased with the results when the manuscripts, both of the Latin original and of the author's own vernacular translation, were finally turned over to them shortly after his death in 1548. The work was properly voluminous: over 800 pages of print in a quarto volume for the twenty-five years between where Sabellico stopped and 1513. It made modern Venetians appeal like ancient Romans to "dii immortales." It turned prayer into "supplicatio ad aras deorum." It expanded Sanudo's rather bare "wanted to come to repossess his kingdom of Naples" into a more copious "The king was all ready to come into Italy with an army to make his own the Kingdom of Naples, which belonged to him by hereditary right"—all preceded in the vernacular version by the resounding conjunction *con-ciò-fosse-cosa-chè*. It added just enough personal references to the author himself to make him appear as a guarantor of the veracity of what he took from his sources. And while one version was impeccably classical, the other was so faithful to Bemban orthodoxy concerning the distinction between written and spoken vernaculars that only the educated could have disentangled any meaning from the tangle of infinitive clauses and ablative absolutes:

> Scritte e fermate queste condizioni, il capitano de' Francesi promise al Re se volea cento libbre d'oro dargli, con le quali egli pagare alle sue genti ciò, di che era loro tenuto, potesse; che fra tre dì gli darebbe la città e partirebbesi.

Better yet, it put into the speeches of leading citizens exactly the ideology that the senators claimed as their own: "This is the true way of life," he proclaimed, "to benefit our country, to defend the republic, to protect its citizens, ... to consider even death better than servitude." It clearly presented the arguments in favor of the current postimperialistic foreign policy, particularly in its account of the debate over intervention in Pisa, while fully justifying, even by reference to human nature, the preceding expansionist policy ("most men are inclined by nature to augment that which they possess"). Finally, it offered as exemplars a proper number of heroes: Andrea Gritti, the expert on Turkish affairs who "easily surpassed all others ... in his physical beauty, his moral gravity, and his liberality," and Paolo Barbo, who emerged from retirement upon hearing the news of Agnadello "with his eyes full of tears" to offer the fruits of a lifetime of experience in the republic's darkest hour.

Unfortunately, the senators were not wholly pleased with what they read. Perhaps they noticed that Bembo frequently betrayed his Latin model by throwing in extraneous details—about a two-headed baby born in Padua, about the visit of a certain "Queen of Dacia," about Frederick III's tour of the Terraferma, about the purchase of a house by the Armenian colony, about the arrest of an official in Treviso on bribery charges. They certainly should have noticed that none of these details was brought to bear on such very real issues as Venice's relations with the Empire, the status of resident foreign populations, and the kind of corruption in public office that Priuli had complained about. They might also have noticed that most of his background asides, which humanist historiographical standards imposed as a way of providing context for an event, turned out to be merely personal-interest stories—like the details about the inheritance of the queen of Cyprus. They might further have noticed that his causal explanations were usually superficial or unconvincing: the "mutable" character of the French, the "perfidious" character of Il Moro, the intransigent character of Paul III. But what seems really to have worried them was Bembo's sarcastic barbs at those of their ancestors who did not quite come up to the ideal of the perfect citizen—or at those whom Bembo happened not to like. Careless of their future reputation as the last island of free thought in Italy, they permitted the Latin version to appear only after the Riformatori of the university had expurgated the objectionable passages. They permitted the vernacular edition to appear only after still other passages had been recast by Bembo's successor as a linguistic authority, Antonio Minturno, and by two Venetian popular historians, Francesco Sansovino and Marco Guazzo—although, fortunately, they then permitted Bembo's successor as the leading verse and prose writer of the day, Giovanni Della Casa, to put back much of what his colleagues had taken out. They then quietly let drop for a while the whole experiment with "official" historiography. They appointed instead an official diarist, LUIGI BONGHI, who, as secretary of the Council of Ten, was charged with summarizing its records in the form of a chronicle to be kept locked up in the Senate archives for the private consultation of the councillors.[57]

Bembo's last great literary effort thus turned out to be somewhat less successful than the others. Most of his followers either ignored it or else joined in the chorus of those who apotheosized him as a great poet, linguist, Latinist, or critic—not as a historian. But the efforts of those who were appointed, or who aspired, to succeed him were even less successful. All of them, of course, had the necessary qualifications. PAULO RAMUSIO, or RANNUSIO was the son of the great chronicler of the overseas discoveries, Giovan Battista, who, as secretary of the Council of Ten, had been largely responsible for the appointment of Bembo. ALVISE, or LUIGI CONTARINI was the nephew of the famous Gasparo, the leading theorist of the early Counter Reformation as well as of the republic, who furthered the cause of the state as well as the cause of letters while serving as captain of Verona and as ambassador to France. PIETRO GIUSTINIANI earned a reputation for "eloquence in all languages" while rising to the position of leader (capo) of the Council of Ten by 1573.[58] AGOSTINO VALIER the successor of Matteo Gilberti as bishop of Verona, was the emulator—and biographer—of Carlo Borromeo and one of the principal representatives of post-Tridentine Catholic culture. DANIELE BARBARO (1513–70) wrote a commentary on his uncle Ermolao's translation of Aristotle's *Poetics,* his own translation of Vitruvius, a dialogue on eloquence, and several "philosophical poems." He was the founder of the botanical garden and cofounder of the Accademia degli Infiammati at Padua. And his career in the service of the republic was rewarded by his appointment first as ambassador to England and then, in 1556, as patriarch.

231

Yet none of these candidates for Bembo's long-vacant post was particularly interested in history—with the exception, perhaps, of Valier, who put history along with the Fathers of the Church at the top of his obligatory reading list and who vainly urged some of his disciples to undertake what he did not have time for.[59] At the same time none of the historians already resident in Venice who were approached unofficially by individual senators was particularly interested in embarking upon a project for which the Senate no longer promised a stipend. Ramusio merely translated parts of Villhardouin's chronicle of the Fourth Crusade from an old-French manuscript discovered years before by the Venetian ambassador to the court of Charles V in Brussels; and he then patched it together with passages taken from the standard humanist historians in order better to demonstrate the "heroic piety and exemplary religion" of the protagonists of that none too pious enterprise. But the results hardly justified the claims of his grandson that he had "consumed years, spent his substance, and neglected his family affairs" while working on it.[60] Similarly, even though he was specifically instructed by Valier on how to write humanist history, even though he had chosen Polybius, Xenophon, Sallust, and Guicciardini rather than Sabellico and Bembo as his models, and even though the Senate finally conferred upon him the office that had been vacant since 1549, Contarini managed to produce only a rough draft before his sudden death, just two years later, in 1579. Valier himself produced—on his own initiative, but for basically the same purposes—what amounted to, not history, but a series of maxims drawn from history, or, more exactly, from the drafts submitted to him by his disciple, Contarini. But even the "utility" of the maxims was impaired by the author's insistence upon ignoring or suppressing the often very real conflicts among the senators themselves and between the Senate and the Papacy. He then put the maxims aside to return to his usual unhistorical collections of moral precepts, which had nothing whatever to do with the history of Venice.[61] And they were duly forgotten until they were rediscovered and translated into Italian in the late eighteenth century.

Giustiniani took the task somewhat more seriously, possibly because he hoped to receive the appointment that was given instead to Contarini.[62] He surveyed the whole of Venetian history from the arrival of the first "Heneti" to the aftermath of Lepanto. And although his survey did not fully satisfy the senators, who made him suppress the last book, it pleased the general reading public enough to warrant its being twice reprinted during his lifetime.[63] It drew a flattering parallel between the Pax Romana under the rule of Augustus and the current Pax Italica under the guardianship of Venice. It quoted at length from documents the author himself had collected—e.g., letters from friends in Rome during the sack. It sometimes included cultural along with political events—e.g., the revival of Greek letters, which is mentioned apropos of the donation of Bessarion's library, and the work of Ermolao Barbaro, which is noted apropos of his son's heroic defense of Brescia. Better yet, it provided a convincing historical justification for the separate peace that the Venetians had recently concluded with the Turks. The business of the republic has always been commerce, Giustiniani pointed out, not war; and Venetian specialists in Turkish affairs had always insisted on the vanity of Christian crusades. Hence, if the sacrifice of Negroponte or Cyprus happened at one moment to be the price of keeping open the routes to the Black Sea and the Levant, Venice should not hesitate to pay it, without regard to the anachronistic dreams of a pope or the empty promises of a king of Spain. Barbaro took the task even more seriously, although his duties as patriarch prevented him from completing any more than two of his many projected books.[64] He reviewed what Bembo had written about Agnadello in order to transfer the moment of Venice's greatest misfortune from the summer of 1509 to the winter of 1513, when

> such was the state of the city, after having all alone supported most justly a war for five continuous years and after having lost the greater part of its mainland possessions, that what little it still had left was all burned and destroyed.

He discovered still another mission for the republic: that of protecting the most helpless and usually the most forgotten victims of the war, the peasants, who repaid its solicitude by readily volunteering for military service thereafter. And a certain Girolamo da Canal was accordingly raised to the rank of a minor hero for having transported several boatloads of peasants over from Mestre at his own expense and then arranging for their lodging in the monasteries of the city.

Yet neither of these two works met the traditional standards of humanist historiography, and neither of them corresponded to recent Senate declarations about the pedagogical value of history for the formation of future patricians. Since his own age was well furnished with "very many praiseworthy writers of history," thought Giustiniani, all he had to do was add a few extra details to what they had already written. Since Venice had always been "most fertile in illustrious men," all he had to do was identify whoever outside of Venice had been responsible for whatever went wrong. His own history thus turned out to be in large part an exposure of the culprits—the perfidious Cretans, who "greatly loathed the Italian name," the "jealous Genoese, the authors of so many misfortunes," the furious Anconitans, "who hurled dishonest insults at the Venetians," the cruel Greeks, who exhibited their captives with their genitals cut off and affixed to their backsides, the imperious Florentines, who were "urged on by a shameless desire to be the lords of all Tuscany," the ambitious Pope Paul III, who was "so disliked by all that what they could not do to him while living they did to him after he was dead." Barbaro, on the other hand, thought of history largely as a means of demonstrating the constant collaboration between the Venetians and Divine Providence. Hence, the "afflictions and persecutions" he wrote about served chiefly the purpose of making more manifest "the prudence of the senators, the love of the citizens for their country," and "the constant and invincible virtue" of them both. The only lessons that an account of the afflictions could yield were those that had been as well known before as after Agnadello: that non-Venetian Italians could be as barbarous as the French and Spanish, that good treatment of subjects is the best way to assure their loyalty, that God punishes those who do not seize the "occasion" he presents to them, that a good pope (Leo X) can betray the republic as easily as a bad pope (Julius II). And since these lessons were already known, there was not much point in repeating them.

Despite these relative failures, the bestowal of, or at least the anticipation of receiving, an official commission continued to be a prerequisite for writing the history of Venice, as PAOLO PARUTA (1540–98) pointed out to his reluctant competitor, Antonio Riccoboni, shortly after succeeding Contarini in 1579.[65] After twenty-five years of teaching Greek and Latin at Padua, Riccoboni's credentials as a humanist were impeccable, and as a citizen of a loyal subject-city, his loyalty to its *dominante,* which happened also to be his employer, was unquestionable. What he modestly referred to as mere "annals" in continuation of Bembo were admittedly superior to those of Giustiniani. And his manuscript was probably worthy of the offer made him by a prospective publisher in Frankfurt. Still, Riccoboni could never hope to be given access to documents from which even most senators were barred. And without the documents *(le scritture pubbliche),* he would never be able to penetrate the "causes and the deliberations" *(le cause et i consigli)* upon which the explanation if the single events he read about in Natale Conti depended.

Moreover, the qualifications laid down by the Senate at the moment of Navagero's appointment were still a prerequisite for receiving a commission. Both Paruta and his brother-in-law and successor, ANDREA MOROSINI (1558–1618), were, in Paruta's words, "noble persons of this *patria,*" and they could thus be entrusted with "employing [their] labors in the service of this most noble and dear country."[66] Paruta had sought his first office, as a member of an embassy to Emperor Maximilian II in 1567, for the specific purpose of adding from observation to what he had already learned about politics from books. But he was apparently successful enough even as a man of action to merit being elected to important offices for the rest of his life—as *provveditore agli imprestidi* in 1580, as *savio di Terraferma* in 1582, as ambassador to Pope Clement VIII during the delicate negotiations for the reconciliation of King Henry IV, and, finally, as *procuratore di San Marco,* one of the highest positions in the state, in 1596. Morosini was admitted to the Senate soon after he succeeded Paruta in 1598 by a special decree waiving the prohibition against seating more than five members of the same family; and he was three times thereafter elected to the Council of Ten. Both were also among the leading men of letters of their generation. Paruta was the author of the *Perfezione della vita politica,* which was twice published in his lifetime and often thereafter; and his *Discorsi politici* are still recognized as a classic of late Renaissance political thought.[67] Morosini was the sponsor of the famous literary circle that bore his name *(Ridotto Morosini),* a friend and correspondent of its distinguished members and guests—Galileo Galilei, Giordano Bruno, Alvise Lollini, Paolo Sarpi—and the author of numerous treatises and orations on many different subjects, from the relics of St. Mark to the constitution of the republic.

What finally made possible the emergence of a Venetian historiography fully consonant with humanist standards, however, was the coincidence of a commission and a prior commitment to history as a discipline. Unlike his predecessors, Paruta had already demonstrated his skill as a historian—first in his public oration on the victory at Lepanto and then in his three-book commentary on the Cyprus War;[68] and the commentary was already good enough as history that it might well have been incorporated into the text of the history had his premature death not cut his narrative short at 1552. To be sure, Paruta was still willing to pay occasional tribute to his predecessors' campaign to justify Venetian political actions in moral and religious terms, at least in his preface. The Republic of Venice, he admitted, "by the duration . . . and the excellence of its government is justly reputed to be the most fortunate and the most magnificent of any that has ever existed in the world." It acquired its possessions not from "an appetite for dominion" but from "a desire to protect its freedom." It conscienciously served the cause of peace in Italy—even to the point of patching up a quarrel between the pope and the duke of Urbino in which it had no interest. And it occasionally served the cause of *Cristianità* abroad by defending it against "the barbarous, enemy nations [that were constantly being] called against it." Some of Paruta's defects, on the other hand, were merely exaggerations of those of his humanist models—in particular, his rigorous restriction of history solely to political and diplomatic affairs. The arts, letters, and even the architecture and urban development for which Venice was widely admired in the age of Palladio, were downgraded to the rank of "things of little moment" *(cose molto leggieri)*. Religion and the Church—even the Council of Trent, at which Venetian bishops played so important a role—were reduced to what little Paruta could find in them of political interest. Commerce and banking, which he knew to be the chief strength of the republic, were limited to an occasional aside—one and a half pages in Book IV followed by a "Now let us return to the interrupted narrative." And years of peace received far less attention than years of war: an average of seventy-one pages for each year between 1513 and 1516, and only three and a half pages for 1518.

On the other hand, Paruta learned how to exploit fully the humanist technique of joining the narratives of several contemporary events with such phrases as "While this was happening here, there . . ."; and he thus overcame one of the greatest obstacles posed to historians of a state which was engaged simultaneously in so many different places. He omitted, in typically humanist manner, whatever might have detracted from a tight exposition of the causal link between one event and another: no storms, no monsters, no ceremonious receptions for visiting princes. After demonstrating, in the first four books he submitted to the Senate in 1580, that he could imitate Sallust's prose as well as anyone, he reverted to the linguistic medium that even Bembo had sanctioned as the most appropriate one for municipal historiography: Italian. And he did so for the reasons put forth by the vernacularists in the Accademia degli Infiammati and the Accademia Fiorentina: that his work would thus be accessible beyond the narrow circle either of the learned or of the purely local audience accustomed to Sanudo's dialectical peculiarities. Above all, he dismissed all explanations of Venetian political actions other than the one he thought to be correct: the preservation and the expansion of the state. The sultan was just as capable of "grave and important thoughts" and "magnificent deeds" as any Christian prince, said Paruta, and he was far more willing than any Christian king or pope to "make courteous and friendly gestures" toward the republic "in the hour of its greatest adversity." Moreover, all Christian princes were just as willing as infidels to act "according to their own convenience" when pretending to act "in the service of others" *(il servitio commune)*. Hence, taking seriously such slogans as the common cause of Italians against barbarians or of Christians against Turks led as certainly to disaster as did permitting the choice of allies to be determined by notions of honor or fidelity. Paruta accordingly recast the Senate debate of early 1525—a debate that by then had become a classical *locus* of humanist historiography and political philosophy[69]—in terms solely of practical utility: whether Venice could gain more by respecting its alliance with Charles V or by responding favorably to the overtures of Francis I. He also abandoned his predecessors' attempt to soothe modern consciences concerning what they presented as occasional aberrations before 1509 from Venice's current policy of peace and liberty. Venice could have possessed a state as great as Rome's, he pointed out, if it had not waited until the fifteenth century to start doing to Italy what it had done so gloriously to the Greek Empire in the thirteenth century. Agnadello and "the manifest inclination of the times" in favor of the Ottomans had forced it recently to concentrate first on recovery and then on conservation. "But if one day the condition of the times ever permits it [once again] to aspire to a wider dominion and a greater glory of rule," there was no reason why it should not do so.

Morosini had not yet written any history at the time of his appointment. But he was already convinced that history was the most important element in the education of responsible patricians. He had studied the historiographical style of the most recent addition to ancient historical models, Tacitus. And he frequently interrupted his major work thereafter in order to study particular moments of the past in greater detail: the war in Istria, the Fourth Crusade, the life of Leonardo Donà. Hence the *Historia Veneta,*[70] which first appeared just four years after his death in 1621, may still have exhibited some of the exaggerations of his humanist predecessors. It used established formulas in the place of accurate descriptions of particularly tragic events. It resorted to platitudes in summary character sketches. It skipped over "uneventful" years (only five pages for 1586, only thirteen for 1589). And it replaced modern with classical names (Poland = "Sarmatia"). Thus what the Papal troops did at Ottolengo near Brescia in 1521 was exactly the same as what every other sacking army had done before and after ("non aetati, non sexui parcitum...."). Leo X was "vir excellenti ingenio." Charles IX was "pietate...ac religione insignis," just like all other rulers. Lorenzo Bragadena had the same "sapientiae studia cum eloquentia conjuncta" as all other speakers in the Senate. And all the speeches were equally divided into pro and con arguments, without consideration of the various shades of opinion that were undoubtedly expressed at the same time.

But the very different circumstances of the decades in which he was an actor as well as an observer ("vel in Patrum collegio vel in Senatu interfui") led Morosini to go well beyond the example left him by Paruta, whose text he nevertheless followed closely in preparing his own. The controversy over the Interdict of 1606 may have been inferior to the Cyprus War in "the gravity...and variety of events." But it ended not in defeat with honor but in victory, one comparable to the victories that had made possible the recovery of the Terraferma a century earlier. Moreover, the victory had been accomplished without resort to physical violence. Hence, glorious acts did not have to be identified solely with military events. They could be artistic events (although Morosini could not figure out how to qualify them aesthetically), like Palladio's contract for a votive temple and Tintoretto's murals in the Palazzo Ducale. Or they could be economic events (although Morosini did not manage to demonstrate their political implications), like the establishment of a state bank (*publica mensa*) in 1587.

More important, the victory had been accomplished in part by persuading both subjects and foreigners of the impeccable fidelity of Venice to the true principles of Catholicism[71] in the face of the purely temporal ambitions of Pope Paul V. Hence, some forty-five pages were dedicated to the last sessions of the Council of Trent, which Paruta had barely mentioned. The republic was presented as having been solicitous for the spiritual dignity of the Roman see during the debates over episcopal residency in 1561, for the Catholic orthodoxy of its subjects in 1606, and for the defense of Christendom in all the great struggles against the Turks, which the ambassadors pointedly, and with some justice, recalled in the lecture on history they delivered to the pope. More important still, the victory had been accomplished with the assistance of all the great Catholic powers. Hence, Morosini broadened Paruta's Italian context of Venetian history. The context now included not only France, where the consequences of religious controversy had been particularly pernicious, but even Persia, which turned out to be a mid-eastern version of Venice's tempered aristocracy, equally opposed to the efficient, successful, but nonetheless autocratic regime of the Ottomans.

Yet even this victory had not been complete; and Morosini's arguments were correspondingly weakened by the events that immediately followed it. True, the victory had momentarily restored the unanimity of the patriciate. But it could not guarantee future immunity from the kind of internal conflict that Morosini had described in such detail during the reform of the Council of Ten in 1586. It had gotten rid of the Jesuits. But it had not permanently changed the minds of those many patricians who still admired the Jesuits, at least as educators of their children. It had countered the pope's arguments about the "novelty" of the laws limiting the growth of ecclesiastical property. But then the pope's argument was based on abstract principles, not on historical precedent. And what his chief theologian continued to say to King James I of England could just as easily be addressed to the Venetians whenever the opportunity arose. Worse yet, the victory coincided with the end of the era of peace; and it may have been his experience with the war of Gradisca, the war against the Uscocchi, and the unending war against the Mediterranean pirates that led Morosini to tone down the significance of that favorite date of all the late-sixteenth-century Italian historians, 1559.

Morosini died before he could foresee the consequences of what occurred in Bohemia the year of his death. But his evident nostalgia for the happier years of his youth betrayed a suspicion that what the Venetians might, or did, learn from history would not do them much good. In the work of his successor and cousin, NICCOLÒ CONTARINI, this nostalgia turned into pessimism. An autonomous Venetian Church, protected from the abuses of the Roman Church that it still recognized as its spiritual superior, had been swept away by the centripetal forces of the rest of Counter Reformation Catholicism; and its main psychological support, the austere piety of Leonardo Donà and Morosini's associate Alvise Lollini, had been swallowed up by what modern specialists call "baroque piety," which was unliturgical, individualistic, and therefore totally apolitical. Venice's ability to participate actively in the shifting balance of European powers had been gravely compromised by the unexpected extension of the Thirty Years' War into the plains of Lombardy—which, after fifty years of peace, once again became a European battleground. Venice in 1597 had enjoyed "the confidence . . . and the friendship of all the princes," and it had "abounded in all the things that the fertility of the land, the industry of men, and the advantages of the site generally produce under well-regulated governments." But by 1631, when Contarini died, Venice had lost most of its merchant fleet. It had been decimated by another outbreak of the plague. And it had been forced to stand by helplessly as Spanish soldiers, after some seven decades of playing the role of Italy's policemen, once again vented their fury against an Italian city: Venice's neighbor and protectorate, Mantua. When the official historian finally himself became doge, he found he could do nothing to apply the lessons he had learned and the virtue he had acquired by reading and writing history. Moreover, since current literary standards no longer favored either humanist prose style, which he still tried to imitate, or the humanist principle of the priority of truth, which he adhered to rigorously, the Senate decided to keep his manuscript locked up in the state archives. And it remained all but unknown until Gaetano Cozzi finally published parts of it in 1958.[72]

Independence Regained: Piedmont, Parma-Piacenza, Genoa

The preservation of independence alone, then, could not guarantee the production of historiography. But the recovery of an independence that had once seemed hopelessly lost provided at least a forceful stimulant to its production. To be sure, in a state —or rather in an area—like the domains of the dukes of Savoy in which loyalty to the same ruler formed the only bond of unity, the stimulant did not really become effective until independence had been fully consolidated.[73] PIERRE LAMBERT Seigneur de LA CROIX (b.c. 1480) had faithfully served his dukes as an intimate counselor and as an ambassador. He had followed them into their Italian-speaking domains when, in 1543, they had been chased out of Savoy. And he was aware that the position of all the dominions at "the center of Christendom" had the disadvantage of exposing them to attack from many surrounding "nations"—the Ligurians, the Italians, the Dauphinois, the Bernois, et al. But when he later looked back on the disastrous reign of his former employer, Charles IX, the only solution to the dilemma he could suggest was a policy of benevolent neutrality: unquestioning loyalty to Savoy's "temporal and spiritual sovereigns," the emperor and the pope, and the offering of "all possible services not in conflict with higher duties" toward France and Fribourg.[74] But with all these benevolent neighbors constantly fighting each other back and forth across Savoyard territory, there was not much hope of putting the policy into practice.

When Emanuele Filiberto finally managed to return to his domains—not by molifying his neighbors but by playing them off against each other—he looked about for somewhat more helpful teachers. After failing to attract the well-known Genoese exile Umberto Foglietta, he turned to his subjects—first to GUILLAUME PARADIN of Bresse, then to Guillaume's nephew CLAUDE, and finally to EMMANUEL PHILLIBERTE PINGON (or Pingone, as he was known in Piedmont) of Chambéry; and his son Carlo Emanuele then turned to CLAUDE GUICHARD Seigneur d'ARANDAT (d. 1607). But in vain. Paradin merely repeated the romantic legends of his *chroniqueur* sources, particularly in his fantastic *Chroniques de Savoye* of 1552, which someone strangely thought worthy of being *augmentées* and reprinted fifty years later; and he then went on to write equally fantastic tales about England, Burgundy, and France. Guichard merely edited a collection of real, misread, and fake ancient inscriptions about the burial customs of the ancients; and after several years in jail as the result of the false accusations of a jealous rival, he turned once again to his chief interest, law.

Pingon should have known better. He had studied long enough at Padua to beget three illegitimate children. He was a friend both of the historian Foglietta and of the jurist-statesman Michel de l'Hôpital. He had administered both the university of Turin and the city of Ivrea. And he had become so fascinated with the documents he borrowed from the ducal archives that he neglected to return most of them. But even Pingon managed to produce nothing more than a mass of "sterile virtuosity"—first in a Latin history of Turin (1577) well padded with dubious inscriptions,[75] then in a genealogical table that made the houses of Savoy and Saxony cousins through their common descent from a certain Fetonte who *fl.* 1529 B.C., then in a series of antiquarian rhapsodies about the origins of Chambéry, Aosta, Vercelli, Nice, and the Allobroges. All these rhapsodies served no other purpose than that of fueling an equally futile campaign against the bestowal of a grand ducal title upon Cosimo de' Medici.

Those who tried to write the history of the Savoyard domains on their own initiative did not fare much better. The general and diplomat René de Lucinge composed a Latin chronicle of the years from 1572 to 1584 but never published it. The Gallicized Tuscan bishop of Albi, ALFONSO (or ALPHONSE) DEL BENE (1538–1608) merely repeated for Savoy and the House of Savoy the kind of Latin school-text he had already prepared for Burgundy and the Capetians: a *Descriptio Sabaudiae,* of which a part was published only much later, a treatise *De . . . Vera Ducum Origine,* published in 1581, and a *Sabaudiae Historia* from 636 to 1284, a "huge miscellany without any logical organization," which was never published at all (Castronovo). LOUIS DE BETTET forgot what he had learned of philology from the leader of the French historical school of jurisprudence, Jacques Cujas, when he put out as his own what amounted to a mere transcription of several medieval chronicles. And GIULIO CAMBIANO DI RUFFIA (1544–1611), even though he was a jurist and a judge of some ability, and even though he had studied under the historian Ludovico Della Chiesa, produced no more than *Memoriali*[76]—personal recollections of all the innumerable major and minor events he had witnessed between the locust invasion of 1542 and his retirement in 1590.

Finally, at the end of the sixteenth and the beginning of the seventeenth century, three historians at last succeeded in accomplishing what none of their predecessors had been able even to conceive. The first was GIOVANNI TONSI, a Milanese by birth, who had been a rector of the University of Pisa and a pensionato of Pope Gregory XIII before being invited to join Duke Carlo Emanuele's Consiglio di Stato in 1594; and he brought his literary talents to bear upon his political responsibilities by composing a history of the restoration of the duchy in the form of a biography of its restorer. The second was Giulio's cousin, the artillery commander GIUSEPPE CAMBIANO DI RUFFIA. In 1598 Giuseppe began writing down what he had learned "from the most serious authors, from handwritten memorials, from the reports of wise and trustworthy men," and from what he had "observed, discovered, heard about, and seen" during his twenty-four years of service as a diplomat and a general. In three introductory books he traced the history of Savoy from Noah to Cateau-Cambrésis. Then, in the four books that formed the core of his work, he described in detail the subsequent restoration, consolidation, and expansion of the duchy. And from what he described he drew the political maxim that had inspired the work of his hero, Emanuele Filiberto, namely, "how necessary it is quickly to provide the people with a good and stable government and to reorganize everything that concerns the public good."[77]

The third of the historians of Piedmont was LUDOVICO DELLA CHIESA (1568–1621), a native of the March of Saluzzo, who had been rewarded for his service to the dukes of Savoy with an appointment to the Senate of Turin. Della Chiesa began his literary career with a history of his own country (*Compendio della historia di Saluzzo*—1602) and a series of biographies of the marchesi who had ruled it before its transformation into the principal, and then the last, French outpost east of the Alps (*Vite dei marchesi di Saluzzo*—1598, 1603).[78] When his employers succeeded at last in exchanging what they had come to regard as an uncomfortable enclave in the middle of their Italian domains for the enclave they had long possessed north of the Rhone in France, Della Chiesa began to read "not only the works of the ancient and modern historians" but also "the writings in the archives of the cities, towns, and abbeys" of all Piedmont. And he soon came to the conclusion that most of what had been written about it was either incorrect or incomplete. He found the first defect very difficult to overcome, partially because he was timid. After all, who was he to say that the name Nice (Nizza) did not derive from the Greek word for "victory"? And who was he to prefer the date 1259 clearly inscribed in a contemporary contract when all the authors he consulted put it at 1256? But the second defect he at least remedied by packing in details until the quality of his prose began to break down. It took him some seven years after publication of the first book (1601) to complete the other two. And it took him another ten years to gather the supplementary material that was not fully incorporated in his text until 1777.[79] Better yet, he managed to overcome what had been the greatest obstacle for all his predecessors: the problem of how to write a single history of all the various feudal and communal entities that only recently had been brought together under one ruler. He did so by following each of them separately in chronological order down to the creation of the duchy in 1406 and by following the course of the wars and the acts of the princes that affected them all thereafter.

The works of Giuseppe Cambiano and Della Chiesa thus complemented each other. One described the gradual growth of the duchy and its sudden destruction, the other its remarkable restoration. Together they might have provided the Savoyard dominions with a work of humanist history similar in quality to the one provided Venice by Paruta and Morosini. But unfortunately Duke Carlo Emanuele suddenly recoiled at the thought of sharing his father's political wisdom with others, and he forthwith confiscated all the extant copies of Cambiano's *Historico discorso* for the sole use of the chancery in Turin. That left the wisdom hopelessly buried in the inextricable detail of Della Chiesa's packed verbiage, which broke down into a disorganized chronicle soon after the account of the first French invasion and which petered out as it approached 1585 with the excuse, borrowed from Solomon and Horace, that "it's best not to talk about the actions of the living." Hence, a history that covered all the Savoyard domains, that linked the past with the present, and that offered guidance for the future had to wait until 1616, when PIETRO MONOD became rector of the university, or even until 1650, when SAMUEL GUICHENON became court historian. And by then it no longer could be written according to the standards recognized a half-century earlier by the first, and the last, humanist historians of Piedmont.

On the other hand, in those cities which unexpectedly regained their independence—or which at least regained their status as metropolises of independent states and which also possessed a rich, although forgotten tradition of local history writing—the production of a work of history worthy of their new-found dignity required less effort. Both UMBERTO, or OMBERTO, LOCATI[80] and BONAVENTURA ANGELI[81] took care to assure the citizens of Piacenza and Parma that the restoration of independence did not mean a return to the conditions that had always been associated with independence in the past. Parma, Angeli admitted, had been subject throughout its history to "revolutions, turbulence, fierce civil discord, violent wars among its citizens, impious tyrannies, and the cruelty of usurpers of liberty." Piacenza, Locati pointed out, had been "pitifully sacked by the Goths, put in servitude by the Lombards . . . , reduced to desperation under the yoke of the Visconti, sacked eight times in one year," devastated by an "impious, cruel tyrant" after the death of Giangaleazzo, and finally, in 1527, subjected to a long siege by foreign barbarians. Worse yet, each time it had begun to recover from the ruin visited upon it by outsiders, it was immediately torn apart by its own citizens. Indeed, Locati was so convinced that history up until his time had consisted of an unending succession of "wars, seditions, plagues, and other tragedies," that he subsequently compiled a list of them in fifteen books; and he published it under the appropriate name of *Italy Afflicted* for use by those of his fellow Dominicans who wanted to scare their congregations.[82]

Fortunately, all that was now past. What neither the Visconti nor the Sforza, neither the Venetians nor Pope Leo X, had been able to accomplish had at last been realized by Ottavio Farnese—who "not only has freed [us] from the tyranny of the barbarians," but who also "has cured and purged [us] of civil factions." The accomplishment had not been easy. Ottavio's father had been murdered almost as soon as he had set foot in his new duchy. He himself had had to fight for the preservation of the duchy, first against the emperor, then against Pope Julius III, then against the king of France. And just as he had succeeded in inserting himself within the Papal-Imperial-Medici power structure in Italy, he was suddenly forced to defend himself against the "evil, poisonous spirit" of Pope Paul IV. But by 1568 the accomplishment was complete. It was guaranteed by Ottavio's successor, Alessandro Farnese, who was gloriously stamping out heresy in the Netherlands, and by Alessandro's son, Ranuccio, who, "in complete accord with the Catholic faith, rules and governs his state to the great satisfaction of his subjects and the joy of his people." "No one," Angeli concluded, "could possibly desire [a government] more temperate, more clement," and, he might have added, more durable.

Having thus chronicled what they sincerely hoped would be the abolition of history, the historians were now free to concentrate on two equally important tasks. They had first to correct, with the help of their communal chronicles and archival documents, the gross and prejudicial errors concerning the two cities that had been perpetrated by the new humanist historians of other cities—by that "liar" Bernardino Corio, who had accused Francesco Cotto of having sold Piacenza to the Visconti; by Natale Conti, who "without the support of any authority" had given the ancient name of the Parma River as "Palmula"; by Guicciardini, who had put Girolamo Morone in Trent when he was actually in Brussels; by Strabo, Ptolemy, Biondo ("errori infiniti"), Giovio ("poco costante"), Volterrano, and Leandro Alberti. They had then to isolate the great deeds committed by their ancestors, at home and abroad, so that "the moderns," whom the greatest of all heroes had rescued from the need to create heroes of their own, could have something to imitate. And to facilitate the process of imitation, they presented their works in novel, and never thereafter imitated forms: one as a dialogue between the author and "Gigliota" ("Lady Piacenza"), the other as a historical narrative interspersed with separate histories of the great families of the city and with geographical-historical descriptions of the surrounding country.

Genoa too had inherited a native tradition of historiography. Indeed, it had inherited one of the oldest in all Italy, one to which its future historians were to turn for the kind of continuous, and usually reliable, narrative that was almost wholly unavailable to their colleagues in Piedmont.[83] It had also inherited, as Parma had not, a traditional office of state historiographer, one that went back as far as the twelfth century. But maintaining the office alone could not revive a tradition that had disintegrated into Bracelli's separate monographs and into Senarenga's chaotic chronicle. Battista Fregoso left behind his memoirs of the years between 1478, the beginning of his first violent and short-lived tenure as doge, and 1499, when he was still living, as usual, in exile. But since he chose to imitate Valerius Maximus rather than Livy, the memoirs finally appeared in the form of a *De Dictis et Memorabilibus Collectanea* rather than in the form of history. Benedetto Tagliacarne, who was appointed chancellor in 1514, may have written something, but whatever he wrote disappeared almost immediately. And what Paolo Franchi Partenopeo wrote after becoming professor of humanities in 1528 had to be completely rewritten by his successor.[84]

What finally led to the revival of historiography in Genoa, then, was not the tradition alone, but the tradition combined with what the historians all held to be an event as unexpected and as far-reaching in its consequences as the creation of the Farnese duchy in Parma: the occupation of the city and the reorganization of the government by Andrea Doria in 1528. Unlike their Venetian counterparts, to be sure, those who responded to this event by writing histories of Genoa had very little in common. Only one of them was a resident nobleman, PAOLO INTERIANO, although very little else is known about him.[85] Two of them were Genoese noblemen who spent most of their lives abroad. AGOSTINO GIUSTINIANI (1470–1536) was an exemplary protagonist of the early Catholic Reformation. After a trip to Spain, he had entered the Dominican order at Pavia in 1488. He had learned Hebrew, Aramaic, and Arabic, as well as the standard ancient languages, well enough to publish multilingual editions of the Scriptures and to be appointed to a chair of Hebrew in Paris. He had met Gianfrancesco Pico at Bologna, Erasmus in Flanders, and More and Linacre in England. When one of his rare trips home happened to coincide with another outburst of endemic civil war, one that left him badly wounded, he retired to his diocese in Corsica to translate Xenophon for his sister-in-law and a great quantity of pious literature for his alarmingly unlettered clergy. And he died, appropriately, in a shipwreck while returning to his flock from a mission to Rome.[86] Similarly, UBERTO, or OMBERTO, FOGLIETTA belonged to one of the new noble families admitted to the government by Doria's reorganization. But he had been brought up in Rome; and there he lived as a professional man of letters in the service of Cardinal Ippolito d'Este after the government confiscated his property in response to the attack on the old nobles in his justly famous dialogue *Della Repubblica di Genova* (written in 1555, published in 1559).[87] His several commentaries on various important contemporary events,[88] his contributions to the current discussions of historical theory,[89] and, above all, his general history of his times, which was partially published in 1571 to block the plagiarists, soon made him famous not only as a political philosopher but also as a historian. He was accordingly invited to add his personal glory to the glory of the fatherland he had never seen with the title of official historiographer in 1576, just after the old nobility had finally been forced to treat the new nobility as equals. And there he died, still working on his last, and perhaps greatest, historical work, five years later, at the age of about sixty-three.[90]

Two of the historians of Genoa were not Genoese at all. JACOPO BONFADIO (before 1509–1550) was a pugnacious academic from Lake Garda who had studied with Bembo in Padua, edited the orations of Cicero and a very popular collection of the letters of his famous contemporaries, and traveled up and down Italy in the service of various prelates before accepting a position as professor of philosophy and historiographer in Genoa in 1545. Unfortunately, his status as an ecclesiastic did not prevent his enjoying a very active, and apparently rather varied, sex life; five years after his arrival he was beheaded and then burned as a consequence of an affair, possibly with a wellborn boy, that his biographers did their best to hush up.[91] PIETRO BIZZARRI (b. 1525) was an Umbrian orphan who left Italy at the age of twenty to wander around Europe, from Wittenberg to Venice, from Augsburg to London, frequently in the service of the English government, and to write histories of all the countries he visited and of many that he had barely heard of.[92] And he wrote his monumental, 900-page history of Genoa, properly dedicated to the current doge, in a vain hope of returning once more to Italy after most of a lifetime in exile.[93]

The differences of status and point of view among the historians of Genoa were such that at least once they broke out into open hostility: Foglietta denounced Bizzarri's text as so much *"porcheria,* written in pedantic language, devoid of critical judgment, and full of heresies." Moreover, each of the histories reflected the particular interests and experiences of its author. Giustiniani prefaced his work with a geographical description of Liguria—one that included a sour observation on the quarrelsome nature of the citizens of Savona and a eulogy of the wine of the Cinque Terre. And linguist that he was, he refused to sacrifice Genoese orthographical peculiarities, which are "clear, easy, and intelligible to the moderately educated as well as to the learned," to the strict rules prescribed by the Tuscans. Bizzarri interrupted his narrative with separate disquisitions on subjects he could not fit into it—like the "short treatise on the state and administration of the republic" at the beginning of Book III. And he wrote in the same Latin to which his international audience had been accustomed in all his other historical works. Bonfadio would have preferred to write Livian history; and he showed abundantly that he had mastered the art of piling up long gerundic phrases and inventing fantastic metaphors—like one drawn-out comparison of the republic to a pomegranate. But he felt obliged by his commission to write year-by-year "annals," without regard to the "quality of words or candor of eloquence." Interiano covered all of Genoese history from the beginning to 1505. And Foglietta died while writing about the year 1527, which, fortunately, is where Bonfadio had begun.

Nevertheless, all the historians based their accounts on the same Genoese chronicles since the time of Caffaro and upon the same Genoese and Italian historians since the time of Giorgio Stella. Such was their respect for the sources, indeed, that Giustiniani and Interiano claimed only to be making a "compendium" of them ("ridurre in un corpo"; "ridurre in compendio"), and Giustiniani went so far as to publish one of them—the commentaries of Bracelli—as a model of impeccable Latin historical prose.[94] All of them, however, were careful not to accept uncritically everything they found in the sources; and to the critical standards they inherited from their Quattrocento predecessors—verisimilitude and mutual agreement—they added two more of their own: confirmation by archaeological evidence and the word of recent authorities. That the name of the founder of the city had been lost, said Giustiniani, was proof enough of its "antiquity," and, added Foglietta, there was no need to invent stories about a certain "Ligure, son of Fetonte," in order to justify the already perfectly obvious thesis that the Ligurians, like the Romans, descended from a mixture of Italots and Trojans. Livy provided plenty of information about Genoa in Roman republican times. A recently discovered bronze plaque (now *C.I.L.* V, 7749) testified to the bellicose nature of the Genoese in 209 B.C. (or in 116 B.C.: Bizzarri). Pliny's reports about the wealth of the Roman world in the first century A.D. at least made probable the identification of the emerald vase in the treasury of San Lorenzo with the one Nicodemus used to catch the blood shed by Christ on the Cross. And Procopius guaranteed the accuracy of the rather extraordinary number of Milanese refugees from the Goths. But when the works of reliable historians gave way to "the truncated and broken writings of uncultivated authors who barely touch upon events without giving either the causes or the consequences" (Foglietta), it was better to say nothing; and it was better simply to repeat what had been said by William of Tyre," an absolutely uncorrupted and most diligent writer," than to speculate about the number of ships and the names of the captains sent off on the first Crusades.

Similarly—or perhaps consequently—all the historians presented much the same general view of Genoese history. It began, they agreed, not with the arrival of some Trojan, not with a visit from "Janus," whose name had no etymological connection with that of the city, and not with the Romans, since the Saracens wiped out all traces of the previous Roman city. Rather, it began with the establishment of the consuls in 1102, the first certain date recorded in the documents. The first age was an age of gold, one in which "the hearts of all the citizens were fixed solely upon the public good" (Foglietta in *Della Repubblica*), when they "undertook magnificent expeditions to as far away as Syria and Spain," and when they answered Frederick Barbarossa's demands for money with lectures on the tax structure of the Athenian Empire—or of what they imagined to have been an Athenian Empire.

A decline from this initial apex began in 1190, when the Genoese unwisely modified their original constitution in imitation of the cities of the interior; and by 1170 they had entered a second age—an age of endemic civil war. Glorious deeds still took place—deeds like the defeat of the Pisans, the colonization of the Black Sea, and the capture of Alfonso d'Aragona, which were still to arouse the enthusiasm of romantic storytellers well into the seventeenth century.[95] Virtuous men still set examples for the imitation of their descendants: Pietro Fregoso, "the great ornament and glory of his country," Innocent VIII, "modest, clement, and most desirous of peace and concord," Julius II, "that most brilliant light," and, above all, Christopher Columbus, whose accomplishments seemed to justify even the sober Foglietta as he let biography degenerate into ridiculous patriotic hagiography.[96]

But the effect of these deeds was neutralized by the occurrence of as many needless disasters—like the War of Chioggia and the liberation of Alfonso. Rivalry among the great families prevented the expansion of Genoese dominion into Tuscany and Lombardy; and it gradually infected the entire population with attitudes and habits incompatible with civic life. All measures to cure the malady turned out to be equally inefficacious: the institution of the office of doge, the elevation of the popular leader Simone Boccanegra, the transfer of ultimate sovereignty to powerful foreign monarchs. Incapable of saving themselves, the Genoese were at last saved by a superhuman hero, Andrea Doria, a man "born for glory and great things," inspired by "an incredible love of his country," and graced by all the virtues and none of the vices of all the great statesmen of antiquity. Andrea threw out the French, reannexed Savona, promulgated a new constitution, and thus ushered in a third and final age—one so radically different from the preceding age that the two historians who tried to chronicle it were left with very little to write about.

Or at least so they thought. Unfortunately, the models of humanist municipal historiography they followed made them forget that Genoa was also the *dominante* of a territorial state. It therefore never occurred to them that the citizens of Savona, a city which had produced no less a hero than Pope Julius II and that had been honored by visits from no less distinguished personages than Charles V, Clement VII, and Julius III, might be less than happy at having their monasteries razed to make room for a Genoese fortress in their midst. It never occurred to them that the friends of GIOVAN AGOSTINO ABATE (b. 1495), president of the hat-makers guild and member of the Council of the Anziani, who sat talking to the old-timers on the benches in Piazza San Petro in 1565, might have severe misgivings about the economic consequences of their subject status.[97] Even Giustiniani, who lived there, was unaware of the dissatisfaction that was soon to lead to open revolt in Genoa's largest colony, Corsica—the first of the many revolts that were to end only with the annexation of the island to France in the eighteenth century. Even Bonfadio, who witnessed it, was unable to explain the outbreak of the Fieschi rebellion in Genoa itself—except by recreating Gianluigi Fieschi in the image of Catiline. Even Bizzarri, who lived and published in Antwerp, where most of the money ended up, was oblivious to the fact as well as to the political consequences of Genoa's rise to the position of banker to the Spanish empire. In his work of political theory, Foglietta had poignantly described all the defects of the settlement of 1528—the persistence of antisocial attitudes among the old noble families, the de facto exclusion from power of the Genoese counterpart of the *novi homines* at the time of Cicero, the unjust taxation of the plebeians. But the 664 packed pages of his work of history contain not a word prophetic of the civil war of 1575–76, a war that ended with a constitutional revision almost identical with the one he had proposed twenty years earlier and that made possible his appointment as state historiographer. Thus in the one Italian city that actually benefited from the calamities of Italy as a whole, and in the city that most successfully overcame the problems it had inherited from the past, history was reduced to a role even more modest than the one granted it in other cities. It sought only to present "the events of the past in such a way that no good citizen would not find the very memory of them abhorrent" (Foglietta)—and in such a way that no one would ever question the perfection and the immutability of the regime that had abolished such events once and for all.

Independence Lost

As historiography was stimulated by the restoration of independence in some cities of Italy, in at least one other it was actually stimulated by the loss of independence. Sienese had never before written their own history, explained ORLANDO MALAVOLTI (before 1518–1599), because they had been too busy fighting each other;[98] and none of the various regimes established by violence for the ostensible purpose of ending the violence ever did anything for history except destroy the records of their predecessors.

> The infinite discords and divisions . . . among the citizens and the frequent alterations of the state between one faction and another are the reason why no [historical] writings have survived until now; for everyone has always sought not only to overcome and suppress his enemy, but with all his might to cancel out the memory of his enemy.

Even the most successful of the regimes, the government of the Nove in the fourteenth century, eventually provoked a rebellion among those it excluded from power. Even the external lordship of Giangaleazzo Visconti, which had been voted in with almost unanimous enthusiasm, collapsed within months of the lord's sudden death. And the heroic expulsion of the Spanish garrison in 1552, which had inspired the admiration of some contemporary observers,[99] did nothing but complicate the usual domestic discord with the additional machinations of Florentine exiles and French imperial agents. Cosimo de' Medici did not fool Malavolti when he reinvested his newly conquered subjects with all their traditional magistrates, in the *dominio* as well as in the city; and the work accordingly ended the moment all effective authority was quietly placed in the hands of a Florentine governor responsible solely to the duke of Florence. But Cosimo accomplished what had long been accepted as impossible: an end to the fighting. He also gave official encouragement to the first of his new subjects who was prepared to take advantage of the unprecedented peace for the benefit of historiography. And he was fully repaid when the first complete history of Siena appeared under the eloquently grateful dedication to his son, Ferdinando I, in 1599.

Since history had come abruptly to an end with the capitulation of 1555, and since the prevention of a catastrophic return to historical times was a matter that now pertained solely to an external authority, neither Malavolti nor his successor in the next generation, GIUGURTA TOMMASI (d. before 1625),[100] had any reason to exhort their fellow citizens to do anything. What they had to do, on the other hand, was to reassert the honor of their city, which had been severely compromised during the some three centuries in which its history had been recorded exclusively by foreigners. Giovanni Villani, they found, was an indispensable guide to the history of Siena in the fourteenth century. But like so many other writers who had been "misled by a spirit of emulation or hatred or blinded by ignorance" (Tommasi), he erroneously attributed the foundation of the city to Charles Martel. Biondo may have been "a very well educated person and a diligent investigator of antiquity." But he was "rather negligent" *(poco accorto)* when he put the foundation in A.D. 1007, and he read the pertinent passages in Pliny the Elder in a manner incompatible with the proper interpretation given by Guillaume Budé in *De Asse*. Bruni and his followers were "not very consistent among themselves." Antonino merely swallowed Bruni's errors uncritically. And Poggio and Machiavelli deliberately belittled Siena by back-dating Florence's subsequent territorial dominion to an age in which Florence had actually been enclosed within Charlemagne's six-mile limit. The truth, insisted Malavolti, and then, apparently independently of him, Tommasi, was that Siena is one of the oldest cities in Tuscany, and not, like Florence, a relatively "new" city. Since none of their predecessors had been aware of this truth, they themselves had to dig it out of all the well- and little-known writings of the ancients—not only out of Livy, but also out of a recently discovered agrarian treatise by Aggenus Urbicus and out of the surviving fragments of Clearchus Solensis. They had to dig confirmation of the truth out of the wealth of stones and manuscripts of the Middle Ages that were preserved in the city's collections. Moreover, since what they said about the truth was obviously polemical, they had also to transcribe the documents exactly as they found them, "in order not to give rise to any suspicion that the sense had in any way been altered." Since the documentation they found was far more abundant than they had expected, and since they discovered in the documents much information that had never before been recorded, their volumes became thicker and thicker—until they reached the monumental size, respectively, of 1,555 quarto pages and 340 pages of very small print.

In some subject cities, on the other hand, historiography was stimulated by the acquisition of a new kind of independence, one that had none of the disadvantages of the kind they had experienced before their submission to a *dominante*. PIETRO TERNI assured the glory of the tiny Lombard town of Crema before 1449 by tracing its foundation to the same flight of noble Romans from the barbarians that accounted for the foundation of its *dominante*, Venice. And he assured its glory thereafter by recalling the tenacity with which its citizens had "exposed their lives and possessions to maintain themselves under the shadow . . . of this most happy state" in the dark days after Agnadello. But what persuaded ALEMANIO FINO (d. 1585) to revise Terni's manuscript for publication, to continue it to 1567, and to defend it against the imperialist theses of a certain Cremonese Latin teacher, was first the expectation and then the realization of Crema's elevation to the rank of a bishopric.[101] That the first and all succeeding bishops turned out to be Venetians rather than Cremesi merely confirmed Terni's and Fino's thesis. Venetian patricians could now reside with perfect honor in the city they governed, Fino pointed out; for it was now the equal of their own ecclesiastically, even though, to the delight of all its citizens, it re-mained subject politically.[102]

Similarly, CESARE CLEMENTINI assured the glory of Rimini in antiquity by tracing its foundation back to the year 1,678 B.C. and by collecting all the many flattering references to it contained in the works of Plutarch, Strabo, Appian, Livy, Silius Italicus, Cicero, Caesar, Polybius, Florus, Dio Cassius, Horace, etc. He then saved its rather tarnished glory in the fourteenth and fifteenth centuries by rescuing the good name of the Malatesta from what he found to be the rather misinformed judgments of Antonino of Florence and Pius II. And he earned for himself the reputation of being as great a writer in his own day as his namesake had been a general in antiquity:

> Ecce manu pungens melior cum CAESARE CAESAR
> Scriptores unus vincis ut ille duces.

But what set him to digging through all the public and private archives of the city, what forced him to read through every page of every published and unpublished medieval chronicle and Renaissance history he could lay his hands on, what induced him to send his correspondents on a search through all the Riminese documents that Clement VIII had stored in the Vatican, and what ultimately left his 1,500-page text a mass of undigested quotations, references, and digressions, was the threat of the archbishop of Ravenna to take seriously the Council of Trent's provision for the reestablishment of ecclesiastical provinces. As a city, Rimini could honorably admit its temporal submission to the pope, just as in antiquity it had been obedient to the Roman emperor. But a letter of Pope Gregory the Great, a privilege of Pope Innocent III, and the papal decrees of 1370, 1568, and 1582 all proved that as a church it had never been "of or in the province of Ravenna" and had always been "immediately subject to the Apostolic See" alone. Consequently, the bishop was perfectly justified in ignoring the "notwithstanding" clauses of Trent and in refusing to publish a papal bull sent on to him from Ravenna in 1578 until he received a copy of his own directly from Rome.[103]

Still, where the city-as-church most spectacularly came to the rescue of the city-as-commune was in Bologna. To be sure, Bologna enjoyed several advantages not shared by Crema or Rimini. It had a thriving university, one in which professors of literature could be induced to write history instead of poetry as part of their normal academic obligations. It also had a fairly rich chronicle tradition, one which, in the work of the patrician-professor Giovanni Garzoni, had already adopted at least the external forms of humanist historiography.[104] In fact, the chronicle tradition was still so strong that it overcame the chief historiographical disadvantage of Bologna's status as a subject city: newslessness. JACOPO RAINIERI's nineteenth-century editors deduced from the then current axioms about the nature of papal government the historical thesis that "once Bologna became a thing of the pope, it had no more history, and languished [*sbugiardò*] in silence and unhappy decadence."[105] But Jacopo himself found plenty to write about: the walling up of the door of the communal palace in 1535; one more useless edict against urinating on the columns of the palace of the *podestà* ("che nesuno non pissase a li pilastri del palazo . . . perchè quello pissa roseghava le masegne di pilastri . . .: questo durò pocho como è usanza . . .") the outrages by and the capture and hanging of bandits; the regulation of retail shops;

elaborate ceremonies at the university; and an endless round of distinguished visitors. His successor, the jurist and city official Valerio Rainieri, found even more to write about—enough, that is, to fill some twenty-four manuscript volumes by the time of his death in 1613. And so, apparently, did Valerio's contemporary, Cristoforo Saraceni, whose unpublished chronicle-diary runs from 1471 to 1596.

More important still, no one really thought that Bologna had lost its independence, not even those of its citizens who most resented the forcible capture of the city by Pope Julius II. After all, papal overlordship had always been recognized as an institution of some legal justification, and it had occasionally been voluntarily adopted in practice as a preferable alternative to a government dominated by either domestic or foreign lords. Thus the local representatives of the distant, and tactfully abstemious, papal authority were usually welcomed into the city "with every sign of joy and jubilation," with triumphal arches, and "with several nights of firework displays"—like those put on for Cardinal Giulio Ascanio Sforza in 1536 (Rainieri). For while guaranteeing the protection of the city from external aggression and internal discord, the papal legates left the Senate (Anziani) in virtually complete control of local affairs, and they assured the maintenance of "all the magistracies, in the country as well as in the city, in the hands of citizens" alone. Indeed, to one historian (Alberti), the submission of the city to Leo X really amounted to a restoration of independence, one very similar to the declaration of independence issued upon the expulsion of the last Imperial garrison in the year 1112. Once again, he noted, "we have thrown off the yoke of servitude, so long and with such pain imposed upon our shoulders." After the experience of civil war at the time of the Lambertazzi and the Geremei, after the experience of tyranny at the time of Cardinal Beltrando and Taddeo Pepoli, and after the experience of foreign domination at the time of Giangaleazzo and Filippo Maria Visconti—all of which he described in detail—the charters drawn up "for the maintenance of liberty" in the twelfth century looked very much like a blueprint for the government actually in force in the sixteenth century.

Yet municipal history in Bologna was slow to be born. The first candidate for the role of progenitor, ACHILLE BOCCHI (1478–1562), had all the proper credentials: the title of professor of Greek at the university, the sponsorship of a literary academy at which none other than Guicciardini read passages from his forthcoming history aloud, and a facility for Latin verse that earned his *Symbolicae Quaestiones* the honor of two editions and the applause of several famous men of letters. He also had plenty of time, since the Senate regularly granted him exemptions from his teaching obligations. And he had plenty of money, since the Senate increased his salary each time he turned in another installment of his work. But the history turned out to be a failure.[106] It was so not because he copied some of his sources without acknowledgment, accepted others uncritically, and rewrote still others in anachronistically polished Latin, as one modern critic has proposed after measuring the work according to the standards of the early twentieth century. It failed rather because the author tried to do too much—namely, to include every detail he could find in every chronicle, history, or archival document that had anything to do with Bologna. And it failed because, in the absence of a thesis to sustain or a lesson to illustrate, he lacked the only criteria provided by humanism for emphasis and selection. With one entire book for the years between 1219 and 1223 and another book for those between 1251 and 1256, it is not surprising that the text got no farther than 1263—and that it has remained in manuscript ever since.

The second candidate was not much more successful. LEANDRO ALBERTI (1479–after 1522) had studied under the chief authority on Bolognese history of the previous generation, Giovanni Garzoni, and he was a personal friend of Bocchi.[107] Moreover, he had a clear purpose in mind, as Bocchi had not. Since municipal history was the chief fount of civic morality, he sought to make it available to "the rough peasant, the industrious artisan . . . , and the strenuous soldier" as well as to "the noble citizen . . . and the wise, prudent captain." Since it provided numerous examples of how to live "chastely and virtuously," he sought to make it available "to all classes of women" as well. Yet Alberti ended up with a text that was substantially little more than a vernacular version of Bocchi's.[108] It included all the stories about a certain Fero who, shortly after the Flood, left overpopulated Scythia for the banks of the Reno, where, after his wife had died in a flash flood, he built a wall in honor of his daughter, Felsina. It included all the stories about Bologna's declaration of independence from the Roman Empire during the reign of Gratian, its war with Ravenna in A.D. 356, and its destruction by Theodosius just before he repented of the massacre at Thessaloniki—all of which, it seems, is documented in the letters of Ambrose of Milan. It was based on the same blind faith in any written source, be it a credible ancient historian or an unnamed medieval chronicle, that happened to pop up out of some archive. It maintained the same confusion between chronicle and historical forms ("1251 . . .: the Bolognese passed this year quietly, and so we arrive at the year 1252"). Even its boasted vernacular style frequently broke down into interminable run-on sentences, so that even the best-educated peasant would certainly have gotten as lost as Alberti himself in "the wide, long, lovely garden of the histories of our country." The only lessons it yielded were perfectly obvious even without the addition of historical illustrations: that "the people of Bologna are civil, magnificent, liberal, wise, courageous, strong, virile . . . ," and that "the things of this world are [so] fragile" that everyone should "put his faith and hope in God alone."

What finally succeeded in generating a municipal historiography consonant with humanist standards, and therefore satisfactory to the discriminating senators, was the intervention of the leader of the Counter Reformation in Bologna, Gabriele Paleotti.[109] Even before his elevation as bishop in 1566, Paleotti had persuaded the Senate to give a university chair and the title of historiographer to his old friend, CARLO SIGONIO, who was later to become his adviser on cultural affairs and the leading historian of all Italy in his generation. He did so for the very practical purpose of obtaining specific information about the particular religious and ecclesiastical traditions of the city and of thus facilitating the implementation of the Tridentine decrees in his diocese. The result was first a study of the life of the city's patron, St. Petronius, later expanded into a complete series of biographies of all its bishops,[110] and, second, the *Historiae Bononiensis,* which was finally published, after long delays and after considerable pressure exerted by Paleotti himself in Rome, in 1578.[111] Sigonio began by getting rid of Feto and Felsina, by devoting the equivalent of one paragraph each to the little-known Etruscans and Gauls, by writing no more about the Roman period than what was specifically reported in Roman historical literature, and by stating no more about the medieval period than what "was made plain by [contemporary] diplomas," on which he was a recognized expert. The greatness of Bologna, he insisted, in defiance of long-established assumptions, was a product of its liberty, not of its antiquity. And to make his thesis more convincing, he translated the documents from which he quoted liberally into current humanist Latin Prose.

Unfortunately, even Sigonio's history was still marred by occasional reversions to a purely chronicle form—by the inclusion of material that proved nothing and by the confusion of periods in the city's growth with a system of periodization based on the reigns of emperors. Moreover, it broke off inexplicably with a description of a horse race in 1267. His task was therefore taken up by Alberti's younger colleague, LUCIO CACCIANEMICI. Caccianemici was also inspired by Paleotti, to whom he dedicated Part II of his work, to begin where Alberti had left off.[112] To Alberti's format, however, he added the reproduction of documents in their original form. And he managed to extract from what he wrote the lessons that Alberti had left buried in a mass of detail. Much as they might benefit from imitating the simpler manners of the twelfth century, Caccianemici pointed out, the chief lesson to be derived from history was an appreciation of the incomparable advantages of the present. At one time Bologna had been the scene of constant civil strife, which "led not only to the death of thousands of citizens but also to the extirpation of the very roots and foundations of families and their habitations." Now it was "a public theater of the world," one in which learned men demonstrated their abilities "in all the faculties of the intellectual sciences" while "truly praiseworthy gentlemen" demonstrated their virtue "in their manners and political and civil activities." And all this was made possible by the "benign mantle of Peter, which defends us from the insidious machinations of the common and capital Enemy of mankind and from the powerful hands of tyrants."

Caccianemici got no farther than 1258. His task in turn was taken up by CHERUBINO GHIRARDACCI (1519–98), the Augustinian scholar-artist who had designed the illustrations for Sigonio's *De Episcopis Bononiensibus.* Ghirardacci's theological and liturgical treatises brought him into close association with Paleotti's program of diocesan regeneration. His collection of the proverbs of his Bolognese ancestors gave him an appreciation of the importance of morality, which, humanists had always held to be one of the most useful aspects of historical study. And his *Della historia di Bologna,* of which Part I was published just before his death, Part II a half century after his death,[113] and Part III, finally, in the second edition of the *Rerum Italicarum Scriptores.*[114] demonstrated his ability to master and then to surpass the methods of his predecessors. Since he had no reason to deny them, he confined the latest embellishments of the legends about the foundation of the city to a few introductory pages, and he then devoted proportionately more space—all thirty pages of Book XVI, for example, to the year 1308 alone—to those periods in which he was more certain of the validity of his sources. He reviewed not only all the standard ancient and modern historians, but also many of the recent non-Italian historians whose works had become available in Italy—from Budé to Pedro Mexia. He reproduced verbatim much of the new archival material he discovered—both for the well-accepted purpose of distinguishing his own from the corresponding statements of his predecessors and also for the much more original purpose of providing his readers with concrete illustrations "of the manner in which republics in those times corresponded with other peoples." In accordance with Paleotti's program, he included bishops, saints, and preachers along with *anziani* and *podestà,* and, in deference to Bologna's special character as a university town, he fitted the history of its most famous institution into his account of "the counsels, the wars, the peace [treaties], and the famous deeds of its citizens." And he facilitated the consultation of his enormous text (612 pages in Part I alone, to 1320) with references to his sources in the margins and lists of pontiffs, bishops, and "an infinity of important details" in an appendix.

To the quantity of information supplied by Ghirardacci—as well as several local researchers whose manuscript volumes have been identified by Ghirardacci's modern editor—POMPEO VIZIANI added a historical thesis.[115] Viziani abandoned Ghirardacci's—and Sigonio's—ambitious defiance of humanist historiographical traditions and reverted to the more usual separation of political and ecclesiastical history. He consequently ran into the same difficulty faced by most of his contemporaries when he sought to extend his narrative into an epoch in which the church alone provided the "events." But he managed thereby to present all Bolognese history since the formation of the first commune as the unfolding of a single theme: the conflict between liberty and order. The horror story about Imelda Lambertazzi, who killed herself by sucking poison from the wounds inflicted in the body of her lover by her jealous brothers, illustrated the general problem of civil strife. The constitution promulgated by Taddeo Pepoli illustrated the chief means adopted in the mid-fourteenth century to restore civil peace. And whatever might appear to be an extraneous detail was fitted in as a causal link by such expressions as "It seems to me not inappropriate to write about... in order to make clear that...." Communal independence had been bought at the price of the destruction of all super-communal political authority and, consequently, at the price of an unending round of foreign and civil wars. Thus the city "gradually lost its ancient authority, until it fell into the subjection of others"—namely, of the Visconti; and the collapse of the Visconti empire then exposed it to various forms of tyranny—that of a condottiere, that of the plebeians, that of a small group of oligarchs hiding behind the ineffective authority of Pope John XXIII. A penultimate solution was achieved in the mid-fifteenth century: under the protection of the Bentivoglio, the magistrates governed while the citizens "applied themselves toward increasing their wealth and beautifying the city." A final solution was then achieved in 1530: the coronation of Charles V, which took place appropriately in Bologna, guaranteed the territorial integrity of the Papacy; and the Papacy, which wisely chose to respect the internal autonomy of the city, was thus enabled, as the Bentivoglio had not been after 1494, to protect it from the danger of outside aggression.

The cycle was now complete. Liberty had destroyed order in the twelfth and thirteenth centuries. Order restored liberty in the sixteenth century. And the Bolognese could look forward to living forever "in peace, under the tranquil government of the Holy Church." Moreover, in the monumental works of Ghirardacci and Viziani, the history of the cycle had been completely recorded.

10

THE DIVERSIFICATION
OF MODELS

PATRIOTISM, THEN, OR, AS CESARE OTTONELLI PUT IT IN PRESENTING A HISTORY OF HIS
native city to his Roman friends in 1591, "an innate love of our country, a desire
placed in us by nature by which we are constantly drawn back to our native soil,"[1]
was the principal stimulant of municipal historiography in the sixteenth century; and
this stimulant was strengthened chiefly by a consciousness of having participated in
one or another of the great calamities of the period. But what made this stimulant
effective, what channeled it specifically into the production of works of history, was
the ever greater availability both of literary models and of historical information.

Editions and Translations

Sallust remained, particularly after the publication of Lorenzo Valla's commentary
in 1493, the chief model for the history of single periods in the life of the Italian
cities—as well as for such dramatic orations as those composed by Bonfadio and
Bernardo Segni.[2] After the *editio princeps* of the *Conspiracy of Catiline* and the *Jugur-
than War* in Venice, 1470, editions multiplied: thirty-three of them in Italy alone by
1500. And they continued to lead all the works of ancient history in number of
printings all over Europe well into the following century.[3] Caesar, in turn, remained
the chief model for the history of particular contemporary events as well as for
commentaries. No one before the seventeenth century seems to have noticed the
deliberate falsifications attributed to him by Suetonius and confirmed by scholars in
the twentieth century. Indeed, many of his imitators found his deliberate magnifi-
cation of his own deeds very useful as a guide to magnifying their own domestic
heroes, and many of them were enchanted by the examples of concise yet dramatic
narrative prose that is still today considered one of the greatest of his deeds.[4] Therefore, after the first of 1471, editions of the *Civil Wars* as well as of the *Gallic War*
multiplied until in Italy they finally outnumbered even those of Sallust. Similarly,
the chief model for histories of cities *ab urbe condita* remained the one first adopted by
Bruni: Livy. No one seems to have noticed what Livy himself said about his own
motives; indeed, according to one modern authority, no one was to notice it even
thereafter until the middle of the twentieth century.[5] Nor did anyone notice the
skeptical tone of his account of the origins of Rome, which was systematically
plundered for corroborating evidence of the mythical origins of other cities as well.[6]
And no one noticed Cicero's denunciations of the kind of legendary material that the

Augustan antiquarians made Livy, good Ciceronian though he was, put back in—denunciations that were to become unavoidable after the discovery of the *De Re Publica* in the early nineteenth century.[7] Hence, editions of Livy also multiplied, first in the texts of Valla and Sabellico, of which at least eleven editions appeared between 1469 and 1500, and then in the texts of Henricus Loritus Glareanus and Carlo Sigonio, whose comments were usually printed together in the rest of Europe after 1555. The size of the text also grew, particularly after the discovery of additional fragments of Book XXXIII in the cathedral of Bamberg early in the century.[8]

At the same time, whoever could not, or, in accordance with the linguistic doctrines of the Accademia Fiorentina, whoever chose not to read the classics in the original could now read them in Italian. They could read Sallust in any of the six editions of Agostino Ortica's translation of 1518 or in the two editions of Lelio Carani's translation of 1550. They could read Livy in any of the nine reprintings of the first edition of 1476 or in any of the eleven editions of Jacopo Nardi's translation of 1540, the latter augmented by the explanatory notes, the gazetteer, and the table of measures that the translator deemed "necessary to enable the reader to understand it fully." They could read Caesar in any of the ten editions of the translation by Ortica, of the two by Dante Popoleschi, or of the seven by Francesco Baldelli (1554); and whoever had trouble following the geographical digressions that were one of the more admired peculiarities of Caesar's plan of organization could consult both Raimondo Marliano's index of place names and the charts and battle plans that Andrea Palladio drew for the son of Pope Gregory XIII in the edition of 1575.[9] Whoever might tire of the standard Latin models was invited, in the last decades of the century, to adopt a very different one: the consciously anti-Livian historian Tacitus. To be sure, Tacitus had been used extensively for his theses as well as his information since the time of Bruni and Poggio. But when Jean Bodin and Justus Lipsius declared him to be the best of all the ancient historians—and also the most appropriate in an age that was governed more like the Rome of Augustus and Tiberius than like the Rome of the Scipios—Tacitus acquired a new importance. The expatriate French philologist Marc-Antoine Muret declared to his Roman audiences that Tacitus was a master of historical prose. And the two Florentine translators, Giorgio Dati and Bernardo Davanzati, then showed that his stylistic qualities, brevity and concision, could be realized just as well in the vernacular.[10]

Although the Roman models far outdistanced their modern competitors, many of the works of the early Quattrocento humanist historians became available in print, and many of the others were reprinted. Bruni's *Historiae* could now be read in the Venice, 1560, edition of Donato Acciaiuoli's translation, and his *Commentarius* could be read in the translation of 1561. Poggio could be read in the translation by his son Jacopo, of which at least five editions appeared after the first of 1476. Biondo's *Decades* could be read either in the 1483–84 edition or in the much better known and more frequently printed abridgment by Pope Pius II, while his *Roma Instaurata* and

Triumphans appeared respectively in five and three editions until the originals were replaced by Lucio Fauno's translations (1543 and 1544). Giovanni Albino's histories of Naples, which had been left in manuscript at the time of the invasion of 1495, were finally published by the author's nephew, Ottavio, together with a collection of contemporary documents illustrative of "the many things that are touched upon [only] briefly" in the texts. Francesco Contarini's *De Rebus in Hetruria Gestis* was published in 1562 by Giovan Michele Bruto because, said the editor, it still was found to contain, a century after its composition, "many things suitable to the comfort and embellishment [*commoditates atque ornamenta*] of the life of the reader."[11] Giorgio Merula was printed first in Latin (1527), then in translation (1543). Sabellico was printed first in Latin and then in the translations of Matheo Besconte (1510) and of Lodovico Dolce (1544, 1554, 1558). Corio was printed in three editions after 1503. Fazio and Pontano were printed in Jacopo Mauro's translations of 1540 and 1580.

To the Latin and Renaissance humanist classics were added many more potential models from Greek historical literature. Valla's Latin translation of Thucydides was published together with Ammianus Marcellinus in 1483; and while Giovanni Della Casa, apparently for his own amusement, retranslated several of the more famous passages into Latin, Francesco di Soldo Strozzi composed a vernacular version of the entire text that was republished at least five times after the first edition of 1545. Polybius—even though most Renaissance historians preferred to read what Livy had borrowed from him rather than what he himself had written about the Punic wars—was translated by that most assiduous, although "notoriously incompetent" (Momigliano), of mid-century translators, Lodovico Domenichi, who also provided the standard Italian versions of Plutarch (from the 1517 Giunti edition of the Greek) and of Xenophon (from Francesco Filelfo's Latin version first printed in 1502). Polybius could thus be compared directly with Bruni's paraphrases, which Domenichi also translated and twice published after 1526. At the same time, Eusebius was translated by the same Francesco Baldelli who had translated Caesar. Dionysius of Halicarnassus was translated into Italian (1545) by Francesco Venturi with the help of the first Latin translation by Lapus (Lampugnino) Biragus (1480) as well as of the current one by Glareanus. The 1493 translation of Josephus was reprinted some eighteen times before 1589. And Appian was translated three times: by Alessandro Braccio, by Girolamo Ruscelli, and by Lodovico Dolce, whose versions all then appeared in numerous editions.[12]

Thus by the second half of the sixteenth century a considerable body of ancient and Renaissance historiography had become readily available in print, and to it had been added several of the classics of early and high medieval historiography as well: Paulus Diaconus (1516, 1517, 1521, . . .) and Vincent of Beauvais (1483, 1494, 1591, . . .), Giovanni Villani, Mosè del Brolio, and Ricordano Malispini (1568, 1592, 1598). So much had become available, indeed, that a historian could now "accomplish in one day what once would have taken a whole year," at least in the eyes of Pompeo Pellini, one of the most successful of them.[13] Instead of plunging unaided into the chronicles and the archives, he could begin by looking up what had already been reported about his city in the printed sources. And he could then draw up an outline for an eventual text on the basis of whichever of the several recognized models he thought to be most appropriate.

The Availability of Information

Promising as this procedure might seem, some historians still tried to shortcut it. STEFANO GIONTA read all the ancient historians, all the early Mantuan chronicles, and even the letters of that "most diligent writer," Leonardo Bruni.[14] JACOPO SACCHI should have read all the modern historians, for he was a graduate of the University of Siena, a frequent ambassador to Rome, the first professor of philosophy in the new *studio* of Viterbo, *protomedico generale* for Viterbo and Orvieto, and a personal friend of such eminent humanist prelates as Reginald Pole and Pope Marcellus II—or so he claimed.[15] Both Gionta and Sacchi sought to sustain certain historical theses: that Mantua had maintained its independence and privileges by constantly siding with the pope against the emperor, that popular government invariably brought on civil war, that Paul III was a "loveable benefactor," and that Paul IV was "bellicose, difficult, and avaricious." But both of them thought that they could pile up information and forget about form. Consequently, they produced respectively a chronicle and a diary that were complete anachronisms in the age of humanist histories and commentaries. Gionta wandered off into stories about the Roman soldier at the Crucifixion who brought back to Mantua all the remaining Vinegar and a whole jarful of the Blood that had dripped down his spear. And he failed to notice the obvious contradiction to his theses represented by the career of his main hero, Federico Gonzaga, who served the Venetians, then the French, then the pope, and then the emperor, with equal indifference to anything but the money they paid him. Sacchi refused to attribute the shocking cruelty with which suspected troublemakers were treated in 1529 to anything but the "jealousy" of certain of their unnamed fellow citizens. And he presented the War of Siena, in which he had served as a supplier for the Imperial army, as nothing but a minor rebellion. What is surprising is that Gionta's chronicle was published twice in the sixteenth century and once, along with the continuation by BENEDETTO OSANNA,[16] in the seventeenth—instead of being left in manuscript, like Sacchi's, for the benefit of nineteenth-century document hunters.

Some writers, on the other hand, tried to do just the opposite: to create histories of cities about which the standard texts contained very little information. CESARE NUBILONIO proudly displayed his authoritative sources: Eutropius, Paulus Diaconus, Livy, Plutarch, the "Decade of the Sforza Dukes" (Crivelli? Simonetta?), Corio, and Leandro Alberti—in that order.[17] GIOVAN FRANCESCO ANGELITA pored over Ptolemy, Eusebius, Orosius, Sabellico, and even Francesco Filelfo.[18] GIANGIROLAMO BRON- ZIERO read all these and still more while living leisurely and happily "among his literary delights and friends" at Padua, where he also wrote observations on the antiquities of the other towns of the lower Po Valley.[19] But Nubilonio was forced to rely on a series of *dicono (dicitur)* and the poem of a late-fifteenth-century Dominican friar in order to establish the descent of the first settlers of Vigevano from Noah's descendant, Subres. And he was forced to pad his lists of consuls in Vigevano with imaginary transcriptions of the heroic speeches of the dukes of Milan. Angelita had to turn to the poet Trissino to resolve the question of the ancient name of Recanati, which neither Strabo nor Ptolemy nor Volterrano had bothered to mention. And he had to deduce the destruction of the city by the Goths from what Bruni and Orosius had said in general about the Marche as a whole. Bronziero was even more desperate. Rovigo apparently entered history during the War of Ferrara and left it after its subsequent annexation by Venice. And nothing was left to do but conduct still another inscription-hunting expedition around the Polesine with the help of "Pliny, Livy, Ptolemy, Sigonio, and, not to mention many others, Silius Italicus"—none of whom was really of much help.

The tiny towns of Monte San Savino and Chiusi in the Valdichiana, alas, had escaped history even more completely than Rovigo. To be sure, the first town had produced one pope and one grand master of the Order of St. John, and the other had been captured by an Imperial-Papal army in 1529 and by an Imperial-Florentine army during the War of Siena. But, admitted AGOSTINO FORTUNIO,[20] who found much more to write about in his Latin history of the Camaldolese order, only a tomb recently discovered at Arezzo could guarantee the foundation of Monte San Savino by the inhabitants of the abandoned town founded by Noah-Janus on nearby Monte Iano; and the only event that could be credited to it before the Florentines rescued it from the Sienese and the Perugians in 1385 was a visit by the Virgin Mary in 1155. The only events that could be credited to Chiusi during the two hundred years after the canonization of Thomas Aquinas in 1323 were the rebellion of Genoa in 1478, the capture of Asinalunga in 1553, and the election of Henry III as king of Poland—none of which JACOMO GORI could really blame on his fellow citizens.[21]

The procedure of reworking information extracted from published sources was far more fruitful in the case of a subject city that had already attracted the attention of the historians of the *dominante*—like Como. And Como was even more fortunate in that its historian happened to be BENEDETTO GIOVIO, the older brother and former guardian of one of the most famous historians of all Italy, Paolo.[22] For Benedetto knew Greek well enough to discount the fabulous etymologies upon which Como's supposedly Hellenic origins depended. He also knew Latin well enough to make even the medieval privileges he cited sound like the letters quoted in the *Conspiracy of Catiline,* and he managed to make the speech he heard Il Moro give on his return from exile ("me quoque audiente") sound like Caesar addressing the Senate. He therefore extracted everything that all the authors had said about Como from Pliny to Corio—except whatever consisted merely of questions of proper dating, which he reserved for another, and purely annalistic, catalogue of local bishops.[23] He left out everything in his authorities that did not pertain to Como—even the invasion of Charles VIII, which he mentioned only as background for the siege of nearby Novara. He filled up chronological gaps with lists of emperors and dukes. He restored the importance of what the Milanese historians had regarded as marginal with the standard generalizations about sacks and sieges:

> Quot ploratus & clamores infelicissimi cives edidere sub eorum oculis ruente patria? quis lachrymarum modus & moestitiae finis supremo civitatis fato?

And when the records finally abandoned him, he filled another quarter of his book with his own recollections of the wars that had gone back and forth through Como during the two decades before 1532.

Indeed, the procedure could even be fruitful for an area that had long been politically as well as linguistically and culturally isolated from mainland Italy—like Sardinia. It could be fruitful, that is, providing that the historian was willing to "spurn the delights of his native soil" (which apparently was not fertilized by a single book) and "for the love of virtue to make himself an exile, visiting the schools of Italy and hearing the most learned professors of civil wisdom." Actually, GIOVAN FRANCESCO FARA[24] could have gotten along very well without ever having seen the country of his birth. For he learned all he knew about the fertility of its fields from Polybius and Claudian, all about the character of its inhabitants from Aristotle, all about its adjacent islands from Baldus and Bartolus, and all about its fauna from Strabo and Volterrano. He therefore knew, without having to make any observations of his own, that Sardinia boasted a breed of goats and dogs found nowhere else, that it abounded in boars and horses, and that it was bereft of lions and wolves. He could deduce from Nikeforos Gregoras that St. Peter must have visited Sardinia and from the ruins of "the vast, sumptuous buildings" he had seen elsewhere that such buildings must have existed also in Sardinia during the age of the Antonines. He could reconstruct the Pisan and Genoese conquests from Foglietta and from Gratian, whom he had studied in law school. And when the records gave out completely, as they did after the Aragonese occupation, he could resort to lists of governors and notes about the Sardinian bishops who attended the Council of Trent.

Where the procedure was most productive, however, was in a country that rejoined the mainstream of Italian culture after two centuries of isolation and chaos—namely, in Sicily. To be sure, the historiographical debate over whether Sicily progressed or stagnated in the sixteenth century is still far from being resolved even today. Yet the hundreds of miles of new roads and the some thirty-three new bridges that were built either by local initiative or with viceregal subsidies are a sign at least of a considerable economic recovery.[25] Similarly, the literary careers of TOMMASO FAZELLO (1498–1570), the Dominican prior of Palermo who crossed the whole island four times on foot, and of FEDERICO MAUROLICO (1494–1575),[26] the astronomer, mathematician, poet, theologian, and architect who lectured at the new University of Messina, are a sign, if not of an intellectual revival, at least of their country's ability to generate some of the most learned men of all Europe.

Although they wrote at roughly the same time, and although Maurolico pretended to do no more than correct the errors in Fazello's work, which he otherwise admired, the two texts are not identical. Fazello was better informed about such recent events as the rebellion of Giovan Luca Squarcialupa in 1517–23, of which he had been a witness. Maurolico was better informed about the visit of Charles V, for which he had been commissioned to erect a triumphal arch. And they disagreed with each other somewhat in their evaluation of the Hohenstaufen period, which Fazello portrayed as an unmitigated disaster, and of the Sicilian Vespers, which Maurolico described as nothing more than a terrifying blood bath. But both of them were thoroughly familiar with contemporary cultural activities on the continent, which they occasionally visited. And both of them had read absolutely everything there was to read about almost every imaginable subject.

Like their continental colleagues, moreover, the Sicilian historians often put their literary sources on the same plane: Maurolico cited Sabellico as an authority on the Athenian invasion of 416 B.C., even though he knew that Sabellico had only summarized the account of Thucydides, whom he had read in Greek; and Fazello had to swallow the story about the post-Creation creation of the island of "Hiera" because he had read it in Isidore and Orosius as well as in Eusebius. They also resorted to the etymological arguments sanctioned by their authorities whenever the authorities abandoned them in fact—as Fazello did most notoriously in his interminable digression on the origin of the name of the river Tiber. But unlike Fara, at least, they tried whenever possible to check what was reported in the books by what they themselves observed—especially as archaeologists, since archaeology was then the chief passion of all the learned men of the island. The existence of the Cyclops and monsters reported by Homer and Berosus was confirmed in 1552 when a whole cemetery full of their bones was dug up. The structure of the Ark was confirmed by the testimony of traveling Armenian merchants. The history of the Norman invasion as recorded by Malaterra was confirmed by the edicts of Ruggero and Guglielmo, "which are still preserved uncorrupted in Palermo." Finally, both Maurolico and Fazello found plenty to write about. For Sicily had already enjoyed two periods of splendor in the past—in the age of the Syracusan tyrants and in the age of the Norman dukes. And the final age of splendor inaugurated a century earlier by Alfonso d'Aragona—and by Panormita—had just culminated in the still more splendid age of Charles V—and of Antonello da Messina.

The availability of ancient and humanist models proved to be even more effective as a stimulant to municipal historiography when at least one of the models happened to be directly concerned with the city of which the historians were citizens. To be sure, in some cases the domestic models turned out to be somewhat restrictive.

even in the deplorable conditions of the present ("a period in which there is no observance of either religion, law, or military discipline, and which is stained by every species of the lowest brutality"). The *Discorsi* also provided the author with what was to become one of his leading themes: the contrast between Rome, the most successful, and Florence, the least successful, of republics. They provided him with several of the chief assumptions he was to share with most other humanist historians—for example, that the character of a people is largely determined by its founders (e.g., I, i, on Florence and Alexandria), and that readers are more impressed by examples drawn from the history of their own city (e.g., II, iv, on the ancient and the modern Tuscans). They provided him with some of his chief historical explanations for the events he was to narrate, such as the habit of each succeeding Florentine regime of expelling or disenfranchising the beneficiaries of its predecessor and the proclivity of the great Florentine families for using the state to pursue their own private interests.

Thus when the prospect of an appointment as official historian of the republic first appeared in 1520—the first such appointment to be made, by the way, since the demise of the office of chancellor—Machiavelli took advantage of a trip to Lucca to study the present constitution and to read through a biography of the fourteenth-century lord of the city, Castruccio Castracani—the one written in impeccably humanist prose by the Lucchese jurist NICCOLÒ TEGRIMI and published in Modena in 1496. He then picked out corresponding passages from Villani and Biondo, recast the personages according to formulas borrowed from Diogenes Laertius and Diodorus Siculus, and ended up with a largely fictitious portrait of what seemed to him an anticipation of Cesare Borgia, the hero of *Il Principe*. He then sent the portrait to his friends in the Rucellai Gardens; and they had to admit that, fiction aside, it proved his mastery at least of the external forms of humanist historiography.[38]

When on November 8 the prospect finally became a reality, Machiavelli accepted it gladly—not just because it gave him at last the "rolling stones" government job he had been waiting for since 1513 (Letter to Francesco Vettori of December 10), but also because he was truly interested in proving his worth as a historian. He began immediately to gather documents from the half-century after 1434 and to make extracts from the records of the *Dieci* for the years after 1494. He then reread his two principal predecessors as official historians of Florence, Bruni and Poggio. Noticing, or rather proclaiming, that they had given too little attention to what had long been his main interest, the internal turmoils of the republic, he decided to abandon contemporary history on the model of Bruni's *Commentarius* for a history *ab urbe condita* on the model of Bruni's—and Livy's—*Historiae*. Putting aside his research notes, Bruni's example notwithstanding, he turned instead to the available narrative sources. He read Biondo's *Decades*—in the original, not just in Pius II's abridgment. He condensed Biondo's account, accepted Biondo's main theses (e.g., the Great Age of Theodoric and the formation of an entirely new political order out of the ruins of the Roman Empire), and ended up with an introductory book that was not, as some have claimed, the first history but a paraphrase of the first history of all Italy during Biondo's thousand-year "Middle Age." He then read Frontinus, Tacitus, and Pliny; and he concluded that Poliziano's rectification of the date of the city's foundation proposed by Bruni supported exactly the opposite of Bruni's thesis: Florence was founded not by still uncorrupted republicans, he insisted, but by the victors over Brutus and Cassius—which is one reason why it remained subject to external dominion for its first 1,200 years. He next read Villani, Cavalcanti, Stefani, and Gino Capponi; and they convinced him that the history of the independent commune began not with the capture of Fiesole but with the appearance of the first civic factions. Books II–IV accordingly recount the struggles among the factions down to the advent of Cosimo de' Medici, who succeeded, as the Duke of Athens and the Ciompi had failed, in bringing the factions temporarily under control. After reading Simonetta and perhaps Corio on what had happened in Milan, he abandoned his original scheme and combined external with internal affairs, thus placing Florence more clearly in the context of all Italy. The last four books, accordingly, describe both the imposition of an authoritarian government at home and the establishment of a balance of power abroad down to the death of the chief architect of both the regime and the balance, Lorenzo il Magnifico.[39]

At this point Machiavelli paused, added introductions to the first six books; and, early in 1525, he took the manuscript to Rome for presentation to his patron, who had now become Pope Clement VII. Had his patron not suffered the humiliation of the Colonna rebellion and the sack, and had Machiavelli himself not died soon after the expulsion of his patron's family from Florence, he might well have followed standard humanist practice and reworked his abundant collection of notes into a continuation. Indeed, his terminal date provided a logical conclusion only for the events that reached a dramatic climax with the Pazzi conspiracy, not for those that followed from the initial fatal flaw of 1215.[40]

Yet Machiavelli had reason to be pleased with what he had written so far. True, his work described a tragedy rather than the more customary triumph of a political community. But otherwise it conformed perfectly to the standards of humanist municipal historiography. It was divided into books that emphasized important turning points—like the death of Ladislao of Naples and the return of Cosimo de' Medici—and that enabled him to insert prefatory reflections on political philosophy without interrupting the narrative. It was organized into chapters according to topics: the rise and fall of the Visconti empire, the conquest of the Venetian Terraferma. It presented *consilia* and motivations in the form of elegant orations, and it offered models of political behavior in the form of brilliant character sketches—Gian della Bella, Michele di Lando, Rinaldo degli Albizzi, and, best of all, Cosimo and Lorenzo de' Medici. It provided "a remarkably sophisticated socio-economic analysis of the central phase of the Ciompi revolution," which had elicited little but blanket condemnations from his predecessors.[41] It also expounded at length the principal political lessons that Machiavelli had long sought in the study of history. It proved once again that "men are slower in taking what they can have than they are in desiring what they cannot have" (II, xxxi), that mercenary soldiers are as harmful as citizen soldiers are indispensable, that infractions of one law contribute to the ruin of all law; that peace and quiet usually engender avarice and sedition (VII, xxviii). It showed in still greater detail that Florence's endemic weakness proceeded from an initial error in excluding the nobility from office, that Guicciardini's pre-1434 model regime was little more than an instrument for the aggrandizement of a narrow oligarchy, that Bruni's glorious resistance to the Visconti succeeded more through *fortuna* than through *virtù*. Better yet, it offered still another remedy for these weaknesses. Since the institution of a perfect republic according to the prescriptions of the *Discorsi* was not currently realizable, a republic under the veiled dominion of the Medici was at least capable of preventing the complete extinction of the state. And such a regime was certainly preferable to the kind of aristocratic government that might have been instituted by its opponents, whose purely selfish motives Machiavelli denounced in a speech he put into the mouth of Piero di Cosimo (VI, xxiii):

> You rob your neighbors of their goods. You sell justice. You ignore the civic judges. You oppress peaceful men and exalt the insolent. Indeed, I believe that in all Italy there is not so much avarice and violence as exists in this city.

It was undoubtedly such themes as this, as well as the absence of a rival, that earned for the work its reputation as the definitive history of the republican regime even during the first half-century after the establishment of a regime in Florence totally different from any that the author had envisaged. It was from him, indeed, rather than from his successors, that Bartolomeo Cavalcanti was to take most of the historical references for his *Retorica* of 1559. But Machiavelli was fortunate that his own death and the dispersal of his friends in the Gardens relieved him of having to defend the work when it finally appeared in print in 1532. For he would certainly have faced charges of having plagiarized and misconstrued his sources, of having mixed up the order of the wars of Piccinino and Francesco Sforza, of having made Salvestro de' Medici speak in phrases lifted from Cicero. Indeed, he had called Pope Paul I "Teodoro" and made him, rather than Adrian I, responsible for calling in Charlemagne. He had confused Gregory VII with Alexander II and placed the affair at Canossa in 1080 instead of in 1077. He had made Rudolf of Hapsburg an "emperor" and provided the Duke of Athens with a "council." And his modern editor has consequently charged him with having woven "un tessuto di inesattezze" (Gaeta, p. 92). Moreover, he turned what should have been, according to humanist standards, only a source into a model—which is why much of Book I reads like chronicle rather than history. And he turned what should have been only a model, Sallust, into a source—which is why much of II, vi, is an unacknowledged paraphrase of *Bellum Catilinae,* vii, and why the "golden age" after the return of the Guelfs is almost identical to Sallust's "golden age" after the fall of the monarchy. "In short," as his much more conscientious successor, Scipione Ammirato, was to note, he "altered names, twisted facts, confounded causes, increased, added, subtracted, diminished, and did anything that suited his fancy, without checking, without any lawful restraint; and what's more, he seems to have done so occasionally on purpose."[42]

This insouciance with regard to the humanist criterion of the Truth cannot be attributed, as his anti-Medici disciple Donato Giannotti claimed, to either direct or indirect pressure on the part of his patrons. They left him alone while he was writing and rewarded him when he finished. They did not object to his insistence on the less spiritual qualities of Clement's papal predecessors (e.g., on Sixtus IV: VII, xxxi) nor to his frank recognition of the less commendable aspects of the pre-1494 Medici regime. And they were not at all disturbed by his defiance of eulogistic conventions in admitting both the personal and political defects of the chief architects of that regime. Rather, Machiavelli's shortcomings as a historian were the result of the same preoccupation with the discovery and the illustration of the laws of politics that had frequently distorted the record of history in the *Discorsi.* Hence the *Istorie Fiorentine* should properly be judged, not as a bold new step in the development of Renaissance historiography, as has sometimes been suggested, but rather as an adaptation of the forms and methods he borrowed from Bruni, for the purposes not of history but of political philosophy.

The Remaking of Pandolfo Collenuccio

What Bruni and Poggio bequeathed to Machiavelli, Tristano Caracciolo and the "grave and truthful" Pontano bequeathed to CAMILLO PORZIO (c. 1527–80). Porzio's initial inspiration, it is true, had come from Paolo Giovio, whom he met in Florence in 1551 while his father was teaching law at Pisa, and then from Guicciardini, whose posthumous *Storia d'Italia* he was one of the first to read. For it seems never to have occurred to him, as it occurred to no one else before the nineteenth century, that the Florentines he met were really but a "pale shadow" of those who had effected "the exuberant development of the Renaissance" a few decades earlier.[43] But when he finally found time to put the inspiration into practice—when he had made some money from a law practice in Naples and invested his father's inheritance in a feudal domain in the country—he turned instead to his Neapolitan predecessors. They provided the information necessary to make sense out of trial records of the rebel barons, of which he obtained copies, and thus to fill in what Giovio had identified as a grave lacuna in recent Italian history. They also provided models of historical prose particularly suited to his intended domestic audience. Hence, all he had to do was to put the revolt of the barons against Ferrante I into a pan-Italian context by looking up the relevant passages in the standard humanist histories—and in the most recent addition to available sources for the first invasions, Philippe de Commynes. He had then to translate his text into Italian according to the instructions of that energetic promoter of historiography in the kingdom, Cardinal Seripando, and submit it to him for stylistic correction. The polished, concise, elegant commentary, fully worthy of all its ancient and modern models, was then ready for the press; and it duly appeared in Rome in 1565.

So successful was the commentary, indeed, that Porzio was soon induced to try another one—this time addressed not to a distant event but to the most recent crisis in Naples, the Inquisition revolt of 1547. In form and style the second commentary was as impeccable as the first. It made Gianluigi Fieschi talk as Catiline had in almost identical circumstances, without a trace of anachronistic inconsistency. It went well beyond even Uberto Foglietta, probably one of its chief sources, in connecting the events of Naples with similar contemporary events in Rome, Piacenza, and Genoa. But apparently Porzio was somewhat less than satisfied with his work, and it vanished from sight for the next two and a half centuries. Probably what bothered him was the failure of all the various kinds of causal explanation sanctioned by humanist historiography to account for the events he described. The opposition of the Neapolitan barons to central authority was a persistent problem in Naples, one to which any number of ills could convincingly be ascribed. But the troubles that broke out in several different cities in 1547 could not possibly be attributed to the general conditions of the time, Porzio discovered. Italy was just then reaping the fruits of its accomplishments in "military discipline and the liberal sciences." Its new prosperity was reflected in "a numerous population." Its peace was guaranteed by "powerful and valorous kings." Its role as "the mother of all the noble sciences" was assured by "new instruments for the perpetual defense of writing" (i.e., the press). And, most important of all, the two chief agents of its troubles during the preceding thirty years, the emperor and the king of France, were now exhausted. The fault, he concluded, lay rather with the "heavens," which put into the head of Charles V the ridiculous idea of adding Piacenza and Siena to his already overextended empire. It lay with Pierluigi Farnese, who deliberately provoked the emperor by taking a French wife. It lay with Paul III, whose illegal seizure of the Doria estates in the Kingdom gave the Doria an excuse for seizing all the Papal galleys they could find in the Mediterranean. It lay with Toledo, who was willing to risk a holocaust rather than admit he had made a mistake. But how could such trivial causes have brought about such catastrophic effects? Porzio multiplied "o per ragione . . ." phrases before each irrational decision—but all in vain. The only lesson he could draw from them in the end was that sometimes a statesman needs to be thickheaded (*stolto*) as well as wise (*savio*). For he may thus be better able to protect himself against the all too obvious thickheadedness of so many others.

As Porzio turned back to Caracciolo and Pontano, his compatriots turned back to two of Pontano's contemporaries. Giovanni Albino, whose nephew Ottavio finally published his four monographs along with a documentary appendix in 1589, provided them with still another model for commentaries. It was thanks to Albino, they noted, that Alfonso d'Aragona was spared Caesar's task of writing the history of his own deeds:

> Felice Albino, a cui diedero i fati
> con la persona far notabil opre
> e con l'ingegno libri alti e lodati:
> Qui il nome tuo molt'altri adombra e copre.[44]

Pandolfo Collenuccio, on the other hand, gave them what none of their Neapolitan predecessors had ever managed to write: a model of municipal historiography, or, in this case, of a history of the whole Kingdom, with a chronological breadth similar to that of Corio and Sabellico.

Like Porzio, all the Neapolitan historians were the spiritual heirs of the humanists of the court of Alfonso and Ferrante, although by now humanism had taken such deep roots in Naples that, in an age which some historians still like to describe as court-dominated, they were no longer dependent upon the court. ANGELO DI COSTANZO (1507–after 1590), for instance, the son of an urban nobleman and the heir to a large estate at the foot of Vesuvius, grew up in the literary entourage of Sannazaro and Bernardino Rota. He studied Latin and Italian literature, theology, philosophy, and the sciences. And he learned to write poetry well enough to be included as an interlocutor in one of Antonio Minturno's dialogues, to be resurrected by the Arcadians as a Petrarchan purist, and to be included in post-Risorgimento school anthologies.[45] Similarly, GIOVAN BATTISTA CARAFA was an uncle by marriage of the poet Torquato Tasso and a fellow member, and sometime debating opponent, of Di Costanzo in the Neapolitan Accademia de' Sereni (Soria). They were therefore fully prepared to imitate their model. But as soon as they began to study it, they came to realize that it was all organized in support of an inadmissable thesis—namely, that the congenital rebellious and seditious nature of the Neapolitans had ruined what nature had once made the fairest of all lands, with "healthy air," "clement skies," and "a soil fertile enough to meet all the requirements of human life."[46] That thesis became increasingly dangerous after 1527 as the Venetian printers, responding to the demand for a comprehensive humanist history of Naples, had the text "reduced to the purity of the vulgar language" (Giovanni Ruscelli) and spread all over Italy in six successive editions during the next twenty-five years.[47]

Di Costanzo therefore set out immediately to redo the research Collenuccio had or should have done. Since the only Norman historians he could find had written mostly about Sicily, since the fifteenth-century Neapolitan humanists had written only about their own times, and since the standard Italian historians had treated the

Kingdom only marginally, he turned instead to the chroniclers—the Neapolitans Matteo di Giovenazzo, "Monteleone," and Fazello, and the Florentine Giovanni Villani. And after twenty years of careful research, sure enough, he caught Collenuccio in enough errors to be able to refer generically to his "usual nonsense." "Here Collenuccio makes another error," he proclaimed triumphantly; "and this one is so nasty [*brutto*] and inexcusable that it clearly condemns him of ill-colored [*mal colorita*] lying." Otherwise unspecified "writings of the times" then proved him wrong about Frederick II. "The archives of the Kingdom" proved him wrong about Carlo d'Angiò, notwithstanding the apparent support of Valla and Fazio. And Villani and Boccaccio, who after all had lived in Florence at the time, proved him wrong about Naples' involvement in the affair of the Duke of Athens. To make his point stick, Di Costanzo polished his style in imitation of that of Giovio and Guicciardini. And if he did not always succeed in perfectly balancing all his long strings of gerundic phrases, he certainly ended up with a text far more artful than the "jumble of chronicles and humanistic histories" that has been attributed to him.

Carafa was even more severe.[48] "If only Naples had had a Livy, a Thucydides, or a Bembo," he cried, it would long ago have freed itself from that "malignant liar," who had deliberately misread Livy and Cicero in order to attribute even to the ancient Neapolitans the unflattering qualities he attributed to their modern descendants. Collenuccio had also misread his medieval sources in order to exalt "this Emperor Frederick [II] of his," proclaimed Carafa, and he had purposely, or lazily, overlooked the documents that proved him wrong—like the "record of the trial brought at the time of Carlo I, which is kept in the mint of Naples, and which I have seen and read." Carafa might have succeeded even better than Di Costanzo in vanquishing his adversary. For he went well beyond him in digging up new sources, which he usually transcribed verbatim. But, unfortunately, he often buried his theses in interminable run-on sentences. One of them, for example, begins with the original settlers from Euboea (today called Negroponte), who really landed first on Ischia and then founded Cuma, which is why Naples is called "New Town," although actually there may have been an earlier New Town properly called "Old Town" (Paleopolis), in which lived three prostitutes (hence the name "Parthenope"); and it ends with a comment on the loyalty of the Neapolitans during the Second Punic War, when they donated forty-two silver cups to the Roman treasury without even being asked and offered their lives and goods as well. Carafa also contradicted his theses because he could not resist including such charming stories as the one about Queen Isabella leading her children around the streets to raise money for her beleaguered husband—a story that clearly undermined his efforts to present King Ferrante in a bad light.

Therefore, instead of declining, the prestige of Collenuccio rose. He was soon honored with a continuation by one of the most popular popularizing historians of the century, Mambrino Roseo da Fabiano.[49] And Roseo's continuation was then legitimized by another continuator from Naples itself, COLANELLO PACCA, who carried the narrative down to 1572.

The harshest of all the critics, however, was TOMASO COSTO.[50] Realizing the futility of trying to write a completely new work, Costo decided to edit Collenuccio himself, together with Roseo's and Pacca's continuations, and to make the edition even more attractive by adding still another continuation of his own. Unlike Di Costanzo, Costo did not have to search through the archives. For he could rely instead on the many recent editions of the standard narrative histories that had since become available. Sigonio enabled him to reduce Collenuccio's calculation of the duration of the Lombard kingdom from 232 to 208 years. The "infallible order of the annals of Genoa of Giustiniani" enabled him to correct Collenuccio's date for the pontificate of Adrian IV. Pedro Mexia, Riccardo Malaspina, and Antonino enabled him to reveal Collenuccio's deliberate misreading of Biondo. Pius II enabled him to prove Collenuccio wrong about the earthquake of 1456. The same authorities then enabled him to snipe at Collenuccio's emulator Roseo, particularly since he could turn against him the very sources Roseo had used for his "compendium." His own memory enabled him to elaborate considerably on what Roseo had written "too sparsely, as is his custom," about the Inquisition rebellion, and to reproach Pacca for having "tried to imitate Roseo's dryness and bad order."

Thus Costo finally won the war that had been declared by Di Costanzo a half-century earlier. Whoever wanted to read Collenuccio thereafter—or at least before the new critical edition of the mid-twentieth century—had to read Costo's comments as well, for they were set off from the rest of the text only by barely visible asterisks. Yet correcting Collenuccio was not the only task the Neapolitan historians had to undertake. The other was far graver, for it involved not just saving the reputation of Neapolitans in general but of defining the relationships between them. The challenge had been made as early as 1496 by one of the victims of the Baron's rebellion, FRANCESCO ELIO MARCHESI (d. 1519). Marchesi was also a product of the Pontano-Sannazaro circle. He had taken advantage of his exile in Rome to perfect his humanist education under the guidance of Pomponio Leto and to prepare critical editions of Diogenes Laertius and Horace. He actually had meant to justify the barons. But he was too much of a philologist and a humanist not at the same time to sweep away the mythological origins invented by the baronial families, to reveal the relatively recent origin of most of them, and to redefine nobility in humanist terms as the product not of ancestry but of virtue.[51]

Marchesi thus posed the question: if the barons were nobles and if nobles are virtuous, how is it that they rose up against their legitimate sovereign? They did so, answered Porzio, because they were neither virtuous nor noble. "Those people who these days are called barons" and who attacked Ferrante just as he had exhausted himself defending the Kingdom simultaneously against Turks, French, Florentines, and Venetians, were merely the perpetrators of "innumerable calamities." And the

THE DIVERSIFICATION OF MODELS

calamities that Ferrante then most justly visited upon them should serve as a warning to anyone else who might be tempted to be "somewhat less than observant of the will of the king." Quite the contrary, answered Di Costanzo. Barons have revolted in the past only in order to defend the kingdom against abuses of royal authority—as they did with such sacrifices at the time of the Swabians. Whenever there were good kings, there were no rebellions. Carafa agreed with Di Costanzo. Disorder was caused exclusively by "foreign" kings, among whom "you will find nothing but cruelty, murder, immorality, and tyranny." "Natural" kings, like Charles V and Philip II (!), could safely entrust the defense of the Kingdom entirely to the barons, who as a matter of fact were alone responsible for saving it from the machinations of a foreign king and of a Neapolitan pope. Costo, too, agreed. The barons who sided with the people were really supporting their monarch against a misguided viceroy, he pointed out. The barons who sided with a viceroy in 1585 were defending their monarch against the least stable element in Neapolitan society, the mob. And he fittingly concluded his narrative with an inspiring description of the frantic howls of the plebeian rebel Benedetto Mangone as his body was slowly torn apart on the wheel.

The Neapolitan historians did, then, have a solution for Naples' problems. It consisted in the reestablishment of a strong baronage under the control, or better under the leadership, of a strong and righteous monarchy. Hence their historical studies can be criticized as lacking in a consciousness of "political themes" (Cola-pietra) only to the extent that they overlooked such equally important problems as the relation between church and state. They can not be held responsible for failing to foresee the disastrous consequences of the somewhat distorted form in which their solutions actually were adopted during the following decades: that of an arrogantly omnipotent baronage collaborating with an uninterested, bankrupt monarchy to bleed the country dry. Moreover, it must be admitted that they drew from the example of golden ages in the past—the second century A.D., the early twelfth century, the early fourteenth century, and the mid-fifteenth century—an important political thesis: Collenuccio was wrong in claiming the ills of Naples to be insoluble. They drew from the example of model monarchs, like Roberto d'Angiò, Alfonso d'Aragona, and even the much misrepresented Giovanna I, abundant lessons for the guidance of a modern monarch determined to cure the ills. To make the lessons still more forcible, they then reduced their long narratives to the form of brief compendia, with the theses carefully underlined. And to assist a Spanish viceroy on a three-year term in carrying out the good intentions of the monarch, they compiled political-geographical surveys of the country—like Pacca's *Descrizione delle città, terre e vescovadi* and Porzio's and Costo's lists of provinces, tribunals, and baronial dominions.[52]

The Memorable Events

Even as early as the 1520s, on the other hand, some historians began to have doubts about the utility of humanist historiography as a reliable or adequate source for the history at least of their particular municipalities. For instance, BENVENUTO DI SAN GIORGIO (d. 1527)[53] read through Sabellico, Biondo, Volterrano, Matteo Palmieri, Giorgio Merula, and even Konrad Peutinger and Johannes Naucler, whose *Sermones* and *Chronicon* he seems to have found during a diplomatic mission to Germany. But as court tutor, minister, the ambassador for the marchesi of Monferrato, he soon came to realize that none of them had anything of substance to say about his native country. Similarly, GUIDO PANCIROLI (1523–94)[54] read through all the "histories of the ancients and of our own authors" in what time he had left over from his academic duties at Padua. But he found little more than "fables" in the former and nothing at all after 1352 in the latter that would enable him to express his "singular benevolence and reverence" toward his compatriots in Reggio. These historians therefore turned to other kinds of sources—to the "ancient and authentic instruments" that Benvenuto found in the archives of Casale, to a copy of the articles of the Peace of Constance and to a bill of sale signed by a twelfth-century bishop that Panciroli found in the collection left him by his father. "In my great desire . . . to learn about the origins, the wars, and the deeds of my country," said PIERO GRITIO of Iesi,[55] "I have never ceased to . . . turn over the ancient, dusty writings of our city." "I have not . . . shaken the dust off of every single parchment [I have seen]," confessed GIULIO CESARE TONDUZZI of Faenza.[56] For his compatriots Gregorio Zuccolo and Bernardino Conti had already spent so much time trying to do so that they never got around to putting their huge volumes of notes into publishable form. And anyway, Tonduzzi had already collected enough material to fill some 728 octavo pages.

The almost complete shift from narrative to archival sources did not necessarily rule out the maintenance of at least one of the principal characteristics of humanist historiography, a thesis. Gritio managed to prove to his own satisfaction that Iesi had always been a "faithful, devoted servant of the Apostolic Church," notwithstanding the flagrant misgovernment of the papal sublegates under Alexander VI and Clement VII. Similarly, Benvenuto proved that a long record of good government gave the Paleologo house indisputable rights over Monferrato. And both his vast vernacular original as well as his Latin abridgment were used as evidence in settling the thorny question of succession a few years after his death. But more often the documents provided no more reliable a guide to the truth than the narrative histories. All the bulls and charters that RINALDO CORSO[57] copied out of Sigonio did not prevent him from claiming that none of the lords of Correggio had ever had the slightest fault of character—at least since the Virgin had appeared to their most distant ancestor as he led Charlemagne's armies through Italy. None of the warnings of Dionysius of Halicarnassus about the uncertainty of antiquity prevented Zuccolo and Tonduzzi from following in detail the travels of Noah's grandson Fetonte (or Faetonte) from Egypt through Thessaly to the mouth of the Po. And Panciroli's scoffing at Fetonte did not prevent him from ascribing the Gallic invasions to the jealousy of a cuckolded husband named Arunte Tirreno, about whom he claimed to have read in Plutarch. Worse yet, the connections among the documents quoted at length often disappeared almost completely. The enormous *De Provinciis et Civitatis Regni* of MARINO FRECCIA (b. 1503) of Naples grew to such proportions between 1554 and his death in 1566 that no one but captious lawyers, like himself, could make sense out of it.[58] And Benvenuto surpassed even Panciroli in including whatever he found in his charters regardless of its relevance to his theme. History thus tended to become merely a collection of documents with no other principle of organization than the successive dates of their composition.

The availability of models and of information in the form of narrative histories thus provided a greater incentive to history writing than the presence of nonliterary documents alone. But what most effectively sent historians both to the narratives and to the documents was—as indeed it had since the beginning of humanist historiography—the consciousness of a great event that of itself deserved to be recorded for the admiration of posterity. One such event was the sack of Brescia, in which "many worthy citizens by their great and marvelous valor obtained ample privileges from emperors" as well as, particularly in 1541, from the Venetian Republic. Unfortunately, Cavrioli's history broke off too early to show the sack in proper perspective, and the on-the-spot accounts of what followed were all written in the form of diaries or commentaries. Hence PATRICIO SPINI went back to 1509.[59] He rewrote Cavrioli's account of the initial surrender to the French so as to make it appear to be the result of unfortunate necessity. He rewrote the account of the plot to readmit the Venetians to make it appear as the work of the whole citizenry, not just of the peasants and a pro-Venetian party. He then added an account of the wars that led to the permanent expulsion of the foreigners in 1517 in order to reinforce his favorable comparison of the recovery of Venice after the battle of Agnadello and the recovery of Rome after the battle of Trasimeno. So great were these achievements that they kept him going through the somewhat less glorious events of the succeeding decades. They might then have propelled him into a search for the future ills foretold by the fire in the great hall of the Palazzo Comunale had he not decided to leave the fate of the city thereafter to the "majesty of God" and of "this glorious and immortal [Venetian] Republic, to which"—it is not clear from the syntax whether "which" refers to God or the republic—"be glory and praise *ne'secoli de'secoli.*" Amen.

In the opinion of many sixteenth-century historians, however, and also in the opinion of Mambrino Roseo, who immediately turned it into the subject of a popular epic poem[60]—the greatest of all the great events that took place between the Battle of the Taro and the Peace of Cateau-Cambrésis was the eleven-month siege of

Florence in 1529–30. At least two Florentines found time during the busy, tense period of the siege itself to keep abundant diaries. One was an active participant, the anti-Medici militia captain Lorenzo Martelli.[61] The other was an interested and committed spectator, the Franciscan friar GIULIANO UGHI (d. 1569).[62] Martelli's diary consists, apparently, of a detailed, though rather disorganized, account of all the minute details of all the military engagements from the arrival of the Imperial-Papal army to the aftermath of the capitulation of August 11. Ughi's diary is somewhat more thorough in its reflection of the psychological state of the besieged; and it is prefaced by a brief recapitulation of what had happened since 1501, when the author made his religious profession. Neither of them makes any pretense at literary quality, although Ughi gradually learned to elevate a simple diary into something approaching a humanist chronicle. But both of them consciously weave their narratives around two dramatic climaxes: the duel between Lodovico Martelli and Giovanni Bandini in the first and, in the second, the lightning campaigns of the meteoric chief of the Florentine militia, Francesco Ferrucci.

Not until the 1540s, on the other hand, did historians capable of writing according to humanist standards finally begin to reflect upon the importance of the siege in terms of what had by then been revealed as its more far-reaching consequences. Two of them were members of prominent families who had followed their forefathers into political careers. BERNARDO SEGNI (1504–58) was the nephew of Niccolò Capponi, the *gonfaloniere* elected under the constitution of 1527; and after 1540 he was rewarded for his and his father's acceptance of the principate established after 1530 by being appointed a member of the Council of the Two Hundred and commissioner for Cortona.[63] FILIPPO DE' NERLI (1485–1556) had been rewarded for his loyalty to the Medici regime before 1527 by thrice being chosen *priore;* and he was rewarded for his continuing loyalty during the republican interim by being raised under the Medici duchy to the rank of senator and governor of several subject cities.[64] The third historian had only occasionally been involved in politics, since he did not belong to that class of citizens which usually acceded to political office. Still, the precocious literary talents of BENEDETTO VARCHI (1503–65), a descendant of a modest family of notaries originally from Montevarchi in the Val d'Arno (hence his surname), soon brought him into contact with such active agents in Florentine, and even European, politics as the Pazzi and the Strozzi. He himself was then enrolled in the Florentine militia for three months in 1529; and in 1537 he took part in one of the more disastrous of the military excursions led by his current patron, Piero Strozzi, into Florentine territory.[65]

Yet actually, involvement in politics had very little to do with the historians' dedication to history. True, Nerli had once been an active member of the moderate Medicean party. Segni had been an ardent proponent of the moderate Ottimati party represented by his uncle, whose biography he had written in justification of his acts in office.[66] And Varchi, at least after 1537, had been closely associated with the anti-Medici exiles. But by the time they came to write history, all of them, reluctantly or willingly, had put aside their former political loyalties and had become reconciled with the regime imposed by Clement VII in 1530 and consolidated by Duke Cosimo after 1537. All of them had recognized that what had once been political offices were now purely administrative ones, since all important decisions were made exclusively by the duke. All of them, moreover, had benefited directly or indirectly from the new regime's policy of encouraging the revival of culture in Florence after 1540. It was Duke Cosimo who persuaded Nerli to finish his work. It was he also who brought Varchi back home, assured him a salary as lecturer at the Accademia Fiorentina, and, in 1547, bestowed upon him the title, unclaimed since the death of Machiavelli, of official state historian. It was he, moreover, who guaranteed the historians a large measure of freedom of thought and expression. For while preventing anyone else from interfering with what they wrote, Cosimo himself interfered only when it was reflected in such specifically propagandistic projects as pageants, parades, and the murals in the Sala de' Cinquecento. And he thus enabled them to look with considerable critical detachment upon the previous regimes that they were describing as well as upon the new regime under which they then were living.

What counted, rather, was the historians' commitment to humanism. Nerli had learned Greek and Latin philology from a disciple of Poliziano, who dedicated an edition of Horace to him; and he had been a close companion of Machiavelli, who dedicated one of his *capitoli* to him. Segni had studied law and literature at Padua and had translated the principal works of Aristotle into Tuscan; and in 1542 he was elected consul of the Accademia Fiorentina, the chief institution of Florentine culture in the middle decades of the century. Varchi had become an accomplished poet and critic before embarking, at Duke Cosimo's invitation, on history, the one form of humanist literature he admitted having not yet tried; and he continued thereafter to write frequently on aesthetics, ethics, philosophy, and, above all, vernacular philology, the subject that most concerned his associates in the Accademia Fiorentina. He was also one of the most competent popularizers of his age, an age in which humanism was rapidly being disseminated outside the limits of the bilingual elite that had created it. And he was largely responsible for the introduction into the area of humanism of the discipline of natural philosophy, a discipline that had previously been restricted to the antihumanistic faculties of the universities.[67]

Consequently, all three historians of the siege took care not to violate but rather to develop further what they perceived as the potentialities of the models of historiography they had inherited from their immediate forerunners. Nerli imitated Machiavelli's prose style and adopted his scheme of periodizing Florentine history. Varchi sought to avoid Machiavelli's errors by comparing what he had written with what had been written by all the other Florentine historians, chroniclers, poets (Dante, Boccaccio) and philologists (Poliziano). And both Segni and Varchi departed from Florentine historiographical models only when they could appeal to those whom Bruni and Machiavelli had recognized as their own models. Thus Segni followed Sallust and Thucydides in consistently presenting the opposing views of the leaders of the Florentine government in the form of two set orations. Varchi defended his having written about wars and politics without being a general or a politician by pointing to the example of Livy and Plutarch; and he took courage from Tacitus's doctrine of "the truth at any price" in revealing the full story of Pierluigi Farnese's homosexual exploits.

Similarly, all three historians amended or expanded what they wrote about Florence in accordance with what they read in the latest humanist histories of other parts of Italy and Europe. Segni incorporated supplementary information from Guicciardini and Giovio as soon as their works became available; and Varchi took most of his information about France and Germany respectively from Paolo Emili and Johannes Sleidanus.[68] They also accepted the most recent methodological innovations of sixteenth-century municipal historiography: that is, they turned to archival sources whenever the narrative sources appeared to be unreliable or inadequate. Varchi was particularly diligent in his research. He read through all the records of the governing bodies of the republic and all the reports of ambassadors of foreign courts; and he reproduced verbatim and in toto all those documents that were particularly pertinent to his argument. More important still, he solicited written and oral testimony from surviving eyewitnesses. He thus generated a number of supplementary writings about the siege, some of which—like the series of letters written by GIOVAN BATTISTA BUSINI between 1548 and 1551[69] and the formal commentary composed by the ex-Capponian senator BACCIO CARNESECCHI (b. 1501)—have been recognized as works of historiography in their own right.[70]

Hence, it is not surprising that, in spite of the differences among their previous political commitments, all the Florentine historians agreed on which names to place in the indispensable humanist categories of heroes to be admired and villains to be execrated. The series of heroes began, appropriately enough, with Duke Cosimo's father, Giovanni delle Bande Nere, whom Carnesecchi, perhaps following his model, Machiavelli, portrayed as a candidate for the role of the Moses or Lycurgus of Italy. It included Jacopo Nardi, who saved the Palazzo Vecchio from the Cardinal of Cortona's mercenaries, and Niccolò Capponi, who might have saved the republic from the follies of the Piagnoni. It even included a notable exception from the usual limitation of heroes to generals and politicians, namely, Michelangelo; and Varchi underlined his departure from the norm by inserting his eulogy of Michelangelo not in the midst of his activity as director of the city's fortifications but on the morrow of his flight to Venice. The series of villains began with Clement VII, whose small-minded jealousy the historians held to be primarily responsible for the tragedy of their city. It included such arch-republican hotheads as Jacopo Alamanni and Piero Pandolfini ("a young man of unstable mind": Carnesecchi), the "ambitious and restless" leader of the anti-Capponi faction, Baldassare Carducci, and the self-seeking rabble-rouser Anton Francesco degli Albizzi. It also included—and once again Varchi broke with humanist conventions in the name of humanist principles—groups as well as individuals, groups like the Savonarolan friars, who unjustly persecuted Antonio Bruscioli, and "all these modern prelates," who "recognize no greater good than their own utility." The series ended with Pope Paul III, who was consequently excoriated as the chief obstacle to the creation of the new Florentine state by all the successors of the sixteenth-century Florentine historians for the next 250 years.

It is also not surprising that all the historians ended up with much the same interpretation of the events they described. True, they could not but admire the courage of the defenders, who held out for so long at the cost of such sacrifices against such odds. But Nerli admitted that the siege was also a civil war and that as such it constituted the climax of three centuries of increasingly violent internecine strife. "Considering what trouble our city has always experienced," he reflected, considering "how disunited its chief citizens have always been," and considering that now, for the first time in its history, it was governed pacifically "without the need of arms or any extraordinary force," he could only conclude that "the heavens have decreed that our city will never find peace until it is made subject to one prince." Similarly, Varchi admitted that even the 1512–27 regime had been split within itself, just like the pre-1434 and the pre-1512 regimes; and he was at a loss to explain "how in a single city there could be so many and such diverse opinions so keenly felt about so many issues." Indeed Varchi discovered still another cause for the failure of all the many experiments in constitutional reform with which Florentine history was replete. "The second cause," he noted,

> is the great authority that has always been enjoyed by doctors of law. Almost all people think that, being doctors, they know everything, particularly about governing states; whereas actually they know little about it [for the very reason that] they are doctors. (vi, v)

Hence, those factions and those lawyers who took over the city in 1528 could certainly not be held preferable to the pragmatic politicians who took it over in 1530. They had chopped off heads without trials on the mere suspicion of pro-Medici or "defeatist" sentiments. They had tortured one young Roman as a spy simply because he had once been a member of the papal choir. They had drilled a hole through the tongue of a certain Michele da Prato simply because he had been accused of uttering a phrase they held to be blasphemous. Thus the post-1530 proscriptions, which Varchi described in minute detail, were mild in comparison to the reign of terror instituted by the heroic defenders of the city before 1530. Segni eventually came to agree with Varchi, in spite of his exaltation of the constitution of 1527 as the closest approximation of the political order sanctioned in theory by Aristotle and in practice by the Venetians. The persecution of Niccolò Capponi had been enough to persuade him that "liberty" was irreconcilable with "wisdom." The expulsion of

Luigi Alamanni, the hero of the 1522 anti-Medici plot, proved to him that "it is indeed the custom of the people, particularly... in Florence, to use their liberty perversely against its very authors." And the efforts of the popular government in Florence to overthrow an equally popular government in Siena proved to him that ideological slogans of the self-professed leaders of the people were largely hypocritical. In comparison, the rule even of the "universally hated prince" Alessandro de' Medici was not so bad. At least Alessandro "made justice equal for rich and poor alike."

What made the siege so remarkable, then, was not that it afforded an unparalleled occasion for deeds of individual and collective heroism but rather that it marked, in a very dramatic manner, the end of an entire epoch of Florentine history. Accordingly, the historians felt obliged to extend their accounts beyond the capitulation through its immediate consequences—through the adoption of the constitution of 1532, which is where Varchi originally intended to stop, through the election of Cosimo in 1537, which is where death finally forced him to stop, through the Battle of Montemurlo, which for Segni and Nerli marked the definitive defeat of the last hopes of reversing the effects of the capitulation.

> Since this so glorious victory of Signor Cosimo and this so great ruin of the exiles appear to have put an end to the ancient and modern discord of our citizens, it seems to me no longer necessary to record the civil events of our city; for having been brought under the government of a powerful prince, our citizens no longer have any reason for engaging in civil disputes. (Nerli)

Having arrived at the end of one period, Segni at least was induced to go on to describe the beginning of the next, particularly since it too turned out to be rather full of memorable events. And he wrote at length about the defense of the Tuscan coast against Turkish raiders, about the removal of the Spanish garrisons, about the execution of those patricians still unwilling to abide by Cosimo's policy of honesty in office, about the assassination of Duke Alessandro's assassin, Lorenzaccio, and finally about what served him as a concluding dramatic climax, the War of Siena.

Indeed, enough of interest still occurred within the city to inspire one anonymous diarist to vent his rage against the *plebe* and against their hero, Cosimo, almost weekly from 1543 to 1555—for the entertainment at least of those of his readers who made so many copies of his diary in the 1580s and 1590s.[71] Enough of interest still occurred also to inspire one accomplished humanist into accepting Cosimo's request for a sequel to the history of Varchi. GIOVAN BATTISTA ADRIANI (d. 1579) first conducted a systematic search through the archives, which Cosimo, with his usual passion for order, had inventoried for him. He then rearranged the mass of notes he had taken into the literary form he had learned by studying his model, Guicciardini. He added still another kind of "event" to those prescribed by humanist tradition, namely, administrative reform; and he thus succeeded in describing as the most significant event of his age the transformation of a state run by amateur patricians into a state run by professional administrators. By reading the secret communications of the Florentine ambassadors, he also came to understand the place of Florence in the pan-Italian, or rather pan-European, federation of dependent and semi-independent states that constituted the Empire of Charles V; and he thus credited Cosimo, as the emperor's chief ally in Italy, with having elevated Florence from the first to the second category. His history appropriately concluded with the bestowal upon Cosimo of the just rewards for his efforts: the investiture of Siena and the title of grand duke of Tuscany.[72]

All that remained to be done, then, by the equally accomplished humanists JACOPO NARDI (1476–after 1563) and JACOPO PITTI (1519–89) was to put the siege into a broader chronological context—for Nardi from the revolt of the Ciompi to the revolt of the Sienese in 1552, for Pitti from the end of Florence's first golden age in 1215 to the beginning of the second golden age in 1537.[73] Both these historians descended from old patrician families, the first traditionally anti-Medicean, the second traditionally pro-Medicean. Nardi had held important offices under the Republic of 1527–30, which he had helped to create, and had gone into first forced and then, after 1537, voluntary exile as a consequence of his political commitments. Pitti had held important offices under the Principate, of which he had been one of the earliest proponents. Both were also accomplished men of letters. Nardi had written several comedies and a considerable corpus of free verse as well as what soon became standard Italian translations of Cicero's orations and Livy, and he kept in constant contact with his literary friends in Florence by correspondence. Pitti had built up a famous private library. He had been elected consul of the Accademia Fiorentina (1567). And he had made two important contributions to the still current debate about the nature of the siege that had been launched on the morrow of the surrender by one of the most competent of the future administrators of the Principate, Francesco's brother, Luigi Guicciardini.[74] Indeed, the *Apologia dei Cappuccini* and the *Vita di Antonio Giacomini Tebalducci*[75] of 1570–75 led him to the historical work to which he devoted his last years. And he set forth to reread not the documents, which he supposed to have been studied adequately by his predecessors, but all the chronicles and histories since the earliest times.

Both Nardi's and Pitti's works were to some extent methodologically retrogressive. Nardi threw in what he had forgotten to mention earlier, not at the point where it belonged chronologically, but at the point where he was writing when he recalled it (e.g., IX, 16: "Ma non debbo già mancare di dire . . . che"), and Pitti restricted his narrative almost exclusively to political and military matters. But both of them succeeded in setting forth clearly their theses about the siege. The fortitude of the Florentines during those tragic months was "cosa maravigliosa," proclaimed Nardi. They willingly put up with the starvation rations they had imposed upon themselves, and they were not the least discouraged by "having been abandoned by the princes and lords of Christendom . . . and even by those of our own citizens" who preferred private pleasure to "the public good and the preservation of the city" (IX, 22). "Of all the wars ever fought by the people of Florence," insisted Pitti, "none in my opinion was ever greater or more glorious (although with an unfortunate end) than that of 1529." But, he insisted, its greatness could not disguise its still more unfortunate causes. Those causes consisted not just of the constant quarreling among the leading citizens, as Varchi and Segni had supposed. They consisted above all of the constant mistreatment of all those residents of the city whom none of the republican constitutions had ever enfranchised by all the citizens of all factions and parties. Thus injustice, and not just strife, was the main characteristic of the regimes that had preceded the debacle. And neither the constitution of 1495, which he considered to be the least bad of them all, nor the various schemes entertained by Pope Leo X "to restore the city to its ancient liberty," had succeeded, or could have succeeded, in overcoming this basic defect. Cosimo emerged as the savior of the *plebe* from three centuries of abuse at the hands of the *grandi*. And the proscriptions of 1530 turned out to be a fitting reward for those whose slogan of "liberty" had never applied to any but themselves.

The Definitive Histories

By the 1580s and '90s, the great events of the past had been fully commemorated, and the less pleasant circumstances from which they had arisen—domestic strife and foreign war—had been happily removed. The value of municipal historiography as a means of moral inspiration had been generally accepted, and its traditional locus, the commune, had survived as the center of its citizens' political loyalties even after it had lost much of its political authority. Models of good historical writing and well-organized, elegantly written collections of historical information were more abundant than ever, and the potentialities of archival and archaeological sources as a supplement, even a corrective, to the narrative sources had been frequently demonstrated. It was now possible, therefore, for historians to reflect upon what had been accomplished during the two centuries since the introduction of humanist historiography. Their reflections then led some of them to aspire to perfect what their predecessors, in less fortunate times and with more restricted means, had bequeathed to them. And they set forth to provide their cities with definitive histories according to the highest humanist standards.

Unlike most of their predecessors, however, these "definitive" historians were very rarely connected with the dominant social and economic groups that previously had written or sponsored the writing of history. POMPEO PELLINI (d. 1594),[76] it is true, was born into a prominent Perugian family, and both SCIPIONE AMMIRATO (1531–1601)[77] and GIUSEPPE RIPAMONTI (1577–1641)[78] wrote under commission from their respective governments. But GIROLAMO ROSSI (Hieronymus Rubeus [1539–1607])[79] was the son of a refugee from Parma. CELESTINO COLLEONI (1567–1635)[80] was a Capuchin friar whose religious vows obliged him to express his *amor della patria* in writing from his friary rather than in action from the city hall. GIANNANTONIO SUMMONTE (d. 1602),[81] a descendant through an unknown father of one of Pontano's academic associates, was a notary-lawyer, not a jurist; and the only job he is known to have held, that of procurator to a charitable money-lending agency, was precisely of the kind that most social-climbing members of his professional-forensic class scrupulously avoided. Even Ripamonti was not really a Milanese. He had been born of humble parents in an obscure foothill village ("ex obscuro pago Briantaci collis aspero & confragoso"), educated at the expense of the bishop of Novara, and first employed as a teacher at Monza. He finally settled down in Milan, as a professor at the Collegio Ambrosiano, only after several years of indecision about accepting an offer to accompany the retiring governor to Spain. Ammirato was not even a Tuscan. He had been born at Lecce, on the furthest extremity of the Italian boot. He had been educated at Naples and introduced into high literary circles in Rome and Venice. And all that he knew about Florence before accepting Cosimo I's invitation to come live there in 1570 was what he had learned from the exiled Florentine bishop of his native town (V, 422).

What most particularly characterized these historians was rather their exclusive dedication to the discipline of history. Celestino prepared for his major work by compiling chronicles of his own and another nearby religious community and by composing biographies of local saints. Pellini prepared for his major work by editing Campano's life of Braccio da Montone and by translating Poggio's passages about Piccinino into Italian. The only exception was Ammirato, who began his career as a poet and a critic of poetry and who first made his career profitable by compiling genealogical charts for title-chasing aristocrats from Naples and Florence. Indeed, for over a decade he suspended work on his history, even though that is what the grand duke was supposedly paying him to write, in order to solve Machiavelli's dilemma about the contradiction between politics and Christian morality. And he succeeded in solving it at least to the satisfaction of his associates in the Florentine Accademia degli Apatisti, of which he was the mentor, and of the many readers in France in the following generation who used the translations of his *Discorsi sopra Cornelio Tacito* as a textbook in the theory of *raison d'état*. But once he had discovered the delights of leafing through dusty parchments for what they contained in general, and not just for the information they might yield to a genealogist or a political theorist, he abandoned all his former interests for what he now considered his true vocation. And he divided the last decade of his life exclusively between the archives and his writing desk.

With the exception of Summonte, who made use of Ammirato's history of the Neapolitan nobility, none of these "definitive" historians seems to have known any of the others; and each of them consequently attempted to resolve the traditional organizational and methodological problems of municipal historiography in his own way. Ammirato was the most faithful in his adherence to early sixteenth-century humanist models, from which, after all, he had first learned the substance as well as the art of history. He cited his narrative sources only when he wished to avoid taking responsibility himself ("Machiavelli says that..."), when he suspected them of deliberate falsification (Giovanni Cambi was prejudiced against Lorenzo il Magnifico: V, 325), or when they were manifestly incorrect (Corio's "singular negligence": V, 577); and, following Bruni, he usually referred to them generically as "other writers" (I, 59), or "some diaries" (VI, 191). He paraphrased those original documents he felt obliged to refer to directly, like the treaty with Charles VIII (V, 375); and he quoted verbatim only those documents that could be presented in the form of a speech, like the remarks of Piero di Cosimo to Luca Pitti (V, 171). He introduced dates only when referring to the election of a new pope, as permitted by Mattia Palmieri's universal chronicle form, or when mentioning the names of the new magistrates, which, he, like all his predecessors, took care to list in full for the benefit of ancestor-hunting readers. He drew out descriptions of battles, complete with heroic exchanges of words between the contenders, to the point where they could be appreciated as literary works in their own right (one of the best is the battle of Gavinana). Although the vastly increased bulk of his work forced him to select far shorter time-periods, he still divided his narrative according to the internal connection among the principal events described in each book: from the expulsion of the Ghibellines to the Ordinances of Justice (Book II), the rise and fall of the Duke of Athens (IX), the revolt of the Ciompi (XIV). And he took care to justify his occasional departures from his predecessors' schemes of periodization by reference to a causal connection that they had missed (e.g., XXVI).

Most of these historians, however, insisted upon mentioning all their sources, whether literary or archival, even at the expense of literary quality. Pellini cited Pedro Mexia as well as Orosius and Procopius about Perugia at the time of Belisarius. He cited Villani and Antonino as well as Biondo, Platina, and what "has been left in manuscript by several of our citizens" about Perugia in the fourteenth century. Celestino littered his text with the name of Cesare Baronio the moment each succeeding volume of the *Annales Ecclesiastici* appeared in print. He acknowledged all the passages he borrowed, sometimes rather indiscriminately, from Sigonio, Corio, Pierfrancesco Giambullari, Ariosto, Petrarch, et al. And he usually identified the inscriptions he reproduced by where they were found as well as by their current location ("at Bariano was found a stone that now can be seen on the wall of the house of Clemente Vertona"). Both he and Rossi often put the texts of documents—e.g., the official correspondence regarding the return of Bergamo to Venetian rule—in the place reserved by humanist standards for formal orations; and they both left the language of the documents just as they found it—"ut honesti verbis utar," as Rossi put it. After all, the very words of Charlemagne in an edict of

787, of Otto I in a privilege of 972, and, above all, of the archbishop in a decree of 1308 supported Rossi's thesis about the jurisdiction of Ravenna's metropolitan see far more eloquently than any oration he himself might have composed. Or at least the device succeeded in moving the sixteenth-century reader of the copy that is now in the Regenstein Library to underline all the important passages in ink. The most scrupulous of all the historians was Summonte, who hardly ever dared to make a statement without mentioning all his authorities or to quote a source without giving the entire text—except, alas, when it came to lifting passages out of Tomaso Costo's edition of Collenuccio. His work thus includes the whole of Cassiodorus's version of Theodoric's exhortation to the Neapolitans and all of the Greek inscriptions that apparently confirmed what could be deduced from Aristotle, Cicero, Thomas Aquinas, Dionysius of Halicarnassus, and Sigonio about Naples' earliest constitutions.

Indeed, care in the use of sources was one of these historians' most notable achievements. All of them began by consulting every narrative history that might reflect upon their principal subject. Rossi was fortunate in having before him the chaotic "compendium of things worthy of memory about our ancient city of Ravenna" first published, albeit in an imperfect version, in 1574 by the well-known authority on plagues, TOMMASO TOMAI (d. 1593/95).[82] For several chapters he had only to impose order on Tomai's disorder and to weed out the obvious factual errors. Summonte was more scrupulous. When Carlo d'Angiò stopped in Florence, he looked him up in Bruni. When Giovan Giorgio Trissino said something about Justinian, he compared the statements with what he knew to be Trissino's source, Procopius. To be sure, Summonte, like all the others, frequently succumbed to the general humanist error of supposing one narrative source to be as good as any other—of supposing Orosius to be as authoritative as Livy and Pliny the Elder to be as reliable as Biondo. The consequences of this error became most apparent in their discussions of remote antiquity. Petrarch and Plutarch said one thing about Priso, or Pruso, the brother of the Greek king Diomedes, Pellini found. Dante said another thing about Tirreno, the brother of the king of Lydia, who threw out the Umbrians and renamed their country "Thuscana" from the Lydian word for "incense." And neither Appian nor Sabellico nor the Perugian law professor and antiquarian Cristoforo Sassi were of any help in determining who was right. Indeed, Celestino was often so upset by the "variety of opinions" he encountered that he was tempted "to mention them all [and] let the reader choose which one he prefers."

Yet such a solution, Pellini had to admit, would amount to shirking the historian's responsibility. Ripamonti might well laugh at Galvano Fiamma's vain efforts to create a golden age in the mythical past when it was much easier to find one ready-made in the age of Ambrose and Theodosius. Ammirato might well leave the Etruscans to Bruni and refuse to "put so much effort into a matter about which there is little hope of ever discovering the truth." For the date of the foundation of

Florence had long since been firmly established as a date of comparatively recent times. But the others strictly held to Pellini's axiom—that "two things in particular render a city noble: one is the antiquity of its foundation and the other is the greatness of him who founds it." They therefore had to choose at least one of the stories about the descendants of Noah, even when, like Rossi, they suspected the authenticity of the "authors" published by Annio da Viterbo. They had to maintain Barnabas as the apostle of Bergamo, Peter as the apostle of Naples, and a poor weaver with a dove on his head as one of the electors of St. Theodorus, bishop of Ravenna.

Indeed, they were obliged to accept these stories because all of them had been reported in written records; and the only reason that could be offered for rejecting the veracity of a written record was an ill-defined, instinctive sentiment about what appeared to be true-to-life *(verosimile)*. Only when the records contradicted each other did the historians have a legitimate reason for doubt; and only then could they have recourse to what few principles of documentary criticism were provided by the humanist tradition. One such principle was contemporaneity with the events. Thus Falco Beneventano was wrong and Bishop Fortunato of Naples was right about the life of St. Agnello, because Fortunato was "an author of those time." But Falco was right about Ruggero because, having written "shortly after the events, he could know the truth of the matter much better than Biondo, who lived in the fifteenth century." Another such principle was the word of a modern authority. Thus Summonte followed the chronicles of Montecassino rather than Collenuccio on the marriage of Duke Guglielmo because Ammirato had declared them to be accurate. Rossi established the presence of the emperor Honorius in Ravenna in 399 because one of the greatest archaeologists of the age, Pirro Ligorio, had found what appeared to be a corroborative inscription in the Roman Forum. And Celestino supported his elaborate etymological explanations of Latin place names by consulting "a man very well versed in the Hebrew language"—who, alas, was as unaware as almost everyone else before the mid–eighteenth century that Latin and Hebrew were languages of completely different origins. Still another principle was the priority of nonliterary to narrative sources. The historians of Orvieto were wrong in crediting Otto II with having taken Chiusi away from the Perugians, because Pellini could find no mention of the incident in the archives of Perugia, where a record certainly would have been kept. And Celestino hesitated to accept what he learned from local scholars until he had searched through all the papers in the cathedral chapter of Bergamo and read the "infinite number of ducal letters" supplied to him by two friends in the Venetian chancery. Indeed, the diligent Celestino spent hours trying to decipher the Ottonian handwriting of his mutilated parchments, and he spent days on end trying to put together hundreds of scraps of pottery—all in the hope of discovering "How the Ancients Buried Their Dead," the subject of one of his long digressions.

As these historians agreed about methodology, so also they agreed in accepting, at

288

least implicitly, a modified version of traditional humanist doctrine concerning the purpose of historical writing. History was still useful for inculcating virtue, they insisted. But by virtue they meant private, individual virtue, not the social or political virtues; and that kind of virtue definitely excluded acts of heroism motivated by a desire for glory. They therefore toned down their predecessors' heroes. Bruni's Gian Della Bella was permitted to speak only when he at least realized how much trouble was being caused by the pursuit of his good causes. Machiavelli's Lorenzo il Magnifico was left with only a two-sentence eulogy. Ferrucci was excused of his defects with a reference to the needs of the time. And Alfonso d'Aragona was drowned out in the celebrations held in his honor. Less disturbing heroes were elevated alongside them—heroes like Corso Donati, who, Ammirato observed, would have been still more innocuous had he lived under the rule of a prince, and Giovanna I, who became a model, not of queenly courage but, surprisingly enough, of marital fidelity. Similarly, the traditional villains were deprived of their truly threatening qualities. Summonte hurried over Manfredi's distasteful *scelleraggini* as quickly as possible, and Ammirato turned even Il Moro, whom a half-century of historians had blamed for a half-century of unprecedented disasters, into merely "a good example [to inspire] everyone to moderate better his unreasonable appetites." "The memory of our fathers of old," concluded Pellini, served to promote not the performance of great deeds but "the conservation of those things that tend to the honor of God, the greatness of the city, the maintenance of our families, and the support of our holy places."

Similarly, history was still supposed to present theses about the general course of historical development. Yet in all but two cases, that development had already come to an end. The historical role of Florence, Ammirato pointed out, was to reestablish the political unity of Tuscany which had been briefly realized under the Lombards and under Countess Matilda and which had been finally realized with the creation of the grand duchy.

> This is what we promise to show: ... how ... among the infinite number of bodies that emerged from the corruption of the Roman Empire [the image is borrowed from the theory of spontaneous generation] there was formed the body of the duchy of Tuscany; how this body in turn became corrupted and altered and divided into many smaller parts ... until at last, in modern times, it was reconstituted in another body under the name first of the Republic of Florence and then of the Grand Duchy of Tuscany. (I, 41)

Meanwhile, the "many calamities" perpetrated "in Florence and in all Tuscany" by the murder of Buondelmonte Buondelmonti in 1215, the "variation of spirits" and the "aspiration for new things" that followed the death of Giangaleazzo Visconti in 1402, the plebeian violence that "surpassed the limits of the most barbarous cruelty" even at the time of Savonarola—all that was gradually overcome by an ascending curve of historical development, one which began in 1434, was interrupted in 1494, and reached its climax in the aftermath of the War of Siena. The age of the Medici principate thus differed from the age in which the Medici had ruled as first citizens in that "it was durable." Consequently, "the fruit that is gathered from [the principate] is without any doubt more excellent and more perfect: the cities are more embellished, the population has multiplied, the fine arts are flourishing, religion is held in greater respect, and the state, being restricted to fewer people, is more united and more powerful" (V, 315).

What was accomplished in Florence after 1537 was accomplished in Perugia after 1540. The reign of the Baglioni, insisted Pellini, was only a partial solution to the chronic problem of civil strife. The final solution was provided by Paul III's fortress, which now served as "an honest bridle to whoever might think of machinating against the State of the Holy Church" and whoever might compromise thereby what the State of the Church had made possible: the flourishing of "all the arts necessary to the ornamentation and splendor of civic life," including the pottery works at Deruta. The same was accomplished in Bergamo—after a long, horrible succession of "imprisonments, homicides, conflagrations, and other massacres caused [first] by the infernal factions of our country" and then by the French, German, and Spanish occupying forces—with the restoration of the rule of "the Venetian Republic, the ornament and splendor of Italian dignity, the [modern] image of the authority and greatness of the Roman Republic." What was accomplished in Bergamo in 1517 was accomplished in Milan not by the Visconti, who were not better than the factions that preceded them, and not by the Sforza, whose intrafamily quarrels brought on the ruin of all Italy. Rather it was accomplished by Charles V, who put an end to "tempora plena turbarum," and by Carlo Borromeo and his Milanese uncle, Pius IV, whose "pontificate may be imitated by his successors for all ages." Under their aegis, "the pure rays of the sun . . . and the healthy air uncontaminated by the vapors of the irrigated terrain" gave "abundant harvests" and left "nothing to be desired with regard to what serves to nourish men and render their existence pleasant."

Although the historians hesitated to admit it, moreover, even in Ravenna and Naples the curve of history had come just as conclusively to an end. It was in the best interest of the Roman Curia that the Tridentine prescription for the restoration of ecclesiastical provinces not be carried out; and no arguments that Rossi might induce from history could possibly sway the Curia's decision to recognize the autonomy of the Church of Rimini. Indeed, the *Liber Pontificalis* of Agnello, upon which Rossi's arguments rested, was forthwith removed from Ravenna to the Vatican; and no one heard of it again until Benedetto Bacchini, almost a century later, discovered another copy in the Este library at Modena—to the immense annoyance of the Inquisition.[83] Similarly, it was in the best interests of the Spanish monarchy that it divide the spoils of the Kingdom of Naples with the barons; and nothing that Summonte had to say about the privileges of Ferrante II could possibly restore the long-lost political power of the *popolo*. A term in prison after the publication of the first volume of his history must have convinced him too of the futility of drawing any further political lessons from the example of the past.

That left only one really important purpose for history: the purpose of providing a complete and correct record of everything that had ever happened. Thoroughness became a quality in its own right; and what Ammirato himself missed in the records of the Archivio delle Riformaggioni was later supplied by his equally industrious disciple and heir, SCIPIONE AMMIRATO, JR. To be sure, thoroughness posed a serious problem of organization, and it brought upon Summonte a violent reprimand from Costo for having exceeded the just limitation of history to "gli avvenimenti publici e notabili."[84] All justification for the previous distinction between political and non-political events disappeared now that both had become irrelevant to the present. But the humanist models gave no indication of how to put them all together. Ripamonti managed to incorporate sacred history into political history by placing the arch-bishops Carlo and Federico Borromeo in the role formerly reserved for princes and magistrates; and he managed to describe diocesan synods, sermons, catechisms, and the reform of religious congregations in the terms his predecessors had used for senate meetings, orations, ducal decrees, and reforms of the constitution. Rossi and Ammirato were less successful in incorporating what they recognized as the greatest achievements of their cities: the arts and letters. Such matters could appear only in the funeral eulogy of an artist or a writer ("Florebat hoc tempore Ioannis Ravenna qui cum a Francisco Petrarca multa didicit, tum . . ."); and such eulogies had to be tacked on at the end of the narrative of the "real" events of a particular year. Economics posed the same difficulty for Pellini: his description of the wool industry in Perugia appears as a commentary on the law of 1428, which promised subsidies for immigrant Florentine technicians.

Still worse, thoroughness precluded brevity. As the traditional scheme of organization by chronological periods became increasingly unwieldy, and as bits of information multiplied at a rate far greater than the ability of the historians to absorb them, history tended to break down once again into chronicle; and chronicle became unchronological every time a historian found himself too rushed to bother reinserting a tidbit he had forgotten to mention in its correct year. Summonte tried to mitigate the effects of excessive length by dedicating a separate book to the obligatory humanist category of "site" *(sito)* and a separate chapter to a description of the judiciary system. Notwithstanding his ambition to imitate Thucydides, Celestino extracted from his main category of *storia profana* a separate description of "the territory," twenty-four books of local saints' lives, and almost as many on ecclesiastical institutions. Ripamonti never managed to join his chronicle of the plague of 1630, which the Senate commissioned him to write, to the main body of his work.

And his many volumes were published simply in the order in which he got them ready for the press, often without any indication of their place in the series.

But such organizational difficulties were not considered to be particularly important. After all, the "definitive" histories were not really meant to be read. They were meant to be consulted. They were not intended to inspire action. They were intended to be repositories of information. Consequently, they could well be printed without benefit of paragraph divisions. For the reader was supposed to begin not with the text itself, but with the copious indices of names, places, and subjects that invariably preceded the text. Length thus posed no barrier to whoever wanted simply to find out who had governed Bergamo in 1300 or who had been the archbishop of Ravenna in 1400. Indeed, it was an advantage, not a defect, for it assured the reader of being able to find out all there was to know about a given subject. Better yet, along with correctness and thoroughness, length was largely responsible for winning for the histories the "definitive" character so ardently sought by their authors. There was little chance that anyone would dare to rewrite what Rossi had already spread across 900 pages, what Pellini had committed to 2,251 pages, or what Summonte's eighteenth-century editor and Ammirato's nineteenth-century editor had been obliged to divide into six volumes each. And no one did. Summonte remained the standard historian of Naples until well after the time of Giannone, who freely plagiarized him some 120 years later.[85] And Ammirato was once again confirmed in his role as the standard historian of Florence in 1755, when Domenico Maria Manni's authoritative manual made him required reading for all students of Florentine history during the next half-century.[86]

BOOK V

FROM MUNICIPAL HISTORY
TO WORLD HISTORY

I I

NATIONAL HISTORY

The Present

DURING THE VERY YEARS IN WHICH MUNICIPAL HISTORIOGRAPHY WAS BEING REVIVED all over Italy, at least one historian came to the conclusion that a single city, even one that was formally independent, no longer would provide an adequate framework for historical narration. FRANCESCO GUICCIARDINI was well acquainted with municipal historiography. After all, he had written a minor masterpiece of the genre in his youth;[1] and even though he seems to have forgotten about the manuscript during his busy career as a diplomat and a papal governor after 1511, it was still another history of Florence that first came to his mind when, late in 1527, he temporarily retired from active life. He had returned to Florence just a few months before, for the explicit purpose of saving his country from what he saw to be the imminent ruin of all the rest of Italy. The League of Cognac, a project to which he had been passionately dedicated ever since the Battle of Pavia, had just collapsed; and the sack of Rome had momentarily eclipsed one of the two remaining Italian states still capable of resisting the complete subjection of the rest of them to the empire of Charles V.[2] Further action on the plane of pan-Italian politics was therefore futile. Unfortunately, an active role on the plane of municipal politics was also closed to him, at least for a while, since his many years in the service of two Medici popes had made him suspect in the eyes of the new regime. But if he could not aid his country as a politician, he could still, like Sallust, aid it as a writer. And that is what he set out to do as soon as he had settled down in his villa of Finocchietto in the Mugello.

Guicciardini began by taking up once again the arguments he had put forth many years earlier—first in the treatises of 1513–16 and then in his *Dialogo del reggimento di Firenze* of the early 1520s—in support of an aristocratic solution to the burning problem of the Florentine constitution. He then added to and rearranged the various lessons in practical politics and political wisdom that he had accumulated during his long tenure as papal governor in Emilia and Romagna—the lessons that were discovered and published in the mid-ninteenth century as the *Ricordi*. He also studied what was soon to become the most famous nonaristocratic solution to the problem, Machiavelli's *Discorsi,* which he found to be based on incorrect assumptions about human behavior and thus inapplicable to any real political situation. No solution, Guicciardini realized, could be effective unless the problem were first accurately and completely identified. Hence, in accordance with well-established humanist methods, he reread the standard historians of Florence, particularly Giovanni Villani, Bruni, and Poggio, and the standard historian of all Italy, Biondo, who provided him with a general scheme of organization as well as with an abundance of specific information. He also looked at Machiavelli's *Istorie fiorentine,* although he apparently judged it to be unreliable and soon put it aside. He then made extensive notes from the minor chronicle and commentary writers, like Malispini, Stefani, Neri Capponi, and Buoninsegni. He even made use of one famous medieval chronicle that seems previously to have been unknown in Florence, Froissart ("Il Frossardo"). And he filled in the gaps he found in the narrative sources with long extracts from such nonliterary sources as the *Ricordanze* of Rinaldo degli Albizzi.

Like his predecessors, moreover, Guicciardini went back to the founders of the city, whom he identified, after a careful examination of the texts referred to by Poliziano, as a group of colonists sent directly from Rome. Also like his predecessors, he credited the founders with having impressed certain indelible characteristics upon their descendants: what Florentines had been at the beginning, so would they always be. But unlike Machiavelli, he judged those characteristics favorably. Any people capable of erecting in a short time monuments of the size indicated by their abundant archaeological remains, Guicciardini surmised, must certainly have been endowed with an ability to perform magnificent deeds. Hence, if Florence remained relatively small during the first centuries of its existence, that was simply because of its geographical proximity to the capital of the Roman Empire. If it did not begin to grow as soon as the capital declined and fell, that was because Attila robbed it of much of its accumulation of material goods—without, however, totally destroying it, as Villani had supposed. Then, when Charlemagne's financial assistance enabled it at last to repair the damage wrought by the barbarians, the inherent virtues of its citizens at last became fully manifest. Whatever went wrong thereafter could be explained as the effect of the aberrant wills of individual men—or, occasionally, of the wills of groups of men, like the Ghibellines and the Ciompi. Indeed, had it not been for the "discord" that conflicts of wills so often produced, Florence "would soon have created a great dominion, since it was always formidable to its neighbors, full of excellent talents, and desirous of great things." Whenever the wills of its citizens were duly constrained by a good constitution, as they were in the late thirteenth and in the early fifteenth centuries, the results were invariably felicitous:

> The city abounded in goods and money, and it greatly benefited from good counsel; for the government was in the hands of the wise and the noble, and it is no surprise that they demonstrated such prudence and such generosity.

Yet the follies of the various Florentine governments after the fall of Niccolò Capponi soon convinced Guicciardini that none of the good constitutions he might resurrect from the past and fortify with the political wisdom of the present would ever be implemented. And the disastrous consequences of its unrealistic foreign policy convinced him that Florence could no longer hope to isolate itself from the common fate of all Italy. He added a few more notes after his flight to Lucca in 1529. He made some corrections and composed a dozen or so formal orations for eventual insertion in the narrative after his definitive return to the city in 1534. He then put the manuscript aside, with the later chapters still in the form of a rough draft or of scattered notes. And it remained unknown until it was discovered, but incorrectly identified, in 1737, and then correctly identified and edited in 1930.[3]

Meanwhile, Guicciardini had been experimenting with another form, one which sacrificed the past to the present, but which no longer would have confined him within the now clearly untenable limits of one state. He himself had kept a diary during his first embassy to Spain,[4] and his brothers, to whom he was bound by common business interests as well as by ties of affection,[5] had preserved the tradition that the Guicciardini shared with most other patrician households. That is, they kept a running record of the family's sales, purchases, deaths, births, and marriages, as well as of its growing accumulation of political wisdom. Thus when, in 1527, he extracted a number of entries from the *ricordanze* he too had kept until 1516, and when he added to them a note of all the commissions he had received and all the contracts he had signed,[6] he may well have been planning, as Francesco Sansovino was to insist many years later,[7] to adopt Caesar rather than Livy as a model and to compose an account of his own *res gestae*.

Notwithstanding the high offices he had held, however, and notwithstanding the considerable personal fortune he had accumulated,[8] Guicciardini knew that he was no Caesar. His role in history had always been that of one who, rather than initiating action himself, tried simply to mitigate the more disastrous effects of the actions initiated by others. That was the role he was once again called upon to play, first as governor in Bologna for Clement VII in 1531, and then, in 1534, as tutor, advisor, and *éminence grise* to the undisciplined playboy to whom the pope had turned over the city after its surrender in 1530, Alessandro de' Medici. He therefore decided to abandon Caesar as well for a completely new format: an account of all the political and military events that had occurred in all the various parts of Italy during the preceding decade.

To be sure, this new format had no precedent either in ancient or in modern historiography. It constituted neither a history of a single political entity *ab urbe condita* nor a "commentary" on contemporary events like those of Polybius or Bruni, which were, at least potentially, universal in scope. It was not even a history of a coherent group of political entities, since Italy had by then lost whatever common institutions it may have created before 1494, and much of it had since become subject to non-Italian powers. Hence even the example of Thucydides, of which Guicciardini seems anyway to have been unaware, was inapplicable. Still, this format had some notable advantages. It would have permitted the author to demonstrate the long-range effects of the Battle of Pavia and thus to endow his work with a certain thematic unity. It would have permitted him to draw upon all his own recollections as an eyewitness of what had happened in many different places. It would have permitted him to identify those whose blunders had permitted the collapse of the League of Cognac, the sack of Rome, the siege of Florence, and a score of other major tragedies. And it would have permitted him to wreak vengeance upon those who had forced him to end his days not as a responsible member of a wise aristocracy but as an insecure servant of an incompetent tyrant.

Yet within a year of his return to Florence, Guicciardini came to realize that identifying the culprits in the present was as gratuitous a task as looking for them in the past. For he had watched the tyrant yield control even of the internal affairs of his state to the foreign prince, Charles V, who was now the undisputed master of all Italy. By June of 1537, moreover, he had to admit the failure of one last attempt to institute even a modified version of what he still held to be the model constitution of 1380–1420. For the seventeen-year-old Cosimo de' Medici, whom he had been instrumental in electing, not as the successor to his distant cousin Alessandro but merely as "head" of the "Florentine Republic," had by now proved himself capable of negotiating directly with the emperor's representatives, without any assistance from his patrician counselors.[9] Then, after the Battle of Montemurlo in August he also proved himself capable of stamping out the last flicker of internal opposition. Unaware that Cosimo was well on the way to solving the constitutional problems of Florence once and for all, and even less aware that he had taken the first steps toward elevating Florence from the status of an imperial dependency to that of an independent state, Guicciardini retired for the second, and last, time. He devoted the remaining two and a half years of his life not to lamenting, not to excogitating remedies, not to seeking guidance for the future from the record of the past, but merely to describing and explaining the process by which the rulers of the Italian states had gradually lost, or been deprived of, all control over their own destinies.

The *Storia d'Italia*[10] thus begins not with the Battle of Pavia, in which the chief protagonists were no longer Italians, but with the fatal error that first introduced foreigners into Italy—"when the armies of the French, summoned by our own princes, began to perturb it with great movements." And since the error had been committed by Italians themselves, the first lines of the *Storia* were followed by a survey of Italy during the years immediately preceding the invasion—a period which Guicciardini, developing fully the insight of some of his Florentine predecessors on the morrow of the sack of Prato,[11] turned into a somewhat mythical golden age. Not since the fall of the Roman Empire, he insisted,

> had Italy ever experienced such prosperity nor such desirable conditions of life. It enjoyed perfect peace and tranquility, ... it was subject to no rule but that of its own men, and it abounded in inhabitants, goods, and riches.

But even the golden age was the creation of men—of Innocent VIII, of Alfonso d'Aragona, and above all of Lorenzo de' Medici, who "with all diligence took care that the affairs of Italy were kept in such balance that they could not lean in one direction more than in another." Similarly, the destruction of the golden age was also the work of men—of the Venetians, who "stood ready to take advantage of every accident that might open to them the way to the rule of all Italy," of Alexander VI, who "publicly bought . . . the votes of the cardinals," and, above all, of Lodovico Sforza, the favorite villain of all the historians of the *calamità*. True, Guicciardini occasionally attributed a collective defect to a whole people—for example, to the Romans, whom a half-century of papal tyranny had robbed of the last vestige of civic spirit (XVIII, 8, 10), to the Milanese, who lost a chance to destroy the Spanish army that was despoiling them because of their eagerness to despoil each other (XVII, 1). He occasionally admitted that an institution, like the church, could affect the actions of men by the awe—or contempt—it inspired in them (III, 15). He was even willing to attribute the weakness of Italian armies to faulty organization and inferior technology as well as to the defects of their generals (I, 11). Still, individual men remained the sole agents of historical change. Portents were nothing but purely coincidental signs of what was about to happen, and what occasionally made them historically important was the prophetic quality that men, in their ignorance, attributed to them. The sinking of a Venetian treasure ship and a bolt of lightning in Brescia had no causal connection whatever with the Battle of Agnadello. And the powerful, respected Medici family fell suddenly from power not because of the intervention of some superhuman force but "through the temerity of [one] young man."

Yet individual men act not just from reason and calculation but also from passion, prejudice, blindness, and insight. Julius II seized Modena because he hated the Borgias and because he therefore hated Alfonso d'Este, who had married a Borgia. King Maximilian joined the League of Cambrai not from calculation but because he was filled with *odio* for the Venetians. Hence, as for all the other humanist historians, so also for Guicciardini, the ultimate causes of historical action were psychological. What happened in history, he assumed, was the result not immediately of the will of individual historical agents but of the particular combination of character traits that determined what these agents would will. If they were by nature generous and ambitious, they automatically acted in a manner that they supposed would benefit others and further their own careers. If they were timid and suspicious, they would invariably refrain from acts that might necessitate their confiding in others. And since character traits were independent of the will, men could not become generous if they had been born stingy, or brave if they were by nature cowardly. Accordingly, Guicciardini's work abounds in character sketches, usually as brilliant as they are brief—sketches in which the author displayed all the skill he had acquired during his long experience as a diplomat in trying to predict what men would do from an analysis of what they were. A few sketches are obviously of villains—like that of the duke of Urbino, whom Guicciardini never forgave for failing to rescue the pope from Castel Sant'Angelo. A few are obviously of heroes, like those of Giovanni delle Bande Nere (XVII, 16) and Gonzalo de Córdoba, the "Gran Capitán" (VI, 10; XII, 19). And one, that of Charles VIII, is intentionally derogatory: to have granted Charles any noble qualities would have undermined the force of Guicciardini's thesis, that Italians had none but themselves to blame for their plight.[12] But most of the portraits appear to be as objective and accurate as they are true to life, particularly such famous ones as those of the Marchese di Pescara (XVI, 11), Leo X, Clement VII (XVI, 12), and Francis I (XV, 14). And since Guicciardini is still regarded as the leading authority on most of the persons he portrays, it would be dangerous to accept Jean Bodin's view that the vices artificially outweigh the virtues in those persons.

Still, what resulted from the intervention of individual men in history did not always correspond to their intentions. And the real tragedy of Italy consisted in the increasing inability of Italians to put their intentions into practice. In 1495 the Florentines were able to reorganize their constitution as they saw fit (II, 2), thanks in great measure to Savonarola, "whose work was no less beneficial for the state of the city than it was profitable in spiritual matters."[13] After 1512 they had to accept whatever constitution was dictated to them. Before 1509 the Venetians could bargain with the French over the spoils of Lombardy. After 1509 they could not. Francesco II Sforza would have liked to get rid of the Spanish; but he could have done so only by replacing them with the French, which was the worse of two evils. And Pope Clement would have liked to use the French and the Venetians to get rid of the emperor. But he ended up as the emperor's loyal ally. Eventually Italians gave up trying to be effective politicians. Either they lapsed into lethargy, or they merely adapted themselves to whatever political circumstances seemed to be the most favorable at the moment, or they retired into private life to cultivate purely private virtues—as Guicciardini himself did in 1537. The *Storia* ends with an expression of hope that the new pope would be worthy of the confidence placed in him. But Guicciardini knew that Paul III would never be able to claim credit even for those of his projects that might happen to succeed. And he did not reproach the cardinals for choosing as a successor to the unfortunate Pope Clement a man whose advanced age seemed to preclude his undertaking any projects at all.

The causes of this progressive loss of control were twofold, Guicciardini proposed. First, the variety of intentions multiplied to the point where they invariably canceled each other out. In 1495 the pope, the duke, and the Venetians had at least been able to agree on the advisability of chasing the army of Charles VIII out of Italy; and they managed to agree long enough to accomplish their end. By 1525 the representatives of the same powers were completely unable to agree on even how to chase a far smaller Imperial army out of Milan.

Amid such diversity of wills, such variety of interests and objectives, there easily arose disorder, irritation, disagreement, and diffidence. Hence there was never either celerity in boldly pursuing fortune when it showed itself favorable or in firmly resisting it when it turned unfavorable (XVI, 11).

Second, Italians gradually let the initiative in their own domestic affairs pass into the hands of foreigners. Lodovico il Moro might still legitimately think of Charles VIII as his instrument in securing his power in Milan. The Venetians, Alexander VI, and the Florentines might still believe that they were using Louis XII to ruin Il Moro, to create a state for Cesare Borgia, and to reconquer Arezzo. Leo X might still hope to maintain a balance between the Spanish in the south and the French, Germans, and Swiss in the north and so preserve a certain freedom of action in central Italy. But after 1521 the Germans and the Spanish could no longer be played off against each other, since they were united under the same monarch. After 1525, and particularly after Lautrec's abortive expedition against Naples, the French could no longer be played off against either of them, since they had been driven from all of Italy but Piedmont. And by 1530 almost the whole of the peninsula depended directly upon the authority of one man, a foreign prince who ostentatiously displayed his contempt for his dependents. The result was the destruction of Italy's cities, the devastation of its fields, the demoralization of its citizens. Worse yet, the result was at least the potential ruin of all Christendom. Just at the moment when the pope found himself trapped between a futile campaign in Siena and disastrous rebellion in Rome itself, the Turks began pouring across the Danube and onto the plains of Hungary. And no Italian could do anything at all to stop them.

Unfortunately, Guicciardini's last-minute plea for a continuer, for someone who might "write about the events that occur in Italy" after illness and then death (May, 1540) forced him to break off in the year 1534, went unanswered. Apparently the greatest problem posed to Guicciardini's admirers was his unprecedented format. Even the one of them who dared to adopt it, PATRIZIO DE'ROSSI, was forced to fall back on the history of only one of the Italian powers, the Papacy, as a center about which to organize the actions of all the others.[14] Rossi's organizational principle was then reinforced by the nature of his chief documentary source: the papers left by his forebear Francesco, who had lived in Rome after 1519 and had accompanied the pope to Viterbo in 1527. This source, in turn, enabled Rossi not just to paraphrase Guicciardini, whom he nonetheless respected as "a man of consumate integrity and prudence," but also to alter significantly Guicciardini's scheme of culpability. He thus elevated the two Medici popes to the rank of tragic heroes. It was not Leo's fault, Rossi insisted, that the king and the emperor turned all Italy into a battleground. And it was not Clement's fault that the Battle of Pavia led inexorably to the sack of Rome. The fault lay rather with the decline in religious spirit, which prevented Clement, who "demonstrated a constancy that honors the priesthood," from doing to Bourbon what Leo I had done to Alaric. The fault lay with the Venetians, who "didn't care if all the springs of the earth went dry as long as water continued to flow through their mill." The fault lay with the Florentines, who continued to hold out when "it was a question no longer of citizens dying for their country but of the country bringing death to the citizens." The fault lay with the Colonna, who "infested the streets of Rome, pillaging, destroying, and committing unheard-of atrocities." Indeed, Rossi in the end questioned even Guicciardini's thesis of an unmitigated tragedy. For the Treaty of Barcelona and the Conference of Bologna at least brought peace, which he was better able to appreciate from the vantage point of the quieter years of the mid-sixteenth century. And the absolute dominion that Guicciardini accorded to Charles V alone Rossi granted also to Charles's chief Italian allies, the Medici.

Indeed, it was the format Guicciardini had adopted that aroused much of the subsequent criticism of the *Storia d'Italia.* For by trying to encompass all the states of Italy in one continuous narrative, he inevitably trod on the sensibilities of those who persisted in looking upon history as a way of glorifying that state to which they happened to be subject.[15] The Venetians, for instance, objected to a number of speeches that they found to be "no less false than full of hatred and poison against the Venetian Senate" and disrespctful of "the great prudence of this most wise republic, the ancient and glorious splendor of the Italian name." It was bad enough, said Paolo Paruta, that Guicciardini put into the mouth of one senator a speech that was "not only not true but not even *verosimile*"—"like the truth." He even suggested that Lorenzo de' Medici was a tyrant, and Guicciardini had let his "implacable hatred" of the house of Aragon blind him to the well-known virtues of Lorenzo's ally, Ferrante I. It was bad enough, said GIOVAN BATTISTA LEONE, that Guicciardini had lowered the reputation of all Italians, the Vicar of Christ included, in the eyes of foreigners and heretics.[16] But it was inadmissible that Venice be accused of having ever assumed any other role in Italian politics than that of guardian of Italy's freedom. It was still more inadmissible, Leone continued, that any Venetian be accused of having made a speech like the one Guicciardini put into the mouth of Domenico Trevisan on the eve of the Battle of Agnadello. And Leone did his best to repair the damage by composing reams of pious odes and sermons and by turning Sixtus IV, Julius II, and Francesco Maria Della Rovere into models of political morality.[17]

The Bolognese were even more annoyed. Not only did Guicciardini completely misrepresent the government of the Bentivoglio, said Pompeo Viziani; he "almost never mentions the Bolognesi . . . without biting them in one way or another." "He was rather a partisan of his own city than a good historian," added the leading municipal historian of the following century, Antonio Lamberti; his particularism "made him prejudiced against the glorious reputation of our city" and "annoyingly irreverent toward the Vicar of Christ," its temporal overlord. As late as 1659, indeed, the Bolognese historian Giacomo Certani found it worth his time to fill 305 pages with quotations from those "authorities" who claimed to have found minor errors in the text.[18]

Even some Florentines were not completely happy with what they read. The nostalgic-in-exile Donato Giannotti found the text to be marred by serious lacunae, and he assured Varchi that he need fear no competition in his plan to write a definitive account of the siege. The nostalgic-in-residence Jacopo Pitti blamed Guicciardini's pro-*Ottimati* prejudices for what he decried as an unfair judgment of the popular regime of 1528–30.[19] Some Mediceans were not quite satisfied either, even though they could find nothing in the text contrary to their regime. The philologist Vincenzo Borghini "corrected" a number of words and phrases that were not quite consonant with linguistic orthodoxy as prescribed by the Accademia Fiorentina. Bartolomeo Concini, secretary to the duke, discovered several passages that, coming from a famous Florentine author, might have disturbed the good relations his government had established with the Papacy since the death of Paul III. He therefore toned down many of Guicciardini's stronger adjectives (Alexander VI's *natura facinorosa* became *natura pessima*). He deleted an excursus on the origins of the Temporal Domain. He removed the sarcastic remarks about the role of the Holy Spirit in papal conclaves in Book XVI and the portrait of Leo X in Book XVI.[20] Worse yet, he and Borghini prevailed upon the printer Torrentino to accept their alterations in the first edition of the first sixteen books that appeared in 1561; and that edition unfortunately served as the text for most of the other editions and translations published during the next half-century. What saved the text was that the censors, who acted in a purely private capacity, had only one of the several manuscripts that had been circulating since 1546. Hence two of the suppressed passages were printed separately under the caption "nihil occultum quod non revelatur" by Pietro Perna, the publisher of Curione's Latin translation, in 1569[21] and were incorporated in the Genevan editions after 1621. And all of them were restored in the first complete edition, which was published under the auspices of the grand duke of Tuscany in the eighteenth century.

Actually, the most effective response to the critics was provided, in anticipation, by Guicciardini himself. First, he gave an account of the political, military, and diplomatic history of Italy from 1492 at least to 1529 that was at once more thorough and more comprehensive than any available either then or later. He did so by adding to what he read in a great number of contemporary narratives and to what he himself had learned from his contacts with many of the great personages of the age the vast quantity of information preserved in the records of the Florentine foreign office, the *Dieci*, which he had transported to his own house upon his return to Florence in 1530. And he supplemented what he found himself with special *relazioni* commissioned from well-informed observers in other parts of Italy.[22] Second, he took great pains to make sure that his version of the events was as accurate as possible. He did so by submitting for additions and corrections each chapter as it was ready to those of his friends, like Jacopo Nardi, whose knowledge of the age approached his own. Third, he took care to polish his prose style, in draft after draft; and he did so with a degree of success that can readily be appreciated by comparing the results with the uncorrected prose of his contemporary *Cose fiorentine*. Finally, he scrupulously adhered to the rhetorical requirements of humanist historiography. A high sense of drama is achieved through a basically chronological arrangement, one in which suspense is maintained by interrupting the narration of one event in one part of Italy ("while this was taking place in Lombardy...") to return to the contemporary progress of another event elsewhere. Causal relationships between two events are indicated by their placement one immediately after the other. And the various *consigli* of which each event was the effect are presented in formal orations—some of which are all but verbatim transcripts, others of which (like the controversial debate between Andrea Gritti and Giorgio Corner in XV, 2)[23] are impeccably *verosimili* in accordance with the standards inherited by his fellow humanists from Thucydides.

It may be true, as one modern authority insists, that these rhetorical devices are "heterogeneous with respect to the historical discourse" into which they were inserted. It may even be true that they represent "a shameful bowing to a [humanist] tradition... to which the author did not belong."[24] But in the sixteenth century no one reprimanded him for using them, not even the punctilious Scipione Ammirato, who was afraid of being led astray by what he recognized as the unparalleled beauty of the prose.[25] Indeed, the *Storia d'Italia* was immediately elevated to the rank that Guicciardini himself apparently aspired for it, that of a masterpiece equal to or even greater than the historiographical masterpieces of antiquity. According to Tommaso Porcacchi, it perfectly fulfilled the three Platonic criteria of beauty, measure, and truth. It contained *ragioni* (no "event" without a "cause"), *giudicio* (condemning vices and praising virtues), *descrittioni* (the site of the event), *gravità delle sententie,* and *diversità dell'eloquentia.* And its rather un-Platonically frank evaluations of the persons it portrayed could easily be justified with reference to the examples of Polybius and Josephus. Hence, no one who tasted a part of it could avoid "avidly returning to fill himself to the point of inebriation" on the rest.[26] According to Remigio Nannini, it was so full of concrete illustrations of the rules of practical politics that it could serve the same purpose as Livy had for Machiavelli. He extracted from it a complete textbook of political wisdom for the use of princes, magistrates, ambassadors, and captains.[27] According to Francesco Sansovino, the author of the biography printed thereafter in many of the editions, it was a mine of valuable information set forth with incomparable elegance by an author "without equal in the realm of history." He therefore extracted "the most valuable gems... from the infinitely rich treasure" it contained and published them in a 244-page pocketbook for the benefit of those who might not have time for all twenty books of the original.[28] According to a certain Girolamo Canini, it was full of valuable political aphorisms—1,181 of them, to be exact, which he then dug out ("cavati") of the text for the sake of those who wished "to conduct themselves wisely...in public affairs." According to the heterodox exile Celio Secondo Curione, it was so replete "illustribus & vivis exemplis" of wisdom and so consonant with Cicero's string of sonorous epithets that he took time from his usual theological debates to translate it into Latin.[29] As edition followed edition in the various cities of Italy, with notes, explanations, and summaries by the various editors, it was acclaimed as a classic in other parts of Europe as well. It appeared in French translation in 1568, in German in 1574, in English in 1579, in Spanish in 1581, and eventually even in Dutch, in 1599. It was hailed by Montaigne and Bodin as the greatest work of modern historiography. And it was saved from the attacks of some French historians in the sixteenth century by its inclusion in Bayle's *Dictionnaire historique* (vol. VII of the 1820 edition) in the seventeenth.

"Historia" and "Descriptio"

While Guicciardini produced a masterpiece of national historiography that defied or intimidated imitators, LEANDRO ALBERTI, wholly independently, it seems, composed an inelegant miscellany of fact and fiction that was continued, imitated, and plundered for information for over a century thereafter. Although he was a friar rather than a statesman, Alberti too had traveled rather extensively, usually as an assistant to the master-general of his order—to Rome, Naples, Sicily, as far as Brittany in France, then back to Rome for several years as *vicario* of Santa Sabina—before settling down in 1528 as head of the monastery of San Domenico and, for two years, inquisitor of Bologna. Moreover, he was known to several of the leading humanists of his generation in other parts of Italy; and at least a few of them must have been somewhat sincere in the praise they heaped upon the collection of Dominican biographies he had edited in 1517. Although much of his previous writing had consisted in rather traditional hagiography, he had also composed a municipal history of his own city, one which, while hardly comparable in quality to Guicciardini's *Storie fiorentine,* had at least been partially published.[30] Although he made no use of the kind of archival research upon which so much of the *Storia d'Italia* was based, he had at least read all the available narrative histories and chronicles, ancient and medieval as well as contemporary, and he had kept a private record of principal events since 1500. In order to date the diversion of the Po from its ancient bed, he consulted the *Chronica Parva Ferrariensis.* In order to explain the growth of the delta, he noted a correlation between the recent increase in population and of land under cultivation and the phenomenon of erosion, in accordance with standards that anticipate those of modern geographers. He thus learned to approach Guicciardini's criteria of accuracy, although he chose to do so less by sifting the evidence than by listing his authorities. One point alone, he affirmed, was "demonstrated by Polybius, Thucydides, Strabo, Dionysius of Halicarnassus, Cato, Sempronius, Pliny, Pomponius Mela, Gaius Solinus, Ptolemy, & all the other writers."

Yet Alberti went beyond even the most gullible of his contemporaries in swallowing the patriotic myths of the municipal historians; and his attempts to judge critically among conflicting stories usually ended in his choosing the most fantastic. Dionysius of Halicarnassus was wrong, he proclaimed, in trying to derive the ancient name *Enotria* for Italy from Enotrius, son of Licaone, who emigrated from Arcadia seventeen "ages" before the siege of Troy. For it obviously derived from the Greek word for wine *(enos),* and it therefore accorded with the other ancient name, *Gianicola,* an adaptation of the proper name Janus-Noah, the inventor of wine. Biondo was wrong in setting the number of ancient Italian cities at 264, for Alberti's own number, c. 300, was closer to the 700 identified by Guido Prete of Ravenna. Biondo was also wrong in questioning the existence of Genoa before the Punic wars, simply because of the absence of surviving documentation. For Bracelli had found clear references to the city in what Florus said about the Ligurian tribes and had interpreted a passage in Diodorus Siculus in such a way that a group of Ligurians could be credited with having transported Themistocles to safety in Asia Minor. Moreover, Alberti frequently said in one place the opposite of what he had said earlier. The history of Italy, he insisted, began with the fall of the Roman Empire; and, unlike the Empire, the Italian nation was circumscribed by definite geographical limits. And yet even after the coronation of Charles V, Italians were still "capable & prepared to rule [*signoreggiare*] & to command not only all its neighbors, but all the realms & the nations of the world as well." Since the invasion of Charles VIII, he noted, Italy "has constantly been afflicted and injured." Yet never have Italians, and particularly Genoese, been so happy and so prosperous, occupying themselves no longer with civil and foreign wars, but with "trade and commerce"—*le mercantie & traffichi.* Finally, Alberti never figured out how to get from one subject to another without resorting to rubrics ("Having described the position, . . . I will now enter into the narrative . . .") and cross-references ("Elsewhere I will write more fully of this. For now it is enough to say . . ."). And his attempts occasionally to elevate his plodding style invariably ended in disastrous kettlefuls of scrambled metaphors—like that of the hiker in the introduction who wades deeper and deeper into a swamp until he suddenly transforms it into a "spacious field" and then flies off with "his sails opened to the wind."

But Alberti had one great advantage over Guicciardini: he adhered strictly to a form that had been sanctioned by Strabo and Pomponius Mela in antiquity and by Biondo—in the *Italia Illustrata*—in modern times. This form permitted him to include ancient as well as recent history, description as well as narration, and such subjects excluded from the Livian-Brunian model as institutions (the libraries of Florence), buildings, arts and letters, "famous men, . . . customs, conditions, mountains, lakes, and fountains" (the subtitle). This form also permitted him fully to satisfy the patriotic aspirations of all the municipal historians. For he could display the glories of Siena and Arezzo without infringing upon the glories of Bologna and Cremona—because he confined them to different parts of his text. And he could induce the glories of all Italy from the sum of the glories of all of its single cities. Thus, as he followed Biondo down the Tyrrhenian coast to Lucca, as he zigzagged back and forth through Tuscany and Umbria to Naples, as he headed back up the Adriatic toward Lombardy and Friuli, and as he then took off, in a subsequent edition, on a tour of the islands, Alberti could not but reach the conclusion that "never has there been a province in the whole world where so many deeds [*opre*] worthy of being commended to immortal memory [sic] have been done." Accordingly, the *Descrittione di tutta Italia* went through eight editions within twenty-five years of the appearance of the first (1550). It was translated into Latin and twice published at Köln (1566 and 1567) for the benefit of non-Italian readers. And in 1581 it was expanded, emended, and continued for another twenty years by the professional translator (Thomas à Kempis, Cicero) and editor (Aristotle) for the Della Porta printing firm in Venice, BORGARUCCIO BORGARUCCI.

Meanwhile the same form was adopted by another academic historian, the Pavian patrician-jurist BERNARDO SACCHI (b. 1497), who may have been acquainted with Alberti through his brother, a law professor at the University of Bologna. Sacchi was most familiar with the history of his own city; and in 1565 he put his knowledge in the service of the rebellion of the former communes against the Council of Trent's attempt to revive ecclesiastical provinces.[31] Pavia might today be politically subject to the same state as Milan, he admitted. But Pavians, whose ancestors were "ab ipsa Italia oriundi," had nothing in common with the Milanese, who owed their origins to the Gallic invasion at the time of Tarquinius Priscus. Moreover, whatever moral authority Ambrose might have enjoyed in the province of Liguria in the fourth century was wiped out by the Gothic invasion of the fifth. The Church of Pavia had been totally independent of the Church of Milan ever since it was refounded under Theodoric. And the current bishop had every reason to be "rei novitatem admirandus" when he was issued a completely illegal and unprecedented summons to a provincial synod signed by a certain Carlo Borromeo who, notwithstanding his tender years, had just been made bishop of a completely different diocese.

But Sacchi realized that Pavia was not alone; and that same year he finally published what he had finished of a much larger work begun a decade earlier. Unfortunately, he had not proceeded very far—no more than 115 pages; and his text dwindled off notably as soon as he started down the peninsula from "Insubria." Nor had he managed to free himself from the monographic scheme of the antiquarians: his narrative is constantly interrupted by separate, and often barely relevant, essays *De Lytprandi Regno, De Divi Augustini Tumulo,* et al. Nor had he had time to reorder his material according to its place in a more comprehensive work. An entire chapter under "flora" is thus dedicated to asparagus alone. Still, he wrote enough to prove at least to his own satisfaction that Italy was still associated with Rome as the "Christiani ovilis caput" and that "no kingdom or principality can ever enjoy stability if God is against it." He apparently proved this thesis to the satisfaction of some readers, too; for the first edition (1565) was eventually followed by an expanded second edition (1587).

Together, Alberti and Sacchi provided the inspiration, and much of the information, to those many writers who were looking for shortcuts in order to meet a rapidly growing demand for travelers' guidebooks.[32] Descriptions of single cities, even modern adaptations of the medieval *Mirabilia Urbis,* were no longer adequate at a time when the "grand tour" and the restoration of Rome as the administrative capital of Catholic Christendom were bringing many more, and much better-educated, tourists to Italy. In Italy itself, what Francesco Sansovino launched, first with his *Tutte le cose notabili e belle che sono in Venetia* in 1556 (expanded edition, 1561) and then with his *Ritratto delle più notabili et famose città* in 1575, was complemented, in 1599, by Pietro Bertelli's *Theatrum Urbium Italicarum,* replete with references to Biondo and Alberti and well illustrated with plates. Beyond the Alps, what was inaugurated by the English traveler William Thomas with his *History of Italy* of 1549[33] was complemented in 1587 (Plantin) by the classical scholar Stephanus Vinandus Pighius (Pighe), who added the personal observations he had made while accompanying the son of the duke of Cleve-Jülich in 1574. At the same time, bird's-eye views of individual cities were being transformed into panoramic views, with all the streets and principal buildings clearly marked for the benefit of newcomers; and thanks to such enterprising printers as Paolo Furlani and Donato Rasciotto, they were made available to purchasers all over Italy.[34] Both the maps and the guidebooks in turn prepared for what was to become the greatest of the early predecessors of Baedeker: François Schott's *Itinerarium,* which fortunately came on the market on the eve of the Jubilee of 1600. The *Itinerarium* made such an impression even in Italy that it was soon translated into Italian, filled out for still other "routes" up and down the peninsula by Girolamo de Capugnano and Francesco Bolzetta, illustrated with reduced versions of the larger city maps, and printed over and over again in amended and updated editions throughout the following decades.

The Past

A national history could thus be written by projecting a Caesarian account of "things done in my times" back to the single event in the recent past to which all of them were causally connected. A national history could also be written by arranging the separate histories of all the single parts of the nation in geographical order. But there was still a third way: to go back to a more remote period when what currently consisted merely of a number of distinct political entities had actually been united within a single entity. Modern Italy could then be described as a nation at least to the extent that all its present states were descendants of the same ancestor; and a history of that nation could be justified with reference to the Livian model of a history of a single commonwealth. This kind of national history had been sanctioned a century earlier by Biondo's *Decades*. And in 1561 it still seemed capable of overcoming the limitations of municipal historiography during those ages in the past when the events of a single city were closely interwoven with those of its neighbors. At least so thought CIPRIANO MANENTE, who, in his attempt to reconstruct the history of his native Orvieto, discovered "many things done worthy of memory unrecorded by other writers," not just in Orvieto but also in the rest of what had then been Tuscany and beyond. Since those "things" could not, alas, be presented as anticipations of an autonomous state in the sixteenth century, like Florence or Venice, Manente had to look elsewhere for a principle of unity; and he found it in the Ottonian Empire and its successors, which he treated as if they were solely national and Italian, rather than universal, monarchies.[35]

Unfortunately, Manente's formula rested largely on a happy coincidence: Otto I arrived in Italy in the same year that Orvieto adopted a consular form of government. But how to fit the rise of the Visconti, the career of Castruccio, and the maritime expeditions of the Genoese in between the names of the consuls of Orvieto and the year of reign of a non-Italian "emperor of Italy" was a problem he could solve only by reverting to pure chronicle. And after trying vainly to put meaning into an "empire" during a century and a half in which it withered away even in theory, he simply stopped writing. Still, the formula was a valid one; and in the hands of a master, it proved capable of generating one of the greatest masterpieces of Renaissance historiography, the *De Regno Italiae* by CARLO SIGONIO (1523–84).

Sigonio was neither a statesman, like Guicciardini, nor an administrator of a religious order, like Alberti. Nor was he a municipal historian, like both of them and like Manente. When once he did write a history of one city, its subject was not his native, but his adopted city, and he wrote it not out of patriotic fervor but in response to a request from his patron and close friend, Bishop Paleotti.[36] Rather, Sigonio was an eminent member of what was rapidly becoming a single, pan-Italian academic community. Like his colleagues, he never became attached to the particular city in which he happened to be employed, and he was always willing to move on to any other city that offered him more favorable working and financial conditions.[37] After having learned Greek and Latin letters in his native Modena, and after having studied logic and medicine at the universities of Bologna and Pavia, he worked for a while as secretary to the patriarch of Aquileia before accepting his first teaching position, that of successor to his own teacher, the renowned Hellenist Franciscus Portus of Crete, in Modena. He was appointed professor of classical literature at Venice in 1551, then as successor to his later bitter enemy Francesco Robortello at Padua in 1562, and finally, at double his then current salary, at Bologna, where he remained for the rest of his life. In the course of his academic career, he became a close friend of most of the intellectual and many of the religious and ecclesiastical leaders of post-Tridentine

Italy: Gian Carlo Bosio, the translator of Gregory of Nyssa and archbishop of Brindisi; Girolamo Seripando, general of the Augustinians, archbishop of Salerno, and patron of the Neapolitan historians;[38] the literary theorist Lodovico Castelvetro; the anatomist Gabriele Fallopio; the scholar Onofrio Panvinio.[39] At the same time he managed to consolidate his influence in the academic world by placing his disciples in important university chairs. And he gradually increased his earnings, first by renting rooms in his house to students and then by investing his savings with Bolognese merchants, until he had built up a patrimony of some 12,000 Bolognese *lire*.[40] Not bad for the son of a modest wóol-worker, and a sign that, at least since the admission of humanistic disciplines to the regular curriculum, the universities now provided a means of social mobility similar to that won by the humanist secretaries and artists a century earlier.

Sigonio was originally not a historian either. He had begun his career as a classical philologist—as a specialist, that is, in one of the fields most closely associated with humanism since its beginning.[41] His first major works had been a Latin translation of Demosthenes and an edition of the Roman *Fasti Consulares,* which had earned him his job at Venice, and a life of the younger Scipio, which had almost earned him a job at Pisa. And his reputation thereafter rested largely on his studies of the laws and institutions of ancient Rome, Greece, and Israel. But philology gradually led him to history. After compiling some two hundred dense pages of annotations on that favorite text of so many humanist philologists, Livy, and after successfully correcting, with the help of Roman coins and parallel Greek texts, a good number of passages missed by all his predecessors since Valla, he became convinced of the validity of the platitudes about history that the humanist historians had been repeating over and over for more than a century.[42] History was not the same as annals, he decided, even though it might follow Livy's example in using annals as a source of information. For "history indicates not only what has been done, but why and for what reason it has been done." History was superior to philosophy. For it contained *voluptas* as well as *utilitas.* It was superior to poetry too. For the *varietas* it offered as abundantly as poetry also happened to be true.[43] And it was superior to moral philosophy. For it taught morality not by principles but through the example of great moral men who were also the direct ancestors of the readers—"veterum prudentissimorum hominum egregia instituta, praeclari potentissimorum populorum mores . . ." (Livy: Preface). The study of one historical text then led him to a critical study of many others. Polybius, he found, "seems to neglect the laws of history" with his interminable digressions. Sallust approaches his model Thucydides in "Attic brevity." Tacitus writes with great diligence, but in a style more "grave . . . and harsh than elegant." Ammianus is admirably trustworthy *(optime fide),* but his prose is "inept and utterly barbarous." And Procopius's value as a source must be perceived in spite of his language, which is "more Asiatic than Attic."[44]

If even the ancient historians all revealed defects, or, rather, if even Quintillian and

Trogus had found such defects in their works, then there was no reason why they could not be surpassed in modern times, when the science of historiography had been more fully elaborated. Moreover, if they had furnished their fellow citizens with examples of virtue drawn from their own past, then there was very good reason why the same should be done for Italians of the mid-sixteenth century. Since his fellow citizens had none but histories of single cities to guide them, and since the one previous attempt at a national historiography, Biondo's *Decades,* was now out of date, Sigonio decided to take on the task himself. He purchased a great number of modern editions of ancient and medieval historical texts and at least one edition of almost all the modern historians, transalpine as well as Italian. And he soon accumulated one of the largest libraries of historical scholarship of his day, with some 682 different titles. He also procured copies of the manuscript chronicles of most of the Italian cities and all of the "pontifical, imperial, and royal *diplomata,*" all the contracts, edicts, personal letters, *registri,* and other "more authentic sources" that he or his correspondents could dig out of the archives.[45] He then organized the extensive notes and extracts he had taken from all this material into major periods: from Justinian to Charlemagne, from the dissolution of the Carolingian kingdom to its reconstruction by Otto I, from the investiture controversy to the triumph of Frederick Barbarossa. Before completing the first draft, he was distracted for several years, first by Paleotti's request for a civil and an ecclesiastical history of Bologna, and then by Gregory XIII's request for a continuation of Panvinio's history of the Church universal.[46] But the interruption permitted him to add still more material from several transalpine historians that previously had been unavailable to him: Cuspianus, Nauclerus, Trithemius. It also permitted him to reconsider the history of the national state he had described in the context of his earlier studies of ancient Rome. He therefore set out to collect all the surviving narrative histories of the fourth to sixth centuries and all the nonnarrative sources that might permit him to correct the errors and fill in the gaps he found in them: the homilies of Augustine, the poems of Claudian, inscriptions, and coins. He was thus able, in a separate *Historia de Occidentali Imperio,*[47] to explain the genesis of the Kingdom of Italy as a consequence of the dissolution of the Roman Empire. Rome had fallen, he discovered, because of two major political errors. The first was the transfer of the imperial capital to the East, which gravely compromised the otherwise admirable work of a reconstruction accomplished by Diocletian. The second was the definitive separation of the East from the West at the time of Arcadius and Honorius. The consequence of these errors first became apparent after the abdication of Romulus Augustulus, when Odoacer and Theodoric unintentionally anticipated the kind of political organization that was soon to become common to all Europe. The consequences finally became apparent after the death of Justinian, when the Lombards destroyed once and for all the last attempt to restore the kind of political organization that had prevailed since the time of Augustus.

Sigonio's main purpose in publishing this, the greatest of his works, was patriotism. He intended it, that is, as a stimulus and as a guide to an action for his fellow citizens. And by fellow citizens he meant not just those of his native city, to which he was now bound only by the retirement and vacation house he had bought there, but those of all the cities of Italy, even of Venice, whose chief glory, as he had told his Venetian students in Padua, consisted in protecting the liberties of all the other members of a common *patria*.[48] This purpose could be realized only by a full exposition of the truth. And since the truth could emerge only from faithfully following all the relevant documents, Sigonio did not hesitate to replace the customary orations with long quotations from his sources and even, whenever "verba ipsamet ... inserire non est visum alienum," with entire texts. At times, indeed, the sources threatened to suffocate the narrative that was supposed to be drawn from them. But Sigonio was willing to sacrifice elegance, which he still proclaimed to be an essential element of historiography, in order to accomplish the equally rhetorical aim of persuading his readers of the unquestionable veracity of his theses. And he was fully justified by the results. A few Bolognese might grumble at the obliteration of one of their favorite myths, the one about the destruction of the city by Theodosius.[49] And certain Roman bureaucrats might hold up the publication of the *Historiae Bononiensis* for several years while they worried about its implications for the Temporal Domain. But in the age of Paleotti and Borromeo—in an age, that is, when scholarship was acclaimed as the chief arm of orthodoxy and when scholars were honored as the chief collaborators of the Tridentine bishops—there was not much the censors could do. The Bolognese had to admit that the eminent professor whose salary they paid brought in a good number of students; and the students obviously contributed considerably to the economic prosperity of their city. Similarly, when the *De Regno Italiae* appeared with a dedication to none other than the son of the pope himself, the curial officials simply had to put up with theses that would have shocked Pius V—that Constantine was baptized on his deathbed, in accordance with a practice well documented in the letters of Ambrose, and that Charlemagne owed his imperial crown to the people of Rome rather than to the pope. In fact, the only authorities who succeeded in altering the texts were those of that much-lauded bastion of Italian liberty, the Republic of Venice. By then the author was dead; and the Venetian publisher of the second edition dared not resist their injunction to suppress those words and phrases that seemed to contradict the theses of the official historians of the republic.

Actually, even the Venetian censors were wasting their time. The *De Regno Italiae* was immediately recognized as a definitive work, just as definitive, that is, for the history of all Italy between the seventh and the thirteenth centuries as were the works of Rossi, Ammirato, and Summonte for the histories of their respective cities. So definitive was it, indeed, that even its eighteenth-century editors found it in need only of a few minor additions and corrections; and they decided, rather than to rewrite it, to publish instead the documents upon which it was based. That was a fortunate decision; for the result was the *Rerum Italicarum Scriptores,* which has remained an indispensable instrument for medieval studies ever since.[50] Since the work was definitive, it could be consulted for authoritative answers to disputed questions. But it did not have to be read. Hence, while in Germany, where scholarship was appreciated for its own sake, it was republished four times in the original and once in translation, in Italy it was published only twice. And it was quietly forgotten thereafter for another century and a half. Only then, in the generation of Muratori and Tiraboschi, when it was at last resurrected, edited, and republished along with all the others of Sigonio's works, did it at last succeed in launching the kind of national historiography that Sigonio in his generation had called for in vain.[51]

The limited editorial success of Sigonio's works can also be attributed in part to his mode of presentation. Just at the moment when the vernacularists had triumphed in almost every field of literature, Sigonio persisted in scorning Italian as a regional dialect and in clinging to Latin—an indispensable means, he maintained, of preserving the unity of Christendom.[52] In spite of his admission of the humanist principle of historical causation, moreover, he was unwilling or unable to describe adequately the character of the individual personages from which his events proceeded: even a character so well documented as that of Gregory VII remains a mere shadow. He also proved incapable of giving his relentless succession of events the slightest dramatic quality: even the death of Frederick II, which precipitated the demise of the Kingdom of Italy within a decade of its greatest achievements, is reported in one short, dry sentence.

Still, the main reason for Sigonio's failure to reach a wider audience is probably to be found in his theses, which could not have had much appeal in the late sixteenth century. The Kingdom of Italy never achieved any of the goals expected of political institutions in his own day, Sigonio admitted—neither peace nor stability nor prosperity. Indeed, in its some six centuries of existence it had produced little more than "contention, bloodshed, discord among rulers, sedition among peoples, and various perturbations in the church." It had been imposed by foreign invaders and maintained by violence, often against the will of its subjects. And it had vanished with the last of the Hohenstaufen just as cataclysmically as it had been created by the first of the Lombards. Thus Italy before 1268 was utterly—and happily—dissimilar from Italy after 1494 or 1530. The only connection Sigonio ever succeeded in establishing between the two consisted in a genealogical chart of the Doria family of Genoa. Indeed, most of what he knew about Italy of the sixteenth century consisted of what he read in Giovio and Guicciardini in preparation for a biography of Cardinal Lorenzo Campeggi. And when the patriotism of his greatest modern hero, Andrea Doria, turned out to be wholly municipal, he had to admit that the national state he had studied in the past had not left the slightest trace either on the mentality or on the institutions of the present.[53]

What, then, could possibly be learned from the example of a Berengar or a Henry

IV in a day when "outstanding princes" governed "by high wisdom and singular moderation"? Who could prefer a kind of national unity that opposed the rise of the Italian communes with fire and sword to one in which a beneficent, omnipotent, though happily distant, monarch guaranteed the integrity of what was still left of them? and who would prefer barbarism and desolation to "the splendid conditions of these times, in which, during the pontificate of Gregory XIII, we enjoy a secure and perpetual peace . . . and the flourishing of all the arts?" Certainly not Sigonio. "Illa saepe animum meum cogitatio non iniucunda subierit," he confessed, in words which it would be disrespectful of his memory to translate into any vernacular:

> quanto melior nostra nunc sit, quem avorum, majorumque nostrorum conditio. Nam quam illi aetatem in perpetuis olim barbarorum im-pressionibus, incendiis, direptionibus, principum, civitatumque dissidiis perferendis rerum suarum anxii peregerunt, eam nos quieto nunc animo in ipsis pacis artibus & studiis doctrinae, pietatisque colendis traducimus.

ITALIANS ABROAD AND FOREIGNERS IN ITALY

THE ATTEMPT TO CREATE AN ITALIAN NATIONAL HISTORY WAS THUS ABANDONED SOON after it had inspired two great masterpieces of humanist historiography; and by the end of the century nothing was left of it but a number of tourist guidebooks and manuals, the purpose of which was merely to make more readily accessible information already gathered by others. The reason for this failure is to be found first of all in the inability of the national historians to find in the national past a political organization capable of replacing either the universal state of the ancient Romans or the extended communal state of the modern Venetians as a model worthy of imitation. It is to be found also in their inability to discover in the present any other expression of a united nation than that of an increasingly common language and culture, neither of which was admitted as an organizing principle of historical narration by any of the acceptable models of historiography. But there was still another reason for this failure. Just at the moment when Imperial and Spanish hegemony had succeeded in mitigating some of the more unfortunate consequences of political fragmentation, and just at the moment when a single Italian culture had succeeded in coordinating the various regional and municipal cultures of the peninsula—just at that moment the barriers that had separated Italy spiritually from the rest of Christendom, at least since the advent of humanism, began to crumble. Italians became increasingly aware of what was taking place beyond their increasingly indeterminate borders, and they consequently felt less than ever impelled to search for a common element in what took place inside the borders.

Foreigners in Italy

The events of Italy, particularly such noteworthy events as the Pazzi conspiracy in Florence, had for some time attracted the attention of foreign observers. But after the first foreign army crossed the Alps in 1494, those events could no longer be considered wholly Italian; as non-Italian observers followed the armies, they too began to write about them. The most eminent of these observers, the one Italian historians eventually learned to use as a supplement to the first books of Guicciardini's *Storia d'Italia,* was Philippe de Commynes, or "Argentone," as he was known to his hosts, whose works, after 1544, could be read partially (to the death of Louis IX) in the Italian translation commissioned by Paolo Giovio and completely in the Latin translation of Sleidanus.[1] But there were many others too. Some of these non-Italian historians were rather naive—or at least they were totally unprepared to look beneath the surface of what they observed. One anonymous fellow traveler in the army of Louis XII thought that Alexander VI was a Roman and that the Venetians "held" their mainland and overseas dominions from various feudal overlords. And what he said specifically about Genoa, the city he knew best, demonstrates a complete ignorance of all the Genoese histories.[2] It is no wonder, therefore, that the French governor-general who took over Genoa in 1508 turned to a Genoese emigrant—one who had read the histories and a bit of ancient literature as well and who was fluent in French—to provide his French assistants with a more helpful guide through the jungle of Genoese family rivalries.[3] Similarly, Commynes's unwitting successor as royal historian, the Benedictine poet Jean d'Auton (1466/7–1528) may well have been "simple, droit, bon, doux, très franc, [and] tolérant"; and certainly he took trouble to inform himself at the French court about the origins of the Orléanist claim to the Duchy of Milan after the death of Filippo Maria Visconti. But he was not permitted to see any official documents; and when he got to Italy he proved incapable of seeing anything except the chivalric "oeuvres meritoires de ceulx qui de labeurs recommandables doybent estre celebrés." Hence, his enormous manuscript was put away in the royal library at Blois, where it remained forgotten until it was rediscovered in the still more tolerant nineteenth century.[4] The same is probably true of the diary of Francis I's campaign of 1515 written by his *portier ordinaire:* it is still in manuscript except for a selection of passages published in 1890.[5]

Some observers, on the other hand, confined their reports to the specific events of which they had been eyewitnesses. Conrad Wenger (d. 1501), a canon of the Church of Brixen, described in somewhat pompous Latin the heroic *gesta* "inclyte Germanice nationis" during the Tyrolian campaigns of Archduke Sigismond of Austria against the Venetians.[6] An anonymous German and a Spanish friar named Juan de Oznayo described the triumph of the Imperial army, of which they were members, at the Battle of Pavia—the former rather simply, the latter with some pretense of elegance and thoroughness.[7] Michael Coccinus (b. 1482), a lecturer in humanities at the University of Tübingen who had lived in Modena before 1505 and in Venice after 1508, described what he himself had seen at the siege of Padua and at the Bentivoglio restoration in Bologna. And he described the sack of Brescia and the Battle of Ravenna from the official reports hè had read while a guest of the German governor of Verona. He did so, indeed, with such accuracy that his account of the latter is almost identical with that of the Milanese historian Giovan Andrea Prato. And his chronicle was duly incorporated, after separate editions in 1512 and 1544, in the *Chronicon Uspergense* published at Basel in 1569.[8] Similarly, the Fribourg Franciscan Anton Palliard kept a chronicle of the adventures of his fellow countrymen at home and beyond the Alps from 1499 to 1543; and notwithstanding the unintelligible local dialect in which it was written, it was included in the great compilation of another Franciscan, Franz Katzengran, in the following century. At the same time, at the other end of Switzerland, Ulrich Campell (or Durich Chiampel in Romansh—d. 1576), the son of a soldier in the Italian wars from 1516 to 1531, described the struggles of the Italians of the Valtellina against their former Milanese landlords after the annexation of the area by the Grisons. After settling down as pastor of the Reformed church in Süs in 1548, he also described the activities of the Italian religious refugees who, from 1542 on, gradually turned their hosts from warriors into theologians.[9]

Somewhat more attentive to the affairs of Italy was the French captain Blaise de Monluc, who had been lured there at the beginning of his fifty-five-year military career by "the stories that circulated [in France] about the wonderful feats of arms being performed there" and who returned with almost every successive French campaign between the invasion of Naples in 1528 and the siege of Siena of 1555, which he directed and described in detail.[10] Still more attentive were his Spanish counterparts, since, after all, many more of them served in Italy. The Gran Capitán, Gonzalo Hernandes de Córdoba, was a hero for both nations, as one of his aides realized when, upon his return to Spain in 1550, he read Domenichi's translation of Giovio's biography; and his equally anonymous successor extended the narrative back a century to the arrival of Córdoba's predecessor in Naples, Alfonso I d'Aragona. The house of Aragon had ruled in southern Italy as well as in eastern Spain, as Jerónimo Zurita (b. 1512) discovered after an exhaustive search through the archives of Aragon and Castile, to which he alone among historians of his age had been admitted. After complementing his archival research in Spain with a document- and chronicle-hunting expedition in Naples and Sicily, and after learning about the techniques of historiography by reading the Roman historians, he realized that Naples was as essential a member of the scattered empire of his princes as were Aragon and Catalonia. Accordingly, he devoted to Alfonso's campaigns in Naples between 1431 and 1451 all 488 pages of volume VI of his immense *Annales de la corona de Aragón*.[11]

Except for Zurita, whose rather chaotic mass of information became an indispensable reference book for the later Neapolitan historians, none of these writings circulated in Italy, and many were not even published in the original. Such was the fate even of some histories that had much to say about Italy in the context of the empire of Charles V. The history of the reign by Juan Jinés de Sepúlveda, who had taken Bruni and Giovio as his models, was not published until the eighteenth century. The vast, if chaotic, *Crónica* of the decade of the 1530s by Pedro Girón was not published until 1964. And the works of Alonso de Santa Cruz were never published at all.[12] Much more fortunate was the work of ALFONSO ULLOA (b.c. 1530), largely because of the role he assumed as chief cultural intermediary between Italy and the Iberian peninsula.[13] Ulloa possessed both of the qualifications demanded in Italy of a writer of contemporary history: experience and letters. The first he had acquired as secretary to the Spanish ambassador in Venice and as a soldier in the service of the

governor of Milan. The second he had acquired as an associate of Girolamo Ruscelli's literary circle in Venice and as an employee of the famous and productive
literary firm of the Gioliti de' Ferrari in Venice. Indeed, putting these two qualifications together may have been responsible for his tragic end. A charge apparently of
dealing in illicit publications brought upon him a death sentence from the very
government that he himself had praised as "the preserver of the liberty and reputation of Italy"; and the most that his patron, a wealthy resident Portuguese merchant,
and his sovereign, Philip II, could obtain in his behalf was a commutation of the
sentence to life imprisonment. He also gained for himself still another essential
qualification, one which was rather rare for a Spaniard at a time when the members
of both nations studiously refused to learn each other's language. He acquired an
impeccable command of Italian. He forthwith sought to remedy what he considered
to be the greatest obstacle to better understanding between his native and his
adopted country by composing a guide for Italians to the correct pronunciation of
Spanish.

Consequently, Ulloa was able to make an important contribution to current
Italian historiography in his own name. But since he was by birth neither a Venetian
nor an Italian, he felt no obligation to observe the geographical limits of either
national or municipal historiography. His historical biography of his second employer, the general and governor of Milan, Ferrante Gonzaga, included the great
actions of all the other princes and generals of all the nations involved in the wars of
Italy after 1525. For he had to prove that Ferrante was "the greatest captain in many
years, not only of Italy but of all Europe."[14] His biographies of the emperors
Charles V and Ferdinand I extended his vision from the frontiers of the Ottoman
Empire to Lisbon—and to Africa and the Americas.[15] The various commentaries
that eventually made up his *Historia di Europa* covered even the Turks, as well as the
other great enemies of His Catholic Majesty, the Queen of England and the Prince of
Orange. A history capable of doing for modern men what statues of their ancestors
had done for the ancients demanded an analysis of "the internal workings of the
spirit, the discourses, the counsels, and the prudence" of all the participants in the
events described—those of the Prince of Condé as well as those of the Duke of
Alba.[16]

Moreover, since war, and therefore interesting events, had vanished from Italy
after the Peace of Cateau-Cambrésis, Ulloa was obliged to look to those other parts
of the world where "the diabolical enemy of the human seed and the sower of weeds
and discord" could be more successful—namely, in Tripoli, Hungary, and
Antwerp. That he occasionally misrepresented the causes—that he blamed the personal ambition of Egmont and Horne for the revolt of the Netherlands rather than
Philip II's decision "to reduce [the various] provinces and estates to [a single] kingdom like Naples" did not bother his readers, who would have come to the same
conclusions from reading his sources. And most of his works accordingly went
through several editions within a few years of the publication of the first.

More important still, Ulloa was able to introduce to Italians the best of contemporary Spanish and Portuguese historiography. After 1562 they could read in their own language the first two decades of Joâo de Barros's history of the Portuguese expeditions to the Far East, after 1563 Agustín de Zárate's history of the conquest of Peru, after 1566 the first part of Anton Beuter's history of ancient and medieval Spain, after 1571 the history of Columbus's voyages that was attributed to his son, after 1577 the first seven books of Fernâo Lopes de Castanheda's history of the East Indies. Ulloa thus encouraged still further the program proposed previously by the Italian popularizers of great works: the translation of recent foreign historians as well as of the more common ancient historians. Translation constitutes neither a travesty of the original nor an encouragement to laziness, explained Mambrino Roseo da Fabiano in his version of Antonio de Guevara's life of Marcus Aurelius—even if the original is written, as Giovio claimed this one was, by "a friar in refectorial Latin." If something of value is contained in a language known only to a few, it would be "against the divine law of charity to one's neighbors" not to make it accessible also to the many who otherwise could not read it.[17] Some texts were replete with incredible marvels, admitted Remigio Nannini, who was a bit disconcerted by Olaus Magnus's stories about high tides in Iceland and wars fought on ice in Norway. But even they could be "full of varied and wonderful things"; and, after all, Scandinavians would probably be just as surprised about what were accepted as ordinary occurences in the Mediterranean.[18] Lodovico Domenichi agreed. "An infinite desire to know many things" is innate in all men, he pointed out in his preface to Theodoros Spandougino's *Dell'origine de' principi turchi,* not just in those who know Latin or who can travel abroad.[19] Agostino di Cravaliz made the same point in his translation of López de Gómara. The style might not be wholly consonant with humanist standards, he said; but the matter regards "a people [hitherto] unknown to us, [a people] with religion, customs, and military organization very different from ours," and hence a legitimate object of our curiosity. So also did Camillo Camildi in his version of Peter Cornejo's history of the wars in Flanders. Other Italians too, he thought, might well be inspired by the example of one adventurous Venetian, who left his peaceful, and hence unadventurous, homeland to "display his valor and to gain proficiency in the profession of arms" in those happier parts of the world where there was still some action.[20]

Thus translations multiplied—from the commentary on the recent campaigns of Charles V by Luis de Avila y Zuñiga commissioned by the Imperial ambassador to Venice in 1548 to the account of the fourteenth-century campaigns of Aegidius Alburnoz by Sepúlveda in 1521 (Bologna);[21] from the first part of the *Mémoires* of Philippe de Commynes, which were translated first in 1544 and then again in 1610, to the *Historia di Mexico* (1555) and the *Historia generale delle Indie occidentali* (1556) by Francisco López de Gómara, of which eleven editions appeared between 1557 and 1576;[22] from Niccolò Liburnio's translation of Fernando Cortes (1524) to Agostino de Cravaliz's translation of Cieza de León (1555—and five subsequent editions) to

Giuseppe Horologgi's [Orologgi] translation of André Thévet's *Francia antartica* (1584). The most popular of all was, apparently, the history of China by Juan González de Mendoza, which appeared in nineteen editions between the first edition of 1585 (Venice) and the end of the century, and which made a great impact upon the Italian political philosophers of the age.[23] One of these translations was incorporated directly into the corpus of Italian historiography: Pedro Mexia's (1446–1552) *Historia imperial y cesaria*, first published at Seville in 1547. LODOVICO DOLCE added his own life of Charles V—or rather his own reworking of the life by Ulloa—to the translation of the whole text he published in Venice in 1561; and GIROLAMO DE'BARDI added the lives of Charles's successors through the early years of Rudolf II in the new edition he in turn published in 1583 and again in 1589.

The greatest of all the translation projects was the one planned and carried out by the father of all subsequent European travel literature, GIOVAN BATTISTA RAMUSIO (1485–1557). Ramusio's inspiration seems to have come not from his own occasional trips around Europe as a minor Venetian civil servant but from his association with the leading humanists of Venice and Padua—Pietro Bembo, Andrea Navagero, and above all the philosopher and theorist of history Girolamo Fracastoro, to whom he dedicated the first volume of his *Delle navigationi et viaggi* in 1550.[24] His purpose was to provide "nostri studiosi di geografia" with a full and correct modern version of the now clearly inadequate and incorrect works of the ancient geographers. Accordingly, he selected his texts, often after painstaking explorations, solely with regard to their content, and he accompanied his translations with his own philological and scientific observations and with parallel passages from the ancients. For example, he appended Arrian's letter to the emperor Hadrian about the Black Sea to the rather inelegant, if detail-packed, diary of the Imperial ambassador to Moscow, Sigismund, Freiherr von Herberstein.[25] He thus drew the attention of the Italians to the many previously neglected travel accounts that had been written by their own compatriots since the age of Marco Polo. Better yet, he made available to them a wide selection of contemporary Iberian travel literature: parts of Barros and Tomé Pires on the Far East, much of Duarte Barbosa on Africa and Arabia, most of Pierre Crignon on Sumatra, of Nunno de Gusman and Francisco Xerez on Peru, all of Jacques Cartier and Gonzalo Fernándes de Oviedo y Valdés on America, and all but the first part (which "so far we have not been able to locate") of Fernando Cortes's account of his own achievements in Mexico. His work found such favor that the first enormous folio volume alone was republished five times before 1613; and it was adopted as a model for the still more ambitious program launched shortly afterward by Richard Eden and Richard Hakluyt in England.

Indeed, there seems to have been only one exception to the pattern of translation on behalf of the recognized goals of humanist historiography, namely, the one undertaken by an anonymous Italian refugee in Geneva (Giulio Cesare Paschalli?: Rhodes) of one of the greatest and most influential works of sixteenth-century historiography, the *Comentarii* of Johannes Sleidanus,[26] first published in 1556. Sleidanus had earned the gratitude of Italian historians by translating Froissart and Commynes into a language they could understand.[27] He now offered them an abundance of information about the events of northern Europe collected during his long career as a diplomatic agent in France and Germany and cast in a form consciously adopted from the Latin classics. And he spared them the annoyance of having to put up with his attempt to revive the long discredited Four Monarchies theory by confining it to a student manual he published separately. But Sleidanus also happened to be a convert to Lutheranism—so sincere a convert, indeed, that he all but ignored the Zwinglian and Calvinist forms of Protestantism, about which he was nonetheless well informed. And he made no effort in writing to disguise what he had proclaimed orally before the emperor himself—namely, his conviction that civilization had now fled the lands corrupted by the Papacy and the "papal council" and had taken refuge in the Lutheran states of Germany. The purpose of the translation was thus religious and theological, not historiographical. It was distributed clandestinely without any hint of its real place of publication, Geneva. And except for the bits of specific information it provided those few historians who managed to procure a copy, it bore fruit in Italy chiefly as a source for Paolo Sarpi's historical-theological condemnation of the Council of Trent.

The task of the translators was facilitated, during the course of the century, by the rapid diffusion of the works of the Italian historians beyond the Alps. The first French humanists—Robert Gaguin, Guillaume Budé, and Guillaume Fichet—were already familiar enough with Biondo's scheme of a thousand-year "middle age" to adopt it, in spite of its inappropriateness to the history of their own country.[28] Jean Bodin, a half-century later, was thoroughly familiar with the latest works of Italian historiography, of which he presented an accurate and critical review in his *Methodus;* and in his subsequent *De la République* (II, 1) he used Sabellico exactly as he used Livy—as an authoritative source of information about the state whose history Sabellico had written. By 1576, at least one French historian, Bernard Girard Du Haillan, had completely mastered the Italian art of prefacing historical works with a string of platitudes about the utility of history:

> History is necessary to all sorts of men . . . It is a faithful and bold counselor of princes and accurately indicates their duties, clearly showing them the faults of their predecessors. . . . It shows subjects their duties toward their princes . . . and incites great courage . . . by promises of glory and praise. . . .[29]

This diffusion was in turn encouraged by the work of transalpine printers, who published the works of contemporary Italian historians either in Latin or in vernacular translations. Machiavelli's *Istorie fiorentine* appeared in French in 1577 and in English in 1595. Johannes Badius Ascensius of Paris introduced Bracelli's history of

Genoa to France as early as 1520.[30] Pietro Perna of Basel introduced a whole series of texts to the whole of northern Europe: Biondo's complete works and Sabellico's *Enneades* in the 1530s, Guicciardini, Panormita, Fazio, and Pontano in the 1560s, Giovio, Sigonio, and Collenuccio in the 1570s.[31] Ulloa and Pedro Barrantes Maldonado introduced Giovio into Spain; and their efforts were accompanied by those of the Spanish translators of Galeazzo Capella's history of Milan (Valencia, 1536), Alessandro Andrea's history of the Carafa War, and Mambrino Roseo's continuation of Collenuccio's history of Naples (both Madrid, 1589)—all works of considerable interest to Spanish readers. Finally, in 1600, the Frankfurt printer Andreas Cambierius published a vast anthology of texts concerning the early history of Italy, the *Italiae Illustratae Scriptores,* which in turn set an example for the still greater anthologies of the later seventeenth and early eighteenth centuries.

Stimulated, then, by contact with the work of their Italian contemporaries and, as humanism spread to the rest of Europe, with the historiographical models of antiquity, foreign historians soon began writing according to the same standards demanded of historians in Italy. The Venetian edition (1546) of Sepúlveda's *De Correctione Anni Mensiumque Romanorum* contained only a few minor errors, noted Cardinal Gasparo Contarini after taking time off from his many obligations in the Roman Curia to read it; "in many parts it is [indeed] illustrious." Martin Cromer's *De Origine et Rebus Gestis Polonorum* of 1558 followed Italian literary models successfully enough to warrant Robortello's praise of it as worthy of Caesar.[32] Notwithstanding his tendency to attribute historical phenomena directly to God, Barros followed the precepts of Cicero, noted Ulloa, and he organized his text by decades, like Livy.[33] Notwithstanding his rather unhumanistic training as a theologian, Beuter took all his information from such impeccably humanist sources as Silius Italicus, Livy, Herodotus, Eusebius—and, alas, Annio's "Beroso."[34] Even the works of such nonhumanist writers as Claude Champier and Gilles Corrozet, whose tales about the foundation of Sens and Lyon sound like parodies of popular Italian foundation stories, appeared at least to the papal copyright officials to be serving "the general utility of all students of history," just like all the others of Michele Tramezzino's popular publications.[35]

Indeed, two non–Italian historians went so far in their efforts to conform to Italian standards that they wrote directly in Italian: MAURO ORBINI and GIACOMO DI PIETRO LUCCARI of Ragusa (Dubrovnik).[36] True, they were encouraged in this decision by the rapid adoption of contemporary Italian culture in their native city just at the time when the ethnic composition of its population was becoming increasingly Slavic. Hence, neither of them had much trouble acquiring a thorough familiarity with the classics of ancient and Italian humanist historiography. Orbini did much of his research in Italian libraries; and Luccari's numerous citations actually prove just the opposite of his prefatory thesis: that "the human intellect in this all-but-last age of the universe had been [so] weakened . . . that there are very few poets, very few orators, and almost no historians left." But their real motive was rhetorical: by adopting the leading modern language of culture, just as Italian historians had once adopted the language of Livy and Sallust, they could more effectively magnify the "glory" of the Slavic nation (which, alas, had yet very few historians of its own) and correct the "innumerable errors and many lies" contained in the works of such misinformed modern Italian historians as Francesco Sansovino. It is unfortunate that their books were published too late to permit the humanist cosmographers to review critically their main theses: that modern Slavs were descendants of the ancient Illyrians, that they originally came, like the Goths, from Scandinavia, that their ancestors had beaten the Romans and the Greeks on every occasion, that they had refused to accept Arianism or to betray Piero Soderini to Julius II because of their innate religiosity, that Ragusa "has always been and still is flourishing, with a great number of men most excellent in arms, letters, and government." It is even more unfortunate that their books appeared too late to permit Italian historians to take advantage of the abundance of new information about the Balkans drawn from Slavic language sources that Luccari had uncovered with considerable difficulty during his diplomatic missions into the interior.

Obviously, Italian historians were not wholly dependent upon what was published in one or another of their own states. Pietro Bembo, for instance, did not have to consult any books at all in order to fill up the some twenty pages of Book VI of his history of Venice dedicated to the flora, fauna, and geography of the New World: he obtained the information he needed either orally from Navagero, then Venetian ambassador to Spain, or from his correspondence with Oviedo. After all, on the trade routes of the age, Naples was as close to Seville as it was to Florence, and Milan was as close to Basel as it was to Venice. And although Italian book buyers were eventually forced to observe confessional boundaries, they never paid any attention to linguistic or political boundaries, particularly when the books they bought were written in what was still the official language of European men of letters, Latin. Thus when Mauro Orbini went to Pesaro in search of material for his history of the Slavs, he found not only all the products of the Italian presses but also (to judge from his references) such relative rarities as the histories of Saxony by David Chytraeus, of Bohemia by Jan Dubravius, and of the "Aquilonic Regions" by Albertus Crantius. And when Lodovico Della Chiesa was writing his history of Piedmont, he apparently had no trouble obtaining the works of Robert Gaguin, Joannes Cuspianus, Juan de Mariana, François de Belleforest ("Belloforesto"), and Papire Masson ("Papiro Massone").[37]

Still, the Italian translators and publishers were at least responsible for encouraging the spread of non-Italian historiography in Italy. It is thanks in part to them that Lodovico Dolce could insert so many and such varied entries in his *Giornale* of 1572. that Anton Francesco Doni could double the size of his *Libreria* between the first (1550) and second (1557) editions, and that Michele Poccianti could approach, in his

Catalogus of 1589, the volume and the comprehensiveness of the bibliographical dictionaries then being published beyond the Alps.[38]

Italians in the East

While foreigners came to Italy, so Italians continued to go abroad, just as their ancestors had for some three centuries before them, and to bring back information concerning the lands they had visited. Indeed, as Iosafa Barbaro pointed out, "the world today would be totally unknown if it had not been opened up by the commerce and navigation of the Venetians." Italians also continued to write about what they had seen, as they had since the days of Marco Polo, whose writings, though neglected in the fifteenth century, were rehabilitated and republished by Ramusio in the mid-sixteenth century.[39] This tradition was given added stimulation by the intervention of one of the leading humanists of the age, Poggio Bracciolini, the historian of Florence. While accompanying Eugenio IV in Florence, Poggio happened to meet a merchant from Chioggia named NICCOLÒ DE'CONTI (before 1385–1469), who had come to the papal court seeking absolution for having, during his absence from Italy, conformed outwardly to Islam. Niccolò had left home in 1424, traveled from Damascus to Hormuz, down the west coast and up the east coast of India, then to Java, Borneo, and Cochin-China; and he had returned home twenty-five years later with two sons by an Indian wife to settle down as procurator of the church of San Francesco and as a magistrate and roving ambassador for his native city. Poggio quickly realized that the "admirable things" he heard from Niccolò were just what he needed to supplement his collection of examples of "the variety of things" found in the works of the ancients. He therefore transcribed Niccolò's account into good Latin, producing a work that was eventually to be recognized as "the most lucid account of Indian manners and customs to be prepared by a European since Megasthenes."[40] The Latin text was then translated into Italian and circulated around Italy; and it was in this form that it came into the hands of Columbus a half-century later.[41]

Humanism also provided travelers with literary forms capable of raising their travel accounts to the rank of literature. Ugolino Pisani (1380–1459) of Parma could think of no other way of recording his impressions of "Dacia," which he was one of the first Italians to visit, than making notes in the margin of his copy of Aristotle.[42] Cristoforo Buondelmonti compared his observations of the Greek Islands in 1420 with what Ptolemy had said about them in antiquity. But he did not bother to compare his impressions with what any of his contemporaries had seen; and he left his observations in a literary form that his editor was to find barbarous even five centuries later. Similarly Bartolomeo da li Sonetti (d. 1485) left his experiences in contemporary Greece in the form of a letter to the doge, which was not then deemed worthy of publication, in spite of—or perhaps because of—his efforts to decorate it with irrelevant quotations from Vergil.[43] Ciriaco d'Ancona, who traveled almost solely for scholarly reasons, was better trained as a writer, and the vivacity of the descriptions of the places he visited probably contributed to the interest aroused by the inscriptions he found in those places and provoked the multiplication of copies of his notebooks during the next half-century.[44] GIORGIO INTERIANO of Genoa knew enough about standards of good writing to seek help from Pontano and Aldo Manuzio in finding someone capable of revising his rather rough account of the Christians he had found in the regions beyond the Black Sea.[45] But the authors of the two principal pilgrim guidebooks of the sixteenth century remained wholly innocent of humanism. Like all their predecessors for over a millennium, NOÈ BIANCHI (d. 1565) in 1527 and GIOVANNI ZUALLARDO in 1588 were interested solely in getting to the Holy Land as fast and as piously as possible. And what they saw of the Greek-speaking lands they traveled through on the way back and forth was influenced neither by a desire for accuracy nor by a realization of its past and present importance.[46]

Some travelers, on the other hand, realized that their observations might serve a purpose higher than that merely of satisfying a "natural instinct" for "new things." The lands of the Aqqoyunlu dynasty, for instance, which they referred to indiscriminately as "Persia," were not just an object of curiosity or a source of profit. "Persia" was a potential, and occasionally an active, ally against the Ottomans. It was therefore still as worthy of careful attention to its present and past political conditions as it had been in the days of Herodotus. Even though he admitted to being something less than "accomplished in the art of writing," an anonymous merchant who spent eight years and eight months there in the first decade of the century felt obliged to adhere to the "pure truth." And he claimed to possess the fundamental requisite for being able to do so: a knowledge of Turkish, Arabic, and *Azemina* (Persian). He thus took care to describe in great detail all the places he had visited—the city of Vitlis, the castle inhabited by Armenians on an island in the "Great Salt Sea" (Lake Von), the palace at Tabriz—as well as the customs of the people he met, particularly of the various Christian sects in the Levant. And he did so in order better to explain the campaigns in Karamon ("Caramania") and Erzincan, which he had witnessed, in the context of the previous Aqqoyunlu-Ottoman wars since 1472.[47]

GIOVAN MARIA ANGIOLELLO of Vicenza (1451/2–after 1524) was even more precise in relating his observations—although it is difficult to tell from Ramusio's edition just what is his and what is rather Ramusio's own reworking of his text with other sources. But since what happened could be better explained by a chronological succession of recent events, he began not with his own experiences but with the attempt of the last emperor of Trebizond to maintain the independence of his state by marrying his daughter to the Aqqoyunlu king. And his narrative moves from place to place according to the progress not of his own travels but of the civil wars among the sons of the previous king which ultimately thwarted the emperor's project. By effacing himself, Angiolello managed to create a hero comparable to those of his colleagues in Italy: the Aqqoyunlu general Yusuf ("Iusef"), who had commanded the spearhead of an Aqqoyunlu thrust into Ottoman territory.[48]

The two principal Venetian ambassadors to "Persia" were even more aware of the political importance of their travels. IOSAFA, or GIOSAFAT BARBARO (1413–94) knew that the information he gathered during his voyages around the Black Sea in the years after 1436 could do much more than provide "consolation for those who are amused by reading about new things"—like the fascinating story about the Venetian merchants who tried to dig a treasure out of a frozen mound near the Volga. "I leave it to the reader to decide whether this is possible or probable," he said. "[All I can say] is that it is true." But much of what he wrote about the fur trade between Moscow and Frankfurt-an-der-Oder and about the commercial relations between Persia and India after his retirement from his subsequent government commissions as *provveditore* in Albania and Rovigo in 1485 was immediately recognized as valuable by Venetian statesmen and merchants alike. AMBROSIO CONTARINI realized that the question of how he had gotten to Tabriz after the Turks blocked the Levant route was as important—"dilettevole & utile a' nostri discendenti"—as the question of what he found out upon his arrival. Hence, he preferred a diary-chronicle format. And the result indeed was an account exciting enough to appeal to the most jaded amateur of humanistic *rerum memorabilium* collections. Whoever had the courage to repeat the author's seventeen-month (February 1473–August 1474) trip to Tabriz by way of Nürnberg, Poznan, the Black Sea, and Georgia, and whoever had the ambition to undertake the even more hazardous trip back—by boat across the Caspian Sea, by horseback to Moscow—would certainly be happy to learn how a distinguished patrician cooks his meals in the middle of the treeless, uninhabited plains of Ukraine[49]

Still, Contarini's main purpose was to determine the possibility of establishing a permanent alliance with the Aqqoyunlu king, "Assimbeio," or Uzun Hasan ("Ussun Cassan"). And that purpose was still more fully pursued by his successor, CATERINO ZENO.[50] Zeno was well prepared for his mission. His father had been a merchant in the Levant and had traveled as far as Mecca. His aunt was a princess of Trebizond married to Uzun Hasan. One of his sons remained as a businessman in Damascus until after 1512. He was therefore already familiar with the country; and he knew enough of the language to decorate his prose with transliterations of technical terms and place names. Zeno agreed with Contarini. As the Aqqoyunlu domain was an eastern version of the balanced constitution represented by Venice in the West, so Uzun Hasan was "a warlike, valiant, and above all most magnificently liberal" prince. Unfortunately, Uzun Hasan lost a few crucial battles, and he thus failed to "restore" "Persian" rule over Egypt and Anatolia (and, by implication, restore Venetian rule over its portion of the spoils of 1204). The death of the last of his direct successors in 1501 was followed by a bloody civil war that reminded

Italians of the fights between the Guelfs and the Ghibellines. Thus Contarini's hopes in the long run came to naught.

Still, even though it could not be counted on to help defeat the Turks, Persia could still be used as an important trade route to India. And that route, once they had recovered from the double shock of the Portuguese expedition around the Cape of Good Hope and the War of the League of Cambrai, the Venetians were very anxious to exploit. They were thus particularly interested in the adventures of LUDOVICO DI VARTHEMA, the Bolognese merchant who traveled to India, picking up a knowledge of Arabic as he went, by way of Mecca, Yemen, Hormuz, and the deserts of southern Persia, and who returned by way of the Cape after being knighted by the Portuguese government in recognition of his services to the viceroy. Everyone else was interested, too, at least to judge from the number of editions of his account: five in Italian after the first edition of Rome in 1510, six in German, four in Spanish.[51] His example was followed, in 1529, by a certain ALOIGI DI MESSER GIOVANNI, who dwelt at length on "the marvelous islands that produce gold and precious stones," and a decade later by another otherwise unknown Venetian who, as a captive of the Turks since 1537, witnessed the defeat of the Turkish fleet in the Indian Ocean in 1540. They in turn were followed later in the century, when the eastern trade had again become more profitable than the sea route, by GASPARO BALBI, who organized a commercial expedition from Aleppo to Goa, Burma, and Ceylon from 1579 to 1589.[52]

Most of these later travelers were concerned principally with commerce. Even Balbi, who described Baghdad in detail because he thought it was the same city as ancient Babylon, filled most of his pages with notes about weights, measures, exchange rates, and the location of bandits. But one of them, GIOVAN THOMASO MINADOI of Rovigo, was a physician, one who had spent some nine years in the service of "many *bassa,* ambassadors, and other great men, Persian as well as Turkish," and who had methodologically gathered information both from his clients and from the Venetian consuls and their well-connected interpreter in Syria. Minadoi was also a man of some learning, "Vir ingenio promptus & in optimis cum Graecis tum Latinis scriptoribus perlegendis non modice exercitatus," as his brother and apologist put it.[53] He was therefore interested in correlating modern place names with those given in Strabo, Ptolemy, Herodotus, Procopius, and Zonaras. What had most attracted his attention in the East, however, was the fate of the Levantine Christians, "a people once celebrated for their nobility and famous in all ages for their learning, now either expelled from their homes or forced to live as the vile servants of the enemies of Christ." In order, therefore, to correct the misinformation about the East in general that marred most of the news bulletins *(avvisi)* he found circulating in Rome after his return, and in order to disabuse Western Christians of the hopes they placed in maintaining a balance of power among the persecutors of their Eastern brethren, he went back to the beginning of the most recent war. The progress of the war, he admitted, had not been totally disappointing. The current shah, Isma'il, was well informed about Ottoman military organization, and he had settled the question of religious conflict in his own dominions by imposing the Shi'ite sect of Islam upon all his subjects. Still, the long-run prospects were anything but encouraging. And he concluded that nothing short of a crusade, that favorite project of the Counter Reformation popes, could avert a total disaster.[54]

Those whom Westerners called "Persians" may have been distant and uncertain allies. But the Ottoman Turks were close and certain enemies. Of this Italians gradually became aware, notwithstanding the frequently successful attempts of the Venetians in establishing profitable diplomatic and commercial relations with them. This awareness grew as the last Hellenic despotates, then the autonomous Italian states, and finally most of the Venetian and Genoese possessions in the Aegean surrendered, one after the other, to the new masters of the East. And when parts of the Italian mainland itself—Puglia in the 1480s, Friuli and the Veneto in 1472, 1477, and 1499—were subjected to the murder or enslavement of their inhabitants and the systematic pillage of their property, this awareness turned into hysteria.

Still, Italians were very slow to realize that an effective defense against their enemies depended upon the possession of reliable information concerning their aims, resources, and methods. Cardinal Bessarion (1403–72) could provide them with some reasons for resurrecting the long discredited ideal of a Latin crusade against the infidels. After all, as a native of Trebizond and a former resident of Constantinople and Mistra in their last days, he had been one of the Ottoman's most illustrious victims. But Bessarion was principally interested in saving and transmitting to his hosts the cultural heritage of ancient Greece; and consequently his orations were valued, in the late fifteenth century when they were first delivered and in the late sixteenth century when they were republished, more for their rhetorical value than for their informative qualities.[55] Similarly, Francesco Filelfo, took the trouble, in 1451, to transcribe parts of an account written by the Armenian king Hethum (or Hayton) of his voyage to Mongolia in 1354–55. But he did not bother to corroborate what he transcribed with the information supplied him by another well-known Greek immigrant, Theodore of Gaza; and while Hethum's text was not published until 1562, Filelfo's was never published at all.[56] Enea Silvio Piccolomini, the most dedicated crusader of his age, sought to become somewhat better informed; and he turned for assistance to the two most authoritative experts then resident in Rome. NIKOLAOS SEKOUNDINOS (Saguntinus) of Euboia (1402–64) wrote from personal experience: he had spent some eighteen months as a prisoner of the Turks before escaping to Italy and had accompanied Venetian diplomatic missions to the sultan thereafter.[57] LAMPO, or LAMPUGNINO, BIRAGO of Milan (d. 1472) wrote as a research scholar. What he wrote was based on interviews with Greek refugees and on whatever was then available in Greek-language sources.[58] Both of them were also humanists. Sekoundinos translated Arrian and Plutarch's *De Civili Institutione* into

Latin while serving as secretary to the Council of Ferrara-Florence and as a diplomatic agent for the Venetians and the Papacy. Birago, a pupil of Francesco Filelfo, served as secretary to Filippo Maria Visconti and the Ambrosian Republic before joining the Roman Curia in 1453; and he was best known for a century thereafter as the author of the authoritative Latin translations of Dionysius of Halicarnassus and Plutarch's *Moralia*. The short treatises of both men were therefore eloquent as well as competent. But except for Enea Silvio himself, who incorporated some of their material into his geographical-historical surveys, no one paid much attention to them. The first *(De Origine et Rebus Gestis Turcarum)* was published only a century later, and then in Germany rather than in Italy (Vienna, 1551; Basel, 1556); and the other was not published until the twentieth century.

Thus even as late as the turn of the century, Italian historians were still dependent for their knowledge of the Turks on a very limited number of sources. The long excursus in Sabellico's *Enneades* drew upon a memorial written for Sixtus IV by his legate Martino Segono in 1480 and, for a few details, upon the long account of the decline and fall of Byzantium written by Sekoundinos's acquaintance, the Athenian historian Laonikos Chalkokondylis (1423–90). The somewhat longer *De Origine Turcarum* inserted by Giovan Battista Egnazio in his biographical history of the Roman emperors[59] drew upon the diplomatic reports recorded by Sanudo and upon the reform projects presented to the despot of the Peloponnesus by Giorgios Gemistos. Neither of them seems to have read the informative *Tractatus de Moribus, Conditionibus et Nequicia Turcorum* of the former Turkish slave Georgius de Hungaria, even though it was written in Rome in 1475–80. Certainly neither of them had read the *Reisebuch* of the Bavarian Hans Schiltberger, since it was written in German, a language few Italians could read. Neither of them read the very informative *Pereginationes* of Bernhard von Breydenbach, although it was written in Latin, twice published in Germany after the first edition of 1486, and translated subsequently into French and Spanish. Neither of them seems to have heard of the fact-finding mission of Bertranon de la Broguière of 1423–33. Indeed, Egnazio did not bother even to consult the text of Chalkokondylis, which Sabellico had lent him, although he must have been aware of its importance since the author's cousin Demetrios was well known in Italy as one of the chief associates of Marsilio Ficino in the Platonic Academy. Nevertheless, their sources were at least more numerous than those of Pomponio Leto, whose brief explanation of the rise of Islam had been based mostly on his own imagination.[60] And they were apparently sufficient in the opinion of the German humanist Cuspianus; for he copied long passages from both Sabellico and Egnazio while preparing the memorandum on the Turks that he later inserted into his *De Caesaribus* of 1540.[61]

Gradually, however, much more precise information became more readily available. The eulogy of the Venetian admiral at Negroponte (Euboia), Pietro Mocenigo, by the enthusiastic Venetian patriot from Dalmatia, CORIOLANO CIPPICO (c.

1425–75), provided a very thorough description of the organization and tactics of the Turkish fleet; and it was written in impeccably humanist form, replete with stirring orations and archaeological reminiscences of classical antiquity.[62] The *Historia de Vita et Gestis Scanderbegi* by the Latin-rite priest MARINO BARLEZIO, or BARLETIUS (b.c. 1450), was based on the author's firsthand observations during and between the two sieges of his native city of Scutari in Venetian Albania, which he also described in a polished humanist commentary after his retirement to Venice in 1478. And, as what one modern authority calls "still the most important source for the life of Scanderbeg," the work was read in at least four different languages all over Europe during the following century. Angiolello's history of the Aqqoyunlu-Ottoman wars provided a thorough description of the Ottoman army. For the author, after being captured at Negroponte, succeeded so well in ingratiating himself with his captors that he rose to the rank of a secretary; and in this capacity he accompanied the army on expeditions to Serbia, Wallachia, and eastern Anatolia.[63] JACOPO DE PROMONTORIO provided a still more thorough description of Ottoman political administration. He had been an official representative of the Genoese merchants at the court of Mehmed II both before and after the fall of Constantinople and had accompanied the sultan as far as Belgrade. He was therefore able to give Western equivalents of the salaries and titles ("Jhixinighirbasi [Chashnigir-bāshī?], *id est,* Maestro di Sala") of the officials in the capital and the provinces.[64] And it is unfortunate that his manuscripts were deposited in Bologna and Genoa, where they were soon forgotten. DONALDO DA LEZZE (1479–1524) went beyond all his predecessors. As a Venetian soldier, administrator, and diplomat in the Peloponnesus, in Constantinople, and in Cyprus, he had made numerous observations of his own. As adviser on Eastern affairs to the Dieci, he had access to official diplomatic reports. He went to a considerable effort to obtain little-known accounts of earlier Italian travelers—Andrea Balastro, Cristoforo Buondelmonti, Nicolò Barbaro (on the siege of Constantinople), and Iosafa Barbaro. And he had sent to Rome for copies of the letters addressed by the sultan to popes Innocent VIII and Alexander VI. He was thus able to give a survey of all previous explanations of the origin of the Turks as well as a chronicle of the growth of the Ottomans since 1300. His style was anything but felicitous, and his causal explanations rather frequently reverted to God's wrath over the sins of the faithful—which was visited most visibly when the Venetians lost the well-fortified castle at Argos. But his message was clear. The Turks were the barbarian descendants of illiterate nomads, and their rulers were the uncivilized descendants of the "viscious, bad-natured man" (Osman) who had subjugated Anatolia by the time of his death in 1328. Crusades like that of Pius II ("fu gittata tanta spesa") were a waste of money, negotiations with Persia would produce no more than border squabbles, and the Great Turk would probably succeed in his design "to make himself the lord of all Christendom" as long as the basic cause of the entire series of tragedies was not removed: "the avarice and quarreling of Christians."[65]

Thereafter information increased still more rapidly. Much of it appeared in the form of those sixteenth-century precursors of modern Associated Press releases, *avvisi,* which supposedly consisted of eyewitness reports of some spectacular event. To judge by their numbers and by the number of reprints and translations made of many of them, these *avvisi* must have become a popular form of literature. The earliest of them usually concerned battles on the borders of the Ottoman Empire, and they include such titles as *Letter Sent from Constantinople in Which is Narrated the Horrifying Defeat of the Great Turk by Thomas, called Sophi [Sufi?] King of Persia; All the Things That Have Taken Place in the Levant and How the Turk Took Aleppo and Damascus with Jerusalem; The Siege of Vienna of Austria and the Horrifying Cruelties and Unheard-of Torments Used by the Turks.* As the Turkish expeditions moved westward, so did the *avvisi* writers. A certain Gugliemo Pansa and another Giulio Casare Ripa reported on the war in Tunisia in 1535. A score of writers reported on various moments of the siege of Malta in 1565. And at least twice that number described the Battle of Lepanto.[66]

Not all of these *avvisi* were reliable. Some of them were actually written in Venice rather than in the places indicated in the titles. And some of them sought to stimulate the public's wishful thinking rather than satisfy a quest for information.[67] But the travelers who wrote in the form of humanist *relazioni* generally were reliable. BENEDETTO RAMBERTI learned about the Turkish system of government and about the character of both Turks and Greeks during a long voyage around Greece and a period of residence in Constantinople.[68] LUIGI BASSANO of Zara, a secretary to Cardinal Rodolfo Pio di Carpi, learned about the habits and customs of ordinary Turks after some eight years in various towns of Anatolia; and he could thus tell Westerners what time Turks got up in the morning, how and when they bathed, and how they fed, washed, and exercised their dogs.[69] GIOVANNI ANTONIO MENAVINO of Veletri in Liguria had been brought up in the household of the sultan since his capture at sea at the age of twelve; and thanks to the sultan's conviction that "Christians, and above all those of Tuscany, were by natural instinct people of remarkable intelligence," he became acquainted with its "most intimate and most secret parts." He could therefore give the names and job descriptions of all the officers of the empire from the pasha to the zookeeper. He could give transliterations and translations of Turkish technical terms. He could give many new details about the Turkish institution which most fascinated Christians, the harem, where he had been bathed, perfumed, and dressed upon his arrival at court. And he could point out that, veil-over-the-Truth though it might be, the Islamic religion inspired admirable acts of charity, and it imposed an effective check upon what Christians, too, regarded as vices. If, then, the king of France wished "to undertake an expedition against our common enemy," he would do well to put aside the current myths about his incivility and barbarity and "inform [himself] of the customs of that country."[70]

It was the availability of sources such as these that enabled writers who had never been out of Italy and who had never seen a live Turk to raise the literature on the

Turks to the level of humanist historiography. ANDREA CAMBINI (1455/60–1527) had been successively a disciple of Cristoforo Landino, whose *Disputationes Camaldolenses* he translated into Latin, an admirer of Marsilio Ficino, who inspired his translation of Cicero's philosophical dialogues, a diplomatic agent for Lorenzo il Magnifico, and, finally, after breaking with Piero de' Medici, an ardent follower of Savonarola. The fall of the last of his heroes then barred him from an active life and enabled the vocation first awakened by his translation of Biondo's *Decades* in the early 1490s to begin a fuller development. Spurred apparently by the rapid success of the Ottomans in Syria and Egypt, which he was to describe in detail, he began reading Pius II and Sekoundinos, "a man very learned both in Greek and Latin"; and he interviewed a "Persian" who had been brought to Florence by a multilingual compatriot. He thus discovered that the Turks were descendants not of the ancient Trojans but of the Scythians, and that they had emerged from the lands beyond the Caspian in the eighth century to attack the Avars and then devastate Pontus and Cappadocia. "Barbarian and cruel" though they may be, however, Cambini had to admit that the founder of the Ottoman dynasty had been a man "of great nobility, ... of great intelligence, and of great spirit," that Mehmed the Conqueror had begun his reign by "promulgating new laws and correcting old ones," thus winning "the benevolence and gratitude of all the peoples subject to him." He also had to agree that the sultan had attacked Constantinople for motives that every reader of humanist historiography would find acceptable:

> not content with the very ample state his father had left him and desirous
> of accomplishing some great deed by which he could gain a reputation
> not only equal to, but actually surpassing that of his ancestors. . . .[71]

He then went on to apply the same standards to the French, whose victories in Italy were quite as spectacular as those of the Turks in the Levant. How can anyone call "barbarian," he asked, a people who are evidently not "barbarically organized," and among whom only one out of fifty-nine kings has suffered a violent death? What need is there to invent mythical ancestors for a people whose past exploits, as described by Gregory of Tours, Robert Gaguin, and Paolo Emili[72] ("I have not omitted any writer," he boasted, "Latin or vernacular, eloquent or barbarous"), made their present exploits fully comprehensible? Unfortunately, the present exploits turned out, almost as soon as he had finished writing, to include the Battle of Pavia; and since he died before the French had begun to recover from the calamity, his manuscript was consigned to oblivion, where it has remained ever since.[73]

Similarly, PAOLO GIOVIO[74] and MARCO GUAZZO[75] were as near as anyone came in the sixteenth century to being professional historians; and it was the immediacy, and the popularity, of the subject matter alone that induced them to interrupt their more important historiographical projects to write monographs on the Turks. Both of them confined their narratives to the period after the fall of Constantinople—to the period, that is, in which Ottoman power had seemed the most irresistable. Both of them, however, had a message of hope for their own contemporaries. George Scanderbeg, the Albanian prince who escaped from captivity at the Ottoman court to lead a Christian resistance movement in his homeland, kept an army of 200,000 at bay for some eleven years while his fellow Christians in Italy were busy quarreling among themselves.[76] Alvise Loredan, the Venetian admiral in the first great Veneto-Turkish war, continued to sack Turkish towns in Anatolia while his fellow Christians in Rhodes raided his stray ships. Therefore, advised the historians, the Great Turk would do well to take note of the refutation of the Koran sent him by one of Giovio's Franciscan friends. Christians had finally learned the lesson that GHERARDO BORGONI was once again to repeat, a half-century later, after reading Sekoundinos and Theodore of Gaza: that it was their own "discords which caused the greatness of the Ottoman House."[77] And as soon as Pope Paul III succeeded in getting their two principal leaders to stop fighting each other, the Christians would turn as one body against their common enemy. Christian soldiers, Giovio and Guazzo noted further, had finally learned to choose between certain glory in the next world and certain slavery in this. They would henceforth fight to the death, as they had at Negroponte. Obviously, then, nothing short of a mass conversion to Christianity could save the Turks from total extinction.

Unfortunately, the Peace of Cateau-Cambrésis did not result in the proclamation of a crusade; and the Turks remained as firmly entrenched as ever in Tunis, Tripoli, Djerba, and Hungary, notwithstanding repeated attempts to dislodge them. Thus the next humanist historian to take up the problem, FRANCESCO SANSOVINO,[78] proposed that his compatriots turn to studying what they so far had been unable to destroy, and he suggested that they make history useful to political science if it could no longer be useful to Christendom. Anyway, study was far preferable to fighting, particularly at a time when Italy was at last beginning to enjoy "a most tranquil peace." And what more appropriate object of study could be found than the Turks, who, unlike the ancient Romans, "are living right under our eyes," and whose empire "has grown in such a short time to such heights of glory and renown"? In order to further such a study, Sansovino composed a chronicle of the the Turks and their Arab forerunners from the birth of Muhammad. He then supplemented his chronicle with the texts of his principal sources; and he either translated them into Italian or (as in the case of Cambini, who "did not maintain the stylistic quality required for a history of such an important subject") edited them to fit current aesthetic and linguistic standards. Some of the texts were already fairly well known—like those of Cambini, Bassano, Menavino, like Jacques Fontaine's (Jacopo Fontano) *La guerra di Rodi* and Domenichi's translation of Spandouginos. Some of them were of rather doubtful authenticity, like the otherwise unidentified "lives" of the recent kings of Persia and a biography of Muhammad supposedly translated through the Latin from the Arabic. At least one was really a prophesy based on a deliberately warped presentation of facts: Bartholomew Georgijević's oration to Archduke Maximilian of Austria, which had previously been translated by Domenichi from the first Latin edition of Worms, 1543. Some of the texts were either wholly or relatively unknown: the letters of Pius II and the grand master of Rhodes to the sultan, the letters of a secretary of Sigismondo Malatesta from the Peloponnesus, and the very detailed and reliable history of the fall of Constantinople composed in Latin by the Greek Catholic prelate Leonardos of Chios. Many of them presented contradictory views; and Sansovino left to his readers the task of deciding whether Muhammad was a well-meaning founder of a reasonable religion or the disseminator of "lies, fables, and chimeras," whether the Turks were perpetrators of "unbelievable calamities" or "mortals like us, of the same flesh, and creatures of God." All the texts, however, served his purpose well: that of promoting not crusades but objective inquiry. His lesson was not lost on the two principal Italian political philosophers of the late sixteenth century. Giovanni Botero treated the Ottoman state as a modern equivalent of the model states of antiquity—that is, as one capable of furnishing lessons in political wisdom. Paolo Paruta came to realize, once the euphoria of Lepanto had worn off, that the Ottoman state could easily survive the drain on its resources imposed by the current war with "Persia"; and he warned that only the Venetian policy of vigilant neutrality could save Christian powers from a repetition of the disasters they had suffered in the past.[79]

Still, both Sansovino and the other Italian Turcologues of his age could have greatly strengthened their position had they also taken advantage of the many other sources that were then available, or that could have been made available with a little extra effort. They did, it is true, overcome some of the Ciceronian antipathy of their ancestors toward postclassical Greeks. Besides the texts republished by Sansovino, they could now read Nikiforos Grigoras (Gregoras) and Nikitas Choniatis ("Aconiato") in Lodovico Dolce's translations, and they knew the latter to have been, as his German editor put it, "a man preeminent in his age because of his intelligence and manifold learning."[80] They could also read Ioannis Skylitzis in the translation of Giovan Battista Gabio, a Veronese professor of Greek at Rome. However, they all but ignored the eleventh-century annals of Georgios Kendrinos (Cendrenus), whom Minadoi had consulted,[81] and the history of the last days of Byzantium by the secretary of Manuel II, Georgios Frantzis (Sfrantzis), whom even ZANCARUOLO had read in preparation for his account of the Battle of Gallipoli.[82] They also ignored Doukas, a protégé first of the Turkish emir of Ephesus and then of the Genoese governor of Phocea, even though he was a staunch Uniate and even though an Italian translation, composed around 1517 but never published, could have shielded their classically trained eyes from the demotic character of his prose.[83] Even the most consciously Thucydidean of recent Greek historians, Michail Kritovoulos (Kritobulos) of Imbros and Laonikos Chalkokondylis of Athens, were known only to those specialized scholars who could consult the Latin editions published at Basel. While Chalkokondylis appeared at least twice in French translation, most Italians read him, albeit unwittingly, in the usually unacknowledged paraphrases that Sansovino scattered through his *Annali*.[84] Thus not even Dolce seems to have suspected that Spandouginos, whom he chose to translate from Latin, was really not nearly as original as he thought and that what appeared to reflect a knowledge of Turkish actually consisted of transcriptions of words Spandouginos found in the works of the modern Greek masters.[85]

During the first part of the century, when Italians were busy editing and translating the ancient Greeks, and during the second half of the century, when they were busy procuring definitive editions of the Greek Church Fathers, most of the modern Greeks, who knew more about the Turks than any Italians did, were abandoned to the care of scholars in Germany. Many more Greek sources were known to Hieronymus Wolf and Wilhelm Holtzmann, the editors of the first corpus of Byzantine historiography, published with the financial assistance of Anton Fugger in the 1560s, than to anyone in Italy. And still more were known to Martin Crusius, who made the first survey of emigrant Greek scholars in his *Turco-Graecia* of 1584. When the study of Byzantine letters finally became acceptable in Italy, as it did thanks to the efforts of the Italianized Greek Leone Alatsis, or Allacci (1586–1669), in the early seventeenth century, its motive force was no longer historical. Allacci was interested not in providing information about the Turks or in pleading for the liberation of Constantinople but in assisting the Counter Reformation Papacy to make contact with the Christian churches of the East. And it was solely for theological and ecclesiastical reasons that he persuaded a group of French Jesuits to undertake a project as inconceivable in the age of humanism as it was consonant with the tastes of the succeeding age of ecclesiastical scholarship: an up-dated, vastly expanded edition of the corpus of Wolf and Holtzmann in some twenty-two volumes.[86]

Similarly, Italians gave only passing attention to the literature on the Turks then being published elsewhere in Europe. They owed their knowledge of the history of Díaz Tanco de Fregenal (1547) to its fortuitous inclusion in Ulloa's translation projects (1558); and they owed their belated knowledge of the survey of the Balkans written earlier in the century by the bishop of Dubrovnik, Ludovico Tuberone (Crijeva), to the unexplained publication of one chapter in 1590.[87] Giovio seems to have heard of the work of another Latin-language Ragusan, Feliks Petančić, adviser on Turkish affairs to King Vladislas II of Hungary at the beginning of the century. But no one seems to have heard of the most popular—and most humanistically inspired—book about the Turks written in French, Guillaume Postel's *De la république des Turcs* (1560).

Stranger still, in a country that took pride in its mastery of even the more obscure ancient languages, no one ever bothered to learn Turkish—not even the Venetian diplomats, who generally relied on professional translators until the end of the seventeenth century.[88] Most of the Turkish chronicles, it is true, were not published even in Turkish until the nineteenth century, and most of them consisted only of lists of the *acta* of the sultans. Still, the German scholar Hans Spiegel managed to obtain and to translate the synthesis of previous Turkish chronicles composed in the late fifteenth century by the cultivated and Latin-speaking teacher of Adrianople, Muhyiddin Mehmed; and there is no reason why one of the many humanistically educated Italian merchants at Constantinople could not have obtained the popular handbook of Ottoman history prepared by Mehmed Pasha on commission from Suleimān the Magnificent. In any case, the task of exploiting Turkish sources for the sake of a better understanding of the Turks was left to another German scholar, Hans Löwenklau, or Leunclavius, who launched the scientific, as opposed to the humanistic, study of the Turks in 1598 with his *Annales Sultanorum Othmanidarum,* which no Italian humanist ever bothered to look at.

It is thus not surprising that the Turkish policy of the grand dukes of Tuscany broke down on the question of the Knights of Santo Stefano, and that the Turkish policy of the popes and the Venetians turned out to be less flexible, and hence less efficacious, than that adopted by Henry IV with the help of much better informed experts in France.[89] Nor is it surprising that all Italians mistook as a mortal blow what the Turkish chronicles more correctly presented, on the eve of the recapture of Tunis, as a merely momentary setback at Lepanto.[90] What most Italians knew of the Turks was really a caricature of reality, one more fitting for poems and plays than for political calculation.[91] Thus within a few years of the publication of the sober reflections of the political philosophers, the current expert on the Turks was once again pretending, to the great annoyance of the Venetian government, to have found the secret of how to wipe out the Turks and unite the Maronite and Greek Orthodox churches with Rome, all in one blow. LAZARO SORANZO[92] did not have to go to Constantinople to learn the names of the current officers of the Turkish empire. That he could find out easily enough in Venice. And he did not feel obliged to write his stirring war cry in a library, since it was much more comfortable to do so during a vacation on Ischia. And that the Duke of Mantua, to whom it was dedicated, did not succeed immediately in driving the Turks out of Hungary, he could easily attribute to his not having read the text carefully enough.

These defects notwithstanding, it was from the Italian humanists that most sixteenth-century readers, beyond the Alps as well as in Italy, learned about the Turks. Sansovino's anthology drew forth "letters from many places and favorable comments from many gentlemen" as soon as it appeared, and it was republished some six times before 1600. The abridgment of the accompanying commentary that he prepared in the form of "annals" of the Ottoman princes was republished in an amended edition within two years of the first. Many of its passages were then translated or paraphrased and augmented with additional information by an unknown Greek writer, who might thus have made known to his demotic-speaking compatriots something of the work of their own historians, who wrote only in classical Greek, had his manuscript not been ignored until the twentieth century.

Passages from Giovio were disguised to look like the results of oral interviews (*De Prima Truculentissimorum Turcarum Origine*—1543), and passages from Menavino and Domenichi were translated and rearranged to look like the record of the translator's own *Viaje de Turquia* (1557) by a benefice-collecting Spanish physician named Andrés de Laguna, whose plagiarisms remained sheltered behind the more prestigious name of Cristóbal de Villalón until 1958.[93] Similarly, Cambini's survey was found worthy of being bound with Bruni's paraphrases of Procopius when it first appeared. In the 1541 edition it was bound with Giovio's monograph, which had already been published in Latin (1537), German (1538), and French (1539) editions. And both of them were then translated from Latin into English (1546). Even Soranzo's diatribe was reprinted several times in Italy and translated almost immeditely into English, with due apologies from the translator for the author's papist prejudices.[94] Finally, all the works of these Italian writers were represented in the greatest of the European collections of Turkish material assembled at the end of the century, the library of Liévin Vanderbeecken in Antwerp.[95]

The reasons for this success are not hard to find. They lie not in the intrinsic quality of the works themselves but in the efficacy of the negative version of the humanist formula "what is not well written won't be read" in an age when all Europe was being converted to humanism.

Italians in the West

Most Italian traders, diplomats, and missionaries went east. But some of them also went west. PIERO QUERINI, for instance, left Crete in 1431 for Scandinavia; and his story about being blown in a rudderless ship to some two hundred miles west of Ireland so excited two of his friends at home that they wrote it down in the form of a humanist *relazione*.[96] The brothers NICOLÒ and ANTONIO ZENO were shipwrecked on the Faeroe Islands in the 1380s; and while assisting a local chieftain in his unending wars with the chieftains of the Shetland Islands, they managed to visit Iceland, Greenland, and a number of strange countries that even modern editors cannot identify. Their story so excited their descendant NICOLÒ even in the mid-sixteenth century, when adventurous travelogues had become common, that he printed it along with the account of his uncle Caterino's trip to Persia.[97] Indeed, Italians were among the pioneers not only in leading but above all in writing about the voyages of discovery undertaken under the auspices of the kings of Portugal and Castile and the city fathers of Dieppe in the last decade of the fifteenth century and the first decades of the sixteenth. COLUMBUS's reports of his first voyage were published almost immediately (1493) by Gugliolmo Dati in Rome and Florence.[98] They were then republished with AMERIGO VESPUCCI's letter on his discoveries in an anthology printed in Vicenza in 1507 and often thereafter.[99] GIOVANNI DA VERRAZZANO's famous letter of 1524 about "a new land never before seen either by the ancients or modern men" circulated widely before being included in Ramusio's collection.[100]

The authors of these travel reports were still motivated principally by the prospect of profit. MATTEO DA BERGAMO, who accompanied Vasco da Gama to India in 1502, gave his colleague in Cremona a full list of prices on the markets of the East and instructed him on what to order in advance on the markets of Lisbon.[101] GIOVANNI DA EMPOLI (b. 1483), the son of a rich retailer in Florence, a former member of Savonarola's boy-scout troops, and a friend and correspondent of the gonfaloniere Soderini, made two trips around the Cape to India and China, where he died in 1515. His uncle was so impressed by the potentially profitable information Giovanni had sent home about "the ports, the countries, the cities, and the people, the customs, laws, weights, measures, goods for sale, spices of all sorts . . . , where pearls are gathered and where rubies, diamonds, and other gems are to be found" that he rewrote it for future editing by "some excellent and eloquent man," who fortunately never appeared to rework the fascinating, if a bit naive, original.[102]

It soon became apparent, however, that the "admirable, almost unbelievable" things that the merchant travelers found outside the marketplaces—"parrots and birds of diverse kinds," enchanted horses, ingenious musical instruments—were quite comparable to the strangest of curiosities collected by Pliny, and hence of interest to a much wider reading public. "Having been the first of the nation of the noble city of Venice," proclaimed ALOVISE DE CA DA MOSTO (Alvise da Cadamosto),[103]

> to have navigated the ocean beyond the Straits of Gibralter toward the regions of the south . . . and having there seen many new things worthy of some notice, [I must point out] that truly the customs and places familiar to us, in comparison with what I have seen and heard about, can well be called those of another world.

Consequently, curiosity, or, to use a humanist expression, the desire to know about new things, soon took the place of a desire for profit in the minds both of readers and of writers.

Obviously, this new motive could best be served by a writer capable of satisfying the humanistic tastes of his Italian audiences. And it was undoubtedly a humanist education that roused in ANTONIO PIGAFETTA of Vicenza a desire to "see those things for myself" by joining Magellan's trip around the world and "to gain some renown [in the eyes of] posterity" by writing about what he had seen.[104] His humanist education undoubtedly helped him also in acquiring a rudimentary knowledge of several Philippine languages and a fairly workable knowledge of two Indonesian languages. Unfortunately, the full revision of his diary, which he composed according to humanist historiographical models after his return to Italy, was not published until the late nineteenth century, notwithstanding the encouragement of Isabella d'Este and Clement VII. Except for a privileged few, like the doge and his counselors, who listened with astonishment as he spoke at a dinner party in his honor in Venice in 1523, none of his contemporaries was allowed to read more than a written version of an interview he had given in Paris on his way home. Hence, the honor of being the first to elevate the accounts of the discoveries to the level of humanist historiography fell to a writer who himself never visited most of the lands he wrote about, PIETRO MARTIRE D'ANGHIERA (c. 1459–1526) [105]

To be sure, Anghiera had had no particular subject in mind when he left Rome in 1488 in the train of the Spanish ambassador to look for a more promising career in Spain, and the official position he obtained as chaplain to Queen Isabella obliged him to do no more than offer Latin lessons to the court nobility. But the various missions he undertook with and for King Ferdinand soon gave him an opportunity to put into practice the art of good writing he had learned during his years in the company of Pomponio Leto. The missions took him to Granada during the siege, to Flanders, and in 1501, by way of Venice, to Egypt; and his account of this last mission was eventually judged worthy of an Italian translation.[106] Through the king he also met Columbus. Their long conversations were enough to convince him that he had at last found an interesting subject. And he accordingly reworked the conversations in the form of a humanist *relazione*. What was to become the first two books of his *Decades* begins with his hero's birth, upbringing, and early travels in Portugal and Spain. It pauses, shortly after his arrival in the Canaries to explain why he first went there—with a long excursus on the discovery and the settlement of the islands. By pausing for a long prayer of thanksgiving in the form of a set oration, it underlines the dramatic tension of the moment in which he first sighted land. And it ends, in accordance with humanist prescriptions, with observations about the customs, religion, and languages of the inhabitants of the newly discovered country. Accordingly, much of it was immediately translated into Italian and published at Venice, without the author's knowledge or consent—first in 1504, then in 1507, then in 1534,[107] and finally in Ramusio (vol. III).

The cordial reception of the first books then led Anghiera, five years later, to compose another seven books. By 1510, with encouragement from the Florentine ambassador, the papal legate, and the spiritual leader of the reform party at the Fifth Lateran Council, Egidio da Viterbo, he had decided to make a career of collecting and recording all the accounts of all the voyages executed under the auspices of his employers. And his employers obligingly facilitated the carrying out of his decision, first by providing him with the necessary financial support—in the form of a number of lucrative ecclesiastical benefices—and then by guaranteeing him access to the most abundant stores of information—in the form of appointments to the Council of the Indies and the Casa de Contratación in Seville.

Anghiera may not always have succeeded in fulfilling what gradually became his grand plan. Several important voyages, including Vespucci's, were omitted. Others, like that of Vincenzo Yañez Pinzon, were mentioned only in retrospect. Moreover, much of the text consisted of little more than a paraphrase of the diaries of the voyagers, with vernacular expressions freely mixed with the classical Latin in which he was supposed to be writing. And the historiographical form often broke down into little more than chronicle, particularly when his information started coming in faster than he could digest it. Still, the result constituted a rather spectacular achievement. The author's intention of writing according to the standards of his native rather than of his adopted country was reinforced by his dedication of the later volumes to his former countrymen—Leo X, Clement VII, and Francesco Maria Sforza. His moderate success in living up to those standards has been recognized even by modern critics, who readily admit that "toda la obra respira un ambiente de aristocrático humanismo." And his success in achieving at least one humanist objective—thoroughness—was recognized by many of the subsequent Spanish historians of the Indies, like Bartolomé de Las Casas and Fernando Colombo—who simply copied from him much of what they needed to broaden the scope of their own accounts of still further voyages.

Anghiera's example may well have affected the literary quality of the last of the Italian merchant-adventurers to follow the Spanish and Portuguese overseas, GIROLAMO BENZONI (b. 1519), by whom he was frequently cited. Benzoni admitted to not being a man of letters; and indeed his narrative frequently consists of little more than isolated descriptions of the many places he visited in the order in which he visited them—Puerto Rico, Panama, Guatemala, Quito, Cuzco. But before and after his return to Milan in 1556, he managed to read most of the Spanish literature on the Americas. He cast his personal travelogue in the form of a history of the Spanish settlements since the time of Columbus. He wrote chiefly for the purpose not of showing his compatriots how to make money (having lost most of his in a shipwreck) but of enlightening them about the unspeakable cruelty of the conquistadores: "among those of the Spanish nation are to be found some who are not only cruel, but very cruel" ("non solamente son crudeli, ma ancora crudelissimi"). And whenever his own observations did not wholly suffice toward that end, he borrowed whatever extra information and whatever theoretical force he needed from that most abundant mine of incriminating evidence, Las Casas. His narrative was accordingly absorbed into contemporary "black legend" literature and republished in five different languages some thirty-two times in the following 150 years.[108]

Benzoni's two great successors did not have to read Anghiera. ALESSANDRO VAGLIANO (b. 1539) had been assured a full humanist education by the Society of Jesus, which sent him to India (1574), to Japan (1579), and then back to Goa (1588), where he remained until his death in 1606. And the history of the Jesuit missions in the Far East he wrote in Spanish was fully consonant with the principles of his education, even though, unfortunately for his contemporaries, it was not published until much later.[109] GIOVAN PIETRO MAFFEI of Bergamo (b. 1535) was imbued with humanism from his earliest years, first in the school of a student of ancient history, Giovan Crisostomo Zanchi, then in the company of Varchi and Lelio Torelli in Florence, and finally in the company of Annibal Caro, Paolo Manuzio, and Silvio Antoniano in Rome; and the Society of Jesus, which he entered in 1565, recognized the quality of his education by appointing him professor of eloquence in the Collegio Romano.[110] Maffei became familiar with contemporary travel literature by translating into Latin the first account of India and Japan written by his Portuguese confrère, Emmanuel Acosta,[111] and then the biography of King Manuel of Portugal by Jerónimo Osorio da Fonseca.[112] And he gained experience in putting into practice the rules of good writing in his original biography of Ignatius of Loyola.[113] An eleven-year research expedition to Portugal then confirmed him in the vocation that the translations had awakened; and he divided the rest of his years after returning to Rome in 1581 between a commentary on the pontificate of Gregory XIII, which he wrote in obedience to a specific request from Pope Clement VIII,[114] and what he recognized as his magnum opus, the *Historiae Indicae,* which was reprinted six times in the decade after the first edition of Rome, 1588, and which appeared the very next year in Francesco Serdonati's Italian translation.

Maffei felt obliged to pay at least a nominal tribute to his theological studies in the preface. History, he affirmed, consists of a continuous dialectic in which God responds to man's repeated infidelities with ever new tactics: the Flood, the Exile, the conversion of the Greeks. The most recent instruments of his policy to wipe out "the thickheaded rites of the gentiles and the detestable cult of lying gods" were the Portuguese and the Castilians. But in his text Maffei stuck strictly to what he could extract "from the public archives or from approved writers and men worthy of confidence who have taken part themselves in these undertakings." The causes of the voyages are traced no further than to the heroic nature of certain men—like King John III, "a man certainly great and venerable and worthy therefore of being remembered through all eternity," and Magellan, "who for his strength of character, his knowledge of governing others, and his unheard-of fortune deserves not to have his own name and that of his fatherland obscured either by chance or by length of time." The ancient cosmographers are brought in one by one either to be proved wrong or to supply an ancient, and therefore immediately acceptable, equivalent for a modern place name, or to provide an ancient parallel to a modern curiosity—like the Carthaginian policy of closed frontiers, which was adopted by the Chinese, the guardians of the most recent earthly paradise. Finally, what could be established about the activities of the author's confreres, like Francis Xavier, not according to the wild stories that ran around Europe but according to the objective results of a royal investigation which Maffei had read in Coimbra, is put clearly in the context of an almost two century-long history of the Portuguese discoveries.

The transformation of merchants' diaries into a form of humanist historiography was now complete.

Italians in the North

For many of the same reasons that led their compatriots to go east and west, some Italians also went to transalpine Europe. Like Michele Ricci,[115] VITTORIO SABINO apparently went to France because he sided with the French after the invasion of his homeland. Accordingly, his short chronicle of the kings of France, which begins when the Franks migrated into Germany to escape the Roman occupation of Gaul and which ends when Francis I was captured at Pavia, was intended above all as a demonstration of "the great reputation of the great and wealthy kingdom of France" and a justification of the rights of its rulers over Milan and Naples. All those of his fellow countrymen who denied these rights, Sabino concluded, were responsible for the calamities of their country; and since most of them did indeed deny them, the only Italian to whom he accorded honorable mention was Gian Giacomo Trivulzio, who saved Charles VIII from the Venetian mercenaries at the Taro.[116] Like Machiavelli,[117] PANDOLFO COLLENUCCIO[118] went to Germany on a diplomatic mission—namely, as ambassador of the duke of Ferrara to the emperor in 1500. However, he wrote not to provide his government with politically useful information or to clarify his own theories about the nature of politics but rather to satisfy the curiosity of a personal friend, the poet Tito Strozzi. He used as his standard reference book not Livy or Tacitus but Pomponius Mela. His main purpose, therefore, was to show how the political geography of Germany had changed during the thousand-year period "involuta barbaricis tenebris" between ancient and modern times—how Germany now extended from the Vistula to the Mosel and how ancient Rhaetia and Noricum had now become Bavaria, Carinthia, and Styria.

CERBONIO BESOZZI of Bergamo, on the other hand, went abroad to work as a musician: from Bergamo, where he was born and trained, to Trent, where he won the applause of delegates to the Council, to Spain in the train of the emperor, to Saxony in the service of the elector, and to Bavaria, where he died in 1579, in the service of the duke. He described minutely the customs and physical appearance of all the places he visited as well as the foreign and domestic activities of all his employers, on which he was particularly well informed.[119] VINCENZO SCAMOZZI, a half-century later, went abroad to study architecture—from Vienna to Prague, from Nürnberg to Strassburg. And he illustrated his account of the return trip from Paris to Venice with sketches of Gothic churches, which later provided the empirical basis for his theoretical treatise, *Idea dell'architettura universale,* first published in 1616.[120] PIETRO RUGGIERO of Bologna went abroad as a secretary to the papal nuncio sent in 1560 to summon the Lutheran princes to the forthcoming third session of the Council of Trent. As he followed his master's zigzag voyages from Prague to Liège, from Bremen to "Nanzi," from Trier to Munich, and finally, "not without the special grace of the Lord God after such hardships and perils," to Venice, he noted down the past as well as the present circumstances of all the towns he visited.[121] GIROLAMO FALLETTI (or Faleti) went abroad in the service of Francesco d'Este, who had contributed a regiment to the army of Charles V in the Schmalkaldic War. He too, apparently, knew Pomponius Mela, for he was just as curious as Collenuccio about modern equivalents of ancient place names. But he also read Thucydides, Xenophon, and probably Caesar (*incipit:* "all Germany is divided into four parts"). He therefore knew that soldiers on leave can make good historians. And he was also able to avoid the kind of sweeping generalizations ("the kingdom is full of every sort of heretics") and amusing inaccuracies (in some parts of Brandenburg people still "speak the Vandalic language, now called Schiavona") in which Ruggiero abounded. His geographical survey is thus followed, in impeccable humanist style, by an exposition of the causes of the war he had fought in, starting with Luther's frustrated ambition to become head of the Augustinians and ending with the imperial deposition of Philip of Hessen. The exposition is followed in turn by a detailed account of the war itself, with abundant references to the events elsewhere in Europe that affected the course of events inside Germany. And the work ends, appropriately enough, with a political lesson: that an army, under one leader, no matter how heterogeneous its composition, can always defeat a much larger league of several different armies. Falletti's history of the war in Germany [122] apparently made a good impression on his employer, to whom it was dedicated; for he was subsequently appointed ambassador to the pope, the emperor, the king of Poland ("Sarmatia"), and the Venetians. And success of the history inspired him a few years later to describe the rebellion in the Netherlands, which he had not see, in Latin verse—with all the difficult Flemish place names ingeniously provided with declinable Latin endings. [123]

Some Italians, however, went to transalpine Europe neither to make money, nor to win souls, nor to fight, nor even to seek adventure, but rather to further a career as men of letters in what they hoped would be a more favorable environment. TITO LIVIO FRULOVISI (Titus Livius Foro-Iulensis, c. 1400–after 1456) was a graduate of the pioneering school of Guarino in Ferrara. Unfortunately, his propensity for expressing publicly his rather harsh opinions of others made his subsequent career as a schoolmaster and a playwright in Venice somewhat less than pleasant. He therefore accepted an offer, procured through a former fellow student with English connections, to become secretary to Duke Humphrey of Gloucester. Humphrey was just then engaged in a one-man campaign to introduce humanist letters into his native country; and Tito Livio fulfilled his initial commission by writing several Latin plays and a treatise *De Re Publica*. But Humphrey was also engaged in a campaign, as protector of the realm during the minority of King Henry VI, in support of a more actively interventionist policy on the continent. He therefore charged his secretary with finding an appropriate model in recent English history, procured him letters of denization (1437), and assured him access to state papers. And when Tito Livio left England a few years later to study medicine in Barcelona and then to practice it in Venice, he left behind a biography of the most interventionist of all recent English kings, Henry V, written according to the highest standards of Humphrey's book-buying agent in Italy, Pier Candido Decembrio.[124] DOMENICO MANCINI (c. 1434–c. 1514) followed Tito Livio to England some forty years later. But he went in search of a job offer, not in response to one; and he found himself unexpectedly, in 1483, in the midst of a recrudescence of England's endemic civil wars, this one being precipitated by the death of Edward IV and concluded by the victory of the usurper, Richard III. Disappointed in his search, Mancini returned to France. On the request of his patron, who happened to be the same prelate-diplomat Angelo Cato to whom Commynes was to dedicate his *Mémoirs,* he interrupted work on the moral-philosophical treatise *De Quattuor Virtutibus* that was intended to justify his appointment as a Latin teacher in Paris; and he composed a commentary upon what he had seen or heard during this three months in London.[125]

Like Tito Livio, FILIPPO BUONACCORSI (1437–96), better known by his pen name, CALLIMACO ESPERIENTE, combined a talent for letters with a quarrelsome disposition. Implicated in the plot that brought down the wrath of Pope Paul II upon the circle of his mentor, Pomponio Leto, in 1468, Callimaco fled to Naples, to Cyprus, and then to Chios. His involvement in still another plot in Chios forced him to flee again, first to Constantinople and finally to Poland, where his Tuscan-Venetian family had business connections. There he obtained the protection of Poland's version of England's Humphrey, Gregory of Sanok (Grzegorz z Sanoka), archbishop of Leopolis (Lwów). When the death of Paul II then freed him from fear of persecution, he became tutor to the royal children and counselor and roving ambassador for King Casimir IV and for Casimir's successor, John Albert. It was in this capacity, for the benefit and entertainment of his patrons and charges, that he wrote the moral treatises and verses that won him the recognition he still holds today as "one of the best Latin poets of the Quattrocento."[126] But he soon decided that the principal shortcoming of the culture of his adopted country was the paucity of well-written biographies about morally inspiring heroes—"vitae illustrium virorum." In order to provide moral guidance for Polish ecclesiastics, he wrote a life of his first patron, Gregory of Sanok, which was elegant, eloquent, and, except for certain well-known details about Gregory's preferences in wine and women, faithful to the record. In order to provide political guidance for Polish statesmen, he wrote a biography of King Casimir's immediate predecessor, Vladislas III, the hero and victim of the Polish-Hungarian expedition against the Turks that ended in the disaster of Varna (1444). In order to further the project he had proposed at Venice as well as at Cracow—a grand alliance against the Turks—he wrote a history of the similar projects pursued by the Venetians; and he broadened the scope of the history to include all of eastern and central Europe, from the first embassy to Persia until the aftermath of the War of Ferrara.[127]

While some emigrant men of letters were thus led eventually to concern themselves with history, others went abroad specifically for that purpose. True, ANTONIO

BONFINI (c. 1427–1502) was not solely a historian. He began his career as a teacher of Greek and Latin at Padua, Florence, and Recanati, where he married and bought a house. He edited the works of Philostratus, translated Herodian into Latin, and composed a popular moral treatise on matrimony. But it was the first drafts of his now-lost history of his native Ascoli Piceno that particularly recommended him to Beatrice d'Aragona, queen of Hungary, when he met her at Loreto in 1482. She in turn, after failing to attract the services of the more famous scholar Giorgio Merula, procured from the king, Mattias Corvinus, an offer for Bonfini of a position as royal historian. After a first visit to Hungary in 1468–87, he returned to Italy to begin his research in Italian collections; and after his reappointment by Mattias's successor in 1491, he spent the remaining eleven years of his life in Buda working on his monumental *Rerum Ungaricarum Decades*.[128]

POLIDORO VERGILIO (c. 1470–1555) of Urbino was not solely a historian either. The most immediately popular of his works were a collection of famous sayings, the *Adagia* (1498), a collection of *Prodigia,* and a collection of antiquarian inquiries, the *De Inventoribus Rerum* (1499), all culled from the writings of the ancients according to the *de viris illustribus* and the *de rebus memorabilibus* forms prescribed by Jerome and Petrarch. The first of these works, indeed, rivaled the now more famous collection of the same name by Erasmus through most of the sixteenth century, and the last was reprinted some seventy times in six different languages. It was on the strength of these works that Vergilio was invited to England in 1501 by the Italian bishop of Hereford, given a job as acting papal collector for the absentee incumbent,[129] and showered with favor at court and a number of lucrative sinecures in the church. But soon after his arrival he became curious about the past as well as the present conditions of the country that had welcomed him. Thanks to the encouragement of his English friends in the circle of Thomas More and John Colet, and thanks also to Cardinal Wolsey's forceful warning to stay out of politics, he remained in England until the eve of his death, working almost constantly on what he himself regarded as his masterpiece, a history of England through the reign of Henry VIII.[130]

On the other hand, neither PAOLO EMILI of Verona (d. 1529) nor, with the exception of a few orations and a collection of familiar letters, LUCIO MARINEO of Catania (b. 1444) ever wrote anything but history. Emili began studying Gallic and Frankish antiquities as soon as he arrived in France in 1483, apparently at the invitation of Cardinal Charles de Bourbon; and subsidies from Charles VIII and Louis XII then enabled him to spend his remaining years at work on his only published work, a history of France from the beginning to the marriage of Anne of Brittany.[131] Marineo began traveling around Spain as soon as he arrived to gather observations for his first public work, *De Laudibus Hispaniae*—instead of writing commentaries upon the Greek and Latin poetry he had been brought from Palermo to teach to others at Salamanca. As soon as he had procured a position at court, apparently on the recommendation of his fellow countryman Pietro Martire d'Anghiera, he began collecting materials for a chronicle of the kings of Aragon, which was first published in 1509. And thereafter he spent whatever time was left over from teaching on a vast history of all Spain, which was finally published in 1530.[132]

Fortunately, all these emigrant historians found their work greatly facilitated by the goodwill and understanding of their hosts. Bonfini's reception had been prepared by the several Italian humanists who had visited Hungary since the days of Giovanni Conversino and Pier Paolo Vergerio. His commission had been prepared by Janus Pannonicus, the first Hungarian to be educated in Italian humanist schools, who had proposed it to King Mattias as early as 1467.[133] Such a commission had actually been given previously to GALEOTTO MARZI (Galeotus Martius Nariensis, c. 1427–97), whom Mattias had brought from Bologna as director of his famous library at Buda. But instead of a Livian history, Marzi produced only a collection of deeds and sayings arranged—"Liviana eloquentia," perhaps, but certainly not in Livian form—under such headings as "dictum iocose," "dictum egregie," and "sapienter factum," perhaps in imitation of Panormita's *De Dictis et Factis Alphonsi*.[134] Such a commission might have been given instead to Pietro Ranzano, who was then gathering material for the chapters on Hungary eventually incorporated into his encyclopedia of world history;[135] but Mattias apparently knew nothing of his extracurricular activities.

Callimaco's reception too had been well prepared—by Zbigniew Oleśnicki, a patron of humanism in Poland and vice-chancellor of the kingdom after 1472, by Johannes Roth, bishop of Breslau, who outlined a plan for a history of Poland on the basis of what he had learned as a student of Lorenzo Valla, and by those friends and protégés who formed the "Societas Vistulana" at the University of Cracow. Similarly, Vergilio's reception had been prepared not so much by Tito Livio, who was all but forgotten for a half-century after his departure, but by those Englishmen in Oxford and London who, at the end of the fifteenth century, finally came to realize the value of the library Duke Humphrey had bequeathed to them. Emili's reception had been prepared by the first Italian humanists who settled in Paris in the decade before Mancini and by the first French historian to adopt at least the externals of ancient historiographical models, Robert Gaguin. Marineo's reception had been prepared by the decision of the University of Salamanca to follow recent Italian examples in creating a chair of poetry; and King Ferdinand showed his appreciation of Marineo's work by making him royal chronicler in 1506 and by taking him along on royal tours of his far-flung dominions.

Even more fortunately, the emigrant historians usually had little difficulty in locating an abundance of source materials. To be sure, their intervention was indispensable, for domestic chronicle traditions alone proved no more capable of generating humanist forms of historiography in northern Europe than they had been in Italy—as shown notably by the abundance of chronicles and the absence of history in East Prussia.[136] Moreover, while Italian humanists were willing to learn languages like Spanish and French that related to their own, and while Vergilio took the trouble to master even such an irregular language as English, they found it very difficult to learn languages like Polish and Magyar—quite understandably in a day before the existence of dictionaries or grammars. But happily even native chronicles were often written in Latin, which educated Poles and Hungarians considered to be the only language worthy of literature. Hence Bonfini found most of what he needed in the *Chronica Budense,* whose anonymous author knew enough of humanist standards to decorate his tales of national origins with the names of ancient writers, and in the much longer *Chronica Hungarorum* of Jan Thuróczy (or Thwrocz) whose text showed at least some signs of his having read, besides the *Chronica Budense,* the works of the ancient historians he had brought home with him from Bologna.[137] Callimaco supplemented what he had read in the chronicle of Johannes Długosz (Dluglosseus) with what he learned in conversations with Vincentius Kadłubek and Mattias Drzewicki (Drevitus), then the leading authorities on Polish antiquities.[138] Tito Livio was guided by several earlier accounts of the life of his hero as well as by the *Brut,* which had been finished on the eve of his arrival in England. Vergilio was guided for recent history by interviews with eyewitnesses, for less recent history by the several vernacular chronicles provoked by the War of the Roses, and for more remote history by the ancient chronicles of Britain, one of which, that of Gildas, he himself edited for publication. Emili was guided through the High Middle Ages by Froissart and by the chronicle of Saint-Denis, of which a new version had been published in 1477, and he was guided through the fifteenth century, when the medieval chronicle tradition withered away, by Commynes and Nicole Gilles.

Since they were the first to use any of these sources critically and systematically, and since they continued to follow Italian pratice in relying heavily on the standard ancient and modern Italian historians, it is not surprising that these historians occasionally made mistakes. Emili avoided error only by declining to judge among conflicting reports ("some say . . . others say . . . ; but in any case . . ."). In one case he avoided error only by compounding it—by taking the miracles and the visions out of Nicole Gilles's account of the capture of Pamplona and inserting in their place an equally fictitious Charlemagne addressing his troops in Caesarian periods. Hence one recent authority has demoted him to the rank of a "médiocre instituteur," and another has held him responsible for retarding the development of critical historiography among his French successors.[139] Similarly, Callimaco so misread his Polish sources on the early history of Poland that another modern authority has called him retrogressive with respect to Długosz and generally "schlecht unterrichtet" on the whole subject (Zeissberg). Bonfini got so carried away with his campaign to perpetuate the Corvinian constitution that he traced Mattias's father's family back to ancient Rome, his mother's family back to ancient Greece, and the rest of the Hungarians back to Scita, son of Hercules, the first of the Scythians. And Vergilio became such an enthusiastic naturalized Englishman that he turned Philippe of

Valois into a Hannibal and explained the ascension of Henry VII as the fulfillment of a 797-year-old prophesy.

Nevertheless, all these historians succeeded in imposing history upon cultures that previously had known only chronicles. They began by sweeping away local myths about national origins. Emili refused to speculate on what the ancient Franks might have said if they had not been so busy acting ("propitiores ad faciendum quam ad dicendum"), and he began only with those of the Franks who were specifically mentioned in reliable late-Roman authorities—Orosius, Jerome, Gregory of Tours. His own "Francus" turned out to be not a son of Hector but the author of a letter to Theodoric reporting a victory over the Alamanni; and his Trojan homonym was accordingly reserved thereafter for the poets, to the immense advantage both of history and of French Renaissance poetry.[140] Similarly, Vergilio drove the Knights of the Round Table out of the domain of history, even at the risk of annoying Tudor propagandists. Marineo refused to admit anything about Roman Spain that he could not document with references to Tacitus, Eusebius, Jerome, and, alas, the "Beroso" of Annio da Viterbo. Bonfini refused to admit anything about ancient Scythia that was not reported in Ptolemy or anything about modern Scythia that he could not learn from returning merchants; and he buttressed his thesis of the Hungarians' non-European descent by noting the absence of any similarity between Magyar and the neighboring Slavic languages.

The historians then went on to propose a more accurate and more objective account of succeeding events. Bonfini may have been guilty of European ethnocentrism when he compared Tartar songs to the mooing of cows, and he may have exaggerated somewhat in displaying the virtues of his first imitable hero, St. Stephen; but he avoided any expression of opinion on either side in his much more abundant, because better documented, description of the wars of the Hungarians with various of the Italian states. Tito Livio too may have exaggerated somewhat in maintaining that "no sign of lasciviousness was ever found [in Henry V] after the death of his father"; but he was far less receptive to apocryphal stories about him than any of his English contemporaries. Mancini admitted to some uncertainty about the events he had witnessed; but the rediscovery of his text some four centuries after Emili saw the last known copy forced an important revision even in modern scholarly theses concerning the popularity of Richard III. And much as some of his hosts may have disputed his account of recent history, Vergilio was far less biased than any of his English predecessors or contemporaries—Edward Hall or John Leland, for example (Trimble).

Finally, most of the historians were able to extract from what they had learned about the past some practical advice on what to do in the future. The hope of Poland, concluded Callimaco, lay in institutionalizing the dynastic union with Lithuania and in making the king stronger and the nobles weaker. The hope of England, Vergilio decided, lay in perpetuating the Tudor dynasty, which alone seemed capable of avoiding the errors of the Lancastrians and the Yorkists; and he refused to abandon his conviction even after the Act of Supremacy presented him with a personal conflict of loyalties—a conflict so severe that he could solve it, in the end, only by returning to Italy. The hope of Hungary, insisted Bonfini, lay in maintaining the constitutional reforms of Mattias, whose reign he elevated for rhetorical purposes to the rank of a golden age. When those reforms were instead abandoned, first by Mattias's spineless son and then by the weak foreign prince to whom he voluntarily yielded his crown, Bonfini fell back on gloomy reflections that seem in retrospect to be prophetic of the catastrophe of Mohacz.

These theses were not always agreeable to the audiences to which they were directed. Callimaco was accused of having tried to subvert the Polish constitution, particularly after the king honored him with a magnificent funeral at public expense. Vergilio was assailed as antipatriotic by the latter-day Arthurian, John Leland, and as "that most rascall dogge knave in the worlde" by the vigilant hunter of Papists, John Foxe. But in an age when the stylistic, linguistic, and methodological principles of humanism were rapidly being adopted all over Europe, the historians easily won out over all their enemies. Tito Livio was translated or paraphrased into English at the beginning of the next century, and in this form he provided the standard account of the life of Henry V for the rest of the Tudor period. Vergilio was used as a model for most English historiography throughout the reign of Elizabeth and was an important source for Shakespeare in the composition of his historical plays. Emili was translated into German and Italian as well as into French. His history was reedited and continued at least three times in the course of the century. He served as a model for Bernard Du Haillan and as a source of inspiration and information for many of the other participants in the outburst of historical research during the Wars of Religion. Callimaco's *De Rege Vladislao* remained the standard history of the period, in the Augsburg (1518) and Cracow (1582) editions, well after the publication of the geographical-political survey of Poland by Marcin Kromer (Cromerus, 1512–89) in 1578.[141] Bonfini's *Decades* were reprinted some fifteen times in five languages. And although the Italian humanist hired to continue them, Francesco Pescennio (b. 1452),[142] did not manage to get much farther than some preliminary note-taking, they were accepted as authoritative both by the chief Magyar-language historian of the century, Gaspar Heltai (1575), and by the chief Latin-language historian of Hungary, the Padua-educated counselor of Emperor Rudolf II, Niklós Istvánffy (1538–1615).[143]

Having provided five of the greatest states of Europe with their respective versions of Livy—or Bruni or Sabellico—Italians might well have left the rest to the natives, among whom they succeeded in arousing an appreciation for this new form of literature. But Italians increasingly thereafter came to be valued abroad as artists, technicians, diplomats, and men of letters. This demand in turn created a new social category, one destined to play an important role in European history from the time of Leonardo da Vinci to that of Casanova. It consisted of a number of rootless, restless peripatetics, willing to sell their talents to whomever would pay the price, "men on whom a certain decree of the heavens has imposed a life of wandering about among the provinces of the world," as one of them put it.[144] And now that history had become recognized as a legitimate and useful form of literary expression in provinces other than the one in which they had been born, many of these peripatetics became, among other things, historians.

GABRIELE SIMEONI (or SYMEONI, 1507–c. 1570) and PROSPERO SANTACROCE (1513–89) both originally left home on diplomatic missions, the first on behalf of the beleaguered Florentine Republic, the second on behalf of Pope Paul III. But both remained after their missions were completed—the first thanks to ecclesiastical benefices procured by literary friends at court and subsidies from the bishops of Troyes and Clermont-Ferrand, the second in the service of Henry II and Charles IX. JACOPO STRADA left home to accept a position with Emperor Ferdinand as director of the imperial museum at Vienna, and he remained to become cultural adviser to Maximilian II. ALESSANDRO GUAGNINI (d. 1614) left Verona to accept a position in the Polish army, and he remained long enough as commander of the fortress at Vitebsk to become very familiar with "the language, customs, and laws of the Poles," who had "received him, although a foreigner, into their bosoms." No one knows why LUDOVICO PONTICO VIRUNIO or Simeoni's fellow Florentine PETRUCCIO UBALDINI left home.[145] But after their arrival in England one was employed in some capacity, perhaps as a pedagogue, by Henry Sidney, and the other was employed variously as a miniaturist, a pageant director, an actor, an Italian secretary, and an occasional diplomatic messenger at court under the auspices of William Cecil. None of them, however, even after a long residence abroad, ever severed his ties with his native country. Santacroce returned to Rome when Pius IV made him a bishop and a cardinal. Ubaldini ingratiated himself with the grand duke of Tuscany by compiling a genealogy of the Medici family,[146] and he managed to collect enough information about current political conditions in Naples and Rome as well as Florence to prepare a guidebook for aspiring English diplomats.[147] Simeoni devoted one of his historical works to a comparison of the constitutions of four northern Italian states—a comparison which made Venice the guardian of liberty, Ferrara a model of stability, and Milan the source of most of "the troubles not only of poor Italy but of all Europe." "Had Giangaleazzo only thought more about the public good," Simeoni reflected, "than about decorating his house with Royal insignia," he would not have married his daughter to Charles d'Orléans. Louis XII would then have had no justification for claiming Giangaleazzo's state. Charles V would have had no justification for taking it away from Francis I. And it would still be independent.[148]

Still, their main effort was dedicated to the history of the countries in which they settled. Besides an immense catalogue of the contents of his museum, Strada produced still another biographical compendium of the Roman emperors from Julius

Caesar to Maximilian II.[149] Simeoni produced a bilingual treatise on ancient medals and inscriptions, a dialogue on the location of Vercingetorix's last stand, and studies of the antiquities of Auvergne and Lyon.[150] Santacroce attributed the outbreak of civil war in France to the pent up "hatred and ill-will" of the Bourbons, which was unleashed by the sudden death of Henry II just at a moment when four decades of dynastic wars had left the monarchy exhausted. Religion, he surmised, was just an excuse. Who, after all, even in France, could take seriously a religious creed based on the necessity of the Cup for salvation and first proclaimed by a half-educated monk to curry favor with the Germans, a "populo vini cupidissimo"?[151] Pontico threw the Trojans out of England on the authority of Vergilio, of Thucydides (who declared most of the stories about them to be "fabulous"), and of Diodorus Siculus (who called even Herodotus "pater fabularum"). He then readmitted them in the form of Brutus, great-grandson of Aeneas, Turnus, his nephew and the founder of Tours in France, and Coelus, son of Lucius, whose favors toward the "viros doctos" of his realm Pontico held up as an example for imitation by modern monarchs. If his editor happened to find some of these "truths" a bit "fabulous" in their own right, he had to admit that they were supported by a string of citations from such impeccable authorities as Vergil, Caesar, and Gildas.[152]

Similarly, Guagnini was depressed by the small size of the animals and the squalid appearance of the houses in which they cohabited with people in Lithuania. He was scandalized by the way the Lithuanian lords treated their peasants, making them work as much as six days a week and robbing them at will. And he was horrified by the cruelty of Ivan the Terrible, whose murder of his own brother Guagnini described at length. But he was so faithful to the Polish chronicle tradition in tracing the Lithuanians back to the Italian prince Palaemon and the Poles back to the "most illustrious and magnanimous princes Cechus and Lechus" that his work was published in 1761 under the name of the Polish historian Maciej Stryjkowski, who had once accused him of plagiarism. Ubaldini bewailed "the constantly changing, even unstable, governments" of England and the weakness of Henry VIII for women, the principal cause of his cruel persecution of the monks. But he insisted that England, as well as Scotland, of which he wrote a *descriptio*, had become "great and powerful among Christians," and thus worthy of study by his fellow countrymen. He was finally proved correct by the events of 1588. Accordingly, he put down the results of his interviews with Sir Francis Drake in the form of a humanist commentary, beginning with the queen's first admonitions on the preparation of the Armada in Spain and ending with her proclamation of an annual national holiday in commemoration of its destruction.[153]

Of the two Italian historians of the Netherlands, one went to fight: POMPEO GIUSTINIANI, who served as aid to Ambrosio Spinola, the Genoese general in charge of military operations in Flanders during the last phases of the revolt against the Spanish crown. With the help of his comrade in arms, Giuseppe Gamurino of

Arezzo, Giustiniani narrated the siege of Ostend of 1601 from its inception, through the vain attempts of Spinola's brother Federico to prevent the arrival of reinforcements by sea, to the ceremonious signing of the surrender agreement by Maurice of Nassau. And he narrated it simply as a series of glorious military feats, without a single reflection of the ideological and national issues involved—which may be why he was ignored by the greatest modern historian of Belgium, Henri Pirenne.[154] The other historian went there as the business partner in his cousin's firm in Antwerp: LUDOVICO GUICCIARDINI (1521–84), a nephew of the historian Francesco. When the firm failed a few years after his arrival in 1541, Guicciardini established a new one of his own and rose to the honorable position of consul of the Florentine nation. But his tastes soon shifted from banking to letters and politics—to the detriment of his business, and probably also to the annoyance of Duke Cosimo de' Medici, who had to intercede with the Duke of Alba to get him out of jail. He became a close associate of the men of letters of Antwerp, whom he entertained with stories of "pleasant and grave sayings and deeds" culled from his voluminous reading in French, Latin, Spanish, and Italian literature; and these stories were immediately translated into French by François de Belleforest.[155] He also became an assiduous student of his adopted country: his *Descrittione di tutti i Paesi Bassi*[156] followed the pattern of Biondo and Alberti in covering the country town by town, in comparing the present circumstances of each with those mentioned in previous authors since the time of Caesar, and in preserving local spellings of technical and place names. He then became a student of recent history—somewhat less successfully, since his long reading list did not apparently include his uncle's *Storia d'Italia,* which might have served him as model. His *Commentarii delle cose più notabili seguiti in Europa* sought to put the history of the Netherlands in the context of the history of all Europe between 1529 and 1560. But since it merely listed events instead of establishing connections among them, he was left explaining the coming civil war as the result not of a historical process but of the gloomy prophecies of astrologers.[157]

Several of the most prolific Italian historians of the age went abroad not only in search of a profitable literary career but also because their religious opinions were no longer wholly consonant with what was becoming recognized as minimally acceptable at home. CELIO SECONDO CURIONE (1503–69) of Piedmont had already acquired considerable experience as a teacher of rhetoric in various northern Italian cities when, in 1542, he chose to emigrate rather than to explain to the recently reestablished Roman Inquisition why he had been reading Melanchthon.[158] After settling in Basel, by then one of the capitals of European culture, he rapidly acquired a wide reputation as an editor and commentator of ancient texts and as one of the leading theologians of the Italian religious diaspora. Such was his fame, indeed, that it won a chair of rhetoric also for his son AGOSTINO. GIOVAN MICHELE BRUTO (b. 1517) left his native Venice first in 1555, perhaps to avoid embarrassment after having left his religious order to marry.[159] From Antwerp, where he published his first book, he followed a Venetian ambassador from Madrid to London. In 1560 he visited

Genoa, Florence, and Rome on his way to a long sojourn in Lucca. In 1565 he left Venice again, this time to avoid a summons before the Inquisition, and spent most of the next decade living amid the Florentine colony in Lyon. In 1574 he accepted an invitation to write a sequel to Bonfini's history of Hungary from Stephen Báthory, prince of Transylvania. Two years later he followed Stephen to Cracow; and after his death he procured an appointment, at a nominal salary far higher than the one actually paid him, as court historian to Emperor Rudolf II. He died in 1592 en route to what he hoped would be a more remunerative post, again in Transylvania. PIETRO BIZZARRI (1525–after 1586), who had been brought up in a Capuchin orphanage in Urbino, discovered religious diversity first at Wittenberg in 1545, then at St. John's College, where he met two of the most famous Italian theologians of the age, Bernardino Ochino and Pier Martire Vermigli.[160] His English patron took him to Italy during the reign of Mary, and he remained in Venice for several years as his patron's informer. After shuttling back and forth between England and Normandy, he was hired again as an informer by the elector of Saxony; and after returning for three years to Antwerp, he vanished from sight somewhere in Holland by way of London and Hamburg.

While engaged in such dizzying peregrinations, these emigrant Italians all continued, like the technicians, soldiers, and bankers, to maintain contact with their homeland. Bizzarri wrote a history of Genoa in the hope of being invited to live there—only to have his work put on the Roman Index.[161] Curione assumed the role of propagator of Italian humanist culture in the north, translating Guicciardini and studying Giovio in preparation for a sequel of his own to Sabellico's *Enneades*.[162] Bruto entered the current debate about the origins of Venice with a long appendix to his collection of "Letters of Famous Men" (Lyon, 1561). He also entered the debate over the merits of Giovio by providing the critical notes for Federigo degli Alberti's *Difesa della Repubblica Fiorentina* (Lyon, 1566). Guided by the indomitable anti-Medicean exile, Donato Giannotti, and by the rather biased "Florentine citizens doing business in Lyon," he finally decided that all previous histories of Florence consisted of little more than "perpetual praise of the Medici alone, of lie-filled calumnies, of maledictions, villanies, and shameless falsehoods directed against the entire city." He therefore set out to rewrite them from the beginning, with the intention of exalting Guicciardini's oligarchical constitution and the last of its great representatives, Niccolò Capponi.[163] Unfortunately his research was restricted largely to the works of his predecessors; and instead of rejecting their theses, he ended up confirming them. He exalted Cosimo the Elder as "a most admirable man." He belittled Lorenzo's first declared opponent as an "acer iuvenis." He permitted Piero de' Medici to deliver undisturbed his customary six-page denunciation of the anti-Medician conspirators. But since he never got around to writing a sequel for the years after 1492, his chief villain, Cosimo I, wasted his time and money in trying to buy up and destroy all the available copies of the parts he had written.

Nor was the patriotism of the emigrants marred by their religious heterodoxy.

Bruto's Calvinist sympathies were so vague that even the papal nuncio in Poland had hopes of his imminent reconversion. Even Curione, the most theological of them all, was induced by his own theological hair-splitting to propose practical compromises that earned him repeated denunciations as a Nicodemite;[164] and the increasing intolerance shown by the magistrates of his adopted city toward his deviations from the doctrines to which he had been converted made him increasingly tolerant toward those he had rejected. When faced with what he, like all his colleagues back home, identified as the sole cause of the growth of the Turkish Empire, namely, dissension among the Christians, he was willing for a moment in 1567 to put aside his ever changing religious opinions and proclaim none other than the pope as the leader of Christendom against the common enemy.[165] His son Agostino agreed with him. *Concordia* and *populorum benevolentia,* Agostino pointed out, were the chief instruments of political success, and they had been wielded with as much skill by the modern Turks as they had been by the ancient Romans. *Discordia,* however, was the chief characteristic of Christians today, as it had been of Saracens in the past. And he was ready to enlist Catholics, Lutherans, and even his father's Soccinian friends in the 300,000-man army that he hoped some latter-day Peter the Hermit would soon call forth.[166]

Still, what interested them most was the history of the countries they visited; and since they visited so many of them, they soon set aside the restriction of the scope of history to a single political entity, a restriction that had been observed by the first generation of emigrant historians. To some extent, this universalism was a product of their adaptation of the humanist formula that all history is useful, whatever its particular subject. Northern Europeans too can profit, they proclaimed, from the examples of such eternal heroes as Themistocles, Alexander, and Alfonso d'Aragona. Italians too could profit from Bruto's biographies of Charles V and Archduke Ernst of Austria. And everyone could enjoy following Caesar's campaigns with the help of the maps in Bruto's pocket-book edition of the *De Bello Gallico.* To some extent this universalism was also the product of their study of the ancient historians, whom Bruto analyzed once again in the prefatory epistles he dedicated to Pier Capponi and to Stephen Báthory. Thucydides and Xenophon were all the greater for having overcome Athenian particularism. Philistos of Syracuse probably deserved the censure he received because of his subservience to the ruler of his city. And those famous exiles of antiquity, Polybius and Dionysius of Halicarnassus, owed their greatness to having escaped the control of the "powerful men" of their native countries. Foreigners, he concluded—deducing from the same sources exactly the opposite of the theses of the Italian municipal historians—invariably wrote better history than natives. They may have to "put up with the harshest and gravest burdens imaginable." But they alone are capable of freeing history from the patriotic bombast that almost destroyed it in the days of Isocrates. They alone are able to recognize it not only as a form of rhetoric, one which "teaches, exhorts, and enflames man to good actions," but also as a *scientia,* one which "refuses not only what is false but also what is uncertain, contradictory [*inconstantia*], and dubious." Hence Mattias Corvinus, Henry VIII, and Francis I did very well not to entrust the histories of their countries to any of their own subjects.

It was in accordance with these theses—rather than with the nonsense he put in his preface about "imbecillitate & inconstantia rerum humanarum"—that Curione placed the familiar theme of the Battle of Malta in a context that included "Thracia, Dacia, Moesia, Pannonia," and the whole of the Mediterranean. It was in accordance with such theses—and with the obvious model suggested by the opening lines: "Arabia omnis in tres partes est distributa, quarum una . . ."—that Agostino wrote a history of the Saracens, or rather a history of the Islamic Caliphate from the death of Muhammad to the rise of the Turks, based on everything he could discover about it from Byzantine ("Cendrenus, Zonaras & alii Graeci scriptores") as well as Latin sources. And if he found it hard not to portray the Saracens as the ravishers of Cyprus and Sicily, he also found that the Baghdad Caliphs were rulers who never permitted religious differences to impinge upon their patronage of the arts and sciences and who rescued the cultural heritage of antiquity just at the moment when the Iconoclastic Byzantines were throwing it out of Constantinople. It was also these theses that inspired Bruto to incorporate most of eastern Europe into what he entitled a history of Hungary alone. He could correct Bonfini's negative characterization of the kings of Poland and Callimaco's unfavorable judgment of Mattias Corvinus. He could further explain the ruin of Hungary after Mattias's death as a result of a contest for his crown among the rulers of all the neighboring states as well as the result of the usual moral decay ("a recto cursu gloriae . . . ad mollem et languidum, a labore, duritia . . . ad turpe otium, ad vinum, ad crapulam defluxisse. . . ."). He could describe the atrocities committed by Christians as eloquently as he did those committed by Turks. And after forty pages on the Battle of Mohacz, which he compared for dramatic effect with the battles between Alexander and the Persians and between Caesar and Pompey, he could show Stephen Báthory to be the first agent in an eventual resurrection of the ruined kingdom. He might also have persuaded his contemporaries of the validity of his view of Hungarian history had his manuscript not become a victim of the same dynastic rivalries that had been responsible for much of the tragedy he described— and had not all but censored scraps of it disappeared from sight until the end of the seventeenth century.[167]

Bizzarri's vision was even broader—so broad, indeed, that his most recent student (Firpo) has characterized his work as "a disorganized catalogue of names, dates, episodes, battles, defeats, intrigues, [and] plots . . . without a shadow of analysis or evaluation." Still, Bizzarri was not wholly unworthy of the laudatory sonnets he had solicited from a number of prominent Italian men of letters. For the current wars in Hungary actually were the result of Suleimān's desire to regain prestige after the debacle at Malta, of his pashas' realization that new conquests alone would make them personally wealthy, of Maximilian's attempts to win over the Hungarian nobility, of John of Transylvania's determination to drive Maximilian's soldiers out of Sakmár.[168] That Scotland at the same time was disturbed "turbis ac motibus," that the kings of Sweden and Denmark hated each other, that Charles IX and the Prince of Condé had fallen out: all these details might not have had any apparent relevance for what went on in Hungary, any more than the latest news from America, which Bizzarri could not resist throwing in. But they were included for correct reasons—namely, in response to what Bizzarri had learned from Guicciardini about the ultimate interrelationship among all contemporary political events. These same reasons permitted him then to abandon Giovio's crusading attitude toward the Turks—except for those moments in his history of the Cyprus war when he too succumbed to the excitement of Lepanto.[169] And he consequently portrayed Suleimān as a model prince and recognized in the Turkish Empire an administrative system far more efficent and effective than any known in Christendom. Similarly, modern Persia might not seem to have any apparent relation with what Ptolemy and Herodotus had said about ancient Persia, and it certainly had no relation with the "Eulogy of the German Nation" that Bizzarri inserted out of deference to his current employer, the elector.[170] But at least Bizzarri was able, as none of his Italian predecessors had been, to fill in the many silent centuries between Cyrus and his modern reincarnation, Uzun Hasan, "liberal, magnanimous, strong, prudent, warlike, venerable of sight and of word." And however disparate the contents might become, they were organized at least externally with strict regard for humanist notions of periodization: the Hellenistic empire, the age of Chosroes, the Arab conquest, the Crusades. For Persia, like Famagosta, was a link in the chain of interdependent phenomena that Bizzarri hoped, in spite of his doubtful talent for synthesis, to weld together in the form of a universal history.

To those Italians who went abroad as soldiers, scientists, diplomats, and religious refugees, the advent of the Counter Reformation added still another category: the official representatives of the Roman Church, whose diplomatic reports (the *Nuntiaturberichte*) surpass even those of the Venetian ambassadors for the mass of information they contain about political and ecclesiastical conditions all over Europe. Some of them turned out also to be historians. ALESSANDRO CILLI of Pistoia (b.c. 1565) accompanied his compatriot, the legate Bonifacio Vannozzi, to Poland at the turn of the century; and when he failed to obtain by correspondence a position either in Florence or in Urbino, he remained for another twenty years as court singer and Italian secretary to King Sigismund III and occasionally as a messenger for the grand duke of Tuscany. After returning home in the last years of his life, he published the results of what he had seen or what he had heard from his numerous well-placed friends about the rebellions of the Polish nobles in 1606–8 and about the heroic acts of the king in his running feud with the grand duke of Muscovy.[171] ANTONIO MARIA

GRAZIANI of Borgo San Sepolero (1537–1611) accompanied his guardian and tutor, Cardinal Filippo Commendone, to the imperial court, to Poland, and eventually even to Moscow; and, for the benefit of a young Polish nobleman who had studied at Padua, he wrote an account of what he had heard during his voyage of 1567 about recent events in Wallachia.[172] ANTONIO POSSEVINO (1533–1611) went on several missions to Scandinavia, Poland, Russia, and Transylvania on behalf of Pope Gregory XIII. His secretary and fellow Jesuit, GIOVAN PAOLO CAMPANO of Reggio Emilia (b. 1546), wrote a diary of the (1581) mission to Moscow for the information of the general of the Society.[173] And Possevino himself, after his return to Rome, wrote for the information of the pope historical-political-geographical descriptions of the various countries he had visited.[174]

All these historians were primarily dedicated to the purposes of their missions: to reestablish peace in northeastern Europe, to reunite the Russian Church with Rome, and to contain, if not to repel, the Turks and the Protestants. Not all of them, it is true, conceived of their historical writings solely as a means to these ends. Cilli seems to have appealed principally to those growing numbers of Italian readers in the seventeenth century for whom the exotic was of interest for itself. Even the re-Catholicization of Poland then underway meant little to him next to the more spectacular exploits of his military heroes. Graziani lost sight of religious issues— except to note that there was very little religion of any kind in Wallachia—because of his fascination with the adventures of a Cretan who-would-be-king by the name of John. Having mastered Latin, Italian, French, and Spanish within a few years of being hired as an assistant at the Vatican Library, John managed to persuade, successively, Emperor Charles V, whom he met in Flanders, a band of would-be crusaders, whom he rounded up in Denmark and Sweden, and the king of Poland, whom he met in Wilna, that he was the heir of the last Byzantine despot of the Peloponnesus. He then metamorphosed into a mathematician-magician and learned enough Romanian ("it's just like Latin if you listen carefully") to ingratiate himself with the butcher-prince of Wallachia, Alexander. At an opportune moment he summoned his crusaders, expelled Alexander, and proceeded to transform Wallachia into a Counter-Reformation paradise, free of Calvinists and subject to the rule of law. Just as he had completed his work, he was surprised by a horde of Turks and Tartars, who restored Alexander, butchered him and all his followers, sacked the entire country, and dragged 15,000 of the remaining Christian population into slavery. The story was indeed fascinating, even though it proved no more than what all Italians already knew: that some Greeks were too intelligent even for their own good.[175]

Yet even Graziani had learned about history as well as about the *Nicomachean Ethics* from Commendone's reading lists. Or at least he had learned enough to realize that he could not get away with consistently misreading Villani in order to whitewash the ancestors of his fellow citizens; and he accordingly left his history of his native city as an uncompleted manuscript.[176] He also knew that history could provide moral examples. He therefore brought the horrible Borgias, the good but misunderstood Savonarola, Alessandro de' Medici, John Fisher, et al, to be judged before the bar of Tridentine moral standards.[177] He knew further that good historians present causes as well as effects. After briefly reviewing the history of Cyprus from its occupation by the Romans to its occupation by the Venetians, he traced the Turkish invasion both to the usual divisions among Christians and to the machinations of certain Marranos who managed to capture the sultan's ear.[178]

Possevino, on the other hand, knew exactly what he was doing. After critically surveying all of the ancient, most of the Latin and Greek medieval, and a good number of the modern historians of all the nations of Europe, he concluded that history was one of the chief supports of orthodoxy, because it too recorded the Truth.[179] Before the advent of Christianity, it is true, some non-Christians had been good historians—namely, Tacitus, who could be justified by reference to Augustine, and Herodotus, whose bad reputation he ascribed to Plutarch's offended Boeotian patriotism. But after the fourth century, the best historians were invariably those whose authority had been recognized by the Church ("cui... auctoritatem Ecclesia tribuit"): Eusebius, Orosius, Chalkokondylis, Sigonio, Gilbert Génébrard. For "it is by the light of the Christian religion that they have abstained from falsehood." Error, then, could be explained as the result of two causes. The first was excessive patriotism, Possevino pointed out, unwittingly agreeing with Bruto and unwittingly contradicting his own brother and editor, Giovan Battista, who wrote a history of their native Mantua. For Christ's injunction to "love one another as I have loved you" ruled out any distinction between fellow countrymen and foreigners. And any historian who "preferred his own nation over others" would undoubtedly end in the kind of blasphemous obliteration of the truth committed by that patriot of Viterbo, Annio. The second cause of error was heterodoxy. If Zosimus slandered Constantine, it was because he hated Christianity—and therefore the Truth. If Commynes seemed occasionally to contradict himself, it was because Sleidanus had deliberately mistranslated him. If Vergilio seemed to make questionable remarks concerning Henry VIII, it was because English Protestants had introduced alterations into the text—alterations that were not fully revealed until the Roman censors managed to extract them from the "corrected" edition of Rome (1576).

Difficult as these theses might have been to maintain in the face even of the evidence he himself mustered to their support, Possevino applied them rigorously in his own writing. The only written material then available in Italy about the countries to which he was to be sent consisted of two short memoranda, both of them over a half-century old. The first had been prepared for Pope Clement VII by a certain ALBERTO CAMPENSE on the basis of information supplied him by his father and brothers, whom he claimed had visited Russia several times on business. The other had been prepared by Paolo Giovio on the basis of an interview with the grand duke's legate to the same Pope Clement.[180] Still another had been prepared more recently by one Francesco Tiepolo from secondhand sources; but it did not become known until the mid-twentieth century.[181] Nothing at all was available about Sweden or Transylvania, at least in the form of historical descriptions and historical narratives. But none of these writings was more than minimally adequate, notwithstanding the unquestionable piety of their authors. Campense's judgment of Russian religion did not take into account the refinements of Catholic orthodoxy established at Trent, and Giovio's ambassador admittedly spoke only what little Latin he had picked up during a previous embassy to Sweden.

Possevino therefore did his own research. He interviewed a Florentine merchant named Giovanni Tedaldi, who had been to Russia more recently. He diligently inquired of all the Latin- and Italian-speaking authorities he could find in Poland. He devoured Bruto's history of Hungary—in spite of the danger he knew it posed for his soul. He put up with the shocking behavior of the Russian delegates whom he was charged with escorting from Venice to Rome. He traveled across the plains of White Russia in midwinter. He managed to survive in Moscow even though its entire marketplace offered fewer goods for sale than a single shop in Venice. And he tramped, uncomplaining, around the unhospitable villages of eastern Hungary and the burned-out villages of Livonia.

Obviously, Possevino could not be wholly impartial. He could not bring himself to assist at the Orthodox liturgy that had been arranged for him in Smolensk. He had read too much about the Goths in Rome not to associate them with the Russians in Livonia. He had lived in too many stone palaces to enjoy Russian wooden huts. He was too steeped in humanist theories of causation not to attribute religious pluralism in Transylvania to the evil influence of a certain royal counselor from Saluzzo, and he could understand Anti-Trinitarianism only as a logical consequence of Luther's theological deviation.[182] He was too imbued with Aristotle's *Politics* not to be shocked by a ruler who actually owned all the land and who denied his subjects the slightest freedom of movement. Nevertheless, he managed to rise above the anti-Russian prejudices of the Poles, to which most foreign observers were then exposed. He learned to look upon both the Orthodox and the heterodox as inherently rational men who could be persuaded by rational arguments. All they needed to become civilized was to accept the doctrine of Tridentine Catholicism and recognize the authority of its visible head. This goal could easily be achieved by sending them copies of Thomas Aquinas's *Errors of the Greeks* and of Anselm's *Procession of the Holy Spirit* and by establishing seminaries at Moscow and Kolozsvár (Cluj). And thanks to his efforts, the eventual teachers in these seminaries could have had at their disposal what one modern historian (Giacomo Bascapé) has called "the most accurate picture of the conditions and the life in that region" of any published in the sixteenth century.

13

CONTEMPORARY HISTORY AND UNIVERSAL HISTORY

The Universality of Memorable Events

THANKS TO THE EFFORTS OF ITALIANS WHO WENT ABROAD, OF FOREIGNERS WHO CAME to Italy, and of Italians who imported works written abroad about other countries, it soon became possible to write about almost any part of the world without having to leave home. In the first decades of the sixteenth century, accurate information was still somewhat difficult to procure. GIOVANNI GARZONI had been able to learn something about the tiny town of Ripa in the Marche because one of its citizens happened to have been assigned to a monastery in Bologna, where Garzoni happened to be practicing medicine.[1] But when he tried to distinguish among such mysterious places as Wittenburg, Thuringia, and Lusatia, he had not even the ancient geographers to guide him; and when he tried to recreate the heroic actions of the first elector of Saxony for the moral inspiration of the current elector, he had to rely mostly on his own imagination. All the princes of the Wettin line turned out to possess the same monotonous list of virtues: "sapientia, prudentia, iustitia, magnanimitas." And anyone who ever opposed any of them, from the *Vindeli* to the citizens of Erfurt, were ipso facto held guilty of "scelera."[2]

By the last decades of the century, on the other hand, the quantity of available information was quite sufficient for the purposes of historians raised in the humanist tradition. GIOVAN ANTONIO VIPERANI easily found in the published "writers about Lusitanian affairs" all that he needed to know about the background of the devolution of Portugal to the Spanish crown in 1580. For the rest he could rely on the common knowledge that the inhabitants of "Mauretania" were "unstable and faithless of spirit" and that all Iberia too "in tres divisa est partes"—not Aragon, Castile, and Portugal, to be sure, but "Baetica, Tarraconensis, and Lusitania."[3] Similarly, FILIPPO PIGAFETTA easily found all he needed to know about the kingdom of the Congo from a Portuguese missionary named Orlando Lopez, who had retired to a Roman hospital directed by one of Pigafetta's friends.[4] He probably learned about the defense of Paris against a prince he scrupulously referred to only as "il Navarro" from the papal legate who had supported the defenders; for his perfectly balanced commentary ended with the legate's pomp-filled return to Rome for the conclave of 1590.[5] He could therefore prove conclusively that everything Ptolemy (whom he had read in Greek) had said about Equatorial Africa was wrong and that the pope's subsidies to French Catholics were well spent.

With the exception of Garzoni, who may have been hoping for an appointment in Saxony similar to the one given to Bonfini in Hungary, most of the sedentary Italians who wrote about specific foreign countries did so for one of two reasons. Viperani, LUCA CONTILE, and BERNARDO DAVANZATI (1529–1606) sought principally to demonstrate how well they had mastered the art of historical writing. Contile began just as he should have: with a detailed survey of the controversies over the succession to the English throne on the death of Henry VIII, with a notation of the mileage distance from London of every place mentioned, and with brief character sketches of all the agents.[6] The narrative of events then follows the machinations of the Duke of Northumberland down to the point where they were wrecked by the successful accession of Mary Tudor. Interruptions in the narrative, such as the text of the proclamation as queen of Lady Jane Grey, serve not to document the narrative but simply to heighten its dramatic effect. Similarly, Davanzati began with the event from which all the rest depended: the marriage of Henry VIII and Catherine of Aragon.[7] He then introduced the evil personages responsible for the unhappy consequences of this event: Thomas Wolsey, "an ambitious, audacious man"; the French ambassador, who hoped to marry the king to the daughter of Francis I; and finally Anne Boleyn, whose "spirit was full of . . . pride, jealousy, and lasciviousness," and who "at the age of fifteen let herself be deflowered [*sverginare*] by a cupbearer and a chaplain. . . ." He ended his narrative when the process came to its logical close, with the accession of Mary.

Neither of these two authors could offer any new information about the events they described, for both of them were equally ignorant of the English language, and Davanzati was usually content merely to condense Sleidanus. Neither of them could offer any new interpretations of the events, because both of them were convinced that all faithful Catholics were by definition pious and holy and that everyone else was bad. Rather, Contile sought to demonstrate that he could write a monograph as coherent and as consistent as Sallust's, notwithstanding the introduction of one element, religion, that Sallust had not anticipated. Similarly Davanzati sought to demonstrate that he could surpass the taciturn Tacitus in a composition of his own, just as he surpassed him in his translation of the *Annals* and the *Histories*.[8] As Davanzati's Italian prose, prepositions and all, ended up with fewer words than Tacitus's Latin prose, so the *Scisma d'Inghilterra* (a record-breaking short title in the long-title-loving sixteenth century) compressed a maximum of narration into a minimum of words, even at the expense of such syntactical twisters as this: "sospettante non Cesare gli togliesse lo Stato." It thus proved that historians could write "without all the pomp of various declamations" even in an age dominated by "the fertility and richness of Marcus Tullius." Unfortunately, the work remained the private possession of Davanzati's colleagues in the Accademia degli Apatisti for another four decades, by which time the last traces of Tacitean conciseness had been thoroughly buried in baroque verbosity. And it was not fully appreciated, either for its stylistic or for its substantive qualities, until the mid-eighteenth century, when a Florentine editor dedicated a second edition to Frederick II of Prussia.

CIRO SPONTONE (c. 1552–c. 1610), ASCANIO CENTORIO, and IERONIMO DE FRANCHI CANESTAGGIO, on the other hand, wrote chiefly for the purpose of supplying military and political theorists with empirical data. To be sure, all three of these historians scrupulously observed the stylistic and formal principles of humanist commentaries. Spontone's history of Transylvania begins with a historical and geographical description of the Carpathian paradise he unfortunately never visited: "softly sloping hills [that produce] an abundance of excellent wines," "green [*verdeggianti*] woods [in which] are born diverse animals for hunting," "high mountains with mines rich in gold and silver." It then presents the principal protagonists of the ensuing conflict: the Ottomans, the Tartars, the emperor, and Prince Sigismund. And it would have observed an impeccable topical unity had the author not been tempted into updating his narrative from time to time for the decades between 1588 and 1610.[9] Similarly, Canestaggio's history of the annexation of Portugal begins with the preparations for King Sebastian's invasion of Morocco, and it ends with the execution of the last Portuguese "rebel" against Philip II. His history of the war in the Netherlands, "the most atrocious, most pitiful, most difficult war that has ever been heard of," includes only those external events, like the outbreak of civil war in France, that directly affected the principal subject.[10] And both these works thus fitted very well into the series of books—a discourse on *Fortuna,* a commentary on Plutarch, a volume of rhymes—that he was composing as a member of the Giolito de' Ferrari team of popular writers in Venice. Canestaggio also hoped, with works as formally impeccable as Livy's, to elevate Ottavio Farnese to the rank of Fabius Maximus and to equate Emperor Ferdinand's wars in Hungary with those of the Romans against Carthage. According to his colleague Lodovico Dolce, he succeeded:

> Che vinto è ogni pennello, ogni perfetto
> stile, se'n va da lui molto lontano;
> ne scrisse così ben l'horribil guerra
> che con Carthago hebbe l'antica Roma,
> Com'ei di Ferdinando in quella terra.

And François de Belleforest apparently agreed with Dolce, for he extracted from the narrative the "harangues militaires" and published them separately in French translation.[11]

Yet Spontone's main concern was to reinforce with examples taken from the present the *avvertimenti historici* that he had collected from the age of Lycurgus and the age of the Duke of Athens and thus more effectively to refute "Nicolò Machiavello," who, "with diabolical inventiveness tried to drag hordes of men [*grandi schiere*] into accepting his evil opinions." Since "noble Italy, almost alone among the many provinces of Europe, after . . . horrible and intestine wars, now enjoys the peace it has so long desired," he had to look elsewhere for a subject; and he chose Hungary and Transylvania because the wars fought there were more horrible even than those of France and Flanders.[12] Similarly, Centorio's main interest was to show how a truncated fragment of a ruined kingdom could affirm its independence amid a four-way power struggle; and he appropriately supplemented his history of the wars in Transylvania with a manual for generals.[13] Canestaggio's main interest was to show how "a commonwealth . . . can maintain itself" in the face of both "domestic corruption" and the inherent ambition of all princes "to increase the size . . . of the states they possess." Now that Genoa had successfully settled its problems of domestic discord, the best example of such commonwealths were Portugal and the Netherlands. Portugal, although "a small and sterile country," managed to make itself "the equal of all the [other] kingdoms of Spain . . . , by good institutions, frugality, and the virtues of several of its kings"—only to be corrupted by "overconfidence, that natural vice of the Portuguese," and by the luxuries its merchants brought back from India. The Netherlands, once "a body [so] healthy and strong" that it could hold off "the monarch of half the world," was eventually, through a "malignant illness," made to suffer "the greatest unhappiness imaginable."

All three authors therefore assumed an obligation to supply themselves with oral and written reports by the participants in the wars they wrote about—including, in one case, the emperor himself. All of them willingly sacrificed brevity to thoroughness. And all of them maintained the strictest impartiality with respect to the issues at stake. Centorio recognized that the Christian soldiers in Hungary were more interested in plunder than in the defense of Christendom; and he had not a single word of reproach for the decision of the prince of Transylvania to ally himself with the sultan in order to defend himself against the emperor. Being a foreigner, Canestaggio could state exactly what he had discovered after "diligent investigations" "without respect for those who . . . don't want to hear of their own defects." He criticized the Portuguese Jesuits for filling the young king's head with romantic dreams while abandoning his body to "delizie." He upbraided Centorio's great peacemaker, Philip II, for ignoring the good advice of his own governors and for rescrambling the Belgian dioceses without consulting the bishops. And he had nothing but anathemas for the Spanish soldiers who sacked Antwerp.

Once Italian historians began writing about one foreign country, there was no reason why they should not go on to write about others. Realizing that the sovereign of much of Italy was also the sovereign of much of the rest of Europe, Contile decided to organize his memorable events not around a succession of princes but around a single military captain, Cesare Maggi of Naples, in whom he saw the incarnation of all military virtues. And as Maggi passed from the service of the Venetians to the service of the duke of Urbino, of Prospero Colonna, and finally, during the Schmalkaldic War, of the emperor, Contile's history came to include all the states of Germany, notwithstanding his lack of sympathy for "that strongly armed province, odious to the Italian name."[14] Realizing that what happened in Transylvania depended in large measure upon "the more notable events not only in Europe but in all parts of the world." Centorio frequently interrupted his narration of domestic affairs to determine why, at the same time, the Sienese had expelled an Imperial garrison, why the duke of Suffolk had opposed the accession of Mary Tudor, and why the Viennese were so upset over a bolt of lightning that struck in the middle of a cloudless day. And the second volume of a history of one state thus became the history of a whole continent.[15]

Actually, the format adopted by Contile and Centorio was not one of their own invention. It was implicit in Guicciardini's *Storia d'Italia,* which frequently went outside of Italy for explanations of what went on inside of Italy. It was somewhat more explicit in Francesco Vettori's admission that "the historical events of our times are so closely bound together that you can't speak of those of Italy alone and omit all the others" (Dedication). And it was stated very clearly in FRANCESCO CARPESANI's (or CARPESANO—1441–1528) history of the long-range consequences of the assassination of Duke Galeazzo Maria Sforza in 1476. For the siege of his native Parma in 1521, which Carpesani had witnessed in his old age, as well as the various diplomatic missions he had undertaken on behalf of Ludovico il Moro, had made him realize that the calamities of his own city were somehow (he never figured out just how) connected with the contemporary calamities of all other Italian cities; and he came to realize that these calamities were being perpetrated by forces external to all of the cities. National frontiers thus vanished along with city-state frontiers; and the accession of Francis I in distant France became as important to the citizens of Parma as was his capture at nearby Pavia to all his subjects in his own domains.[16]

Still the main reason for the expansion of the geographical and chronological scope of history lay in the humanist doctrine that memorable events are memorable wherever they occur. ANTONFRANCESCO CIRNI prepared for writing about that most memorable event, the siege and relief of Malta, by interviewing numerous eyewitnesses, by personally traveling to Messina and Malta to check on the sites, and by reading his resulting manuscript out loud to other eyewitnesses to make sure it contained neither errors nor omissions. But.he soon realized that even this event could be understood properly only as a consequence of a chain of events that had begun as early as A.D. 433. And after following this chain through the failure of the Crusades to the division of Christendom into hostile religious loyalties, he perceived that the siege of Malta marked the beginning of an uphill turn after several centuries of steady decline. For it coincided with the settling of the Farnese in Parma, the restoration of Genoese rule in his native Corsica, the end of the Valois-Hapsburg wars, and the successful conclusion of the Council of Trent. Better yet, all these events were followed by the election, "truly by divine inspiration," of Pope Pius V, thanks to whose energetic leadership Christianity could now be expected to "spread so far and wide that the Mohammedan sect will soon be extinguished."[17]

Similarly, EMILIO MARIA MANOLESSO began with a five-page letter demonstrating the ability of the Venetians to defend themselves against the Turks in 1570 as effectively as they had previously defended themselves against the Visconti and the League of Cambrai; and the letter carefully stated the author's qualifications for writing on such subjects by reference to his titles as "doctor of arts, of civil and canon law, and of sacred theology." In several more pages of parallel clauses he traced the history of Cyprus from its prehistoric separation from the mainland to the decision of the sultan to turn it into an endowment for the support of his new mosque at Adrianople. But the war in Cyprus then reminded him of all the other memorable events that had taken place in those same "most unhappy" years—the elevation of Cosimo I to the rank of grand duke, the truce between Charles IX and the Huguenots, the rebellion of Holland, the appointment of Geronimo Mercuriale as professor of medicine at Padua, and the birth to the wife of a Venetian sailor of "a piece of flesh" with the head and feet of a chicken.[18] CESARE CAMPANA of Aquila (c. 1540–1606) began with the siege of Antwerp. For he hoped to turn Alessandro Farnese, the chief protagonist, into another Alexander the Great, and himself into another Arrian—or at least into a well-subsidized protégé of Duke Ranuccio of Parma, Alessandro's son, to whom his brief commentary (72 pages) was dedicated.[19] He accomplished his end by stopping with the articles of surrender, thus overlooking the less agreeable history of the subsequent sack. But this one incident, "the greatest and the most stupendous military action that has ever been heard of in any city," led him to supply the more general context in the form of a "history of the wars of Flanders in defense of the Catholic religion [waged] by the king of Spain during a space of thirty-five years."[20] The wars in Flanders suggested a parallel with the contemporary wars between the Persians and the Turks. And he then sought to establish a connection between Persia and Flanders by giving an account of all the other wars that had taken place in the intervening parts of the world—in all the parts, that is, except Italy, where nothing of note any longer occurred except an occasional parade in honor of a cardinal-legate returning to Rome.

Unfortunately, even Campana, the most committed of the poly-national historians, ran into difficulties when he tried to relate the events of one place with those of another. He himself was well aware of the perils faced by anyone who tried to view the whole world from the vantage point of a comfortable teaching position at Vicenza (1572), at Legnano (1582), at Ferrara (1593), or at Verona.[21] For—as he explained in a long introductory *Discorso* to his *Dell'historie del mondo*—the sedentary historian, unlike Xenophon or Caesar, was dependent wholly upon the reports of others, reports which were inevitably colored by the particular passions of the individual writers.[22] Yet he also had several advantages. First, not being a native of the countries he was writing about, he could be more objective; and he proved his point by referring to other well-known nonnative historians like Paolo Emili, Polidoro Vergilio, Callimaco Esperiente, and, above all, his chief source of inspiration, Dionysius of Halicarnassus, who "surpassed Livy, Tacitus, and all the Latins who wrote before and after him about the affairs of Rome." Second, since the truth was always impossible to determine absolutely, he was better able to decide what was more reasonable—that is, what ought to have been, which was the closest that most men could come to recreating what actually had been. Finally, since the "end of history is principally to be useful and only incidentally to be pleasing," he was better able to cut out of his narrative those things which might be true but which certainly were not useful. And that procedure, he noted, fully accorded with the precept of the philosophers: "What may be damaging ought not to be taught."

Putting these principles into practice, however, was quite a different matter. In order to justify beginning with the arbitrarily selected year 1580, Campana had to imagine a preceding age of absolute peace and tranquility, one in which the only defect consisted of an occasional famine. But what such an uneventful age had to do with the relentless succession of unsettling events that followed he was at a loss to say: the annexation of Portugal, the civil wars in France, the construction of a fortress in Ireland, a riot in Aachen, the death of the brother of the king of Denmark, the presentation by the king of Persia to a Turkish general of a Koran bound in tapestry. He thus left to his son AGOSTINO. the task of providing an introduction and a sequel to his work. But Agostino's solution to the problem of organization was not much better. For by including only those events that had some relation to those personages he deemed the most important of the age, the kings of Spain, he ended up not with a history of the world but with a survey of "l'époque de Philippe II"—and III.[23]

Paolo Giovio and His Successors

Many of these difficulties could more easily have been solved had these historians sought to imitate, rather than just plunder, the *Sui Temporis Historiae Libri* of PAOLO GIOVIO (1483–1553), which appeared in the first complete edition (1550–52)[24] before any of them had begun writing. Giovio too wrote histories of various nations: a *relazione* on Muscovy, a commentary on the Albanian resistance,[25] and a geographical-historical description of the British Isles.[26] The last-mentioned of these works is a good example of his success in the genre. He took his information about ancient times from Caesar, Pliny, Strabo, and Tacitus's *Agricola*. He took his information about modern times from what Vergilio had written and what Reginald Pole, the exiled cardinal of England, had told him in personal interviews. He began each historical section not with the Trojans or with Brutus but with the moment when Britain was first reported in reliable historical records: Caesar's invasion. And he ended with the most recent event about which accurate information could be obtained: the marriage of Henry VIII and Catherine Howard. Such was his success, indeed, that the *Descriptio* was warmly received even in Britain, which Giovio never saw. George Lyly composed a eulogy of the author, whose text he edited; and he filled in its one notable lacuna by adding an appendix about the descendants of Brutus.

Giovio was also something of a municipal historian. He expressed his constant affection toward his fellow citizens of Como by interceding on their behalf with the pope and the governor of Milan. He dedicated much of his time and money to planning and managing a portrait gallery in the museum he established at Como. And he supplemented his brother Benedetto's history of the city itself with his own *descriptio* of the lands around the lake.[27] To some extent, Giovio was a loyal citizen of his greater fatherland as well—that is, of the Duchy of Milan, of which he wrote a history in accordance with the biographical form he inherited from the Lombard historians of the mid-fifteenth century. He rejected what he identified as legendary in the "often uncouth" medieval chronicles as well as in his chief source of information, Tristano Calco. No fictitious Roman ancestors, he insisted, could provide the Visconti any more glory than that which they had acquired by their own virtue; and Ottone himself had scoffed at the "marvelous conjunction of planets" that supposedly accompanied his birth. But at the same time, he accepted the principal theses he found in the historians. Bernabò was indeed "imperious, harsh, and cruel"—and Giovio did not even have to repeat the story about his dogs to prove it. Giangaleazzo was "resplendent in gravity and prudence, . . . more illustrious and more magnificent in the extent of his dominions and the splendor of his life . . . than any prince in Italy since the time of the Goths." Francesco Sforza, even while he was tearing apart the Marche, was "famous for his military prudence and his extraordinary valor." And all his rivals—Braccio da Montone, Paolo Orsini, and Alfonso d'Aragona—were brutes, who fought "with ungrateful spirit and criminal arms."[28]

Moreover, Giovio possessed at least one of the essential qualifications that might have led him to write national history on the model of a Guicciardini or a Sigonio: a deep patriotic affection for all of Italy and a profound bitterness over its recent calamities. Better yet, he possessed an ability to grasp the personalities of individual men that enabled him to explain the tragedies according to the humanist scheme of causation he shared with all his contemporaries. Best of all, he possessed a vivacity of style and a conciseness of expression that made his work as exciting to read in Latin as in Italian translation; and, unlike Sigonio, he succeeded in being both comprehensible and pleasing to transalpine as well as to Italian readers. He also possessed an appreciation of the better things of life—good wine, handsome women, and colorful pageants. He was thus able (as Guicciardini, with his "unadorned, economical" prose [Chabod], was not) to give his readers occasional relief from the tragedy presented in his narrative; and he was able at the same time to appeal to the love of display so characteristic of the age of Paolo Veronese. The shape of Vittoria Colonna's breasts, the brilliance of a wedding feast in Casa Trevisan, the color of Francis I's armor at Pavia, the designs of the brocaded vestments at the Congress of Bologna—all those, for Giovio, were part of history. So also was the taste of the various sauces served with the forty-one different kinds of fish eaten by ancient and modern Romans, for which he gave recipes during a series of delightfully learned conversations among his high-ranking literary and ecclesiastical friends in the Curia in 1524.[29]

Yet the project to which Giovio had been chiefly dedicated ever since his arrival in Rome in 1514 was neither a municipal, nor a regional, nor a national, nor even a poly-national history. It was rather a "history of his own times, one that is universal and that includes the whole world" (preface). Everything else was secondary: his training in philosophy at Padua, to which he seldom again referred even after Leo X made him a lecturer in philosophy at Rome, his official position as physician to Cardinal Giulio de' Medici, which he seems never to have exercised, his duties, after 1527, as bishop of the remote southern diocese of Nocera dei Pagani, which he seldom visited and which he administered through a vicar for the sole purpose of making a living from it. His *elogia* of famous men of letters and arms,[30] his widely acclaimed biographies of illustrious contemporaries,[31] his contribution to that highly popular academic parlor game, the composition and the explanation of mottoes *(imprese)*—all these he considered merely as momentary distractions from his main task. They required no further research. They could be supported by references to what "we have written more fully in our *Historiae*" (*Vita del Gran Capitano,* p. 40). They enabled him to analyze in greater detail the personalities of some of his major protagonists. And they permitted him to work out more fully those elements of his theses that were barred by humanist limitations on the subject matter of history—such as the cultural as well as the political golden age of the pontificate of Leo X, which was to be one of his more influential bequests to European historiography in general during the next four centuries.

Giovio prepared himself for a career as a world historian by becoming acquainted with the leading historians of his generation—with Bembo and Navagero in Venice and Padua, with Varchi and Nerli in Florence, with Guicciardini in Bologna. In fact, he was one of the first to read all of Machiavelli's works at a time when most of them were still unpublished; and it was thanks to him—and to his conversations with the leaders of Neapolitan culture during his temporary residence at Ischia—that those works became known and appreciated at Naples as early as 1527–28.[32] At the same time, he began systematically to collect information. He read all the chronicles, *relazioni,* and histories he could get his hands on in any of the many languages he could understand—including those parts of Commynes that were omitted from Sleidanus's Latin translation. He took full advantage of the particularly favorable circumstances of his long residence in Rome, where diplomats, merchants, petitioners, and favor-seekers from all over the world gathered to exchange views and news—not only in the Vatican, where Giovio normally resided, but also in the Campo de' Fiori, where he lived in the 1540s. He took full advantage of his position in Rome as a favorite of the first Medici pope and as a secretary of the second. It was through them that he met many of the eminent princes, generals, and men of letters of his age. As he pointed out in his preface.

> I have acquired a considerable knowledge of places, things, and men,
> . . . having come to know that the center of the whole world, the Court
> of Rome, having acquired the familiarity and the friendship of great
> kings, popes, and famous captains . . . [and having] seen battles, battle-
> fields, armies, sieges and the capture of cities, [and] fields full of
> dead bodies. . . .

It was particularly through Cardinal Giulio, who became Pope Clement VII in 1523, that he became acquainted with other cities as well. In 1515 he followed his patron to Bologna, where he first met King Francis I. In 1522 he followed him to Venice, where he first learned to admire a regime dedicated specifically to favoring "men of genius and the study of letters." In 1523 he followed him to Florence, where he first met the makers of the last republican regime. In 1529 he followed him again to Bologna, where he met the emperor Charles V.

Everyone Giovio met he interviewed; and he did so with such effectiveness that even Guicciardini was hesitant to receive him for fear of letting slip a state secret (Dionisotti). He thus managed to supplement what others knew through Spanish and Italian sources about the conquest of Tunis with what had been told him by the exiled king of Tunisia, by the Imperial admiral, Andrea Doria, and by several former officials in the fleet of the Turkish pirate-admiral, Barbarossa (Khayr al-Din). He was able to add to what he read about the Turks in Menavino with what he heard about them from the Greek scholar Janus Lascaris, to correct the accepted story of the death of Francesco Ferrucci with what he learned directly from the Spanish captain who had killed him, and to elaborate upon the version of Cosimo's election given by the Florentine historians with what he heard "from the mouth of the duke." He also knew how to put pressure on the reluctant: an order from Cosimo forced Varchi to refresh his memory concerning the exiles' rain-soaked march through the Mugello and the Casentino, which Varchi by then would have preferred to forget. Those he could not interview he solicited by letters, which were to remain one of the chief sources of information about contemporary affairs until the advent of periodicals late in the following century.[33] Sanudo regularly reported to him the news he was transcribing into his diaries. The Venetian ambassador Mario Foscarini kept him informed about Rome during his absence at the time of Pope Adrian VI. And the letters he sent and received from as far away as Constantinople soon came to form a sort of epistolary history in their own right, one that paralleled and illum- inated the work for which they were intended to be instruments of research.[34] To make sure his information was complete, Giovio then submitted the first drafts of the various books, as they were ready, to eyewitnesses and authorities: the first books to Leo X, Book VIII to the duke of Ferrara, Book IX to Equicola,[35] the secretary and the historian of the duke of Mantua. Those for which his information was not yet complete he postponed until such time as he could consult the latest authorities—which is why he wrote the books on the seige of Florence after he had written those on the events of 1537. And those for which his information remained incomplete at the time of his death, or for which his notes had been destroyed during the sack of Rome (e.g., Books V–X and XIX–XXIV), were finally published only in the form of outlines. So thorough and so meticulous was his research, indeed, that he soon became known as the best-informed man of his age; and even representatives of governments—like the Venetian ambassador at Milan who transmitted his letters to the Dieci—occasionally applied to him for assistance.

This abundance of information, as well as his wide reputation for being well informed, enabled Giovio to attain and to maintain a degree of objectivity considerably greater than that achieved by most of his contemporaries. To be sure, he too recognized that the purpose of history was also to denounce villains and exalt heroes—so that "the negligent and lazy, after reading the valorous acts of illustrious men, will be inflamed to act in a good and praiseworthy manner" (*Gran Capitano*, dedication); and, particularly in his biographies, he did not shy from using his customary abundance of morally charged adjectives in describing the personalities he judged. Alexander VI "stained the Papacy with infamous scandals," he insisted. Baldassare Carducci was inspired by no more noble a goal than that of "acquiring reputation and wealth." The election of Adrian VI was "shameful." Gonzalo de Córdoba gave "infinite proofs of virtue worthy of being imitated by the most valorous captains" (p. 25). The Marchese di Pescara surpassed all others for "the honored virtues of body and soul."[36] The Venetian Republic deserved more praise than the Roman because it recovered faster than had Rome from a blow greater than the battle of Cannae.

Giovio's distribution of praise and blame was certainly not always devoid of self-interest. After all, writing history was an expensive undertaking, especially for one like himself whose tastes were something less than Spartan and whose relatives were numerous and poor. He therefore did not refrain from occasionally tempting prospective patrons by reminding them that he, as one of the best-known historians of his age, held the keys to future glory or ignominy. Yet even for those heroes he most admired, or to whom he was most obliged, the laudatory epithets were frequently followed by an account of somewhat less than laudable acts. Leo X may have been the greatest pope of modern times. But, Giovio had to admit, his seizure of Urbino was as unjust as it was impolitic; and his failure to check the rapacity of his finance officials was one of the chief reasons for the success of the Lutheran revolt. The Venetians may have been the guardians of liberty in all Italy and of justice among their subjects. But they acted contrary to that role when they let Louis XII buy them off with the offer of Cremona and when they let their judges consistently favor patricians in civil cases.[37] Even the Marchese di Pescara was culpable, not perhaps for permitting his soldiers to sack Como in spite of the articles of surrender, but certainly for not punishing the ringleaders afterwards.

Moreover, Giovio refused to accept the judgments even of his most reliable informants whenever he found them irreconcilable with information at his disposal. That, in any case, is why he reversed Du Bellay's judgment about the conduct of Anne de Montmorency.[38] He similarly refused to alter his own judgments even when they were clearly contrary to those of his most influential friends and patrons. He came to the conclusion that Machiavelli was the greatest vernacular writer of his age just at the moment when everyone else in Rome was condemning him as the most pernicious. And he defied them all by honoring Machiavelli as one of only three non-Latin writers admitted to his series of *Elogia*. Indeed, it was principally this refusal to compromise in any way his freedom of expression that led him, on the eve of the publication of his life's work, to move to Florence, where he had been invited as a collaborator in Duke Cosimo's campaign to rebuild the Florentine intellectual community. While reminding Giovio that he was now too old to bargain for favors with anyone, Cosimo shielded him from the intense political as well as moral pressure exerted by the emperor's committee of censors. And Giovio accordingly accepted only the most insignificant of the "corrections" that Charles V sought to impose on his manuscript (Zimmermann). True, he sometimes made mistakes—as he apparently did when he accused Gian Matteo Giberti of trying to denigrate the Marchese di Pescara.[39] He may also have been unjust, as he certainly was when he questioned the sincerity of Egidio da Viterbo's religious commitment.[40] But at least he sought conscientiously to live up to the standard he set for himself:

> I have not embarked on this most grave undertaking of writing history in order to accommodate myself to the wishes of others. Rather I have given my judgments with a sincere and truly open mind. [For only thus can I fulfill] my purpose of being useful both to those who are still alive and to those who will come after us. (Part II, dedication)

And he usually succeeded in doing so.

Objectivity, however, did not preclude the statement of theses. For Giovio too recognized the obligation of the humanist historian to interpret as well as to record the events he had verified. At least one of these theses, to be sure, seems to have been ideological rather than historical in origin—namely, that politics, the chief instrument for achieving the humanists' twin goal of peace and prosperity, was generally most effective when it was least influenced by religious or theological considerations. For Giovio, Catholic Christianity was simply one of the essential components of the culture into which he happily had been born—like Latin poetry and Brianza wine. While he was intensely dedicated to the promotion of this culture, and while he was willing to consider even a political version of a crusade to defend it against its avowed enemies, he was convinced that exaggerating the importance of one of the components of the culture would result in the weakening of the others. He was therefore incapable of recognizing that religion was increasingly becoming the chief preoccupation of ever greater numbers of his contemporaries. He distrusted the Catholic reformers. He abhorred the Protestant reformers. And he had very little sympathy for anyone who wanted substantially to modify, to say nothing of destroying, that venerable institution in which Catholic Christianity had always been most visibly manifest—the Papacy. Still, even this shortcoming had one notable advantage for his work as a historian. It enabled him to recognize the remarkably Christian behavior of many infidels and the notoriously barbarous behavior of some Christians. And it enabled him to surpass most of his colleagues in overcoming the Christian, Hellenic, or Latin ethnocentricity that had limited the visions of the vast majority of his predecessors since the time of Herodotus.

Nevertheless, most of Giovio's theses emerged from his study of the events themselves, and they were fully formulated only when, after moving to Florence, he at last had time to put in final form the results of a lifetime of research and reflection. The first of these theses regarded the scope of contemporary history. The invasion of 1494, Giovio decided, was the first step in what soon became a series of causally related historical events that extended all over the world. For the intervention of the French in Italian affairs had provoked the intervention of the Spanish and the Germans, and it was conditioned in turn by pressures exerted on France by its northern neighbors. Hence, the Iberian peninsula and the British Isles had to be brought within the range of the history of Italy. Similarly, the intervention of the Germans was conditioned by the relations of the German princes to the emperor and by the emperor's dynastic ambitions in Eastern Europe. Hence Poland, Hungary, and Russia, as well as Saxony and Hessen, had to be included too. The main beneficiaries of the resulting quarrels among Christians were the Turks, who were frequently kept from taking what was offered to them only by the threat of aggression from the east. Hence, Persia and Tartary had to be included along with the whole of the Ottoman Empire.

To be sure, this chain of events was not yet wholly universal. Since the voyages of discovery could in no way be traced back to Charles VIII, the Americas could be included only as a source of revenue for the Spanish armies; and India, Africa, and the Far East could be omitted altogether. In seeking causal connections among historical events, Giovio did not see fit to look for the causes of the first cause; and he was thus forced to imagine an age of universal tranquillity before the invasion of Charles VIII, a time as mythical as Guicciardini's age of Lorenzo. Yet he succeeded better than most of his colleagues in realizing the potentially universal scope that had been an essential characteristic of contemporary history, *historia ipsius temporis,* ever since its resurrection by Bruni, if not since its formulation by Polybius. He also succeeded in discovering among geographically separate events connections far more substantial than mere contemporaneity. He could thus finish the account of a series of events in one place before beginning an account of another series elsewhere; and he could interrupt his narrative to present the peculiar geographical and historical conditions that determined the singular course of events in each place without losing sight of the general causes that bound them all together. He was able, in his own words,

> to accommodate [himself] to history in such a way that those who read will have the substance of the narrative not interrupted, with its members dispersed, but complete and with the parts perfectly joined together.

The second of Giovio's theses regarded the nature of the course of events in that part of the universe known as Christendom. Not because of fate, not because of divine wrath, Giovio pointed out, but solely because of the stupidity of its leaders, Christendom had entered a period of decline, if not actually in 1494, at least after the death of Leo X in 1521. The first tragic manifestation of this decline was the sack of Rome. The second was the defeat of the Veneto-Imperial navy in 1538, which clearly portended a definite shift in the world center of political and military power from the Tiber to the Bosporus. So far had this decline gone by the 1540s, thought Giovio, that not much could be done to halt it—particularly not by the Council of Trent, which he regarded as a fruitless discussion among ineffectual enthusiasts.

The third of these theses regarded the course of events in one part of Christendom: Italy. Within Italy Giovio discovered a pattern of historical change that could be defined not as a decline but as progress—as progress, that is, from chaos to order. The chief instrument of this progress had been the institution of the principate, which had first been launched by Ottone Visconti in the thirteenth century and which had been brought to perfection by Cosimo de' Medici in the mid-sixteenth. The disastrous consequences of all attempts to revert to an oligarchical or a popular constitution were amply illustrated in the experience of the Florentines. They had enjoyed their greatest prosperity in the second half of the fifteenth century, when Lorenzo il Magnifico had made them stop fighting each other and dedicate themselves to making money, reading philosophy, and building palaces. They reached the nadir of their ill fortune in 1528–30, when the deposition of Niccolò Capponi removed the last effective check on their natural character.

> They are full of such ambition and jealous pride that each of them desires to control the government by any means, to dominate the common fatherland, and to divert public wealth to his own private use. They all burn with such insatiable greed...that they cannot bear to have any other citizen superior to them either in property or in dignity.

And the inevitable consequence of this unbridling of their natural character was the folly of the siege and the tragedy of the capitulation.

The popularity of Giovio's published biographies, together with the reputation he gained as the leading authority on contemporary history during the same thirty-five years in which his chapters circulated in manuscript, assured for the *Sui Temporis Historiae* a widespread notoriety the moment it finally appeared. The original was reprinted at least three times and Domenichi's translation at least four times before the end of the century. A Spanish translation appeared in 1562, a German translation in 1570, and a French translation, which was reprinted five times thereafter, in 1552. Camillo Porzio hailed the author as the "father of modern history." Giovan Battista Gelli proclaimed his "elegance" and other "rare qualities" to be worthy of "reverence." Pietro Giustiniani judged "the abundance [*copia*] and beauty of his style" to be "not very distant from that of Livy's . . . and worthy of comparison with [the best of] the ancients."[41] VINCENTIO CARTARI of Reggio could only find one slight fault: two huge tomes were too much to read for busy citizens like his patron, the procurator of San Marco. Yet the patron could hardly be expected to carry on his political responsibilities without some acquaintance with the contents of Giovio's history; and he accordingly "reduced" the forty books of the original to the more manageable dimensions of a 422-page pocket-book.[42] CARLO PASSI, who had gained some familiarity with historiography while translating Anghiera's treatise on Egypt, found nothing that needed abridging. But the important political lessons contained therein might be more apparent, he thought, particularly to the busy commander-in-chief of the Venetian armies for whom he wrote, if the corresponding passages were accompanied by explanatory notes. To Giovio's reference to the antipodes he therefore supplied a brief discourse on ancient geography; to his mention of Attila, an excursus on the Huns, to his introduction of the duke of Burgundy, a genealogy of the current duke's predecessors. And at the end he added a very helpful index of all "the provinces, cities, castles, lakes, and mountains" mentioned in Giovio's text.[43]

Unfortunately, this favorable reception was countered almost immediately by a storm of protest. The Florentine exiles were infuriated by what they perceived to be a thesis exactly the opposite of their own: that the Savonarola-Soderini constitution as perfected by the patriots of 1528 represented the greatest political achievement since the establishment of the Roman tribunate and that it had been violently destroyed by a ruthless tyrant with the help of a few mercenary traitors and a foreign army. And Federigo degli Alberti, with the help of Florentine bankers in Lyon and their current protégé, Pietro Bizzarri, tore the author to pieces in his *Difesa della Repubblica Fiorentina* of 1566.[44] The resident Florentine historians, even those who fully supported the new regime, were upset by what seemed to them a serious stain upon the unqualified heroism of the city's defenders in 1529–30. They were also annoyed by the favors showered by their own prince upon a mere Lombard, who, not being a Florentine, could not possibly understand the intimate workings of

Florentine history. Varchi vented his annoyance upon the intruder by withholding his critical annotations as long as Giovio was alive and then, as soon as he was dead, compiling a long list of factual errors. He then arranged the list in such a way as to give added authority to his dissent from the author's judgments of the various authors. And it is thanks in part to this list, which was published in the early years of the Italian Risorgimento, that, right up until the present, Filippo Strozzi's daughter has been acclaimed as a ladylike patriot incapable of calling a cardinal a "peasant" or militiamen "bastards," that the murder of the Volterrans has been dismissed as a minor tactical error, and that Francesco Ferrucci has been praised as "a bit proud, but fully committed to justice and moderation."[45]

But the greatest obstacle to a favorable reception of Giovio's work lay in the confusion inherent in humanist historiography between the historian's role as a recorder of facts and his role as the bestower of fame. Giovio himself did nothing to allay this confusion. Notwithstanding his efforts to determine exactly what happened, he entrusted to the same great personages whom he recognized as the agents of history the task of "supporting, assisting, and elevating the noble disciplines," including his own; and to the historians he entrusted the task of perpetuating the memory of "the honorable deeds of [the] illustrious captains and kings" who employed them (Part II: Dedication). Worse yet, he permitted the circulation, as examples of imitable epistolography, of some of his applications for subsidies, in which, for rhetorical purposes, this dependent relationship was emphasized to the point of jeopardizing the interests of the truth.[46] Many readers therefore felt justified in complaining that the honorable deeds of their own particular heroes or the nobility of their own particular political or religious causes had been slighted. And they sought to right the wrong done to them by questioning the author's honesty as well as his accuracy. Giovio was accused of "praising the valor, the power, the prudence, and every other virtue of the Turks" in response to a bribe from the sultan. He was accused of denigrating Paul III out of revenge for not having been given the see of Como and of misrepresenting the defenders of Chieri (Book XXVIII) because they had refused to buy him off. He was accused of obscuring the role of Piero Strozzi at Serravalle in order to please Piero's archenemy, Cosimo I, of making insinuations about the predilections of Spanish soldiers for young boys in order to exalt their Italian rivals, of taking revenge upon Charles V for what he considered an insufficient subsidy by crediting Charles's glorious deeds to his lieutenants. The storm of protest grew louder and louder until it could be heard even as far away as Bogotá, where the retired governor of New Granada spent the last years of his life collecting Giovio's "infamous" blots on the honor of Spain into forty-five long chapters.[47]

So loud was the storm, indeed, that not much could be done to quiet it, not even when Giovio's champion turned out to be the poet and critic GIROLAMO RUSCELLI, whose authority in matters of literary taste was recognized even by Tasso. Having successfully elevated a number of his contemporaries to the rank of imitable letter writers and poets, Ruscelli turned to the historians, with an annotated translation of Collenuccio's history of Naples. He then trained himself in the art of contemporary history by "conversing with every sort of person, private and public, French, Spanish, Italian, and of every other nation" during an eleven-year residence in Venice. Having plundered Giovio's biographies in preparation for his own biographical dictionary, he selected some passages from Giovio's *Historiae* as *exempla* of crusade rhetoric. But in the light of the still current controversy, he had to justify his selection in terms of all of Giovio's historical work. He first demonstrated the conformity of Giovio's practice with the theory of historiography of Dionigi Atanagi. He next answered all the critics, one by one. But then he could not resist the temptation of boasting that he too could find errors. And he thus ended by unwittingly confirming the critic's main contention: that the text was untrustworthy.[48]

What Ruscelli failed to do by argument, NATALE CONTI (c. 1520–c. 1582) tried to do by example—in a continuation of the *Historiae* for another thirty-five years after 1545.[49] Conti did his best to carry out Giovio's program. He did not let his religious commitments prevent him from admitting that Catholics could match Huguenots in barbarity. He extended Giovio's geographical scope to include Peru, Ethiopia, and Japan. And he matched Giovio's length: two large volumes totalling over a thousand pages. He was even willing occasionally to suspend his own principles of political philosophy. Although he held that princes could not be judged by mere mortals and that they were always right in disputes with their subjects, he nonetheless reprimanded Charles V for not paying the Italian troops sent to assist him in Germany, and he blamed Paul IV himself for the popular uprising that followed his death. Indeed, he sought to update his model according to the new standards of the late sixteenth century: he quoted some of his supporting documents verbatim even when their wording was not stylistically consonant with his own prose.

Yet Conti turned out to be far better at composing Latin verse and at translating Greek orations than he was at writing history. He was far less successful than Giovio in discovering an intelligible pattern among all the events he recounted. For the two organizing principles he adopted, the glories of Charles V and Philip II and the progress of Tridentine Catholicism, turned out to be still less universal than Giovio's Hapsburg-Valois wars. He was thus forced to fall back on the assumption that war alone was of interest, wherever it might occur; and he had to excogitate such wholly artificial links between one war and another as this: "Nor were affairs in a turbulent state and full of dissension only in Gaul. They were so also in that country commonly known as Japan." Moreover, his notion of Protestantism was so misinformed (Bucer, it seems, denied the doctrine of the Trinity), and his notion of the German character was so misled by stock Italian commonplaces ("an uncouth, light-minded people, naturally desirous of new things"), that he could explain the failure of pope and emperor instantly to wipe out all their enemies only by reverting to an unfathomable divine will or to pure chance: "nothing on this earth is durable or happy; rather, things are continuously fluctuating and undulating." What was left, then, was a miscellaneous jumble of single facts—the arrival of Mary Stuart in France, the acceptance of the Interim in Saxony, the death of the pirate Barbarossa, the outbreak of war on the Turco-Persian frontier, the refusal of Ottavio Farnese to give up his claim to Piacenza. And as these facts had no relation among themselves, so they had no relation either to the fictitious universal peace announced in the first lines or to the arrival of the king of Poland in Wilna recounted in the last lines.

After receiving its most perfect expression at the hand of Giovio, contemporary world history thus reverted to chronicle. Instead of reinforcing a modern model with ancient models, instead of reexamining Polybius, who had been published in Niccolò Perotti's elegant Latin translation in 1529, instead of studying the less-known Velleius Paterculus, who had been discovered and edited by Beatus Rhenanus as early as 1520,[50] instead of reconsidering Giovio's most immediate predecessor, Pope Pius II, historians of the contemporary world turned to that favorite ancient text of their medieval predecessors, Valerius Maximus. As a collection of illustrious deeds, contemporary history could certainly yield *exempla* for the political philosophers. Conti accordingly interrupted his narrative at every occasion to point out that "whoever believes in the pleasing flattery of his enemy" will certainly suffer misfortune, that freedom and riches are easier to acquire than a lost reputation, and that popular uprisings serve "to recall princes to a just moderation of their desires." But history treated in this manner could not reveal any pattern of historical development. What was useful in Conti could therefore more easily be looked up in Botero. Hence, the Renaissance master of contemporary history was abandoned to his enemies. He was scorned in the eighteenth century for "capricious inventions" (Tiraboschi). He was denounced in the nineteenth century for "selling himself out of avarice and ambition to the house of the Medici." He was dismissed in the mid-twentieth century for "caring little about writing the truth and often taking care not to write it."[51] And he remained all but unread until 1954, when he was finally rescued, and resuscitated, by Federico Chabod.[52]

Historia Ab Orbe Condito

As the historians *ipsorum temporis* sought to put municipal and national history into a spatial context of the whole world, so another group of historians sought to put contemporary history into a temporal context *ab orbe condito,* from the beginning; and they sought thus to replace the great medieval world chronicles, which were no longer consonant with current standards of historical writing. The first to do so was JACOPO FILIPPO FORESTI (1434–1520), usually known as Jacopo Filippo DA BERGAMO, whose immense *Supplementum Chronicarum* first appeared at Bergamo in 1483; and he did so with a degree of success sufficient to warrant his twice adding continuations, first from 1480 to 1490 and then from 1490 to 1502. So successful, indeed, was the work that it discouraged competitors. It was translated into Italian in 1505 and reprinted either in the original or in translation frequently thereafter— 1513, 1520, 1524, 1535, 1540.... And just as its popularity began to wane, or just as its defects became too apparent to justify its retention as the standard world history of the age, it was resurrected by the famous popularizer of humanist literature, FRANCESCO SANSOVINO, who revised the translation in accordance with the new linguistic and historiographical tastes of the late sixteenth century. Sansovino "amplified" some passages and abbreviated others, corrected a certain number of factual and orthographic ("nomi guasti") errors, and added two lengthy continuations of his own down to the year 1580.[53]

Not until 1553 did anyone have the courage to challenge Jacopo Filippo's monopoly. Inspired by the success of his revision of Sanudo's history of the invasion of 1494–95 and by his short treatise on the origins of Islam,[54] MARCO GUAZZO decided to expand his previous account of the great men of his own time, one which he had augmented and republished several times since its first appearance in 1540, in order to include the great men of all times.[55] And he did so sufficiently to the taste of the current editors of Jacopo Filippo that they included long extracts from his work along with those they had taken from Bembo and Giovio in the expanded Italian edition of 1564. Guazzo was followed less than a decade later by GIOVANNI TARCAGNOTA (d. 1566), whose *Delle historie del mondo* first appeared in Venice in 1562. Tarcognota was then continued from 1513 to 1582 by MAMBRINO ROSEO, the polymath continuer of Collenuccio;[56] and Roseo's continuation was then continued still further by the editor of Panvinio's ecclesiastical history, BARTOLOMEO DIONIGI of Fano.[57] In 1570, just as Sansovino was finishing his expanded revision of Jacopo Filippo, GASPARO BUGATI, or AMBIGATO, of Milan published what had probably begun as a history of Milan under the more appropriate title of a "Universal History" from the beginning to 1559, which he himself then continued in successive editions.[58] Fifteen years later, GIROLAMO DE' BARDI added many more sources to those he had found mentioned in Sansovino's edition of Jacopo Filippo and composed a new "Chronological Summary of the Ages of the World" down to 1581.[59] In the last decade of the century GIOVAN NICOLÒ DOGLIONI expanded his studies of the history of Venice and of his native Belluno into a "Universal Historical Compendium," which he then continued for another seven years after the first edition of 1594.[60] And MICHELE ZAPPULLO of Naples (b. 1548) expanded what appears to have begun as a history of his native city into a history of all the other great cities and regions of the world.[61]

All these works together represent a not inconsiderable accomplishment, at least quantitatively. To be sure, none of them claimed to do more than simply "reduce all the notable events scattered through so many books into a compendium of a single volume; for by reading [such a compendium] one can learn about many events with little time and effort and at a modest price." Still, Doglioni managed to fill some 562 pages, Bardi some 780 pages, and Tarcagnotta and Roseo over 1,500 pages in fine print. These works also represent a considerable effort toward the goal of bibliographical thoroughness. The list of authors from which Jacopo Filippo "dug out" *(cavato)* his information included almost all the known historians of ancient Greece and Rome and most of the classics of medieval and early Renaissance historical writing, including a good number that at the time he could have read only in manuscript. Sansovino added to the list all the writers he had consulted when writing about the Turks and Arabs. Bardi, the most thorough of them all, read Paulus Diaconus, Procopius, and Jordanus as well as Biondo on the early Middle Ages, and the "chronicles of Nürnberg," "Saxony," and "Bremen," as well as Johannes Trithemius and Pietro Della Vigna on the High Middle Ages. Indeed, almost alone of his generation, he took the trouble to learn German, and he quoted at length in the original from the chronicles procured for him by correspondents in Germany and by friends at the Fondaco de' Tedeschi in Venice.

Admittedly, the ideal of bibliographical thoroughness was not always attained. For instance, none of the universal historians seems to have noticed what might have provided them with several new theses and a provocative scheme for organizing their material: PIERFRANCESCO GIAMBULLARI's (1495–1555) *Storia d'Europa* since 887.[62] True, by the time of his death Giambullari had managed to cover only the first half-century of the history of what he defined as Europe: a system of separate but interdependent "nations," the antithesis of the universal Christendom recently revived by the ideologues of Charles V. But the manuscript was edited posthumously by the well-known Florentine man of letters, Cosimo Bartoli, in 1566—in plenty of time, that is, for the universal historians to have made use of it. Giambullari observed all their most exacting requirements. He justified his initial date with an excursus on the fall of Rome and the rise of Charlemagne, the last truly universal Christian-Roman monarch. He read and extracted passages from some seventy printed historical works, and he went well beyond the bibliographical canon of ancient authorities to include recent German and Spanish sources either previously unknown or only recently republished in Italy: Sebastian Münster's *Cosmografia* (1550), Olaus Magnus's *Historia de Gentibus Septentrionalibus* (1555), Beatus Rhenanus's *Rerum Germanicarum Libri Tres* (1531). But he continued to be classified not as a historian but as a Dantist, a philologist, and a linguist; and this, his sole excursion into history, remained forgotten until the nineteenth century. Nevertheless, at least one universal historian, Doglioni, took the trouble to put together what information was available about one hitherto unknown part of the world, Hungary, in anticipation of including it into a worldwide synthesis.[63] And another, Bardi, set out to counter what he had found to be anti-Venetian biases in the sources he had used when writing about the times of Pope Alexander III. He accordingly reprinted in a separate volume all the documents in Sigonio that proved Venice to have been "the front-line defender of the Christian religion" throughout its long history, and he denounced as flagrant misrepresentations everything that the contemporary German chronicles had suggested to the contrary.[64]

Notwithstanding the universal scope of their major works, all these historians were as attached as any of their contemporaries to their own families, fatherlands, and, occasionally, religious orders. Jacopo Filippo interrupted his account of the scientists of the fourteenth century to discourse on "the privileges of the noble house of the Foresti," and he carefully repeated the official Venetian thesis about "voluntary submission" every time he mentioned one of the cities of the Terraferma. Doglioni and Bardi demonstrated their reverence for their adopted cities by also publishing, respectively, a eulogy of "Venice triumphant and ever-free" and a tourists' guidebook on its present and past wonders.[65] Bugati proclaimed the Milanese Giovanni Simonetta to be the most elegant historian before Giovio. He minimized the crimes usually attributed to Lodovico il Moro. He wholeheartedly endorsed the traditional Milanese contrast between the noble Giangaleazzo and the hypocritical Florentines. And he did not hesitate to admit "the great delight I have in always showing my reverence for my most noble and ancient fatherland." Nevertheless, all of them tried hard to view the ideas and institutions to which they were personally attached from the universal perspective to which they were professionally committed. Bardi recognized the sultan as "emperor of the East" and thus worthy of being included with the pope and the "emperor of the West" in his dating scheme. Bugati began his supplement with a favorable description of Turkish military and civil administration, and he ended it with a very unfavorable judgment of the recent acts of his own sovereign, in Flanders and in Castile as well as in Milan. Zappullo sorrowfully admitted that the Venetians he otherwise admired had let their soldiers throw away victory at the Taro, and he even more sorrowfully conceded that the litigious passions of his fellow Neapolitans were ruining the efforts of the Spanish viceroys to make their country in fact what it obviously was potentially: the richest in Italy.

These historians also tried hard to solve what had been, and what was long to remain, one of the most difficult problems of their discipline: chronology. "Nothing is more important for the understanding of Roman history," Sigonio had observed, "than the correct description of years and times."[66] And nothing is more dangerous, added the theologian Roberto Bellarmino some years later, than getting dates mixed up: for anachronism is often a sign of heresy.[67] Indeed, the problem of chronology became particularly urgent after the adoption of the Gregoran calendar—so urgent, indeed, that Doglioni's scheme for coordinating the new and the old calendars sold out almost as soon as it was printed.[68] The problem was threefold. First of all, it involved transferring onto the B.C.–A.D. Christian calendar the various chronological systems used by the ancient Greeks and Romans—Olympiads, consulships, years before and years after a significant event. Second, it involved coordinating the resulting Greco-Roman calendar with one extracted from the Old Testament. Finally, it involved connecting both of the calendars of antiquity with the series of dates recorded in the A.D. system by the more consciously chronological historical writers of the Middle Ages. From the beginning, the historians' main guide had been Mattia Palmieri's updated version of Eusebius, Jerome, and Prosper of Aquitaine.[69] But they also made use of the more recent emendations to Jerome's texts proposed by such contemporary transalpine experts as Gilbert Génébrand and Johannes Lucidus Samotheus, the second of whom Bardi edited and republished in 1575.[70] One of them composed a new chronological chart of his own, namely, Sansovino, who had consulted astronomers and antiquarians in correcting the dates in Jacopo Filippo and who then wrote a short history of the work of all his predecessors from Julius Africanus to Hermann Contractus (1549).[71] As a result, all the universal histories were replete with dates, sometimes inserted directly into the narrative, sometimes printed in parallel columns according to the various systems—*Anno Orbis, Anno Urbis, Anno Incarnationis,* and the year of the reigning pope, emperor, or doge.

Like most of their non-Italian colleagues of the sixteenth century, and like most of their successors before the early eighteenth century, the Italian universal historians assumed that the history of mankind and the history of civilization had both begun at the same determinable moment in time. They thus wasted considerable effort in attempts to date the undatable—the Flood, the birth of Abraham, the foundation of Trier, the invention of water wells. Unlike most of their contemporaries beyond the Alps, however, they failed to recognize Joseph Scaliger's *De Emendatione Temporum* for what it was, an epoch-making contribution to the ancient science of chronology.[72] They were therefore unaware of Scaliger's rejection of the forgeries of Annio da Viterbo as a basis for chronological computation; and since the forgeries better supported their assumption than did the authentic Hellenic and Hellenistic texts that Annio had sought to discredit, they continued to accept them as authentic, notwithstanding the increasing skepticism of many of their compatriots in other fields of historiography. Still, their efforts were not wholly without positive results. They occasionally made important errors, to be sure—as did Sansovino when he shifted the entire Roman calendar two years ahead of the Christian calendar. But at least they avoided the metaphysical and astrological by-products of chronology that still distracted many chronologers elsewhere in Europe. And, even if for the wrong reasons, they often arrived at dates that were eventually accepted, for the right reasons, as correct. The conspiracy of Catiline actually did take place in Anno Urbis 690, as Bardi declared, and the Council of Nicaea actually did meet in Anno Domini 325.

As they expanded the temporal and geographical scope of municipal history, so also the universal historians managed to introduce subjects other than those to which the municipal historians had generally been confined. When wars vanished, as they did for much of the second century A.D., they filled in the gap with personal anecdotes—about Hadrian, who fooled a suitor who tried to fool him by wearing a wig, about Albinus, who ate 100 Campania peaches, 10 Ostia melons, 500 figs, and 400 oysters in a single meal (Bugati). When heroic captains abandoned them, they turned to equally heroic, and sometimes equally fictitious, inventors—to a certain Dionysius, who taught Greeks to make wine and Germans to make beer, to a certain Cain, who established the first system of weights and measures. When statesmen were wanting, they wrote about men of piety and letters—about Peter Lombard, "a very excellent man, highly esteemed in Paris for his doctrine and good morals," about "Lorenzo Valla of Rome, who awakened Italians and incited them to the study of good letters" (Guazzo). They thus came close at times to defining ages by their cultural and religious as well as by their political accomplishments: the age of the Greek artists and philosophers for Tarcagnota, the age of the scholastics and the age of the humanists for Bardi, the age of Ariosto and Vesalius and the age of the Church Fathers for Bugati:

> The lifetime [of Ambrose] was one in which flourished a group of men highly distinguished for sanctity, letters, and morals, like Anastasius of Alexander, Eusebius of Caesaria, Basil of Cappadocia, and Gregory of Nazianzen, not to mention Augustine and Ambrose himself.

The Rejection of Humanism

In general, however, universal history failed to attain the standards demanded of humanist historiography in other kinds of historical writing. First of all, with the exception of Bardi, who as an artist collaborated in the vast project to redecorate the Palazzo Ducale in Venice,[73] the universal historians all worked not, like most humanists, in close contact with their colleagues but as isolated scholars, in contact only with the texts they were studying. Jacopo Filippo was an Augustinian friar who looked upon his private library in Bergamo just as he looked upon the religious communities he governed in Forlì and Imola: as a place of retreat from the world. For him, scholarship meant simply rearranging the passages he culled from his books according to the subjects that from time to time happened to arouse his curiosity: the life of the Virgin, the practical problems of confessors, the Gospel of Luke, and the feats of the various historical and fictitious women mentioned in the Bible and the Decameron.[74] Guazzo was a soldier who spent "the flower of the years of my life in the wars."[75] For him, reading and writing were simply a way of avoiding idleness after he had retired to a farm inherited from his father outside Padua.

Of their own individual personalities, even in an age that was passionately interested in individual personality, almost nothing remains except what is only occasionally revealed in the books the universal historians wrote. Tarcagnota was the son of a Greek refugee who was born and who died equally distant from the centers of humanist culture, in Gaeta and Ancona. Bugati was a Dominican who seems to have spent his whole adult life inside a monastery in Milan. But otherwise, nothing is known of them. They were remembered by the bibliographies of the eighteenth century merely as names opposite titles; and they have been completely forgotten by the diligent editors of the *Dizionario biografico degli Italiani* in the twentieth century. Some of them, it is true, picked up some humanist conventions—like set orations, prefatory platitudes about the nature of history, and, later in the century, documents quoted in the original. But they usually misunderstood the purpose of these conventions. They treated the historical works they were "epitomizing" merely as collections of single episodes upon which they could draw freely in compiling their own collections. They did not distinguish even among the different genres of the historical writings they used as sources: to Jacopo Filippo, Bruni was just another "chronicler," no different in kind from Benzo of Alessandria. The nearest they came to criticism of sources was an occasional admission that conflicting accounts existed of the same episode. And they invariably left to their readers the task of deciding which of the accounts was the most plausible.

The popularizers, it is true, might have done something to correct these defects, for they were much more closely tied to the mainstream of humanism. Roseo was a magistrate of his native Fabiano and a resident of Perugia during the crises of the siege of Florence and the Salt War.[76] Sansovino was the son of the famous Florentine architect Jacopo and a welcome member of the literary circles in Venice, Padua, and Rome.[77] But it was usually their publishers, not they themselves, who selected the texts they edited or translated; and they intervened in the original only to the extent of recasting it according to the then current standards of good Tuscan prose. The form and the substance they left untouched, whether their author was an ancient Greek (Diodorus Siculus), a modern Spaniard (Guevara), a Frenchman (Guillaume du Bellay), or a late medieval Fleming *(De Imitatione Christi)*—all of whom Sansovino translated with equal fidelity. Indeed, they continued to follow the style and organization of their authors even in composing their own supplements and additions. And they flatly refused to let the value of the texts they edited be compromised by the intrusion of humanist philology. Tommaso Porcacchi, for instance, the chief editor of the Giolito de' Ferrari popular series of historical works in translation, insisted upon identifying that favorite source of medieval legends, Dares of Phrygia, as a classical Greek historian, rather than as the somewhat clumsy fifth-century A.D. forger he actually was. He closed his eyes to the enormous discrepancies between Dares and the authentic historians of the fifth century B.C. And he declared Dares's language to be impeccably Attic, even though he admitted to having read him only in Latin translation.[78]

Secondly, none of the universal historians ever managed to find for themselves what the humanists insisted upon as a prerequisite to a successful literary enterprise: an appropriate ancient model. Writers of commentaries had Caesar. Municipal historians had Livy. Historians of the contemporary world had Polybius. But the best the universal historians could come up with was Orosius, and Orosius's own model, Justinus. Even the translator of Justinus could not hide what Justinus himself admitted: that he was merely abridging a much longer work in order to fill up his own leisure time and to enable his still less industrious compatriots to "talk and argue about the histories of the Greeks" with relatively little effort.[79] Nor could the rather incompetent translator of Orosius hide what modern critics have fully demonstrated: that Orosius had written a compendium not of histories but of other compendia and that he had completely ignored some of the sources which should have been among his most important ones.[80] Moreover, neither Justinus nor Orosius was wholly universal in scope. The first left out the Romans, the second left out the Christians. And the most they could provide in the way of a system of organizing such a vast quantity of material was that of Orosius, which was based on various multiples of the divine number, seven.

One possible alternative was offered as early as 1516 by GIOVAN BATTISTA EGNAZIO, or EGNATIUS CIPELLI (1475–1553), who was soon to become justly famous as the editor of Aulus Gellius and Lactantius—namely, an organization of world history according to emperors or groups of emperors (the Antonines, the successors of Constantine, the Carolingians . . .).[81] This format was to some extent sanctioned by two ancient models, both of which Egnazio also edited: Suetonius and the *Scriptores Historiae Augustae,* which everyone still believed to have been written by second- and third-century continuers of Suetonius. The format received further support in 1561, when Lodovico Dolce published his translation of Pedro Mexia, which he himself and then Bardi subsequently continued through the reigns of the more recent emperors.[82] It received still further support in 1564, when Dolce published his translation of Zonaras's world chronicle that extended from Julius Caesar to the eleventh century.[83] It was then shorn of its most apparent weakness—that of having to ignore all history before the foundation of the Roman Empire—by Roseo, in 1570. For Roseo's fusion of passages translated from Plutarch and Diodorus Siculus pushed the chronological limits back three centuries, since it elevated Alexander and his successors to the same level of importance as the first Roman emperor. And his fusion of passages from Dio Cassius, Herodian, Eutropius, and the *Scriptores Historiae Augustae* proved also that history organized by rulers was particularly capable of yielding bits of practical political wisdom, which he accordingly inserted in almost every paragraph.[84]

Unfortunately, this alternative turned out to be somewhat less than satisfactory. The fault was partially Egnazio's. He allotted the same space to each emperor without regard for the length of the reign. He thus made Augustus, who had to share his short paragraph with Jesus, just half as important as the most ephemeral third-century emperor, and he made him one-fourth as important as Frederick III, who, just because he was the last on the list, was accorded a whole page. Moreover,

Egnazio took all his information solely from narrative sources. He thus identified Trajan simply as the organizer of two military expeditions and as the builder of a column, and he completely omitted what Pliny had said and what the biographical form permitted him to repeat about Trajan as an administrator and a lawgiver. Finally, he separated all the Eastern from all the Western emperors after the time of Theodosius I. He was thus unable to coordinate such mutually significant landmarks as the Fourth Crusade and the Council of Ferrara-Florence. He was forced to introduce his discourse on the Turks as a wholly irrelevant aside. And he failed to recognize what his most immediate, though much more modest, predecessor, GIOVANNI STELLA, had recognized over a decade earlier: that by the time of Maximilian I, the empire had disappeared completely in the East and "now possesses only a small part of the West."[85] How then could emperors serve as a framework for universal history? Egnazio himself apparently decided that they could not. He subsequently retreated from history altogether and dedicated himself to collecting miscellaneous information about anything and anyone without any apparent order at all.[86]

The fault was also to some extent that of Zonaras and Roseo. Zonaras belied his, and his translator's, claim to have drawn upon "all the writers, Greek as well as Latin, whose histories have survived." For he left out all of classical as well as Hellenistic Greece. He omitted all the emperors after Constantine, even Charlemagne, who had not resided in Constantinople, and he was even less equitable in his allocation of space than Egnazio: one short paragraph to all of Hadrian's accomplishments, and two whole pages solely to the death of Alexios Comnenus. Obviously, what a Byzantine monk chose to write about during the idle hours between prayers could be "profitable to those who are busy with public affairs" only because of its "brevity." Similarly, Roseo never managed to decide which of Alexander's successors might serve as the focal point around which to organize the *gesta* of all the others. He devoted most of one of his four books to Agathocles of Syracuse, who certainly did not qualify for so central a position in history. He abandoned Antigonus, who might have qualified for it, in the midst of nothing more significant than showing his generosity to the defeated Pyrrhus. And he could not discern, amid the jumble of events spread out across the Mediteranean from Rome to Antioch, any unifying characteristics in what neither he nor his successors for another three centuries even had a name for, the Hellenistic age.

Given the inadequacies of post-classical Roman and Greek historians as models, and given the inability of Egnazio and Roseo to develop a new model on the basis of the classical biographers, some of the universal historians turned for help to their more recent colleagues across the Alps, particularly to Hartmann Schedel, Johannes Naucler, and Johannes Carion. Alas, in vain. Notwithstanding his frequent borrowings from the Italian humanists, Schedel really did—indeed, he pretended to do—little more than to transpose Jacopo Filippo's scheme to the particular requirements of a wholly traditional world chronicle of his native city, Nürnberg.[87] Notwithstanding his intention to break away from the same tradition, Naucler wrote in a language that proved to be as unacceptable in Italy as it was popular in Germany—at least to judge by the number of reprintings that continued well into the following century.[88] Notwithstanding the efforts of the professional translator Pietro Lauro to render Carion accessible to his compatriots, not even Bardi, who most frequently cites him, could have overlooked Carion's chief purpose: to present history in a manner consonant with the Confession of Augsburg.[89]

That left the universal historians right back where they had started—with Jacopo Filippo and with the great medieval world chronicles that had served him as models. Following Jacopo Filippo's example, they too repeated, with no more than an occasional *dicono* or *dicitur,* whatever they found in the chronicles, even when it was clearly contradicted by those very historians, ancient or Renaissance, whom they elsewhere cited as authorities. The Greeks lost 870,000 men at Troy and the Trojans lost 660,000, said Doglioni, quietly forgetting that Thucydides, his main source for the "War of the Morea," had relegated such statistics to the realm of poetic license. Semiramis invaded India in A.O. 1,988, said Tarcagnota, with an army of 1,300,000 foot soldiers and 100,000 horse. The night Matteo Visconti was born, said Bugati, all the domestic animals in Milan broke their chains and wandered freely about the city. A miraculous rain of fire caused the outbreak of three simultaneous conflagrations in Troyes in 1525, said Guazzo. The conversion of the American Indians, concluded Zappullo, could be attributed largely to the many miracles wrought by the piece of the True Cross that Columbus had the foresight to bring with him.

Thus vanished the line between truth and legend, between the reasonable and the fantastic, between human and divine initiative, which the first humanist historians had made such efforts to establish. So also vanished the humanist schemes of periodization based solely on the causal relationships among the events themselves. Except for Zappullo, who divided all history into parallel chronologies according to four representative cities, all the universal historians reverted to some combination of Isidore of Seville's Four Monarchies and Six Ages, all of which they knew had been banished by the humanists from all other branches of historical writing.[90] Some readers may be surprised, confessed Bugati, at

> the division of times that I have adopted into six ages, four monarchies, and four metallic ages. I must therefore remind [them] that this order has been judged to be the best of all and the one most certain in overcoming the discordances among the various authors concerning the numeration of years.

When this scheme failed them, as it invariably did sometime between the Incarnation and Constantine, they fell back either on the death dates of arbitrarily selected emperors (Bugati's Book III: from the death of Charlemagne to the death of Frederick II), or merely on single years identified by the reigns of the current pope, emperor, *signore,* or *podestà* ("In the year 1396, Giangaleazzo being duke of Milan, Boniface IX governing the See of Peter, and Wenceslaus Caesar the Roman Empire..."). All the humanists' great watersheds—312, 410, 1095, 1402, 1494, 1509, 1530, 1559—were flattened out into an interrupted mass of miscellaneous events, often undistinguished even by paragraph divisions. The relative importance of single events became merely a function of the number of lines dedicated to each one. Causal connections gave way merely to chronological coincidence—or to whatever Doglioni's bee happened to pick up as it buzzed about among the flowers planted by his predecessors. And since the historian could no longer perceive any patterns of historical development, he could no longer advise his readers on how they might affect the future course of history—or even how they might most painlessly accommodate themselves to a course over which they had no control.

To be sure, universal history could still serve one of the purposes, albeit a minor one, that the humanists had recognized for historiography: that of providing a storehouse of information. And the universal historians emphasized this purpose by perfecting another humanist technical innovation, indices of names, places, and subjects, which forthwith took the place of the narrative as the guide through the storehouse. Indeed, the indices now included not only generals and battles but also natural phenomena and moral qualities, like Doglioni's "Sceleratezze di Heliogabalo," "Sdegno di Solimano," and "Segno notabile apparso a Roma." But storehouses of information did not have to be presented in chronological order. Indeed, if they were presented rather in the order of the day of the year on which each event occurred, the busy reader would find them far more accessible. When he opened Lodovico's Dolce's calendar on January 1, he would immediately learn that on the very same day the Romans used to sacrifice to the Lares, that Marius had beaten Jugurtha, that Ovid, Livy, and King Louis XII had died, and that King Sigismund of Poland had been born. And when, toward the end of the year, he opened it on Christmas day, he would discover that on what the Romans called IIX KAL. JAN., Charlemagne had been crowned emperor, William of Normandy had been crowned king, and God, according to Eusebius, Orosius, Augustine, Bede, and "several modern authors," had started creating heaven and earth.[91]

But these storehouses of knowledge could be arranged in still other ways. For instance, the various items could be placed under the respective kinds of "famous deeds and sayings" according to the scheme borrowed from Valerius Maximus, Petrarch, and Giovanni da Ravenna. Accordingly, BATTISTA FREGOSO read through scores of ancient and modern authors, from Pliny and Strabo to Pontano and Simonetta, and he distributed all that he found under such headings as "religious piety," "dreams," and "fortitude," which better comforted him in his exile from Genoa and more effectively trained his son in the art of "living well and happily."[92] They could be arranged by geographical location, as they were by Doglioni himself in his "theater of the princes of the world," or according to symbolic representations of the virtues, or *imprese,* as they were by Girolamo Ruscelli on the basis of his reading of Giovio and Collenuccio.[93] They could also be arranged, for easy consultation by preachers, under such headings as "the unhappy end of many illustrious men" and "the marvellous example of great women," as were "the infinite number of beautiful flowers" gathered from Corio, Paulus Diaconus, Philo, et al., by the reverend father Luigi Contarini for his nephew, the vicar-general of the Crociferi.[94]

Better yet, the storehouses could be arranged according to Polidoro Vergilio's categories of great inventions, although GUIDO PANCIROLI of Reggio, a professor of law at Padua and Turin, claimed to have borrowed the arrangement from Plutarch. Under "linen" he placed Nero's tablecloth, the *asbetino* of the Greeks, and the shroud of Francis Xavier; under "signatures" he placed what Pliny had said about Caesar, what Dio Cassius had said about Commodus, and what Antonino of Florence had said about Gregory I.[95] Best of all, the storehouses could be arranged under the subtopics that even the humanists admitted to be principal subjects of history: wars and battles. GIOVAN CARLO SARACENI "dug out [*cavato*] from all the historians with great diligence" a collection of narratives representing all the centuries from the third to the sixteenth;[96] and TOMMASO PORCACCHI,[97] following the example of BERNARDINO ROCCA of Piacenza,[98] dug out of the authentic and apocryphal histories he was editing for Giolito a great number of "jewels" *(gioie)* concerning "the causes of war." Each battle could then be lined up next to similar battles in order to emphasize the practical lessons they all illustrated—that "imprudent and ambitious princes are harmful to the public good," that "anger is contrary to prudence." Moreover, since each war was presented in isolation from its temporal context, explanations could be kept at a minimum. The Peloponnesian War broke out, said Porcacchi, because the Corinthians unjustly attacked the Athenians; the Carafa War broke out because Marcantonio Colonna and Giulio Orsini needed a chance to show off their valor. Since the purpose of writing about battles was to entertain the lay reader and to inspire the professional reader, the accuracy of the account was less important than its rhetorical effect. After all, Alexander the Great did not check what Homer had said about Achilles, nor did Alfonso d'Aragona and Charles V question Livy and Philippe de Commynes. Hence Porcacchi, with his usual disregard for the relative value of his various sources, could reconstruct the naval battles of the First Punic War solely from Orosius, Florus, and Silius Italicus. And he did not have to bother with Polybius, from whom he had previously extracted all his "reasons for the first Roman expedition outside of Italy."

What might, and what should, have constituted the highest achievement of humanist historiography thus ended by rejecting—or at least by ignoring—the scientific as well as the aesthetic principles of humanism. One victim of this rejection was humanist historiography as a whole, since the various forms in which it had been most successful were left without a more general framework to measure the relative importance of their single subjects. But the other victim was universal history itself. For, unlike the works of the humanist historians in general, those of the Italian universal historians never won recognition as models of historical writing outside of Italy. And inside of Italy they never achieved anything like the popularity enjoyed by similar works in other parts of Europe, particularly in those countries like Spain, France, and Germany, where the medieval roots of Renaissance culture were far more visible.

BOOK VI
THE LATERAL DISCIPLINES

14

BIOGRAPHY

BY THE END OF THE SIXTEENTH CENTURY AND THE BEGINNING OF THE SEVENTEENTH, humanist historiography in Italy had reached an impasse. It was faced, that is, with a threefold problem: a problem of content at the level of municipal history, of organization at the level of regional and national history, and of methodology at the level of world and universal history. This problem was not insoluble. Indeed, an important step toward an eventual solution could easily have been found within the very humanist tradition that was largely responsible for having generated the problem. The historians had only to borrow certain elements that had been developed independently of them within several other, parallel humanist disciplines. At a time when the joining of formerly independent disciplines was producing such spectacular novelties as the opera and the natural sciences, such borrowing would not have been at all unusual.

Series of Biographies

One of these disciplines was biography. Of the two forms of biography that the Renaissance inherited directly or indirectly from antiquity, the first to be adopted consisted of a series of short notices concerning one or more categories of persons whom the author or compiler held to be "illustrious." The principal model for this form was the elaboration of Suetonius's notes on the lives of the philosophers composed by Jerome with the help of the biographical literature of the early empire, much of which was subsequently lost. This model was popular enough in the three centuries after Jerome to inspire several imitations and continuations, of which the best known thereafter were those of Gennadius of Marseilles and Isidore of Seville. It was revived in the early twelfth century by Honoré of Autun (Honorius Augustodunensis) and Sigibert of Gembloux, whose work was continued into the fourteenth century by Petrarch's close friend Giovanni Colonna.[1] It was then adapted to the exigencies of a single political community by Filippo Villani. And it was widened again in scope to include personages throughout Latin Christendom by Enea Silvio Piccolomini.[2]

Since the subject of Book VI does not regard historiography itself, but rather the disciplines that remained separate from historiography, and since each of these disciplines is represented by a vast number of texts that have not yet been studied systematically, I herewith renounce any pretension to the bibliographical completeness that I have sought to achieve in the preceding books. The theses I here propose should be taken as purely provisional, subject to modification or correction in the light of further investigation.

These series of biographies provided historians of the Renaissance with one valuable service: that of a guide to proper names parallel to the guide to dates compiled, also on a model inherited from Jerome, by Matteo and Mattia Palmieri. Indeed, the late-fourteenth-century catalogue of famous ancients by GUGLIELMO DA PASTRENGO was still considered useful enough two centuries later to warrant its being once again "e tenebris eductus in lucem," with only a few emendations and additions.[3] For it included not only the names Pastrengo had found in Jerome but also those he had found in what remained of Jerome's sources and those whose own writings he knew of only by references in the writings of others. This form might have provided historians with still another important service: that of overcoming the limitation of Livian historiography to the actions of men of state and arms. For it placed "inventors of things" on the same plane as "founders of cities" (Pastrengo). It considered shady street-prowlers like Serafino Aquilano to be as worthy of treatment as Constantine and Guidobaldo da Montefeltro, with whom VINCENZO COLLI planned to begin and end his series.[4] It admitted astrologers—like the one mentioned by Dante and added by Filippo Villani after his appointment as lecturer on the *Divine Comedy*—along with patricians.[5] It even admitted women, who were granted, like Boccaccio's Griselda, a list of virtues all of their own—although it is unfortunate that TOMASO GARZONI so emptied the illustrious women he found in the Bible of the virile virtues ascribed to them by his source that they could not have tempted even the most lascivious of his fellow preachers.[6] In some cases, indeed, series of biographies seem to have been written in conscious opposition to Livian topical limitations. At least ANTONIO MANETTI omitted any mention of the well-known political activities of some of the "singular men" of his age, since he had chosen them solely on the basis of their contributions to the arts and letters.[7]

The series of biographies according to the model of Jerome was considerably enriched in the middle of the fifteenth century by the revival of another ancient model: the most complete surviving version of the once abundant genre of "lives of the philosophers" written in the third century A.D. by the meticulous collector of details and doctrines, Diogenes Laertius. Diogenes soon became one of the more popular ancient writers in the Renaissance, with some eleven editions of Ambrogio Traversari's new Latin translation[8] (1480) and still more editions of the Italian translations of 1480 and 1545.[9] For the biographers, he was also one of the more instructive. He taught them that the private lives of their subjects were as important as the titles of the books they wrote, that fullness of information and documentation was more important than literary cohesiveness, and that statements of fact should always be backed up by accurate references to the sources. Better yet, he taught them that single lives within a series should be arranged not in alphabetical or in topical order but according to the relation of masters to disciples and according to progressive innovations and elaborations within continuing schools of thought.

By combining the Jerome model with the Diogenes model, Renaissance biographers were able to propose a completely new scheme of historical periodization—one based not on the usual succession of dominant powers, political regimes, or decisive battles but on what today would be called "culture." Such a scheme was first suggested by Petrarch's disciple SICCO POLENTONE (1375/76–1447).[10] Even though Sicco separated historians from poets according to the precepts of Cicero, and even though he put Josephus before Curtius Rufus simply because he believed Jews to be superior to Macedonians, he reduced all his categories to a single standard of judgment: eloquence. The presence or absence of eloquence in various periods of time thus permitted him to distinguish qualitatively among them. Antiquity, he suggested, came to an end not with the sack of Rome by the Goths, nor with the invasion of Italy by the Lombards, but with the death of Juvenal, the last truly eloquent Roman; and the modern great age began not with the rise of the Visconti or the fall of the Ghibellines but with Bruni, "the first to restore its former ornateness to the Latin language." Sicco's scheme was then developed still further by CRISTO-FORO LANDINO in the preface to his edition of the *Divine Comedy*.[11] Landino too arranged his subjects by professional categories: Cosimo de' Medici was a "statesman," and Bruni was an "orator." But he added far more evidence in support of an expanded version of Sicco's thesis. Since the founding of hospitals and the composition of treatises were deeds just as illustrious as fighting battles and signing treaties, Landino insisted, the age which had produced Alberti, Antonino, and Brunelleschi was qualitatively diferent from the age which had produced only the Bianchi and the Neri.

What Landino accomplished in a few pages for Florentines of his own day, four other authors accomplished, in volumes ranging from several hundred to over a thousand pages apiece, for all the writers of the Renaissance and for all the poets of antiquity. These authors were BENEDETTO ACCOLTI, PAOLO CORTESI (1456–1510),[12] PIETRO CRINITO (1465–1505),[13] and LELIO, or LILIO, GREGORIO GIRALDI (1475–1552).[14] Since the chief value of the Jerome model had been its utility as a reference work, these authors too took pains to be thorough. So thorough were they, indeed, that in order to account for every obscure reference in their sources, they included Pythagoras as a lyric poet and Plato as a tragedian, and they made Achille Bocchi, whose historical work was still known only to a few Bolognese, into a colleague of Pontano and Bembo. To make sure that all the names they mentioned could be found easily, they usually reprinted them, first in the margin opposite the corresponding entries, and then in an exhaustive index. Since the chief value of the Diogenes model was readibility, they rearranged their single articles into well-established Renaissance literary forms. Cortesi wrote Ciceronian dialogues. Crinito "imitated Suetonius Tranquillus . . . in the books he composed about the grammarians and rhetoricians." And Giraldi had his students pose questions to him as they sat, "Platonis et Ciceronis exemplo," "under the wide branches of a plane tree by the murmuring waters of a rivulet" in the garden of his patron at the time, Alberto Pio da Carpi.

Since none of their models prescribed the unification of all genres of literature within a single chronological sequence, none of these authors was fully aware of the historiographical implications of his work. Crinito failed to explain why Romans of the late third century B.C. decided to give up swords for pens or why Christians of the late third century A.D., the spiritual descendants of Giraldi's first poets, should have been apathetic toward poetry. Giraldi separated the poets into three categories, with separate, two-millennia chronologies for each; and in his desire to show off the truly remarkable erudition he had acquired while still "pene puer," he frequently forgot that not every ancient author was necessarily an authority on all subjects—Ammianus on the sophist Hippias, Ausonius on Plato's lost dithyrambs, Aulus Gellius on the moral qualities of Draco. But each of them, about the same time (from the last decade of the fifteenth century to the first decade of the sixteenth) but independently (Giraldi borrowed some details from Crinito only in a later revision), came up with patterns of historical development that were at least complementary, if not identical. Poetry—by which Giraldi meant imaginative literature in general—began among the Hebrews at the time of the Exodus; hence "poets are the most ancient of all writers." It was taken over by the Greeks well before the destruction of most early Hebrew literature by the Assyrians—as proved by the transliteration of the name "Moses" as "muses." A string of pioneers before and after Homer then prepared the way for its perfection in the age of the great Athenian dramatists. Poetry was soon afterwards brought to Rome by the Hellenized Roman Livius Andronicus, and it was perfected in its Latin form by Horace and Vergil in the age of Augustus. It then declined after the death of Antoninus Pius; and by the time of Theodosius nothing was left of it but the corrupt, and hence unpoetic, Latin of Sidonius Apollinaris. Along with other forms of literature, poetry was resurrected a millennium later by Manuel Chrysoloras, the modern Livius Andronicus, who reintroduced Greek, and by Leonardo Bruni, who used Greek to polish Latin. And it reached perfection for the third time in the age of the modern Augustus, Lorenzo de' Medici, to whom Cortesi accordingly dedicated his work in 1492.

The scheme of periodization proposed by these biographers for the history of literature proved to be much more difficult to sustain when it was applied to *viri illustres* in general. BARTOLOMEO FAZIO included generals and princes as well as orators and poets. But since a series of biographies for him was merely a way of relaxing after the exhaustive labor required by the first ten books of his history of contemporary Naples, the ten-line paragraphs he allotted to each of his subjects were really not capable of achieving Fazio's rhetorical purpose: that of "arousing our spirits [to strive for] dignity, honor, and glory." And since the paragraphs were arranged without regard to chronological order, they could in no way be read as "a literary history of his times"—except, perhaps, by a scholar as disorganized as Giovanni Lami, who reviewed the book upon the apprearance of the first edition in 1745.[15] PAOLO GIOVIO included rogues, like Charles of Bourbon ("a cruel and impious man . . . who took up arms against his king and his country"), as well as heroes, like Giovanni delle Bande Nere ("the most valorous of all the Italian captains"); and he included the kings of Persia and Morocco as well as Charles V and Ferrante Gonzaga. But since a biographical dictionary for him served solely to illustrate the portraits he was collecting for his museum, he felt no need to iron out the numerous contradictions among his entries—even after they were rearranged in chronological order and presented to the public in Domenichi's Italian translation. Dante turned out to have been a Platonist in spite of what Giovio had said about his Aristotelian predecessor, Thomas Aquinas, in the preceding article. Petrarch was presented as nothing but a vernacular poet. Bruni was accused of plagiarizing Procopius. And both Chrysoloras and Valla were given the same credit for having first awakened Italians from the "sleep" of the "Gothic ages."[16]

The search for a pattern of historical development turned out to be no more fruitful in the case of several single categories of *viri illustres*. What might have become a history of Renaissance philosophy was cut short in the form of separate biographies of only the Platonists among Renaissance philosophers; and the philosophers in turn were portrayed not as contributors to an ongoing philosophical inquiry but solely as citizens or teachers.[17] What might have become a history of ancient and modern jurisprudence was compromised by GUIDO PANCIROLI's inability to recognize the importance of the innovations introduced into the discipline by his own teacher, Andrea Alciati. The only "schools" of jurisprudence he could distinguish were purely chronological in nature: from the Twelve Tables to Justinian, from the eleventh century to the sixteenth century. And the Cultists were lumped together with the Bartolists, the *Mos Gallicus* with the *Mos Italicus,* as integral parts of the same, unbroken medieval tradition.[18]

Emperors fared no better than philosophers and jurists. The principal difficulty lay in the nature of the empire itself. Trajan, Otto I, and Ludwig of Bavaria could be placed in the same category only at the risk of reviving the medieval concept of the empire as the changeless, eternal embodiment of temporal power—a concept that was at least implicit in the two sentences that Boccaccio's companion BENVENUTO DE' RAMBALDI accorded to all the emperors he had heard of, both Eastern and Western, until the time of Charlemagne and to all the Western emperors down through the fourteenth century.[19] But this difficulty could easily have been overcome by the first Renaissance Italian to embark on a series of lives of the emperors, GIOVAN BATTISTA CIPELLI, or EGNAZIO. For Egnazio was one of the most honored and best-paid Latin teachers of the early sixteenth century, and he had edited the two ancient texts that were most pertinent to his task, Suetonius's *Lives of the Caesars* and the *Scriptores Historiae Augustae*. But he had already learned to put aside what might have served him as models when he chopped up the lives of famous Venetians under such headings as "miracles" and "triumphs."[20] And he had no trouble putting them aside once again in favor of the medieval imperial lives from which he took, uncritically, much of his information for his own series from Julius Caesar to Maximilian II. All that even his translator could say about the work, except to note its utility as a list of names and dates, was that it represented "an inestimable effort in gathering together information from many [different] books, both Latin and Greek."[21] The difficulty could have been overcome even more easily by MAMBRINO ROSEO. For Roseo was one of the most prolific translators and editors of historical works in the whole sixteenth century. But when he embarked upon the much more modest project of continuing Suetonius from Trajan to Alexander Severus—apparently supposing, incorrectly, that additional biographies by Suetonius himself would eventually come to light—he did no more than paste together passages from Plutarch, Dio Cassius, and Herodian. And he consequently failed to notice the political crisis in the Roman Empire corresponding to the crisis in Roman culture that Sicco and Giraldi had discerned in the century after the death of Marcus Aurelius.[22]

Popes fared somewhat better as subjects for series of biographies than emperors—except when they were occasionally put back together with emperors in a revival of the medieval format of a *Compendium Vitarum Summorum Pontificum Imperatorumque Romanorum*—like that of MARINO BARLEZIO (1555).[23] For just as the Peace of Augsburg and the retirement of Charles V dispersed the last hopes of reasserting the universal character of the Empire, the Papacy was emerging as one of the strongest and most determined institutions of all Christendom. Moreover, the principal biographer of the popes, ONOFRIO PANVINIO (d. 1568), discovered that the model Egnazio had rejected, Suetonius, was very well suited to his subject, since modern popes were not all that different from first-century emperors. He also discovered that his ancient model could be combined with a very successful Renaissance model, that of his fifteenth-century predecessor, Platina. Panvinio's task was thus immensely shortened. He had only to correct the spelling of a few proper names, add the new details he himself had run across while preparing a four-volume history of Gregory VII, identify as such all the many passages that Platina had lifted without acknowledgment from his sources, and otherwise simply reprint the text as it stood.[24] So faithfully did he follow his models, indeed, that he maintained in his judgments of the popes of the sixteenth century the same frankness with which they had judged Tiberius and Paul II. And the same judgments were faithfully repeated, for the benefit of those who could not read the entire work, in Tomaso Costo's popular, and authoritative, abridgment.[25] The cardinals who elected Urban VI really did act under constraint, Costo insisted. Sixtus IV really did prefer wars and palaces to peace and religion. Alexander VI really was a "horrible monster" whose sole virtue consisted in not keeping his election promises. And the stories about Sylvester and Constantine were indeed fabrications worthy of Platina's wrath, however comforting they might have been to certain neo-Gregorians in the Roman Curia.

The necessity imposed by the biographical form of going back in time to the birth of each successive pope prevented Panvinio from clearly formulating a thesis about the progressive change in the nature of the Papacy he had witnessed in his own day. Nonetheless, he managed at least to suggest such a thesis by giving more space to those individual popes who came the closest to his ideal. What Marcellus II might have done had he reigned for more than a few days is contrasted with what Paul IV unfortunately did do during his four-year reign. The magnificent projects launched by Pius V are summarized in the heroic but fatal pilgrimage he made on foot to the basilicas of Rome while planning a still more magnificent follow-up to Lepanto—and while running a fever. The magnificent projects by which Gregory XIII was assured of "being remembered for all the centuries" are underlined by long series of anecdotes illustrative of his "pleasant and majestic bearing" and his "mild and benign disposition." Indeed, the pontificate of Gregory XIII might have maintained its place in the final redaction as the culmination of some 1,600 years of papal history had not Panvinio's continuer accorded three times as much space to Clement VIII—and had not the whole project then been transformed from an individual into a collective enterprise entrusted not to humanist laymen but to non-Italian monks.

Mathematicians proved to be even more susceptible to consideration from a historical point of view than were popes—or at least they became so when, in the last decades of the sixteenth century, mathematics was finally recognized as an independent discipline, and when the accomplished humanist BERNARDINO BALDI of Urbino (1553–1617) decided to include it in his humanist curriculum. Baldi was even more of a universal man—in an age when there was far more to learn—than had been the predecessor he most consciously imitated, Leon Battista Alberti. He mastered not only Greek and Latin but also French, German, Persian, and Arabic. He studied all the Italian poets and, under the direction of Carlo Borromeo, all the Church Fathers. And he visited all the major centers of learning in northern Italy. He then turned to history. He put together a series of the current formulae about how history ought to be written. He read through all the ancient and most of the modern historians. And he managed both to correct what he found to be an error in Biondo's reading of Procopius and to shift the usual date for the "emergence of good letters" from the early fifteenth to the early sixteenth century.[26] He next turned to biography; and he wrote the first two large installments—each of them some 500 pages long—of what he planned as a complete series on the dukes of Urbino.[27] Finally, after settling down in Urbino with a lucrative ecclesiastical sinecure, he returned to mathematics, the favorite subject of his youth. And it was probably at the request of his former teacher, Federico Commandino, court mathematician at Urbino, that he took on the project Commandino had had time only to sketch out: a historical survey of mathematics.[28] The established forms of historiography did not permit the historical consideration of literature, as Baldi remembered from having been able to refer only in passing to Castiglione in his account of Urbino at the time of Guidobaldo. Or rather, they permitted mention of it only in set orations attributed to princes and generals. But orations—like the one he probably read in the 1537 edition of the works of Regiomontanus (Johannes Müller)—were too brief for a proper treatment of his subject. Baldi therefore compiled an alphabetical list of some 366 mathematicians he had found mentioned by ancient authors.[30] And between 1588 and 1596 he carefully arranged the mass of reading notes he had accumulated according to the format prescribed by Diogenes Laertius—that is, in chronological order, with the length of each entry determined by the relative importance of the subject in the development of the discipline.

True, Baldi often let his taste for scholarly minutiae lead him astray: whole paragraphs are given over to figuring out the sources of a single statement in Tommaso Fazello and to establishing the exact connotation of the term "grains of sand" at the moment when Archimedes decided to count them. Moreover, he was more interested in the individual genius of each mathematician—which was a matter not subject to historical interpretation—than he was in the connections among them. And he may have doubted that any of his contemporaries shared any of his interests, for his manuscript remained relatively unknown during his lifetime and was not published until almost three centuries later.[31] But his theses were made clear by the very arrangement of the biographies. For Baldi, the progress of mathematics in antiquity culminated in the career of Archimedes, to whom he accorded four times as much space as to his nearest competitor, Vitruvius; for Vitruvius's merits as an applied mathematician were to some extent offset by his sloppiness as a writer. The progress of mathematics in modern times culminated in the work first of Copernicus, who applied mathematics to astronomy,[32] and then of Guidobaldo Del Monte, who resurrected the texts of Archimedes.

From Biography to Art History: Giorgio Vasari

The most amenable of all the professions to the transformation of biography into history was the arts. It was so in part because the artists of antiquity had been honored in their own times with a place next to the philosophers and because they had been arranged according to a pattern of progressive historical development by an authoritative ancient writer, Pliny the Elder. It was so also because the artists of the early Renaissance had been made the equals of the *viri illustres* of arms and letters ever since the time of Filippo Villani. In recognition of this respectability, the Florentine novelist GIAMBATTISTA GELLI traced the origins of Florentine art in the early sixteenth century to the aesthetic innovations of Giotto in the early fourteenth century. The Neapolitan humanist Pietro Summonte traced the introduction of this same artistic tradition into Naples in the mid-fifteenth century to the cultural policies of Alfonso d'Aragona. And Summonte's Venetian correspondent MARC' ANTONIO MICHIEL made extensive notes on the location and the attributions of works of art in the homes and churches of Padua, Cremona, Milan, Bergamo, and Venice—notes that might have served as a precious research guide for an eventual historan of art had they been discovered in the early sixteenth rather than in the early eighteenth century.[33]

But the chief responsibility for promoting this transformation lies with the most successful of the biographers of artists of the High Renaissance, GIORGIO VASARI. Vasari had begun his career as a painter, one who took pride in being able to cover more wall space in less time than any of his competitors; and he ended his career not only as a painter but also as an architect, a stage and float designer, and director of public works for Duke Cosimo I de' Medici. But the commissions that constantly took him away from his home in Arezzo and from the houses of his patrons in Florence soon made him acquainted with all the principal works of art in Italy, past as well as present. The fear that what he had observed might eventually be ruined or forgotten and that future art students might no longer be able to "imitate" their masters in accordance with humanist theories of pedagogy led him to compile a series of notes: who did what, when, with what degree of skill, and where it was currently located.

Meanwhile, the most famous historian and biographer of the day, Paolo Giovio, had acquired considerable recognition as an art critic as well as some experience as a biographer of artists. Probably while collaborating with him in the program for the frescoes in the Cancelleria in Rome in 1546, Giovio suggested that Vasari follow his example and rearrange his notes in the form of a series of biographies; and Vasari at least went so far as to reorder, to mount—and, alas, to "edit"—the collection of drawings he had inherited from a descendant of Lorenzo Ghiberti in 1528. At the same time, his own master in painting, Michelangelo, assured him that writing was more properly his vocation than painting: and Vasari accordingly sought help from the current master of good literary style, Annibal Caro, in perfecting his natural talent for writing ("Move the verbs from the end to the middle of your sentences," Caro admonished, "and make sure you use the correct nouns").[34] When the first edition of his *Vite de' più eccellenti pittori, scultori e archetettori* was hailed for having indeed done "honor to those who are dead" and for being "beneficial to those who are now engaged in these three excellent arts," he turned even more seriously to his task.[35] He decided not to follow the advice of his antiquarian friend—and research assistant—Vincenzo Borghini, that he leave out the artists and stick to art. He decided rather to follow Giovio's advice and to describe acts in their relation to the particular character of each agent, just as the historians did:

> Seeing that the writers of histories . . . have not been content simply to narrate what has taken place, but with all diligence [have sought to] investigate the means, ways, and manner which valiant men have used in carrying out their undertakings . . . and to ascertain the judgments, counsels, and opinions of those who act, since these are in fact the causes of the happy or unhappy consequences of what is done. . . . (*Proemio* to Part II)

He then took research expeditions to the cities of northern Italy where he had not previously worked. He solicited information from correspondents in those cities he was unable to visit. And, in order to remember what he had seen or heard of, he put together a vast collection of drawings, sketches, and prints—the latter thanks to the recent inventors of copper engraving, whom he accordingly honored with a place among the painters and sculptors.

To be sure, even the second, and vastly expanded, edition of 1568 was still basically a collection of single biographies. The chronological order generally observed for the fourteenth century ran into serious difficulties in the fifteenth century, since many of the artists could not clearly be fitted into a single pattern of stylistic development. And it broke down completely in the sixteenth century, to which over half of the whole work was devoted (five out of eight volumes in the Club del Libro edition). Vasari occasionally resorted to geographical order (Lombardy, Venice, Verona...), to an institutional order (all the younger Florentines are lumped together as members of the newly founded Accademia del Disegno), or to no order at all: Michelangelo's disciple Daniele da Volterra comes before Michelangelo himself. Furthermore, Vasari assumed about artists what Giraldi and Baldi assumed about poets and mathematicians: that their particular accomplishments were essentially manifestations of their own particular genius. Less talented disciples, he admitted, were usually worthy of consideration for having continued or elaborated upon the works of their masters, and he accordingly emphasized such connections by including them at the end of their masters' own biographies. Even the masters, he found, were frequently encouraged to realize their potential by associating with a community of collaborators, critics. and competitors. After all, it was the hope of profiting from such a community that had led Donatello to turn down a lucrative offer at Padua[36] and that had induced Vasari himself to accept a lucrative offer from Duke Cosimo. But genius itself—and thus major changes in styles and techniques—could be explained only by invoking the intervention of divine forces:

> in order to save us from such great errors... the Most Benign Ruler of Heaven turned his eyes clemently toward earth ... and consented to send down a Spirit. ...

That such explanations bordered on the blasphemous, that they resorted to the kind of supernatural causes that the historians had banned from history, and that they contradicted Vasari's own expressions of adherence to the historians' theses about the effects of "a great desire for glory"—all this bothered no one. For neither Vasari nor any of his readers took them at all seriously.

Nevertheless, the attempt to judge all the works of art still visible in his own day according to the principles set forth in his introductory essay convinced Vasari that what he held to be the full realizaiton of the principles in the mid-sixteenth century had been the result of a long historical process. At the same time, his humanist upbringing—and his reading of Pliny—persuaded him that the same principles had also been realized in antiquity. With the help of the accomplished historian Giovan Battista Adriani, whose reasearches in the written records of ancient art he then published along with his own abridged version of them,[37] he traced the evolution of Greek art to the age of Apelles and of Roman art to the age of Augustus. He then documented the decline of ancient art in general (it never occurred to him that what is today called "Byzantine" might designate an original and autonomous art style) with a detailed analysis of the Arch of Constantine. And he traced this decline to the same cause identified by Giraldi for the decline of ancient literature: the Christians.

> The fervent zeal of the new Christian religion not only . . . threw to the ground all the marvelous statues . . . and paintings of the fallacious gods of the gentiles, but also [wiped out] the very memory of the infinite number of worthy persons who had made them.

Although Vasari found traces of the "good manner" of the ancients even in the darkest moments of the Middle Ages, he attributed its recovery in the late thirteenth century wholly to the spontaneous initiative of two artists, Cimabue and Giotto—the same two artists identified as the founders of modern art over a century earlier in one of Vasari's chief sources, the *Commentarii* of Lorenzo Ghiberti.

After this promising beginning, however, the progress of art slowed down. Instead of imitating nature and searching for ever closer approximations to his "regola, ordine, misura, disegno e maniera," Vasari discovered, the artists of the late fourteenth century merely copied Giotto. The resumption of progress thus required a second revolution—the revolution which Leon Battista Alberti, Vasari's chief predecessor in art theory, had credited to Masaccio, Donatello, and Brunelleschi.[38] Vasari then hit upon a way of introducing a scheme of historical periodization without infringing upon the literary and topical unity of each biography. He divided the whole work into three parts, each one corresponding to a chronologically successive age of art history. And he then justified the division in the critical and historical essays that served as introductions to each of the parts. The third age, he insisted, began with Leonardo da Vinci, who fully incorporated all the technological and aesthetic improvements of the preceding two ages. And it culminated in the painting of Raffaello and Tiziano and in the painting, sculpture, and architecture of the greatest artist of all times, the "divine" Michelangelo.[39]

Having reached "perfection," however, art was not then condemned to repeat some form of the "cycle" that Vasari had referred to in passing—and without taking it at all seriously—in his account of post-Constantinian art ("la fortuna, quando ella ha condotto altri al summo della ruota . . ."). Nor was it endangered by the intrusion of "celestial influences," like the ones he thoughtlessly evoked in his introduction to the biography of Leonardo. At the same time, further progress in art was not dependent upon the discovery of still other aesthetic principles. Indeed, Vasari never seems to have suspected that his much-admired friends Parmigianino and Salviati would ever be classified as "mannerist" rebels against their "High Renaissance" masters—not even when he had to admit his inability to comprehend Pontormo's frescoes in San Lorenzo. What Vasari foresaw in the future, then, was neither an improvement in quality nor a new definition of quality. Rather, he looked forward to an unlimited application of the infallible rules taught through example by Michelangelo and by precept in the new Accademia del Disegno that Vasari himself founded in Florence. These rules guaranteed the maintenance of perfect quality while permitting a rapid increase in quantity:

> art . . . has now been reduced to such perfection and made so easy for whoever possesses [its three basic elements], design, invention, and color, that while past masters did one work in six years, masters of today can do six in one year. (Part 3, Preface)

The task of artists in the incipient fourth age of the history of art was therefore to carry to the four corners of the earth what in the third age had been realized only in a few cities of Italy. Painters would cover wall after wall with beautiful canvases and frescoes. Sculptors would fill halls and public squares with beautiful statues. And architects would "render the habitations [of all mankind] comfortable, safe, healthy, pleasuresome, well-proportioned, and rich in various ornaments" (Club del Libro ed., vol. VII, p. 107).

The Renaissance biographers who sought to apply a combination of the literary forms inherited from Jerome and Diogene Laertius to one or another profession or discipline seldom knew each other, and none of them seems ever to have tried to coordinate the historical theses drawn from his particular series with those drawn from the others. Nevertheless, all of them came up with patterns of historical change that were similar, at least in their sharp contrasts with the patterns proposed by the Livian and Caesarian historians. The decline of ancient mathematis preceded, and that of ancient law followed, the decline of literature and art, they found; and the decline of all these aspects of ancient culture was not necessarily dependent upon the decline of the Roman Empire as a political institution. The successive partial revivals of the Papacy after the great age of the Fathers—those corresponding to the pontificates of Gregory VII, Innocent III, and Pius II—prepared for the perfection of the Papacy as an institution a half-century after a three-century development of art culminated in the work of Michelangelo. And the first stirrings of a revival of good letters in the ages of Dante, Petrarch, and Bruni prepared the way for their triumph in an age that coincided almost exactly with what the political historians bewailed as Italy's calamity.

Had the historians of the late sixteenth century taken the trouble to reflect on these alternate chronologies, they might indeed have found a way out of the dilemma posed by their living in an age devoid of political and military events. And they might have discovered that history had not stopped after all.

The Suetonian-Plutarchan Tradition

The other principal form of biographical writing adopted by the Renaissance from classical antiquity was the autonomous, comprehensive life of a single individual. This form of biography was originally based on one of the favorite ancient models of the medieval biographers, Suetonius's *Lives of the Caesars*. It was also based on an early Renaissance model, Petrarch's *De Viris Illustribus,* which was inspired by Petrarch's reading, in 1340 or 1341, of what today is known as the Berlin codex. It was based as well on the other ancient model that Petrarch had joined to Suetonius in breaking with the medieval biographical tradition, Sextus Aurelius Victor. This form of biography enabled the biographer to include many different categories: Old Testament patriarchs (Adam, Noah), kings (Numa), statesmen (Scipio Africanus), and foreigners (Hannibal, Pyrrhus). It permitted him to distribute space according to the degree of "illustriousness" of each personage as well as to the quantity of available information about him (Petrarch gave 156 pages to Scipio in the modern edition and only two to Romulus). It forced him to go back to the sources—in Petrarch's case to Livy, Pliny, Cicero, and Valerius Maximus—rather than to just copy his predecessors, as Giovanni Colonna had done. It therefore came to be called not biography—a term neither Petrarch nor his successors ever used—but "history." "Historiam narrare propositum est," insisted Petrarch in the preface to his *Lives.* For even history, in the words of Matteo Palmieri, "is nothing other than the celebration of illustrious men." Thus what Petrarch began, others soon continued. He himself composed an *Epitome* of his *Lives* in order to assist his last patron, Francesco da Carrara, in planning a cycle of murals for his palace. And Petrarch's Paduan disciple LOMBARDO DA SERIGIO supplemented what his master had written with lives of still other illustrious Romans from the time of Caesar until the time of Trajan.[40]

The single biography as a genre of humanist literature was reinforced in the course of the fifteenth century by the introduction of several other ancient models: those of Cornelius Nepos, of Quintus Curtius Rufus, of Arrian of Nicomedia, and, above all, of Plutarch, which, after it had aroused the curiosity of Coluccio Salutati in the 1390s, became, in the words of a modern authority, "one of the most clamorous discoveries of humanism."[41] To be sure, many of these models actually consisted of series of connected biographies rather than single, autonomous biographies. But Renaissance readers seldom had the opportunity of reading them all together. Suetonius's *Lives of the Caesars* were generally presented one at a time, even after Poliziano's lectures on them and the appearance of the first critical edition of 1494. Petrarch's lives of illustrious men were generally presented in the same form, since Petrarch had composed and revised them one at a time and had never made up his mind about the order in which they should appear. Plutarch's *Lives* were translated and circulated separately by different translators. The first attempts at complete editions of Plutarch, those of Pier Candido Decembrio and Giovannantonio Campano, simply reproduced the previous translations without attempting to impose a uniform Latin style on all of them. And none of the subsequent Italian translators and epitomizers—Achille Bocchi, Lodovico Domenichi, and Dario Tiberti of Cesena[42]—ever noticed the subtle contrast between pairs of Greeks and Romans that provides most of what there is of a unifying principle among them all. Even Cornelius Nepos's *Lives of the Excellent Generals* were published without a hint that they had originally formed part of a larger collection. Indeed, both in the original Aldine edition (1491) and in Remigio Fiorentino's standard Italian translation (reprinted as late as 1746), they were attributed erroneously to an obscure fourth-century copyist named Emilius Probus; and neither the original nor the translation included the two surviving lives of Cornelius's nonmilitary heroes, Atticus and Cato. Others of the models, on the other hand, had once been parts of more general historical works. But Sextus Aurelius Victor's *Illustrious Men of the City of Rome* was published in the Italian translation of 1544 as a complement not of his own *Origins of the Roman People* but of Suetonius. Neither of the first two editors of the Latin text of Quintus Curtius Rufus, Pomponio Leto and Bartolomeo Merula, nor the two Italian translators, Decembrio and Porcacchi, noticed the importance of his text as a historiographical link between Sallust and Tacitus. Neither Bartolomeo Fazio, the first of several Latin translators of Arrian, nor the Italian translator—the same Pietro Lauro who also wrote an epitome of Plutarch—realized that Arrian's biographical history of Alexander's Asian campaigns had been intended as a supplement to the author's longer work of narrative history; and Lauro associated it not with the work of Quintus Curtius, with which it shared common sources, but with that of Xenophon.[43]

Since it was necessarily restricted to one moment in time, the single biography could not, like a series of biographies, suggest to historians an alternate scheme of historical periodization. It could, however, offer them a deeper perception of the relationship between a single individual and the historical circumstances in which he lived—as Giovio showed in his reflections on the "age" of one of his heroes, Leo X. It could show, that is, that the "very great virtues" of many very great men were in part the product of the "very troubled times" after 1494.[44] Even more effectively than history, where chronological narrative inevitably involved a number of extraneous events, the single biography could preserve the memory of a great man for the moral guidance of his posterity. Best of all, it could make possible a much deeper understanding of what the historians held to be the ultimate cause of all historical events: the peculiar character of individual historical agents. For it admitted a consideration not just of the public acts and virtues of its subjects but also of their private habits, tastes, and idiosyncracies. And to illustrate various aspects of a subject's character, it could make use not only of set speeches and battlefield pronouncements but also of such anecdotes as those in Plutarch about Alcibiades' dog and those in Giovio about young Giangaleazzo's recognition of Petrarch.

It was these peculiar qualities of the Suetonian-Plutarchan model that had permitted its combination with certain elements of Livian historiography in the many "biographical histories" devoted to the lives and times of the great princes of the Quattrocento: lives of Alfonso d'Aragona, Paul II, or Filippo Maria Visconti that became substantially histories of Naples, the Papacy, or Milan during their respective reigns. It was these same qualities that then encouraged its adoption in the Cinquecento by the biographers of the traditional heroes of historiography, men of state and of arms. With the help of this model, PIETRO SPINI was able to eliminate noble blood as a cause of the great deeds of a wellborn general like Bartolomeo Colleoni: it was rather the deeds, he insisted, that brought glory to his hero's lineage and that gave fame to the city in which both hero and biographer had been born.[45] And with the help of the same model, LORENZO CAPELLONI was able to add two more to the usual lists of heroic virtues: moderation in the face of opportunities for self-aggrandizement and sagacity in picking the right moment for changing sides in a war. Indeed, the career of Andrea Doria was so packed with examples of these virtues that Capelloni was occasionally obliged to depart "from the brevity used by Suetonius and Plutarch."[46]

By far the most successful biographer of princes and generals in the sixteenth century was PAOLO GIOVIO,[47] notwithstanding his insistence that biography was marginal to his chief vocation as a historian. Giovio was attracted to Plutarchan-Suetonian biography—as opposed to series of biographies, which served him only as decoration for his portrait gallery[48]—principally because of its potential as a means of presenting readers with examples of good deeds to imitate and bad deeds to avoid. But this prospect eventually led him to reevaluate the usual definition of "deeds" that he had accepted in his role as a historian. In order to stigmatize once again that traditional villain, Bernabò Visconti, and to exalt Bernabò's traditional opposite, Giangaleazzo, Giovio had to admit that the role of an administrator—one who imposed "a marvelous order . . . on all the offices" of his state—was just as productive of glory as the role of a military commander. In order to emphasize the glorious achievements of a hero as poorly endowed in political and military skill as Pope Leo X, he had to examine more closely the relationship of an individual to the family from which he descended; and he consequently presented Leo as the heir of his great-grandfather's abilities as a diplomat and of his father's abilities as a patron of the arts and letters. In order to explain the apparent anomaly of the modest circumstances in which so great a general as the Marchese di Pescara had ended his days, he had to add moderation and abstinence to bravery as qualities required of a great warrior. Giovio's biographies were therefore recognized as "necessary for a full understanding of his histories"; for they obviously included many more "illustrious examples of virtue" than "would have been permitted in a work of history."[49] And Giovio himself suggested that they might serve temporarily to fill the gaps that still remained in his major work.

This perception of the historiographical function of biography was still further deepened by two of Giovio's most able successors, GIROLAMO MUZIO (or MUTIO)

(1493–1576)[50] and GIOVAN BATTISTA LEONI.[51] Neither by birth nor career, did Muzio and Leoni have much in common. The first was a peripatetic polygraph whose various jobs as a soldier, a secretary, and a diplomat took him to most of the cities of Italy, France, and Germany, and whose skill as a popular writer was effectively employed in making Counter Reformation theology intelligible to humanist-educated laymen. The second was a sedentary, well-to-do Venetian who enjoyed a considerable reputation as a historian of his native country. The problem they faced as biographers were very different, too. Muzio's task was relatively easy: all he had to do was restate the well-known virtues of Federico da Montefeltro, who had spent most of his active life in the service of such unquestioned humanist heroes as Alfonso d'Aragona and Pius II. Leoni, on the other hand, was obliged to defend Julius II, one of the least popular predecessors of the Counter Reformation popes, to rehabilitate Francesco Maria Della Rovere, whom a generation of historians had accused of abandoning Rome to Bourbon, and to turn Giovio's hero, Leo X, into a "scandalously ungrateful" nepotist.

In spite of these differences, however, both Muzio and Leoni faithfully followed Giovio's example in making biography conform to the formal and methodological standards of humanist historiography: the use of orations and dialogues for the exposition of *consilia,* the appeal to ancient standards of credibility ("this event cannot be dismissed as a fable because such horrors are [also] reported by various [ancient] historians"), and the insistence upon "legitimate and authentic writings" as the primary source of historical truth. Better yet, both of them succeeded as well as the best historians in identifying their heroes not just as performers of imitable deeds but as representatives of particular moments in historical time. Federico was one of the captains most responsible for rescuing central Italy from the political chaos of the mid-fifteenth century, Muzio pointed out. And Francesco Maria Della Rovere, according to Leoni, was among the most glorious of "the great number of glorious princes" who made the early sixteenth century "one of the most famous and exemplary" eras in all history.

The biographical form that Giovio, Muzio, and Leoni applied so successfully to the standard heroes of humanist historiography could also be applied to men of letters, particularly to the three great men of letters of the fourteenth century whom all succeeding vernacular writers looked to as the founders of literature in their language. The series of such biographies was inaugurated by Boccaccio and Filippo Villani, although still according to prehumanist criteria of how poets and philosophers should behave. It was then radically altered by LEONARDO BRUNI, who insisted that romance yield to documentable proof and who turned Dante into a prototype of Civic Humanism. It was then promoted to the dignity of the language of the Quattrocento scholars by the historian GIANNOZZO MANETTI, who rejected Bruni's linguistic distinction between biography and history and translated his own *Lives and Manners of the Three Illustrious Florentine Poets* into Latin, and by the "poet and doctor of the arts and of both laws," as he called himself in the prologue, GIOVAN MARIO FILELFO, who wrote his *Life of Dante* directly in the humanist Latin of which he was then a recognized master. It was broadened in scope to include the philosophical and critical as well as the poetic work of its heroes and refined in method to overcome the remaining "inconvenientia" by GIROLAMO SQUARCIALUPO (1501), an editor of Plutarch and Sallust as well as of Petrarch's *Trionfi*. It was rendered still more historical in approach by GIOVAN ANDREA GESUALDO (1533), who supported his theses with frequent citations of Petrarch's works and gave dates for the principal events of Petrarch's life. It was rid of the last remnants of "favole" by ALESSANDRO VELLUTELLO (1535), who added "the others of his works" and "the histories of his times" to what Petrarch said about himself in the *Letter to Posterity*. And many of these biographies were then broadcast throughout Italy in one after the other of the innumerable editions of Petrarch's *Rime* that poured from the presses throughout the sixteenth century.[52]

This form could also be applied to individual citizens of republics—to those, that is, whom the historians usually referred to collectively as "the Venetians" or "the Florentines," without distinguishing among them as individuals. So, in any case, thought the Maecenas of late-sixteenth-century Florentine culture, Baccio Valori, who was afraid that the stable regime and the "quieter conditions" introduced by the principate might lead his compatriots to question traditional moral ideals.[53] Some of the virtuous citizens proposed by the Florentine biographers as exemplary happened also to have been princes or generals: Lorenzo de' Medici, Francesco Ferrucci, Giovanni delle Bande Nere, Cosimo I.[54] But even they came to be appreciated more for their private than for their public virtues. Cosimo was commended for his "benignity," his "mildness," and the "firmness of spirit" that kept him, as a boy, from revealing the Cardinal of Cortona's secrets even to his mother. Lorenzo was commended for his piety, his clemency, and his proficiency in philosophy and poetry—qualities that enabled him to conquer his enemies not by force, which NICCOLÒ VALORI found rather distasteful, but by generosity and love, which he found to be far more effective in an age of peace and prosperity.

Occasionally the sixteenth-century Florentine biographers let Plutarchan anecdotes overwhelm their theses—as did DOMENICO MELLINI in his anxiety to present Cosimo's plain brown clothes, his predilection for popular ball-games *(palla a corda)*, and his "modest, grave, dignified bearing" as antidotes for current Spanish mannerisms.[55] Occasionally they forgot the man they were supposedly writing about in an effort to complete the list of abstract virtues he supposedly incarnated—as did the faithful bureaucrat PIERO USIMBARDI, whose heavy administrative responsibilities apparently prevented him from consulting the standard biographical models.[56] Occasionally they confused biography with eulogy, notwithstanding the clear distinction between the two genres prescribed by the ancient theorists and exemplified in LODOVICO DOLCE's frankly nonbiographical *encomia* of the "rather divine than human" emperors, Charles V and Ferdinand I.[57] For a time when the recitation of eulogies had become a regular function of the literary academies and when eulogy disguised as biography could procure university chairs for candidates with publication records as weak as that of ALDO MANUZIO JR. (1547–97), [58] the temptation to tolerate such a confusion was often difficult to resist.

Still, the chief purpose prescribed for biography by Valori—that of adapting the moral standards of the republic to the new circumstances of the principate—was generally realized. Lelio Torelli, Cosimo's chief legal adviser, was accepted as a model public servant, one for whom the good of the people took precedence over the hallowed formulae of academic law texts.[59] Filippo Strozzi, Cosimo's most determined and wealthiest opponent, was turned into a model of a cultivated businessman, one who combined the strictest honesty in his financial transactions with an ability to compose madrigals and translate Polybius. Bartolomeo Valori, Piero di Gino Capponi, Pier Vettori the Elder, Antonio Giacomini Tebalducci, and Niccolò Capponi were exalted as model private citizens—citizens who kept strictly to their own affairs until such time as they were called upon to take charge of public affairs, and who then devoted "hard work, sweat, blood, tears, and their very lives to the good of [their] country."[60] Thus those Florentines whose virtues had been called forth in a happily bygone age of war, famine, and civil strife could still serve as moral examples for those of their descendants whom peace, order, and prosperity had deprived of the ability to generate new examples of their own.

Giovio's version of Suetonian-Plutarchan biography was found to be applicable also to prelates, partially because the personal and professional requirements for ecclesiastical office remained much the same in the sixteenth century as the requirements for civil and military office. Gasparo Contarini, Pietro Bembo, Reginald Pole, and Filippo Commendone were all men of noble birth, humanist education, and literary accomplishment.[61] Consequently, the "example of [their] well-known virtues" could be "of great benefit to [all] others" regardless of differences in vocation, as Beccatelli pointed out, and the occasional defects that made a few of them somewhat less acceptable by post-Tridentine standards could easily be excused with reference to the "licence and permissiveness" that had prevailed in the decades before Trent. There were differences among the prelates' biographers, to be sure. GIOVANNI DELLA CASA was somewhat more generic, even when writing about his personal friends, whereas LODOVICO BECCATELLI was "more diligent, better organized, and much better informed," at least according to his eighteenth-century editor. But most of them belonged to the same social group as the prelates they wrote about. Della Casa, who learned to write history and biography by paraphrasing Fazio's history of Alfonso d'Aragona, was a papal nuncio and Bembo's successor as the leading authority on the Italian language. Beccatelli, who also wrote a biography of Petrarch, was Della Casa's successor as nuncio to Venice. And ANTON MARIA GRAZIANI (1537–1611), after a busy life as a papal diplomat, settled down to writing and to implementing the Tridentine Reformation in a quiet diocese of the Papal State.

Moreover, all the prelates' biographers agreed in extracting from their biographical works much the same historical theses: that Lorenzo de' Medici and Poliziano rather than Petrarch or Chrysoloras were responsible for the rebirth of good letters in modern times, and that the reform of the church, of which they were active protagonists, resulted from the application to ecclesiastical affairs of the same virtues applauded by the historians in civil and military affairs. Gregory XIII, for instance, could boast of deeds as glorious as those of any prince or general: he rebuilt old churches in Rome, he built new seminaries in Poland and Hungary, he organized the jubilee of 1575, he uncovered the bones of famous martyrs, he burned relapsed heretics, and he issued the first new calendar since that of Julius Caesar.[62] What was later to be called the Catholic or the Counter Reformation was thus seen to be not the negation but the logical continuation of what was even then called the Renaissance. And the church was proposed as a promising source of memorable events to write about just at the moment when historians were beginning to despair of finding any in the traditional areas of the state and the battlefield.

Biography thus had much to contribute to historiography in the way of new theses, new kinds of material, and new schemes of periodization; and that it might well have made such a contribution is suggested by several striking similarities between the two genres. Both biography and historiography sought to "constrain" the reader "to fill himself with the same virtues as those possessed by him who has been proposed as a guide." Both of them were committed, in the words of no less an authority than Claudio Tolomei,[63] to presenting "not just the things done by great men, . . . but also the roots and the foundations." Both of them observed the same distinction between fiction and truth, and both of them prescribed the same means for distinguishing the one from the other.

In the light of these similarities, Giovannantonio Campano was not wholly unjustified in referring to Plutarch not as a biographer but as "historiographus."[64] CESARE CAMPANA was fully justified in transforming what started out as a life of Philip II into a history of "every part of the world" between the date of Philip's birth and the date of his death.[65] PAOLO PANSA could legitimately deduce from his life of Innocent IV the proposition that "the Genoese have always produced excellent popes," a proposition very pleasing to the current pope, Sixtus V.[66] The rector of the Spanish College in Bologna could conclude from Sepúlveda's life of Cardinal Albornoz that the Church alone was able to protect the Bolognese "from the hands of cruel tyrants."[67] And GUIDO MELLINI could extract information from "several handwritten books not previously known to anyone" about the Countess Matilda to show that Biondo, Sabellico, Sigonio, Sardi, and Pigna had erred in their judgment of what he held to be an exemplary relationship between lay and ecclesiastical authority.[68]

Nonhumanist Biography and the Ancient Models

In spite of these similarities, however, and in spite of the potential advantages to both, a fusion, or even a reciprocal exchange, between the two genres became increasingly difficult to realize. First of all, biography lacked the support of a nonhumanist tradition of biographical writing similar to the nonhumanist chronicles and diaries that continued to supply the historians with information well after the advent of humanism. Or rather, what little there was of such a tradition had so little in common with the humanist literary models that not much could be learned from it. To be sure, most of the nonhumanist biographers of the Renaissance knew at least something about humanism. VESPASIANO DA BISTICCI was a personal friend of the many fifteenth-century humanists who bought books from him. ALESSANDRO CEC-CHEREGLI was sufficiently welcome in the humanist circles of mid-sixteenth-century Florence to enable him to introduce Giovio's translator, Lodovico Domenichi, as an interlocutor in one of his dialogues.[69] ASCANIO CONDIVI (1525–74) had heard enough about good writing from Michelangelo's literary friends to realize that it was beyond his competence.[70] And GIROLAMO CATENA was aware that his personal recollections of his employer and hero, Pope Pius V, could be of interest only if they were corroborated by references to "the letters written by nuncios and princes . . . and by the pope himself."[71]

But some of the nonhumanist biographers consistently confused fact and fiction in a manner that would never have been admitted by the most credulous of the medieval chroniclers. Indeed, Ceccheregli may well have been following the example not of the ancient biographers but of the contemporary translation of Boccaccio's *Casi de gli huomini illustri* by Giuseppe Betussi, whose *novelle* were appropriately republished in the same edition with his own in the nineteenth century. For the concrete illustrations of the "divinity of spirit, piety, and humanity" he attributed to Duke Alessandro de' Medici were no less incredible than those that Boccaccio attributed to Nemrod and Dante.[72] Others of the nonhumanist biographers apparently equated good style with worn-out metaphors—like Condivi's "Mercury having received Venus into the house of Jupiter with a benign expression." All of them freely piled up anecdotes with so little concern for the historians' distinction between the important and the trivial that Catena's readers could not but suppose Pius V's greatest achievement to have been not the Battle of Lepanto but "having remained a virgin throughout his [whole] life." One of them, GIROLAMO, or HIERONIMO, GARIMBERTO, frankly admitted his inability "to put [the lives of the popes] on paper in the order of a continuous history."[73] He chopped up his life of Innocent III into separate compartments labeled "religion and liturgy," "love of the Apostolic See," etc., and he credited Ippolito de' Medici with such unlikely qualities as "greatness of spirit," "goodness of character," and "most gracious appearance." Since such procedures were utterly incompatible with humanist principles, the works that incorporated them were quickly forgotten—with the one exception of Ceccheregli's, which may have served some political purpose during the last years of Cosimo I and the first years of Francesco de' Medici. Vespasiano was not rediscovered for another two centuries.[74] And Condivi's sole sixteenth-century edition remained eclipsed by Vasari, who had read it, until it was finally reevaluated as a supplementary historical document by modern art students.

One potentially promising variant of biography, autobiography, remained wholly untouched by humanism and hence incapable of being incorporated into either biography or history. None of the Renaissance autobiographers ever thought of using as a model the most obvious autobiographical work of antiquity, Augustine's *Confessions*. None of them could have followed one of the most potentially useful Renaissance models, that of Leon Battista Alberti, for it was not discovered until much later. None of them bothered to notice the other Renaissance model, Petrarch's *Metrical Letters* and his *Letter to Posterity,* even though the first had been imitated by Machiavelli in his famous letter of 10 December 1514, and even though the second was all but copied in the biographies of such sixteenth-century editors of Petrarch's works as SILVANO DA VENAFRO.[75] And those of them who tried to follow the model of the traditional personal or family diaries usually ended up with little more than lists of events—as did even the famous Tridentine reformer GIROLAMO SERIPANDO, whose *Diarium de Vita Sua* tells almost nothing about the author's intense spiritual life but gives an abundance of detail about his administrative and diplomatic activities.[76] Ignoring both ancient and Renaissance models, Renaissance autobiographers never learned to engage in an objective examination of their own personalities. They were reduced instead merely to recounting the memorable feats that they had, or would like to have, accomplished.

Unfortunately, not all these feats were equally historical in nature. MARC' ANTONIO MALTEMPI claimed to have been dropped into a deep well, hung from a bell rope, swept a mile down a flooding river, and thrown from a horse in front of a charging regiment of Turkish cavalry. But his readers could have accepted these claims only if they happened to be totally ignorant of what Giovio, Ulloa, Pellini, and the other historians Maltempi cited ostentatiously had said about the nature of truth.[77] GIROLAMO CARDANO (1501–76) claimed to have crushed every one of his innumerable debating opponents. But his readers could have believed him only if they were willing to accept his other claim: that he was following the example of Caesar, Augustus, Josephus, Galen, and Suetonius. And at least the Holy Office was unwilling to accept all the personal qualities he arranged under such un-Suetonian headings as "the good things of my life," "small dogs," and "birds" in support of his candidacy for a chair at Bologna.[78]

BENVENUTO CELLINI might have been more careful about what he said concerning his own great deeds and the despicable deeds of his enemies had he bothered to check his own account with those of Giovio, Varchi, and Adriani.[79] But he apparently read no more than the two books given him while he was a prisoner in Castel

Sant'Angelo, the Bible and Giovanni Villani, for he thought the latter still to be the current authority on Florentine history. One of the autobiographers, on the other hand, happened to have been accurate: FRANCESCO PATRIZI; and his autobiographical epistle of 12 January 1587 to his friend and possible patron, Baccio Valori, tells much about his activities as a businessman that most modern students of his works do not seem to have thought relevant to his activities as a philosopher. But only one of them made a concerted effort to be accurate: Cardinal GIULIO ANTONIO SANTORO (b. 1432). After all, Santoro's father had been a historian, and he too consciously "tried to find out the truth about what happened in order to compose a brief history [*historietta*]" of his own. Still, most of what Santoro related about himself regarded the books he read, and the interminable pious practices that he, and his mother, constantly engaged in. And what might have been an autobiography became instead a chronicle—albeit a full and fascinating one—of the author's efforts to implement the spirit and the letter of the Tridentine Reformation.[80]

The transformation of biography into history was even more seriously impeded by the inability, or unwillingness, of the Renaissance biographers to judge their ancient models in the light of the historical circumstances in which they had been composed. They were apparently unaware that Cornelius Nepos and Plutarch reflected the antihistoriographical bias of the fourth-century B.C. Hellenic biographers they imitated.[81] They did not realize that Suetonius knew nothing about philosophy, that he was interested in specific details at the expense of general theses, and that he was writing for the benefit solely of the nonpolitical administrators who in his day had succeeded the politicians as guardians of the empire.[82] They did not notice that he viewed the age of the Julian-Claudian emperors with the same ahistorical spirit that allowed Arrian to isolate Alexander from "the traditional virtues of the provincial bourgeoisie" of the ahistorical second century A.D.[83] They were thus unaware that the separation of biography and history in antiquity had been the result of a conscious decision on the part of the authors of their models. And they continued to suppose that the separation was rooted in the very nature of biography itself.

Moreover, the Renaissance biographers assumed that all the complete biographical texts that happened to have survived from antiquity were equally authoritative as models. They were therefore obliged to accept at least as possible the wholly improbable feats attributed to the first-century thaumaturge Apollonius by his gullible third-century hagiograph, Philostratus—particularly after Philostratus's first translator proposed him as a "most elegant" writer dedicated to the pursuit of "a happy and blessed life"[84] and after his second translator, Lodovico Dolce, rendered him into elegant Italian prose. The biographers also assumed a definition of "ancient" that for Greek texts extended as far down the tenth century. They therefore had no reason to doubt the assurances of the authoritative Hellenist Dimitrios Chalkokondylis that the Byzantine lexicographer Suidas (or Suda) was a model of "brevity" as well as a reliable source of information about a great number of otherwise unknown ancient writers—as he still is today. And they never suspected that Suidas had taken most of his information not from the writings he cited but from late Roman compendia.[85]

The limitations imposed by the models were reinforced by the pronouncements of both the ancient and the modern theorists. Biography, said Quintillian—who was the schoolmaster of the Renaissance as well as of the age of the Antonines—should begin not with a survey of the age in which the hero was born, like history, nor with a survey of the specific historical circumstances in which he had to operate. It should begin rather with an exposition of the "nobility" of his ancestors and his *patria* and with quotations from prenatal prophesies about his future greatness. Accordingly even Sigonio, when he turned momentarily from history to biography, felt obliged to begin his life of Onofrio Zarrabini with a panegyric of an insignificant village in the Romagna.[86] History, said Scipione Miccio—who fortunately forgot what he had said when he wrote his own history of the life and times of Pedro de Toledo—was "a narration of things done" by many men acting together. Biography, on the other hand, was "a collection of the particular attributes of the body and soul" of one man alone.[87] "Writing history is one thing," said Marc-Antoine Muret, who knew as much about the historical and biographical literature of antiquity as anyone of his generation; "writing lives is quite another."[88] In other words, history and biography had always been and should continue to remain different in form. And Sigonio accordingly omitted or moved to an appendix the explanatory notes and illustrative documents that would have distracted nonscholarly readers from being inspired by the exemplary qualities of Scipio Aemilianus and Andrea Doria.[89] History and biography had always been and should continue to remain different in subject matter as well, proclaimed the Cinquecento theorists, heedless of what their predecessors had said in the days of Petrarch and Fazio. It thus never occurred to Giovambattista Giraldi's Venetian editor that what Giovio had said about Alfonso d'Este in his *Vita* might be redundant in the light of what Giraldi said about him in his "history" of the Este. And they accordingly added the *Vita* as an appendix to the history.[90]

Still, the main responsibility for the failure of biography to develop into history lay not with the nonhumanist biographers and autobiographers, not with the ancient models, but with the humanist biographers themselves. They continued to assume, in spite of abundant evidence to the contrary, that the character of an individual person was indelibly established at the moment of birth, or even, as in the case of Giovio's Bernabò Visconti, at the moment of conception. They continued to assume that character was independent of will—that Charles VIII invaded Italy and that Lodovico il Moro invited him in not because they wanted to or decided to after careful political calculations but because they were driven by forces over which they had no control, forces such as "avarice, ambition, . . . and an insatiable desire for new dominions."[91] They permitted individual personality to be broken up into lists of abstract qualities, even in the case of so colorful a personality as Ferrante Gonzaga, and even in the hands of GIULIANO GOSELLINI (d. 1587), who had been Ferrante's personal assistant since the age of seventeen.[92] Some of them went even so far as to renounce the chief purpose attributed to biography ever since the advent of humanism: that of providing useful moral examples. The virtues of princes were inherited, they noted, not acquired. The Este princes of the sixteenth century were "inclined to virtuous and praiseworthy actions" not because they tried to emulate Caesar, Augustus, or the Este princes of the fifteenth century but because of "the nobility of their blood."[93] Having nothing to learn from their predecessors, they had nothing to teach their contemporaries, either noble or nonnoble. Thus the purpose of biography became merely decorative or celebrative. And biographers could compile lists of the kings of Spain, the dukes of Mantua, and the lords of Rimini, replete with elaborate initials and engraved coats of arms, fully assured that none of their readers would dream of trying to go and do likewise.[94]

Genealogy and Hagiography

With biography shorn of its original purpose, the prominent position it had long enjoyed was soon usurped by genealogy. This usurpation was facilitated by certain apparent similarities between the two disciplines. Like biography, genealogy too required research and hard work, as Paolo Mini discovered while plowing through chronicles, letters, and archival documents in search of Baccio Valori's Florentine ancestors.[95] It too had the merit of being useful. It could obtain for one of Antonio Feltrio's (d. 1562) clients admission to the Sedile di Capua in Naples over the solid opposition of the current members.[96] It could comfort the heirs of a recently departed relative with the assurance that they had indeed inherited "the form of a true prince" or of "a Christian soldier" as defined by Antonio Possevino.[97] It could turn the merchant-patricians of Lucca into feudal barons and thus shield them from the tax collector.[98] But otherwise genealogy had very little in common with biography. It was expected not to inspire readers with historically accurate moral exemplars but to assure paying customers of an elevated social rank in return for a fee. It had even less in common with history, as Francesco Sansovino learned when he first encountered "the vain ornaments of false and pestiferous adulation" with which it was replete. But once he moved definitely from one discipline to the other, even Sansovino had no trouble adjusting himself to the Boccaccian standards of his main, although unacknowledged, source of information, Giuseppe Betussi; and he "transfused . . . most ancient blood" into "the most florid and noble [modern] provinces" as easily as the most callous of his new colleagues.[99] If a Roman senator or a Lombard chieftain were needed to keep one customer abreast of another, then a bit of etymological juggling could easily make up for inexplicable lacunae in the archives, as an obscure Brescian patrician named Alfonso de' *Lantieri* found out when he became the descendant of a former *Landherr* of all Lombardy. If one customer objected to the multiplication of ancient ancestors on the family tree of another, then all the customers could be arranged in strictly alphabetical order; and Scipione Ammirato—one of the most accomplished historians as well as one of the best-paid genealogists of the age—thus extinguished that last flicker of communal fratricide, "quarrels of precedence."[100] So great was the gulf between genealogy and history that Vincenzo Carrari was forced to drop all the ancient historiographical models he had displayed on the first three pages of his "history" of the Rossi of Parma as soon as he reached page four. Since all the members of the family had been equally illustrious in all ages, the only scheme into which all of them could be fitted was one borrowed not from the historians but from the chroniclers: one date followed by one wholly isolated and completely atemporal "great deed."[101]

Moreover, humanist biography never succeeded in encompassing several important areas of human experience. One such area was institutions. The biographers all assumed—as did just about everyone else then and for a century thereafter—that an institution consisted merely of a fortuitous collection of individuals, and that it was always the object, never the subject, of action. Hence, the few attempts to write histories of such prominent institutions as universities seldom amounted to more than series of disconnected biographies of individual professors—even the history of the greatest of all the late Renaissance universities, Padua, by that most devoted of its members, ANTONIO RICCOBONI.[102] The only attempts to write histories of another flourishing institution of the time, the academies, were those of their secretaries, like ROMANO ALBERTI of the Roman academy of fine arts, who merely transcribed the diary he had kept of the election of officers and the titles of lectures.[103] The several attempts to put into the histories of single cities the classes of citizens the historians had excluded failed to generate even the notion of a single body of citizens: neither ALEMANIO FINO of Crema nor BARTOLOMEO DI GALEOTTO of Bologna could think of any better way to avoid "confusion" than to divide the citizens under such headings as church, letters, and arms, or prelates, senators, and knights.[104] The same division was observed as well in the guide to Italian literature composed by GIOVAN MATTEO TOSCANI for the benefit of visiting foreigners: the grammarians, the historians, the jurists, et al., were each placed in separate chronological sequences running from the time of Dante to the time of Sperone Speroni.[105]

Another such area was religion, as opposed to the administration or direction of a church or diocese—an area that traditionally had been relegated to the separate discipline of hagiography. Some of the sixteenth-century hagiographers were not humanists at all, and they were thus completely unaware of the stylistic and methodological requirements of humanist biography. Paolo Rossi, for example, was wholly concerned with events that by their very nature could not be subject to historical verification: trees that bloomed in January, rivers that could be crossed solely with the aid of holy water, and figs that could nourish three thousand men apiece.[106] Similarly, neither the author of the anonymous Latin life of Savonarola nor the author of the vernacular version of it attributed to a certain Fra Pacifico Burlamachi could find any other explanation for their hero's mission in Florence than the direct intervention of God; and they could find no other explanation for the eventual failure of his mission than the utter perversity of his enemies.[107]. Some hagiographers, on the other hand, were at least acquainted with humanism. Both GIOVAN BATTISTA POSSEVINO and GIOVAN PIETRO GIUSSANO knew that biography should "propose examples of righteous living," that it should be based on research in "authentic writings" (like the *Acta* of the Church of Milan), and that it should approach the "very grave style" they admired in the Latin prose of their humanist predecessors, CARLO BASCAPÈ (1550–1615) and AGOSTINO VALIER.[108] Still other hagiographers were actually accomplished humanists. Giovanni Pico della Mirandola's nephew GIOVAN FRANCESCO knew that a biography of a writer was supposed to mention everything the writer had written,[109] and GIOVAN PIETRO MAFFEI knew that the motives even of so taciturn a hero as Ignatius of Loyola should properly be expressed in the form of set speeches.[110] Two of the most prolific hagiographers of the late sixteenth century happened to be not only humanists but also historians and biographers: SERAFINO RAZZI (1531–after 1613) and his brother SILVANO.[111] Serafino walked nine hundred miles around northern Italy in search of documents in Dominican monasteries, and he wrote a three-book history of Ragusa during his two years there as rector of the Dominican college. Silvano read through the historical works of Guicciardini, Nardi, and Varchi (of whom he also wrote a biography) for the impeccably humanist purpose of defending the honor of his fellow Florentines from the unflattering judgments of Jean Bodin.

Yet even the humanist hagiographers recognized that hagiography had very little to do with biography and nothing at all to do with history. They found themselves bound by ancient models that had been consciously written in oppostion to prevailing biographical and historiographical models—like Eusebius's *Life of Origen*. They thus quietly abandoned the promising experiments of their Quattrocento predecessors, from Alberti and Vegio to Volterrano, aimed at transforming hagiography in accordance with humanist standards of style, language, and method.[112] And not until the eighteenth century—not until it came to be considered "a great misfortune that saints, unlike Alexander and Caesar, Plato and Marcus Tullius, have been given over to vain and false writers who deform their acts with hundreds of little stories"—not until then did any of their Italian successors question the wisdom of their decision.[113]

Consequently, sixteenth-century hagiographers continued to write for purposes very different from those of the biographers and the historians. They sought not to gain or to bestow praise but to perform one more "exercise in devotion" (Maffei) for "their own [personal] consolation" (Possevino). They strove not to inspire virtue by describing virtuous men in this world but to procure wholly gratuitous favors from the powerful advocates they managed to locate in the next world. They considered themselves members not of a city or a commonwealth but of a religious order; and they served their order not by separating truth from fiction in its past but by exalting its ability to generate saints and by rehabilitating occasional aberrant members—like the Theatines' unfortunate Pope Paul IV.[114]

Moreover, the sixteenth-century hagiographers chose to write about a very different kind of hero. As children, their heroes were supposed not to read Cicero and listen to their fathers' political debates but to "construct little altars, sing lauds," and deliver sermons to their playmates.[115] As adults they were supposed not to serve princes or to lead armies, but to sleep on bare ground, "macerate their bodies with twisted ropes," and, above all, "preserve intact the flower of virginal integrity."[116] They could admit to having noble ancestors (which many of them happened to have) only on the condition that they qualify noble descent as a gift from God. And they could accept appointment to ecclesiastical offices only when they were certain of a special divine vocation—as had been, to Serafino Razzi's delight, some two popes, twelve cardinals, and over a hundred bishops of his own Order of Preachers. The heroes did not have to be courteous: St. Paul the Hermit most certainly was not when he bit off his tongue just in order to have something to spit at a whore, and neither was a detached head that kept talking until one harassed pilgrim took it to Rome, at his own expense, so that it could receive communion from the hand of the pope.[117] They did not have to be ecclesiastics, either. The "glorious and magnanimous actions" of the Countess Matilda "in the service of the Holy Roman Church" were sufficient to make her a "resplendent star, the friend of all virtues and the enemy of every vice." And Tealdo of Mantua, apparently undisturbed by his obligations as lord of the city, no sooner finished "building many holy places" than he "turned his thoughts to another undertaking worthy of his greatness," like erecting a dormitory for the Benedictines.[118] As Maffei (or Giustiniani) succinctly put it, the heroes of the biographers and the historians strove for "magistracies, honors, wives, children, riches, and all the goods this world can provide." But the heroes of the hagiographers took refuge in "vigils, poverty, discomfort, cold and heat, and the negation of themselves in perpetual servitude."

Hagiographers also adopted a completely different set of rules governing the distinction between truth and fiction. They could admit that portraits of Francis and Dominic had actually been painted before the subjects' birth, that a brilliant light had indeed illuminated a dark classroom in Pavia when Carlo Borromeo took his doctoral examination, that a mad woman had instantly become sane upon eating a piece of bread blessed by St. Romoaldo. They could accept as authentic all the "written documents" of the past centuries in which such phenomena had been reported. They could forget humanist literary standards and write in "a common, easy style proper to the capacity of uneducated [volgari] persons" (Giussano). They could dispense with the historical circumstances in which their heroes had acted—

419

thus diminishing the contingent character of such acts and increasing the possibility of their being repeated. They could rearrange the acts of several different heroes—who all came to resemble each other almost to the point of identity—in such catalogues for preachers as Serafino Razzi's *Garden of Examples, or Flowers from the Lives of the Saints,* to which a hundred new "examples" were added with each successive edition.[119] Finally, they could include as equally historical the acts performed by a hero after his death—which were generally more numerous and more spectacular than those performed during his lifetime. But no such liberties were permitted in biography. Hence, the biographers were forced to ignore the religious motive that was in fact becoming increasingly important in the lives of their own heroes during the course of the sixteenth century. And since they were barred from mentioning either a *Turmerlebnis* or the doctrine of Justification, they were at a loss to explain why Gasparo Contarini willingly wore himself out in those endless debates at Regensburg.

From Biography to Biographical Dictionaries

While thus continuing to neglect some areas of human experience, the biographers of the late sixteenth century also retreated from others that had once represented their most promising departure from the topical restrictions of humanist historiography: the arts and letters. Increasingly, lives of writers came to be compressed within the narrower scope imposed by the exigencies of prefaces to editions of the writers' works. Since each writer was isolated from all the others, his works could no longer be seen in relation either to others in the same genre or to the history of literature as a whole. Sannazaro could thus be portrayed as a philosopher, and the *Orlando furioso* could be described as a poem for the learned alone—as it was even by the accomplished historian GIOVAN BATTISTA PIGNA in a momentary vacation from his principal literary occupation.[120] One serious attempt was made in the half-century after Giraldi to write a history of one branch of literature: GIAMBATTISTA BARBIERI's (1519–74) *Dell'origine della poesia rimata.* But Barbieri abandoned the biographical form altogether, and hence any possibility of describing the works in relation to their authors; and, for all its admirable erudition in Provençal poetry and Spanish history, his work actually amounted to little more than an introduction to a manual on how to compose rhymes.[121] Similarly, one attempt was made at a series of lives of authors within a single literary genre: the lives of the Greek historians that TOMMASO PORCACCHI wrote for the Giolito de' Ferrari series of ancient historians in translation. But Porcacchi wrote his biographies not in the chronological order in which the historians themselves had written but in the order in which his publisher chose to publish their works. And, distracted as he always was by a dozen other occupations, he often forgot while writing one biography what he had previously written in another. He thus repeated the fantastic figures given by "Dares of Phrygia" about Trojan War casualties (676,000 Trojans and 886,000 Greeks), indifferent to what Thucydides had said about the reliability of prehistorical statistics and to what any philologist could have told him about the reliability of fifth-century A.D. forgers. And he made Thucydides himself into a disciple of Herodotus on the authority not of Dionysius of Halicarnasus, whom he should have remembered, but of Cicero and Quintillian.[122]

. Lives of the artists, on the other hand, vanished altogether. And they did so, unfortunately, just at the moment when two historians, Tomaso Costo and Giannantonio Summonte, had managed to incorporate enough of the specific subject matter of such lives into their works of political and military history to make them invaluable sources for modern art historians.[123] True, Vasari was still ransacked for bits of specific information—even by Ludovico Dolce, notwithstanding the declared purpose of Dolce's *Aretino* to correct Vasari's slighting of Tiziano in favor of Michelangelo. But he was no longer read from cover to cover; and his prefaces, where his historical reflections were most explicitly stated, ceased to be read at all. What counted, in the age of the late mannerist art theorists, was the extent to which single works incorporated abstract aesthetic principles, not where they fitted into a pattern of progressive stylistic development. Since the critics agreed in restricting good art wholly to Vasari's "third age" of art history, even such an ardent collector of historical miscellany as Giovan Paolo Lomazzo felt free to push the first two ages back into an undifferentiated night between Constantine and Charles V. He accordingly rearranged his specific examples of good art under categories that corresponded not to different or successive styles but to the seven planets.[124] And he ignored, as did almost everyone else at the time, one rather acid warning that art was declining rapidly under the impact of Vasari's campaign to perpetuate it.[125] The next step in the emergence of art history from biographies of the artists had to wait for another half-century—that is, until Giovanni Baglione took on the task of continuing Vasari to 1642, and until Filippo Baldinucci and Carlo Cesare Malvasia put all the artists of all the preceding centuries back into chronological order.

Thus by the end of the sixteenth century humanist biography was no longer able to contribute very much to historiography. For little was left of it but Anton Maria Graziani's catalogue of "cases" and Girolamo Ruscelli's "Index" to "the men and women celebrated by the poets, historians, and philosophers." Graziani's "cases" were wholly divorced from the individual persons brought forth to illustrate them; and they could yield theses that were no more applicable to history than was his assertion of the unmitigated "sensuality and luxury" of all the ages before his own and of the "weakness and fragility" of "what we call wealth, force, and power." Similarly, Ruscelli's single entries did not provide even the relevant biographical information about the corresponding personages. They simply told where the information could be found: On Mutius Scaevola: see Volterrano, Book XVII; On Labireto, king of Babylon: see Herodotus, Book I; On a certain Miagro": see Plato, XXXIV, 1.[126]

Humanist biography thus yielded before its most lasting offspring, the biographical dictionary. Biographical dictionaries served far better than biography to augment "the glory of those of whom we have been called to be descendants."[127] But they lost whatever they may once have possessed of a historical character. And they still remained, in 1976 as in 1620, basically "portrait galleries," in which the individual portraits were presented "without a trace of effective continuity" between one portrait and the next.[128]

15

ANTIQUITIES

What the Study of Antiquities Could Have Contributed to Historiography

THE STUDY OF ANTIQUITIES, OR *ANTIQUITATES*—A TERM WHICH WAS USED IN THE sixteenth century to refer to an autonomous discipline dedicated to the study of all aspects of the ancient world—had even more to offer history than biography.

First of all, the antiquarians—or *antiquari,* as they called themselves, without a trace of the negative connotation the term was later to acquire—could have contributed as much as the biographers to breaking down the topical limitations of Livian historiography.[1] They too were interested in political and military events, to be sure. But they also studied the way in which political life was organized—its constitutional bases, its legal expressions, its public ceremonies and festivals, its system of administration. They studied the way in which armies were organized: the methods of warfare, the plans of battle, the routes of marching legions, the relations between soldiers and captains. They studied the physical environment in which ancient people had lived—the planning, building, and expansion of cities, the layout of streets, squares, and marketplaces, the functions of temples, theaters, and arches. They studied religion—the gods, the liturgies, the ceremonial calendars, and the obligations of religious officials. They studied economics, particularly in the numerous treatises "on moneys" that sought to establish the value of ancient currencies in terms of modern ones. They descended even into the private affairs of individual persons—of ordinary persons as well as of those recognized as "historic" by the historians. They clarified the legal and social relationships of slaves, masters, freedmen, plebeians, *equites,* and senators. The reconstructed—over two centuries before the discovery of Pompei and Herculaneum—the plan of a typical ancient house, from the *atrium* and the *vestibulum* (or *propylaia* in Greek) to the *hortus,* the *stabulum,* and the *aviarum;* and they tried to imagine how real people would actually have lived in such a setting.[2] Some of them studied all these subjects at once. Paolo Manuzio "concerned himself particularly with the city and the countryside of Rome, with the tribes, centuries, *classes,* and orders of the citizens." Carlo Sigonio, in the words of his eighteenth-century editor, "wrote not only about all of these subjects, but also about the laws regarding families, religion, marriage, testaments, the status of minors, tributes, and taxes, about the priests, magistrates, triumphs, senators, publicans, and many other things without which the organization [*disciplina*] of the Roman Republic cannot accurately be discussed.[3]

Secondly, the antiquarians added several other kinds of sources to those generally used by the historians. One of the most important of their written sources, especially for the study of Roman legal institutions and practices, were the law codes of Theodosius II and Justinian. That is where ANDREA ALCIATI, the chief proponent of the application of humanist philological methods to the study of Roman law, found most of the information he presented in his description of the Roman magistracies;[4] and that is where CARLO SIGONIO discovered many of the most ancient laws concerning the rights of citizens and the administration of Italy and the extra-Italian provinces.[5] Still other written sources became available in the course of the century: the epitome of Stephanus Bizantius's index to ancient place names, which Alessandro Sardi copied from his father's translation of the first Greek edition of 1502,[6] the fourth-century A.D. history of Zosimus, which Panvinio had translated by his Veronese compatriot Giovan Battista Gabbia, professor of Greek at Rome,[7] and the description of ancient Greek military organization by Aelian, which Francesco Robortello published with additional charts and diagrams from the fifteenth-century translation by Theodoros of Thessaloniki in 1552.[8] The most spectacular novelty in this category was the list of late empire officials known as the *Notitia Dignitatum,* which was first printed at Basel in 1552 and then reprinted in 1593 in Guido Panciroli's corrected and emended edition with four hundred pages of commentary.[9]

More important still were epigraphic sources. The interest in ancient inscriptions awakened by Ciriaco d'Ancona in the early fifteenth century and nurtured by Felice Feliciano in the late fifteenth century led in the early sixteenth century to the publication of several large *corpora,* of which one of the most complete was the *Epigrammata Antiquae Urbis* by Mariangelo Accuri and Jacopo Mazzocchi (Rome, 1521). True, the earlier of these collections usually lacked the kind of explanatory apparatus that would have made them amenable to historical study. Torello Sarayna gave little more information about the inscriptions he copied than the names of the citizens of Verona in whose houses they were then located. BERNARDINO SCARDEONE freely mixed ancient and medieval funeral epitaphs in the 56-page appendix to his 381-page study of Paduan antiquities; and he arranged them solely by the names of the churches in which he had found them.[10] But by the middle of the sixteenth century, inscriptions were generally produced, thanks to the perfection of the art of copper engraving, exactly as they appeared *in situ,* and often with the decorative elements of the corresponding monument carefully drawn around them. And the engraved designs were invariably accompanied by the author's conjectures concerning the missing or omitted letters and the meaning, purpose, and epoch of the whole text. Thus PAOLO MANUZIO was able to confirm his thesis about the continued division of Roman citizens into thirty-five tribes as late as the second century A.D., for he found an inscription from the time of Trajan in which they were mentioned.[11] Similarly, BARTOLOMEO MARLIANI was able to prove, in his authoritative guidebook to the antiquities of the city of Rome, that the city walls had been rebuilt at the time of

Arcadius and Honorius; for he found an inscription bearing their names affixed to one of the gates.[12]

The recognition of the historiographical significance of epigraphic sources was further enhanced by two major archaeological events. The first was the discovery of fragments of ancient Roman calendars of religious observances, which Fulvio Orsini identified with the help of passages in Columella, Ovid, and Pliny.[13] The other was the discovery, in 1546, of the *Fasti Consulares* and *Triumphales* (or at least of the late-first-century B.C. and early-third-century A.D. copies made from the destroyed originals), which consisted of lists of magistrates and triumphs from the foundation of the city until the end of the republic. The tablets themselves were immediately lodged in the walls of Michelangelo's new Palazzo dei Conservatori on the Capitoline. The texts were then published with explanatory notes first by Marliani (1549), then by Sigonio (1550) and Robortello (1555), and finally, along with the other fragments that subsequently came to light, by Panvinio (1555–58). And since they seemed to provide a solution to the old problem of the discrepancy between Cato's and Varro's computations of the number of years *ab urbe condita,* their publication set off a scholarly war between two of the editors, Sigonio and Robortello, that resulted in the further publication of several thousand pages of packed annotations.[14]

Still, the real novelty of the antiquarians was that they elevated to the rank of historical documents wholly nonliterary remains of the past. GIOVANNI GIOVANE searched for traces of the Hellenic origins of Taranto not only in the well-known passages of Livy and Dionysius of Halicarnasus but also in the remnants of Greek still present in the local dialect.[15] GIOVAN FRANCESCO LOMBARDI, SCIPIONE MAZELLA, and many others surveyed the ruins at Pozzuoli and lined up the visible remains with corresponding passages in scores of ancient and modern authors—from Tacitus and the Acts of the Apostles to Panormita and Pontano.[16] ANTONIO FERRI identified, with the help of many other authors, the statues recently discovered at Cuma.[17] ALESSANDRO CANOBBIO reconstructed on paper the original appearance of the amphitheater at Verona from the decorative fragments then scattered among the private collections of the city.[18] VINCENZO MIRABELLA spent over ten years comparing what Thucydides and Plutarch had said about ancient Syracuse with those of its remains that were still visible.[19] ENEA VICO discovered in late imperial coins the names of emperors who were not mentioned in the written sources.[20] And SEBASTIANO ERIZZO discovered in late republican medals many new details concerning the shape of military insignia, the manner in which military captains took oaths of allegiance, and the way in which captives and spoils of war were exposed in triumphal processions.[21]

Such, indeed, was the excitement aroused by the new appreciation of ancient archaeological remains that some antiquarians were tempted into anticipating future discoveries. PIRRO LIGORIO induced the grandiose size he attributed to some ancient temples not from what little was left of them but from his conviction that a personage as important as Augustus would not have bothered visiting anything smaller; and he accordingly drew what *should* have been left of them into his famous sketchbook, more for the admiration than for the instruction of present and future antiquarians.[22] A judge in Sarteano dug up an "earthenware jar" containing—so he said, "a memorial [signed by] fifty young leaders of the rebellion of Selva [the Etruscan name for San Gimignano] against King Porsena."[23] Panvinio "discovered"—and published—ancient inscriptions that were actually his own transcriptions into epigraphic language of well-known passages in the literary sources. One clever stonecutter remodeled a genuine first-century B.C. placque into a "No Crossing" sign, which he set up on the banks of the Rubicon River, and he did so with such skill that it took the well-trained eye of Antonio Agustín to identify it as a forgery.[24]

To be sure, archaeological objects were also valued for their aesthetic qualities; even the archaeologists preferred those of the late republic and early empire, which came closer to the artistic standards of the sixteenth century. These objects were valued as well for the prices they commanded on the market. One bronze imperial coin that had been bought for 15 *scudi* a few years earlier was sold in 1558 for 30 *scudi*. Three second-century medals cost as much as 75 *scudi* (the equivalent of a year's salary for a beginning university lecturer). And the patriarch of Aquileia had to pay over 3,000 *scudi* to acquire the collection left by his own brother.[25] Still, the main value of such objects derived from the insights they provided into the life and times of ancient Rome. Vico studied "the admirable ruins, the arches, the inscriptions, the medals, the statues, the cameos, and the carved jewels" he collected, not just because he admired them, but because they provided him with "manifest testimony" of the veracity of what he had read in "diverse authors" about the "marvelous deeds" of the ancient Romans.

The third major contribution that the antiquarians might have made to history consisted in the close relationships they established with colleagues in the rest of Europe. The history of Italy was of interest mainly to Italians, and the history of Verona and Genoa was of interest almost solely to Veronese and Genoese. But ancient Rome belonged to all Europeans—to all of them, that is, except for those transalpine legal antiquarians, like Jean du Tillet, who rejected their Roman for their national heritage.[26] As their ancestors for centuries had composed guides to the *mirabilia* of what was also their *urbs,* so transalpine scholars of the Renaissance were accepted as equals by their Italian counterparts in the study of ancient texts and stones. Sigonio acknowledged his debts to Erasmus, Guillaume Budé, and Beatus Rhenanus. He argued politely—"non gloriae quaerendae sed antiquitatis illustrandae causa"—with Nicolas Gruchius (de Grouchy), whose work on the same subject as his own *De Comitiis Romanorum* was published twice in Venice within four years of the first Paris edition of 1555. And he argued somewhat less politely with Henricus

Glareanus (Heinrich Loriti), who resented having Sigonio use the *Fasti Consolares* to correct the corrections he himself had made in Livy on the basis of other epigraphic evidence he had procured directly from Rome.[27] Transalpine scholars returned the compliments. Sigonio was recognized as one of the two leading antiquarians of the age in Bodin's *Republic* (III, 3). Arezzo's *Chorographia Siciliae,* which won the author the honorary title of "imperial historiographer" in 1540, was published in Basel within two years of the second edition of Messina, 1542, and again in Lyon four years later.[28] The works of the early-sixteenth-century Sicilian antiquarians were reprinted at Frankfurt in Andreas Schottus's *Sicularum Rerum Scriptores* of 1579 and those of the principal late-sixteenth-century continental antiquarians were reprinted in his *Italiae Illustratae Scriptores* of 1600. The theses of the late-sixteenth-century Sicilian antiquarians were still accepted as authoritative by Philip Clüver in the early seventeenth century—so authoritative, indeed, that quotations from them far out-numbered the usual quotations from the ancient sources.[29] Almost all the major works of the continental as well as the Sicilian antiquarians were then republished early in the eighteenth century, in that greatest of all tributes to the lasting value of their achievements, the several *Thesauri* of Joannes Georgius Graevius.

Modern Rome also belonged at least to all Catholic Europeans, particularly after the Counter Reformation cleansed it of its Boccaccian reputation. During the four decades after the visit of Joachim du Bellay in the 1550s, some of the best-trained scholars of Europe came to Rome for business or study and remained to write about the results of their investigations. MARC-ANTOINE MURET, or MURETO, as the Italians called him, a disciple of the emigrant Italian Julius Caesar Scaliger, taught at Venice and Padua for almost a decade before settling down in Rome for the last twenty-one years of his life; and his Ferrara *Disputationes* on the origins of Roman law assured him a reputation as an antiquarian almost as great as his unrivalled reputation as a classical philologist.[30] After touring the principal Italian universities, Jean-Jacques Boissart (Ianus Iacobus Boissardus, 1533–1602) of Besançon read through all his Italian predecessors, from Biondo to Marliani, in order to respond properly to the repeated requests of visiting compatriots that he show them the sights of the city; and his own compact *(succincte et breviter)* guidebook departed from his predecessor's plan of organization only in that it began not with the Campidoglio but with the gate through which most transalpines entered the city.[31] Pope Gregory XIII was responsible for bringing two of the principal Spanish antiquarians to Rome—as he was responsible for outbidding the king of Poland in order to keep Muret there. Pedro Chacón (1527–81) came principally to help with the pope's projects of pub-lishing definitive editions of the Church Fathers and of reforming the calendar; but he also found time to write a number of treatises on ancient Rome, either alone or in collaboration with the native antiquarian, Fulvio Orsini.[32] Alonso Chacón (1540–99) who, like his homonymous compatriot, was renamed "Ciaccone" by his hosts, came from Seville to teach scriptural theology; but he also found time to retrace Trajan's Dacian campaigns with the help of the friezes on Trajan's column—and to resolve favorably the age-old question about the salvation of Trajan's soul.[33] The greatest of all the Hispano-Italian scholars, Antonio Agustín (1517–86), was first attracted to antiquarian studies by the university lectures of the father of Italian humanist jurisprudence, Alciati. He was further inspired by a perusal of Pirro Ligorio's sketchbooks, of which he found a copy in Bologna. Most of his time thereafter was taken up with official responsibilities—as papal nuncio to France, as an editor of the Tridentine decrees, and as one of the chief promoters of the Tridentine reform in Spain. But he still managed, during his years in Rome, to collaborate with Orsini in several treatises and text editions and with Sigonio on the reconstruction of Sextus Pompeius Festus's *Epitome* of Verrius Flaccus's lost *De Verborum Significatione*.[34]

The most important lesson the historians could have learned from the antiquarians was the art of longevity. Although coeval in origin—Ciriaco d'Ancona and Leonardo Bruni were almost contemporaries—antiquities developed much more slowly than historiography during the first century of humanism. According to Graevius, who is still to some extent the current authority on the subject, Pomponio Leto, Volterrano, and even Biondo should be considered only precursors, "since they were not yet furnished with the abundance of learning and the many ancillary disciplines that are required by this kind of writing."[35] But after the appearance of what Graevius defined as its first great monuments— Panvinio's *De Civitate Romana* in 1558 and Sigonio's *De Antique Iure Romanorum* in 1560—the growth of antiquarian studies proceeded rapidly. Their growth was encouraged in part by one contemporary movement with which the historians were very little concerned: the Counter Reformation. As the Tridentine Index specifically exempted ancient literature from the control of ecclesiastical censors, so pagan antiquity was recognized as a field in which anyone could say anything, not only without fear of harming the Church, but with the assurance of augmenting the prestige of the modern descendants of the ancient *pontefices maximi*. Moreover, as the Tridentine Reformation looked for inspiration to the Church Fathers, so the reformers could not avoid Augustine's commendation of the greatest of their ancient models, Varro. Indeed, one professor at the Collegio Romano turned what was supposed to be an explanation of Cicero's *Pro Sesto* into a complete survey of the political institutions, the tribunals, the army, and the theaters of the late republic. "I am accustomed," he said, "whenever I come upon a passage of which the understanding requires a knowledge of antiquity, to expand upon history at length."[36] And he carefully heeded the admonition Augustine had copied from Cicero about the moral value of *commemoratio antiquitatis*—all while ignoring, to be sure, the un-Ciceronian theses that Augustine drew from the passage. The growth of antiquarian studies was also favored by the very change in the political conditions of Italy that proved to be unfavorable to history. Historians thrived on war. But antiquarians needed time, leisure, and security in order to assemble the requisite mass of inscriptions, vases, and texts; and they could begin their work only after Padua, Brescia, and all the other cities of Italy had once and for all been freed from "the troubles of war and civil factions" and assured a "most happy tranquillity."[37] War had almost ruined good letters in the first half of the century, explained Paolo Manuzio,—"eas labefactavit omnes atque pervertit." Only "now, after a long interval"—i.e., the ten years between Cateau-Cambrésis and the composition of his *De Legibus Romanis*—"when some hope of a [lasting] peace has begun to shine," could they once again be profitably cultivated.[38]

At the same time, the antiquarians were untouched by the crisis of content that was just then beginning to afflict historians. If they tired of the all too abundant wars and battles of ancient times, they could change the subject and talk about menus and circuses. Since each new archaeological discovery required still another run through all the ancient written sources, they could never relax beneath the shade of one "definitive" interpretation of them. Since research into the antiquities of any one part of Italy required reference to the same literature that was used in all the other parts, they learned to cooperate with each other. Antiquities thus became, much more than historiography, a collaborative endeavor. It was also a cumulative endeavor. Since the methods and standards remained the same, each new generation of antiquarians continued to recognize the lasting value of the work of their teachers. And even those writers like GIUSEPPE CARNEVALE who merely copied or summarized the work of their predecessors could justly claim to be making a positive contribution to the field as a whole.[39]

Consequently, the proponents of the new historical school in the age of Muratori did not have to resurrect a dormant tradition in antiquities as they did in historiography. For a tradition was still very much alive. The work of Marliani and Fulvio Orsini had been carried on, with ample acknowledgment of its sixteenth-century masters, by Famiano Nardini and Ottavio Falconieri in the mid-seventeenth century.[40] Robortello's study of the baths at Pisa had been continued by Enrico Noris in the late seventeenth century. Even ANTONIO SANFELICE's (c. 1515–70) *Campania* of 1562 was reprinted in 1636 and in 1726, and as late as 1781 it was still considered to be "written with such polish that Pliny himself would not have been ashamed to call it his own."

The Renaissance antiquarians were not always found to be free of error, to be sure. GIROLAMO MARAFIORI had included some "apocryphal and imaginary books" in his *Croniche et antichità di Calabria* of 1596, noted his eighteenth-century critic. CESARE MOLEGNANO occasionally committed "grossi svarioni" in his *Descrizione dell'origine, sito e famiglie antiche della città di Sorrento* of 1607.[41] Marliani was deemed worthy of still another edition less because of his intrinsic scientific merits than because of the recognition accorded him as a pioneer throughout the seventeenth century.[42] And ANDREA FULVIO was quietly put aside: eighteenth-century antiquarians were not at all interested in the Rome of Sixtus V, which Fulvio's posthumous editor had consistently compared favorably with the Rome of Augustus; and they were no longer willing to tolerate either fantastic etymologies ("Rome" = *ruma,* the archaic word

for "wolf's breast") or superficial causal explanations (Rome grew "because it maintained liberty and justice above all else").[43] But generally the praise—or at least the
reverence and respect—of the eighteenth for the sixteenth-century antiquarians was
unanimous. Scipione Maffei referred his readers to Sigonio and Paolo Manuzio "for
an explanation of some difficult points" in his authoritative *Istoria diplomatica* of
1727. Sigebertus Havercampus was "very delighted" by the "various vestiges of
remote antiquity" he read about in FILIPPO ANTONINI's *Dell'antichità di Sarsina* of
1606—even though, for a town that was mentioned only three or four times in the
ancient written sources and that numbered less than five thousand inhabitants even
in 1971, the vestiges were rare indeed.[44] Ezechiel Spannheim marveled at the "incredible, never sufficiently praised industry" of all his Italian predecessors and at the
even more productive spirit of cooperation—*studiorum communione*—in which they
had worked.[45] And the Hamburg professor Johann Albertus Fabricius accordingly
made no distinction in quality among successive generations of scholars during the
preceding two centuries when he drew up his detailed survey of Italian literature in
1730.[46]

What the Study of Antiquities Shared with History

Antiquarians, then, had much to offer historians. And historians might have been
encouraged to accept what was offered them by noting some of the striking
similarities between the two disciplines. First of all, the study of antiquities in the
Renaissance had been launched by the first of the humanists himself, Petrarch,
although his wanderings about the ruins of Rome were obviously inspired more by
the medieval *Mirabilia* tradition than by Varro. It was also indebted to some of the
same scholars of the fifteenth century who had been responsible for the birth of
humanist historiography, particularly to Biondo and to Pomponio Leto. Indeed, as a
reminder of this common origin, several of the more important fifteenth-century
antiquarian works were republished in translation on the very eve of the appearance
of the first great antiquarian works of the mid-sixteenth century. Biondo's *Roma
Triumphans*, translated by Lucio Fauno, was published in 1543, and Pomponio
Leto's *L'antiquità di Roma*, was edited by Gianluca Papera, in 1550. Even LEONARDO
PORZIO was still respectfully remembered, a half-century after the publication of his
De Sestertio in 1516, as "the first to have shed light on the subject" of numismatics,
of which Sebastiano Erizzo was then the current authority.[47]

Second, the study of antiquities was held to be as much of a humanistic discipline
as Livian historiography. It too was motivated by a "quest for glory": why else,
asked Sigonio, would anyone undertake such a difficult task with so little hope of
material reward? It too could be "useful to the *patria*." If only his fellow citizens of
Nola "had an adequate conception of themselves and of their country," insisted the
former Nolan AMBROGIO LEONE (1459–1525) after settling down in the studious
circle of Manuzio and Egnazio in Venice, if only they realized that their own past
contained names as illustrious as the Athenians' Isocrates and Aristides, then "they

could treat more freely with foreigners; for a consiousness of belonging to an obscure *patria* seems to be an obstacle to speaking freely."[48] The study of antiquities also taught morality. "The abundant selection of excellent examples" and the "portraits of the admirable ancients" it proposed could not but "arouse men's spirits to embrace all the honest things of life"—at least so thought Alessandro Alessandri's German editor, who was probably thinking more of Alessandri's model, Aulus Gelius, than of Alessandri's own 580 pages of "multiplex eruditiones elegantia."[49]

Third, the antiquarians too believed that information in itself was useless. And at least one of them drew out of the mass of information collected by his colleagues a thesis that the historians would have found very provocative. The city of Rome was not destroyed by the barbarians, said PIER ANGELIO of Barga (hence his nickname, BARGEO—1517–96), for neither Jordanes nor Cassiodorus nor Procopius nor any other contemporary witness ever mentioned their having torn down buildings or statues. Rather, it was destroyed by Christians, who abandoned many monuments out of indifference, wrecked others on the pretext of their being "idolatrous," and let many of the rest burn down during their interminable civil wars. Anyone who might wish to forget the seriousness of Gregory I's anticlassical tirades, Bargeo added, need only look at what his modern emulators, the Jesuits, were just then doing to "idolatrous" art in Japan.[50]

The antiquarians also paid occasional tribute to the historians' insistence upon the union of substance and eloquence, and many of them tried to make their treatises somewhat more palatable to a wider audience. Andrea Fulvio described the ruins of Rome in Latin hexameters, for the delight as well as for the instruction of Leo X's courtiers.[51] Alessandri rearranged his endless strings of citations in such a way that they might seem to have been recited after dinner in "the most pleasant garden of Giovanni Pontano" near Naples. GAUDENZIO MERULA (1500–1555) was hopeful that Alciati's law students, "nonnulli Ciceronianarum elegantiarum sectantes," would enjoy spending afternoons on a meadow outside Pavia exchanging recondite quotations with the "most florid lights of all Cisalpine Gaul." He even permitted them to vary their Ciceronian Latin with an occasional borrowing from the dialect of Novara and from "the paternal woods of Borgolavizario on the river Agonia." And the moment they showed the least sign of boredom, he was ready to regale them with stories about a fountain in America that made old people young again and about a spring in Ethiopia that froze at noon and boiled at midnight.[52] Several of the antiquarians wrote directly in Italian or had their Latin treatises translated; and Francesco Patrizi even rearranged the passages he himself had translated in order to make them fit smoothly into his own Italian style.[53] At least one of them, Guido Panciroli, who was a historian and biographer as well as an antiquarian, rearranged the contents of his Latin tomes in the form of a popular vernacular miscellany, one "embellished with greater variety" for the greater "pleasure of *virtuosi* [who wish to] read in a few pages what otherwise they would have to search for in many volumes."[54]

That these efforts failed, in the long run, to produce prose of literary as well as of scientific value made little difference. The books sold very well anyway, both at home and abroad. Alessandri's *Dies Geniales* was reprinted at least seven times in Paris, five times in Frankfurt, and twice each in Köln and Lyon. FRANCESCO MARIO GRAPALDI's *De Partibus Aedium* was reprinted in 1501, 1506, 1516, 1517, etc. Even BENEDETTO DE FALCO's monograph on Naples was published four times after the first edition of 1539,[55] notwithstanding the lyrical asides on the woods of Bactria and the hills of Media, backed up with citations of Petrarch and Boccaccio, that would have been ruled out by the antiquarians of the next generation.

Like the historians, moreover, the antiquarians accepted as one of their primary obligations the exposition of the truth—or, as GIROLAMO ALEANDRO (1574–1629) put it, "praeclarem animis hominum instillare veritatem." NICCOLÒ ZENO established "the truth" about the first settlers of Venice, and he did so with such skill that Sigonio followed him almost line by line in his *De Regno Italico*.[56] CESARE ORLANDINI established "the truth" about the origins of Siena, even though it obliged him to deprive his fellow citizens of their favorite legends about Remus and Brenno.[57] Enea Vico used numismatic evidence to establish definitively the length of Trajan's reign, even though he was thus obliged to throw out the calculations of such distinguished authorities as Eusebius, Orosius, Platina, and Egnazio.[58] VINCENZO BORGHINI (1515–80) was the most uncompromising herald "of the concrete, of objectivity, of adherence to reality [and] of an empiricism that kept him far away from intellectual abstractions and schemata." Borghini first submitted the text of Frontinus to the same careful scrutiny he had applied to those of Petrarch and Cicero. He then proposed several critical principles: that an occasional interpolation does not destroy the authenticity of a text as a whole, that the revelation of a few fake inscriptions does not rule out the use of epigraphic evidence, and that orthographic errors were as possible in antiquity as they were in the sixteenth century. Hence, the testimony of Frontinus could be accepted without question. And the letters COION on the stone recently found by Pier Vettori should be read as COLON. The conclusion was then binding, however unpleasant it might be for nostalgic patriots. Florence was originally a *colonia*, not a *municipium*. It was founded by Octavian in the name of the Triumvirate in 40 B.C., not by Sulla or Caesar. And it was no more the heir of the Roman Republic or the Empire than were the hundreds of other identical colonies scattered throughout the Mediterranean basin.[59]

The antiquarians also shared with the historians the same methods for arriving at the truth. Indeed, they were even more insistent upon the priority of nonliterary to literary sources, and they were even more hesitant to accept the testimony of the latter until they had subjected them to careful philological scrutiny. It was thus they who first presented conclusive evidence for what several historians had long suspected: that the texts published late in the fifteenth century by Giovanni Annio (or Nanni) da Viterbo (c. 1432–1502) were forgeries. Annio was a Dominican friar with a nose for the profitable side of erudition. He had begun his scholarly career as a

Latin teacher at Genoa and had gone on to master Greek and, with the help of a local Talmud scholar, at least the rudiments of Hebrew. He had then learned some theology and a good bit of astrology. But Annio was also a patriotic citizen of Viterbo; and in order to compensate for what he judged to be a culpable omission of information in the known sources about the past glories of his native city, he decided to "discover" several new sources. He "translated" into Latin what the Egyptian Manetho and the Chaldean Berosus must written in the lost works mentioned by Josephus. He filled out the extant fragments of the Roman historians Fabius Pictor and Cato into complete narratives. And he recomposed what must have been an important decree of the Lombard king Desiderius. To these texts he added lengthy commentaries in which he vented his wrath against both ancient and modern Greeks and in which he proved the chronological priority, and hence the qualitative superiority, of Italians to all Greeks through an identification of Noah, the common parent of all men, with Janus, the euhemeristic first king of Italy. When Pope Alexander VI showed himself to be impressed, or at least amused, by the presentation of these theses in the form of lectures during a visit to Viterbo in 1493, Annio realized that making the Spanish prior even to the Italians might better serve his ambitions for a successful career at the Hispanophile papal court. His texts were accordingly published in 1498 with a dedication to the Spanish ambassador at Rome, who obligingly paid for the publication.[60]

The reception of Annio's texts was not universally favorable. Volterrano, Sabellico, and Crinito in Italy, and Jacques Lefèvre d'Etaples, Juan Luis Vives, Beatus Rheanus, and the geographer Gherardus Mercator in northern Europe all expressed severe reservations about their authenticity. But in an age when the expectation of new discoveries was constantly nourished by their very frequency, the doubters were all but silenced amid the horde of municipal and national historians, poets and rhetoriqueurs (e.g., Jean LeMaire des Belges), and philosophers on both sides of the Alps who joyously plundered Annio in support of their own mythological reconstructions of the distant past. The texts circulated among the learned in edition after edition of the original. They were offered to the general public in the somewhat more elegant version of the well-known translator Pietro Lauro. And they led even so skeptical a critic of modern Florence as GIAMBATTISTA GELLI to push back the earliest date of ancient Florence "much farther than has been believed until now," even by Gelli himself, on the basis of Poliziano's texts and of the mosaics discovered under the floor of S. Maria degli Alberighi.[61]

Not until the middle of the sixteenth century were Annio's *Antiquitates* finally made the object of a general attack. The first was launched by the Spanish theologian Melchior Cano in what was to become one of the chief theological textbooks of the Counter Reformation; and it was soon followed by another attack by the Portuguese scholar Gaspar Barreiros, in a *Censura* of Annio's "historical" justification for Castilian hegemony published in Rome in 1565. To what Barreiros and "the most religious, prudent, and learned" Cano, as he called him, had written, the Florentine antiquarian Vincenzo Borghini then added irrefutable philological arguments.[62] Annio's texts, Borghini pointed out, were full of "childish errors in time, persons, and substance" that no wise Egyptian and no cultivated first-century Roman would ever have committed. And the "decree" of "Desiderius" was written in a Plinian vocabulary that no known seventh-century author had ever approximated. Not only, then, were the texts forgeries; they were not even very skillful forgeries. Borghini's arguments were then reinforced by those of his Hispanophobe colleague OTTAVIO FERRARI (1518–86), who showed that what two of Barreiros's compatriots had deduced from Annio about the foundation of Rome could be accepted only at the price of throwing out such undeniably trustworthy authors as Plutarch and Dionysius of Halicarnassus.[63] The arguments were broadcast to the Jesuit schools by Antonio Possevino in his official guide to the study of history. They were augmented by still further observations of linguistic anachronisms in the texts of "Fabius Pictor" and "Cato" by the Veronese municipal historian GIOVAN FRANCESCO TINTI.[64] And they were finally confirmed by the still more detailed demonstrations of the greatest scholar of all Euope in the last decades of the century, Joseph Scaliger.

This campaign would have been much more effective had it been accompanied by a thorough exposure of the causes of the well-established fact of forgery. To be sure, Borghini was aware of one of the reasons for the acceptance of the forgeries: the inability of modern scholars to recognize that the ancients, too, fabricated myths for patriotic purposes. The Romans made up stories about Mars and the Wolf, said Borghini, thus anticipating the attack upon them by Johannes Temporarius in his *Chronologicarum Demonstrationum Libri III* in 1596, because they were ashamed of having descended from "two shepherds born in the woods of an uncertain father and a simple, uncautious girl [*feminella*]." But not until 1638 was anyone willing to attribute both the making and the acceptance of the myths to the almost universal belief in the transmission of glory from ancestors to posterity and to the equally universal reluctance to admit that the origins of an obviously glorious modern city were "wrapped in darkness, hidden from our eyes."[65] No one in either the sixteenth or the seventeenth century was willing to denounce what most encouraged the forgers: the supposition that a successful forgery constituted the supreme test of philological skill. And no one before the eighteenth century was willing to question the authoritative testimony of Thucydides and Dionysius of Halicarnassus in support of the belief that cities could be founded only by single men equipped with all the intellectual refinements expected of educated citizens in the fifth and first centuries B.C.

Hence some antiquarians and many municipal historians continued to accept Annio's text and to ignore the critics. The authority of "the most ancient historian Manetho" was evoked in 1598 in order to trace the origins of Bologna back to "Tiberius, son of Capetus, king of the Latins."[66] The authority of "Berosus the

Chaldean, to whom the Athenians erected a statue," was still evoked as late as 1617 in order to trace the origins of Rimini back to Osiris, who liberated Italy from the giants five hundred years after the Flood.[67] Even those who rejected Annio's texts were still willing to follow his methods. Tinti found in Vergil, Justinus, and Diodorus Siculus all the evidence he needed to support his thesis about the priority of the "Eugenei" as residents of the Veneto. LORENZO MARUCCINI needed no more than a recently discovered inscription to demonstrate the derivation of the place name *Bassano* from the same Trojan word for "prince" preserved in the modern Turkish *bassa* ("pasha"). And Tommaso Mazza exonerated Annio himself by making him the unwitting victim of the real forgers.[68] Even Ferrari was perfectly willing to use Homer, Strabo, and Stephanus Byzantius in the same way that Annio had used "Berosus." He put together phrases lifted arbitrarily out of texts that had been written over the course of some thirteen centuries; and he came up with irrefutable proof of what "everyone knows—*ut nemo ignorat*": that long before the Trojan War the Hellenes took their name from Hellen, the son of the first king of Thessaly and a direct descendant of Pelasgian immigrants from Italy. Thus historians and antiquarians went on constructing fantastic genealogies based on fabulous etymologies, fabricated documents, and detached fragments of authentic sources for another century and a half—at least until as late as 1747, when Etienne Fourmont's charming reconsideration of the sources he accused Eusebius of misreading was thought worthy of still another edition. And they continued to forge documents in support of their theses—and to pass off the forgeries to respectable journalists and news agencies—at least until just after World War I, when a skillful archivist in Rome "discovered" a number of scabrous dispatches in the Vatican for the enlightenment of the United Press.[69]

What the Study of Antiquities Did Not Share with History

The study of antiquities thus shared with history many common elements. But it also preserved many characteristics that were peculiarly its own.

For one thing, its basic motivation was different. Some antiquarians were stimulated primarily by contact with their sources, and particularly by the many archaeological discoveries which, some two centuries before the inauguration of systematic excavations, were all the more spectacular for being unexpected. GIOVANNI BONIFACCIO began writing after a trench-digger's shovel struck the artfully decorated sarcophagus of the supposed founder of Treviso in 1493. FRANCESCO ROBORTELLO began writing after his first academic appointment placed him in proximity to the site of the Roman baths near Pisa. FERRANTE LOFFREDO began writing after bad health forced him to spend his days wandering among "all the marvelous things" at Pozzuoli. ANTONIO DEL RE began writing after he had toured the *prodigia* at Tivoli with Marliani's guidebook in hand. Antonio Ferri began writing after he had tried to catalogue the newly uncovered statues at Cuma.[70]

Other antiquarians were originally inspired by one or another of the great—and equally unsystematic—collections of objects taken from the sites, like those of Benedetto Rizzoni in Verona, of Federico Contarini in Venice, of Sebastiano Ajello in Naples, and of the Sicilian numismatist Filippo Paruta in Rome.[71] Still others turned to antiquities for the purpose of elucidating passages in the written texts they were charged with editing or explaining to students. It was his doubts about the relative accuracy of Polybius's and Livy's accounts of Hannibal's route through Tuscany that led the greatest Florentine philologist of the day, PIER VETTORI, to inspect the remains of Roman roads in Tuscany.[72] It was apparent discrepancies between Polybius and Dionysius of Halicarnassus that led Ferrari to reconstruct from supposed fragments the lost text of Antiochus of Syracuse.[73] It was the hope of presenting a still more accurate reading of Livy that led Sigonio to study inscriptions—rather than the hope of being able to pass off as authentic one of his expert falsifications.[74] It was the desire to provide still further commentaries on all the major Roman historians that led FULVIO ORSINI (with unacknowledged help from Scaliger) to separate out the fragments of Marcus Verrius Flaccus contained in the third-century epitome by Sextus Pompeius Festus and to add in his own edition a line-by-line transcription of the new fragments he himself had found in the collection of his patron, Alessandro Farnese.[75] None of the antiquarians, on the other hand, was particularly interested in inspiring virtue, promoting the political advantage of his city, or contributing to a better understanding of the world he lived in.

For another thing, antiquarians generally belonged to social categories different from those of the historians. There were exceptions, to be sure. Municipal antiquarians were often municipal historians as well, or at least they associated with municipal historians in the same circles and institutions. For example, the architect-antiquarian of San Gimignano, BERNARDO GAMUCCI, was a close friend both of the antiquarian Borghini and of the historian Varchi.[76] Some antiquarians with national reputations were also active in other humanist disciplines. Giraldi was also a fairly good second-rate Latin poet. Francesco Maria Grapaldi, Parma's "true storehouse of learning," served his city as senator, chancellor, and roving ambassador.[77] Girolamo Aleandro was the great-nephew of Girolamo Sr., a well-known theologian and papal diplomat of the early sixteenth century; and after his presentation to Clement VIII and his appointment as secretary to Cardinals Odoardo Bandini and Francesco Barberini, he wrote sacred and secular poetry, treatises on ecclesiastical and legal antiquities, and an influential defense of the poet Giambattista Marino, as well as studies on antiquities in general and on classical philology.[78] MARCO GRIMALDI (d. 1544), the son of a doge and the nephew and brother of patriarchs of Aquileia, was kept so busy with his duties first as *procuratore* of San Marco and then as governor of Avignon (1529) that his works were published only posthumously. And Bonaventura Castiglione (1487–1565) compiled his enormous collection of Lombard antiquities while serving as *proposto* of Sant'Ambrogio and as inquisitor-general of Milan. At least one antiquarian led as busy a political and military life as could be expected of the most ardent exponent of *vita activa:* GIACOMO ANTONIO FERRARI (1507–87). Ferrari began writing his *De Situ Corinthi* while accompanying his military superior from Brussels to Speyer. And he began his study of vestal virgins while preparing proposals for judicial reforms in the kingdom of Naples based on his experience as a fiscal officer and a judge in Calabria.[79]

Most of the antiquarians, however, were of much more modest origins. Some of them came from very poor families. FELICE FELICIANO (1433–79) had to support himself during his student days by copying texts and inscriptions for clients in the libraries of Verona.[80] ONOFRIO PANVINIO (1529–68) could obtain an education only by entering the Augustinian order, since his father could not afford to hire a teacher. Before he was "discovered" and loaded with benefices by Gian Matteo Giberti and the future Pope Clement VII, Giovan Pietro Valeriani had to support himself doing odd jobs in patrician households. Indeed "the poverty of his family did not permit him to begin [even] the first elements of [formal] education" (Tiraboschi) until, at the age of fifteen, his uncle Urbano Bolzani, by then a well-known Greek teacher, brought him from Belluno to Venice and introduced him to Giorgio Valla and Sabellico. A few of them were born into families of scholars. Paolo Manuzio was the son and heir of the famous editor and printer Aldo, and ALESSANDRO SARDI began his career studying the still unpublished works of his father, the historian Gasparo.[81]

Like almost none of the historians, moreover, many of the antiquarians were professional teachers. Pier Angelio Bargeo—after a number of adventures that included correcting Greek manuscripts for the French ambassador in Venice and murdering a Frenchman who spoke ill of Italians—became successively professor of Greek at Reggio and of letters, ethics, and Aristotle's *Politics* at Pisa. Ambrogio Leone, true to the interests he had acquired after exchanging an environment of local merchants at his native Nola for an environment of academic philosophy at Padua, dedicated most of his life to commenting on Aristotle, castigating Averroës, and translating Greek medical treatises. What these academics wrote was thus frequently a by-product of what they were required to teach; and their verbal battles, particularly such famous battles as the one between Sigonio and Robortello,[82] followed the pattern of traditional academic debates, which the historians professed to abhor. Even more of the antiquarians were members of religious orders—and usually of the pre-Tridentine religious orders that had traditionally been the least receptive to humanism. MARIANO VALGUARNERA of Palermo was the abbot of S. Anastasio. BENEDETTO COCCORELLA of Vercelli was a canon-regular of the Lateran.[83] GIOVAN CRISOSTOMO ZANCHI of Bergamo was an Augustinian canon.[84] LUIGI CONTARINI of Venice belonged to the order of the *Cruceferi;* and it was thanks to his order that he was able to live for several years in a house it owned in Rome—a house supposedly built, he discovered to his delight, by none other than Belisarius.[85]

Antiquarian studies thus came to be associated with a life not of action, to which most historians were committed, but of contemplation. Indeed, CLAUDIO MARIO AREZZO (or ARETIUS) (d. after 1575) gave up a successful career in the Neapolitan army when he realized that the *Coreographia Siciliae* he planned to write was the reflection of a completely different vocation.[86] Indeed, the only other vocation that was considered at all compatible with antiquarian research was religion—and in particular the religion of Counter Reformation Catholicism, which was still further removed from the political and military vocations thought proper for historians. Thus GIULIO CESARE CAPACCIO (1552–1634) divided his time almost equally between the "delights" of Neapolitan antiquities, on which he was recognized as the greatest authority of his generation, and the Lenten sermons and "scriptural conceits" that were expected of him as a disciple of the Dominicans and a professor of theology.[87] Even this external commitment involved a certain risk, however: it encouraged such intrusions of theological concerns into scholarship as that admitted by Luigi Contarini when he reintroduced the story about Constantine waiting eight days in white robes for an interview with Sylvester—stories as comforting to certain curial ecclesiologists as they were incompatible with Platina's and Panvinio's notion of history. Hence, most antiquarians agreed in defining their discipline as a full-time occupation. And many of them were consequently able at least to approach the amazing record of publications realized by Panvinio in the barely two decades of his active life.[88]

More important still, antiquarian studies were based on completely different ancient models. To be sure, many of what would have been the most appropriate models were no longer available: the voluminous production of the Hellenistic and early Roman antiquarians, who were known only through references in the works of their successors.[89] Also not available was the model Augustine recommended to them, Varro, whose *Antiquitates* survived only in a few fragments. And one of their principal sources of information could not be used as a model, namely, Dionysius of Halicarnassus, who was recognized as a rhetorician and a historian, not as an antiquarian, and who was consequently included in Michele Tramezzino's collection of ancient historians in translation.[90] But there were still enough texts left to make possible a reconstruction of the basic form: Aulus Gellius, Varro's *De Lingua Latina,* Strabo—and also, alas, Diodorus Siculus, whom Giraldi, forgetting Poggio's warnings, declared to be a "most diligent and reliable writer."[91] These models were sufficient to make clear the strict separation that had pertained between antiquities and history in antiquity; and none of the Renaissance emulators of the ancients was prepared to reject such authoritative precedent.[92] Even the polished Poliziano entitled his imitation of Aulus Gellius a *miscellanea;* and he insisted that its quality be judged solely according to the quantity and accuracy of the sources cited, not according to the beauty or the persuasive force of the prose.[93]

Hence the antiquarians did not have to bother, like the historians, with unity of subject: what counted, said Giovan Crisostomo Zanchi, was *diversitas,* since man himself was a *microcosm* (Zanchi wrote the word in Greek) which reflected "the great diversity of all things" in the *macrocosm*—trees, plants, animals, stones.[94] They did not have to bother with Ciceronian standards of good style either: what made Giraldi's *De Annis et Mensibus* "not unpleasant reading," the author insisted, was precisely that its style "crawled in the dirt."[95] They could take off on any asides that might occur to them. After all, Strabo had done so in accordance with his "philosophic" or "encyclopedic" definition of geography;[96] and CESARE BRISSIO, who followed Strabo's example in touring Cesena, did not hesitate to throw in at random all the passages he had "collected" from the many "illustrious writers" he read.[97] They could ignore the warnings of the vernacularists and the popularizers—without any visible infringement upon the sale of their books. Indeed, GABRIELLE BARRIO (c. 1510–75) openly defied them. "The honor of the Latin language," he insisted, was essential to "the glory of Italy"; and he refused to write in what was, after all, no more of a "vernacular" in his native Calabria than the Latin and Greek he spent all day reading.[98] They could—in fact, they were obliged to—put accurately transcribed passages or inscriptions in the places reserved by the historians for orations, and they could then let what they transcribed grow in size until it chased their own prose off the page. Thus what held BONAVENTURA CASTIGLIONE's *Gallorum Insubrum Antiquae Sedes* together was not what he himself wrote, which consisted of little more than a running commentary, but the series of inscriptions he reproduced ("ex hac inscriptione colligimus . . .": p. 254).[99]

Even organization, to which historians gave such attention, was unimportant to the antiquarians. They could—and they generally did—forget about chronological order, to the point, indeed, of giving the impression that all the ten or fifteen centuries of "antiquity" constituted a single moment in time. Varro had apparently arranged his material topically. Accordingly, Panvinio too divided the "one hundred books" he planned to write by "men," "things," "times," "what pertains to the gods," "circuses," "theaters," etc.[100] Sextus Rufus however had arranged his guidebook to the city of Rome topographically. Accordingly, Marliani, who could have read Rufus in any of the many editions of Angelo Tifernate's original Latin (1472) and of Ludovico Dolce's Italian translation (1550), began with the Campidolio and did the rounds successively of the walls, the gates, and the hills, quoting inscriptions and texts as he went.[101] Given these liberties in form and style, it is not surprising that the study of antiquities attracted the attention of representatives of just that profession that had long been the least amenable to humanist writing standards. ALESSANDRO ALESSANDRI (1461–1523) had learned to pile up citations in law school. When he tired of law, he found that he could ignore the rhetorical prescriptions of his humanist teachers, Filelfo and Perotti, and of his humanist friends, Platina, Volterrano, and Pontano. In the name of Aulus Gellius, he produced what his eighteenth-century critics described as "an enormous universal warehouse containing goods of all kinds arranged with no discernible order at all.''[102] Similarly, GUIDO PANCIROLI found, as soon as he turned to antiquities, that he could put aside the clear prose and chronological succession that had been required in his other experiments in nonlegal writing.[103] He could jump back and forth from the Twelve Tables to a decree of Valentinian II when describing the Roman magistrates. He could jump from the Arch of Constantine to one of Vitruvius's archaic temples when describing the "fourteen regions" of Rome—which thus became, if not an eternal, at least a timeless city.[104] And he could write page after page of periods as charming as these:

> Allectionem, ubi quis in curiam legitur, vocat: quod Ulpianus in or-
> dinem allegi dixit, in l. *generaliter,* 8 s. spurius, ff. eo. Lex tamen Pompeia
> ex aliena civitate decurionem legi prohibebat, quam desuetudine anti-
> quitatem Trajanus restituit, ut in ult. lib. epist. 80 & seq. Plinius nepos
> est auctor.

To these differences in practice and tradition corresponded even more rigorous distinctions in theory between the two disciplines. History, said Paolo Manuzio, was concerned with time. Antiquities was concerned with space. Since space was prior to time, so Varro was superior to Livy:

> Patet enim, tempus esse non posse, nisi locus sit. Quia tempus est men-
> sura motus, & omnis motus est in loco. Locus autem ut cum tempore sit,
> necesse non esse. Quia nihil ad definitionem loci tempus affert. Quod si
> tempus a loco pendet, locus autem a tempore non item, non tempus loco,
> sed locum tempore natura priorem esse constat. . . .

Therefore Manuzio thought himself perfectly justified, after a brief aside on Romulus, in describing "the Senate" without paying any attention at all to what Tacitus had said about the changes in its role under the principate.[105] Moreover, history could be written only about those places and times that had not yet been written about—like contemporary Italy, Spain, or Flanders, and like the past centuries of those Italian cities that had not yet been graced with an Ammirato or a Summonte. That was a principle that could easily be deduced from the surviving works of ancient historiography; for, as a matter of fact, they seldom did overlap with each other. Since, therefore, the history of antiquity had already been written by the ancient historians, modern historians could write nothing new about it. All they could do was compile manuals, like that of GEORGIOS GEMISTOS,[106] which, because they "reduced" the original texts to a more manageable size, were translated and reprinted over and over again during the course of the century. The same principle held true in biography. AMBROSIO SCHIAPPALARIA never pretended to write a new biography of Julius Caesar, just as he never pretended to write anything more than a summary of the history of the Roman Republic.[107] For a definitive biography had already been written by Plutarch; and no one, as Paolo Manuzio pointed out after swallowing even his stories about Romulus, was "a better witness than Plutarch."[108] All Schiappalaria dared write was a compendium of what Plutarch had written with the addition of a few details from Suetonius and Suidas. Thus the separation of antiquities from history according to subject matter implied a corresponding separation according to time. Everything before the Lombard invasion was turned over to the antiquarians, on the understanding, which they strictly observed, that they write nothing but footnotes. Everything after the Lombard invasion was reserved to the historians, on the understanding that they go on writing history until all the subsequent centuries had been "covered."

In an age when originality was still highly esteemed in most humanist disciplines, this relegation to a field from which originality was excluded might have placed the study of antiquities in a hierarchical position inferior to that of history. The antiquarians were thus obliged to widen still further the gulf between the two disciplines by vociferously reaffirming the superiority of ancient to modern times—a proposition which the historians had consistently denied. "There is no doubt," said Giovan Francesco Tinti, "that the age of an object renders it more valuable." After all, he pointed out, a figure by Apelles costs twice as much even today as one by Raffaello or Tiziano, and "the histories of Bembo, Sabellico, and Panvinio cannot be compared in reputation or authority with those of Sallust and Livy." Sigonio agreed. "There has never been any nation or people," he insisted, "that has been more diligent in cultivating the arts of war and peace than the Romans."[109] Since these were judgments that no one in the sixteenth century was prepared to question, the tactic was a complete success. The antiquarians maintained both their self-esteem and the esteem of the general public for over a century after humanist historiography had disappeared.

To be sure, this victory brought with it one notable disadvantage. It obliged the antiquarians to continue to identify "antiquity" with those of the ancients whose behavior was still recognized as normative: the Romans and the Greeks. One of the few attempts to go beyond the borders of Greco-Roman civilization was stillborn: Sigonio's *De Republica Hebraeorum*. For it was immediately relegated to the domain of biblical exegesis, even by the author himself.[110] Another such attempt, the treatise on Egyptian hieroglyphics by GIOVAN PIETRO (or PIERIO, as Sabellico rebaptized him) VALERIANI (b. 1477),[111] fell victim to the still universal belief in the unsurpassed wisdom of the ancient Egyptians. Giovanni Pico della Mirandola may once have accused the Egyptians of being "ingenia rudissima." But since the whole school of Renaissance Platonism rested upon the assumption that the Egyptians had possessed a *prisca theologia,* of which certain elements had been "robbed" by Moses and of which certain others had been revealed in the writings of one Hermes Trismegistus, Pico was ignored. When the Aristotelians—most notably one Teodoro Angelucci of Treviso—tried to answer the Platonists by questioning the authenticity of the Hermetic texts, and when the philologists—most notably the French chronographer

Gilbert Génébrard and the Dutch physician-linguist Jean van Gorp—threatened to move them in time from remote antiquity to the age of the Ptolemys, they were vigorously and effectively restored to their traditional place by the greatest of the late Renaissance Platonists, Francesco Patrizi.

Valeriani was thus fully supported in his supposition that the invention, or rather the revelation, of phonetic alphabets preceded the invention of hieroglyphics. The latter must therefore have been a means not of communicating ideas but rather of expressing abstract or arcane wisdom in such a way that it could be comprehended only by an initiate. His task thus became one of figuring out, with the help of Homer, Aristophanes, St. Basil, and any other ancient author who had ever said anything about the nature of symbols, what the hieroglyphics symbolized. The symbol *lion* must have meant "greatness of spirit," because all the authorities agreed on identifying that as the chief attribute of lions. The symbol *dog* must have meant theology, prophecy, faithfulness, and immodest love, because the authorities had observed the way dogs bark, follow their masters, and sniff each other's genitals.

So convincing, indeed, was Valeriani's argument, that not even the doubts put forth by one Michele Mercati in 1589 succeeded in undermining it. Aroused by the spectacular discovery of Caligula's obelisk in Rome,[112] Mercati admitted that Tacitus and Ammianus may have been right in asserting that the Egyptians had used hieroglyphics in their ordinary written transactions, just as the Chinese were known to do in theirs in modern times. Hieroglyphics thus served the same purpose for them as did phonetic alphabets among those peoples fortunate enough to have them. But Mercati's doubts went unheeded. Valeriani's treatise was republished in Italian translation thirteen years later without a murmur of protest, and Tasso's *Gerusalemme* was republished again and again without arousing a single question concerning the signs on the cypress in the Enchanted Garden (XXXI, 38) that were supposedly

> simili a quei che in vece usò di scritto
> l'antico già misterioso Egitto.

In fact, these doubts continued to go unheeded, at least in Italy, until Giambattista Vico finally turned the whole traditional history of the origins of civilization upside down.

Similarly, even the pre-Roman peoples of Italy failed to stir up much more than a brief mention of their political sagacity in Panciroli's history of Reggio and of their artistic achievement in the historical prologue to Vasari's *Vite*. No one seems any longer to have remembered what Bruni had once said about the superiority of their political institutions. Indeed, the one attempt of the early seventeenth century to study them systematically, that of the refugee Scots professor Thomas Dempster, went wholly unnoticed until his work was discovered and published in 1723.[113] The one attempt of the mid-seventeenth century to fit into the context of late Renaissance world history the "many remains of the antiquities of Tuscany that . . . by the Providence of God . . . have come up from the bowels of the mountains . . . in these times" provoked little more than the scoffing suggestion that the antiquities had been planted in the mountain by none other than the discoverer himself.[114] And the Etruscans were left to slumber in Curzio Inghirami's "tombs" until the dawn of Etruscology a century later.

There was still one other important difference between history and antiquities. The antiquarians seldom claimed for their own discipline what the historians unanimously claimed for theirs: practical utility; and when occasionally they did so, they themselves did not take the claims seriously. LELIO GREGORIO GIRALDI wrote his *De Re Nautica* solely in order to decide who was right: Aristotle, who said that seaborne commerce was essential to human life, or Plato, who warned that "uncouth and immoral" sailors might corrupt the state. It never occurred to him to ask Duke Ercole II, to whom the book was dedicated, to solve the question on the basis of the advantages derived by his state from the port of Comacchio.[115] Similarly, Borghini proved that aqueducts and public baths had been "of great benefit in those times for keeping bodies healthy and robust." But neither he nor anyone else before the time of Pietro Leopoldo thought of actually constructing an aqueduct and a public bath for the use of the citizens of Florence.[116] Fulvio Orsini suggested that Agustín's study of Roman legions might be of help in elucidating the text of the *Corpus Iuris Civilis,* which was still the common law of the Italian states. But he then showed how little he understood of either ancient or modern law by supposing the Twelve Tables to be a complete code, one, indeed, that "surpassed in the weight of its authority and the fertility of its usefulness the libraries of all the philosophers."[117] Guido Panciroli insisted that his *De Magistratibus* could serve as an instrument for correcting the errors of the fourteenth-century commentators. But then he did nothing to stop the lawyers and jurists of his day from quoting the commentators—uncorrected—as authorities on the law. Manuzio and Panvinio both raised questions of considerable interest to contemporary political philosophers: how Rome grew from an obscure village to be the capital of a world empire, and how it subsequently fell victim to corruption.[118] But since neither of them had ever read Machiavelli and Botero, they thought they could solve the question merely by repeating the same old platitudes lifted indiscriminately out of Sallust and Livy. FRANCESCO PATRIZI hoped that Giacomo Buoncompagni might learn something from the example he propsed of the Roman army, which, he noted, had won 437 out of the 550 battles it had fought; and indeed, the example was taken seriously by a number of eminent generals of the day, who used his antiquarian work as a textbook in military strategy. But Patrizi himself admitted what Robortello had once proudly affirmed: "I have never been a soldier and have never seen a military camp."[119] By calling, he was neither a military strategist nor an antiquarian, but a philosopher. And he took up the study of antiquities late in his career not in order to be of service to generals but simply because he was tired of arguing with Holy Office bureaucrats about the orthodoxy of his version of Platonic philosophy.

Thus, the study of antiquities was found to serve only very limited practical purposes. It could, if properly and abundantly indexed, provide handy reference books for those who needed to decorate their treatises and orations with bits of ancient lore—which almost everyone did. It could enable artists to make historically accurate visual reconstructions of ancient figures—like the arch of triumph erected by Parmigianino's antiquarian pupil Vico for the entry of Charles V into Augsburg in 1550, and like the symbolic matrons copied by Tiziano from one of Vico's printed coins.[120] It could add some force to the ineffective campaign to stop the continuous destruction of ancient monuments in the city of Rome.[121] It could provide foreign tourists with "brief" guidebooks based on "everything that has been written in ancient and modern times."[122] But not even this limited degree of utility went unchallenged. Most of what the archaeologists dug up, said the art theorist Gregorio Zuccolo, was of little artistic merit, and now that Michelangelo had brought the arts to their perfection, not much could be learned from it.[123] Even Sebastiano Erizzo admitted that he had undertaken the study of ancient moneys "for no other reason than [that of increasing] my own understanding."[124] He never seems to have heard of inflation, devaluation, and the fragility of the Besançon money fairs, which constituted the real monetary and financial problems of his age.

Consequently, the fusion of antiquarianism and historiography never took place. Municipal historians continued to write according to the rules of the antiquarians—with a great display of citations and learned asides—until they reached the fifth or sixth century A.D.; thereafter they wrote according to the rules of the historians—prose narratives in chronological sequence interrupted only by formal orations. Regional historians—like GIUSEPPE CARNEVALE of Sicily[125]—continued to isolate their theses about the conditions of their representative regions in the distant past from any suggestion about the amelioration of the conditions in the present; indeed, Carnevale based his estimate of the wealth of Sicily in his own day on what he discovered about the size of its grain exports in antiquity. Even Sigonio, who was a master in all of them, kept the genres of historical writing carefully distinct. His life of Scipio Aemilianus, which proposed for imitation "a man illustrious in doctrine, eloquence, and all humanity," contains not a single footnote. His life of Andrea Doria, which exalts the example of a prince who refuses to become a tyrant of his country, was published with the supporting documents relegated to an appendix.[126] For footnotes and documents did not belong in biographies. But his treatises on ancient Roman law and institutions, which were not meant to inspire or stimulate anyone, are so crowded with footnotes and documents that they could not possibly serve any other purpose than that of storing, or making available, information. And information, for the antiquarians, was its own reason for being.

16

SACRED HISTORY

HUMANIST HISTORIOGRAPHY ALSO FAILED TO INCORPORATE STILL ANOTHER LATERAL discipline: sacred history, or *historia sacra,* a discipline better known since by the other term that was even then applied to it, ecclesiastical history.

The Tridentine Reformation

To be sure, sacred history was by no means a novelty in the Renaissance.[1] In the Middle Ages, when no theoretical distinction was usually made between the realms of the sacred and the profane, all history was really sacred history. But the advent of humanism sanctioned a secession already initiated in the fourteenth-century chronicles. When the profane came to be recognized as a separate realm of human experience with independent values of its own, and when the humanists turned for models of historical writing to works composed in an age when the sacred was subordinate to the profane, all history became instead profane history. What little was left of medieval sacred history thereafter was confined to those matters that even the humanists recognized to be solely religious. And it remained untouched by humanist stylistic and methodological standards. The history of the founding of the Gesuati by the Florentine poet FEO BELCARI (d. 1484), for example, was inspired by "the sacred, modest muses," not by Clio, and it was accordingly relegated to the exclusive domain of the literary heritage of the Savonarolans and of the linguistic heritage of the Cruscan lexicographers.[2] The six large volumes compiled by AMBROGIO TAEGIO (d. after 1517) about the first three centuries of his Order of Preachers consisted almost wholly of passages extracted from medieval chronicles, and it followed the same standards used by the chroniclers themselves in borrowing from each other.[3] The acts of the patriarchs of Aquileia set forth by ANTONIO BELLONE of Udine, the chancellor of the most recent of them, were set forth in exactly the same format as that adopted by his anonymous fourteenth-century predecessor.[4] The building projects of the archbishops of Amalfi from 912 to 1542 were recorded by FERDINANDO DE ROSA in complete innocence of the historical thesis that any historian would certainly have induced from them: the transformation of archbishops from communal into royal officials. And De Rosa admitted to knowing about "humane letters" only enough to assure his readers that the current archbishop was "satis eruditus" in them.[5] So isolated were these remnants of medieval sacred history, indeed, that the one humanist who ventured into the field quickly withdrew: AMBROGIO TRAVERSARI. And his attempt to rewrite a *Chronica* of the Benedictines of

445

Montecassino in a style suitable to the cultivated ears of the abbot of S. Giustina of Padua was not republished in Italy after the first edition of 1513 until 1616.[6]

The particular forms of sacred history characteristic of the Renaissance cannot, then, be explained as a survival or even a revival of medieval sacred history. By the time they appeared, toward the middle of the sixteenth century, the latter had all but vanished. Rather, the genesis of Renaissance sacred history is to be found first of all in a happy coincidence, on the one hand, of an energetic campaign to implement the Tridentine religious reformation in several Italian cities and, on the other, the usual crisis of content among the local municipal historians. The aims of some of these municipal sacred historians were basically practical. CARLO BASCAPÈ, bishop of Novara and a devoted follower and biographer of Carlo Borromeo,[7] sought to preserve what Carlo had striven against such odds to create: an ecclesiastical province in accordance with the historical model of the Ambrosian Church and with the juridical norms of Trent. He therefore had to prove that the city of Milan had enjoyed a position of "praecipua dignitas" over most of northern Italy at the time of the Gauls as well as at the time of the Christian emperors. He had to prove also that the Church of Milan had been established by none other than the apostle Barnabas and that both the city and the church "so excelled [in holiness] that [they] yielded not even to Rome." And although he had to abandon Turin and Genoa in the face of the specific legislation of popes Innocent III and Sixtus IV, he could at least maintain the authority of the Milanese metropolitan over Pavia, Brescia, and Bergamo, of which the foundation dates could be traced back with certainty only to the time of Constantine.[8] On the contrary, BERNARDO SACCHI sought to preserve the independence of a local church as it had emerged from the dissolution of the ancient provinces in the Middle Ages. He therefore had to prove that the Church of Pavia had been founded in A.D. 50 by a certain Syro of Aquileia, whose missionary voyage, he insisted, was at least better documented than that of Barnabas, even if he was not actually an apostle. He could then pick out the passages in the Milanese historians that suggested a recognition by the archbishops themselves of Pavia's status as an immediate dependency of the Church of Rome.[9]

The aims of other sacred historians were more properly historical: they sought to fill what they perceived as a gap in municipal history. Having already written about the famous captains and jurists of Bologna,[10] GIOVAN NICOLÒ PASQUALE ALIDOSSO added still another series dedicated to "the supreme pontiffs, cardinals, patriarchs, archbishops, and bishops" who had been born in the city since the year 270.[11] Having begun work on a catalogue of former men of letters capable of serving as "exemplars" for their current descendants, MICHELE POCCIANTI then delivered a discourse on the great representatives of "devout and pure religion in the city of Florence," hoping thus to provide exemplars as well for another field of human activity not included in his catalogue.[12] Having written about the nobles and politicians of Florence, SCIPIONE AMMIRATO felt obliged to write about the bishops too, beginning with those of Fiesole, who, he found, descended spiritually from a Roman nobleman converted by St. Peter himself. And his episcopal genealogy might eventually have covered all of Tuscany had it not been compromised by his inability to differentiate between episcopal and noble virtues. The only virtue specifically recognized in the current bishop, Francesco da Diacceto, was the not specifically Christian virtue of hospitality, even though Ammirato, his close friend, knew him to be above all an ardent Savonarolan and a hardworking Tridentine reformer.[13]

Still, the main purpose of municipal sacred history was religious. Now that all their political problems had been solved, announced BARTOLOMEO DE PEREGRINO in 1553, the citizens of Bergamo could at last devote themselves entirely to the task of becoming holy, of "cultivating justice and piety" and "turning with all their hearts to God." So could the citizens of Milan. In fact, GIAMBATTISTA CASALE simply ignored the conflicts between his bishop and his civil governor in his eagerness to describe the constant round of pious exercises that kept the Milanese out of mortal sin for some forty years as well as his own tireless activities as a volunteer catechist; and his compatriot PAOLO DE' MEDICI filled the lacunae left in his eleven-year diary (1584–95) by the dearth of political affairs with interminable accounts of such ecclesiastical affairs as the funeral of Archbishop Gaspare Visconti. So also, for that matter, could the residents of a mountain parish near Pistoia, who hitherto had been left out of history altogether: their pastor, GIROLAMO MAGNI, enobled their occasional quarrels with a careful description of the incessant projects for the repair and redecoration of their church as well as with frequent news of what occurred in the world beyond.[14]

The most effective way of bringing about such a conversion, Bartolomeo noted, was to make the citizens conscious of being members of a holy community, one that, as his successor ANTONIO BENAGLIO proudly observed, "far surpasses other peoples and nations in piety and religion."[15] Sacred history was the most effective means for inspiring such a consciousness, declared Benaglio's successor, MARIO MUTIO. "Profane history is held to be useful," he conceded,

> even though it is concerned solely with human events, and even though these events are often mendacious and immoral. How much more beneficial, then, is sacred history, which is concerned with the memorable and exemplary acts of the favorite courtiers of the High Emperor God and of the valorous and triumphant warriors of Christ![16]

Profane history has already shown, noted PIETRO DE STEFANO, probably in deference to the profane historian Colantonio Pacca,[17] who contributed the prefatory sonnet to his book, that "Naples has always been the home of wise, illustrious, and worthy men." It is now the task of sacred history to show it "to have been no less religious [religiosissima]" by drawing attention to "the abundance of its holy places."[18] The happiest commonwealth, insisted GUGLIELMO BALDESANO, or BALDESSANO, is one in which the citizens most completely incarnate the virtues of the age of the apostles and martyrs—an age in which "the holy pastors and prelates of the Church were perfect reflections of Christ." If, as in the case of the Duchy of Savoy, it could not trace its own history directly to that age, it could adopt those holy ancestors of other countries whose earthly remains it happened to possess—which is what Duke Carlo Emanuele did in assuming the grand mastership of the Order of Saints Mauritius and Lazarus. A holy commonwealth is also a strong commonwealth, Baldesano continued. The example of holy noblemen who threw away their possessions, of generals who "lived in chastity and purity without soiling themselves with women," and of soldiers who "preserved their virginity even in marriage" might seem to produce nothing but passive celebates capable only of being butchered. But no! Now that the duke had acquired St. Mauritius's relics at the very reasonable price of a few fortresses ceded to the Valdesi, and now that Baldesano's researches had made him live again in the hearts of whoever was willing to wade through three books of heavy erudition, the Savoyard army had an invincible protector; and he was sure to heed their pleas and turn them into his equally invincible instruments for clearing the heretics out of Geneva.[19]

At least two of these historians were actually bishops: Carlo Bascapè, at least in his historical survey of his own (since 1593) see of Novara, and OTTAVIANO PASQUA (1542–91) of Genoa. When Gregory XIII rewarded him for years of service in the Roman Curia by appointing him to the tiny, remote diocese of Geraci in the Kingdom of Naples, Pasqua responded, in good Tridentine style, by going to live there. And he spent much of his remaining days proposing to his subjects the pious examples of their own spiritual leaders in former ages.[20] Others of the historians were close collaborators of bishops. CARLO SIGONIO was the historical adviser of Bishop Gabriele Paleotti, and the history of Bologna's bishops which he wrote as a sacred history to complement his history of its politicians and soldiers formed an essential element in Paleotti's program of adapting the Tridentine decrees to the particular historical traditions of his diocese.[21] RAFFAELLE BAGATA was an assistant to Bishop Agostino Valier; and Valier, well prepared by his study of current Venetian historiography,[22] assisted Bagata in turn by contributing some articles to Bagata's project—a hagiographical history of Verona written in accordance with the admonitions of that patron saint of the Counter Reformation, John Chrysostom.[23] One of the most prolific of the sacred historians, PIER MARIA CAMPI (1569–1649), was first introduced to historical research by a commission from his bishop to straighten out the calendar of the saints of Piacenza, whose biographies he published one at a time from 1608 on. He was then commissioned to prepare a historical dossier for the canonization of one of Piacenza's most prominent holy heroes, Pope Gregory X. And he spent the rest of his life reorganizing the immense number of documents he had assembled on every aspect of ecclesiastical life in all the centuries of Piacenza's history.[24] Campi's still more prolific contemporary, GIOVAN ANTONIO CASTIGLIONE (d. 1630), was a devoted follower of Archbishop Federico Borromeo, as well as a noted jurist and theologian. He took on the task of providing the necessary historical research in support of the campaign Federico had taken over from his uncle, Archbishop Carlo—that of digging up and properly identifying the bodies of third- and fourth-century Milanese martyrs.[25]

Whether bishops themselves or collaborators of Tridentine bishops, all these historians agreed that the cause of holiness in the various churches of their own day could best be promoted by proving the existence of holiness in the same churches in the past. Just as his fellow Theatines stood to benefit from his reassurances about the Theatine pope, Paul IV,[26] reflected ANTONIO CARACCIOLO (d. 1642), so his fellow Neapolitans could more easily be persuaded to behave like St. Janarius if they knew that he too had been born in Naples; and his cousins in Salerno could more profitably adopt in their own lives the virtues of the patron saint of their city if they were better informed about who he was.[27] Milan may have been humbled by the "Gauls" in 1500 and robbed of "all its former glory" by the "Lutherans" in 1529, admitted Castiglione. But after exploring the archives of every parish in the city and after reading the works of all the writers who ever mentioned the city, he was convinced that the great age inaugurated by Carlo Borromeo in 1565 was destined to last forever. Who cares whether Milan is ruled by a Spanish governor rather than by a Sforza duke! he reflected. With such a treasure of martyrs' bodies and saints' relics, with so many well-endowed and handsomely constructed churches and monasteries, and with such indomitable heroes as Quirinus, Nicodemus, and Ambrose among its forefathers, who could doubt that it had already taken the place of Rome as the Christian Jerusalem?

The Religious Orders

The second major source of Renaissance sacred history were the new and reformed religious orders of the Counter Reformation. One of the most urgent tasks faced by these orders on the morrow of Trent was the defense of the validity of monastic life, which some of them felt—without daring to say so explicitly—had been brought into question by the Council's emphasis on the role of the secular clergy. The principal argument put forward first by PAOLO MORIGIA, the future historian of Milan,[28] and then by AGOSTINO, or AUGUSTINO, FORTUNIO of Florence,[29] within five and thirteen years respectively of the conclusion of the Council, was one that no Renaissance reader could ignore: antiquity. If the first monasteries could be traced back only as far as the age of Benedict and Basil, then the former role of monks and friars as religious leaders could legitimately be taken over by priests and bishops. Morigia and Agostino made up for the want of documents by denouncing Valla and Erasmus for having incorrectly moved Dionysius the Areopagite from the first to the fifth century, by following the root of Jerome's term *monachus* back to the Gospel of Mark, and by identifying as monastic the various groups mentioned by Philo of Alexandria. They thus discovered that Jesus had been "the first founder of a religious order" and that Mary had been "a true and perfect nun." That closed their case against "those who so foolishly judge and speak badly of religious orders" and against the *vituperatores vitae monasticae,* whom Agostino denounced in a special *Apologeticon.* All he and Morigia had now to do was to sustain the antiquity of their respective orders, the Gesuati and the Camaldolesi, which were notoriously of medieval, not of apostolic, origin. This they accomplished by producing long catalogues of bulls and privileges that recognized the orders as the direct heirs of all the Tridentine normative centuries. This method was so attractive that it was adopted even for an order that needed to apologize to no one for modernity: the Carmelites. CAMILLO D'AUSILIO added to all the evidence for their "antiquity" a long list of "indulgences, privileges, and graces accorded [to them] by many popes." The method was then adopted still more effectively by IACOPO, or GIACOMO, BOSIO, who finally succeeded in producing the 1,200 closely printed pages that his superiors had sought in vain from the scholarly members of his order for over a half-century. The Order of St. John of Jerusalem, Bosio found, was "the most noble and the most ancient . . . of all the military orders . . . , the one in imitation of and according to the example of which all the others have been founded." It could be said even to antedate the First Crusade. For Bosio, who served his order as Flavius Vegetius had served his commonwealth, that is, with his pen, made the knights the heirs of the entire religious experience of the city of Jerusalem, which he traced back etymologically to Sem, the son of Noah, and Salem, the son of Artaxat.[30]

Another urgent problem faced by the religious orders was that of defending their reputations against rivals. This problem was particularly urgent among the Capuchins, who lived in constant fear of being forcibly reunited with the Observant Franciscans. The argument generally brought forth against them was that they had been founded not by Matteo da Bascio and Lodovico da Fossombrone, both of whom were universally recognized as holy men, but by a lesser-known Paolo da Chioggia, or *incredibile dictu,* by the notorious Capuchin apostate, Bernardino Ochino. So worried were both the generals and the cardinal-protectors about these accusations that they ordered one MARIO DA MERCATO SARACENO (b. 1512/13), whose job as an itinerant inspector had taken him around to all the provinces of Italy, to set forth the truth as he could gather it from his own memory and from that of the surviving companions of Matteo and Lodovico. When in 1579, the Paolo da Chioggia thesis was advanced in print by none other than GIOSEFFO ZARLINO (1517—90), the famous mathematician-musician from Chioggia and then director of music at San Marco in Venice, they ordered him to include a fully documented life of Paolo himself in still a third *relazione.*[31] Still not satisfied, the general then "wrote to the older brothers in all the provinces requesting that they put down on paper all the more important things they remembered having happened in our congregation." The resulting information was then put at the disposal of one of the most industrious respondents, BERNARDINO COLPETRAZZO (1514–94), who spent the last fifteen years of his life reconstructing the history of the order from its foundation in 1525 to his own time.[32]

A still more urgent task, particularly for the orders founded in the late medieval and early Counter Reformation periods, was that of keeping alive the spirit of the founders among their heirs—among those, that is, who were called upon not so much to innovate as to consolidate what had already been accomplished. The task was especially urgent, according to the first historian of the Society of Jesus, NICCOLÒ ORLANDINI (1554–1606), in the light of the experience of the two preceding centuries, when the "invidious enemy" had succeeded in "extinguishing the cult of holy religion" in the very organizations charged with maintaining it.[33] History, Orlandini insisted, was by far the most effective means "of preventing either us or our descendants from departing from the rules and customs of our Society." That this means had not previously been adopted was no surprise to Orlandini's Theatine colleague, GIOVAN BATTISTA DEL TUFO (d. 1622).[34] The founders had been too busy performing great deeds to reflect upon what they were doing, Del Tufo explained. Indeed, they often performed these deeds with such rapidity that even their secretaries could do little more than record hastily what they observed from one day to the next. That had been the experience of Juan Polanco, the diarist and secretary of the first two generals of the Society of Jesus; and it had also been the experience of Orlandini himself during the three years in which he was charged with editing the Society's annual newsletter. Moreover, the political conditions of the age in which the founders had lived were not such that they could have engaged in the necessary historical research. Not until he had solved the problems of his southern diocese and not until he had properly formed the conscience of the wife of its feudal overlord could Del Tufo finally retire to the studious tranquillity of Clementine Rome and begin writing. Not until the religious reformation so ardently promoted by the Theatines had at last been fully carried out could GIUSEPPE SILOS expand what Del Tufo had ably begun into a multivolume history of the order during the whole first century of its existence.[35] Not until "peace, by divine grace," had definitely replaced "the troubled times of war and plague" could the Olivetan of Perugia, SECUNDO LANCELLOTTO, undertake the laborious task of extracting all the relevant information "from pages corroded and consumed by age" and "from fragments of stone and bronzes" scattered about in twenty-five different monasteries all the way from southern Italy to Hungary.[36]

Just how laborious such a task could be became all too evident in the case of the historians of the largest of the new orders, and the one most productive of written administrative records, the Society of Jesus. Orlandini began his historical career with a project of more manageable proportions: a biography of one of the founders.[37] But when, in 1598, he started to work on the history he was commissioned to write

of the order as a whole, he was soon overwhelmed with the quantity of documentation preserved in the Society's archives; and by the time of his death eight years later
he had completed only a first draft covering only the lifetime of the first general. His
successor, FRANCESCO SACCHINI (d. 1626) of Perugia, followed Orlandini's example
by beginning with a biography of the Jesuit apostle, Stanislas Kostka. But when he
then undertook to continue the text of Orlandini he had edited for publication, he
soon found himself so busy poring through the Society's written records, conduct-
ing oral interviews with its more authoritative members, and recreating from a long
list of contemporary historical works the general context in which its multiform and
widespread activities had taken place, that he arrived only at the beginning of the
generalship of Claudio Aquaviva when he too was surprised by death.[38]

The other of the principal generators of Renaissance sacred history was the Roman
Oratorio—or, more precisely, the interest stirred up by the founder of the Oratorio,
Filippo Neri, in the physical remains of what Trent had defined as the great age of
Christianity.[39] Filippo himself was an apostle, not a historian, and his own cultural
inheritance was made up of a combination of Florentine popular traditions and
Savonarolan piety, not of humanist historiography. Still, he was by far the most
popular preacher and confessor in Rome during the middle decades of the century,
and whatever he did immediately attracted the attention of cardinals and scholars as
well as of bank clerks and artisans. One of Filippo's most successful liturgical innovations was the pilgrimages he led to the ancient churches of the city. The main
purpose of these pilgrimages, notwithstanding the lavish picnics that accompanied them, was to engender in the pilgrims a feeling of direct contact with their
forefathers in the faith. This purpose, Filippo realized, could best be realized if the
pilgrims were provided with adequate and correct information about what he was
taking them to look at. He therefore appealed to the Roman scholarly community.
And since the scholars of Rome had just recently begun to dedicate themselves
seriously to antiquarian studies, he had no difficulty in obtaining very competent
assistance. Realizing that the scientific methods of the antiquarians could now be
made to serve the very lofty end of "kindling in souls . . . a desire more fervently to
honor and revere" the sites they visited, ONOFRIO PANVINIO set to work reshuffling
his immense collection of written and epigraphic sources; and he soon produced a
large volume of "true and legitimate" facts concerning the seven basilicas, complete
with historically accurate prayers to be recited in each one of them. Indeed, he
became so engrossed in this project that he soon began planning a much vaster
one—one which, had he lived a little longer, might have done for ancient Christian
Rome what Biondo's *Roma Triumphans* had done for ancient pagan Rome.[40] POMPEO
UGONIO then followed Panvinio's model for the station churches. After wading
through all the relevant documentation, he managed to solve to his satisfaction the
questions of what the churches had looked like when they were first built, why they
were called "stations," and how the early Christians worshiped in them. And he
published the results of his researches in a thick, but still pocketable, guidebook that

could conveniently be carried around by the faithful as they followed the processions on each successive day of Lent.[41]

Another of Filippo's liturgical innovations was his pilgrimages to ancient cemeteries—pilgrimages which attracted even greater attention after 1544, when he experienced one of his most exhausting ecstasies in one of them. Panvinio went through his documents once again—James, V, 14–15, Eusebius, VI, 47, Gregory Nazianzen, Gregory of Tours, Einhard, et al.—in order to find out just how ancient Christians had prepared for death and how they were then buried.[42] ANTONIO GAL-LONIO pored over all the extant "acts" of the martyrs as well as the relevant passages in the Latin Church Fathers and the early Christian historians in order to establish just how some of the early Christians had actually died—or, in this case, been put to death. After writing about a number of specific martyrs individually, he rearranged his mass of information under the headings of the instruments of their martyrdoms; and he hired an artist to make woodcuts of each of them so that the pious faithful could see still more graphically how their forefathers had been burned, mutilated, or torn to pieces.[43] The most productive of all the Filippine antiquaries was ANTONIO BOSIO (1575–1629). Bosio mastered all the written sources under the direction of the scholars who frequented the Oratorio in the 1580s. He learned to apply what he read to the concrete problems raised by the restoration projects of popes Sixtus V and Clement VIII—first in supervising the reconstruction of two ancient churches that had been initiated and subsidized by his uncle, and fellow historian, Iacopo Bosio,[44] and then in directing the rebuilding of Santa Cecilia, where he was·called upon as well to identify the bones and relics that the workmen dug up.[45] He then learned to apply his learning to the interpretation of those archaeological sites that most interested Filippo when Ugonio took him on a tour of the catacomb of Domitilla—or of what was known of it before he himself discovered the rest. Often these discoveries were made at no little risk to the discoverers. "One of the largest and most magnificent [catacombs] that has ever been seen"—one with fourteen well-furnished rooms and several inscriptions corresponding exactly to passages in Cassiodorus—came to light only after Bosio, Alonso Chacón, Cesare Baronio, and "several other illustrious men," all of them as advanced in age as they were in dignity, ventured into a bandits' lair near the Via Prenestina and, armed with ropes and lamps, crawled down the thousand-year-old steps of a deep, rectangular hole that Bosio had located on the basis of some parchments in the chaotic archives of S. Giovanni Laterno. But the effort was fully repaid. For what they found was exactly what Filippo had told them to look for: "the image of the primitive Church" and the visible expression of "the fervor of the first Christians." And with the help of an artist who faithfully reproduced whatever he was placed in front of, Bosio put together a huge volume which, after it had been edited and published posthumously by his fellow Oratorian Giovanni Severani da S. Severino, admirably fulfilled the Filippine aim of augmenting "the devotion and veneration due to these holy places."[46]

The Aims of Sacred History

The historical scholarship inspired by the Oratorio was by no means limited to the role of illustrating Filippo's liturgical innovations. It soon came to be recognized as a fundamental discipline by all the many scholars whom the publishing projects of the Counter Reformation popes had brought to Rome. It was actively promoted by the former boy wonder, Silvio Antoniano, the editor of Terence, the censor of Tasso, and an authoritative member of the commission charged with the revision of the Martyrology, whom Filippo obliged to say Mass every day and deliver a sermon every week.[47] It was prescribed as a required subject in the Jesuit colleges by the general, Claudio Aquaviva: "after the Sacred Scriptures," Aquaviva pointed out, history is "the basis of all Christian doctrine."[48] It was incorporated into Tridentine diocesan reform by the most famous of the Tridentine bishops, Carlo Borromeo, whose third provincial synod obliged his Lombard colleagues to have copied into readily accessible volumes whatever they could find in their archives about "the earliest times of their churches" and about "the names, families, and pastoral activities" of their predecessors. Such information, Carlo noted, contains "the perpetual norm of ecclesiastical discipline," and it is of great "assistance in properly administering the church."[49]

Sacred history thus came to be endowed with much broader purposes. First of all, it could be made to complement the traditional role of profane history as a practical guide to morality. That was the thesis of TOMMASO BOZIO (1548–1610), the Oratorian jurist who, at Filippo's insistence, returned to historical research after having refuted all the theses of "that impious writer, Machiavelli," and who was accordingly admitted to Traiano Boccalini's Parnassus (Ragg. II, xiv) "with extraordinary expressions of love." Sacred history was prior in time to profane history, Bozio pointed out, Moses having lived long before the Hellenic Egyptian Manetho. Better yet, it instructs positively "in good morals, healthy doctrine, and the worship of one God," rather than negatively, as did profane history, in showing by example only "how weak the human mind is when it is deprived of the light of faith." Bozio first resolved, at least to his own satisfaction, the outstanding discrepancies in chronology between the two histories. He cleared up the remaining doubts about the dates of Jesus' birth and death. He reconstructed the main moments in the life of Mary. He then went on to compose a sacred history of the whole world, one parallel in time and structure to the profane histories which Dionysius of Halicarnassus and Josephus had devoted respectively to the Romans and the Jews alone. To emphasize his point that profane history was the complement, not the contradiction, of sacred history, he used the sources of both interchangeably: a verse from Ovid in support of the biblical account of the creation of dry land, and a passage from Pliny the Elder on the construction of the first houses by the descendants of Sem.[50]

Sacred history could even replace profane history, according to PAOLO REGIO, bishop of Vico Equense and the "unquestioned protagonist of Neapolitan cultural life at the end of the century,"[51] even for those persons who previously had most profited from the example of the heroes of the profane historians. Now that peace had been established once and for all "in most Catholic Spain and in most faithful Italy," there was no longer any need for princes to read about Julius Caesar or Alfonso d'Aragona. What remained to be corrected in their behavior, said Regio, was their excessive "preoccupation with mundane affairs." For unless they kept constantly before them "true examples of the sacred and moral virtues," their subjects could "easily be seduced by the servants of Satan or by their [own] sensual appetites" into "vice, disobedience, and infidelity"—with disastrous consequences that anyone could observe in "afflicted Flanders, tormented France, and unhappy England." Regio therefore prepared for the princes, with all the energy he had previously dedicated to theoretical poetics and Petrarchan poetry, a monumental *Historia Catholica,* one which contained the lives not of great captains and rulers but of the Apostles, the Evangelists, and the first popes. In order to emphasize the current applicability of what could be learned about the distant past, he added to his lengthy elaborations upon the often inadequate information about the lives of his heroes all that he could find about the subsequent veneration accorded to them after their deaths.[52]

What Bozio did for the ages before the Incarnation and what Regio did for the first generation after the Incarnation, GIROLAMO MUZIO did for the whole first century of the history of the Church. He read all the Church Fathers and all the ancient and medieval sacred historians in order to reconstruct an exact chronicle of the years between the Ascension and the death of Pope Alexander I, and he decorated the margins with pertinent rubrics: "There's an example [of the practice] of virginity"; "note how the holy followers of Christ [observed] abstinence from foods."[53] FAUSTO TASSO did the same for the years between 1566 and 1580, at least for those parts of the world in which he himself had traveled or about which he could subsequently procure the latest news from traveling fellow Franciscans. Fortunately, those parts of the world happened to be the ones in which the experiences of modern Catholics most strikingly resembled those of pre-Constantinian Catholics—with the exception that now Catholics like Philip II and the Duke of Alba were partially responsible for the sufferings of their companions in the faith. It was in France, Tasso noted, that "many brothers of St. Francis have been subjected to cruel torments and bitter death for having confessed the Catholic faith." It was in Friesland that a Carmelite preacher had been roasted alive. It was in Gascony that a whole group of priests "went meekly like lambs to their death" during a massacre in 1567.[54]

What remained to be done was to rewrite profane history in such a way that it fulfilled the role assigned to it by the sacred historians. And this task fell to no less competent and industrious a writer than the Roman Jesuit ORAZIO TORSELLINI, or TUR-SELLINI (1544–99). Torsellini was first of all an accomplished sacred historian. He wrote a biography of one of the most popular modern sacred heroes, Francis Xavier, based largely on Francis's own letters, which Torsellini himself had translated into Latin. During his term as director of the Jesuit college in Loreto, he had collected in five books a mass of information about the origins of and subsequent devotions to the famous shrine. And both these works spread rapidly all over Catholic Europe in a steady stream of Latin and vernacular editions.[55] Better yet, Torsellini was professor of Latin literature at the most prestigious undergraduate school of his age, the Collegio Romano; and he demonstrated his mastery of Latin eloquence with a steady stream of poems, tragedies, anthologies of model texts, and technical treatises on grammar and rhetoric. Just how he then found time to embark on the immense reading list required by what was to become the greatest and most popular of his works is an unanswerable question. For the two most thorough catalogues (after that of Bodin, which Jesuits avoided) of the immense historical literature made available by sixteenth-century printers, Possevino's *Apparatus* and Roberto Bellarmino's *De Scriptoribus Ecclesiasticis,*[56] had not yet been published; and he could not therefore take advantage of the qualities that to some extent made up for the occasional reflections of theological narrow-mindedness in these works: the comprehensiveness of the first and the philological observations of the second.

Although he did not admit it explicitly, Torsellini seems to have chosen as a guide to the distinction between profane and sacred history the very work of ancient historiography that had most consciously made such a distinction, Orosius. He at least followed Orosius's example when he left out all the favorite stories of the Italian patriots about the wandering descendants of Noah. He rushed over the favorite stories of the Counter Reformation theologians about Constantine and Sylvester with a *vi è che scrive* ("some say"), and he did not even mention the Donation. He accepted one author who was anathema to the theologians, Zosimus, in his account of the murder of Constantine's son. He followed Thucydides on ancient Greece, Livy on republican Rome, and Biondo, Sigonio, and Platina on the Middle Ages, just as the profane historians did. Thanks to an implied definition of profane history as simply all that was not sacred history, he surpassed the humanist historians in including culture along with politics as a·measure of an age. The Athenians did not disappear from history after "they lost their wealth and power," Torsellini insisted. They turned instead to the equally praiseworthy occupation of "acquiring the sciences." Dante, Villani, Nikeforos, and John Duns Scotus (at least "for sharpness of mind") were even greater heroes of the age that had begun with Frederick II than was the "perverse" Frederick himself. And literary heroes like Guicciardini, Paolo Emili, Giovio, and Tasso did far more "to make illustrious the [present] century" than did such political heroes as Julius II, a man "of perhaps more warlike nature than is suitable in an ecclesiastical prince."[57] Tiraboschi could not understand, a century and a half later, why anyone ever read Torsellini's work. But Torsellini's fellow Jesuits understood immediately. It was exactly what they needed to provide the students in their schools with an underpinning of profane history before going on to study sacred history. It was therefore twice continued in the fifty years after the first edition, reprinted at least every other year during the second two decades of the seventeenth century, and translated into all the major European languages. It remained the official history text of the German Jesuit schools until 1736.[58] And it had the honor of being banned by the anti-Jesuit Parlement of Paris as late as 1761.

The Truth versus the Heretics: Cesare Baronio

The second major purpose with which sacred history came to be endowed was that of combating heresy. This purpose was suggested as early as 1522 by the humanist ecclesiastical lawyer turned Benedictine monk, Gregorio Cortesi. The challenge of the Lutherans, Cortesi told Pope Adrian VI, was one that concerned more a historical than a theological question; for it involved the destruction of what had "consistently been received and passed on, obviously with divine inspiration," about the beliefs of the early Church. All that apologists needed to do, then, was to demonstrate with authentic documents the historical truth—for instance, about Peter's residence in Rome; and at least one Lutheran doctrinal innovation would collapse automatically.[59] A similar proposal was made again in 1551. Heretics would of their own accord abandon their doctrines, said ALOISE (or LUIGI) LIPPOMANO of Verona, the successor of the first model bishop of the pre-Tridentine reformation, if it could be shown that none of their doctrines had been held by the early Church. And he accordingly collected all the passages from all the Church Fathers and even from some medieval theologians that stated exactly what Christ and the Apostles actually had taught—without realizing that the Lutherans denied his authorities any particular competence in such matters.[60] Even those who eventually gave up trying to convert the heretics were emphatic on the utility of history in preserving Catholics from the temptation of heresy. All his popular theological tracts had been a waste of time, admitted Girolamo Muzio, because they had taken seriously doctrinal formulations that were really just a cover-up for the only real Protestant doctrine: "Eat, drink, sleep, and satisfy all the most base [instincts of] the flesh, and your soul will be carried to heaven anyway, without even so much as repentance and absolution."[61] And that was the main reason why Muzio in his later years abandoned theology altogether for history.

These observations were correct to the extent that the Lutherans and Calvinists did in fact make certain assumtions, and occasionally some explicit statements, concerning the history of the Church that were apparently antithetical to those generally held by Catholics even before the appearance of Renaissance sacred history.[62] But what finally drew attention to the antitheses, and what finally made Catholics aware of the necessity of adding historical demonstrations to doctrinal formulations, was the publication, between 1559 and 1574, of the major historical manifesto of the radical Lutherans under the leadership of Matthias Flacius Illyricus (Mattia Vlačič), a manifest usually known, from the name of the seat of the collective enterprise, as the *Magdeburg Centuries*. The challenge was particularly grave, for the Centurians, as the editors were called, backed up their version of the events with a large number of ancient documents, some of which they themselves had unearthed during research expeditions around Germany and Denmark. Therefore, the response had to be conducted on the basis of scholarship, not on the basis of personal invective, as the first Catholic apologists in Germany had supposed. It also had to be historical in form, not merely a refutation of specific theses, like the one by the Spanish Jesuit Franciscus Turrianus, or Torres (1509–86), published at Florence in 1572.[63] It had to demonstrate that the Centurians had been misled by apocryphal documents, that they had misread authentic documents, and that they had ignored, or had not properly taken account of, all the other documents from which theses different from theirs might emerge.

The Catholic scholar best equipped to take on such a responsibility was, everyone agreed, the already world-famous antiquarian, Onofrio Panvinio. But Panvinio died before he could finish anything but an ecclesiastical version of Palmieri's chronology and a monograph on the position of Peter among the Apostles.[64] The next candidate, at least in the mind of Pope Pius V, was the Dutch-born Jesuit Peter Canisius, who, being the leading Catholic expert on German affairs, could be counted on to see the polemic in its national as well as in its theological context. But although he was reported to be still working on a refutation as late as 1597, Canisius was too busy founding and directing Jesuit colleges in Germany to give much attention to it, and nothing appeared in print except a purely introductory book entitled *De Verbi Dei Corruptelis* in 1571. Still another candidate was the greatest living master of all branches of profane history, Carlo Sigonio. But Sigonio was by then too occupied with the local sacred history commissioned by his bishop; and he managed to write no more than a general outline for the first four centuries.[65]

The search for a candidate was thus left to a commission of scholars nominated by Pius V in 1571; and its choice eventually fell on one of the two "oldest, most assiduous, and most productive [*profittevoli*] of the companions of Filippo . . . in the Oratorio," CESARE BARONIO, or BARONIUS (1518–1607).[66] To be sure, Baronio was then and continued to be thereafter engaged in a number of other time-consuming occupations. He was charged with pastoral (and housekeeping) duties in the Oratorio from 1577 to 1581. He was sent to Naples to organize a branch of the Oratorio there in 1583. He was made librarian of the Oratorio's Vallicelliana Library in 1584 and of the Vatican Library in 1597. He succeeded Filippo as head of the Oratorio in 1593. He was raised to the cardinalate in 1593, a position that obliged him, among other things, to finance and supervise the execution of Pomerancio's stark martyrdom scenes on the walls of his titular church, SS. Nereo e Achilleo. He worked continuously to secure the support of the Curia on behalf of his close friend Federico Borromeo in his efforts to block the encroachment of the local and Spanish political authorities in Milan on his authority as bishop. And had it not been for the opposition of the king of Spain, he might even have been elected pope in the conclave of 1605.

Nevertheless, Baronio had already been introduced to historical studies by Guglielmo Sirleto, then director of the Vatican Library and a member of Pius V's search commission. He had adopted the three principles of historical scholarship that were to guide him ever thereafter: "Assert nothing that has not been thoroughly explored; follow the Truth as the first law of history; set down everything in chronological order [*per annorum et temporum seriem*]."[67] And he had shown himself capable of applying what he learned in the historical lectures Filippo ordered him to deliver in the Oratorio. Indeed, Baronio soon came to be recognized as an expert in sacred history, one who could solve current disciplinary and liturgical questions according to the Tridentine principle that what was done in the first five centuries of the Christian era ought also to be done in the sixteenth century. For Carlo Borromeo he collected the opinions of the earliest Church Fathers on the question of whether priests might wear beards. For the future Pope Sixtus V he wrote a biographical introduction to the definitive Catholic edition of the works of Ambrose, apparently a complement to the biography of Gregory Nazianzen he had written two years earlier (1580).[68] For the Martyrology commission, in which he served as a colleague of Silvio Antoniano and Roberto Bellarmino, he edited the supporting documents and wrote the explanatory notes that were to appear in all the editions of the Martyrology even after the successive revisions ordered by Pope Urban VIII.[69] For Popes Clement VIII and Paul V he wrote authoritative opinions on such critical current problems as the reconciliation of King Henry IV, the annexation of Ferrara, the Interdict of Venice, and the rights of the king of Spain over the Church of Sicily.[70]

Still, from the late 1570s on Baronio was known chiefly as the future author of what everyone on either side of the confessional iron curtain expected to be the definitive Catholic response to the *Magdeburg Centuries*. It was toward this end that he dedicated every extra moment to searching through the printed and manuscript treasures of the Vatican Library and writing for assistance to the leading scholars of all Europe. And it was toward this end that he obtained the support and collaboration of the entire Roman community of scholars. Sigonio sent him all that he had written and collected on the project he himself had been unable to carry out. Fulvio Orsini aided him in exploring the Farnese collection of incunabula and inscriptions. Several Roman philologists provided him with translations of those sources still available only in Greek, a language he never had time to master. A pension from Sixtus V enabled him to hire as research assistants two of the most able Oratorian scholars,

Antonio Gallonio and Tommaso Bozio.[71] And orders from Filippo enabled him to enlist the whole Oratorio in the painstaking work of checking references and correcting proof.

The expectations of Baronio's collaborators and correspondents were not disappointed when the first large folio volume of the *Annales Ecclesiasticae* finally appeared in 1588.[72] The text began, to be sure, not with Abraham or Moses, but with the Incarnation; for Baronio, like most ecclesiologists of the age, assumed that the Old Testament had nothing directly to do with the Church. It then proceeded with relentless thoroughness. Every conceivable document, numismatic and epigraphical as well as written, of pagan as well as of Christian provenance, was brought to bear on every successive moment in the Gospel narratives: Origen, Epiphanius, Scholasticus, Justin, Eusebius, and Jerome on the exact place of the Nativity; Pliny, Josephus, Suetonius, Herodian, Ammianus, and an inscription in the Farnese collection on the Temple of Peace at Rome, which, Baronio decided, could not possibly have collapsed at the moment of the Nativity; and as many other authors on the kinds of animals and the number of shepherds who had been witnesses to the Nativity. Whatever still seemed doubtful after such a thorough study of the sources Baronio presented as such—like the supposed visit of Peter to Byzantium. Whatever "rested on tradition rather than on written records," like Barnabas's visit to Milan, was put clearly in the category of the unknown, no matter how important it might be to such of Baronio's close friends as Archbishop Federico Borromeo; "De rebus tam antiquis & incertis," Baronio insisted, "quid potissimum affirmare debeamus non satis constat" (51, liv). Whatever the ancient ecclesiastical historians or the Church Fathers had said to be untrue or apocryphal, like the Acts of Pilate and Peter, Baronio declared to be so too. Whatever they declared to be authentic he accepted unless it was contradicted by other written or archaeological sources closer to the event—like Justin's reading of an inscription to "Simon Magus" at Rome repeated by Eusebius, which only subsequently discovered evidence proved to be a misreading of "Semon," an Etruscan deity. But he occasionally caught the Fathers themselves in historical error: Tertullian was clearly wrong, for instance, in attributing to Barnabas Paul's letter to the Hebrews. And he frequently had to make up his own mind on the basis solely of his own philological investigations. The correspondence between Seneca and Paul had to be rejected, he said, even though Augustine had not specifically denounced it, because what it said about the burning of Rome did not accord with the account in Tacitus. The correspondence between Mary and Ignatius also had to be rejected, because Jerome did not mention it in his complete catalogue of Ignatius's writings. What was attested only by medieval or modern authors, like the apostolic foundation of the churches of Bergamo and Venice, could be passed over in silence—since setting forth the truth did not yet include, as it was to for his eighteenth-century successors, the corresponding obligation to denounce error. Baronio simply washed his hands of reponsibility for what he knew to be the legends of local patriots with the laconic remark: "tracing the history of single [*privatarum*] churches is not our concern" (51, liv).

All this mountainous scholarship was not intended, as it would have been in a purely antiquarian work, as an end in itself. It was intended rather as a support for certain theses that were of crucial importance in the confessional controversies of the time. These theses became ever more evident as one huge volume followed the other during the remaining eighteen years of Baronio's life. What the Roman Church held to be orthodox in the late sixteenth century, Baronio pointed out in one example after the other, is exactly what it held to be orthodox in the first century. What the Centurians claimed to be a disastrous inversion in ecclesiastical history between the fourth and the sixth centuries was merely a continuation of what had gone before. What Protestants in general condemned as antiapostolic novelties in the centuries that followed—or at least until the beginning of the twelfth century, where Baronio's work was cut short by his death—were actually clarifications, or faithful applications, of what had been taught by Christ, the Apostles, and their immediate successors. The institution of Holy Orders was explicitly defined as a sacrament by Tertullian, Baronio insisted; the hierarchical structure of the seven orders of the clergy was clearly reflected in the writings of Ignatius, Cyprian, and Pope Cornelius as quoted by Eusebius. "The Church of God has always been one and the same in all times: one faith, one Christ, and one God," as Panigarola put Baronio's thesis in his summary.[73]

To be sure, Baronio occasionally accepted as authentic texts that were later proven to be apocryphal, like several of the *acta* included in the Martyrology. He even accepted some—most notoriously the *Acta* of Sylvester— that such illustrious predecessors of his as Biondo, Valla, Volterrano, and Sigonio had already proven to be apocryphal. He was also guilty at times of forcing the evidence to fit his theses—of admitting what Panvinio had already shown to be forgeries in support of Gregory V's authorship of the German electoral system and of dismissing the opponents of Gregory VII, without a trace of documentary support, as mere "innovators" maddened by an "implacable hatred for the Roman pontiff" (1073, i). He also made a number of errors of fact, and he was accordingly chided by the Calvinist scholar Isaac Casaubon[74] and corrected by the Franciscan scholar Antonio Pagi, whose extensive notes were duly appended to all the editions after the mid-seventeenth century. Still, the process by which he arrived at even erroneous assertions was generally in accord with sixteenth-century standards of philology—and often with twentieth-century standards as well. What Eusebius said in his *Life of Constantine* was indeed not always the same as what he said in his *Ecclesiastical History* (324, xli). What he said about the Council of Nicaea was indeed colored by Arian sympathies. What Zosimus wrote about Constantine was indeed more "philippics" than history—or, as Pauly puts it, "Märchen."[75] Baronio was ever willing to bow before new evidence or a reconsideration of old evidence: "Here an error that slipped into the first edition must be corrected," he said on more than one occasion; "after more diligently inspecting the original exemplar, I must now say . . ." (312, lxx). Thus the piles of contemporary coins he methodically had reproduced in woodblock, the absence of any contradictions in the literature of the next two centuries, and his own study of all the codices available in Rome erased most of the doubts he himself had entertained about the Acts of Sylvester. That their testimony supported the thesis he found more amenable—that Constantine had been baptized in Rome by the impeccably orthodox Sylvester rather than at Constantinople by the doubtfully orthodox Eusebius—surprised no one, for it corresponded to the current Catholic axiom that the truth of history would always support the Catholic cause. When the document upon which an equally amenable thesis rested turned out upon examination to be a forgery, Baronio left the thesis out: for example, of the famous Donation of Constantine there is not a word in the narrative of Constantine's conversion. Even the distortions were not always the fault of Baronio alone. Practically all the documents then available from the time of Gregory VII did indeed support the position of Paul V on the place of the Papacy in relation to church and state. And Baronio had no trouble in proposing the thesis he happened to favor without ever forgetting his promise "to say nothing about Gregory that cannot be backed up by the writers of those times."

Thus one of the original purposes of the *Annales* was fully realized—not, to be sure, that of converting the heretics, for only a very few Protestant scholars actually abandoned their faith after reading them, but rather that of strengthening the conviction among Catholics of the correctness of their belief. The *Centuries* caused more dissent than harmony among Protestants, and they were reprinted only once after the financially unfortunate first edition. The *Annales,* on the other hand, were received with almost unanimous applause among Catholics. The first edition of 800 copies of the first volume sold out immediately and had to be reprinted, in Antwerp, a few months later. And it was followed within two years by the abridged Italian translation by the famous preacher Francesco Panigarola, duly fortified with "annotations" for the guidance of the translator's colleagues in the pulpit.[76]

The *Annales* then came to fulfill still another purpose: that of assuring a place for history among the disciplines called upon by the Counter Reformation Church to support the doctrinal decrees of Trent. In the company of Panvinio's definitive version of Platina's history of the popes, of Bellarmino's definitive statement of Tridentine theology, of the Gregorian calendar and the Clementine Vulgate, the *Annales* were raised to the position of a definitive version of the history of the Church. Like the Martyrology and the Breviary, they too could be emended, expanded, added on to, abridged,[77] and translated—as they were, indeed, by Pagi, by the four successive scholars who continued them from the twelfth to the seventeenth century, by the compilers of the three-volume index,[78] and by Alonso Chacón[79] and Ferdinando Ughelli in their immense biographical dictionaries of the cardinals and the Italian bishops.[80] But in substance and in basic theses, the *Annales* were expected to stand. They were accordingly reissued in some twenty-one complete and fifteen partial editions. They were hailed as the foundation of all ecclesiastical history by Muratori, the founder of critical ecclesiastical history in Italy, over a century later.[81] And they still occupy an honored place alongside the much briefer, but no less partisan or more attractive, modern manuals on the reference shelves of students of church history even today, after four intervening centuries of intense scholarly activity.

At the same time, the *Annales* succeeded in preserving for history a role in Tridentine Catholicism that had been denied it among Lutherans from the time of Melanchthon's theological and pedagogical settlement:[82] that of an autonomous and indispensable element in the ongoing process of the clarfication of doctrine. Notwithstanding the indifference, if not the outright hostility of some religious orders and of some members of the Curia even in the sixteenth century,[83] notwithstanding the Liguorian reaction against the Muratorians in the mid-eighteenth century, notwithstanding the elevation in the late nineteenth century of the most unhistorical of all philosophical systems to the apex of a hierarchy of disciplines, notwithstanding the constant appeal of speculative theology for its efficiency in furnishing quick answers in doctrinal emergencies, notwithstanding the constant fear that what has once been defined might prove instead to be contingent or transitory, the *Annales* could never be gotten rid of. And the historical point of view they represented has been vindicated over and over again during the some five hundred years since they first appeared—by Tillemont and Muratori, by Ludwig von Pastor and Henri de Lubac, and by the theologians of Vatican II.

The Sacred and the Profane

Within a half-century of its inauguration, then, sacred history had already developed to the point where it was able to offer the humanist historians a promising remedy for their current crisis of content—namely, the incorporation into history of an area of human experience that was becoming increasingly important to all Italians during the half-century after the Council of Trent. Such a proposal might well have been taken seriously. For one thing, some of the leading sacred historians were, if not actually humanist historians, at least humanists. For example, the two historians of the Society of Jesus were diligent products of the humanist curriculum of the Jesuit schools, and they accepted as normative the rhetorical and historiographical texts they had studied there. They were thus able to present "celestial Rome" as the complement of "Rome of the Capitoline" and to define both as essential, parallel components of "the whole world of human affairs" (Sacchini). For another thing, many of the sacred historians were, if not principally antiquarians, like Panvinio, at least thoroughly familiar with the methods and standards of the equally humanist field of antiquarian studies. SILVESTRO MAUROLICO was the nephew of the historian-archaeologist of Sicily, Francesco, and he followed his uncle's example in mastering all the languages appropriate to his subject and in traveling all over Spain in search of relevant documents.[84] Antonio Bosio and Pompeo Ugonio wrote their descriptions of Christian Rome in exactly the same form that their master Panvinio had used in describing pagan Rome. They even adopted his predilection for interminable digressions: the etymology of the word *cemetery* (a "place of sleep" in Greek) had to be supported by long quotations on everything that Homer, Vergil, Isaiah, John the Evangelist, John Chrysostom, and Augustine had said about the nature of sleep; and the question of whether ancient Christians stood or knelt in prayer had to be solved even at the cost of interrupting the course of the exposition for several pages. The sacred historians also accepted one of the antiquarians' major practical commitments: that of preserving ancient ruins from further destruction; and Bosio's tomes seem to have been partially effective in stopping the kind of desecration he had observed at S. Ermete, where German seminarians had whitewashed over the paleo-Christian frescoes.[85] Moreover, they too were disposed to forget this commitment whenever they beheld the glorious urban programs of the Counter Reformation popes—straight streets built across potential archaeological sites, ancient shrines covered with baroque domes, and "altars, temples, monasteries, charitable institutions, and a thousand other very religious structures" (Ugonio), all of which were rapidly burying what was left of the Rome of the principate and the martyrs beneath the brick and marble of the Rome of the Counter Reformation.

Sacred history even surpassed humanist historiography and antiquarian studies in its dedication to one of their basic principles: that of discovering and broadcasting the truth. And it fully accepted the means prescribed by the humanists for discovering the truth: the objective examination of the sources. "The main reason [*occasio*] for my writing," said ROCCO PIRRI (1577–1651), "is my determination [*studium*] to find the truth"; and he accordingly read all of Fazello's notes and all the documents in all the public and private archives of Palermo in order to clear away the lies (*mendacio*) with which his fellow Sicilians for centuries had obscured "the faith of our forefathers."[86] Some of Lancellotto's Olivetan brothers feared that his history might "diminish, rather than increase, the reputation of the congregation," and they tried to prevail upon him to lock it up in their safe for consultation by them alone. Not so the cardinal-protector, Paolo Sfrondato, who cited Tacitus on the obligation of historians to keep alive, not hidden, the memory of their ancestors; and the history was accordingly made available to the general public. The only time a historian should refrain from stating explicitly what he had found, according to Del Tufo, was when he is unable to reach "that complete . . . certainty required for the truth in history." Only heretics had to cover up or deform the historical record, continued Paolo Regio. Catholics can best combat them by pulling up "the infinite weeds which they have sown" in the record. For Catholicism was true. Hence the truth would always support it, even in those cases when it was not particularly flattering to some well-known Catholics. And Silos advanced the cause of Catholicism not by trying to hide Guicciardini's famous judgment of Clement VII but by repeating it almost verbatim. In warning his readers about the "immanem silvam errorum" he found in the volumes of Ughelli, Muratori was attacking only what might be expected when one man takes on too big a task and then fails to proofread it.[87] For Muratori recognized that Ughelli's, as well as Baronio's, purposes and methods were fully consonant with the philological standards of the sixteenth century. They were therefore unacceptable by eighteenth-century standards only to the extent that they did not anticipate the *ars critica* of the late seventeenth century. Thus Renaissance sacred history can be called un- or pre-scientific, as it sometimes is, only if the word *wissenschaftlich* is restricted solely to its nineteenth-century connotation.[88]

To be sure, not all Catholics were ready to accept the historians' creed about the automatic convergence of theological and historical truth. The Dominicans certainly were not; and they, alas, were often in charge of ecclesiastical censorship. They thought that particular terms even in such an impeccably orthodox writer as Sulpicius Severus should be explained in the context not of late Roman Latin but of their own brand of thirteenth-century philosophy; and since they were rather hazy about the difference between ancient and modern heresies, they thought that the former should be mentioned only as an excuse for heaping abuse on the latter.[89] The Dominicans were not alone. Even Cardinal Sirleto, scholar though he was, tried to keep hidden what he thought to be the only surviving text of the "anti-Catholic" ancient historian, Zosimus. And the Spanish Jesuits—that is, the Spanish members of one of the orders most amenable to humanism and hence to history—tried to suppress what they held to be "false and ignominious" information about the ancestry of the Spanish general, Diego Laynez.[90]

But the historians held fast to what they regarded not just as one of the rules of a particular discipline but as a religious obligation binding in conscience. Sigonio refused to withdraw his philological annotations or to modify the text of his history of the Church, even at the risk of having all subsequent editions published outside of Italy—and thus far away from the Bolognese seminary students for whom he had written them. Baronio could not read Greek anyway. So he simply waited until Leunclavius had published his Latin translation of Zosimus at Basel and then quoted from it extensively, right under the nose of his former mentor. And after confronting Zosimus's account with those of other historians of the late Roman Empire, he may have wondered what Sirleto was so worried about. Similarly, Sacchini categorically rejected the principle of his Spanish brethren—"etiamsi fuisset illa pars vera, nullus illius est usus"—just as he rejected their un-Italian racism and their antihumanistic social snobbery. "Great virtues are not dishonored by birth," he reminded them in true humanist terms; "rather, birth is honored by virtue." If his opponents could show him to be wrong on the basis of authentic documents, he would piously retract. Otherwise they would just have to put up with a bit of Jewish blood in their spiritual veins, even if that meant yielding a few religious vocations to their rival orders in Spain.

Sacred and humanist historians thus agreed on one end, the truth, and on the means for getting there, authentic documents. But on the further question of what constituted an authentic document, they parted company—or, to be more precise, the sacred historians answered the question in a way that the humanist historians would have found unacceptable had they ever bothered to pose it, which they did not. If Catholicism equalled the Truth, then Possevino was right: modern heretical historians were automatically unreliable. Baronio was also right: the *Acta Passionis Petri* attributed to Pope Linus could not be authentic because no bishop of the See that never erred could have committed the theological errors it contained (64, vi). Catholic historians should avoid both, not because of danger to their souls, but because of the threat such writings posed to the scientific validity of their work. Conversely, if a master of orthodoxy pronounced a document to be authentic, his judgment could be accepted without question. The Council of Trent had declared the Fathers of the Church to be such masters. Hence, while he might find them singly in historical error, the Tridentine historian could safely assume as authentic or accurate whatever was "passed on and written, not by one of them or another, but by almost all of the ancient Fathers" (Baronio, 34, cx). Since Muzio—and everyone else at the time—thought that Orosius had written under Augustine's direct supervision, he had no reason not to accept Orosius's story about Tiberius's recognition of Christ as a god. Since John Chrysostom occasionally used anachronistic terms for the sake of his historically ignorant audiences, Muzio was justified in doing so as well. Peter thus became a "pontiff" and James a "bishop of Jerusalem." Since many of the Fathers referred to the considerable number of *acta* of the pre-Constantinian martyrs that circulated in post-Constantinian times, there was no reason why Antonio Bosio should not take them seriously too. Anyone who has doubts about the story of the crow that guarded St. Vincent's body in Spain, he admonished, need only look it up in the *Acta Sancti Vincentii*. Anyone who has doubts about the *Acta* need only look them up in Prudentius, Augustine, Leo I, "and many other Holy Fathers," who accepted them without question. Anyone who had doubts about any aspect of this critical principle could fall back on the assurances of that authoritative modern theologian, Melchior Cano: "Si cui historico auctoritatem Ecclesia tribuit, hic dubio procul dignus est. . . . Contro vero, cui Ecclesia derogavit fidem. . . ."[91]

For events or documents that the Fathers had said nothing about, or that had occurred chronologically after the patristic age, the sacred historians could fall back on what Trent admitted as a complement to the Fathers' authoritative statements: the universal consent of the Church. As Baronio put it, "Since the Universal Church . . . both Greek and Latin . . . has always held [Constantine] to have been a pious man, and since no one [i.e., no Christian] has ever found his life to have been stained with impiety, it is necessary to affirm that . . ." (324, xlvi). This principle permitted Giacomo Bosio to recount soberly the charming story about the sultan's daughter who was flown to Picardy in order to recover the luminous statue given her by the Virgin as a conversion present. It permitted the serious Florentine scholar FRANCESCO BOCCHI to publish an account, fully guaranteed by two centuries of Servite storytellers, of the flames that turned from a Christian captive and rushed toward his Turkish torturers the moment he invoked the name of the Virgin of the Annunziata in Florence.[92] It permitted the faithful Baronian Panigarola to ignore all that Baronio had induced from Josephus about the life and customs of first-century Palestinian Jews and to have Joseph make a vow of celebacy upon hearing that his Fiancée had made one behind the backs of the temple priests who were her wards during the first fourteen years of her life. It permitted that careful synthesizer of humanist historiography Torsellini to publish what "the memory of the *Schiavoni* [i.e., Dalmatian Slavs], the citizens of Recanati, the authority of the Roman pontiffs, the constant consent of so many years, and the concourse of peoples from all over the world" had established as "so certain and unquestionable" about the miracles of the Virgin of Loreto "that it would be a sin to entertain the least contrary thought."[93] Possevino was thus justified in suspecting that heretics had tampered with the German edition of Bodin he read. For no good historian would have said such nasty things about historians like Eusebius, Nikeforos, and Sozomenus, whom the Church had always accepted.

As sacred historians were concerned with an order of events that had no place in humanist historiography, so the heroes they proposed for imitation were as different from those of the humanist historians as were the heroes of the hagiographers from those of the biographers.[94] The heroes of sacred history were not responsible men who drew upon their own *virtù* in order to overcome, organize, oppress, or benefit others. Rather, they were men who "by their own volition trample on the world and its delights and give up all worldly power and eminence [*grandezze*] for the love of Christ" (Morigia). They were women who deliberately threw aside the advantages of noble birth and who feigned bad health in order to avoid marriage (Gallonio)—a pious lie, according to Counter Reformation standards, being preferable to a degrading sacrament. Better yet, they were men and women who happily let their bodies be torn apart by lions or roasted on grates rather than abandon an eternal Savior for an all too ephemeral stooge of the Praetorian Guards. And just to assuage the inferiority complexes of modern Romans, who never had an opportunity to make such decisions, an anonymous student at the English College in Rome added his bit to the historians' ample collection of martyr stories with what appears to be an expanded version of Thomas Alfield's account of the death of the English Catholic martyrs. And he emphasized the implied thesis that the age of the martyrs was fortunately here again by drawing frequent parallels between the behavior of ancient heretics and that of those in his own day who unjustly accused Catholics alone of being intolerant.[95] Such heroes were not even the causes of historical events, as were by definition the heroes of the humanist historians. They were merely passive instruments in the hand of the sole cause, immediate as well as ultimate, of all historical events: God. And the most heroic action they could perform was to remain "all alone for four years in a cell" doing absolutely nothing but "fasting on bread and water" (Colpetrazzo). Whoever, indeed, tried to act on his own initiative inevitably became the instrument of "the enemy who never sleeps."

The task of sacred history was thus to describe the feats not of men but of God acting through men. And the pattern of historical periods it presented was one marked by certain extraordinary acts of divine intervention—acts that alone were capable of reversing the natural tendency of all things human toward lethargy and corruption. Such a pattern was discernible not only in the church but also in "cities, kingdoms, and empires," which God establishes "so that men under civil law will follow justice and the other virtues," but which "he permits to be destroyed" whenever they then fail to do so (Campi). That no one but God made these historical periods was demonstrated by the kind of human instruments he used in making them: not kings or popes, not established leaders of established orders, but a minor pharisee from a non-Palestinian Hellenistic city, the son of a pagan captain in a peripheral Roman province, the son of a middling merchant in an insignificant Umbrian town, a wounded soldier not even of Spanish but of Basque background (Orlandini).

Renaissance sacred history was in no way a continuation or a resurrection of medieval sacred history. Nevertheless, it arrived at an explanation of historical causality very similar to the one which humanist historiography had begun by rejecting. Indeed, it carried this explanation to its logical conclusion in denying even to historians themselves the rights of authorship to their own works. The chief qualification of a future historian was "animi simplicitas [et] vitae innocentia"; and the best preparation for history was knowledge that "came rather from divine than from human wisdom" (Colpetrazzo). The future historian then became an actual historian not because he wanted to, not because he wished to enlighten or instruct others, and certainly not because he hoped thereby to confer or gain glory. Indeed, there was not one of them who would not have preferred to "be patient and humble, not contending with anyone [and] living in holy peace [*sancta pace*]," as Mario da Mercato Saraceno vainly tried to do. Some of them would even have preferred to spend their days suspended over their desks in ecstatic levitation rather than sitting at their desks working. Historians, then, wrote history for one reason alone: because their superiors ordered them to do so. But even the superiors were not free agents. Had they been so, they would never have picked as a historian one so little inclined to such a career as Baronio. Superiors acted "divino afflatum spiritu," like Filippo Neri, who "saw the [*Magdeburg*] *Centuries* emerging from the gates of hell"—not in letters he received form Germany, not in the texts of the *Centuries* themselves, which he never read, but in a "prophetic vision." Or at least so said Gallonio, and Gallonio knew Filippo very well.[96] Hence, God not only initiated directly each individual work of sacred history. He was also directly responsible for initiating and sustaining the entire school of Renaissance sacred history. For he alone could see what had to be done. And he alone was willing to take the necessary steps to have someone do it.

A still more noticeable peculiarity of Renaissance sacred history was its almost complete disregard for one of the most essential ingredients of humanist historiography: eloquence. To be sure, the sacred historians had as good reasons as the humanist historians for being eloquent. Eloquence, after all, was the only means known at the time for making their "true examples of sacred and moral virtues" (Del Tufo) effective in the practical lives of their readers. Accordingly, the Carmelites entrusted their history to a "concionator eloquens," GIUSEPPE FALCONE of Piacenza (d. 1597), who could write about pigs, chickens, and the delights of country life with the same "admirable elocution" that won him "the applause of the public" for the sermons he delivered in Naples, Rome, Pisa, and Florence.[97] The Society of Jesus entrusted the continuation of Orlandini not to the greatest scholar of the mid-seventeenth century, but to one of the most elegant writers, Daniello Bartoli.[98] Even the Capuchins, who had long shunned what the world called eloquence after one unfortunate experience with an eloquent preacher, were finally converted; and ZACCARIA BOVERIO (1568–1637) opened the first of his two huge volumes with a typically humanist commonplace about "praeclarum apud omnes historiae nomen ac dignitatem."[99]

But most of the sacred historians actually wrote in a manner exactly the opposite of what they promised in their prefaces. They wrote not humanist historical prose but brief observations and rubrics that served no other purpose than that of linking one long quotation and the next:

> doceat tum s. Iacobus Apostolus tum alii patres Apostolorum temporibus vicini. Ille quidem Epistolae Catholic. cap. v, 14. 15. sic poenitentiam et extremam unctionem commemorat:

and after another interminable quotation:

> De sacramento Eucharistiae paullo ante obitum sumpto extat exemplum apud Eusebium in Historia Ecclesiastica lib. vi, cap. xlix . . .; verba sunt haec: . . . (Panvinio)

They indulged in hopelessly tangled run-on sentences like this one by Baldassano:

> Ma niuna di quelle [a whole list of the various cities called *Thebes*] diede il nome alla Legione Thebea eccetto la Thebe di Egitto, la quale di tutte l'altre fu la più antica, potente e celebratissima [*pace* the double superlative], posciacche ella fu edificata non dal tiranno Busiri, infame per la crudeltà e altre sue sceleratezze, ma come con altri auttori scrive Eusebio, dal principe Osiri, celebrato tra i più antichi e più famosi heroi, del quale tratterremo più a lungo nella nostra historia ecclesiastica di Piemonte e de' paesi vicini [*sic passim*].

Even Orlandini, who followed humanist precepts to the point of dividing his books not by year but by important turning points in the history of the Society, wrote what amounted to a heavily footnoted record of daily events, with paragraph interruptions only when one *Annus Domini* or *Annus Societatis* gave way to the next. Even Sigonio, that master of historical prose, observed the same practice as soon as he turned from the history of Italy to the history of the Church: "Copiosissime apud Cyprianum loquutus est," he announced; and then followed a very copious quotation. "Firmilianus sic scribens," he went on; and then followed a whole page from that authority.

These stylistic peculiarities cannot be attributed solely to ignorance. Except for the Capuchins and for the members of one or two of the more obscurantist religious orders,[100] most of the sacred historians were fully aware of the "elegance" and the "noble, ornate style" (Poccianti) of the ancient as well as of the modern humanist historians, whom, after all, they used as sources of information. Even Baronio, who associated daily with the best writers of Rome, showed himself to be capable of the loaded, vituperative epithets characteristic of humanist polemics whenever he was called upon to write "exhortations" rather than history.[101] Nor can these peculiarities be attributed solely to haste—to "not wanting to take away from writing [on so vast a subject] the time necessary for achieving a more elegant and polished style," as Guido Bentivoglio, that master of good historical prose, supposed.[102] Rather, they were the consequence of a deliberate choice of literary models. The sacred historians also accepted the humanist precept according to which works of quality could be created in the present only by remaining within the confines of the literary genres sanctioned by the ancients: "I have done nothing," Baronio insisted, "that would not have been pleasing to the great ancient writers."[103] Since Livy and Sallust were obviously inappropriate to the subjects they had chosen, the sacred historians were faced with two possibilities. They could turn for a model to the discipline nearest their own, antiquarian studies, and write like Varro or like Varro's modern counterpart, Panvinio. Or else they could turn to the model followed by Sozomen, Rufinus, Socrates, Theodoret, and most of the other ecclesiastical historians from whom they took their information regarding the golden age of the Church. That model was Eusebius, "easily the prince of all those who write ecclesiastical history," according to Baronio.

To be sure, Baronio did not imitate Eusebius in every detail—for example, in the garbled sentences that even modern philologists cannot make sense of and in the dragged-out metaphors that serve only to demonstrate the author's insensitivity to the rules of rhetoric. But otherwise he followed him faithfully. He too indulged in long martyrdom stories of pietistic rather than historical value. He too reproduced whole documents when only parts of them were relevant to his argument. He too included many texts simply because of their inherent rarity, novelty, or contemporaneity, not because they had anything to do with what he himself was saying. Indeed, such was the bond of empathy between the research librarian of Renaissance Rome and the research librarian of Roman Caesarea that one simply let the other do the talking whenever he found he had nothing to add—which is why almost half the volume on the early fourth century of the *Annales Ecclesiasticae* is actually a transcription of the *Historia Ecclesiastica,* interrupted only by an occasional "This is what Eusebius says on this matter...."

Having chosen Eusebius as a model, however, Baronio became the unwitting victim of Eusebius's conscious choice to write a kind of history totally different from that of the classics of Greco-Roman historiography. As Eusebius borrowed information from Tacitus and Josephus while rejecting the example of their style and form, so Baronio learned to study Ammianus, Procopius, and Biondo for what they wrote, without being in the least influenced by how they wrote. Similarly, since Eusebius's ancient imitators carefully avoided mentioning political affairs, or at least since they apologized for doing so whenever they found that the course of ecclesiastical affairs made no sense without some mention of Stilicho, Alaric, and the successors of Theodosius I, so Baronius's Renaissance colleagues scrupulously kept saints and bishops separate from princes and generals. Renaissance sacred history thus continued to observe the same distance from Renaissance humanist historiography that ancient sacred history, of which it was a conscious revival, had established between itself and the historiography of Thucydides, Sallust, and Livy.[104]

Just how difficult it was to bridge this thousand-year-old gulf had been indicated as early as 1559, when a minor Brescian humanist named FLAVIO ALESSIO, or FLAVIUS ALEXIUS, UGONI tried to apply the standard humanist form of a dialogue to the history of the Order of St. Benedict. As a result, a religious order was turned into a civil republic, the "Respublica Casinensis." The best that could be said of this republic was that it achieved the goal of all other republics: "it holds an empire [*imperium*] subject to no one ... ; it enjoys liberties and privileges; it holds dominion [*sub se habet*] over many towns and even some cities; and it has custody of many communities of holy virgins."[105] All this may have been perfectly true; but it did not correspond to the image the Benedictines were trying to project of themselves in the midst of the unworldly Counter Reformation. The same difficulty became apparent once again in 1585, when TOMASO COSTO, in the last years of his life, decided to extend his much-applauded skill as a profane historian from things temporal to things spiritual. "If the lives of emperors and great captains can be described with all the well-known [*che si sa*] ornaments," he asserted, "so much more should one whose spirit is inclined to what belongs to God and his saints write beautifully as well as diligently." But all he actually managed to accomplish toward this goal was a translation into humanist Italian of the very unhumanist string of incredible miracles loyally attributed by the Neapolitan monk VINCENZO VERACE to the rather mythological founder of his monastery.[106]

Paolo Sarpi

Yet the most eloquent example of the incompatibility between sacred and profane history is furnished by the attempts to write about the one great event of recent history in which both were intimately involved: the Council of Trent. That the Council constituted an important subject of historical study, for theological as well as for political purposes, was a proposition that first occurred to one of its chief protagonists, Gabriele Paleotti, bishop of Bologna and patron of Sigonio. Soon after his arrival at Trent, indeed, Paleotti began recasting the diary he kept of day-by-day activities into a work of humanist historiography. But a history of so important an event by so authoritative an author would automatically have assumed the character of an official history, one which would need the approval of the Papacy, just as an official history of Venice needed the approval of the Senate. Unfortunately Paleotti was too busy governing his model Tridentine diocese to push his text through the Congregation of the Council, which in turn was in no mood to have its authoritative interpretations of the conciliar decrees undermined by the suggestion that any of them were the products of particular passions or compromises. And the text remained largely unknown until the middle of the following century, when much of it was incorporated into the official continuation of Baronio and into what eventually did become the official history of the Council by Sforza Pallavicino.[107]

The task of writing the history of the Council thus fell to the Venetian Servite, PAOLO SARPI (1562–1623). Of all the writers of his generation, Sarpi was undoubtedly the one who most completely spanned all the various fields and circles of late Renaissance Italian culture. He was a man of intense, and typically Counter Reformation, religiosity—one who seldom spoke, seldom smiled, and "ate so little that it is amazing how he stays alive," according to his first, and still authoritative, biographer, Fulgenzio Micanzio.[108] He was one of the severest proponents of reform in the order of medieval origin that he joined at the age of fourteen—so severe, indeed, that some of his less reformable brothers tried to ruin his reputation before the Holy Office. He also became, first as an assistant to Carlo Borromeo in Milan and then, after 1585, as the procurator of the order at the Curia, a close associate of the leaders of the Roman world of scholarship and piety. He fully shared their belief in the normative values of the first centuries of church history. He agreed with them that "the principal foundation of every . . . [civil] dominion is true religion and piety" and that the true mark of a pious dominion was the number of "magnificently adorned sacred edifices" it contained.[109] And that he gladly returned to Venice in 1589 can be attributed less to homesickness or to traditional Venetian anti-Roman prejudices than to his pessimism about the possibility of realizing his associates' program of religious regeneration in a city as heterogeneous and disorderly as Rome.

At the same time, Sarpi was a devoted citizen of the most powerful independent state of Italy—or, more correctly, a loyal subject of the small group of Venetian patricians to whom God had entrusted the exclusive right to govern the state. Such was his loyalty, indeed, that it alone figured as a qualification in the petitions he presented for nomination to an episcopal see in Dalmatia. And he eventually came to modify his thesis about the religious aim of political authority by admitting as an equally valuable aim that of promoting the wealth and protecting the property of the authority's subjects—even when that aim came into obvious conflict with the multiplication of outward signs of piety. Sarpi was also a humanist. Like Bruni and Alberti before him, he was occasionally willing to suspend his religious commitments in order to contemplate an ethical system based solely on the teachings of the ancient moral philosophers. He mastered all the languages required of late Renaissance humanists, including Hebrew. He was insatiably curious about all the exciting new fields that late Renaissance humanism was opening up: the geography and anthropology of overseas lands, speculative metaphysics, higher mathematics, medicine, and, most of all, natural science. And he learned enough about all these fields to ask intelligent questions and offer perceptive suggestions to all the learned men—from Giordano Bruno to Galileo Galilei—who frequented the university at Padua and the *Ridotto* of Andrea Morosini in Venice in the last decade of the century. Indeed, he even surpassed his fellow humanists in Italy in his appreciation of the universal scope of letters and scholarship; and the many contacts he established in the years after 1607 with colleagues in France, England, and the Netherlands, Protestant as well as Catholic, made him a forerunner of the international, supraconfessional "Republic of Letters" that was to save learning in Europe from the consequences of religious schism in the following century.[110]

The idea of writing a history of the Council—the "Iliad of our times," as he was later to call it—seems first to have occurred to Sarpi shortly after it had occurred, albeit independently, to Paleotti, that is, in 1566, when he was given to read the diary of the Council kept by Cardinal Ercole Gonzaga, the former secretary of the papal legate. The idea then occurred to him again during his years in Rome, when he met several of the surviving protagonists and made long extracts from the memoranda and records they procured for him. But what finally led him back to history after his long tour through all the other disciplines of the age was the Interdict hurled at the republic by Pope Paul V in 1606. The first arguments put forth by Sarpi in his new position of official theologian of the republic were of the same kind as those of his opponents: arguments from theological principles and arguments from historical precedents. Since the latter rested on the assumption that particular decisions in the past were eternally binding without regard to the particular circumstances that had provoked them, both kinds of argument were equally unhistorical in nature.[111] But no sooner had the resolution of the controversy put an end also to the theological polemics than he received a request from Jacques Auguste de Thou, then the leading writer of humanist contemporary history in all Europe, for full information about the recent events in which he had been a leading participant. Sarpi immediately agreed to do for de Thou what Pliny had done for Tacitus. But by December 1607, when the first draft was finished, it became clear that he had rather done what Caesar had done for himself. He had produced not a *Istoria del-l'Interdetto,* as the work is incorrectly called today, but a *commentario,* which is what he himself called it, one which observed perfectly all the rules of that well-established genre of humanist historical writing.[112] It began with a character sketch of the human agent without whom the whole event would never have occurred, Paul V. It then proceeded to a chronological exposition of the diplomatic negotiations, with ample extracts from the diplomats' reports and with speeches written in indirect discourse ("The Senate having reflected at length . . . , replied to the nuncio that . . ."). After the negotiations had foundered on the intransigence of the pope, the hero was introduced in the person of the newly elected doge, Leonardo Donà, a man "esteemed without question . . . for the integrity of his life, adorned with all the heroic virtues that are so rare in this century." And it was Donà alone, unaided by institutions, which are not mentioned, uncircumscribed by the constitutional structure of the state, of which there is not a word, without the help of jurists and theologians, who, not being men of state could not be true historical agents, who brought the event to a happy conclusion—which is where, appropriately, the commentary ends.

Even though it was formally complete in itself, the commentary posed for Sarpi a series of historical questions that went far beyond the single historical event to which it was dedicated. How is it, Sarpi wondered, that the Church of Paul V was so different from the Church of Paul, Polycarp, Ambrose, and Constantine—that is, of the Tridentine normative age? How is it that an institution in which bishops, princes, and laymen collaborated toward a common spiritual end had become one in which one bishop alone sought to reduce everyone to the rank of his personal servants in the pursuit of the very worldly ends of temporal power and material possessions? How is it, finally, that the united Christendom of the past had become the divided Christendom of the present, one in which the right of a sovereign state to defend itself with alliances was supposedly limited by the particular religious confessions of other Christian states?

During the following years, Sarpi was kept busy with one after another political problem presented to him in his capacity as an officer of the republic: how to defend it against the threat of encirclement by Hapsburg powers, how to defend its dominion of the Adriatic against the Uscocchi pirates, how to maintain direct land communications with northern Europe, how to build a new set of alliances to replace the one with France that had been compromised by the assasination of Henry IV. As a historian, his work was thus limited to polishing the text of the commentary, trying in vain to get it either approved by the Senate or smuggled out of the country, and warning his superiors about the "prejudicial" passages in the contemporary historical writings of others—such as the *relazione* of the war of Grandisca published under the pseudonym of one Pompeo Emigliani of Milan.[113] In the meantime, his interest in the history of the Council was aroused once again by the publication in France of a

French edition of the *Actes,* by an encounter with the former French ambassador at Trent, and above all by a meeting with the cousin of the English ambassador, who had written a tract on papal interference in temporal affairs. And what started in 1613 as a collection of documents became, by 1619, when the first edition appeared under a pseudonym at London, one of the most famous works of history of all time, the *Istoria del Concilio tridentino.*[114]

Sarpi approached the history of the Council in exactly the same way as Guicciardini had approached the invasion of Charles VIII, Giovio the pontificate of Leo X, and Adriani the principate of Cosimo I. They, after all, together with Sleidanus, were his principal sources of information for the political history of the decades preceding and during the Council. He began with a brief sketch of the history of the Church and of ecumenical councils from the time of Constantine to the time of Leo X; and he presented the latter, with only a slight adaptation of the theses of Giovio and Panvinio, as a high point in church history. It was in the age of Leo X, he noted, that the thousand-year-old problem of internal heresy had finally been overcome, that the question left hanging by the Church Fathers about the relation of Christianity to pagan culture had finally been solved, and that history, therefore, had come to an end. He then located the fatal flaw that set off another historical process: first one character trait—Leo's lack of religious piety—and then one act—Leo's decision to redress the depleted papal treasury by selling indulgences. From this one act flowed all the others that eventually ended up in the Council. It awakened the avarice of the pope's favorite and set off a feud between the German Augustinians and Dominicans. A counterattack by the Augustinian Luther brought on another attack by the Dominican Eck, who thus provoked an even more serious counterattack by Luther. And one by one, Sarpi noted, the contrasting theses became more and more extreme until a reconciliation appeared to be all but impossible.

When at last, in Chapter 2 of Book II, Sarpi arrived at the Council itself, the narrative continued strictly on the basis of the enormous number of documents that he had collected and arranged in chronological order. In fact, most of the text thereafter consists of paraphrases of the documents—paraphrases, that is, not verbatim transcriptions, since Sarpi was consciously following historical rather than antiquarian models. True, it contains a number of errors of fact and attribution and some notable gaps: after all, many of the more important documents were so tightly locked up in the archive of the Congregation of the Council that even Sforza Pallavicino had difficulty gaining access to them several decades later. But many of what have been denounced as errors actually turn out to have been substantially, if not verbally, exact reproductions of documents that have only recently been rediscovered, like the Cervini papers.[115] What once seemed to have been distortions aimed at emphasizing the role of the Papacy in conciliar affairs turn out to be a reflection of the imbalance of the documentation at his disposal, much of which happens to have been written by papal sympathizers. And his own opinions have to be induced from the accurately transcribed discourses of those of the participants he approved of or from the opinions he attributed to a typically humanist "chorus" of "pious men."

Sarpi thus managed to incorporate sacred history into humanist history or, rather, to apply humanist historiographical standards to sacred history. He did so by the simple device of substituting disputations for battles, sermons for orations, colloquies for *consilia,* and prelates' reports for diplomats' letters. He then divided his chapters not by declarations of war or successions of kings, but by major turning points in the preparation for and the subsequent progress of the Council: The Peace of Crespy, the transfer to Bologna. And he placed the events of one kind of history in causal relation to those of the other with the help of introductory sentences very similar to those used by Guicciardini for parallel political events in different places: "While the princes were all busy with the war, the affairs of religion proceeded in this manner...."

Still, the gulf between the two kinds of history was only partially breached. Sacred history for Sarpi meant exclusively the history of theology and of ecclesiastical politics, and within that limit his synthesis was successful. But to most of the sacred historians, sacred history meant primarily the history of religion—of that spiritual force, that is, which created martyrs in the third century and that sent missionaries to India in the sixteenth. And of that, Sarpi said barely a word. What led Luther to his doctrine of Justification, what led Zwingli to his doctrine of the Eucharist, and what led the Fathers at Trent to many different formulations of the same doctrines, was not an inner conviction that these doctrines were correct or a personal spiritual experience of which they were the most satisfying theological expression. The doctrines were merely the result of a concatenation of abstract theological arguments and of impersonal diplomatic maneuvering among theologians and politicians. If the Augustinians rather than the Dominicans had been given the privilege of selling indulgences, and had Eck kept his mouth shut in 1517, the Protestant—and therefore the Tridentine—reformation would never have taken place. And the happy age of Leo X, Sarpi might well have concluded, would have gone on forever.

Moreover, the restriction of the subject matter of the work as a whole to these two elements of sacred history had the further consequence of eliminating individual persons from an active role in history. All that was left of them, indeed, at least from Book II on, was a certain number of proper names attached as labels to a corresponding number of theological or ecclesiological positions; and the proper names of two of the most active participants in the last sessions, Carlo Borromeo and Gabriele Paleotti, are not mentioned at all.[116] Even the bold theses announced on the first page about the Council's responsibility for the division of Christendom eventually got lost in the morass of detail about what exactly was said and done one day after another. And Sarpi's decision to end his narrative with the closing session, as if he were writing a commentary rather than a history, ruled out the possibility of sustaining that half of his thesis which regarded the Council's long-range effects. Pius IV is presented not as the last of a line of villains who cemented the schism and "caused the greatest deformation [in the state and church] that there has ever been since the name of Christian was first heard." He is presented rather just as the final conciliar decrees present him: a deus ex machina who brought eighteen years of often fierce debate to a happy and productive conclusion. And the unwary reader who does not continually turn back to the beginning, or who falls asleep in the midst of interminable discussions of theological minutiae, may well think that the Council represented a triumph, not a tragedy, in the history of Christianity.

Thus the *Istoria del Concilio tridentino* turned out to be only partially sacred history. And without individual historical agents, without clearly stated and sustained theses, and without any concession to the limited patience of the lay audience for which humanists were supposed to write, it turned out to be only superficially humanist history as well. In fact, it was really not a work of Renaissance historiography at all. It was rather the unwitting forerunner of the scholarly historiography that was to take the place of humanist historiography in the late seventeenth century—a historiography which deliberately forsook both the rhetorical restrictions and the moral purposes of its predecessor in order to include every bit of information, trivial or important, charming or dull, about a given subject, all for the sole purpose of being useful to whoever wished, for reasons that were none of the historian's business, to be informed. Since the *Istoria* was first published under a very provocative preface written by the momentary renegade from Catholicism Antonio De Dominis, and since ecclesiastical prohibitions in Italy made it necessary that all subsequent editions also be printed abroad,[117] it could not even serve as one of the great scholarly monuments of the Counter Reformation Church. It could serve only to provoke—to the annoyance of the Curia, which thought that all the necessary monuments had already been published—the monument that was indeed recognized as the official Roman version of the events: the still more fully informed, still more thoroughly documented, and still more somniferous history of the Council by Sforza Pallavicino. And no one in Italy paid much attention to Sarpi's version, or for that matter to anything else that might open up questions that everyone thought to have been definitely settled, until the revival of interest both in Sarpi and in the Council in the middle of the eighteenth century.

Thus profane history, both in its humanist and in its subsequent baroque forms, remained a discipline completely separate from sacred history. The one regarded "the goods of fortune" and gave lessons in how "to promote those things which concern the body." The other regarded "the qualities of the soul" and provided "examples of holy life." So said no less authoritative a sacred historian than Ferdinando Ughelli; and Ughelli's definition was backed up by the thorough knowledge of profane history he had acquired through his reading of the "praestantissimus historicus" Scipione Ammirato and his conversations with Ammirato's heir and editor, the "eruditus, candidusque scriptor mihi amicissimus," Scipione Ammirato, Jr.[118] One kind of history could perhaps be of help, or at least amusement, to princes. The other was an indispensable source of positive theology, "without which," according to the faithful Baronian Alessandro Burgos, O.F.M. (b. 1666), later bishop of Catania, "it is all but impossible to talk about divine things."[119] Indeed, the two disciplines remained separate throughout the seventeenth century, thanks to the choice of Eusebius as a model by the greatest of the sacred historians of the age, Sébastien Le Nain de Tillemont. They remained separate in the late nineteenth century, thanks to the decision of the editors of the *Corpus Inscriptionum Latinarum* in Germany to leave all Christian inscriptions to the editors of the *Inscriptiones Christianae Urbis Romae* in Rome.[120] They were still separate in 1929, when Wilhelm Weber complained about barriers between *Kaisergeschichte* and *Kirchengeschichte*.[121] They were still separate in 1974, when a prominent Dominican historian, with an abundance of citations to the great twentieth-century sacred historian Etienne Gilson, reported as historically true the "miraculous cure" of a thirteenth-century Dominican whose feet were anointed by the Virgin.[122] And the separation has now been formally sanctioned by the most ambitious manifesto of modern Italian historiography, the Einaudi *Storia d'Italia*. Sacred history, translated as *la storia religiosa*, and Livian–Sallustian history, translated as *la storia politica*, have been given to two different authors. And still another Renaissance lateral discipline, *le vite degli huomini illustri*, has been assigned a distinct compartment all its own under the title of *la cultura*.

EPILOGUE

Ars Historica

BY THE BEGINNING OF THE SEVENTEENTH CENTURY, HUMANIST HISTORIOGRAPHY—THAT is, the form of historical writing that had constituted an essential element in Italian culture ever since it was launched by Bruni, Biglia, and Biondo in the early fifteenth century—was suffering from several grave weaknesses. It was suffering from a conviction that the history of the major and of many of the minor cities of Italy had already been definitively written. It was suffering from the increasingly apparent failure of the experiments aimed at overcoming its topical limitation to the Renaissance equivalent of the ancient polis. It was suffering from the scarcity, in the decades after the pacification of the peninsula in the mid-sixteenth century, of the kind of political and military events with which it had always been chiefly concerned; and it was now threatened with the loss of what few were left of such events, which at least two critics, Pietro Lauro and Cesare Campana, sought to remove from the eyes of subjects and confine within the cabinets of princes.[1] Humanist historiography was also suffering from the continued isolation of three lateral disciplines—biography, the study of antiquities, and sacred history—that might have provided it with other subjects to replace those that were disappearing. And it was suffering from the inability of the historians to regard critically—as historically conditioned phenomena rather than as models of eternal value—the works of their ancient predecessors in which many of these same limitations were enshrined.[2]

To some extent, the plight of history can be attributed to pressures exerted from outside the discipline. In Venice, domestic history remained a state monopoly, one which could be entrusted only to historians already fully committed to whatever "myth of Venice" was then sanctioned by the majority of senators. In Lucca, domestic history was a matter of such political delicacy that not even such an apparently innocuous project as the publication of Lucca's greatest medieval chronicler, Tolomeo, could be tolerated; and Thomas Dempster, the editor, had to look for a publisher in distant Lyon.[3] Even in the more liberal states, powerful personages could frequently harrass a historian they suspected of presenting their ancestors in a less than favorable light; indeed, Robortello and Sansovino both complained bitterly about the self-censorship practiced by many of their colleagues in order to avoid offending "this one or that."[4] Baldi was required to cross out all his references to the humble origins of the forerunners of the reigning duke of Urbino, his employer.[5] Sigonio had to make a special trip to Parma, armed with letters from his bishop, in order to protect himself from the demands of certain Parmesan nobles that he be excluded from the ducal archives.[6] And at least one historian, Summonte, got into serious trouble when he broke the unwritten rule: that historians refrain from criticizing the government of which they were subjects.

Since, however, the vast majority of the historians in the late sixteenth century were ardent supporters of the current civil and religious establishment, they were generally left alone. In Medicean Florence, which is sometimes held up as the exact antithesis of a liberal-democratic regime, they could say what they pleased even about such staunch republican heroes as Francesco Ferrucci, Piero Strozzi, and Antonio Giacomini, as Jacopo Nardi discovered when his nostalgic biography of the latter was published with the special blessings of the grand duke.[7] Indeed, if they had any complaint at all, it was that the censors were not strict enough. They should search all the houses in the city, said Francesco Bocchi, in order to rid it once and for all of the scourge of lewd pictures; and he held up as an example of good government the case of the pornographic engraver in Rome who had finally been let out of jail only through the special intervention of the pope.[8] In Piedmont, according to Ludovico Della Chiesa, the historians were permitted "to think anything [they] wish and to express whatever [they] think," thanks to a religion "that loves the truth above all else," and thanks to "the goodness and prudence of the reigning princes," who allowed them the same freedom that Trajan had guaranteed to Tacitus.[9]

The ecclesiastical censors behaved much like the civil censors—except that they were generally more consistent. They may well have "strangled at birth every free manifestation of thought . . . with sequestrations and persecutions" in the several fields examined by one modern historian—like theology, morality, and metaphysics.[10] But they respected the integrity of the sacred historians, most of whom were either leaders themselves or protégés of leaders of the Counter Reformation. And they respected the autonomy of profane history in accordance with the Tridentine principle of reconsecrating the sacred by removing it from the profane. The only Italian profane historians who fell even into Possevino's category of those whose works might undermine the faith of the readers ("derogherebbe appresso i buoni molta fede") were those who, like Bruto, had left Italy for religious reasons.[11] Even Sigonio's arguments with his timid fellow-scholar Sirleto were concerned more with linguistic and philological than with historical or theological matters.[12] And since neither Sirleto nor Possevino were ecclesiastical censors anyway, what they said counted only as advice, not as injunctions.

Moreover, censorship in the realm of history was no more severe at the end of the sixteenth century, when Italian culture was supposedly being suffocated, than it had been in the middle of the fifteenth, when the Renaissance was supposedly flourishing. In the years after 1434, only one Florentine chronicler dared to write any more than "brief, bland" accounts of the events that marked the exile and recall of Cosimo de' Medici; and he subsequently crossed out what he had written so thoroughly that it can be read today only under an ultraviolet lamp. Similarly, in 1465 one of Pius II's nephews got the duke of Milan to place the famous scholar Francesco Filelfo under house arrest as punishment for what he had written about the late pope.[13] Nor was censorship in the late sixteenth century more severe in most of Italy than it was in France, where De Thou found himself as much at the mercy of the king as of the Church.[14] And it was much less severe in Italy than it was in England. There, one historian was thrown into the Tower for writing even about "men long since dead, and whose posteritie is cleane worne out" in a manner displeasing to the queen. Another was forced to express his judgments even about the distant past only "between the lines or by omission." An edict of 1599 specifically banned, with "reasonable effectiveness," all histories of England that had not been previously approved by the archbishop of Canterbury or the bishop of London and by the commission established by the censorship decree of 1559. And the Society of Antiquaries, whose deliberate avoidance of contemporary political issues rivaled that of their Italian counterparts, was finally dissolved by order of James I.[15]

Thus the Italian historians could not justifiably blame the censors for the crisis of their discipline. Nor could they blame their colleagues in other disciplines, who continued to respect the autonomy of history just as they had once asserted the autonomy of ethics, aesthetics, and political philosophy. Only one man of letters ever seriously questioned the value of history. That was Lionardo Salviati, who, carrying to a logical conclusion the traditional doctrine of the moral utility of history, suggested that what historians could persuade their audiences to accept as true might be more effective than what actually was true.[16] But Salviati's suggestion could not approach the violence of the charge made by Philip Sidney, with no great damage to the vigor of Elizabethan historiography, that exposure to "the trueth of the foolish world is many times a terror from well doing and an incouragement to unbridled wickedness";[17] and it was quickly forgotten among the many other orations on many other subjects of which the sole purpose was to show off the orator's ability to compose pompous orations. Only one philosopher ever openly attacked history. That was the iconoclastic physician Girolamo Cardano, who denied the exemplary quality of all the traditional heroes of antiquity and proclaimed the age of Nero and Nerva to be too remote from his own to warrant serious study. But Cardano's observations were scattered about in works dedicated to other subjects and hence attracted no attention. Only one philosopher ever questioned the epistemological bases of history. That was not Francesco Patrizi, as some recent scholars have thought after reading nothing but Book V of his dialogues. It was rather the *Urfaust* occultist from Köln, Heinrich Cornelius Agrippa (1486–1535), whose *On the Vanity of the Sciences,* written in a fit of depression in 1526, might never have been known in Italy had not Domenichi, for reasons unexplained, decided to translate it. But Agrippa's Pyrrhonism went no deeper than one not very profound proposition: since Cicero had found fault with Theopompos, Biondo with Orosius, and Martial with Livy, no historian at all was capable of distinguishing between fact and fable.[18]

And that form of Pyrrhonism, which none of his Italian readers took any more seriously than he seems to have taken it himself, bore no relation at all to the violent ejection of history from the realm of science perpetrated by Descartes and the Cartesians in France less than a century later.[19]

Some philosophers, in fact, made suggestions that might have been rather helpful, particularly after 1542, when formal treatises on history, or *Ars Historica,* were elevated to the rank of a subdiscipline of philosophy parallel to the other flourishing subdiscipline of literary criticism.[20] True, most of the philosophers took their examples exclusively from the works of the ancient historians. None of them knew enough about the works of modern historiography to perceive what were its most important problems. And they devoted most of their writings to repeating the same platitudes about the purpose and place of history that the historians already knew by heart.[21] Still, Sperone Speroni (1500–1588) performed one valuable service by undermining the authority of one notorious fabricator of platitudes, Lucian, whom he reproached for not having stuck to fables.[22] Francesco Robortello at least tried to substitute Aristotle, whose *Poetics* was at that moment the most exciting and productive novelty in the field of literary criticism, for Cicero, who, as everyone should by then have realized, had reduced history to the role of a grab bag of examples for moral philosophy.[23] And this substitution led him to suggest that historians stop wasting their time with moral asides. Just say that the Corinthians threw urine on the Roman ambassadors, he admonished. Your reader will easily be able to form his own opinion about the morality of such acts.

Francesco Patrizi (1529–97)—almost five decades before he himself turned, if not to historical, at least to antiquarian, studies—made some even more promising suggestions. He did so not because "the courts had taken the place of republics," which was the case neither in Padua nor in Ferrara, where he was then living, nor because "the Council of Trent was moving toward a close," which, in the years in which he was writing his dialogues, it most certainly was not, but rather because he could explicitly contrast what he had recently learned from the Neo-Platonists with what he had learned earlier from his Aristotelian academic mentor, Robortello.[24] Patrizi sometimes contradicted himself, for he was still only at the beginning of his career as a philosopher. He told historians that they should identify the causes of the events they described, which is what they had been doing since the time of Bruni; and he then turned around and told them to forget about causes, to "dir nè meno nè più di quanta à la cosa." He told them to bother with biographies only of great generals and princes—a lesson just the opposite of the one they should have been learning from contemporary biographers. He then told them that history had to present applicable examples of civil life ("a vivere vita civile") to everyone, ruled as well as rulers. But he also told them, rather forcibly, to get rid of their rhetorical and philosophical authorities altogether. And he told them to write not just about "the great deeds of great princes and republics" (III), but also about the acts of private persons, about geography and topography (II), and about "the source of food supplies, public revenues, and the strength and mode of governing" (VI)—without realizing, apparently, that the antiquarians had already begun to do just that.

After Patrizi, the philosophers gradually lost interest in the problems of the historians. Except for Tommaso Campanella, who much later—too much later, indeed, to be of any help—reelaborated the thesis first proposed by Valla about history as the foundation of all other disciplines,[25] they turned *Ars Historica* over to the rhetoricians. And the rhetoricians, instead of looking for new ideas in the vivacious speculations of their colleagues abroad—François Baudouin, Jean Bodin, Henri de la Popelinière, et al.[26]—went back to the well-worn pages of their ancient progenitors. The poet Ventura Cecchi (or Cieco) padded most of his slim, wide-margined dialogue with superfluous epithets ("the most grave author," Cicero; "the writer of Roman affairs," Livy), for he had no other advice for historians than that they should concern themselves with the things of the earth rather than with those of heaven.[27] The poet and free-lance editor Dionigi Atanagi (c. 1504–73) threw out Aristotle and insisted, on the authority of Cicero and Aulus Gellius, that "ornament" alone distinguished history from annals—as if Aulus Gellius's distinction between the two genres had not since been replaced by the distinction between history and chronicle. What made Caesar and Sallust better than all their predecessors and successors, he said, was the "quantity and frequency of [their] conceits and the matter [*cose*] they expressed in well-selected words and pleasant and exquisite locutions."[28] The professional translator Remigio Fiorentino insisted that the value of history consisted in the prudence and the delight it generates in the reader and in the "greatness of the matters it treats of"—as if no one had ever said that before.[29]

Only one of these rhetoricians actually tried to put his theories into practice: the "insignis theologus et eruditus vir clarus" (Ughelli) Sicilian, Giovan Antonio Viperani, bishop of Giovinazzo (d. 1610). The essence of history, Viperani proclaimed, was *utilitas,* which in turn is the measure of what of the whole truth the historian ought to include. But in order to be fully useful, he admitted, history also had to be enjoyable; and most of his treatise thereafter is involved in wholly external questions of style and form—which were, after all, the only ones he kept in mind in his own purely celebrative commentary on the siege of Malta.[30] With the possible exception of Lorenzo Ducci, whose attacks on Aristotle and Cicero may have been inspired by his meeting Patrizi in Ferrara, only one of these writers paid any serious attention to Patrizi: Giacomo Aconcio (1492–1566), the former secretary to the prince-bishop of Trent. But Aconcio spent his most productive years in religious exile, and his principal contribution to the debates in Italy consisted in making them known in England.[31] Only one of them ever tried to put in the form of a principle what modern historians actually did: Girolamo Ruscelli. But the only principle Ruscelli managed to identify, after reading Giovio and Alessandro Andrea, was that of the necessity of full information for the perception of truth. The diligent writer of contemporary history, he enjoined, should "go to every part of Europe, live some time in the principal towns, converse with all kinds of people, . . . and procure letters written by diligent persons."[32] Even the vociferous linguistic iconoclast Paolo Beni (1552–1625) had nothing to add, in the first decades of the next century, except a few more nasty words about Livy's style ("horrendus, inaequalibis"), which meant very little after Possevino's much more perceptive inquiry into the reliability of Livy's content.[33] Even that resounding Hispanophobe Traiano Boccalini[34] was able to do no more than to defend Tacitus against the accusation of fomenting tyranny, as if Ammirato and Davanzati had not long since cleared him of that charge, and to recommend him as a more eloquent model than Livy, as if Alciati had not done that a century earlier. And he was left with castigating Cesare Campana for having omitted what Patrizi had said was unnecessary: "elegance, gravity, political conceits. . . ."[35]

Just when they most needed help, then, the historians were abandoned to their own devices. Most of them preferred to follow the traditional format of confining their critical remarks to prefaces and dedications. History, said MICHELE ZAPPULLO in dedicating the third edition of his *Sommario storico* to the Spanish ambassador in Rome, is the remedy God gave man in order to compensate somewhat for the absence in this world of the immediate perception of reality enjoyed by the blessed in the next world.[36] It was thus on the same level as theology. History, said GIROLAMO DELLA CORTE in dedicating his *Istoria di Verona* to the city councillors, is the key to prudence, which "is nothing other, according to the testimony of the divine Plato, than the science of things that should be followed or avoided."[37] History, said POMPEO PELLINI's editor in presenting his *Dell'istoria di Perugia*,[38] is above all the science of getting straight the record of the past—of "resolving discordant [accounts] and of placing before the eye in an orderly manner all the facts pertinent to a republic or a kingdom according to the times in which they took place." Since history is "a perpetual possession, according to the saying of Thucydides," said CHERUBINO GHIRARDACCI in dedicating the first part of his *Della Historia di Bologna* to Pope Clement VIII,[39] it need not be "adorned with stylistic beauty." If its accuracy was necessarily limited by the human weaknesses of the individual historian, it could at least approach the truth whenever the historian followed Ghirardacci's own example: never consciously tell a lie, never "silence the truth for the love or dislike of anyone," consult all the living authorities on a particular subject, and thoroughly explore all the pertinent archival collections.

Some of the historians, on the other hand, actually wrote *Ars Historica* treatises of their own. CARLO SIGONIO anticipated Campanella in giving history the function of providing raw material for orators, poets, and grammarians as well as for philosophers; and he put it on top of the hierarchy of disciplines in accordance with the etymological principle: it is easier for the human mind to proceed from the single to the general than from the universal to the concrete.[40] GIOVAN MICHELE BRUTO proposed a similar scheme in the name of public utility. Philosophy was as necessary as religion, he noted, in order to turn men from the barbarians they are by nature into citizens. But history is both the source of philosophy and the means by which it teaches—which is why the invention of history in ancient Greece followed immediately upon Socrates's invention of moral philosophy. And without bothering to check his chronology, he went on to proclaim Livy, Polybius, and Dionysius of Halicarnassus much more appropriate reading for ordinary citizens than the dull political treatises of Plato and Aristotle.[41] UBERTO FOGLIETTA insisted that truth alone distinguished history from epic poetry; and in a long Pauline sentence he summed up the principle he claimed to have extracted from Polybius:

> Even if the narrative is ornate, elegant, and copious of words,
> Even if persons, places, and times are conveniently displayed,
> Even if the shape of towns and the site and order of battles are fully described,
> Even if the mind of the reader is [artfully] attracted to the material, . . .
> If the truth is missing, it can never be called history.[42]

CESARE CAMPANA agreed, although he qualified his agreement with the proposition that the truth of history was always "probable," not "demonstrative"; and he went on to propose the practical corollary that was to provoke the fury of Boccalini: "History should be seen in public rather as a modest virgin than as a whore dressed up in rich ornaments."[43] ALESSANDRO SARDI—after discoursing like a rhetorician on beauty, nobility, poetry, earthquakes, and "the qualities in general"—tried to determine finally the relation of history to other similar disciplines according to the scheme handed to him by his teacher, Marc'Antonio Teobaldi. History in general, he said, was divided into natural and accidental, the accidental into the fictitious (poetry) and the true; the true again into collections of "nude" events (annals) and events-plus-causes; and the latter was further divided according to the object to which it was directed: persons (biography), places (histories of one country), and time (histories of one event). And to provide this scheme with a veneer of empiricism, he placed a list of ancient authors under each of the categories.[44]

Whether in prefaces or in separate treatises, however, the historians of the late sixteenth century found very little to add to the definitions of history already put forth by their fifteenth-century predecessors. Guarino da Verona had already elaborated upon everything the ancient rhetoricians had said about the distinction between history and poetry and about the utility of the former in getting generals to fight harder. Lorenzo Valla had already proved history to be more effective than poetry in stimulating moral behavior and had shown how historical truth could be extracted from conflicting testimony. Giovannantonio Campano had already assured for history a place of dignity among the other *studia humanitatis*. Bartolomeo Fonzio had already shown how to moderate the forms of historical discourse in accordance with the kinds of subject matter. And Giovanni Pontano had already summarized all the views of his predecessors in his defense of history exclusively as a form of literature.[45] Indeed, most sixteenth-century historians countinued to approach the whole question of the theoretical foundation of history just as their predecessors had. As Poliziano had taken his definitions not from Suetonius, whom he was supposed to be commenting upon, but from Cicero, Pliny, Quintillian, and Lucian, so they derived their theoretical considerations not from a study of actual works of history, ancient or modern, but from the precepts of the ancient rhetoricians, none of whom had ever written a line of history. Even when they accidently hit upon a new idea, they soon reverted to the same resounding phrases: "testimonianza de' tempi, luce della verità, vita della memoria, maestra della vita...."

Unfortunately, the attempts of several non-historians to apply some of these phrases in practice were beginning to show the phrases to be quite other than the innocent bombast they had been when they were first pronounced in the first century B.C.[46] If history was really the foundation of oratory, then there was no reason why readers should wade through the works of historians now that the best orations had been extracted, translated, and summarized "for the better understanding of what they contain" by Remigio Fiorentino.[47] If history consisted of "memorable deeds," then there was no reason why they should not be content with Lodovico Domenichi's 830-page collection of the more memorable of them.[48] If history was the record of the imitable deeds of ancestors, then the essence of Venetian or Neapolitan history could be found much more easily in the deed-collections of Pancrazio Giustinian or of Cornelio Vitignano (d. 1613/14) than in the works of Sabellico or Summonte, where they were buried in thousands of pages of extraneous detail.[49] If history was a guide to civic behavior, then there was no reason to read even what Boccalini and Ammirato recommended as the most reliable guide, Tacitus. For Ascanio Piccolomini had already extracted all the "civic lessons" from the *Annals* and Fabio Frezza had pulled out *(cavato)* "the principal rules and precepts of government and war" from the *Histories* and the *Life of Agricola* as well.[50] If, on the other hand, history was the record of "the customs, ways of living, and wars" of bygone ages that no longer bore any relation to the age of peace and happiness inaugurated by Cosimo I, by Philip II, or by Sixtus V, then the only reason left for reading history was the entertainment of the reader[51]—a reason that no historian or theorist in the sixteenth century was prepared to accept.

In other words, taking seriously the rhetoricians' precepts was threatening to destroy history, or at least to reduce it to a few ahistorical manuals and anthologies. What saved history during most of the sixteenth century was the universal practice of the historians themselves in forgetting completely what they had said in their prefaces as soon as they turned to their texts. There is not a line, for instance, in Girolamo Bardi's *Sommario del mondo* that could possibly "persuade [anyone] to act well and virtuously"; and there is not a word in Cesare Nubilonio's history of

Vigevano that could possibly "awaken spirits to glory" or "incite generals and captains to magnanimous undertakings."[52] When historians wrote history, they followed instead the only rule that was ever actually applied, even if it was seldom stated explicitly: write history just as it has been written by any of several ancient historians or by any of several of their successful modern emulators.

That rule, however, made the historians the slaves of their models. If Sallust had said nothing about the introduction of Greek philosophy into Rome in the first century B.C., they could not mention Telesio or Patrizi in the sixteenth. If Livy had written independently of Varro, they could safely ignore Panvinio and the rest of the Renaissance antiquarians. If Tacitus had preferred the generals and princes who almost wrecked the Roman principate to the bureaucrats who actually saved it, they had to stick to Francesco Ferrucci and forget about the hardworking lawyers who were laying the foundations of modern bureaucratic states right under their noses. If Guicciardini did not mention Pontormo or Andrea del Sarto, they did not have to read Vasari. If Thucydides had deliberately turned his back on the gods, they had to consult Baronio only when they were unsure of a date. If both ancient and modern model historians respected the mutual isolation of the theory and the practice of history, they did not have to take the modern *Ars Historica* writers any more seriously than the *Ars Historica* writers had taken the historians. And they accordingly paid no more attention to them throughout the sixteenth century than did their successors in 1977, when one historian noted that "the multiplication of treatises on historical method . . . in recent years" had taken place with very little regard for "the actual methods of research characteristic of historians [themselves], either past or present."[53]

The sixteenth-century humanist historians were thus deprived of any kind of external vantage point from which they might examine critically either their own works or those they regarded as models. They were therefore wholly unaware that their discipline was suffering from anything at all. And that was the most important reason for the sudden demise of their discipline just at the moment when the appearance of a number of its greatest monuments seemed to have guaranteed it a long life.

The Demise of Humanist Historiography

How rapidly humanist historiography actually disappeared is a question that will finally be known only when the cliometricians study the publication lists not only of the sixteenth century, some of which have been published, but also of the seventeenth century, which are all but unexplored. Still, the few statistical approximations that can be hazarded at present indicate that history never achieved the popularity of some other humanist disciplines, not to mention the traditional academic disciplines, even at the height of its popularity in the first half of the sixteenth century. Even though he hired Tommaso Porcacchi specifically for the purpose of supervising his history offerings, Gabriele Giolito actually published no more than

25 titles (11.26 percent) that could qualify as historical in the broadest sense of the term between 1536 and 1550, as compared with 52 (23.42 percent) for Italian classics and 100 (45.04 percent) for contemporary Italian prose and verse.[54] Yet Giolito was exceeded only by Michele Tramezzino, who specialized in history: 29 out of 71 (40.84 percent) in history between 1539 and 1577 as compared with 12 (29.57 percent) in that perennially best-selling field, law. And he was consistently above the Giunti of Florence, that center of historiographical productivity, with an average of 9.93 percent for the years 1497–1519 and 1540–50.[55] He also surpassed all the known Roman publishers whose collective record between 1502 and 1536 was 29 out of 308, or 9.42 percent.[56]

A general average of somewhere around 10 percent, then, was not very high; and the most successful history texts could not rival the publication record of a local versifier like Giovanni Bonifacio of Rovigo, whose "desolately banal" rhymes were reprinted five times after the first edition of 1576.[57] But even these modest percentages had crumbled by the first decades of the seventeenth century. Although he was the chief printer for the principal historians of Naples just at the time when they were completing their major works, Giovanni Giacomo Carlino published only 14 historical titles, or 5.60 percent, out of a total of 251 between 1593 and 1616—all 14 of them before 1610. If two antiquarian guidebooks and a genealogical treatise are excepted, Carlino's nearest competitor, Tarquinio Longo, the chief printer for the Neapolitan Jesuits, published none at all.[58] And of the 442 books licensed by the state censors of the Venetian Republic *(Riformatori)* between 1609 and 1627, only 13, or 2.94 percent, were historical.[59] These indications of a sharp fall in quantity are corroborated by the disappearance from the market of many of the principal works of ancient historiography. The next Italian translation of Livy after the fifth edition of Jacopo Nardi's in 1568 appeared only in 1804, the next translation of Ammianus after Remigio Fiorentino's of 1559 only in 1829; and Tramezzino's *collana* was not reprinted until the eighteenth century. The figures become even more impressive when they are compared with those in France at roughly the same period: from 5.94 percent for Simon Colinaeus of Paris between 1529 and 1530 and 7.65 percent for the Grypho of Lyon between 1528 and 1574 to 13 out of 88, or 13.64 percent, for Henri Estienne between 1572 and 1598;[60] and historical publications for six Parisian publishers during the second half of the sixteenth century take up four and a half pages in an eighteenth-century catalogue in which six and a half are dedicated to rhetoric and seven and a half to poetics.[61]

History did not completely disappear in seventeenth-century Italy, to be sure. But what there was of it was of a very different character from the history that had been written during the two preceding centuries. This difference consisted not in the replacement of an interest exclusively in "facts" with a search for "the intimate rhythm of life stirred up in things by Bruno's incarnate divinity"; for seventeenth-century historians were as indifferent to metaphysical speculation as their predecessors had been, and none of them seems to have heard either of Bruno or of Neoplatonism. Nor did the difference consist in the replacement of narrative with an analysis of "the organicity of the real" and an appreciation of the "toned down, diffused light" in which events take place, particularly if these metaphors refer to an interest in the geographical setting and the immediate causes of events, which was one of the principal marks of all Renaissance historiography.[62] Rather, the difference consisted in the separation of the two chief aspects of historical writing that, in fact if not always in theory, had coexisted throughout the Renaissance: history as literature and history as research. It consisted also in the complete detachment of either from the concrete political and moral problems of the age. *Utilitas,* in other words, gave way to *delectatio* alone as the purpose of history as literature, and it gave way to a combination of *distractio* and *campanalismo,* local flag-waving, as the exclusive motivation of history as research.

To some extent, this change can be attributed to the ahistorical mentality that the seventeenth century inherited from the decades after Cateau-Cambrésis—a mentality which was "incapable of meditation and detachment, completely caught up in a vortex of contemporaneity and immediacy," in the words of one modern authority.[63] But it can also be attributed to the fortuitous decision of the sixteenth-century founders of Jesuit pedagogy, to which most upper-class Italians were exposed in the seventeenth century, to eliminate modern historians from their program ("pleros... esse... qui a prisca sapientia et disciplina tantum degeneravint") and to read ancient historians not for what they said but only for how they said it.[64] History thus presented as literature by the Jesuits became the sole concern of the seventeenth-century successors of the *Ars Historica* writers—Sebastiano Macci, Famiano Strada, and, the most famous of all, Agostino Mascardi. And they put aside Possevino's reservations and made Livy alone the master of good history-writing.[65] It was then taken up by those many seventeenth-century historians who, unlike their predecessors, paid attention to or collaborated with the theorists: Guido Bentivoglio, Enrico Caterino Davila, Alessandro Zilioli, Maiolino Bisaccioni, and Famiano Strada himself.[66] Since Livy left them with little to write about but wars, they were forced to go abroad for their subjects—to Flanders, to Catalonia, to Poland, to England, to France. And since most of the wars they chose were civil wars, rather than the international wars that had once again begun spilling over the Alps, the histories they wrote could be read solely for the "vigor of [their] language," for "the acumen with which the character of [their] personages were delineated," and for their "sentences, neither too short nor twisted, but carefully adjusted in proportion to the subject."[67] Only one or two of these historians ever suggested that his polished prose might also serve princes in keeping their subjects ("animos subditorum") in line; but then none of the very rare perpetrators of civil disturbances in seventeenth-century Italy could possibly have gotten around to reading the works in which the suggestions were made—like Agostino Aldoini's ponderous *Athenaeum Romanum*.[68]

History as literature was generally written by authors of a national, if not a pan-European, reputation. History as research, on the other hand, was left completely in the hands of the local or municipal historians. And they—the "Tuscan Varro" Carlo Roberto Dati in Florence, the tireless inscription hunter Antonino Amico in Messina, Antonio Beatillo in Bari, Giovan Battista Villanova in Lodi, et al.—were not obliged to pay the least attention to the stylists. What they wrote consisted largely of masses of undigested documents interspersed with inextricably tangled sentences the only apparent purpose of which was to fill as many pages as possible. Nor did they have to pay attention to the Renaissance criteria of discerning truth from falsehood. They went on fabricating stories about Sem and Noah and deducing "extravagant absurdities" from whatever they found in the archives,[69] fully knowing that no one in their times would ever bother to contradict what they wrote. And they invariably ended up with "a bundle tossed together without any criterion of selectivity and with none but purely external bonds" between one part and the next.[70] Even those municipal historians who tried to escape from the confines of their municipalities carried the defects with them. Emanuele Tesauro's "History of Italy under the Barbarians" was little more than a series of uncritical biographies, one which could have earned the author "an honorable place in the Republic of Letters" only on the condition that he free himself from "the prejudices of his century"—which he never did. Girolamo Briani's "History of Italy" was "a history without a problem, two thousand pages of chaos in which [Giambattista] Marino figures as a historical source for the birth of Christ and Tasso for the Crusades."[71] So engrossed, indeed, were these archive hunters in the real or forged scraps of the distant past that they overlooked the opportunities offered by occasional reappearances of the kind of *calamità* that had roused their ancestors in the decades after 1494. Even so spectacular a *calamità* as the Masaniello insurrection at Naples was abandoned to the diarists, whose abundant accounts were not incorporated into history until much later.[72]

Renaissance historiography thus disappeared in the country that had generated and nourished it. But north of the Alps it was not forgotten. Its principal products were all made available to students at the University of Leiden, either in the original Italian editions or in the Basel and Antwerp editions that were designed specifically for the diffusion of Italian humanism abroad. Many even of its minor products were included in the great German and Dutch anthologies that were eventually to lead up to the greatest of them all, Graevius's *Thesaurus*. And many of them are mentioned or described in such bibliographical guides as Paulus Bolduarus's *Bibliotheca His-*

torica[73] and Gerard Vossius's collection of Latin historians. Some of these works were remembered from time to time even in Italy. Giovan Francesco Palladio degli Olivi was inspired to go on with his history of Friuli in the 1650s by the memory of "the Piccolominis, the Bembos, the Giovios, and others," even though he carefully discarded the memory as soon as he started pouring documents into his own illegible tomes.[74] Giacomo Certani was still upset enough a hundred years after their publication to attempt another defense of Bologna against the slighting remarks of Guicciardini, and he did so for the same reasons that had guided his sixteenth-century predecessors: "the duty of a good citizen not to refuse to spill not only ink but his blood as well in the service of his fatherland."[75] What inspired the seventeenth-century chronicle hunters of Naples was still the conviction that history was "lux veritatis & vitae magistra," as well as the admonition of Diodorus Siculus that chronicle salvaging was a particularly fitting occupation for priests.[76]

In the early eighteenth century, when Italians once again became interested in the practical application of history—as a means, that is, for effecting progressive changes in the realms of politics and economics—it was to the Renaissance classics that they turned for models of historical writing as well as for information. And, notwithstanding the new concept of history as a science that they had learned from the Benedictines of Saint-Maur, they were delighted with what they found. For just as the sixteenth-century Petrarchans were ranged on the side of the Arcadian poets against the Marinists, so the Renaissance historians, notwithstanding their occasionally outdated methodology, provided an example of how history could be both scientifically sound and rhetorically effective, both satisfying to scholars and inspiring to reform-minded state officials, jurists, and political economists. Muratori himself learned how to write history not from Cammillo Peregrino, to whom he probably owed the original project for his *Rerum Italicarum Scriptores,* but from Carlo Sigonio, whose works he republished for the first time in a century and a half. "This is a most worthy work, one deserving of many editions," exclaimed Francesco Antonio Soria as he prepared still another edition of Panormita's history of Naples for publication.[77] "These are works still much esteemed by good writers," said Giovanni Gravier as he republished Pontano, Porzio, and Albino, "both for their elegance and for their accurate and judicious narration of the events."[78] "Neither for style nor for a prudent [reconstruction of the past] can anything more be desired," confessed Giovan Bernardino Tafuri as he made his own Pietro Giannone's opinion of De Costanzo: "a grave and judicious historian who put into shadows everything previously written on the subject."[79] Zagata's chronicle of Verona, said Giambattista Biancolini, could teach "not only those who govern but also those who live privately how to follow the good and acquire prudence."[80] And Giovanni Molina and Giambattista Verci returned to the example of the Renaissance municipal historians in order to "ennoble their cities [with the records] of the many good writers, citizens, and men of letters who ... flourished" in them in the past and to find inspiration in the actions of their ancestors for proposing new ways to improve the lives and fortunes of their fellow citizens in the present.[81]

Even in the late twentieth century, when historians have learned to ask new questions, to study new subjects, and to adopt methods of research unheard of four centuries earlier—even in the twentieth century certain of the peculiar traits of Renaissance historiography may still occasionally be observed, even in the works of those historians who are the least conscious of a debt to Renaissance humanism. The ancients are still held up as models for imitation—not only Tacitus, who "was (and is) a great man," but also Livy, whose style, according to one well-known classicist, "is so elevated and attractive as to put his work ... in the front rank of literature."[82] Individual personalities are still identified as the chief causes of historical events. "Movements [and] regimes are indeed real things," admits a noted authority on the history of Fascism; "but what provides unity and synthesis [in this case] is the personality [of one man]."[83] The personal motives of individuals are still induced from their subsequent actions whenever specific documentation of the motives is wanting. "Either out of sincere conviction or with demagogical intentions," states a popular history of modern Greece, "many deputies voted...."[84] Geography is still considered to be the first foundation, or part of the *structure,* upon which historical events take place; and one of the most important products of *Annales* historiography begins accordingly with a chapter on "la ville, son site, ses fonctions."[85] Chronology is still considered to be the second foundation of history. "Careful dating is an obligation of historians," says one authority, doubtlessly unconscious of echoing Baronio and Bellarmino. "For a consciousness of the succession [of events] in time" is the best defense of the truth against the mythmaking of Marxist philosophers.[86] Biography is still considered to be a form of literature separate from historiography—or at least it was until it got into the hands of what one critic calls "neither gentlemen nor scholars."[87]

Moreover, history is still distinguished from chronicle—or from journalism, which has now taken the place of chronicle—particularly in the case of such events as Watergate, where one is emerging only with difficulty from the other.[88] It still accepts the obligation of recording the names of all persons associated with a particular event: one modern historian lists forty-three of them in a sentence governed by the simple verb-phrase *basta citare* ("I need only mention").[89] It is still directed not just to the initiate but to "engineers and notaries"—that is, to the same general public for which the humanists themselves wrote.[90] It is still used as a means of conferring glory: "All my actions," says a historian of the Italian Communist Party, are aimed at "encouraging Socialists ... to study their history and make manifest its glorious pages."[91] It is still used as a source of practical political wisdom: "There are times," concludes a historian of early modern Europe after a study of charitable institutions, "when radical reform proves to be more permanent than moderate reform";[92] And there are others, adds one of his colleagues, when "we must think less about pacifying 'deviants' and more about changing . . . central values."[93] Even Annio da Viterbo still has a few disciples, although the mathematical calculations they now use in the place of forged Egyptian texts have led them not to Mount Arat but to Mexico.[94]

Yet the lasting effects of the accomplishment of the Renaissance historians go far deeper than just a few, perhaps fortuitous, similarities. It was they who first resurrected what had been an almost accidental invention of a fifth-century Athenian, one that might have vanished amid the rhetorical and philosophical interests of his immediate successors had it not been almost as accidently rediscovered three centuries later in a very different part of the ancient world. It was they, moreover, who, almost a thousand years after the demise of the last Thucydidean historian of antiquity, first made clear the radical difference between the past and the present and who then divided the former into comprehensible periods in accordance with similarities among the phenomena they discovered in each of them. It was they who first distinguished between myth and fact and who eliminated the transcendent and the supernatural as active forces in human affairs. It was they who first distinguished between history and record-keeping and who presented the former as a series of causally as well as chronologically related events in time. It was they who first perceived that a knowledge of what men had done in the past could be of use in informing and directing the decisions of men in the future and who incorporated into the writing of history at least one means, eloquence, by which this knowledge could be impressed upon the minds of the decision-makers. It was they, finally, who first realized that a knowledge of the past was not something that could be merely copied and then passively transmitted. It had to be acquired, with the expenditure of considerable labor, from a study of the remnants of the past that were often nonhistorical in nature and that were frequently incomprehensible to an investigator without very refined philological skills.

Thus only a few of the works of the Renaissance historians may any longer be read by any more than a few specialists in Renaissance studies. But, in the age of computors, conventions, journals, and university chairs, their more significant innovations are as much a part of the discipline they founded as they were in the age of secretaries, chancellors, *in-folio* tomes, and literary academies. Renaissance historiography may have vanished, then. But its heritage is still very much alive.

ABBREVIATIONS

AASTor	*Atti dell'Accademia delle Scienze di Torino,* Classe Scienze Morali
Agostini	Giovanni Degli Agostini, *Notizie istorico critiche intorno le vite e le opere degli scrittori viniziani* (Venice, 1752–54)
AIVSLA	*Atti e memorie dell'Istituto Veneto di Scienze Lettere ed Arti*
AM	*Archivio muratoriano*
AMAcPat	*Atti e memorie dell'Accademia Patavina*
AMDSPMarche	*Atti e memorie della Deputazione di Storia Patria per le Marche*
AMMod e Parm	*Atti e memorie della Deputazione di Storia Patria per le provincie modenesi e parmensi*
AMRom	*Atti e memorie della Deputazione di Storia Patria per le provincie della Romagna*
Argellati	Philippi Argelati Bononiensis *Bibliotheca Scriptorum Mediolanensium* (Milan, 1745) (or in the offset by Gregg Press, 1965)
ASI	*Archivio storico italiano*
ASL	*Archivio storico lombardo*
ASLigSP	*Atti della Società Ligure di Storia Patria*
ASNapSP	*Atti della Società Napolitana di Storia Patria*
ASPN	*Archivio storico per le provincie napolitane*
ASS	*Archivio storico siciliano*
Atti Pont	*Atti dell'Accademia Pontaniana*
AV	*Archivio veneto / Nuovo archivio veneto*
BDSPUmb	*Bollettino della Deputazione di Storia Patria per l'Umbria*
BHILomb	*Bibliotheca Historica Italica* cura et studio *Societatis Longobardicae Historiae Studiis Promovendis* (Milan, 1911 ff.)
BHR	*Bibliothèque d'humanisme et renaissance*
BISIme	*Bullettino dell'Istituto Storico Italiano per il Medio Evo*
BSPiac	*Bollettino storico piacentino*
DBI	*Dizionario biografico degli Italiani*
Di Giovanni	Vincenzo Di Giovanni, ed., *Cronache siciliane dei secoli XIII, XIV, e XV* (Bologna, 1865)
DSI	*Documenti di storia italiana* pubblicati per cura della Deputazione sugli Studi di Storia Patria per le provincie di Toscana, dell'Umbria e delle Marche.
Forni	*Historiae Urbium et Regionum Italiae Rariores,* a series of texts published in offset by Forni in Bologna; the number in the series is given whenever it appears on the title page, which it often does not.
Foscarini	Marco Foscarini, *Della letteratura veneziana libri otto* (Padua, 1752)
FSI	*Fonti per la storia d'Italia*
GCFI	*Giornale critico della filosofia italiana*
Giordano	Domenico Giordano, ed., *Collectio Scriptorum Rerum Napolitanarum* (Naples, 1735)
Graevius	*Thesaurus Antiquitatum et Historiarum Italiae,* ed. Joannes Georgius Graevius (1704–25). The continuations are referred to separately as *Thes. Ant. Rom.* and *Thes. Ant. Sic.* (below).

Gravier	Giovanni Gravier, ed., *Raccolta di tutti i più rinomati scrittori dell'istoria generale del Regno di Napoli* (Naples, 1769–70)
Gregorio	Rosario Gregorio, ed., *Bibliotheca Scriptorum Rerum Napolitanarum* Naples, 1735)
GSLI	*Giornale storico della letteratura italiana*
IMU	*Italia medioevale e umanistica*
JHI	*Journal of the History of Ideas*
JMH	*Journal of Modern History*
JWCI	*Journal of the Warburg and Courtauld Institutes*
Lincei Rendiconti	*Rendiconti dell'Accademia Nazionale dei Lincei,* Classe Scienze Morali
Martène-Durand	*Veterum Scriptorum et Monumentorum Historicorum . . . Amplissima Collectio . . .* studio et opere Domni Edmundi Martene & Domni Ursini Durand (Paris, 1724–33)
MASTor	*Memorie dell'Accademia delle Scienze di Torino*
Mazzuchelli	Giammaria Mazzuchelli, *Gli scrittori d'Italia* (Brescia, 1753 ff.)
MGH	*Monumenta Germaniae Historica*
MHP	*Monumenta Historiae Patriae:* Scriptores
MHP Par Plac	*Monumenta Historica ad Provincias Parmensem et Placentinam Pertinentia* (Parma, 1862)
Mon ist Romagna	*Dei monumenti istorici pertinenti alle provincie della Romagna:* Serie di cronache
Mongitore	Antonio Mongitore, *Bibliotheca Sicula* (Palermo, 1708–14)
Monumenta Neap.	*Monumenta ad Neapolitani Ducatus Historiam Pertinentia,* ed., Bartolomeo Carpasso (1881)
MSI	*Miscellanea di storia italiana*
MSLig	*Miscellanea di storia ligure*
MSPP Modena	*Monumenti di storia patria delle provincie modenesi:* Serie di cronache
Muratori, *Antiquitates*	Muratori, *Antiquitates Italicae Medii Aevi* (Milan, 1737–43)
NRS	*Nuova rivista storica*
Pauly	*Paulys Realencyclopädie der classischen Wissenschaft*
Pelliccia	Alessio Aurelio Pelliccia, ed., *Raccolta di varie cronache, diari et altri opuscoli appartenenti alla storia del Regno di Napoli* (Naples, 1780–82)
Querini	Angelo Maria Querini, *Specimen Variae Literaturae quae in Urbe Brixia Florebat* (Brescia, 1739)
Quétif-Echard	Jacobus Quétif-Jacobus Echard, *Scriptores Ordinis Praedicatorum* (Paris, 1721)
Racc CDS Lomb	*Raccolta di cronisti e documenti storici lombardi*
Ramusio	Giovan Battista Ramusio, *Navigationi e viaggi* (see Chapter 12, n. 24)
RIS[1]	*Rerum Italicarum Scriptores,* 1st ed., by Ludovico Antonio Muratori
RIS[2]	*Rerum Italicarum Scriptores,* 2d ed.
RLI	*Rassegna della letteratura italiana*
RQ	*Renaissance Quarterly / Renaissance News*
RSCI	*Rivista di storia della chiesa in Italia*
RSI	*Rivista storica italiana*
SBBayAW	*Sitzungsberichte der Bayerischen Akademie der Wissenschaften:* Philosophische-Historische Klasse
Schottus	Andreas Schottus, ed., *Italiae Illustratae Scriptores* (Frankfurt-am-Main, 1600)

Soria	Francesco Antonio Soria, *Memorie storico-critiche degli scrittori napolitani* (Naples, 1781–82) (Forni, 1967)
SR	*Studies in the Renaissance*
SV	*Bollettino dell'Istituto di Storia della Società e dello Stato Veneziano / Studi veneziani*
Tafuri	Gio. Bernardino Tafuri, *Istoria degli scrittori nati nel Regno di Napoli* (Naples, 1744–53)
Tartini	Giuseppe Maria Tartini's appendix to Muratori's *RIS*[1]
Thes. Ant. Rom.	*Thesaurus Antiquitatum Romanorum,* ed. Graevius, 2d ed. (Venice, 1732)
Thes. Ant. Sic.	*Thesaurus Antiquitatum Siciliae* (continuation of Graevius)
Tiraboschi	Girolamo Tiraboschi, *Storia della letteratura italiana* (I cite it in whichever edition happened to be handy when I consulted it.)
Zeno, *Istorici*	Apostolo Zeno, *Degl' istorici delle cose veneziane* (Venice, 1718–22)
Zeno: Voss	*Dissertazioni vossiane, cioè, Giunte e osservazioni intorno agli storici italiani che hanno scritto latinamente rammentati dal Vossio nel III libro De Historicis Latinis* (Venice, 1752)

NOTES

PROLOGUE

1. Felix Gilbert in his review of J. G. A. Pocock, *The Machiavellian Moment, Times Literary Supplement*, 19 March 1976.

2. Antonio Ceruti in *MSI*, vol. XVII, p. 116 (a similar statement by the editors of the *Cronache e statuti di Viterbo, DSI*, vol. V [1872], 276); Agostino Sagredo in preface to Domenico Malipiero, *ASI*, VII¹ (1843), xii; Luigi Simeoni in preface to *RIS*², vol. XX², p. viii.

3. Raffaello V. Chiantella, *Storiografia e pensiero politico nel Rinascimento* (Turin: Società Editrice Internazionale, 1973).

4. *Historia de la historiografía española* (Madrid: Consejo Superior de Investigaciones Científicas, 1944), p. 62.

5. "Medioevo barbarico e Cinquecento italiano," in Vittore Branca, ed., *Concetto, storia, miti e immagini del Medio Evo* (Florence: Sansoni, 1973), pp. 25–26; *Niccolò Machiavelli: Colloquio* (Accademia Nazionale dei Lincei, *Quaderno*, No. 34) (Rome, 1970), p. 22; *IMU*, XI (1968), 158: "Quando si pensa allo scempio che della storiografia umanistica italiana fu fatto poi in quel libro del Fueter...."

6. "The Swathes and Tunnels," *Times Literary Supplement* (22 September 1978).

7. Milan-Naples: Ricciardi.

8. I have presented a much more thorough treatment of this question in a separate paper entitled "The Transition from Renaissance to Baroque: The Case of Historiography," to appear in *History and Theory*, XIX (1980). Here I refer specifically to Karl H. Dannenfeldt, "The Italian Renaissance," in Matthew A. Fitzsimons et al., eds., *The Development of Historiography* (Harrisburg: Stackpole, 1954); Augustin Renaudet, "Humanisme, histoire et politique au '400," in his *Humanisme et Renaissance* (Geneva: Droz, 1958); Giovanni Previtali, *La fortuna dei primitivi* (Turin: Einaudi, 1964), p. 5; Eugene Rice, *Foundations of Early Modern Europe, 1450–1559* (New York: Norton, 1970), p. 71; Hugh Trevor-Roper on Camden in his *Queen Elizabeth's First Historian* (London: Jonathan Cape, 1971); and Felix Gilbert in "The Renaissance Interest in History," in Charles Singleton, ed., *Art, Science, and History in the Renaissance* (Johns Hopkins University Press, 1967). To all these works, as well as to the interesting selection of programmatic statements published in Peter Burke, *The Renaissance Sense of the Past* (New York: St. Martin's, 1969) I am indebted for introducing me to this subject. Similar opinions are expressed by Benjamin C. Kohl and Ronald G. Witt apropos of Poliziano's *Congiura dei Pazzi* in the edition cited below, Chapter 1, n. 109.

9. Gilbert, "Machiavelli's *Istorie fiorentine*," now reprinted in his *History, Choice and Commitment* (Cambridge: Harvard University Press, The Belknap Press, 1977), here quoted from pp. 137, and in *RQ*, XXXI (1978), 608; Denys Hay, *Annalists and Historians: Western Historiography from the VIIIth to the XVIIIth Century* (London: Methuen, 1977), Chapter 6. A very similar point of view is expressed in Franco Gaeta's introduction to the Feltrinelli edition of the *Istorie fiorentine*, cited below, Chapter 10, n. 30.

10. Ruggiero Romano, *La storiografia italiana* ("Espresso Strumenti") (Rome, 1978).

11. Herbert Weisinger, "Ideas of History during the Renaissance," *JHI*, VI (1945); Frank Manuel, *Shapes of Philosophical History* (Stanford University Press, 1965), chap. 3; Myron Gilmore, "Freedom and Determinism in Renaissance Historians," *SR*, III (1956). Similar theses in August Buck, *Geschichtsdenken der Renaissance* (Krefeld: Scherpe, 1957).

12. Luigi Malagoli, *Seicento italiano e modernità* (Florence: La Nuova Italia, 1970), pt. II. A similar point of view is suggested by Ferdinando Vegas in his long essay, "La concezione della storia...," in Michele Federico Sciacca, ed., *Grande antologia filosofica* (Milan:

Marzorati, 1964), vol. X: after Guicciardini he mentions no actual writers of history in Italy, only theorists of history.

13. Tenenti, "La storiografia in Europa dal Quattro al Seicento," in *Nuove questioni di storia moderna* (Milan: Marzorati, 1964), vol. II; E. Lugnani Scarano, "Storiografia e pubblicista minori," in *Il Cinquecento* = vol. IV² of the Laterza series, *La Letteratura italiana: Storia e testi*. A similar format is followed in two other very helpful selections of texts: Chapter 8 of Arturo Pompeati's *Storia della letteratura italiana* (Turin: UTET, 1962), and vol. II² and vol. III¹ of the Rizzoli (1966) *Antologia della letteratura italiana,* ed. Maurizio Vitali.

14. E.g., Sergio Bertelli, *Ribelli, libertini e ortodossi nella storiografia barocca* (Florence: La Nuova Italia, 1973).

15. Georges Lefebvre in *La naissance de l'historiographie moderne* (Paris: Flammarion, 1971), which I happen to have read in the Mondadori Oscar series as *La storiografia moderna.*

16. Donald R. Kelley, *Foundations of Modern Historical Scholarship: Language, Law, and History in the French Renaissance* (Columbia University Press, 1970); George Huppert, *The Idea of Perfect History* (University of Illinois Press, 1970).

17. Gerald Strauss, *Sixteenth Century Germany: Its Topography and Topographers* (University of Wisconsin Press, 1959); Werner Goez, "Die Anfänge der historischen Methoden: Reflexion in der italienischen Renaissance und ihre Aufnahme in der Geschichtsschreibung des deutschen Humanismus," *Archiv für Kulturgeschichte,* LVI (1974); Adalbert Klempt, *Die Säkularisierung der universal-historischen Auffassung* (Göttingen: Musterschmidt, 1960).

18. F. Smith Fussner, *The Historical Revolution: English Historical Writing and Thought, 1580–1640* (London: Routledge and Kegan Paul, 1962); Arthur Ferguson, "Circumstances and the Sense of History in Tudor England: The Coming of the Historical Revolution," *Medieval and Renaissance Studies,* III (1968).

19. Baron, *The Crisis of the Early Italian Renaissance,* cited below, Chapter 1, n. 46; Garin in his "Leggi, diritto e storia nelle discussioni dei secoli XV e XVI," in *L'età nuova:*

Ricerche di storia della cultura dal XII al XVI secolo (Naples: Morano, 1969).

20. Krzysztof Pomian, "L'histoire de la science et l'histoire de l'histoire," *Annales,* XXX⁵ (1975).

21. Amos Funkenstein, "Periodization and Self-Understanding in the Middle Ages and Early Modern Times," *Medievalia et Humanistica,* V (1974).

22. Rudolf Pfeiffer, *The History of Classical Scholarship from 1300 to 1850* (Oxford: Clarendon, 1976).

23. Robert Nisbet, *Social Change and History* (Oxford University Press, 1969); Ricardo J. Quinones, *The Renaissance Discovery of Time* (Harvard University Press, 1972).

24. Frank L. Borchardt, *German Antiquity in Renaissance Myth* (Johns Hopkins University Press, 1971).

25. My more general guidance in medieval historiography—rather than in the specific or local aspects of it considered separately in the several chapters of Books I and II—comes from Benoît Lacroix, *L'Histoire au Moyen-Age* (Paris: Vrin, 1971) as well as his article in the volume edited by Fitzsimons et al. cited above at n. 8; from Werner Kaegi, *Grundformen der Geschichtsschreibung seit dem Mittelalter: Drei Vorträge* (Utrecht, 1948); from Herbert Grundmann, "Grundzüge der mittelalterlichen Geschichtsanschauung," an essay of 1934 reprinted in Walther Lammers, ed., *Geschichtsdenken und Geschichtsbild im Mittelalter* (Darmstadt: Wissenschaftliche Buchgesellschaft, 1961); from Hanno Helbling, "L'Ecclesia Spiritualis e la storiografia alla fine del medioevo," in "L'attesa dell'età nuova nella spiritualità della fine del Medioevo (Centro di Studi sulla Spiritualità Medievale, Convegno No. 3) (Todi: Accademia Tudertina, 1962); from William J. Brandt, *The Shape of Medieval History* (Yale University Press, 1966); from Krzysztof Pomian, "Le passé, objet de la foi," *Organon,* VIII (1971); from Denys Hay, "History and Historians in France and England during the Fifteenth Century," *Bulletin of the Institute of Historical Research,* XXXV (1962); and from Jean-Pierre Bodmer, "Die französische Historiographie des Spätmittelalters und die Franken," *Archiv für Kulturgeschichte,* XLV (1963).

26. Ernesto Sestan, "La Storiografia del-

l'Italia longobarda," and Arnaldo Momigliano, "L'età del trapasso fra storiografia antica e storiografia medievale," in *La Storiografia altomediovale* (Settimane di Studio del Centro Italiano di Studi sull'Alto Medioevo, vol. XVII) (Spoleto, 1970).

CHAPTER ONE

1. All references hereafter are to the edition (with a long introduction) by Emilio Santini in *RIS*[2], vol. XIX[1].

2. On Livy, I follow P. G. Walsh, *Livy, His Historical Aims and Methods* (Cambridge University Press, 1961), and Mario Mazza, *Storia e ideologia in Tito Livio* (Catania: Bonanno, 1966). On Bruni, I take account of what Santini says in his *Leonardo Bruni Aretino e i suoi 'Historiarum,'* reprinted from the *Annali della Scuola Normale di Pisa* (Pisa, 1919), since his theses are accepted by B. L. Ullmann in "Leonardo Bruni and Humanistic Historiography," *Medievalia et Humanistica,* IV (1946), now in his *Studies in the Italian Renaissance* (Rome: Edizioni di Storia e Letteratura, 1955), and by Eugenio Garin in "La storia nel pensiero del Rinascimento" in his *Medioevo e rinascimento* (Bari: Laterza, 1954), as well as the very informative article by Cesare Vasoli in *DBI.* I have also taken note of what Nancy Struever says, about Poggio as well as Bruni, in *The Language of History in the Renaissance* (Princeton University Press, 1970), although with the reservations expressed by Sergio Bertelli in *Il pensiero politico,* VI (1973), 113, and of Donald J. Wilcox in *The Development of Florentine Humanist Historiography in the Fifteenth Century* (Harvard University Press, 1969), although Wilcox's approach to the problem is obviously very different from my own; see F. Smith Fussner in *RQ,* XXIII (1970), 439–41. By far the most authoritative guide to Bruni is now Riccardo Fubini's "Osservazioni sugli *Historiarum Florentini Populi Libri XII* di Leonardo Bruni" (although it contains much more than the title suggests), which the author kindly let me read in manuscript in anticipation of its inclusion in a festschrift in honor of Ernesto Sestan. At least one detail of Bruniana has recently been settled as definitely as it ever will be: "The year of Leonardo Bruni's Birth," by Hans Baron, in *Speculum,* LII (1977).

3. Antonio La Penna, "Die Bedeutung Sallusts für die Geschichtsschreibung und die politischen Ideen Leonardo Brunis," *Arcadia,* I (1966).

4. R. F. Hathaway, "Cicero's *De Re Publica II* and His Socratic View of History," *JHI,* XXIX (1968).

5. Arnaldo Momigliano in *Polybe* (Geneva: Vandoeuvres, 1974), p. 357.

6. I take this detail from a letter of Palla to Orsino Lanfredini (BNF II, V, 10, fol. 218r), a copy of which was kindly given me by Gene Brucker.

7. I use the edition of Acciaiuoli's translation by C. Monzani (Florence, 1861). See Emilio Santini, "La fortuna della *Storia fiorentina* di Leonardo Bruni nel Rinascimento," *Studi storici,* XX (1911). The observations that follow, on Bruni's treatment of the guilds, are from John M. Najemy, "*Arte* and *Ordini* in Machiavelli's *Istorie,*" in Sergio Bertelli and Gloria Ramakus, eds., *Essays Presented to Myron P. Gilmore* (Florence: La Nuova Italia, 1978), vol. I.

8. Nicolai Rubinstein, "The Beginnings of Political Thought in Florence," *JWCI,* V (1942); Pietro Santini, *Quesiti e ricerche di storiografia fiorentina* (Florence: Seeber, 1903); Alberto Del Monte, "La storiografia fiorentina dei secoli XII e XIII," *Bullettino dell'Istituto Storico Italiano per il medio Evo,* LXII (1950); Raffaello Morghen, "La storiografia fiorentina del Trecento," in Libera Cattedra di Storia della Civiltà Fiorentina, *Secoli vari* (Florence: Sansoni, 1953) (a somewhat chatty speech rather than a serious monograph). I have followed carefully Louis Green, first in his prefatory article, "Historical Interpretation in Fourteenth-Century Florentine Chronicles," *JHI,* XXVIII (1967), and then in his thorough study of the published texts of the chronicles in *Chronicle into History: An Essay on the Interpretation of History in Fourteenth-Century Chronicles* (Cambridge University Press, 1972), with assurances from Donald Kelley in *Speculum,* XLIX (1974), 334–36, and John C. Barnes in *Italian Studies* XXVIII (1973), 112–13, although having taken into account the reservations expressed by Anthony Molho in *American Historical Review,* LXXX (1975), 957, and by Lauro Martines in *RQ,* XXVII (1974) ("no method apart from textual analysis"), and

my own: it isolates the Florentine chronicle tradition from that of the other northern Italian cities—which I describe in the following chapters. Lists, though not complete, of chronicles can be found in Domenico Maria Manni's *Metodo per istudiare con brevità e profittevolmente le storie di Firenze* (Florence, 1755), pp. 34 ff. (more evidence for a revival of interest in the chronicles in the eighteenth century), in G. G. Gervinus, *Geschichte der florentinischen Historiographie bis zum 16ten Jahrhundert* (Vienna, 1871), and in Ovidio Capatini, "Motivi e momenti di storiografia medievale italiana," in *Nuove questioni di storia medievale* (Milan: Marzorati, 1969), pp. 774 ff.—an article I follow also in the next chapters. Selections from several of the more important chronicles are edited by Roberto Palmarocchi in *Cronisti del Trecento* (Milan: Rizzoli, 1935), without scholarly apparatus, but with brief biographies of the chroniclers in appendix. Sanzanome's *Gesta Florentinorum* is most conveniently found in the edition of G. Milanesi in *DSI*, vol. VI. It is also published with *Chronica de Origine Civitatis* and several other early chronicles by Otto Hartwig, with a long introduction, in his *Quellen und Forschungen zur ältesten Geschichte der Stadt Florenz* (Marburg, 1878). On Morelli, Pitti, Gino Capponi, Dati, and in general on all Florentine chronicle writing in the fourteenth and early fifteenth centuries, the fundamental work is that by Christian Bec, *Les marchands écrivains: Affaires et humanisme à Florence (1375–1434)* (Paris: Mouton, 1967).

9. Ed. Ernst Eherenfeuchter, *MGH*, vol. XXII.

10. Malispini's chronicle *ab urbe condita* to 1281 is edited, with a continuation by his nephew to 1286, by Ludovico Antonio Muratori in *RIS¹*, vol. VIII. Compagni's chronicle to 1324 is edited in *RIS²*, vol. IX², by Isidoro Del Lungo. Two other editions have recently appeared: the first with a long introduction by Gino Luzzatto (Turin: Einaudi, 1968), the second with abundant footnotes by Bruna Cordati (Turin: Loescher, 1969). In general, see Gaetano Salvemini, *Magnati e popolani in Firenze,* 2d ed. by Ernesto Sestan (Turin: Einaudi, 1960), p. 150.

11. Ernst Mehl, *Die Weltanschauung des*

Giovanni Villani (Leipzig: Teubner, 1926), as well as the relevant chapter of Green, *From Chronicle to History*. The text of the chronicle was published imperfectly in Venice in 1537 and then in a complete version by Torrentino in Florence, 1554. I use the edition of Florence, 1844–45, and that of Trieste (Lloyd), 1857–58, which also includes the continuation by Matteo and Filippo Villani. A modern critical edition is badly needed; the one promised for Laterza by Giorgio Bruscoli in *Giornale italiano di filologia,* X (1957), has not yet appeared. Further biographical details I have taken from Michele Luzzati, "Ricerche sulle attività mercantili e sul fallimento di Giovanni Villani," *BISIme,* LXXXI (1969). Luzzati disagrees with the usual favorable judgment of Villani's literary qualities in *Giovanni Villani e la compagnia dei Buonaccorsi* (Rome: Istituto dell'Enciclopedia Italiana, 1971); and he supports his judgment by showing how much of the last book is made up solely of transcriptions of merchant letters. The question of the priority of Villani and Malispini has been raised recently by C. T. Davis and is discussed at length by Maria Consiglia De Matteis in *BISIme,* LXXXIV (1972–73).

12. That is the thesis of Marvin Becker in "Individualism in the Early Italian Renaissance," *SR,* XIX (1972), esp. p. 284.

13. E.g., *Il libro di ricordanze dei Corsini (1362–1457),* ed. Armando Petrucci in *FSI,* vol. C (1965).

14. Ser Naddo, *Croniche fiorentine,* ed. Ildefonso di San Luigi in *Delizie degli eruditi toscani,* vol. XVII (Florence, 1764), and Nofri, ed. Giuseppe Odoardo Corazzini in *L'assedio di Pisa* (Florence, 1885).

15. Romolo Caggese, "Una cronica economica del secolo XIV," *Rivista delle biblioteche e degli archivi,* XII (1902).

16. P. J. Jones, in an article from which most successive studies on this subject derive, "Florentine Families and Florentine Diaries in the Fourteenth Century," *Papers of the British School of Rome,* XXIV (1956).

17. Julius Kirshner in *Archiv für Begriffsgeschichte,* XIX (1975), 19 (apropos of Giovanni di Bernardo Buongirolami), and in *Journal of Modern History,* XLVII (1975), 715.

18. E.g., Lorenzo di ser Tano da Lutiano, *Cronica ovvero Memorie attenenti alla nobilissima*

famiglia de' Signori da Lutiano (1366–1403), ed. Giuseppe Maria Brocchi (Florence, 1748).

19. *Il libro degli affari proprii di casa di Lapo di Giovanni Niccolini de' Sirigatti,* ed. Christian Bec (Paris: SEVPEN, 1969).

20. As in Francis William Kent, *Household and Lineage in Renaissance Florence* (Princeton University Press, 1977), which in turn contains a mine of information.

21. Namely, in *Two Memoirs of Renaissance Florence,* ed. Gene Brucker (Harper Torchbook, 1967), with an introduction that I rely on in the following paragraphs. My own references to the two diaries of which selections are translated in this book are to the standard editions of the originals: Gregorio (or Goro) Dati, *Il libro segreto,* ed. Carlo Gargiolli (Bologna, 1865), and Buonaccorso Pitti, cited below at n. 28. Of the other diaries I refer to here, one of the earliest is the *Cronaca domestica* of Donato Velluti (1313–70), first edited by Domenico Maria Manni in 1731 and more recently by Isidoro Del Lungo and Guglielmo Volpe (Florence, 1914). One of the best known is the *Libro di ricordi* of Bernardo Machiavelli (Florence: Olschki, 1954).

22. *Diario di anonimo fiorentino, 1358–1389,* ed. Alessandro Gherardi in *DSI,* vol. VI (1876).

23. Maria Pisani, *Un avventuriero del Quattrocento: La vita e le opere di Benedetto Dei* (Genoa: Perrella, 1923), further discussed by Dale Kent in "The Florentine *Reggimento* in the Fifteenth Century," *RQ,* XXVIII (1975).

24. *Andata di Giannozzo Manetti cittadino fiorentino a Vinegia,* ed. Nadia Lerz, *ASI,* CXVII (1959).

25. Ettore Bonora, "I *Ricordi* di Giovanni di Pagolo Morelli nella prosa del Quattrocento," in his *Retorica e invenzione: Studi sulla letteratura del Rinascimento* (Milan: Rizzoli, 1970).

26. I refer here to the introduction to Giovanni Odoardo Carozzini's edition of the chronicle in *ASI,* ser. 5, vol. XIV (1894).

27. Mannelli is published by Domenico Maria Manni in *Cronichette antiche di vari scrittori del buon secolo della lingua toscana* (Florence, 1738).

28. Morelli, *Ricordi,* ed. Ildefonso di San Luigi in *Delizie degli eruditi toscani* (above, n. 14), col. 19 (1770); Pitti, *Cronica,* ed. Alberto Bacchi della Lega with an interminable introduction, in the series published by the Commissione pe' Testi di Lingua (Bologna, 1905).

29. Gene Brucker, *The Civic World of Early Renaissance Florence* (Princeton University Press, 1977)—one of my principal sources also for information about the chroniclers.

30. Note Marvin Becker, "Un avvenimento riguardante il cronista M. di Coppo Stefani," *ASI,* CXVII (1959).

31. *Memorie* (1398–1411), in *Delizie degli eruditi toscani* (above, n. 14). vol. XVIII.

32. For example, the one published by Manni in *Cronichette antiche di vari scrittori,* cited above at n. 27. Another anonymous chronicle, which Robert Davidsohn attributed to the great-grandfather of Niccolò Machiavelli, was published by Alessandro Gherardi in 1876; selections of it are republished by Palmarocchi in *Cronisti del Trecento* (above, n. 8).

33. Manni is responsible for the original attribution. The most recent edition is that of Elinda Bellendi in *RIS²,* vol. XXVII², as *Cronaca volgare già attribuita a Piero di Giovanni Minerbetti.*

34. Raffaello Morghen seemed to have solved one such dilemma (above, n. 8); but his solution has been called into question by Charles T. Davis in his article in *Studi medioevali,* X (1969). See Ivo Mattezzi, "La questione malispina," *Il pensiero politico,* IV (1971), and the article by De Matteis cited above at n. 11.

35. The texts in this case are edited by Gino Scaramella in *RIS²,* vol. XVIII³.

36. Published by Manni in *Cronichette antiche* (above, n. 27).

37. Published with the chronicle of Giovanni cited above at n. 11.

38. Edited by Niccolò Rodolico, after an interminable preface, in *RIS²,* vol. XXX¹.

39. *Istorie pistolesi,* 1824 edition, p. 1. The most recent edition is that of Silvio Adrasto Barbi in *RIS²,* vol. XI⁵.

40. "Minerbetti": "M'è molto per l'addietro dilettato di ragionare e diletto ancora.... Ma oggi è tanto indebilita la memoria...." Morelli: "ciò per passare tempo e che i nostri alcuna cosa ne sappino." Morelli, *Ricordi,* ed. Vittore Branca (Florence: LeMonnier, 1956), on which: Claudio

Varese, "Premesse alla Cronaca del Morelli," *RLI*, LVIII (1954), and Leonida Pandimiglio, "Giovanni di Pagolo Morelli e la ragion di famiglia," *Studi sul medioevo cristiano offerti a Raffaello Morghen* (Rome: Istituto Storico Italiano per il Medio Evo, 1974). Several biographical passages from this diary have been translated for the purpose of psychoanalyzing the author by Richard Trexler in *History of Childhood Quarterly*, III (1975). Compagni here quoted by Palmarocchi, *Cronisti del Trecento*, p. 23. The sharp distinction made here between history and prehumanist chronicle is somewhat at variance with the theses of Marvin Becker in "Towards a Renaissance Historiography in Florence," In *Renaissance Studies in Honor of Hans Baron*, ed. Anthony Molho and John A. Tedeschi (Northern Illinois University Press, 1971); but Becker claims only to "suggest" his theses, not to sustain them.

41. Giovanni Villani, I, lxi.

42. Brucker, *The Civic World of Early Renaissance Florence*, pp. 250 ff. On Cavalcanti, see below, n. 78. On the accuracy of Villani's and Stefani's demographic figures: Alberto Benigno Falsini, "Firenze dopo il 1348: Le conseguenze della Peste Nera," *ASI*, CXXIX (1972); on Goro Dati and Cavalcanti: Anthony Molho in *Florentine Public Finance in the Early Renaissance* (Harvard University Press, 1971), pp. 13 and 82.

43. B. L. Ullmann, "Filippo Villani's Copy of His History of Florence," in his *Studies in the Italian Renaissance*, cited above at n. 2.

44. *Caso o Tumulto de' Ciompi*, ed. L. A. Muratori in *RIS¹*, vol. XVIII. On Capponi, see the series of articles by Ida Masetti Bencini in *Rivista delle biblioteche e degli archivi*, from vol. XVI (1905) to vol. XX (1909). The twenty-seven articles of political wisdom, detached from their possible origins in historical narratives, which Gino dictated on his deathbed, have been published as *Ricordi* (a literary form completely different from *Ricordanze*) by Gianfrancesco Folena in a recent version of the traditional Italian literary "wedding present," *Miscellanea di studi offerti a Armando Balduino e Bianca Bianchi* (Padua: Seminario di Filologia Moderna, 1962). Renzo Sereno says the work "belongs to the great political literature of the times," even

though the printed version is only five pages long: *American Political Science Review*, LII (1958).

45. Marisa Mariani, "La favola di Roma nell'ambiente fiorentino dei secoli XIII–XV," *Archivio della Società Romana di Storia Patria*, LXXXI (1958).

46. *L'istoria di Firenze dal 1380 al 1405*, ed. L. Pratesi (Norica, 1904), on whom see Hans Baron, *The Crisis of the Early Italian Renaissance*, 2d ed. (Princeton University Press, 1965), Chapter 8. Baron's argument for a slightly earlier date is in Chapter 3 of his *Humanistic and Political Literature in Florence and Venice at the Beginning of the Quattrocento*, 2d ed. (New York: Russell and Russell, 1968). The one given here is the more recent one he proposed in *From Petrarch to Leonardo Bruni* (Newberry Library and University of Chicago Press, 1968), which is accepted by Green in the chapter dedicated to Dati of his *From Chronicle to History*.

47. For Salutati's relations with Petrarch and Boccaccio, see his letters of 16 August 1374 and 24 December 1375 in *Epistolario*, ed. Francesco Novati (Rome: Forzoni, 1891), nos. 15 and 223.

48. For example, Salutati instructed his friend Juan Fernandez de Heredia in February 1392 to buy any manuscript of ancient historiography he could find, but to forget about "the nonsense of the moderns" *(modernorum nugas)*, such as Vincent of Beauvais, Martinus Polonus, "and others of the same kind published in the last two centuries": *Epistolario*, no. 11.

49. *Ep. Sen.*, X, 2, quoted in Eckhard Kessler, "Geschichtsdenken und Geschichtsschreibung bei Francesco Petrarca," *Archiv für Kulturgeschichte*, LI (1969), now expanded in his book, *Petrarch und die geschichte* (Munich: Fink, 1978), which I follow in this and the following paragraph. Similar observations in Arnauld Tripet, *Pétrarque, ou la connaissance de soi* (Geneva: Droz, 1967), pp. 117–25.

50. Salutati in the letter to Heredia cited above at n. 48. See Kessler, *Das Problem des frühen Humanismus: seine philosophische Bedeutung bei Coluccio Salutati* (Munich: Fink, 1968), as well as Alfred von Martin, *Coluccio Salutati's Traktat "Vom Tyrannen"* (Berlin-Leipzig: Rothschild, 1913), and B. L.

Ullmann, *The Humanism of Coluccio Salutati* (Padua: Antenore, 1963). On the importance of periodization, see A. Funkenstein, in the article cited in the Prologue, n. 21, and T. E. Mommsen, "Petrarch's concept of the Dark Ages," in his *Medieval and Renaissance Studies* (Cornell University Press, 1959), to which may be contrasted the more typically medieval view described by Giovanni Soranzo in "Il senso storico di Dante Alighieri," *AMAcPat,* LXXII (1956).

51. See B. L. Ullmann, "The Post-Mortem Adventures of Livy," in his *Studies in the Italian Renaissance,* cited above at n. 2; Giuseppe Billanovich, *I primi umanisti e le traduzioni dei classici latini* (Fribourg: Ed. Universitaires, 1953), and "Il Petrarca e gli storici latini," in *Tra Latino e volgare: Per Carlo Dionisotti* (Padua: Antenore, 1974); Maria Teresa Casella, "Nuovi appunti attorno al Boccaccio traduttore di Livio," *IMU,* IV (1961), and Albinia de la Mare, "Florentine Manuscripts of Livy in the Fifteenth Century," in T. A. Dorey, ed., *Livy* (University of Toronto Press, 1971).

52. Ed. Giuseppe Billanovich (Florence: Sansoni, 1945), on which see also Giuseppe Kirner, "Sulle opere storiche di Francesco Petrarca," *Annali della scuola Normale di Pisa,* VII (1890).

53. Ed. Guido Martellotti (Florence: Sansoni, 1964), which I read also in the Renaissance translation of Donato degli Albanzani as *Le vite degli uomini illustri,* ed. Luigi Razzolini (Bologna: Romagnuoli, 1874–79). The significance of these two works for the beginning of humanism is fully brought out in Martellotti's introduction to the Ricciardi (1955) volume of Petrarch's *Prose,* which contains selections from both of them.

54. *La vita di Scipione l'Africano,* ed. Guido Martelloti (Milan-Naples: Ricciardi, 1954).

55. Quoted by Franco Simone in "Il Petrarca e la sua concezione ciclica della storia," in *Arte e storia: Studi in onore di Lionello Venturi* (Turin: Giappichelli, 1965), which takes up from an earlier study (1942) by Carlo Calcaterra in preparation for his own further studies of early French humanism.

56. *Fam.,* XXIV, 8, translated by Mario Emilio Cosenza in *Petrarch's Letters to Classical Authors* (University of Chicago Press, 1910), pp. 101–2.

57. See Eugenio Garin, "La fortuna dell'etica aristotelica nel Quattrocento," Part I, Chapter 3 of his *La cultura filosofica del Rinascimento italiano* (Florence: Sansoni, 1961), and, on Bruni in general and on his successors, "I cancellieri umanisti della Repubblica fiorentina," Part I, Chapter 1, of the same volume, now in English translation by Victor and Elizabeth Valen as Chapter 1 of his *Portraits from the Quattrocento* (Harper Torchbook). Ludwig Bertalot, "Zur Bibliographie der Übersetzungen des Leonardus Brunis Aretinus," *Quellen und Forschungen aus italienischen Archiven und Bibliotheken,* XXVII (1936), adds several titles to the list of translations already given in Baron's edition of Bruni, *Humanistische-Philosophische Schriften* (Berlin-Leipzig: Teubner, 1928). See, further, Chapter 5 ("Bruni's Development as a Translator from the Greek") in Baron's *Humanistic and Political Literature.* The 219 manuscript and 5 printed editions surviving from the fifteenth century makes the *Economics* (Book I translated from Greek, Books II and III adapted from earlier Latin translations) one of the "best sellers" of the age—well above the popular *Metamorphosis* of Ovid (113) according to the calculations made by Joseph Soudek in "L. B. and His Public," *Studies in Medieval and Renaissance History,* V (1968).

58. I compare Bruni's *Historia Rerum Gestarum in Graecia succinta Interpretatione Librorum Xenophontis* (Leipzig, 1546) with Rex Warner's modern English translation (Penguin, 1966).

59. *De Bello Italico Adversus Gothos,* first published at Venice in 1470, then in 1471, with later editions at Basel, 1531, and Paris, 1534.

60. On the *De Bello Punico,* first published at Brescia in 1498 as a work of Polybius himself, *Latine Leonardo Arretino interprete,* see Beatrice Reynolds, "Bruni and Perotti Present a Greek Historian," *BHR,* XVI (1954). I read the text as *La seconda e la terza Guerra Punica,* ed. Antonio Ceruti (Bologna: Romagnoli, 1875).

61. "Illa enim amplior ac diligentior est, haec contractior et minus explicita": Bruni in Book IV, no. xx of his *Epistolae,* ed. Lorenzo Mehus (Florence, 1741), vol. I, p. 135.

62. "Est autem haec non translatio, sed

opus a me compositum . . .": ibid., vol. II, p. 150. (IX, v). Hence the charge of plagiarism made by, among others, Alessandro Sardi in his *Discorsi* (Venice, 1587), p. 141, is unfounded.

63. Cino Rinuccini made fun of the passion for ancient history in an "invective" written just before his death in 1417. See George Holmes, *The Florentine Enlightenment, 1400–40* (New York: Pegasus, 1969), p. 2.

64. There are ten separate editions of the *De Bello Gothico* in the Bibliothèque Nationale of Paris alone, including the Italian translation by Lodovico Petioni (Venice, 1528). I have examined the copy of the Italian translation of *De Bello Punico* made by a certain Jachopo di Francescho de Soci di Casentino in 1467, now in the Newberry Library.

65. Now edited, with notes and an introduction, in the appendix to Hans Baron, *From Petrarch to Leonardo Bruni*, cited above, n. 46. What I say about Bruni in general is heavily indebted to this and to the other essays in the same volume, although I cannot but be influenced by those who have since reexamined Baron's thesis concerning the causal relationships between the Visconti wars and the intellectual revolution of the 1410s. On one aspect of Bruni's career in papal service, see Gordon Griffiths, "Leonardo Bruni and the Restoration of the University of Rome (1406)," *RQ*, XXVI (1973).

66. Lauro Martines, *The Social World of the Florentine Humanists* (Princeton University Press, 1968), pp. 117–23 (with pertinent bibliography).

67. *Vite di uomini illustri del secolo XV* I read in the edition of Paolo d'Ancona and Erhard Aeschlimann (Milan: Hoepli, 1951); here cited on p. 253.

68. *Le vite di Dante* scritte da Giovanni e Filippo Villani, da Giovanni Boccaccio, Leonardo Aretino e Giannozzo Manetti, ed. G. L. Passerini (Florence: Sansoni, 1917), of which those by Boccaccio and Bruni were translated into English by James Robinson Smith (New York, 1901). This subject is treated only briefly in Hermann Gmelin, *Personendarstellung bei den Florentinischen Geschichtsschreibern der Renaissance* (Leipzig-Berlin, 1927). For the historiographical

significance of these works, see below, Chapter 14.

69. Ed. Carmine de Pierro, *RIS*[2], vol. XIX[3]. Twenty-six manuscript copies are still extant.

70. The last Latin edition of the Renaissance period is that of 1539; an Italian edition was published in Padua in 1545. On the commentary in antiquity, I follow Chapter 1 of F. E. Adcock, *Caesar as a Man of Letters* (Cambridge University Press, 1956).

71. The eulogies by Giannozzo Manetti and Poggio Bracciolini are published in appendix to vol. I of Mehus's edition of the *Epistolae* cited above at n. 61.

72. Anon., *Istorie di Firenze dall'anno 1406 fino al 1438, RIS*[1], vol. XIX.

73. Pitti cited above, n. 28, on which see Varese, *Storia e politica*, Chapter 1.

74. Both parts of the chronicle are published together under the name of Piero as *Historia fiorentina* (Florence, 1581); on Domenico, see the article by Anthony Molho in *RQ*, XXIII (1970).

75. *Summa Theologica* (Verona, 1740), vol. III, p. 166.

76. I use the 1st edition of Nürnberg, 1485. For other editions and for biographical information, I follow James Bernard Walker, *The "Chronicles" of Saint Antoninus* (Catholic University of America Press, 1933), and A. D'Addario in *DBI*. On the stories about Dominic, see Sergio Bertelli, *Ribelli . . .* (above, Prologue, n. 14), pp. 121 ff.

77. Giorgio Merula quoted by Ferdinando Gabotto in *Vita di Giorgio Merula* (Alessandria, 1893), p. 272.

78. Cavalcanti, *Istorie fiorentine*, ed. Filippo Luigi Polidori (minus the first fifteen chapters, which are mostly cribbed uncritically from previous chronicles, and with the spelling "modernized" for the benefit of nineteenth-century readers) (Florence, 1838). For a full analysis of this work, see the relevant chapter in Varese's *Storia e politica* and his special article on "Giovanni Cavalcanti, storico e scrittore" in *RLI*, LXXVII (1959), as well as Gian Mario Anselmi, "Contese politiche e sociali nelle 'Prime storie' del Cavalcanti," *ASI*, CXXXIV (1977), which arrives independently at a judgment almost identical to that of Gene Brucker.

79. The passages on the return of Cosimo

de' Medici are published, with commentary, by Varese in *Prosatori volgari del Quattrocento* (Milan-Naples: Ricciardi, 1955).

80. Published as a sequel to Gino's chronicle of the Ciompi revolt cited above, n. 44, preceded by a typical humanist biography by Bartolomeo Platina edited by Anton Francesco Gori. See Ida Masetti Bencini, "Neri Capponi," in *Rivista delle biblioteche e degli archivi*, XVI (1905)–XX (1909), who accepts Muratori's attribution of the commentary not to Gino but to Neri.

81. *La cacciata del conte di Poppi ed acquisto di quello Stato pel popolo fiorentino* and *Commentari* di Neri di Gino Capponi published by Muratori in the same volume referred to in the last note, *RIS¹*, vol. XVIII.

82. *Chronicon Universale*—or rather that portion of it from 1411 to 1455—ed. Guido Zaccagnini in *RIS²*, vol. XVI², on which see Zaccagnini's "Uno storico umanista pistoiese," *Studi di letteratura italiana* (a periodical edited by Erasmo Pèrcope and Nicola Zingarelli in Naples), II (1900), and Sebastiano Ciampi, *Notizie del canonico Sozomeno* (Pisa: Prosperi, 1810).

83. *RIS²*, vol. XXVI¹, minus the dedication to Piero de' Medici, which Gino Scaramella published subsequently in *RIS²*, vol. XIX², p. viii. I have also consulted some of the earlier editions in the Newberry library: Venice, 1483, Paris, 1512 and 1518, Basel, 1529 and 1549—the number of which gives some idea of its lasting popularity. Most of Scaramella's biographical information comes from the article by Apostolo Zeno in *Giornale de' letterati*, X (1712).

84. Vespasiano da Bisticci in *Le vite degli uomini illustri*, p. 302.

85. The *Chronicon*, also called *De Temporibus*, was not published until 1529. It was republished by Giuseppe Maria Tartini in 1748 (Tartini, vol. I). See Luigia Lanzani, "L'umanista Mattia Palmieri e la sua storia *De Bello Italico*," *Studi storici*, XIV (1905). The passages concerning Pius II at Ancona, which are based on the author's own experience, were published by Arsenio Frugoni in *Bollettino storico pisano*, n.s., vol. IX (1940), from the manuscript in the library of the University of Pisa.

86. *Annales* (part in Latin, part in Italian), *RIS¹*, vol. XXVI¹.

87. *Annales Suorum Temporum ab Anno 1448 ad Annum 1483*, first published by Giovanni Lami in the eighteenth century and more recently in appendix to Filippo Villani's *Liber de Civitatis Florentinae Famosis Civibus* (Florence, 1847), in the edition of Gustavo Camillo da Galletti. On the author: Concetto Marchesi, *Bartolomeo della Fonte, Contributo alla storia degli studi classici in Firenze nella seconda metà del Quattrocento* (Catania: Giannetta, 1900); more recent biographical information in Chapter 2 of Stefano Caroti and Stefano Zamponi, *Lo scrittoio di Bartolomeo Fonzio, umanista fiorentino* (Milan: Il Polifilo, 1974), most of which is dedicated to his innovations in calligraphy. His *Oratio in Historiae Laudationem* was published with his other *Orationes* in Florence, 1490.

88. *RIS¹*, vol. XXI. On his other work, a history of the kings of Naples, see below, Chapter 6, n. 95. Mark Philips has promised to publish still another humanist chronicle in his "A Newly Discovered Chronicle by Marco Parenti," *RQ, XXXI* (1978), covering the years 1464–67.

89. Ed. G. Scaramella in *RIS²*, vol. XIX². On Palmieri as a historian I take account of what Apostolo Zeno says in *Dissertazioni vossiane* (Venice, 1752), vol. I, and of what August Buck says in "M. P. als Repräsentant des Florentinischen Bürgerhumanismus," *Archiv für Kulturgeschichte*, XLVII (1965). Donald Wilcox's essay in *Studies in the Italian Renaissance in Honor of Hans Baron* (above, n. 40) is less helpful for my purposes, since it consists of a running commentary on the text rather than a historical-philological examination of it.

90. *RIS¹*, vol. XIX. For biographical information, see Naldo Naldi's contemporary biography in *RIS¹*, vol. XX, and Vespasiano da Bisticci in *Le vite degli uomini illustri*, pp. 159–91. A complete list of Manetti's published and unpublished works is given by Francesco Pagnotti in "La vita di Niccolò V scritta da G. M.," *Archivio della Società Romana di Storia Patria*, XIV (1891).

91. The work is usually known as *Historia Gotefridi* and was first published in Venice in 1532. The most recent edition is that in vol. V of *Recueil des histoires des Croisades*, published by the Académie des Inscriptions et Belles Lettres (Paris 1895), although I use the

edition by the exiled Scots antiquarian Thomas Dempster entitled (more accurately) *De Bello a Christianis contra Barbaros Gesto* (Florence, 1623). I am indebted for most of my information on Accolti to Robert Black, who kindly permitted me to read the dissertation he was preparing for the University of London. A section of the dissertation is published as an article, "Storia della Prima Crociata . . . ," *ASI,* CXXXI (1973). Further information in the article by A. Petrucci in *DBI.*

92. I read the text published at Basel in 1535. The only study I know about Fiocchi is Giovanni Mercati, "Andreas de Florentia segretario apostolico," in his *Ultimi contributi alla storia degli umanisti* (Vatican City, 1939), vol. I. Pauly absolves Fiocchi of any responsibility for the mistaken attribution.

93. Fiocchi accused Livy of confusing two separate offices, the *sacerdos patris patrati* and the *pater fetialis.* The *Oxford Classical Dictionary* ignores Fiocchi and his arguments and puts the offices back together on the sole authority of Livy.

94. Ed. I. E. I. Walchius (Leipzig, 1752).

95. Alessandro Perosa, *Giovanni Rucellai ed il suo Zibaldone* (London: Warburg Institute, 1960). The best authority on this subject is Roberto Weiss, in his packed but elegantly written *The Renaissance Discovery of Classical Antiquity* (Oxford: Blackwell, 1969).

96. Tartini, vol. II. On Rucellai, see Guglielmo Pellegrini, *L'umanista Bernardo Rucellai e le sue opere storiche* (Livorno: Giusti, 1920) and Felix Gilbert, "Bernardo Rucellai and the Orti Oricellari: A Study on the Origins of Modern Political Thought," *JWCI,* XII (1949).

97. See Preface to *Historiae Florentini Populi* (written 1453–58) in the offset edition of Poggio's *Opera Omnia* published with a preface by Riccardo Fubini (Turin: Bottega d'Erasmo, 1964)—which is where I read Poggio's other semihistorical works: *Utrum Priscis Romanis Latina Lingua Omnibus Communis Fuerit* and *De Fortunae Varietate.* The *Historiae* were not published in the original Latin text until 1715; but the Italian translation by his son Jacopo was published in 1476 and frequently thereafter, usually bound together with Donato Acciaiuoli's translation of Bruni. There are no modern biographies

of Poggio. R. Roedel's article in *Rinascimento,* XI (1960), merely rehashes what had been said before, and Domenico Bacci's *Cenni biografici e religiosità di P. B.* (Florence: Arte della Stampa, 1963) is taken mostly from an old article in the *Enciclopedia cattolica.* Francesco Tateo's *Tradizione e realtà nell'umanesimo italiano* (Bari: Dedalo, 1967) discusses Poggio at length, but only in the form of a history-of-ideas analysis of his works, removed from their personal or historical context. Students of Poggio's history writing must therefore rely largely on Fubini's preface (a mine of erudition, like everything else Fubini writes), Nicolai Rubinstein's "P. B., cancelliere e storico di Firenze," in *Atti e memorie dell'Accademia Petrarca di Arezzo,* n.s., vol. XXXVII (1958), and Chapter 6 of Santini's *Leonardo Bruni Aretino.*

98. In appendix to Mehus's edition of Bruni's *Epistolae.*

99. Carlo di Capodimonte, "Poggio Bracciolini, autore delle anonime *Vitae Quorundam Pontificum,*" *Rivista di storia della chiesa in Italia,* XIV (1960).

100. As noted by John W. Oppel in "Peace vs. Liberty in the Quattrocento," *Journal of Medieval and Renaissance Studies,* IV (1974).

101. Nicolai Rubinstein, "Bartolomeo Scala's *Historia Florentinorum.*" in *Studi di bibliografia e storia in onore di Tammaro de Martinis* (Verona, 1964), vol. IV. Biographical information by Domenico Maria Manni in *Bartolomae Scalae Collensis Vita* (Florence, 1768) and by G. B. Benvenuti in *Quaderni storici fiorentini,* 2d ed. (Florence: LeMonnier, 1889). At the moment of the last revision of my manuscript (November 1978), unfortunately, I knew only the title of Alison Brown's *Bartolomeo Scala, 1430–1497, Chancellor of Florence,* which had just been announced by Princeton University Press for publication in 1979.

102. "Qui primus Florentinam historiam totam prope e tenebris . . .": from the preface to *Historia Florentinorum* published in Graevius, vol. VIII[1].

103. E.g., the *Ricordanze* of Francesco Gaddi, referred to by Christian Bec in *BHR,* XXXIV (1972), 140, in the article "La bibliothèque d'un gran florentin," which also gives at least negative evidence (the paucity of titles) for the relatively small place accorded to

history (3 out of 40 titles, and none of them contemporary) in the otherwise broad culture of the "haute bourgeoisie florentine" at the end of the fifteenth century.

104. Palmieri, *Vita Nicolai Acciaioli,* ed. Gino Scaramella, *RIS²*, vol. XIII²; Manetti, *Vita Nicolai V, RIS¹*, vol. III (from a text provided by Anton Francesco Marmi—on which see the article by Pagnotti cited above at n. 90), and *Vitae Dantis, Petrarcae ac Boccacci* in Lorenzo Mohus, ed. *Specimen Historiae Litterariae Florentinae Saeculi Decimiterti ac Decimiquarti* (Florence, 1747); Naldi, cited above at n. 90; Accolti, *Dialogus de Praestantia Virorum Sui Aevi,* and Paolo Cortesi, *De Hominibus Doctis,* both published in Galletti's edition of Filippo Villani, *De Famosis Civibus.* On biography as a lateral form of historical writing, see below, Chapter 14.

105. Nicolai Rubinstein, "Il Poliziano e la questione delle origini di Firenze," in *Il Poliziano e il suo tempo* (Florence: Sansoni, 1957), and Vittore Branca, "Il metodo filologico del Poliziano," in *Tra Latino e volgare,* cited above at n. 51. The translation of Herodian and the prolusione on Suetonius I read in the *Opera Omnia* (Basel, 1553).

106. *De Bello Italico* (London, 1733), with a prefatory *vita.* It is bound with *De Bello Pisano,* which is admittedly nothing but a Latin translation of Neri Corsini's *Dell'acquisto di Pisa* (above, n. 80). Leon Battista Alberti's *De Porcaria Conjuratione, RIS¹*, vol. XXV, might be included in this list of commentaries, but it is only two pages in length. Rucellai also started working on a *Bellum Mediolanense* concerning the wars of the Florentines against the Visconti; but he got no farther than extracting the relevant passages from Bruni. Cf. Chapter 5 of Mario Santoro, *Fortuna, ragione e prudenza nella civiltà letteraria del Cinquecento* (Naples: Ligouri, 1967).

107. Fonzio, in a letter of 1509, *Epistolarium Libri III,* ed. Ladislaus Juhász (Budapest, 1931), vol. III, pp. 47–48.

108. So notes Momigliano in "Storiografia greca," *RSI,* LXXXVII (1975). See also Giorgio Brugnoli, "La *Praefatio in Suetonium* del Poliziano," *Giornale italiano di filologia,* X (1957), which demonstrates the high quality of the scholarship devoted by Poliziano to reconstructing the life of Suetonius, even

though it does not then analyze the *Laus Historiae* that accompanied the "Prolusione" of 1490.

109. "Ex hac tanta rerum commutatione saepe ego de humanae fortunae instabilitate sum admonitus": Poliziano, *Coniurationis Commentarium,* ed. Alessandro Perosa (Padua: Antenore, 1958). The work has recently been translated, for reasons that are not very clear, by Elizabeth B. Welles and published in Benjamin C. Kohl and Ronald G. Witt, eds., *The Earthly Republic* (University of Pennsylvania Press, 1978).

110. Guido Battelli, "La corrispondenza del Poliziano con il re don Giovanni II di Portogallo," *La rinascita,* II (1939).

111. See below, Chapter 2, n. 18.

112. *Commentariolus de Bello Volterrano,* first published in *RIS¹*, vol. XXIII, and then with the title *Historia de Volterrana Calamitate* with an introduction by Francesco Luigi Mannucci in *RIS²*, vol. XXIII⁴. On which I follow Giovanni Targioni Tozzetti in *Relazione d'alcuni viaggi,* 2d ed. (Florence, 1779), vol. XII, pp. 96 ff., Carlo Braggio in "Antonio Ivani, umanista del secolo XV," *Giornale ligustico,* XII (1885), Ruffo Landucci in "L'epistolario di Antonio Ivani," *Rinascimento,* VI (1965), Gabriella Airaldi, "Qual è la patria di Antonio Ivani?" in *ASI,* CXXIX (1972), and above all, Riccardo Fubini in a long essay full of new information and provocative theses entitled "Antonio Ivani da Sarzana: Un teorizzatore del declino delle autonomie comunali," which the author has buried away, as is his custom, in the *atti* of a *convegno* (Pistoia, 1975) published as *Egemonia fiorentina ed autonomie locali nella Toscana nord-occidentale* (Pistoia: Centro Italiano di Studi di Storia e d'Arte, 1978).

113. Manetti's *Vita* is published among his *Operette storiche* by Gaetano Milanesi (Florence, 1887), and now in English translation edited by Howard Saalman (Pennsylvania State University Press, 1971). Antonio should not be confused with Giannozzo Manetti. The correctness of the traditional attribution has now been established by Giuliano Tanturli in two articles that contain much other information about Manetti, one published in *Rinascimento,* XXI (1970), the other in *Studi medievali,* XIV (1973). The standard edition of Vespasiano is that of Aulo

Greco (Florence: Istituto Nazionale per gli Studi sul Rinascimento Italiano, 1970), which I follow, paying heed to the warning of M. Cagni in an important article devoted to Quattrocento biography, "Agnolo Manetti and Vespasiano da Bisticci," *IMU*, XIV (1971). What I say here about biography in general is indebted to Carlo A. Madrignani, "Di alcune biografie umanistiche di Dante e Petrarca," *Belfagor*, XVIII (1963).

114. See below, Chapter 6. A good example of late fifteenth-century historiographical theory in Florence is the *prolusiones* of Fonzio to his lectures on ancient historians, which are partially analyzed by Charles Trinkaus in *SR*, VII (1960). This subject is more fully considered in the Epilogue.

115. See E. H. Gombrich, "The Renaissance Conception of Artistic Progress and Its Consequences" (1952), now in his *Norm and Form* (London: Phaidon, 1966). On the importance of Philostratus for the later development of Renaissance biography, see below, Chapter 14.

116. *De Hominibus Doctis*, in Filippo Villani, *De Famosis Civibus*, p. 225, on which see below, Chapter 14.

117. "Villula ipsa devia in media sylva delitescat": quoted by Emilio Bigi in *La Cultura del Poliziano e altri studi umanistici* (Pisa: Nistri, 1967). In general, see Eugenio Garin, "L'ambiente del Poliziano," in *Il Poliziano e il suo tempo*.

118. Garin, "Donato Acciaiuoli, cittadino fiorentino," in his *Medioevo e Rinascimento* (Bari: Laterza, 1954), now in English in *Portraits from the Quattrocento* (Harper Torchbooks). See also the article by Arnaldo D'Addario in *DBI*. The *Vita Caroli Magni* was published with his edition of Plutarch in Rome in 1470 and reprinted in *Scriptores Rerum Germanicarum* (Leipzig, 1720–30), vol. I, pp. 818–31, on which see Ian Short in *Mittellateinisches Jahrbuch*, VII (1972), 142. What I say about Acciaiuoli is indebted to Margery Ganz of Le Moyne College in New York, who kindly supplied me with an exhaustive bibliography of Acciaiuoli's works. I also read what appears to be a section of a *tesi di laurea* by Daniella Gatti, "La *Vita Caroli* di Donato Acciaiuoli," *BISIme*, LXXXIX (1972–73).

119. Cesare Vasoli, "L'attesa della nuova era in ambienti e gruppi fiorentini del Quattrocento," in *L'attesa dell'età nuova nella spiritualità della fine del Medioevo* (Todi: Accademia Tudertina, 1962) (a very packed and learned essay). See also Felice Battaglia in *Il pensiero pedagogico del Rinascimento* (Florence: Sansoni, 1960), p. 104, Garin in *La cultura filosofica del Rinascimento italiano* (Florence: Sansoni, 1960), pp. 188 ff., and Donald Weinstein, both in "The Myth of Florence," in Nicolai Rubinstein, ed., *Florentine Studies* (London: Faber & Faber, 1968), and in *Savonarola and Florence* (Princeton University Press, 1970). On the *Liber Pontificalis*, see below, Chapter 2, n. 94.

120. Sermon on Job of 1496, quoted by Romeo De Maio in *Riforme e miti nella chiesa del '500* (Naples: Guida, 1973), p. 41.

121. Fonzio, *Epistolarum*, pp. 47–48: letter to Simone Cinozzo, c. 1500.

122. Described by Vasoli in "Temi mistici e profetici all fine del Quattrocento" in his *Studi sulla cultura del Rinascimento* (Manduria: Lacaita, 1968). Reflections of this attitude in popular pageantry as early as 1491 are recorded by Francesco Tateo in his *Lorenzo de' Medici e Angelo Poliziano* (Bari: Laterza, 1972), p. 64.

CHAPTER TWO

1. Biographical information in the introduction to Bartolomeo Nogara, ed., *Scritti inediti e rari di Biondo Flavio* (Vatican, 1927) and in the long, very informative article of Riccardo Fubini in *DBI*. The humanist character—as well as the political independence—of Biondo's work is further sustained by Eugenio Marino in "Eugenio IV e la storiografia di Flavio Biondo," *Memorie domenicane*, n.s., IV (1973). On Biondo I also read the Ph.D. dissertation (Berkeley, 1973) of Angelo Mazzocco, kindly lent me by the author.

2. Published by Nogara in *Scritti inediti*. See also below, Chapter 3, n. 56. I first read the text, with the relevant dedication to Francesco Foscari, in the edition bound with his *Roma Instaurata*, cited below at n. 18. It is also published in Graevius, vol. V[1].

3. *De Verbis Romanae Locutionis*, also published by Nogara.

4. Published with an introduction as Chapter 2 of Massimo Miglio's *Storiografia*

pontificia del Quattrocento (Bologna: Patron, 1975), a book I use extensively in the following pages, taking account, needless to say, of Fubini's review in *RSI,* LXXXIX (1977), 172–74. Brief biographical notes in the introduction to Lapo's *Dialogus de Curiae Commodis* published by Eugenio Garin in the Ricciardi *Prosatori latini del Quattrocento.* Fubini's article on Lapo for the *DBI* was in proof, but not yet published, when I rewrote this page.

5. I follow the text of *Historiarum ab Inclinatione Romanorum Imperii Decades* (Venice, 1484) as well as the modern translation by Achille Crespi (Forlì, 1964), with the help of Denys Hay, "Flavio Biondo and the Middle Ages," *Proceedings of the British Academy,* XLV (1959), the article by Fubini cited above at n. 1, and G. Romano, *Degli studi sul medio evo nella storiografia del Rinascimento in Italia* (Pavia, 1892).

6. Arnaldo Momigliano, "La caduta senza rumore di un impero nel 476 DC," *RSI,* LXXXV (1973). Biondo's concept of historical periods is put into a broad historiographical context in the still useful essay of Giorgio Falco, *La polemica sul Medio Evo* ("Biblioteca della Società Storica Subalpina," vol. CXLIII [Turin, 1932]).

7. Leodrisio Crivelli (on whom see below, n. 62, and Chapter 4), in his *De Vita Sfortiae, RIS¹,* vol. XIX, col. 627.

8. The abridgment was usually read in the sixteenth century in the translation of Lucio Fauno as *Le historie del Biondo de la declinazione ... ridotte in compendio da Papa Pio,* of which I used the edition of Venice, 1547—one of many.

9. What follows is largely dependent upon Roberto Weiss's *The Renaissance Discovery of Classical Antiquity,* cited above, Chapter 1, n. 95.

10. The relevant texts down to the mid-fourteenth century are partially edited by Roberto Valentini and Giuseppe Zucchetti in vol. III, and those through the fifteenth century in vol. IV, of *Codice topografico della città di Roma = FSI,* vols. XC–XCI (Rome, 1953).

11. On which see Braxton Ross, "Giovanni Colonna, Historian at Avignon," *Speculum,* XLV (1970).

12. On whom see F. Babinger, "Notes on Cyriac of Ancona and Some of His Friends," *JWCI,* XXV (1962). Full surveys of the abundant modern bibliography on Ciriaco, together with much valuable new information, is given by Roberto Weiss in "Ciriaco di Ancona in Oriente," in *Venezia e l'Oriente fra tardo Medio Evo e Rinascimento* (Florence: Sansoni, 1966), and by Gian Paolo Marchi in *IMU,* XI (1963), 317–18. The text of his brief *Itinerarium* was published by Lorenzo Mehus, with a long introduction, in Florence, 1742, from the original manuscript of 1443. Note also Carlo Claudio van Essen, "I *Commentaria* di Ciriaco d'Ancona," in *Il mondo antico nel Rinascimento* (Florence: Sansoni, 1958) (Atti del V Congresso Internazionale di Studi sul Rinascimento, 1956), and for one particular iconographical problem, Augusto Campana, "Giannozzo Manetti, Ciriaco d'Ancona e l'Arco di Traiano," *IMU,* II (1959).

13. See above, Chapter 1, n. 97.

14. Signorili's *Descriptio Urbis Romae* is published in vol. IV of the *Codice topografico* cited above at n. 10, along with the relevant passages from Petrarch, Dondi, and Vergerio.

15. "Primus omnium ex recentioribus": Onofrio Panvinio in preface to *Centum Libros Antiquitates,* published by Angelo Mai in *Spicilegium Romanum,* vol. VIII (Rome, 1843); on whom see below, chapters 15 and 16.

16. The first edition of Sextus Rufus I have found reference to is that of 1468 under the title of *De Historia Romae.* There are many fifteenth- as well as sixteenth-century editions and at least two Italian translations, those of Florence, 1550, and of Venice, 1560.

17. The text is published in vol. IV of the *Codice topografico* (above, n. 10).

18. I consulted *Roma Instaurata* in the edition of 1481 (no indication of place) and in the Venice, 1558, edition of Lucio Fauno's Italian translation. It has been studied in detail by Roberto Weiss in "Biondo Flavio archeologo," *Studi romagnoli,* XIV (1963), and by Dorothy Robathan in "Flavio Biondo's *Roma Instaurata,*" *Medievalia et Humanistica,* n.s., vol. I (1970).

19. I use the edition of Verona, 1482, as well as the Rome, 1558, edition of the translation by Lucio Fauno. For the details on its

genesis I follow Augusto Campana in "Passi inediti dell'*Italia Illustrata* di Biondo Flavio," *La rinascita,* I (1938).

20. Cited below, Chapter 3, n. 48.

21. On which see Gerald Strauss, *Sixteenth-Century Germany,* cited in the Prologue, n. 21.

22. I here follow Aulo Greco, "Monumenti e figure dell'umanesimo | romano," in *Aspetti dell'umanesimo a Roma* (Rome: Istituto di Studi Romani, 1959), and Pio Paschini, *Roma anel Rinascimento* (Bologna: Cappelli, 1940).

23. Monaldesco, *Annali, RIS*[1], vol. XII (a note in the text says the author lived for 115 years, which makes me suspect the accuracy even of the one date mentioned for him, 1327); *Historiae Romanae Fragmenta* (1327–55) in Muratori, *Antiquitates,* vol. III, on which: Francesco A. Ugolini, "La prosa degli *Historiae Romanae Fragmentata* e della cosiddetta *Vita di Cola di Rienzo,*" *Archivio della Società Romana di Storia Patria,* LVIII (1935), and, on the style, Natalino Sapengo in the 3d ed. of his *Il Trecento* in the Vallardi "Storia Letteraria" series, p. 557; *Diario attribuito a Gentile Delfino,* ed. Francesco Isoldi, *RIS*[2], vol. XXIV[2].

24. *Diarium Romanum, RIS*[1], vol. XXIV, and reedited by Isoldi as *Il diario romano di . . .* in *RIS*[2], vol. XXIV[5].

25. Ed. Isoldi in *RIS*[2], vol. XXIV[2].

26. Ed. Isoldi in appendix to the text cited in the preceding note; on which: M. Pelaez, "Paolo di Benedetto di Cola della Maestro," *Archivio della Società Romana di Storia Patria,* XIV (1893).

27. Ed. Oreste Tommasini in *FSI,* vol. V.

28. Ed. Diomede Toni (with a helpful survey of several other chronicles of the time) in *RIS*[1], vol. III[2].

29. Edited respectively by Giuseppe Chiesa and Paolo Piccolomini in *RIS*[2], vol. XXIII[5], appendix.

30. That is the chief reason why Riccardo Fubini told me to leave them out altogether. But since I mention chronicles in every other part of Italy, and since I had already taken the trouble to look these up, I have instead greatly abridged the description of them presented in my penultimate draft. This abridged version at least permits me to sus-

tain my. thesis concerning the very peculiar relationship that obtained between chronicle and history in Rome.

31. *Diario romano,* ed. Enrico Carusi, *RIS*[2], vol. XXIII[3].

32. *Liber Notarum,* ed. Enrico Celani, *RIS*[2], vol. XXXII[1] (two enormous volumes). Its widespread diffusion is indicated by the existence of two copies at Padua located by Giovanni Soranzo and described in *AMAcPat,* LXXI (1958–59), 140–56.

33. Giuseppe Calamari, *Un confidente di Pio II: Cardinale Iacopo Ammannati* (Rome-Milan: Augustea, 1932), which is drawn mostly from his extensive correspondence, as well as the article by Edith Pásztor in *DBI.*

34. I here refer to the dedication to Platina's *De Optimo Cive* printed along with his other minor works in the Venice, 1511, edition of his *De Vitis Maxi. Ponti. Historia Periocunda,* which is described below. Further information in the prefatory biography by the most recent editor of *Liber de Vita Christi ac Omnium Pontificum,* Giacinto Gaeda, in *RIS*[2], vol. III[1], which is the text I use henceforth.

35. Giuseppe Lesca, *Giovannantonio Campano, detto l'Episcopus Aprutinus* (Pontadera, 1892) and the much larger and more recent work by Flavio Di Bernardo, *Un vescovo umanista alla corte pontificia: Giannantonio Campana* (Rome: Gregoriana, 1975), which is put into a still broader context in the indispensable article by Riccardo Fubini, "Umanesimo curiale del Quattrocento: Nuovi studi su Giovann'Antonio Campano," *RSI,* LXXXVIII (1976), upon which I depend heavily in the rest of this chapter. I have also consulted Franz Rutger Hausmann's "Giovanni Antonio Campano" in *Römische historische Mitteilungen,* XII (1970), as well as his article in the *DBI* and the notes in Zeno: Voss, vol. II, pp. 196–202.

36. All the details in the rather disorganized but immense mine of information about the literary life of Rome in the late fifteenth century, Vladimiro Zabughin, *Giulio Pomponio Leto* (Rome: La Vita Letteraria, 1909).

37. In a letter to Paul II published in his *Opera Omnia* (Venice, 1502), pp. xxxv[v]–xxxvii[r].

38. Letter of Jacobus Antiquarius to Michele Ferno of 1494 about Campano inserted in the preface to the *Opera* cited in the preceding note.

39. Toward the end of Platina's *Proemium* as it appears in the 1511 edition cited above at n. 34.

40. *Descriptio Adventus Friderici III Imperatoris ad Paulum Papam II* in *RIS*[1], vol. XXIII.

41. *Sallustiana Recognitio... Explanatio Historieque* in Sallust, *Opera* (Lyon, 1526).

42. In Campano's *Opera Omnia*, cited above at n. 37, translated by Marc'Antonio Arrojo (identified only as a "spagnolo") as *Del modo et ordine nel governare* (Florence, 1574).

43. Benedetto Falconcini, *Vita del nobil' uomo e buon servo di Dio Raffaello Maffei detto il Volterrano*, written at the time of Urban VIII and published in Rome in 1722. On his translation of Procopius: Pio Paschini in *Rivista di storia della Chiesa in Italia,* VII (1953), 344–55.

44. Roberto Weiss, "Andrea Fulvio, antiquario romano," *Annali della Scuola Normale di Pisa,* ser. 2, vol. XXVIII (1959).

45. I take the biographical information from Soria. See below, n. 94 and Chapter 6, n. 92.

46. Biographical information in the preface to his *Le storie de' suoi tempi,* with an Italian translation on facing pages (Rome, 1883).

47. I follow the common practice of referring to him as Enea Silvio before his election and as Pius II thereafter except where the distinction might be confusing or inelegant. The most recent biography, R. J. Mitchell, *The Laurels and the Tiara* (London: Harvill Press, 1962), mentions the works only as sources for the life; but it includes a very helpful list of them in the appendix. Somewhat wider in scope is Berthe Widmer, *Enea Silvio Piccolomini in der sittlichen und politischen Entscheidung* (Basel-Stuttgart: Helbing & Lichtenhahn, 1963). The most succinct is Eugenio Garin, "Ritratto di Enea Silvio Piccolomini," in his *La cultura filosofica del Rinascimento italiano* (Florence: Sansoni, 1961).

48. I follow Remo Ceserani in "Note sull'attività di scrittore di Pio II," in

Domenico Maffei, ed., *Enea Silvio Piccolomini, Papa Pio II: Atti del Convegno per il V Centenario della morte* (Siena: Accademia degli Intronati, 1968), and Ceserini's review of Mitchell and Widmer in *GSLI,* CXLI (1964), 265–82.

49. Published in *Bibliothek des Literarischen Vereins in Stuttgart,* I (1843).

50. I read the text in the Basel edition of Pius II, *Opera Omnia* (Basel, 1551). See now Nicola Casella, "Pio II tra geografia e storia," *Archivio della Società Romana di Storia Patria,* XCV (1972).

51. See Constance Head, "Pope Pius II as a Student of English History," *Archivum Historiae Pontificiae,* IX (1971).

52. Note Fausto da Longiano's preface to his translation dated Padua, 1543, and published in Venice in 1544.

53. I use the edition with translation by Denys Hay and W. K. Smith (Oxford: Clarendon, 1967) with a very helpful introduction. The *De Rebus Basileae Gestis* is published in *Fontes Rerum Austriacarum,* ser. 2, vols. LXI–LXVIII (1908–18).

54. *De Situ, Ritu, Moribus et Conditione Germaniae Descriptio* I read in the edition (with German translation) by Adolf Schmidt (Köln-Graz: Böhlau, 1962) rather than in the edition (with Italian translation) by Gioacchino Paperelli (Florence: Fusi, 1949) for the reasons given by Schmidt in his long and informative preface; but I read it taking account of the reservations of Ceserini in the article cited above at n. 48.

55. Victor Bayer, *Die 'Historia Friderici III Imperatoris' des Enea de' Piccolomini* (Prague, 1872). The famous description of Vienna contained therein has recently been published separately as *Vienna nel '400* with an Italian translation by Baccio Ziliotto (Trieste: Ed. dello Zibaldone, 1958). I read the *Historia Bohemica* in Italian translation as *Le historie, costumi et successi della nobilissima provincia delli Boemi* (Venice, 1545). The original text is in the Basel edition of the *Opera Omnia.*

56. André Desguine, *L'incunable 'De Captione Urbis Constantinopolitanae'...* (Paris: D'Argences, 1963).

57. The passages here quoted in English come from the translation of the *Commentaries of Pius II* by F. A. Gragg and L. C.

Gabel in the Smith College Studies in History, now available in an abridged paperback edition (Capricorn Giant). The only modern Italian edition is that of Giuseppe Bernetti (Siena: Cantagalli, 1973), in four volumes.

58. P. J. Jones, *The Malatesta of Rimini and the Papal State* (Cambridge University Press, 1974), p. 235.

59. By Leodrisio Crivelli in the work cited below at n. 62, p. 3. His suggestion of Augustine as an ancient model equivalent to Caesar is not so surprising in the light of what Tito Orlandi writes in "Il *De Civitate Dei* di Agostino e la storiografia di Roma," *Studi romani,* XVI (1968).

60. Above, n. 2.

61. Above, Chapter 1, n. 91.

62. *De Expeditione Pii Papae II adversos Turcos,* first published by Muratori in 1733 and more recently by Giulio C. Zimolo in *RIS²,* vol. XXIII⁵. On which, see L. F. Smith, "Lodovico Crivelli of Milan and Aeneas Sylvius, 1457–64," *SR,* IX (1962).

63. Described by Rino Avesani in *RSCI,* XXVIII (1974). On the sequel to this episode, see below, Epilogue, n. 12.

64. On which, see below, Chapter 4, n. 42.

65. *De Origine Maomethis* published together with Robertus Mamachius, *Bellum Christianorum contra Saracinos* (Basel, 1533).

66. I follow the text in his *Epistolae et Commentarii* (Milan, 1506). On the author, see above, n. 33.

67. Cited above, n. 46.

68. Cited above, n. 40.

69. Above, n. 43.

70. *De Institutione Christiana ad Leonem X P. M. Libri VIII* (Rome, 1518).

71. *De Bello Persico . . . et Vandalico,* which I found together with other translations and adaptations (including Bruni's) in a collection with a dedicatory letter by Beatus Rhenanus to Bonifacius Amerbach printed in Basel in 1531. I also consulted the Rome, 1509, edition of *De Bello Persico* with Volterrano's letter in praise of Belisarius and Justinian.

72. The *Epitome* was first published at Basel in 1557; but I consulted it in the edition of Ludovicus Dindorfius in the *Bibliotheca Scriptorum Graecorum et Romanorum* (Leipzig, 1868).

73. I use the edition of Lyon, 1552.

74. See above, Chapter 1, n. 112.

75. Alberti's *Vita S. Politi* is published by Cecil Grayson in *Opuscoli inediti di Leon Battista Alberti* (Nuova collezione di testi umanistici inediti o rari, ed. A. Mancini and P. O. Kristeller, vol. X) (Florence: Olschki, 1954). My main source of information on Agli is the article by Arnaldo D'Addario in *DBI;* the relevant texts are published in the book by Miglio cited above at n. 4.

76. Fubini in *Studi medievali,* XVIII (1977), 340.

77. Agostino Sottili, "Zur Biographie Giuseppe Brivios und Matteo Vegios," *Mittellateinisches Jahrbuch,* IV (1967). Luigi Raffaele in *Maffeo Vegio* (Bologna: Zanichelli, 1907) says that Vegio's *Vita B. Monicae* (unlike the *Vita B. Augustini*) was printed; but he does not say where, and I have been unable to find it. The life of Bernardino (c. 1543) I read in *Acta Sanctorum,* May, *die* 20; and I read about it in Remo L. Guidi, "Maffei Vegio agiografo di s. Bernardino da Siena," in his *Aspetti religiosi nella letteratura del Quattrocento* (Studi e testi francescani, vol. LIV) (Vicenza: L.I.E.F., 1974), vol. II.

78. Volterrano's *Vita* is published in Sivano Razzi's *Le vite de' santi e beati dell'Ordine di Camaldoli* (Florence, 1600). My information on Diedo comes from Zeno: Voss, vol. II, pp. 56 ff.

79. Therefore, see Chapter 15 below.

80. See above, Chapter 1, n. 92.

81. Among the many surviving editions, I happen to have used his *De Re Magistratibus, Sacerdotiis et Legibus . . . Libellus* (Basel, 1535), bound (as it almost always was) with Fiocchi's *De Magistratibus.* I read the *Compendio del'historia romana* (sic) in the translation of Francesco Baldelli (Venice, 1549) and the *Antiquità di Roma* in the translation of Gianluca Papera (Venice, 1550).

82. J. Ruysschaert's article on Albertini in *DBI* is based largely on the article by C. Olschki in *Roma,* II (1924). I therefore follow rigorously the *DBI* rule of using initials in the place of first names.

83. I use the modern offset edition of the original (1510) with dedication to the king of Portugal—unfortunately without indication of date or place of publication—in the Biblioteca Nazionale of Florence.

84. The *Memoriale* I also read in an anonymous offset edition of 1932.

85. Published along with the *Septem Mirabilia* in Jacopo Mazochi, ed., *De Roma Prisca et Nova Varii Auctores* (Rome, 1523).

86. Published in the same *De Roma* cited in the preceding note.

87. Discovered, described, and partially published by Giovanni Mercati in his *Opere minori* (Vatican, 1937–41), vol. IV, pp. 437–59.

88. I read the *Antiquitates* in the translation of Paolo dal Rosso (Venice, 1543). I quote Weiss on Fulvio from the article cited above at n. 44.

89. Above, chapter 1, n. 90 and n. 113.

90. On whom I follow the authorities cited above at n. 35. On what follows, my main guide is the collection of essays by Miglio cited above at n. 4, which are put into historical context by Fubini in his fundamental "Papato e storiografia nel Quattrocento: Storia, biografia e propaganda in un recente studio," *Studi medievali*, XVIII (1977), from which I have already quoted several times.

91. First published in Rome, 1495; but I use the modern edition by Roberto Valentini in *RIS²*, vol. XIX⁴, as *Bracii Perusini Vita ac Gesta*.

92. Both are published by Giulio C. Zimolo in *RIS³*, vol. III², and discussed further in Zimolo's articles, "Il Campano e il Platina come biografi di Pio II," in the *Atti . . . Convegno* cited above at n. 48, and "La *Vita Pii II P. M.* del Platina," in *Studi in onore di Carlo Castiglioni* (Milan: Giuffrè, 1967).

93. Published together by Giuseppe Zippel in *RIS²*, vol. III¹⁶ and discussed at length in several of Miglio's essays.

94. I consulted the *Liber Pontificalis* in the edition of L. Duchesne (Paris, 1886–92) and the introduction to Louise Roper Loomis's English translation (Columbia University Press, 1966). On the humanist historians' use of it, I read Giuseppe Billanovich, "Gli umanisti e le croniche medioevali," *IMU, I* (1958). For background: Ottorino Bertolini, "Il *Liber Pontificalis*," in the volume *La Storiografia altomedioevale*, cited above in the Prologue, n. 26. Lignamine's continuation of Riccobaldo (on which see below, Chapter 4,

n. 35) was first published in Rome, 1474, and reprinted in *RIS¹*, vol. IX, with a preface by Muratori. On Zeno, see below, Chapter 3, n. 58.

95. I read the *Vita di Vittorino da Feltre* in the edition of Giuseppe Biasuz (Padua: Liviana, 1948) and the *Vita Nerii Capponi*, discovered and published as an original work by Anton Francesco Gori in Florence, 1722, in *RIS¹*, vol. XX, where Muratori correctly identifies it as a translation.

96. I compared Platina with Marco Tabarrini's edition (with a very informative introduction) of the *Annales Ptolomaei Lucensis, DSI*, vol. VI. The editor notes the passages that Tolomeo borrowed from Martinus. On this see below, Chapter 5, n. 5. That Platina's methodological and substantive problems have not yet been solved is indicated by Karl Bosl, "Papstgeschichte als Problem historischer Theorie," *Zeitschrift für bayerische Geschichte*, XXX (1970).

97. I compared Platina with Paulus Diaconus in William Dudley Foulke's English translation (University of Pennsylvania Press, 1907), which refers to preceding scholarly editions.

98. I use the English rather than the Latin or the Italian title here because the latter varies considerably from one edition to the next. I originally read the text in the edition cited above at n. 34, which contains Volterrano's continuation, and then in the modern *RIS²* edition cited in the same note. A *Vita* of Platina by Nicol'Angelo Caferri (the source of much of my biographical information) is included in the edition with the continuations published in Venice in 1685.

99. All fully described below in Chapters 14 and 16.

100. John Headley, *Luther's View of Church History* (Yale University Press, 1963), p. 45.

101. Virginia F. Stern in *RQ, XXV* (1972), 12.

102. *Historia Urbis Mantuae Gonziacaeque Familiae, RIS¹*, vol. XX; on which see below, Chapter 4.

103. The relevant passages from the *Lives* are given by Eugenio Garin in *Prosatori latini del Quattrocento*, p. 695.

104. Letter to Panormita in the introduction to Panormita's *De Dictis et Factis*

Alphonsi, cited below, Chapter 5, n. 85; but I read it in Pius's *Opera Omnia,* p. 490.

105. In the introduction to his *Compendio dell'historia romana,* cited above at n. 81.

106. See John O'Malley, "Historical Thought and the Reform Crisis of the Early Sixteenth Century," *Theological Studies,* XXVIII (1967).

107. O'Malley, "Fulfillment of the Christian Golden Age under Pope Julius II," *Traditio,* XXV (1969).

CHAPTER THREE

1. Quoted by Roberto Cessi in *Storia di Venezia,* which I read both in the first edition (Milan-Messina: Principato, 1944) and in the second (Centro delle Arti e del Costume, 1957). On the relations between the two cities, I follow Francesco Surdich in his *Genova e Venezia fra Tre e Quattrocento* (Genoa: Bozzi, 1970). I would have followed it more easily had it been furnished with an index.

2. The most recent text is that of Luigi Tommaso Belgrano in *FSI,* vol. XI, which is based on the more authoritative Paris MS rather than on the defective copy used by Muratori (whom the Genoese government barred from the archives) for the first edition. In general: Girolamo Arnaldi, "Uno sguardo agli annali genovesi," in appendix to his *Studi sui cronisti della Marca Trevigiana,* cited below at n. 17, and "Il notaio cronista e le cronache cittadine in Italia," in *La storia del diritto nel quadro delle scienze sociali* (Atti del I Congresso Internazionale della Società Italiana di Storia di Diritto) (Florence: Olschki, 1966), pp. 293–309. The role of Caffaro and his successors in Genoese society of the late Middle Ages is made clear by Giorgio Costamagna in *Il notaio a Genova tra prestigio e potere* (Rome: Consiglio Nazionale del Notariato, 1970); but the reader should keep in mind what Anthony Molho says about the book in *RQ,* XXVI (1973), 53–54. An indispensable guide to the subject treated in the next pages is Giovanna Petti Baldi, "La storiografiia genovese fino al secolo XV," in *Studi sul medioevo cristiano offerti a Raffaello Morghen* (cited above, Chapter 1, n. 40), vol. II.

3. Ed. Luigi Tommaso Belgrano and Cesare Imperiale di Sant'Angelo in *FSI,* vol. XII.

4. Ed. Imperiale, *FSI,* vols. XIII–XIV, but according to Leopoldo Valle in *Per una nuova edizione veramente critica degli Annali di Iacopo D'Oria* (Genoa: Artigianelli, 1933), with numerous errors of transcription inherited from the earlier Pertz edition in *MGH,* vol. XVIII.

5. Or even until 1941, to judge from the many pages dedicated by his most recent editor, Giovanni Monleone, to the question of how to spell his name in the padded 516-page introduction to the chronicle in *FSI,* vols. LXXXIV (Introduction)–LXXXV (text).

6. These paragraphs are based largely on the thorough monographic researches of Gina Fasoli, Giorgio Cracco, Antonio Carile, and Girolamo Arnaldi (especially with regard to Andrea Dandolo), edited by Agostino Pertusi in *La storiografia veneziana fino al secolo XVI* (Florence: Olschki, 1969) (a volume far broader in scope than the title suggests), of which see the long review by Silvana Collodo in *AV,* CI (1970), 12–30; on Hans Baron, "Early Renaissance Venetian Chronicles," in his *From Petrarch to Leonardo Bruni;* and on Roberto Cessi, "Studi sopra la composizione del cosiddetto *Chronicon Altinate,*" *BISIme,* XLIX (1933). Further bibliography of recent scholarship is given by David Robey and John Law in "The Venetian Myth and the *De Republica Veneta* of Vergerio," *Rinascimento,* XV (1975). On Alberto Limentani's recent edition of Martino, see the editor's own "Martino da Canal e l'Oriente," in Agostino Pertusi, ed., *Venezia e l'Oriente fino al secolo XV* (Fondazione Cini, Studi no. 27) (Florence: Olschki, 1974), vol. II.

7. Edited by Ester Pastorello in *RIS²,* vol. XII¹, on which Enrico Simonsfeld, "Andrea Dandolo e le sue opere storiche," *AV,* ser. 1, vol. XIV (1887) (mostly a philological study of the variants). Dandolo's sources are listed, and the abundant borrowings from Paulus Diaconus are revealed, by Girolamo Tartarotti in *RIS¹,* vol. XXV.

8. On Dondi: Ezio Franceschini in his *Scritti di filologia latina medievale.* The numbers are given by Maria Zannoni in "Le fonti...di Giorgio Dolfin," *AIVSLA,* CI² (1942) (see also n. 39 below). On this and on what follows: Hans Baron, "A Forgotten

Chronicle of the Early Fifteenth Century," in *Essays in History and Literature Presented to Stanley Pargellis,* ed. Heinz Bluhm (Chicago: The Newberry Library, 1965). On the decree of the Maggior Consiglio of 18 December 1291, which shows that "the governing class of the republic already had a mature sense of history," see Carile in *SV,* LX (1967), 103.

9. *Venetiarum Historia,* ed. Roberto Cessi and Fanny Bennato (Monumenti storici pubblicati dalla Deputazione di Storia Patria per le Venezie, n.s., vol. XVIII; Venice, 1964).

10. On Morosini, see the biography by G. Lefèvre-Pontalis in vol. IV of his edition of Léon Dorez's translation (the only published version) of those parts of the chronicle that regard France: *Chronique d'Antoine Morosini: Extraits rélatifs à l'histoire de France* (Paris, 1898–1902). On Dolfin, see below, n. 40.

11. Carile, "Note di cronachista veneziana: Piero Giustinian e Nicolò Trevisan," *SV,* IX (1967).

12. Raphaynus de Caresinis, *Chronica,* ed. Ester Pastorello, *RIS²,* vol. XII².

13. Vincenzo Joppi, ed., "Chronachetta veneziana dal 1402 al 1415," *AV,* XVII (1879).

14. Alberto Ghinato, *Fra Paolino da Venezia, OFM* (reprinted from *Le Venezie francescane,* XVI [1949] and XVII [1950], in Rome, 1951), and Dora Franceschi, "Fra Paolino da Venezia," *AASTor,* XCVIII² (1963–64), as well as Ester Pastorello's resume of the earlier studies of Simonfeld in her preface to Andrea Dandolo cited above at n. 7.

15. Marin Sanudo (often called "Il Vecchio" to distinguish him from the later chronicler-historian of the same name), *Liber Secretorum Fidelium Crucis* in offset reproduction of the 1st ed. in Bongartii, *Gesta Dei per Francos* of 1611 by Joshua Prawer, with an introduction (University of Toronto Press, 1972). Much pertinent information is in Aldo Cerlini's edition of "Nuove lettere di Marin Sanudo il Vecchio," *La bibliofilia,* XLII (1940). Selections from Sanudo's unpublished history of Romania (Greece) are edited by Carlo Hopf (Naples, 1862). Hopf seems never to have fulfilled his promise to publish the whole work. On all this, see Raymond-J. Loenerts, "Pour une édition

nouvelle...," *SV,* XVI (1974). On what follows concerning the Fourth Crusade, the latest study is by Donald Queller and Gerald Day, "Some Arguments in Defense of the Venetians..." *American Historical Review,* LXXXI (1976), as well as Queller and Susan Stratton, "A Century of Controversy on the Fourth Crusade," *Studies in Medieval and Renaissance History,* VI (1969).

16. "Cronaca di Giovan Antonio di Faie," discovered by accident by Jacopo Bicchierai in his family's house in Bagnone in 1860 and edited by him in *ASLigSP,* X (1874), 513–605. The names of the two chroniclers of Savona are mentioned by G. B. Spotorno in vol. II of his *Storia letteraria della Liguria* (Genoa, 1825); but even Spotorno could find no trace of the texts.

17. My chief authority for the paragraphs that follow is Girolamo Arnaldi in his papers printed in *Studi ezzeliniani* and in his *Studi sui cronisti della Marca Trevigiana,* both published (with frequent repetitions of the same passages) in the "Studi storici" of the Istituto Storico Italiano per il Medio Evo, vols. XLV–XLVII and XLVIII–L (1963).

18. *Cronica Dominorum Ecelini et Alberici Fratrum de Romano,* ed. Giovanni Soranzo in *RIS²,* vol. VIII².

19. I use the edition of Muratori in *RIS¹,* vol. VIII. On the identification of the author: Luigi Alfredo Botteghi, "Degli 'Annales Sanctae Justinae Patavini'" (which is the name incorrectly given the chronicle in the *MHG* edition, vol. XIX [1866]), *BISIme,* I.

20. Rolandini Patavini *Cronica Marche Trivixane,* ed. Antonio Bonardi, *RIS²,* vol. VIII¹—on whom, and on other Paduan chroniclers: Giuseppe Vedova, *Biografia degli scrittori padovani* (Padua, 1832) (in alphabetical order). All the Paduan chronicles are listed in the Appendix to vol. I of Attilio Simioni, *Storia di Padova* (Padua: Randi, 1968).

21. Alberti Mussati paduani..., *De Gestis Henrici VII Caesaris, Historia Augusta, XVI Libris Comprehensa, RIS¹,* vol. X; *Il principato di Giacomo da Carrara...: Narrazione scelta dalle storie inedite di Albertino Mussato,* ed. anon. *per nozze* (Padua, 1891), and *Sette libri inediti del 'De Gestis Italicorum Post Henricum VII',* ed. Luigi Padrin in the series Monumenti storici of the Deputazione Veneta di Storia Patria, ser. 3, vol. III. For bio-

graphical information: the long-winded *Della vita e delle opere di A.M.* by Michele Minoia (Rome, 1884), and other titles given at n. 36 below.

22. *Le opere di Ferreto de'Ferreti,* ed. Carlo Cipolla, *FSI,* vols. XLII–XLIII (1908–12). For biographical information: the 43-page essay with numerous repetitions of Guido Manera, *Ferreto dei Ferreti, preumanista vicentino* (Vicenza, 1949), and Giovanni Mantese, "Nuovi documenti su F. de' F.," *AV,* XCII (1971).

23. Another example: much of the anonymous *Vita et gesti d'Ezzelino terzo da Romano,* which Arnaldi has now shown actually to have been written in the fourteenth century and merely polished, not forged (as Muratori thought), by Fausto da Longiano in 1543 and which he has published in an appendix to his *Studi sui cronisti* cited above at n. 17, is simply translated from Rolandino.

24. *Chronicon Veronense, RIS¹,* vol. VIII.

25. Note William Bouwsma in "Lawyers and Early Modern Culture," *American Historical Review,* LXXVIII (1973), esp. p. 325. On notaries and jurists "as guardians of an ancient and cosmopolitan legal *ordo,*" see Julius Kirshner, "Some Problems in the Interpretation of Legal Texts," *Archiv für Begriffsgeschichte,* XX (1975).

26. Guillelmi de Cortusiis *Chronica de Novitate Padue et Lombardie,* ed. Beniamino Pagnin, *RIS²,* vol. XII⁵.

27. *Frammenti di storia vicentina,* ed. Carlo Steiner, *RIS²,* vol. XIII¹. On Conforto—and on the other chroniclers of Vicenza from Gerardo Maurisio on, I have taken note of Lodovico Gonzati, "Delle cronache antiche di Vicenza," *Atti dell'Accademia Olimpica di Vicenza,* II (1872), and the various biographies in alphabetical order in the still standard *Biblioteca e storia di quei scrittori . . . di Vicenza* by Angiolgabriello di Santa Maria (Vicenza, 1782).

28. No one seems to know anything about Pier Zagata—not even Scipione Maffei, who does not mention him in the biographical sections of his *Verona illustrata* (Verona 1731–32), vol. II. But the first part of the chronicle written by him and then continued by others was written apparently shortly after 1375 and was edited and published by Giambattista Biancolini (Verona, 1745) in 3 vols.

29. I consulted Smeregli's *Annales Civitatis Vincentiae,* which is essentially a continuation of Maurisio, and Godi's *Cronaca* in the editions of Soranzo in *RIS²,* vol. VIII⁵ ᵃⁿᵈ ². The thesis of Clemente Miari (b.c. 1360) is much the same, according to the description of his still unpublished chronicle of Belluno by Francesco Pellegrini in *AV,* II (1871).

30. The results of modern criticism of Pagliarini since the first researches of Domenico Bortolan are presented by Soranzo in his preface to Goldi cited in the preceding note. But some of his errors were already obvious to Gonzati (above, n. 27). I follow the text of *Chroniche di Vicenza* published in Vicenza in 1663. Biographical information is in Zeno: Voss, vol. I, pp. 124–27.

31. *Cronaca di anonimo veronese (1446–1448),* ed. Soranzo (Venice: Deputazione Veneta di Storia Patria, 1915).

32. Gatari's *Cronaca carrarese* is published by Antonio Medi and Guido Tolomei in *RIS²,* vol. XVII¹, together with the fourteenth-century *Gesta Domus Carrariensis,* ed. Roberto Cessi. I follow Vittorio Lazzarini in "Il diario della Guerra di Chioggia e la cronaca di Galeazzo Gatari," *AV,* XII (1896). The *Liber Memorialis* (1174–1399) is published by Muratori in *Antiquitates,* vol. IV. I read Savonarola's *Commentariolus de Laudibus Patavii* in *RIS¹,* vol. XXIV, which is the first edition. A further note on the discovery of Livy's body is given in Cesira Gasparotto's article in *AMAcPat,* LXXX (1967–68), 125–38; the official report of the discovery is in appendix to Paolo Sambin's *Ricerche di storia monastica medioevale* (Padua: Antenore, 1959), p. 164. All my information about Giovan Michele Alberto da Carrara comes from Zeno: Voss, vol. II, pp. 27–31, which, on pp. 61–62, also mentions Michele Cavicchia's "raccolto cronologico delle cose di sua patria."

33. *Memorie delle guerre contro la signoria di Venezia, 1437–1468, RIS¹,* vol. XXI (Italianized version).

34. Rizzoni's continuation of Zagata, cited above at n. 28, *ad annum* 1405. On Rizzoni's education and career as a humanist, I consulted Gian Paolo Marchi, "Due corrispondenti veronesi di Ciriaco d'Ancona," *IMU,* XI (1968).

35. Daniele di Chinazzo, *Cronica de la guerra da Veniciani a Zenovesi*, ed. Vittorio Lazzarini in the *Monumenti storici* of the Deputazione di Storia Patria per le Venezie, n.s., vol. XI (1958). On Manelmi's *Commentariolum de Obsidione Brixiae* I follow Gianni Zippel in "Lorenzo Valla e le origini della storiografia umanistica a Venezia," *Rinascimento*, VII (1956) (below, n. 57). Malvezzi's *Chronicum Brixianum* is published in *RIS¹*, vol. XIV. Andrea de Redusiis, *Chronicon Tarvisinum*, *RIS¹*, vol. XIX (only the years after 1368 are published in this edition). Similar problems of attribution are presented by Soranzo in "Cronaca sconosciuta del secolo XV," *AV*, ser. 3, vol. XIII (1907).

36. On Boncompagno: Antonio Pini in *DBI*, and Giulio Zimolo, "Di un nuovo codice dell' *Assedio di Ancona* di Maestro Boncompagno," *BSISme*, LV (1941). On Mussato as a prehumanist: Manlio Dazzi, "Il Mussato storico," *AV*, ser. 5, vol. VI (1929), now republished with his other subsequent studies of Mussato in *Il Mussato preumanista* (Venice: Neri Pozza, 1964); in the context of the whole Paduan environment, the last pages of J. K. Hyde, *Padua in the Age of Dante* (University of Manchester Press, 1966), with a list of all the contemporary chronicles in appendix; Baron, *The Crisis of the Early Italian Renaissance*, 1st ed., vol. I, pp. 101–20; Giuseppe Billanovich, *I primi umanisti e le tradizioni dei classici latini* (Freibourg, 1953); and Attilo Simioni, *Storia di Padova dalle origini alla fine del secolo XVIII* (above, n. 20). Prehumanist elements are also observable in the Paduan chronicles that succeeded and drew on Rolandino and Mussato in the fourteenth century—e.g., the Latin dedication to Francesco II of the judicial notary Bernardo da Caselle (ca. 1300–after 1376) for his compilation of earlier chronicles entitled *Gesta Magnifica Domus Carrariensis* (to 1350) and of the chancellor Nicoletto di Alessio, a friend of Petrarch and Vergerio, for his *Storia della guerra per i confini* (almost a humanist commentary in form). But that the fifteenth century represented a break with the past and not a necessary development of the chronicle tradition is demonstrated once again by the retrogressive character of Nicoletto's continuer, the anonymous author of the *Ystoria de mesier Francesco Zovene*, who, as soon as he stops copying Nicoletto and takes off on his own, breaks down into the usual choppy paragraphs with no continuity among them: "Chomo fo presa Yoza [Chioggia]," "Chomo fo habù Trieste." All are edited by Roberto Cessi in the many *fascicules* of *RIS²*, vol. XVII¹.

37. First published in Graevius, vol. VI³, then in *RIS¹*, vol. XVI, and most recently by Attilio Gnesotto in *AMAcPat*, XLI (1925), 327–475, with preface and index. The latest word on the question of sources, date, and authenticity is by Carmela Marchente, *Ricerche intorno al "De Principibus . . . attribuito a Pier Paolo Vergerio* (Padua: CEDAM, 1946), which draws biographical data from the article by Leonardo Smith, editor of Vergerio's published correspondence, in *AV*, ser. 5, vol. IV (1928), 82–141. It should be noted, however, that Pertusi puts the date of composition at 1412, which would seriously undermine the interpretation I present here, and that Cessi questions the attribution (he speaks only of "l'autore del componimento vergeriano") and denies its historiographical value ("privo di ogni originalità storica"), *RIS²*, vol. XVI¹, part 2, p. xxviii. The chronicle source mentioned in the next sentence is described by Sante Bortolani in "Per la storia della storiografia comunale: Il *Chronicon de Potestatibus Paduae*," *AV*, CVI (1975).

38. Note his letter of presentation of December 1352 printed on p. civ of the edition of Andrea Dandolo cited above at n. 7. On the plagiarization of the *Gesta* (above, n. 32): Cessi in "Alcune osservazioni critiche sulle cronache carraresi prima e seconda del secolo XIV," *AM*, I (1904).

39. Maria Zannoni, "Giorgio Dolfin, cronista veneziano del sec. XV," *AMAcPat*, LVIII (1941–42). Other references are given above at n. 8. Part of Zorzi's chronicle is edited by G. M. Thomas (with a brief explanatory postscript) as "Die Eroberung Constantinopels aus einer venetianischer Chronik," *SBBayAW*, II¹ (1898).

40. Pietro Dolfin, *Annali Venetorum*, ed. Roberto Cessi and Paolo Sambin in the series Diarii veneziani del secolo decimosesto (Venice: Istituto Veneto di Scienze, Lettere ed Arti, 1943).

41. *RIS¹*, vol. XVI. Adrianna Razzolini,

"Sulla inedita cronaca veneziana attribuita a Filippo di Domenico," *AIVSLA,* CXXIX (1970–71). On the primacy of patriotism as a motive among Venetian historians even in the late sixteenth century, note Foscarini, vol. I, p. 266, apropos of Luigi Contarini.

42. Quoted from Platina's *Vita di Vittorino da Feltre,* ed. Giuseppe Biasuz (Padua: Liviana, 1948).

43. Remigio Sabbadini, *Giovanni da Ravenna* (Como, 1924). Giovanni's comments on the paucity of historiography in Venice are noted by Labalme on p. 253 of the book cited below at n. 61. The beginnings of an interest in humanism among the patricians are described by Percy Gothein in "Zaccaria Trevisan il Vecchio, La vita e l'ambiente," Deputazione di Storia Patria per le Venezie, *Miscellanea di studi e memorie,* vol. IV (1942). The appropriate remarks of Guarino are to be found in his letters of XIV Kal. Mar. 1428, which is no. 439 in Sabbadini's edition of his *Epistolario* (Deputazione Veneta di Storia Patria, 1915): "Adde quod cum historia lux veritas esse debeat...."

44. Bruno Nardi in "Letteratura e cultura veneziana del '400," in *La civiltà veneziana del Rinascimento* (Florence: Sansoni, 1958), and more extensively in his *Saggi sulla cultura veneta del Quattro e Cinquecento* (Padua: Antenore, 1971).

45. From Book I, Chapter 1 of Giorgio Stella, *Annales Genuenses, RIS¹,* vol. XVII (with the continuations). On the author: Giovanna Balbi, "Giorgio Stella e gli *Annales Genuenses, MSLig,* II (1961).

46. Quoted from letter no. 27, published with the other letters to Biondo et al. by Giovanna Balbi in *L'epistolario di Iacopo Bracelli* (Genoa: Fratelli Bozzi, 1969). The absence of personal diaries in Genoa is noted by Jacques Heers on p. 5 of his *Gênes au XVe Siècle* (Paris: SEVPEN, 1961). The importance of the example of the Florentines, and especially of Giannozzo Manetti, in attracting the Genoese to historiography is emphasized by Giangiacomo Musso in "Politica e cultura in Genova alla metà del Quattrocento," *Miscellanea di studi liguri in onore di Giorgio Falco* (Milan: Feltrinelli, 1962).

47. Carlo Braggio, "Giacomo Bracelli e l'umanesimo dei Liguri al suo tempo,"

ASLigSP, XXIII (1890). For a much briefer but also more comprehensive biographical sketch, see that by Cecil Grayson in *DBI.*

48. *Orae Ligusticae Descriptio* (above, Chapter 2, n. 20) and *De Claris Genuensibus* are printed together in the same slim but elegant volume with *Hispaniensis Belli Libri,* edited by Bracelli's admiring successor of the following century, Agostino Giustiniani (Paris, 1520), which is the edition (one of many) that I use.

49. All the works are printed together with *De Rebus Genuensium,* ed. Emilio Pandiani, *RIS²,* vol. XXIII¹.

50. Franz Babinger, "Die Aufzeichnungen des Genuesen Iacopo de Promontorio- de Campis über den Osmanenstaat um 1475," *SBBayAW* (1956)¹.

51. Quoted by Emilio Pandiani in his preface to the now standard edition of the *De Rebus Genuensibus Commentaria, RIS²,* vol. XXIV⁸.

52. Mario Poppi, "Ricerche sulla vita e cultura del notaio e cronista veneziano Lorenzo de Monacis, cancelliere cretese," *SV,* IX (1967), contains all that can possibly be discovered about his little-known life and a complete bibliography on previous studies of him, although the article in Foscarini (vol. I, p. 230–39) is still valuable, particularly with regard to De Monacis's sources. His anti-Hellenic prejudices are noted by Deno J. Geanakoplos in *SR,* XXI (1974), 131, as well as in his *Greek Scholars in Venice* (Harvard University Press, 1962), p. 39.

53. Above, n. 19.

54. The parts on Ezzelino were prepared for publication by Felice Osio in the early seventeenth century and published in *RIS¹,* vol. VIII. The complete text exists only in the very rare edition of Venice, 1758.

55. Agostino Pertusi, "Le fonti greche del *De Gestis," IMU,* VIII (1965), of which the main theses are presented again in his essay on "Gli inizi della storiografia umanistica nel Quattrocento," published in the volume he edited cited above at n. 6, which I follow closely in the following paragraphs.

56. On Biondo: above, Chapter 2, n. 2. J. Marius Philelphus, *Vita Dantis Aligherii,* ed. (the first) Domenico Moreni (Florence, 1828), dedicated to Dante's descendant, Pietro Alighieri.

57. *Commentariolus de Quibusdam Gestis in Bello Gallico . . . , seu De Obsidione Brixiae . . . ,* ed. Giannandrea Astezati (Brescia, 1728). On the author, see also above, n. 35. Every possible archival document (and not much else) regarding Manelmi is collected as part of an interminable argument about the authenticity of the text in Angiolgabriello di Santa Maria, *Biblioteca* (above, n. 27), pp. xliv ff.

58. Jacopo Zeno's life of Albergati is published in *Acta Sanctorum,* May, vol. II, pp. 469–77; his *Vita Caroli Zeni* is in *RIS¹,* vol. XIX. See above, Chapter 2.

59. *De Rebus in Hetruria a Senensibus Gestis,* ed. Giovan Michele Bruto (Lyon, 1562).

60. Letters of Kal. Sept. 1483 and 8 Kal. Quint. 1484, vol. I, pp. 43–44 and 54 of Barbaro's *Epistolae, Orationes et Carmina,* ed. Vittore Branca (Florence: Bibliopolis, 1943).

61. Ample biographical notices in the sixteenth-century *Vita* by Antonio Stella (Venice, 1553) as well as in Foscarini and Zeno: Voss, vol. II, pp. 154–62. Still more (although without a critical assessment of his work) in Patricia H. Labalme, *Bernardo Giustiniani, a Venetian of the Quattrocento* (Rome: Edizioni di Storia e Letteratura, 1969), which has the particular advantage for my purposes of being chronicle rather than history.

62. Bernardo Giustinian, *Vita di s. Lorenzo Giustinian,* which I read in the anonymous Italian translation of Venice, 1712.

63. I follow Lodovico Domenichi's translation as *Historia . . . dell'origine di Vinegia e delle cose fatte da Vinitiani* (Venice, 1545).

64. *De Divi Marci Evangelistae Vita . . . ,* in Graevius, vol. V¹ (where the Latin text of the Historia is also conveniently printed).

65. *Itinerario . . . per la terraferma veneziana nell'anno 1483,* ed. Rawdon Brown (but with errors in transcription) (Padua, 1847). The current authority on Sanudo is Gaetano Cozzi, whose principal study, "Marin Sanudo il giovane: Dalla cronaca alla storia," is published in Pertusi's anthology cited above at n. 6.

66. *Commentarii della guerra di Ferrara,* ed. Leonardo Manin (Venice, 1829).

67. *Le vite dei dogi,* ed. Giovanni Monticolo, *RIS²,* vol. XXII⁴. Says Giorgio Cracco on p. 45 of the same *La storiografia veneziana* edited by Pertusi and cited above at n. 6: "La storia [of Sanudo] . . . si muove . . . entro un sistema politico-sociale perfettamente consolidato . . . le cui strutture restano indiscusse e costituiscono anzi motivo di vanto e di celebrazione."

68. *Petri Mocenici Imperatoris Gestorum Libri III* (Venice, 1477), reprinted at least three times (1544, 1556, 1611) and translated as *Delle cose fatte da m. Pietro Mocenico* (Venice, 1570).

69. *De Bello Ferrariensi, RIS¹,* vol. XXI, with several harsh attacks on Sabellico ("Qui sua barbarie notissimis mendaciis omnia confundit . . .").

70. *De Laudibus Historiae in Titum Livium* (1493), which, along with all the others of Sabellico's works that I do not cite specifically in other editions I read in his *Opera Omnia,* ed. Celio Secondo Curione (Basel, 1560), vol. IV. The errors in the still standard biography by Apostolo Zeno in *Scrittori veneziani* are noted by Giovanni Mercati in *Ultimi contributi* (Vatican City, 1939), vol. II, p. 9.

71. From *Dialogus qui et Latinae Linguae Reparatio Inscribitur* (1493) in *Opera Omnia,* vol. IV. The most complete biography is still that of Zeno, *Istorici,* in the preface.

72. *De Vetustate Aquileiae, Opera Omnia,* vol. IV.

73. "Squalida, foedaque barberie." I also read the *Rerum* in the Italian translation as *Le historie vinitiane* (Venice, 1554). I here follow Ruggero Bersi, "Le fonti della prima decade delle *Historiae Rerum Venetarum* di M.A.S.," *AV,* XIX (1910), 422–60, et seq.

74. Letter of Kal. Mai 1486 to Merula, *Epistolae,* p. 98.

75. Noted by Vittore Branca in J. R. Hale, ed., *Renaissance Venice* (London: Faber & Faber, 1973), p. 223.

76. Franz Babinger, "Johannes Barius (1414–1494), Sachwalter Venedigs im Morgenland und sein griechischer Umkreis," *SBBayAW* (1961), Heft 5; *Traité d'Emmanuel Piloti sur le passage en terre sainte,* ed. Pierre-Herman Dopp (Louvain: Neuwelaerts, 1958), of which the parts referring specifically to Egypt were previously published by Dopp in *L'Egypt au commencement du quinzième siècle d'après le traité . . .* (Cairo, 1950). All the literature hereafter referred to that Sabellico ignored is considered below in Chapter 12.

77. For this and for most of what I say about Sabellico I am indebted to Gaetano Cozzi, "Pubblica storiografia veneziana del '500," *SV,* V–VI (1963–64), and to Felix Gilbert, "Biondo, Sabellico, and the Beginnings of Venetian Official Historiography," in *Florilegium Historiae: Essays Presented to Wallace K. Ferguson,* eds. J. G. Rowe and W. H. Stockdale (University of Toronto Press, 1971), which I also use extensively in later chapters.

78. Giorgio Cadoni in *Storia e politica,* XV (1976), 11.

79. *Rapsodiae Historiarum ab Orbe Condito Enneades Quinque* (1st ed.: pt. 1, 1498, pt. 2, 1505), which I read in *Opera Omnia* (but there are many other editions). The section on *Historia Hebraeorum* was printed separately in Basel, 1515.

80. I read it in Domenichi's translation as *Vite de' prencipi di Vinegia* (Venice, 1557).

81. All described by Gaetano Cozzi in "Intorno all'edizione dell'opera di Marcantonio Sabellico curata da Celio Secondo Curione...," in *Venezia e la Polonia* (Venice: Istituo per la Collaborazione Culturale, 1963). Sabellico's saving of some of the Carolingian legends is given as one reason for his popularity in France by Ian Short in "A Study in Carolingian Legend and its Persistence in Latin Historiography," *Mittellateinisches Jahrbuch,* VII (1972).

CHAPTER FOUR

. *RIS*[1], vol. IV. On what follows: Giuseppe Martini, "Lo spirito cittadino e le origini della storiografia communale lombarda," *NRS,* LIV (1970).

2. Ed. Alessandro Cutolo, *RIS*[2], vol. IV[2].

3. Ed. Alessandro Cutolo and Giuseppe Colombo, *RIS*[2], vol. I[2]. All the previous datings are demolished one by one in the 118-page preface, and the date of composition is placed at A.D. 789. But Martini (n. 1, above) restores it to the late tenth or early eleventh century.

4. Ed. Carlo Castiglioni, *RIS*[2], vol. V[3].

5. *Annales Mediolanenses* (1154–1230) (but the additions after 1177 are very sparse, and there are no entries at all between 1202 and a brief weather report of 1230), and *Notae Sancti Georgii* (1061–1157), ed. Philip Jaffé, *MGH,* vol. XVIII. "Sire Raoul" is in *RIS*[1],

vol. XV. His name is correctly established by Gerolamo Biscaro in "Note biografiche di due antichi cronisti milanesi," *ASL,* XXXIV[2] (1907), where he also gives information about another early chronicler, Antonio da Retenate, whose work disappeared soon after it was used as a source by Corio.

6. "Anon. XII" to 1346 is published in *RIS*[1], vol. I[2]; for the rest, the "Anonimo" entries in Pietro Paolo Ginanni, *Memorie storiche critiche degli scrittori ravennati* (Faenza, 1769).

7. Alessandro Testi Rasponi in the very sparse and exclusively textual introduction to his edition in *RIS*[2], vol. II[2].

8. Published by E. Monaci in *FSI,* vol. I (1887).

9. Published together by Philip Jaffé and Ludwig Bethmann in *MGH,* vol. XVIII. Two very short, very rudimentary chronicles of Brescia and Bergamo, respectively, dating from the ninth century were published by Muratori, one by an anonymous monk (568–883) in *Antiquitates,* vol. IV, the other by Andrea Prespyter (573–874), ibid., vol. I. Most of the diaries and chronicles of Bergamo are listed by Bortolo Belotti in *Storia di Bergamo e dei Bergameschi* (Bergamo: Banca Popolare, 1959), vol. II, Book II, Chapter 2.

10. *Breves Chronicae Bergomenses,* ed. Giovanni Finazzi, *MSI,* vol. V.

11. *Chronicon Bergomense Guelfo-Ghibellinum,* (1378–1407), ed. Carlo Capasso, *RIS*[2], vol. XVI[2], with everything that has been said or possibly could be said about the chronicles of Bergamo stretched out into a preface that fills two entire *fascicoli.*

12. *De Bello Mediolansium Adversus Comenses, RIS*[1], vol. V.

13. On *Sicardi Episcopi Cremonensis Cronica,* ed. O. Holder-Egger, *MGH,* vol. XXXI, see below, n. 35. The preface contains references to Siccardo's local chronicle sources.

14. *Annales Cremonenses,* ed. Philip Jaffé, *MGH,* vol. XVIII, and again, more fully, by Holder-Egger in *MGH,* vol. XXXI.

15. *De Rebus Laudensibus,* ed. Jaffé, *MGH,* vol. XVIII.

16. *De Laudibus Civitatis Ticinensis,* ed. Rodolfo Maiocchi and Ferruccio Quintavalle, *RIS*[2], vol. IX[1]. The authorship was

established by Giovanni Borsio in 1857 in an obscure provincial review that the editors apparently overlooked. Borsio's conclusions were restated authoritatively by Francesco Novati in a footnote to p. 8 of *BISIme*, XX (1898).

17. *Cronache cremonesi dall'anno 1399 al 1525*, ed. Francesco Robolotti in *BHILomb*, vol. I; Albertus de Bezanis, *Chronicon Magnum Universale Pontificum et Imperatorum*, *MGH*, vol. XXXI.

18. *Cronicon Modoetiense* (from origins to 1349), *RIS¹*, vol. XII.

19. The connection between the feudal constitution and the poverty of Piedmontese historiography is suggested by Valerio Castronovo in *Samuel Guichenon e la storiografia del Seicento* (Turin: Giappichelli, 1965), which also, in chapter 4, provides a thorough survey of Piedmontese chroniclers through the seventeenth century based to some extent on the still more thorough monograph of Gaudenzio Claretta, "Sue principali storici piemontesi," *MASTor*, ser. 2, vol. XXX (1878), which I use extensively in the following paragraphs. See further, Francesco Cognasso, *Storia di Torino* (Milan: Martello, 1961), and Lino Marini, *Savoiardi e Piemontesi nello Stato sabaudo (1412–1601)* (Rome: Istituto Storico Italiano, 1962). The latter is "straight" political history with much of its mass of information confined to lengthy footnotes.

20. *MHP*, vol. III.

21. Giuseppe Sergi, "La produzione storiografica di San Michele della Chiusa," *BISIme*, LXXXI (1969).

22. Ed. Domenico Promis, *MHP*, vol. I.

23. *Chronicon Parvum Ripaltae seu Chronica Pedemontana Minora*, ed. Ferdinando Gabotto, *RIS²*, vol. XVII³.

24. Ed. Gustavo Avogadro, *MHP*, vol. III.

25. All these chronicles are published in *MHP*, vol. I, except for *La ribellione di Filippo senza terra* (but the text is in French) edited by Emanuele Bollati in *MSI*, vol. XVI.

26. *Les grans croniques des gestes et vertueux faits des très-excellens catholiques illustres et victorieux ducz et princes des pays de Savoye et Piémont* (Paris, 1516).

27. Since the first reference to Pius II appears right in the beginning, I cannot agree

with the modern editor in *MHP*, vol. III, that Gottfredo stopped writing in 1440.

28. *Libro de la genealogia et vite de gli illustrissimi principi et excelsi marchesi di Monferrato*, ed. Gustavo Avogardo, *MHP*, vol. III.

29. Ferdinando Gabotto, *Asti e la politica sabauda in Italia al tempo di Guglielmo Ventura* (= *Biblioteca della Società Storica Subalpina*, vol. XVIII) (Pinerolo: Tip. Chiantore-Moscarelli, 1903).

30. A still earlier chronicle attributed to Raimondo Turco (1003–92) is really a forgery of the seventeenth century, as Giacomo Gorrini shows in *Il comune astigiano e la sua storiografia* (Florence, 1884), which I follow in the rest of this paragraph. The one here referred to is published by Vincenzo Promis in *MSI*, ser. 1, vol. IX.

31. Olgerio Alfieri, *Fragmenta de Gestis Astensium* (1090–1294), in *MHP*, vol. III, and as *De Chronica Civatatis Astensis*, ed. Quintinio Sella, in *Codex Astensis* = *Atti dell'Accademia Nazionale dei Lincei*, ser. 2, vol. V (1875–76; but actually published in 1880). In the original: "Dominus noster Yhesus Christus custodivit eam et facit omnia suprascripta mala omnimodo superare et etiam ampliavit terram Astensem et multiplicavit bona ipsius in personis et hominibus, castris villis terris. . . ."

32. *De Gestis Civium Astensium et Plurium Aliorum*, *MHP*, vol. III, together with that of Secondino Ventura referred to below. See Axel Goria, "Studi sul cronista astigiano Guglielmo Ventura," *BISIme*, LII (1937).

33. *Antonii Astesani De eius Vita et Fortuna Varietate Carmen*, ed. A. Tallone, *RIS²*, vol. XIV¹.

34. Both edited by Vincenzo Promis in *MSI*, ser. 1, vol. IX (1870).

35. Siccardo is cited above at n. 13. Salimbene's *Cronica* is edited most recently by Giuseppe Scalia (Bari: Laterza, 1966). Besides showing what was later borrowed from him, Aldo Cerlini points out the "unpardonable errors" in the earlier *MGH* edition of Salimbene in "Fra Salimbene e le cronache attribuite ad Alberto Milioli," *AM*, I (1904). Mariano D'Alatri identifies some of his sources in "*Clerici e magni clerici* nella cronica di Salimbene da Parma," *Rivista di storia della Chiesa in Italia*, XXX (1976), and in "S. Francesco nella cronica di Salimbene," *Ar-*

chivum *Franciscanum Historicum*, LXIX (1976).
The current authorities are Augusto Sainati
in a study now republished in his *Studi di
letteratura latina, medievale e umanistica* (Padua:
Antenore, 1972), and Cinzio Violante in
"Motivi e carattere della cronica di Salim-
bene," *Annali della Scuola Normale Superiore di
Pisa*, ser. 2, vol. XXII (1953). Riccobaldo's
*Pomarium Ravennatis Ecclesiae sive Historia
Universalis* is in *RIS¹*, vol. IX.

36. Nino Scivoletto, *Fra Salimbene da
Parma e la storia politica e religiosa del secolo
decimoterzo* (Bari: Laterza, 1950). Riccobaldo's authorship of the *Chronica Parva* and
the *Historia Romana* has been established by
Aldo Francesco Massèra in "L'autenticità
della *Chronica Parva Ferrarensis*," *AM*, I
(1904).

37. Antonio Boselli and Ferdinando Ber-
nini, "La fortuna della cronica di Salimbene,"
BISIme, LII (1937.

38. Edited by O. Holder-Egger in *MGH*,
vol. XXXI.

39. *Liber de Temporibus et Aetatibus* and
Cronica Imperatorum (usually referred to
together as the *Doppelchronik*), also ed.
Holder-Egger, *MGH*, vol. XXXI; but note
the reservations of Cerlini in the article cited
above at n. 35.

40. *Polyhistoria*, *RIS¹*, vol. XXIV, appendix.

41. *RIS¹*, vol. IX.

42. Tolosano, ed. Francesco Torraca,
RIS², vol. XXVIII². Ferdinando Güterboch,
"Studi sulla cronaca faentina del Tolosano
con un nuovo esame dei manoscritti,"
BISIme, LII (1937). Cantinelli, ed. Francesco
Torraca in the same volume; on whom I
follow—in this as well as in much of this
section—Gherardo Ortalli, "Aspetti e motivi
di cronachistica romagnola," *Studi romagnoli*,
XXIV (1973), with a wealth of bibliographical information. The title notwithstanding,
Nino Tamassia's "Le cronache romagnole ed
emiliane dei secoli XV e XVI," *AMRom*, ser.
3, vol. XVII (1899), is of little help because
it gives no specific evidence to support its
generalizations.

43. *Annales Caesenates* (1162–1362), *RIS²*,
vol. XIV. On which I follow Ortali in "Gli
Annales Caesenates tra la cronachista
canonicale trecentesca," *BISIme*, LXXXV
(1974–75).

44. *Chronicon Foroliviense*, ed. Adamo Pasini, *RIS²*, vol. XIX⁵.

45. Francesco Lanzoni, "La cronaca del
convento di Sant'Andrea in Faenza," *AM*, I
(1904).

46. Ed. Giuseppe Mazzatinti, *RIS²*, vol.
XXII².

47. Giovanni di m. Pedrino depintore,
Cronica del suo tempo, ed. Gino Borghezio and
Marco Vattasio (Biblioteca Apostolica Vaticana: Studi e testi, vols. L and LXII [Vatican
City, 1929 and 1934]). That part of Cobelli's
chronicle that regards an incident
in the *Divine Comedy* was published by
Giovanni Casali in *ASI*, VII appendix (1849);
the rest was published by Giosuè Carducci
and Enrico Frati in *Mon ist Romagna*, vol. I
(1874).

48. All but those with another reference
are published by Aldo Francesco Massèra—
with no preface but with countless
footnotes—in *RIS²*, vol. XV².

49. Edited, together with the continuation, by Massèra in *RIS²*, vol. XVI³.

50. In the same *RIS²*, vol. XVI³, which
includes as well the chronicle of Broglia di
Tartaglia referred to in the next paragraph.
The work of Desiderio Spreti also referred
to in the next paragraph, *Libri III De
Amplitudine, De Vastatione, De Instauratione
Urbis Ravennae*, I read in the edition by
Bonifacio Spreti (Venice, 1588), while consulting Camillo Spreti's Italian translation,
*Della grandezza, della ruina e della restauratione
di Ravenna*, first published at Pesaro in 1574
and republished, with a biographical introduction, at Ravenna in 1793–96. The
political background is given by P. J. Jones in
"The Vicariate of the Malatesta of Rimini,"
English Historical Review, LXVII (1952). The
current authority on all the foregoing is Ortalli in the article cited above at n. 42.

51. *Annales Parmenses Minores*, ed. Giuliano Bonazzi, *RIS²*, vol. IX⁹, which corrects
the earlier edition by Jaffé in *MGH*, vol.
XVIII. An important distinction between the
chroniclers of Romagna (canons) and those of
Emilia (notaries) is made by Ortalli in a study
that contains much other valuable information about all the chronicles, "Tra passato e
presente: La storiografia medioevale," in
Storia dell'Emilia-Romagna (Bologna: University Press, 1977).

52. Muratori's edition of the *Chronicon Regiense, RIS*[1], vol. XVIII, is far from adequate. But instead of correcting it, the *RIS*[2], editor, Aldo Cerlini, expended all his energy in several hundred pages of polemics against all his predecessors. More helpful is his article cited above at n. 42 and "Le *Gesta Lombardiae* di Sagacino Levalossi e Pietro della Gazata," *BISIme,* LV (1941).

53. Ed. L. Vischi in *MSPP Modena,* vol. XV.

54. *Chronicon Mutinense,* ed. Tommaso Casini, with a lengthy introduction regarding all the chronicles of Modena, in *RIS*[2], vol. XV[4].

55. *RIS*[1], vol. XV.

56. Both in *MGH,* vol. XVIII.

57. *Chronicon Placentinum* and *Placentiae Urbis Descriptio,* both in *RIS*[1], vol. XVI. That this repetition of the well-established anti-Temporalist line had nothing to do with a proposal for the political unification of Italy, even in the form in which it appears in Giangaleazzo's propaganda, is made clear by "M. N." in "Il concetto dell'unità politica italiana nel *Chronicon Placentinum,*" *BS Piac,* XXXII (1937).

58. That part of the chronicle successive to the terminal date of Mussi is published in *RIS*[1], vol. XV.

59. Ruinagia's Latin text is printed under the title *Del Sacco di Piacenza del 1447* by Luciano Scarabelli in *ASI,* vol. V, appendix (1847); Marliano's is published in *RIS*[1], vol. XVI. A complete list of the Piacenza chronicles is given by Emilio Nasalli Rocca in "Agli albori della storiografia piacentina," *Storia e storiografia: Studi in onore di Eugenio Duprè Theseider* (Rome: Bulzoni, 1974).

60. Edited (rather superficially) by G. Bonora in *MHP Par Plac.*

61. *Breve Chronicon Mantuanum,* ed. Carlo D'Arco in *ASI,* ser. 2, vol. I[2] (1885), on which, and on what follows: G. B. Intra, "Degli storici e dei cronisti mantovani," *ASL,* V (1878). My reading of the chronicle, which tapers off in the last few years, leads me to disagree with the editor's thesis that it was all written after the terminal date. For the historical context: Giuseppe Coniglio, *I Gonzaga* (Mantua: Dall'Oglio, 1967).

62. Both are published by Orsini Begani in *RIS*[2], vol. XXIV[13], on which see the rather

nasty remarks, as well as the additional information, by Pietro Torelli in *ASI,* ser. 4, vol. XV (1911).

63. His history of the families of Mantua is still unpublished. His *Cronaca di Mantova* is published in *Racc CDSLomb,* which is where I read it; it has since been republished by Carlo D'Arco with a preface by Giuseppina Pastore in Mantua (Baldus) 1976. Strangely, none of this material was used by Coniglio in preparing the book cited above at n. 61.

64. *RIS*[1], vol. VIII.

65. Ed. Giulio Bertoni and Emilio Paolo Vicini in *RIS*[2], vol. XV[3]; but the new edition breaks off at 1354. Since the modern editors never got around to either finishing the text or writing the preface they promised, the rest of the chronicle and the relative critical information must be sought in Muratori's first edition in *RIS*[1].

66. Published by Muratori in sequel to the *Chronicon Estense,* cited in the preceding note, under the title: *Varia Anonymorum Diversis Characteribus Conscripta.*

67. Ed. Giuseppe Pardi in Deputazione di Storia Patria per l'Emilia e la Romagna, Sezione di Ferrara, *Monumenti,* vol. I (1938). Caleffini also wrote a "poco felice" rhymed chronicle in honor of Este, which is published by A. Cappelli in *AMMod e Parma,* ser. 1, vol. II (1864).

68. Ed. Giuseppe Pardi, *RIS*[2], vol. XXIV[7], appendix.

69. Ed. Pardi, *RIS*[2], vol. XXIV[7].

70. Eugenio Garin, "Motivi della cultura ferrarese nel Rinascimento," in his *La cultura filosofica del Rinascimento italiano* (cited above, Chapter 1, no. 57). Giuseppe Venturini, *Un umanista modenese nella Ferrara di Borgo d'Este* (Ravenna: Longo, 1970).

71. Published in appendix to *RIS*[1], vol. IX (above, n. 35).

72. *Memorie istoriche de' letterati ferraresi* (Ferrara, 1792). The only historians mentioned are Pigna and Bentivoglio.

73. Werner Gundesheimer, *Ferrara: The Style of a Renaissance Despotism* (Princeton University Press, 1973).

74. Cecilia May Ady, *The Bentivoglio of Bologna* (Oxford University Press, 1937), as well as her review of the chronicles in "Materials for the History of the Bentivoglio Signoria in Bologna," *Transactions of the Royal*

Historical Society, ser. 4, vol. XVII (1934). For most of what follows: Albano Sorbelli, *Le croniche bolognesi del secolo XIV* (Bologna: Zanichelli, 1900), and, above all, the complete and authoritative study by Gherardo Ortalli, "Notariato e storiografia in Bologna nei secoli XII–XVI," in *Notariato medievale bolognese* ("Studi storici sul notariato italiano," vol. III) (Rome: Consiglio Nazionale del Notariato, 1977), vol. II.

75. Augusto Gaudenzi, "La cronaca bolognese di Floriano da Villola e le fonti della *Storia miscella* del Muratori," *AMRom,* ser. 3, vol. X (1892).

76. The *Corpus Chronicorum Bononiensium,* ed. Albano Sorbelli, *RIS²,* vol. XVIII¹, is a good example of the defects of the new *RIS.* The publication extends through several *fascicoli,* which are not numbered consecutively, and most of which begin somewhere in the middle of a text with no preface or other indication of where the rest of the text is printed. The general preface to the whole series has not yet been published. The texts for the first half of the fifteenth century are still missing. Even after a diligent search I was unable to locate the texts to which the index in *fasciolo* 25 refers. Hence, this edition is unusable for anyone not prepared just to jump in and start reading on his own—and to figure out unaided what the editor means by his references to "A," "B," et al. Anyone else, myself included, must constantly fall back on Muratori's amalgamation of the separate chronicles in *RIS¹,* in spite of its editorial defects, in order to understand the context of what he is reading in *RIS².* And he must constantly keep before him the article by Ortalli cited above at n. 74 as well as Gianfranco Orlandelli's "La vicenda editoriale del *Corpus Chronicorum Bononensium*" in *Storiografia e storia: Studi in onore di E. Dupré Theseider* (above, n. 59), vol. I. On Bartolomeo della Pugliola: Orlandelli's article in *DBI.* On Biancetti: Sorbelli, "Un direttore d'archivio del secolo XIV," *Miscellanea di studi storici in onore di G. Sforza* (Lucca, 1920), and the unsigned article in *DBI.* One still unpublished chronicle of the early fifteenth century is described by Lodovico Frati in *L'arte,* XIII (1910), 466.

77. Frati in *AM,* I (1904), 121–16.

78. *Il compendio della storia di Bologna,* ed. Frati, *BISIme,* XXXII (1912), and XXXIII (1913).

79. Griffoni, *Memoriale Historicum,* ed. Frati and Sorbelli, *RIS²,* vol. XVIII².

80. *Diario bolognese,* ed. Corrado Ricci and Olindo Guerrini (Bologna, 1887).

81. *Cronaca bolognese,* ed. Ricci (Bologna, 1855).

82. Ed. Domenico Promis in *Cronache anteriori al secolo XVIII concernenti la storia di Cuneo, MSI,* vol. XII.

83. Above, Chapter 2, n. 102.

84. Benedetto Morandi: editions of Bologna, 1481, Rome 1589, Bologna, 1640. Cf. Zeno: Voss, vol. I, pp. 159–62.

85. Cf. Section 2 of Cesare Vasoli, "Copernico e la cultura filosofica italiana del suo tempo," *Giornale di fisca,* XIV (1973).

86. *RIS¹,* vol. XXI.

87. See below, n. 96.

88. *Annales Bononienses,* ed. Sorbelli, along with Vincenzo Spargiati's continuation, in *RIS²,* vol. XXIII². Sorbelli's evaluation is very different from that of Muratori in *RIS¹.*

89. Cf. Julius Kirshner's biographical essay in *DBI. Annales Estenses* (1393–1409), *RIS¹,* vol. XVIII. The several additions for the years 1450–52 are in another hand.

90. Antonio Rotondò, "Pellegrino Prisciano," *Rinascimento,* XI (1960), 69–110. I hope to persuade Danilo Aguzzi Barbagli, who is currently editing Prisciano's poetics, to edit his historical work as well. On Prisciano's interests in mathematics, see Paul Lawrence Rose, *The Italian Renaissance of Mathematics* (Geneva: Droz, 1975), p. 123.

91. *Annales Principum Estensium* have been published only for the period 1409–1454, first by Muratori and then by Simeoni in *RIS²,* vol. XX².

92. Above, n. 3.

93. *De Magnalibus Urbis Mediolani,* ed. Francesco Novati (with a long preface) in *BISIme,* XX (1898), and most recently, with an Italian translation, by Angelo Paredi, in the "Fontes Ambrosiani" (vol. XXXVIII) (Milan: Bompiani, 1974). For bibliographical and biographical information: Filippo Argellati, *Biblioteca degli volgarizzatori* (Milan, 1767), *sub nomine,* and the article by d'Arco Silvio Avalo in *DBI.* On Antonio da

Retenate, one of Bonvesin's prececessors and sources, see Gerolamo Biscaro, "Note biografiche di due antiche cronisti milanesi," *ASL*, XXXIV² (1907).

94. *De Mediolano Civitate* is edited partially by L. A. Ferrai in *BISIme*, IX (1890), and by Joseph R. Berrigan in "Benzo d'Alessandria and the Cities of Northern Italy," *Studies in Medieval and Renaissance History*, IV (1967). For further information: Ferrai, "Benzo d'Alessandria e i cronisti milanesi del secolo XIV," *BISIme*, VII (1889), and Berrigan, "The Prehumanism of Benzo d'Alessandria," *Traditio*, XXV (1969), as well as Biscaro, "Benzo da Alessandria e i giudizi contro i ribelli dell'Impero a Milano nel 1311," *ASL*, XXXIV¹ (1907), and Eugenio Ragni (who shows Benzo not to have been a priest) in *DBI*. On Benzo's importance for the subsequent development of humanist historiography: Baron, *From Petrarch to Leonardo Bruni*, p. 160.

95. Novati in his introduction to Bonvesin cited above, n. 93. Parts of his many chronicle writings are published by Muratori in *RIS¹*, vols. IX and XII. The *Chronicon Extravagans* and the *Chronicon Maius* are published by Antonio Ceruti in *MSI*, vol. VII (1869). Parts of the *Cronaca maggiore dell'Ordine domenicano* are published by Gundisalvo Odetto in *Archivum Fratrum Praedicatorum*, X (1940).

96. As John Larner observes in *Culture and Society in Italy, 1190–1420* (London: Batsford, 1971).

97. One particular example: Guglielmo de Pastrengo, *De Originibus Rerum Libellus . . . , in quo Agitur de Scripturis Virorum Illustrium, de Fundatoribus Urbibus . . .*, ed. (and "expurgatus omni errore") by Michelangelo Biondi (Venice, 1547).

98. *Historia de Situ, Origine et Cultoribus Ambrosianae Urbis . . . sub Imperio Henrici VII* (1307–13), *RIS¹*, vol. IX.

99. See above, n. 18.

100. *Synchroni Autoris Chronicon* (Milan, 1771); *Liber Gestorum in Lombardia*, ed. Francesco Cognasso, *RIS²*, vol. XVI⁴. On the author: Anna Maria Nada Patrone in *DBI*.

101. Ed. Alfio Roseo Natale, *Acta Italica*, I (1962). On which note Vincent Ilardi in *RQ*, XXXI (1978), 335–37.

102. Argellati gives publication dates as 1492 and 1592 respectively.

103. "Una inedita cronachetta degli Sforza," published anonymously in *ASNapSP*, XIX (1894).

104. *RIS¹*, vol. XVI.

105. Published by Giulio Porro Lambertenghi in *MSI*, vol. VIII, and analyzed critically by Giacinto Romano in *ASL*, XIX (1892), 245–60.

106. On which see the unsigned article in *DBI*. For one aspect of Biglia's career: Diane Webb, "Andrea Biglia at Bologna, 1424–27," *Bulletin of the Institute of Historical Research*, XLIX (1976).

107. *Historia . . . in Novem Libros Digesta*, *RIS¹*, vol. XIX.

108. Ed. Porro Lambertenghi, *MSI*, vol. VII (1869).

109. Ernst Ditt, *Pietro Candido Decembrio: Contributo alla storia dell'umanesimo italiano* (Milan: Hoepli, 1931), and Vittorio Zaccaria, "Sulle opere di Pier Candido Decembrio," *Rinascimento*, VII (1956).

110. Both edited, with an interminable preface and long footnotes, by Attilio Butti and Felice Fossati in *RIS²*, vol. XX¹. Both were translated into German and published in an elegant edition by Philipp Funk as *Leben . . . und Taten* (Jena, 1913).

111. Above, Chapter 2, n. 7.

112. Crivelli, *De Vita Rebusque Gestis Sfortiae Bellicosissimi Ducis ac Initiis Francisci Sfortiae Vicecomitis eius Filii* (1359–1424), *RIS¹*, vol. XIX, on which see the discussion of the date of composition by Giovanni Soranzo in *RIS²*, vol. XXI, *fascicolo* 6, pp. xxxiii ff., and Ferdinando Gabotto, "Ricerche intorno allo storiografo quattrocentista Leodrisio Crivelli," *ASI*, ser. 5, vol. VII (1891). Simonetta, *Rerum Gestarum Francisci Sfortiae Commentarii*, ed. Soranzo (without textual notes but with a long and helpful essay at the end), *RIS²*, vol. XXI². Its orthodox humanist character is demonstrated by Cristoforo Landino in his *prohemio* to his translation as *Historia delle cose facte dallo invictissimo duca Francesco Sforza* (Milan, 1490).

113. What follows is largely based upon Ferdinando Gabotto's very thorough *Vita di Giorgio Merula* (Alessandria, 1893). I also follow A. Goria's remarks in *BISIme*, LII

(1937), 178–79, the full bibliography in Zeno: Voss, vol. II, pp. 62 ff., and Annalisa Belloni, "Tristano Calco e gli scritti inediti di Giorgio Merula," *IMU*, XV (1972).

114. Graevius, vol. III[1]. The first edition was published by Calco in Milan in 1500. On Calco: Franca Petrucci in *DBI*.

115. Graevius, vol. II[1]. For the ideological context of their theses: D. M. Bueno de Mesquita, "The Place of Despotism in Italian Politics," in J. R. Hale et al., eds., *Europe in the Late Middle Ages* (Northwestern University Press, 1965).

116. The lives of Nerva, Trajan, and Hadrian, translated from Dio Cassius, were edited by Calco. I read them in a collected volume published in Milan, 1503. See Manfredi Liberanome, "Per le idee politiche e sociali di storici greci dell'Impero Romano," *Il pensiero politico*, IV (1971).

117. *Acta Sanctorum*, April, vol. III, pp. 694–727.

118. On Biglia in this regard, see Baron, *Crisis* (in the first edition), pp. 450–51.

119. *Storia di Milano*, ed. Egidio De Magri (Milan, 1855), now reprinted by the Istituto Editoriale Cisalpino (Milan, 1974), for the modest price of Lit. 80.000.

120. One example of Corio's care for accuracy is given by Attilio Portioli in "La morte di Jacopo Piccinini," *ASI*, V (1878). I do not think that Aldo Cerlini's harsh judgment in *BISIme*, LV (1941), 21, is wholly justified: "rozza e infarcita di latinismi, la parte antica è piena di favole e manchevole di critica."

CHAPTER FIVE

1. *Diario dal 1299 al 1320*, ed. Luigi Passerini, in *DSI*, vol. VI. For the latest word on the still current debate about the connection between communes and chronicles, see the remarks of Gigliola Soldi Rondini in *NRS*, LVII (1973), 505.

2. *Cronachetta di San Gimignano*, ed. E. Sarteschi (Bologna, 1865).

3. D. M. Faloci Pulignani, "Le cronache di Spello degli Olorini," *BDSPUmb*, XXIII (1918).

4. Gottfriedi Viterbiensis *Speculum Regum*, or *De Genealogia Omnium Regum et Imperatorum*, ed. Georg Waitz, *MGH*, vol. XXII. The borrowings from Otto are noted by Charles Christopher Mierow in his trans-

lation of *The Two Cities* (New York: Octagon Books, 1966), p. 45.

5. *Annales* Ptolemaei Lucensis, ed. Marco Tabarrini with an "avvertimento" by Carlo Minutoli in *DSI*, vol. VI, on which see Bernhard Schmeidler, ed., "Die Annalen des Tholomeus von Lucca in doppelter Fassung," *MGH*, vol. VIII. All the relevant current bibliography is given in the article from which I take much of my information: Charles T. Davis, "Ptolemy of Lucca and the Roman Republic," *Proceedings of the American Philosophical Society*, CXVIII (1974). Tolomeo's role as a precursor of Bruni's reassessment of the Roman Republic is recognized by Baron in *Crisis*, 2d ed., p. 55. On his relations with Aquinas: Thomas Gilby, *The Political Thought of Thomas Aquinas* (University of Chicago Press, 1958), p. 95.

6. Leonis Urbevetani *Chronicon Summorum Pontificum et etiam Summorum Imperatorum*, published by Giovanni Lami, with one of his usual lengthy prefaces, in *Deliciae Eruditorum*, vol. I (Florence, 1737).

7. *Le croniche di Giovanni Sercambi*, ed. Salvatore Bongi, *FSI*, vols. XIX–XXI.

8. All the earlier chronicles are listed in Daniel Waley's pre-Herlihyian political history of the period, *Mediaeval Orvieto (1157–1334)* (Cambridge University Press, 1952). One of them is published by G. F. Gamurrini, "Le antiche cronache di Orvieto," in *ASI*, ser. 5, vol. III (1889). The *Discorso historico*, the various fragments of the *Cronica urbevetana*, the *Cronica antiqua* (1161–1313), the *Cronica Potestatum* (1194–1322), the *Cronaca* of Francesco di Montemarte e Corbara, the *Cronaca* of Luca di Domenico Manenti (1174–1413), and the *Ricordi* of Ser Matteo di Cataluccio are edited by Luigi Fumi in *RIS*[2], vol. XV[5], t. I. Fumi and Aldo Cerlini edited the "Continuazione orvietana della cronaca di Martino Polono" in *AM*, XIV (1914). Filippo Antonio Gualterio edited the *Cronaca ... degli avvenimenti d'Orvieto* of Francesco Montemarte, conte di Corbara (Turin, 1846).

9. *Diario* (1482–1514), ed. Fumi, *RIS*[2], vol. XV[5], t. II.

10. Selections from the chronicle of Giovanni da Iuzzo and the diary of the Sacchi are published by Ignazio Ciampi with a long

introduction from the earlier Viterban chronicles in Niccola Della Tuccia, *Cronache di Viterbo e di altre città,* in *DSI,* vol. V.

11. Paltroni, *Commentari,* ed. Walter Tommasoli (Urbino: Acc. Raffaello, 1966). On Porcelli, see below, Chapter 6, n. 70. Filelfo's *Vita* was published by Giovanni Zannoni in *AMDSPMarche,* V (1895).

12. Giovanni Zannoni,' "Federico II di Montefeltro e G. A. Campano," *AASTor,* XXXVII (1901–2), with long quotations from Campano. See above, Chapter 2, n. 91.

13. René Dubos, *Giovanni Santi: Peintre et chroniqueur à Urbin au XVme siècle* (Bordeaux: Samie, 1971).

14. *Cronaca* (1350–1472), dedicated to Duke Federico, ed. Giuseppe Mazzatinti, along with several sixteenth-century chronicles and one earlier *Gesta Eugubinorum ab aedificatione civitatis,* which Guerrieri could not have used because it survives only in a sixteenth-century compilation, in *RIS²,* vol. XXI⁴.

15. *Annales Reatini,* ed. L. C. Bethmann, *MGH,* vol. XIX.

16. *Fragmenta Fulginatis Historiae,* ed. Michele Faloci-Pulignani, *RIS²,* vol. XXVI².

17. Included in the chronicle of Lazaro de' Bernabei, cited below at n. 20.

18. *Memoriale* of Petruccio di Giacomo degli Unti, also ed. Faloci-Pulignani, *RIS²,* vol. XXVI².

19. *Cronache della città di Fermo,* ed. Gaetano de Minicis and Marco Tabarrini, with a long introduction on the history of later Fermo chronicles, in *DSI,* vol. IV (1870).

20. Ed. Carisio Ciavarini in *Collezione di documenti storici antichi inediti ed edite delle città e terre marchigiane,* vol. I (Ancona, 1870).

21. Above, Chapter 3, n. 26, Chapter 2, n. 12, and Chapter 1, n. 59.

22. Christopher Black, "The Baglioni as Tyrants of Perugia," *English Historical Review,* LXXXV (1970).

23. The history of earlier and later chronicle writing in Perugia is given in the preface to Ariodante Fabretti, Francesco Bonaini, and F. L. Polidori, eds., *Cronaca della città di Perugia dal 1309 al 1491, ASI,* XVI¹ (1850), which happens to be the same diary that Oscar Scalvanti attributed not to "Graziani" but to Antonio dei Guarneglie in the article

cited in the next note. Fabretti also published three *cronichette* of the fourteenth century and that part of a longer anonymous chronicle regarding the years 1308–1398 from a copy made in the mid-sixteenth century by Mariano del Moro in *Chronache della città di Perugia* (Turin, 1887), vol. I.

24. Scalvanti, ed., *Cronaca perugina inedita di Pietro Angelo di Giovanni . . .,* in *BDSPUmb,* IV (1898), and IX (1903), previously described in his "Sul ritrovamento di un codice di cronaca perugina," ibid., II (1896).

25. Published by Fabretti in *ASI²* (1851).

26. *Cronichetta volterrana,* ed. Marco Tabarrini in *ASI,* vol. III, appendix (1846). Paris and Zagata in the edition of Giambattista Biancolini (Verona, 1747).

27. Above, Chapter 1, n. 112.

28. *Seconda calamità volterrana,* ed. Tabarrini, in the same volume of *ASI* cited at n. 26.

29. All the Aretine chronicles here mentioned are edited by Arturo Bini and Giovanni Grazzini in *RIS²,* vol. XXIV¹.

30. For a thorough treatment of these chronicles: Ottavio Banti, "Studio sulla genesi dei testi cronistici pisani del secolo XIV," *BISIme,* LXXV (1963), and Craig Fisher, "The Pisan Clergy and the Awakening of Historical Interest in the Medieval Commune," *Studies in Medieval and Renaissance History,* III (1966). One of the earliest, the *Annales Pisani Antiquissimi,* is edited by F. Novati in *Centenario della nascita di Michele Amari* (Palermo, 1910).

31. See *Fragmenta Historiae Pisanae . . .* (1191–1337), *RIS¹,* vol. XXIV, appendix.

32. Ed. Carlo Calisse in *FSI,* vol. XXIX.

33. Bernardo Maragone (continued by his son Salem to 1192), ed. Michele Lupo Gentile, *RIS²,* vol. VI², together with the *Gesta Triumphalis* (c. 1120), an anonymous *Chronicon* (688–1136), and another continuation of Maragone from 1182 to 1268.

34. Muratori put the original *Chronicon Breve* (1004–1188), together with its continuations up to 1268, in the form in which they were then copied by Michele de Vico in 1838, in *RIS¹,* vol. VI.

35. Above, Chapter 1, n. 10.

36. E.g., in the anonymous chronicle of 1084–1389, continued to 1406, in *Monumenta Pisana, RIS¹,* vol. XV.

37. *Cronaca di Pisa,* ed. Ottavio Banti, *FSI,* XCIX (1963).

38. Both chronicles are published by Giuseppe Odoardo Corazzini in *L'Assedio di Pisa* (Florence, 1885).

39. Above, Chapter 1, n. 80.

40. Tartini, vol. I.

41. *Annales Senenses,* ed. Johann Friedrich Boehmer, *MGH,* vol. XIX. Siena also produced at least one family diary: that of Mattasala di Spinello from 1231 to 1243, ed. N. Tommaseo in *ASI,* vol. V, appendix (1847).

42. Uberto Benvoglienti calls him Neri di Donato di Neri in his edition, published together with the chronicles of Andrea Dei and Agnolo da Tura, in *RIS¹,* vol. XV; but the editors of the Sienese chronicles (published together with a long introduction in *RIS²,* vol. XV⁶), Alessandro Lisini and Fabio Iacometti, call him Donato di Neri. The modern editors have also cleared up the true nature of Agnolo's diary.

43. What Muratori published as genuine *Annales Senenses (1385–1422)* in *RIS¹,* vol. XIX, are actually a series of notes and extracts compiled by Muratori's collaborator in Siena, Uberto Benvoglienti, as Anna Maria Chiavacci Leonardi has shown in "Gli *Annali senesi . . . ,*" in *Studi sul medioevo cristiano offerti a Raffaello Morghen* (above, Chapter 1, n. 40), vol. I.

44. This and the next two chronicles are published in *RIS²,* vol. XV⁶, along with the others cited above at n. 42.

45. *Diari delle cose sanesi del suo tempo,* ed. Benvoglienti, *RIS¹,* vol. XXIII. This edition is not complete because Muratori admittedly took out some of the material that he considered to be "nullam utilitatem, nullam delectationem," in accordance with the humanist principles to which he still adhered.

46. Roberti Ursi, *De Obsidione Tiphernatum Liber,* ed. Giovanni Magherini Graziani, *RIS²,* vol. XXVII³.

47. All these texts are published in *RIS¹,* vol. XX. They are described, with the usual eighteenth-century prejudice in favor of "naive" writing, in Benvoglienti's introduction to the Sienese chronicles in *RIS¹,* vol. XV.

48. Essential biographical data can be found along with much padding in Giovanni Niccolò Bandiera's *De Augustino Dato Libri*

Duo (Rome, 1733). The *Fragmenta Senensium Historiarum* (minus the passages that his son and editor feared might "confodere auriculas teneras" in the liberty-loving republic) and the *Plumbinensis Historia,* are published with all his other works in *Opera* (Siena, 1503), which I read in the 2d ed. of Venice, 1516.

49. Paolo Piccolomini, *La vita e l'opera di Sigismundo Tizio* (Siena, 1903). Long quotations from Tizio are included in the appendix to G. Rondini. "Una relazione senese su Girolamo Savonarola," *ASI,* ser. 5, vol. I² (1888). More information on the author in Romeo De Maio, *Riforme e miti nella chiesa del Cinquecento* (Naples: Guida, 1973), pp. 58 ff.

CHAPTER SIX

1. The chronicles of Amalfi are published in Muratori, *Antiquitates,* vols. I and VI. On the first, see Michelangelo Schipa, *La cronaca amalfitana* (Salerno, 1882); on the second, the critical comments of P. Egidi in *ASPN,* XXXIII (1908), 160–68. Fonticolano's *Belli Bracciani Aquilae Gesti Fidelis Narratio* I read in Graevius, vol. IX³, from the 1st ed. of Aquila, 1580. For biographical information: Tafuri, vol. II², p. 196 (which gives titles of his still unpublished works), and Alfonso Dragonetti, *Le vite degli illustri Aquilani* (Aquila, 1847).

2. The best guide to the early chronicles is Bartolomeo Capasso, *Le fonti della storia delle provincie napolitane dal 568 al 1500,* ed. E. O. Mastrojanni (Naples, 1902), and the best guide to all the histories and chronicles alike is Soria. Pelliccia provides critical prefaces only to the chronicles published in vol. I. A brief summary of historiography through the Swabian period is given by Nicola Cilento in Chapter 6 of his "La cultura e gli inizi dello Studio," in *Storia di Napoli* (Naples: Edizioni Scientifiche Italiane, 1969), vol. II. Also useful is Pietro Napoli Signorelli's classic *Vicende della cultura nelle Due Sicilie* (Naples, 1784–86) under the rubric "istorici."

3. *Il 'Chronicon' di Benedetto di Sant'Andrea,* ed. Giuseppe Zucchetti, *FSI,* vol. LV. Notes the editor, "In mezzo al vecchio che si dissolve, non troviamo molti segni del nuovo" (p. xlvi).

4. *Il 'Chronicon Farfense' di Gregorio di Catino . . . ,* ed. Ugo Balzani, *FSI,* vol. XXXIII.

5. *MGH*, vol. III.

6. *Chronicon Episcoporum Sanctae Neapolitanae Ecclesiae*, first published by Muratori in *RIS*[1], vol. I[2], and now by Capasso in *Monumenta Neap.*

7. *MGH*, vols. III and VII, and *RIS*[1], vol. IV. See Hartmut Hoffmann in a very thorough "Studien zur Chronik von Montecassino," *Deutsches Archiv für Erforschung des Mittelalters*, XXIX (1973), and, in general, Nicola Cilento, "La storiografia nell'Italia meridionale," in *La storiografia altomedievale,* cited above in the Prologue, n. 26.

8. *RIS*[1], vol. V.

9. *MGH*, vol. III; on which: Ottorino Bertolini, "Gli *Annales Beneventani*," *BISIme*, XLII (1923).

10. *Chronicon Sancti Benedicti, MGH*, vol. III; *Chronicon Ducum et Principum Beneventi, Salerni et Capuae et Ducum Neapolis*, ed. Capasso, *Monumenta Neap.* Cf. P. Bertolini, "Studi per la cronologia dei principi langobardi di Benevento," *BISIme*, LXXX (1968).

11. An example: Bartolomeo Capasso, *La 'Cronaca Napoletana' di Ubaldo edita dal Pratilli nel 1751 ora stampata nuovamente e dimostrata una impostura del secolo scorso* (Naples, 1855). The text was supposedly rescued from the wreckage of the house of the Tafuri in Nardò. Another chronicle published by Pratilli, that of Santa Trinità of Cava (below, n. 18) as well as that of Mattheo di Giovenazzo (below, n. 22) were also called into question; but their authenticity seems now to be generally accepted. Several lost or fragmentary chronicles of the late fourteenth century are mentioned by Giuseppe De Blasiis in his introduction to the *Chronicon Siculum* (below, n. 38), p. viii; and Muratori records his frustration in trying to determine the authorship of several known manuscripts in *Antiquitates*, vol. IV, p. 949: "Quis fuerit, nemo a me petat, non minus mihi quam lectori ignotus est." Further reference to eighteenth-century forgeries in Sergio Bertelli, *Erudizione e storia in Ludovico Antonio Muratori* (Naples: Istituto Italiano per gli Studi Storici, 1960), p. 356.

12. *RIS*[1], vol. V.

13. *RIS*[1], vol. IV.

14. *Chronicon Sublacense*, ed. Rafaello Morghen, *RIS*[2], vol. XXIV[6], on which see Morghen's "Gli *Annales Sublacenses* e le note obituarie...," *BISIme*, XLV (1929), and Pietro Egidi, *I monasteri di Subiaco* (Rome, 1904), whose phrase is "disordinato, incerto, infarcito di nomi spuri." Capisacchi's new chronicle has never been published, but its continuation by Cherubino Mürtz, or Miritus, of Trier, down to 1626 was published by Leone Allodi in Rome, 1885.

15. Chronicon Vulturense, ed. Vincenzo Federici, *FSI*, vols. LVIII–LX. Federici is also the author of the critical article, "Ricerche per l'edizione del *Chronicon Vulterense*," *BSISme*, LIII (1939). On the *Liber Pontificalis*, see above, Chapter 2.

16. *MGH*, vol. XIX, and *Annales Siculi*, ed. E. Pontieri, *RIS*[2], vol. V[1].

17. *Vitae Quatuor Priorum Abbatum Cavensium*, ed. Leone Mattei Cerasoli, OSB, *RIS*[2], vol. VI[5].

18. *Chronicon Cavense, RIS*[1], vol. VII.

19. *RIS*[1], vol. VII, and *MGH*, vol. XIX.

20. *Breve Chronicon Atinensis, RIS*[1], vol. VII.

21. The first is published in appendix to vol. III[3] of Tafuri; the second in Muratori, *Antiquitates*, vol. I.

22. *Gli diurnali*, ed. Hermann Pabst, *MGH*, vol. XIX.

23. Stephano monacho benedictino, *Brevis Historia Monasteri Neritini* (1090–1368), continued anonymously to 1412, *RIS*[1], vol. XXIV. On the retreat of Greek culture in the South under the Angevins: Roberto Weiss, "Greek Culture of Southern Italy in the Later Middle Ages," *Proceedings of the British Academy*, XXXVII (1951).

24. *Chronicon de Rebus in Apulia Gestis*, ed. Albano Sorbelli, *RIS*[2], vol. XII[3]

25. Both published in Latin translation in *RIS*[1], vol. I[2].

26. Michele Amari and C. Schiaparelli, eds., *L'Italia descritta nel 'Libro del Re Ruggero'* compilato da Edrisi (Rome, 1883).

27. Amari, ed., *Bibliotheca Arabo-Sicula* (Leipzig, 1856), and "Frammenti di testi arabi sulla storia della Sicilia musulmana," *ASI,* IV, appendix (1847). Considerable information on Ibn Giubayr in Umberto Rizzitano, *Storia e cultura nella Sicilia saracena* (Palermo: Flaccovio, 1975).

28. Amatus = Aimé, *Ystoire de li Normant*, ed. O. Delarc (Rouen, 1892). Cf.

Michelangelo Schipa, "A proposito della prossima edizione delle 'Istorie' d'Amato," *ASPN*, XVIII (1893). The translator apparently did not understand the original very well, as Schipa points out in *ASPN*, XXXIII (1908), 545–48.

29. Malaterra, *De Rebus Gestis Rogerii Calabriae et Siciliae Comitis et Roberti Guiscardi Ducis Fratris Eius,* ed. Ernesto Pontieri, *RIS²*, vol. V¹. On this and on what follows: Robert Lopez, "La Sicilia al tempo della conquista normanna," in vol. II of *Ricerche storiche ed economiche in memoria di Corrado Barbagallo* (Naples: Edizioni Scientifiche Italiane, 1970).

30. Gregorio, vol. II. But now in a philologically more critical edition by G. Rossi-Taibbi as *La conquesta di Sichilia fatta per li Normandi* (Collana di testi siciliani dei secoli XIV e XV) (Palermo: Centro di Studi Filologici e Linguistici Siciliani, 1954).

31. *La historia o Liber de Regno Sicilie,* ed. G. B. Siragusa, *FSI,* vol. XXII, on which see Marco Vattasso, "Del codice benedettino di San Nicolò dell'Acena di Catania contenente la 'Historia'...," *AM,* I² (1913).

32. *Romoaldi II Archiepiscopi Salernitani Annales,* ed. Wilhelm Arndt, *MGH,* vol. XIX, and by C. A. Garufi in *RIS²,* vol. VII¹—but with such endless footnotes that I, for one, soon got bored reading them.

33. Ed. Garufi, *RIS²,* vol. VII².

34. *Historia Sicula ab Ingressu Normannorum in Apuliam usque ad Annum 1282, RIS¹,* vol. VIII. The debt of the medieval historians to late Roman historiography can be noted in comparing their work to what Benoît Lacroix says in *Orose et ses idées* (Montréal-Paris: Vrin, 1965).

35. *RIS¹,* vol. VIII.

36. Nicolai de Jamsilla *Historia de Rebus Gestis Friderici II Imperatoris eiusque Filiorum, RIS¹,* vol. VIII.

37. Gennaro Maria Monti, "Una inedita Cronica Dominorum Regni Sicilie," *BISIme,* LVII (1941).

38. *Chronicon Siculum Incertis Auctoris* (340–1396), ed. Giuseppe De Blasiis, *Monumenta Neap.*

39. On the *Cronaca di Partenope,* first published by Lionardo Astrino in 1526 and again at Naples in 1680, see Nicola Cilento, "Di Marino Freccia erudito napolentano del Cin-

quecento e di alcuni codici di cronache medievale a lui noti," *BISIme,* LXVIII (1956).

40. Denis Mack Smith, *A History of Sicily* (London: Chatto and Windus, 1968), p. 71.

41. "L'ira d'un popolo ferocemente oppresso ... reprova della fierezza indomita del siciliano": Enrico Sicardi in introduction to his edition of the *Ribellamentu* in *RIS²,* vol. XXXIV¹.

42. Sicardi in the same volume of *RIS²* cited in the preceding note: *Due cronache del Vespro in volgare siciliano del secolo XIII.* But see Francesco Giunta in *Repertorio storico critico dei testi in antico siciliano* (Palermo, 1949), vol. II. The most recent authority on the question is Helene Wieruszowski in two important articles published in her *Politics and Culture in Medieval Spain and Italy* (Rome: Edizioni di Storia e Letteratura, 1971). Her position is generally accepted by Stephen Runciman in *The Sicilian Vespers* (Cambridge University Press, 1958), which draws upon earlier editions of the articles.

43. Published by Di Giovanni, along with Frate Atanasio and the *Cronica Cavellorum,* et al.

44. Ed. Giuseppe Paladino in *RIS²,* vol. XIII³, and in Gregorio, vol. I.

45. Gregorio, vol. II. Di Giovanni's title is *Chronichi di quistu Regno di Sicilia,* which is the text I follow. In general, see the remarks of Giunta in the work cited above at n. 42, and Venanzio Todesco, "Appunti su una traduzione catalana del 'Chronicon Siciliae'," *BISIme,* LVII (1941).

46. *Historia Sicula* (1282–1337), in Gregorio, vol. I.

47. On all this and on the relevant chronicles: Francesco Giunta, *Aragonesi e Catalani nel Mediterraneo* (Palermo: Manfredi, 1953).

48. Salvatore Tramontana, "Una fonte trecentesca nel 'De Rebus Siculis' di Tommaso Fazello e la battaglia di Lipari del 1339," *BISIme,* LXXIV (1962), with much information about the chronicles in general as well.

49. Michaelis Platiensis *Historia Sicula,* in Gregorio, vol. I; on which: Tramontana's *Michele da Piazza e il potere baronale in Sicilia* (Florence-Messina; D'Anna, 1963), as well as Girolamo Arnaldi's review in *Belfagor,* XX (1965).

50. *Cronica di Sicilia per epitome* (827–1432), in Di Giovanni.

51. Angelo de Tummulillis da Sant'Elia, *Notabilia Temporum,* ed. Costantino Corvisieri, *FSI,* vol. VII.

52. Nicola Vacca, "Sull'autore della 'Cronaca napoletana figurata del Quattrocento'," *Atti Pont,* n.s. vol. IX (1960). The editor of the text itself is Riccardo Filangieri, who also edited Leostello's *Ephemeridi de le cose fatte per el Duca di Calabria* in vol. I of *Documenti per la storia delle arti e le industrie delle provincie napoletane* (Naples, 1883).

53. Francesco Torraca, "Antonio de la Salle e la storia napoletana," *ASPN,* LVII (1932).

54. *Annales* (1468–85), *RIS¹,* vol. XXIII, described in the general introduction to the Neapolitan chronicles in vol. XXI.

55. *RIS¹,* vol. XXIII.

56. Cf. Francesco Tateo, *L'umanesimo meridionale* (Bari: Laterza, 1972), p. 82, and Benedetto Croce, *Storie e leggende napoletane,* 4th ed. (Laterza), p. 126. Loise's text is published in appendix to G. Petrocchi's edition of *Il novellino* of Masuccio Salernitano (Florence, 1957). Cardami's is published in appendix to Tafuri, vol. III¹.

57. *Diurnali detti del Duca di Monteleone* (because the manuscript was discovered in 1535 by Ettore Pignatelli, duke of Monteleone and viceroy of Sicily), ed. Nunzio Federico Farfaglia in *Monumenta Neap.,* vol. I, and also in *RIS¹,* vol. XXI. On which, as well as for other fifteenth century chronicles: Francesco Sabatini, "La cultura a Napoli nell'età angioina," in *Storia di Napoli,* vol. IV².

58. *Istoria del Regno di Napoli,* ed. Giuseppe De Blasiis in *ASPN,* XVI (1891)–XVII (1892).

59. Both published in vol. I of Pelliccia.

60. Giacomo Gallo, *Diurnali,* ed. S. Volpicella (Naples, 1846).

61. *Ragionamento delle guerre de' signuri viniziani contro la cettate di Gallipoli, RIS¹,* vol. XXIV.

62. *Cronica di Napoli,* ed. Paolo Garzilli (Naples, 1845). Many long passages are reproduced in Tommaso Pedìo, *Napoli e Spagna nella prima metà del Cinquecento* (Bari: Cacucci, 1971).

63. "Annotazioni critiche del sig. Gio. Bernardino Tafuri . . . sopra le croniche di m.

Antonello Coniger leccese," in Calogerà, *Raccolta d'opuscoli,* VIII (1733), upon a text published by Giusto Palma in Brindisi in 1700.

64. *Vita Nicolai Acciaioli,* written about 1440 and now edited by Gino Scaramella in *RIS²,* vol. XIII²; on the author, see above, Chapter 1, nn. 83 and 84.

65. On Porcelli as well as Panormita (and the group in general): Antonio Altamura, *L'umanesimo nel mezzogiorno d'Italia* (Florence: Bibliopolis, 1941), along with the article by Gianvito Resta ("Beccadelli") in *DBI* and Resta's edition of *L'epistolario del Panormita* (Messina: Università, 1954). What I say here about the place of the historians at the court of Alfonso is not completely in accord with the thesis of Alan Ryder in *The Kingdom of Naples under Alfonso the Magnanimous* (Oxford: Clarendon, 1976); but then he does not pay much attention to them. More on Porcelli below at n. 70.

66. The most helpful of the recent studies of Valla for my purposes are Salvatore Camporeale, *Lorenzo Valla: Umanesimo e teologia* (Florence: Olschki, 1972), and Pompeo Giannantonio, *Lorenzo Valla, filologo e storiografo dell'umanesimo* (Naples: Liguori, 1972), which, together with those of Mario Fois and Giovanni Di Napoli are reviewed critically by Eugenio Marino in *Memorie domenicane,* III (1972), and by Franco Gaeta in *Rivista di storia della chiesa in Italia,* XXIX (1975), 559–77—a long review article; but I still follow Gaeta's *Lorenzo Valla: Filologia e storia nell'umanesimo italiano* (Naples: Istituto Italiano per gli Studi Storici, 1955) very closely.

67. Claudio Marchiori, *Bartolomeo Facio tra letteratura e vita* (Milan: Marzorati, 1971) does not add much that is not already in Ubaldo Mazzini, "Appunti per servire alla biobibliografia di B. F.," *Giornale storico e letterario della Liguria,* IV (1900). On one aspect of his career: P. O. Kristeller, "The Humanist B. F. and his Unknown Correspondence," in *From Renaissance to Counter Reformation: Essays in Honor of Garrett Mattingly* (London: Jonathan Cape, 1966). On Fazio as a biographer: below, Chapter 14, n. 15.

68. *Gestorum per Alphonsum Aragonum et Siciliae Regem Libri V,* ed. Raffaele Atarabba

in *Aneddoti storici e letterarii siciliani,* vol. I (Palermo, 1904). On the literary quality of the verse, see N. F. Faraglia in *ASPN,* XXX (1905), 81–85.

69. *De Urbis Interamenae seu Terami Situ et Iucunditate* (Teramo, 1765). On Campano, see above, Chapter 2, n. 4.

70. Altamura (above, n. 65) is more useful than Ugo Frittelli, *Giannantonio de' Pandoni detto il "Porcellio"* (Florence: Paravia, 1900).

71. Alberto Boscolo, "Ferdinando I e Alfonso il Magnanimo nella storiografia," in *Medioevo aragonese* (Padua: Milani, 1958). See also the article on Alfonso by Felice Scifoni in *DBI,* and Andrés Soria Ortega, *Los humanistas de la corte de Alfonso el Magnánimo* (Granada: Universidad, 1956).

72. Vespasiano da Bisticci, p. 266 of the Hoepli edition of the *Vite.*

73. *Historiarum Ferdinandi Regis Aragoniae Libri Tres,* in vol. II of *Opera Omnia,* ed. Eugenio Garin (Turin: Bottega d'Erasmo, 1962), on which see Buscolo in the article cited above at n. 71 and in his "Dei *Gesta Ferdinandi Regis Aragonum* del Valla," *IMU,* IX (1966), with complete relevant bibliography. The most recent edition is by Ottavio Besomi (Padua: Antenore, 1973).

74. *Fatti d'Alfonso d'Aragona,* tr. Giacomo Mauro (Venice, 1579). The Latin original is in Graevius, vol. IX³, as *De Rebus Gestis ab Alphonso Primo.*

75. *Liber Rerum Gestarum Ferdinandi Regis,* ed. Gianvito Resta, with a long preface that surveys all the historical literature of the age (Palermo: Centro di Studi Filologici e Linguistici Siciliani, 1968).

76. *Commentarii,* pt. I, in *RIS¹,* vol. XX, with relevant comments by Apostolo Zeno in the Venetian *Giornale de' litterati,* IX (1712), 148–53.

77. According to Wolfram Setz in his edition of *Lorenzo Vallas Schrift gegen die Konstantinische Schenkung* (Tübingen: Max Niemeyer, 1975).

78. In both Latin and English as *The Treatise of Lorenzo Valla on the Donation of Constantine,* ed. Christopher B. Coleman (Yale University Press, 1922).

79. So says Donald Kelley in "Clio and the Lawyers," *Mediaevalia et Humanistica,* V (1974), esp. p. 38.

80. Gerhard Laehr, "Die Konstantinische Schenkung in der abendländischen Literatur...," *Quellen und Forschungen aus italienischen Archiven and Bibliotheken,* XXIII (1931–32); Domenico Maffei, *La Donazione di Costantino nei giuristi medievali* (Milan: Giuffrè, 1958, and several subsequent editions); Joseph Levine, "Reginald Pecock and Lorenzo Valla on the Donation of Constantine," *SR,* XX (1973); and Massimo Miglio, "L'umanista Pietro Edo e la polemica sulla Donazione...," *BISIme,* LXXIX (1968).

81. The first draft is published in the appendix to the very important article by Gianni Zippel, "Lorenzo Valla e l'origine della storiografia a Venezia," *Rinascimento,* VII (1956).

82. R. Valentini, "Le *Emendationes* in T. *Livium* di Lorenzo Valla," *Studi italiani di filologia classica,* XV (1907). The texts of the translations from Greek I consulted in Conrad Heresbachius' edition of 1527 and in Estienne's edition of Frankfurt-a-M., 1594, neither of which contains Valla's prefaces. See R. I. Wilfred Westgate, "The Text of Valla's Translation of Thucydides," *Transactions and Proceedings of the American Philological Association,* LXVII (1936). Valla's commentaries on Sallust, given as lectures in the University of Rome, were published at Padua in 1470. For a good example of Valla's philological methods: Anna Morisi, "La filologia neotestamentaria di Lorenzo Valla," *NRS,* XLVIII (1964).

83. Fully described by Ottavio Besomi in "Dai *Gesta Ferdinandi Regis Aragonum* del Valla al *De Orthographia* del Tortelli," *IMU,* IX (1966), and by Roberto Valentini in "Le invettive di Bartolomeo Facio contro Lorenzo Valla," *Lincei Rendiconti,* XV (1906). Valla's response is in volume I of his *Opera Omnia* (above, n. 73). The texts have not, therefore, been ignored by recent scholarship, as has been claimed. They are reviewed once again by Linda Gardiner Junk in "Valla on Rhetoric and History," *History and Theory,* XII (1973), who says they, not the prefaces to his historical work, contain Valla's real ideas on the nature of history.

84. *De Bello Veneto Clodiano* (Lyon, 1568).

85. The first is cited above at n. 74; another edition by Janus Gruterus in *Thesaurus Criticus* (Palermo, 1793), on which Vincenzo

Laurenza in "Il Panormita a Napoli," *Atti Pont.*, XLII (1912). The second is published by Resta in the same collection also cited above at n. 74 (Palermo, 1968), with a very informative philological introduction.

86. Contrast Pertusi's view: "Una ben povera cosa" on p. 290 of his *La Storiografia veneziana*, cited above, Chapter 3, n. 6. For what follows: G. B. Picotti, "Dei *Commentari del secondo anno* di Porcellio Pandoni e di un codice marciano che li contiene," *AM*, I⁶ (1913).

87. *Quattro opuscoli inediti . . . intitolati, Della educazione, Della ipocrisia, Del beneficio, Degli apparecchi militari de' Turchi . . .* (Naples, 1744). Pelliccia in preface to vol. I, p. vii, calls Ferrante an "amante della storia patria." The latest studies of the pedagogical and philological aspects of Neapolitan humanism are by Michele Fuiano, *Insegnamento e cultura a Napoli nel Rinascimento* (Naples: Edizioni Scientifiche Italiane, 1971), and Mario Santoro, "La cultura umanistica," in *Storia di Napoli*, vol. VI², esp. Chapter VI on "L'impegno politico ed etico nella storiografia e nella trattatistica."

88. For Pontano in particular and on Aragonese humanists in general, I follow Francesco Tateo in *L'umanesimo meridionale* (Bari: Laterza, 1972) and Cesare Vasoli in his article on Pontano in *La letteratura italiana: I minori* (Marzorati), vol. I. A complete survey of the writings of Galateo is given by Claudio Griggio in "Tradizione e rinnovamento nella cultura del Galateo," *Lettere italiane*, XXVI (1974). Considerable biographical information about all these historians is given by Pietro Giannone in *Stora civile del Regno di Napoli* (Milan, 1844–47), vol. V, e.g., on Ricci, pp. 563–64.

89. All of Lignamine's faults of judgment about Ferrante are explained in the footnotes of his editor, Ernesto Pontieri, in *Per la storia del regno di Ferrante I d'Aragona, re di Napoli,* 2d ed. from the 1st of 1946 (Naples: Morano, 1969).

90. *De Gestis Regum Napolitanorum,* in Gravier, vol. V, with the diplomatic correspondence upon which much of it is based published in appendix. The work actually consists of four parts, which were first published by the author's great-nephew in 1589, and which he himself never got around to revising as chapters of the more general history indicated in Gravier's title.

91. *Historiae Napolitanae Libri Sex,* in Gravier, vol. V.

92. See above, Chapter 2, n. 94.

93. The first is published as *Epitome Rerum Ungaricarum, cura et studio* Matthiae Belli [&] Ioannis Georgii Schwandtneri, in *Scriptores Rerum Hungaricarum Veteres ac Genuini* (Bibliopolae Vindobonensis, 1746); the second, which Ranzano himself copied out as a separate piece from Book XXIX of his huge opus in 1470, in vol. IX (1767) of *Opuscoli di autori siciliani.* For critical and biographical details: Ferdinando Attilio Termini, "Ricostruzione cronologica della biografia di Pietro Ranzano," *ASS*, XLI (1916), and *Pietro Ranzano, umanista palermitano del secolo XV* (Palermo: Trimarchi, 1915), and now Tibor Kardos (who knows much more about Hungary than he does about Italian humanism), in *Studi e ricerche umanistiche italo-ungheresi*, vol. I ("Studia Romanica Universitatis Debreceniensis," Fasc. iii [1967]).

94. *Acta Sanctorum,* 5 April and 4 December.

95. Partially published by Muratori in the same vol. XII of *RIS*¹ that contains his other work cited above, Chapter 1, n. 88.

96. Graevius, vol. X⁵, as *De Regibus Siciliae et Apuliae Liber.*

97. E. Pontieri, "Napolitani alla corte di Carlo VIII: Giovani de Candida e due suoi compendi di storia del Regno di Napoli," = section viii of the 2d ed. of his *Per la storia del Regno di Ferrante I* cited above at n. 89.

98. Ed. Alfredo Saviotti in the Laterza Scrittori d'Italia series (Bari, 1929). Much biographical information both in the older *Pandolfo Collenuccio umanista pesarese del secolo XV* by Saviotti (Pisa, 1888) and in the more recent *P. C. umanista* by Claudio Varese (Pesaro: Olivieri, 1957). The French translation by Denis Sauvage was published in Paris in 1546, 1553, and 1586. The Latin was published in Basel in 1572 and 1618, and the Spanish in Seville in 1584.

99. *The Summa Rerum Germanicarum* was first published in Rome in 1546 (see below, Chapter 12, n. 118).

100. On Fonzio: Charles Trinkaus, "The Humanist's Image of Humanism: The In-

augural Orations of B. F.," *Studies in the Renaissance,* VII (1960). Poggio on Diodorus Siculus in *D. S. Bibliothecae Historicae Libri XV* (Basel, 1578).

101. Zeno: Voss, vol. I, p. 56, and vol. II, pp. 55–56.

102. Guarino on history from his *Epistolario,* ed. Remigio Sabbadini (Venice: Deputazione Veneta di Storia Patria, 1916), vol. II, nos. 458, 465, 796.

103. Preface to *Historiarum Sui Temporis* (Rome, 1883), cited above in Italian translation in Chapter 2, n. 46.

104. Francesco Tateo, "Per l'edizione critica dell'*Actius* di Giovanni Pontano," *Studi mediolatini e volgari,* XII (1964). The current text is in *I dialoghi,* ed. Carmelo Previtera (Florence: Sansoni, 1943).

105. Eugenio Garin, ed., *Il pensiero pedagogico dell'umanesimo* (Florence: Giuntina, 1958), pp. 490–92, 454, et al.

106. Ladislao Reti, "Two unpublished Manuscripts of Leonardo da Vinci," *Burlington Magazine* (February, 1968), 81–89.

107. My calculations are based on the information provided by Giovan Battista Audiffredi, O.P., *Specimen Historico-Criticum Editionum Italicarum Saeculi XV* (Rome, 1794); Robert Alexander Peddie, *Printing at Brescia in the Fifteenth Century* (London: Williams and Norgate, 1905); Alberto Serra-Zanetti, *L'arte della stampa in Bologna nel primo ventennio del Cinquecento* (Bologna: Comune, 1959); and Giuseppe Antonio Sassi, "Historia Literario-typographica Mediolanensis, 1464–1500," published as the preface to Filippo Argellati's *Bibliotheca Scriptorum Mediolanensium.*

108. *De Situ Iapygie,* ed. Giovan Bernardino Tafuri in Calogerà's *Raccolta d'Opuscoli,* VII (1732), from the edition of Basel, 1553. See Ezio Savini, *Un curioso poligrafo del Quattrocento, Antonio de Ferrariis* (Bari: Macrì, 1941).

109. *De Re di Napoli et di Sicilia* is vol. IV of the series (but not in order of composition), which I read in the translation of Giovanni Tatti (Venice, 1543), as well as in the original, *De Regibus Neapolis & Siciliae* (Rome, 1505), which is republished in Graevius, vol. X.

110. *De Inquisitione* (1510), published along with the other works referred to in the following paragraphs: *Vita Joannae Primae ...*, *Vita Serzannis Caraccioli, De Ferdinando Qui Postea Aragonum Fuit Eiusque Posteris, Nobilitatis Neapolitanae Defensio,* and *De Varietate Fortunae,* by Giuseppe Paladino in *RIS²,* vol. XXII¹; but without a preface, so that it is still necessary to refer back to Muratori's preface in *RIS¹* as well as to the recent monographs: Carlo De Frede, "L'umanista Tristano Caracciolo e la sua 'Vita di Giovanna I'," *ASI,* CV (1947), and Mario Santoro, *T. C. e la cultura napoletana della Rinascenza* (Biblioteca del Giornale Italiano di Filologia, vol. VII) (Naples: Armanni, 1957).

111. In the long run, this attempted rehabilitation did not succeed. Carlo de Frede calls Giovanna "illetterata" and blames her in part for the rapid eclipse of the literary movement sponsored by Roberto, in *Storia di Napoli,* vol. III, p. 203 (above, n. 2).

CHAPTER SEVEN

1. *Cronaca modenese di Tomasino de' Bianchi,* ed. Carlo Borghi in *MSPP Modena,* vols. II–XIII. On Jachopino, see above, Chapter 4, n. 51. Much information about Tomasino in particular and on Emilian chronicles of the period in general was presented by Alberto Biondi in "La figura di Alberto Pio nella pubblicità minore," a paper delivered at a *convegno* held at Carpi in 1978.

2. Villa, *Chronica Civitatis Placentiae* (1511–56), ed. Giuseppe Bonora in *MHP Par Plac,* vol. III; Papazzoni, *Cronaca della Mirandola,* ed. Felice Ceretti in *Memorie storiche della città e dell'antico ducato di Mirandola,* vol. I (1872).

3. *Le due spedizioni militari di Giulio II,* tratte dal diario di Paride Grassi, ed. L. Frati (Bologna, 1886).

4. *Diario romano* (1485–1524), ed. Paolo Piccolomini, *RIS²,* vol. XXIII³. On Infessura, see above, Chapter 2, n. 27.

5. *Memorie perugine* (1502–27), ed. F. Bonaini in *ASI,* XVI² (1851).

6. *Cronache modenesi di A. Tassoni, di G. da Bazzano e di B. Morano,* ed. L. Vischi in *MSPP Modena,* vol. XV (1861). Tiraboschi mentions a continuation of Tassoni by Alessandro Tassoni, Jr., in *Biblioteca modenese* (Modena, 1784), vol. V, p. 210; but I have found no trace of it in print.

7. This and the following chronicles are published together by Gaetano da Minicis in *DSI,* vol. IV (on which see above, Chapter 5, n. 19)—all of them, that is, except the anonymous diary of Cesena, which I read in Latin translation in appendix to Cesare Brissio's *Urbii Caesenatae Descriptio,* in Graevius, vol. IX³ (cols. 65–77).

8. An example of the abundance of still unpublished chronicles and diaries regarding merely one incident is to be found in the huge footnotes and the bibliography of the nineteenth-century chronicle by Gaetano Giordani, *Della venuta e dimora in Bologna del sommo pontefice Clemente VII per la coronazione...di Carlo V imperatore* (Bologna, 1842). The three other chronicles here referred to are all published by Giovan Battista Moriondo in *Monumenta Aquensia* (Turin, 1789–90); but they can be found in the editor's chaotic pages only with the help of the index published sometime in the nineteenth century by Fedele Savio and included as vol. III of the Forni reprint. On Della Chiesa, see above, Chapter 4, n. 27.

9. Tiraboschi, pt. III, vol. VII, p. 953. I am not the first to have perceived a connection between the *calamità* and the increase in the quantity of history writing during the first decades of the sixteenth century. The credit belongs to Michele Maria Vecchioli in a passage in his introduction to Giuliano Passero's diary (below, n. 23) in 1785. On p. 9 he says: "si vide il mondo da tai, e tante novità...che dappertutto si vide sorgere...negl'ingegni più eletti...un desiderio di comporre storie...."

10. *Diaria de Bello Carolino* (Latin and English on facing pages), ed. and tr. Dorothy M. Schullian (New York: Ungar, 1967) (Renaissance Society of America, Renaissance Text Series, vol. I), with all the relevant information in the preface and with the letter from Valla on p. 28.

11. *Chroniche del marchese di Mantova,* ed. Carlo E. Visconti in *ASI,* VI (1879).

12. *Historie di messer Marco Guazzo ove se contengono la venuta & partita d'Italia di Carlo Ottavo re di Franza* (Venice, 1547), 239 pp. in 16º.

13. Sanudo, *La spedizione di Carlo VIII in Italia,* ed. Rinaldo Fulin in *AV,* III (1873); on Sanudo's earlier works, see above, Chapter

3, p. 81. Malipiero, *Annali veneti,* ed. Francesco Longo and Agostino Sagredo in *ASI*¹, VII, in 2 vols. The importance of Malipiero's documents for modern Near Eastern studies is demonstrated in John Woods, *The Aqquyunlu: Clan, Confederation, Empire* (Minneapolis-Chicago: Bibliotheca Islamica, 1976), p. 18. Dolfin is cited above, Chapter 3, n. 40. The slowness of other Italians as well as Venetians to understand the significance of the first French invasion is further documented by Giovanni Pillinini in Chapter 1 of his *Il sistema degli Stati italiani, 1454–1494* (Venice: Libreria Universitaria, 1970).

14. *I diarii,* ed. Rinaldo Fulin et al., for the Deputazione Veneta di Storia Patria (Venice, 1879–1902).

15. Above, Chapter 4, n. 47.

16. All the Forlì chronicles, published as well as unpublished, are listed by Ernst Breisach in his delightful biography, *Caterina Sforza: A Renaissance Virago* (University of Chicago Press, 1967), which gives all the pertinent background information.

17. *Cronache forlivesi...dal 1476 al 1517,* ed. Giuseppe Mazzatinti in 3 vols., published in *Mon ist Romagna* in 1895.

18. Coniger's chronicle is printed in Pelliccia, vol. V. See above, Chapter 6, n. 63.

19. *Diario (1492–1507)* in Pelliccia, vol. I. Cf. Agostino Pascale, *Racconto del Sacco di Capua dato...su'l 24 di luglio...1501* (Naples, 1682).

20. Reflections of this same sentiment are described by Pasquale Alberto De Lisio in *Gli anni della svolta* (Salerno: Società Editrice Salernitana, 1976).

21. Anonymous chronicle from 1434 (but really from 1494) to 1496, in Pelliccia, vol. I. All the published chronicles and histories of sixteenth-century Naples are listed in Tommaso Pedìo's catalogue-cum-commentibus, *Storia della storiografia del Regno di Napoli nei secoli XVI e XVII, Note e appunti* (Chiaravalle: Frama, 1973). There is another such list in Giovanni Gravier's Introduction to the diary of Gregorio Rosso (see below, n. 90) in vol. III of his *Raccolta* and still another in vol. III¹ of Tafuri.

22. Anonymous chronicle, 1495–1519, in Pelliccia, vol. I.

23. *Prima pubblicazione in istampa*

che . . . delle storie in forma di giornali le quali sotto nome di questo autore finora erano andate manoscritte . . ., ed. Vincenzo Maria Altobelli and Michele Maria Vecchioni (Naples, 1785). On the Inquisition affair, see the sources cited by Luigi Amabile in "Il tumulto napoletano dell'anno 1510 . . . ," *Atti Pont*, XIX (1888).

24. *Istorie*, ed. Ildefonso di San Luigi in *Delizie degli eruditi toscani* (Florence, 1770–89), vols. XX–XXIII. The biographical introduction is in the preface to vol. XXIII.

25. Partially published by G. Aiazzi in *ASI*, IV² (1853).

26. *Libro debitori e creditori e ricordanze*, partially published by Joseph Schnitzer in *Quellen und Forschungen zur Geschichte Savonarolas* (Munich, 1902), vol. I.

27. Published in appendix to *Riccordi storici di Filippo di Cino Rinuccini*, cited above, Chapter 1, n. 78.

28. *Storie fiorentine dal 1378 al 1509*, ed. Roberto Palmarocchi (Laterza, 1931). Passages here cited in English are taken from Mario Domandi's translation *(The History of Florence)*, which also contains a good introduction (Harper Torchbooks), largely based on the standard critical study by Nicolai Rubinstein, "The *Storie fiorentine* and the *Memorie di famiglia* by Francesco Guicciardini," *Rinascimento*, IV (1953), with other current bibliography in the appendix. A partial English edition translated by Cecil Grayson is published as *History of Italy and History of Florence*, ed. John Hale (New York: Washington Square Press, 1964).

29. *Diario de' successi più importanti seguiti in Italia & particolarmente in Fiorenza dall'anno 1498 in sino all'anno 1512* (Florence, 1568). The *Ricordi* are published in appendix to the chronicle of his life by the scholar who discovered them, Denis Fachard, in *Biagio Buonaccorsi: Sa vie, son temps, son oeuvre* (Bologna: Boni, 1976).

30. Partially published by Schnitzer (above, n. 26), vol. IV, with a long introduction. Despite Schnitzer's promise and the plea of Guido Pampaloni in *ASI*, CXVII (1959), 147–53, the full text has never been published (but Newberry Library has a microfilm of the manuscript). Much information on Parenti can be found in Donald Weinstein's *Savonarola and Florence* (Prince-

ton University Press, 1970). Still unpublished are also many other important chronicles of this period, e.g., that of Piero Vaglienti, the "modesto mercante-cronista" cited by Michele Luzzati in *RSI*, LXXXVI (1974), 442, and used extensively by Sergio Bertelli in "Pier Soderini 'Vexillifer Perpetuus . . .'," *Renaissance Studies in Honor of Hans Baron* (above, Chapter 1, n. 40). A fragment of Parenti on the Pazzi conspiracy, left complete and isolated from the body of the diary by the author, is published in appendix to Perosa's edition of Poliziano's *Coniurationis Commentarium*. cited above, Chapter 1, n. 109.

31. *Ricordanze di Bartolomeo Masi calderaio fiorentino dal 1478 al 1523*, ed. Giuseppe Odoardo Corazzini (Florence: Sansoni, 1906).

32. *Diario fiorentino dal 1450 al 1516*, with an anonymous (but probably by his son) continuation to 1542, ed. Iodoco Del Badia (Florence: Sansoni, 1883), upon which is based an English translation by Alice de Rosen Jervis (New York: Dutton, 1927).

33. Above, Chapter 1, p. 23 ff.

34. Vittorio De Caprariis, *Francesco Guicciardini: Dalla politica alla storia* (Laterza, 1950), upon which I depend frequently for what I say about Guicciardini elsewhere.

35. *Ricordanze di Tribaldo de' Rossi*, partially published by Ildefonso di San Luigi in *Delizie degli eruditi toscani*, vol. XXIII.

36. *Delle cose fatte da Luca di Antonio degli Albizzi*, ed. Filippo Luigi Polidori, *ASI*, IV² (1853). Cf. above, n. 29.

37. Marino Berengo calls it "la più memorabile resistenza che i contemporanei, pur cresciuti in un'età di guerre e di assedi, avessero conosciuto": *RSI*, LXXXVII (1975), 172. The details are now in Michele Luzzati, *Una guerra di popolo: Lettere private dal tempo dell'Assedio di Pisa (1494–1509)* (Pisa: Pacini, 1973).

38. All three Pisan chronicles are published together in *ASI*, VI² (1845): an anonymous *Guerra del Millecinquecento*, the *Ricordi* of Ser Perizolo da Pisa, and the *Memoriale* of Giovanni Portoveneri. A humanist commentary on these events by Leonardo Sfrenati, *De Bello Italico*, written in Sallustian prose, has never been published, probably for the good nineteenth-century reason that it is a "his-

tory," not a chronicle. But several pages are quoted in the article dedicated to it by Michele Lupo Gentile in *ASI*[5], XXXII (1903).

39. *Commentarius de Platonicae Philosophiae post Renatas Litteras apud Italos Instauratione, sive Marsilli Ficini Vita*, ed. Angelo Maria Bandini (Pisa, 1771), on which see Raymond Marcel, *Marsile Ficin* (Paris: Les Belles Lettres, 1958), p. 21. The authority on the "golden age" myth is Felix Gilbert, the result of whose previous studies into the political ideology of this period are brought together in his *Machiavelli and Guicciardini: Politics and History in Sixteenth-Century Florence* (Princeton University Press, 1965) (since 1973 also available in paperback), upon which I rely heavily in these pages. On Guicciardini's *Storia d'Italia*, see below, Chapter 11. Other formulations of the thesis are given in the work by Pillinini cited above at n. 13.

40. *Il miserando sacco dato alla terra di Prato*, published in *Tre narrazioni del sacco di Prato* in *ASI*, I (1842).

41. Boccineri, *Riccordi*, published in the same *Tre narrazioni*.

42. From the poem by Stefano Guizzalotti, in *Tre narrazioni*, p. 265.

43. *Priorista* of Paolo di Girolamo di ser Paolo Paoli, published in appendix to Rinuccini's *Ricordi storici* cited above in Chapter 1, n. 78.

44. His diary is published along with that of Modesti (above, n. 40). Still another diary by Antonio Benemati in the city archives of Prato is mentioned by the editor.

45. *Recitazione del caso di Pietro Paolo Boscoli e di Agostino Capponi*, *ASI*, I (1842).

46. *Storia fiorentina*, partially published by Schnitzer in *Quellen und Forschungen*, above, n. 26, vol. III. On Rucellai, above, Chapter 1, n. 106.

47. *Vita di Lorenzo de' Medici*, published by Enrico Niccolini in *Scritti storici e politici* (Laterza, 1972).

48. The best text of the *Sommario della istoria d'Italia* is that published in the *Scritti storici e politici* cited in the preceding note, for reasons given in the ample bibliographical appendix. But the older edition by Alfred von Reumont in *ASI*, appendix, vol. VI (1848), is still useful for its introduction. Full biographical information in the somewhat

wordy *Un ami de Machiavel, François Vettori* by Louis Passi (Paris: Plon, 1913). A chronicle of Vettori's *res gestae* is to be found in Rosemary Devonshire Jones's *F. V.: Florentine Citizen and Medici Servant* (London: Athlone Press, 1972). Vettori's political reflections on these events are described by Furio Diaz in *Il Granducato di Toscana: I Medici*, vol. I (Turin: UTET, 1976), pp. 35 ff.

49. *Cronaca milanese dall'anno 1476 al 1515*, ed. Antonio Ceruti, *MSI*, vol. XIII. On the author: Giuseppe Martini in *DBI*.

50. *Annalia*, ed. Pietro Luigi Donini (Milan, 1861).

51. Ed. Cesare Cantù in *ASI*, III (1842). On the author: Franco Petrucci in *DBI*.

52. Described by Carlo Marcora in *ASL*, XC (1966), 330–32.

53. Above, Chapter 4, n. 120.

54. *De Bello Italico et Rebus Gallorum Praeclarae Gestis Libri VI*, in Graevius, vol. IX[6].

55. Published together with Cagnola (above, n. 50). He and Burigozzo are the only ones of the Milanese historians and chroniclers of this period mentioned by Gian Luigi Barni in "La vita culturale a Milano dal 1500 alla scomparsa dell'ultimo duca Sforza" in *Storia di Milano* (Treccani), vol. VIII.

56. On Sanudo, see above, nn. 13 and 14. Priuli, *I diarii (1494–1512)*, *RIS*[2], vol. XXIV[3], of which vol. I (to 1500), corresponding to vol. I of the autograph, is edited by Arturo Segre, while vols. II (1500–1506) and IV are edited by Roberto Cessi. Vol. III of the autograph (1506–June 1509) has been lost, according to Cessi; and vol. V, which is promised in the last lines of vol. IV, has not yet been published (to my knowledge). For biographical information, I rely on R. Fulin, "G. P. e i suoi diarii," *AV*, XXII (1881), and for some details about Priuli's reports of foreign policy debates after the calamity, on Lester J. Libby's article in *RQ*, XXII (1975). Libby could have saved himself the trouble of reading the autograph had he realized that vols. II and IV had indeed been published, the latter as early as 1938.

57. See Corrado Vivanti's discussion of Gaetano Cozzi's edition of Domenico Morosini's *De Bene Instituta Re Publica* (in which the policy is advocated) in *RSI*, LXXXIV (1972).

58. *Cronaca della città di Verona,* ed. by Giambattista Biancolini (Verona, 1747), as a continuation of Zagata (above, Chapter 3, n. 28), which it is not: Zagata wrote in the years 1453–54, while Rizzoni began writing only after 1503 and then seriously only about events since the outbreak of the War of Ferrara. The *Diarii udinesi . . . di Leonardo e Gregorio Amaseo e Giovan Antonio Azio* (Venice, 1884–85) may be relevant at this point, to judge from what Rino Avesani says about the relatives of Romolo Quirino Amaseo in *DBI.* But the volume (ser. 3, vol. I) of the *Monumenti storici* of the *Deputazione Veneta di Storia Patria* was missing from the libraries I consulted.

59. All the Paduan chronicles are mentioned by Andrea Gloria in *Di Padova dopo la lega stretta in Cambrai* (Padua, 1863). A few pages of Jacopo Bruto's diary are published in the appendix. None of these chronicles is mentioned in Polibio Zanetti's chronicle of "L'assedio di Padova del 1509," *AV²,* II¹ (1891), since its main purpose is to demonstrate that Venetian patriotism was still not dead in the late nineteenth century. Here is the closing sentence: "Venetia usciva da codesta lotta più gloriosa di prima e colla speranza di nuovi trionfi poteva prepararsi ai futuri cimenti." But they are carefully examined by Innocenzo Cervelli in his *Machiavelli e la crisi dello Stato veneziano* (Naples: Guida, 1974), pp. 336 ff. The chronicles of Friuli are mentioned in the preface to the *Lettere* of Luigi Da Porto (below, n. 61).

60. Caprioli (the editor calls him Cavrioli) I read first in the Italian translation by Patricio Spini (below, Chapter 10, n. 59) and then in *Dell'istorie della città di Brescia* (Venice, 1744). The quotation is from Vittore Branca in a note to p. 520 of his edition of Boccaccio's *Decameron* (Florence: LeMonnier, 1965).

61. *Lettere storiche dall'anno 1509 al 1528,* (but really only through 1513: the letter of 1528 is separated from the other letters), ed. Bartolomeo Bressan (Florence, 1851), on which see Achille Olivieri, "Dio e 'fortuna' nelle *Lettere storiche* di Luigi Da Porto," *SV,* XIII (1971).

62. Brief passages from three of the still unpublished chronicles of the sack, those by Clemente Zamara, Jacopo Melga, and Tommaso Carcanda, are published by Federico Ororici in *I congiurati bresciani del MDXII* in *Raccolta di cronisti lombardi inediti* (Milan, 1856), vol. II.

63. *De Exterminio Brixianae Civitatis* and *De Calamitatibus post Excidium Passis Libellus,* both published by Paolo Guerrini in *Le cronache bresciane inedite dei secoli XV–XIX,* vol. II (Brescia, 1922) (= "Fonti per la storia bresciana," vol. III).

64. *Della congiura de' Bresciani per sostrarre la patria alla francese dominazione,* ed. Giovanni Labus and published in Carlo Rosmini's *Dell'istoria di Milano* (Milan, 1820), vol. IV. So strong was the memory of these events still a century later that the *congiurati* were accorded by far the longest articles in Ottavio Rossi's *Elogi historici di Bresciani illustri* (Brescia, 1620), on which see below, Chapter 14.

65. *Descrizione del sacco di Brescia,* published in appendix to Caprioli, cited above, n. 60.

66. The petition of the Brescians is published by Agostino Zanelli in *ASL,* XXXIX (1912), pp. 66 ff.

67. *Diario del campo tedesco nella guerra veneta dal 1512 al 1516,* ed. Vincenzo Joppi, *AV,* XXXIV (1887), et seg.

68. The diary of Ascanio Cantieri da Paratico (1496–1545) is published together with that of Benvenuto Brunelli, which covers the years 1514 to 1530, by Paolo Guerrini along with Casari in the volume cited at n. 63.

69. Bernardi Arluni iureconsulti patricii mediolanensis *De Bello Veneto,* Graevius, vol. V⁴.

70. Andreae Mocenici *Belli Memorabilis Cameracensis adversus Venetos Historia,* Graevius, vol. V⁴. What I say here will probably have to be modified when someone finally publishes Tommaso Donato's chronicle to 1528 from the MS Marciana, cl. VII Italiani CCCXXXIII.

71. See Lester J. Libby, Jr., "History and Political Thought after 1509," *SR,* XX (1973), esp. p. 31.

72. *Cronache cremonesi dall'anno 1399 al 1525,* of which the second here referred to begins in 1494, ed. Francesco Robolotti in *BHI Lomb,* vol. I. See above, Chapter 4, n. 17.

73. *Commentaria Suorum Temporum Libri X,* ed. Edmund Martène and Ursinus

Durand in *Veterum Scriptorum et Monumentorum... Amplissima Collectio* (Paris, 1729), vol. V.

74. The anonymous and still unpublished *Vite* of the bishops of Ravenna to 1517, quoted by Pietro Paolo Ginaiani in *Memorie storico-critiche degli scrittori ravennati* under "anonimi."

75. *De Bello Rhodio Libri III* auctore Iacopo Fontano brugensi iurisconsulto, first published in Rome in 1524, but which I read in the 2d edition of Paris, 1540. The author was not an Italian by birth, but his writing is fully in the tradition of his adopted Italian and Rhodian compatriots. Much of the work is the result of firsthand observation.

76. Antonio Grumello; see below, n. 79.

77. Martino Verri, *Relazione delle cose successe in Pavia dal 1524 al 1528*, ed. Giuseppe Müller in *Racc CDS Lomb*, vol. II (1856).

78. *Cronaca di Milano, 1500–1544*, published together with Cagnola (above, n. 51). Burigozzo says he was six years old in 1500. Hence, the earlier entries are all based on what he remembered, none too well, many years later (Pope Julius II, it seems, died in 1514). Still, according to Gaspare De Caro in *DBI*, this chronicle is a very valuable reflection of popular religious attitudes, even though little is known about the author himself.

79. *Cronaca... dal MCCCCLXVII al MDXXIX* (but it really starts in 1494), ed. Giuseppe Müller in *Racc CDS Lomb*, vol. I. His position as captain of Pavia is proven by a letter published by E. Motta in *ASL*, XXXIV (1907), 478–79.

80. *Historia Rerum in Insubribus Gestarum sub Gallorum Dominio, BHILomb*, vol. I.

81. *De Bello Mediolanensi*, Graevius, vol. II², and *De Bello Mussano*, Graevius, vol. III², translated by Francesco Philipopoli of Florence as *Delle cose fatte per la restituzione di Francesco Sforza secondo, duca di Milano* (Venice, 1539) from the first two editions: *De Rebus Gestis pro Restitutione Francisci II* (Milan, 1531) and *De Rebus nuper in Italia Gestis...* (Nürnberg, 1532).

82. *De Bello Gallico Commentarii*, ed. A. Ceruti, *BHILomb*, vol. I.

83. *L'anthropologia*, which I have found only in Part II (Venice, 1533).

84. *Suae Aestatis Rerum Gestarum Libri IV*, ed. Ceruti, *BHILomb*, vol. I. On the author, see also below, Chapter 15, n. 52.

85. *La ossidione di Pavia per il Cambiago cremonese volgarmente descritta* (Cremona, 1525).

86. First published by Domenico Orano as *Il Diari* (Rome, 1895); but the relevant passages are republished, albeit with errors of transcription and without the aid of a critical apparatus, in Vicente de Cadenas y Vicent, *El Saco de Roma* (Madrid: Instituto Salazar y Castro, 1974).

87. Buonaparte, *Ragguaglio storico di tutto l'occorso giorno per giorno nel sacco di Roma* ("Colonia" [Lucca], 1756); Guicciardini, *Sacco di Roma* (Paris, 1664).

88. The controversy over the authenticity of these chronicles began in the review articles of the *Novelle letterarie* in 1756 and 1758, and the arguments were then summarized by Giuseppe Torra in his edition of Patrizio de' Rossi's early nineteenth-century *Memorie storiche* (Rome, 1837). De' Rossi's account is based on the still unpublished account by his ancestor, Francesco, who had been in Rome since 1519. Both the chronicles were reprinted by C. Milanese in *Il sacco di Roma...: Narrazioni di contemporanei* (Florence, 1867). The attribution of the second to Guicciardini is certified by Bono Simonetta in the biographical preface to his edition of Guicciardini's *Del Savonarola, ovvero Dialogo... il giorno dopo la battaglia di Gavinana* (Florence: Olschki, 1959). The authenticity of both chronicles is accepted by Judith Hook in *The Sack of Rome* (New York: Macmillan, 1972). I do not here include Francesco Vettori's *Sacco di Roma*, published in the volume cited above at n. 47, because it is a discussion, rather than a description, of the events.

89. See above, n. 47.

90. *Istoria delle cose di Napoli sotto l'impero di Carlo V*, Gravier, vol. VIII.

91. *Dei successi del sacco di Roma e guerra del Regno di Napoli sotto Lotrech* (Naples, 1858).

92. Above, n. 23.

93. *Racconti di storia napoletana* (from the accession of Alfonso d'Aragona to 1535), discovered by Bartolomeo Capasso in the 1870s and published anonymously in *ASPN*, XXXIII (1908) and XXXIV (1909).

94. Giuseppe Marinella da Molfetta, *Conpendio del Dominio di Napoli.... Sacco della città di Molfetta*, in Pelliccia, vol. IV.

95. *Cronaca del soggiorno di Carlo V in Italia,* ed. G. Romano (Milan, 1892).

96. *Breve trattato e discorso di quello che successe di bene al Regno di Napoli per l'andata del magnifico Giovan Paolo Coraggio alla corte di Carlo Quinto,* written in 1571 and published in Gravier. Some passages are republished, along with passages from other diaries of the period, in Pedìo's *Napoli e Spagna nella prima metà del Cinquecento* (Bari: Cacucci, 1971). After checking it with other sources, Carlo De Frede declared it to be "molto precisa e veritiera": *ASPN,* XCII (1975), 126.

97. These are the words of Geronimo de Spenis da Frattamaggiore (d. 1605) in an untitled chronicle of festivals and crimes covering the years 1543–1547 printed in *ASPN,* II (1877).

98. Cited above at n. 93.

99. *Vita di don Pietro di Toledo,* ed. Francesco Palermo in *Narrazioni e documenti sulla storia del Regno di Napoli dall'anno 1522 al 1667,* which is the title of the whole vol. IX (1846) of *ASI.*

100. *Dell'istoria di notar Antonio Castaldo libri quattro, ne quali si descrivono gli avvenimenti più memorabili ... sotto il governo del vicerè d. Piero di Toledo,* Gravier, vol. VI.

101. *Ex Universa Historia Rerum Europae Suorum Temporum ...; Coniuratio Ioannis Ludovici Flisci; Tumultus Neapolitani ...* (which is also published separately in Gravier, vol. VI); *Caedes Petri Ludovici Farnesii Placentiae Ducis* (Naples, 1571). More on Foglietta below, Chapter 9, nn. 87–90.

102. *Della guerra di Campagna di Roma e del Regno di Napoli nel pontificato di Paolo IV l'anno MDLVI e LVII; tre ragionamenti,* which I read in Gravier's reprint (vol. VII) of Girolamo Ruscelli's first edition of Venice, 1560.

103. *Della Guerra carafesca,* ed. Luigi Volpicella, *ASPN,* XXXV (1910).

104. On the insurrection of 1585, see below, p. 275.

105. Collection of Antonio Feltrio (d. 1562) and *Croniche antiquissime* of Tommaso di Catania, both in Pelliccia, vol. 1.

106. Anon., *La morte di Giovan Vincenzo Starace, eletto del popolo di Napoli nel maggio 1585, ASPN,* I (1876). For the background: Rosario Villari, *La rivolta antispagnola a Napoli,* vol. I: *Le origini* (Laterza, 1967),

which cites all the relevant chronicles. On the unpublished "Corona" chronicle, see Michelangelo Mandella, *Il moto napolitano del 1585 e il delitto Storace* (Naples: Giannini, 1967). Giuseppe Marenello, *Presa e sacco della città di Molfetta,* and *Il compendio del Dominio di Napoli e successione di Filippo II,* both written just before the dedication of the second to Ferrante Gonzaga, prince of Molfetta, in 1596, and both published in Pelliccia, vol. IV.

CHAPTER EIGHT

1. Partially published in the transcription of Lazaro de' Bernabei in *Collezione di documenti storici antichi inediti ed editi rari delle città e terre marchigiane,* ed. C. Ciavarini (Ancona, 1870), vol. I.

2. Several of the Perugian chronicles are described by Francesco Bonaini in a proposal to the editors of the *ASI,* appendix, vol. VII (1849); and Bontempi and Frolliere were accordingly published in the same *ASI,* XVI² (1851), along with Alfani (above, Chapter 7, n. 5). The others are published by Ariodante Fabretti in vol. IV of *Cronache della città di Perugia* (Turin, 1892).

3. Above, Chapter 2, n. 73.

4. Anon., *Diario della ribellione d'Urbino nel 1572,* ed. Filippo Ugolini, *ASI,* n.s., III¹ (1856).

5. *Libro di ricordi di Iacopo di Maccario di Gregorio Catani, cittadino aretino,* ed. Arturo Bini in appendix to *RIS²,* vol. XXIV¹; Spadari, *Racconto della ribellione aretina del 1529,* ed. Giovanni Rondinelli in his *Relazione sopra lo stato antico e moderno della città di Arezzo* (Arezzo, 1755).

6. Benedetti's speech is cast in the form of a commentary in the anonymous *La cacciata della guardia spagnola da Siena, ASI,* II (1842). Lodovico Domenichi in the dedicatory preface to his translation of Giovambattista Giraldi's *Commentario delle cose di Ferrara* (below, Chapter 10, n. 29), dated 9 October 1556.

7. *Racconti delle principali fazioni della guerra di Siena, ASI,* II (1842), written in the form of an on-the-spot *relazione.* Roffìa also wrote a commentary on the siege of Volterra of 1530, a history of San Miniato, and an account of another "caso notabile seguito in Firenze" (1557); but I have not found that

they were ever published. His most successful casting of historical materials in the form of *novelle* on the model of Franco Sacchetti is his *Ghiribizzi di mess. Bernabò Visconti, signore di Milano* (Modena, 1868). All of the historically documented tales were meant to prove that Bernabò was "di natura aspra e ruvida e di ghiribizzosa crudeltà, mescolata talvolta con alcuna ridicola piacevolezza." His *Narrazione della presa di Golfanara in Piemonte* was published by L. Scarabelli in *ASI*, XIV (1847).

8. Anon., *Notizie della vittoria riportata dagl'Imperiali presso Marciano*, also in *ASI*, II (1842).

9. *Il successo delle rivoluzioni della città di Siena d'imperiale franzese e di franzese imperiale, colle guerre venute contro a detta città*, in the same *ASI*, II (1842).

10. Ed. Antonio Cerugi, *MSI*, vol. XVII.

11. *Cronica*, ed. Giuseppe Vernazza, *MSI*, vol. I.

12. *Memoriale dal 1482 al 1528*, ed. Vincenzo Promis, *MSI*, vol. VIII.

13. *Cronache anteriori al secolo XVII concernenti la storia di Cuneo e di alcune vicine terre*, ed. Domenico Promis, *MSI*, vol. XII.

14. *Memorie di un terrazzano di Rivoli dal 1525* [but it actually starts earlier] *al 1586*, ed. "D. P." (Promis), *MSI*, vol. VI.

15. *De Gestis Antonii Torresani Brevis Narratio*, ed. D. Promis, *MSI*, vol. XII.

16. Agostino Dutto, *Le relazioni sull'assedio di Cuneo del 1557 con appendice, MSI*, vol. XLI, describes all the texts. "P" was published in *ASI*, appendix, vol. II (1845), by C. Promis.

17. *Histoire mémorable de la guerre faite par le duc de Savoye Emanuel Philebert contre ses subjectz des Vallées*, first published in 1561, and now by Enea Balmas and Vittorio Diena in the Collana Storici Valdese (Turin: Claudiana, 1972). *Histoire des persécutions et guerres faites depuis l'an 1555 jusques en l'an 1561* ... (Geneva, 1562); and Lentolo, *Historia delle grandi e crudeli persecutioni*, written in 1562 (not in 1595), both soon to appear in the same series. On Lentulo, see Emilio Comba, "La storia inedita dei Valdesi ...," *Bulletin de la Société d'histoire vaudoise*, XIV (1897). On all three and on Miolo (next note), I follow the apparently authoritative study by Giovanni Gonnet, "Note sulla

storiografia valdese dei secoli XVI e XVII," *Rivista di storia e letteratura religiosa*, X (1974). For the background, see Raffaele de Simone, *Tre anni decisivi di storia valdese* ... (Analecta Gregoriana, vol. XCVII) (Rome, 1958).

18. *Historia breve e vera de gl'affari de i Valdesi delle Valli*, ed. Enea Balmas, published in 1971 in the same series cited in the preceding note.

19. *De Bello Melitensi Historia* (Perugia, 1567).

20. Marcantonii Montiflori *De Pugna Navali Cursularia Commentaria* (Genoa, 1577).

21. *De Bello Cyprio Libri V*, ed. C. Graziani (Rome, 1624); published also in French translation as *Histoire de la guerre de Chypre* (Paris, 1685). On Graziani, see also below, Chapter 14.

22. *Commentari della guerra di Cipro e della lega dei principi cristiani contro il Turco*, ed. "per cura de' Monaci della Badìa Cassinese" in *Archivio cassinese*, I (Montecassino, 1845). My biographical information comes from Marcello Turchi, "Vitalità eroica e tensione tragica nella memorialistica di Bartolomeo Sereno," *RLI*, LXXVII (1973).

23. *Historia delle cose successe dal principio della guerra mossa da Selim Ottomano a' Venetiani fino al dì della gran giornata vittoriosa contra Turchi* (Venice, 1572), dedicated to Giovanni Grimani, patriarch of Aquileia. A full list of Venetian chronicles of the war, published and unpublished, is given by Gino Benzoni on pp. 409 ff. of *Il Mediterraneo nella seconda metà del Cinquecento alla luce di Lepanto* (Florence: Olschki, 1974)—a volume which also contains a very helpful article by Carlo Dionisotti, "Lepanto nella cultura italiana del tempo." The still unpublished chronicle of Giovanni Antonio Venier is described by M. Brunetti in "La crisi finale della Sacra Lega," *Miscellanea in onore di Roberto Cessi* (Rome: Edizioni di Storia e Letteratura, 1958), vol. II.

24. *Successo della guerra fatta con Selim Sultano Imperator de' Turchi e giustificazione della pace con lui conclusa*, ed. Agostino Sagredo in *ASI*, appendix, vol. IV (1847) (written in 1573 according to internal evidence).

25. *La battaglia di Lepanto* ... *e la dispersione della invincibile armata di Filippo II* (vol. VII of G. Daelli's Biblioteca rara) (Milan, 1863).

26. *Estratto dal libro nono tuttora inedita della*

historia manoscritta di Georgio Pilone dottore (Belluno, 1881, *nozze*).

27. *Historia de Salamina captá et m. Antonio Bragadeno excoriato . . .*, Latin and dialect texts on facing pages (Venice, 1843).

28. *Della historia vinitiana parte secondo, nella quale in libri tre si contiene la guerra fatta dalla lega de' prencipi christiani contro Selino ottomano* (Venice, 1605). On Paruta as a historian, see below, Chapter 9.

29. Caracciolo, *I commentarii delle guerre fatte co' Turchi da don Giovanni d'Austria dopo che venne in Italia*, ed. Scipione Ammirato (the historian of Florence, on whom see below, Chapter 10) (Florence, 1581). Costo (also in Chapter 10, below), *La vittoria della Lega* (Naples, 1582). My biographical information on Caracciolo comes from the unsigned article in the *DBI*. On the importance of Lepanto in literature, see Marcello Turchi, "Riflessi letterari in Italia della battaglia di Lepanto," *Nuovi quaderni del Meridione,* IX (1971).

30. See Aldo Stella, "Le pubbliche entrate' e la crisi veneziana del 1582," *Miscellanea in onore di Roberto Cessi,* vol. II.

31. Described (but not published) by Aldo Landi in *NRS,* LIX (1975), 576 ff.

32. Described in the introduction to Book I of Palladio's *Historie della provincia del Friuli* (Udine, 1660).

33. Mario Brunetti, "Il diario di Leonardo Donà, procuratore di San Marco," *AV,* ser. 5, vol. XXI (1937).

34. *Relazione dell'ingresso della infanta Caterina d'Austria in Torino, MSI,* vol. XV.

35. *Estratti del diario delle cose avvenute in Sabbioneta dal 1580 al 1600,* ed. Giuseppe Müller in *Racc CDS Lomb,* vol. II.

36. *Cronaca,* ed. Adamo Pasini in *Fonti della storia forlivese* (Forlì, 1929).

37. *De Origine atque Historia Civitatis Alexandriae,* ed. Moriondo in *Monumenta Aquensia* (above, Chapter 7, n. 8), vol. I.

38. *Castrensium Depredationis Historia* (1575), in Graevius, vol. VIII³.

39. *Compendio delle croniche di Milano,* ed. Massimo Fabi (Biblioteca storica italiana, vol. II) (Milan, 1853).

40. The chronicles of Cornelio di Ascanio Lantieri de Paratico, Bernardino Vallabio (also published in four previous editions, from 1555 to 1637), Tito Luzzago, Francesco Robacciolo, and Giovanni Pluda di Castenedolo are edited by Paolo Guerrini in *Le cronache bresciane inedite dei secoli XV–XIX* (cited above, Chapter 7, n. 63).

41. Published by Ariodante Fabretti in *Cronache della città di Perugia* (above, n. 2), vol. IV.

42. *Gonzagarum Mantuae et Montisferrati Ducum Historia* (Mantua, 1617). On which I follow Mario D'Addio in *Il pensiero politico di Gaspare Scippio* (Milan: Giuffrè, 1962), pp. 131–32. On Antonio Possevino, see below, Chapter 12.

43. *Cronaca modenese (1588–1636),* ed. G. Bertoni, T. Sandonnini, and E. P. Vicini in *MSPP Modena,* vols. XIV–XVIII (i.e., in several volumes, which alone gives an idea of the quantity of *petits détails* that Giambattista Spaccini managed to pile up). Similar entries are to be found, notwithstanding the author's exposure to the standard humanist historians of the first decades of the century, in the *Cronichetta breve e dilettevole . . .* of "B. V., cittadino bresciano" (Brescia, 1584). On Spaccini in particular: Tiraboschi in *Biblioteca modenese* (cited in Chapter 7, n. 6), vol. V, pp. 136–37.

44. Roberto Ridolfi, "Lorenzo Poggio e le sue sconosciute istorie," *Bibliofilia,* LXV (1963).

45. *Diario fiorentino . . . dal 252 al 1596,* ed. Giuseppe Odoardo Corazzini (Florence, 1900).

46. *Diario di Firenze e di altre parti della cristianità, 1574–1579,* ed. Roberto Cantagalli (Florence: Istituto Nazionale di Studi sul Rinascimento, 1970), on which see Giorgio Spini in *RSI,* LXXXII (1970), 232–35.

47. *Cronaca (1532–1606),* ed. (in exemplary fashion) Giuliana Sapori (Milan: Ricciardi, 1972), with further biographical and critical remarks by the editor in *Studi in onore di Armando Sapori* (Milan: Cisalpino, 1957), vol. II, and in "Giuliano de' Ricci e la polemica sulla stampa nel Cinquecento," *NRS,* LVI (1972). Christian Bec places the chronicle in the context not of the times but of the tradition of Renaissance *ricordanze,* in "L'Historiographie bourgeoise à Florence à la fin du XVIe siècle," *Revue des études italiennes,* XX (1974).

CHAPTER NINE

1. Dedication to Benedetto Giovio, *Historiae Patriae,* on which see below, Chapter 10, n. 22.

2. Emilio Garba, "Storiografia greca e imperialismo romano," *RSI,* LXXXVI (1974).

3. *Annali della città dell'Aquila* (Rome, 1570) (but written in 1535).

4. Renzo Negri in *DBI.*

5. *De Origine et Temporibus Urbis Bergomi* (Venice, 1532), subsequently translated as *Il libro delle origini...* (Bergamo, 1556). The historians and antiquarians of Bergamo are listed by Belotti in *Storia di Bergamo* (above, Chapter 4, n. 9).

6. Mario Giovannelli, nobile volterrano dell'Ordine Eremitano di Sant'Agostino, *Cronistoria dell'antichità e nobiltà di Volterra cominciando dal principio della sua edificazione infin'al giorno d'hoggi* (Pisa, 1613).

7. Ludovici Cavitellii Patritii Cremonenses *Annales* (from the "foundation" to 1583), Graevius, vol. III², from the 1st ed. published as *Annales quibus res urbique gestas memorabiles* (Cremona, 1583).

8. *Cremona fedelissima città et nobilissima colonia de Romani rappresentata in disegno col suo contado et illustrata d'una breve historia delle cose più notabili appartenenti ad essa...* (Cremona, 1585), with dedication to Philip II.

9. Anon., *Cronaca di Casale, 1530–1582,* ed. Luciano Scabarelli, *ASI,* XIII (1847)—a long selection from a much longer original.

10. *Della città di Udine,* partially published by Francesco Tomadini and Giuseppe Bonturini in *Monografie friuliane offerte a monsignore Zaccaria Bricito arcivescovo d'Udine* (Udine, 1848), and *Descrittione de' passi e delle fortezze che si hanno a fare nel Friuli,* ed. Sebastiano Lampertico and C. A. Combi (Venice, 1876), with a description of all his other works, published and unpublished, in the introduction; further biographical information in Gian Giuseppe Liruti, *Notizie delle vite ed opere scritte da' letterati del Friuli* (Venice, 1762), vol. II, p. 204. The antiquities of Friuli inspired one Belmonte Cagnoli to compose 272 pages of verse entitled *Di Aquileia distrutta,* which I found, but needless to say did not read, in the 2d edition (Venice, 1628) of the translation.

11. *De Rebus in Civitate Firmana Gestis Fragmentorum Libri Duo* (Rome, 1591), also

in Graevius, vol. VII². Another edition was issued in 1772.

12. *De Bello Balearico Commentariolum,* first published by Domenico Moreni in 1810 (Florence).

13. Giovannelli, cited above at n. 6.

14. In an undated letter printed at the end of his *De Praeclaris Venetae Aristocratiae Gestis Liber* (Venice, 1527).

15. Ludovico Della Chiesa, from the preface to the work cited below at n. 79.

16. As is pointed out in the work cited below at n. 23.

17. *Caesenae Urbis Historiarum ab Initio Civitatis ad Annum 1640...* (Cesena, 1641), and in Graevius, vol. VII².

18. *La historia di Vicenza,* 2d ed. (Venice, 1604). On his preparation and on the support he received from his fellow citizens: Angiolgabriello di Santa Maria, *Biblioteca e storia di quei scrittori... di Vicenza che pervennero fin' ad ora a notizia,* 6 vols. (Vicenza, 1772–82), vol. V, pp. 215 ff.

19. Liruti, *Notizie* (above, n. 10), vol. II, pp. 218 ff., gives all the details; quoted here from p. 223.

20. *Commentarii dei fatti d'Aquileia,* ed. Michele Tramezzino (Venice, 1544), from the original *Commentariorum Aquileiensium Libri VIII* (Venice, 1521), on which see Roberto Ricciardi in *DBI.*

21. *Istoria di Trivigi,* 2d ed., "molto emendato ed accresciuta di copiose correzione... dall'autore stesso" (Venice, 1744) (Forni, 1968), with a biographical preface by the editor, from the 1st ed. of Treviso, 1591, published as *Historia Trivigiana.* On the author: Gino Benzoni's note in *DBI* greatly expanded in his "Giovanni Bonifacio, erudito uomo di legge...," *SV,* IX (1967).

22. *Verona illustrata* (above, Chapter 3, n. 28), pt. II: *Istoria letteraria o sia La notizia degli scrittori veronesi,* Book IV.

23. *Le historie e fatti de' Veronesi ne i tempi del popolo e signori Scaligeri,* revised edition of Venice, 1549, from the 1st ed. of 1542, reprinted in 1586 and 1649. A Latin translation is published in Graevius, vol. IX⁷.

24. *L'istoria di Verona* (Verona, 1596) (but finished by 1586). Another edition by A. Savioli was published in Venice in 1744. An *Adversaria Historica Praesertim Veronensia* by Michele Cavicchia is mentioned by Adriano

Prosperi in *Tra evangelismo e Controriforma: G. M. Giberti* (Rome: Edizioni di Storia e Letteratura, 1969), p. 153; but it appears never to have been published.

25. In *Breve trattato sopra le accademie* (Venice, 1571). Canobbio also wrote a *Historia di Verona* from which was *cavato* a *Breve compendio* published in Verona in 1598 as well as several other antiquarian and religious works, on which see below, Chapter 15, n. 18, and Gino Benzoni in *DBI*.

26. Above, n. 8.

27. See *RIS²*, vol. XXVIII³, particularly the comment of Giuseppe Rossini in vol. I of this tome, pp. lxxv ff., and Francesco Lanzoni in *AM*, I (1907), 511.

28. The story about Montaperto is told by Mario Scaduto in *Rivista di storia della Chiesa in Italia*, XXVIII (1974), 564; on Malaterra: above, Chapter 6, n. 29. The story about Syndicis is told by Muratori in his introduction to Falco (above, Chapter 6, n. 12).

29. *Cronache cortonesi di Boncitolo e d'altri cronisti* (Cortona, 1896).

30. Bartolommeo Capasso's introduction to *Le croniche de li antiqui ri del Regno di Napoli*, in *ASPN*, I (1876).

31. Astrino to Troiano Mormile, 18 May 1526, published by Carlo Porsile in the introduction to his edition of the "Villani" chronicle (Naples, 1680).

32. *La vera istoria dell'origine e delle cose notabili di Montevergine...*, raccolta dal R. P. D. Vincenzo Verace et ordinata e ridotta ...da Tomaso Costo (Naples, 1585). On Costo, see below, Chapter 10, n. 50.

33. Described by Nicola Cilento in *BISIme*, LXVIII (1968), 289. The current authority on Cardinal Seripando is Hubert Jedin, particularly in *Papal legate at the Council of Trent: Cardinal Seripando*, tr. Frederic Eckhoff (St. Louis: B. Herder, 1947).

34. Giuliano Bonazzi in *RIS²*, vol. IX⁹, p. vi.

35. *Croniche de la inclyta cita de Napole* (Naples, 1526).

36. The editions are listed by Giuseppe Vedova in *Biografia degli scrittori padovani* (above, Chapter 3, n. 20) under "Gerardo."

37. In dedication of the 1568 edition of the diary of Buonaccorsi.

38. *Istorie pistolesi*, published under the title of *Istoria delle cose avvenute in Toscana dall'anno 1300 al 1348* (Florence, 1578). See also the introduction to the Marescotti (Florence) edition of Piero Buoninsegni's *Historia fiorentina*.

39. Marino Berengo's *Nobili e mercanti* (Turin: Einaudi, 1965), a model of modern municipal historiography, gives all the details.

40. On Lorenzo Trenta's *Cronaca della guerra che fecero i Fiorentini alli Lucchesi al tempo di Paolo Guinigi*, written in the second half of the sixteenth century, see F. P. Luiso, "Una cronaca manoscritta di L. T.," *Bollettino storico lucchese*, IX (1937). I have searched through all the volumes of this review for some mention of other historians, but in vain.

41. Above, Chapter 7, n. 69.

42. *Historia dell'antichità di Milano* (Venice, 1592) (Forni, XLVIII). On Morigia as an ecclesiastical historian: Chapter 16, n. 28.

43. *Historia della nobiltà e degne qualità del Lago Maggiore* (Milan, 1603) (Forni, II).

44. See below, Chapter 10, n. 78. The *Historia delle vite de duchi et duchesse di Milano* (Milan, 1642), by Antonio Campo of Cremona (above, n. 8), is really nothing but a picture book.

45. *Della letteratura veneziana*, vol. I: *Cronache* (Padua, 1752).

46. Above, Chapter 3, p. 85.

47. The continuations are published together with Domenichi's translation of Marcello's *Vite de' prencipi di Vinegia*, "Nelle quali s'ha cognitione di tutte le istorie venetiane fino all'anno MDLVIII" (Venice, 1557). For what follows, I am indebted to Gaetano Cozzi, "Cultura politica e religione nella 'pubblica storiografia' veneziana del '500," *SV*, V–VI (1963–64).

48. *Andreae Mocenici Artium Doctoris Pentateuchon* (Venice, 1511).

49. The relevant documents are printed in the 1809 edition of Pietro Bembo, cited below at n. 56. The documents of the Senate stating its criteria for the selection of a historian are quoted at length by Cozzi in the article cited above at n. 47, pp. 225–26.

50. Emanuele Antonio Cicogna, *Della vita e delle opere di A. N.* (Venice, 1855), and Ernesto Lemma, "Saggio di una bibliografia intorno a A. N.," *L'ateneo veneto*, XLIX (1927).

51. Deno John Geanakoplos, *Greek Schol-*

ars in Venice (above, Chapter 3, n. 52), p. 35, but with the reservations about the "Aldine Academy" expressed by Carlo Dionisotti in *RSI,* LXXV (1963), 169.

52. Letter-preface to his edition of Livy, Decade I, quoted on p. 121 of his *Opera Omnia,* ed. Jo. Antonio et Cajetano Vulpiis [Volpio] Bergomensibus Fratribus (Padua, 1718), which also contains a number of his poems and orations.

53. *Historia veneta,* ed. Muratori, *RIS*[1], vol. XXIII. The title page on the manuscript was Muratori's only evidence for admitting the possibility of Navagero's authorship. The text bears no similarity whatever to contemporary references to the Latin historical work mentioned in several of the letters printed in the *Opera Omnia,* of which the bibliographical preface by Giovan Antonio Volpio accepts Bembo's story about the destruction of the manuscript. The *Viaggio fatto in Ispagna ed in Francia ... con la descrizione particolare de' luoghi e costumi* is included in his *Opera Omnia.*

54. In preface to Bembo's commentary on Pier Paolo Vergerio's *De Nobilium Puerorum Educatione* ([Venice], 1560), which I found in a Leipzig edition of 1604.

55. All the details about the composition of the history are to be found in Carlo Lagomaggiore, "L'*Istoria Viniziana* di M. Pietro Bembo," *AV,* ser. 3, vol. IX (1905), in two parts. But Lagomaggiore's judgments must be accepted in the light of what Mario Santoro says in his *Pietro Bembo* (Naples: Morano, 1937) and what W. T. Elwert says in his "Pietro Bembo e la vita letteraria del suo tempo," in *La civiltà veneziana del Rinascimento* (Venice: Istituto per la Collaborazione culturale, 1958). The most recent, and most authoritative, biography is by Carlo Dionisotti in *DBI.* For a full bibliography: Mario Marti's introduction to the *Opere in volgare* (Florence: Sansoni, 1961). Carlo Dionisotti apparently agrees with my judgment of this work, for he passes over it with the brief note (p. 51) that "non era di suo gusto" in his introduction to his edition of *Prose e rime* (Turin: UTET, 1960).

56. Bembo's response to the secretary of the Council of Ten, the historian Giovan Battista Ramusio, printed by Jacopo Morelli, who edited the standard edition of the vernacular version (Venice, 1791), reprinted in the "Classici Italiani" edition of *Della istoria veneziana ... da lui volgarizzata,* which is vol. III of his *Opere* (Milan, 1809).

57. Parts of the chronicle are published in appendix to the work of Barbaro, to whom it was once attributed, cited below at n. 64.

58. Quoted from dedication to him of Paolo Ramusio's translation of Villhardouin, cited below at n. 60.

59. *Ricordi per scriver le historie della Republica di Venetia,* ed. G. B. M. Contarini in *Anecdota Veneta,* vol. II (Venice, 1757).

60. *De Bello Constantinopolitano et Imperatoribus Comnensis* (Venice, 1573), which I read in Girolamo Ramusio's translation as *Della guerra di Constantinopoli* (Venice, 1604).

61. *De Politica Prudentia cum Christiana Pietate Coniungenda ex Venetorum Potissimum Historiis,* which I read in the translation of Niccolò Antonio Giustiniani as *Dell'utilità che si può ritrarre dalle cose operate dai Veneziani Libri XIV* (Padua, 1778). On Venier's work as a biographer, see below, Chapter 15, n. 108. One of his unhistorical manuals is *Institutione d'ogne stato lodevole delle donne christiane* (Venice, 1575), a delicately decorated purse-size pocketbook.

62. *Le historie venetiane,* tr. Giuseppe Horologgi and Remigio Fiorentino (Venice, 1576) from *Rerum Venetarum ab Urbe Condita ... Historia.* I read the 2d ed. of Venice, 1598.

63. See note of F. Stefani in *AV,* II (1871), 220.

64. *Storia veneziana,* ed. Tomaso Gar, *ASI,* VII[2] (1844), with biographical introduction. For what follows, cf. William J. Bouwsma, *Venice and the Defense of Republican Liberty* (University of California Press, 1968), which follows Cozzi in the article cited above at n. 47. Further biographical information in P. Pennato, "Nuove notizie intorno ad Andrea Navagero e Daniele Barbaro," *AV,* III (1872).

65. "Lettere passate tra Antonio Riccobono e il procuratore Paruta d'intorno allo scrivere le historie venete," ed. Antonio Favaro, *AV,* ser. 2, vol. II (1891).

66. From dedication to Doge Marin Grimani by Paruta's son and editor, Giovanni, in Paruta's *Historia Vinetiana,* which I read in Zeno, *Istorici,* together with the *vita,* as well

as in the 1st ed. of Venice, 1605. The importance of historiography in sixteenth-century Venetian culture is emphasized by Oliver Logan in his *Culture and Society in Venice, 1470–1790* (London: Batsford, 1972), pp. 112 ff. See further below, Chapter 12, n. 79, and the bio-bibliographical essay on Paruta by Carlo Curcio in vol. II of *I minori* of the Marzorati *Letteratura italiana*.

67. The current edition is that of Giorgio Candeloro (Bologna: Zanichelli, 1943), although the judgments of the author given in the preface must be read in the light of what Cozzi has said subsequently.

68. See above, Chapter 8, n. 28.

69. The significance of this debate is brought out by Cozzi in the article cited above at n. 47, and by Paolo Preto (who shows how Paruta turned what Bembo had passed over discreetly into a magnanimous gesture and how he passed on this "pious lie" to Alvise Contarini) in *Venezia e i Turchi* (below, Chapter 12, n. 79), pp. 51–52. According to Felix Gilbert, passing on the "myth of Venice" was an integral part of the commission given to the official historians: "Venetian Diplomacy before Pavia: From Reality to Myth," in J. H. Elliott and H. G. Koenigsberger, eds., *The Diversity of History. Essays in Honour of Sir Herbert Butterfield* (London: Routledge and Kegan Paul, 1970), esp. p. 115. Paruta has recently been relieved of the burden imposed upon him by those historians who associate him with Machiavelli as a proponent of a "Republican ideology": Angelo Baiocchi, "Paolo Paruta: Ideologia e politica nel Cinquecento veneziano," *SV*, XVII–XVIII (1975–76). Unfortunately the article is written in a style so difficult that few readers will get much past the first pages.

70. Which I read in Zeno, *Istorici*. It was later translated by Girolamo Ascanio Molino as *Storia della Repubblica Veneziana* (Venice, 1782–87).

71. To the immense annoyance of the ecclesiastical censors, who got it put immediately on the Roman Index: F. Stefani in *AV*, above, n. 63.

72. In appendix to his *Il doge Nicolò Contarini: Ricerche sul patriziato veneziano agli inizi del Seicento* (Venice: Istituto per la Collaborazione Culturale, 1958).

73. Most of what follows is taken from Gaudenzio Claretta, "Sui principali storici piemontesi," *Memorie della Accademia delle Scienze di Torino*, ser. 2, vol. XXX (1878), and Valerio Castronovo, *Samuel Guichenon*, cited above, Chapter 4, n. 19.

74. *Mémoires sur la vie de Charles duc de Savoye neuvième*, *MHP*, vol. I.

75. *Augusta Taurinorum* (Turin, 1577), which I read in Graevius, vol. IX⁶.

76. *MSI*, vol. IX. Biographical information in Francesco Agostino Della Chiesa, *Catalogo de' scrittori piemontesi, savoiardi e nizzardi* (Carmagnola, 1660), in alphabetical order of *first* names.

77. Tonsi, *De Vita Emanueli Philiberti*... (Turin, 1596), analyzed almost line-by-line in Aldo Garosci's *dispensa, Storiografia piemontese tra il Cinque e il Seicento* (Turin: Tirrenia, 1971), a very helpful work which, however, does not pretend to be thorough (several of the names mentioned here are not there). Cambiano, *Historico discorso, MHP*, vol. I. Giuseppe does not have a separate entry in the *DBI*. He is just briefly mentioned in the one for Giulio cited in the preceding note. The *Memorie* of Carlo Francesco Manfredi di Luserna (1551–1631), ed. Vincenzo Promis in *MSI*, vol. XVIII, is merely a personal notebook by a member of the court and cannot be classified under any of the categories of historical writing.

78. E.g., *De Vita ac Gestis Marchionum Salutientium* (Turin, n.d.).

79. *Dell'istoria di Piemonte...Libri III* (Turin, 1777, from the 1st ed. of 1608) (Forni, XXXIII). It actually includes a fourth book on the origins and descent of the House of Savoy. All the details on composition and publication are in Castronovo, *Samuel Guichenon*, p. 96.

80. *Cronica dell'origine di Piacenza*, translated by the author from the original Latin, published the same year and then again in Graevius, vol. IV².

81. *La historia della città di Parma et la descrittione del fiume Parma* (Parma, 1591) (783 pp. in 8°).

82. *Italia travagliata* (Venice, 1576).

83. See above, Chapter 3.

84. Giovan Battista Spotorno, *Storia let-*

teraria della Liguria (above, Chapter 3, n. 16), vol. III, "Epoca terza," under *Storici*.

85. *Ristretto delle historie genovesi* (Lucca, 1551) (reprinted in 1558).

86. Spontorno's introduction to his edition of Giustiniani's *Annali della Repubblica di Genova* (Genoa, 1854), and the additional biographical information under his name in Quétif-Echard.

87. Most recently published in Carlo Curcio's *Utopisti e riformatori sociali del Cinquecento* (Bologna: Zanichelli, 1941).

88. See above, Chapter 8.

89. See the Epilogue, Part 1.

90. *Dell'istorie di Genova,* tr. Francesco Serdonati (Genoa, 1597) (Forni, 1969).

91. Biographical information by Giammaria Mazzuchelli in his edition of Bonfadio's *Lettere* (Piacenza, 1763), who says he came from Piacenza, and by Rossana Urbani, in *DBI*. I read the *Annali delle cose de' Genovesi* in the translation of Bartolomeo Paschetti, first published in Genoa in 1597 (which is the edition reproduced by Forni) and then in Capolago, Canton Ticino, in 1836. On his poetic works: Querini, vol. II, pp. 204 ff; on his work in general: the Treccani *Storia di Brescia* (Brescia: Morcelliana, 1961), vol. II, pp. 587–88.

92. Massimo Firpo, *Pietro Bizzarri, esule italiano del '500* (Turin: Giappichelli, 1971), which I also follow in describing Bizzarri's other works below in Chapter 12, as well as the article by Silvana Seidel Menchi in *DBI*.

93. *Senatus Populique Genuensis Rerum Domi Forisque Gestarum Historiae atque Annales* (Antwerp, 1579).

94. Jacobi Bracellei *Genuensis Lucubrationes* (Paris, 1520).

95. Gio. Agostino della Lengueglia wrote a great number of poems and sermons, which are listed in the biography written by Michele Giustiniani in his *Gli scrittori liguri* (Rome, 1667) (which also contains a biography of Agostino Giustiniani). His short, elegantly printed, coffee-table volume entitled *Guerre de' Genovesi contro Alfonso rè di Aragona* was published in Genoa in 1643.

96. In his *Degli huomini chiari della Liguria,* translated by Lorenzo Conti from the original Latin (published in Rome, 1573) (Genoa, 1579).

97. *Cronache savonesi dal 1500 al 1570,* ed. G. Assereto (Savona, 1879), in dialect.

98. *Historia de' fatti e guerre de' Sanesi, così esterne come civili* (Venice, 1599).

99. See above, Chapter 8, p. 200.

100. *Dell'historie di Siena* (Venice, 1625).

101. Fino, *La historia di Crema raccolta . . . da gli annali di M. Pietro Terni* (Venice, 1566), republished, together with the continuation, the defense, and a biographical introduction, by Giuseppe Racchetti and Giovanni Solera (Crema, 1844–45), with further information on previous editors.

102. Fino, *Scielta de gli huomini di pregio uscite da Crema dal principio della città fin' a' tempi nostri* (Brescia: 1581).

103. *Raccolto istorico della fondazione di Rimini e dell'origine e vite de' Malatesti* (Rimini, 1617–27) (Forni, XXXVIII).

104. See above, Chapter 4, pp. 104–9. For biographical information on the historians mentioned below, I refer to Pellegrino Antonio Orlandi, *Notizie degli scrittori bolognesi* (Bologna, 1714), and Gino Fasoli, "La storia delle storie di Bologna," *AMRom,* XVII–XIX (1965–68). On Romagna chronicle writing in general, see Giorgio Cencetti and Gina Fasoli, "Gli studi storici sulle signorie romagnole," *AMRom,* IV (1938–39).

105. *Diario bolognese,* eds. Olindo Guerrini and Corrado Ricci in *Mon Ist Romagna* (1887), quoted from p. vii of the introduction. On the unpublished diary of Vincenzo Spargiati (c. 1576–84), see Albano Sorbelli in his introduction to the chronicle of Girolamo Borselli, *RIS*², vol. XXIII².

106. A thorough description of the text (but not the context) is given by Gisella Ravera Aira in "Achille Bocchi e la sua *Historia Bononiensis,*" *Studi e memorie per la storia dell'Università di Bologna,* XV (1942), which I read in a copy kindly sent me by Giuseppe Alberigo. Bocchi's *Symbolicarum Quaestionum Libri V* were published in Bologna, in 1555 and 1574; his Latin translation of Plutarch in Rome in 1555. On his possible involvement with heretical movements in Bologna: Carlo Ginsburg, *Il nicodemismo* (Turin: Einaudi, 1970), pp. 179–80.

107. See below, Chapter 11.

108. *Historie di Bologna* (Bologna, 1541) (Forni, XLIV).

109. All the details in Paolo Prodi, *Il cardinale Gabriele Paleotti,* vol. II (Rome: Edizioni di Storia e Letteratura, 1967), pp. 245–62.

110. *De Episcopis Bononiensibus* (Bologna, 1584).

111. I read the text printed in vol. III of Filippo Argellati's edition of the *Opera Omnia* (Milan, 1733). On Sigonio's other works, see below, Chapter 11.

112. His *Historie di Bologna* are published as a continuation of Alberti in the edition of Bologna, 1589.

113. Rome, 1596, and Bologna, 1657.

114. Ed. Albano Sorbelli, *RIS*[2], vol. XXIII[1]; the preface describes also the work of Ghirardacci's successors in the seventeenth century.

115. *Diece libri delle historie della sua patria* (Bologna, 1596–1608).

Chapter Ten

1. In preface to Francesco Adami, *De Rebus in Civitate Firmana Gestis* (Rome, 1591).

2. Ezio Bolaffi, *Sallustio e la sua fortuna nei secoli* (Rome: Perrella, 1949).

3. I take these estimates in part from my own rough count in the catalogues of the Biblioteca Nazionale Centrale of Florence, in the printed catalogues of the British Museum and the Bibliothèque Nationale, and from Peter Burke, "A Survey of the Popularity of Ancient Historians, 1450–1700," *History and Theory,* V (1966). They should therefore be considered merely as general indications. Even Burke's figures are based on what he admits to be the incomplete lists published in 1830–34 by F. L. A. Schweiger for Europe as a whole. Much more accurate are the figures concerning the period before 1500, which I extract from L. M. Guarnaschelli and E. Valenziani, *Indice generale degli incunabili delle biblioteche d'Italia* (Rome: Libreria dello Stato, 1943 et seq.). Except for the few rare cases noted below, the history of the recovery and adaptation of ancient historiography in the Renaissance is almost wholly unknown.

4. Michel Rambaud, *L'Art de la déformation historique dans les "Commentaires" de César* (Paris: Les Belles Lettres, 1966); F. E. Adcock, *Caesar as a Man of Letters* (above, Chapter 1, n. 70).

5. Mario Mazza, *Storia e ideologia in Tito Livio* (Catania: Bonanno, 1966).

6. J. Briscoe, "The First Decade," in Dorey, ed., *Livy* (above, Chapter 1, n. 51).

7. Michel Rambaud, *Cicéron et l'histoire romaine* (Paris: Les Belles Lettres, 1953).

8. B. Doer, "Livy and the Germans," in Dorey, ed., *Livy.*

9. These figures, and those for the other translations referred to below, are mostly taken from the admirably thorough but understandably incomplete lists compiled by Filippo Argellati in *Biblioteca dei volgarizzatori* (above, Chapter 4, n. 93). Carani was a good friend of Domenichi, as is pointed out in the dedication of his *Historia di G. Crispo Sallustio nuovamente tradotta* (Florence, 1550). Nardi's phrase from the 1547 edition is quoted by Carlo Nardi in his "Della vita di Jacopo Nardi, gentiluomo, poeta e istorico fiorentino," written in 1735 and published in Calogerà's *Raccolta d'opuscoli,* XIV (1737). On translations of Caesar I follow J. R. Hale, "Palladio, Polybius, and Caesar," *JWCI,* XL (1977).

10. All fully explained by Kenneth Schellhase in *Tacitus in Renaissance Political Thought* (University of Chicago Press, 1976), and in Leandro Perini, "Un Patrizio fiorentino e il suo mondo: Bernardo Davanzati," *Studi storici,* XVII (1976).

11. Ottavio Albino's preface to Giovanni's works are reproduced in the edition in Gravier, vol. V. Bruto in the edition cited above, Chapter 3, n. 59.

12. On Livy vs. Polybius, see J. Briscoe, *A Commentary on Livy, Books XXXI–XXXIII* (Oxford: Clarendon, 1973); on Domenichi, Momigliano in "Polibius' Reappearance in Western Europe," in *Polybe* (Fondation Hardt, *Entretiens,* vol. XX), cited above, Chapter 1, n. 5. The information on editions of Polybius is from Pauly and Zeno: Voss, vol. I, pp. 262–63. Della Casa's translations are in vol. VI of the Naples, 1733, edition of his *Opere.* The translations of Thucydides are described in the reprint by Dionisio Ramanzini of the 1563 edition of the volume published in the Collana Historica Greca of Gabriel Giolito de' Ferrari (Verona, 1735). Thucydides was the third "ring" *(anello)* in the "chain," Plutarch the ninth. On Di-

onysius: Massimo Miglio, "Le versioni di Lampugnino Birago delle Antichità...," *Annali della Scuola Speciale per Archivisti e Bibliotecari,* VII (1968).

13. Publication information from Gina Fasoli, "Medio evo e storiografia nel Cinquecento," in *Storia e storiografia,* cited above, Chapter 4, n. 59. Pellini is quoted from the work cited below at n. 76.

14. *Il fioretto delle cronache di Mantova* (Mantua, 1587—from the 1st ed. of 1585). For the details: G. B. Intra, "Degli storici e dei cronisti mantovani," *ASL,* V (1878), which I follow also below for other Mantuan historians and chroniclers.

15. Ed. Ignazio Ciampi in *Cronache e statuti di Viterbo, DSI,* vol. V.

16. I read it in the "ampliata" version republished with the continuation by Agnello Maffei in Mantua, 1741.

17. *Cronaca di Vigevano, ossia Dell'origine e principio di Vigevano* (1584), ed. Carlo Negroni, *MSI,* vol. XXIX (without preface).

18. *Origine della città di Ricanati e la sua historia* (Venice, 1601), which I read in Latin translation in Graevius, vol. VII².

19. *Istoria delle origini e condizioni de' luoghi principali del Polesine di Rovigo,* ed. Carlo Pecora (Venice, 1748).

20. *Cronichetta del Monte San Savino in Toscana* (Florence, 1583).

21. *Istoria della città di Chiusi in Toscana,* Tartini, vol. I.

22. *Historiae Patriae Libri Duo...emendati...,* ed. Sigismondo Boldoni of Pavia and dedicated to Senator Domenico Molino (Venice, 1626) (although the terminal date is 1532), with a short *vita* in the preface by Paolo; on whom see below, Chapter 13. The nineteenth-century translation by Francesco Fossati, published in Como in 1887 and 1890, adds nothing to the original.

23. *De Episcopis Novocomensibus,* published as appendix to the *Historiae.*

24. *De Rebus Sardois,* dedicated in 1579, first published at Cagliari in 1580, and republished along with his *De Chorographia Sardiniae Libri Duo* by Luigi Cibrario in Turin, 1835.

25. Carmello Trasselli, "Les routes siciliennes du Moyen-Age," *Revue historique,* DIX (1974).

26. Fazello, *Dell'historia di Sicilia,* tr. Remigio Fiorentino (Venice, 1573), from *De Rebus Siculis Decades II,* published in 1558, 1560, and 1568; Maurolico, *Sicanicarum Rerum Compendium sive Sicanicae Historiae Libri Sex,* ed. Etienne Baluze from the 1st ed. of Messina, 1562, in Graevius, vol. X⁴. Biographical information on Maurolico from L. Perroni-Grande in *CCCL Anniversario dell'Università di Messina* (Messina, 1900), and Francesco Guardione, "F. M. nel secolo XVI," *Archivo storico siciliano,* n.s., vol. XX (1895), and on both in Santi Correnti, *Cultura e storiografia nella Sicilia del Cinquecento* (Catania: Istituto Siciliano di Cultura Regionale, 1972), where their other works are listed as well. The most recent authority on Maurolico is Paul Lawrence Rose in *The Italian Renaissance of Mathematics* (above, Chapter 4, n. 90), Chapter 8.

27. Equicola, *Dell'istoria di Mantova, libri V,* revised and edited by Benedetto Osanno, printer to the duke, and published in Mantua in 1607. Sardi, *Historie ferraresi* (Ferrara, 1556). The last two books were published posthumously in 1646.

28. Louis Berthé de Besaucèle, *J.-B. Giraldi: Etude sur l'évolution des théories littéraires en Italie au XVIe siècle* (Paris: Picard, 1920).

29. *De Ferraria...commentariolum* was republished in Graevius, vol. VII¹, and was based in part on the uncompleted and unpolished research notes gathered by Lelio, who wrote the dedication, also printed in Graevius, to Ercole II in 1561. The work was translated by Lodovico Domenichi as *Commentario delle cose di Ferrara et di principi da Este* (Florence, 1566; republished in Venice, 1597).

30. *Historia de principi di Este* (Venice, 1572).

31. Sardi's efforts to ascertain the veracity of his accounts are well illustrated in a letter of 1548 to Vincenzo Maio and in an undated letter to Robortello, both published in his *Epistolarum Liber* (Florence, 1549).

32. Hence the *continuazione* of Gianandrea Barotti's still indispensable *Memorie istoriche de' letterati ferraresi* (Ferrara, 1792) is misleading when it mentions only Pigna among the historians of his age. It omits even Girolamo

Falletti's *De Genealogia Marchionum Estensium et Ducum Ferrariae* (1581), from which Pigna admits to have borrowed extensively. Another *relazione* of Ferrara, written apparently in 1584 by Agostino Mosti, is mentioned by Angelo Solerti in *AMRom,* ser. 3, vol. X (1892); but it seems never to have been published.

33. *Rerum Patriae seu Historiae Mediolanensis,* in Graevius, II[1]. For all pertinent bibliography on Alciatus himself, I refer to the recent articles by the current authorities: Roberto Abbondanza, "The Methodology of Andrea Alciato," in my *Late Italian Renaissance,* and Hans Erich Troje, "Alciats Methode der Kommentierung des *Corpus Iuris Civilis,*" in August Buck and Otto Herding, eds., *Der Kommentar in der Renaissance* (Bonn: Kommission für Humanistenforschung, 1975), although neither takes note of Alciato's historical work. I hesitate to accept the precise date proposed by Gian Luigi Barni in the introduction to his edition of *Le lettere di Andrea Alciato* (Florence: LeMonnier, 1953) simply because I find it hard to ascribe so scholarly and polished a text to a sixteen-year-old boy. No date appears in the 1st ed. of 1625. Abbondanza avoids the issue in his article in *DBI.* A previously little known historical-antiquarian work by Alciati has recently been published as *Antiquae Inscriptiones Veteraq. Monumenta Patriae* (Milan: Cisalpino, 1976).

34. The most thorough biography of Machiavelli is still that of Roberto Ridolfi, *Vita di Niccolò Machiavelli* (Rome: Belardetti, 1954), translated by Cecil Grayson (University of Chicago Press, 1963). I have dedicated somewhat more space to Machiavelli than may seem justified by the context of this book, first because of the vast amount of current scholarship devoted to him, and second because of the failure, apparent in most of the judgments pronounced upon his work, to see him in relation to other historians of the time. My references are occasionally to *Tutte le opere* (but they are not all there), ed. Guido Mazzoni and Mario Casella (Florence: Barbèra, 1929), but more often to those edited by Sergio Bertelli and Franco Gaeta in the Feltrinelli Biblioteca di Classici Italiani. This series contains Gaeta's edition of the *Istorie fiorentine* (1962), with an ample introduction. This edition supercedes that of Mario Bonfanti (Milan: Ricciardi, 1954), which contains little but lexical observations in the notes; but still another, still more thoroughly annotated, edition would be most welcome. Translations are sometimes my own, sometimes those in Max Lerner's edition of *The Prince and the Discourses* (Modern Library).

35. The "genesis" of Machiavelli's method is traced by Gennaro Sasso in *Niccolò Machiavelli: Storia del suo pensiero politico* (Naples: Istituto Italiano per gli Studi Storici, 1958), and *Studi su Machiavelli* (Naples: Morano, 1967). The diplomatic reports are now being published by Fredi Chiappelli as *Legazioni, commissarie, scritti di governo* (Laterza, 1971–). See also Guido Parazzoli, *Niccolò Machiavelli e la lezione liviana* (Milan: Goliardica, 1955). The second half of this paragraph is totally dependent upon Sergio Bertelli, first in his "When Did Machiavelli Write *Mandragola*?" *RQ,* XXXIV (1971), and then in the typescript of his introduction to the forthcoming *Opere* of Machiavelli to be published by Salerno in Milan, which the author kindly permitted me to read. The novelty of Bertelli's thesis, which I accept, is made clear by the statement of his colleague, Gaeta, in "Machiavelli storico," in the *aggiornata* version of 1968 published in *Machiavelli nel V centenario della nascita* (Bologna: Boni, 1973): "A scrivere storia, Machiavelli giunse tardi e forse non lo avrebbe mai fatto se la necessità non lo avesse incalzato." Bertelli proves just the opposite: that Machiavelli first thought of becoming a historian and only subsequently turned to political theory.

36. On Plutarch, see especially Thomas Flanagan, "Machiavelli and History: A Note on the Proemium to Discourses II," *Renaissance and Reformation* (University of Toronto), VIII (1971), and Peter E. Bondanella, *Machiavelli and the Art of Renaissance History* (Detroit: Wayne State University Press, 1973). I accept Hans Baron's revision of Federico Chabod's dating of the principal works as expounded in his "Machiavelli: The Republican Citzen...," *English Historical Review,* LXXVI (1961). That Baron's chronology is often ignored in Italy can perhaps be attributed to the disappearance of

English as a language requirement among younger Italian historians—e.g., Giovanni Cipriani in *Ricerche storiche*, II (1975), 279, where it is completely ignored, even in its reflections in the polemical articles of Sasso. But it is amazing that, simply on the basis of one article by J. H. Whitfield, it should have recently been demoted to the rank of a "minority opinion"—though without any explanation of why the "majority" should have returned uncritically to Chabod's chronology—even in the United States, where English is still fairly well known: e.g., John Geerken in "Machiavelli Studies since 1969," *JHI*, XXXVII (1976).

37. The relation between the *Arte della guerra* and the *Istorie* is demonstrated by Felix Gilbert in the chapter by that name in his *Machiavelli e il suo tempo*, which contains, among other pertinent essays, Gilbert's introduction to the Harper Torchbook edition of Christian E. Detmold's translation of the *History of Florence* (1960).

38. Besides Gaeta's introduction cited above in n. 34, see Alessandro Montevecchi, "La *Vita di Castruccio Castracani* e lo stile storico di Machiavelli," *Letterature moderne*, XII (1962). This work has been translated into English by Allan Gilbert in his *The Chief Works* (Duke University Press, 1965), and into German by Helga Legers and Arrigo Benedetti as *Das Leben . . .* (Köln: Böhlau, 1969). The *Sommario delle cose della città di Lucca* is edited by Bertelli in the Feltrinelli edition of *Arte della guerra*. I read Tegrimi's *Vita Castrucci Antelminelli Castracani Lucensis Ducis* in *RIS*[1], vol. XI; an Italian translation was published at Lucca in 1556. Another biography of Castruccio written in Italian by Aldo Manuzio, Jr., was published in Rome, 1590, on which see below, Chapter 14.

39. Here I follow, besides the studies already cited, Aldo Garosci's course outline on *Le 'Istorie fiorentine' di Niccolò Machiavelli* (Turin: Giappichelli, 1973); Felix Gilbert, "Machiavelli's *Istorie fiorentine*: An Essay in Interpretation," in Myron Gilmore, ed. (with the collaboration of Sergio Bertelli), *Studies on Machiavelli* (Florence: Sansoni, 1972); Franco Gaeta's "Machiavelli storico" cited above, n. 35; Nicolai Rubinstein, "Machiavelli e le origini di Firenze," *RSI*,

LXXIX (1967); Delio Cantimori, "Niccolò Machiavelli: il politico e lo storico," in vol. V of the Garzanti *Storia della letteratura italiana;* Innocenzo Cervelli in the work cited above in Chapter 7, n. 59 (on the evolution of Machiavelli's judgments of Venice during the twenty years preceding the composition of the *Istorie*); and, especially for its careful identification of Machiavelli's sources, Marina Marietti's "Machiavel historiographe des Médicis," in *Les Ecrivains et le pouvoir en Italie à l'époque de la Renaissance*, vol. II (no. 3), ed. André Ruchon (Paris: Sorbonne Nouvelle, Centre de Recherche sur la Renaissance Italienne, 1974). Machiavelli's debt to Domenico Buoninsegni for the internal affairs of Florence between 1450 and 1560 is demonstrated by Gian Mario Anselmi in "Machiavelli e l'*Istoria fiorentina* di Domenico di Leonardo Buoninsegni," *Studi e problemi di critica testuale*, IX (1974). The same issue of this review also contains Anselmi's important warning to those who would judge Machiavelli without undertaking the laborious task of checking his sources: "Prolegomeni al Machiavelli storico."

40. I have examined the views of both Gilbert and Dionisotti (*Niccolò Machiavelli: Colloquio* [cited in the Prologue, n. 5], pp. 19–32) on this matter. But I am incapable of judging between them, particularly when the debate degenerates into incivility. I do not agree with Dionisotti's thesis that Machiavelli "umanista non era mai stato nè era," and I follow Gilbert in accepting the results of the study of the autograph copies by Eugenia Levi, "Due nuovi frammenti degli abbozzi autografi . . . ," in *La bibliofilia*, LXIX (1967). I also follow Gilbert in his "Guicciardini, Machiavelli, and Valori on Lorenzo il Magnifico," *RQ*, XI (1958). Dionisotti presents his arguments against Gilbert in "Machiavellerie (III)," *RSI*, LXXXV (1973); and he responds to Gilbert's defense in *RSI*, LXXXVII (1975), 720–22, after having continued his philippic in *RSI*, LXXXVI (1974).

41. Najemy in the article cited above, chapter 1, n.7.

42. I have slightly altered (without changing the meaning) the translation from Ammirato's *Istorie fiorentine* (below, n. 77) quoted in the English translation by Linda

Villari of Pasquale Villari's still indispensable *Life and Times of Niccolò Machiavelli*, 7th ed. (London: E. Benn, 1929). Cavalcanti's usually unacknowledged borrowings are identified by Dionisotti, in *RSI*, LXXXVII (1975), 25.

43. I follow the biographical preface of Agostino Gervasio to the only edition of the *Historia d'Italia*, *Atti Pont.*, IV (1851), which is described in the following paragraph, and of Ernesto Pontieri to the currently authoritative edition of the *Congiura de' baroni*, 2d ed. (Naples: Edizioni Scientifiche Italiane, 1964). The quotation here is from Fabio Pittorru's preface to the Rizzoli edition (1965) of *La congiura*, which is most certainly not authoritative.

44. Angelo Di Costanzo in his *Lettere e istruzioni de' re aragonesi*, quoted in Gravier, vol. V, p. 4. See above, n. 11.

45. Benedetto Croce, "Angelo Di Costanzo, poeta e storico," in his *Uomini e cose della vecchia Italia*, ser. 1, 2d ed. (Bari: Laterza, 1943), and Gio. Bernardino Tafuri, "Vita di Angelo Costanzo," in the preface to the Gravier edition (vol. III) of the *Istoria* cited in the following note. Giannone expresses his appreciation of Di Costanzo's accuracy and thoroughness in *Storia civile del Regno di Napoli* (above, Chapter 6, n. 88), vol. IV, p. 295. The judgment of Di Costanzo's work quoted at the end of the next paragraph—"un'accozzaglia di cronache e storie umanistiche"—is that of Giorgio Petrocchi in "La letteratura del pieno e del tardo Rinascimento," in *Storia di Napoli*, vol. V[1]. Petrocchi underlines Di Costanzo's subtle anti-Toledo biases.

46. Di Costanzo paraphrasing Collenuccio in the preface to his *Istoria del Regno di Napoli*, which I usually read in the 3d ed. (Turin, 1886) based on the first complete edition of 1572–81.

47. The editions are listed by Raffaele Colapietra in *Belfagor*, XV (1960), 420. Ruscelli's judgment is quoted in appendix (pp. 134 ff.) to Varese's *Pandolfo Collenuccio umanista*, cited above in Chapter 6, n. 98.

48. *Dell'historie del Regno di Napoli* (Naples, 1572). The negative judgments of Di Costanzo are those of Giorgio Petrocchi in "La letteratura del pieno e del tardo Rinas-

cimento," *Storia di Napoli* (above, Chapter 6, n. 2), vol. V[1].

49. See below, Chapter 13.

50. *Compendio dell'istoria del Regno di Napoli di Pandolfo Collenuccio da Pesaro, di Mambrino Roseo da Fabriano . . . e di Tomaso Costo napolitano. Diviso in tre parti, con le annotationi del Costo*, which I read in the edition of Venice, 1613, from the lst ed. of 1557–58.

51. On whom see Croce in *Uomini e cose della vecchia Italia*, cited above at n. 45. His *Dialogo* was first published in Naples in 1569. I read his *Origine e nobiltà di Napoli* in the *Raccolta di varii libri, ovvero opuscoli d'historie di varii et approbati autori* (Naples, 1678) and his *Giardino istorico poetico e geografico* in the edition of Vicenza, 1616.

52. *Memoriale delle cose più notabili accadute nel Regno di Napoli dall'incarnazione di Cristo per tutto l'anno 1586 . . . cavato da . . . il testo del compendio . . . da Tomaso Costo . . .* (Naples, 1618, from the 1st ed. of 1592), and Costo, *Nomi delle provincie, città, terre e castelli . . .* (Naples, 1563 and 1595). My futile quest for mention of contemporary historians in Puglia finally bogged down at the letter 'B' of the interminable hodgepodge of every scrap of manuscript paper on every conceivable subject by Luigi Volpicella, *Bibliografia storica della provincia di Terra di Bari* (Naples, 1884).

53. *Ragionamento familiare dell'origine, tempi, e postumi de gl'illustrissimi principi e marchesi di Monferrato*, *RIS*[1], vol. XXIII. The standard edition is that of Giuseppe Vernazza (Turin, 1780), with a biographical preface. The Latin *Chronicon* is edited by Gustavo Avogadro in *MHP*, vol. III.

54. *Storia della città di Reggio*, tr. Prospero Viani (Reggio, 1846–48).

55. *Ristretto dell'istorie di Iesi* (Macerata, 1578) (Forni XII).

56. *Historie di Faenza*, op. post., ed. Girolamo Minacci (Faenza, 1675) (Forni).

57. *Vita di Giberto terzo di Correggio detto Il Difensore*, published with *Vita di Veronica Gambara* and *Gli honori della Casa di Correggio* (Ancona, 1566).

58. Nicola Cilento, "Di Marino Freccia erudito napoletano del Cinquecento e di alcuni codici di cronache medievali a lui noti." *BISIme*, LXVIII (1956).

59. On Cavrioli, see above, Chapter 7, n. 60. Spini's translation, revision, and continuation were first published in 1585; but I use the Venice, 1744, edition entitled *Dell'historie della città di Brescia*.

60. *Lo assedio et impresa di Firenze* (Venice, 1531).

61. This and the other unpublished diaries are described by Michele Lupo Gentile in "Sulle fonti inedite di Benedetto Varchi," *Studi storici*, XIV (1905), which I follow elsewhere in the following paragraphs.

62. *Cronica di Firenze*, ed. Francesco Frediani, *ASI*, appendix VII (1849).

63. Biographical information is given by Andrea di Lorenzo Cavalcanti in the preface to the 1st ed. of the *Storie fiorentine* ("Augusta," 1723; reprinted in 1778). Still more information in Roberto Ridolfi, "Novità sulle *Istorie* del Segni," *Belfagor*, XX (1960). On all the historians here mentioned, I follow Lupo Gentile's still indispensable "Studi sulla storiografia fiorentina alla corte di Cosimo I de' Medici," *Annali della Scuola Normale di Pisa*, XIX² (1905), also printed separately by Nistri. Further bibliographical indications on pp. 512–13 of my *Florence in the Forgotten Centuries*. On what follows, and on Machiavelli and Guicciardini as well, one of the best guides is Rudolf von Albertini, *Das Florentinsche Staatsbewusstsein im Uebergang von der Republik zum Prinzipat* (Bern: Francke, 1955).

64. A *Vita* is published in the preface to Nerli's *Commentari de' fatti civili occorsi dentro la città di Firenze* (Augsburg, 1728), which is still the standard edition. Ample biographical information in Ivo Biagianti, "Politici e storici del Cinquecento: Filippo de'Nerli," *ASI*, CXXXIII (1976).

65. The first biography of Varchi, by his associate and correspondent Giovan Battista Busini, was published by Gaetano Milanesi in Florence, 1864. That and other sixteenth-century as well as more recent biographies, e.g., Guido Manacorda, *B. V.* (Pisa, 1903), are reviewed critically and substantially augmented with new information in a dissertation presented by Richard Samuels to the Department of History of the University of Chicago in 1976, upon which I depend heavily in the following pages. Of the *Storia*

fiorentina, I follow the text printed in Trieste, 1858, along with the rest of Varchi's *Opere*. On Varchi's literary career: Samuels, "Benedetto Varchi, the Accademia degli Infiammati, and the Origins of the Italian Academic Movement," *RQ*, XXIX (1976).

66. Published in the same edition of the *Storie* cited above at n. 63.

67. This is the thesis of the most recent (and most thorough) study of Varchi available in print, Umberto Pirotti's *Benedetto Varchi e la cultura del suo tempo* (Florence: Olschki, 1971), of which one essay is available in English in my *Late Italian Renaissance*. What Francesco Bruni says, apparently independently, about Varchi in his *Sistemi critici e strutture narrative: Ricerche sulla cultura fiiorentina del Rinascimento* (Naples: Liguori, 1969) differs substantially from what is said by Pirotti and Samuels; and what he says about the culture of the age in general differs significantly from what I say here. My version of the relation between Cosimo and the Florentine historians is somewhat at variance with the one generally accepted, of which one recent expression is that of J. R. Hale in *Florence and the Medici, a Pattern of Control* (London: Thames and Hudson, 1977), a very readable if brief guide to cultural movements of the period.

68. On Emili, see below, Chapter 12, n. 131. The accuracy of Varchi's observations is confirmed by Luigi Passerini in *Giornale storico degli archivi toscani*, I (1857), 106, and by Furio Diaz in the work cited above, Chapter 7, n. 48, on p. 39.

69. Also published in the edition of Varchi's *Opere* cited above at n. 65.

70. Published by Lupo Gentile in appendix to his article cited above at n. 61.

71. I used the clearest of the many copies of the "Marucelli" diary, Biblioteca Nazionale, Firenze, MSS Capponi, 105, in preparing Book I of my *Florence in the Forgotten Centuries*.

72. On Adriani's *Istoria de' suoi tempi* (Prato, 1872), dedicated by his son Marcello to Grand Duke Francesco in 1583, see Giovanni Miccoli in *DNB* (Adriani) and Ridolfi in *La bibliofilia*, LXV (1963), 183–94, as well as Carlo Nardi's biography cited above at n. 9 and the acute analysis of the

Istoria in Diaz, *Il Granducato di Toscana,* pp. 219 ff.

73. I read Nardi's *Istorie della città di Firenze* in the edition, with a biographical preface, of Agenore Gelli (Florence, 1888), and Pitti's *Dell'istoria fiorentina* in the edition of Filippo Luigi Polidori, *ASI,* I (1842).

74. *Del Savonarola, ovvero Dialogo . . . il giorno dopo la Battaglia di Gavinana,* ed. Bono Simonetta (Florence: Olschki, 1959).

75. Published by Polidori in, respectively, *ASI,* I (1842) and IV¹ (1853). For the latter, see below, Chapter 14, n. 60.

76. *Dell'historia di Perugia, parte prima* [e *seconda*]; the third part appeared in the 1670 edition, which is very rare; and some copies still contain only the first two parts (Venice, 1664, from the 1st ed. of 1627). Alessandro Bellucci, "Pompeo Pellini, ambasciatore della città di Perugia a Papa Gregorio XIII," *BSUmbSP,* II (1896), has confirmed Pellini's accuracy by comparing many of his statements with the documents upon which they are based.

77. I use the Florentine edition of 1846 of the *Istorie fiorentine,* with the passages added by Ammirato's heir, Scipione Ammirato, Jr., ed. F. Ranalli; the volume and page numbers given in the text are those of this edition. The most recent studies of Ammirato are those by Rodolfo De Mattei, e.g., *Il pensiero politico di S. A.* (Milan: Giuffrè, 1963), and William J. Bouwsma, "Three Types of Historiography in Post-Renaissance Italy," *History and Theory,* IV (1965); but essential for biographical information is still Umberto Congedo's *La vita e le opere* (Trani, 1904), all of which, and many others, are listed in the Bibliographical Note of my *Florence in the Forgotten Centuries* (pp. 520 ff.), of which Book II is dedicated largely to Ammirato. A biography by a contemporary has recently been discovered; and it is explained by Maurizio Manetti in "una biografia inedita di Scipione Ammirato," *Studi secenteschi,* XIV (1973). On one aspect of Ammirato's view of his own times, see Franco Meregalli, "La Espagña de Felipe II en Italia según Scipione Ammirato," *Hispania,* XXXIII (1973).

78. The most complete biography is that by Francesco Cusani in the introduction to his tranlation of the last part of Ripamonti's history published as *La peste di Milano del 1630, Libri V* (Milan, 1841). Vol. II (Milan, 1643) of the *Historiae Patriae* (the 1641 volume, the first to be printed, actually begins with the third decade, in the year 1313) contains a eulogy by Girolamo Legnani.

79. Hieronymi Rubei *Historiarum Ravennatum Libri Decem,* 2d ed. with the addition of Book XI (Venice, 1589). Rossi may well have been indebted to the local scholar Giovan Pietro Ferretti, who died in 1553 at the age of seventy and whose three decades of the history of Ravenna, ordered burned in his will, Rossi describes in his Book IX at p. 723.

80. *Historia quadripartita di Bergamo et suo territorio* (Bergamo, 1617) (Forni). Bibliographical notes are in the *Lexicon Capuccinum* (Rome: Bibliotheca Collegii Internationalis S. Laurentii Brundisini, 1951).

81. The *Vita di Giannantonio Summonte* by Scipione Di Cristoforo is published in appendix to vol. II of the 3d ed. (Naples, 1748) of Summonte's *Historia del Regno di Napoli,* which is the one I use. I am much indebted to what Rosario Villari says in Part III of his *La rivolta antispagnola a Napoli* (Laterza, 1967), to Raffaele Sirri in "Di Gio. Antonio Summonte e della sua *Historia,*" *ASPN,* LXXXVIII (1971), and, for Summonte's assessment of the reign of Ferrante II, to Giuseppe Galasso in *RSI,* LX (1978), 519.

82. Tomai quoted by Filippo Mordani in *Vita di Ravegnani illustri* (Ravenna, 1837), p. 118. *Historia di Ravenna* (Pesaro, 1574); revised and corrected edition, Ravenna, 1580, reproduced by Forni (1976).

83. The details are in Arnaldo Momigliano's article on Bacchini in the *DBI.* I am very grateful to him for reminding me of them.

84. Costo's objections are given in his preface "ai lettori" to his *Compendio dell'istoria del Regno di Napoli,* cited above at n. 50.

85. See Chapter III of Giuseppe Ricuperati's *L'esperienza civile e religiosa di Pietro Giannone* (Milan-Naples: Ricciardi, 1970).

86. See Chapter V of my *Tradition and Enlightenment in the Tuscan Academies* (Rome: Edizioni di Storia e Letteratura, and University of Chicago Press, 1961).

CHAPTER ELEVEN

1. Above, Chapter 7.

2. The most complete biography is that of Roberto Ridolfi, translated into English as *The Life of Francesco Guicciardini* (New York: Knopf, 1968). I also consulted the briefer biographical summaries by Federico Chabod in his *Scritti sul Rinascimento* (Turin: Einaudi, 1967) and by Pieter E. Bondanella, *Francesco Guicciardini* (Boston: Twayne, 1976).

3. *Le cose fiorentine,* ed. Roberto Ridolfi (Florence: Olschki, 1945). I have taken much of the matter of the following paragraphs from the preface. Except in certain details, I also follow Vittorio De Caprariis in *Francesco Guicciardini: Dalla politica alla storia,* cited above, Chapter 7, n. 34, which relies, as do most other modern studies, on Ridolfi's *Genesi della "Storia d'Italia" guicciardiniana* (Florence: Olschki, 1939). I do so notwithstanding the rather sharp attack on De Caprariis in Mark Phillips, *Francesco Guicciardini: The Historian's Craft* (University of Toronto Press, 1977), which, being largely a series of the author's own personal reflections on, rather than a philological analysis of, the text, is less useful for my purposes. Emanuella Lugnani Scarano also follows De Caprariis, although pointing out that his conversion to history was not as sudden as he thought: *Guicciardini e la crisi del Rinascimento,* an offprint of her chapter in *Il Cinquecento* cited above in the Prologue, n. 13, issued separately by Laterza in 1973.

4. *Diario del viaggio in Spagna,* ed. Paolo Guicciardini (Florence: LeMonnier, 1932).

5. Randolph Starn, "Francesco Guicciardini and His Brothers," in *Renaissance Studies in Honor of Hans Baron.*

6. *Ricordanze inedite di Francesco Guicciardini,* ed. Paolo Guicciardini (Florence: LeMonnier, 1939).

7. See below, Chapter 12.

8. On Guicciardini's finances and on his diary, see Richard A. Goldthwaite, *Private Wealth in Renaissance Florence* (Princeton University Press, 1968), pp. 137 and 269.

9. I here follow my own description of the events in *Florence in the Forgotten Centuries,* Book I.

10. Of the many current editions, the most authoritative is the one by Silvana Seidel Menchi (Turin: Einaudi, 1971). The first books have been translated by Cecil Grayson and published together with parts of the *Is-*

torie fiorentine with an introduction by John Hale in a Washington Square paperback edition. Parts of the whole work are translated by Sydney Alexander as *The History of Italy* (New York: Macmillan, 1968). Alexander is currently working on a full translation. An indispensable guide to the *Storia* is Felix Gilbert's *Machiavelli and Guicciardini,* cited above, Chapter 7, n. 39.

11. See above, Chapter 7.

12. And not some supernatural being or divine plan, as R. Vitiello points out in his review of the Italian translation of Gilbert's *Machiavelli and Guicciardini* in *Il pensiero politico,* V (1972), 184.

13. Quoted by Enrico Gusberti in an article as full of specific references as it is difficult to read, "Il Savonarola del Guicciardini," *NRS,* LIV (1970).

14. *Memorie storiche dei principali avvenimenti politici d'Italia seguiti durante il pontificato di Clemente VII,* ed. C. G. degli Ancarani (Rome, 1837). The last book is incomplete; the first three are published also in French translation by J. L. O. Puÿ de Labastie as *Mémoires historiques* (Lyon, 1867).

15. Most of the details are in Vincenzo Luciani, *Francesco Guicciardini e la fortuna dell'opera sua,* ed. Paolo Guicciardini (Florence: Olschki, 1949).

16. *Considerationi sopra l' "Historia de' Italia" di M. Francesco Guicciardini,* which I read in the 2d edition, expanded and corrected, of Venice, 1599. Leoni's political motives are explained by Paul Grendler in Sergio Bertelli and Gloria Ramakus, eds., *Studies Presented to Myron Gilmore* (Florence: La Nuova Italia, 1978), vol. I, p. 107.

17. Some of his opinions are to be found in his *Lettere familiari,* which I read (given my taste for narrow-minded *camicie gonfiate*) in the 2d ed. of Venice, 1593; the others are to be found in his *Vita di Francesco Maria di Montefeltro Della Rovere, IIII Duca d'Urbino* (Venice, 1605).

18. *La verità vendicata, cioè Bologna difesa dalle calunnie di Francesco Guicciardini; Osservazioni storiche* dell'abate Giacomo Certani, professor of theology and moral philosophy (which, of course, made him an authority on history too) (Bologna, 1659).

19. On Pitti, see above, Chapter 10, n. 73. The relevant passages from the *Apologia dei*

Cappucci are cited by F. L. Polidori in *ASI, I* (1842), 280–81.

20. All this from Paolo Guicciardini, *La censura nella storia guicciardiniana* (Florence: Olschki, 1954).

21. On Perna, see Peter Bietenholz, *Der italienische Humanismus und die Blutezeit des Buchdrucks in Basel* (Basel-Stuttgart: Helbing & Lichtenhahn, 1959), p. 90. Why the editor of the anthology entitled *Respublica Romana* (Leiden, 1629) decided to include several pages "Historiarum Lib. IV celebri loco qui in vulgatis editionibus expunctus et nuper restitutus est" escapes my understanding, for they have nothing whatever to do with the texts of Andrea Domenico Fiocchi, Raffaello Volterrano, Andrea Alciati, et al., that occupy the rest of the volume.

22. E.g., *Chronichetta sopra le ultime azioni di Lorenzo de' Medici duca d'Urbino,* published, alas, without preface, in the supplement to *Delizie degli eruditi toscani,* vol. XXIII (1786). The author held the *offitio del paghare* to the duke and wrote in response to Guicciardini's request for information.

23. I here follow Felix Gilbert in "Venetian Diplomacy before Pavia," first published in *The Diversity of History,* cited above, Chapter 9, n. 69.

24. Lugnani Scarano, cited above, n. 3.

25. Ammirato in his *Ritratti* quoted by Foscarini in *Storia della letteratura veneziana,* vol. I, p. 263, which is where Foscarini once again berates Guicciardini for fabricating speeches that are contained neither in the published histories nor in manuscript records, an opinion consonant with an age in which humanist standards were no longer accepted.

26. *Giudicio . . . sopra l'historia di M. Francesco Guicciardini, nel quale si discoprono le bellezze di questa historia* (Venice, 1574).

27. *Considerationi civili sopra l'historia di M. Francesco Guicciardini . . . trattate in modo di discorso . . . , dove si contengono precette e regole per principi . . .* (Venice, 1582).

28. *Dell'epitome dell' "Historia d'Italia" di M. Francesco Guicciardini* (Venice, 1580).

29. On Canini's *Aforismi politici cavati dall'Historia d'Italia . . .* (Venice, 1615), see Benzoni in *SV,* XVI (1974), 286. Curione in Guicciardini, *Historiarum Sui Temporis Libri XX* (Basel, 1566).

30. See above, Chapter 9, n. 108. The tributes to his *De Viris Illustribus Ordinis Praedicatorum* (Bologna, 1517) are printed in the preface to the 1st edition of the *Descrittione di tutta Italia* (Venice, 1550). All his works are listed by A. L. Redigonda in *DBI.* Some details in the following paragraph are taken from Lucio Bambi, "Per una rilettura di Biondo e Alberti," in *Il Rinascimento nelle corti padane* (Bari: De Donato, 1977).

31. See above, Chapter 8, p. 250. *De Papiensis Ecclesiae Dignitate Nulli Metropolitano Suppositae* and *De Controversia Exorta . . .* are bound together with *De Italicarum Rerum Varietate et Elegantia Libri X* (Pavia, 1565). On the author: Emilio Gabba, "La storiografia pavese del secolo XVI e le origini di Pavia," *Athenaeum* (Pavia, Università), *fascicolo speciale* (1976), an article lent me by Riccardo Fubini.

32. Most of what follows is taken from E. S. Beer, "François Schott's *Itinerario d'Italia,*" *The Library,* ser. 4, vol. XXIII (1942).

33. *The History of Italy* (really a *descriptio* according to the Biondo-Alberti model), ed. George B. Parks (Cornell University Press, 1963).

34. Juergen Schulz, *The Printed Plans and Panoramic Views of Venice, 1456–1797* (Fondazione Giorgio Cini: Saggi e memorie di storia dell'arte, no. 7) (Florence: Olschki, 1970). The considerable body of late-sixteenth-century guidebook and *descriptio* literature merits a special study. Some of it is listed by Vittorio Zaccaria in his review of G. P. Marchi's edition of Adriano Valerini's *Bellezze di Verona* (1974) in *Lettere italiane,* XXVIII (1976), 391–94. Those specifically of Naples are introduced by Mario Rotili in *L'arte del Cinquecento nel Regno di Napoli* (Naples: Libreria Scientifica Ed., 1972), where he emphasizes the importance of these works as sources for the history of art. One of the most interesting of them is Marc'Antonio Surgente's *Aureus Tractatus . . .* (Naples, 1597), which I consulted in the Latin translation with notes by the author's brother Muzio in Graevius, vol. IX³, based on the expanded 2d ed. of 1602. That this is a phenomenon of the late, rather than the early, sixteenth century is supported by the case of Benedetto di Falco, whose *Luoghi antichi di Napoli* of 1535 did not attract much attention

until it was republished in 1598; on all this see Benedetto Croce, "Il primo descrittore di Napoli," in vol. I of the 2d ed. of his *Aneddoti di varia letteratura* (Bari: Laterza, 1953).

35. *Historie ... nelle quali partitamente si raccontano i fatti successi dal DCCCCLXX quando cominciò l'Imperio in Germania in sino al MCCCC* (Venice, 1561).

36. See above, Chapter 9, nn. 110–11.

37. The most complete biography is still that of Muratori, published in Filippo Argellati's edition of the *Opera Omnia* (Milan, 1732), vol. I.

38. See above, p. 271.

39. See below, Chapter 15.

40. All from Luigi Simeoni, "Documenti sulla vita e la biblioteca di Carlo Sigonio," *Studi e memorie per la storia dell'Università di Bologna,* X (1930), and from Giovanni Franciosi, *Della vita e delle opere di Carlo Sigonio,* 2d ed. (Modena, 1872). On the relation between Biondo and Sigonio, I follow Carlo Dionisotti in "Medioevo barbarico e Cinquecento italiano," cited in the Prologue, n. 5.

41. See below, Chapter 16.

42. *Historiarum ab Urbe Condita Libri qui Extant* (Venice, 1555).

43. *De Laudibus Historiae,* in *Orationes Septem* (Venice, 1560).

44. *De Rei Romanae Scriptoribus Judicium,* which I read in *Opera Omnia.*

45. Alfred Hessel, *"De Regno Italiae Libri Viginti" von Carlo Sigonio: Eine quellenkritische Untersuchung* (Berlin, 1900) (Kraus reprint, 1965), which is based on Sigonio's own bibliography of his sources printed as *Catalogus Historiarum et Archivorum* in 1576. On which: Carlo Calcaterra in *Alma Mater Studiorum: L'Università di Bologna nella storia della cultura e della civiltà* (Bologna: Zanichelli, 1948). A good example of Sigonio's archive-hunting is given by Amadio Ronchini on p. 285 of *AMMod e Parm,* IV (1868).

46. See below, Chapter 16.

47. Which I read both in the 1st ed. (Bologna, 1578) and in the *Opera Omnia,* with notes by Gennaro Salinas, vol. I, pt. 2.

48. In *De Laudibus Historiae,* cited above at n. 43.

49. Described by Vincenzo Borghini in his *Discorsi* (Florence, 1584–85), vol. II, p. 256.

50. As I explain in my "L. A. Muratori e gli storici italiani del Cinquecento," in *L. A. Muratori, Storiografo* (Atti del Convegno Internazionale di Studi Muratoriani, Modena, 1972) (Florence: Olschki, 1975). The story of the censors is told by Giuseppe Antonio Sacchi in his introduction to *De Regno* in *Opere Omnia,* vol. II.

51. Tiraboschi admitted that "Io non so se altr'uomo ci abbia dato il secolo XVI a cui con maggior ragione convegna il titolo d'uomo dotato di profonda dottrina e di vastissima erudizione," *Biblioteca modenese* (above, Chapter 7, n. 6), vol. V, p. 76.

52. *De Usu Linguae Latinae Retinendo* (pronounced in 1556), in *Oratione Septem,* cited above at n. 43.

53. *De Vita et Rebus Gestis Andreae Auriae Melphiae Principis Libri Duo* (Genoa, 1586).

CHAPTER TWELVE

1. On the earlier literature: Pierre Jodogne, "La Conjuration des Pazzi racontée par les chroniqueurs français et bourguignons du XVe siècle," *Culture et politique en France à l'époque de l'humanisme et de la Renaissance* (Turin: Accademia delle Scienze, 1974). *La historia di mons. Filippo d'Argenton delle guerre di Lodovico XI* I consulted in the edition of Venice, 1559, with a dedication to "mons. Giovio, padre delle historie." It was published under a slightly different title in 1544. Neither Auda Prucher, *I 'Mémoires' di Philippe de Commynes e l'Italia del Quattrocento* (Florence: Olschki, 1957) nor Lidia Cerioni, "L'Italia ed i suoi problemi visti da Filippo di Commynes...," *ASL,* ser. 9, vol. VII (1968), are of help in this context, since they do nothing but translate or paraphrase the passages that apply to Italy, without comment or explanation. More on Commynes below, n. 22, and on Sleidanus, below, n. 26.

2. *La cronaca di Genova pubblicata in Parigi nei primi anni del secolo XVI,* ed. Vincenzo Promis, *ASLigSP,* X (1874).

3. *Cronaca di Genova scritta in francese* da Alessandro Salvago, ed. Cornelio Desimoni, *ASLigSP,* XIII³ (1886).

4. *Chroniques de Louis XII,* ed. R. de Maulde la Clavière (Paris, 1889); on which: Alberto Tenenti in *Il senso della morte e l'amore della vita* (Turin: Einaudi, 1957), pp. 189 ff.

5. By Beltrami in *ASL,* XVII (1890).

6. Conrad Wenger, *De Bello inter Venetos et*

Sigismundum Austriae Archiducem Gesto (Basel, 1544).

7. *Anzeig warhafftiger newer Zeytung wie es sich eygentlich mit der Schlacht vor Pavia zwischen Keyserlicher Maiestät und des Königs von Frankreich kriegsvolck auff xxiii Februarii begeben hat* (n.d., 1525); *Relacion sacada de la que escribió fray J. O. . . . de la prision del Rey de Francia,* published in *Colección de documentos inéditos para la historia de España,* vol. IX (1846).

8. *De Variis Venetorum & Archiducum Austriae Aliorumq. Principum Bellis in Italia Gestis* (Basel, 1544; bound with Wenger, n. 6, above, from the 1st ed. of Tübingen, 1512). On which: Albert Krieger, in a typically neo-Rankian dissertation, *Ueber die Bedeutung des 4. Buches von Coccinus' Schrift "De Bellis Italicis"* (Karlsruhe, 1886).

9. Palliard's chronicle is published by Th. von Liebenau in *Anzeiger für Schweizerische Geschichte,* XVIII (1887); Campell's *Historia Raetica* by P. Plattner in *Quellen zur Schweizer Geschichte,* vols. VIII–IX (1887–90). This chronicle was apparently unknown to Alessandro Pastore, since he does not mention it in his *Nella Valtellina del tardo Cinquecento* (Milan: Sugar, 1975); nor do Ettore Mazzali and Giulio Spini in their *Storia della Valtellina e della Valchiavenna* (Sondrio: Bissoni, 1968). I owe the reference to that tireless and perspicacious document-hunter, Antonio Rotondò, in his "Esuli italiani in Valtellina nel '500," *RSI,* LXXXVIII (1976).

10. *Commentaires de Blaise de Monluc, maréchal de France,* ed. Paul Courteault (Paris: Picard, 1911–25) (from the 1st ed. by Florimond de Raemond of 1592).

11. The texts of both the Gran Capitán and his continuer are published by Antonio Rodriguez Villa in *Crónicas del Gran Capitán = Nueva biblioteca de auctores españoles,* vol. X (Madrid, 1908). Zurita was published first in 1562, then in 1585 and 1610. I read the text in the edition by Angel Canellas López (Zaragoza: Institución Fernando el Católico, 1967), with the help of Giuseppe Coniglio in "Il regno di Carlo I d'Angiò nell'opera di Jeronimo Zurita," in *Storiografia e storia . . . Dupré Theseider,* cited above, Chapter 4, n. 59, and of Alonzo Sánchez in his *Historia de la historiografía*

española, cited in the Prologue, n. 4, upon which I depend in the following paragraphs.

12. All this from Alfred Morel-Fatio, *Historiographie de Charles-Quint* (Paris: Champion, 1913), except for the detail on Girón, which comes from the introduction to the edition of the *Crónica del emperador Carlos V* by Juan Sánchez Montes (Madrid: C.S.I.C., 1964).

13. What follows is dependent upon Antonio Rumeu de Arras, *Alfonso de Ulloa, introductor de la cultura española en Italia* (Madrid: Ed. Gredos, 1973) (Biblioteca Románica Hispánica, II: Estudios y Ensayos, 180), which contains a full bibliography of his works.

14. *Vita del valorisissimo e gran capitano don Ferrante Gonzaga . . . , nella quale oltre i suoi fatti & di molti altri principi & capitani si descrivono le guerre d'Italia* (Venice, 1563).

15. *Vita dell'invitissimo imperator Carlo Quinto* (Venice, 1560), republished in 1562, 1574, 1575, and 1606. *Vita del . . . imperatore Ferdinando Primo* (Venice, 1565).

16. *Commentari . . . della guerra che il sig. don. Fernando Alvarez di Toledo duca d'Alva . . . ha fatto contro Guglielmo di Nansau* [sic] *principe di Oranges . . . l'anno 1568. Insieme con le cose occorse tra la reina d'Inghilterra, l'ambasciatore catolico appresso quella maestà . . . e quel che più avvenne fino alla morte del Principe di Condè in Francia questo anno 1569* (Venice, 1570). *La historia dell'impresa di Tripoli di Barbaria* (Venice, 1566), 2d ed. "alla quale sono state aggiunte le cose fatte in Ungheria l'anno 1566"* (Venice, 1569). *Le historie di Europa . . . principalmente . . . la guerra ultimamente fatta in Ungheria . . .* (Venice, 1570).

17. *Vita di M. Aurelio imperadore* (Rome, 1542, and Venice, 1544), on which I consulted Joseph Jones, *Antonio de Guevara* (Boston: Twayne, 1975); Giovio cited by Costantino Panigada in a note to Domenichi's translation of *Le vite del Gran Capitano e del Marchese di Pescara* (Bari: Laterza, 1931), p. 483.

18. Olaus Magnus = Olaf Mansson, d. 1558, *Historia delle genti et della natura delle cose settentrionali* (Rome, 1555; Venice—with a slightly different title—1561 and 1565), from the Rome, 1555, edition of the Latin, *Gothorum, Sveonumque Historia,* ed. J. M. de Viottis (Rome, 1555). For the broader con-

text of "popularization," to which there are many references in the following pages, I have taken note of Paul Grendler, "Francesco Sansovino and Italian Popular History, 1560–1600," *SR,* XVI (1969), although with the reservations expressed by Salvo Mastellone in *RSI,* LXXXII (1970), 1022 ff.

19. *I commentari di Theodor Spandugino Cantacuscino, gentilhuomo costantinopolitano, Dell'origine de' principi turchi & de' costumi di quella natione* (Florence, 1551).

20. Pietro Cornelio, *Historia di Fiandra* (Brescia, 1582).

21. Zuñiga, *Commentario . . . nelle guerra della Germania fatta da . . . Carlo V* (Venice, 1549) (the circumstances of the translation are described in the preface). The translation of Sepúlveda follows the Latin edition, *De Vita et Rebus Gestis Aegidii Albunotii . . . Libri III,* which I read in the edition of Bologna, 1559).

22. The Venetian edition of 1576 is the one cited by Montaigne, *Essais,* I, 30. Full information (on other related subjects as well) in Franco Meregalli, *Presenza della letteratura spagnola in Italia* (Florence: Sansoni, 1974). On Commynes, see above, n. 1.

23. Donald Lach, *Asia in the Making of Europe,* vol. I (University of Chicago Press, 1965), upon which I rely heavily in the following pages, here cited at p. 744. I am very grateful to the author personally for his advice and assistance on these matters for which he is the current expert. See also E. van Kley in *American Historical Review,* LXXVI (1971), 363.

24. I cite the first volume of Ramusio's *Navigationi et Viaggi* in the 2d ed. of 1554, "in molti luoghi corretta et ampliata"; vol. II in the edition of 1574; vol. III in the edition of 1565, simply because those were the ones most easily available. I cite them all hereafter simply as "Ramusio." Much information about the contents, scope, and purpose of the collection is given in Lach, *Asia in the Making of Europe,* pp. 205–9 and elsewhere. For biographical information: Tommaso Giunta's preface to the 4th ed. (1588) of vol. I and Antonio de Piero, "Della vita e degli studi di G. B. R.," *AV,* n.s., IV (1902).

25. The Latin translation was published as *Rerum Muscoviticarum Commentarii* (Vienna, 1549, et seq.). The Basel edition of 1556 is bound together with selections from Giovio.

The original German was published at least twice after the 1st ed. of Vienna, 1557.

26. On Sleidanus himself, I follow Walter Friedensberg, *Johannes Sleidanus: der Geschichtesschreiber und die Schichtsalsmächte der Reformationszeit* (Schriften des Vereins für Reformationsgeschichte, Jahrgang LII, Heft 2) (Leipzig: Heinsius, 1935), in spite of its ridiculous nationalistic biases, and Johann Gottlieb Boehmius in the preface to the Frankfurt edition (1785) of the *Commentarii,* rather than Richard Fester, "Sleidan, Sabinus, Melanchton," *Historische Zeitschrift,* LXXXIX (1902), which is plodding and not very clear. Dennis Rhodes, "La traduzione italiana dei *Commentarii* di Giovanni Sleidano," *La bibliofilia,* LXVIII (1966), is a very persuasive piece of detective work.

27. *Duo Gallicarum Rerum Scriptores . . . ambo a Ioan. Sleidano e Gallico in Latinum Sermonem Conversi,* which I found in the edition of Hannover, 1619. The dedication is dated 1537. Earlier editions appeared in 1562, 1576, 1578, 1582, and 1594.

28. Franco Simone, "Une entreprise oubliée des humanistes français," in A. H. T. Levi, ed., *Humanism in France at the End of the Middle Ages and the Early Renaissance* (New York: Barnes and Noble, 1970).

29. I adopt the translation of William F. Church in Orest Ranum, ed., *National Consciousness, History, and Political Culture in Early Modern Europe* (Johns Hopkins University Press, 1975), pp. 47–48.

30. Jacobi Bracellei Genuensis *Lucubrationes* (Paris, 1520). On Machiavelli: the exhaustive *Bibliografia machiavelliana* of Sergio Bertelli and Piero Innocenti (Verona: Edizioni Valdonega, 1979).

31. Bietenholz, *Der italienische Humanismus und die Blutezeit des Buchdrucks in Basel,* cited above, Chapter 11, n. 21.

32. Contarini letter of vii Kal. Maii 1539 in G. M. Bruto, ed., *Epistolae Clarorum Virorum* (Lyon, 1561). On Bonfini and Callimaco, see below, notes 126–28. On Cromer, see below, n. 141.

33. *L'Asia del s. Giovanni di Barros,* from the 1st Portuguese ed. of Lisbon, 1552 (Venice, 1562); also in Ramusio. On this question I follow C. R. Boxer in *Three Historians of Portuguese Asia* (Macao: Instituto Português, 1948).

34. *Cronica general d'Hispagna et del Regno di Valenza* (Venice, 1566). On Annio, see below, Chapter 15.

35. *La historia di tutte le città, ville, fiumi, fonti, et altre cose notabili della Franza et di tutti i re di quella* (Venice, 1558); the "privilegio" (copyright) is of 1555.

36. Orbini, *Il Regno de gli Slavi hoggi corrottamente detti Schiavoni, Historia* (Pesaro, 1601); Luccari, *Copioso ristretto de gli annali di Ragusa . . . fino all'anno presente; . . . Insieme si narra il sito, i costumi, gli abiti, il governo, i magistrati, le famiglie nobili . . .* (Venice, 1605). Bariša Krekíc, *Dubrovnik et le Levant au Moyen-Âge* (Paris: Mouton, 1961) lists still other chronicles in Latin and Italian; but none of them was published until much later. When these chroniclers are viewed in the light of current Italian municipal historiography, with which most of them were familiar, the judgment passed on them by Francis W. Carter in his *Dubrovnik: A Classic City-State* (New York-London: Seminar Press, 1972), p. 509, seems a bit harsh.

37. Above, Chapter 9, n. 78.

38. On which see Theodore Bestermann, *Les débuts de la bibliographie méthodique*, which I read in the 3d ed. (Paris: La Palme, 1950).

39. On Ramusio and Barbaro, see above, n. 24, and below, n. 49.

40. Lach, *Asia in the Making of Europe*, p. 63, where still more bibliography is given.

41. Poggio's text was reprinted by Ramusio in vol. I. The Italian translation is reprinted with an introduction by Mario Langhena as *Viaggio in Persia, India e Giava* (Milan: Alpes, 1929). The history of the text is given, rather wordily, by Vincenzo Bellemo in *La cosmografia e le scoperte geografiche nel secolo XV e i viaggi di Nicolò de' Conti* (Padua: Seminario, 1908).

42. Alexandru Marcu, "Riflessi di storia rumena in opera italiane dei secoli XIV e XV," *Ephemeris Dacoromana*, I (1923).

43. Buondelmonti's *Liber Insularum Archipelagi* was nevertheless printed in the fifteenth century and extensively cited by geographers until the middle of the seventeenth century. Bartolomeo also wrote a *Descriptio Insule Candie*, which was printed in 1755. I follow the most recent editions, both by Emile Lagrand (Paris, 1897).

44. The most recent example is the edition of his *Journeys in the Propontis and the Northern Aegean, 1444–1445* by Edward W. Bodnar and Charles Mitchell, published in the *Memoirs* of the American Philosophical Society, CXII (1976). On the importance of Ciriaco for the genesis of humanist historiography, see above, Chapter 2. Much of what follows was written with the valuable assistance of my colleague Walter Kaegi.

45. *Della vita de Zychi chiamati Ciarcassi*, in Ramusio, vol. II.

46. A full description with bibliography is given by Kyriakos Simopoulos (Σιμόπουλος), Ξένοι Ταξιδιώτες στὴν Ἑλλάδα, vol. I (Athens, 1970), which is difficult to use for my purposes because the voyagers are listed by places visited. But it is helpful because the author points out all the travelers' errors. Bianchi's *Viaggio da Venezia al Santo Sepolcro* I cite both in the Venice, 1566, and in the Treviso, 1791, editions. Zuallardo's *Devotissimo viaggio di Gerusalem* was published in Rome, 1588. Still other reports are presented by Democratia Hemmerdinger Iliadou in "La Crète sous la domination vénetienne," *SV*, IX (1967).

47. *Viaggio d'un mercante che fu nella Persia*, in Ramusio, vol. II. On the importance of the Near East in Venetian diplomacy of the time, see Guglielmo Berchet, *La Repubblica di Venezia e la Persia* (Turin, 1865). I never would have been able to puzzle my way through these texts had it not been for the precious assistance of my colleague John Woods, who has studied them all carefully along with the literature in a score of other languages in preparation for his work on Near-Eastern culture and politics of this little-known age (cited above, Chapter 7, n. 13).

48. Ramusio, vol. II, on which I follow Niccolò di Lenna, "Ricerche intorno allo storico G. Maria Angiolello . . . ," *Archivio veneto-tridentino*, V (1924). A partial English translation is published in *A Narrative of Italian Travels in Persia* (= Hakluyt Society Publications, vol. XLIX) (London, 1873). Further information on Angiolello and his successors in Preto, *Venezia e i Turchi*, cited below at n. 79, pp. 287 ff, and in Franz Babinger's article in *DBI*.

49. Ramusio, vol. II. The *Viaggio* was subsequently translated into Latin by Jacopo Guadero and printed in Frankfurt-am-Main

in 1601. The Italian original was first published in Venice in 1543. I read the texts in Ramusio before coming across the most recent edition ("Il nuovo Ramusio," vol. VII) (Rome: Istituto Poligrafico dello Stato, 1973). For further information: Zeno: *Istorici*, vol. I, pp. 140–42, and Roberto Almagià on Barbaro in *DBI*.

50. Ramusio, vol. II, also published in the edition of Nicolò Zeno, Jr., as *De i commentarii* [the term is correct: the form is that of a humanist historical commentary] *del viaggio in Persia.* together with the voyage of Nicolò and Antonio Zeno to Iceland cited below at n. 97 (Venice, 1558). That Zeno was at least successful in turning the king into a rather mythological hero is evident from Ramusio's introduction to the text, where he is portrayed as a modern Darius. It is only unfortunate, adds Ramusio, unaware that he was a Turk and not a "Persian" at all, that he "non have avuti scrittori [of his own] c'habbian celebrato le [sue] cose."

51. I use the English edition with introduction and scholarly apparatus by Richard Carnac Temple (London: Argonaut Press, 1938).

52. Aloisi and the anonymous Venetian are published along with Barbaro and Contarini ("Contareno") in one of the earliest popular anthologies of travel literature, *Viaggi fatti da Vinetia all Tana, in Persia, in India et in Costantinopoli* (Venice, 1545). Balbi I read in the Latin translation of the first Italian edition published in pt. VII of Ioannes Theodorus and Ioannes Israel de Bry, eds., *Indiae Orientalis...* (Frankfurt-am-Main, 1606), together with the edition of Cesare Federici in *Viaggi... nelle Indie orientali*, ed. Olga Pinto (Rome: Istituto Poligrafico dello Stato, 1962) (in the same Il Nuovo Ramusio series cited above at n. 49). On Balbi: Ugo Tucci in *DBI*.

53. *Pro Sua de Bello Persico Historia adversus ea quae Illi a Ioanne Leunclavio Obiiciuntur Disputatio* (Venice, 1595). Leunclavius's objections regard solely the identification of ancient place names, not the substance of the narration, even though his work as the editor of a translation of the Ottoman chronicle by Muhammed ibn Hasanján (1588 et seq.) made him a leading authority on recent Turkish history (see below, n. 99).

54. *Historia della guerra fra Turchi et Persia... con una descrittione di tutte le cose per-* *tinenti alla religione, alle forze, al governo & al paese del Regno de Persiani*, with a continuation to the year 1586 (Venice, 1588).

55. Bessarion's orations were republished by Scipione Ammirato in appendix to his own literary efforts on behalf of a crusade in the last decade of the sixteenth century (Florence, 1598). The standard modern edition is that in Migne, *P. G.,* vol. 161: *Ad Illustrissimos Inclytosque Italiae Principes contra Turcos Exhortatio.*

56. All the relevant data is in Agostino Pertusi, "I primi studi in occidente sull'origine e la potenza dei Turchi," *SV,* XII (1970), which I follow also in the following paragraphs.

57. I follow P. D. Mastrodimitis, Νικόλαος Σεκουνδῖνος. . .Βιός καὶ ἔργον (Πανεπιστήμιον ᾿Αθηνῶν: Βιβλιοθήκη Σοφίας Ν. Σαρινόλου, vol. IX), which contains a survey of all previous bibliography, as well as Franz Babinger, "Nicolaos Sagoundinos: ein griechische-venedischer Humanist des 15. Jahrhunderts," in vol. I of Χαριστήριον εἰς ᾿Αναστάσιον Κ. ᾿Ορλάνδον (Athens, 1965).

58. Pertusi, "Le notizie sulla organizzazione amministrative e militare dei Turchi nello 'Strategion adversum Turcos' di Lampo Birago," in *Studi sul medioevo cristiano offerti a Raffaello Morghen* (Rome, 1974), vol. II. On Birago: Massimo Miglio in *DBI*.

59. On Chalkokondylis' brother Demetrios, see Giuseppe Cammelli, *I dotti Bizantini e le origini dell'umanesimo* (Florence: LeMonnier, 1954), vol. III. On Egnazio, see below, Chapter 13, n. 80. Some of Chalkokondylis' blind spots are pointed out by Apostolos E. Vakalopoulos on p. 98 of vol. II of his monumental ᾿Ιστορία τοῦ Νέουͺ῾Ελληνισμοῦ (Thessaloniki, 1968) (the part translated into English is cited below, n. 87).

60. *De Origine Turcarum*, published with Robertus Monachus, *Bellum Christianorum contra Saracinos* (Basel, 1533).

61. In addition to the autorities given in the preceding notes, I also follow in this paragraph Agostino Pertusi, *Storiografia umanistica e mondo bizantino* (Palermo: Istituto Siciliano di Studi Bizantini e Neoellenici, 1967) and "Giovan Battista Egnazio e Ludovico Tuberone tra i primi storici occidentali del popolo turco," in Vittore Branca,

ed., *Venezia e Ungheria nel Rinascimento* (Florence: Olschki, 1973). My biographical information on Greek historians here and elsewhere comes from the introduction to the collection of sources edited by Apostolos E. Vakalopoulos, Πηγές τῆς ἱστορίας τοῦ νέου Ἑλληνισμοῦ (Thessaloniki: Πανεπιστήμιον, 1965), from the indispensable handbook of Gyula Moravcsik, *Byzantinoturica*, vol. I, 2d ed. (Berlin: Akademie Verlag, 1958), and from I. E. Karagiannopoulos, Πήγαι τῆς Βυζαντινῆς Ἱστορίας, 2d ed. (Thessaloniki: Κέντρον Βυζαντινῶν Ἐρευνῶν, 1971). Sanudo's *Istoria del Regno di Romania* is published by Carl Hermann Hopf in *Chroniques gréco-romanes inédites* (Berlin, 1873), pp. 94–170. On Georgius, whose *Tractatus* was published in Basel in 1543, see J. A. Palmer, "Fr. Georgius de Hungaria, O. P.," *Bulletin of the John Rylands Library*, XXXIV (1951). On Breydenbach, see Robert Schwoebel, *The Shadow of the Crescent: The Renaissance Image of the Turk (1453–1517)* (New York: St. Martins Press, 1967), Chapter VII, which should be read in the light of the comments of William Monter in *Bibliothèque d'humanisme et renaissance*, XXX (1968), 634.

62. Coriolani Cepionis Dalmatae *De Petri Mocenici Imperatoris Gestis Libri III* (Basel, 1544).

63. On Barlezio, whose principal work I consulted in the English translation of the French translation by Jacques de Lavarin as *The Historie of George Castriot . . .* (London, 1596), I follow (and here quote) Franz Babinger in *DBI*, where he refers to all previous studies. On Angiolello, above, n. 48.

64. Babinger, "Die Aufzeichnungen des genuensen Iacopo de Promontorio-de Campis über den Osmanenstaat um 1475," *SBBayAW*, 1958, Heft 8 (1957), which is also full of information about the other Western observers of the Turks.

65. *Historia turchesca, 1300–1514*, ed. I. Ursu (Bucharest: Editiunea Academiei Romane, 1909). The preface is, alas, in Romanian, which I cannot read. I have therefore followed instead Ursu's long article in Italian published as "Uno sconosciuto storico veneziano del secolo XVI," *AV*, XIX (1910).

66. A few other titles I have encountered: *Risposta del seren.mo Sigismondo Battori prencipe di Transilvania al ragionamento di Amurath Bassà . . . tradotta nella volgar lingua* (three leaves) (Bologna, 1596; reprinted from the 1st ed. of Ferrara); *Relationi della guerra contra Turchi, così in Ungheria come in altre parti . . .* (Ferrara, 1595). Still more are listed by Charles Göllner in *Turcica: Die europäische Türkendrucke des XVI. Jahrhunderts* (Bucharest: Editura Academiei R.P.R./ Berlin: Akademie Verlag G.M.B.H., 1961). Even this two-volume catalogue is not complete, according to Schwoebel (above n. 61), p. 174. Those published in Venice about the wars in France are listed by Gino Benzoni in *SV*, XVI (1974), 388. Those concerning the Levant and Constantinople are considered by Ioannis Chasiotis (Giovanni Hassiotis) in "Venezia, i domini veneziani e i Turchi," in *Venezia centro di mediazione tra oriente e occidente* (Florence: Olschki, 1977), esp. on p. 120. Those published in Rome are fully described by Tullio Bulgarelli in *Gli avvisi a stampa in Roma nel Cinquecento* (Rome: Istituto di Studi Romani, 1967). Their importance in the development of new forms of literature in Italy is evaluated by Valerio Castronovo in "I primi sviluppi della stampa periodica . . . ," in V. Castronovo and N. Tranfaglia, eds., *La stampa italiana dal '500 al '800* (Bari: Laterza, 1976). Their importance in French seventeenth-century historiography is pointed out by Krzysztof Pomian in "De la lettre au périodique," *Organon*, X (1974).

67. As pointed out by Marcel Bataillon in "Mythe et connaissance de la Turquie en occident au milieu du XVI siècle," in *Venezia e l'oriente*, cited above, Chapter 3, n. 12.

68. Bibliography in the work by Simopoulos cited above, n. 46. Ramberti's *Libri tre delle cose dei Turchi* was printed in Venice, 1539 and 1541. On the author: Agostini, vol. II.

69. *Costumi e modi particolari della vita de' Turchi* (Rome, 1545), reproduced in offset in Babinger's *Texte und Widerdrucke zur Geschichte und Landeskunde Südeuropas und des nahen Ostens*, vol. I (Munich: Hueber, 1967). On Bassano: Babinger in *DBI*.

70. *I costumi et la vita de Turchi*, tr. Domenichi (Florence, 1551).

71. *Commntario della origine de Turchi et imperio della casa ottomanna* (Florence, 1538—and not 1528, as erroneously printed on the title

page to the volume, nor 1529, as given in the catalogue of the British Museum). For biographical information: M. Giansante in *DBI,* according to whom a first edition was published in 1529.

72. See below, n. 131.

73. *Storia di Francia dall'anno 1470* (but actually *ab origine*), written, according to the preface, when the author was seventy-five years old, which corroborates internal evidence in favor of a date of composition just before the Battle of Pavia. None of the authorities mentions this work, not even Giansante. I found it in the Newberry Library, Case MS fF. 3910. 146.

74. *Commentario delle cose de Turchi et del s. Georgio Scanderbeg, principe di Epyrro* ([Naples?], 1541) (the dedication date is 1539). On Giovio, see below in Chapter 13.

75. *Historie . . . ove si conteneno* [sic] *le guerre di Mahometto imperatore de Turchi per quindeci anni continui con la Signoria di Venetia . . .* (Venice, 1545). More on Guazzo in Chapter 13.

76. Of whom still another biography was published in 1584 (2d ed., Venice, 1590) by Giovanni Maria Monardo, *Gli illustri et gloriosi gesti . . . fatti . . . da Giorgio Castriotto detto Scanderberg.* Whoever wishes to know who "Scanderbeg" really was, rather than what Western myth-makers imagined him to be, are referred to the article under his real name, Iskender, by Halil Inalcik in vol. III of the *Encyclopedia of Islam.*

77. *Le discordie christiane le quali causarono la grandezza di Casa ottomana, insieme con la vera origine del nome turco* (Bergamo, 1590).

78. *Dell'historie universale dell'origine et imperio de Turchi* (Venice, 1561; 2d ed., 1564). On Sansovino, see also above, n. 18, and below, Chapter 13. On some of the sources he might have used and on some he could not have used because they were discovered only later: Marie-Louise Concasty, "Les informations de Jacques Tedaldi sur la siège et la prise de Constantinople," *Byzantion,* XXIV (1954), and C. J. G. Turner, "Pages from Late Byzantine Philosophy of History," *Byzantinische Zeitschrift,* LVII (1964).

79. Botero, *Della ragion di Stato,* VIII, 17. On Paruta: Paolo Preto, "Paruta e i pubblici storiografi," in his *Venezia e i Turchi* (Pubblicazioni della Facoltà di Magistero del-

l'Università di Padova, vol. XX) (Florence: Sansoni, 1975), with special reference to his memorandum, *Se la guerra fatta a' Persiani da Amurat secondo imperator de' Turchi sia stata di benefizio alle cose della Cristianità,* published by Giovanni Pillinini in *AV,* ser. 5, vol. LXXIV (1964). More on Paruta above, Chapter 9. Sansovino's role as a forerunner of a political rather than a religious view of Islam is recognized by Francesco Gabrieli in *La storiografia arabo-islamica in Italia* (Naples: Guida, 1975), p. 15. For the further development of this view in the following century: the long introduction of Marziano Guglielminetti to his *Viaggiatori del Seicento* (Turin: UTET, 1967).

80. Wolf's preface to the edition of Augsburg, 1557, reproduced in the Bonn, 1835, edition of *Corpus Scriptorum Historiae Byzantinae.* What follows is indebted to Pertusi's *Storiografia umanistica e mondo bizantino* (above, n. 61) and to Steven Runciman, *The Last Byzantine Renaissance* (Cambridge University Press, 1970).

81. Obviously before it was printed in Holtzmann's edition of Basel, 1566, as *Annales sive Historiae ab Exordio Mundi ad Isacium Comnenum usque Compendium.*

82. Sophia Antoniadis, "Le récit du combat naval de Gallipoli chez Zancaruolo en comparaison avec le texte d'Antonine Morosini et les historiens grecs du XV siècle," in *Venezia e l'oriente,* cited above, Chapter 3, n. 12, with references to her earlier studies on the same subject.

83. See the preface by Harry J. Magousias to his translation of Doukas as *The Decline and Fall of Byzantium to the Ottoman Turks* (Detroit: Wayne State University Press, 1975), which also contains a useful survey of late Byzantine historiography. Another very useful summary is "Byzantine Historians and the Ottoman Turks," by Steven Runciman, in Bernard Lewis and P. M. Holt, eds., *Historians of the Middle East* (Oxford University Press, 1962).

84. All this, together (Chapter III) with a survey of Italian literature on the Turks in the sixteenth century, in an excellent piece of detective work in philology by Elizabeth A. Zachariadou, Τὸ Χρονικὸ τῶν τούρκων Σουλτάνων καὶ τὸ Ἰταλικὸ τοῦ πρότυπο (Thessaloniki: Ἑταιρία Μακεδονικῶν

Σπουδῶν, 1960). On Italian attitudes toward Greeks of their own age, see Deno J. Geanakoplos, *Interaction of the "Sibling" Byzantine and Western Cultures* (Yale University Press, 1976), p. 284.

85. That is what Babinger says about him in *Die Aufzeichnungen des genuesen Iacopo de Promontorio,* cited above at n. 64.

86. On Crusius: Chapter I of Nicolae Iorga, *Byzance après Byzance* (Bucharest, 1971). Among Allacci's editions is a work by another Greek historian unknown during the previous century, Giorgos Akropolitis. See Carmela Jacono in *Bibliografia di Leone Allacci* (Palermo: Accademia, 1962), as well as the corresponding article by Domenico Musti in *DBI.*

87. All the bibliographical information is given by Pertusi in *Venezia e Ungheria nel Rinascimento,* pp. 486–87. Many of the many other non-Italian writings on the Turks at the time are given in the notes to Vakalopoulos, *The Greek Nation, 1453–1669,* which is the English translation of vol. II of the original (Rutgers University Press, 1976) (above, n. 59).

88. What follows is based on Babinger, *Die Geschichtsschreiber der Osmanen und ihre Werke* (Leipzig, 1927). On the knowledge of Turkish in Italy, see Chapter III, sec. 1 of Preto, *Venezia e i Turchi,* cited above at n. 79.

89. Rodica Giocan Ivanescu, "Les débuts des recherches byzantines en France à l'époque du Grand Dessein (1598–1609)." *XIIme Congrès des Sciences Historiques* (Vienna, 1965), vol. III.

90. Robert Mantran, "L'écho de la bataille de Lépante à Constantinople," *Annales,* XXVIII (1973).

91. Carlo Dionisotti, "La guerra d'oriente nella letteratura veneziana del Cinquecento," in his *Geografia e storia della letteratura italiana* (Turin: Einaudi, 1967) gives many examples.

92. *L'Ottomanno,* which I read in the edition of Ferrara, 1607. The date on the first dedication is 1598. On which see Preto, *Venezia e i Turchi,* chap. IV, sec. 2.

93. Sansovino, *Gl'annali overo le vite de principi et signori della casa othomano* (Venice, 1571, 1573). The author is quoted here from the preface to pt. IV of the 2d ed. of the *Historie universali,* on which see below, Chapter 13. The Greek chronicle analyzed by

Giorgos Zoras in Χρονικὸν πέρι τῶν Τούρκων σουλτάνων (Athens: Πανεπιστήμιον, 1958) has now been correctly dated and traced to Sansovino's text by Zachariadou in the work cited above at n. 84. Credit for identifying the text of Laguna belongs in part to Marcel Bataillon and in part to Anna Corsi Prosperi, in "Sulle fonti...," *Critica storica,* XIV (1977).

94. Abraham Hartwell's translation (London, 1603) includes also that of Achille Tarducci of Ancona, *Il Turco vincibile in Hungheria,* which also shows "how the Christian princes may combyne & confederate together in this Sacred War."

95. Léopold Dupont, "La bibliothèque de Torrentinus...," *De Gulden Passer,* L (1972).

96. Ramusio, vol. I.

97. Above, n. 50. *Dello scoprimento dell'isole Frislanda, Eslanda..., fatto sotto il Polo artico da due fratelli Zeni* (Venice, 1558). The version in the 2d ed. of Ramusio, vol. II, contains a map.

98. All the bibliographical information is in Giuseppe Fumagalli and Pietro Amat di S. Filippo, *Bibliografia degli scritti italiani o stampati in Italia sopra Cristoforo Colombo* (Rome: Ministero della Pubblica Istruzione, 1893) (= Raccolta di documenti e studi pubblicati dalla Commissione Colombiana per il Quarto Centenario della Scoperta dell'America, vol. VI).

99. *Paesi nuovamente retrovati & novo mondo da Alberigo Vesputio fiorentino intitulato.* I read the facsimile reprint of the Milan edition of 1508 of Gian Jacobo di Legnano by Princeton University Press, 1916: *La navigatione del Re de Castiglia dele isole & paesi....* Vespucci's report was first published as *Mundus Novus* in 1503 in the Latin translation of Giovanni Giocondo of Verona, who also edited Caesar and Vitruvius: Raffaelle Brenzoni, *Fra Giovanni Giocondo* (Florence: Olschki, 1960). Further bibliographical information is given in the well-known essay (which I follow in the next paragraphs) of Rosario Romeo, *Le scoperte americane nella coscienza italiana del Cinquecento* (Milan-Naples: Ricciardi, 1954).

100. In vol. III (Venice, 1565).

101. *Una lettera inedita di Matteo da Bergamo,* ed. Augusto Zeri, offprint from *Rivista marittima* (Rome, 1894).

102. Girolamo da Empoli, *Vita di Giovanni*

da Empoli, ed. Iacopo Gråberg da Hemso, *ASI*, appendix, vol. III¹ (1846).

103. In *Paesi nuovamente retrovati,* cited above at n. 99. On the author: Charles Verlinden, "Venise entre Méditerranée et Atlantique," in *Venezia centro di mediazione* (above, n. 66).

104. A full description with complete bibliographical references is in Lach, *Asia in the Making of Europe,* vol. I, pp. 173 ff. The Italian text appeared at Venice in 1536 and was republished in Ramusio, vol. I. After reading the texts in the editions here cited, I found that they had recently been republished as *Viaggi e scoperti* by Alpes in Milan.

105. Henceforth I follow Giuseppe Pennesi, *Pietro Martire d'Anghiera e le sue relazione sulle scoperte oceaniche* (Rome: Ministero della Pubblica Istruzione, 1894), and Edmundo O'Gorman (who is here quoted), *Cuatro historiadores de Indias* (Mexico: Sep/setentas, 1972), of which the relevant Chapter I was first published in O'Gorman's edition of the Spanish translation of Anghiera's *Décadas del Nuevo Mundo* (Mexico: Porrúa, 1964). Considerable information about the first editions and the Italian translations of the work are to be found in the bibliographical appendix by Joseph H. Sinclair to the edition of the *Décadas* by D. Joaquín Torres Asensio (Buenos Aires: Bajel, 1944). Some important information is buried in the rhapsodic prose of Lorenzo Riber, *El humanista Pedro Martir de Angleria* (Barcelona: Barna, 1964). The generally favorable view of Anghiera among modern scholars is not shared by Margaret Hodgen, who calls him an "inveterate gossip" in her *Early Anthropology in the Sixteenth and Seventeenth Centuries* (University of Pennsylvania Press, 1959), pp. 30–31.

106. *Relationi . . . delle cose notabili della provincia d'Eggitto,* tr. Carlo Passi (Venice, 1564).

107. *Libro primo [et seq] del summario della generale historia delle Indie occidentali cavato de libri scritti dal signor don Pietro Martyre* (Venice, 1534) is mostly a reprint of the *Libretto de tutta la navigation de Re de Spagna . . . ,* which I read in the edition of Venice, 1504.

108. *La historia del nuovo mondo,* which I read in the modern edition by Alfredo Vig (Milan: Giordano, 1965), from the 2d revised ed. of the 1st (Venice, 1565).

109. All my information and bibliographical references are to be found in various parts of Lach, *Asia in the Making of Europe.*

110. Biographical information here comes from Pierantonio Serassi's preface to the Bergamo, 1747, edition of *Opera Omnia Latine Scripta.* His magnum opus I read in Serdonati's translation as *Le historie delle Indie orientali* (Florence, 1589).

111. *Commentarius* Emmanuelis Acostae *De Rebus Indicis usque ad Annum MDLXVIII* (Rome, 1570) (reprinted in Paris, 1572, Naples, 1573, Köln, 1574).

112. Hieronymi Osorii Lusitani *De Rebus Emmanuelis Lusitaniae Regis* (Köln, 1586, from the 1st ed. of 1574).

113. *De vita et moribus Ignatii Loiolae* (Köln, 1585).

114. The only edition I have found is *Degli annali di Gregorio XIII* (Rome, 1742).

115. See above, Chapter 6, n. 109.

116. *Le vite di tutti gli re di Francia . . .* (Rome, 1525).

117. See above, Chapter 10.

118. *Descriptio seu potius Summa Rerum Germanicarum Regionum Populorumque ac Urbium, Oppidorum & Amnium seu Fluviorum Vocabula,* written in 1500; I read the 2d ed. of Rome, 1546). On Collenuccio, see above, Chapter 6, pp. 155 ff. Only as this volume was going to press did I secure a copy (for the outrageous price of $24) of *The Travel Journal of Antonio de Beatis,* ed. J. R. Hale (London: The Hakluyt Society, 1979), from which still more evidence could be drawn in support of my thesis.

119. *Die Chronik des* Carbonio Besozzi, *1548–1563,* ed. Walter Friedensburg in *Fontes Rerum Austriacarum,* pt. 1, vol. IX¹ (1904). On the author: Gerhard Rill in *DBI.*

120. *Taccuino di viaggio da Parigi a Venezia,* ed. Franco Barbieri (Venice: Istituto per la Collaborazione Culturale, 1959).

121. *Delle guerre di Alamagna* (Venice, 1552).

122. The text is published by Adam Wandruszka in appendix to pt. 2, vol. II of *Nuntiaturberichte aus Deutschland, 1560–1572* (Graz-Köln: Böhlaus, 1953). Since I have (rightly, I think) excluded nuncios' and ambassadors' reports from the category of travel literature, I would not have noticed this text had my attention not been drawn to it by

Vaclav Laska of the Regenstein Library, who was then translating the passages on Bohemia into Czech for the enlightenment of the world's second largest Czech city.

123. *De Bello Sicambriae Libri IIII* (Venice, 1557), with biographical information in the dedication.

124. *Vita Henrici Quinti,* which I read in the edition of Thomas Hearne together with a *Sylloge Epistolarum* (Oxford, 1716), with the help of Roberto Weiss in *Humanism in England during the Fifteenth Century,* 3d ed. (Oxford: Blackwell, 1967), and of Remigio Sabbadini in "Tito Livio Frulovisio," *GSLI,* CIII (1934). The most recent edition is that by C. W. Previté Orton as *Opera* (Cambridge University Press, 1932). Parts of the English version done by "The Translator" apparently for the purpose of inspiring the young King Henry VIII, are published in Elizabeth M. Nugent's *The Thought and Culture of the English Renaissance* (Cambridge University Press, 1956).

125. Biographical information in preface to C. A. J. Armstrong's English-Latin edition of *De Occupatione Regni Angliae per Riccardum Tercium* (Oxford University Press, 1936). Armstrong's translation is not always accurate, according to Alison Hanham, who gives still further biographical information and critical judgments on other chroniclers and historians of the period, including Vergilio, in *Richard III and His Early Historians, 1483–1535* (Oxford: Clarendon, 1976).

126. Gioacchino Paparelli, *Callimaco Esperiente (Filippo Buonaccorsi)* (Salerno: Beta, 1971); but I supplement Paparelli, who says very little about Callimaco's writings, with the article by D. Caccamo in *DBI* and with the prefaces to the works cited in the next note. A full bibliography is given by Józef Garbacik in the corresponding article (1964) in *Polski Słownik Biograficzny.*

127. *Vita et Mores Sbignei Cardinalis,* ed. Irmina Lichońska; *Historia de Rege Vladislao,* ed. Lichońska and Thaddeus Kowalewski; and *De His quae a Venetis Tentata sunt Persis ac Tartaris contra Turcos Movendis,* ed. Kowalewski and Andreas Kemp, all published in Warsaw by the Academia Scientiarum Polona in 1961–63, with prefaces in Latin.

128. I follow the most recent biographies: the article by Gerhard Rill in *DBI,* the articles

by Ladislao Tóth and Mario Battistrada in *Antonio Bonfini,* ed. by the Brigata Ascolana Amici dell'Arte (Ascoli Piceno, 1928), Tibor Kardos's Chapter VII ("Bonfini, storiografo di Mattia Corvino") in *Studi e ricerche umanistiche italo-ungheresi,* cited above in Chapter 6, n. 93. A considerable body of recent scholarship in Magyar, which I unfortunately cannot read, is cited in the notes in these studies. The chief merit of Giulio Armadeo's *La vita e l'opera di Antonio Bonfini,* published appropriately by the Tipografia Sisto V in Montaldo Marche (1930), is that it bears an ecclesiastical imprimatur and that the author is praised as "tanto meritamente caro alla S. Sede" by no less an authority on history than Pope Pius IX. I read the *Rerum* in the modern edition of I. Fógel, B. Iványi, and L. Juhász in *Bibliotheca Scriptorum Medii Recentisque Aevorum* (Leipzig-Széged: B. G. Teubner, 1936). For the more general context I follow Vittore Branca, "Mercanti e librai fra Italia e Ungheria," and Péter Kulcsár, "Venise dans l'historiographie en Hongrie," both in *Venezia e Ungheria* (above, n. 61).

129. Details from Pio Paschini, in *Tre illustri prelati del Rinascimento* (= *Lateranum,* n.s., vol. XXIII, nos. 1–4) (Rome, 1957), p. 57, and T. D. Kendrick, *British Antiquity* (London: Methuen, 1950).

130. The last part of the *Anglicae Historiae Libri* (from the 1st ed. of Basel, 1546) dedicated to the years after 1485 has been republished with an introduction and a translation by Denys Hay in the Camden Series (vol. LXXIX) (London: Royal Society, 1956), which I read with the help of Hay's *Polydore Vergil, Renaissance Historian and Man of Letters* (Oxford University Press, 1952), William Trimble, "Early Tudor Historiography," *JHI,* XI (1950), and John Ferguson, "Polydore Vergil's *De Inventoribus Rerum,*" *Isis,* XVII (1932). Brian Copenhaver is now preparing a new edition of the *De Inventoribus;* see his "The Historiography of Discovery in the Renaissance: The Sources and Composition of Polydore Vergil's *De Inventoribus Rerum,* I–III," *JWCI,* XLI (1978).

131. Unfortunately the only biographical information I have been able to find on Emili is in a Ph.D. dissertation submitted to the University of Edinburgh by Katharine Davies, which I read in Xerox copy in the

Newberry Library; and there is not much of it. But the dissertation is very informative with regard to Emili's sources, predecessors, and French colleagues. I read the *De Rebus Gestis Francorum* in the Basel, 1601, edition as well as in the Paris, 1566 (from the 1st of 1517), edition, which has a continuation by Arnauld Ferroni, *De Rebus...Gestis Gallorum Libri IX*, as well as in Michele Tramezzino's edition of the Italian translation published at Venice in 1549 as *Historia delle cose di Francia*, which contains a brief continuation in Italian "da le croniche de le cose istesse de la Francia" by an anonymous author to 1515.

132. All my biographical information comes from Caro Lynn, *A College Professor of the Renaissance: Lucio Marineo Siculo* (University of Chicago Press, 1937), and from Tiraboschi, vol. III, pp. 1020 ff. I consulted the Spanish translation of the history of Spain published without a title and in Gothic letters in 1539. The British Museum lists separately a *Summario de la serenissima vida y heroyces hechos de los catholicos reyes* (Valladolid, 1533), which I take to be an extract from the larger work. I also consulted the edition of *De Hispaniae Laudibus*, of *De Aragoniae Regibus* (which appeared in a Spanish translation by Juan de Molina in Valencia in 1524). and of *De Rebus Hispaniae Memorabilibus Libri XXV* republished from the 1st ed. of Alcala, 1533, in Frankfurt-am-Main, 1603, edited by Andreas Schott. All these and the other works were republished by Nicolao Antonio Hispalensi in vol. II of the *Bibliotheca Hispana Nova* (Madrid, 1780).

133. The extent of humanist influence in Hungary is fully described by Tibor Klaniczay in *Mattia Corvino e l'umanesimo italiano* (Accademia Nazionale dei Lincei, Quaderno No. 202) (Rome, 1974)—another reference I owe to the kindness of Vaclav Laska—and in *Rapporti veneto-ungheresi all'epoca del Rinascimento* (Akadémiai Kiadó: "Studia Humanitatis," vol. II) (Budapest, 1948).

134. *De Dictis ac Factis Mathiae Regis* is published in *Scriptores Rerum Hungaricarum*, vol. II (1786), from the first edition of Vienna, 1563), where the original dedication to Maximilian II is also included. On Panormita, see above, Chapter 6, n. 85.

135. See above, Chapter 6, n. 93.

136. These chronicles are cited by Walter

Hubatsch in *Albrecht von Brandenburg-Ansbach, Deutschordens-Hochmeister und Herzog in Preussen* (Köln-Berlin, 1960).

137. I consulted the first of these in the 2d ed. by Iosephus Podhradczsky (Buda, 1838).

138. All this and much more in the still indispensable work of Heinrich Zeissberg, *Die polnische Geschichtsschreibung des Mittelalters* (Leipzig, 1873). Luckily, Zeissberg's "Mittelalter" extends into the sixteenth century.

139. Corrado Vivanti, "Paulus Aemilius Gallis Condidit Historias?" *Annales*, XIX (1964), upon which I also rely for Emili's influence on subsequent French historiography, and George Huppert in the work cited in the Prologue, n. 16, pp. 16–17.

140. For this influence on French Renaissance poetry, I consulted David Maskell, *The Historical Epic in France, 1500–1700* (Oxford University Press, 1973).

141. *Polonia sive De Situ, Populi Moribus, Magistratibus et Republica Regni Polonici Libri II* (Köln, 1577), reprinted with introduction by Wiktor Zermak in *Biblioteka Pisarzów Polskich*, LX (1901).

142. See Giovanni Mercati in *Ultimi contributi*, vol. II, p. 108.

143. *Regni Hungarici Historia post Obitum Gloriosissimi Mathiae Corvini Regis...Libri XXXIV* (Köln, 1724), with a brief *Vita* in the preface. On the fortune of Bonfini in the sixteenth century: M. Kaposi on p. 175 of M. Horányi and T. Klaniszay, *Italia e Ungheria: Dieci secoli di rapporti letterari* (Budapest: Akadémiai Kiadó, 1967), and R. J. W. Evans, *Rudolf II and His World* (Oxford: Clarendon, 1973), p. 124.

144. Petruccio Ubaldini, *Le vite delle donne illustri del regno d'Inghilterra* (London, 1591).

145. Not even Frank Smith Fussner, the current authority on Elizabethan historiography, mentions Pontico in his *The Historical Revolution* (London: Routledge and Kegan Paul, 1962). What I say about Guagnini is based on what little Maffei (*Verona illustrata*, pt. II, p. 413, of the 1731 edition) and Tiraboschi could find out about him. The quotations are from his dedication to the 1578 edition of his *Sarmatiae Europae Descriptio quae Regnum Poloniae, Lituaniam, ...Complectitur* (Cracow, 1630). On Ubaldini: Anna Maria Crinò, "Come Petruccio

Ubaldini vede lo schisma d'Inghilterra," *Studi offerti a Roberto Ridolfi* (Florence: Olschki, 1973), and Giuliano Pellegrini, *Un fiorentino alla corte d'Inghilterra nel Cinquecento* (Università di Pisa, Facoltà di Lettere e Filosofia, "Studi di Filologia Moderna," n.s., vol. VII) (Turin: Bottega d'Erasmo, 1967).

146. Some passages of the still unpublished manuscript are printed in appendix to the article by Crinò cited in the preceding note. A similar work, the *Militia del gran duca di Thoscana,* was printed in London in 1597.

147. *Lo stato delle tre corti . . . relationi di alcune qualità politiche . . . ritrovate nello Stato della corte Romana, nel Regno di Napoli et nelli Stati del gran duca di Thoscana* (London, 1594).

148. *Commentarii alla tetrarchia di Vinegia, di Milano, di Mantova et di Ferrara* (Venice, 1546).

149. All the biographical information is given in Evans, *Rudolf II* (above, n. 143), pp. 129 ff.

150. *Description de la Limagne d'Auvergne,* tr. (with biographical-bibliographical preface) by Antoine Chappuys, ed. Toussaint Renucci (Paris: Didier, 1943), from the 1st ed. of the original published in Lyon in 1561.

151. *De Civilibus Galliae Dissensionibus Commentariorum Libri III* (a fourth book was begun but never finished). The text was found by Mabillon and is published in Martène-Durand, vol. V (1729).

152. *Britannicae Historiae Libri VI* (London, 1585).

153. Guagnini, *De Lituana Gentis Origine & Moribus, De Ducatu Samogitiae,* published in *Respublica sive Status Regni Poloniae, Lituaniae, Prussiae . . .* (Leiden, 1642); *Omnium Regionum Moscoviae Monarchiae Subiectarum Morum & Religionis Descriptio,* in *Rerum Moscoviticarum Auctores Varii* (Frankfurt-am-Main, 1600). Ubaldini, *Relatione delle cose del Regno d'Inghilterra,* which I read in the London, 1590, translation and in *The Harleian Miscellany,* I (1808), as *A Discourse Concerning the Spanish Fleet Invading England in the Year 1588.* His *Descrittione del Regno di Scotia* was published at Antwerp in 1588.

154. *Bellum Belgicum sive Belgicarum Rerum . . . Libri VI* (Köln, 1611). I do not count a *Istorie delle Fiandre* by Giulio Carafa, cited by Ammirato and Costo, because it seems never to have been published.

155. *Detti e fatti piacevoli et gravi di diversi principi filosofi & cortigiani* (Venice, 1596).

156. Finished in 1560, dedicated to Philip II in 1566, and published first at Antwerp in 1567 and then, with numerous maps, at Antwerp again in 1581 and 1588.

157. I read the Venice, 1565, edition, dedicated to Cosimo I, as is the 2d ed. of 1566. In the same year it was published at Antwerp in Latin translation. All the pertinent biographical information is in Melchiorre Roberti, "Il Belgio descritto da un fiorentino del Cinquecento," *ASI,* LXXIII[1] (1915), and, together with interminable polemics against all its predecessors, in R. H. Touwaide, *Messire Lodovico Guicciardini* (Nieuwkoop: De Graaf, 1975).

158. I take all these biographical details from various passages in Delio Cantimori, *Eretici italiani del Cinquecento* (Florence: Sansoni, 1939; reprinted in 1967).

159. The following is based on Andrea Veress, "Il veneziano Giovanni Michele Bruto e la sua *Storia d'Ungheria,*" *AV,* ser. 5, vol. VI (1929); Mario Battistini, "Jean Michel Bruto, humaniste historiographe, pédagogue," *De gulden Passer,* XXXII (1954); and the article by D. Caccamo in *DBI.* Bruto's confessional position is made clear in an unpublished paper on "Heretics in Poland" kindly lent me by the author, Lech Szczucki.

160. I follow the very full biography by Massimo Firpo, *Pietro Bizzarri, esule italiano del '500,* and the article in *DBI* by Silvana Seidel Menchi, both cited above, Chapter 9, n. 92.

161. See above, Chapter 9, n. 93.

162. Gaetano Cozzi, "Intorno all'edizione dell'opera di Marcantonio Sabellico curato da Celio Secondo Curione," in *Venezia e la politica nei secoli dal XVII al XIX,* ed. Luigi Cini (Venice: Istituto per la Collaborazione Culturale, 1965).

163. I read *Delle historie fiorentine* in the Italian translation of Stanislao Gatteschi (Florence, 1838), from the Lyon, 1562, edition of *Florentinae Historiae Libri VIII,* also published in Graevius, vol. VIII[1].

164. Carlo Ginzburg, *Il Nicodemismo: Simulazione e dissimulazione religiosa nel-*

l'Europa del '500 (Turin: Einaudi, 1970), pp. 187–91.

165. *De Bello Melitensi Historia Nova* (Basel, 1567).

166. Caelii Augustini Curionis *Sarracenicae Historiae Libri III...* (Basel, 1563). I see no sign that Agostino actually took any of his information "ex Arabum, Maurorumque annalibus," as he claims; he undoubtedly took most of it "ex multis Graecorum, Byzantinorumque & Latinorum voluminibus."

167. *Ungaricarum Rerum Libri qui Extant,* including the prefatory *De Historiae Laudibus,* ed. in three volumes by Toldy Ferencz in *Monumenta Hungariae Historica Scriptores,* vols. XII–XIV (Pest, 1863–76).

168. *Historia della guerra fatta in Ungheria dall'invittissimo Imperatore de Christiani contra quello de Turchi* (Lyon, 1569), which I read together (since the two are not identical) with *Pannonicum Bellum sub Maximiliano II...et Solymano...Gestum* (Basel, 1573). On which see Massimo Firpo, "P. B. e la storia della guerra d'Ungheria," in Vittore Branca, ed., *Venezia e Ungheria nel Rinascimento* (above, n. 61).

169. *Cyprium Bellum, inter Venetos et Selymum Turcarum Imperatorem Gestum* (Basel, 1573).

170. *Rerum Persicarum Historia* (Frankfurt-am-Main, 1601), published together with Callimaco's *Oratio de Bello Turcis Inferendo,* Barbaro's and Contarini's itineraries, and a translation of Minadoi as *Belli Turco-Persici Historia.*

171. Angiolo Danti, "Alessandro Cilli e la sua *Historia di Moscovia,*" *ASI,* CXXVI (1968), and Jan Władyslaw Woś, "Per la storia dei rapporti culturali tra Italia e Polonia...: La corrispondenza del pistoiese don Alessandro Cilli...," *Annali della Scuola Normale di Pisa,* ser. 3, vol. I (1971).

172. *De Despota Valachorum Principe Libri III,* ed. Angelo Mai in *Spicilegium Romanum,* vol. VIII (Rome, 1842).

173. Campana's diary stayed in the Jesuit archives in Rome until 1773, when it turned up in Bavaria. The only text I have seen is the German translation by A. M. Ammann, S.J., published as "Ein russischer Reisebericht aus dem Jahre 1581," in *Ostkirchliche Studien,* X (1961).

174. *Commentarii di Moscovia et della pace seguita fra lei e 'l Regno di Polonia colla restitutione della Livonia* (Mantua, 1596); Giacomo Bascapé, *Le relazione fra l'Italia e la Transilvania nel secolo XVI* (Rome: Anonima Romana, 1931). Full bibliographical information concerning the Latin originals of his works are given by Stanislas Polčin, S.J., *Una tentative d'union au XVIe siècle: La mission religieuse du père Antoine Possevin, S. J.,* (Orientalia Christiana Analecta, no. 150) (Rome, 1957), Domenico Caccamo, "Conversione dell'Islam e conquista della Moscovia nell'attività diplomatica e letteraria di Antonio Possevino," in *Venezia e Ungheria nel Rinascimento* (above, n. 61). On Possevino's earlier career: Mario Scaduto, *L'epoca di Giacomo Lainez: L'azione* (Storia della Compagnia di Gesù in Italia, vol. IV [Rome: La Civiltà Cattolica, 1974]), pp. 672 ff. and 749 ff.

175. This version of the story is, not surprisingly, rather different from the one given by the current authority on the history of Romania, Nicolae Iorga, who in *Byzance après Byzance* (Bucharest, 1971), pp. 45–47, refers also to his fuller notes in Romanian published elsewhere.

176. Discovered and published by Girolamo Lagomarsini, S.J., in *De Scriptis Invita Minerva* (Florence, 1745).

177. *De Casibus Virorum Illustrium* (Paris, 1680).

178. *De Bello Cyprico Libri Quinque,* ed. Carlo Graziani (Rome, 1624), of which Book III on Commendone's mission to persuade the emperor to join the league against the Turks is largely autobiographical. On the Cyprus war, see above, Chapter 8.

179. *Apparato all'historia di tutte le nationi et il modo di studiare la geografia,* which I read both in Possevino's own Italian translation (Venice, 1598) and in the original *Apparatus ad Omnium Gentium Historiam* in the Venetian edition of 1597.

180. Both are published in Ramusio, vol. II.

181. Charles Halperin, "Sixteenth-Century Foreign Travel Accounts to Muscovy, A Methodological Excursus," *Sixteenth-Century Journal,* VI (1975), which omits all the relevant Italian scholarship. It is

based instead on a considerable body of Russian scholarship which, alas, I cannot read.

182. Rotondò in *Studi e ricerche di storia ereticale*, pp. 164–65.

CHAPTER THIRTEEN

1. *De Rebus Ripanis Libellus,* ed. Teodoro Quatrini (Ancona, 1576) (but written in 1477). This edition is reproduced in the 2d ed. of Rome, 1781. Garzoni didn't get very much information, however; the history is only some twenty pages long.

2. *De Rebus Saxoniae Thuringiae Libonotriae Misnae et Lusatiae Libri II* (Basel, 1518). Some sixteenth-century Germans thought more highly of the work than I do. It was republished in Latin under a somewhat different title in Frankfurt-am-Main in 1580, and it was twice (1546 and 1606) translated into German.

3. *De Obtenta Portugalia a Rege Catholico Philippo Historia* (Naples, 1588).

4. *Relatione del Reame del Congo et delle circonvicine contrade,* dedicated to the hospital director, Antonio Migliore (Rome, 1591).

5. *Relatione dell'Assedio di Parigi* (Rome, 1591). It is bound together with the contemporary work cited in the preceding note, although under a separate title page.

6. *Historia delle cose occorse nel Regno d'Inghilterra . . . dopo la morte di Odoardo VI* (Venice, 1568).

7. *Scisma d'Inghilterra* (Padua, 1754, from the 1st ed. of Florence, 1638).

8. I give a fuller account of this project in my *Florence in the Forgotten Centuries,* pp. 119–21.

9. *Historia della Transilvania* (Venice, 1588) (but Book XII contains the date: 1607; which indicates that it was added to the original text without a corresponding change of title page). I was not able to read his other historical works: *Ragguaglio fedele et breve del fatto d'arme seguito nell'Africa tra d. Sebastiano re di Portogallo et Mulei Auda Malucco* (Bologna, 1601) and *Attioni de re dell'Ungaria brevemente descritte* (Bologna, 1602; Venice, 1685) (British Museum). What little Argellati and Zeno could find out about the author is summarized in Tiraboschi.

10. *Dell'unione del Regno di Portogallo alla corona di Castiglia* (Genoa, 1585); *Delle guerre della Germania inferiore* (Venice, 1614).

11. *Harangues militaires et concions de princes, capitaines . . .* (Paris, 1572).

12. I quote here from his *Dodici libri del governo di Stato* (Verona, 1599) and *La corona del principe* (Verona, 1590).

13. *Commentari della guerra di Transilvania . . . fino all'anno 1553* (Venice, 1566), reproduced in offset with an introduction by Ladislao Gáldi (Budapest: Athenaeum, 1940); *Il primo discorso . . . sopra l'ufficio d'un capitano generale di essercito* (Venice, 1558) (finished in 1557: dedication).

14. *La historia de fatti di Cesare Maggi di Napoli, dove si contengono tutte le guerre successe nel suo tempo in Lombardia e in altre parti d'Italia e fuori d'Italia* (Pavia, 1564).

15. *La seconda parte de' commentari delle guerre et de' successi più notabili avvenuti così in Europa come in tutte le parti del mondo* (from 1553 to 1560) (Venice [or Milan?], 1568). I have not found the third volume promised at the end of the second.

16. *Commentaria Suorum Temporum ab Anno circiter 1470 ad Annum 1526,* in Martène-Durand, vol. V. On the author: Tiziano Ascari in *DBI.*

17. *Comentarii* [sic] *ne quali si descrive la guerra ultima di Francia, la celebratione del Concilio Tridentino, il soccorso d'Orano, l'impresa di Pignone, e l'historia dell'assedio di Malta . . . , con altre cose notabili* (Rome, 1567).

18. *Historia nova, nella quale si contengono tutti i successi della guerra turchesca . . . e finalmente tutto quello che nel mondo è occorso da l'anno 1570 sino all'hora presente* (Padua, 1572).

19. *Assedio e racquisto d'Anversa fatto dal sereniss. Alessandro Farnese . . . con una breve narratione delle cose avvenute in Fiandra dall'anno 1566 fino al 1584* (Vicenza, 1595).

20. *Della guerra di Fiandra fatta per difesa di religione da' catholici re di Spagna . . . per lo spatio di anni trentacinque* (Vicenza, 1602).

21. All biographical information from the preface of Campana's *Arbori delle famiglie le quali hanno signoreggiato con diversi titoli in Mantova* (Mantua, 1590) and from the article by Gino Benzoni in *DBI.*

22. *Delle historie del mondo, libri XIII* (Venice, 1596).

23. *Supplimento all'historia della vita del catolico* [sic] *re delle Spagne . . . d. Filippo II d'Austria, cioè, Compendio di quanto nel mondo è avvenuto dall'anno 1583 sino al 1596, et His-*

toria universale di quant' è occorso dal 1596 sino al 1599 (Venice, 1599).

24. I follow the two-volume modern edition, based on the first Torrentino edition of 1550–52 (Florence) by Dante Visconti, published as vols. III and IV of the still incomplete *Opera* (Rome: Istituto Poligrafico dello Stato, 1964), as well as Domenichi's translation as *Delle istorie del suo tempo,* which I read in the Venetian editions of 1555 and 1565. On Giovio as a man and a writer, I follow Federico Chabod in an article which marks the beginning of the recent reevaluation of Giovio, "Paolo Giovio," now reprinted in his *Scritti sul Rinascimento* (Turin: Einaudi, 1967), Carlo Dionissotti, "Machiavellerie (IV)," *RSI,* LXXXVII (1975) (a mine of information), the two published articles, "A Note on Clement VII and the Divorce of Henry VIII," *English Historical Review,* LXXXII (1967), and "The publication of Paolo Giovio's Histories," *La bibliofilia,* LXXIV (1972), as well as the forthcoming critical biography, which the author kindly let me read in a first draft, by T. C. Price Zimmermann, as well as on other more specialized studies cited below. V. J. Parry arrives independently of Chabod at the same positive evaluation in "Renaissance Historical Literature in Relation to the Near and Middle East (with Special Reference to Paolo Giovio)," in Bernard Lewis and P. M. Holt, eds., *Historians of the Middle East,* cited above in Chapter 12, n. 83—still another reference I owe to the kindness of John Woods.

25. Above, Chapter 12, nn. 74 and 180.

26. *Descriptio Britanniae & Scotiae, Hybernae & Orcadum* (Venice, 1548).

27. I read the *Descriptio Larii Lacus* in the Venice, 1559, edition, which includes also the other *Descriptiones.* It is reprinted in the *Italiae Illustratae Scriptores* of Frankfurt-am-Main (1600).

28. *Le vite dei dodeci Visconti* I read in Domenichi's translation in the new edition of Milan, 1645, and the *Vite degli Sforzeschi* in the edition of Massimo Fabi (Milan, 1853).

29. *De Romanis Piscibus* (Rome, 1524 and 1527), translated into Italian as *De' pesci romani* (Venice, 1560).

30. *Elogia Veris Clarorum Virorum Imaginibus Apposita* (Venice, 1546), translated by Domenichi as *Gli elogi: Vite brevemente*

scritte d'huomini illustri (Florence, 1554).

31. *Le vite di dicenove huomini illustri* (Venice, 1561), all translated by the same tireless Domenichi except for that of Alfonso I d'Este, which is by Giovan Battista Gelli. This edition includes the *vite* cited above at n. 28 and below at n. 36.

32. All the relevant information in Ezio Raimondi, "Machiavelli, Giovio e Aristofane," in *Saggi di letteratura italiana in onore di Gaetano Trombatore* (Milan: Goliardica, 1973), which is on Giovio's *Dialogus de Viris Litteris Illustribus* first published by Tiraboschi in appendix to his *Storia della letteratura italiana.*

33. Pomian in "De la lettre au périodique," cited above, Chapter 12, n. 66, which I keep in mind for the purposes of comparison.

34. Now published in the first two volumes of the *Opera* (above, n. 24).

35. Above, Chapter 10, n. 27, on Equicola.

36. *Le vite del Gran Capitano e del Marchese di Pescara,* in Domenichi's translation, first published in Florence, 1551 and 1550, now in a modern edition by Costantino Panigada (Bari: Laterza, 1931).

37. This and much else from Carlo Volpati, "Paolo Giovio e Venezia," *AV,* LXIV (1934).

38. This and other information from Franca Bevilacqua Caldari, "Un brano delle *Historiae* in una lettera inedita del cardinale Jean du Bellay," *Studi romani,* XIX (1971).

39. Prosperi, *Tra Evangelismo e Controriforma,* p. 59.

40. John O'Malley in *RQ,* XX (1967), 3.

41. Porzio in dedication to the *Congiura dei baroni;* Gelli in introduction to his translation of the *Vita di Alfonso;* Giustiniani in his *Dell'historia venetiana* (1598 edition of the translation).

42. *Dell'historie di mons. Paolo Giovio* (Venice, 1562). Cartari is mentioned as a mythologist by Jean Seznec in *The Survival of the Pagan Gods,* tr. Barbara Sessions (Princeton University Press, 1972), pp. 233 ff.

43. *La selva di varia istoria,* 2d ed. from the 1st, which was published as *Annotationi dell'Infortunio nella prima e seconda parte delle istorie di monsig. Giovio* (Venice, 1564).

44. Above, Chapter 10, n. 162. Sleidanus

says, "Ubicunque de rebus germanicis loquitur, praesertim de religione, morbum animi prodit; nam . . . falsa et calumniosa quaecunque scribit"—in the dedication (1555) to the *Commentarii* on pp. 11–12 of the Frankfurt edition of 1785. Zeno carries on the diatribe in *Istorici*, pp. xxxvii ff.

45. Varchi, *Errori di Paolo Giovio nella storia,* ed. Vincenzo Follini (Dalla Badìa di Fiesoli, 1821).

46. Some of them were published by Domenichi in 1560 (Venice) as *Lettere volgari.*

47. Gonzalo Jimenez de Quesada, *El antijovio,* ed. with a long preface by Manuel Ballesteros Gaibrois (Bogatà: Istituto Caro y Cuervo, 1952).

48. The translation of Collenuccio, *Storia del Regno di Napoli* (Venice, 1552) is prefaced by a *Breve discorso sopra l'autore.* Giovio is one of the main sources for Ruscelli's *Le imprese illustri* of 1566 (I read the 2d ed. of Venice, 1572). A good review of the debate over Giovio is in the preface to his *Supplemento . . . nell'istorie di monsignor Paolo Giovio* (Venice, 1572). Ruscelli describes his Venetian experience in a letter of 8 November 1559 published in Gravier, vol. VII.

49. I have consulted the Latin original published as Natalis Comitis Veneti *Universae Historiae Sui Temporis Libri XXX* (Strasbourg, 1612, from the 1st ed. of Venice, 1581), and the translation by Giovan Carlo Saraceni as *Delle historie de' suoi tempi* (Venice, 1589). More information on the author in the work of Seznec cited above at n. 42.

50. All explained in the preface of F. Portalupi to the edition of Turin (Giappichelli), 1967. On Polybius: Alfonso de Petris, "Le teorie umanistiche del tradurre . . . ," *BHR,* XXXVII (1975), esp. p. 21.

51. Stanislao Gatteschi in introduction to Bruto's *Dell'historie fiorentine* (above, Chapter 12, n. 163). Roberto Ridolfi quoted by Dionisotti in the article cited above at n. 24.

52. The article cited above at n. 24 was first published in this year in the *Periodico della Società Storica Comense,* vol. XXXVIII.

53. I thus read the "continued" version of the earlier Italian translation by P. Francesco Fiorentino published as *Croniche universale* [sic] . . . *cominciando dal principio della creatione*

del mondo . . . (Venice, 1564), as well as the 1st ed. of *Supplementum Chronicarum . . .* (Bergamo, 1483), which alone includes the original dedication. I read Sansovino's version in the Venice, 1581, edition of the 1st ed. of 1574. On Sansovino's earlier works, see above, Chapter 12, n. 78.

54. See above, Chapter 7, n. 12, and Chapter 12, n. 75.

55. *Cronica . . . ne la quale ordinatamente contiensi l'essere de gli huomini illustri antiqui & moderni, le cose & i fatti di eterna moria degni, occorsi dal principio del mondo sino a questi nostri tempi* (Venice, 1553), which actually forms a single work with his earlier *De le cose degne di memoria . . . successe dal 1524 sino all'anno 1552,* the last updating (Venice, 1552) of the work first published in 1540. A full bibliography of Guazzo's works is given by Salvatore Bongi in *Annali di Gabriele Giolito de' Ferrari* (Rome, 1890), vol. I, pp. 115–16.

56. Above, Chapter 10, n. 50.

57. *Delle istorie del mondo di Giovanni Tarchagnota, con l'aggiunta di m. Mambrino Roseo* [e] *del reverendo m. Bartolomaeo Dionigi da Fano* (Venice, 1592). I also consulted the edition of Venice, 1585, of Tarcagnota and Roseo.

58. *Historia universale nella quale . . . si racconta brevemente & con bell'ordine tutto quello ch'è successo dal principio del mondo fino all'anno 1569* (Venice, 1570); *L'aggiunta dell'Historia universale et delle cose di Milano, . . . nella quale si leggono i più memorabili fatti* (Milan, 1587).

59. *Sommario overo Età del mondo chronologiche . . . ne le quali . . . si racconta le origini di tutte le genti, il principio di tutte le monarchie, di tutti i regni, republiche & principati . . .* (Venice, 1581). On Bardi: above, Chapter 12, p. 320.

60. *Compendio historico universale di tutte le cose notabili,* which I read in the 2d ed., "da lui medisimo riveduto e corretto & ampliato con aggiunta sino all'anno 1600," from the 1st ed. of 1595 (Venice, 1601).

61. *Sommario istorico,* 2d ed. from the 1st of Vicenza, 1599, "ampliato e migliorato" (Naples, 1602). The 3d ed. of 1609 was further "ampliata" to include "the kingdoms of Japan, China, Egypt, and Syria, all the peoples formerly subject to the Roman Empire as well as the Saracens, the Turks, and the Tartars," in order to present "with

no less clarity than brevity . . . almost all the histories [i.e., the histories of all the countries] of the world."

62. Florence, 1566. On which: Eugenio Mele, "Le fonti spagnuole della *Storia d'Europa* del Giambullari," *GSLI*, LIX (1912), Giuseppe Kirner, "Sulla *storia d'Europa* di Pierfrancesco Giambullari," *Annali della Scuola Normale Superiore di Pisa,* VI (1889), Pietro Fiorelli, "Pierfrancesco Giambullari e la riforma dell'alfabeto," *Studi di filologia italiana,* XIV (1956), and, on the German sources, Gustavo Costa, *Le antichità germaniche nella cultura italiana da Machiavelli a Vico* (Naples: Bibliopolis, 1977), pp. 55–65. Giambullari's historical work may have been neglected at the time because of the unusual nature of his subject, which is what led Riccardo Fubini to object to my placing it within the category of "universal history." But neither he nor I could think of a more appropriate collocation.

63. *L'Ungheria spiegata, ove si leggono tutte le cose successe in quel regno . . . sino all'anno corrente 1595* (Venice, 1595).

64. *Vittoria navale ottenuta dalla Republica Venetiana contra Othone figliuolo di Federigo Primo . . .* (Venice, 1584).

65. Doglioni, *Venetia trionfante et sempre libera, dove per ordine de' tempi si legge la sua origine et augmento* (Venice, 1613); Bardi, *Delle cose notabili della città di Venezia,* which I read in the 2d ed. of Venice, 1606, from the 1st ed. of 1581.

66. In preface to his edition of Livy, *Historiarum ab Urbe Condita Libri qui Extant* (Venice, 1555).

67. *Brevis Chronologia ab Orbe Condito,* which I read in the edition of Köln, 1654.

68. As he points out in the preface to *L'Ungheria spiegata,* cited above at n. 63, concerning his *L'anno, dove si ha perfetto et pieno ragguaglio . . . d'intorno alle cose del mondo celeste ed elementare . . .* (Venice, 1587).

69. Above Chapter 1, n. 85.

70. Ioan. Lucidi Samothei *Chronicon seu Emendatio Temporum ab Orbe Condito usque ad Annum Christi 1535* (Venice, 1575), with a preface by the editor, Giovanni Maria de Tholosanis of Colle Valdelsa.

71. *Chronologia del mondo* (Venice, 1580).

72. All this is based on the forthcoming study of Scaliger by Anthony Grafton and on Pietro De Rosa, "Denis Petau e la cronologia," *Archivum Historicum Societatis Iesu,* XXIX (1960).

73. See Bouwsma, *Venice* (above, Chapter 9, n. 64), pp. 224–25.

74. *De Claris Mulieribus Scelectisque* [sic] *Mulieribus . . . ,* which I read in the edition of Ferrara, 1497. Laura Torretta called it a "Lavoro di arida, poco intelligente compilazione" in *GSLI,* XL (1902), 55–56.

75. Guazzo inserted a brief autobiography right in his text under "Mantua."

76. Romualdo Canavari, "Sulle opere di Mambrino Roseo," in preface to Canavari's *L'assedio di Firenze* (Florence, 1894).

77. See above, Chapter 12, pp. 333–34, and Giovanni Sforza, "Francesco Sansovino e le sue opere storiche," *MAS Tor,* ser. 2, vol. XLVII (1897).

78. Ditte Candiotto et Darete Frigio, *Della Guerra troiana* (Venice, 1570), on which see Momigliano, *Secondo contributo alla storia degli studi classici* (Rome: Edizioni di Storia e Letteratura, 1960), pp. 46–47.

79. Iustino historico clarissimo *Nelle historie di Trogo Pompeo, nuovamente in lingua toscana tradotto* (Venice, 1542); on which: Otto Seel, *Eine römische Weltgeschichte* (Nürnberg: Hans Carl, 1972).

80. *Paolo Orosio tradotto . . .* per Giovanni Guerini da Lanciza (Venice, 1571); on which: Eugenio Corsini, *Introduzione alle "Storie" di Paolo Orosio* (Turin: Giappichelli, 1968).

81. I read the *Romanorum Principum Liber* (= Libri III) in the Paris, 1544, edition from the 1st ed. as *De Caesaribus Libri III* (Venice, 1516), as well as the 2d ed. with the same title as the 1st published in Florence, 1519, and the French translation as *Summaire des chroniques contenans les vies, gestes & cas fortuitz* of Geofroy Tory de Bourges (Paris, 1529).

82. On Dolce's Mexia, see above, Chapter 12, p. 320. The *Scriptores* were first published in Milan, 1475, then in Venice, 1489, 1516, and 1519, and they were edited by Erasmus in 1518. On which see Momigliano, "An unsolved Problem of Historical Forgery . . . ," in his *Secondo contributo* (above, n. 78).

83. *Historie di Giovanni Zonara monaco, diligentissimo scrittore greco, dal cominciamento del mondo insino all'imperadore Alessio Comneno*

(Venice, 1564) (another in the historical text series of Gioliti de' Ferrari).

84. *Historia de' successori di Alessandro Magno et della disunione del suo imperio . . . raccolta da diversi auttori et in gran parte da Diodoro Siculo* (Venice, 1570), published together with Plutarch's life of Alexander; *Le vite dei diece imperatori incominciando dalla fine di Suetonio* (Venice, 1564).

85. Joh. Stellae *Vita Romanorum Imperatorum* (Venice, 1503), to which was added two years later a supplement, *Vite Ducento Triginta Summorum Pontificum a Beato Petro . . . Usque ad Julium Secondum* (Venice, 1505).

86. *De Exemplis Illustrium Virorum Venetae Civitatis* (Venice, 1554). But it is by no means limited to Venice—or to any particular *viri*.

87. See Henry Lewis Bullen, *The Nuremberg Chronicle,* printed in a luxurious format by the Book Club of California in 1930, and Frank L. Borchardt, *German Antiquity in Renaissance Myth* (Johns Hopkins University Press, 1971), pp. 84–86. The 1st ed. is of Nürnberg, 1493.

88. So said Erich Joachim in *Johannes Nauclerus und seine Cronik* (Göttingen, 1874). On Naucler's unsuccessful attempt to free himself from medieval models, and on the medieval models themselves: Anna-Dorothee von den Brincken, "Die lateinische Weltchronistik," in Alexander Randa, ed., *Mench und Weltgeschichte. Zur Geschichte der Universalgeschichtsschreibung* (Salzburg-Munich: Antono Pustet, 1969). The other articles in this volume add further evidence in support of my thesis, that in the genre of universal historans the Italians fell far behind their foreign colleagues.

89. Above, n. 71.

90. On the acceptance of these schemes elsewhere in Europe (but not in Italy, which the author does not mention): Adalbert Klempt, *Die Säkularisierung der universalhistorischen Auffassung* (Göttingen: Musterschmidt, 1960). The text of another Italian Dominical follower of Martinus Polonus, Leo Urbetanus, is edited by Giovanni Lami in vols. II–III of *Deliciae Eruditorum* (Florence, 1737) (Riccardiana, 3138).

91. *Giornale delle historie del mondo* (Venice, 1572).

92. Baptiste Fulgosi *De Dictis Factisque Memorabilibus Collectanea,* tr. Camillo Ghilini (1490–c. 1535), which I read in the edition of Paris, 1518.

93. Doglioni, *Del theatro universale de' prencipi . . .* (Venice, 1606); Ruscelli, *Le imprese illustri* (Venice, 1572), on which: above, n. 48.

94. *Il vago e dilettevole giardino, ove si leggono: Gli infelici fini di molti huomini illustri . . .* (a long list follows) (Vicenza, 1602).

95. *Raccolta breve d'alcune cose segnalate c'hebbero gli antichi e d'altre trovate da moderni* (Venice, 1612).

96. *I fatti d'arme famosi successi tra tutte le nationi del mondo da che prima han cominciato a guerreggiare sino ad hora* (Venice, 1600).

97. *Il primo volume delle cagioni delle guerre antiche . . . tratte da gl'historici antichi greci a beneficio di che vol'adornarsi l'animo delle gioie dell'historie* (Venice, 1565); and *Paralleli o essempi simili . . . cavati da gl'historici accio che si vegga come in ogni tempo le cose del mondo hanno riscontro o fra loro o con quelle de' tempi antichi* (Venice, 1567).

98. *De' discorsi di guerra . . . libri quattro, dove s'insegna a' capitani e soldati il modo di condurre esserciti, di far fatti d'arme, espugnare e difendere città* (Venice, 1580).

Chapter Fourteen

1. On Giovanni Colonna, I read Braxton Ross's preface to his forthcoming edition of the *De Viris Illustribus,* which the author kindly permitted me to read in manuscript.

2. On Villani and Piccolomini, see above, Chapters 1 and 2.

3. *De Originis Rerum Libellum,* ed. Michelangelo Biondi (Venice, 1547).

4. Since the rest of this series was never written, the life here referred to is published separately with Colli's *Prose e lettere edite e inedite,* ed. Cecil Grayson (Bologna: Commissione per i Testi di Lingua, 1959).

5. Talbot R. Selloy, "Filippo Villani and His *Vita* of Guido Bonatti," *RQ,* XI (1958).

6. *Le vite delle donne illustri della Sacra Scrittura* (Venice, 1588).

7. See Peter Murray, "Art Historians and Art Critics," *The Burlington Magazine,* XCIX (1957).

8. Charles Stinger, *Humanism and the*

Church Fathers: Ambrogio Traversari (Albany: State University of New York Press, 1977), p. 77.

9. Incipit: Incomincia el libro . . . D. Lahertio . . . (Venice, 1480); Le vite de gli illustri filosofi di Diogene Laertio da 'l greco idiomata ridutte ne la lingua commune d'Italia ("a commun'utilità de chi non sà lettere ne grece ne latine"—sic) (Venice, 1545). The rest of my information here comes from the very informative preface of Marcello Gigante (who ought to know, juding from the length of the list of his own publications) to his new Italian translation as Vita dei filosofi (Bari: Laterza, 1976).

10. Scriptorum Illustrium Latinae Linguae Libri XVIII, ed. B. L. Ullmann (Rome: American Academy, 1928). The distinction made in the Renaissance between a scheme of periodization based on politics and one based on "culture" is noted by Nicolai Rubinstein in "Il Medio Evo nella storiografia italiana del Rincascimento," in Concetto, storia, miti e immagini, cited in the Prologue, n. 5.

11. Commedia del divino poeta Danthe Alighieri con la dotta & leggiadra spositione di Christophoro Landino, which I read in the edition of Venice, 1536. On the date and circumstances of the commentary, see Roberto Cardini, the modern editor of Landino (Scritti critici e teorici [Rome: Bulzoni, 1974]), in La critica del Landino (Istituto Nazionale di Studi sul Rinascimento: Studi e Testi, vol. IV) (Florence: Sansoni, 1973), chap. 2.

12. Accolti, De Praestantia Virorum Sui Aevi, which I read in Graevius, vol. IX⁶; on his historical work, see above, Chapter 1, n. 91. Cortesi, De Hominibus Doctis Dialogus, ed. with commentary (unfortunately better informed about the text than about the literary and cultural context) by Maria Teresa Graziosi (Roma: Bonacci, 1973). On Cortesi's less-known De Cardinalatu, see Dionisotti in Geografia e storia (above, Chapter 12, n. 91), pp. 80 ff., and Paschini in Tre illustri prelati (above, Chapter 12, n. 129).

13. De Poetis Latinis I read in the edition of Lyon, 1554, bound with his De Honesta Disciplina.

14. I read the Historiae Poetarum tam Graecorum quam Latinorum Dialogi Decem in the first edition of Basel, 1545, from the text

dedicated the year before to Duchess Renata of Ferrara. I read the De Poetis Nostrorum Temporum in the edition of Karl Wotke in vol. X of Lateinische Literaturdenkmäler des XV. und XVI. Jahrhunderts (Berlin, 1894) as well as in Giraldi's Operum Quae Extant Omnia (Basel, 1580), vol. II. For biographical information I rely on Tiraboschi, vol. VII, pp. 849, ff., of the Modena, 1792, edition, which draws on and adds to the longer biography in Barotti, Memorie de' letterati ferraresi (above, Chapter 4, n. 72), vol. I, pp. 265 ff.

15. On Fazio's historical work, see above, Chapter 6, n. 67. For his statements about biography, see the article by Miglio cited below, n. 40. Several of the lives with full commentary are published with English translation by Michael Baxandall in "Bartholomaeus Facius on Painting," JWCI, XXVII (1964). I consulted the De Viris Illustribus in the first edition of Lorenzo Mehus (Florence, 1745), which is preceded by Mehus's Vita. Lami's review appeared in Novelle letterarie, VI (1745), cols. 385 ff.

16. I used the Antwerp, 1557, edition of Elogia Doctorum Virorum ab Avorum Memoria, and the translations of Hippolito Orio as Le iscrittioni poste sotto le vere imagini (Florence, 1551) and of Domenichi as Vite brevemente scritte d'huomini illustri . . . (Venice, 1559)—among the many partial and whole editions of the sixteenth century—as well as Elogia Virorum Illustrium, ed. Renzo Meregazzi (= Opera, vol. VIII) (Rome: Istituto Poligrafico dello Stato, 1972).

17. I here follow Antonio Banfi in "Concetto e sviluppo della storiografia filosofica," republished in his La ricerca della realtà (Florence: Sansoni, 1959), and Raymond Marcel, Marsile Ficin (Paris: Les Belles Lettres, 1958), pp. 15 ff. on Giovanni Corsi (above, Chapter 7, n. 39) and on Pietro Caponsacchi. My other references here are to Frosino Lapini in the biographical preface to Cattani's Opera Omnia (Basel, 1564), and to Varchi's Vita, which is published in his edition of Francesco Cattani da Diacceto, Tre libri d'amore (Venice, 1561).

18. I read De Claris Legum Interpretibus in the edition of the author's nephew Ottavio Panciroli (Venice, 1637), which contains a very informative Vita Auctoris. Panciroli's

history of Reggio is cited in Chapter 10, n. 54.

19. I read the *Augustalis Liber* in appendix to vol. I of the Basel (1554) edition of Petrarch's *Opera,* now in a Gregg Press offset edition (1965).

20. *De Exemplis Illustrium Virorum Venetae Civitatis atque Aliarum Gentium* (Venice, 1554). On the author: above, Chapter 13, n. 81.

21. I consulted the Venice, 1517, and the Florence, 1519, editions entitled *De Caesaribus Libri III,* as well as the *Romanorum Principum Liber [-ri]* bound with the author's edition of Suetonius and published at Lyon in 1539. The latter made such an impression upon one reader of the copy in the Palatina collection of the Biblioteca Nazionale of Florence that he ripped out the first ten pages. I also use the anonymous Italian translation, *Le vite de gl'imperadori romani* (Venice, 1540); and on Egnazio's life and works I consulted James Bruce Ross, "Venetian Schools and Teachers, Fourteenth to Early Sixteenth Century: A Survey and a Study of Giovanni Battista Egnazio," *RQ,* XXXIX (1976).

22. *Le vite dei diece* [sic] *imperatori incominciando dalla fine di Svetonio* (Venice, 1544).

23. On whom see above, Chapter 12, n. 63.

24. I use the complete edition with all the continuations published in Venice, 1730, as *Le vite de' pontefici di Bartolomeo Platina . . . con le annotazioni del Panvinio e con la cronologia ecclesiastica dello stesso ampliata . . . da altri fino all'anno MDCCXXX* (Venice, 1730), which contains a *Vita di Platina* by Nicol'Angelo Caferri of Rome. Full biographical information on Davide Aurelio Perini, *Onofrio Panvinio e le sue opere* (Rome, 1899).

25. *Le vite di tutti i pontefici . . . ridotte in epitome* (Venice, 1592).

26. *Breve trattato dell'istoria,* dedicated to the duke of Urbino in 1611. I read the text in *Spicilegium Romanum,* vol. I (Rome, 1839), and the *Difesa di Procopio contro le calunnie di Flavio Biondo* in the 2d ed. of Urbino, 1627.

27. *Vita e fatti di Federico di Montefeltro duca d'Urbino,* edited with a very informative *Vita* of Baldi by Francesco Zuccardi (Rome, 1824); *Della vita e de fatti di Guidobaldo I da Montefeltro . . .* (Milan, 1821). Further bio-

graphical information in Irenio Affò, *Vita di mons. B. B.* (Parma, 1783), Guido Zaccagnini, *B. B. nella vita e nelle opere,* 2d ed. (Pistoia, 1908), and Raffaele Amaturo in *DBI.*

28. In preface to *De gli elementi d'Euclide* (Urbino, 1575).

29. The importance of Baldi's innovations is eloquently demonstrated by Paul Lawrence Rose in the work cited above, Chapter 4, n. 90.

30. *Cronica de matematici, ovvero Epitome dell'istoria delle vite loro* (Urbino, 1707).

31. *Vite inedite di matematici italiani,* ed. Enrico Narducci, in vol. XIX (1886) of the *Bullettino di bibliografia e di storia delle scienze matematiche e fisiche* (Rome), also published separately (Rome, 1887).

32. On which see Bronisław Bilinski, *La 'Vita di Copernico' di Bernardino Baldi dell'anno 1588 alla luce dei ritrovati manoscritti* (Accademia Polacca delle Scienze, Roma: *Conferenze,* no. 61) (Warsaw: Wydawnictwo Polskiej Akademii Nauk, 1973), and Rose in *Isis,* LXV (1974), 387–89. The life of Vitruvius was published separately in appendix to Baldi's analysis of the text of *De Architectura* in 1612 (but I consulted the edition of Amsterdam, 1649), which puts the blame for the difficult passages on Vitruvius himself, not on later copyists. See Paolo Galluzzi, "I traduttori di Vitruvio nel '500," *Annali dell'Istituto e Museo di Storia della Scienza di Firenze,* I (1976).

33. On Villani: Giuliano Tanturli, "Le biografie d'artista prima del Vasari," in *Vasari storiografo e artista: Atti del Congresso Internazionale nel IV centenario della sua morte* (Florence: Istituto Nazionale di Studi sul Rinascimento, 1976). Gelli's *Vite de' primi pittori di Firenze* are published in *ASI,* ser. 5, vol. XVII (1896), on which see Armando De Gaetano, *Giambattista Gelli and the Florentine Academy* (Florence: Olschki, 1976), pp. 46 ff. On Summonte (not to be confused with the historian Giannantonio) and on Michiel, I follow Luigi Grassi, *Teorici e storia della critica* (Rome: Multigrafica, 1970), pt. I, and Ferdinando Bologna, *I pittori alla corte angioina di Napoli* (Rome: Bozzi, 1969). Michiel's text, which was first discovered by Apostolo Zeno, I read in the bilingual edition by Theodor Frimmel as *Der 'Anonimo Morelliano'* (Quellenschriften für Kunstgeschichte

und Kunsttechnik, N.F., vol. I) (Vienna, 1896); an English translation by Paolo Mussi was published in London in 1903.

34. All this from Bernard Degenhart and Annegrot Schmitt, "Methoden Vasaris bei der Gestaltung seines 'Libro'," in Wolfgang Lotz and Lise Lotte Möller, eds., *Studien zur Toskanischen Kunst: Festschrift Ludwig Heinrich Heydenreich* (Munich: Prestel-Verlag, 1964); Paola Barocchi in the *premessa* to Rosanna Bettarini's edition of the *Vite* and of subsequent commentaries published in Florence by Sansoni from 1967 on (a project that may never be completed); Alessandra Bonsanti in "Vasari scrittore," in *Unione fiorentina: Il Cinquecento* (Florence: Sansoni, 1955), and T. C. Price Zimmermann, "Paolo Giovio and the Evolution of Renaissance Art Criticism," in Cecil H. Clough, ed., *Cultural Aspects of the Italian Renaissance: Essays in Honour of Paul Oskar Kristeller* (Manchester University Press, 1976).

35. The title here given is the one used in the edition cited in the preceding note as well as in the most complete modern edition of all Vasari's works, that of the Club del Libro, ed. Giovanni Previtali et al. (Milan, 1962–), and the Della Valle edition of the eighteenth century. But the word *architettori* was often modernized as *architetti*. The Berrarini-Barocchi edition has the advantage of including the texts of the 1st and 2d editions side by side. Here I rely on Zygmunt Waźbiński, "L'idée de l'histoire dans la première et la seconde édition des *Vies*," in *Vasari storiografo e artista* (above, n. 33), which presents in brief the theses of the author's *Vasari et son histoire des arts du dessin* (Toruń, 1972) and has the great advantage of bypassing the usual divisions of modern academia between "history" and "art history." Jean Alazard, "Quelques notes sur le sens historique . . . ," in *Studi vasariani: Atti del Congresso Internazionale . . .* (1950) (Florence: Istituto Nazionale per gli Studi sul Rinascimento, 1952), does little more than give the impressions of a "historien français" of a "foreign" phenomenon—a relic of an epoch in which nationalism still reigned unchecked in certain universities of Europe.

36. Vasari's explanation on this point is the same as that recently proposed by E. H. Gombrich in "The Leaven of Criticism in Renaissance Art," in *Art, Science, and History in the Renaissance,* ed. Charles Singleton (Johns Hopkins University Press, 1967).

37. *Lettera . . . nella quale brevemente si racconta i nomi e l'opere de' più eccellenti artefici antichi,* published in all the editions of the *Vite.* Vasari changed Adriani's collection of data into history by rearranging it in chronological rather than in the original topical order.

38. Cf. Eugenio Garin, "Giorgio Vasari e il tema della 'Rinascita'," in *Vasari storiografo e artista* (above, n. 33), and E. H. Gombrich, "The Renaissance Conception of Artistic Progress," in his *Norm and Form* (1966), now in Italian translation as *Norma e forma* (Turin: Einaudi, 1973).

39. The definitive edition of the life of Michelangelo is that of Paola Barocchi (Milan-Naples: Ricciardi, 1962), with exhaustive notes.

40. I here follow Kessler in *Petrarch und die Geschichte* (above, Chapter 1, n. 51), Guido Martellotti, "Il *De Gestis Cesaris* del Petrarca nel *Corpus Caesarianum*," IMU, XVII (1974), as well as in his introduction to his edition of Petrarch's *De Viris Illustribus* cited above, Chapter 1, n. 53, and Giuseppe Billanovich, "Uno Sventonio della biblioteca del Petrarca," *Studi petrarcheschi,* VI (1956). Petrarch's *Epitome* and Lombardo's (Lombardus Sirichius) continuation I read in vol. I of the edition of Petrarch's *Opera* cited above at n. 19. For the role of the *De Viris Illustribus* in the genesis of humanist historiography, see above, Chapter 1, pt. 3. The quotation from Palmieri is taken from p. 169 of the important article by Massimo Miglio, "Biografia e raccolte biografiche nel Quattrocento italiano," *Atti della Accademia delle Scienze dell'Istituto di Bologna, Rendiconti,* LXIII (1974–75), an article upon which I depend frequently in these pages. It contains a long statement by Fazio, from 1451, on the nature of biography (pp. 170–73).

41. Gianvito Resta in "Cassarino traduttore di Plutarco e Platone," IMU, II (1959). For the detail on Salutati: Ronald Witt, "Salutati and Plutarch," in *Studies Presented to Myron Gilmore,* cited above, Chapter 11, n. 16.

42. *Plutarco ridotto in compendio* da Dario Tiberto da Cesena (Venice, 1543).

43. The origin of the confusion of Cornelius Nepos and Emilius Probus is explained by Arnaldo Momigliano in pp. 96–97 of *La storiografia alto-medievale,* cited in the Prologue, n. 26. What I say about Suetonius comes from Gianna Gardenal, *Il Poliziano e Svetonio* (Università di Padova, Pubblicazioni della Facoltà di Lettere e Filosofia, vol. LIII) (Florence: Olschki, 1975), and the long review by Emilio Bigi in *GSLI,* CLIII (1976), 450–55. What I say about Plutarch comes from Resta's *Le epitomi di Plutarco nel Quattrocento* (Padua: Antenore, 1962) and Philip A. Stadter, *Plutarch's Historical Methods* (Harvard University Press, 1965). On Fazio's translation of Arrian I follow the observations of Ubaldo Mazzini in the article cited in Chapter 6, n. 67. Lauro's translation was published as *De i fatti del Magno Alessandro* (Venice, 1544).

44. Giovio in the *Vita del Gran Capitano* in the editions cited above, Chapter 13, n. 36, in the introduction to Book I.

45. *Istoria della vita e fatti dell'eccellentissimo capitano di guerra Bartolomeo Colleoni,* ed. Giovanni Santini (Bergamo, 1732).

46. *Vita del prencipe Andrea Doria,* which I read in the 2d ed. of Venice, 1569 (from the 1st of 1564).

47. I read Giovio in the Laterza edition of the two *Vite* cited above, Chapter 13, n. 36, the lives of Leo X and Adrian VI in the translation of Lodovico Dolce (Florence, 1551), and the rest in *Le vite di dicenove huomini illustri* both in the edition cited above, Chapter 13, n. 28, and in the edition of Giovan Maria Bonelli and Girolamo Ruscelli (the publisher of the Venetian edition of the *History* [Venice, 1561]). The Latin original of the lives of the Visconti is in Graevius, vol. III¹, with portraits of the subjects at the beginning of each life.

48. Above, n. 16.

49. Bonelli in introduction to the edition of *Le vite* cited in n. 47.

50. *Historia de'fatti di Federico di Montefeltro, duca d'Urbino* (Venice, 1605). Biographical information in Tiraboschi.

51. *Vita di Francesco Maria di Montefeltro Della Rovere, IIII duca d'Urbino* (Venice, 1605), bound with the *Historia* of Muzio.

52. All these texts are published by Angelo Solerti in *Le vite di Dante, Petrarca e Boccaccio scritte fino al secolo decimosesto,* in the Vallardi series (Milan) Storia letteraria d'Italia. On Bruni, above, Chapter 1, n. 68. On Manetti, Chapter 1, n. 90.

53. The program is described in detail in the dedication to Valori of Antonio Benivieni's *Vita di Piero Vettore l'Antico, gentil'huomo fiorentino* (Florence, 1585).

54. Francesco Vettori's *Vita* of Lorenzo is cited above, Chapter 7, n. 47. Niccolò Valori, *Vita del magnifico Lorenzo de' Medici il Vecchio* (Florence, 1586). Baccio Baldini, *Vita di Cosimo Medici, primo granduca di Toscana* (Florence, 1578). Filippo Sassetti, *Vita di Francesco Ferrucci,* ed. C. Monzani in *ASI,* IV² (1853). Gerolamo Rossi (no relation, as far as I know, to the historian of Ravenna mentioned above in Chapter 10), *Vita di Giovanni de' Medici,* ed. Massimo Fabi in the Milan, 1853, edition of Giovio's *Vite degli Sforzeschi.*

55. *Ricordi intorno ai costumi, azioni e governo del sereniss. gran duca Cosimo I,* written at the request of Grand Duchess Cristina di Lorena (m. Ferdinando I) and published by Domenico Moreni in Florence in 1821.

56. *Istoria del Gran Duca Ferdinando I,* ed. G. E. Saltini in *ASI,* ser. 5, vol. VI (1880).

57. *Vita dell'invitiss. e gloriosiss. imperador Carlo Quinto* (Venice, 1561—and at least four more editions by 1567); *Vita di Ferdinando I imperadore* (Venice, 1566). On Dolce as a historian, see above, Chapter 12, p. 320.

58. *Vita di Cosimo I,* written in 1586; I use the edition of Pisa, 1823, with a biographical introduction. Manuzio also wrote *Le azioni di Castruccio Castracane* (Rome, 1590) on the basis of documents he found in Lucca while on vacations from the chair his eulogy of Cosimo had won him at Pisa.

59. Baccio Valori, *Vita di Lelio Torelli* (Bologna, 1886).

60. Lorenzo Strozzi, *Vita di Filippo Strozzi,* in appendix to Varchi, *Istoria fiorentina* (Leiden, 1723). Vincenzo Acciaiuoli, *Vita di Piero di Gino Capponi* (written c. 1550) (the author also of a life of Giannozzo Manetti); Jacopo Pitti, *Vita di Antonio Giacomini Tebalducci* (written in 1574); and Luca Della Robbia, *Vita di Bartolomeo Valori,* all published in *ASI,* IV² (1853). Jacopo Nardi, *Vita d'An-*

tonio *Giacomini Tebalducci Malespini* (Florence, 1577 and 1597). Bernardo Segni, *Vita di Niccolò Capponi,* which I read in the "Classici Italiani" edition of Milan, 1805, as an appendix to Segni's *Storie fiorentine.*

61. Della Casa, *Vita Petri Cardinalis Bembi,* edited by Apostolo Zeno in *Degli'istorici delle cose veneziane,* vol. II (1718); his *Gasparis Contareni Vita* (first published in preface to his *Latina Monumenta* (Florence, 1567) and *Alphonsi Regis Vita* I read with his life of Bembo in the Naples, 1738, edition of his *Opere,* vol. II—on which see Antonio Santosuosso, "On the Authorship of Della Casa's Biography of Cardinal Gasparo Contarini," *RQ,* XXVIII (1975). Beccatelli, *Vita di Bembo,* published in the same volume of Zeno, *Istorici; Vita di Petrarca,* published in the Padua, 1722, edition of Petrarch's *Rime,* and *Vita del cardinale Gasparo Contarini* and *Reginaldo Pole,* published by Angelo Maria Querini along with a biographical introduction to all the biographical writings of Beccatelli and of his secretary Antonio Gigante of Fossombrone in the beginning of Querini's edition of Pole's *Epistolae,* which appeared without indication of date or place, but probably in Brescia, 1748. Della Casa's biography of Contarini, which was commissioned by Contarini's heirs, was not finished at the time of his death. It was completed by Pier Vettori, largely by lifting whole passages from Beccatelli—as shown on the basis of page after page of parallel passages with frequent criticisms of Santosuosso in Gigliola Fragnito's *Memoria individuale e construzione biografica* (Pubblicazioni dell'Università di Urbino; Urbino, Argalìa, 1978). Beccatelli's life of Petrarch is in the volume of Solerti cited above at n. 52. On Beccatelli in general, see Giuseppe Alberigo in *DBI.* On the biography of Pole, see Paolo Simoncelli, *Il caso Reginald Pole* (Rome: Edizioni di Storia e Letteratura, 1977), pp. 33 ff. Anton Maria Grazzini (on whom, see above, Chapter 8, n. 124, and Chapter 12, pp. 357–58), *La vie du cardinal Commendon,* which I read in the French translation of the Paris, 1669, Latin original, published for the fourth time in Lyon, 1702. I have not found any edition of this work published in Italy.

62. Marc'Antonio Ciappi, *Compendio delle*

heroiche *et gloriose attioni et santa vita di papa Gregorio XIII* (Rome, 1596).

63. *De le lettere,* 2d ed. (Venice, 1549), pp. 15–16 (dated 1529).

64. In the dedication to his edition of Plutarch (Rome, 1470), referred to above, p. 52.

65. *Vita del catholico & invitissimo re don Filippo Secondo* (Vicenza, 1608). On Campana, see above, Chapter 13, n. 19 et seq.

66. *Vita del gran pontefice Innocenzio Quarto,* ed. Tomaso Costo . . . *co' nomi de' pontefici e cardinali stati nella Liguria . . .* (Naples, 1601).

67. *Historia della vita et gesti dell'illustriss. et reverendiss. cardinal Alburnotio* (Bologna, 1590). On the importance of translations of Sepúlveda in Italy, see above, Chapter 12.

68. *Trattato . . . dell'origine, fatti, costumi e lodi di Matelda* [sic] *la gran contessa d'Italia* [!] (Florence, 1589).

69. *Delle attioni et sentenze del s. Alessandro de' Medici primo duca di Fiorenza* (Venice, 1544, with three subsequent printings through the 1580s). For Vespasiano, see above, Chapter 1, n. 113.

70. I read the *Vita di Michelangelo* in the text published by Paolo D'Ancona in the introduction to the collectively edited *Michelangelo: Architettura, pittura, scultura* (Milan: Bramante Editrice, 1969). It has recently been published in a new English translation by Alice Sedgwick Wohl (Louisiana State University Press, 1976). That Condivi did not borrow from Vasari is demonstrated once again by Robert Clements in his review of the translation in *RQ,* XXX (1976), 56–58.

71. *Vita del gloriosissimo papa Pio Quinto* (Rome, 1586).

72. *I casi de gli huomini illustri,* published by the translator, Giuseppe Betussi (on whom see G. Mutini in *DBI*) in his edition of Boccaccio's *Opera* in translation (Venice, 1545). Betussi's motives are reflected in his subsequent *Ragionamento . . . sopra il Cathaio, luogo dello ill. sig. Pio Enea Obizzi* (Padua, 1573). On Boccaccio as a biographer, I follow Massimo Miglio in "Boccaccio biografo," in *Boccaccio in Europe* (Proceedings of the Boccaccio Conference, Louvain, December 1975), ed. Gilbert Tournoy (Leuven University Press, 1977).

73. *La prima parte delle vite, ovvero Fatti memorabili d'alcuni papi et di tutti i cardinali passati,* published, surprisingly, by Giolito de' Ferrari (Venice, 1586).

74. I follow here Helène Wieruszowski in "Jacob Burckhardt and Vespasiano da Bistici," in Mahoney, ed., *Philosophy and Humanism: Renaissance Essays in Honor of P. O. Kristeller.*

75. See Riccardo Fubini and Anna Menci Gallorini in "L'autobiografia di Leon Battista Alberti," *Rinascimento,* XII (1972). Venafro's *Vita* was published in the preface to his edition of the *Canzoniere* (Naples, 1533). Among the several modern editions of Petrarch's *Posteritati,* I use that in the Ricciardi edition of the *Prose,* ed. Martellotti et al. (1955).

76. Ed. D. Gutiérrez in *Analecta augustiniana,* XXVI (1963). In general: Marziano Guglielminetti in *Memoria e scrittura: L'autobiografia da Dante a Cellini* (Turin: Einaudi, 1977), p. 309. I rely on this book for general orientation as well as for a number of details in these paragraphs.

77. *Notabili avversità a lui accorse con alcune historie de suoi tempi,* published in his *Trattato diviso in quattro libri* (Orvieto, 1585).

78. *Autobiografia,* ed. Paola Franchetti (Universale Einaudi, vol. LVII) (Turin, 1945). My judgment here differs somewhat from that of Mario Gliozzi in *DBI:* I see no trace of any classical model, not even Suetonius. Karl Joachim Weintraub gives a somewhat different version of the circumstances of the composition of the *De Vita Propria.* But he uses editions both for Cardano and for Cellini different from the ones I use, and he is interested not so much in form as in the personalities revealed in the works: *The Value of the Individual: Self and Circumstance in Autobiography* (University of Chicago Press, 1976), esp. p. 143.

79. Of the several modern editions, I use that in the Universale Einaudi series (1977) edited by Guido Davico Bonino, with help from Guglielminetti (above, n. 76) and from Carlo Cordil in his introduction to the Ricciardi edition of the *Vita.*

80. Patrizi's letter is published by A. Solerti in *Archivio storico per Trieste l'Istria e il Trentino,* vol. III. Santoro's *Vita* is edited by C. Cugnoni in *Archivio della Società Romana di*

Storia Patria, XII (1889), et seq. On Leonardo Santoro, see above, Chapter 7, pp. 191–93.

81. Here and elsewhere I rely upon Arnaldo Momigliano in *The Development of Greek Biography* (Harvard University Press, 1971).

82. All this from Chapter 9 of Francesco Della Corte, *Svetonio Eques Romanus,* 2d ed. (Florence: La Nuova Italia, 1967), and Helmut Gugel, *Studien zur biographischen Techkik Suetons* (Wiener Studien, Beiheft 7) (Vienna: Böhlaus, 1977)—the latter being particularly useful in demonstrating "wie stark die Biographie gegenüber der Geschichtsschreibung geöffnet sein kann" in Tacitus too (p. 145).

83. That is the expression used by Alfred and Maurice Croiset in the section on Arrian in *Histoire de la littérature grèque* (Paris, 1899), vol. V.

84. "Filostrato greco scrittore elegantissimo," *Della vita del mirabile Apollonio Tyrneo* (Venice, 1549) (but the dedication is dated 1541).

85. My information comes from the introduction to Ada Adler's edition of Leipzig, 1928, in four volumes, of the *Lexicon.* Chalkokondylis's *editio princeps* is of Milan 1499. Similar judgment in Pigna on pp. 70–71 of the biography of Ariosto cited below at n. 120. Several of Suidas's individual lives were published in introductions to the works of the respective authors—e.g., in the Venice, 1549, edition of Isocrates.

86. Quintillian, *Institutio Oratoria,* III, 7, 10–18. Sigonio, *Vita del p. don Onofrio Zarrabini* in his *Opera Omnia,* vol. VI.

87. In the *Vita di don Pietro di Toledo* cited above, Chapter 7, n. 98.

88. *Opera Omnia* (Leiden, 1789), vol. IV, p. 281, from Oratio X delivered III non., Nov. 1578: "Aliud est enim vitas scribere, aliud historiam."

89. Both published in the same volume cited above at n. 86.

90. *Commentario delle cose di Ferrara,* cited above, Chapter 10, n. 29.

91. *Della vita e dei fatti di Guidobaldo,* cited above at n. 27.

92. *Vita dell'illustrissimo et generosissimo sig. d. Ferrando Gonzaga* (Milan, 1574), republished in Pisa, 1821, for reasons I fail to comprehend.

93. Giovan Battista Gelli in dedication to

his translation of Giovio's *Vita di Alfonso d'Este*, n. 49. As a reminder that barbarism has not yet disappeared in the twentieth century, someone tore the title page out of the copy of this work in the Regenstein Library.

94. E.g., Cesare Campana, *Arbori delle famiglie le quali hanno signoreggiato* (Mantua, 1590), and *Arbori delle famiglie reali di Spagna* (Verona, 1591); Tommaso Porcacchi, *Historia dell'origine e successione dell'illustrissima famiglia Malaspina*, edited posthumously by his wife, Aurora Bianca (Verona, 1585).

95. All about it in J. R. Woodhouse, "Una storia della nobiltà fiorentina inedita," *Studi secenteschi*, XIV (1973).

96. Introduction to his chronicle in Pelliccia, vol. I, p. xxxiii.

97. *Vita et morte della serenissima Eleanora archiduchessa d'Austria et duchessa di Mantova* (Mantua, 1594); *Il soldato christiano con nuove aggiunte et la norma del vero principe et principessa...* (Venice, 1604).

98. Marino Berengo, "Patriziato e nobiltà, il caso veronese," *RSI*, LXXXVII (1975).

99. *Della origine et de' fatti delle famiglie illustri d'Italia* (Venice, 1582)—one of the longest (810 pp.) of the usually long works of collective genealogy. On Betussi, see above, n. 72.

100. Lantieri's case is described by Paolo Guerrini in his introduction to *Le cronache bresciane* (Brescia, 1927), p. 55. Ammirato, *Delle famiglie nobili fiorentine*, ed. Scipione Ammirato, Jr. (Florence, 1615): "le quali per levar ogni gara di precedenza sono state...posto in confuso & senza ordine alcuno." On Ammirato: above, Chapter 10, n. 77.

101. Carrari, *Historia dei Rossi parmigiani* (Ravenna, 1583).

102. *De Gymnasio Patavino...Commentarium* (Padua, 1598). On Riccoboni as a historian: above, Chapter 8, n. 27.

103. *Origine et progresso dell'Academia* [sic] *del Disegno de' scultori & architetti di Roma* (Pavia, 1604) (the dedication is of 1599). As Alberto Asor Rosa points out in *DBI*, Alberti is best known for his work as a theorist of art.

104. Fino, *Scielta de gli huomini di pregio usciti da Crema* (Brescia, 1581); Galeotti, *Trattato degli huomini illustri in Bologna* (Ferrara, 1590). Similarly, Antonio Stella, *Elogia Ven-*

etorum Navali Pugna Illustrium (Venice, 1558), Onofrio Panvinio, *De Urbis Veronae Viris Doctrina et Bellica Opusculum* (Verona, 1621), and Francesco Bocchi, *Elogi degli uomini dotti di Firenze* (Florence, 1607–9).

105. I read the work in the edition of Paris, 1578, as *Peplus Italiae*.

106. *Vita e miracoli di s. Francesco di Paola* (Venice, 1597).

107. *Vita del beato Ieronimo Savonarola*, ed. Piero Ginori Conti (Florence: Olschki, 1937), with a long and very informative introduction. On biographies of Savonarola in general, see De Maio, *Riforme e miti* (above, Chapter 5, n. 49), pp. 81 ff.

108. Possevino, *Discorsi della vita et attioni di Carlo Borromeo* (Rome, 1591); Giussano, "nobile milanese della Congregatione delli Oblati di S. Ambrogio," *Vita di s. Carlo Borromeo* (Rome, 1610); Bascapè, *De Vita et Rebus Gestis Caroli Cardinalis Borromaei*, which I read first in the edition of Ingolstadt, 1592, and then in the elegant bilingual edition published by the Veneranda Fabbrica del Duomo in Milan, 1965 (with imprimatur). On Bascapè, see Paolo Prodi in *DBI;* on Valier, above, Chapter 9, pp. 231 ff.

109. *Vita R. P. Fr. Hieronymi Savonarolae Ferrariensis* (Paris, 1674).

110. *De Vita et Moribus...Ignatii Loyolae,* in vol. II of Maffei's *Opera* (Bergamo, 1747), and *Vita di s. Lorenzo Giustiniano...tratta da quella che scrisse Bernardo Giustiniano* (c. 1560) *dal padre Gio. Pietro Maffei* (Venice, 1819); on whom, see above, Chapter 12, pp. 340–41.

111. Serafino (on whom see Quétif-Echard, vol. II, pp. 386–87), *Istoria de gli huomini illustri...del sacro ordine de gli Predicatori* (Lucca, 1596) (but dedicated in 1592); I read his *Vita del rev.do padre fra Girolamo Savonarola* in the beautifully bound manuscript in the Biblioteca Nazionale, Florence, MS II.III.172. Silvano, *Le vite de' santi e beati dell'Ordine di Camaldoli* (above, Chapter 2, n. 78) and *Vite de' santi e beati toscani* (Florence, 1593). I read his *Vita di Piero Soderini* in the edition of Padua, 1737, and the other "lay" biographies in *Vite di cinque huomini illustri* (Florence, 1602).

112. Above, Chapter 2, pp. 50–51. I follow here Robert Grant in "Eusebius and His Life of Origen," in *Forma Futuri: Studi in*

onore del cardinale Michele Pellegrino (Turin: Bottega d'Erasmo, 1975).

113. Giovanni Lami I quote from p. 527 of my edition of his *Charitonis et Hippophili Hodoeporicon* (1741), published in *Politici ed economisti del primo Settecento,* vol. V: *Dal Muratori al Cesarotti* (Milan-Naples: Ricciardi, 1978).

114. Antonio Caracciolo, *De Vita Paoli Quarti* (Colonia Ubiorum, 1612).

115. Giovan Battista Castaldo, "suo ultimo confessore," *Vita di Elisabetta Bonsi Capponi nobile matrona fiorentina,* written in Naples before 1619 and published in Florence in 1624.

116. Orazio Torsellini, *De Vita Francesci Xaverii* (Antwerp, 1596), from the 1st ed. of Rome of the same year.

117. *Le vite de' santi Padri insieme con prato spirituale,* "Nuova edizione purgata da infinitissimi errori" (Venice, 1623), with all respect to the author for excogitating a superlative form of the adjective "infinite."

118. P. D. Benedetto Lucchino da Mantova, *Cronica della vera origine et attioni della ...contessa Matilda et de' suoi antecessori & discendenti...* (Mantua, 1592).

119. *Giardino d'essempi, o vero Fiori delle vite de i santi* (Florence, 1594); 2d ed.: "con aggiunta di cento cinquanta esempi" (Florence, 1597), and a 3d ed. with another hundred "esempi" (Venice, 1599).

120. Giovan Battista Crispo, *Vita di Giacomo Sannazaro* (Rome, 1593), reprinted in Rome in 1594 and in Naples in 1633), on which see Domenico De Angelis in *Le Vite de letterati salentini* (Naples, 1713), vol. I; Simon Fornari, *Vita di m. Lodovico Ariosto,* which I read in the Venice, 1566, edition of *Orlando furioso;* Giovan Battista Pigna, *I romanzi...ne quali della poesia & della vita dell'Ariosto con nuovo modo si parla* (Venice, 1554). Pigna's life of Ariosto is reprinted by Angelo Solerti in *Autobiografie e vite de' maggiori scrittori italiani* (Milan: Albrighi, Segati, 1903).

121. I read this work in Tiraboschi's first edition of Modena, 1790. On the author I follow the biography by Giulio Bertoni, *Giambattista Barbieri e gli studi romanzi nel secolo XVI* (Modena, 1905).

122. The lives of the historians were published first in the 1550s–70s and again in the 2d ed. of the whole *collana* published in the eighteenth century. Porcacchi's other biographies are written in the same manner, e.g., *Attioni d'Arrigo terzo re di Francia* (Venice, 1574) and the life of Sannazaro published in the Giolito edition of 1568 of the *Arcadia.*

123. See Mario Rotili, *L'arte del Cinquecento nel Regno di Napoli* (Naples: Libreria Scientifica Editrice, 1972), p. 12, and De Lisio in *Gli anni della svolta* (above, Chapter 7, n. 20), pp. 168–69.

124. On Dolce, I follow Mark Roskill, *Dolce's "Aretino" and Venetian Art Theory of the Cinquecento* (New York University Press, 1968). On Lomazzo, I follow the long preface of Roberto Paolo Ciardi to his edition of *Scritti sulle arti* (Florence: Marchi & Bertolli, 1973), and on the general context, Martino Capucci, "Dalla biografia alla storia: Note sulla formazione della storiografia artistica nel Seicento," *Studi secenteschi,* IX (1968). The latest critical edition of Lomazzo's *Idea del tempio della pittura* is that of Robert Klein, with a French translation on facing pages (Florence: Istituto Nazionale di Studi sul Rinascimento, 1974).

125. Giovan Andrea Giglio, *Dialogo nel quale si ragiona degli errori e degli abusi de' pittori circa l'istorie,* written in 1561 and now published in Paola Barocchi's edition of *Trattati d'arte del Cinquecento* (Bari: Laterza, 1961), vol. II.

126. Graziani, *De Casibus Virorum Illustrium,* which I read in the edition of Paris, 1670; Ruscelli, *Indice degl'uomini illustri* (Venice, 1572).

127. Ottavio Rossi in *Elogi historici di Bresciani illustri,* cited above, Chapter 7, n. 64.

128. Mario Rosa on p. 82 of his *Religione e società nel mezzogiorno tra Cinque e Seicento* (Bari: De Donato, 1976).

CHAPTER FIFTEEN

1. Even though it is "one of the most interesting chapters in the history of modern culture," said Santo Mazzarino almost two decades ago, "the history of early modern historiography dedicated to the Roman world today still remains, in large part, to be written." The statement is just as true today, at least for Italy, which has escaped the attention of most recent historians of antiquarianism. I cannot pretend to fill this

lacuna. For the writings of the Italian antiquarians are almost as voluminous as those of the historians. They are far more difficult and far less pleasant to read. None of them has appeared in a modern critical edition. And they cannot be properly understood without a knowledge of the ancient sources and of the corresponding studies of modern classical scholars that I do not possess. Hence, my theses in this chapter should be considered even more tentative than those in the last one. Mazzarino's statement is in his "Gli studi romani dal Rinascimento alla *Storia dei Romani* del De Sanctis," in vol. II of Vincenzo Ussani and Francesco Arnaldi, eds., *Guida allo studio della civiltà romana antica* (Napoli: Istituto Editoriale del Mezzogiorno, 1961). For general orientation in this still all but unknown field, I have taken note of Roberto Weiss's summary of the theses of his *The Renaissance Discovery of Classical Antiquity* (above, chapter 1, n. 95) that he published as "Lineamenti per una storia degli studi antiquari in Italia," *Rinascimento,* IX (1958), and H. J. Erasmus, *The Origins of Rome in Historiography from Petrarch to Perizonus* (Leiden, 1962). Still the most thorough and dependable surveys of sixteenth-century Italian antiquities are Panvinio's introduction to his unpublished "Centum Libros Antiquitatum" published in *Spicilegium Romanum,* vol. VIII (1842), pp. 653 ff., and the introduction of Petrus Burmannus to Graevius, vol. IX[1], as well as the relevant sections of Tiraboschi and the studies of Mandowsky and Mitchell cited below at notes 22 and 24. A useful and, considering that it was first published in 1927, surprisingly accurate survey is U. von Wilamowitz-Moellendorff's *Geschichte der Philologie,* which I read as *Storia della filologia classica* in the Piccola Biblioteca Einaudi edition of 1967, esp. pp. 33–48. The promising titles notwithstanding, neither Leighton D. Reynolds and Nigel G. Wilson's work, which I read in Mirella Ferrari's translation as *Copisti e filologi,* 2d ed. (Padua: Antenore, 1973), nor Rudolf Pfeiffer's *History of Classical Scholarship* (Oxford: Clarendon, 1976), are particularly useful for my purposes. The first dedicates no more than half a page to only one Italian; the second assumes that Italy became a wasteland as soon as "humanism

and scholarship spread to other countries" and accordingly barely mentions only three Italians.

2. The work referred to here is Francesco Maria Grapaldi, *De Partibus Aedium,* of 1494. I read it in the edition of Turin, 1517.

3. Graevius in preface to vol. I of *Thes. Ant. Rom.,* p. 3.

4. *De Magistratibus et Officiis Romanorum,* published in *Respublica Romana* (Basel, 1626). On Alciati's historical work, see above, Chapter 10, n. 33.

5. I read it in the text of 1574, republished in vol. V of his *Opera Omnia.*

6. On which I follow Kristeller in *Catalogus Translationum et Commentariorum* (Catholic University of America Press, 1960 ff.), vol. II, pp. 221–24.

7. *De Urbis Veronae* (Verona, 1621), pp. 33–34.

8. *Aeliani De Militaribus Ordinis Instituendis* (Venice, 1552); the first Latin translation, by Theodoros of Thessaloniki, was published in Rome in 1487.

9. I consulted the edition of Venice, 1602. More on Panciroli below, nn. 103 and 104.

10. Sarayna, *De Origine Veronae,* in Schottus. Scardeone, *De Antiquitate Urbis Patavii* (Basel, 1560), which is the edition I use; it is also published in Graevius, vol. VI[3]. On Sarayna: above, Chapter 9, n. 23.

11. *De Comitiis Romanorum,* in *Thes. Ant. Rom.,* vol. I.

12. *Urbis Romae Topographia* (Rome, 1544).

13. *Kalendarium Rusticum in Bibliotheca Farnesiana,* in *Thes. Ant. Rom.,* vol. VIII. On Orsini, see further, below, n. 75.

14. Sigonio's *Disputationum Patavinarum adversas Franciscum Robortellum,* which I read in the edition of Padua, 1562, until I got tired of the repeated "maledicentia & obstrectatio," is also published in vol. VI of his *Opera Omnia* along with his edition of the *Fasti.*

15. *De Antiquitate et Varia Tarentinorum Fortuna Libri VIII,* republished from the edition of Naples, 1589, in Schottus.

16. Lombardi, *De Balneis Putolanis* (Venice, 1566), also in Schottus and in Graevius, vol. IX[4], and Mazzella, *Sito et antichità della città di Pozzuolo* (Naples, 1596). More on the baths at n. 70, below.

17. *Apparatus Statuarum Novissime in Destructis Cumis Inventorum,* in Graevius, vol. IX[4], form the original Italian published at Venice in 1606.

18. *Notizie dell'antico teatro . . . tolte dagli "Annali" di Alessandro Canobbio,* published in appendix to G. B. Biancolini's edition of the *Cronaca della città di Verona* of Pier Zagata, vol. II, cited above, Chapter 3, n. 28. On Canobbio: above, Chapter 9, n. 25.

19. *Dichiarazioni della pianta dell'antiche Siracuse e d'alcune scelte medaglie d'esse e de' principi che quelle possedettero* (Naples, 1613). This edition, alas, does not include the maps.

20. *Discorsi sopra le medaglie de gli antichi . . . ove si dimostrano notabili errori di scrittori antichi e moderni* (Venice, 1558).

21. *Discorso sopra le medaglie antiche con la particolare dichiarazione di molti riversi* (Venice, 1559), with a long appendix of wood-block prints in chronological order.

22. *Descriptio . . . Villae Tiburtinae Hadrianae,* which I read in Graevius, vol. VIII[4]; in general: Erna Mandowsky and Charles Mitchell, *Pirro Ligorio's Roman Antiquities* (London: Warburg Institute, 1963). More on Ligorio's fakes by Christian Hülsen in *Römische Mitteilungen,* XVI (1901), 130.

23. In the chronicle of Tommaso Brogi of 1555 as reported in Giovan Vincenzo Coppi, *Annali, memorie ed huomini illustri di San Gimignano* (Florence, 1695).

24. On Agustín, see below, n. 34.

25. The quotation and the prices are from the work of Vico cited above at n. 20.

26. On which: Donald Kelley, "Jean du illet, Archivist and Antiquary," *Journal of Modern History,* XXXVIII (1966).

27. The quotation is from Gruchius in col. 817 of the edition I read of his treatise in *Thes. Ant. Rom.,* vol. I, from the edition of Venice, 1559. Sigonio in turn called Gruchius "doctus vir in primis & Graecis Latinisque literis eruditus, cuius ab auctoritate . . . non levissimis . . . rationibus discessissem": ibid., col. 838. Sigonio's own *Disputationes* are in his *Opera Omnia,* vol. VI. His last word on the subject, *De Binis Comitiis & Lege Curiata,* was published in 1566. The controversy with Glareanus is described by Denis van Berchem in his *Tito Livio nella Svizzera del Rinascimento* (Rome: Reale Istituto di Studi Romani, 1943).

28. The information is in Mazzatinti under the name of the author, on whom see below, n. 86.

29. *Sicilia Antiqua* I read in the edition of 1659. Fazello (above, Chapter 10, n. 26) is accorded two page-long quotations apropos of ancient Aegesta, while Livy is given only five lines and Thucydides only seven lines. On the particularly productive school of Sicilian antiquities, I am indebted to Santi Correnti, *Cultura e storiografia nella Sicilia del Cinquecento,* also cited in the same n. 26 of Chapter 10.

30. I follow the biographical introduction by the ambassador of the world of Italian antiquarians in Germany, Andreas Schottus, published in Muret's *Orationes et Epistolae,* ed. Joannes Erhardus Kappius (Hannover, 1825–26).

31. *Romanae Urbis Topographia* (Frankfurt-am-Main, 1597), organized as a guided tour of four days. The book was translated into German six years later.

32. E.g., *De Triclinio, sive De Modo Convivendi apud Priscos Romanos* (Rome, 1590) and *Opuscula in Columnae Rostratae Inscriptiones: De Ponderibus, De Mensuris, De Nummis* (Rome, 1608).

33. *Historia Utriusque Belli Dacici a Traiano Caesare Gesti ex Simulacris Quae in Columna . . . Visuntur* (Rome, 1576); *Istoria . . . nella quale si tratta esser vera la liberazione dell'anima di Traiano . . . ,* Italian tr. by Francesco Pifferi (Siena, 1595).

34. The principal treatises "cum notibus Fulvii Ursini" are reprinted from the edition of 1583 in *Thes. Ant. Rom.,* vol. II. On Agustín, see Luisa Ceretti, "I precedenti e la formazione dell' *Editio* di S. Pompeo Festo di Antonio Agustín," *AIVSLA,* CXI (1952–53), and Charles Mitchell, "Archaeology and Romance in Renaissance Italy," in E. F. Jacob, ed., *Italian Renaissance Studies: A Tribute to the Late Cecilia M. Ady* (London: Faber & Faber, 1960).

35. In his preface to vol. I of *Thes. Ant. Rom.*

36. My translation of François de Dainville's translation on p. 132 of his "L'enseignement de l'histoire et de la geographie et le *Ratio Studiorum,*" *Analecta Gregoriana,* LXX (1954). See further, Tito Orlandi, "Il *De Civitate Dei* di Agostino e la storiografia

di Roma," *Studi romani*, XVI (1968).

37. Ottavio Rossi, *Le memorie bresciane* (1616) I read in the edition "accresciuta di considerabil numero di marmi non più stampati" of Fortunato Vinaccesi (Brescia, 1693), which is the edition reproduced in Graevius, vol. IV²; Scardeone, *De Antiquitate Urbis Patavii*, cited above at n. 10.

38. *De Senatu Romano* (Venice, 1580) republished in *Thes. Ant. Rom.*, vol. I, in the preface.

39. *Historia et discrittione del Regno di Sicilia* (Naples, 1591). Carlo Padiglione gives much information about the immense quantity of antiquarian research in Naples that was never published in his *La Biblioteca . . . S. Martino in Napoli e i suoi manoscritti* (Naples, 1876). On the equally great quantity of lost or unpublished antiquarian studies of Sicilian scholars, see Guido Libertini, "L'indagine archeologica a Catania nel secolo XVI e l'opera di Lorenzo Bolano," *Archivio storico per la Sicilia orientale*, XVIII (1921).

40. I refer to Falconieri's introduction to his edition of Nardini's *Roma Vetus, Libri VIII* of 1666, which I read in the Latin translation published in *Thes. Ant. Rom.*, vol. IV: "Iam duo saecula sunt, decus peperunt illustres doctrina viri Fulvius, Boissardus, Blondus, Marlianus. . . ." On antiquities at the time of Alexander VII, see my *Florence in the Forgotten Centuries*, pp. 265–66.

41. The opinions are those of Soria (see above, Chapter 6, n. 2).

42. So says Graevius in the introduction to vol. III of *Thes. Ant. Rom.*

43. *L'antichità di Roma. Di nuovo con ogni diligenza corretta & ampliata . . . con le aggiuntioni & annotationi* di Girolamo Ferrucci romano (Venice, 1588).

44. His introduction to the Latin translation in Graevius, vol. VII².

45. His introduction to Ligorio's *Villae Tiburtinae Hadrianae*, in Graevius, vol. VIII⁴.

46. *Conspectus Thesauri Litterarii Italiae* (Hamburg, 1730).

47. In his *Discorso sopra le medaglie antiche* (Venice, 1559). Porzio's work was republished in Basel in 1520 and 1530, again by Gronovius, and finally in vol. IX of the *Thesaurus Graecarum Antiquitatum*. On the debt of the sixteenth to the fourteenth and fifteenth centuries, I have followed Roberto

Weiss in "Petrarch and the Antiquarians," in Charles Henderson, ed., *Classical, Medieval, and Renaissance Studies in Honor of Berthold Louis Ullmann* (Rome: Edizioni di Storia e Letteratura, 1964), vol. II, and Angelo Mazzocco, "The Antiquarianism of Francesco Petrarca," *Journal of Medieval and Renaissance Studies*, VII (1977).

48. Sigonio quoted in *Opere Omnia*, vol. I, p. 33, from his dedication to the *Fasti Consulares;* Leone in *De Nola Patria* (Venice, 1514), which I read in the Italian translation by Paolino Barbati printed privately in Naples in 1934 as well as in Latin in Graevius, vol. IX⁴.

49. Preface to the Köln, 1552, edition of *Genialium Dierum Libri VI;* on Alessandri, see below, n. 102.

50. *De Privatorum Publicorumque Aedificiorum Urbis Romae Eversoribus Epistola*, dedicated in 1587 and published in Florence in 1589. Biographical information in Tiraboschi.

51. *Antiquaria Urbis* (Rome, 1527); Italian prose version by Paolo Dal Rosso, *Delle antichità della città di Roma* (Venice, 1543).

52. *De Gallorum Cisalpinorum Antiquitate ac Origine* (Lyon, 1538). The bits of entertainment I take from his *Memorabilium Liber* (Venice, 1550); there are many more of them in the same book. On Merula's other work, see above, Chapter 7, n. 84.

53. On Patrizi, see below, n. 119.

54. *Raccolta breve d'alcune cose più segnalate c'hebbero gli antichi e d'alcune altre trovate da moderni* (Venice, 1612). Quoted from the dedication to Carlo Emanuele di Savoia.

55. Grapaldi is cited above at n. 2. Further information is given below at n. 78. My publication figures come from Burmannus's introduction to the Latin translation of Benedetto's *Descrittione de' luoghi antichi di Napoli*, first published in Naples in 1535, in Graevius, vol. IX¹, and from Mazzuchelli's entry on Alessandri. Mazzuchelli is incomplete: he does not include the edition I used in the Biblioteca Nazionale of Florence.

56. Aleandro, *Antiquae Tabulae Marmoreae Solis Effigie Symbolisque Exculptae Accurata Explicatio*, which I read in the 2d ed. (1st: Rome 1616) of Paris, 1617; Zeno, *Dell'origine di Venetia* (Venice, 1558).

57. *De Urbis Senae Eiusque Episcopatus Antiquitate*, which I read in Schottus.

58. *Discorso sopra le medaglie de gli antichi,* cited above at n. 20.

59. *Discorsi,* which I read not in the 1st edition (1589) but in that of Florence, 1755, which contains the biographical introduction by Domenico Maria Manni. The passage quoted is from Mario Pozzo, "Il pensiero linguistico di Vincenzo Borghini," *GSLI,* CXLVIII (1971), at p. 223.

60. *Antiquitatum Variarum Volumina XVII* (Venice, 1489) and *De Commentariis Antiquitatum* (Rome, 1498). On Annio and his fortunes, I follow the cautious biography in Quétif-Echard, Argellati in *Biblioteca dei volgarizzatori* (above, Chapter 4, n. 93), under "Nannio," Roberto Weiss in "An Unknown Epigraphic Text by Annio of Viterbo," in *Italian Studies Presented to E. R. Vincent* (Cambridge: Heffer & Sons, 1962), and in "Traccia per una biografia di Annio da Viterbo," *IMU,* V (1962), Erasmus in the work cited above at n. 1, pp. 41 ff., together with Momigliano's review essay first published in *RSI,* LXXV (1963), 390 ff., and then in his *Terzo contributo* (Rome: Edizioni di Storia e Letteratura, 1966), Albano Biondi, "Annio da Viterbo e un aspetto dell'orientalismo di Guillaume Postel," in *Melchior Cano: La storia come locus theologicus = Bollettino della Società di Studi Valdesi,* XCIII (1972), Cesare Vasoli in Chapter 1 of his *I miti e gli astri* (Naples: Guida, 1978), and, on one aspect of the question, E. N. Tigerstedt, "Ioannes Annius and Graecia Mendax," in *Classical, Medieval and Renaissance Studies,* cited above at n. 47. The story of Annio and LeMaire is told by Georges Doutrepont in *Jean LeMaire des Belges et la Renaissance* (Brussels: Académie Royale, 1934).

61. Lauro, tr., *I cinque libri de le antichità... con lo commento di Giovanni Annio...* (Venice, 1550). I cite Gelli on p. 77 of the only edition of *Dell'origine di Firenze,* ed. Alessandro D'Alessandro in *Atti e memorie dell'Accademia... La Colombaria,* XLIV (1979). On Gelli as a biographer: above, Chapter 14, n. 33.

62. In the work cited above at n. 59; here quoted from pp. 237–38.

63. *De Origine Romanorum,* 2d ed. from the 1st of Pavia, 1589 (Milan, 1607), the latter being the edition reproduced in Graevius, vol. I.

64. Possevino in *Apparato all'historia di tutte le nationi,* which I read in the author's own Italian translation in the edition of Venice, 1598; Tinti, *La nobiltà di Verona* (Verona, 1592).

65. G. B. Agocchi, *Fundatio et Dominum Antiquum Urbis Bononiae,* which I read in the Latin translation of the 1638 original in Graevius, vol. VII[1].

66. Ghiarardacci, *Della historia di Bologna, Parte terza,* cited above in Chapter 9, n. 113.

67. Cesare Clementini, *Raccolto istorico della fondazione di Rimini e dell'origine e vite de' Malatesti* (Rimini, 1617–27) (Forni XXXVIII).

68. Maruccini, *Bassanum sive Dissertatio de Urbis Antiquitate et de Viris eiusdem Illustribus,* Latin translation from the Italian original of Venice, 1577, in Graevius, vol. IX[8]; Mazza (under the pseudonym Didimo Ropaligero Liviano), *I Goti illustrati* (Verona, 1677).

69. *Reflexions sur l'origine et la succession des anciens peuples* (Paris, 1747). The second case is reported by Robert A. Graham in *Catholic Historical Review,* LIX (1974), 719–21.

70. Bonifaccio cited above in Chapter 9, n. 21; Robortello, *Laconici, seu Sudationis Quae adhuc Visitur in Ruina Balnearum Pisanae Urbis... Explicatio,* bound with the Florence, 1548, edition of his *De Historica Facultate Disputatio* (on which, see below, chapter 16); Loffredo, *L'antichità di Pozzuolo,* reprinted from the 1st edition of 1580 in vol. VI of Summonte's *Historia,* cited above at Chapter 10, n. 81; Del Re, *Antiquitates Tiburtinae,* reprinted from the 1610 edition in Graevius, vol. VIII[4]; Ferri cited above at n. 17.

71. On Rizzoni: Gian Paolo Marchi in "Due corrispondenti veronesi di Ciriaco d'Ancona...," *IMU,* XI (1968) (which contains many other details relevant to this subject); on Contarini: Gaetano Cozzi, "Federico Contarini, un antiquario veneziano tra Rinascimento e Cóntroriforma," *SV,* III (1961); on Ajello, the detailed aside on the Neapolitan collectors in Summonte's *Historia,* book VIII, p. 135. Paruta's collection of numismatic prints was published by Leonardo Agostino as *La Sicilia* in Rome, 1649, long after the collector's death.

72. *Viaggio di Annibale per la Toscana,* a report addressed to Cosimo I in 1559 and published by Francesco Saverio Gualtieri in

Naples, 1780. On this and on what follows, the indispensable guide is Anthony Grafton in his forthcoming book on Scaliger.

73. Above, n. 63.

74. The story of Sigonio's "discovery" of Cicero's *De Consolatione* is told by Jacopo Facciolati in *Fasti Gymnasii Patavani* (Padua, 1757), vol. II, p. 216.

75. Festus's *De Verborum Significatione,* was frequently republished after the first edition of 1471. Orsini's edition with the fragments was first published in Florence, 1582; but his notes are included with those of Scaliger in the edition of Amsterdam, 1700, which is the one I consulted. On Orsini: Anet Marie de Nolhac, *La bibliothèque de Fulvio Orsini* (Bibliothèque de l'Ecole des Hautes Etudes, Sciences Philologiques et Histoire, fasc. 74) (Paris, 1887).

76. Biographical information in the preface of his translator, Tommaso Porcacchi, which I read in the 2d ed. of the translation of his *Le antichità della città di Roma* (Venice, 1569). Gamucci's wide range of humanist associates is amply illustrated in the sections of the book dedicated to modern Rome.

77. Elvira Magri in "I carmini latini di L. G. G. nel codice I...," *Lettere italiane,* XXVI (1974). A future biographer of Giraldi should take note of the autobiographical material in the dedications to the successive *syntagmata* of his *De Deis Gentium,* which I read in his *Operum quae Extant Omnium,* cited above in Chapter 14, n. 14. Biographical information on Grapaldi in the corresponding entry in vol. III of Ireneo Affò, *Memorie degli scrittori e letterati parmigiani* (Parma, 1791).

78. All about Aleandro in the article by Alberto Asor Rosa in *DBI.* See below, n. 56.

79. Biographical information in Domenico De Angelis, *Le vite de' letterati salentini,* vol. II (Naples, 1713).

80. What is said here in particular and in general at the end of this paragraph is well documented by what Feliciano said about himself in the dedication to his *Alphabetum Romanum,* ed. Giovanni Mardersteig (Verona: Ed. Bodoni, 1955). I am also dependent on Mardersteig's article, "Leon Battista Alberti e la rinascita del carattere lapidario romano nel Quattrocento," *IMU,* II (1959).

81. Dionisotti, "Aldo Manuzio umanista," *Lettere italiane,* XII (1960). I cannot cite Di-

onisotti's introduction to Giovanni Orlandi, ed., *Aldo Manuzio editore* (Milan: Il Polifilo, 1975), about which I read in Francesco Barberi's review in *La bibliofilia,* LXXXIX (1977), 160, because neither I nor any of the libraries to which I presently have access can afford to buy the book. On Sardi: Barotti in *Memorie istoriche di letterati ferraresi,* vol. II, pp. 199 ff. On Panvinio, below, n. 88.

82. Above, n. 14. Tiraboschi corrects what he says are errors in Liruti's biography of Robortello in his own article in vol. VII of his *Storia della letteratura italiana.*

83. See prefaces to their works, respectively *Dell'origine ed antichità di Palermo* (Palermo, 1614) by Valguarnera and *Tremitanae Insulae Descriptio* (Milan, 1604) by Coccorella, both reprinted by Graevius in *Thesaurus Antiquitatum Siciliae,* vol. XIV.

84. I read his *De Orobiorum sive Cenomanorum Origine,* first published in Venice in 1531, in Graevius, vol. III[1].

85. *Dell'antichità, sito, chiese, corpi santi, reliquie et statue di Roma* (Naples, 1569), reprinted by Carlo Porsile in his *Raccolta di varii libri* (with separate pagination) *d'historie del Regno di Napoli* in 1678. On Contarini, see above, Chapter 9, p. 36.

86. I follow the article by Roberto Zapperi in *DBI.* The *Chorographia sive De Situ Siciliae Libellus* was first printed in Palermo in 1537 and subsequently in Messina (1537 and 1542), in Basel (1544), in Schottus, and in Graevius, vol. X[1]. He applied the same formula to a *Hispaniae Descriptio,* or *De Situ Hispaniae* (Lyon, 1552), also reprinted in vol. I of *Hispania Illustrata* (Frankfurt-am-Main, 1603).

87. I follow both the *vita* by Lorenzo Crasso published in Capaccio's *Antiquitates et Historiae Neapolitanae,* translated from the first Italian edition of Naples, 1607, in Graevius, vol. IX[2-3], and the article by Salvatore Nigro in *DBI.* A survey of all of Capaccio's antiquarian writings in the context of his many other works is presented by Amedeo Quondam in *La parola nel labirinto* (Bari: Laterza, 1975), pp. 203 ff.

88. A complete bibliography of Panvinio's published and unpublished works is given by the publisher of his *De Urbis Veronae,* Angelo Tami (above, n. 7), pp. 48–49, and in the corresponding biographical note by Scipione Maffei in his *Verona illustrata,* pt. II. On his

biography of the popes, see above, Chapter 14, n. 24.

89. Cf. Momigliano in *RSI,* LXXXVII (1975), 34.

90. As is made clear in the privilege of Paul III to the first edition of Venice, 1545. The titles of all the books in this series are included in the complete list published by Alberto Tinto in *Annali tipografici dei Tramezzino* (Florence: Olschki, 1966).

91. I follow, besides Paully, Russell Meiggs on pp. 10–12 and in appendix 2 of his *The Athenian Empire* (Oxford: Clarendon, 1972). Giraldi is here quoted from p. 5 of his *De Deis Gentium,* cited above at n. 75.

92. See Francesco Della Corte, *La filologia latina dalle origini a Varrone* (Turin: Vincenzo Bona, n.d.).

93. Anthony Grafton, "On the Scholarship of Politian and Its Context," *JWCI,* XL (1977).

94. Cited above at n. 84.

95. Written in 1593 (as indicated on p. 9) and published with *Calendarium & Romanum & Graecum* (Basel, 1541).

96. As is clear both from the Lyon, 1557, edition of the Latin translation by Guarino da Verona and Gregorio Tifernate and in the Venice, 1562, edition of Alfonso Buonacciuoli's Italian translation from the Greek *(Geografia di Strabone . . . in volgare italiano).*

97. *Urbis Caesenae Descriptio,* translated from the Italian original of 1598 in Graevius, vol. IX[8]. Brissio did not make it into the *DBI.*

98. Besides his immense *De Antiquitate et Situ Calabriae,* consisting of 222 folio pages in tiny print in the Rome, 1571, edition (which is reprinted in Graevius, vol. IX[5], and again, with corrections and emendations by Sertorio Quattromani, in Rome, 1737). Barrio also wrote *Pro Lingua Latina, De Aeternitate Urbis,* and *De Laudibus Italiae,* all first published in the same year, 1571 (after he failed to get Pier Vettori to have them published in Florence). The quotation is from the *prooemium* of *De Antiquitate.*

99. Milan, 1541, reprinted in Graevius, vol. I[1].

100. Panvinio in the volume of *Spicilegium Romanum* cited above at n. 1, pp. 653 ff.

101. *Urbis Romae Topographia,* cited at n. 12. A list of editions of the Latin original, as well as a full bibliography, is given by Argellati.

102. That is what Mazzucchelli says in vol. I, p. 36, where publication data are also given. I read the Köln, 1552, edition of his work cited above at n. 49.

103. See above, Chapter 14, n. 19.

104. *De Magistratibus Municipalibus* (1593) and *De Quattuordecim Urbis Romae Earundemque Aedificiis . . . ,* in *Thes. Ant. Rom.,* vol. III. Panciroli recognized his debt to his teacher by including Alciati's *De Magistratibus* (above, n. 4) in his edition of the *Notitia Dignitatum* (above, n. 9). On Panciroli as a historian, see above, Chapter 10, n. 54.

105. *De Senatu Romano* in *Thes. Ant. Rom.,* vol. I. Needless to say, I find Manuzio's theory wholly ridiculous, and I am at a loss to understand how it fits into any of the recognized philosophic systems of the late sixteenth century.

106. I read the most recent edition in *Storici minori volgarizzati e illustati,* vol. I (Milan, 1826).

107. *Della vita di Caio Giulio Cesare* and *Sommario dell'acquisto e Stato dei Romani* were published in the same volume in Verona, 1600.

108. In *Antiquitatum Romanarum . . . Liber de Civitate Romana* (Rome, 1585).

109. Tinti cited above at n. 62; Sigonio in *De Antiquo Jure Italiae* in vol. VI of his *Opera Omnia.*

110. That is the substance of what he says in his dedication to Gregory XIII of 1582, in *Opera Omnia,* vol. IV.

111. I have consulted both the Latin original, *Hieroglyphicorum ex Sacris Aegyptiorum Literis* (Florence, 1556), and Celio Agostino Curione's expanded Italian translation of Venice, 1602. Both are equally amusing. Most of this and the following paragraph depends upon Frederick Purnell, Jr., "Francesco Patrizi and the Critics of Hermes Trismegistus," *Journal of Medieval and Renaissance Studies,* VI (1976) (a fascinating article) and on Chapter 2, "La religione dei geroglifici e le origini della scrittura," in Paolo Rossi, *Le sterminate antichità* (Pisa: Nistri-Lischi, 1969), a study which builds on and adds to the well-known *The Myth of Egypt* by Erik Iversen (Copenhagen: Gad, 1961).

112. See Karl H. Dannenfeldt, "Egypt and Egyptian Antiquities in the Renaissance," *SR*, VI (1959).

113. *De Etruria Regali*, ed. Thomas Coke (Florence, 1723), on which see my *Tradition and Enlightenment in the Tuscan Academies* (above, Chapter 10, n. 86), pp. 165 ff.

114. *Discorso di Curzio Inghirami sopra l'opposizioni fatte all'antichità toscane* (Florence, 1645), in response (endless pages of it!) to his *Etruscarum Antiquitatum Fragmenta . . .* of 1637. The cool reception accorded to these works may in part be a consequence of the impossible prose in which they were written.

115. I read it in the edition of his *Opera Omnia . . .* cited above in Chapter 14, n. 14.

116. *Discorsi*, vol. I, p. 136.

117. In *Thes. Ant. Rom.*, vol. II.

118. Panvinio, *Imperium Romanorum* (1558), Chapter 1, and Manuzio in *De Comitiis Romanorum*, both in *Thes. Ant. Ro.*, vol. I.

119. *La militia romana di Polibio di Tito Livio e di Dionisio Alicarnasso* (Ferrara, 1583), and *Paralleli militari . . ne' quali si fa paragono delle milizie antiche . . . con le moderne* (Rome, 1594); Robortello in the dedication to his edition of Aelianus, cited above at n. 8.

120. From the biography in Affò, *Memorie degli scrittori . . . parmigiani*, vol. III.

121. See Roberto Weiss in *Rinascimento*, IX (1958), 171, and Robert Gaston, "Vesta and the Martyrdom of St. Lawrence . . . ," *JWCI*, XXXVII (1974).

122. Lucio Mauro, *Le antichità de la città di Roma, brevissimamente raccolte da chiunque ne ha scritto o antico o moderno*. I cite the edition of Venice, 1556.

123. *I discorsi . . . ne i quali si tratta della nobiltà, honore . . . et anticaglie . . .* (Venice, 1575).

124. *Discorso sopra le medaglie antiche* (Venice, 1559), cited above, n. 21.

125. *Historie et descrittione del Regno di Sicilia* (Naples, 1594).

126. Both published in his *Opera Omnia*, vol. III. The *De Vita . . . Scipionis* was first published in Florence in 1549.

CHAPTER SIXTEEN

1. That the subject of this chapter is relatively unknown is suggested by the contents of Peter Meinhold's authoritative *Geschichte der kirchlichen Historiographie* (Freiburg-Munich: Karl Alber, 1967), which, while giving considerable space to contemporary Protestant historians, all but ignores their Catholic counterparts and leaves the Italians out altogether. Harald Zimmermann's "Ecclesia als Object der Historiographie," Oesterreichische Akademie der Wissenschaften, Philosophische-historische Klasse, *Sitzungsberichte* 235, vol. IV (1960), refers briefly to only three Italians, Panvinio, Sigonio, and Baronio; and even they are rather lost in the shadow of the *Magdeburg Centuries*. A broad context is provided by Paolo Brezzi in a mimeographed course outline entitled "La storiografia ecclesiastica," distributed by the Libreria Scientifica of Naples (1959). Important remarks on the seventeenth-century successors of the sixteenth-century ecclesiastical historians are given in the first chapter of Denys Hay's *The Church in Italy in the Fifteenth Century* (Cambridge University Press, 1977). And abundant information on several individual historians is to be found in chapter 3 ("Gli ortodossi") of Sergio Bertelli's *Ribelli, libertini e ortodossi*, cited above in the Prologue, n. 14.

2. *Vita del beato Giovanni Colombini da Siena . . . con parte de la vita di alcuni altri de li Jesuati: cosa molto divota et utile all'edificazione de l'anima* (Rome, 1556), from the Italian translation first published at Siena in 1541 of the Latin original first published in Florence around 1480 and thereafter at Brescia in 1505 (and not in 1500, as Negri says on p. 162, on whom I nevertheless rely for biographical information). On Feo's verse, see Roberto Ridolfi, *Vita di Girolamo Savonarola* (Florence: Sansoni, 1974), pp. 503 and 663, and for further biographical and bibliographical information, the article by Mario Marti in *DBI*.

3. On Taegio I follow Quétif-Echard, vol. II, p. 36, and G. Onetto in *Archivum Ordinis Praedicatorum*, X (1940), 317–18.

4. *De Vitis ac Gestis Patriarcarum Aquilensium*, *RIS¹*, vol. XVI.

5. *Chronicon Archiepiscoporum Amalphitanorum*, in Pelliccia, vol. V.

6. Zeno: Voss, vol. I, p. 77. For details on publication: Hartmut Hoffman in *Deutsches Archiv für Erforschung des Mittelalters*, XXIX (1973), 84.

7. Above, Chapter 14, n. 108.

8. *De Metropoli Mediolanensi* (Milan, 1596). Full biographical information is given in the article on Bascapè in Giuseppe Boffito, *Scrittori barnabiti* (Florence: Olschki, 1933).

9. *De Papiensis Ecclesiae Dignitate* (1566), which I read in appendix to his *De Italicarum Rerum Varietate et Elegantia Libri X*, in the 2d (from the 1st of 1565) ed. of Pavia, 1587. On Sacchi as a municipal historian, see above, Chapter 11, n. 31. For biographical information, below, n. 83.

10. Above, Chapter 9, n. 118.

11. *I Sommi pontefici, cardinali, patriarchi, arcivescovi e vescovi bolognesi...* (Bologna, 1621).

12. *Catalogus Scriptorum Florentinorum Omnis Generis*, op. post., ed. Luca Ferrini (like Poccianti, a Servite) (Florence, 1589); *Vite de' sette beati fiorentini institutori del sagro Ordine de' Servi di Santa Maria, con un discorso intorno alla devota e pietosa religione della città di Fiorenza con sommario poi di tutte le chiese & luoghi pii di quella* (Florence, 1575) (2d ed. 1589).

13. *Vescovi di Fiesole, di Volterra e d'Arezzo*, ed. Scipione Ammirato Jr. (Florence, 1637) (but written before 1598, when Francesco da Diacceto died).

14. Bartolomeo De Peregrino, *Opus Divinum de Sacra ac Fertili Bergomensi Vinea ex Diversis Authenticis Catholicisque Libris et Scripturis Diligenti Cura Collectum* (Brescia, 1553); Casale and Medici are both edited by Carlo Marcora in *Memorie storiche della Diocesi di Milano*, vols. XII and II; Antonio Paolucci, "Arte e storia nelle memorie di un parrocco di montagna," in *Scritti di storia dell'arte in onore di Ugo Procacci* (Milan: Electra, 1977), vol. II.

15. *De Vita et Rebus Gestis Sanctorum Bergomatum Commentarii*, op. post., ed. Giovan Antonio Guarneri (Bergamo, 1584).

16. *Sacra historia di Bergamo*, 2d ed. (Bergamo, 1621).

17. Above, Chapter 10, p. 37.

18. *Descrittione de i luoghi sacri della città di Napoli* (Naples, 1560).

19. *La sacra historia di S. Mauritio arciduca della Legione thebea* (Turin, 1604), from an earlier edition mentioned in the title that I was unable to locate. On the author, who is to be found neither in Tiraboschi nor in the *DBI*, and on his other published works, see Francesco Agostino, *Scrittori piemontesi savoiardi e nizzardi*, ed. Andrea Rossotto (Turin, 1790), *sub nomine*.

20. Bascapè (above, notes 7 and 8), *Novaria seu De Ecclesia Novariensi* (Novara, 1612); Pasqua, *Vitae Episcoporum Ecclesiae Hieracensis* (Naples, 1755).

21. Above, Chapter 9, n. 110.

22. Above, Chapter 9, n. 59.

23. *SS. Episcoporum Veron. Antiqua Monumenta et Aliorum Sanctorum Quorum Corpora... Habentur Veronae* (Venice, 1576).

24. *Dell'historia ecclesiastica di Piacenza*, op. post., ed. by Campi's nephew Pietro (Piacenza, 1651). Tiraboschi's comments are based on the edition of 1659. On Campi I have consulted Giorgio Fiori, "La storia ecclesiastica piacentina di Pier Maria Campi alla luce di nuovi documenti," *BS Piac*, LXIV (1969), as well as the article by Armando Petrucci in *DBI*.

25. *Mediolanenses Antiquitates ex Urbis Paroeciis Collectae* (Milan, 1625), of which the first part is published in Graevius, III[1]. A complete bibliography in Argellati.

26. Above, Chapter 14, n. 114.

27. *Historica Demonstratio quod s. Ianuarii Patria Neapolis Fuit*, published in his *De Sacris Ecclesiae Neapolitanae Monumentis Singularis*, op. post. (Naples, 1645), on which I consulted Severino Gori, "Le lettere inedite di Luca Wadding," *Archivum Franciscanum Historiae*, LXVI (1973), and the considerable biographical and bibliographical information in the corresponding article in Giuseppe Silos, *Catalogus Scriptorum Congregationis Clericorum Regularium*, published in appendix to vol. II of his work cited below at n. 35.

28. *Historia dell'origine di tutte le religioni che sino ad ora sono state*, 2d ed. from the 1st of 1569 (Venice, 1581), which also includes his *Historia degli huomini illustri per santità di vita e per nobiltà di sangue che furono Giesuati*. On Morigia's history of Milan, see above, Chapter 9, n. 42. The chapters on the Capuchins are reprinted in appendix to vol. I of the *Monumenta Historica Ordinis Fratrum Minorum Capp.* (below, n. 31).

29. *Historiarum Camaldulensium Libri III*, which includes Agostino's life of his predecessor, Ambrogio Traversari (Florence, 1575).

30. D'Ausilio, *Sommario dell'antichissima origine della religione carmelitana, con le indulgenze, privilegi e gratie* (Naples, 1559); Bosio, *Dell'institutione della sacra religione et illustrissima militia di san Giovanni Gierosolimitano* (Rome, 1594). All the information about his predecessors is given in his own *proemio*. Much information about the author himself is given by Gaspare De Caro in *DBI*.

31. All three *relazioni* (the first is of 1569) are published with an ample introduction by Melchiorre a Pobladura as *Relationes de Origine Ordinis Minorum Capuccinorum* (= *Monumenta Historica Ordinis Fratrum Minorum Capuccinorum*, vol. I) (Assisi, 1937). Zarlino's *Informatione...intorno la origine della Congregatione dei reverendi frati Cappucini*, first published at Venice in 1579, is included in the appendix to the same volume.

32. *Una simplice et divota historia dell'origine della congregatione de' frati Cappuccini*, ed. Melchiore a Pobladura, in vols. II–IV of the same series (Assisi, 1939).

33. *Historia Societatis Iesu Prima Pars*, ed. Francesco Sacchini (Roma, 1615).

34. *Historia della Religione de' padri Cherici Regolari* (Rome, 1609). Full biographical and bibliographical notices in the *Catalogus Scriptorum Congregationis Clericorum Regularium* (above, n. 27).

35. *Historiarum Clericorum Regularium a Congregatione Condita* (Rome, 1650).

36. *Historiae Olivetanae Libri II* (Venice, 1623).

37. *Vita Petri Fabri* (Lyon, 1617).

38. *Vita B. Stanislai Kostkae* (Rome, 1612); *Historiae Societatis Iesu Pars Secunda* (to *IV*[1]) (Antwerp, 1620 ff). Much on both Orlandini and Sacchini in both Tiraboschi and Sommervogel. I was unable to locate several other histories of religious orders to which I have references, e.g., Panvinio's *Augustiniani Ordinis Chronicon* (Rome, 1550); Giuseppe Panfili, *Chronica Ordinis Fratrum Eremitarum* (Rome, 1581) (the copy in the Biblioteca Nazionale of Florence is still, twelve years after the flood, "alluvionata").

39. Carlo Cecchelli, *Il cenacolo filippino e l'archeologia cristiana* (Quaderni di Studi Romani) (Rome, 1938).

40. *Le sette chiese principali di Roma*, tr. Marco Antonio Lanfranchi (Rome, 1570).

41. *Historia delle stationi di Roma che si celebrano la Quadragesima* (Rome, 1588).

42. *De ritu sepeliendi mortuos apud veteres Christianos et Eorundem Coemeteriis Liber*, ed. Iohannes Georgius Ioch (Frankfurt & Leipzig, 1717).

43. E.g., *Historia delle sante vergini romane...e de' gloriosi martiri Papia e Mauro soldati romani* (Rome, 1591) and *De SS. Martyrum Cruciatibus* (Rome, 1594). A complete bibliography in Cecchelli, above, n. 39.

44. Cf. above, n. 30.

45. All described by Antonia Nava Cellini while castigating all her predecessors for having overlooked the relevant documents, in "Maderno, Vanni e Reni a Santa Cecilia," *Paragone* 227 (January, 1969).

46. *Roma sotterranea* (Rome, 1650); on the author: Nicola Parise in *DBI*.

47. I follow the article by Paolo Prodi in *DBI*.

48. Quoted by Harald Dickerhof in *Historisches Jahrbuch*, LXXXVIII (1968), 356.

49. I happen to have read the appropriate passages quoted at length in the *ad lectorem* of Pirri's *Sicilia Sacra* (below, n. 86)—another example of the effectiveness of the Milanese reforms as a Counter Reformation model.

50. *Annales Antiquitatum*, ed. Francesco Bozio (Rome, 1637). On the author: Pietro Craveri in *DBI*.

51. The phrase is that of Amadeo Quondam in "Dal manierismo al Barocco," in *Storia di Napoli* (above, Chapter 6, n. 2), vol. V[1], of which pp. 434–37 are my chief sources of relevant biographical information.

52. *Della historica catholica libro primo e secondo...* (Vico Equense, 1588).

53. *Della historia sacra* (Venice, 1570). On Muzio as a literary critic, see Bernard Weinberg, *A History of Literary Criticism in the Italian Renaissance* (University of Chicago Press, 1961), pp. 729–31.

54. *Le historie de' successi de' nostri tempi* (Venice, 1583).

55. *De Vita Francisci Xaverii*, cited above, Chapter 14, n. 116; *Laurentae Historiae Libri V* (Rome, 1595), which I read in the Italian translation of Bartolomeo Zucchi as *De l'historia lauretana libri cinque* (Milan, 1600). All my biographical information comes from Sommervogel.

56. Possevino, *Apparato*, cited above,

Chapter 15, n. 64. Bellarmino I consulted in André du Saussay's "continued" edition (a sign of its lasting popularity) of *De Scriptoribus Ecclesiasticis* (Köln, 1684), with the help of Edward Ryan, *The Historical Scholarship of Robert Bellarmine* (Louvain: Bibliothèque de l'Université, 1936). The only major reservations made by eighteenth-century scholars about Possevino was his occasional failure to cite his sources—for instance, the paragraph on p. 494 of vol. I, which is lifted without acknowledgment from Poccianti: Zeno: Voss, vol. I, p. 365.

57. *Ristretto dell'historie del mondo* I read in the translation and continuation by Lodovico Antelli and Bernardo Oldoino (Venice, 1662).

58. Ansgar Philipps, *Die Kirchengeschichte im Katholischen und Evangelischen Religionsunterricht* (Vienna: Herder, 1971), p. 86. Alas, Philipps begins only in the eighteenth century.

59. *Adversus Negantem Petrum Apost. Romae Fuisse,* published in appendix to his *Epistolarum Familiarum Liber* (Venice, 1573).

60. *Sanctorum Priscorum Patrum Vitae Numero Centum Sexagintatres per Gravissimos et Probatissimos Auctores Conscriptae* (Venice, 1551).

61. *Della historia sacra,* cited above at n. 53.

62. Cf. Headley, *Luther's View of Church History,* cited above, Chapter 2, n. 100, and Heinrich Berger, *Calvins Geschichtsauffassung* (Zürich: Zwingli Verlag, 1955).

63. On the Centurians, I follow Wilhelm Preger, *Matthias Flacius Illyricus und seine Zeit* (Erlangen, 1861), and Franz Peter Sonntag, "Matthias Flacius Illyricus und die *Magdeburge Centurien,*" in *A Cesare Baronio: Scritti vari* (Sora, 1963) (published without title page). Turrianus's title is *Adversus Magdeburgenses Centuriatores . . . Libri V* (Florence, 1572).

64. I read *La cronologia ecclesiastica* in the *aumentata* translation by Bartolomeo Dionigi da Fano (Venice, 1592). On Panvinio's activities as an ecclesiastical historian, by far the fullest account is that given by José de Orella y Unzue on pp. 276–302 of his *Respuestas católicas a las Centurias de Magdeburgo* (Madrid: Fundación Universitaria Española, Seminario "Suarez," 1976), a work which is a mine of information about the questions posed in the following paragraphs. It contains long summaries of all the works of all the protagonists in this quarrel backed up by extensive archival research in both Italy and Spain.

65. *Historia Ecclesiastica . . . ad Annum CCCXI,* in *Opera Omnia,* vol. IV. On this preparatory work, and on much else, I follow Angelo Walz, "Il Baronio, 'Pater Annalium Ecclesiasticarum'," in *A Cesare Baronio,* cited above at n. 63, and Sergio Bertelli, in the Garzanti *Storia della letteratura italiana,* vol. V¹, *Il Seicento* (Milan, 1977), p. 341, of the article "Storiografi, eruditi, antiquari e politici," of which I take account also in other parts of this chapter.

66. The most complete biography is that of Cyriac K. Pullapilly, *Caesar Baronius, Counter-Reformation Historian* (University of Notre Dame Press, 1975); but I have also taken note of the biographical introduction by E. Vaccaro to *A Cesare Baronio* and the article by Alberto Pincerle in *DBI.* The quotation is from Guido Bentivoglio, *Memorie e lettere,* ed. Costantino Panigada (Scrittori d'Italia) (Bari: Laterza, 1934, p. 63). Much information about Baronio's ecclesiastical-political activities in the packed erudition of A. D. Wright, *Federico Borromeo and Baronius* (University of Reading, Department of Italian Studies, 1974).

67. Quoted from the preface to his life of Ambrose cited in the next note.

68. I read the text in vol. VI of Ambrosius, *Opera* (Rome, 1587), pp. 1–64. Why Baronius himself never got around to publishing his life of Gregory is explained in the preface to the first edition in the *Acta Sanctorum,* May II (1680), pp. 369 ff.

69. *Martyrologium Romanum Gregorii XIII pont. Max. Iussu Editum et Urbani VIII Auctoritate Recognitum* (Rome, 1630), on which see Sergio Mottironi, "Cesare Baronio agiografo," in *A Cesare Baronio.*

70. *Paraensis ad Rempublicam Venetam* (Rome, 1606), also in Italian translation by F. Serdonati as *Esortatione alla Republica Venetiana* (Siena, 1606); *Tractatus de Monarchia Siciliae,* in *Thes. Antiq. Sic.,* vol. III.

71. Above, pp. 453 and 454, on Gallonio and Bozio.

72. But I read the edition of Lucca, 1738, with notes by Antonio Pagi and introduction by Enrico Noris. Since the division of this edition into volumes does not correspond to that of the first, my references to the text between parentheses follow the system used in the index: AD + chapter number.

73. See below, n. 76.

74. Sigonio on this matter: above, Chapter 11, p. 312. Casaubon in *De Rebus Sacris et Ecclesiasticis Exercitationes XVI* (London, 1614), and *Animadversiones in Annales Baronii Ineditae,* in *Casauboniana* (Hamburg, 1710). Baronio's favorable view of the *Acta* of Sylvester can be explained in part by the evidence presented by Fausto Parente in *RSI,* XV (1978), 878–97: they had just been published in translation from the Greek edition of Gentien Hervet (Venice, 1556) by Aloise Lippomano, bishop of Verona, and one of the presidents of the Council of Trent.

75. *Neue Bearbeitung, Zweit Reihe,* vol. XIX (1972), col. 805.

76. *Il compendio de gli Annali ecclesiastici* (Rome, 1590).

77. On the Italian abridgment by Alessandro Tassoni, see Tiraboschi in *Biblioteca modenese,* vol. V, p. 209. The first Latin abridgment was that by Henri de Sponde (Spondanus), bishop of Pamiers, first published in 1614.

78. *Indici de' sommi pontefici, degl'imperadori e de' consoli con la tavola copiosa de' nomi e delle materie historiche e morali* (Rome, 1643).

79. *Vitae et Res Gestae Pontificum Romanorum et S.R.E. Cardinalium ab Initio Nascentis Ecclesiae usque ad Urbanum VIII,* continued from the 1st ed. of 1601 by Francisco Cabrera Morali and Andrea Victorello and edited by Girolamo Aleandro (Rome, 1630). The work was often continued and republished through the mid-eighteenth century. On Chacón, see above, Chapter 15.

80. I cite the *Italia Saccra* not in the 1st (1643 ff.) but in the 2d ed. (Venice, 1717 ff.).

81. Muratori in *RIS*[1], vol. VII, p. 853. On Muratori's "running dialogue" with Baronio, see Bertelli, *Erudizione e storia,* cited above, Chapter 6, n. 11, pp. 198–99, 250, and 254.

82. Cf. Leonard Krieger on p. 69 of Ranum, ed., *National Consciousness . . . ,* cited above, Chapter 12, n. 29.

83. A good example of Dominican antihistorical attitudes is given by Gensette Epiney-Burgard in "J. Eck and la théologie mystique," *BHR,* XXXIV (1972). Even those orders which did produce historians were not necessarily historically minded—e.g., the Servites, whose constitutions of 1580 required preachers to be masters only of theology and required ordinary members to have only enough education to be able to follow ecclesiastical chants: Pacifico Branchesi, "Gli 'studia' delle provincie italiane . . . ," *Studi storici dell'Ordine dei Servi di Maria,* XXIII (1973).

84. *Historia sagra intitolata Mare oceano di tutte le religioni del mondo* (Messina, 1613). A full bibliography of his works is in Mongitore, vol. II, p. 226, as well as in Tiraboschi. On Federico Maurolico, see above, Chapter 10, n. 26.

85. Sandro Carletti, "Un malinteso fra Antonio Bosio e 'alcuni Giesuiti antichi' di S. Ermete," *Rivista di archeologia cristiana,* XLV (1969).

86. *Sicilia Sacra Disquisitionibus et Notiis Illustrata . . . a Christianae Religionis Exordio ad Nostra Usque Tempora,* which I read not in the 1st (Palermo, 1630) or in the 2d (*Thes. Antiq. Sic.,* vols. II–III) but in the 3d ed. of Antonino Mongitore (Palermo, 1733), which has the advantage of including the *Vita* by Vito Maria Amico. More information on the author in Tiraboschi, in Mongitore, and in Alessio Narbone, S.J., *Bibliografia sicola* [sic] *sistematica* (Palermo, 1850–55), vol. I, p. 279.

87. *RIS*[1], vol. VII, p. 853, and vol. XV, pp. 98–99.

88. Harald Zimmermann, "Über das Anfangsdatum der Kirchengeschichte," *Archiv für Kirchengeschichte,* XLI (1971). To be sure, Zimmerman pays no attention to the Italian "Catholic" historians. Hence, his sole sixteenth-century predecessor of the "scientific" church historians of the nineteenth century is Johannes Pappus of Strassburg.

89. The whole story is told by Paolo Prodi in "Storia sacra e controriforma: Nota sulle censure al commento di Carlo Sigonio a Sulpicio Severo," *Annali dell'Istituto Storico Italo-Germanico in Trento,* III (1978), which the author kindly let me read in manuscript.

90. All fully documented in the text of the *postulata* of the Toledo province and in Sacchini's *Responsio* published in *Lainii Monumenta*, vol. VIII (Monumenta Historica Societatis Iesu) (Madrid, 1917), the latter being one of the most eloquent defenses of the freedom of historical investigation I have found in Renaissance literature. (Then what becomes of the thesis about the Counter Reformation, of which Sacchini was an illustrious representative, suffocating "lay" culture in the Renaissance?) I am very grateful to Mario Scaduto, S.J., for having pointed it out to me. The tale about Zosimus is in Pauly, *sub nomine*.

91. Quoted by Girolamo Cotroneo on p. 272 of his *I trattatisti*, cited in the Epilogue, n. 21.

92. *Opera... sopra l'imagine miracolosa della santissima Nunziata di Fiorenza* (Florence, 1592).

93. Cited above at n. 55.

94. See above in Chapter 14, pp. 417–20.

95. *Historia del glorioso martirio de' sedici sacerdoti martirati in Inghilterra...* (Milan, 1584). For the probable identification of the original, I am indebted to my friend William Trimble of Loyola University in Chicago, a well-known expert on English Catholics.

96. Gallonio's *Vita* of Filippo Neri was first printed in Rome in 1600; but I read it in *Acta Sanctorum*, May VI, pp. 463–524. The quotation is from p. 483.

97. *La cronica carmelitana dall'origine di Santo Elia profeta...fino al dì d'hoggi* (Piacenza, 1595). His *La nuova vaga et dilettevole villa* (Brescia, 1597) I read in the edition of Treviso, 1649. It seeks to turn an agricultural enterprise into a combination of a Carmelite monastery, a Campanellian utopia, and a profit-making business. The judgments here quoted are those of the *Bibliotheca Carmelitana* cura et labore unius è Carmelitis Provinciae Turoniae (Aurelianis, 1752), vol. II, under "Josephus Falconius."

98. On the qualities of Bartoli's prose: Renato Bertacchini, "Tre scrittori gesuiti del Seicento," *Studium*, LXIV (1968), as well as Ezio Raimondi's introduction to Mario Scotti's edition of the *Prose* of Bartoli and Paolo Segneri (Turin: UTET, 1976). On the deliberate choice of an "eloquent" rather than

an "erudite" historian, see John Renaldo, "Antecedants of Vico: The Jesuit Historians," *Archivum Historicum Societatis Iesu*, XXXIX (1970).

99. *Annalium...Ordinis Minorum S. Francisci qui Capuccini Nuncupantur* (Lyon, 1632), translated by Benedetto Sanbenedetti as *Annali dell Ordine de' Frati Minori Cappuccini* (Turin, 1641–45).

100. Note Tiraboschi's unfavorable judgment of several other histories of religious orders: vol. VIII, p. 143, of the 1793 edition.

101. An example: p. 15 of his *Esortatione alla Republica Venetiana*, apropos of the Venetian bishops. Poccianti quoted from *Catalogus Scriptorum Florentinorum*, cited above, n. 12, under Scala and Guicciardini.

102. *Memorie e lettere*, p. 64.

103. This and the following quotation are from Baronio's introduction to his *Vita S. Ambrosii* (above, n. 68).

104. Cf. Arnaldo Momigliano, "Pagan and Christian Historiography in the Fourth Century," reprinted in his *The Conflict between Paganism and Christianity in the Fourth Century* (Oxford: Clarendon, 1963). On the efforts of Sozomenus and Socrates to maintain the separation, I follow R. A. Markus, "Church History and the Early Church Historians," in Derek Baker, ed., *The Materials, Sources and Methods of Ecclesiastical History* (Oxford: Blackwell, 1975).

105. *De Dignitate atq. Praestantia Reipub. Casinensis*, dedicated to Reginald Pole and published along with his other dialogues in his *Academia Veneta* (Venice, 1559). Since I found no mention of this Ugoni in Tiraboschi, Querini *(Specimen Variae Literaturae)*, or Ottavio Rossi *(Elogi historici di Bresciani illustri* [Brescia, 1620]), I can only suppose that he descended from what Rossi calls "one of the noblest families of Brescia" and that he may have been related to the late-sixteenth-century poet Gian Andrea Ugoni.

106. *Istoria dell'origine del sagratissimo luogo di Montevergine*, 2d ed., corrected from the 1st of 1585 (Venice, 1591).

107. Much of the foregoing is from Paolo Prodi, "Le prime riflessioni storiografiche sul Tridentino negli *Atti di Gabriele Paleotti*," in *Reformata Reformanda*, eds. Erwin Iserloh and Konrad Repgen (Festgabe Jedin)

(Münster-i-w: Aschendorff, 1965), vol. I.

108. *Vita del padre Paolo dell'Ordine de' Servi* (Leiden, 1646), to which I have added for biographical information the prefaces by Renzo Pecchioli to his edition of the *Istoria del Concilio Tridentino* (Florence, Sansoni, 1966), by Gaetano and Luisa Cozzi to their edition of the *Opere* (Milan-Naples: Ricciardi, 1959), as well as the prefaces of the individual selections included in the volumes, and by Corrado Vivanti to his edition of the *Istoria* (Turin: Einaudi, 1974), which includes the latest edition of Micanzio's *Vita*. These editions summarize all the immense quantity of previous studies dedicated to Sarpi.

109. In *Considerazione sopra le censura,* which I read in the Cozzi's edition of the *Opere*. On the subjects of this paragraph, I am still indebted to a classic of my student days: Federico Chabod, *La politica di Paolo Sarpi,* most recently republished by the Fondazione Cini (Venice: Istituto per la Collaborazione Culturale, 1962), and Luigi Salvatorelli, *Le idee religiose di fra Paolo Sarpi,* which I read in the *Atti* of the Accademia Nazionale dei Lincei, Classe Scienze Morali, ser. 8, vol. V (1954).

110. Cozzi's studies are basic on this point too, particularly his "Fra Paolo Sarpi, l'anglicanesimo e la *Historia del Concilio Tridentino,*" *RSI,* XLVIII (1956). Morosini himself was also a historian, of course: above, Chapter 9, n. 66.

111. As Paolo Prodi observes on p. 411 of his "Structure and Organization of the Church," in J. R. Hale, ed., *Renaissance Venice* (London: Faber & Faber, 1973).

112. I read the full text in the edition of M. O. Busnelli and Giovanni Gambarini (Bari: Laterza, 1940).

113. *Guerre d'Italia tra la sere.ma Rep.ca di Venetia e gli arciducali d'Austria* ("In Poistorf per Peter Gat," [1617]). Neither Sarpi nor any of his modern editors has identified the author. The uncomfortable question brought up by "Emigliani" was whether the Venetian emissaries in France had exceeded their commissions and then prevailed upon the king to cover up for them—a question of some embarrassment to the Senate.

114. I happen to have read it in the edition

of Giovanni Gambarini (Bari: Laterza, 1935), but I have taken note of the textual comments of the more recent editions, particularly that of Vivanti cited above, n. 108.

115. Corrado Vivanti, "Una fonte dell'*Istoria del Concilio tridentino…,*" *RSI,* LXXXIII (1971).

116. As Prodi notes in the article in *Reformata Reformanda* cited above at n. 107, vol. I, pp. 729–30.

117. All the particulars are given by Frances Yates in "Paolo Sarpi's *History of the Council of Trent,*" *JWCI,* VII (1944), and then used effectively to strike horror in Anglophone ears over "the Hispano-Papal tyranny which was swallowing up all Italy" at the time (p. 134).

118. Preface to the edition of *Italia Sacra* cited above at n. 79.

119. *De Ecclesiasticae Historiae in Theologia Auctoritate* I found in a miscellany entitled *Opusculi di autori siciliani* (Palermo, 1759) in the Biblioteca Nazionale of Florence. It is not mentioned by Mongitore.

120. See p. 81 of Henri I. Marrou, "Philologie et histoire dans la période du pontificat de Léon XIII," *Aspetti della cultura cattolica nell'età di Leone XIII* (Rome: 5 Lune, 1961).

121. I take this from Santo Mazzarino in *Guida allo studio della civiltà romana antica,* eds. V. Ussani and F. Arnaldi (Naples: Istituto Editoriale del Mezzogiorno, 1954), vol. II, p. 585.

122. James A. Weisheipl, *Friar Thomas d'Aquino* (New York: Doubleday, 1974), pp. 57–58.

EPILOGUE

1. Pietro Lauro in *De le lettere* (Venice, 1553), vol. I, pp. 66 ff. (in between praises of matrimony, patriotism, and commerce); Cesare Campana in the letter-preface to the secretary of the Pregadi of his *Delle historie del mondo* (1607), cited above, Chapter 13, n. 22; on which, see Gino Benzoni in *SV,* XVI (1974), 288.

2. On the presence of these same limitations in the ancient historians: W. Robert Conner, *The New Politicans of Fifth-Century Athens* (Princeton University Press, 1971), p. 9; Robert Drews, *The Greek Accounts of East-*

ern History (Harvard University Press, 1973), esp. pp. 137–39; Sallust, *Bellum Iugurt.*, 77 ("novis rebus studere . . .").

3. P. 26 of Marco Tabarrini's introduction to *Annales Ptolemaëi Lucensis*, in *DSI*, vol. VI; on which, see above, Chapter 5, n. 5.

4. Robortello in *Lettera . . . intorno al modo di scrivere la storia*, cited below at n. 23, p. 1; Sansovino in the 2d ed. (Venice, 1581) of his *Ritratti delle più nobili e famose città d'Italia*.

5. Editor's preface to Baldi, *Della vita e de' fatti di Guidobaldo da Montefeltro*, cited above, Chapter 14, n. 27.

6. Amadio Ronchini in "Carlo Sigonio," *AMMod e Parm*, IV (1868).

7. Cited above, Chapter 14, n. 60. In general on freedom of speech under Ferdinando I, see Book II of my *Florence in the Forgotten Centuries*.

8. From pp. 1–2 of the work cited in Chapter 16, n. 92.

9. Proemio to the work cited in Chapter 9, n. 79.

10. Castronovo in the work cited in Chapter 12, n. 66, p. 13.

11. Quoted with comment by Andrea Veress in *AV*, ser. 5, vol. VI (1929), p. 161.

12. Sirleto's criticisms and Sigonio's responses are published in appendix to Sigonio's *Historia Bononiensis*, cited above, Chapter 9, n. 110.

13. My detail about the Florentines comes from Dale Kent, *The Rise of the Medici* (Oxford University Press, 1978), p. 3. On Filelfo: Rino Avesani in *RSCI*, XXVIII (1974), 526.

14. Alfred Soman in *RQ*, XXIV (1971), 1–2.

15. All this comes from Herschel Baker, *The Race of Time* (University of Toronto Press, 1967), Chapter 1; Trevor Roper in the book cited in the Prologue, n. 8; Frederick Seaton Siebert, *Freedom of the Press in England, 1476–1776* (University of Illinois Press, 1952) (a work that can serve as a model for what should be done to investigate the same problem in Italy), and Wallace MacCaffrey in his introduction to William Camden, *The History of Princess Elizabeth* (University of Chicago Press, 1970).

16. See Salviati's application for a position as historian of the house of Este in a letter to the Este ambassador in Florence quoted at

length by Peter M. Brown in *GSLI*, XXX (1956), 545, and Salviati's *Il Lasca, Dialogo* (Florence, 1584), where he proves that "non importa che la storia sia vera"—on which, Brown in *Lionardo Saviati: A Critical Biography* (Oxford University Press, 1974), pp. 184–85.

17. Quoted by Denys Hay in the preface to his edition of Vergilio cited above in Chapter 12, n. 130.

18. Antonio Corsano, "Per la storia del pensiero del tardo Rinascimento: Il Cardano e la storia," *GCFI*, XV (1961); Arrigo Cornelio Agrippa, *Della vanità delle scienze* (Venice, 1547).

19. Cf. Lucien Lévy-Bruhl, "The Cartesian Spirit and History," in Raymond Klibansky and H. J. Patton, eds., *Philosophy and History: Essays Presented to Ernst Cassirer* (Oxford: Clarendon, 1936).

20. "Il Cinquecento fece orge di teoria, non solo per la letteratura, ma per tutte le arti": Cesare Segre in *Lingua, stile e società* (Milan: Feltrinelli, 1974), p. 370.

21. The most recent study of the theoreticians is by Girolamo Cotroneo, *I trattati dell'Ars Historica* (Naples: Giannini, 1971), which benefits from the author's previous studies of Bodin. It should be read, however, bearing in mind the observations of Margherita Isnardi Parente in *RSI*, LXXXV (1973), 473–77. Giorgio Spini's "I trattatisti dell'arte storica" is also very informative and is much more fun to read, since the author freely expresses his personal antipathies toward most of the authors he cites. The article, first published in 1948, should now be read in my translation, corrected and updated by the author himself, in my *The Late Italian Renaissance*. Strangely enough, this pioneering work is not even mentioned by Rüdiger Landfester in *Historia Magistra Vitae: Untersuchung zur humanistischen Geschichtstheorie des 14. bis 16. Jahrhunderts* (Geneva: Droz, 1972)—another sorry sign of the persistence of nationalism in modern historiography. Many of the more important texts were published in another of the many German anthologies of current authors, Johann Wolf's (Joannes Wolfius) *Artis Historicae Penus* (Basel, 1579). They and still others have recently been reproduced in offset, with a very informative introduction, by Eckhard

Kessler, *Theoriker humanistischer Geschichts-schreibung* (Munich: Fink: 1971); these are the texts I read unless I indicate otherwise. That my opinions differ somewhat from those of the authorities is not surprising, since none of them has yet been interested either in the persons who wrote the treatises or in the relation between the theory of history and what was actually written as history at the time.

22. It was first published in vol. II of his *Opere* (Venice, 1740).

23. *Lettera . . . intorno al modo di scrivere la storia particolarmente veneziana,* ed. Emanuele Cicogna (Venice, 1843); *De Historica Facultate Disputatio* (Florence, 1548). On Cicero, Hathaway in the article cited in Chapter 1, n. 4. On the unpublished treatise of Robortello's disciple Flaminio Filonardi, see De Maio in the work cited in Chapter 5, n. 49, pp. 123 ff.

24. Patrizi was also, to be sure, an agricultural entrepreneur, as he himself makes clear in the autobiographical letter he wrote to Baccio Valori on 12 January 1587, published by A. Solerti in *Archivio storico per Trieste, l'Istria e il Trentino,* vol. III, which I read in an unmarked offprint in the Biblioteca Nazionale, Florence (Misc. Morpurgo 8254.20). On his antiquarian researches, see above, Chapter 15, n. 119. Besides the authorities already mentioned in n. 21, I have consulted Franz Lamprecht, *Zur Theorie der humanistischen Geschichtsschreibung: Mensch und Geschichte bei Francesco Patrizi* (Zürich: Artemisverlag, 1950), and Raffaello Franchini, "Francesco Patrizi teorico della storiografia," *Atti Pont,* n.s., vol. XV (1966), which has the advantage of being written by a philosopher capable of pointing out those elements that can still be considered "pensieri fecondi" today. John Charles Nelson in "L'amorosa filosofia di Francesco Patrizi," *Rinascimento,* II (1962), does not mention the *Ars Historica* at all, which is probably why he misses the significance of Patrizi's introduction of Carlo Sigonio as an interlocutor in the philosophical dialogues. I read *Della historia diece dialoghi* in the 1st ed. of Venice, 1560. One chapter of Julian H. Franklin's *Jean Bodin and the Sixteenth-Century Revolution in the Methodology of Law and History* (Cambridge University Press, 1963) is devoted to

Patrizi (whose name he consistently spells Patrizzi"); but I agree with Cotroneo's reservations: one dialogue of Patrizi is lifted out of the context both of the other dialogues and of the rest of contemporary Italian *Ars Historica* writing. The causal explanations here quoted are those of Cotroneo in *I Trattati . . . ,* pp. 210–11.

25. Nicola Petruzzellis, "La metaphysique et l'historiographie de Campanella," *Organon*(Warsaw), X (1974); Raffaello Franchini, "Campanella teorico della storiografia," in *Miscellanea di studi nel quarto centenario . . . di Tommaso Campanella* (Naples, 1969); and Rodolfo De Mattei in *Storia e storiografia* (above, Chapter 4, n. 59), p. 872.

26. On which, see especially Huppert, *The Idea of Perfect History* (above, Prologue, n. 16).

27. *De Conscribenda Historia Dialogus,* bound with his *Laelii sive Monarchi Due ad Cosmum Medicem* (Bologna, 1563).

28. *Ragionamento della istoria fatto . . . l'anno 1559 in Venetia* I read in appendix to Girolamo Ruscelli's *Supplemento nell'istorie di monsignor Paolo Giovio* (1572), cited above, Chapter 13, n. 48. Further biographical information in the article by C. Mutini in *DBI.*

29. Remigio in preface to his translation of Fazello (1573), cited above in Chapter 10, n. 26.

30. *De Scribenda Historia* I read in the copy of the 1st ed. of Antwerp, 1569, in Kessler, in the work cited above at n. 21. Viperani's historical works are cited above, Chapter 8, n. 19.

31. On Aconcio, see also the article by Delio Cantimori in *DBI.* His *Delle osservationi et avvertimenti che haver si debono nel legger delle historie* (Kessler) was incorporated, together with most of Patrizi's theses, into Thomas Blundeville's *The True Order and Methode of Wryting and Reading Hystories* (1574). It was republished by Giorgio Radetti in 1944 (Florence: Vallecchi). See further, Charles Donald O'Malley, *Jacopo Aconcio,* tr. Delio Cantimori (Rome: Edizioni di Storia e Letteratura, 1955). I read about Ducci's *Ars Historica* on pp. 119–20 of the article by Spini cited above at n. 21, from the edition of Ferrara, 1604. Since Tiraboschi judged it to be "not worthy of mention," and since he judged Ducci's treatises on nobility and on

how to win the favor of a prince not worthy of mention at all, I stopped looking for it after the single copy I finally located at the Biblioteca Nazionale of Florence turned out to be still "alluvionata" in June, 1978.

32. Letter to Pietro Afan de Rivero in preface to his edition of Alessandro Andrea published in Gravier, vol. VII.

33. *De Historia Libri IV* (Venice, 1611), on whom see Giancarlo Mazzacurati in *DBI.* Possevino from vol. II of the *Apparato* (above, Chapter 1, n. 8), p. 16.

34. *Ragguagli di Parnaso,* ed. Luigi Firpo (Bari: Laterza, 1948), vol. II, Rag. xvii, and vol. III, Rag. xxxv.

35. In the dedicatory letter to his *Annotationes* of 1517: above, Chapter 10, n. 33.

36. Cited above, Chapter 13, n. 61.

37. Cited above, Chapter 8, n. 24.

38. Cited above, Chapter 10, n. 76.

39. Cited above, Chapter 9, n. 113.

40. *De Laudibus Historiae Oratio Sixta,* in *Opera Omnia,* vol. VI.

41. *De Historiae Laudibus,* first published in his *Selectarum Epistolarum Libri V* (Cracow, 1583); but I read it in his *Opera Varia Selecta* (Berlin, 1698).

42. *De Ratio Scribendae Historiae,* published among his *Opuscula Nonnulla* (Rome, 1574); I quote here from his *De Similitudine Normae Polybianae* published in Graevius, vol. I[1].

43. *Discorse intorno allo scrivere historie,* in preface to his *Delle historie del mondo,* in Venice, 1607, edition, rather than that of 1596 cited above in Chapter 13, n. 22.

44. *De i precetti historici,* published together with his other *Discorsi* (Venice, 1587). I might have added here the *Avvertimenti della historia* (Bergamo, 1608) by Ciro Spontone (on whom: above, Chapter 13, n. 9) had I been able to find a copy; all I know about it is what I read in Benedetto Croce, *Storia dell'età barocca in Italia* (Bari: Laterza, 1946), p. 75.

45. Most of the relevant passages have been cited in the first two books of this volume and are more fully explained in the first three chapters of Cotroneo's *I trattati* (above, n. 21). My specific references here are to Guarino's letter to Tobia del Borgo and his dedication to his translation of Plutarch's life of Themistocles reprinted in Garin, *Il pensiero pedagogico* (above, Chapter 6, n. 105), pp. 320 and 382–94, to Salutati's letter to Guarino

quoted by Carlo Pincin in his "Osservazioni sui *Discorsi* di Machiavelli," in *Renaissance Studies* (chapter 1, n. 40), to Lorenzo Valla as quoted from his history of Ferdinando d'Aragona by Cardini in *La critica del Landino,* pp. 97–99, to the eulogy of Campano by Jacobus Antiquarius (1494) in the preface to Campano's *Opera* (1502), to Fonzio in his letters of 1509 and 1512 apropos of Rucellai's *De Bello Gallico* published in his *Epistolarum Libri III,* ed. Ladislaus Juhász (Bibliotheca Scriptorum Medii Recentisque Aevorum [Budapest, 1931]). On Poliziano, see Gardenal, *Il Poliziano e Svetonio* (above, Chapter 14, n. 43), p. 12. His *Oratio in Historiae Laudationem* is cited above, Chapter 1, n. 87.

46. *Orationi in materia civile e criminale tratte da gli historici greci e latini* (Venice, 1561).

47. Just how vague these phrases must have been is suggested by M. L. W. Laistner in *The Greater Roman Historians* (University of California Press, 1971), pp. 30–31.

48. *Historia varia ... nella quale si contengon molte cose argute, nobili e degne di memoria di diversi principi & huomini illustri* (Venice, 1565) (but dated by the author as Florence, 1563).

49. *Pancratii Iustiniani Patritii Veneti ... De Praeclaris Venetae Aristocratiae Gestis Liber* (Venice, 1527); Vitignano, *Cronica del Regno di Napoli ... ove si contiene una breve e sostantial cognitione di molte cose successe ...* (Naples, 1595).

50. *Avvertimenti civili estratti* da mons. Ascanio Piccoluomini ... *dai sei primi libri degli Annali di Cornelio Tacito,* ed. Daniello Leremita, "gentiluomo del gran duca di Toscana" (Florence, 1609); Frezza, *Massime, regole e precetti di Stato & di guerra cavati ... Cornelio Tacito* (Naples, 1616).

51. Filippo and Jacopo Giunti in their dedication to their edition of Matteo Villani (Florence, 1562). Filippo di Soldo Strozzi says the same thing in the dedication of his translation of Thucydides to Cosimo I (1545), which I read in the Ramanzini reprint of Verona, 1735.

52. Bardi's *Sommario* cited above, Chapter 13, n. 59, here quoted from p. 1; Nubilonio cited from the edition in *MSI,* vol. XXIX, p. 207.

53. Momigliano in *RSI,* LXXXIX (1977), 605.

54. Salvatore Bongi, *Annali di Gabriel*

Giolito de' Ferrari (Rome, 1890). These and all the following figures are based on my own count from the published lists of titles and should not be taken as scientifically accurate. The total history production for the Giolito firm for the whole sixteenth century is given by Amedeo Quondam in "Mercanzia d'onore, mercanzia d'utile: Profusione libraria e lavoro intellettuale a Venezia nel Cinquecento," in Armando Petrucci, ed., *Libri, editori e pubblico nell'Europa moderna* (Bari: Laterza, 1977).

55. Alberto Tinto, *Annali tipografici dei Tramezzino* (above, Chapter 15, n. 90); Angelo Maria Bandini, *De Florentina Iuntarum Typographia* (Lucca, 1781); Domenico Bernoni, *Dei Torresani, Blado e Ragazzoni, celebri stampatori a Venezia e Roma nel XV e XVI secolo* (Milan: Hoepli, 1890); Claudia Di Filippo Bareggi, "Giunta, Doni, Torrentino: Tre tipografi fiorentini fra repubblica e principato," *NRS,* LVIII (1974).

56. Wolfgang Panzer, *Annales Typographici ab Anno MDI ad Annum MDXXVI* (Nürnberg, 1793–1803).

57. Gino Benzoni in *SV,* IX (1967), 258.

58. My calculations from the titles published by Pietro Manzi in *La tipografia napoletano nel '500* (Florence: Olschki, 1975).

59. Paolo Ulvioni in *AV,* CIV (1975), 57.

60. J. Baudrier, *Bibliographie lyonnaise* (Lyon, 1910), vol. VIII. Antoine Augustin Renouard, *Annales de l'imprimérie des Estienne* (1843), which I consulted in a recent (but without date) Burt Franklin reprint (New York).

61. Michel Maittaire, *Historia Typographorum aliquot Parisiensium Vitae et Libros Complectans* (London, 1727).

62. This is the thesis of one of the few recent historians to give much attention to the question, Luigi Malagoli, in his *Seicento italiano e modernità* (Florence: La Nuova Italia, 1970), pt. II: "La 'storia' del Rinascimento e la 'storia' della controriforma." Like Bertelli, Malagoli separates the "Counter Reformation" from the "Renaissance" and annexes it to the "Baroque"; but unlike Bertelli, he confines his illustrations almost wholly to the Florentine historians. He puts the dividing line of Baroque from Renaissance between Varchi and Segni and not, as I do, after Ammirato.

63. Gino Benzoni in *SV,* XVI (1974), 284.

64. This is Spini's thesis, too. But I have taken my specific information from vol. I of *Monumenta Paedagogica Societatis Iesu,* where all the relevant documents are printed. The quotation is from Benedetto Perera's *Brevis Ratio Studendi* of 1564.

65. Besides the work of Cotroneo and Spini cited above, see also Spini's earlier "La istorica del barocco italiano," *Belfagor,* I (1946), and Chapter 1 of Bertelli's *Libertini e ortodossi.*

66. All these historians have been the object of monographic study by Spini, Benzoni, Raffaele Belvederi, Domenico Caccamo, and others. Still further titles are given by Valerio Castronovo in the work cited above at n. 10 and in Chapter 12, n. 66. However, the most complete guide through the forest of Baroque historiography is still Tiraboschi. I offer a much more detailed exposition of the subject treated in the following paragraphs in the paper cited in the Prologue, n. 8.

67. Bentivoglio quoted by Anna Maria Crinò in *Studi secenteschi,* IX (1968); Fulvio Testi on Bentivoglio's *Relazione* on Flanders quoted by Marina Castagnetti, ibid., XIV (1973), 15–16.

68. (Rome, 1676), from the dedication to Giulio Spinola.

69. That is Soria's judgment concerning Francesco De' Petris, *Della historia napolitana libri II* (Naples, 1634).

70. Carlo Capasso apropos of Celestino in *RIS²,* vol. XVI², p. v.

71. Tiraboschi quoted from vol. VIII of the 1812 edition, p. 392, with reference to Tesauro's *Del Regno d'Italia sotto i barbari* (Turin, 1663) (2d ed.; Venice, 1667); Ernesto Sestan quoted from *RSI,* LXII (1950), 187, with reference to Briani's *Dell'istoria d'Italia* (Venice, 1624).

72. Many of them were published or republished in the 1930s.

73. I consulted the edition of Leipzig, 1620. What I say about Leiden is based on my own tour through the library catalogue.

74. *Historie della provincia del Friuli* (Udine, 1660) (Forni VIII).

75. *La verità vendicata, cioè, Bologna difesa dalle calunnie di Francesco Guicciardini* (above, Chapter 11, n. 18).

76. Quoted by Muratori in *RIS*[1], vol. V, p. 5.

77. Soria, pp. 77–78.

78. Gravier, vol. III (1759), p. xiii.

79. From the preface of his *Istoria degli scrittori nati nel Regno di Napoli* (cited in the Abbreviations).

80. Preface to his edition of Zagata, cited above, Chapter 5, n. 26.

81. Molina, *Notizie storiche profane della città di Asti* (Asti, 1774) (Forni XXXVII); Verci in *Degli scrittori bassanesi* (pt. V) in Calogerà *Nuova raccolta*, XXIX (1776).

82. Norman P. Miller, "Style and Content in Tacitus," in T. A. Dorey, ed., *Tacitus* (London: Routledge and Kegan Paul, 1969), p. 115; Dorey himself, in his introduction to *Livy* (above, Chapter 1, n. 51), p. xi.

83. Renzo De Felice, *Intervista sul Fascismo*, with Michael A. Ledeen ("Saggi Tascabili Laterza") (Bari, 1976), p. 37.

84. My specific example is from Ἱστορία τοῦ Ἑλληνικοῦ Ἔθνους, nos. 11–12, Τόμος ΙΔ' (Athens: Ἐκδοτικὴ Ἀθηνῶν [1977]), p. 160.

85. Marcel Couturier, *Recherches sur les structures sociales de Châteaudun* (Paris: SEVPEN, 1969).

86. Pierre Vilar, apropos of Louis Althusser on p. 185 of "Histoire marxiste, histoire en construction," in *Faire de l'histoire*, eds. Jacques Le Goff and Pierre Nora (Paris: Gallimard, 1974), vol. I.

87. Marino Berengo and Corrado Vivanti in *Belfagor*, XXXI (1976), 235–36, citing Arnaldo Momigliano: "Quando ero giovane, i dotti scrivevano storia e i gentiluomini biografia."

88. "Writing 'hot history'," *Saturday Review*, 29 May 1976.

89. Paolo Spriano, *Storia del Partito Comunista Italiano* (Einaudi Reprints, 77), vol. I, p. 44.

90. Ruggiero Romano, in *Quaderni storici*, XXVI (1974), 541.

91. Giorgio Amendola, cited in Piero Melograni, ed., *Intervista sull'antifascismo* (Bari: Laterza, 1976), p. 16.

92. Robert Kingdon, in *American Historical Review*, LXXVI (1971), 69.

93. Natalie Zemon Davis, in *Past and Present*, no. 59 (May, 1973), 891.

94. I read not Cyrus H. Gordon's *Before Columbus* (New York: Crown, 1971) but the review essay by R. C. Padden in *American Historical Review*, LXXVIII (1973), 987–1004.

INDEX

INDEX